# ILLUSTRATED
# FAMILY
# ENCYCLOPEDIA

Indonesian bank note
*see* MONEY

Colt Peacemaker
*see* WEAPONS

Straw boater *see* SAILING AND
OTHER WATER SPORTS

Shipping signal
*see* FLAGS

1970s platform shoes
*see* CLOTHES AND FASHION

Postage stamps
*see* STAMPS AND
POSTAL SERVICES

Yu'pik family, Alaska
*see* ARCTIC OCEAN

King and Queen
*see* CHESS

Picture book
*see* CHILDREN'S
LITERATURE

Tenor horn
*see* MUSICAL
INSTRUMENTS

Gecko *see* LIZARDS

Honey fungus
*see* MUSHROOMS

Monarch butterfly
*see* EVOLUTION

Clown fish *see*
ECOLOGY

Hoverfly
*see* INSECTS

Paradise riflebird egg
*see* EGGS

Kiwanos
*see* FRUITS AND SEEDS

Duckling
*see* DUCKS, GEESE, AND SWANS

Bloodhound *see* DOGS

SLR camera
*see* CAMERAS

Personal stereo
*see* RADIO

Hubble space telescope
*see* SPACE
EXPLORATION

Light bulb
*see* INVENTIONS

Mobile phone
*see* TELEPHONES

DNA double helix
*see* GENETICS

Chemical reactions
*see* CHEMISTRY

Ethane molecule
*see* ATOMS AND MOLECULES

Jaguar XK120
*see* CARS AND TRUCKS

Dagger
*see*
WEAPONS

Amulet
*see* EGYPT, ANCIENT

Board Game
*see* VIKINGS

Throwing dice
*see* ROMAN EMPIRE

Thumbscrew
*see* WITCHES AND WITCHCRAFT

Portable sextant *see* EXPLORATION

Flint arrowhead
*see* STONE AGE

Clasp *see* CHINA, HISTORY OF

Ceremonial dress
*see* NORTH AMERICA,
HISTORY OF

Ancient coins
*see* SUMERIANS

Sabaton *see* ARMS AND ARMOUR

*The Dorling Kindersley*

# ILLUSTRATED
# FAMILY
# ENCYCLOPEDIA

## VOLUME 1 · A-I
*Aboriginal Australians* to *India, History of*

A DK PUBLISHING BOOK

LONDON, NEW YORK, MUNICH,
MELBOURNE AND DELHI

**Senior Editor** Jayne Parsons     **Senior Art Editor** Gillian Shaw

**Project Editors**
Marian Broderick, Gill Cooling,
Maggie Crowley, Hazel Egerton,
Cynthia O'Neill, Veronica Pennycook,
Louise Pritchard, Steve Setford, Jackie Wilson

**Project Art Editors**
Jane Felstead, Martyn Foote,
Neville Graham, Jamie Hanson,
Christopher Howson, Jill Plank, Floyd Sayers,
Jane Tetzlaff, Ann Thompson

**Editors**
Rachel Beaugié, Nic Kynaston, Sarah Levete,
Karen O'Brien, Linda Sonntag

**Art Editors**
Tina Borg, Diane Clouting,
Tory Gordon-Harris

**DTP Designers**
Andrew O'Brien, Cordelia Springer

**Managing Editor** Ann Kramer     **Managing Art Editor** Peter Bailey

**Senior DTP Designer** Mathew Birch

**Picture Research** Jo Walton, Kate Duncan, Liz Moore

**DK Picture Library** Ola Rudowska, Melanie Simmonds

**Country pages** by PAGE*One*: Bob Gordon, Helen Parker,
Thomas Keenes, Sarah Watson, Chris Clark

**Cartographers** Peter Winfield, James Anderson

**Research** Robert Graham, Angela Koo

**Editorial Assistants** Sarah-Louise Reed, Nichola Roberts

**Production** Louise Barratt, Charlotte Traill

First published in the United States in 1997.
This edition published in the United States in 2002
by DK Publishing, Inc.,
375 Hudson St., New York, NY 10014

A CIP catalogue record for this book is available from the Library of Congress

ISBN 0 7894 8865 5

Color reproduction by Colourscan, Singapore
Printed and bound in China by Toppan Printing Co. (Shenzhen) Ltd.

**See our complete product line at www.dk.com**

# CONTRIBUTORS AND CONSULTANTS

**Simon Adams BSc MSc**
Historian and writer

**Norman Barrett MA**
Sports writer and consultant

**Dr Martin R. Bates BSc, PhD**
Institute of Archaeology
University of London

**David Burnie BSc**
Science and natural history writer

**Jack Challoner BSc, ARCS, PGCE**
Science writer, formerly with the Education
Unit, Science Museum, London

**Julie Childs BSc**
Zoologist and natural history writer,
former Head of Public Affairs, Zoological
Society of London

**Neil Clark BSc**
Paleontologist, Hunterian Museum and
University of Glasgow

**Paul Collins MA**
Institute of Archaeology
University College, London

**Dr Gordon Daniels**
Reader in History,
University of Sheffield

**Veronica Doubleday**
Lecturer, Historical and Critical Studies,
University of Brighton

**John Farndon**
Writer and consultant

**Roger Few BA**
Author on natural history and the
environment

**Theresa Greenaway BSc, ARCS**
Botanist and natural history writer

**Frances Halpin BSc**
Science consultant and teacher at
Royal Russell School

**Dr Austen Ivereigh D Phil**
Lecturer in Latin American History
University of Leeds

**Robin Kerrod FRAS**
Science writer and consultant

**Bruce P. Lenman**
Professor of Modern History
University of St Andrews

**Nicky Levell**
Curator Collections History,
The Horniman Museum

**John E. Llewellyn-Jones BSc**
Zoologist and botanist; writer and lecturer

**Miranda MacQuitty BSc, PhD**
Zoologist and natural history writer

**Kevin McRae**
Writer and consultant

**Haydn Middleton MA**
Historian and author

**Mark O'Shea BSc, FRGS**
Curator of Reptiles, West Midland Safari
Park; tropical herpetologist and zoologist;
natural history author

**Chris Oxlade BSc**
Writer and consultant, specializing in
science and technology

**Douglas Palmer BSc, PhD**
Writer, lecturer, and Open University tutor
specializing in palaeobiology

**Steve Parker BSc**
Zoologist, science writer and scientific
fellow of the Zoological Society

**Tom Parsons MA**
Art historian and writer

**James Pickford BA**
Writer and
electronic editor FT Mastering

**Richard Platt BA**
Writer and consultant

**Matthew Robertson**
Senior invertebrate keeper, Bristol Zoo

**Theodore Rowland-Entwistle BA, FRGS**
Writer and consultant

**Noel Simon**
Member emiritus of the Species Survival
Commission of IUCN; original compiler
mammalia volume, Red Data Book

**Carole Stott BA, FRAS**
Astronomy and space writer;
formerly Head of the Old Royal
Observatory, Greenwich, London

**Jonathan Stroud BA**
Writer and consultant: literature

**Barbara Taylor BSc**
Environmental scientist and
natural history writer

**Louise Tythacott**
Writer and consultant Southeast Asia

**Richard Walker BSc PhD**
Human biology and natural history writer

**Marcus Weeks B Mus**
Composer and writer

**Philip Wilkinson MA**
Historian and writer

**Elizabeth Wyse BA**
Writer and consultant

**Dorling Kindersley Cartography**
in conjunction with leading cartographic
consultants, embassies, and consulates

# LIST OF MAIN ENTRIES

## See index for further topics

Jupiter, the largest planet, comparative to the Sun

Sun *see* Sun and solar system

## COMPARATIVE PLANET SIZES

Uranus *see* PLANETS

Neptune *see* PLANETS

Pluto
*see* PLANETS

Mars
*see* PLANETS

Earth
*see* EARTH

Mercury
*see* PLANETS

Venus
*see* PLANETS

Saturn
*see* PLANETS

Jupiter
*see* PLANETS

# HOW TO USE THIS ENCYCLOPEDIA

THE FOLLOWING PAGES WILL HELP YOU get the most out of your copy of the *Dorling Kindersley Illustrated Family Encyclopedia*. The encyclopedia consists of three volumes. Volumes 1–2 contain nearly 700 main entries organized alphabetically, from Aboriginal Australians through to Zoos. To find the entry you want, simply turn to the correct letter of the alphabet.

If you cannot find the topic you want, then turn to Volume 3. This volume includes an index and gazetteer for the whole encyclopedia, which will direct you straight to the page you need. In addition, Volume 3 contains hundreds of reference charts, fact boxes, lists, and tables to supplement the information provided on the main entry pages.

## MEASUREMENTS AND ABBREVIATIONS

Most measurements are supplied in both metric and imperial units. Some of the most common abbreviations used in the encyclopedia are shown below in **bold** type.

**°C** = degrees Celsius
**°F** = degrees Fahrenheit
**K** = degrees kelvin
**mm** = millimetre; **cm** = centimetre
**m** = metre; **km** = kilometre
**in** = inch; **ft** = foot; **yd** = yard
**g** = gram; **kg** = kilogram
**oz** = ounce; **lb** = pound
**ml** = millilitre; **l** = litre
**pt** = pint; **gal** = gallon
**sq km (km²)** = square kilometre
**sq ft (ft²)** = square foot
**kmh** = kilometres per hour
**mph** = miles per hour
**mya** = million years ago
**BC** = before Christ
**AD** = anno Domini (refers to any date after the birth of Christ)
**c.** = circa (about)
**b.** = born; **d.** = died; **r.** = reigned

## THE PAGE LAYOUT

The pages in this encyclopedia have been carefully planned to make each subject as accessible as possible. Main entries are broken down into a hierarchy of information – from a general introduction to more specific individual topics.

### Alphabet locators

Letter flashes help you find your way quickly around the encyclopedia.

### Sub-entries

Sub-entries provide important additional information and expand on points made in the introduction.

*This sub-entry explains how rainbows are caused by raindrops in the air.*

### Diagrams

Clear diagrams help explain complex processes and scientific concepts.

*The diagram here shows how a raindrop splits sunlight into its constituent colours.*

### Introduction

Clear introductions are the starting point for each entry. The introduction defines and provides an overview of each subject.

*In the main entry on COLOUR, the introduction explains that colours are different forms of light, and that sunlight contains light of many different colours.*

---

COLLEGES see SCHOOLS AND COLLEGES • COLOMBIA see SOUTH AMERICA, NORTHERN

# COLOR

A WORLD WITHOUT COLOR would be dull and uninspiring. Color is a form of light. Light is made up of electromagnetic waves of varying lengths. The human eye detects these different wavelengths and sees them as different colors. White light – like that from the Sun – is a mixture of all the different wavelengths. Objects look colored because they emit or reflect only certain wavelengths of light.

### White light spectrum

Passing white light through a transparent triangular block called a prism separates the different wavelengths of light. The prism refracts (bends) each wavelength by a different amount, forming a band of colors called a white light spectrum, or visible spectrum. The seven main colors are red, orange, yellow, green, blue, indigo, and violet. Red has the longest wavelength and violet the shortest. Here, a convex lens combines the colors back into white light.

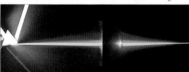

### Rainbow

If it rains on a sunny day, you may well see a rainbow if you stand with your back to the Sun. A rainbow is a curved white light spectrum that forms when light is reflected and refracted by raindrops in the sky.

A rainbow at dawn

### How a rainbow forms

The white sunlight passes through a raindrop, the raindrop acts like a tiny prism, refracting the light and splitting it up into its separate colors. The colors fan out and emerge as a spectrum. A rainbow is made up of spectra from millions of raindrops.

Sunlight
Spectrum
Colors refract again
Light refracts
Colors reflect off back surface.

### Color and temperature

Objects at room temperature emit (give out) electromagnetic waves, but these waves are too long for human eyes to see. Heating an object, such as this steel bar, makes the waves short enough to be seen, and the bar begins to glow. As the bar's temperature rises, it glows with different colors.

Steel bar at 1,170°F (630°C)

Steel bar at 2,790°F (1,530°C)

### Spectroscope

An instrument called a spectroscope is used to analyze the light emitted by hot substances. Inside the spectroscope, a prism or diffraction grating (a glass slide scored with fine lines) splits light from a glowing substance into its component wavelengths.

Light source
Diffraction grating

### Emission spectrum

Each chemical element gives out a unique range of light wavelengths when heated. Seen through a spectroscope, these wavelengths appear as a set of bright lines on a dark background. This is the element's emission spectrum. A compound's emission spectrum is a combination of spectra from the elements that make up the compound.

Emission spectrum of a sodium flame

Sodium flame

### Cone cells

At the back of the eye are special cells called cones that enable humans to see colors. There are three types of cones, called red, green, and blue cones. Each type of cone is sensitive to a different range of light wavelengths. White light stimulates all three types of cones.

Cone cells

Sensitivity of red cones
Sensitivity of green cones
Sensitivity of blue cones

Visible spectrum

Sensitivity of cone cells in the human eye

### Red hot and white hot

Glowing white
Glowing red
Visible spectrum

As the steel bar gets hotter, it emits more and more of the visible spectrum. At about 1,170°F (630°C), it is "red hot" and emits light from the red end of the spectrum. At about 2,790°F (1,530°C), the "white hot" bar emits the entire white light spectrum.

### Hot stars

The color of a star gives a clue to its age. To the naked eye, most stars look white, but their true colors can be seen through a telescope. Young stars are hot and glow with white light. Older stars are relatively cool and glow red or orange.

A cluster of young stars

### Joseph von Fraunhofer

The German physicist Joseph von Fraunhofer (1787–1826) became interested in the nature of light while training as a mirror maker and lens polisher. His training enabled him to make spectroscopes of great precision. From 1814–17, he used them to make the first scientific study of the Sun's emission spectrum.

### Munsell color system

Describing colors exactly using words alone is not easy. To avoid confusion, manufacturing industries use standard color-identification systems. The Munsell system is used to specify colors for dyes and pigments. It defines a color by its value (brightness), its chroma (strength), and its hue (position in the spectrum).

### Color matching systems

Graphic designers use swatches of color cards to match the colors in their work with those available from printers. The designer supplies the printer with the reference number of the color, so the printer knows exactly what is wanted.

*Each color has a reference number.*

226

---

*Labels help to identify images.*

### King Penguin

act as rudders.

*Strong chest muscles pull down the wings.*

*Penguin rises through the water to break through the surface.*

*Huddling reduces heat loss.*

*emperor penguins carry chicks around on their feet.*

## KING PENGUIN

**SCIENTIFIC NAME** *Aptenodytes patagonica*

**ORDER** Sphenisciformes

**FAMILY** Spheniscidae

**DISTRIBUTION** Islands and ocean north of Antarctica

**HABITAT** Coasts and open sea

**DIET** Fish and squid

**SIZE** Length, including tail 95 cm (37.5 in)

**LIFESPAN** About 20 years

### Natural history data boxes

On the natural history pages, data boxes summarize essential information about a key animal featured in the entry. The box contains information about the animal's size, diet, habitat, lifespan, distribution, and scientific name.

*This data box gives you key facts about the King Penguin.*

### Biography boxes

Most main entry pages have biography boxes that tell you about key people who have contributed to our knowledge of the subject. The encyclopedia also has single-page entries on the life and work of more than 50 major historical figures.

*This biography box describes the work of the physicist Joseph von Fraunhofer.*

### Headings

The topic headings enable you to see at-a-glance which subjects are covered within the main entry.

*The heading Colour matching systems refers to the way designers use reference numbers to match the colours on their work to the colours of printers' inks.*

HOW TO USE THIS ENCYCLOPEDIA

## INDEX

Volume 3 contains an index and a gazetteer. The index, which comes first, lists all the topics mentioned in the encyclopedia and the pages on which they can be found. The gazetteer follows on, with references to help you find all the features included on the maps.

• page numbers in **bold** type (eg Knights and heraldry **495-6**) show that the subject is a main A–Z entry in Volumes 1–2.
• page numbers in plain type (eg armour 69) send you to sub-entries, text references, and the reference section.
• grid references (eg Cremona Italy 475 C3) are letter-number combinations that locate features on maps.

Knights and heraldry **495-6**
    armour 69
    feudalism 329
    Crusades 247, 883
Knights of Malta 70
Knights of St John 247
Knossos, Crete 557
Knowledge, epistemology 651

Craiova Romania 727 C7
Cremona Italy 475 C3
Crcs *Island* Croatia 105 B4
Crete *Island* Greece 403 E11
Crete, Sea of Mediterranean Sea 403 E10
Crimea *Peninsula* Ukraine 727 I7
Croatia *Country* SE Europe 105
Crotone Italy 475 G8

*This two-page entry discusses the main types of primate.*

## Running head
There is an A–Z running head at the top of most pages to help you find important topics that are not main entries within the encyclopedia.

*The running head on PRINTING tells you that although there is no main entry on primates, you can find the topic on MONKEYS AND OTHER PRIMATES.*

## Illustrations
Each main entry is heavily illustrated with models, photographs, and artworks, adding a vibrant layer of visual information to the page.

*This annotation tells you how different colours can be produced by mixing red, green, and blue light.*

## Annotation
The illustrations are comprehensively annotated to draw attention to details of particular interest and to explain complex points.

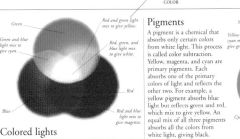

## Colored lights
Different amounts of red, green, and blue light can be mixed to form light of any other color. This process is called color addition. Unlike paints, red, green, and blue are the primary colors of light. Equal amounts of any two primary colors give a secondary color (yellow, cyan, or magenta). When all three primaries are mixed in equal amounts, white light is produced.

### Color television
The principle of adding colored lights is used in color television. The screen is covered with tiny strips that glow with red, green, or blue light. They are so small that, at normal viewing distance, the human eye mixes the light coming from them. By adjusting the intensity of these three colors, the sensation of any other color is produced.

*Image is formed by tiny glowing strips.*

### Painting with dots
"Pointillism" is a style of painting in which an artist uses thousands of tiny colored dots to build up a picture. When viewed close up, the colors of the individual dots are clearly visible. Like the colored strips on a television screen, the dots are too small to be seen from farther away. When viewed from a distance, the dots seem to merge, giving areas a single color.

### Thomas Young
The English doctor and physicist Thomas Young (1773–1829) carried out many experiments to prove that light travels in waves. He realized that colors are light waves of different lengths and that interference colors occur when light waves meet and combine. Young also investigated color vision. In 1801, he proposed that the human eye contains three types of color sensors (now called cone cells), sensitive to blue, red, and green light.

## Pigments
A pigment is a chemical that absorbs only certain colors from white light. This process is called color subtraction. Yellow, magenta, and cyan are primary pigments. Each absorbs one of the primary colors of light and reflects the other two. For example, a yellow pigment absorbs blue light but reflects green and red, which mix to give yellow. An equal mix of all three pigments absorbs all the colors from white light, giving black.

### Color printing
To print a color picture, three single-color images are printed on top of each other – one in cyan, one in magenta, and one in yellow. Each picture is made up of tiny colored dots. The dots overlap and absorb the right wavelengths of light to give all the other colors required. A black image is then added to make the picture sharper.

*Picture is made up of tiny ink dots.*

### Mixing paints
Paints are pigments mixed with water or oil. Any color except white can be made by mixing the three primary pigments. Mixing paints has the effect of evenly mixing the pigments, and absorbing more of the white light spectrum.

## Scattering and interference
Two other processes, called scattering and interference, can remove colors from the spectrum. Interference occurs when light from two sources meets and combines. In scattering, some parts of the spectrum are briefly absorbed by particles of matter and then radiated out again in all directions.

### Blue sky
Sunlight includes all the colors of the spectrum. The sky appears blue during the day because air molecules in the atmosphere scatter blue light from the blue end of the spectrum in all directions.

### Soap bubble
When white light strikes a soap bubble, it reflects off both the inner and outer surfaces of the bubble. The reflected light rays interfere, canceling out some colors but making others appear bright.

*Interference creates a pattern of bright colors and dark bands.*

### Using interference
Stress is a force that can stretch or bend objects. Engineers shine light through plastic models of their designs to test their ability to withstand stress. The plastic molecules make the light rays split up and interfere. The interference patterns show the points of greatest stress.

*High stress*

## Reflecting colors
Objects have color only when light falls upon them, because colors do not exist in total darkness. An object that appears one color in white light may look different when illuminated by colored light. The yellow pot in this sequence of pictures appears yellow only in white light.

### White light
The yellow pot reflects the red and green parts of the white light spectrum, but absorbs the blue part.

### Red light
The yellow pot reflects red light, and therefore appears red when illuminated by red light.

### Green light
When illuminated by green light, the yellow pigment reflects the green light and appears green.

### Blue light
When only blue light is available, the yellow pot absorbs the blue light, making it look black.

| FIND OUT MORE | DYES AND PAINTS | EYES AND VISION | LIGHT | PHOTOGRAPHY | PRINTING | TELEVISION |

227

## Timelines
An entry may include a timeline that gives the dates of key events in the history or development of the subject.

*The PRINTING timeline stretches from the printing of the first books in ancient China to the computerization of modern printing.*

## COLLECTION PAGES
There are more than 70 pages of photographic collections, which follow main entries and provide a visual guide to the subject. They are organized under clear headings.

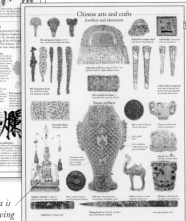

## Find out more
The Find Out More lines at the end of each entry direct you to other relevant main entries in the encyclopedia. Using the Find Out More lines can help you understand an entry in its wider context.

*On COLOUR, the Find Out More line directs you to the entry on PRINTING, where there is a detailed explanation of the colour printing process and how printing presses work.*

*PRINTING'S Find Out More line sends you to CHINA, HISTORY OF, which lists ancient Chinese inventions, including printing.*

*The entry on the history of China is followed by a collection page showing Chinese jewellery and ornaments.*

9

## CONTINENT AND COUNTRY PAGES

The encyclopedia contains entries on all the world's continents and countries, each containing a detailed map. Continent entries focus on the physical geography of the region; country entries provide information about the society and economy of the country. Below is the single-page entry on the Netherlands

*The country's flag appears by its name.*

### Locator map

A small map in the top left-hand corner of the page shows you where the region lies within a continent or in relation to the rest of the world.

*Map of Netherlands' position in Europe.*

*The introduction defines the region and provides an overview to the entry.*

*Compass points north*

*Scale bar*

### Scale bar and compass

Each map has a scale bar that shows how distances on the map relate to actual miles and kilometers. The compass shows you which direction on the map is north (N).

### Grid reference

The numbers and letters around the map help you find all the places listed in the index.

*The index gives Amsterdam's grid reference as C4, so you can find it on the map by locating the third square along (C) and the fourth square down (4).*

### Population density

A population density diagram shows how many people there are to every square mile or square kilometer.

*The Netherlands is a very densely populated country*

---

### KEY TO MAP

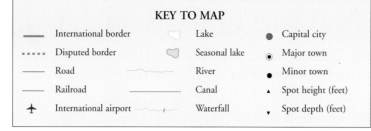

| | | |
|---|---|---|
| International border | Lake | ● Capital city |
| Disputed border | Seasonal lake | ◉ Major town |
| Road | River | ● Minor town |
| Railroad | Canal | ▲ Spot height (feet) |
| ✈ International airport | Waterfall | ▼ Spot depth (feet) |

---

NETBALL see BALL GAMES

# NETHERLANDS

ALSO CALLED HOLLAND, the Netherlands straddles the deltas of five major rivers in northwestern Europe. The Dutch people say they created their own country because they have enclosed about one-third of the land from sea, swamps, and marshland with earth barriers, or dikes, and drained the water from it. Despite being one of the most densely populated countries in the world, the Netherlands enjoys high living standards. Amsterdam is the official capital, although the government is based at The Hague.

**NETHERLANDS FACTS**

CAPITAL CITY Amsterdam (seat of government The Hague)
AREA 14,413 sq miles (37,330 sq km)
POPULATION 15,612,000
MAIN LANGUAGE Dutch
MAJOR RELIGION Christian
CURRENCY Guilder
LIFE EXPECTANCY 78 years
PEOPLE PER DOCTOR 410
GOVERNMENT Multiparty democracy
ADULT LITERACY 99%

**Amsterdam**
The Dutch capital is built on 70 islands, linked by about 500 bridges that span its many canals. The best way to get around is by bicycle, and more than half a million people cycle to school or work each day. Today, Amsterdam is a center for tourism and diamond cutting.

*One of Amsterdam's many canals*

**People**
The Dutch see their society as the most tolerant in Europe, with relaxed laws on sexuality, drugs, and euthanasia. The country has a long history of welcoming immigrants, often from former Dutch colonies. Most immigrants are now assimilated as Dutch citizens. However, members of the small Turkish community, which makes up just one per cent, do not enjoy full citizenship.

**Canals**
The Netherlands is a land of canals, which drain the land and serve as waterways for people and freight. The capital, Amsterdam, alone has more than 100 canals.

**Windmills**
For centuries the Dutch landscape was dotted with 10,000 windmills, which powered pumps to drain water from the land. Electric pumps now do this work in the battle to keep the sea back.

**Climate**
The Netherlands has mild, rainy winters and cool summers. In winter northerly gales lash the coast, damaging dikes and threatening floods. Frosts sometimes freeze canals.

**Physical features**
The Netherlands is mainly flat, with 27 percent of the land below sea level. The land is protected from the sea by natural sand dunes along the coast, and by artificial dikes. Wide, sandy plains cover most of the rest of the country, falling into a few low hills in the eastern and southern parts of the country.

99°F (37°C) -13°F (-25°C)
62°F (16°C) 36°F (2°C)
23 in (580 mm)

**Land use**
Almost one-third of the land has been reclaimed from the sea. These areas are known as polders and are extremely fertile. The country has large natural gas reserves in the north, and there is some offshore oil drilling in the North Sea.

Forest 3.5% Farmland 84.5%
Built-up 12%

**Farming and industry**
The Dutch economy is one of the most successful in Europe. Most imports and exports travel through Rotterdam, the world's biggest port. In addition to high-tech sectors such as electronics, telecommunications, and chemicals, the Netherlands has a successful agricultural industry. Productivity is high, and products such as vegetables, cheese, meat, and cut flowers are significant export earners.

*Street scene, Amsterdam*

1,083 per sq mile (418 per sq km)
89% Urban
11% Rural

*Dutch tulips*

FIND OUT MORE | CANALS | DAMS | EMPIRES | EUROPE | EUROPE, HISTORY OF | EUROPEAN UNION | FARMING | NETHERLANDS, HISTORY OF | PORTS & WATERWAYS

601

---

### Country file

On each country page there is a fact box containing key details about the country, such as its population, capital city, area, currency, political system, and main language and religion. Other categories of information include:

**Literacy** – the percentage of people over 15 years old who can read and write.
**People per doctor** – a rough guide to the availability of medical facilities.
**Life expectancy** – how long an average person can expect to live.

### Climate

A climate diagram gives details of rainfall levels and temperatures in the country, region, or continent.

*Average summer temperature*   *Average winter temperature*   *Average rainfall*

**Single country's average in capital city**

*Average summer temperature*   *Average winter temperature*   *Average rainfall*

**Regional average is the average of all capital cities on map**

*Concise explanation of the country's main physical characteristics.*

### Land use

The land-use diagram tells you how much of the the country's total land area is taken up by, for example, woodland, agriculture, and urban developments such as villages, towns, and cities.

*Most of the land in the Netherlands is used for farming.*

### Urban/rural split

A small diagram shows the percentage of people living in urban (built-up) areas and rural (country) areas.

*The majority of people in the Netherlands live in urban areas.*

---

## REFERENCE PAGES

Volume 3 of the Encyclopedia contains an illustrated reference section with essential facts, figures, and statistical data, divided into the five main strands described here.

### International world

This strand contains a double-page map showing all the countries of the world, and data on the world's population, economy, and resources.

### History

The history strand features a timeline of key historical events, stretching from 40,000 BC to the present day, together with the dates of major wars, revolutions, battles, and great leaders.

### Living world

The centerpiece of this strand is a detailed guide to the classification of living things, supported by lists of species in danger, and many other facts about the natural world.

### People, arts, and media

This strand is crammed full of information about television, theater, music, art, philosophy, architecture, literature, dance, and much more besides.

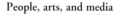

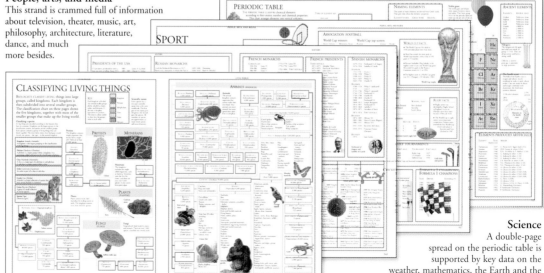

### Science

A double-page spread on the periodic table is supported by key data on the weather, mathematics, the Earth and the Universe, and measurement conversion tables.

# ABORIGINAL AUSTRALIANS

THE ABORIGINALS settled the Australian continent more than 40,000 years ago. They lived in total isolation from the rest of the world, existing by hunting and gathering. In the 18th century, the Europeans arrived and forced the Aboriginals off their territories. Today, many feel isolated from white society, but still try to preserve their tribal identity.

*Some early peoples crossed by means of a land bridge.*

*Settlers stayed near the coast and rivers where more food was available.*

### Aboriginal history
Aboriginals first reached Australia during the last Ice Age. Sea levels were low, and they were able to cross from Southeast Asia over land bridges and small stretches of water. When the ice melted and sea levels rose again, the continent was completely cut off. Initially, the settlers clung to the coasts and rivers, but gradually moved across the continent. By the time Europeans arrived, there were about 500 different tribal groups living in Australia.

## Ways of life
Traditionally, Aboriginals lived by hunting and gathering. They were nomadic, roaming over large stretches of territory, setting up temporary camps near watering places, and moving on when food supplies were exhausted. They traded with other tribes, exchanging goods such as spears.

### Hunting and gathering
Aboriginals lived by hunting animals such as kangaroos, and supplemented their diet with wild plants, nuts, and berries. The hunters used spears with stone blades and wooden boomerangs, a type of missile that flies back to the thrower. Some tribes developed an elaborate sign language so that they could send silent messages to each other when they were stalking game.

**Aboriginal hunters** used silent signals so they would not disturb game. The sign for kangaroo starts with a closed hand and moves to an open shape.

### Corroborees
Aboriginal peoples have handed down stories, songs, and traditions from generation to generation. This culture is kept alive at corroborees, ceremonial dances where tribes gather together to retell the tales of Australia's past through songs, music, and dance.

## Dreamtime
The Aboriginals believe that Dreamtime is a period when Ancestral Beings shaped the land, creating all species and human beings. These beings are thought to live on eternally in spirit form. Human beings are believed to be a part of nature, closely associated with all other living things. Images of spirits of Dreamtime, such as Lightning Man, cover sacred cliffs and caves in tribal areas.

**Lightning Man** was believed to have created thunder and lightning.

*Barrkinj – wife of Lightning Man*

*Lightning Man, also known as Namarrgon*

## Aboriginals today
European colonists arrived in Australia in 1788 and displaced Aboriginal tribes from their territory. Today, there are about 250,000 Aboriginals in Australia, many of whom live in urban areas. Although there is still discrimination, Aboriginals are beginning to benefit from government aid, and to assert their civil rights.

### Land rights
When the Europeans arrived in Australia, they claimed that the land was *Terra nullius*, that it belonged to no one, and that they were entitled to occupy it. More recently, the Aboriginals have campaigned to regain their lost territory and sacred sites. In 1993, the Australian government reversed its *Terra nullius* policy.

### Uluru (Ayers Rock)
Aboriginals believe that the Ancestral Beings created the Australian landscape and established customs and traditions still followed today. They have left evidence of their presence in the many sacred places, such as Uluru in central Australia. This is revered as a sacred place by the local Aranda people. Once called Ayers Rock by the Australian government, the rock regained its Aboriginal name in 1988.

### Education
During early contact with the Europeans, Aboriginal languages were lost or fell into disuse. In 1972, the government established a bilingual education program. Many children are now taught in their tribal languages before learning English. Books, radio, and television broadcasts are all available in many Aboriginal languages.

**FIND OUT MORE** ART, HISTORY OF • AUSTRALASIA AND OCEANIA • AUSTRALIA • AUSTRALIA, HISTORY OF • COOK, JAMES • MYTHS AND LEGENDS • RELIGIONS • SOCIETIES, HUMAN

# ACIDS AND ALKALIS

LEMON JUICE AND VINEGAR taste sour because they contain weak acids. An acid is a substance that dissolves in water to form positively charged particles called hydrogen ions ($H^+$). The opposite of an acid is an alkali, which dissolves in water to form negatively charged ions of hydrogen and oxygen, called hydroxide ions ($OH^-$). Alkalis are "anti-acids" because they cancel out acidity. Toothpaste, for example, contains an alkali that cancels out acidity in the mouth that would otherwise damage teeth.

*Hydrochloric acid*

*The mixture bubbles fiercely as hydrogen gas is given off.*

*Zinc replaces the hydrogen in the acid to form zinc chloride.*

*Zinc nuggets*

## pH scale

The concentration of hydrogen ions in a solution is known as its pH. Scientists use the pH scale to measure acidity and alkalinity. On the pH scale, a solution with a pH lower than 7 is acidic, and a solution with a pH greater than 7 is alkaline. Water is neutral, and has a pH of 7. A solution's pH can be tested with universal indicator solution or paper, which changes color in acids and alkalis.

**Universal indicator pH color chart**

*Universal indicator paper*

1
Strong acids

*Digestive juices: pH 1*

*Lemon juice: pH 3*

**Hydrochloric acid (pH 1)**

*Acid rain: pH 5*

**Vinegar (pH 4)**

7
Neutral

*Human blood: pH 7.4*

**Liquid soap (pH 8–9)**

*Oven cleaner: pH 13*

14
Strong alkalis

**Household cleaner (pH 10)**

## Strong acids

The more hydrogen ions an acid forms in water, the stronger it is, and the lower its pH. Strong acids such as sulfuric acid and nitric acid are very dangerous and must be handled carefully.

*Sulfuric acid*

*Carbon*

*Sugar*

**Sulfuric acid**
Concentrated sulfuric acid will dehydrate (remove water from) any substance with which it comes into contact. For example, the acid dehydrates sugar, a carbohydrate, to leave a mass of smoldering black carbon.

*Cork*

*Nitrogen dioxide gas and smoke are given off as acid reacts with cork.*

*Nitric acid*

**Nitric acid**
Organic matter, such as paper, cork, rubber, fabric, and skin, is rapidly decomposed by nitric acid. The acid is so corrosive because it oxidizes (supplies oxygen to) any material it touches.

### Svante Arrhenius
Swedish scientist Svante Arrhenius (1859–1927) won acclaim for his research into how compounds form ions in solution. This work led him to realize that it is hydrogen ions that give acids their special properties.

## Acids and metals

Even the weakest acids cannot be stored in metal containers because acids are corrosive to most metals. When an acid reacts with a metal, hydrogen gas is given off and the metal dissolves in the acid to form a compound called a salt. The reaction is very violent with metals such as potassium and sodium, and quite vigorous with metals such as magnesium and zinc.

**Salts**
When the hydrogen in an acid is replaced by a metal during a chemical reaction, a neutral compound called a salt is formed. For example, when copper reacts with nitric acid, the copper takes the place of the hydrogen to make the salt copper nitrate. Like other metals, copper forms a variety of salts when mixed with different acids. Most salts are crystals, and many are colored. Some salts, such as sodium chloride (table salt), occur naturally.

*Copper turnings*

*Nitric acid*

*Sulfuric acid*

*Hydrochloric acid*

*Copper nitrate*

*Copper sulfate*

*Copper chloride*

## Acid industry

Acids are widely used in industry because they react so readily with other materials. For example, sulfuric acid is used in the production of dyes and pigments, artificial fibers, plastics, soaps, and explosives. The acid is made by mixing sulfur and oxygen together.

**Sulfuric acid chemical plant**

### Acid rain
Burning fossil fuels to produce energy for use at home and in industry releases polluting gases into the air. The gases dissolve in water in the clouds to form nitric acid and sulfuric acid. This water falls as acid rain, which erodes stone buildings and statues, kills trees and aquatic life, and reduces the soil's fertility.

# Bases and alkalis

The acidity of vinegar (ethanoic acid) can be neutralized, or canceled out, by adding chalk (calcium carbonate). Any substance that neutralizes acidity, such as chalk, is called a base. An alkali is a base that dissolves in water. An alkali's strength is measured by the number of hydroxide ions it forms in water. Strong alkalis, such as sodium hydroxide, are just as corrosive as strong acids.

*Chalk and vinegar react together and release carbon dioxide gas.*

*The product of the reaction is a salt called calcium ethanoate.*

*The mixture spills out of the flask.*

*Testing the mixture with universal indicator solution proves that it is now neutral – the acidity has been canceled out.*

# Soaps and detergents

Alkalis are good at dissolving oil and grease, so they are widely used in soaps and detergents. Most dirt is bound to skin, clothes, or eating utensils by grease. The grease makes it difficult to remove the dirt with water alone, because it does not mix with water. A detergent or soap breaks the grease up into tiny drops, allowing the water to wash away any remaining dirt.

*Once the liquid soap has broken down the grease, the water can wet the plate and dissolve the rest of the dirt.*

### Oil slicks
Accidents with oil tankers at sea can create huge oil slicks (spillages) on the water's surface. Strong detergents called dispersants may be used to break up the oil. Wildlife experts use weaker detergents, such as liquid soap, to clean the feathers of oil-coated seabirds. If the birds' feathers – which usually keep them warm and dry – become clogged with oil, the birds may lose their buoyancy and drown, or die of exposure to the cold.

### Batteries
Acids, alkalis, and salts are electrolytes, meaning that they conduct electricity when in solution. Batteries consist of an electrolyte – usually in the form of a moist paste or liquid – between two rods or plates called electrodes. The most common battery is the dry cell, which uses the salt ammonium chloride as an electrolyte. Long-life batteries contain alkaline electrolytes, such as potassium hydroxide; car batteries have electrolytes of sulfuric acid.

*Car battery*

*Long-life battery*

*Dry cell*

# Alkali industry

The main raw material in the alkali industry is brine (saltwater). Sodium hydroxide, which is used to make soap and paper, is produced from brine by electrolysis (passing electricity through it). Brine will also absorb carbon dioxide to make sodium carbonate, which is used in textile treatment, photography, and glassmaking.

*Electrolysis of brine to make sodium hydroxide*

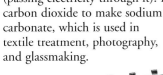

# Neutralizing acids

An alkali and an acid react together to give a neutral salt. In addition, hydroxide ions ($OH^-$) in the alkali combine with the acid's hydrogen ions ($H^+$) to produce water ($H_2O$). In daily life, problems of unwanted acidity are solved by adding an alkali of the appropriate strength.

### Soil acidity
The pH of soil varies from area to area. Few crops grow well in highly acidic soil, because the acid dissolves vital minerals that the plants need for healthy growth and allows them to be washed away. Farmers treat acidic soil by spreading lime (calcium oxide) over their fields. This alkali made from limestone neutralizes the acid in the soil, making it more fertile.

**Farmer liming acidic soil**

### Curing indigestion
The human stomach uses hydrochloric acid to break down food. Some foods cause your stomach to produce so much acid that you feel uncomfortable. The "ache" is cured with antacid tablets, powder, or liquids. Antacids contain weak alkalis that neutralize the acidity, but do not harm your stomach, or react too vigorously with the acid.

*An antacid fizzes as it reacts with lemon juice (citric acid).*

### Bee and wasp stings
A bee sting is painful because it is acidic. Treating the sting with a weak alkali, such as soap or baking soda, relieves the pain by neutralizing the acid. In contrast, a wasp sting is alkaline, so it can be neutralized by a weak acid, such as vinegar or lemon juice.

*Wasp*

*Bee*

## Fritz Haber

In 1908, the German chemist Fritz Haber (1868–1934) developed a process for making the alkali ammonia, which is used to make fertilizers and explosives. The Haber process involves mixing nitrogen from the air with hydrogen at high pressure and temperature. Haber later devised a way of making nitric acid by heating ammonia in air.

## Timeline

**c.600 BC** The Phoenicians use alkaline wood ash to make soap.

**11th century AD** Arab chemists make sulfuric, nitric, and hydrochloric acids.

**1780s** World's first sulfuric acid factory opens in France.

**1865** Ernest Solvay, a Belgian chemist, develops the first commercially successful process for making the alkali, sodium carbonate, on a large scale.

**Sodium carbonate**

**1887** Svante Arrhenius proposes that it is hydrogen ions that give acids their special properties.

**1908** Fritz Haber invents a process for making ammonia.

**1909** The Danish chemist Søren Sørensen (1868–1939) devises the pH scale.

**FIND OUT MORE**    ATOMS AND MOLECULES   BEES AND WASPS   CHEMISTRY   DIGESTION   ELECTRICITY   MIXTURES AND COMPOUNDS   POLLUTION   ROCKETS   SOIL

# ADVERTISING AND MARKETING

A

WHEN A COMPANY WISHES TO SELL or improve the sales of its products or services, it may decide to advertise. Newspapers and magazines carry advertisements, as do billboards, television, and radio. Marketing is the wider process of creating a product or service, advertising it, and selling it. Advertising and marketing are vast industries that affect all our lives.

**Copy line** gives us product information. Here, the tire company Pirelli uses humor and an eye-catching image to advertise its tires' road-holding ability.

CHANEL

## How advertising works

Advertisements use humor and strong images to get our attention. Short, memorable catchphrases called slogans become associated with the product. An advertising campaign often combines posters and television advertisements, so repetition ensures that people remember the product.

*Well-known athlete*

POWER IS NOTHING WITHOUT CONTROL.

*The striking image of an athlete in high heels grabs our attention.*

PIRELLI — *Product name*

### Image
Advertisers try to create a product image that will appeal to particular customers. An advertisement for perfume, for example, may project an image of beauty and sophistication. Well-known personalities may be shown endorsing a product to strengthen its image.

## Marketing

A company's marketing strategy includes market research, product development, publicity, advertising, and point of sale displays. The marketing department researches the products people want and works with other departments to make sure that the products meet consumers' expectations.

### Market research
The purpose of market research is to find out what sort of people are likely to buy a product, and what will make them buy one product rather than a similar product. Researchers get this information from interviews, questionnaires, and government statistics.

### Public relations
Many companies use public relations, or PR, to improve their standing with the people who buy their products. The two main branches of PR are research and communication. Research tries to find out what people think about the company and its products. Companies communicate with people through press coverage, advertising, and sponsorship.

**Pepsi-Cola painted the Concorde blue to gain publicity.**

### Point of sale
Stores use posters and display units to encourage people to buy products. Point of sale displays try to catch the customer's eye where he or she can buy the product immediately. Store window displays aim to draw customers into a store.

OILILY

## Advertising agencies

Companies use advertising agencies to advise them on their advertising strategy. Advertising agencies conduct market research, plan which forms of media the client's advertisements should appear in, and finally prepare the client's advertisements.

*The film is combined with a sound track, and then edited.*

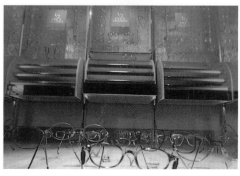

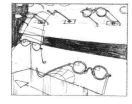

### Storyboards
The first stage of producing a television advertisement is to present a storyboard of ideas to the client, showing how the final advertisement will look. A storyboard looks rather like a comic strip, with a series of pictures showing how the action will run. If the client approves the storyboard, production can go ahead.

### Production
The advertising agency hires a production team to film the advertisement. The team includes a producer, who supervises the rehearsal schedule, and a director, who directs the action when the commercial is being filmed. Once the film has been shot, a sound track is added. The sound track may be a voice-over repeating the product name and a catchy tune called a jingle.

### Advertisement
Once the advertisement has been completed, it is shown to the client. If the client approves the film, it is taken to the television stations to be aired. Television advertising is by far the most expensive form of advertising, but it is the most effective since it reaches people in their own homes.

FIND OUT MORE | DESIGN | FILMS AND FILM-MAKING | MONEY | SHOPS | TELEVISION | TRADE AND INDUSTRY

# AFRICA

THE SECOND LARGEST CONTINENT after Asia, Africa is dominated in the north by the vast Sahara Desert and in the east by the Great Rift Valley. A rain forest lies along the equator, and open grasslands provide grazing for herds of wild animals. Africa is home to many different peoples, each with their own distinctive languages and customs. Islam and Christianity are widespread, but many Africans adhere to their own traditional beliefs.

## Physical features

Most of Africa is a high plateau covered with deserts, lush rain forests, and dry grasslands. Rivers crossing it bring water to dry regions and provide a means of transportation. Although they lie on the equator, the high peaks in the east are snowcapped all year. Africa has several volcanoes.

### Sahara

The world's largest desert, the Sahara covers much of northwestern Africa. It has an area of 3,263,400 sq miles (9,065,000 sq km) and is rapidly expanding as land at its edges is overgrazed. With less than 4 in (100 mm) of rain a year and daytime temperatures of up to 122°F (50°C), only a few specially adapted plants and animals survive here.

### Nile River

The Nile is the world's longest river. From its source in Lake Victoria it flows 4,160 miles (6,695 km) north through Uganda, Sudan, and Egypt to the Mediterranean Sea. Africa's third longest river, the Niger, flows 2,597 miles (4,180 km) in a big loop through western Africa, ending in Nigeria in a delta bigger than that of the Nile.

*Mountains rise from the Great Rift Valley.*

**Nile River at Aswan in Egypt**

### Great Rift Valley

The mountains of Ethiopia are divided by the Great Rift Valley, which stretches 3,750 miles (6,000 km) north from Mozambique through east Africa and the Red Sea into Syria. The valley is formed by massive cracks in the Earth's crust. It is up to 55 miles (90 km) wide, and in millions of years will eventually divide the African continent.

**Simen Mountains, Ethiopia**

### Okavango Delta

Many rivers end in deltas at the sea, but the Okavango River in southern Africa has a delta that forms a swamp in the Kalahari Desert. The Okavango rises in Angola and flows 605 miles (974 km) to Botswana, where its delta and swamps cover more than 8,500 sq miles (22,000 sq km).

## Cross-section through Africa

Africa rises sharply from the Atlantic Ocean to 3,280 ft (1,000 m) before dropping down into the marshes of the Zaire Basin. The Ruwenzori Mountains and Great Rift Valley lie to the east, and the plateau falls gradually to the Indian Ocean.

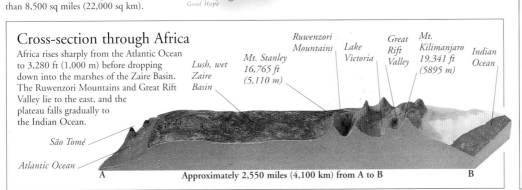

Approximately 2,550 miles (4,100 km) from A to B

### AFRICA FACTS

**AREA** 11,712,434 sq miles (30,335,000 sq km)

**POPULATION** 783,800,000

**NUMBER OF COUNTRIES** 53

**BIGGEST COUNTRY** Sudan

**SMALLEST COUNTRY** Seychelles

**HIGHEST POINT** Kilimanjaro (Tanzania) 19,341 ft (5,895 m)

**LONGEST RIVER** Nile (Uganda/Sudan/Egypt) 4,160 miles (6,695 km)

**BIGGEST LAKE** Lake Victoria (East Africa) 26,590 sq miles (68,880 sq km)

15

# Climatic zones

Although most of Africa is warm or hot all year round, the climate varies greatly because of the wide range of landscapes. Parts of the north coast have hot, dry summers and cooler, damp winters. Desert regions have cold nights, scorching hot days, and almost no rain at all. On the equator the climate is hot and humid, with high rainfall. Mountain regions have warm summers and cool winters.

*Scrubland*  *Desert*  *Grassland*  *Tropical rain forest*  *Wetland*  *Mountain*

## Scrubland

Much of the northern coast of Africa has a warm Mediterranean climate. Coastal cliffs and hills are covered in sparse, low-growing, often fragrant plants and shrubs that are able to thrive in the poor, stony soils. Many of the plants have thorns and small, leathery leaves to prevent them from drying out in the fierce heat of the sun and frequent sea breezes.

Baie de Souhalias, Algeria

*Evergreen plants are able to retain their moisture in the heat.*

*Fantastically shaped dunes are formed by strong desert winds.*

## Deserts

About 40 percent of Africa is desert. The Erg of Bilma in Niger is part of the vast Sahara. In Arabic, *erg* means a sandy expanse. The sand is blown by the wind into ripples and into huge dunes, some of which may be nearly 650 ft (200 m) high. Two other main desert areas are the Kalahari and the Namib, both in southern Africa.

## Savanna

About 40 percent of Africa is covered with savanna, the name given to grassland with scattered trees and shrubs. This type of land forms a wide loop around the Zaire (Congo) basin. Vast herds of grazing animals, such as antelope and zebras, move around the savanna seeking fresh grass to eat.

Masai Mara, Kenya

*Occasional stunted trees offer animals some protection from the harsh sun.*

*Many streams and rivers cross the rain forest.*

## Tropical rain forest

Dense, tropical rain forest covers less than 20 percent of Africa. The most extensive areas lie close to the equator in West Africa and in central Africa's Zaire (Congo) Basin. Thousands of species of trees flourish in the hot, humid climate, which produces rain all year round. However, large-scale felling of trees for timber hardwoods, such as teak and mahogany, threatens to destroy this environment.

Mahogany leaf

*Low shrubs cover some of the mountains' lower slopes and foothills.*

## Mountain

Africa's highest ranges include the Drakensberg, in southeastern Africa, which runs for about 70 miles (1,130 km) through South Africa and Lesotho and forms part of the rim of the great South African Plateau. The highest point is Thabana Ntlenyana at 11,424 ft (3,482 m). Even higher mountain ranges are the Atlas range in Morocco, and the Ruwenzori on the border between Uganda and Congo (Zaire).

## People

One in eight of the world's people lives in Africa, mostly along the north and west coasts and in the fertile river valleys. Although traditionally people live in small villages, a growing number are moving to towns and cities to look for work. Birth rates in many countries are high and families are large. About half the population is under 15 years old.

Ghanaian girls    Tanzanian girl    Egyptian boy

## Resources

Africa has many resources, but they are unevenly distributed among the countries. Libya and Nigeria are leading oil producers, southern Africa is rich in gold and diamonds, and Zambia is a leading copper producer. Tropical forests yield valuable timber but are being felled at an alarming rate. Africa is a leading producer of cocoa beans, cassava, bananas, coffee, and tea.

Oil

Cocoa beans and pod

Diamond

 FIND OUT MORE    AFRICA, HISTORY OF    AFRICAN WILDLIFE    CLIMATE    CONTINENTS    DESERTS    FORESTS    GRASSLAND WILDLIFE    MOUNTAINS AND VALLEYS    OIL    RAIN FOREST WILDLIFE

A

# AFRICA, HISTORY OF

CIVILIZATION IN AFRICA BEGAN TO appear more than 5,000 years ago with the rise of ancient Egypt. From about 2,500 years ago in sub-Saharan Africa, many other kingdoms also developed. The Sahara acted as a barrier to keep this area separate from the rest of the world until the arrival of Arab traders in the 8th century. From the 15th century, the arrival of Europeans, the subsequent slave trade, and European imperialism had a profound effect on the continent. Since the 1950s, all African nations have reclaimed independence, although modern Africa continues to struggle with its postcolonial legacy and with environmental problems.

## Early inhabitants

Humans have inhabited Africa for 4 million years. The Sahara was once a fertile land rich in plants and animals. But thousands of years ago, it dried up, and people moved south to the savanna to farm there.

*Vegetable dye*

*Animals*

**Painted bone**

**Rock paintings**
Rock and bone pictures often depicted everyday events, such as dancing, hunting animals, and fishing. Painters used animal fat colored with vegetable dyes.

### Nok culture
The earliest evidence of Iron Age settlement is called the Nok culture (500 BC–AD 200), which existed in what is now central Nigeria. Nok people lived in farming communities. They produced iron weapons and tools for farming, and also made fine terra-cotta sculptures.

**Terra-cotta head, Nok culture**

## Ancient empires

North Africa was in a good position to trade with western Asia, giving rise to rich empires to develop, including Meroë (modern Sudan, c.600 BC–AD 350) and Aksum (a trading state in northern Ethiopia, c.100 BC–AD 1000). Ghana (in West Africa, c.500–1300) developed for similar reasons.

Meroë
Ghana
Aksum

### Meroe
From the city of Meroë, the Kushites controlled trade in the Red Sea and the Nile River from 600 BC. They exported luxury goods, such as ostrich feathers and leopard skins, and built fine temples and flat-topped pyramids over the graves of their dead.

**Ruined temple, Meroë**

### Ghana
Ghana (located on the borders of modern Mali and Mauritania), one of Africa's most important empires, controlled the trans-Saharan trade in gold. Ghana's kings wore gold jewelry, and gold-embroidered clothes and turbans. Surviving gold artifacts show the incredible wealth of this kingdom.

**Heads of gold,** often of royalty, played an important part in rituals.

*Carving was made of wood and coated with gold.*

*Head weighs 3 lbs (1.5 kg).*

*Figures were attached to royal thrones.*

**Bird ornament**

*Rings were often decorated with flowers.*

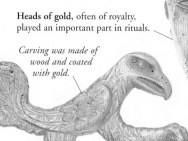

**Finger rings**

**Stela, Aksum**

### Aksum
From c.300, Egyptian scholars introduced Christianity to Aksum, which then became known as a holy city. During this period, Aksum took over the empire based at Meroë. Aksum's people built tall, stone stelae (monuments) to mark the tombs of dead kings.

## Spread of religions

From the 8th century, trade, conquests, and colonialism spread religions such as Islam in Africa. In North Africa, Islam completely replaced traditional religions, which often included the worship of ancestors.

**Festival mask**

### Ancestor worship
In many parts of Africa, communities had sacred shrines where they placed offerings for the spirits of their dead ancestors. Today, during certain annual festivals, members of the community wear special masks, sing, dance, and tell stories in honor of their ancestors.

### Islam
By c.800, Middle Eastern Arabs had taken Islam to North Africa. From the 11th century, trade helped spread Islam across the Sahara into West Africa and up the Nile River into Sudan.

**Ait Benhaddou, Morocco**

### Slave trade
By the 1470s, the Portuguese were trading copper, brass, gold, and slaves with Benin in West Africa. In the 1480s, the Portuguese arrived on the islands of Principe and São Tomé in the Gulf of Guinea, just off the west African coast. They established sugar plantations and forced African captives (mainly kidnapped in Senegal and Gambia) to work as slaves on the plantations. This was the beginning of European domination in Africa.

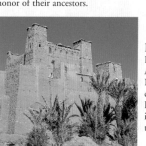

**Plaque showing Portuguese soldier, 1500s**

A

## Colonialism

During the 1800s, Europeans colonized areas in Africa, introducing Christianity and taking economic control. They used African workers to grow or mine precious raw materials, but sent the materials to be manufactured in Europe and America – where profits stayed. During this period, slavery was at its height with Europeans kidnapping Africans to work in the Americas.

### African Diaspora

The slave trade scattered more than 20 million Africans throughout the Americas and Europe, undermining African culture in the process. Over the centuries, the dispersal of these slaves and their descendents became known as the African Diaspora.

African carving of a European

Traditional witch doctors

Voodoo voice disguiser

### Voodoo

In 19th-century Caribbean colonies, traditional ancestor worship combined with Christianity to produce a religion called voodoo.

### Christianity

Europe sent missionaries to Africa to set up schools and churches, and to convert Africans to Christianity. They also tried to abolish African traditional religions by punishing those who still practiced them.

## Scramble for Africa

In 1884, European leaders decided that their countries could claim African territories as colonies when occupied by Europeans. They started scrambling to the interior in search of new lands. By 1902, all of Africa was colonized except Liberia and Ethiopia.

Carving of Queen Victoria

Morocco
Tunisia
Egypt
Algeria
Libya
Liberia
Nigeria
British Somaliland
Sierra Leone
Ethiopia
British East Africa (Kenya)
Angola

French
British
German
Portuguese
Belgium
Spanish
Italian
Anglo-Egyptian

## World Wars I and II

Although both world wars were European, thousands of Africans lost their lives as colonial rulers forced them to join the army. One cause of World War I was German resentment against other European countries during colonization. In World War II, North Africa became a battleground, as German and Italian forces invaded British- and French-ruled territories.

Troops at El Alamein, Egypt

### World War I

When World War I broke out in 1914, the Ottoman Empire controlled North Africa. The Egyptians colluded with the British to overthrow Turkish rule, and they were helped from 1916 to 1918 by the eccentric soldier and author Thomas Edward Lawrence (1888–1935), who became famous as Lawrence of Arabia. After the war, Egypt became a British protectorate but signed a treaty for independence in 1922.

### El Alamein

In 1941, Italian and German forces invaded North African territories held by the British. The British recruited soldiers from their colonies of Nigeria, Ghana, and Sierra Leone to join the fight on their behalf. In 1942, the British defeated the Germans at the historic battle of El Alamein. This battle was a turning point in the war.

Herero and Nama tribes fight German colonialists, Namibia, 1904

## African resistance

Africans strenuously resisted colonialism. The Ethiopians fought to stay independent and won (1896); Zimbabwe and Sudan rebelled against the British (1896 and 1920); tribes in Angola tried to overthrow the Portuguese (1902); in Namibia and Tanzania, thousands were killed in uprisings against the Germans (1904–1908); and in Nigeria, tribes revolted against French rule (1920s).

African Front

### Operation Torch

In 1942, American and British soldiers landed in Morocco and Algeria in an invasion called Operation Torch. Joined by the French, the Allies attacked the German and Italian armies, forcing them into Tunisia. After a bloody battle, Germany's Afrika Korps surrendered. The war on African soil was over by May 1943.

T.E. Lawrence

### Haile Selassie

Emperor Haile Selassie of Ethiopia (r.1930–74) led his troops against the Italian invasion of 1935. The Italians forced the emperor into exile in 1936, but he returned in 1941. Haile Selassie instituted reforms, suppressed slavery, and worked with the Organization of African Unity. In 1974, the army overthrew the emperor, and set up military rule. He died in exile in 1975 aged 84.

Ghanaian
Independence
Day stamps

# Independence

After World War II, many Africans wanted to end colonial rule and govern their own countries. Colonial powers such as France, Portugal, and Britain fought to prevent this, and there were bloody wars of independence in Algeria, Mozambique, Angola, and Zimbabwe. By the late 1960s most African countries had gained independence, but political and economic problems remained.

Returning refugees, Angola

## Gold Coast

One of the first colonies to become independent was the former British colony of the Gold Coast. After World War II, anticolonial feeling had intensified, and, in 1957, the state of Ghana (which was named after a powerful West African medieval empire) became independent. A leading nationalist, Kwame Nkrumah (1909–72), became the new country's first prime minister. In 1960, Nkrumah declared Ghana a republic and himself president for life. He became increasingly dictatorial and distanced his country from the West. In 1966, a police-military coup overthrew Nkrumah.

*OAU member states now number 50.*

OAU
summit, Tunisia

## Organization of African Unity

In 1963, the heads of 30 independent African states met to form the OAU (Organization of African Unity). Its goal was to promote political and economic cooperation between states, and help colonies attain independence.

## Angola War

In 1961, Angola's people rose in revolt against the Portuguese colonial government. The Portuguese army crushed the rebels, who fled into exile in Zaire. While in exile, the rebels formed liberation movements and waged guerrilla warfare in Angola. In 1974, the liberation forces staged a military uprising and overthrew the Portuguese, who finally granted independence in 1975. After independence, a bitter civil war erupted between two political groups, both of whom wanted to govern Angola. One side was backed by South African troops; the other by Russian troops. The Angolan factions agreed to a ceasefire in 1994.

A taxi stand for whites, South Africa, 1967

## Apartheid

By the 1980s, only South Africa was still trying to retain white-minority power. The white government had passed the Apartheid (separateness) Policy in 1948, which classified people according to race. Under apartheid, those classified as black, colored, or Asian had few rights. Apartheid was abolished in 1994.

Electronics technician

Game park, Kenya

# Modern Africa

Mineral-rich Africa has a thriving mining industry. More recently, new African electronics plants specialize in assembling equipment from imported components.

## Tourism

A century ago, East African governments established game reserves and parks to protect wildlife from hunters. Today, tourists pay to stay in the parks and go on safari to see the wild animals. Kenya now makes more money from tourism than from any other source.

## Village cooperatives

Agricultural workers (mainly women) set up village cooperatives to grow food crops, which they sell at the local market, reversing policy that existed under colonial governments. Then, small-scale farmers were forced to grow cash crops (coffee, peanuts, cocoa, and cotton) to sell to large European companies. The farmers could not grow food crops for themselves and had to buy expensive imports, such as rice.

Women's agricultural
cooperative, Niger

*Women are the main agricultural workers.*

*Food crops*

Deforestation, Somalia

## Environmental devastation

In semiarid areas of Africa, such as Somalia, land is gradually turning into desert. Since the 1950s, there has been a fall in the average annual rainfall, and much of the land has become very dry. The people have often overused the land for cash crops, and cut down the trees for firewood.

## Ken Saro-Wiwa

Ken Saro-Wiwa (1941–1995), a human rights campaigner, was hanged along with eight others by Nigeria's military government. His "crime" was to speak out against the pollution of tribal lands by government-backed international oil companies.

## Timeline

**2500 BC** Climatic changes in the Sahara region force people to move southward.

**c.600 BC** Kushite people of Sudan expand and base their capital at Meroë.

**c.AD 320–25** King Ezama of Aksum becomes Christian.

African carving

**500–1300** The kingdom of Ghana controls trans-Saharan trade.

**641** Arabs conquer Egypt and convert it to Islam.

**600s** The empire based at Aksum begins to decline.

**1497** Portuguese explorers land on east coast, after sailing around Africa.

**1900** Most of the Sahara region comes under French colonial rule.

**1940** Italian forces invade North Africa; Germans follow one year later.

**1945** League of Arab States is founded; it includes eight African nations.

**1973–75** Horn of Africa suffers a severe drought.

**1994–95** In Rwanda 800,000 Hutus are massacred by Tutsis; millions flee the country.

FIND OUT MORE   BENIN EMPIRE   GREAT ZIMBABWE   MALI EMPIRE   MANDELA, NELSON   RELIGIONS   SLAVERY   SONGHAI EMPIRE   SOUTH AFRICA, HISTORY OF

# AFRICA, CENTRAL

THE EQUATOR RUNS THROUGH central Africa, affecting not only climate but also peoples' lives. There are ten countries. All were European colonies with a history of a cruel slave trade. Although they were all independent by the end of the 1960s, these countries have experienced mixed success. Cameroon is stable, while Democratic Republic of Congo (Zaire) and the Central African Republic have suffered dictatorships. Most central Africans live by subsistence farming.

## Physical features

The landscape varies according to its distance from the equator. Much of the region is rolling hills and valleys, with craggy mountains in the north and east. The arid Sahara Desert and Sahel cover the extreme north. Farther south is the vast equatorial basin of the Congo River, surrounded by some unspoiled tropical rain forest.

**Dry woodland**
Tropical rain forests give way to woodland, where the climate is much drier. Acacia and baobab trees grow in this region. The baobabs have very thick trunks that can hold water to feed themselves. Some baobabs on Cameroon's central plateau live for 1,000 years.

**Congo River**
One of the longest rivers in the world, the Congo, formerly the Zaire, flows in a great curve for 2,900 miles (4,666 km), crossing the equator twice. It drains an area of about 1,400,000 sq miles (3,630,000 sq km).

**Tibesti**
The dramatic cliffs of the volcanic Tibesti Mountains dominate the border between Chad and Libya in the Sahara Desert. At 11,204 ft (3,415 m) above sea-level, Emi Koussi is the highest peak.

**Equatorial rain forest**
The hot, humid basin of the Congo River is Africa's largest remaining region of tropical rain forest. Competing for light, a wide variety of trees grow tall, forming a protective canopy that teems with plant and animal life.

**Regional climate**
The north of the region, the Sahara and Sahel area, is a broad band of dry, dusty land that is starved of rain. By contrast, in the steamy equatorial forests more than 1.5 in (38 mm) of rain falls every day in places. The south experiences the monsoon season between May and October.

84°F (29°C)   81°F (27°C)

56 in (1,434 mm)

## Ethnic diversity

There are hundreds of different peoples in central Africa, each with their own customs and languages. Large groups include the Kongo and Luba, and there are several pygmy groups, including the Twa, BaKa, and Mbuti, who live in clearings deep in the rain forests. A growing number of people are moving to towns to escape war, drought, or famine, and because larger centers offer more jobs and food.

**Village chief, Brazzaville, Congo**

# Chad

The landlocked republic of Chad is one of the world's poorest countries. Nearly half of the land is desert or lies in the Sahel, where rainfall is erratic. More than half of the people work on farmland near the Chari River in the south, but lack of food is still a problem. Chad has some valuable mineral deposits, but they are unexploited.

### Muslim nomads
More than 100,000 nomadic Muslims live in the desert and northern Sahel regions of Chad. They include the Kanimbo people, who are related to the Arabs and Berbers of North Africa. Every day, Kanimbo women must walk long distances in the heat to fetch water for their families.

### Camels
One of the only ways to cross the vast Sahara desert is by camel. Camels are used as pack animals to transport forest products and minerals from Lake Chad, as well as for farming, pumping water, and carrying people. Herders value their milk, meat, and hides.

*Dried gourds used as bowls for making butter.*

### Fulani
Throughout Africa a nomadic group called the Fulani herd cattle and roam wherever there is grazing land. They drink the cows' milk and use it to make butter and cheese. Bottle-shaped gourds, a type of fruit, are dried and decorated for use as water carriers and bowls.

## CHAD FACTS

| | |
|---|---|
| CAPITAL CITY | N'Djamena |
| AREA | 486,177 sq miles (1,259,200 sq km) |
| POPULATION | 7,700,000 |
| MAIN LANGUAGES | French, Arabic, Sara |
| MAJOR RELIGIONS | Muslim, Christian, traditional beliefs |
| CURRENCY | CFA franc |

A

# Cameroon

On Africa's west coast, Cameroon was once a colony divided between the French and the British. The two parts gained independence in 1961 and became a united country. Despite initial troubles, Cameroon now has one of the most successful economies in Africa, exporting oil, bauxite, and a range of natural products including cocoa, coffee, and rubber. The country has a diverse culture with more than 230 ethnic groups.

### Timber
Like many other African countries, Cameroon sells hardwood logs, including mahogany, ebony, and teak from its rain forests to earn foreign currency. Although the trade represents one tenth of the country's total exports, it poses a serious threat to the future of the forests.

*Dried gourds amplify sounds made by strings.*

### Music
*Makossa* is a popular style of African folk music that originated in Cameroon. It is played on traditional instruments, including this one, known as a *mvet*. It is made using a wooden stick, horsehair strings, and hollowed-out gourds. *Mvet* players are specially trained and highly regarded in the community.

*Several strings are stretched along the stick and plucked to make a range of sounds.*

### Soccer
One of Cameroon's leading amateur sports, soccer is widely enjoyed and people play it whenever they have time. Games draw large crowds of spectators. Cameroon's national soccer team has been acclaimed as one of the best in Africa after displaying its skills in the 1990 World Cup.

## CAMEROON FACTS

| | |
|---|---|
| CAPITAL CITY | Yaoundé |
| AREA | 179,691 sq miles (465,400 sq km) |
| POPULATION | 15,100,000 |
| MAIN LANGUAGES | French, English, Fang, Duala, Fulani |
| MAJOR RELIGIONS | Traditional beliefs, Christian, Muslim |
| CURRENCY | CFA franc |

# Central African Republic

Lying in the very heart of Africa, the Central African Republic, or CAR, has a complicated history. Drought and 13 years of repressive government have made the CAR one of the poorest nations in the world. Only two percent of the people live in the semiarid north, and the majority are clustered in villages in the southern rain forests.

*Bantu woman*

### Cotton
Coffee and cotton together form about 13 percent of the country's exports. Grown on large plantations, all parts of the cotton plant are used. The fiber, known as a boll, is spun into yarn to make fabric. The seed's oil forms the base of many foods; whilst the plant's stalks and leaves are plowed back into the soil to fertilize it.

*After drying in the sun, cotton bolls are sorted by hand.*

*Millet*

### People
Seven major Bantu language groups and many smaller ones make up the population of the CAR. Several thousand hunter-gatherers live in the rain forests in harmony with nature. They survive by eating forest fruits and build their homes from banana leaves.

### Food
The people of the CAR grow nearly all their own food by subsistence farming. Root crops, such as cassava, yams, and vegetables, are cultivated alongside grains, including millet, corn, and sorghum. Fish from the CAR's rivers, including the Chari and Ubangi, is a vital source of protein.

*Cassava*

## CENTRAL AFRICAN REPUBLIC FACTS

| | |
|---|---|
| CAPITAL CITY | Bangui |
| AREA | 240,530 sq miles (622,980 sq km) |
| POPULATION | 3,600,000 |
| MAIN LANGUAGES | French, Sango, Zande, Banda, Sara, Arabic |
| MAJOR RELIGIONS | Traditional beliefs, Christian, Muslim |
| CURRENCY | CFA franc |

# Congo

The Republic of Congo was a French territory until 1960. It is a hot, humid land, and its densely forested north has few inhabitants. Nearly half the country's people are members of the Kongo group; the rest include Batéké, M'Bochi, and Sangha. The mineral and timber industries have made Congo wealthy, but many people are still subsistence farmers, growing barely enough food to survive.

**Coffee beans**

*Each cocoa pod contains about 30 beans for use in chocolate and cosmetics.*

**Cocoa pods**

**Crops**
About 50 percent of the workforce farms, growing cassava, corn, rice, peanuts, and fruit. Much food is imported. The steady export of coffee and cocoa beans has enabled Congo to remain solvent.

*Animal skin is stretched across the drum.*

**Drum**
An essential part of African life, drums are used for signaling as well as for music. Most drums are intricately carved out of a solid piece of wood and can be decorated with different woods and hides. Drums are made in all shapes and sizes – this one is almost as tall as the player.

**Industry**
Oil from the Atlantic Ocean accounts for 90 percent of Congo's exports, contributing largely to the country's wealth. Changing oil prices have caused some economic problems, but Congo's crop exports have remained strong. The felling of forests to export tropical timber is a pressing environmental concern. Huge barges on the Congo and other rivers carry timber goods as far as Brazzaville; from there the Congo Ocean Railway takes them to Pointe-Noire, Congo's only port.

## CONGO FACTS

**CAPITAL CITY** Brazzaville

**AREA** 131,853 sq miles (341,500 sq km)

**POPULATION** 2,900,000

**MAIN LANGUAGES** French, Kongo

**MAJOR RELIGIONS** Christian, traditional beliefs,

**CURRENCY** CFA franc

# Gabon

A palm-fringed sandy coastline 500 miles (800 km) long and lush tropical vegetation dominate Gabon's landscape. The country earns 80 percent of its foreign currency from oil and also sells timber, manganese, and uranium ore. Gabon has the potential to be wealthy, but mismanagement by the government has led to continued poverty.

**Libreville**
The bustling port city of Libreville was founded in 1849 by French naval officers. Meaning "free town" in French, Libreville was a new home for liberated slaves. It is now a modern, growing city and a center of culture, industry, and government. Many citizens are wealthy, but poverty still exists.

## GABON FACTS

**CAPITAL CITY** Libreville

**AREA** 99,486 sq miles (257,670 sq km)

**POPULATION** 1,200,000

**MAIN LANGUAGES** French, Fang

**MAJOR RELIGION** Christian

**CURRENCY** CFA franc

*Woman in Libreville, Gabon's capital*

**People**
Although Gabon is one of Africa's most thinly populated countries, it contains more than 40 different ethnic groups. The indigenous Fang people form the largest group. Once fierce warriors, they now dominate the government. Most Gabonese are Christians, and 90 percent of their children attend primary schools. The Gabonese traditions of dance, song, poetry, and storytelling remain an important social and cultural part of daily life.

*The Trans-Gabon Railway runs from Libreville to Franceville.*

**Trans-Gabon Railway**
Opened in 1986 to transport gold and manganese, the Trans-Gabon Railway has caused much controversy because it cut through rain forest, destroying many valuable and rare trees.

# Equatorial Guinea

Two former Spanish colonies make up the country of Equatorial Guinea, located close to the equator. Río Muni, also called Mbini, is on mainland Africa, and Bioko Island, which has fertile, volcanic soil that is ideal for growing cocoa beans, is situated to the northwest, off the coast of neighboring Cameroon.

**Traditional healing**
Like other Africans, many people in Equatorial Guinea believe that illness is due to the influence of bad spirits. Professional healers use dancing and chants to drive out the evil spirits. They keep a range of animal bones, shells, sticks, and other plant parts in their medicine bags for use in group ceremonies.

**Hippopotamus tooth**

**Cowrie shell**

**Tree root**

**Animal bone**

**Extended families**
Among the people of Equatorial Guinea there is a strong tradition of large, extended families, which cling together and help one another in times of hardship.

## EQUATORIAL GUINEA FACTS

**CAPITAL CITY** Malabo

**AREA** 10,830 sq miles (28,050 sq km)

**POPULATION** 453,000

**MAIN LANGUAGES** Spanish, Bubi, Fang

**MAJOR RELIGION** Christian

**CURRENCY** CFA franc

# Dem. Rep. Congo (Zaire)

Formerly known as Belgian Congo and then as Zaire, this country was renamed Democratic Republic of the Congo in 1997 after the overthrow of the corrupt military government. The country consists of a plateau 3,900 ft (1,200 m) above sea-level, through which the Congo River flows. The land is fertile and rich in minerals, but spendthrift governments and civil war, including conflict with Rwanda in 1996–97, have kept it poor.

*Cowrie shells are sewn on to decorate the mask.*

### Mask
Among the many peoples of Dem. Rep. Congo are the Kuba, a small ethnic group that has lived there for many years. Their chief wears a hunting mask, known as a Mashamboy mask, made of shells, beads, and raffia, to symbolize the power of the Great Spirit.

| DEM. REP. CONGO FACTS | |
|---|---|
| CAPITAL CITY | Kinshasa |
| AREA | 875,520 sq miles (2,267,600 sq km) |
| POPULATION | 51,700,000 |
| MAIN LANGUAGES | French, English, Kiswahili, Lingala |
| MAJOR RELIGIONS | Christian, traditional beliefs |
| CURRENCY | Congolese franc |

**Creole woman selling diamonds**

### Farming
Dem. Rep. Congo has much potentially cultivable land. Sixty percent of the population are subsistence farmers, producing palm oil, coffee, tea, rubber, cotton, fruit, vegetables, and rice. Here, on the border of volcanic Virunga National Park, the land is rich and fertile.

### Mining
Copper ore, cobalt, and diamonds provide 85 percent of national exports. Dem. Rep. Congo rates second in world diamond exports, with most mining activity in the Shaba province.

### River ports
The Congo River and its tributaries give the country 7,000 miles (11,500 km) of navigable waterways. There are many river ports with boatbuilding and repair yards, bright crafts shops, and lively markets that sell cassava, fruits, and fish, and delicacies like monkey and snake meat. Traders take their produce to sell at river markets in dugout canoes made by local craftsmen.

### Ethnic strife
The present country boundaries in central Africa date back to European colonialism, and cut across logical ethnic groupings. In some places there is actual ethnic warfare, for example that between the Hutus and the Tutsis of Rwanda and Burundi. For hundreds of years, Rwanda has been dominated by the Tutsis, who ruled the Hutus. In 1959, the Hutus rebelled, and widespread fighting broke out. In the mid-1990s the violence escalated, resulting in 800,000 Hutu deaths and a massive refugee exodus into other countries.

**Refugee camp, Tanzania**

# Sao Tome and Principe

This tiny country, formed by the main volcanic islands of Sao Tome and Principe and four smaller islands, lies 120 miles (200 km) off the coast of Gabon. Its mountains are covered with forests, and rich soil supports farms that grow cocoa beans and sugarcane. Sea fishing has potential for development.

### Pepper
The pepper plant's small, green berries redden as they ripen. Harvested quickly, the half-ripe berries are cleaned, dried in the sun, ground, and sifted to make ground black pepper.

# Rwanda

One of Africa's most densely populated countries, Rwanda has been made poor by ethnic strife that has forced many thousands of people to flee to Dem. Rep. Congo for safety. Rwanda makes its money by exporting coffee, tea, and tin and tungsten ores. Most of its people just manage to feed themselves.

### Volcanoes Park
The *Parc des volcans* is a scenic reserve dominated by volcanic mountains, two of which are active. The park is the last refuge of the mountain gorillas, which now number around 630.

| RWANDA FACTS | |
|---|---|
| CAPITAL CITY | Kigali |
| AREA | 9,633 sq miles (24,950 sq km) |
| POPULATION | 7,700,000 |
| MAIN LANGUAGES | Kinyarwanda, French, Kiswahili |
| MAJOR RELIGIONS | Christian, Traditional beliefs |
| CURRENCY | Franc |

# Burundi

Like Rwanda, its neighbor, Burundi has been torn by conflict between the Tutsis and the Hutus, which has led to riots and thousands of deaths. Burundi has massive oil and nickel reserves beneath Lake Tanganyika, but lacks the funds to begin extraction. Most people are subsistence farmers.

### Farming
Most farmers grow cassava and corn to feed their families. Some grow coffee, tea, cotton, and bananas for export. Overplanting fertile land is causing soil erosion.

| BURUNDI FACTS | |
|---|---|
| CAPITAL CITY | Bujumbura |
| AREA | 9,903 sq miles (25,650 sq km) |
| POPULATION | 6,700,000 |
| MAIN LANGUAGES | Kirundi, French, Swahili |
| MAJOR RELIGIONS | Christian, Traditional beliefs |
| CURRENCY | Franc |

### Creole culture
Nobody lived on these islands until Portuguese explorers landed in 1470. The Portuguese peopled the islands with slaves from the mainland. Their mixed descendants created a culture called creole, but now only ten percent are creoles because over 4,000 left the country when it became independent.

| SAO TOME AND PRÎNCIPE FACTS | |
|---|---|
| CAPITAL CITY | São Tomé |
| AREA | 371 sq miles (960 sq km) |
| POPULATION | 159,900 |
| MAIN LANGUAGE | Portuguese |
| MAJOR RELIGION | Christian |
| CURRENCY | Dobra |

 FIND OUT MORE — AFRICA, HISTORY OF • EMPIRES • FARMING • FORESTS • MONKEYS AND OTHER PRIMATES • MUSIC • OIL • PORTS AND WATERWAYS • SLAVERY • TRAINS AND RAILROADS

# AFRICA, EAST

ONE OF THE WORLD'S OLDEST civilizations, Egypt, occupies the northeastern corner of East Africa, while Kenya, Tanzania, and Uganda sit farther south. Along the Horn of Africa, a piece of land that juts out into the Indian Ocean, are four of the world's poorest countries – Eritrea, Somalia, Ethiopia, and Djibouti. In recent years, Somalia, Sudan, and Ethiopia have been devastated by drought and war. Most East Africans scrape a living from farming, and some rely on food aid from abroad.

## Physical features
Running through eastern Africa is the Great Rift Valley, a huge gash in the Earth that continues north through the Red Sea. Other features include the Nile, the world's longest river, and Lake Victoria, Africa's largest lake. The varied landscape includes deserts, grassland, mountains, and swamps.

### Nile River
At 4,160 miles (6,695 km) long, the Nile supports the thousands of people who live on its fertile banks. The river flows north from Lake Victoria to the Mediterranean Sea. The Blue Nile Falls is on an important branch of the Nile in Ethiopia.

### Savanna
The southern countries of East Africa contain large areas of savanna, or grassland scattered with acacia and baobab trees. This region is home to much of Africa's wildlife, including antelope, giraffes, and zebras, and their predators, such as lions and hyenas.

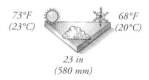

### Kilimanjaro
Africa's highest peak at 19,341 ft (5,895 m), the snowcapped Mount Kibo is one of the Kilimanjaro group of three volcanoes. The group dominates Arusha National Park in Tanzania, on the border with Kenya. Steam and fumes smoking from Kibo's crater indicate that the volcano is not yet extinct, adding to the attraction for mountaineers.

### Regional climate
East Africa's climate is affected by altitude. Dominated by desert, Djibouti and parts of Egypt, Eritrea, Sudan, Ethiopia, and Somalia are plagued by droughts. Southern Sudan and western Ethiopia receive seasonal rainfall, while parts of Tanzania, Kenya, and Uganda are hot and dry; their highlands are wet.

73°F (23°C)    68°F (20°C)
23 in (580 mm)

### Map labels

A, B, C, D, E, F, G, H — 1, 2, 3, 4, 5, 6, 7, 8, 9, 10, 11, 12

Mediterranean Sea
Alexandria, Matrûh, Nile Delta, ISRAEL, Port Said, Isma'iliya, JORDAN
Monkhafad el Qattâra, Tanta, CAIRO, El Gîza, Suez, Helwân, Beni Suef
El Minya, Hurghada
EGYPT, Asyût, Sohâg, Qena, Luxor
Tropic of Cancer, El Khârga, Isna, Idfu, Aswân, Buheiret Nâsir
LIBYA, Libyan Desert, Wadi Halfa
Nubian Desert, Port Sudan, Dongola, Nile, Atbara, Red Sea
CHAD, SUDAN, Khartoum North, Karora, ERITREA
Omdurman, KHARTOUM, Kassala, Massawa, ASMARA
Geneina, El Fasher, Wad Medani, Gedaref, Teseney, Himora, Ed
Darfur, El Obeid, Singa, Mek'ele, Aseb
Nyala, Dilling, Blue Nile, Gonder, Desê, DJIBOUTI, Gulf of Aden
Kadugli, Bahir Dar, DJIBOUTI, Berbera, Boosaaso
Malakal, Kurmuk, Bure, Ethiopian, ADDIS ABABA, Hargeysa
Sudd, White Nile, Debre Zeyit, Nazret, Dirê Dawa, Garoowe
CENTRAL AFRICAN REPUBLIC, Wau, Gore, Jima, Highlands, Oganden, Gaalkacyo
Rumbek, Jonglei Canal, ETHIOPIA, Dila, SOMALIA
Yambio, Juba, Elemi Triangle, Negêlê, Shebeli, Beledweyne
Arua, Gulu, Lokitaung, Lake Rudolph, Moyale, Baydhabo, Wanlaweyn
Lake Albert, Lira, KENYA, Buurhakaba, Marka, MOGADISHU
DEM. REP. CONGO (ZAIRE), Masindi, Mbale, Eldoret, Meru, Jamaame, INDIAN OCEAN
KAMPALA, UGANDA, Entebbe, Nakuru, Nyeri, Garissa, Kismaayo
Equator, Lake Edward, Kabale, Lake Victoria, Kisumu, NAIROBI, Machakos
RWANDA, Mwanza, Arusha, Moshi, Malindi
BURUNDI, Shinyanga, Mombasa
Kigoma, Tabora, Tanga, Zanzibar
Lake Tanganyika, TANZANIA, DODOMA, Morogoro, Dar es Salaam
Sumbawanga, Iringa, Mbeya
0 km 400, 0 miles 400, Lake Nyasa, Lindi
Songea, Mtwara
Great Rift Valley, ZAMBIA, MALAWI, MOZAMBIQUE

### Nomadic herding
Many of the original people of East Africa, particularly the Dinka of Sudan, are nomads, who move from place to place with their herds of cattle in search of water and grazing land. However, competition for land is forcing many nomads to seek alternative lifestyles. Some men now take occasional work in cities or on construction sites.

Dinka cattle camp, Sudan

# Egypt

 Today, as throughout its 5,000-year history, Egypt depends on the Nile River for much of its water, food, transportation, and energy, now generated at the massive Aswan Dam. Egypt controls the Suez Canal, a vital shipping route that links Africa, Europe, and Asia, and brings money into the country. About 99 percent of Egypt's people live along the lush, fertile banks of the river, and most are farmers, although the oil industry and tourist trade provide a growing number of jobs.

*Water is drawn up to feed pipes that lead into the fields.*

## People
Several ethnic groups live in Egypt. Most people speak Arabic, but there are Berber and Nubian minorities. Women who live in the cities are among the most liberated in the Arab world, but, in rural families, men go to market and organize the planting and harvesting, while women cook and fetch water for the family.

## EGYPT FACTS

**CAPITAL CITY** Cairo

**AREA** 384,343 sq miles (995,450 sq km)

**POPULATION** 68,500,000

**DENSITY** 154 per sq mile (60 people per sq km)

**MAIN LANGUAGE** Arabic

**MAJOR RELIGION** Muslim

**CURRENCY** Egyptian pound

**LIFE EXPECTANCY** 67 years

**PEOPLE PER DOCTOR** 625

**GOVERNMENT** Multiparty democracy

**ADULT LITERACY** 55%

A

## Farming
Egypt is one of the world's leading producers of dates, which are mostly grown in oases, along with melons. While some farmers use modern methods, many *fellahin*, or peasant farmers, use centuries-old techniques such as this one, where the donkey drives a wheel that scoops up water for irrigation.

## Food
Reputed to be as old as the Pyramids, the traditional Egyptian dish of *ful medames* is made by boiling broad beans with garlic, onion, olive oil, and spices. The beans are served with hard-boiled eggs, lemon, and unleavened bread. Food is often accompanied by sweet tea and coffee.

Ful medames

## Tourism
Millions of people flock to Egypt every year to see the Pyramids and other remains of the country's ancient past, such as the tombs in the Valleys of the Kings and Queens, and the temples at Karnak and Luxor. The oldest pyramid is the Step Pyramid at Saqqara, which was built about 2650 BC as a tomb for King Zoser.

*Soft dusters on poles are used to clean the delicate sandstone.*

**Ramesses II statue, Temple of Luxor**

Cotton plant

## Cairo
Egypt's ancient capital is the largest city in Africa, with a population of more than 6,000,000. It has at least 1,000 mosques, some built with stone looted from the Pyramids. Old Cairo's narrow streets heave with bustling bazaars, while the wealthy west bank has modern casinos and hotels.

**The Sultan Hassan Mosque and surrounding area**

## Suez Canal
More than 20,000 cargo ships sail through the Suez Canal each year. The canal, built by French engineers in 1869, is 118 miles (190 km) long and provides a shortcut for ships between the Gulf of Suez and the Mediterranean Sea.

## Cotton
Although only five percent of Egypt's land can be farmed, the country is a leading producer of cotton. Quality cloths are sold abroad or made into tunics, or *jelebas*, worn by locals.

Cotton boll

# Sudan

Sudan is the largest country in Africa, measuring 1,274 miles (2,050 km) long from north to south. Desert in the north gives way to a central, grassy plain. Marshland covers much of the south. Two branches of the Nile (the White Nile and the Blue Nile) meet at the capital, Khartoum, providing fertile soil for farming. The country has good oil and mineral resources, but war and drought have weakened it.

## People
There are more than 500 Sudanese ethnic groups, speaking about 100 languages and dialects. Some are nomadic herders, many of whom have now settled on farms. Most own their own plot, and live in villages of mud huts along the Nile, where farming is combined with fishing. The produce is sold at markets. Civil war and famine in the south of Sudan have created refugees.

## SUDAN FACTS

**CAPITAL CITY** Khartoum

**AREA** 917,374 sq miles (2,376,000 sq km)

**POPULATION** 29,500,000

**MAIN LANGUAGE** Arabic

**MAJOR RELIGIONS** Muslim, traditional beliefs, Christian

**CURRENCY** Sudanese pound or dinar

## Religious conflict
The ruling people of the north are Arab Muslims, and the tall minarets of their beautiful mosques dominate the landscape. Farther south, the majority are divided into many ethnic groups and follow Christianity or traditional African religions. The religious, cultural, and language differences between north and south have caused bitter fighting.

# Eritrea

A small, hot country on the Horn of Africa, Eritrea won independence from Ethiopia in 1993 after a 30-year war with Ethiopian troops that has left a legacy of destruction. Vast, but as yet unexploited, copper resources around the rugged mountains have potential for development. Eritrea's strategic Red Sea coastal position gives it access to the sea's oil fields, rich fishing grounds, and useful trade routes.

## ERITREA FACTS

**CAPITAL CITY** Asmara

**AREA** 45,405 sq miles (117,680 sq km)

**POPULATION** 3,920,00

**MAIN LANGUAGES** Tigrinya, Arabic

**MAJOR RELIGIONS** Christian, Muslim

**CURRENCY** Nakfa

### Subsistence farming
More than 80 percent of Eritreans live by subsistence farming, many of them as nomadic herders. Farmers depend on September rains to create seasonal rivers that water the harvest, but recurring droughts have meant that Eritrea has been forced to rely on food aid from overseas.

### People
The long war of independence developed a strong sense of nationalism among the people, although they belong to several ethnic groups speaking different languages. Women, 30,000 of whom fought in the war, many at leadership level, have been pressing the government for equal rights in the country's new political constitution.

# Somalia

An arid, flat country bordering the Indian Ocean, Somalia has some of the longest beaches in the world. The country gained independence in 1960, but since the late 1980s there has been no effective government and the south has been in the grip of civil war waged by wealthy rival warlords. Most people are poor, and live in coastal towns in the north and in the south near rivers.

## SOMALIA FACTS

**CAPITAL CITY** Mogadishu

**AREA** 242,216 sq miles (627,340 sq km)

**POPULATION** 10,100,000

**MAIN LANGUAGES** Somali, Arabic

**MAJOR RELIGION** Muslim

**CURRENCY** Shilling

### Mogadishu
Conveniently situated on Somalia's coastline, Mogadishu has long been an important port. Arabs founded the capital more than 1,000 years ago and sold it to the Italians in 1905. In 1960, it was returned to Somalia. The city's buildings are a mixture of older Arab architecture and 20th-century Italian design, but many have been damaged by war.

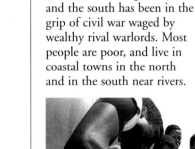

### Civil war
Traditionally, the Somalis were organized in clans, or loyal family groups that were controlled by elder members. The government destroyed the clan system in the 1980s, provoking bitter wars. Many people are now dependent on overseas aid.

# Ethiopia

The Great Rift Valley, a high plateau, and an arid desert dominate Ethiopia. The country has suffered famine, drought, and civil war, but farming reforms and good seasonal rains have enabled Ethiopians to depend less on aid from abroad. Four-fifths of the population makes a living through farming. Traditions such as storytelling, music, and dance are an important part of everyday life.

### Food
Spicy foods are standard in Ethiopia. A hot sauce known as *wat* is served with beef or chicken and mopped up with bread. Usually, a soft, flat bread called *enjera* is eaten, which is made from teff, a field crop grown mainly in Ethiopia. A wide range of fish is available to those with money. Ethiopian *kaffa*, coffee flavored with rye, is known as "health of Adam."

## ETHIOPIA FACTS

**CAPITAL CITY** Addis-Ababa

**AREA** 428,571 sq miles (1,110,000 sq km)

**POPULATION** 62,600,000

**MAIN LANGUAGE** Amharic

**MAJOR RELIGIONS** Muslim, Christian, traditional beliefs

**CURRENCY** Birr

*Vegetable dish made from cabbage, carrots, garlic, and red lentils*

*Hard-boiled egg*

*Chicken stew with egg and red peppers*

*Enjera*

*A stew of beef, cinnamon, peppers, red chili, and tomatoes*

*Red onions, chilies, garlic, and ginger make* wat, *a spicy sauce.*

### Orthodox church
The Ethiopian Orthodox Church is the chief Christian faith in the country. The pilgrimage center of Lalibela, in Ethiopia's central highlands, is known for its Christian churches, which date from the 10th century. *Timkat*, a yearly festival, is celebrated by Christians throughout Ethiopia.

**Orthodox priests**

# Djibouti

A desert country on the Gulf of Aden, Djibouti serves as a port for Ethiopia. The two ethnic groups, the Afars and Issas, have a tradition of nomadic herding, but now half of them live in settled homes in the capital, Djibouti.

## DJIBOUTI FACTS

**CAPITAL CITY** Djibouti

**AREA** 8,958 sq miles (23,200 sq km)

**POPULATION** 638,000

**MAIN LANGUAGES** Arabic, French

**MAJOR RELIGIONS** Muslim, Christian

**CURRENCY** Franc

### Shipping and fishing
The 19th-century city of Djibouti is one of the key Red Sea ports in the area and generates much of the country's income. The fishing industry thrives on its rich waters.

# Kenya

Lying on the equator, Kenya has a varied landscape. The arid north is hot, but there is a rich farming region along the coast, and the south western highlands are warm and wet. The country has a stable, prosperous economy based on agriculture. More than 90 percent of the Kenyan people are under the age of 45 and belong to about 70 ethnic groups. Kenya is noted for its wildlife and its spectacular national parks.

### Nairobi
Founded by British colonists as a railroad town in 1899, Nairobi is Kenya's capital and a center of business and communications. Home to 2,564,500 people, the city's high-rise buildings contrast with the surrounding plains where elephants and lions roam.

### Tourism
National parks are the main attraction for the thousands of tourists who visit Kenya every year. Ten percent of all Kenya is designated parkland, and there are more than 40 major national reserves. Amboseli, where many African animals (including lions, antelope, and leopards) live, enjoys a spectacular view of Kilimanjaro.

Coffee beans

Tea leaves

Green beans

### Crops
About 85 percent of the population works on the land. Kenya is the world's fourth largest producer of tea, which, together with coffee, is grown on plantations. Kenya leads the world in the export of pyrethrum, a pink flower that is dried to make insecticides.

# Uganda

Independence from Britain in 1962 led to ethnic conflict and poverty in Uganda, but since 1986, when peace was restored, the economy has been recovering slowly. Agriculture is still the main activity, with coffee, cotton, and cane sugar the main exports. Uganda also has good mineral deposits, including copper, gold, and cobalt. Most Ugandans live in rural villages.

Sweet potatoes

Market in Kampala

### Farming
About 80 percent of the workforce farms 43 percent of the land. Most people own small farms, producing enough cassava, corn, millet, and sweet potatoes for themselves and to trade at market.

### Kampala
Uganda's capital, Kampala, stands on hills overlooking Lake Victoria. The ancient palace of the former Buganda kings stands alongside the modern Makerere University. The 953,400 people of Kampala experience violent thunderstorms on an average of 242 days a year, and rain nearly every day.

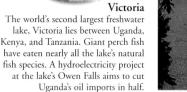

### Lake Victoria
The world's second largest freshwater lake, Victoria lies between Uganda, Kenya, and Tanzania. Giant perch fish have eaten nearly all the lake's natural fish species. A hydroelectricity project at the lake's Owen Falls aims to cut Uganda's oil imports in half.

# Tanzania

The islands of Zanzibar united with mainland Tanganyika in 1964, creating Tanzania. More than half the country is covered by forests, and it has a long Indian Ocean coastline. Dar es Salaam, the largest city and chief port, was until recently the capital. Farming is the main activity, but oil, diamonds, and gas have been discovered.

### Cotton
Tea, tobacco, and cotton account for two-thirds of Tanzania's exports. Most cotton is produced on government-operated farms in the north and south highlands and around Lake Victoria. Workers carry the cotton to the factory to be spun and woven into cloth.

### People
The 120 ethnic groups of Tanzania live together in harmony, as no single group is dominant. More than two thirds of the people live in small, scattered villages, but the state *Ujamaa* policy has tried to resettle them into larger communities to provide more facilities.

Sisal bags

### Zanzibar
The island of Zanzibar and its small companion island of Pemba lie off the east coast of Tanzania. Zanzibar is one of the world's leading producers of cloves and sisal, a plant grown for making rope and bags for export.

FIND OUT MORE

AFRICA, HISTORY OF    CHRISTIANITY    DAMS    EGYPT, ANCIENT    EMPIRES    FARMING    ISLAM    PORTS AND WATERWAYS    RIVERS    WARFARE

# AFRICA, NORTHWESTERN

MOROCCO, ALGERIA, TUNISIA, and Libya, plus the disputed territory of Western Sahara, make up the northwestern corner of Africa. The region has been dominated by Arabs and their religion, Islam, for more than 1,300 years. Algeria and Libya are huge countries, but much of the land is desert. However, they and Tunisia have abundant reserves of oil and natural gas. Farming, made possible by irrigation projects, is still important in the region. Many people lead nomadic lives roaming the land with their herds of animals.

**Mediterranean coast**
Once occupied by the Phoenicians, Greeks, and Romans, northwestern Africa's Mediterranean coast has many ancient ruins that are particularly popular with tourists in Morocco, Algeria, and Tunisia. Most people live on the coastal plain, which has fertile land and a warm climate.

## Physical features

Along the Mediterranean and Atlantic coasts is a fertile strip where most of the people live. The Atlas Mountain chain runs across Morocco and continues as rolling hills in Algeria and Tunisia. The rest of the land is desert, broken by oases and bleak mountain ranges.

**Atlas Mountains**
The Atlas Mountains consist of several chains of mountains that stretch 1,500 miles (2,410 km) from the Atlantic coast of Morocco to Cape Bon in eastern Tunisia. The highest peak is Djebel Toubkal at 13,665 ft (4,167 m), which lies in the High Atlas range in southern Morocco.

**Sahara**
The Sahara Desert covers about 3,500,016 sq miles (9,263,400 sq km). Only about one-fifth is sand. The rest includes vast, flat expanses of barren rock and gravel and mountains such as Algeria's Ahaggar range, peaking at 9,573 ft (2,918 m). Crops are grown in 90 large oases.

77°F (25°C)    -53°F (12°C)

17 in (434 mm)

**Regional climate**
Along most of the coast and on high ground, summers are hot and dry and winters are warm and wet. Daytime desert temperatures average about 100°F (38°C); at night they are low. Desert rainfall may be as little as 1 in (2.5 cm) a year, and irregular.

### Berbers

The original people of northwestern Africa are the Berbers. Today, about 15,000,000 Berbers still live in the mountains and deserts of the region. Most are Muslim, but retain their own language and dialects. The Tuareg are a group of nomadic Berber herders who roam the North African desert.

**Berber man and child**

[Map of Northwestern Africa with grid reference numbers 1–7 and letters A–L]

1 — Ceuta (Spain), ALGIERS, Blida, Annaba, Béjaïa, Constantine, Bizerte, TUNIS, Tanger, Melilla (Spain), Oran, Tiaret, Sétif, Kairouan, Monastir, Mediterranean Sea, Tétouan (Spain), Tlemcen, Sidi Bel Abbès, Biskra, Gafsa, Sfax

2 — Kénitra, RABAT, Fès, Oujda, Laghouat, Tozeur, Gabès, Médenine, Az Zāwiyah, Al Baydā', Darnah, Casablanca, Meknes, TUNISIA, Gharyan, TRIPOLI, Banghāzī, Al Marj, Tubruq, Khouribga, Ben Mellal, Figuig, Touggourt, Al Khums, Misrātah, Safi

3 — ATLANTIC OCEAN, Ghardaïa, Ouargla, Yafran, Surt, Gulf of Sirte, Ajdābiyā, Al Jaghbūb, Marrakech, Béchar, Grand Erg Occidental, Agadir, MOROCCO, Canary Islands (Spain), La Palma, Lanzarote

4 — Tenerife, Fuerteventura, Gran Canaria, Tan-Tan, Hamada du Dra, Grand Erg Oriental, Ghadāmis, Birāk, Libyan Desert, Great Sand Sea, LAÂYOUNE, Tindouf

5 — WESTERN SAHARA (occupied by Morocco), Smara, Erg Chech, Reggane, In Salah, Awbāri, Sabhā, Ayn ath Tha'lab, Murzuq, Ghāt, LIBYA, Al Kufrah, Ad Dakhla, Tropic of Cancer, Tassili-n-Ajjer, Fazzān, Sahara

6 — Lagouira, MAURITANIA, MALI, Ahaggar, Tamanrasset, NIGER, Tibesti, CHAD, SUDAN, EGYPT

7 — 0 km 400, 0 miles 400

# Morocco

 A mix of African, Islamic, Arab, Berber, and European influences, Morocco attracts more than four million tourists each year. The country's strengths are farming and phosphate mining. Founded in Fès, in AD 859, Karueein University is the oldest in the world.

## MOROCCO FACTS

| | |
|---|---|
| CAPITAL CITY | Rabat |
| AREA | 172,316 sq miles (446,300 sq km) |
| POPULATION | 28,400,000 |
| MAIN LANGUAGES | Arabic, Berber, French |
| MAJOR RELIGION | Muslim |
| CURRENCY | Moroccan dirham |

### Mint tea

The traditional drink in Morocco is a refreshing mint tea, served in glasses or pots, with plenty of sugar and a sprig of mint. It is often offered free of charge in the *souks* (markets) when bargaining is about to begin.

### Carpets

Hand-knotted wool carpets are one of Morocco's great craft industries. The leading carpet factories are in Fès and Rabat. The carpets have bold colors and symbolic, abstract Islamic patterns. Though sold by men, most rugs are made by women.

Polisario soldiers keep watch.

### Western Sahara

Morocco has occupied the ex-Spanish colony of Western Sahara since 1975. Polisario Front guerrillas began fighting for independence in 1983, to resist mass settlement of the area by Moroccans keen to hold on to the phosphate-rich territory.

# Tunisia

 A former French colony, Tunisia is the smallest country in the region and one of the more liberal Arab states. Although not admitted into politics, Tunisian women make up 31 percent of the workforce. Tourism is being developed.

*Couscous is steamed in a special pot that sits above the stewing meat.*

## TUNISIA FACTS

| | |
|---|---|
| CAPITAL CITY | Tunis |
| AREA | 59,984 sq miles (155,360 sq km) |
| POPULATION | 9,600,000 |
| MAIN LANGUAGES | Arabic, French |
| MAJOR RELIGION | Muslim |
| CURRENCY | Tunisian dinar |

### Couscous

The staple food in Tunisia is granules of semolina called couscous. Originally a Berber dish, couscous is served with a meat or vegetable sauce. Tunisians like their food spicy. After the main course, dates stuffed with almond paste, or sweet pastries filled with honey and nuts are served.

### Souk

A feature of Tunisian cities – and indeed all northwestern African cities – is the *souk*, or market. This is traditionally a tangle of narrow streets flanked by open stalls where people can buy anything from food to carpets or handmade jewelry.

# Algeria

Under French rule from 1830, Algeria won independence in 1962. The country has a high birth rate and a young population: 86 percent is below the age of 44. Crude oil and natural gas are an important source of income. Increasingly, fundamentalist Islamic groups pose a threat to non-Muslims.

## ALGERIA FACTS

| | |
|---|---|
| CAPITAL CITY | Algiers |
| AREA | 919,590 sq miles (2,381,740 sq km) |
| POPULATION | 31,500,000 |
| MAIN LANGUAGES | Arabic, Berber, French |
| MAJOR RELIGION | Muslim |
| CURRENCY | Algerian dinar |

### Overpopulation

Since more than four-fifths of Algeria is desert, 90 per cent of Algerians live in the far north of the country, where it is cooler. However, as Algeria's population continues to increase at a rate of more than 1.7 percent a year, many northern towns, like Constantine, are struggling to house everybody, and slum areas are growing.

*Houses are built on every available piece of land.*

Black dates

Yellow dates

### Dates

Algeria is the world's sixth largest producer of dates. They are grown in the fertile north as well as in the many oases of the Sahara and provide a main source of income. Date palms also yield timber; their leaves are used to thatch buildings.

# Libya

Since 95 percent of Libya is desert, the Great Man-made River Project was set up to irrigate farming land. Water is piped from beneath the Sahara to populated coastal regions.

## LIBYA FACTS

| | |
|---|---|
| CAPITAL CITY | Tripoli |
| AREA | 679, 358 sq miles (1,759,540 sq km) |
| POPULATION | 5,600,000 |
| MAIN LANGUAGES | Arabic, Tuareg |
| MAJOR RELIGION | Muslim |
| CURRENCY | Libyan dinar |

### Oil and gas

The discovery of oil and natural gas in 1959 transformed Libya into a wealthy nation, and many people moved to the towns in search of work. In 1992, trade with the West was severely disrupted when the UN imposed sanctions because of leader Colonel Gaddafi's alleged links with international terrorist groups.

Oil workers at Calanscio

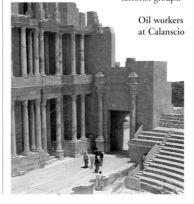

### Roman ruins

Libya was abandoned by the Romans after the Arab conquest of AD 643 and was an Italian colony between 1911 and 1951. Today, some of the finest Roman ruins outside Italy can be seen at Leptis Magna, now called Labdah, to the east of the capital, Tripoli.

FIND OUT MORE    AFRICA, HISTORY OF    DESERTS    EMPIRES    FARMING    ISLAM    ISLAMIC EMPIRE    MOUNTAINS AND VALLEYS    OIL    ROMAN EMPIRE    TEXTILES AND WEAVING

A

# AFRICA, SOUTHERN CENTRAL

SOUTHERN CENTRAL AFRICA is made up of seven countries that form part of the African mainland, and the islands of Madagascar and Comoros in the Indian Ocean. Farming is still an important source of income in these countries, but major deposits of minerals such as diamonds, copper, uranium, and iron have led many people to move to the towns and cities in search of work. Different tribal groups, each with its own language, customs, and beliefs, live in the southern central region.

### Namib Desert
The Namib Desert extends for 1,100 miles (1,900 km) in a narrow strip from southwestern Angola, along the Skeleton Coast of Namibia, and down to the South African border. Although it rarely rains, the climate on the coast is humid with cold, morning fogs. Sand dunes reach down to the edge of the Atlantic and the only practical transportation is the camel.

## Physical features
Although lowlands fringe the coast, most of the region lies 1,200–4,500 ft (400 m–1,500 m) above sea level. The landscape includes the Namib and Kalahari deserts in the west and center, dry savanna, and humid, subtropical forests in the north.

Acacia trees, Madagascar

### Savanna
Much of the region is covered by grassland, or savanna. The most common trees in these areas are thorn trees, especially acacias. They are suited to the dry conditions and grow on the edges of the Kalahari and other semidesert regions.

### Regional climate
Most of the region lies in the tropics, where the climate is always hot, but there are two seasons: wet and dry. Rain is heavy in the wet season. Most of Botswana and Namibia has a semiarid climate, and much of Namibia is desert. Eastern Madagascar has a tropical wet climate.

74°F (23°C)   61°F (16°C)

38 in (964 mm)

### Women's role
The traditional role of African women was to look after the home and bring up the children. Many were also expected to cultivate the crops, and some built their own houses. Today, many women in southern central Africa have additional responsibilities, because their husbands are away working in mines and cities. Despite the domestic power of women, few have official jobs or own property.

Zimbabwean woman with her baby

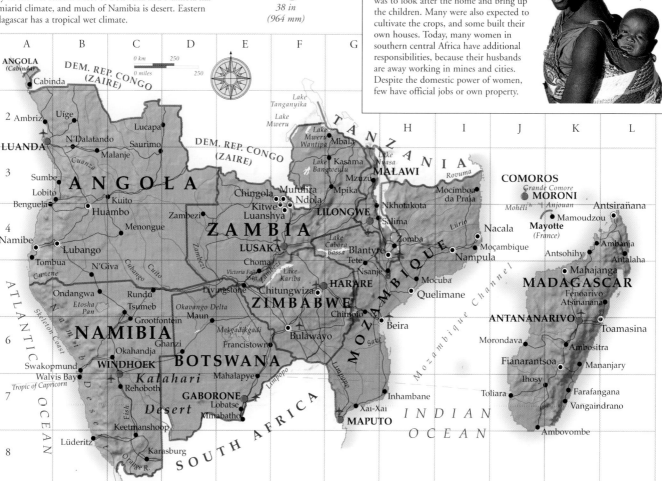

# Angola

In 1975, after a long war, Angola became independent of Portuguese colonial rule. With fertile land and huge reserves of diamonds, oil, and natural gas, the country should have become prosperous. However, the fighting that continued after independence as a civil war between rival ethnic groups tore Angola apart and limited economic development. A truce began in 1996.

### ANGOLA FACTS

**CAPITAL CITY** Luanda

**AREA** 481,351 sq miles (1,246,700 sq km)

**POPULATION** 12,900,000

**MAIN LANGUAGE** Portuguese

**MAJOR RELIGIONS** Christian, traditional beliefs

**CURRENCY** Readjusted kwanza

**Oil and diamonds**
Most of Angola's oil is produced in Cabinda, a tiny Angolan enclave in Democratic Republic of Congo. Petroleum provides 90 percent of Angola's exports. Angola also ranks highly in world output of diamonds.

**Luanda**
Founded by the Portuguese in 1575, Angola's capital and largest city is home for about a million people. Once used for shipping slaves to Brazil, it is still a major seaport. Modern Luanda is an industrial center with its own oil refinery.

# Zambia

Bordered to the south by the Zambezi River, Zambia is a country of upland plateaus, 80 percent of which are grassland and forest. About 50 percent of the people live by subsistence farming, constantly threatened by drought. Tobacco is the main exported crop. Hydroelectric power provides much of Zambia's energy. Low copper prices in the 1980s upset finances.

### ZAMBIA FACTS

**CAPITAL CITY** Lusaka

**AREA** 285,992 sq miles (740,720 sq km)

**POPULATION** 9,200,000

**MAIN LANGUAGES** English, Bemba, Tonga, Nyanja, Lozi, Lunda

**MAJOR RELIGIONS** Christian, traditional beliefs

**CURRENCY** Zambian kwacha

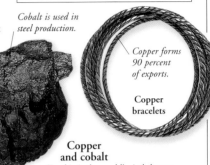

*Cobalt is used in steel production.*

*Copper forms 90 percent of exports.*

**Copper bracelets**

**Copper and cobalt**
Zambia is the world's sixth largest producer of copper. The seam of copper ore where the metal is mined, the Copperbelt, is 200 miles (320 km) long. The second largest producer of cobalt, Zambia also mines lead, silver, and zinc.

**Urban living**
About half of Zambia's people, a mix of more than 70 different ethnic groups, live in towns and cities. The most populated area is the Copperbelt, where most of them work. The capital, Lusaka, a thriving industrial and business center, is home to one in 12 Zambians.

# Namibia

An ex-German colony, and ruled for 70 years by South Africa, Namibia won its independence in 1990. Rich mineral resources make mining the country's leading industry. One in seven people lives on the land, mainly rearing livestock, although drought and the expanding desert make farming difficult. Fishing is good off the Atlantic coast.

### NAMIBIA FACTS

**CAPITAL CITY** Windhoek

**AREA** 317,260 sq miles (823,290 sq km)

**POPULATION** 1,739,000

**MAIN LANGUAGES** English, Afrikaans, Ovambo, Kavango

**MAJOR RELIGION** Christian

**CURRENCY** Namibian dollar

*Himba woman*

**Uranium**
The Rössing Uranium Mine in the Namib Desert is the world's largest, producing 2,200 tons (2,000 tonnes) of uranium every year. Namibia is the world's fifth largest producer of uranium and one of the largest producers of diamonds.

**People**
Namibia has a peaceful multiracial society. The white minority lives mostly in Windhoek, in European-style houses. Black Namibians include many groups, the largest of which are the northern Ovambo. To the west the seminomadic Himba raise cattle.

*Hair is braided and beaded.*

# Botswana

Southwestern Botswana is covered by the Kalahari Desert. To the north is the marshy delta of the Okavango River, a haven for wildlife. Despite this wetland, however, Botswana suffers droughts. Most people live in the more fertile east. Botswana is the world's third largest producer of diamonds.

### BOTSWANA FACTS

**CAPITAL CITY** Gaborone

**AREA** 218,814 sq miles (566,730 sq km)

**POPULATION** 1,600,000

**MAIN LANGUAGES** English, Tswana, Shona, Khoikhoi, Ndebele

**MAJOR RELIGIONS** Traditional beliefs, Christian

**CURRENCY** Pula

*Beef stew with dried spinach*    *Savory porridge*

**San**
The original inhabitants of Botswana are the nomadic San people, once known as Kalahari Bushmen, one of Africa's only remaining groups of hunter-gatherers. There are fewer than 50,000 San today, but small groups still roam the Kalahari Desert hunting small animals and eating edible plants and insects. Many San now work on cattle ranches.

**Food**
The Tswana people, who make up the majority of Botswana's population, live mostly by subsistence farming, raising cattle, and growing enough corn, sorghum, and millet for their own use. Their staple diet consists of meat stews served with a kind of porridge made from grain. Fresh vegetables are rare.

# Zimbabwe

In 1980, the former British colony of Rhodesia became independent and took the name Zimbabwe, after the ancient city of Great Zimbabwe. About 70 percent of Zimbabweans live from farming. Coal, gold, asbestos, and nickel are mined for export. Zimbabwe has recently suffered great disruption over the issues of government and land re-distribution.

## ZIMBABWE FACTS

| | |
|---|---|
| CAPITAL CITY | Harare |
| AREA | 150,293 sq miles (390,580 sq km) |
| POPULATION | 11,700,000 |
| MAIN LANGUAGES | English, Shona, Ndebele |
| MAJOR RELIGIONS | Traditional beliefs, Christian |
| CURRENCY | Zimbabwe dollar |

**Tourism**
Zimbabwe's main tourist attractions are the spectacular Victoria Falls, the Kariba Dam, national parks, and the ruins of the city of Great Zimbabwe. Tourists enjoy active vacations, such as canoeing and rafting, on the Zambezi.

**Harare**
Formerly called Salisbury, the capital is Zimbabwe's commercial and industrial center and home for almost a million people. It is a clean and sophisticated city that is characterized by flowering trees, colorful parks, and modern buildings.

# Madagascar

The fourth largest island in the world, Madagascar is home to some unique wildlife because of its isolated position off Africa's east coast. A high plateau runs the length of the island, dropping to a narrow, fertile strip in the east, where most people live. The country's economy is based on growing crops and raising livestock.

## MADAGASCAR FACTS

| | |
|---|---|
| CAPITAL CITY | Antananarivo |
| AREA | 224,533 sq miles (581,540 sq km) |
| POPULATION | 15,900,000 |
| MAIN LANGUAGES | Malagasy, French |
| MAJOR RELIGIONS | Traditional beliefs, Christian |
| CURRENCY | Malagasy franc |

**Vanilla**
Madagascar is the world's largest exporter of vanilla. The pods of the plants are used to flavor ice cream and chocolate. Other important cash crops are cloves, sisal, cocoa, and butter beans.

*Vanilla pods grow 10 in (25 cm) long.*

**Rural society**
Most Madagascans are descended from Asians from Malaysia and Indonesia, who began to settle on the island almost 2,000 years ago. Later waves of mainland Africans intermixed to produce a uniquely multiracial society. Three-quarters of the Madagascan labor force works on the land, growing subsistence crops, such as cassava and rice.

# Mozambique

As a result of years of civil war, flooding, and drought, Mozambique is now one of the world's poorest countries, with a high birth rate. The land, though largely unexploited, is fertile and rich in minerals. The ports and railroads provide a trade link for landlocked Swaziland, Malawi, and Zimbabwe.

## MOZAMBIQUE FACTS

| | |
|---|---|
| CAPITAL CITY | Maputo |
| AREA | 302,737 sq miles (784,090 sq km) |
| POPULATION | 19,700,000 |
| MAIN LANGUAGE | Portuguese |
| MAJOR RELIGIONS | Traditional beliefs, Christian, Muslim |
| CURRENCY | Metical |

**Fishing**
Mozambique's main industry is fishing, and shrimp accounts for more than 40 percent of export earnings. The country's total annual fish catch totals 26,643 tons (24,170 tonnes). Cotton, tea, and sugar are also exported.

# Malawi

With few natural resources, Malawi has a rural society, despite the constant threat of drought. Light industries, such as food processing, textiles, and manufacturing farm tools, are developing. Fish from Lake Malawi, which covers one-quarter of the country, is a source of food.

## MALAWI FACTS

| | |
|---|---|
| CAPITAL CITY | Lilongwe |
| AREA | 36,324 sq miles (94,080 sq km) |
| POPULATION | 10,900,000 |
| MAIN LANGUAGES | Chewa, English |
| MAJOR RELIGIONS | Christian, Muslim |
| CURRENCY | Malawian kwacha |

*Tea grows well in the tropical climate of Malawi's hillsides.*

**Farming**
Almost 86 percent of the Malawi labor force works in agriculture, growing cash crops, such as tea, tobacco, coffee, cotton, and sugar, as well as subsistence crops of corn, rice, cassava, and plantains. The country is self-sufficient in food.

# Comoros

The three islands and few islets of the Comoros archipelago lie north of Madagascar in the Indian Ocean. They were governed by France until 1975. The economy is underdeveloped, and most of the people live by subsistence farming.

## COMOROS FACTS

| | |
|---|---|
| CAPITAL CITY | Moroni |
| AREA | 861 sq miles (2,230 sq km) |
| POPULATION | 694,000 |
| MAIN LANGUAGES | Arabic, French, local languages |
| MAJOR RELIGIONS | Muslim |
| CURRENCY | Comoros franc |

**Ylang-ylang**
Comoros is the world's largest grower of ylang-ylang, an aromatic tree with greenish-yellow flowers that produce a pleasantly scented oil used to make perfume.

**FIND OUT MORE**   AFRICA, HISTORY OF   AFRICAN WILDLIFE   DESERTS   EMPIRES   FARMING   FISHING INDUSTRY   GREAT ZIMBABWE   OIL   ROCKS AND MINERALS   SOCIETIES, HUMAN

# AFRICA, WEST

THE ATLANTIC OCEAN borders all but three of the 15 countries that make up West Africa. Much of the area is dominated by the Sahara and the Sahel, a vast area of semidesert that the Sahara is slowly invading. Despite their potential wealth and rich resources, most of the countries are desperately poor. Long-established trade routes across the Sahara link West Africa with the Mediterranean coast to the north. For millions of West Africans, life is a perpetual struggle against a hostile climate, the threat of drought, and political instability.

**Sahel**
Immediately south of the Sahara Desert, stretching across West Africa, is a broad band of hot, arid, semidesert grassland called the Sahel. In Arabic, the word Sahel means "shore" of the desert. Rainfall in this region is sporadic and droughts are common.

**Regional climate**
There are four main climate regions in West Africa. From north to south, they are desert, Sahel, grassland, and tropical rain forest. Rain is rare in the northern desert and Sahel regions. The south is humid and tropical with a distinct rainy season that can last for four to six months.

78°F (25°C)    80°F (26°C)
74 in (1,879 mm)

## Physical features

Most of West Africa lies 600–1,200 ft (200– 400 m) above sea level. The Sahara dominates Niger, Mauritania, and Mali, and the Sahel extends south into Senegal, Burkina Faso, and Nigeria. The Senegal, Gambia, Volta, and Niger rivers irrigate the west and south.

**Niger River**
Africa's third longest river, the Niger flows in a great arc for 2,597 miles (4,180 km) from Guinea through Mali, Niger, Benin, and Nigeria to a vast delta on the Gulf of Guinea. A valuable source of fish and water, it is navigable for more than half its length.

**Harvesting peanuts**

### Peanuts
Peanuts are widely grown in West Africa as a source of edible oil and as a foodstuff that is rich in protein and vitamins. Peanuts develop underground; for this reason they are also called groundnuts. The plants were introduced into West Africa from South America.

# Mauritania

The northern two-thirds of Mauritania is desert. The only farmland lies in a narrow fertile strip along the bank of the Senegal River in the southwest. This area is scattered with small villages and oases. Nomadic Moors of Arab descent, from the north, live in Mauritania. They have often clashed with black farmers in the south.

## MAURITANIA FACTS

**CAPITAL CITY** Nouakchott

**AREA** 395,953 sq miles (1,025,520 sq km)

**POPULATION** 2,700,000

**MAIN LANGUAGES** Arabic, French, Hassaniya, Wolof, Soninké

**MAJOR RELIGION** Muslim

**CURRENCY** Ouguiya

## Fishing
The waters off Mauritania have some of the richest fish stocks in the world and attract many foreign fishing fleets. All catches must be sold through the state fishing company. Fishing provides more than half of Mauritania's export earnings.

## Desertification
Successive years of drought and overgrazing in the Sahel region have caused the desert to expand southward, killing livestock and forcing many nomads to move into towns.

*Government schemes are attempting to reclaim the land by reducing soil erosion.*

## Mineral wealth
The Mauritanian desert contains the largest deposits of gypsum – used for making plaster – and some of the largest reserves of iron ore in the world. The country also exports gold. A single railroad connects mines with Nouakchott, the country's capital and main port.

**Gypsum crystal**

# Senegal

The flat, semidesert plains of Senegal are crossed by four rivers – the Senegal, Gambia, Saloum, and Casamance – which provide water for agriculture, the country's main source of income. Tourism is also developing. Senegal has a mix of ethnic groups, the largest of which are the Wolofs.

## Music
At festivals and ceremonies, or *griots*, a mix of historians, musicians, and poets, sing and recite traditional stories, often to the accompaniment of a *kora*.

**Kora**

*Musicians pluck the 21 strings to give a wide range of muted sounds.*

*Many of Senegal's fruits and vegetables are imported and expensive.*

## SENEGAL FACTS

**CAPITAL CITY** Dakar

**AREA** 74,336 sq miles (192,530 sq km)

**POPULATION** 9,500,000

**MAIN LANGUAGES** French, Wolof, Fulani, Sérèr, Diola, Mandinka

**MAJOR RELIGIONS** Muslim, Christian, traditional beliefs

**CURRENCY** CFA franc

## Dakar
Senegal's capital and major port, Dakar is a bustling industrial center with good restaurants, shops, and markets. However, many of the 2,500,000 people who live here are poor and live in suburban slums.

*Gourd soundbox*

## Farming
About 65 percent of Senegalese laborers work on the land growing cotton and sugarcane for export, and rice, sorghum, and millet for their food. Until droughts in the 1970s damaged yields, peanuts were the main cash crop. Fish is now the main export.

# Gambia

One of the most densely populated countries in Africa, Gambia occupies a narrow strip on either side of the Gambia River and is surrounded on three sides by Senegal. With little industry, 80 percent of the people live off the land. Peanuts make up 80 percent of exports. The main ethnic groups are the Mandingo, Fulani, and Wolof.

## GAMBIA FACTS

**CAPITAL CITY** Banjul

**AREA** 3,861 sq miles (10,000 sq km)

**POPULATION** 1,300,000

**MAIN LANGUAGES** English, Mandinka

**MAJOR RELIGIONS** Muslim, Christian, traditional beliefs

**CURRENCY** Dalasi

## Tourism
Gambia is an attractive destination for winter sun-seekers from Europe. Tourism, the country's fastest-growing industry, employs one in ten Gambians. About 10,000 of those work on a seasonal basis.

# Guinea-Bissau

Rainfall in Guinea-Bissau is more plentiful than in the rest of Africa, enabling the country to be self-sufficient in rice. However, flooding is common along the coast because farmers have cut down mangroves to plant rice fields. Most people travel around by riverboat.

**Cashew nuts**

*Grated coconut*

**Coconut**

## GUINEA-BISSAU FACTS

**CAPITAL CITY** Bissau

**AREA** 10,857 sq miles (28,120 sq km)

**POPULATION** 1,200,000

**MAIN LANGUAGES** Portuguese, Crioulo

**MAJOR RELIGIONS** Traditional beliefs, Muslim, Christian

**CURRENCY** Peso

## Cashew nuts
Farming employs 85 percent of the workforce. Rice, cotton, peanuts, and dried coconut are produced as cash crops, as are cashew nuts, which make up nearly 60 percent of the country's exports.

# Guinea

With more than 30 percent of the world's known reserves of bauxite, and deposits of diamonds, iron, copper, manganese, uranium, and gold, Guinea could be a wealthy country. However, years of poor government and lack of support from former French rulers have made Guinea's economic development difficult.

## GUINEA FACTS

**CAPITAL CITY** Conakry

**AREA** 94,926 sq miles (245,860 sq km)

**POPULATION** 7,400,000

**MAIN LANGUAGES** French, Fulani, Malinke, Susu

**MAJOR RELIGIONS** Muslim, traditional beliefs,

**CURRENCY** Guinea franc

**Coffee beans**

**Bananas**

**Pineapple**

### People

Three-quarters of Guineans belong to one of three main ethnic groups – the Malinke and Fulani, who live in the north and center, and the Susu, who live closer to the coast. Two-thirds live in small rural communities, where the standard of living is one of the lowest in the world. Average life expectancy is low, at only 47 years, and only about 41 percent of people can read.

### Fruit growing

Bananas, plantains, and pineapples grow well in the fertile Fouta Djalon hills (Guinea Highlands). Farmers cultivate coffee, palm nuts, and peanuts as cash crops and sorghum, rice, and cassava for their families.

# Sierra Leone

Sierra Leone was founded by the British in the early 1800s as a colony for freed slaves. Its name is Spanish for "Lion Mountains" and refers to the constant roar of thunder. Of the 12 ethnic groups, the biggest are the Mende and the Temne. A ceasefire halted civil war in 2000.

## SIERRA LEONE FACTS

**CAPITAL CITY** Freetown

**AREA** 27,652 sq miles (71,620 sq km)

**POPULATION** 4,900,000

**MAIN LANGUAGES** English, Krio (Creole)

**MAJOR RELIGIONS** Traditional beliefs, Muslim, Christian

**CURRENCY** Leone

### Industry

Mining is the mainstay of Sierra Leone's economy. The chief exports are diamonds, some of which are still mined by hand, as well as gold, bauxite, and titanium ore. Farming employs more than two-thirds of the workforce, growing coffee, cocoa, palm kernels, ginger, and cassava.

*Uncut diamond looks like any other stone.*

### Freetown

Surrounded by green hills, Sierra Leone's capital, Freetown, is a colorful and historic port and home to 700,000 people. The name is a reminder of the country's former status as a haven for freed slaves. Among Freetown's attractions are a 500-year-old cotton tree, and West Africa's oldest university, built in 1827.

# Côte d'Ivoire

With 370 miles (600 km) of Atlantic coastline and three main rivers, Côte d'Ivoire is fertile and arable. It is among the world's top producers of coffee and cocoa. Food makes up half of all exports. Most people work in farming and forestry. Nearly all the tropical forests have been sold off as timber to pay foreign debts.

## CÔTE D'IVOIRE FACTS

**CAPITAL CITY** Yamoussoukro

**AREA** 122,780 sq miles (318,000 sq km)

**POPULATION** 14,891,000

**MAIN LANGUAGES** French, Akan

**MAJOR RELIGIONS** Muslim, Christian, traditional beliefs

**CURRENCY** CFA franc

*Farmers use pesticides on cocoa plantations, but their health is at risk because they don't wear protective clothes.*

### Yamoussoukro Basilica

Although only 29 percent of the population is Christian, Côte d'Ivoire has one of the world's largest Christian churches. Able to seat 7,000 people, it dominates the city of Yamoussoukro, which replaced Abidjan as the country's capital in 1983.

### Cocoa

Côte d'Ivoire is the world's leading producer of cocoa beans. Cocoa trees need humid conditions, and many cocoa plantations lie in moist, tropical regions where rain forests were felled for timber. Factories have been set up in Côte d'Ivoire to make cocoa butter, which is the basic ingredient of chocolate and some cosmetics.

# Liberia

Founded by the US in the 1820s as a home for freed black slaves, Liberia has never been colonized. About five percent of the people descend from former slaves and American settlers. The rest are a mix of ethnic groups. About 70 percent of Liberians work on the land, growing palm trees, coffee, and cocoa, and rubber for export. Civil war has damaged trade.

## LIBERIA FACTS

**CAPITAL CITY** Monrovia

**AREA** 37,189 sq miles (96,320 sq km)

**POPULATION** 3,200,000

**MAIN LANGUAGES** English, Kpelle, Bassa Vai, Grebo, Kru, Kissi, Gola

**MAJOR RELIGIONS** Christian, traditional beliefs, Muslim

**CURRENCY** Liberian dollar

### Civil war

Since 1990, Liberia has been torn by a chaotic and bloody civil war, and its once prosperous economy has collapsed. The war, which began as clashes between various ethnic groups, has made thousands of people homeless and many are forced to live in large refugee camps where food shortages are a part of everyday life.

### Monrovia

Reputedly the world's wettest capital city, with more than 183 in (4,560 mm) of rain per year, Monrovia is a sprawling city and major port. Liberia has the world's largest commercial fleet of ships. Almost all are foreign owned but registered in Monrovia, where taxes are low.

A

# Mali

Desert and semidesert cover the northern two-thirds of Mali, and only two percent of the land can be cultivated. Most people live in the south, in farming settlements close to the Niger and Senegal rivers. Droughts, poor food, and an average life expectancy of only 51 years make Mali one of the world's poorest countries. Some gold is mined, but cotton is the biggest export.

*Buildings such as this granary are made from sand bricks.*

## MALI FACTS

**CAPITAL CITY** Bamako

**AREA** 471,115 sq miles (1,220,190 sq km)

**POPULATION** 11,200,000

**MAIN LANGUAGES** French, Bambara, Mande, Arabic, Fulani, Senufo, Soninke

**MAJOR RELIGIONS** Muslim, traditional beliefs

**CURRENCY** CFA franc

**Making "mud cloth"**

### People

Mali's ethnic groups include the Bambara, Fulani, Tuareg, and Dogon, and smaller numbers of Songhai, and Bozo. Bozo artists, mostly women, are noted for their "mud cloth," made by painting abstract designs onto cloth using soil of various colors.

### Tombouctou

Lying on the edge of the desert, Tombouctou is a city of sand still visited by camel caravans carrying salt from mines in the north for shipping up the Niger River to Mopti. This historic city is a center of Islamic learning.

# Burkina

Landlocked in the arid Sahel region and threatened by the Sahara, which is expanding southward, Burkina (formerly Upper Volta) is one of West Africa's poorest and most overpopulated countries. Faced with droughts and lack of work, many young people are forced to leave to find jobs abroad.

## BURKINA FACTS

**CAPITAL CITY** Ouagadougou

**AREA** 105,714 sq miles (273,800 sq km)

**POPULATION** 11,600,000

**MAIN LANGUAGES** French, Mossi, Mande, Fulani, Lobi, Bobo

**MAJOR RELIGIONS** Traditional beliefs, Muslim, Christian

**CURRENCY** CFA franc

**Fulani children**

### Fulani

The Fulani are nomadic cattle herders who roam West Africa with their animals. In Burkina, where they number about 75,000, they are one of more than 60 ethnic groups. Fulani herders traditionally tend cattle for local farmers in exchange for sacks of rice.

### Cotton

Burkina most valuable cash crop is cotton, which brings in about 25 percent of its export earnings. However, the country's farming is threatened by the mass emigration of young workers, who send money home to their families. The country has deposits of silver and manganese, and exports gold.

# Ghana

Once called the "Gold Coast" by Europeans who found gold here 500 years ago, Ghana still has reserves of gold that have recently replaced cocoa as the country's major source of income. The country is still one of the world's largest cocoa producers. Lake Volta, formed by a dam on the Volta River, is the world's largest artificial lake.

## GHANA FACTS

**CAPITAL CITY** Accra

**AREA** 88,810 sq miles (230,620 sq km)

**POPULATION** 20,200,000

**MAIN LANGUAGES** English, Akan, Mossi, Ewe, Ga, Twi, Fanti, Gurma

**MAJOR RELIGIONS** Christian, traditional beliefs, Muslim

**CURRENCY** Cedi

**Eseye (a kind of spinach)**

**Plantains**

### Food

A popular food in Ghana is *banku*, a mixture of cornmeal and cassava. Ghanaians mix leaves of *eseye*, a type of spinach, with palm oil to make a sauce that is eaten with boiled fish or vegetables.

### People

Family ties are strong in Ghana, and the extended family is important. About half of Ghanaians are Ashanti people whose ancestors developed one of the richest and most noted civilizations in Africa. Other groups include the Mole-Dagbani, Ewe, and Ga. About 38 percent of the people live in cities and towns.

**Ghanaian family**

# Togo

A long, narrow country, just 68 miles (110 km) at its widest point, Togo has a central forested plateau with savanna to the north and south. Nearly half the population is under 15 years of age, and few people are more than 45. Although most people are farmers, Togo's main export is phosphates, used for making fertilizers.

## TOGO FACTS

**CAPITAL CITY** Lomé

**AREA** 21,000 sq miles (54,390 sq km)

**POPULATION** 4,600,000

**MAIN LANGUAGES** French, Kabye, Ewe

**MAJOR RELIGIONS** Traditional beliefs, Christian, Muslim

**CURRENCY** CFA franc

### Farming

Togolese farmers produce cocoa, coffee, cotton, dried coconut, and palm kernels, mainly for export. New products include herbs, tomatoes, and sugar. For their own use, they grow millet, cassava, and corn, and fish in coastal areas.

**Corn**

### Market women

Although politics and formal employment remain the domain of men, many Togolese women work informally in part-time jobs. The Nana Benz, wealthy women traders so-called because they all prefer to own Mercedes Benz cars, dominate Togo's markets and taxi businesses. Based in the market at Lomé, these formidable women fight hard for business and have a legendary capacity for haggling.

# Nigeria

With large reserves of oil, natural gas, coal, iron ore, lead, tin, and zinc, and rich, fertile farmland, Nigeria looked set to prosper when it became independent from Britain in 1960. However, the country's economy has experienced difficulty due to falling oil prices, ethnic conflicts, and corrupt government. After 16 years of military dictatorship, civilian rule was restored in 1999.

## Abuja

Begun in 1980, the new, planned city of Abuja replaced Lagos as Nigeria's capital in 1991, because the government believed Lagos was too influenced by the Yoruba people. By the late 1990s, much of Abuja was unfinished as money ran low during construction.

**Central mosque, Abuja**

## People

Nigerian society consists of an uneasy mix of more than 250 ethnic groups. Two-thirds of the population belongs to one of three groups – the Hausa in the north, the Ibo in the east, and the Yoruba in the west. About 57 percent of people live in small tight-knit villages where communal life is important.

*Nigerian oil has a low sulfur content and is ideal for aircraft fuel.*

## Oil

Nigeria's oil production, which ranks first in Africa and highly in the world, accounts for 95 percent of all its exports. Almost totally dependent on this new industry, which began in the 1960s, Nigeria is vulnerable to changes in world oil prices.

## Plantations

Agriculture employs more than 40 percent of all Nigerian workers. Although most farmers work on small plots with simple tools, vast plantations have been established to cultivate cash crops on a commercial scale for export, using modern machinery. Crops include cotton, coffee, cocoa beans, and palm oil.

*The best cloth is a mix of cotton and silk.*

## Cloth

Nigeria's Yoruba and Hausa peoples produce many attractive patterned textiles, hand-dyed using natural plant colors. In the Hausa town of Kano, in the north, men dye the cloth in ancient dye pits.

## NIGERIA FACTS

| | |
|---|---|
| CAPITAL CITY | Abuja |
| AREA | 351,648 sq miles (910,770 sq km) |
| POPULATION | 112,000,000 |
| DENSITY | 317 per sq mile (122 per sq km) |
| MAIN LANGUAGES | English, Hausa, Yoruba, Ibo |
| MAJOR RELIGIONS | Muslim, Christian, traditional beliefs |
| CURRENCY | Naira |
| LIFE EXPECTANCY | 52 years |
| PEOPLE PER DOCTOR | 5,000 |
| GOVERNMENT | Multiparty democracy |
| ADULT LITERACY | 64% |

# Benin

A former French colony, Benin took its name from an ancient empire, in 1975, 15 years after becoming independent. It is a long, narrow country with a short coastline on the Gulf of Guinea. Most of the land is flat and forested, with a large marsh in the south. Most people live off the land producing yams, cassava, and corn. Cotton brings in about three-quarters of the country's export income.

## BENIN FACTS

| | |
|---|---|
| CAPITAL CITY | Porto-Novo |
| AREA | 42,710 sq miles (110,620 sq km) |
| POPULATION | 6,100,000 |
| MAIN LANGUAGES | French, Fon, Bariba, Yoruba, Adja, Fulani |
| MAJOR RELIGIONS | Traditional beliefs, Muslim, Christian |
| CURRENCY | CFA franc |

## Fishing

Every year, fishermen catch about 42,990 tons (39,000 tonnes) of fish in the lagoons along the coast of Benin.

## Betamaribé

One of five main ethnic groups in Benin, the Betamaribé, or Somba, live in the northwest near the Atakora Mountains. One of the first peoples to settle in Benin, they have lived free from Western influence for hundreds of years and have managed to keep many of their traditions intact.

# Niger

Although it is the largest country in West Africa, Niger is two-thirds desert. The people, who are very poor, live in the dry Sahel region, or in the southwest close to the Niger River, where they plant crops and herd animals. The country is one of the world's top producers of uranium.

## NIGER FACTS

| | |
|---|---|
| CAPITAL CITY | Niamey |
| AREA | 489,188 sq miles (1,267,000 sq km) |
| POPULATION | 10,700,000 |
| MAIN LANGUAGES | French, Hausa, Djerma, Fulani, Tuareg, Teda |
| MAJOR RELIGION | Muslim |
| CURRENCY | CFA franc |

## Fighting the desert

The people of Niger are waging a battle against the advance of the desert into the dry Sahel where they live. They plant trees and grass in an attempt to stop soil erosion.

## Male beauty contest

Every year, in a festival known as the *gerewol*, young Wodaabé men make themselves up to try and attract a wife in an unusual beauty contest. After much dancing, the women make their choice. If a marriage proposal results, the man arranges to kidnap the woman and they set off into the desert for a nomadic life together.

FIND OUT MORE | AFRICA, HISTORY OF | BENIN EMPIRE | CONSERVATION | DESERTS | FARMING | FISHING INDUSTRY | OIL | ROCKS AND MINERALS | SLAVERY | TEXTILES AND WEAVING

A

# AFRICAN WILDLIFE

NO OTHER CONTINENT matches the wealth of wildlife found in Africa. Covering the full climatic spectrum from intense heat to bitter cold, its variety of vegetation supports a wide range of animals, including mammals, birds, reptiles, fish, and insects. Among them are more than 40 species of primates, ranging from tiny galagos to huge gorillas, many different antelope, gazelles, and other hoofed animals, and 70 species of carnivores. Bird life, too, is extraordinarily rich; more than 1,500 species live south of the Sahara. In addition, Africa is inhabited by the world's fastest land animal, the cheetah; the biggest bird, the ostrich; and the largest land animal, the elephant.

### Giraffe
The giraffe's great height – males reach up to 18 ft (5.5 m) – gives it the advantage of being able to spot danger from a distance and then escape quickly. It also enables the giraffe to feed on acacia leaves that are out of the reach of most other grassland animals, giving it a near monopoly of its principal food supply.

*Patterned coat provides camouflage.*

*Long tail with coarse hair is used to deter flies.*

## Grassland wildlife

African grasslands (savannas) sustain over 20 species of grazing animals, from the giant sable antelope to the tiny pygmy antelope. The herds of plains game and their predators, including lions, are pursued by scavengers such as hyenas and vultures. Grassland birds include the guinea fowl and hornbills.

*Long tail feathers help it balance when running.*

### Secretary bird
Among the most striking of Africa's grassland birds is the secretary bird, with its long legs and feathered crest. It rarely flies, preferring to walk, nodding its head with each step. It attacks snakes, spreading its wings over its body to shield itself from venomous bites, while using its feet to stamp them to death.

*Long legs let it run through grass after snakes and frogs.*

*Zebras call to each other while grazing.*

### Lion
The lion is the principal predator of the African savanna. Lionesses hunt together, preying on large animals such as buffalo, zebras, and wildebeest.

### Aardvark
The aardvark is a solitary, nocturnal animal. It uses its powerful claws to break into the nests of ants and termites, which it extracts with its long, sticky tongue. The aardvark can dig at an astonishing speed – faster than a person with a shovel.

### Zebra
Zebras usually live in family groups of 5–20 animals, but in the dry season, they may gather in herds of a few hundred for protection against predators such as lions. Male zebras defend themselves by kicking out with their legs and hooves. Zebras eat the tough tops of the grasses.

### Papyrus
The most common plant in African swamps is papyrus. It grows in clumps, often dense enough to support the weight of large animals.

*Papyrus may reach 15 ft (4.5 m) in height.*

## Wetland wildlife

Africa's wetlands are teeming with wildlife, such as crocodiles, hippos, floodplain species such as lechwes, and fish, including the Nile perch and tiger fish. The wetlands also provide stopping places for migratory birds flying south to winter in Africa.

### Lesser flamingo
Three million flamingos gather at Lake Nakuru, in Kenya, forming an amazing spectacle. They feed on the plentiful algae that flourish in the salty water, sunlight, and high temperatures in and around the lake.

### Hippopotamus
Hippos spend most of the day submerged in water, with only their ears, eyes, and nostrils above the surface. They become active at dusk when they emerge from the water to graze on nearby grassland.

### Cichlid fish
Lakes Malawi and Tanganyika contain 265 different species of cichlids (mouth-brooding fish); all but five are unique to Africa. Great depth, isolation, and few predators have resulted in this proliferation.

*Long legs for wading through water.*

*Webbed feet*

A

## Addax

The addax lives in the driest and hottest parts of the Sahara – conditions few other animals could tolerate. It rarely drinks: it gets liquid from the succulent plants and tubers that it eats.

*Pale coat provides camouflage in the desert.*

## Desert wildlife

The African deserts include the Sahara, the world's largest desert, and the deserts of the Horn of Africa, Kalahari, and Namib. Though the deserts seem barren, they are home to many animals such as bustards, sandgrouse, and the scimitar-horned oryx.

## Fennec fox

The fennec lives in small colonies among sand dunes, into which it burrows to avoid the heat. It burrows so quickly, it disappears from sight in seconds.

*Fox obtains all its liquid from its prey.*

## Sand skink

The sand skink spends most of its life underground in its burrow. It uses its flattened tail to propel itself through the sand. It preys on small mammals such as mice, as well as birds' eggs. If attacked, the sand skink can shed its tail, confusing its attacker and enabling it to get away.

## Sandgrouse

Despite living in the open desert, sandgrouse must drink regularly, so they often fly many miles for water. Sandgrouse obtain water for their young by immersing themselves in water and carrying droplets back to their nests in their feathers.

## Rain forest wildlife

Rain forests dominate western Central Africa. The warm, wet environment is home to many animals. Herbivores such as gorillas feed on leaves. Fruit that falls from the canopy provides food for pigs and porcupines, while animals such as tree pangolins forage in the trees.

## Yellow-backed duiker

Standing 3.3 ft (1 m) at the shoulder, the yellow-backed duiker is the largest of the forest duikers. In West Africa it lives in the densest parts of the rain forest; in East Africa it lives in bamboo forests.

*Yellow back patch*

## Red colobus monkey

The red colobus is one of five species of specialized leaf-eating primates throughout Africa. It lives in the forest canopy in family groups of about 20 animals, rarely descending to the ground.

## Small spotted genet

This catlike animal spends the day asleep in the branches of a tree, becoming active at night. An agile climber, it stalks its prey – birds, small mammals, and insects – like a cat, before seizing it with a sudden pounce.

*Gorillas eat many types of rain forest vegetation.*

## Mountain gorilla

The mountain gorilla is confined to a small area of rain forest, at a point where the boundaries of Uganda, Zaire, and Rwanda meet. It is a massively built animal, but is not normally aggressive. The females build nests where they sleep with their young.

## Gelada

The gelada is the sole survivor of a group of ground-dwelling primates now found only in Ethiopia. It lives in open country at high altitude, close to cliffs and rock faces, where it retreats if alarmed. It eats seeds, roots, grass, and fruit.

## Mountain wildlife

The mountains of Ruwenzori, Kenya, and Kilimanjaro have distinctive plants and animals. Rodents inhabit moorland, while the scarlet-tufted malachite sunbird lives in close association with giant lobelias.

## Giant plants

Africa's mountain plants include some of the most extraordinary vegetation in the world. Plants small elsewhere have grown into giants, including the giant lobelia, tree heath, and giant groundsel, which reaches 30 ft (9 m) in height.

*Geladas have a patch of red skin on the chest.*

*Hyraxes bask in the sun for much of the day.*

*Flower spikes of the Giant Lobelia are more than 3.3 ft (1 m) tall.*

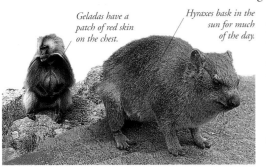

## Rock hyrax

Rock hyraxes live in colonies of 50 or more among rocky outcrops. They remain alert for signs of danger, such as eagles and leopards.

## Crowned hawk eagle

One of the largest eagles, the crowned hawk eagle is widely distributed throughout the mountainous regions of East Africa and Zaire, wherever there are suitable forests containing the monkeys that are its chief food.

**FIND OUT MORE**    BIRDS    BIRDS OF PREY    DEER AND ANTELOPES    GIRAFFES    HIPPOPOTAMUSES    LIONS AND OTHER WILDCATS    LIZARDS    MONKEYS AND OTHER PRIMATES

# AIR

WE LIVE, MOVE, AND BREATHE at the bottom of an immense ocean of air called the atmosphere. Air is an invisible mixture of gases, made up of a teeming mass of millions of tiny gas molecules that move randomly and at high speed. Without air, the Earth would be a lifeless planet – the gases air contains are vital to plants and animals.

## Fractional distillation

The gases in air have many uses. For example, divers use tanks of oxygen to enable them to breathe underwater, and nitrogen is used in explosives. Gases are extracted from air by a process called fractional distillation. Air is cooled and compressed until it forms a blue liquid. When the liquid expands and warms up, each gas boils off at a different temperature and is collected separately.

**Divers with oxygen tanks**

## Composition of air

Any volume of pure, dry air is 78.09% nitrogen, 20.95% oxygen, 0.93% argon, and 0.03% carbon dioxide and other gases. These colored balls represent the proportions of the different gases in air.

Candle burns in jar of air

Flame goes out and water level rises as the oxygen is used up

### Carbon dioxide ($CO_2$)

Carbon dioxide is vital for plant life. Plants absorb carbon dioxide from the air and combine it with water gathered by their roots to help form the food they need for growth.

*Tablets of nitrogen fertilizer*

### Nitrogen ($N_2$)

Every living cell contains nitrogen. Plants cannot take nitrogen from the air, so they get it from the soil. Fertilizers contain nitrogen to replenish what plants remove from the soil.

*Black ball represents carbon dioxide and other gases.*

Red balls represent oxygen.

Green balls represent argon.

Blue balls represent nitrogen.

### Oxygen ($O_2$)

Burning is a chemical reaction of a substance with oxygen, as this experiment shows. The candle burns in the jar of air until it has used up all the oxygen. Humans and other animals use oxygen from the air to "burn" food inside their bodies and produce energy.

### Argon (Ar)

The gas argon is called an "inert" gas because it does not react with other substances. Electric lightbulbs are often filled with argon. It prevents the bulb's filament from burning up as it would in pure air, giving the bulb a much longer life.

## Air pollution

Air is not naturally "pure" and contains varying amounts of other substances, such as dust, water vapor, bacteria, pollen, and polluting gases. Air pollution from industry and traffic can cause serious health problems in towns and cities, as well as long-term damage to the environment.

### Smog
Hazy air pollution that hangs over an urban area is called smog. Sulfurous smog is the result of burning fuels with a high sulfur content, such as coal. Photochemical smog occurs when sunlight causes car exhaust fumes to react together.

### Water vapor
Up to 4 per cent of the volume of air may be water vapor. Warm air can hold more water vapor than cool air. A cold drink can absorb heat from the air around it. As the air cools, water vapor condenses out of the air to form droplets on the outside of the can.

## Air pressure

Air exerts a force on objects because its moving molecules are constantly colliding with them. Air pressure is a measure of this force. The pressure of the open air is called atmospheric pressure. It is lower at high altitudes where the air is less dense.

### Barometer
A device that measures atmospheric pressure is called a barometer. It is used to forecast changes in weather – air pressure varies slightly from day to day with changes in the air's temperature and humidity.

### Sucking
When a person sucks on one end of a drinking straw, air pressure is reduced inside the straw. Atmospheric pressure on the liquid's surface pushes down on the liquid and makes it rise up the straw.

### Compressed air
The pressure of air can be increased by compressing it – that is, pumping more and more of it into a limited space. Bicycle tires are filled with air that becomes compressed to give a smooth ride.

## Weight of air
Air has weight, as this simple experiment proves. Identical empty balloons are attached to both ends of a stick. The balloons balance when the stick is suspended from its middle. Inflating one of the balloons tips the balance, because the balloon full of compressed air weighs more than the empty balloon.

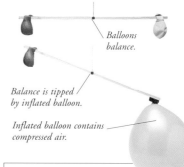

*Balloons balance.*

*Balance is tipped by inflated balloon.*

*Inflated balloon contains compressed air.*

## Joseph Priestley
English scientist and clergyman Joseph Priestley (1733–1804) discovered oxygen in 1774. He also discovered many other gases, including nitrous oxide (laughing gas) and ammonia. Priestley studied carbon dioxide and devised a way to make carbonated (fizzy) drinks.

**FIND OUT MORE**   ATOMS AND MOLECULES   CELLS   FRICTION   GASES   LUNGS AND BREATHING   POLLUTION   PHOTOSYNTHESIS   PRESSURE   WEATHER

# AIRCRAFT

ANY VEHICLE THAT travels through the air is called an aircraft. The ability to soar over obstacles such as oceans and mountains makes aircraft the fastest form of travel. An airliner (a large passenger plane) can fly a passenger thousands of miles in hours. The same journey would take several days by boat or car. Airliners and military aircraft are complex machines. Their frames are built with lightweight metals such as aluminium, and hi-tech materials such as plastics. Inside, their sophisticated electronic controls help pilots fly efficiently and safely. Smaller aircraft, such as gliders and hot-air balloons, are often used for sport and leisure.

## Types of aircraft

The word "aircraft" covers all flying machines – from balloons to helicopters. Most aircraft are airplanes, which have wings, and jet engines to give them speed. Other types of aircraft are gliders, which have no engine, helicopters, balloons, and airships. An aircraft's function determines its size and shape.

A

### Biplanes
Many planes before World War II (1939–1945) had two pairs of wings and were called biplanes.

### Transport aircraft
Armies need aircraft to transport troops and equipment. Special aircraft are designed to carry very heavy objects, such as tanks.

### Balloons
Lighter-than-air craft are known as balloons. A bag is filled with gas or hot air that is lighter than the atmosphere.

### Gliders
Currents of air move up and down. A glider has no engine, but flies by the effects of air currents on its wings.

### Concorde
Supersonic airliners such as Concorde can travel faster than the speed of sound – about 770 mph (1,240 kmh). They can cross the Atlantic twice as fast as any other airliner, but are very noisy and need lots of fuel.

## Anatomy of an airliner

Most airliners, such as this Boeing 747-400, have the same basic design. The main part is the fuselage, which is similar to a long, thin, metal tube. The wings are attached to the middle of the fuselage, and the tailplane and fin are attached at the back. A floor separates the passenger cabin from the baggage compartment.

**The Boeing 747-400** can fly more than 8,451 miles (13,600 km) without stopping for fuel.

*Upper deck with business-class seats*

*Fuselage*

*Forward cabin with first-class seats*

*Main cabin, with economy-class seats*

*Fin*

*Tailplane*

*Fuel for engines in fuel tanks inside wings*

*Turbofan engines hang from wings on pylons.*

*Engine controls and navigation instruments*

*Pilot's control column*

### Freighters
Airplanes that carry cargo are called freighters. The cargo is loaded through a huge door in the aeroplane's nose. The *Boeing 747* can be converted from a passenger plane to a freighter, then back again.

### Cockpit
The aircraft is controlled from the cockpit. The pilot and co-pilot fly the plane using control columns, and instruments show the status of all the plane's equipment. The cockpit also contains radar and radio controls.

### In-flight food
Pre-prepared meals are stored in trolleys, which lock into spaces in the aircraft's galleys until it is time for the flight attendants to serve them.

### Entertainment
Some airliners feature video screens and headphones that can be tuned to music channels.

### Howard Hughes
Hughes (1905–76) was an American industrialist, film-maker, and aviation enthusiast. He founded the airline TWA, and broke a number of aviation records in aircraft of his own design. Not all were successful; the *Spruce Goose* (1947) only flew once.

# Forces of flight

An aircraft needs two forces to fly: lift to keep it up and thrust to propel it forward. Lift overcomes the plane's weight, and thrust overcomes the drag caused by the air flowing past the plane. When an aircraft is cruising, lift is equal to weight and thrust is equal to drag.

Lift

Thrust

Drag

Weight

# Wings

An aircraft's wings create lift. To do this, they need air to flow over them.

**The airfoil shape**
If you cut an aircraft wing in two and looked at the end, you would see a special cross section called an airfoil. The top surface is longer and more curved than the bottom surface.

**The airfoil at work**
The air pressure beneath the wing is greater than above it, and lifts the wing up.

Lift

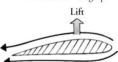

**Angle of attack**
Tilting the angle of the blades gives extra lift.

Lift

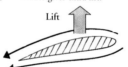

# Flying controls

An aircraft is steered through the air by way of three main control surfaces – the elevators on the tailplane, the ailerons on the wings, and a rudder on the fin.

**Elevators** make the aircraft's nose tilt up and down.

**Ailerons** make the aircraft roll from side to side.

**The rudder** makes the aircraft "yaw" to left or right.

# Airplane engines

An aircraft's engines drive it through the air by producing thrust. Different types of engines produce thrust in different ways. Piston and turboprop engines drive propellers that screw into the air, just as a ship propeller bites into water. Turbojet and turbofan engines produce a fast-moving stream of gas that pushes the aircraft forward.

**Piston engines**
These work in the same way as car engines. Petrol and air vapour are mixed in the engine's cylinders and they cause an explosion. The explosions push pistons, which turn a shaft. The shaft then turns a propeller.

*Shaft*

**Turboprop engines**
The simplest type of jets – a turbojet engine with a propeller is called a turboprop engine. A motor turns the compressor and the propeller, which provides the main engine thrust.

*Propeller spins to provide engine thrust.*

**Turbojet engines**
Air is drawn in and compressed, then sent to a chamber where fuel burns. The gases produced are shot out of the back of the engine, which pushes the aircraft forwards, like a deflating balloon.

*Gas shoots out*
*Air drawn in*

**Turbofan engines**
A hybrid of turbojet and turboprops, the turbofan engine sucks in air, which is combined with the backdraft from a fan, and also sends air around the engine, producing the same effect as a propeller.

*Turbo fan*

*Exhaust*

# Helicopters

Unlike most aircraft, which have fixed wings, a helicopter has a spinning rotor with two or more long, thin blades attached. When the blades spin, they lift the helicopter straight up into the air. A helicopter can take off from almost anywhere and does not need to use airport runways. It can hover in one place, and fly backward, forward, and sideways. It is the most versatile of all aircraft; it is very useful for transportation, surveillance, and rescue missions.

**Rotor blades** twist to control the helicopter's direction.

*Turboshaft engine*

*Main rotor*

**Tail rotor** stops fuselage spinning in opposite direction to main rotor.

*Landing skids in place of wheels*

**Flying controls**
A helicopter pilot has three flying controls. The collective pitch lever changes the amount of lift produced by the main rotor. The cyclic pitch control makes the helicopter move forward, backward, or sideways. Rudder pedals make the helicopter turn left or right.

**Lifting off**
Before takeoff, the main and tail rotors are speeded up. When the main rotor is turning fast enough, the pilot lifts the collective pitch lever to increase the tilt of the rotor blades. The tilt produces lift and the helicopter takes off. The higher the lever is lifted, the faster the aircraft rises.

**Moving away**
The cyclic pitch control makes the helicopter move in the direction the control is pushed. It tilts the main rotor so that some of the rotor's lift pulls the helicopter along. Here, the pilot has pulled the control back to make the helicopter move backward.

## Igor Ivan Sikorsky

Sikorsky (1889–1972) was born in Ukraine. where he became an aeronautical engineer. In 1919 he moved to the United States where he set up an aircraft factory. He designed the first practical helicopter, the *VS-300*, which first flew in 1939. The design had to be modified many times: at one point, the helicopter flew in every direction except forward.

**FIND OUT MORE** | AIRSHIPS AND BALLOONS | ATMOSPHERE | ENGINES AND MOTORS | FLIGHT, HISTORY OF | TRANSPORT, HISTORY OF | WARPLANES | WORLD WAR I | WORLD WAR II

# Types of aircraft
## Military

*Twin tail fins*

**Fighter/strike aircraft,** McDonnell Douglas F/A-18E Super Hornet

*Harrier can take off and land vertically.*

**Naval strike aircraft,** McDonnell Douglas AV-8B Harrier II

*Wings fold back for supersonic flight.*

**Swing-wing bomber,** General Dynamics F-111A Aardvark

*The A-10's huge array of weapons gives it a massive firepower.*

**Ground-attack "tankbuster" aircraft,** Fairchild A-10 Thunderbolt II

*Radar dome*

**Refueling/electronic countermeasures aircraft,** Boeing EC-135 Stratotanker

*Hinged nose is raised to allow loading.*

**Heavy transport aircraft,** Lockheed C-5A Galaxy – one of the world's largest aircraft

*Twin propellers* / *Radar bulge*

**Radar aircraft,** Fairey Gannet AEW-3, gives early warning of air attacks.

*Extended wings for high-altitude flight.*

**High-level reconnaissance aircraft,** Lockheed U-2

## Passenger and cargo aircraft

*777's engines are the most powerful aircraft engines ever built.*

**Wide-bodied, long-haul airliner,** Boeing 777-200

*737 is the world's best-selling jet airliner.*

**Medium-range airliner,** Boeing 737-300

*Low-noise engines*

**Short-range airliner,** British Aerospace Bae 146-RJ85

*More than 1,800 727s were built.*

**Freight transporter aircraft,** Boeing 727

*Seating for 8-14 passsengers*

**Business jet,** British Aerospace Bae 125-600

*Turboprop engines*

**Commuter aircraft,** Fairchild Metro II

*Cabin holds four people.* / *Single engine*

**Leisure aircraft,** SOCATA TB-20 Trinidad

*Rear-mounted engines* / *Wing float*

**Flying boat,** Beriev A-50 Mermaid

## Helicopters

*Wings carry armaments such as rockets and guns.*

**Attack helicopter,** Bell AH-1 Cobra

*Five-bladed main rotor* / *Tail rotor* / *Radar*

**Passenger helicopter,** Sikorsky S-61

*Twin rotors*

**Transport helicopter,** Boeing CH-47 Chinook

*Osprey can fly like both a helicopter and a plane.* / *Rotors can tilt 90°.*

**Tilt-rotor aircraft,** Boeing V-22 Osprey

## Sports

*Glider soars on warm air currents.* / *Pilot launches glider by running downhill.*

**Hang glider** is like a huge wing with a harness below to hold the pilot.

*Fabric-covered wings and fuselage*

**Biplane training/leisure aircraft,** De Havilland Tiger Moth DH8A

*Wing of light woven fabric over metal frame* / *Propeller* / *Motor* / *Hand grip* / *Wheels allow microlight to take off and land like a normal aircraft.*

**Microlight** is a kind of motorized hang glider, with a strong frame and a streamlined fiberglass "tricycle" underneath to carry the pilot.

# AIRPORTS

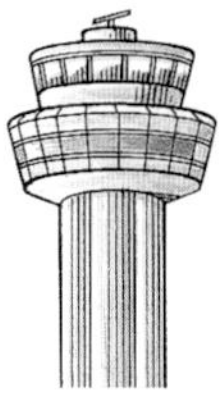

TODAY, MORE PEOPLE TRAVEL by air than ever before. Whether they are business people off to visit clients or families going on vacation, all air travelers leave from airports, which range in size from small local facilities to enormous international terminals. A large airport is like a city. It contains shops, offices, and hotels, in addition to all the buildings, runways, and taxiways needed to service the aircraft and their passengers. Airport security is always tight, because airports and aircraft have often been the targets of terrorist attacks.

## Features of an airport

Airplanes take off and land on runways, which are linked to the terminal buildings by routes called taxiways. The passengers embark and disembark at the terminal buildings. For the aircraft, the airport has repair workshops, refueling facilities, and storage hangars.

**Runway**
To take the biggest jet aircraft, runways have to be 1.8–2.5 miles (3–4 km) long and some 165 ft (50 m) wide. They need a specially toughened surface to take the pounding they get when large jets take off or land.

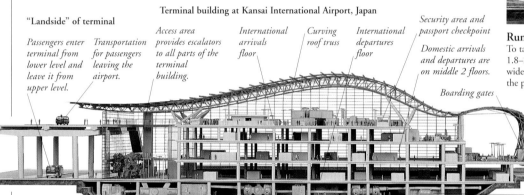

Terminal building at Kansai International Airport, Japan

"Landside" of terminal
Passengers enter terminal from lower level and leave it from upper level.
Transportation for passengers leaving the airport.
Access area provides escalators to all parts of the terminal building.
International arrivals floor
Curving roof truss
International departures floor
Security area and passport checkpoint
Domestic arrivals and departures are on middle 2 floors.
Boarding gates
"Airside" of terminal
Bridge connects boarding gate to airplane
Waiting airplane
Service area contains boilers, ventilation equipment, and other building services.

## Air traffic control

At the heart of an airport is the control tower, where air traffic controllers monitor every moment of an aircraft's arrival and departure. They make sure that each pilot follows the correct flight path, that all aircraft land in the right place, and that there is a safe amount of time between each takeoff and landing.

*Air traffic controllers in the control tower*

**Radar display screen**
Airport radar tracks each aircraft as it lands, giving the controllers precise details of its position. All aircraft within 12 to 30 miles (20 to 50 km) of the airport can be tracked by radar and shown on the controllers' display screens.

**Flight path**
Air traffic controllers tell pilots when it is safe to land. They guide a pilot to a specific path, which the pilot must then follow as the aircraft descends to the runway. Navigation aids, such as high-frequency radio beacons, give the pilot accurate bearings.

How an aircraft lands

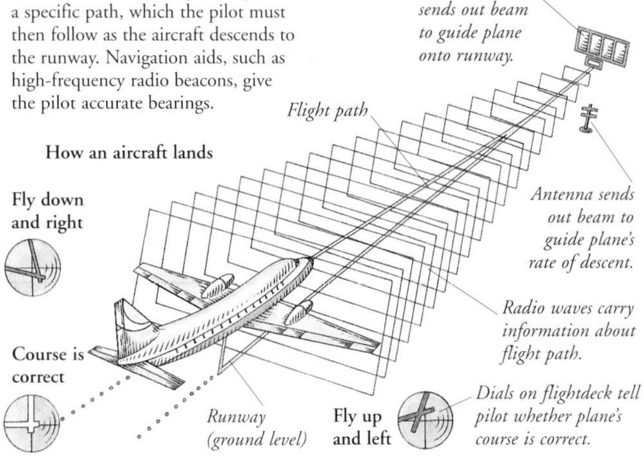
Radar antenna sends out beam to guide plane onto runway.
Flight path
Antenna sends out beam to guide plane's rate of descent.
Radio waves carry information about flight path.
Dials on flightdeck tell pilot whether plane's course is correct.
Fly down and right
Course is correct
Runway (ground level)
Fly up and left

## Security

Airport security staff are always on their guard, trying to spot terrorists or smugglers. Metal detectors and other electronic devices alert staff when a passenger is carrying a gun or other type of weapon. There are also "sniffer" dogs that have been trained to detect the scent of explosives or illegal drugs.

*An X ray reveals a gun.*

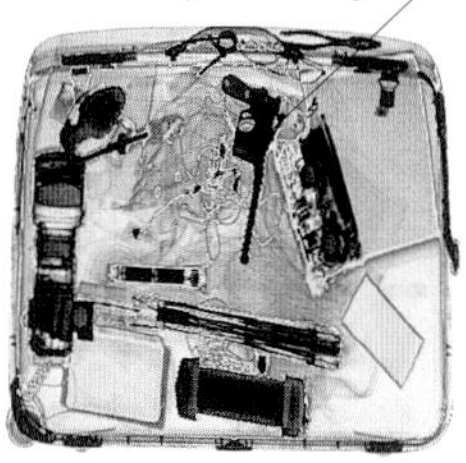

**X ray scanner**
Airport staff use X ray machines to scan the contents of passengers' luggage. A screen on the side of the X ray machine shows what is inside each bag. Different materials show up in different colors, enabling items such as guns to be found with ease.

**Passports**
A person traveling from one country to another usually carries a passport, an official document that identifies the owner and his or her place of origin. Passports are inspected at international airports.

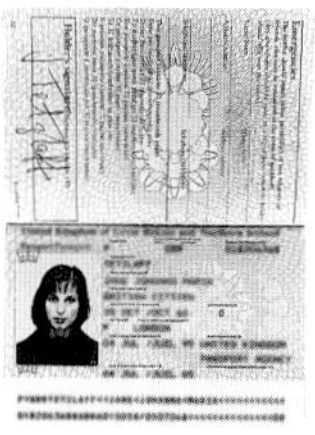

EU passport

## Airports and the environment

A large airport can have a devastating impact on the local environment. Clearing the land to build an airport destroys carefully balanced ecosystems, while the air pollution can harm wildlife, and the noise may scare some animals away.

Kestrel

**Airport ecosystems**
Since airports cover such vast areas, birds and animals can also move into these areas and establish new ecosystems, undisturbed by people.

*Animals can live in the large green spaces around a big airport.*

FIND OUT MORE
AIRCRAFT
ECOLOGY AND ECOSYSTEMS
RADAR AND SONAR
TRAVEL

# AIRSHIPS AND BALLOONS

AIRSHIPS AND BALLOONS are known as lighter-than-air aircraft because instead of wings, they use a large envelope, or bag, full of gas or hot air that is lighter than the air in the atmosphere around it. The air pushes the envelope upward, just as water pushes a submerged air-filled ball upward. In 1783, the Montgolfier brothers achieved the first manned flight ever by sending a hot-air balloon over Paris. Balloons fly where the wind blows them; airships have engines and can be steered. Today, airships are used for aerial photography and coastguard patrols, and ballooning is a popular sport.

## Anatomy of a modern airship

The main part of an airship is its envelope, which contains bags of helium gas. The gas is slightly pressurized to keep the envelope in shape. A fin and tailplane keep the airship steady as it flies slowly along. The crew travels in a gondola attached to the underside of the envelope.

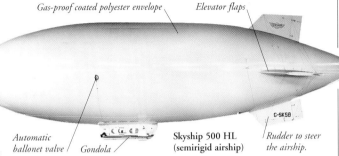

*Gas-proof coated polyester envelope*    *Elevator flaps*

*Automatic ballonet valve* / *Gondola*    **Skyship 500 HL (semirigid airship)**    *Rudder to steer the airship.*

## Airship disasters

The Hindenburg, 1937

Several terrible disasters made people lose trust in airship travel. Airships were usually lost for two reasons: either they were uncontrollable in bad weather; or the highly inflammable hydrogen gas used inside the envelope exploded. Today, airship pilots use the much safer helium gas in special nylon envelopes. However, they still have to be careful in bad weather.

## Types of airships

Practical airships could be built only after the lightweight internal-combustion engine had been developed. The earliest airships were "nonrigid" (they are still used today). These were followed by the "rigid" and the less usual "semirigid" types of airship.

Nonrigid airships have a flexible fabric envelope, from which the load hangs, suspended by ropes.

Rigid airship's envelope is built around a rigid framework. This skeleton contains bags of the lifting gas – helium.

## Balloons

Balloons were first used for aerial reconnaissance during the French Revolution, and used again during the Civil War. During World Wars I and II, balloons were used to spot targets for artillery attacks, and barrage balloon defended cities against aircraft.

### Weather and research balloons

To study what is happening in the upper reaches of the atmosphere, pilots send up helium-filled weather balloons carrying measuring instruments, but not people. The instruments measure temperature, wind speed, and so on, and send their results to the ground or to satellites by radio.

### Balloon festivals

Today, ballooning is a popular sport. During the summer, ballooning enthusiasts gather at festivals to enjoy the dazzling prospect of dozens of brightly colored balloons flying together. Some of the balloons are owned by companies and are made in the shapes that advertise theri products.

## Ferdinand von Zeppelin

German count Ferdinand von Zeppelin (1838–1917) began experimenting with air travel in 1891. In 1900, he devised the first airship, a 128-m (420-ft) rigid craft named the LZ1. During World War I, some 100 Zeppelins were built for military use.

## Flight

Hot-air ballooning requires a perfectly clear day with a gentle breeze. Too high a wind puts the balloon at risk on takeoff and landing. After take-off, a ground crew follows the balloon in a vehicle to recover both it and the crew after landing.

1 The balloon is laid on the ground. Burners heat air to fill the balloon.

2 The balloon's envelope expands as the hot air starts to inflate it.

3 The expanding balloon becomes buoyant and rises into the air.

4 Guy ropes hold the balloon down until the crew boards.

5 The crew blasts hot air into the envelope to keep the balloon afloat.

FIND OUT MORE    ATMOSPHERE    GALILEO GALILEI    GASES    FLIGHT, HISTORY OF    JOHNSON, AMY    RENAISSANCE    WEATHER FORECASTING

# Airships and balloons

## Balloons

*False basket*

**Lavishly decorated** character from *The Thousand and One Nights*

**Easter egg** envelope is decorated to celebrate Easter.

**Golf ball**, an uncomplicated, yet realistic balloon shape

**Upsidedown balloon** has a false basket that is attached to the top.

**Fabergé egg**, the trademark jewel of a famous Russian jeweler

*Basket*

*Part of this balloon hangs below the basket.*

**Red, blue, and yellow panels** of this balloon's envelope represent the exotic plumage of a parrot.

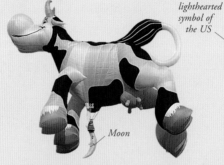

*Uncle Sam, a lighthearted symbol of the US*

*Moon*

*Upturned eaves*

**Modern tractor** has its basket hanging where the back axle would be.

**Carmen Miranda**, a 1940s' singing star

A "**cow jumps over the moon**" is a very complicated balloon shape inspired by the famous nursery rhyme.

**Face-shaped** balloons are relatively simple to create.

**Japanese temple** whose envelope comes complete with authentic upturned eaves and balcony rails.

**Soda can**, the first nontraditional balloon shape

**Santa Claus**, an aerial Christmas decoration

**NASA rocket** celebrates space exploration.

**Elephant**, complete with trunk and a surprised look!

## Airships

**Spectacular eagle** has a very complicated and realistically painted envelope.

**Aerial tours** are often run by companies that have both airships and balloons.

**Modern airships**, because of their visibility and size, are often used to advertise products or services.

**Rupert the Bear** is a favorite fictional character for children all over the world.

# ALEXANDER THE GREAT

IN LESS THAN FOUR YEARS, a brilliant young general created the largest empire the world had ever seen. The empire was the creation of Alexander the Great of Macedon, a gifted leader who inspired tremendous loyalty from his troops. It stretched from Greece in the west to India in the east. Alexander's sudden death at age 33 led to the empire's collapse, but it lived on in a series of towns that spread Greek culture eastward. These cities, all called Alexandria after their founder, opened a trade route between Asia and Europe that lasted for centuries.

A

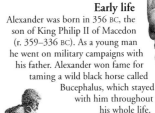

### Early life
Alexander was born in 356 BC, the son of King Philip II of Macedon (r. 359–336 BC). As a young man he went on military campaigns with his father. Alexander won fame for taming a wild black horse called Bucephalus, which stayed with him throughout his whole life.

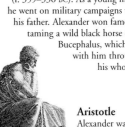

### Aristotle
Alexander was taught by the Athenian philosopher Aristotle (384–322 BC). Aristotle's interests ranged from politics and morality to biology and literature. He shared his enthusiasm for new ideas with his young pupil.

## Alexander's empire

When Alexander became king of Macedon in 336 BC, Greece was dominated by Persia. In a series of brilliant military campaigns, Alexander defeated Persia and created his vast empire.

### Greece
The heartland of Alexander's empire was his home state of Macedon, in northern Greece. Before Alexander became king, Greece was divided into rival city states and was threatened by the powerful Persian Empire.

Terra-cotta figure of the Greek love goddess, Aphrodite

### Persia
The rich empire of Persia occupied much of modern Iraq, Turkey, and Iran. After Alexander had conquered the area, he tried to unite Macedonia and Persia by encouraging his generals to marry Persians. Alexander himself married Roxana, a princess from eastern Persia.

Stag from palace at Persepolis.

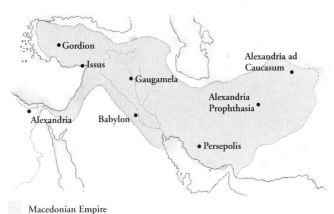

- Gordion
- Issus
- Gaugamela
- Alexandria ad Caucasum
- Alexandria Prophthasia
- Alexandria
- Babylon
- Persepolis

Macedonian Empire

Persian silver stag ornament

### Egypt
In 332 BC, Alexander conquered Egypt and was accepted as the new pharaoh. He founded the city of Alexandria in northern Egypt, which became the most important city of the Greek-speaking world. When Alexander died in 323 BC, he was buried in a vast tomb in the center of the city.

Alexander wears the pharaoh's crown

### Battle of Issus
In 333 BC, the Macedonian army overwhelmed the more powerful Persian army led by Darius III (r. 336–330 BC) at the battle of Issus, Syria. The Persians were defeated again in 331 BC at Gaugamela near the Tigris River. After this battle, the Persian capital, Persepolis, was destroyed and the empire collapsed.

Relief of the Battle of Issus

### Eastern empire
By 326 BC, Alexander had marched through Persia and had conquered Afghanistan and the Punjab. Although his troops were very loyal to him, they refused to go farther than the Indus River.

Coin from Indus area

## Death of Alexander

In 323 BC, Alexander caught a fever in the city of Babylon. Although he was only 33, he died. This sudden death meant that Alexander did not have time to consolidate his rule or even name his successor. Within a few years of his death, the huge Macedonian Empire had collapsed.

Alexander's sarcophagus

Carved relief shows Alexander leading his troops.

Sarcophagus from the royal cemetery of Sidon, said to be the tomb of Alexander.

### ALEXANDER THE GREAT

| | |
|---|---|
| 356 BC | Born in Macedon |
| 336 BC | Succeeds his father to the Macedonian throne; quells rebellions in Greece |
| 334 BC | Leads his army into Persia and defeats a Persian army at the Granicus River |
| 333 BC | Defeats Darius III at Issus |
| 331 BC | Defeats Darius III again at Gaugamela, completing his conquest of the Persian Empire |
| 326 BC | Reaches the Indus, but is forced to turn back by his troops |
| 323 BC | Dies of fever in Babylon |

**FIND OUT MORE**    ASIA, HISTORY OF    EGYPT, ANCIENT    GREECE, ANCIENT    PERSIAN EMPIRES    PHILOSOPHY

# AMERICAN CIVIL WAR

LESS THAN 80 YEARS after independence, the US split in two over the issue of slavery. The richer, industrial northern states had banned slavery, but slaves were used on plantations in the south. When Abraham Lincoln became president in 1860, the southern states, fearing he would ban slavery, seceded from the Union, and established the Confederate States of America. Fighting began in 1861 and lasted four years. At first the sides were evenly matched, but the strength of the Union wore down the Confederacy. Upon the Confederate surrender, slavery was abolished throughout the country.

## Divided nation

Eleven southern slave states left the Union of states, declaring independence as the Confederacy. Four other slave states refused to break away; West Virginia split from the rest of the state and stayed in the Union.

Slave states in the union

Confederate states

Union states

Washington

Charleston

## First modern war

The American Civil War was the first recognizably modern war. Railroads transported men and supplies to the battlefield, and iron ships were used for the first time. Commanders talked to each other by field telegraph, and the war was photographed and widely covered in newspapers.

*Much of the fighting was trench warfare, but troops were also prepared for a pitched battle.*

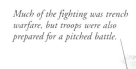

Union soldiers and guns

*Gunner*

*Field gun*

### Soldiers
More than three million people fought in the two opposing armies, most of them as infantrymen (foot soldiers).

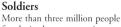

*Officer*

*Percussion musket*

Union infantry sergeant

*Chevrons*

*Shell jacket*

*Sergeant's sash*

*Sergeant's pant stripe*

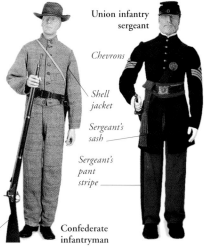

Confederate infantryman

## Abraham Lincoln
Lincoln was born in Kentucky in 1809. He was elected to the state legislature in 1834, was elected president in 1860, and led the Union states to victory in the civil war. He was assassinated in 1865.

### Merrimack and Monitor
The Confederate ironclad ship *Merrimack* (renamed *Virginia*) fought the Union's vessel *Monitor* on March 9, 1862. The outcome of the battle was inconclusive, but the encounter marked the first use of iron ships in naval warfare.

### Gettysburg Address
Lincoln was an inspired orator. In 1863, he dedicated a cemetery on the site of a battlefield in Gettysburg, Pennsylvania. In his speech, he hoped that "these dead shall not have died in vain; that this nation, under God, shall have a new birth of freedom, and that government of the people, by the people, for the people, shall not perish from the earth."

### Appomattox
On April 9, 1865, at Appomattox, Virginia, Confederate general Robert E. Lee surrendered to Union general Ulysses S. Grant. More than 600,000 Americans died in the four years of fighting, and many more were injured.

Signing the surrender documents

## Timeline

**April 1861** After 11 states leave the Union, war breaks out when Confederate troops fire on the Union garrison at Fort Sumter, South Carolina.

**1861** Confederates under generals Jackson and Beauregard win the first major battle against Unionists at Bull Run, near Washington.

Ulysses S. Grant

**1862** Confederates win Seven Days' Battle (near Richmond, Virginia) and Battle of Fredericksburg, Virginia.

**1863** Union wins its first major battle at Gettysburg; Lincoln's Emancipation Proclamation frees slaves.

**1864** Ulysses S. Grant becomes Union commander-in-chief.

**1864** General Sherman's Union army marches through Georgia, destroying the state capital and weakening the Confederacy.

Civil War cannon

**April 1865** Lee's Confederate army surrenders at Appomattox, Virginia.

**May 1865** Last Confederate army surrenders.

**December 1865** Slavery is banned throughout the US by the 13th amendment.

FIND OUT MORE  AMERICAN REVOLUTION  ARMIES  NORTH AMERICA, HISTORY OF  SHIPS AND BOATS  SLAVERY  UNITED STATES, HISTORY OF  WARFARE  WASHINGTON, GEORGE

# AMERICAN REVOLUTION

Maine (to Massachusetts)
New Hampshire
Massachusetts
New York
Pennsylvania
Rhode Island
Connecticut
New Jersey
Virginia
Delaware
Maryland
N. Carolina
S. Carolina
Georgia

**Thirteen colonies**
After the Revolution, Britain's 13 original colonies formed the first 13 states of the new United States.

IN 1783, A NEW NATION WAS BORN – the United States of America. Its struggle for independence is called the American Revolution. It began in 1775, when 13 American colonies went to war against Britain. Britain governed the colonies and imposed high taxes. The colonists, who were not represented in the British Parliament, resented the taxes. Protests and demonstrations broke out, and the colonists formed a Continental Congress to negotiate with Britain. A skirmish led to war, and in 1776, the American colonists, inspired by ideals of freedom, declared independence. The British surrendered in 1781, and two years later recognized the new country.

## Stamp tax

The colonists set their own taxes. But in 1765, Britain introduced a stamp tax on legal documents. The angry colonists stated that "taxation without representation is tyranny." They refused to buy British goods.

### Boston Tea Party
Britain withdrew the stamp tax, but set tax on glass and tea. Three groups of protesters, dressed as Mohawk Indians, boarded tea ships in Boston Harbor and threw their cargo into the water.

Colonists pour tea into Boston Harbor, in protest at British taxes

## Lexington and Concord

In April 1775, the war began with skirmishes near Lexington and Concord. American patriots forced the British to withdraw at Lexington. They marched back to Boston under continuous fire.

### Paul Revere
Paul Revere (1735–1818) rode through Massachusetts on the night of April 18, 1775, to warn that the British were coming. He was part of an anti-British group called the Sons of Liberty.

Revere on horseback

## Thomas Jefferson
A planter from Virginia, Thomas Jefferson (1743–1826) attended the Continental Congress in 1775. He drafted the Declaration of Independence, reformed the laws of his native state, and went on diplomatic missions to Europe. He became the third president of the US in 1801 and served until 1809.

## George Washington
The commander of the colonial army was George Washington (1732–99). He was an inspiring general, who kept the morale of his troops high in spite of several defeats at the beginning of the war. When France joined the war on the colonial side in 1778, followed by Spain in 1779, victory was assured.

Washington

## Surrender at Yorktown
The fighting lasted until spring 1781, when the colonists cut the British off from their supplies at Yorktown. They finally surrendered on October 19.

## Declaration of Independence
On July 4, 1776, the 13 colonies signed the Declaration of Independence. This document stated that "all men are created equal..." and its belief in "Life, Liberty, and the Pursuit of Happiness" later inspired the French Revolution.

**American soldier**
- Cocked hat
- Cartridge box belt
- Backpack strap
- Brush for musket lock
- Musket
- Gaitered pants
- Musket

**British infantryman**
- Cocked hat
- Crossbelt
- Red coat
- Bayonet
- Brush for musket lock
- Breeches
- Leather spatterdash
- Shoe

## Revolutionary war

The war lasted for six years. Washington's leadership played a vital part in the American victory. He led his troops to victories at Brandywine (1777) and Yorktown (1781).

### The opposing armies
The British were well trained but poorly led. Their orders came from 2,500 miles (4,000 km) away. The Americans were less well trained, but knew the terrain and had good leaders.

## Timeline
**1765** Britain introduces the stamp tax. Protests break out. Britain withdraws the stamp tax, but other taxes remain.

**1773** Boston Tea Party. Americans, dressed as Mohawks, dump tea in Boston Harbor as a protest against heavy taxes.

**1774–75** Continental Congress. Representatives draft a petition to Britain insisting on no taxation without representation.

**1775** Battle of Lexington. Congress takes over government of the colonies, and appoints Washington Commander-in-Chief.

**1777** British general John Burgoyne (1722–92) forced to surrender at Saratoga.

**1778** France joins the war on the American side.

**1781** British surrender at Yorktown.

**French private soldier**

FIND OUT MORE — FRENCH REVOLUTION, UNITED KINGDOM, HISTORY OF, UNITED STATES, HISTORY OF, WARFARE, WASHINGTON, GEORGE

# AMPHIBIANS

COLD-BLOODED animals, amphibians are vertebrates (animals with a backbone) that evolved from fish. They are adapted for life on land, but most must return to water in some form to breed. Amphibians undergo a process known as metamorphosis in their development from larvae to adult, hence the Greek origin of their name: *amphi* meaning "double"; *bios* meaning "life." There are three groups of amphibians and more than 3,000 species.

## Amphibian features

Apart from the caecilians and a few species of salamander, adult amphibians have four legs, each with four or five digits. Most species take to the water to mate and produce their eggs, but some make nests on land, occasionally in burrows in the ground or in moss.

European common frog

*Long legs for leaping.*

*Frog leaps after prey such as an insect.*

*Webbed toes for swimming.*

Marbled newt

*"Marbled" color extends along the tail.*

### Newts and salamanders

The tailed amphibians – newts, salamanders, and the eel-like sirens of North America – live in tropical forests, temperate woods, mountain streams, and lakes. Some have very specialized life styles: a few even live in the total darkness of caves.

Couch's spadefoot toad

## Amphibian groups

There are three groups of amphibians: the wormlike caecilians; the tailed amphibians, including newts and salamanders; and the tailless frogs and toads, probably the most diverse group.

### Caecilians

Caecilians are legless, carnivorous amphibians most of which live in the tropics. Some species burrow in the ground; others are aquatic. They have small eyes and ears and sensory tentacles on the head.

### Frogs and toads

In temperate regions, frogs are more aquatic than toads, have slimier skin and longer legs. In the tropics, some species of frogs and toads are fully aquatic and live in trees or underground.

### Distribution of amphibians

Amphibians live everywhere. Desert species survive the driest season by staying underground inside a membranous sac, which they secrete themselves. Some temperate species hibernate in pond mud in the winter.

## Skin

Amphibian skin is thin and scaleless. It is usually kept moist with mucus to increase the flow of oxygen through the skin for breathing. Skin can be smooth or rough. It secretes certain chemicals: pheromones can attract potential mates; poisons deter predators. As they grow, amphibians shed the top layer of skin.

White's tree frogs

### Color

Amphibians may have skin colors that absorb or reflect heat. Color also varies with temperature, becoming pale when warm and darker if cold and damp.

Camouflaged tree frogs

Great crested newt    Square marked toad

Mandarin salamander    Tree frog

### Texture

Many frogs and toads have smooth skin covered by mucus. Other amphibians, such as the mandarin salamander and many dry-skinned toads, have raised nodules.

### Camouflage

Many frogs and toads are camouflaged to avoid detection by predators. Most have a combination of forest colors and disruptive patterning. Some rain forest species are shaped to look like dead leaves.

### Defense

The bright colors of Colombian poison-dart frogs warn predators of their highly toxic skin. The tadpoles develop their skin poisons as their colors develop. Marine toads secrete a strong toxin through large glands behind the head.

Poison-dart tadpoles

## Metamorphosis

The development from an aquatic larva that breathes through gills, or spiracles, to an air-breathing adult is called metamorphosis. It involves the growth of legs and the loss of the tail in frogs and toads.

Newt egg

Frog spawn

### Eggs

Amphibian eggs are laid singly, in clumps, or in strings of clear "jelly" called spawn. They have no shell and require a moist environment to survive.

### Tadpoles

Larvae, or tadpoles, hatch from the eggs. Salamander tadpoles have limbs, but frogs and toads develop these during metamorphosis. Salamander larvae are carnivorous, but most frog and toad tadpoles are herbivorous.

Frog tadpole

*Gills*

Salamander tadpole

### Axolotl

Some salamanders may stay as larvae all their life. The axolotl is a form of the Mexican tiger salamander.

| FIND OUT MORE | EVOLUTION | FROGS AND TOADS | POISONOUS ANIMALS | SALAMANDERS AND NEWTS |

# ANGLO-SAXONS

BY THE END of the 8th century, Britain's people, known as the Anglo-Saxons, had created a rich culture that included masterpieces of jewelry, architecture, and literature. Originally these people had come from northern Germany and southern Denmark, where they were known as the Angles, Saxons, and Jutes. In the 3rd and 4th centuries, these tribes traveled to various parts of the Roman Empire, including Gaul, or present-day France, where their influence was short-lived. They traveled to Britain in the 5th century, where they settled and formed several separate kingdoms. Eventually the kingdom of Wessex became the dominant power.

## Kingdoms

There was always a struggle for supremacy among the kingdoms formed by the settlers. Northumbria was the earliest one to dominate under Edwin (d. 633). Then it was Mercia's turn under Aethelbald (d. 757) and Offa (d. 796). Finally Wessex dominated under Alfred the Great. When Vikings from Denmark attacked and occupied northern England, Alfred stopped them from pushing farther south, and the Anglo-Saxons reconquered the north in the 10th century.

### King Canute and King Edward

By 1016, the Danes ruled all England under the popular Canute (c.995–1035). Canute's sons inherited England, but the Anglo-Saxon Edward the Confessor (c.1003–1066) regained the country in 1042. He had no children and, when he died, an unsettled England was vulnerable to conquest by the Normans.

Edward the Confessor     Canute the Great

## Culture

Cultural life centered on the monasteries and on the royal court. Alfred the Great gathered scholars and artists around him, and himself translated many of the Latin classics into Anglo-Saxon, or Old English.

*Possible image of Alfred the Great*

## Written records

In the 7th century, missionaries from mainland Europe, such as St. Augustine of Canterbury, converted the Anglo-Saxons to Christianity. The creation of monasteries meant that more people learned to read and write. Monks produced historical works, such as the *Anglo-Saxon Chronicle*, which today give insights into the events of the period.

### Alfred the Great

Ruler of Wessex and Mercia, Alfred (c.849–c.899) was an able soldier who defended his kingdom against the Vikings. He loved learning and education, and arts and crafts flourished in his reign. He could not drive the Vikings from northern England, but most people saw him as their protector. He was the first English king to become a national symbol.

### Architecture

Anglo-Saxon churches, like the one at Earls Barton, England, often have square towers decorated with stone relief. This pattern may be based on timber buildings of the period, which have all perished.

### Jewelry

This jewel is inscribed "Alfred ordered me to be made" and may have belonged to Alfred the Great. The inscription and animal-head decoration are finely worked in gold; the portrait, perhaps of the king himself, is made of enamel.

### Decorated manuscripts

Monks produced quality manuscripts. One monk wrote the work, while a second illustrated it with figures, such as St. Dunstan (c.909–988) kneeling before Jesus, and a third decorated it.

### Anglo-Saxon Chronicle

In the ninth century, Alfred the Great ordered the *Chronicle*, a year-by-year account of the history of England. It covers the lives of kings and church leaders, military history, and major events, such as the Viking invasions, and was last updated in 1154.

### Bede (c.673–735)

Bede, an English monk and teacher in Jarrow, wrote *A History of the English Church and People*, one of the most important sources of our knowledge of Anglo-Saxon times.

## Timeline

**450** Angles, Saxons, and Jutes from northern Germany and Denmark begin to arrive in England. They settle mainly along the eastern coast – East Anglia.

**802–39** Reign of Egbert of Wessex. There are many Viking attacks.

**871–99** Reign of Alfred the Great, famous for law-making, translating books into Old English, and defeating the Vikings at Edington in 878.

**1016** Canute the Great, a Dane, is elected king by the British; he rules until 1035.

Anglo-Saxon buckle

**1042** Anglo-Saxons regain power under Edward the Confessor.

**1066** Last Anglo-Saxon king, Harold II, is killed by William of Normandy at the Battle of Hastings.

**FIND OUT MORE**    CELTS    EUROPE, HISTORY OF    MONASTERIES    NORMANS    UNITED KINGDOM, HISTORY OF    VIKINGS

# ANIMAL BEHAVIOR

ALL ANIMALS RESPOND to their surroundings. A cat, for example, will arch its back when threatening a rival, but lower its body when stalking a mouse. Everything that an animal does, and the way in which it does it, makes up its behavior. An animal's behavior enables it to increase its chances of survival and find a mate so that it can pass on its genes to the next generation. Some behaviors are instinctive; others are learned during the animal's lifetime.

**Egg-rolling**
Greylag geese nest on the ground. If an egg rolls out of the nest, the female goose automatically reaches out with her neck and pulls the egg back in. By being in the wrong place, the egg acts as a sign stimulus that causes the female to carry out the fixed-action pattern of egg-rolling.

## Instinctive behavior

"Instinct" is a term used to describe behavior that an animal performs automatically without having to learn it. Instinctive behavior is programmed by an animal's genes. It consists of unchanging components called fixed-action patterns. The fixed-action pattern often begins when an animal responds to a feature in its surroundings or on another animal, called a sign stimulus.

**Web spinning**
Many species of spiders, including this black widow, spin webs in order to trap their insect food. Web spinning is purely instinctive. A spider would not have time in its limited life to learn how to construct such a complex structure.

**Sign stimulus**
In the spring, when these freshwater fish breed, the male's throat and belly turn red. If one male intrudes into the territory of another male, its red color acts as a sign stimulus that produces a fixed-action pattern: the occupying fish drives out the intruder.

*Bright spring colors*

*Bright colors fade after the breeding season.*

## Learned behavior

Learning occurs when an animal adapts to its surroundings by changing its behavior. By responding to experiences and adapting to changing conditions, an animal increases its chances of survival. Learning takes time, and animals that are dependent on learned behavior have long lives and large brains.

**Learning tool use**
Some animals learn to use simple "tools" in order to feed. Sea otters, found off the coast of California, US, swim on their backs with a stone on their chests on which they smash the shells of clams and mussels to get at the juicy contents. Young otters learn tool use from their parents.

**Trial-and-error learning**
An animal will associate an action it carries out with a successful result, such as getting food or defeating a rival. This "reward" motivates the animal to alter its behavior to improve the result of future actions.

*Puppies play-fight and perfect their hunting skills.*

*Young ducklings follow their mother.*

**Imprinting**
Some young animals make a strong bond with their parent soon after hatching or birth. Young ducklings, for example, stay close to their mother and improve their chances of survival under her protection.

**Insight learning**
This involves a form of reasoning. Some animals can solve new problems by drawing on past experiences. Chimpanzees, having learned to extract termites or ants from a nest with a stick, can exploit other nests of any shape.

## Communication

Animals communicate by sending out signals that are recognized by other animals and alter their behavior in some way. The signals can be sights, sounds, or scents. Communication is used, for example, to find a mate, threaten rivals or enemies, defend a territory, warn of danger, or hold a group together.

*Song thrush sings from a perch.*

**Visual signals**
Animals may use visual signals to threaten or to attract a mate. This puss moth caterpillar adopts a warning posture if threatened. An enemy that ignores the warning is rewarded with a stinging squirt of formic acid.

**Puss moth caterpillar**

*Bright colors add to the warning.*

**Sound**
Many animals – including crickets, bullfrogs, peacocks, and whales – use sound to communicate. This male song thrush sings to proclaim his territory, to warn rivals to stay away, and to attract a female.

**Chemicals**
Some animals release chemicals called pheromones, which, when detected, affect the behavior of other members of the same species. Female gypsy moths release pheromones that attract males from several miles away.

**Gypsy moth**

A

# Courtship

Mating in most mammals and birds takes place only at certain times of the year. Courtship describes the behaviors used by a male animal to attract a female and mate with her. It informs a potential mate that the intention is breeding and not aggression. During courtship, males usually compete with one another to attract females, advertise that they are ready to mate, and encourage females to be sexually responsive. Females select males by the quality of their courtship display.

*Male is aware that the female may lash out at him.*

*Male is attentive to the female.*

*Female is sexually responsive and rolls.*

### Domestic cats
A female cat comes into heat, or is sexually responsive, about twice a year. She produces scents and calls loudly to attract males. Several males may compete for her by fighting. The successful male encourages the female by touching her and calling softly.

### Bird of paradise
Most birds have fixed courtship displays that make sure they attract a mate of the same species. Male birds often have brighter plumage than females, and this is especially true of the emperor bird of paradise. Males compete for females by quivering their long feathers and calling loudly.

# Territorial behavior

Many animals defend their territory to maintain access to food, water, shelter, and somewhere to reproduce. Territories can be large or small and held by one animal or by a group. Birdsong or the marking of territorial boundaries may deter rivals from entering a territory and avoid conflict and possible fatal injuries.

### Cats
Most cats are solitary and maintain a territory on their own. Cheetahs patrol their territory and mark its boundaries by spraying urine on trees and other landmarks. The scent warns neighboring cheetahs not to intrude.

### Kittiwakes
Like many gull species, kittiwakes nest in colonies on narrow cliff ledges. Each pair of birds defends a small territory on the ledge just large enough for the female to lay eggs and raise their young.

# Aggression

Animals show aggression to other members of their species when competing for food, water, shelter, or mates. Some animals use horns, some use teeth or claws, and others kick. In many cases, animals signal their aggressive intent. This may defuse the situation and prevent injury.

*Fighting bighorn sheep*

*Inflated porcupine fish*

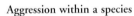

### Aggression within a species
These bighorn sheep use their horns to clash head-on in competition for mates. The winner of the fight gains higher social ranking and more females. Aggression like this is highly ritualized, and neither male is likely to be injured.

### Aggression between species
Animals may be aggressive toward members of other species that are threatening or attacking them. Some animals use a threat display, often making themselves bigger to deter enemies. This porcupine fish inflates its body like a balloon and erects its spines.

# Social behavior

Social animals live in groups. Individuals cooperate to find food, defend themselves, and look after the young. Social groups range from shoals of fish, that form for protection, to societies of honeybees, whose social organization affects all aspects of each animal's life.

### Helping others
African wild dogs are social animals and often help one another. Male dogs will look after pups that are not their own but were fathered by a brother or close relative. In this way, they help pups survive.

### Living in large numbers
Many fish species swim close together in large groups called shoals. A shoal moves and turns in a coordinated manner that mimics a single large living organism. Predators find it difficult to focus on one individual within the shoal.

*Worker bee*

*Male bee, called a drone*

*Section of a beehive*

# Konrad Lorenz

Austrian zoologist Konrad Lorenz (1903–89) pioneered the study of animal behavior. As part of his work on individual and group behaviour, Lorenz discovered imprinting. Lorenz shared a Nobel Prize in 1973 for his work.

### Social insects
Within a colony of social insects, such as bees, there are groups that carry out certain tasks. In a bee colony, a single queen lays eggs while sterile female workers look after the young, collect food, and defend the colony. Male bees fertilize the queen.

**FIND OUT MORE**   BIRDS   FISH   GENETICS   INSECTS   MAMMALS   SONGBIRDS

# ANIMALS

Large eyes enable the leopard to see in dim light.

The body is covered with insulating fur and supported internally by a skeleton.

Long tail is a balancing aid.

MORE THAN a million and a half species of animals have been identified, and there are many millions more yet to be discovered. Animals are living organisms found in nearly all of the Earth's habitats, including the depths of the oceans, the freezing Arctic, and even inside other animals and plants. The animal kingdom is divided into animals without backbones, (invertebrates), such as snails and lobsters, and animals with backbones, (vertebrates), such as frogs and monkeys. Invertebrates make up 97 percent of all animal species.

Air is breathed in through nostrils.

### Black leopard
The leopard is a mammal. Its well-defined head is equipped with sense organs including eyes, nose, tongue, and whiskers. Sharp teeth in the mouth allow the leopard to kill prey and tear off flesh. Muscular legs enable it to walk, run, and pounce.

## What is an animal?
Animals are made up of many cells. Most move actively, and those that are fixed in one place, or sedentary, move their body parts. Animals live by taking food into their bodies. They have sensors and nervous systems that enable them to detect what is happening around them and respond appropriately.

## Animal classification
Animals are classified into groups according to their similarities and whether they have common ancestors. There are 35 major groups called phyla (singular phylum). Each phylum is divided into subgroups. The smallest of these is the species, which contains animals of just one type.

Giant land flatworm

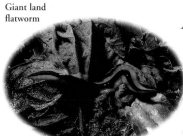

Sponge processed for human use

Sea anemones

### Sponges
The simplest animals are sponges (phylum Porifera). There are about 5,000 species, most of which live in the sea attached to rocks and other objects. Water is drawn in through holes, or pores, in the sponge's body wall, and bits of food are filtered out and eaten by the sponge's cells.

### Cnidarians
There are more than 9,000 species of cnidarians (phylum Cnidaria), most of which are found in the sea. They include jellyfish, sea anemones, hydras, and corals. Cnidarians catch food using tentacles armed with stinging threads called nematocysts.

### Flatworms
These worms (phylum Platyhelminthes) have a flattened body with one opening, the mouth, on the underside. There are about 18,500 species including those, such as tapeworms, that are parasites of humans and other animals.

### Nematodes
Roundworms, or nematodes (phylum Nematoda), have a thin, cylindrical body that is pointed at both ends. Free-living nematodes are found in many habitats and occur in very large numbers in soil. Many nematodes are parasites of plants and animals.

Threadworm

Stalked eye

Coiled shell protects the soft body.

### Annelids
Animals in the phylum Annelida include earthworms, marine bristleworms, such as ragworms, and leeches. There are about 12,000 species, each of which has a body made up of segments with a mouth at one end and an anus at the other.

King ragworm

Snail emerging from its shell

### Mollusks
Mollusks (phylum Mollusca) form a highly diverse group of about 50,000 species. These include snails and slugs, mussels and clams, and squids and octopuses. They are soft-bodied animals that may be protected by a shell. Most live in water, but some, such as snails, are found on land.

Snail moves on a muscular foot.

Sensory tentacle

Head and foot fully extended

### Echinoderms
All echinoderms (phylum Echinodermata) live in the sea. The 6,500 or so species include sea urchins and starfish. Most have five parts radiating from a central point, hard plates under the skin, and many tube feet.

Cushion star

Bloody Henry starfish

Cushion star

### Arthropods
With at least one million known species, Arthropods (phylum Arthropoda) are the largest group of animals. They include insects, crustaceans (such as crabs), arachnids (such as spiders), and centipedes.

Arthropods have hard, jointed external skeletons.

Sharp teeth grasp food.

### Chordates
There are about 48,000 species of chordates (phylum Chordata). Most are vertebrates, such as fish, amphibians, reptiles, birds, and mammals. Vertebrates are the most advanced animals.

Tail used for movement or balance is typical of many vertebrates.

Caiman

Tarantula

# Animal skeletons

The skeleton is a supportive framework that maintains the shape of an animal and enables it to move. Most skeletons are hard structures, either inside or outside the animal's body, to which muscles are attached. The skeleton may also protect internal organs and, in the case of an insect's external skeleton, prevent the animal from drying out.

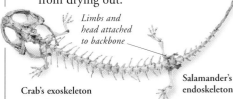

*Limbs and head attached to backbone*

**Crab's exoskeleton**

**Salamander's endoskeleton**

### Internal skeletons
A skeleton found inside the body is called an endoskeleton. Most vertebrates have a skeleton made of cartilage and bone. Joints between the bones allow the animal to move. The endoskeleton grows with the rest of the body.

### External skeletons
A hard outer skeleton that covers all or part of the body is called an exoskeleton. An insect's outer cuticle and a snail's shell are examples of an exoskeleton. An insect's exoskeleton does not grow and must be shed, or molted, periodically to allow the animal to grow.

**Earthworm**

### Hydrostatic skeleton
The hydrostatic skeleton is an internal skeleton found in soft-bodied animals such as earthworms. It consists of a fluid-filled core surrounded by muscles, and maintains the shape of the worm.

*Worm gets longer when it contracts its muscles.*

# Animal movement

**Movement of an eel through water**

*Eel moves by throwing its body into curves that push against the water.*

The ability to move is characteristic of animals, which move to find food, escape from predators, and find a mate. The way in which an animal moves depends on its complexity, lifestyle, and where it lives. The wide range of movement includes swimming through water, walking and creeping on land, and flying or gliding in air.

*Wings sweep downward to produce forward thrust.*

### Movement in air
Insects, birds, and bats are capable of powered flight using wings. Birds have lightweight, streamlined bodies. They use energy to flap their wings, which pushes them forward. As air passes over the wings it creates the lift that keeps the bird in the air.

**Young chaffinch in flight**

**Moving in water**
Many aquatic animals are adapted for movement in water by having streamlined bodies. Most fish move by pushing their tail fin from side to side. This pushes the water backward and sideways, and propels the fish forward. Whales move in a similar way, except that the tail moves up and down.

**Asian elephant**

*Feet expand under the elephant's weight as they are put down.*

### Movement on land
Animals move on land in a variety of ways. Many have limbs that raise the body off the ground, support it, and enable the animal to walk, run, or hop. The animals move forward by pushing the ends of their legs, or feet, backward against the ground.

# Animal senses

The main senses are vision, hearing, taste, smell, and touch. Animals use their senses to find out what is going on around them. A stimulus from outside, such as a sound, is detected by a sense organ, such as the ear. Nerve impulses from sense organs are interpreted by the animal's brain which "decides" how to respond.

### Eyes
**Dragonfly eyes**

Eyes contain sensors that are sensitive to light. When stimulated they send nerve impulses to the brain, which enable it to build up a picture. Insects have compound eyes made up of many separate units, or ommatidia.

### Antennae
These are found on the head of arthropods such as insects. They are used to detect odors and may detect chemicals called pheromones released by insects to communicate with each other. Antennae also detect vibrations and movements in the air or in water.

# Feeding

All animals feed by taking in food. They use a range of feeding strategies and can be grouped accordingly. Some animals kill and eat others, some graze or browse on plants, others filter food particles from water. After feeding, or ingestion, food is digested so that it can be used by the body.

**Mormon caterpillar consuming a leaf**

### Herbivores
Animals that feed solely on plants are called herbivores. Many use specialized mouthparts, such as grinding teeth, to break up tough plant tissues. Plant material is not a rich food source, and most herbivores eat a lot to obtain the necessary nutrients.

**Longhorn beetle**

**Giant clam**

### Filter feeders
These are animals that feed by sieving food particles from water that flows into their body. Many are sedentary and draw in a current of water. Some whales are filter feeders that eat small animals called krill.

### Carnivores
These types of feeders are adapted to detect prey animals, to catch and kill them, and to cut them up to eat them. They include cats, eagles, and some insects. Dragonfly larvae live in water and they can catch small fish to eat.

**Dragonfly larva with stickleback**

*External ear flaps channel sounds into the ear.*

### Ears
Some animals can detect sounds with ears. The ear converts sounds into nerve impulses that can be interpreted by the animal's brain. Animals use sounds to communicate with each other and to detect approaching predators or prey.

**Domestic Basenji dog**

**FIND OUT MORE**

AMPHIBIANS • ANIMAL BEHAVIOR • BIRDS • FISH • FLIGHT, ANIMAL • INSECTS • MAMMALS • REPTILES • SNAILS AND OTHER MOLLUSKS

# ANTARCTICA

WITH THE SOUTH POLE at its heart, Antarctica is the world's windiest, coldest, and most southerly continent. The last region on Earth to be explored, this huge landmass is not divided into countries, but seven countries claimed territories there. In 1959, however, the Antarctic Treaty suspended those claims and stated that the continent is to be used for peaceful purposes only. Antarctica's sole inhabitants are visiting scientists, working in research stations.

## Physical features

Antarctica is almost entirely covered by a vast sheet of ice, in places 4.8 km (3 miles) deep. It contains 90 per cent of the Earth's ice, and 80 per cent of the world's fresh water. The vast Ronne and Ross ice shelves are formed where the ice sheet extends over the ocean.

### ANTARCTICA FACTS

**AREA** 13,900,000 sq km (5,366,790 sq miles)

**POPULATION** 4,000 international researchers

**NUMBER OF COUNTRIES** None

**HIGHEST POINT** Vinson Massif, 5,140 m (16,863 ft)

**AVERAGE THICKNESS OF ICE CAP** 2,450 m (8,000 ft)

### Icebergs

Currents beneath Antarctica's vast ice shelves cause giant slabs of ice to break away, the largest of which may be 200 km (124 miles) long. As these enormous icebergs drift north they slowly break up and melt. Only the top third of an iceberg shows above the water.

[Map of Antarctica with grid coordinates A–J (columns) and 1–8 (rows). Labels include: ATLANTIC OCEAN, Scotia Ridge, Brazilian zone of interest, Queen Maud Land (Norway), Lutzow-Holm Bay, Enderby Land, South Shetland Is. (UK), South Orkney Is. (UK), British Antarctic Territory (UK), Riiser-Larsen Ice Shelf, Weddell Sea, Antarctic Peninsula, Chilean Claim, Argentina Claim, Berkner I., ANTARCTICA, Cape Darnley, Mackenzie Bay, Lambert Glacier, Prydz Bay, Princess Elizabeth Land, Bellingshausen Sea, Ronne Ice Shelf, Graham Land, South Polar Plateau, Australian Antarctic Territory, Antarctic Circle, Vinson Massif 5140m, Ellsworth Land, Transantarctic Mountains, South Pole, Greater Antarctica, Shackleton Ice Shelf, Amundsen Sea, Pine Island Bay, Marie Byrd Land, Lesser Antarctica, Cape Poinsett, Ross Ice Shelf, Australian Antarctic Territory, Terre Adélie (France), Wilkes Land, Cape Colbeck, Limit of permanent pack ice, Mt. Erebus 3794m, McMurdo Sound, PACIFIC OCEAN, Ross Sea, Ross Dependency (NZ), Cape Adare, Victoria Land, INDIAN OCEAN, 0 km 750, 0 miles 750]

### Mount Erebus

Antarctica contains volcanic areas. An active volcano, Mount Erebus, lies on Ross Island on the edge of the Ross Ice Shelf. It forms part of the Transantarctic mountain chain that includes peaks up to 4,570 m (15,000 ft) high.

## Cross-section through Antarctica

The Transantarctic mountains divide the continent of Antarctica into Greater and Lesser Antarctica. Although the land itself is low, the depth of the ice on top of it makes Antarctica the highest continent, with an average height of 2,100 m (6,900 ft). The ice-cap was formed by the build up of snow over the last 100,000 years and contains 90 per cent of the world's ice.

West Antarctic Ice Sheet (Lesser Antarctica)

Ross Ice Shelf

Transantarctic Mountains

East Antarctic Ice Sheet (Greater Antarctica)

A — Approximately 6,000 km (3,728 miles) from A to B — B

## Tourism

Cruise ships now bring around 9,000 people each year to see Antarctica's dramatic coastline and wildlife. Tourists who venture on to the ice are instructed to wear insulated clothing and goggles to protect their eyes from the glare.

Tourists shelter in a whale skull

**FIND OUT MORE** | ATLANTIC OCEAN | CLIMATE | GLACIATION | INDIAN OCEAN | PACIFIC OCEAN | POLAR EXPLORATION | POLAR WILDLIFE | POLLUTION | VOLCANOES

# ANTEATERS, SLOTHS AND ARMADILLOS

A BIZARRE GROUP of animals makes up the order of mammals known as the edentates. They include anteaters, armadillos, and sloths, all of which, except the nine-banded armadillo, live in the tropical regions of South and Central America. The name "edentate" means "without teeth," but it is a misleading term since only the anteaters are toothless. In fact, some armadillos have more teeth than any other land mammal.

### Tongue
Anteaters have long, sticky tongues that can be pushed deep into termite nests. The tongue is covered with little spines that point backward, making it very difficult for ants and termites to escape.

*Curved spines on tongue*

*Giant anteater breaking into a termite mound*

### Young
A female anteater gives birth to a single young. The young anteater travels on its mother's back for the first year of its life, by which time it is almost half the size of its mother.

A

### Anteater
There are four species of anteaters. The giant anteater lives in grasslands; the other three species live in forests and have prehensile (grasping) tails with which they hang from trees. Anteaters have long snouts and tongues to enable them to collect the termites and ants on which they feed. They locate their prey with their acute sense of smell. Their foreclaws are so large that they need to walk on their knuckles. The claws are used to break open termite nests and for defense. If threatened, they rear up on their hind legs and try to rip their opponent with their claws.

*Long, bushy tail*

**Giant anteater**

## Armadillo
Of the 21 species of armadillos, the largest is the giant armadillo, which is 3 ft (91.5 cm) long. It has up to 100 peglike teeth – twice as many as most mammals – that are shed when the animal reaches adulthood. The smallest species, the fairy armadillo, is less than 6 in (15 cm) long. Armadillos give birth to up to four young. The nine-banded armadillo, from North America, gives birth to quadruplets of the same sex.

### Claws
Armadillos have large, curved claws. They use them to dig into the ground to make burrows, to escape predators, and to find food. The giant armadillo's middle claw is the largest claw in the animal kingdom, measuring 7 in (18 cm) around the curve.

**Nine-banded armadillo**

*Bony plates*

*Large claws*

*Hairy stomach*

**Nine-banded armadillo**

### Body armor
Armadillos are encased in "body armor" formed by separate plates made of bone. Soft skin links the plates together, giving them flexibility. In most species the plates cover only the upper part of the body. If threatened, some species, such as the three-banded armadillo, roll into a ball, while others head for their burrow or dig themselves into the ground.

## Sloth
Adapted to living upside down, sloths hang by their claws from the branches of trees. They can rotate their heads through a 270° angle, allowing them to keep their heads upright while their bodies remain inverted. They eat, mate, give birth, and spend their entire life-cycle upside down. Sloth's fur lies in the opposite direction from other animals' to allow rain to run off. Only when asleep do they adopt a more normal position, by squatting in the fork of a tree. There are seven species of sloths; all are herbivorous.

**Female three-toed sloth with baby**

*Green algae cover the sloth's coat.*

### Movement
Sloths are very slow movers. They rarely descend to the ground and can only just stand. They cannot walk, but drag themselves along with their claws. However, they are good swimmers.

**Sloth swimming**

### Camouflage
Because of high humidity levels in the rain forest, infestations of green algae grow within a sloth's fur and cover its coat. This acts as a camouflage and makes the sloth less conspicuous. As the seasons change, the algae change color to match the color of the trees.

### Pangolin
There are seven species of pangolins, or scaly anteaters. They have much in common with edentates, but they belong to a different order – the Pholidota. They are covered with scales attached to the skin. Some species have a long, prehensile tail that is used to grasp branches and also to lash out at predators. They feed on termites, ants, and larvae, which they catch with their long tongues.

**Malayan pangolin**

### GIANT ANTEATER

| | |
|---|---|
| SCIENTIFIC NAME | *Myrmecophaga tridactyla* |
| ORDER | Edentata |
| FAMILY | Myrmecophagidae |
| DISTRIBUTION | South America |
| HABITAT | Grasslands and savannas |
| DIET | Termites, ants, and larvae |
| SIZE | Length, including tail: 6 ft (1.83 m ) |
| LIFESPAN | 25 years (in captivity) |

**FIND OUT MORE**

ASIAN WILDLIFE    CAMOUFLAGE AND COLOR    CONSERVATION    GRASSLAND WILDLIFE    MAMMALS    RAIN FOREST WILDLIFE    SOUTH AMERICAN WILDLIFE

# ANTS AND TERMITES

FOR EVERY HUMAN, there are 1,000,000 ants. Ants and termites are social insects that live in large colonies and have developed complex systems of communication. Ants are found worldwide, but, like termites, most of the 9,500 species of ants live in the tropics. There are more than 2,400 types of termites; many are blind, spending their lives inside nests, never seeing the light of day.

## Ants

Ants have two pairs of compound eyes, three single eyes, or ocelli, two antennae, and three pairs of legs. Only queens and males have wings. A narrow waist connects the thorax and abdomen. Ants undergo complete metamorphosis, from an egg to larval and pupal stages, before emerging as adults. They live in huge groups and each ant has a particular role. The queen runs the nest and mates with male ants. Workers are female and gather food and nurse the eggs, larvae, and pupae. Soldier ants, also female, guard the nest.

Bull ant

*Antennae are used to pick up the scent of pheromones.*

*Eyes*

*Spiked jaws used to attack prey and predators*

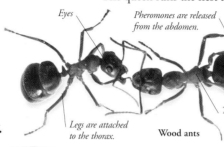
*Eyes*
*Pheromones are released from the abdomen.*
*Thorax*
*Legs are attached to the thorax.*
**Wood ants**

### Communication
Ants lay trails of pheromones – chemicals that smell – so that other ants can follow them by using their sensitive antennae to pick up the smell. This helps foraging teams find food.

### Defense
If a nest is attacked, the ants release pheromones to warn each other. Most run for cover, but soldier ants get aggressive and defend the colony. They attack enemies with their large jaws, or sting them with formic acid, which causes extreme pain. Some ants even explode to shower an attacker in venom.

## Ant nest
Most ants live in nests or colonies, usually underground. However, weaver ants build nests out of leaves in trees, and army ants build "live nests" of worker ants. Normally, there is one queen in a nest, but there are sometimes several. Nests of Australian bull ants contain up to 600 ants, while some wood ants' nests can house more than 300 million.

"Live nest" made by army ants

## Feeding
Many ants are omnivores and eat seeds, nectar, and invertebrates. Army and driver ants are more carnivorous, and kill and eat prey such as worms, spiders, and even some lizards. Leaf-cutting ants are one of a few species of herbivorous ants. They feed on a type of fungus, which grows on the chewed-up remains of leaves and flowers that the ants take back to their nests.

*Ants carry pieces of leaves back to their nest.*
**Leaf-cutting ants**

## Termites

Although often called white ants, termites belong to a totally different order, the Isoptera. Like ants, termites live in large colonies. Unlike ants, termites do not have waists, and the male, called a king, does not die after mating, but lives with the queen. They do not go through complete metamorphosis, but grow up gradually through several nymphal stages.

### Soldiers
Like ants, termites have soldiers. Termites cannot sting, but defend themselves in other ways. Some soldiers have large jaws that can cut through flesh; others squirt a poisonous sticky liquid from a special nozzle on their heads. Some nests have no soldiers – the termites defend themselves by vibrating their bodies against the side of their nest, making the sound of a hissing snake.

*Pincers*

### Queen and king
A queen termite can reach more than 6 in (15 cm) in length. Her ovaries make her so large. She can lay up to 30,000 eggs a day. The king remains by the queen's side and mates with her several times to fertilize all the eggs.

*Queen*

### Fungus gardens
are areas where fungi grow on termites' feces and break down the cellulose within them. The termites feed on the products released and the fungi itself.

*"Chimneys" allow warm air to rise and escape.*
*Solid outer walls are up to 20 in (50 cm) thick.*
*Air channel*
*Living quarters*
*Soft inner walls*
*Food stores*
*Ground level*
*Nurseries*
*Royal chamber*
*Thick pillar supports nest.*
*Termites spread water on walls to cool the nest.*

### Termite mounds
Each species of termite has its own type of nest. Some build towers more than 20 ft (6 m) tall, which help maintain the correct temperature and humidity of the nest at the base. Others build mushroom-shaped mounds – the domed top deflects the rain away from the nest below and has given these insects their name of umbrella termites. Many termites do not build nests above ground, but live below the soil or inside logs. Termites that live in trees build their nests on branches.

### Workers
Worker termites build the nest, collect food, and feed the soldiers, king, and queen. The nest is made from saliva, soil, and their own feces. Most workers feed on wood and have microscopic organisms in their guts to break down the wood into a more easily digested form.

| WOOD ANT | |
|---|---|
| SCIENTIFIC NAME | *Formica rufa* |
| ORDER | Hymenoptera |
| FAMILY | Formicidae |
| DISTRIBUTION | Europe |
| HABITAT | Woods and forests |
| DIET | Omnivorous, feeding on seeds and invertebrates |
| SIZE | Workers 0.24–0.31 in (6–8 mm) in length; queen 0.4–0.5 in (10–13 mm) in length |
| LIFESPAN | Workers live for 3–4 months; the queen lives for about 15 years |

| FIND OUT MORE | ANIMAL BEHAVIOR | ARTHROPODS | INSECTS | MONGOOSES AND CIVETS | MUSHROOMS AND OTHER FUNGI | NESTS AND BURROWS | WOODLAND WILDLIFE |

# ARCHAEOLOGY

HUMANKIND HAS ALWAYS been fascinated by the question of who we are, where we came from, and how we used to live. Archaeology is the study of our past, from early prehistory onward, using the material remains of our ancestors and the possessions they left behind. Over thousands of years, evidence of human activity, such as artifacts, burial sites, and monuments, becomes buried. Archaeological teams discover these sites and uncover this evidence by careful excavation. The material is then preserved and studied in order to help the archaeologist piece together a picture of how people lived and died in the past.

Iron Age fort, England

## Discovery
Archaeological sites are found during construction work, through reading historical documents, geophysical surveys (the study of the soil's structure), and field walking (recording above-ground objects).

**Aerial photography**
Horizontal and vertical lines seen from the air often show medieval strip fields, ancient roads, walls, and ditches. Aerial photography done when the sun is low shows varying surface levels, moisture levels, and vegetation most clearly.

## Excavation
Archaeological sites are excavated by layers. Workers remove the top, most recent layer, and work down, uncovering older, deeper levels. The study of these layers and the items they contain is called stratigraphy.

**Stratigraphy**
By revealing features such as ditches, post holes, and floors, stratigraphy gives information about the history of a site and the people who lived there. In urban areas, ground levels rise as landfill is used as a foundation for rebuilding. Because it shows a chronological sequence, stratigraphy was used to date sites before radiocarbon dating was invented.

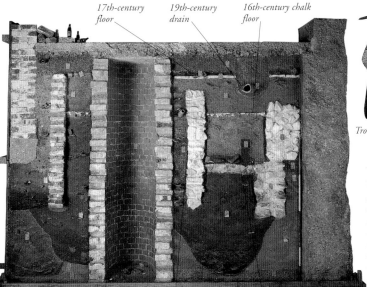
17th-century floor
19th-century drain
16th-century chalk floor
Cross-section of a dig, City of London
Brick-lined well, c.1800
14th-century cesspit
Roman tiled floor

## Tools
Archaeologists use shovels and handpicks to remove the topsoil. Then smaller hand tools, such as dental picks, teaspoons, and trowels, are used to excavate delicate objects.

Pick ax
Trowel
Measuring tape

## Finds
Archaeologists usually draw or photograph the artifacts (objects) to make a visual record. They carefully measure and record the shapes, colors, decorations, and ages of any artifacts or features. These details help archaeologists link different objects and sites.

## Investigation
Buried objects are fragile and decay quickly after excavation. To stabilize them, they are cleaned and preserved. After preservation, an object can be studied. Archaeologists then record the material of the object, its use, and its date. It may then be photographed and displayed in a museum.

Salt water has caused corrosion.
Pewter jug

A cradle hoisted the ship from the seabed.

## Underwater archaeology
Sites beneath the sea or in lakes are more difficult to excavate than those on land because shifting silt or sand causes poor visibility. However, marine sites often preserve materials, such as the wood of the 16th-century ship the Mary Rose, which would usually be lost on dry land. Preservation may involve treatment with water, sealing with chemicals, or careful drying.

To preserve the wood, chilled water is sprayed on the ship 20 hours a day.
Mary Rose, in dry dock

## Timeline

**1748** Pompeii discovered.

**1799** An officer in Napoleon's army discovers the Rosetta Stone, which features 6th century BC hieroglyphs.

**1812** Abu Simbel discovered.

**1822** Scholars decipher Egyptian hieroglyphs.

**1861** Evans and Prestwich confirm the antiquity of humans and humans' association with extinct animals.

**1891** *Homo erectus* material found.

**1922** Howard Carter discovers the tomb of Tutankhamun.

**1931** Louis Leakey begins excavations at Olduvai Gorge.

**1940** Archaeologists discover prehistoric Lascaux cave paintings.

**1949** Radiocarbon dating is developed.

**1974** Donald Johanson discovers "Lucy," an early hominid.

*Australopithecus*, an early human ancestor

## Mortimer Wheeler
Wheeler (1890–1976), a field archaeologist, set up the Institute of Archaeology, London. Worldwide, modern field archaeology stems from the new excavation techniques he pioneered. In 1944, India made him director-general of archaeology. While there, he investigated the Indus Valley Civilization.

FIND OUT MORE
ASIA, HISTORY OF
BRONZE AGE
EUROPE, HISTORY OF
HUMAN EVOLUTION
PREHISTORIC PEOPLE
STONE AGE

# Archaeological finds from the *Mary Rose*

## Weapons

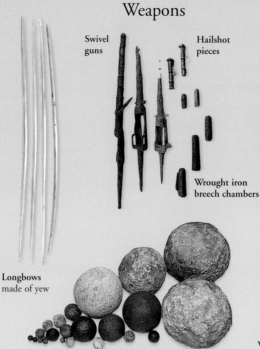
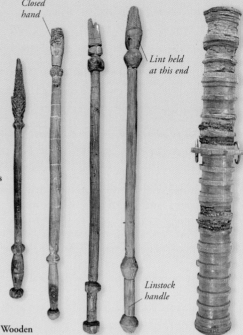

Swivel guns

Hailshot pieces

Closed hand

*Lint held at this end*

Wrought iron breech chambers

Longbows made of yew

Linstock handle

**Demi cannon,** a cast bronze muzzle loader

**Culverin,** a cast bronze muzzle loader

**Stone, iron, and lead shot,** used for cannon

**Wooden linstocks** held the slow match (lint), which the crew used to light gunpowder in cannons.

**Breech loader gun,** made of wrought iron

## Shipboard equipment

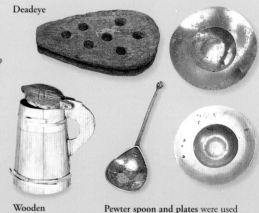

Wooden razor handles

Apothecary's balance

Deadeye

**Personal sundial**

**Ceramic** medicine jar

**An angel,** a 1545 gold coin worth about a dollar

**Bronze cooking pot,** used for communal meals

**Wooden tankard**

**Pewter spoon and plates** were used at the captain's dinner table.

## Clothing and personal

**Inkpot,** made of horn

**Manicure set,** made of bone

**Wooden comb**

**Leather jerkin**

**Backgammon set**

*Yew and spruce inlay*

**Leather flask** for storing wine or water

**Leather book cover**

# ARCHITECTURE

FROM A TOWERING SKYSCRAPER to a functional factory, architecture is the art of planning a building. The word also refers to the different building styles seen throughout history. Looking at changes in architecture tells us about earlier societies: the materials that were available to their builders, the skills mastered by their engineers, and the social ideals that they wished to express in their public buildings.

### Ornamentation
Early in the 20th century, many Western architects abandoned the use of all forms of building ornamentation. This is rare: most buildings from other periods and cultures use it extensively, and even a simple building would have some decoration to reflect the taste of its owner. The ancient Greeks, for instance, carved the tops, or capitals, of columns to dignify their most prestigious buildings. The distinct decorations were based on styles called orders.

*Doric order*

*Ionic order*

*Corinthian order*

## Architectural features
The main structural and functional features of a building are the roof, arches and walls, doors, and windows. The architect combines the practical knowledge of how to construct these features with a sense of shape, space, and light to enhance the function of the building itself.

*Groin*

*Vault*

**Groin vault, where two barrel vaults intersect**

### Arch and vault
An arch is a curved or pointed structure that bridges a gap; it must carry the weight of the wall, floor, or roof above. Its structure allows it to support greater weight than a flat slab can. A vault is simply an arched ceiling.

*Main arch*

*Barrel vault*

**Round arch**

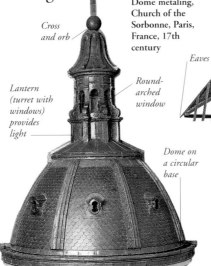

*Cross and orb*

*Lantern (turret with windows) provides light*

**Dome metaling, Church of the Sorbonne, Paris, France, 17th century**

*Round-arched window*

*Dome on a circular base*

*Eaves*

**Pitched roof, supporting frame**

*Main rafter (inclined beam)*

*Horizontal beams add strength to structure.*

### Dome
Domes – curved, solid roofs – were first built on palaces and religious buildings as symbols of the building's importance. They are often difficult to build, and have been constructed in various shapes: the Dome of the Rock in Jerusalem is hemispherical; the "onion"-shaped dome is a popular feature of many Russian and Bavarian buildings.

### Roof
All roofs are designed to provide protection from the weather. The design and covering used reflects the local climate: for instance, in a rainy area a sloping (pitched) roof will let the water run off easily. Apart from being practical, roofs can also be ingenious and beautiful, such as those of an ornate castle.

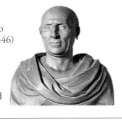

### Brunelleschi
Italian architect Filippo Brunelleschi (1377–1446) returned to the use of Classical features, rejecting the Gothic style. Architects all across Europe followed his example.

## Classical Europe
Classical architecture is that of the ancient Greeks and Romans. Both built by laying stones on top of each other, or by resting beams on columns. The Romans also developed the arch, vault, dome, and the use of concrete to develop curved spaces.

### Use of concrete
Cheap and durable, this material allowed Roman architects to cover vast curved spaces that were impossible to construct before.

### Symbolism
The Pantheon is a temple built to all the Roman gods. Light comes through an opening in its vast dome and moves around the interior, lighting the curved walls. It is as if even the Universe turns around the center of the building, symbolizing the power of the Roman deities.

## Gothic
This distinctive, ornate European style emerged in the 12th century and was used mainly in cathedrals and churches. Features include pointed arches and windows, and elaborate stone tracery used to divide the openings in window arches.

### Building innovations
The pointed arch and flying buttress were innovations that allowed Gothic churches to soar higher than buildings built earlier. Pointed arches can support heavier, taller structures than round arches. The flying buttress is a stone rib that extends down and away from the walls, transferring weight to the ground and giving extra support to a roof or walls.

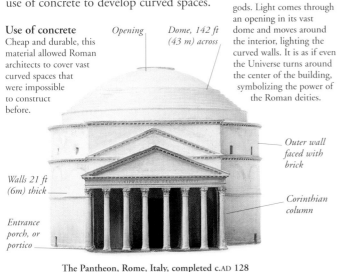

*Opening*

*Dome, 142 ft (43 m) across*

*Outer wall faced with brick*

*Corinthian column*

*Walls 21 ft (6m) thick*

*Entrance porch, or portico*

**The Pantheon, Rome, Italy, completed c.AD 128**

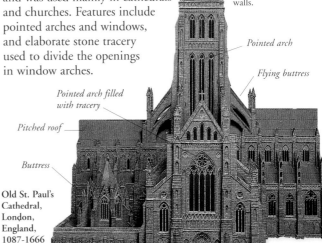

*Eight-sided spire, built using scaffolding and wooden cranes*

*Turretlike pinnacle*

*Pointed arch*

*Flying buttress*

*Pointed arch filled with tracery*

*Pitched roof*

*Buttress*

**Old St. Paul's Cathedral, London, England, 1087-1666**

**A**

*Pagoda in Burmese style, 9th–10th century*

*Gilded crown*

# Southeast Asia and the Middle East

The traditional architectural styles of Asia and the Middle East changed very little for centuries, and were heavily influenced by religious belief: Buddhism and Hinduism in southern Asia, and Islam in the Middle East. The style of buildings was determined by climate and by the materials available to local builders. As early as the 7th century, wooden temples and monasteries were being built in China and Japan.

*Islamic decoration uses geometric patterns and calligraphy.*

*Minaret*

### South and East Asia
Many of the distinctive features of this area's architecture originated in Buddhist India. An example is the multistoried pagoda, a temple that seems to stretch toward Heaven. It was developed initially in Japan and China, but based on the spires found on early Indian temples. An important feature of many traditional Asian buildings is their imaginative roof forms.

### Islamic architecture
The most important buildings in Islamic countries are usually mosques and tombs. The mosque is the center of a Muslim community and provides space for group worship. It contains a prayer hall, often with a domed roof, and a minaret, from which the faithful are called to prayer. It may also have a courtyard.

# Early American civilizations

The Aztecs, who ruled in what is now Mexico from the 14th to 16th centuries, built stone pyramids to their gods. The remains of five separate temples have been found at Tenochtitlan, built one on top of the other as new rulers erected bigger temples on the same site.

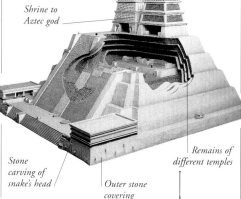

*Shrine to Aztec god*

*Remains of different temples*

*Stone carving of snake's head*

*Outer stone covering*

# Baroque and Neoclassical

The Baroque style emerged in early 17th-century Europe and was noted for its ornate decoration, complex shapes, and dramatic lighting. It was followed by the Neoclassical style, which revived the more restrained Classical traditions. This was partly as a reaction to Baroque excess.

*Greek-style portico*

*Neoclassical church, France, 1764*

# The 19th and 20th centuries

The development of new and stronger materials made it possible to construct buildings that were often highly original in style and owed little to the past. With advanced technology, architects turned to glass, steel, and concrete to express their vision of modern architecture.

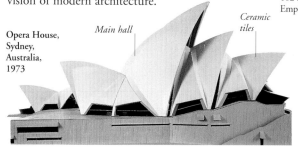

*Opera House, Sydney, Australia, 1973*

*Main hall*

*Ceramic tiles*

### Steel
Following the invention of reinforced steel, tall structures could be built for the first time. An internal steel skeleton supports the weight of a skyscraper, such as the 102 stories of the Empire State Building.

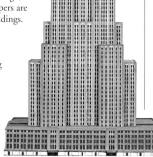

*Empire State Building, New York, 1931*

*Very plain decoration*

*Limestone and granite facing*

### Interlocked vaults
The dramatic profile of the Opera House dominates Sydney Harbour. The building's roof of interlocked vaults, made from reinforced concrete covered with gleaming tiles, resembles the sails of a ship.

### Skyscrapers
The invention of elevators during the 19th century made it practical to build skyscrapers. The first skyscrapers appeared in Chicago, Illinois, in the 1880s. Today, skyscrapers are built as offices and as apartment buildings.

## Le Corbusier

Le Corbusier was the name used by Swiss-French Charles-Édouard Jeanneret (1887–1965), the most influential 20th-century architect. Le Corbusier promoted the use of new materials and construction techniques. His most innovative designs used plain, often severe, geometric forms.

*Proposed design*

### Architects
An architect designs a building and oversees its construction. Successful architects become very well-known. Until recently, architects drafted their building plans, called blueprints, by hand. Much of this work is now carried out on computer.

## Timeline

**2650 BC** The Step Pyramid in Egypt is designed.

**c.300 BC** Buddhist temple mounds appear in India.

**AD 82** Colosseum built in Rome. Dozens of stone arches support the walls of this arena.

**690–850** Early Islamic buildings are designed around courtyards.

**1100–1500** Europe: Gothic churches built.

**c.1420** Renaissance begins in Italy; architects return to the elegant, ordered values of Classical builders.

**19th century** Industrial Revolution: mass-produced materials transform construction.

**1920s** International Modernism begins, typified by glass-and-steel towers and flat-roofed, white houses.

**1970s** Postmodernism develops. It refers to past styles, in a humorous way. Strong colors are popular.

**1990s** Eco-friendly architecture reflects environmental concerns about energy-saving and recycling.

FIND OUT MORE

BUILDING AND CONSTRUCTION  CHURCHES AND CATHEDRALS  CITIES AND TOWNS  MOSQUES

# Architecture
## Gothic, Renaissance, and Baroque

*Carved stone lantern*

*Magnificent Gothic cathedral*

*Two lions flank the entrance.*

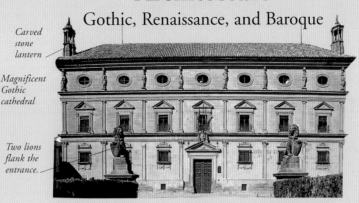

**Notre Dame**, Paris, France, built from 1163 to 1250

**Palacio de las Cadenas**, Ubeda, Spain: built during the mid-16th century. The Classical facade shows the elegance of Renaissance buildings.

**St. Paul's Cathedral**, London, Britain: built in the Baroque style

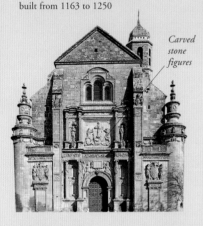

*Carved stone figures*

*Ribbed dome designed by Michelangelo*

*Facade by Carlo Maderno (c.1556–1629)*

*135 spires crown the roof*

**Capilla del Salvador**, Ubeda, Spain: one of Spain's finest Renaissance churches, it was designed by three 16th-century architects.

**St. Peter's**, Rome, Italy, took 108 years to build (1506–1614). It involved all the great architects of the Roman Renaissance and Baroque, including Michelangelo Buonarroti (1475–1564).

**Milan Cathedral**, Italy, is one of the largest Gothic churches in the world. Building began in the 14th century, but was not completed for 500 years.

## Modern architecture

*Windows give the effect of glass curtains.*

*Two towers, linked by means of a central atrium*

*Framework*

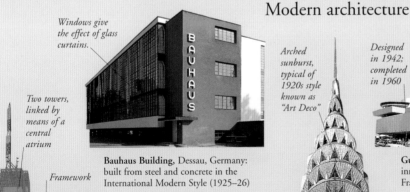

*Arched sunburst, typical of 1920s style known as "Art Deco"*

*Designed in 1942; completed in 1960*

*Descending spiral gallery*

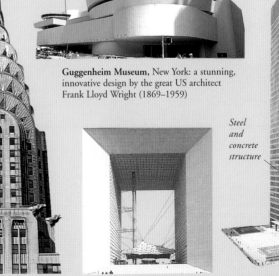

*Steel and concrete structure*

**Bauhaus Building**, Dessau, Germany: built from steel and concrete in the International Modern Style (1925–26)

**Guggenheim Museum**, New York: a stunning, innovative design by the great US architect Frank Lloyd Wright (1869–1959)

**Century Tower**, Tokyo, Japan: completed in 1991

**Palace of the Statues**, Rome, Italy: completed during the 1950s

**Spire of the Chrysler Building**, an office tower in New York: completed in 1930

**Great Arch**, Paris, France: completed in 1989, houses an exhibition gallery

**The Seagram Building**, New York: completed in 1958

# ARCTIC OCEAN

ONE OF THE COLDEST places on Earth, the Arctic Ocean is surrounded by the northern parts of Europe, Asia, North America, and Greenland. These icy lands are rich in minerals and wildlife, but are home to few people. In summer, when temperatures reach 32°F (0°C), warm currents from the Pacific and Atlantic melt some of the ice. With the help of icebreakers to clear their path, ships are able to sail along the coasts of Asia and North America.

## Physical features

The Arctic is the smallest and shallowest of the world's oceans. Much of its surface is covered by a frozen mass of floating ice about 6 ft (2 m) thick. The north pole lies in the center of the ocean on drifting pack ice.

### ARCTIC OCEAN FACTS

**AREA** 5,440,000 sq miles (14,089,600 sq km)

**AVERAGE DEPTH** 4,360 ft (1,330 m)

**AVERAGE ICE THICKNESS** 4.9–9.8 ft (1.5–3 m)

**LOWEST TEMPERATURE** -94°F (-70°C) on northeastern tip of Greenland

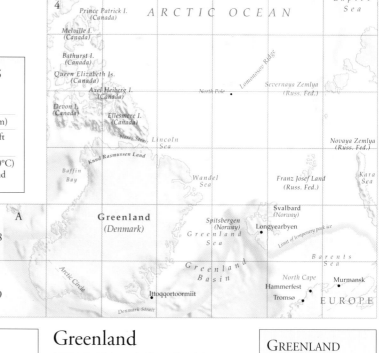

### Icebergs
Giant icebergs break off glaciers in Greenland and drift south into the North Atlantic Ocean. They rise up to 400 ft (120 m) above sea level. As only a fraction of an iceberg shows above water, they are a shipping hazard.

### Northern lights
On dark nights, spectacular colored lights, or Aurora, can be seen in the sky. Caused by electricity in the upper atmosphere, they are brightest in mid-winter when the sun never rises and invisible in summer when it does not set.

## Arctic peoples
About 800,000 indigenous people live in the Arctic. The Yu'pik of Alaska are part of the Eskimo group that includes Inuit in Canada and Greenland, and Yuit in Siberia. Many have given up nomadic life and live in villages. The Arctic is the workplace of 2,000,000 engineers and traders from the south.

Yu'pik family from Alaska

## Greenland

Although Greenland is the world's largest island, its permanent ice cover means few people live there. Most people live on the southwestern coast, where the climate is less extreme than the bleak center. The island is a self-governing territory of Denmark.

Halibut

Haddock

Cod

### GREENLAND FACTS

**CAPITAL CITY** Nuuk (Godthaab)

**AREA** 840,000 sq miles (2,175,600 sq km)

**POPULATION** 56,000

**MAIN LANGUAGES** Danish, Greenlandic

**MAJOR RELIGION** Christian

**CURRENCY** Danish krone

### Fishing
Cod, haddock, halibut, and shrimp fishing are the mainstay of Greenland's economy. Fish-processing factories freeze and can the fish for export to Europe and the US. Much of the cod is made into fish sticks.

**FIND OUT MORE**

ATMOSPHERE   CLIMATE   FISHING INDUSTRY   GLACIATION   NATIVE AMERICANS   OCEANS AND SEAS   POLAR EXPLORATION   POLAR WILDLIFE   TUNDRA

# ARGENTINA, CHILE, AND URUGUAY

THE SOUTHERN PART of South America is occupied by three countries: Argentina, Chile, and Uruguay. Lying between the Pacific and Atlantic Oceans, South America's southernmost point, Cape Horn, is only about 640 miles (1,000 km) from the northern tip of Antarctica. Once part of the Spanish Empire, all three countries still show strong European influences. Their vast mineral resources have resulted in some prosperity, but all have agricultural economies and have suffered under a series of unstable governments.

## Physical features

Dominating the west of the region, running north to south, the Andes Mountains form a rugged frontier between Chile and Argentina. The hot, humid land of the Gran Chaco covers the northeast, turning to rolling grassland, known as pampas, in the center. South of this and the arid plateau of Patagonia, lie the windy islands of Tierra del Fuego.

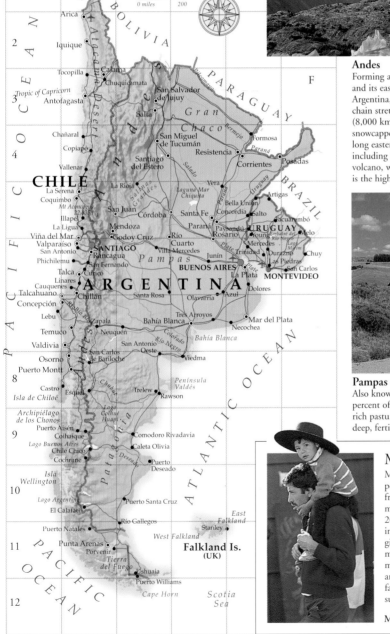

### Andes
Forming a barrier between Chile and its eastern neighbors, Bolivia and Argentina, the vast Andes mountain chain stretches for about 5,000 miles (8,000 km). Nearly half of its mighty snowcapped peaks lie along Chile's long eastern border with Argentina, including Mount Aconcagua, an extinct volcano, which, at 22,835 ft (6,960 m), is the highest peak in South America.

### Atacama Desert
The hot Atacama Desert is one of the world's driest places. It covers the northern 600 miles (965 km) of Chile's long coastal strip and receives less than ½ in (13 mm) of rain in a year. By contrast, the Patagonian Desert, in the far south of Argentina near Antarctica, is a vast, icy-cold expanse of windswept rocks.

### Pampas
Also known as the Entre Rios, the vast natural grasslands of the pampas cover about 20 percent of Argentina and extend north into Uruguay, where three-quarters of the land is rich pasture. Much of the pampas has hot summers, warm winters, plenty of rain, and deep, fertile soil, making the area ideal for growing crops and for raising cattle and sheep.

### Mestizos
More than three-quarters of the people in this region are descended from Europeans, most of whom moved from Spain or Italy in the 20th century. Many Europeans intermarried with Native Americans, giving rise to *mestizos*, people of mixed ancestry. Like their ancestors, most people are Roman Catholic and are close to their extended families. Many of them run successful businesses.

**Man and child at an Easter festival**

70°F (21°C)    48°F (9°C)

30 in (762 mm)

### Regional climate
Chile's long, narrow shape gives it an extremely varied climate. Desert and mountains in the north give way to fertile valleys, with hot, dry summers and mild, moist winters. Argentina's southern Andean peaks and Patagonian glaciers have year-round snow; the north is hotter and wetter. Uruguay is mild and pleasant.

# Argentina

After Brazil, Argentina is the second largest country in South America. It is separated from Uruguay by the Río de la Plata estuary, on which its capital, Buenos Aires, stands. Argentina is one of the wealthiest countries in South America, with fertile soil, a wealth of mineral resources, and a skilled workforce. However, years of political instability have left huge overseas debts, which caused the economy to collapse at the end of 2001.

Couple dancing the tango

## People

More than 89 percent of Argentina's people live in towns and cities and most enjoy a high standard of living. However, city slums, or *orillas*, illustrate the sharp contrast between the country's rich and poor. It was in the slums that the tango, the traditional dance of Buenos Aires, originated, in the late 1800s. Many tangos contain lyrics that express the frustrations of the immigrants who came from Spain, Italy, Austria, France, Germany, and Britain. The tango is now danced worldwide.

**35 per sq mile**
**(14 per sq km)**

**89%**
**Urban**

**11%**
**Rural**

## ARGENTINA FACTS

| | |
|---|---|
| **CAPITAL CITY** | Buenos Aires |
| **AREA** | 1,056,636 sq miles (2,736,690 sq km) |
| **POPULATION** | 37,000,000 |
| **MAIN LANGUAGE** | Spanish |
| **MAJOR RELIGION** | Christian |
| **CURRENCY** | Argentinian peso |
| **LIFE EXPECTANCY** | 73 years |
| **PEOPLE PER DOCTOR** | 370 |
| **GOVERNMENT** | Multiparty democracy |
| **ADULT LITERACY** | 97% |

## Buenos Aires

Situated on the South Atlantic coast, Argentina's capital has been an important trade port since it was founded by the Spanish in 1536. Buenos Aires is a wealthy, sophisticated city, with expensive shops, fine avenues, and modern buildings, as well as a spectacular old cathedral. The city is the center of government, industry, and culture. Almost 40 percent of Argentinians, numbering about 14,000,000, live in the metropolitan capital, referred to as "Baires."

**Government buildings**

*Clarin is Argentina's best-selling newspaper.*

## Food

High-quality beef, which is produced throughout Argentina, is used as a base for many local dishes, such as *empanadas*, or savory mince pies. Every restaurant has a barbecue grill, or *parillada*. As a cheaper alternative to meat, many people eat small potato dumplings called *noquis*, which were introduced by Italian immigrants.

*Noquis*

## Newspapers

More than 180 daily newspapers are published every day in Argentina. Most are in Spanish, but English, French, and German papers are widely available. In the past, dictatorships have imposed censorship on the media, and today's government withdraws advertising from those that do not support its policies.

## Schooling

Literacy is high in Argentina, and free state primary and secondary education is provided. Schooling is compulsory for all children between the ages of six and 14, and more than one-third of all students go on to one of Argentina's 45 universities. Buenos Aires has the largest university in South America, with 140,000 students.

## Farming

Agriculture accounts for about 60 percent of Argentina's export earnings. The country is a major producer of wheat, barley, and corn, which flourish on the pampas, and is the world's third largest producer of soybeans. Fruit, especially oranges, grows well in the warm climate, and grapes are produced for wine-making.

*Harvesting barley on the fertile pampas*

*Bolas rope used to slow down cattle*

*These women work in a fish-packing plant and must wear hats for hygiene.*

*The Falkland Islands lie 300 miles (480 km) east of Argentina.*

## Gauchos

Tough, independent gauchos, or cowhands, have roamed the pampas on horseback for more than 300 years, tending cattle and horses. Modern gauchos work mainly on huge *estancias*, or ranches, owned by wealthy landlords, where they rear animals and mend fences. Gauchos are experts in handling herds and are the national heroes of Argentina.

*Wool poncho, or cloak, for warmth at night*

*Strong boots have heels to fit into stirrups.*

## Industry

About 30 percent of the labor force works in industry. Textiles, food production, and chemical products dominate business. The country is self-sufficient in oil and gas, and rich in minerals.

## Falkland Islands

Britain and Argentina have fought over ownership of the Falkland Islands, or Islas Malvinas, since the British claimed the islands from the Spanish in 1833. In 1982, an Argentine invasion of the islands was overthrown, and the British continue to hold them.

# Chile

A long and extremely narrow country, Chile measures, at most, only about 267 miles (430 km) wide. Most Chileans live in cities and towns in the Central Valley between the low coastal mountains on the west and the towering Andes on the east. The cold, stormy southern coast is flanked by thousands of islands. The waters provide rich fishing grounds. Chile has a strong economy rooted in its natural resources: minerals, fruit, sea products, and timber.

## Santiago

Located in the heart of Chile, the capital, Santiago, is a bustling, modern city. The city and suburbs house about five million people. Santiago is known for severe traffic congestion, and has one of the highest taxi densities in the world, with one per 100 inhabitants. About 2,236 miles (3,600 km) of the Pan-American Highway run through Santiago, but high smog levels over the city concern environmentalists.

Some of Santiago's 14,500 buses on Avenue Campama

## Mapuche Indians

Descended from the original inhabitants of South America, the Mapuche Indians are also known as the Araucanians. About 800,000 Mapuche Indians live in reservations in the south of Chile, which were established during the 1880s. They are Roman Catholics and speak their own language as well as Spanish. The Mapuche people have fought for independence since the 16th century and are still at odds with the Chilean government. Quechua and Aymara Indians also live in Chile, in the north.

53 per sq mile (20 per sq km)

84% Urban    16% Rural

The Chuquicamata copper mine, 2,200 ft (670 m) deep

## Copper

Chile leads the world in the production of copper ore, of which it owns about 20 percent of known reserves. The Central Valley, which extends for 994 miles (1,600 km), has the world's largest underground copper mine, located at El Teniente. Chuquicamata, in the bleak Atacama Desert, is one of the largest opencast copper mines in the world. The country also mines iron, gold, and silver.

## Wine

Vineyards first planted by Spanish colonists in the 1500s have benefited from the hot, dry summers in the Central Valley. Today, about 350,000 tons (320,000 tonnes) of Chilean wines, red from Cabernet Sauvignon grapes and white from Chardonnay grapes, are exported all over the world.

Cabernet Sauvignon grapes and wine

Crabs are put into small baskets.

## Fishing

Although less than one percent of the people work in the fishing industry, Chile leads the world in fishmeal production. An average 6,502 tons of sardines, anchovies, mackerel, and salmon are caught and processed each year. Punta Arenas, on the Strait of Magellan, is the industry's center.

## CHILE FACTS

| | |
|---|---|
| CAPITAL CITY | Santiago |
| AREA | 289,112 sq miles (748,800 sq km) |
| POPULATION | 14,436,000 |
| MAIN LANGUAGE | Spanish |
| MAJOR RELIGION | Christian |
| CURRENCY | Chilean peso |
| LIFE EXPECTANCY | 75 years |
| PEOPLE PER DOCTOR | 909 |
| GOVERNMENT | Multiparty democracy |
| ADULT LITERACY | 96% |

A

# Uruguay

One of the smallest countries in South America, Uruguay is also one of the most prosperous and harmonious. More than 40 percent of its people, about 1,348,000, live in Montevideo, the capital, chief port, and largest city. The rest are scattered over the vast lowland pastures. Uruguay has a high tourist rate, mainly because of its sandy beaches and fine weather.

## People

There are 11 times as many sheep, cattle, and horses as people in Uruguay. Most Uruguayans are of Spanish or Italian descent, enjoying considerable prosperity, largely due to the wealth from earlier cattle ranching in the country.

## Hydroelectricity

More than 90 percent of Uruguay's power is generated through hydroelectricity. The main hydroelectric plants are situated on the country's major rivers, the Uruguay and its tributary, the Río Negro, which both widen into the Río de la Plata estuary. Huge turbines have been built across the rivers, so that as the water rushes through, it turns the turbines and makes electricity.

## URUGUAY FACTS

| | |
|---|---|
| CAPITAL CITY | Montevideo |
| AREA | 67,494 sq miles (174,810 sq km) |
| POPULATION | 3,300,000 |
| MAIN LANGUAGE | Spanish |
| MAJOR RELIGION | Christian |
| CURRENCY | Uruguayan peso |

## Wool

Three-quarters of Uruguay is rich pasture that provides excellent grazing land for its 25,000,000 sheep and 10,000,000 cattle. The land provides work for nearly half the population. Uruguay is the world's second leading wool producer, and textiles made from wool account for about 20 percent of the country's exports.

Handmade scarf

FIND OUT MORE    CHRISTIANITY    DANCE    DESERTS    ENERGY    FARMING    GRASSLAND WILDLIFE    NATIVE AMERICANS    SOUTH AMERICA, HISTORY OF    TEXTILES AND WEAVING

# ARMIES

FROM ANCIENT TIMES to the present day, the role of an army has always remained the same – to attack enemy territory and defend the country from attack. Armies usually work in close partnership with air and naval forces. Throughout history, foot soldiers called infantry have done most of the fighting, supported by troops on horseback called cavalry. Today, cavalry have been replaced on the battlefield by armored tank units.

**Ancient Greece**
Each Greek city-state had its own army. Greek soldiers were so well regarded that other countries hired them to fight on their behalf.

## History of armies
The world's first armies, raised in Assyria, Egypt, China, and India, were poorly trained civilians forced to fight for their leaders. The ancient Greeks introduced compulsory military service and rigorous training for their civilian army. Later, the Romans established the first professional (paid) army to protect its empire.

## The modern army
Combat troops fighting in the front line need plenty of support. Engineers, for example, repair damaged roads and bridges to help troops cross rough terrain. Other support staff includes doctors and nurses to treat wounded soldiers, cooks to feed the army, and communications experts.

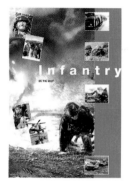

**Recruitment**
In some countries, the army is made up entirely of volunteer recruits who willingly join the army for a fixed period of time. In other countries, the army is made up largely of conscripts – that is, young people required by law to spend a number of years in the army.

**British Army recruitment poster**

British SAS personal equipment — Gas mask, Knife sheath, Leather glove, Body armor, Balaclava, Grenade pocket, Belt loop, Magazine pouch, Thigh strap, Leather boots, Reinforced toe cap

**SAS survival kit** — Miniature harpoons, Wire saw, Steel fire lighter, Fire-kindling tin

## Specialized units
Most armies have units of troops trained to carry out specialized tasks, such as reconnaissance missions and sabotage raids behind enemy lines, tackling terrorists, and rescuing hostages. These units include the US Army's Green Berets and the British Special Air Service (SAS).

**British officer's shoulder strap** / **Italian officer's cap badge**

## Officers
An army needs a strong chain of command, from the highest to the lowest ranks, so that orders are passed on quickly and clearly. Officers receive training in leading and inspiring their troops. Officers' ranks are shown by special symbols on their uniforms.

**Training**
Modern weapons use advanced technology, so troops need to be not just physically fit but also able to make split-second decisions and operate highly complex computerized equipment. For this reason, technical instruction is just as important a part of a soldier's training as exercise and marching drills.

## Terrorist armies
Sometimes armies are set up by groups of people struggling to overthrow the existing government or achieve independence for their country or region. Their supporters call them freedom fighters, but those who oppose them call them terrorists. Such groups often stage spectacular bomb attacks to gain publicity for their cause.

**Terrorist bomb damage**

## Noncombat roles
When a nation is at peace, its army still has a vital role to play. For example, when natural disasters occur – such as earthquakes, floods, or famines – an army can bring in medical supplies and food, and restore communications links and electricity and water supplies. Armies can also help establish peace in other war-torn countries.

**Peacekeeping**
To separate warring sides in a civil war or to keep the peace once a ceasefire has been negotiated, the United Nations (UN) often sends multinational forces consisting of troops from many different armies.

**Crisis response**
Armies need to react quickly and efficiently in times of crisis. Huge cargo planes carry supplies, trucks, and even small tanks to the crisis area, while passenger planes take troops and other personnel.

 **FIND OUT MORE** — ARMS AND ARMOR · COLD WAR · FEUDALISM · GREECE, ANCIENT · KNIGHTS AND HERALDRY · ROMAN EMPIRE · UNITED NATIONS · WARFARE · WARPLANES · WARSHIPS · WEAPONS

# ARMS AND ARMOR

WARRIORS OF THE PAST attacked with slashing swords, sharp spears, flying arrows, deadly axes, and crushing clubs. All of these arms, or weapons, could kill, so fighters protected themselves with armor: tough coverings of wood, leather, or metal. The invention of firearms in the 14th century made armor useless, because metal plates thick enough to deflect bullets were too heavy to wear. By the 16th century, arms and armor were strictly for show. Modern soldiers may still wear shiny breastplates and carry swords or spears on parade, but they swap them for guns and bulletproof vests on the battlefield.

## Arms

The simplest arms – clubs – are extensions of a fighter's fist, delivering a knock-out punch from a greater distance. Most hand arms, however, aim to wound by cutting the body. Swords, daggers, and lances do this for hand-to-hand combat; arrows and boomerangs do it from a distance, killing or injuring foes that may be out of sight.

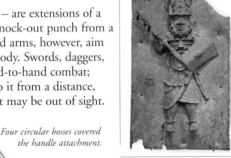

Four circular bosses covered the handle attachment.

### Defensive weapons
Shields are used for defense. Prehistoric hunters may have invented them as camouflage when hunting. Later, fighters strapped shields to their left arms to fend off sword cuts. Wood and leather shields were light and strong enough to deflect all but a direct sword thrust.

**Indian shield**

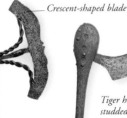

Boomerang

Parrying shield

Crescent-shaped blade

Tabars, Indian steel axes

Tiger heads studded with gems

**Mughal dagger**

Sheath

Aboriginal weapons

Club

**Shamshir, a classic Indian saber**

### Attacking weapons
Over the centuries, warriors have used various weapons for different kinds of fighting. Sabers (curved swords) delivered the deadliest cuts, but straight swords were better for thrusting strokes. Clubs and axes had to be heavy and sharp, yet short enough to swing easily. Small, easily hidden daggers were often used for secret assassinations.

## Armor

A suit of armor had to protect against weapons, yet also had to be comfortable enough to wear all day. Different cultures used various materials, such as leather or metal, to achieve these goals.

Horns

Iron mask

**Samurai, 1300s**

Pauldron and besagew protect shoulder and armpit.

Bevor protects lower face.

A mace was effective against plate armor.

### Benin warrior
Soldiers of this great 15th-century African empire wore heavily quilted garments as armor. Light bamboo shields were easy to carry and protected warriors from glancing blows from iron-tipped spears or javelins.

**Benin bronze plaque**

### Japanese samurai
Samurai armor was made of many small metal or leather scales laced together with silk ties. Armor became more decorative when firearms removed its protective value.

### European knight
Knights wore chain mail (linked metal rings) to protect them. In the 14th century, armorers introduced metal plates (plate armor) for extra protection.

**European knight, 1300s**

Full armor for a horse weighed 75 lbs (34 kg).

Spike

**Italian horse armor, 1570**

Tassels on headpiece protected the horse's face from flies.

Gilt

Charm made of copper bells

Leather saddle

### Animal armor
African horse armor, such as that of the Fulani people of West Africa, was quilted cotton stuffed with kapok. During battle, horses also wore chain mail across the flanks and around the head. In Europe, metal horse armor was expensive, and knights often armored only their horses' heads.

**Fulani horse armor**

### Modern armor
Artificial fabric, such as nylon, provides soldiers and police officers with more protection than thick metal armor. Bulletproof vests are made of 16 or more layers of nylon. A bullet flattens when it hits the outer layer; lower layers slow it down so that the wearer is bruised, rather than killed or seriously injured.

**Riot police**

FIND OUT MORE

| ABORIGINAL AUSTRALIANS | BENIN EMPIRE | EUROPE, HISTORY OF | GUNS | INDIA, HISTORY OF | JAPAN, HISTORY OF | METALS | WARFARE | WEAPONS |

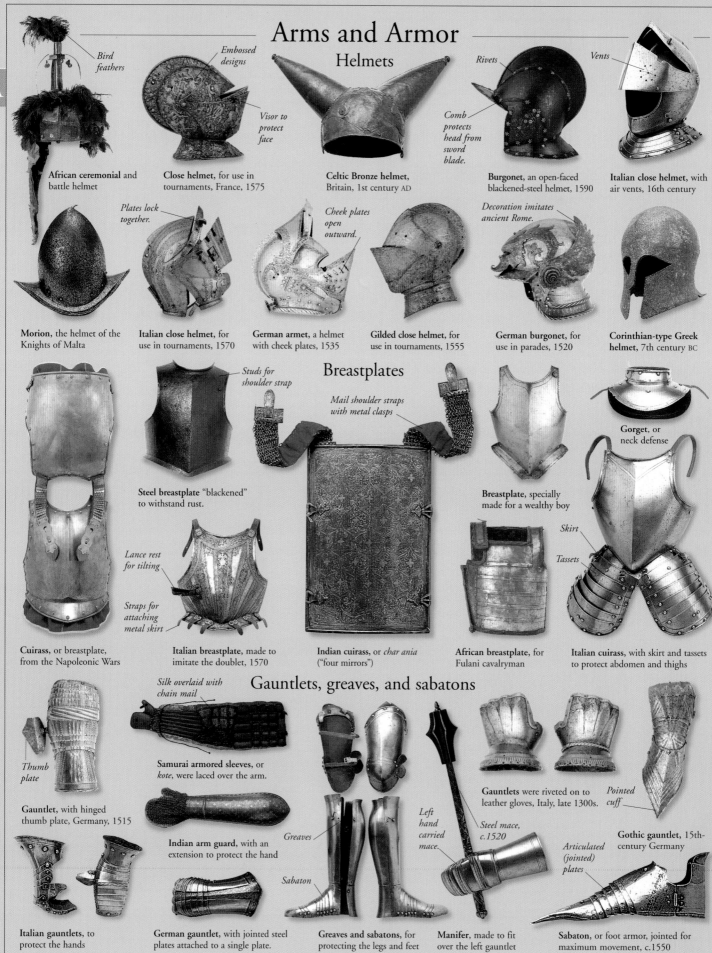

# Arms and Armor
## Helmets

*Bird feathers*

**African ceremonial** and battle helmet

*Embossed designs*

*Visor to protect face*

**Close helmet**, for use in tournaments, France, 1575

**Celtic Bronze helmet**, Britain, 1st century AD

*Rivets*

*Comb protects head from sword blade.*

**Burgonet**, an open-faced blackened-steel helmet, 1590

*Vents*

**Italian close helmet**, with air vents, 16th century

*Plates lock together.*

**Morion**, the helmet of the Knights of Malta

**Italian close helmet**, for use in tournaments, 1570

*Cheek plates open outward.*

**German armet**, a helmet with cheek plates, 1535

**Gilded close helmet**, for use in tournaments, 1555

*Decoration imitates ancient Rome.*

**German burgonet**, for use in parades, 1520

**Corinthian-type Greek helmet**, 7th century BC

## Breastplates

*Studs for shoulder strap*

**Steel breastplate** "blackened" to withstand rust.

*Mail shoulder straps with metal clasps*

**Breastplate**, specially made for a wealthy boy

**Gorget**, or neck defense

*Skirt*

*Tassets*

*Lance rest for tilting*

*Straps for attaching metal skirt*

**Cuirass**, or breastplate, from the Napoleonic Wars

**Italian breastplate**, made to imitate the doublet, 1570

**Indian cuirass**, or *char aina* ("four mirrors")

**African breastplate**, for Fulani cavalryman

**Italian cuirass**, with skirt and tassets to protect abdomen and thighs

## Gauntlets, greaves, and sabatons

*Silk overlaid with chain mail*

*Thumb plate*

**Gauntlet**, with hinged thumb plate, Germany, 1515

**Samurai armored sleeves**, or *kote*, were laced over the arm.

**Indian arm guard**, with an extension to protect the hand

*Greaves*

*Sabaton*

*Left hand carried mace.*

*Steel mace, c.1520*

**Gauntlets** were riveted on to leather gloves, Italy, late 1300s.

*Pointed cuff*

*Articulated (jointed) plates*

**Gothic gauntlet**, 15th-century Germany

**Italian gauntlets**, to protect the hands

**German gauntlet**, with jointed steel plates attached to a single plate.

**Greaves and sabatons**, for protecting the legs and feet

**Manifer**, made to fit over the left gauntlet

**Sabaton**, or foot armor, jointed for maximum movement, c.1550

# ART, HISTORY OF

FROM THE EARLIEST TIMES, people have tried to express their thoughts, feelings, and understanding of the world around them by creating art. Over the centuries, styles in the visual arts (sculpture, painting, and drawing) have changed. These differences reflect the changing beliefs and traditions people held as their societies developed. Materials have changed as well, allowing artists to try new ways of reflecting the world around them.

## Early art

The earliest works of art seem to have had a religious or magical purpose: to represent a god, for example, or to bring a hunter luck as he hunted animals.

**Sumerian sculpture**
A rich artistic tradition grew up in ancient Sumer (now southern Iraq) during the 3rd millennium BC. This statue, which shows a Sumerian ruler, is carved from stone. It represents the strength and dignity of a good leader.

**Caves at Lascaux**
These extraordinary pictures of wild animals were painted in French caves more than 17,000 years ago. The outlines were painted by hand and the vivid colors were filled in by spraying pigment through tubes of bone.

## Classical art

Western art derives from the traditions of the ancient Mediterranean world and especially the art of ancient Greece and Rome. Sculpture from these civilizations is remarkably lifelike, or naturalistic, and concentrates on the human figure.

*Fresco from Pompeii*

**Roman wall painting**
Most ancient paintings have not survived. This one was preserved by volcanic ash at Pompeii. It shows figures from Roman mythology, and was painted on a wall to decorate the interior of a Roman house.

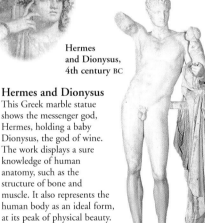

**Hermes and Dionysus, 4th century BC**

**Hermes and Dionysus**
This Greek marble statue shows the messenger god, Hermes, holding a baby Dionysus, the god of wine. The work displays a sure knowledge of human anatomy, such as the structure of bone and muscle. It also represents the human body as an ideal form, at its peak of physical beauty. It is believed to be by Praxiteles, the most famous ancient Greek sculptor.

*The painted vault gives a sense of space.*

*Skeleton, a symbol of mortality*

**Masaccio, *The Holy Trinity*, 1428**

**Perspective**
The Italian Tomaso Masaccio (1401–28) was the first painter to use perspective since classical times. Perspective creates the illusion that depth exists behind the flat surface of a painting.

## The Renaissance

After the fall of the Roman Empire, classical art was considered too pagan for the Christian civilizations that developed in Europe. By the 15th century, painters, sculptors, and architects began to revive the classical tradition, creating highly lifelike works of art. This revival is called the Renaissance, from the French for "rebirth." It began in Italy and spread through Europe. Influential artists included the painter and sculptor Michelangelo (1475–1564).

**Nonreligious art**
During the Renaissance, European painters broke with earlier tradition. Although religious subject matter was still important, artists also began to record everyday events, such as a market day or a wedding.

**Jan Van Eyck, *The Arnolfini Marriage*, 1434**

## Early paint making

The materials used to produce a painting affect the way it looks. Before the 15th century, artists painted on wet plaster with tempera, a mixture of egg and paint pigment. Oil paints arrived in the 15th century. They were more flexible and gave a more realistic finish, so they soon became the favorite medium.

*Mineral, ground into pigment*

**Egg tempera**
Egg (either the yolk or both yolk and white) provides a strong medium for colors, but is quick-drying, making it difficult to apply.

*Egg yolk*

**Oil paint**
As a medium, oil has the advantage of being slow to dry, allowing artists to make changes while they work.

*Oil for binding paint pigment*

**Value of color**
Certain colors, such as gold, have always been more expensive than others. Until the 17th century, dark blue was the most costly because it was made from lapis lazuli, a semiprecious stone.

*Lapis lazuli*

*Scales weigh the pigment.*

# Baroque art

The term "Baroque" describes a style of 17th-century European art. Rome, the centre of the Catholic church, was its birthplace. During the 16th century, the Christian church split into Roman Catholic and Protestant factions. By the 17th century, the Catholic church was using art to spread its teachings. To appeal to the viewer, it promoted a style of art that was theatrical and emotional. Painters were encouraged to use light and shade for dramatic contrasts, sculptors to show figures in dynamic poses. To achieve these effects, artists had to develop great technical skills.

*Dramatic facial expression*

*Arrow is a symbol of God's love.*

Bernini, *The Ecstasy of St. Teresa, 1652*

### Bernini
The Italian painter, sculptor, and architect Gianlorenzo Bernini (1598–1680) was an outstanding influence on Baroque art. He had an exceptional ability to convey great emotion and drama in stone, designed to inspire those who saw his work to greater faith. This sculpture depicts the vision of St. Teresa, in which an angel pierced her with an arrow.

Caravaggio, *The Calling of St. Matthew*, c.1598–99

### Light and shade
The Italian painter Michelangelo Caravaggio (1573–1610) shows the moment when Christ calls Matthew to become a disciple. A ray of light illuminates Matthew but Christ is hidden by shadow.

# Romanticism

The early 19th century in Europe is known as the Romantic Age. It was in part a reaction to 18th-century art, which had emphasized balance and order. Romantic artists questioned the place of human beings in the Universe. They stressed the importance of human emotion and the imagination, and celebrated the wild power of nature in dramatic landscape paintings.

*Friedrich,* Wanderer among the Mists, *1818*

### The lonely universe
The German artist Caspar David Friedrich (1774–1840) was spiritually inspired by natural landscapes. There is an intense mysticism to this painting, as a solitary figure contemplates the mighty Alps.

*A powerful landscape, shrouded in mist, conveys the strength and mystery of nature.*

# Change in the 19th century

From the mid-19th century, artists broke with the tradition established by earlier generations. Where they were once told what to depict by patrons who paid them, they now produced what they wanted, and then tried to sell their work.

Camille Pissarro, *Place du Théâtre Français, 1898*

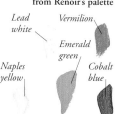

*Selection of colors from Renoir's palette*

*Lead white* — *Vermilion* — *Emerald green* — *Naples yellow* — *Cobalt blue*

### Impressionism
This school of painting grew up in France in the late 19th century. Artists such as Camille Pissarro (1830–1903), Claude Monet (1840–1926), and Auguste Renoir (1841–1919) painted their impressions of a brief moment in time, in particular, the changing effects of sunlight. They were criticised at first, for viewers expected paintings to look more realistic, but have been very influential.

# 20th-century art

During the 20th century, artists explored new theories about the world, religion, and the mind. They asked the public to confront things that they might wish to ignore, and explored many different styles. After nearly 2,500 years, the grip of Classical art seemed to have been broken.

### Surrealism
During the 1920s, the fantastical art made by the Surrealists explored theories about the way the brain works. New ideas had suggested that people consciously used only a tiny part of their brains, and that they were unaware of subconscious activity over which they had no rational control. The bizarre, dreamlike paintings of Surrealists, such as the Spanish artist Salvador Dali (1904–89), were inspired by these ideas.

Salvador Dali

### Abstract art
Abstract artists do not represent objects as we see them every day. Color and shape alone suggest ideas or emotions. In this way, abstract art is like music: neither describe anything that can be defined in words, but both can be expressive and moving. The artists Jackson Pollock (1912–56) and Mark Rothko (1903–70) are two of the most famous abstract painters.

Jackson Pollock, *The Moon, Woman Cuts the Circle, 1943*

### Modern art
Much modern art is specially created to be seen in a museum or gallery, and not for houses, palaces, or churches as in the past. It often prefers to baffle, tease, and provoke its audience rather than make its meaning obvious.

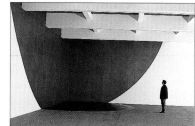

Yoki Terauchi, *Air Castle, 1994*

# Ambroise Vollard

The French art dealer Ambroise Vollard (1865–1939) made a living buying, selling, and exhibiting modern art. He gave early 20th-century artists unprecedented financial and creative freedom to paint as they wished. Artists such as Paul Cezanne and Henri Matisse achieved success in Vollard's gallery in Paris in the 1900s.

A

# Art in Africa

African art has a long tradition, although a lack of written records make its history hard to trace. Sculpture and masks are major art forms. Most art seems to have been made for religious or ritual purposes. Wood-carving and bronze-casting techniques were highly developed.

## Sculpture

The rich tradition of sculpture in West Africa begins with the pottery figures made by the Nok people from 500 BC. Around the 13th century AD, the Ife of Nigeria began to cast outstanding bronze heads and figures in a highly realistic style. These may have influenced sculptures made in Benin, Nigeria, from the 16th to 19th centuries.

Ife sculpture, 13th century

## Masks

African masks may represent a spirit or ancestor, or be purely decorative. Their meaning comes from the masquerade (dance, drama, and music) of which they are a part. Wood, beads, ivory, and shells are important materials. This capped mask, carved in a bold, vital style, is from Cameroon.

Wooden mask, 20th century

# Asia

Traditionally in Asian art the symbolic meaning behind the subject of a painting, sculpture, or carving is more important than the illusion of realism. In China, for instance, landscape paintings are stylized to express the ideals of religious thought: natural harmony, peace, and grace. In China and Japan, calligraphy was seen as a high form of art. The inscriptions are usually of short, poetic situations.

*Brief poetic description of the scene*

T'ang Yin, *Dreaming of Immortality in a Thatched Cottage*, Ming dynasty

## Chinese landscape

In China the art of painting developed from calligraphy. Landscape artists painted on paper or silk, using brush and ink. They did not paint from real life. The flow and vigor of the brush strokes were more important.

16th-century Mughal manuscript

*Vividly colored*

*High level of detail*

## Miniatures

During the Mughal Empire (16th–17th centuries), figurative miniature painting flourished in India. These artworks were richly colored and exceptionally delicate. This illustration comes from a chronicle of the emperor's exploits.

## Hokusai

Katsushika Hokusai (1760–1849) is perhaps the best-known Japanese printmaker. His famous wood-cuts include landscapes as well as scenes of daily life (called *ukiyo-e*). They are dramatically colored and composed.

*The Great Wave of Kawagawa*, 1831

# Native American art

Sophisticated Native American societies, such as the Aztec and Maya in Mexico and the Inca in Peru, created distinct artistic and architectural styles. Nearly 3,000 years ago, nomadic peoples in North and South America marked awe-inspiring "sculptures" on to the land, or created vast earthworks whose shapes can only be seen from high in the air.

Tlingit totem pole

## Totem poles

Complex in design, and carved with great skill, totem poles showed the status of many Native North American chiefs.

## Sand paintings

In the Southwest, Native North Americans trickled colored sand and ground stones on to a smooth background to create temporary symbolic paintings with a ritual importance.

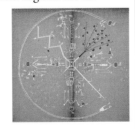

Navajo sand painting shows mythological figures.

## Easter Island statues

Between AD 400 and 1680, the people of Easter Island carved huge heads, up to 40 ft (12 m) high, from volcanic rock. They commemorate the divine ancestors of tribal chiefs.

# Pacific art

Contact with European Christian cultures from the 18th century onward had a destructive effect on ancient local lifestyles in the Pacific islands. Much art has been lost, although some remarkable sculptures have survived, because of their durability. Wood and stone carvings, bark cloth paintings, spirit masks, and intricate body tattoos are among the important art forms of the Pacific area.

*Statues face out to sea.*

Statues, Easter Island

# Timeline

**30,000 BC** Earliest known works of art produced.

**30,000–10,000 BC** Cave paintings made in France.

**c.500 BC** Lifelike human figurines produced by the Nok in West Africa.

**100 BC–AD 300s** Roman Empire spreads Classical art around Europe.

Warrior, Greece, 520 BC

**618–907** T'ang dynasty, China: great tradition of landscape painting develops.

**15th century** Beginning of the Renaissance in Europe.

**16th century** Mughal dynasty holds power in India.

**17th century** Dutch Golden Age of painting.

**19th century** Photography invented.

**1860s–90s** Impressionism develops in France. It is very influential.

*Metal tubes are invented in the 1840s.*

19th-century oil paints

**20th century** Time of incredible diversity of styles in the visual arts, including Cubism (1907–20s), abstract art (1910–50), surrealism (1920s), and Pop Art (mid-1950s).

**FIND OUT MORE**   AFRICA, HISTORY OF   ARCHITECTURE   MONET   NATIVE AMERICANS   PAINTING AND DRAWING   PHOTOGRAPHY   PICASSO   RENAISSANCE   SCULPTURE

# ARTHROPODS

MORE THAN ONE MILLION species of arthropods exist, making them the largest group in the animal kingdom. They live in almost all habitats, from mountaintops to ocean depths. Arthropods are invertebrates – animals without backbones. They come in many shapes and sizes, from tiny mites to large crabs. Their bodies are divided into segments, and they have distinct heads with antennae or eyes. Rigid exoskeletons encase their bodies, but flexible leg joints allow them to move around, and give them their name.

## Types of arthropods

Arthropods vary in size, from minute creatures a fraction of an inch long to oversized sea dwellers weighing several pounds. There are four main types of arthropod – insects, arachnids, crustaceans, and myriapods. Insects are the largest group, accounting for almost 90 percent of all arthropods.

*Spiders have 8 legs.*

*Delicate wings*

*Large compound eyes helps it to catch prey in flight.*

**Red-kneed tarantula**

**Broad-bodied chaser dragonfly**

### Arachnids
Arachnids include spiders, scorpions, and mites. They have eight legs; scorpions use the front pair as claws. Spiders and scorpions are carnivores that live mainly on land. Spiders often kill their prey with poisonous fangs; scorpions use their venom-filled sting.

### Insects
Insects are the most diverse group of arthropods. They live in all kinds of land and freshwater habitats. All adult insects have six legs, and most have wings – they are the only arthropods that can fly.

**Asian giant millipede**

*Two pairs of legs on each body segment*

*Antenna*

### Myriapods
Myriapods include millipedes and centipedes. They have more legs than other arthropods – as many as 200 in some species. Their bodies are long and tubular. They live in the soil or in piles of leaves.

**European lobster**

*Hard exoskeleton*

### Crustaceans
Crustaceans include crabs, shrimps, and lobsters. Most live in the ocean or in freshwater and have five pairs of legs. Lobsters and crabs have very thick exoskeletons and some grow extremely large.

*Exoskeletons are made mainly of a substance called chitin.*

**Exoskeleton of a fiddler crab**

## Exoskeleton

The exoskeleton of an arthropod is a tough outer layer covering the entire body, including the eyes, antennae, and legs. It protects and supports the muscles and soft organs within the body and helps retain moisture.

## Molting and metamorphosis

Exoskeletons are fixed in size. In order to grow, an arthropod must shed, or molt, this rigid layer. Its body then rapidly expands before a new exoskeleton hardens in place of the old one. Molting is part of a process called "incomplete metamorphosis". The young, called nymphs, emerge from eggs looking like tiny adults. They molt many times before reaching adult size. In "complete metamorphosis", the animal changes form as well as size.

### Molting

1 An emerging adult grasshopper has cracked open its old exoskeleton and is starting to wriggle its body free, headfirst. Before this final molt, the nymph will already have been through four previous molts.

*Nymph on twig*

*Adult is almost free of the nymph's skin.*

2 The adult has pulled its legs and most of its body out of the old skin. It is already expanding in size now that it is free from its shell.

*Old, empty exoskeleton*

*Adult waits as blood pumps into its wings before it flies away.*

3 Molting is now complete. The adult rests while its new exoskeleton hardens and its wings unfurl. Its old exoskeleton, now empty and brittle, still clings to the twig.

## Reproduction

Reproduction is diverse among arthropods. Fertilization may take place inside or outside the female's body. Normally eggs are laid; some are guarded, others are hidden and left alone. The young of some arthropods, such as garden spiders, are tiny versions of adults called nymphs; others start life as larvae and look different from the adults.

**Cluster of young garden spiders**

## Feeding

Arthropods feed on plant and animal matter, both living and dead. Some arthropods, such as praying mantises, have pincers to gather food; others use their front legs. Many have cutting and chewing teethlike structures, while those that feed on fluids, such as true bugs, have mouths modified for sucking. Small aquatic arthropods eat by filtering food particles from water.

### Herbivores
Some arthropods, such as chafer beetles, eat only plant matter. Adults feed on stems, leaves, and buds, while larvae eat plant roots.

**Field chafer beetle**

### Carnivores
Many arthropods feed on other animals. Garden spiders, for example, feed mainly on insects. Some meat eaters also eat dead animals and are called scavengers. Sand crabs scavenge on dead birds and other debris found on the beach and ocean floor.

*Web spun around wasp*

**Garden spider feeding on a wasp**

## Defense

Since arthropods are generally small in size, they are the target for a great many predators. Their hard exoskeleton, which acts as a tiny suit of armor, provides the first line of defense. Some arthropods, such as pill millipedes, take a passive form of defense and roll up into a ball if danger threatens. Other arthropods have special protective weapons, including stings and pincers. Many ant species have glands on their abdomens from which they secrete formic acid to drive off enemies.

### Stings and pincers
Some arthropods have pincers and stings, which they use to defend themselves against attackers. Scorpions also use their large pincers to catch animals. They then use their venom-filled stings to paralyze their prey.

*Sting*

*Eyes*

**Fat-tailed scorpion**

**FIND OUT MORE** | ANTS AND TERMITES | BEETLES | CAVE WILDLIFE | CRABS AND OTHER CRUSTACEANS | FLIES | GRASSHOPPERS AND CRICKETS | INSECTS | POISONOUS ANIMALS | SPIDERS AND SCORPIONS

# ASIA

STRETCHING from the frozen Arctic to the equator, Asia is the world's largest continent. It is also a continent of extremes, containing the world's highest point, Mount Everest, as well as its lowest, the Dead Sea. China has the world's greatest population, while Asia's largest country, the Russian Federation, extends into Europe. Asia is separated from North America by the Bering Sea, and from Europe by the Caspian Sea, Turkey, and the Ural Mountains. In the southeast, it breaks into a mass of tiny islands.

## Physical features

Much of Southwest and Central Asia is covered with barren desert, such as the Gobi and Syrian deserts. The Himalayan Mountains separate the bleak north from the fierce heat of the Indian subcontinent and the tropical rain forests of Southeast Asia. Asia has many great rivers, including the Huang He, Mekong, and Indus, flanked by fertile plains and valleys.

### Lake Baikal
Siberia, the northern region of Asia, has the oldest and deepest lake in the world. At its deepest point, Lake Baikal, which contains more than 20 percent of the world's unfrozen freshwater, reaches a depth of 5,371 ft (1,637 m). Covering an area of 12,150 sq miles (31,468 sq km), Baikal is the world's eighth largest lake.

### Himalayas
The snowcapped Himalaya Mountains, the highest range in the world, form a massive natural barrier between the Indian subcontinent and northern Asia. They were pushed up millions of years ago when the Indian plate collided with the Asian plate.

### Island countries
Two Southeast Asian nations, Indonesia and the Philippines, have more than 20,000 islands between them. Most were formed by volcanic activity in the ocean, and there are several active volcanoes in the region. Southeast Asia is prone to earthquakes.

## Cross-section through Asia

From the Indian Ocean, the land rises to the Vindhya Range in central India, descending to the Ganges Plain, watered by the Himalayas. In the east, the mountains drop to the Great Plain of China. Across the Yellow Sea, the Korean Peninsula juts out close to Japan in the Pacific Ocean.

*Labels:* Ganges Plain · Mt. Everest · Himalayas, Nepal · Vindhya Range · Great Plain of China · Red Basin, China · Korean Peninsula · Yellow Sea · Mt. Fuji, Japan · Sea of Japan · Indian Ocean

Approximately 4,027 miles (6,480 km) from A to B

## ASIA FACTS

| | |
|---|---|
| AREA | 17,251,315 sq miles (44,680,718 sq km) |
| POPULATION | 3,700,700,000 |
| NUMBER OF COUNTRIES | 49 |
| BIGGEST COUNTRY | Russian Federation |
| SMALLEST COUNTRY | Maldives |
| HIGHEST POINT | Mt. Everest (China/Nepal) 29,029 ft (8,848 m) |
| LOWEST POINT | Dead Sea shore, 1,312 ft (400 m) below sea level |
| LONGEST RIVER | Yangtze (Chang Jiang) (China) 3,965 miles (6,380 km) |
| BIGGEST LAKE | Caspian Sea 146,100 sq miles (378,400 sq km) |

75

# Climatic zones

Asia has every kind of climate and landscape. In the far north, Siberia is covered in tundra, where part of the ground is permanently frozen. South of the tundra are coniferous forests and open grasslands (steppes). Central and southwest Asia are mostly desert and mountains, while the east has deciduous forests. Tropical rain forests cover much of the south and southeast.

Coniferous forest
Tundra
Mountain
Scrubland
Deciduous forest
Grassland
Desert
Wetland
Tropical rain forest

## Tundra

In the bitterly cold and treeless tundra region of Siberia, the subsoil remains frozen – a condition known as permafrost. With temperatures of less than 14°F (-10°C) and covered by snow for six to ten months of the year, the topsoil thaws only briefly in the summer. The tundra has rich mineral resources.

*Mosses, lichens, and a few flowers appear briefly during the warmer months.*

*The steppes are the Asian equivalent of the pampas and prairies of the Americas.*

## Taiga

The Siberian taiga, which lies to the south of the tundra, is the world's largest coniferous forest. The main trees are fir, larch, pine, and spruce. In the spring, much of the taiga becomes flooded as the lower reaches of the north-flowing rivers thaw, while their mouths remain frozen. In summer, some ground remains swampy; in winter it freezes.

## Steppes

The wide, open grasslands that cover Mongolia and southern Siberia are known as the steppes. Livestock is grazed on these broad, treeless plains, which, in places, merge into semidesert. The soil is mostly fertile and, with irrigation, many areas have become productive farmland.

*Harsh conditions make trees stunted and sparse. Ice and snow cover the region for half the year.*

*Dunes form as sand drifts in the prevailing wind.*

Taklimakan Desert, China

*Temperatures average 70°F (21°C) with 79 in (2,000 mm) of rain per year.*

*Trees lose their leaves in winter as a means of protecting themselves from wind and cold.*

## Deserts

Asia has both hot and cold deserts, as well as many regions of semidesert where animals can be grazed. Middle Eastern deserts are hot and dry all year, with cold nights. The Gobi and Taklimakan deserts of central Asia have scorching summers, but are bitterly cold in winter.

## Wetlands

Mangrove swamps are found along many coasts of southern Asia, from India to the Philippines. The mangrove trees have long, spreading roots, producing a forest that looks as if it is on stilts. Logging and pollution are destroying many mangroves.

*Mangrove roots help stop coast eroding in storms.*

## Tropical rain forest

There are tropical rain forests in India, Southeast Asia, and the Philippines. They flourish on the southern slopes of the Himalayas, and in Burma (Myanmar), the Malay Peninsula, and the western part of the island of Irian Jaya. Home to 40 percent of all plant and animal species, the world's rain forests are threatened as people cut down trees for the timber industry and to clear space for farming.

## Deciduous forest

Asia has comparatively few broadleaf forests of deciduous trees that shed their leaves in winter. They occur mainly in eastern Asia – China, Japan, and the Koreas – or in cooler upland areas such as the mountains of Nepal.

## People

Asia contains two-thirds of the world's population, and the birth rate is still rising in many countries. Most people live in the southern and eastern regions and in the fertile river valleys. Many are farmers, although increasing numbers are moving into expanding cities in search of work.

Israeli boy    Vietnamese girl    Japanese boy

## Resources

Asia's natural resources include farmland, which provides work for 60 percent of the people, and the fishing grounds of the Pacific Ocean. Minerals include oil and natural gas from the Gulf States, as well as bauxite, copper, coal, diamonds, gold, iron, lead, manganese, mercury, tin, and titanium.

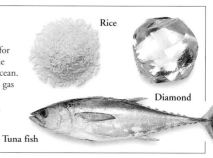

Rice
Diamond
Tuna fish

**FIND OUT MORE**    ASIA, HISTORY OF    ASIAN WILDLIFE    CLIMATE    CONTINENTS    DESERTS    FORESTS    GRASSLAND WILDLIFE    LAKES    MOUNTAINS AND VALLEYS    RAIN FOREST WILDLIFE    TUNDRA

# ASIA, HISTORY OF

ASIA IS THE WORLD'S LARGEST continent and the birthplace of the world's earliest civilizations, such as Sumer, China, and India. The emergence of these civilizations had a profound impact on history, both ancient and modern, as did the emergence of three major world religions: Hinduism, Buddhism, and Islam. Colonial interference affected Asia's development over the centuries, but after decades of independent growth, today's Asian economies are booming. There are still conflicts, however, and those in Southeast Asia and the Middle East affect world politics.

### Early development
Early civilizations in Asia were largely isolated from each other and from the rest of the world by barriers of deserts, mountains, and oceans. Only the Middle East had strong connections with Europe. Therefore Asian civilizations and cultures developed independently for thousands of years. Over time, major civilizations, such as those of India and China, began to affect other Asian countries.

Swat, Pakistan

## Central Asia
For centuries the only travelers in the inhospitable landscape of Central Asia were traders using the Silk Road. In 1398, the Mongolian warrior Timur (1336–1405) swept down from the steppes and founded a Central Asian empire.

**Samarkand**
In 1369, Timur moved his capital to the prosperous city of Samarkand, in modern Uzbekistan. The city experienced a golden age and became the architectural jewel of Central Asia, as Timur and his descendants built palaces, astronomical observatories, and Islamic colleges. In the early 1500s, nomadic Uzbeks attacked the city.

*Typically tiled Samarkandian roof*

**Uleg Beg Medrasa, Uzbekistan**

### Kushan Empire
In c.170 BC, a northern Chinese clan, the Yuezhi, moved west to Central Asia. By the 3rd century AD, they had founded an empire that stretched from eastern Iran to the Ganges in India. The Kushans controlled fertile river valleys and were at the center of the silk trade. They encouraged Buddhism and religious art, but declined in the 4th century.

## Padmasambhava
A legendary sage and yoga expert from Swat, modern Pakistan, Padmasambhava founded Tibetan Buddhism. He and his consort, Yeshe Tsogyal, arrived in Tibet in 747, and established the first Buddhist monastery. The sage then spent his life writing and lecturing on the religion.

*Semiprecious stones*

## Ancient civilizations
The Sumerians of western Asia evolved the world's first civilization, but it was the early civilizations of India and China that affected Asia the most. Their religions had special impact: Hinduism (the religion of the people of India) and Buddhism (founded by Siddhartha Gautama and one of the three great religions of China) spread over Asia.

**Chola dynasty**
From 850–c.1200, a powerful dynasty known as the Cholas began to dominate much of India. Cholas built many Hindu temples and spread their religion to Sri Lanka. They extended their naval power over the seas of Southeast Asia, spreading Hinduism as far as Sumatra and Bali.

**Kogyuro openwork cup**

### Kogyuro dynasty
By the 7th century, China's influence was increasing, and Chinese monks converted Korea to Buddhism. The Kogyuro rulers (1st century BC–AD 7th century) were the last native Korean dynasty. From Korea the missionaries went to Japan, which adopted not only Buddhism but also Chinese script, architecture, and culture.

## Southeast Asia
For 1,000 years, India was the major shaping force of this region and provided a mold for Southeast Asian culture, art, and religion. Its influence declined after c.1300.

### Sea routes
From c.300, Indian traders sailed to Thailand, Malaysia, Indonesia, and the Philippines. From the 1200s, Arabian merchants spread Islam along sea trade routes. From c.1500, the region also traded with Europe.

**Dhow leaving Muscat, Oman**

### Siam
Over centuries, waves of migrants from the north entered Siam (Thailand) and inter-married with the native tribes. In the 13th century, one tribe, the Thais, unified Siam into a single nation with one monarch and one religion – Buddhism.

**Thai tribal woman**

A Hindu temple in Bali, Indonesia, attests to the great influence of the Chola dynasty.

A

# Trade and culture

During the 17th, 18th, and 19th centuries trade thrived, though some Asian countries were closed to outsiders. Russia and European countries bought silk, tea, and porcelain from China. India traded with the world and was noted for its handmade textiles, such as "paisley," which was a traditional Indian pattern. During this period, Western powers became increasingly interested in annexing Asian territories for trade purposes.

### Manchu Dynasty

China's Manchu Dynasty (1644–1911) was expansionist and spread its culture by acquiring other territories, such as Mongolia (1697), Tibet (1751), and eastern Turkestan (1760). At home, however, economic conditions worsened.

*Yellow lotus is a sacred flower.*

### Asian resistance

In the 17th and 18th centuries, China, Japan, Korea, and Siam (Thailand) resisted European expansion. China confined European trade to Macao and Canton, Japan traded only with Holland at Nagasaki, and Korea remained closed to the west. In 1688, a revolution in Siam ended French attempts to gain influence in Bangkok.

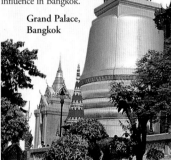

*Gold-coated roof*

**Grand Palace, Bangkok**

### Great Game

During the 1800s, Russia expanded into Central Asia. The British feared the Russians were aiming to take over India, and both sides began to spy on each other. The British called this the Great Game; to the Russians it was known as the Tournament of Shadows.

Mountains of Lake Baikal, Russia

A rich woman's silk robe, 19th century

---

# Nineteenth-century colonization

In the 19th century, European powers colonized much of Asia. The British took over Burma, Malaya, North Borneo, and Hong Kong; France dominated Indochina; the Dutch controlled Indonesia; and Russia annexed Central Asian provinces.

Britain
Russia            Netherlands
France            Japan

### Conversion of the Philippines

In the late 1500s, the Spanish colonial government encouraged Filipinos to become Roman Catholics, and gave financial support to missionaries. By the 18th century, most Filipinos in towns and lowland areas had converted to Catholicism. The island of Mindanao, however, embraced Islam, which was brought to them by Muslim traders.

Paoay church, Ilocos Norte Province, Philippines

---

Engraving of Anglo-Burmese wars, 1824

### Anglo-Burmese wars

In 1886, Burma lost its independence to Britain after a series of wars. This takeover was strategic rather than trade-based: the British wanted to prevent the French from gaining too much influence in Asia.

### Golden East

As Europe gained in military and industrial strength in the 19th century, it expanded, and Asia became a rich source of food and raw materials. European planters developed tea, coffee, and rubber plantations, founded tin mines, exploited Asian timber, and prospected for gold, silver, and precious stones.

Indian tea

Vietnamese mahogany

### Rama V

Chulalongkorn (1853–1910) became Rama V, King of Siam, in 1868. He traveled widely throughout Asia, and was determined to strengthen his country by a process of modernization. In the 1880s, he created a modern army, civil service, and education system. Although Thailand lost some provinces to Britain and France, it managed to preserve its prestige and independence.

The king and queen of Siam

---

# Rebellion

From the 1850s, there were rebellions against European interference in Asian affairs. In 1857, the Sepoy Rebellion took place in India, and, in 1900, there was the Boxer Rebellion in China. Both revolts were protests against Western strength and culture. They were crushed by Western or colonial government forces.

Cover of *Le Petit Parisien*, 1900, "Death to Foreigners"

## Timeline

**4000–c.2500 BC** The world's earliest civilization flourishes in Sumer, western Asia.

**c.2500 BC** Indus Valley period, India's earliest civilization.

**1800 BC** Shang period: China's earliest civilization starts to build its first cities.

**c.330 BC** Alexander the Great destroys the Persian Empire.

**138 BC** First recorded journey on the Silk Road.

**c.50** Buddhism reaches China from India.

**206 BC– AD 220** Height of the Chinese Han Empire.

 **FIND OUT MORE** ARCHITECTURE    ART, HISTORY OF    CHINA, HISTORY OF

*Living quarters*

## Growth of nationalism

After World War I, Asian nationalism (a belief in independence) grew. In 1918, Arab leaders overthrew Turkish rule. The desire of Jews to create an independent state in Palestine gained support. By 1933, 238,000 Jews had settled in Palestine, and, in 1948, the state of Israel was created.

**Jewish settlers in Palestine, 1930s**

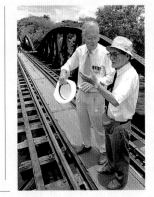

## World War II

In 1941–42, Japan occupied Burma, Indochina, and Indonesia. After the horrors of occupation, these areas rejected all foreign rule. In China, communist guerrillas resisting the Japanese, gained popular and political support.

**Two war veterans on the Death Railroad, Kwai River, Thailand, 1990s**

### Death Railroad
During World War II, the Japanese built a railroad to link Burma and Thailand to supply Japanese troops in Burma. Many thousands of Asian workers and Western prisoners died from malnutrition, disease, and exhaustion building the 260-mile (420-km) railroad, and it became known as the Death Railroad.

A

## Independence movements

After 1945, many Asian countries threw off colonial rule. In 1947, India and Pakistan struggled for and won independence from Britain. In 1948, a Jewish homeland, Israel, came into being. Indonesia won independence from the Netherlands in 1949, after a four-year battle. France also tried to prevent Vietnamese independence, but was defeated in 1954; the other French colonies, Laos and Cambodia, became independent in 1954 and 1953 respectively.

**With the decline** of European empires, there were eventually 48 independent countries in post-war Asia.

## Dragon economies

In the 1980s, Singapore, Taiwan, Hong Kong, and South Korea used their well-educated populations and high investment to become prosperous "dragon" economies. In the 1990s, Thailand, Malaysia, and Indonesia also developed rapidly.

**Taiwanese factory**

### Taiwanese exported goods
Taiwan traditionally exported agricultural products, such as sugar, pineapples, and bananas; but by the 1980s it also exported advanced electronic products, such as personal computers, televisions, and portable phones.

## Communist Asia

In 1949, the communists established the People's Republic of China – the world's largest communist state. In 1954, the North Vietnamese created an independent communist state. From the 1960s, communist movements in Indonesia and Malaysia threatened to overthrow existing governments.

*US troops carry wounded soldiers from a helicopter.*

**Oil rigs, Middle East**

### Middle East conflicts
Since 1948, Arab-Israeli territorial conflict, such as the war of 1973 (when Egypt and Syria attacked Israel), has dominated the Middle East. There have also been conflicts between Arab countries, such as the Iran-Iraq war (1980–88). Although the oil boom has eased conflict somewhat by lessening poverty, the situation in the Middle East remains unstable.

### Vietnam War
From 1954, communist North Vietnam sought to reunite with non-communist South Vietnam by force. Originally a civil war, the Vietnam War escalated into an international conflict with the gradual intervention of the United States in the 1960s. Following defeats and heavy casualties, the US agreed to withdraw in 1973. In 1975, northern forces unified both halves of Vietnam.

### Chaim Weizmann
Weizmann (1874–1952) was born near Pinsk in Belarus and studied chemistry in Switzerland. In his youth he became a passionate Zionist and eventually was made head of the World Zionist Movement. After World War II, Weizmann campaigned for the creation of Israel, and in 1948, became the state of Israel's first president.

## Timeline
c.618–907 The sophisticated T'ang dynasty dominates China.

1211 Mongol warrior Ghengis Khan invades China.

1300s Silk Road is shut.

1368 Ming dynasty expels Mongols from China.

1397 Mongols invade India.

1350–1460 Collapse of Khmer Empire, Cambodia.

1453 Fall of Constantinople to the Turkish Ottoman Empire.

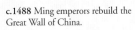
**Toy dog, Thailand, 1926**

c.1488 Ming emperors rebuild the Great Wall of China.

1526–1707 Domination of Mughals in India.

1600–1614 British, French, and Dutch form East India companies.

1757 British take control of Bengal, India.

1839–42 First Opium War.

1736–96 Manchu China prospers under Emperor Qianlong.

c.1750 Cultural and artistic peak in Japan.

1907 Anglo-Russian agreement ends the Great Game in Central Asia.

1949 Chinese Revolution.

1950–53 Korean War.

1954–75 Vietnam War.

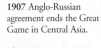
**Toy robot, Japan, 1956**

**FIND OUT MORE**    CONFUCIUS    EMPIRES    EXPLORATION    GANDHI, MOHANDAS    INDIA, HISTORY OF    JAPAN, HISTORY OF    MUHAMMAD    PERSIAN EMPIRES    WARFARE

# ASIA, CENTRAL

MAINLY ARID DESERT and mountainous, central Asia is made up of five countries. The Silk Road, an ancient trade route between China, the Middle East, and Europe, once passed through the region, boosting the textile industry, and making handwoven rugs from central Asia world famous. From 1922 until 1991 the whole area, apart from Afghanistan, was part of the Soviet Union. Under communist rule, the countries were partly modernized. Today, however, as independent nations they face an uncertain future. In 2001 Afghanistan was linked to the terrorist attacks of September 11 in the US and was devastated by US-led reprisal bombings.

## Physical features
Much of central Asia is covered by two hot, dry deserts: the Karakumy and the Kyzyl Kum. The rest is largely rugged mountain chains. There is a small area of farmland that has been expanded by irrigation.

**Kyzyl Kum**
The name Kyzyl Kum means "red sands." This desert region lies south of the Aral Sea between the rivers Syr Daria and Amu Darya, mostly in Uzbekistan. Few people apart from nomads live here. Much of it is covered by low hills and sandy wasteland.

**Tien Shan**
The literal translation of Tien Shan is "Heavenly Mountains." This range of ice-capped peaks runs for 1,864 miles (3,000 km) from eastern Kyrgyzstan into China. The highest point is Pobeda Peak, 24,406 ft (7,439 m). Mountain rivers form broad, fertile valleys, which are used for farming.

**Karakumskiy Ship Canal**
The Karakumskiy Ship Canal is being built from the Amu Darya, one of central Asia's main rivers, across the Karakumy Desert. It will link the river with the Caspian Sea, 870 miles (1,400 km) away.

## Nomads
Many central Asian people are nomads who roam the land with their animal herds, constantly searching for new pastures. They live in traditional tents usually made of animal skins. Their animals – mainly sheep and goats – provide them with meat, milk, skins, and wool, some of which they sell.

Kyrgyz nomad at home with horse

81°F (27°C)    23°F (-5°C)

12 in (316 mm)

## Regional climate
Most of this region is cold in winter and very hot and dry in summer. Rainfall is uniformly low, which hampers farming. The mountain regions are always cooler than the lowlands, and many of the peaks are permanently covered by snow and ice.

# Turkmenistan

Only two percent of Turkmenistan's arid land can be farmed. With irrigation, cotton, fruit, wheat, and vegetables are produced. Many people live in nomadic tribes, and there is much tension between groups. Turkmenistan is the world's fifth largest producer of natural gas.

## TURKMENISTAN FACTS

| | |
|---|---|
| CAPITAL CITY | Ashgabat |
| AREA | 188,455 sq miles (488,100 sq km) |
| POPULATION | 4,500,000 |
| MAIN LANGUAGES | Turkmen, Russian |
| MAJOR RELIGION | Muslim |
| CURRENCY | Manat |

**Saddlecloths**

### Akhal-Teke
Known as the "wind of heaven," Akhal-Teke race-horses have been bred in the south of the Karakumy Desert for centuries. Fast, hardy, and well suited to the hot, harsh climate, Akhal-Tekes compete in traditional horse races at the Ashgabat hippodrome.

**Akhal-Teke**

### Carpets
For centuries, Turkmenistan has produced beautiful, velvety carpets in deep, varying shades of red, brown, and maroon. Women hand-knot each carpet using fine wool from karakul sheep. They make several sizes, including *khali* (large) and *ensi* (welcome mats), as well as weaving curtains, sacks, bags, and pouches.

# Uzbekistan

More than two-thirds of Uzbekistan is dry steppe and desert, but its areas of fertile land and resources of oil, gas, gold, copper, and coal make it one of central Asia's wealthier countries. Fruit, silk cocoons, and vegetables are exported to Moscow. Uzbekistan has the world's largest single gold mine.

## UZBEKISTAN FACTS

| | |
|---|---|
| CAPITAL CITY | Tashkent |
| AREA | 447,400 sq miles (172,741 sq km) |
| POPULATION | 24,300,000 |
| MAIN LANGUAGES | Uzbek, Russian |
| MAJOR RELIGION | Muslim |
| CURRENCY | Som |

### Cotton
Uzbekistan is the world's fourth largest producer of cotton. However, the irrigation system used to water crops has seriously depleted the Aral Sea.

*The Tillya-Kari is an Islamic seminary in Registan Square.*

*An intricate mosaic covers building.*

### Samarkand
Home to 370,000 people, the ancient city of Samarkand was once the center for trade in silk from China. Today, the production of silk and cotton textiles is still the city's main industry. Samarkand's Registan Square contains some magnificent 14th-century Islamic architecture.

# Kyrgyzstan

Dominated by the arid Tien Shan mountains, Kyrgyzstan is a mainly rural country. Only seven percent of the land is cultivable. Half is used for growing fodder for livestock; the rest supports vegetables, wheat, fruit, cotton, and tobacco.

## KYRGYZSTAN FACTS

| | |
|---|---|
| CAPITAL CITY | Bishkek |
| AREA | 76,640 sq miles (198,500 sq km) |
| POPULATION | 4,700,000 |
| MAIN LANGUAGE | Kyrgyz, Russian |
| MAJOR RELIGION | Muslim |
| CURRENCY | Som |

### People
The population of Kyrgyzstan is made up of 57 percent Kyrgyz people. The rest are mainly Russians and Uzbeks. Many Russians are leaving as a result of the strong nationalist feelings that have grown in the country since the end of Soviet rule. Ethnic tension also exists with the Uzbeks.

**Gold**

### Resources
Gold and mercury are mined for export, as well as smaller amounts of other minerals including iron ore, tin, lead, copper, zinc, and bauxite. Kyrgyzstan also has reserves of oil, coal, and gas, and its many rivers and lakes give it great potential for hydroelectric power.

# Tajikistan

The poorest of the former Soviet republics, Tajikistan has been torn by civil war ever since independence. The main conflict is between ethnic Tajiks, who make up about two-thirds of the population, and Uzbeks, who make up one-quarter. Tajikistan has rich mineral resources.

## TAJIKISTAN FACTS

| | |
|---|---|
| CAPITAL CITY | Dushanbe |
| AREA | 55,251 sq miles (143,100 sq km) |
| POPULATION | 6,200,000 |
| MAIN LANGUAGES | Tajik |
| MAJOR RELIGION | Muslim |
| CURRENCY | Somoni |

### Uranium
Tajikistan has 14 percent of the world's uranium, used as nuclear fuel. It is a major export, but the end of the nuclear arms race has reduced its value.

**Watermelon**

### Farming
Only about six percent of Tajikistan is suitable for farming. The main farming areas are in the northwest, near Khudzhand, and the southwest, south of Dushanbe. Melons, grapes, and peaches are grown in fertile soils washed down from the mountains into the valleys.

# Afghanistan

Afghanistan has a long history of war. After years of civil strife, Afghanistan was further destroyed by a US-led war on terrorism in 2001–02. Pashtuns are the majority ethnic group. Afghanistan is one of the world's poorest countries.

### Taliban
An Islamic sect called the Taliban took power in 1996 and created a hardline regime which banned many freedoms. Women suffered heavily under Taliban rule as they were forbidden to receive an education, hold a job, or show their faces in public. The Taliban fled power in 2001 during western bombing reprisals for the September 11 attacks.

## AFGHANISTAN FACTS

| | |
|---|---|
| CAPITAL CITY | Kabul |
| AREA | 251,770 sq miles (652,090 sq km) |
| POPULATION | 26,800,000 |
| MAIN LANGUAGES | Persian, Pashto |
| MAJOR RELIGION | Muslim |
| CURRENCY | Afghani |

**FIND OUT MORE**   ASIA, HISTORY OF   DESERTS   FARMING   HORSES   ISLAM   MOUNTAINS AND VALLEYS   NUCLEAR POWER   ROCKS AND MINERALS   TEXTILES AND WEAVING   TRADE AND INDUSTRY

A

# ASIAN WILDLIFE

ASIA STRETCHES FROM frozen Arctic in the north to warm tropics in the south. Although much of Asia is undulating plain, it also boasts the awesome mountain range of the Himalayas. Much of the interior receives little rain, but parts of India hold the world record for annual rainfall. This continent of contrasts provides many habitats, each with its own characteristic plants and animals. Many of the world's best known endangered species, such as giant pandas and tigers, live in Asia. But many less publicized, smaller animals and plants are also threatened by the steady spread of human population.

## Temperate forest wildlife

Asian temperate woodlands are rich in broad-leaved trees. Summers are mild, but winters can be cold, and after the leaves have fallen, there is little food or shelter. Some animals migrate or hibernate; others, such as the Japanese macaque, are adapted to the cold.

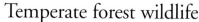

*Monkey eating snow*

*Thick, shaggy coat*

### Japanese macaque
Living throughout most of Japan, the Japanese macaque lives in a more northerly climate than any other monkey. In winter it grows a thick coat for protection, and some troops sit in hot springs to avoid the chill of a snowstorm. Roots, buds, and shoots form its winter diet.

### Japanese emperor butterfly
Only the male Japanese emperor has an iridescent purple sheen, but both sexes have spotted wings. This pattern breaks up their outline, making it difficult to see where they land on sun-flecked foliage. Their caterpillars are leaf green, to camouflage them on the leaves of celtis trees, on which they feed.

*Purple iridescence of male*

*White spots*

## Rain forest wildlife

Asia's rain forests are warm all year round, but they do have short dry seasons. They are festooned with lianas and epiphytes. The rain forest provides homes for animals at all levels, from fruit bats in the canopy to tigers on the forest floor.

### Saltwater crocodile
Large reptiles, such as saltwater crocodiles, lie out on the shores of rain forest rivers in the morning sun to warm up their bodies. Later on, when the Sun gets too hot, the crocodiles return to the water to cool down.

*Bill is used to kill snakes and scorpions.*

*Long aerial roots*

### Banyan tree
Some fig trees, such as the banyan tree, start life as a tiny seedling that grows in the crown of another rain forest tree. The banyan tree sends aerial roots down to the ground that enmesh and kill the host tree.

*Striped coat provides camouflage in forest.*

### Tiger
The tiger spends much of its day roaming through its rain forest territory, stalking prey. Tigers love water, and to avoid the heat of the day, they cool down by basking in shallow pools.

### Rhinoceros hornbill
With its loud call and noisy wingbeats, the rhinoceros hornbill is a very noticeable rain forest inhabitant. It uses its huge bill with great dexterity to pick fruit and kill prey.

## Grassland wildlife

Asia has both tropical savannas and vast plains of temperate steppes with hot, dry summers. However, grasses and drought-resistant shrubs do grow there. Large animals have adapted to conserve moisture; smaller ones shelter in burrows.

*The papery orange lanterns enclose berries.*

### Chinese lantern
The Chinese lantern is a drought-resistant plant. Its roots spread deep into the soil to reach any available water. New shoots appear each spring, that bear flowers and edible fruits.

*Heavy snout*

### Saiga antelope
Herds of saiga antelope migrate south in winter to escape severe weather. They return north in summer, when the grasses are more plentiful. Saigas have a mucus-lined sac in their snout that warms inhaled air in winter and filters out dust in the hot, dry summer.

### Tawny eagle
The tawny eagle nests in shrubs and trees by watercourses. It flies long distances over steppes and semi-arid deserts in search of food. The tawny eagle is a skillful hunter, but it increases its chances of getting enough food by feeding on carrion and stealing other predators' prey.

*Hooked beak for tearing flesh of prey*

*Eagle has pushed off ground to launch itself into the air.*

# Mountain wildlife

The steep crags and valleys of the Himalayas provide many refuges for wildlife. Forests on the lower slopes become high altitude meadows, then snowfields. Animals of the higher slopes, such as the yak, are adapted to survive the winters; others migrate to warmer, lower slopes.

### Himalayan griffon
The Himalayan griffon is a large, aggressive vulture that soars over some of the highest mountain slopes in search of food. The diet of vultures is almost entirely restricted to carrion. The Himalayan griffon's powerful hooked bill is strong enough to rip open the leathery hide of a dead yak to feast on the entrails.

*Hooked beak helps pull apart prey.*

A

*Sharp spines on head and neck provide protection.*

### Rhododendron
When in flower, rhododendrons set the mountainside ablaze with a riot of color. Their tiny seeds are readily spread by wind or water.

### Yak
Domesticated for centuries, the yak is still found living wild in some parts of its mountain range. With its long, shaggy coat, a yak can survive temperatures as low as −40°F (−40°C). It grazes on whatever plants are available, including mosses and lichens, and can use snow as a source of water.

### Armored pricklenape agama
This lizard lives in the treetops in mountain forests. Its greeny-brown scales conceal it among twigs and leaves. Pricklenape agamas have sharp claws that give them a sure grip, as they run and leap through the branches.

*Long toes and claws grip when climbing.*

---

### Northern bat
In summer, this hardy bat forages for insects in the forest and even up into the Arctic Circle. To survive the winter, it hibernates in caves or buildings. Its distribution is dictated by the availability of suitable roost sites.

# Boreal forest wildlife

Just south of the Arctic tundra is a vast forest of conifer trees. In Asia, this boreal forest is called the taiga. Wildflowers, and animals such as the sable are adapted to exploit the brief summers and withstand the long, harsh winters.

### Norway spruce
Narrow-crowned spruces are a characteristic feature of the taiga. Snow slides easily from their curved branches without breaking them. Norway spruce grows at the western reaches of the taiga, soon giving way to Siberian spruce. The seeds of both trees provide food for birds and rodents.

*Fur for warmth*

### Sable
The sable hunts all year round for nestlings and rodents. It also eats shoots and berries if prey is scarce. The sable sleeps, shelters, and gives birth in hollow logs or tree holes.

*Thick fur covers the whole body and even the soles of the feet.*

### Great gray owl
To find enough food, including voles, lemmings, and other small rodents, the great gray owl hunts by day as well as night. It may travel far to a good source of food, but returns to the dense boreal forest to breed. It chooses a secure nest site in a tree, or may use another large bird's old nest.

# Desert wildlife

Not all deserts are hot all year round. Temperate deserts, such as the Gobi in Central Asia, have scorching hot summers, but icy cold winters. Nights are cold even in summer, as there is no vegetation to trap the heat. To survive here, animals must be adapted both to the dry environment and extremes of temperature.

### Onager
Onagers live in small herds in the desert. There is little vegetation here for grazing animals, but the onager can cope by eating tough desert grasses and straw. Wolves, although uncommon, are their main predators. To defend themselves, onagers can run fast for long distances.

### Mongolian gerbil
Like many small desert animals, these gerbils escape from temperature extremes by digging underground burrows. Living below ground also helps conserve bodily moisture. Gerbils nibble roots, shoots, seeds, and buds, and drink water if it is available. In a drought, they can get enough water from the early morning dew on their food.

### Bactrian camel
Few of these desert creatures remain in the wild. A Bactrian camel has a very thick woolly coat to protect it from severe cold in winter. Fat stored in two humps on its back enables it to survive with little food or water for long periods of time.

*Almost all-around vision helps them spot danger.*

*Pale fur for camouflage in desert*

*Cheek pouches stretch so gerbil can carry food in its mouth.*

---

FIND OUT MORE      ASIA      BATS      BIRDS OF PREY      BUFFALO AND OTHER WILD CATTLE      CAMELS      DEER AND ANTELOPES      LIONS AND OTHER WILDCATS      RATS AND OTHER RODENTS      TREES

# ASSYRIAN EMPIRE

THE GRAND CITY OF ASHUR, beside the Tigris River in northern Mesopotamia (present-day Iraq), developed as an important trading center; by 2000 BC, it had become the capital of a great Assyrian kingdom. From 1400 BC, Assyrian armies were marching north and west to secure trade and obtain booty and taxes. Feared for their military strength, they soon came to dominate the Near East. Assyrian kings built several capital cities after Ashur, of which Nimrud and Nineveh were the most magnificent. Assyrian civilization and culture, however, were heavily influenced by Babylonia to the south. The Babylonians eventually absorbed the Assyrians into their empire.

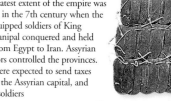

**Extent of the empire**
The greatest extent of the empire was reached in the 7th century when the well-equipped soldiers of King Ashurbanipal conquered and held lands from Egypt to Iran. Assyrian governors controlled the provinces. They were expected to send taxes back to the Assyrian capital, and recruit soldiers for the army.

**Bronze armor**

## Army

The Assyrian army was the most efficient fighting machine of its time. Its reputation alone was often enough to frighten rebellious states into surrender. At first, the army consisted of native Assyrians, but Tiglath-Pileser III (745–727 BC) recruited men from other areas of the empire. They were armed with iron helmets, armor, spears, swords, and shields. The Assyrians also used chariots and siege engines (battering rams on wheels), the most advanced weapons of the time.

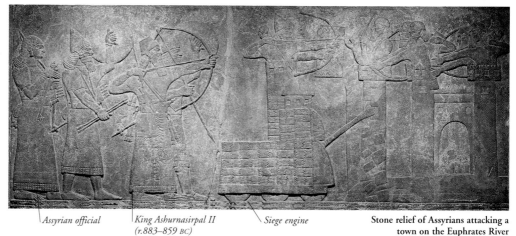

*Assyrian official* | *King Ashurnasirpal II (r.883–859 BC)* | *Siege engine* | **Stone relief of Assyrians attacking a town on the Euphrates River**

**Nimrud and Nineveh**
By 900 BC, the city of Ashur was overcrowded. Nimrud was built in the following century; Nineveh was constructed in the 7th century BC. These cities were famous for their splendid palaces and temples.

**Exotic animals** from all over the empire, such as elephants and lions, filled the wildlife parks and gardens that surrounded the city of Nineveh.

## Politics

At his coronation, the Assyrian king swore to expand the empire. The Assyrians believed their god, Ashur (after whom the first city was named), chose each king, so he had absolute power. He appointed all the governors of the various parts of his empire, led the army, and was responsible for all the temples. The king demonstrated his power and wealth by initiating many ambitious building projects. A network of spies reported to the king on all matters within the empire.

**Gold earrings**

*Precious stones*

**Queens of Assyria**
Some Assyrian queens were so powerful they became legendary. One was Sammu-rammat (Semiramis), who dominated court for 42 years in the 9th century BC. Some royal jewelry has been found in tombs at Nimrud.

## Art and literature

Brightly painted stone relief carvings, the most spectacular of all Assyrian art forms, decorated palace walls from 900 BC. Artists decorated royal furniture with carvings of real or mythical animals, such as sphinxes.

**Ivory-winged sphinx**

## Timeline

**2400 BC** The city of Ashur dominates trade routes; by 1900 BC, Assyrians establish trading colonies in Anatolia (modern Turkey).

**1250 BC** Kings of Assyria campaign as far afield as the Mediterranean and the city of Babylon.

**879 BC** Ashurnasirpal II builds a new capital at Kalhu (Nimrud).

**744–727 BC** King Tiglath-Pileser III creates an empire.

**721–705 BC** Sargon II builds palace at Khorsabad (Dur-Sharrukin).

**Gold earring**

**701 BC** Sennacherib leads his army to Jerusalem from his new capital at Nineveh.

**689 BC** Sennacherib destroys Babylon.

**664 BC** Ashurbanipal attacks and conquers Egypt.

**612 BC** Median and Babylonian armies destroy Nineveh.

**609 BC** Crown prince Nebuchadnezzar of Babylon finally defeats the Assyrians.

**606 BC** The Medes from Iran sack Nineveh.

## Sennacherib

Sennacherib (704–681 BC), a strong king, spent many years building Nineveh. He established control over the coast of the Mediterranean and destroyed Babylon, but he was murdered by his jealous sons.

**FIND OUT MORE** | ARMS AND ARMOR | ASIA, HISTORY OF | BABYLONIAN EMPIRE | HITTITES | PHOENICIANS | SUMERIANS | WARFARE

# ASTROLOGY

FOR CENTURIES, people have believed that the positioning of the stars and planets has an influence on human life. The study of this influence is known as astrology. It began about 4,000 years ago in Mesopotamia (modern Iraq), and eventually spread throughout the ancient world. In most cultures, astrology was regarded as a science, and many rulers used astrology when making important political decisions. Today, many people still believe in astrology, although there is no scientific proof of its accuracy.

## Casting a horoscope
To draw up your horoscope, or birth chart, astrologers need to know the exact date, time, and place of your birth. They then use careful calculations to plot the position of the Sun, Moon, and planets. Astrologers claim that they can interpret the finished chart to reveal your character.

*This line represents the horizon at the time of birth.*

*The chart is divided into 12 houses, one for each zodiac sign.*

*Complicated calculations are now done with calculators.*

## Astrology and astronomy
The scientific study of stars and planets is known as astronomy. For thousands of years, astronomy and astrology were closely linked. Beginning in the 17th century, however, leaps in scientific knowledge resulted in astronomy becoming increasingly important, while belief in astrology began to wane.

An early telescope

Astrological map showing the Universe in 1660

Twelve signs of the zodiac

Aries
Taurus
Gemini
Cancer
Leo
Virgo
Libra
Scorpio
Sagittarius
Capricorn
Aquarius
Pisces

### Celestial spheres
Ancient astrologers believed that the Universe was a gigantic sphere, with the Earth at the center and the stars circling around it. They divided this sphere into 12 sections, each of which was named after a constellation of fixed stars – the signs of the zodiac.

### Signs of the zodiac
Each zodiac sign takes its name from ancient mythology. Early astrologers chose names to suit the shapes formed by the constellations – the stars that make up Leo, for example, were thought to resemble a lion.

## Astrological wheel
Chinese astrology features 12 animals, each representing a different personality type. For example, people born in the year of the snake are said to be sociable, confident, and energetic.

*The black and white bands represent the Universe's balancing forces of yin and yang.*

*Each animal sign is linked to one of the five elements.*

### The five elements

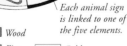

| | |
|---|---|
| Water | Wood |
| Earth | Fire |
| Gold | |

## Chinese horoscopes
Unlike Western astrology, which is based on the movement of the Sun and planets, Chinese horoscopes are based on the cycle of the Moon. Each Chinese year is named after a different animal – the Rat, Ox, Tiger, Rabbit, Dragon, Snake, Horse, Ram, Monkey, Rooster, Dog, and Pig.

### Associations
Each astrological animal is associated with a certain food, color, and symbol. The Rat's symbol is the set of balances, its color is black, and it is linked with salty foods.

## Fortune-telling
People's desire to predict the future has taken many forms that vary from culture to culture. They include crystal ball gazing, dream interpretation, palmistry, divination sticks, tarot reading, runes, numerology, and the *I Ching*, an ancient Chinese oracle.

### The role of chance
Many fortune-telling systems use dice, coins, or cards to introduce an element of randomness.

*Throwing dice is an ancient way of making predictions.*

*Consulting a fortune-teller in Hong Kong*

I Ching coins

### Palmistry
Each person's palm is unique, with its own distinctive pattern of lines. Palm readers believe these markings reveal the owner's character, past, and future. As well as both palms, the palmist examines the fingers and nails.

Palmistry hand

### Tarot cards
Tarot cards are found worldwide. They can be dealt in many different ways and are thought to answer specific questions, as a guide to the future.

 **FIND OUT MORE**  ASTRONOMY  CHINA, HISTORY OF  SCIENCE, HISTORY OF  STARS  SUN AND SOLAR SYSTEM

# ASTRONAUTS

MORE THAN 350 PEOPLE have traveled into space; 26 on missions to the Moon and the rest in orbit around Earth. For journeying into space, astronauts must be physically and mentally fit. They must also be trained to prepare them for living and working in the hostile environment of space.

## Spacesuit

When astronauts work outside the spacecraft, they need to wear a suit that keeps their body at the correct temperature and protects them from fast-moving micrometeoroids. The suit must also provide oxygen for breathing and be pressurized because there is no air or atmospheric pressure in space.

*Pressure helmet*

*Visor*  *Cap*

*Communications headset*

*Communications input socket*

*Oxygen inlets and outlets*

*Liquid-cooled undergarment*

*Water inlet and outlet*

*Pressure glove*

*Extravehicular glove*

*Wrist clamp*

*Urine transfer connection*

*Snap-on fastener*

**Apollo 9 spacesuit**

*Integrated thermal micrometeoroid garment*

*Lunar overshoe*

### MMU
To move away from the spacecraft, an astronaut wears a powered backpack, the Manned Maneuvering Unit (MMU). Mini nitrogen thrusters, operated from arm rests, propel the astronaut at about 65 ft/s (20 m/s).

### Yuri Gagarin
The first person to fly into space was a Russian, Yuri Gagarin (1934-68). His flight on April 12, 1961, orbited him once around the Earth and lasted 108 minutes. No one knew how the space flight would affect a human, so Gagarin's spacecraft, *Vostok 1*, was controlled from the ground.

## Living in space

Daily life for an astronaut includes all the usual things, such as breathing, eating, sleeping, and going to the bathroom. The big difference, however, is living in weightless conditions. Sleeping astronauts float around the spacecraft unless strapped down, and using the toilet has to be carefully controlled.

Astronauts need daily exercise to keep fit in the weightless conditions of space.

*Meal tray strapped to leg.*

*Vacuum-wrapped food pack*

*Rubber grips stop items floating away.*

### Space food
Meals on the space shuttle are prepared from 70 foods and 20 drinks. The meal tray is strapped down and the food eaten with the hand or utensils. Liquids are sucked from cartons or tubes.

### Space toilet
The astronauts' spacesuits collect waste materials when worn outside the spacecraft. Inside the craft, the astronauts use a space toilet by firmly strapping themselves to the seat. The waste is sucked away by the toilet and collected in a secure unit.

*Rubber suction cups*

### Suction shoes
Staying in one place in a spacecraft can be a problem. Suction-cup shoes allow astronauts to grip surfaces tightly.

## Working in space

Each member of a space crew has specific tasks. These may include flying the craft, releasing a satellite into orbit, or testing new equipment. The weightless conditions of space mean that astronauts can also perform experiments not possible on Earth.

### Repair work
Once a satellite is in space, it is left to work on its own. But sometimes one needs repairing. The cargo bay of the space shuttle is equipped with a robotic arm, which specially trained astronauts use to recover the satellite. They can then repair the satellite and release it back into orbit.

### Experiments
Astronauts have carried out many experiments in space. These include observing how living things such as bees are affected by weightlessness.

*Astronaut anchored to a foot restraint, to prevent him floating off into space.*

An astronaut works on the *Syncom IV-3* satellite.

### Endurance record
Most astronauts spend only a few days in space, but some stay for months. Russian cosmonaut Sergei Avdeyev holds the overall endurance record (748 days). Russian Valeri Poliakov holds the record for longest single stay (438 days).

**Valeri Poliakov**

### Space animals
Humans are not the only space travelers; early ones included dogs, rats, and mice. Animals are no longer sent into space alone, but flies, frogs, and tadpoles occasionally accompany human astronauts.

Chimpanzee Ham returned safely from his 1961 flight.

**FIND OUT MORE**   EXPLORATION   GRAVITY   HEALTH AND FITNESS   MOON   ROCKETS   SPACE EXPLORATION

# ASTRONOMY

ASTRONOMY IS THE STUDY OF SPACE and everything it contains. It is a subject that has been studied since ancient times when humans used their eyes to gaze out at the stars and planets. Today's astronomers use sophisticated equipment to collect information about space and how the Universe as a whole works.

## Astronomers' tools

Astronomers collect data from space by analyzing a range of electromagnetic radiations; light and radio waves as well as wavelengths such as X ray, infrared, and ultraviolet. Astronomers use specialized telescopes with various attachments for collecting and studying the data.

### Telescope
The finest and most powerful telescopes use one or more mirrors to collect light from a distant object and form an image. Electronic devices or photographic plates rather than the eye collect the data. Other attachments, such as spectroscopes and photometers, help analyze light emitted by stars.

Kitt Peak Observatory

*The largest optical telescope at Kitt Peak is the 13-ft (4-m) Mayall.*

## Observatories

An astronomer's telescopic equipment is housed and used in an observatory. The atmosphere distorts light and electromagnetic radiation from space, so many observatories are located at high altitudes.

### Space observatory
Telescopes in space collect data 24 hours a day and transmit it back to Earth. The *Hubble Space Telescope*, launched in 1990, orbits Earth, collecting data from optical and ultraviolet wavelengths.

**Hubble Space Telescope**

*Cameras and instruments located inside.*

*Solar panel*

*Antenna for sending data*

### Optical observatory
The world's biggest optical observatories are on mountaintops, away from city lights and where the atmosphere is clear and dry. The Kitt Peak National Observatory, which has 22 major telescopes, is on a 6,900-ft (2,100-m) mountain in Arizona. Observatories sited in such inaccessible places need support services for the astronomers and their equipment, including housing, laboratories, and transportation.

### Radio observatory
Radio waves are largely unaffected by the atmosphere, so radio telescopes can be virtually anywhere. The 1,000-ft (305-m) Arecibo radio dish (above) is in a natural hollow on the island of Puerto Rico. It is the world's largest single radio dish.

*Antenna for sending data*

*Lander under cover*

*Solar panel*

### Space probe
Objects in the Solar System have been studied at close range by space probes. Instruments perform a host of investigations, including making detailed images of planets and their moons, and analyzing what they are made of. Two identical Viking probes investigated Mars in 1976.

**Viking probe**

## Astronomer at work

Most astronomers specialize in one area of research, such as planetary geology, interplanetary dust, stellar development, galaxy formation, or quasars. Whatever the subject, an astronomer can be found in one of two main locations: in universities and observatories.

### Observation
Only a fraction of an astronomer's time is spent observing. Instead, most of the data comes from observations made and recorded by big telescopes tied to computers, or from automatic equipment on space probes. The observations are used to help build theories or to confirm an established theory, such as how stars form.

### Data collection
The CCD, an electronic chip that records data from space, can collect enough data in a few hours to keep an astronomer busy for years.

**Charge-coupled device (CCD)**

### Fred Hoyle
The British astronomer Fred Hoyle (1915–2001) helped solve some of the most baffling questions facing 20th-century astronomers. A major breakthrough was explaining nucleosynthesis – how chemical elements are produced from the hydrogen inside stars.

### Analysis
Data can be collected directly onto a computer and then transferred to other computers for analysis. Computers can process images and handle large amounts of information much more quickly than an astronomer.

## Timeline
**1609** First use of the telescope for the systematic study of space.

**1781** Discovery of Uranus doubled the diameter of the known Solar System.

**Uranus**

**1863** Analysis of starlight shows stars are made of the same elements as those on Earth.

**1923** Astronomers observe galaxies other than the Milky Way.

**1963** Quasar is discovered.

**Supernova**

**Quasar**

**1987** Supernova 1987A explodes.

**1999** Hubble telescope sights 18 other galaxies up to 65 million years away.

FIND OUT MORE ATMOSPHERE GALAXIES SPACE EXPLORATION STARS TELESCOPES UNIVERSE

# ATHLETICS

ATHLETICS IS A GROUP of sports which take place mainly in a stadium and are divided into two main categories: track and field. Track includes running and hurdling races; field includes jumping and throwing. Some athletic events involve more than one discipline – 10 in the decathlon for men; seven in the heptathlon for women. Other events are road and cross-country running. Major competitions are the Olympics and world and continental championships.

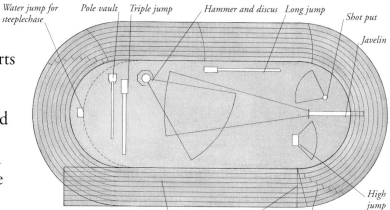

Water jump for steeplechase · Pole vault · Triple jump · Hammer and discus · Long jump · Shot put · Javelin · High jump

**Athletics stadium**
In an athletics stadium, there is a 437-yd (400-m) running track, usually marked with eight lanes. The field events take place in special areas on the grass area inside the track.

*The 100-m sprint, 100-m hurdles, and 110-m hurdles are the only races run in a straight line.*

*The finish line is in the same place for all races.*

*Races around bends have a staggered start, which means athletes do not start in a straight line.*

## Track events

Racing takes place on the flat and over hurdles. Competitors in events up to 400 m have to stay in their lane for the whole race. The 800 m is run in lanes until the end of the first bend. A photo-finish camera is used to determine final places, and runners are timed to 0.01 second.

*Athlete stays in the air as short a time as possible.*

*Weights in the base of the stand keep the hurdle upright.*

### Carl Lewis
In 1984, American Carl Lewis (b. 1961) won Olympic golds in the 100 m, 200 m, 4-by-100-m relay, and long jump. He won five more gold medals in later Olympics and retained his long-jump title three times (1988–96), becoming only the second athlete in history to win four golds in one event.

### Hurdling
Athletes have to negotiate 10 hurdles in all the races – 100 m for women, 110 m for men, and 400 m for men and women. In the 3,000-m steeplechase, runners take four hurdles and the water jump on each full lap. They all use the same, fixed hurdles.

### Running
Races on the track range from 100 m to the 25-lap 10,000 m. Runners use starting blocks for races from 100 m to 400 m. There are two standard relay races: 4 by 100 m and 4 by 400 m, with team members passing a baton.

## Throwing events

In the shot put, discus, and hammer, competitors throw from special circles. In the javelin, they throw from behind a curved line at the end of a runway.

## Jumping events

There are four jumping events. In the high jump and pole vault, the bar is gradually raised. Competitors are eliminated if they have three consecutive failures. In the long jump and triple jump, competitors have a set number of attempts, the best one counting. The triple jump is a hop, step, and jump.

### Pole vault
Poles, usually made of fiberglass, may be of any size. The vaulter plants the pole in a sunken box at the end of the runway before taking off. The pole bends and then straightens as the vaulter tries to clear the bar feet first, releasing the pole.

### Long jump
Competitors must take off before reaching the end of a wooden takeoff board sunk into the runway. The jump is measured from the end of the board to the nearest part of the sand disturbed by the competitor with any part of the body, hands, or legs.

**Javelin** distances are measured to where the tip first hits the ground. It does not have to stick.

**Shot** is a metal sphere weighing 16 lb (7.26 kg) for men and 8.8 lb (4 kg) for women. It is "put" with one pushing action.

**Hammer** is a metal sphere fixed to a handle by steel wire. Most people turn three or four times before releasing the hammer.

**Discus** has a metal rim with a weight at the center. Like the hammer, the discus is thrown from a cage for safety reasons.

Javelin

Shot

Discus

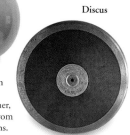

### High jump
Most high jumpers use the Fosbury flop technique, which involves turning at takeoff to pass head first and face up over the bar. Competitors are not allowed to take off from both feet.

### The marathon
This road race is 42.195 km (26.2 miles) long. Some major races start and finish in the stadium. It derives from the Battle of Marathon in 490 BC, when a messenger ran to Athens with news of the Athenian victory over the Persians.

 **FIND OUT MORE**    GREECE, ANCIENT    HEALTH AND FITNESS    HUMAN BODY    OLYMPIC GAMES    OWENS, JESSE    SPORT

# ATLANTIC OCEAN

THE ATLANTIC IS THE WORLD'S second largest ocean, covering about one-fifth of the earth's surface. It separates the Americas in the west from Europe and Africa in the east. The Arctic Ocean lies to the north, and Antarctica to the south. There are several seas around the edges of the Atlantic, including the Baltic and the Mediterranean seas in the east, and the Caribbean in the west. The Atlantic contains some of the world's richest fishing grounds, but it is also the most polluted ocean because of the industry around its shores.

| ATLANTIC OCEAN FACTS | |
|---|---|
| AREA | 31,831,000 sq miles (82,442,000 sq km) |
| AVERAGE DEPTH | 12,000 ft (3,660 m) |
| GREATEST DEPTH | 28,372 ft (8,648 m) Puerto Rico Trench |
| LENGTH | 9,900 miles (16,000 km) |
| GREATEST WIDTH | 4,900 miles (8,000 km) |

## Physical features

The waters of the Atlantic are never still. They move in huge belts of water or currents, such as the Gulf Stream. These affect the world's climate. The currents can be as warm as 86°F (30°C) or as cold as 30°F (-2°C). Many of the islands in the Atlantic are volcanic and lie on the Mid-Atlantic Ridge. Greenland and Iceland are the largest islands, bordered by the Greenland Sea in the north Atlantic.

**Gulf Stream**
Although the Scilly Isles lie just off the coast of Britain, in the northern Atlantic, winters there are mild due to the influence of the Gulf Stream. This warm current, which flows at about 5.6 mph (9 kmh), starts in the Caribbean, circles the Gulf of Mexico, and then heads north and east. Winds that blow over it pick up heat and raise the temperature of northern Europe, keeping ports free of ice in the winter.

**Mid-Atlantic Ridge**
An underwater mountain chain called the Mid-Atlantic Ridge runs down the middle of the Atlantic, where the ocean floor is splitting. Lava oozes up from the seabed and hardens, forming the mountain range. Many of the peaks surface as mid-ocean islands, such as Ascension Island. The ocean is growing wider at a rate of about 1.5 in (4 cm) a year.

**Salmon**

**Fishing**
Although Atlantic fish stocks have run low over the past 20 years because of overfishing, salmon fishing is a thriving industry, and salmon hatcheries are increasingly common.

### Map labels

1 — ARCTIC OCEAN
Ellesmere I., Svalbard (Norway), Limit of permanent pack ice

2 — Baffin Bay, Baffin I., Greenland (Denmark), Greenland Sea, Jan Mayen (Norway), Barents Sea

3 — Davis Strait, Hudson Bay, Labrador Sea, Denmark Strait, ICELAND, REYKJAVIK, Faeroe Is. (Denmark), Rockall (UK), Scandinavia, Arctic Circle

4 — NORTH AMERICA, Great Lakes, St Lawrence, Grand Banks, NORTH ATLANTIC OCEAN, Newfoundland (Canada), Newfoundland Basin, West European Basin, British Isles, North Sea, Baltic Sea, Rotterdam, EUROPE, Alps, Danube, Black Sea

5 — New York, Bermuda (UK), North American Basin, Mid-Atlantic Ridge, Azores (Portugal), Madeira (Portugal), Canary Is. (Spain), Iberia, Gibraltar, Atlas Mts., Mediterranean Sea, Port Said, Suez Canal

6 — Gulf of Mexico, West Indies, Puerto Rico Trench -28,372ft, Sargasso Sea, Canary Basin, CAPE VERDE, Sahara, AFRICA, Niger, Tropic of Cancer, Nile, Red Sea

7 — Panama City, Panama Canal, Caribbean Sea, Cape Verde Basin, Guiana Basin, ATLANTIC OCEAN, Amazon, Lagos, Gulf of Guinea, Lake Chad, Equator, Lake Victoria, Congo

8 — SOUTH AMERICA, Andes, Fernando de Noronha (Brazil), Brazil Basin, Mid-Atlantic Ridge, Ascension I. (UK), St Helena (UK), Angola Basin, Lake Nyasa, Madagascar

9 — PACIFIC OCEAN, Rio de Janeiro, Trindade (Brazil), Paraná, Rio Grande Rise, Walvis Ridge, Tropic of Capricorn, Cape Basin, Cape Town, INDIAN OCEAN, Cape of Good Hope

10 — Buenos Aires, Argentine Basin, Tristan da Cunha (UK), Gough I. (UK)

11 — Cape Horn, Falkland Is. (UK), Scotia Ridge, South Georgia (UK), Scotia Sea, SOUTH ATLANTIC OCEAN, South Sandwich Is. (UK), Atlantic-Indian Ridge, Bouvet I. (Norway), 0 km 1500, 0 miles 1500

12 — Bellingshausen Sea, South Shetland Is. (UK), South Orkney Is. (UK), Weddell Sea, Atlantic-Indian Basin, ANTARCTICA, Antarctic Circle

A  B  C  D  E  F  G  H

# Iceland

The island country of Iceland lies far north in the Atlantic, midway between Europe and North America, and is increasingly important for international communications. Its position on the Mid-Atlantic Ridge means it has many volcanoes and is prone to earthquakes. Iceland has been a republic since 1944.

## Climate

Owing to the Gulf Stream, Iceland's southern lowlands are mild and breezy, and snow is rare. The north is colder, but less windy.

86°F (30°C)    -33°F (-36°C)
52°F (11°C)    34°F (1°C)
34 in (860 mm)

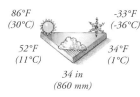

## Land use

Built-up 1%
Barren 75%
Farmland 24%

The Icelandic people live in the more fertile coastal areas. Eleven percent are employed in farming, mainly raising sheep. Only about one percent of the land is used for growing crops. No one lives in the rocky center.

## Reykjavik

Heated by geothermal water from boreholes, Reykjavik is a clean, modern city and home to about 100,000 people. It is a bustling hub of culture, industry, commerce, and government.

Brightly colored houses in Reykjavik's old town

## Physical features

Iceland is a land of fire and ice, where steaming hot volcanic springs bubble up through glaciers. The center consists of uninhabitable plateaus and mountains. In the south are farmlands. There are many rivers, lakes, and spectacular waterfalls.

## Volcanoes

The island of Little Surtsey is a volcano that rose from the sea close to Iceland in spring 1965, but disappeared again the following winter. Mainland Iceland has at least 20 active volcanoes that could erupt at any time.

## Glaciers

Europe's largest ice-caps cover over one-tenth of Iceland. The biggest is Vatnajökull, which covers 3,149 sq miles (8,133 sq km) in the southeastern part of the country.

## Geothermal power

Every year, thousands of people visit the Blue Lagoon, a natural pool of healing, geothermal, mineral-rich sea water. Vast resources ensure that hydroelectric and geothermal power stations generate almost all of Iceland's electricity.

## Fishing

Iceland relies on exporting fish to pay for all the necessities of modern living that must be imported from abroad. Fishing and fish processing are Iceland's leading industries and employ around 20 percent of the workforce.

## People

The first settlers in Iceland arrived from Norway in the 9th century. Today, Iceland is a prosperous society, and 80 percent of Icelanders own their own home. Most people live in towns where the standard of living is high, with extensive social security, health services, and free education.

8 per sq mile (3 per sq km)

92% Urban    8% Rural

## ICELAND FACTS

| | |
|---|---|
| CAPITAL CITY | Reykjavik |
| AREA | 38,707 sq miles (100,250 sq km) |
| POPULATION | 281,000 |
| MAIN LANGUAGE | Icelandic |
| MAJOR RELIGION | Christian |
| CURRENCY | Icelandic króna |
| LIFE EXPECTANCY | 79 years |
| PEOPLE PER DOCTOR | 307 |
| GOVERNMENT | Multiparty republic |
| ADULT LITERACY | 99% |

# Cape Verde

The volcanic Cape Verde Islands are divided into the Windward and Leeward Islands. They lie in the Atlantic, off Africa's west coast. Until 1975, they were a Portuguese colony. Poor soil and lack of fresh water forces Cape Verde to import 90 percent of its food.

## CAPE VERDE FACTS

| | |
|---|---|
| CAPITAL CITY | Cidade de Praia |
| AREA | 1,556 sq miles (4,030 sq km) |
| POPULATION | 428,000 |
| MAIN LANGUAGES | Portuguese, Creole |
| MAJOR RELIGION | Christian |
| CURRENCY | Cape Verde escudo |

## São Nicolau

The island of São Nicolau in the Windward Islands has many Portuguese colonial-style buildings. Most of the people here are Portuguese-African Creole. Where they can, they grow bananas and sugarcane.

# Atlantic Islands

The Atlantic Ocean contains hundreds of islands. Some, such as the British Isles, are part of a continent. Others, like the Azores and the Canaries, are volcanic. Ascension, Bermuda, St. Helena, and other small islands are the summits of undersea mountains and volcanic in origin.

## Falkland Islands

The Falklands, with an area of 4,617 sq miles (11,960 sq km), are a British territory off the coast of Argentina. That country calls them Las Malvinas and claims ownership. Until oil was discovered, most people made a living sheep farming.

## Canary Islands

The Canary Islands, off northwestern Africa, are governed as two provinces of Spain. Popular with tourists, the seven islands and six islets have a total area of 2,807 sq miles (7,270 sq km) and a population of 1,445,000.

FIND OUT MORE    ARGENTINA, CHILE, AND URUGUAY    CLIMATE    CONTINENTS    ENERGY    FISHING INDUSTRY    GLACIATION    ISLANDS    OCEANS AND SEAS    TUNDRA    VOLCANOES

# ATMOSPHERE

LIFE ON EARTH could not exist without Earth's atmosphere. The atmosphere is a colorless, tasteless, odorless blanket of gases that surrounds the Earth. It gives us air to breathe and water to drink. It not only keeps us warm by retaining the Sun's heat, it also shields us from the Sun's harmful rays. The atmosphere is approximately 440 miles (700 km) deep, but it has no distinct boundary. As it extends into space, it becomes thinner, eventually fading out. Human activity is upsetting the atmosphere's natural balance, with damaging results.

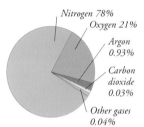

Nitrogen 78%
Oxygen 21%
Argon 0.93%
Carbon dioxide 0.03%
Other gases 0.04%

Pie chart showing the composition of the atmosphere.

## Composition of the atmosphere

Earth's atmosphere is made mainly of two gases – nitrogen and oxygen. It also contains small amounts of argon and carbon dioxide, with tiny traces of other gases. The oxygen is made primarily by green plants, which maintain the balance of gases.

## Ozone layer

The thin layer of ozone gas within the stratosphere protects us by absorbing harmful ultraviolet rays from the Sun. But the buildup of man-made gases called chlorofluorocarbons (CFCs) has depleted the ozone layer and holes have started to appear in it every spring over the poles.

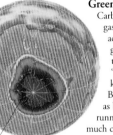

Ozone hole over Antarctica is shown as violet and pink.

**Greenhouse effect**
Carbon dioxide and other gases in the atmosphere act like glass in a greenhouse, trapping the Sun's heat. This "greenhouse effect" keeps the Earth warm. But human activity, such as burning forests and running cars, releases too much carbon dioxide into the air and may cause global warming.

**Some aerosol sprays use CFC gases.**

## Layers of the atmosphere

The atmosphere is divided into five different layers. The composition of gases varies within these layers, as does the temperature, which drops in the troposphere, the lowest layer, and rises in the stratosphere above.

*Satellite*

**Exosphere is the** outer layer of the atmosphere. Here lighter gases drift into space.

**In the thermosphere,** gases are very thin but they absorb ultraviolet light from the Sun, raising temperatures to 3,632°F (2,000°C). The ionosphere (layer within the thermosphere) is made of gases electrically charged or ionized by the Sun's light. Radio signals can be bounced off these ionized gases.

*Aurora – lights in the night sky, possibly caused by charged particles from the Sun striking atoms*

*Space shuttle*

*Meteorites*

*Stratopause is the boundary between stratosphere and the mesosphere.*

**In the mesosphere,** gases are so thin that temperatures drop rapidly to less than -166°F (-110°C). However, the air at that height is still thick enough to slow down meteorites.

*Sonar balloon*

**Stratosphere contains** 19 percent of the atmosphere's gases, but little water vapor. It is very calm, so jets fly up here.

*Tropopause borders troposphere and stratosphere.*

*Ozone layer shields the Earth from dangerous radiation.*

*Sea level*

**Troposphere extends** about 7.5 miles (12 km) above the ground and is the only layer in which living things can survive naturally. It contains 75 percent of the atmosphere's gases, water vapor, and clouds. Changes here create the weather.

Oxygen used in burning fossil fuels

Oxygen given off by marine plants

A large amount of oxygen is stored in the atmosphere.

Oxygen used up by marine animals

Oxygen used up by humans and animals

Oxygen given off by plants and trees

## The oxygen cycle

Gases continually circulate between the atmosphere and living things. Animals breathe in oxygen to help them release energy from food, and breathe out carbon dioxide. Green plants release oxygen back into the air and take in carbon dioxide as they absorb energy from the Sun. Oxygen is also used in burning fossil fuels.

## James Glaisher

English meteorologist James Glaisher (1809–1903) was one of the many balloonists who, during the 19th century, took great risks when they ascended to extraordinary heights to discover more about the atmosphere. Glaisher went up almost 7.5 miles (12 km) into the troposphere without oxygen or protective clothing. Such research led to the discovery that air becomes cooler with altitude.

**FIND OUT MORE** | CLIMATE | FORESTS | GASES | LUNGS AND BREATHING | PLANETS | POLLUTION | SUN AND SOLAR SYSTEM | WEATHER

# ATOMS AND MOLECULES

TINY PARTICLES CALLED ATOMS are the basic building blocks of all matter. Forces called bonds effectively "cement" the atoms together. A molecule is a cluster of atoms linked by bonds. There are just over a hundred different types of atoms, which are themselves made up of even smaller "subatomic" particles, such as protons, neutrons, and electrons.

## Atomic structure

The center, or nucleus, of an atom contains particles called protons, which carry a positive electric charge, and neutrons, which carry none. Arranged around the nucleus in layers called shells are negatively charged particles called electrons. The atom has no charge of its own, because it contains equal numbers of electrons and protons, so the positive and negative charges are balanced.

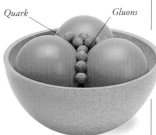

*Nucleus of carbon-12 atom*
*Six protons*
*Six neutrons*

### Isotopes

All the atoms of an element have the same number of protons in the nucleus, but some atoms, called isotopes, have different numbers of neutrons. For example, the carbon isotope carbon-12 has six protons and six neutrons, but the isotope carbon-14 has two extra neutrons.

### Quarks

Both neutrons and protons consist of three smaller particles called quarks stuck together by tiny particles called gluons. Quarks, in turn, may contain even smaller particles.

## Electron shells and valency

Atoms can have up to seven shells of electrons. An atom with eight electrons in its outermost shell is very stable. Bonds form when atoms gain, lose, or share electrons in order to achieve this stable arrangement. An atom's valency is the number of bonds it can form with other atoms.

*When sodium bonds, it loses an atom, leaving an outer shell of eight electrons.*

**Sodium**
(3 shells, valency 1)

*A carbon atom can form up to four bonds with other atoms.*

**Carbon**
(2 shells, valency 4)

*Nucleus* *Proton (red)* *Neutron (green)*
*Electron shells*

*Electrons move around the nucleus in paths called orbits.*

**Atom of carbon-12 cut in half**

*Quark* *Gluons*

**Inside a neutron**

## Ionic bonds

When an electron transfers from one atom to another, the atoms become charged particles called ions. The atom losing the electron becomes a positively charged ion, and the atom gaining the electron becomes a negatively charged ion. The force of attraction between the ions' opposite charges is called an ionic bond.

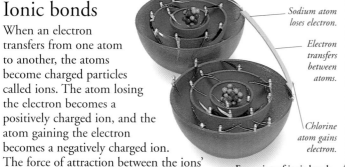

*Sodium atom loses electron.*
*Electron transfers between atoms.*
*Chlorine atom gains electron.*

**Formation of ionic bonds in sodium chloride (NaCl)**

## Covalent bonds

A covalent bond forms when two atoms link up by sharing electrons. Each atom supplies an electron, and the pair of electrons orbits the nuclei of both atoms, holding the atoms together as a molecule.

**Covalent bonds in ammonia molecule ($NH_3$)**

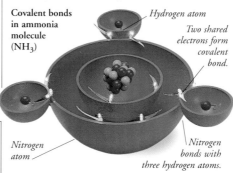

*Hydrogen atom*
*Two shared electrons form covalent bond.*

*Nitrogen atom*
*Nitrogen bonds with three hydrogen atoms.*

### Double bonds

Sometimes atoms form covalent bonds by sharing two pairs of electrons. This is called a double bond. A triple covalent bond forms when atoms share three pairs of electrons.

*Atoms share four electrons.*
**Oxygen molecule ($O_2$)**

*Double bond links two oxygen atoms.*

## Chemical formula

Scientists use a kind of code called a chemical formula to describe a substance. The formula uses letters and numbers to show which elements are present in the substance, and in what proportions. Methane, for example, has a chemical formula of $CH_4$, which shows that it contains carbon (C) and hydrogen (H) combined in the ratio of one carbon atom to every four hydrogen atoms.

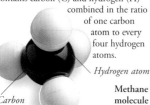

*Hydrogen atom*
*Carbon atom*

**Methane molecule ($CH_4$)**

## Linus Pauling

The American chemist Linus Pauling (1901–94) won the 1954 Nobel Prize for chemistry for his work on chemical bonds and the structure of molecules. He calculated the energies needed to make bonds, the angles at which bonds form, and the distances between atoms. He also won the 1962 Nobel Peace Prize for his efforts to stop the testing of nuclear weapons.

### Bonds between molecules

The molecules of covalent compounds are held together by weak bonds called Van der Waal's forces. Some hydrogen-containing compounds, such as water, have stronger forces called hydrogen bonds between their molecules. In water, these bonds form because each oxygen atom in a water molecule is attracted to hydrogen atoms in two nearby molecules.

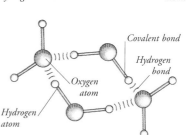

*Covalent bond*
*Hydrogen bond*
*Oxygen atom*
*Hydrogen atom*

**Hydrogen bonds between water molecules**

**FIND OUT MORE** ELEMENTS MIXTURES AND COMPOUNDS NUCLEAR POWER RADIOACTIVITY

# AUSTRALASIA AND OCEANIA

AUSTRALIA, New Zealand, Papua New Guinea, and the nearby islands are collectively called Australasia. The wider area known as Oceania also includes the island groups of Melanesia, Micronesia, and Polynesia and spans a huge area in the South Pacific Ocean. Australia is the largest country and a continent in its own right. Although many Pacific islands were once European colonies, the region now has closer trade links with Asia.

**Coral islands**
Many of the thousands of tiny islands in Oceania are the peaks of undersea volcanic mountains that are just breaking the surface of the Pacific Ocean. Reefs of coral, teeming with tropical fish, often build up close to the islands' sandy shores.

## Physical features

Australasia and Oceania include a range of landscapes, from tropical rain forest in northern areas, to the arid desert of central Australia. Many islands are volcanic, with sandy beaches, high mountains, and a constant threat of earthquakes.

**Geysers**
These occur in New Zealand where hot rock heats water in an underground chamber. As the water boils, a fountain of scalding water and steam shoots 1,640 ft (500 m) into the air.

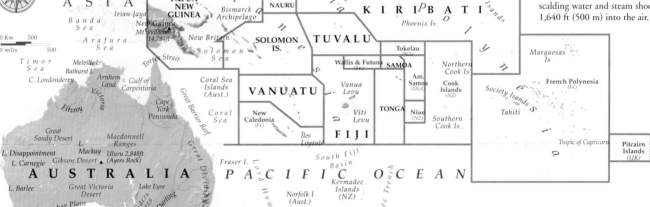

**Pinnacles Desert**
Tall pinnacles of limestone rise from the sand in parts of Australia's hot, dry Western Desert. These unusually shaped rocks have been sculpted by the eroding action of plant roots and harsh winds over the last 25,000 years.

## Cross-section through Australasia

Australia is a largely flat continent, with low mountains in the southwest and a central desert. The highest mountains are the Great Dividing Range in the east. The Pacific Ocean between Australia and New Zealand dips to 16,405 ft (5,000 m). The Southern Alps run down New Zealand's South Island.

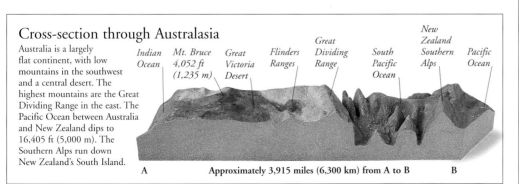

Indian Ocean — Mt. Bruce 4,052 ft (1,235 m) — Great Victoria Desert — Flinders Ranges — Great Dividing Range — South Pacific Ocean — New Zealand Southern Alps — Pacific Ocean

A                    Approximately 3,915 miles (6,300 km) from A to B                    B

### AUSTRALASIA AND OCEANIA FACTS

**AREA** 3,285,048 sq miles (8,508,238 sq km)

**POPULATION** 29,700,000

**NUMBER OF COUNTRIES** 14

**HIGHEST POINT** Mt. Wilhelm (Papua New Guinea) 14,794 ft (4,509 m)

**LONGEST RIVER** Murray Darling (Australia) 2,330 miles (3,750 km)

**BIGGEST LAKE** Lake Eyre (Australia) 3,700 miles (9,583 sq km)

# Climatic zones

With a wide range of landscapes and spanning a vast area, Australasia and Oceania experience many different climates. Northern Australia and Papua New Guinea are always hot with wet and dry seasons, the east has hot summers and mild winters, and the center is dry desert. New Zealand is mild and damp. The most westerly of the Pacific islands have a wet, tropical climate.

*Wetland*

*Desert*

*Tropical rain forest*

*Deciduous forest*

*Scrub*

*Grassland*

*Mountain*

*Many species of insects and animals live in the canopy.*

## Tropical rain forest

Steamy tropical rain forest covers most of the Solomon Islands, the mountains of Papua New Guinea, and northern Australia. Often shrouded in mist, these dense, lush forests are a haven for wildlife and contain more than 600 species of tree. As a measure to protect the environment, logging is controlled in Queensland.

## Scrub

At the edges of the four major deserts that make up the interior of Australia are areas of arid brush where there is little, often unreliable, rainfall. These areas support coarse grass, scattered shrubs, and low trees.

*Small, stunted shrubs*

*After rain, flowers burst into bloom.*

*Bushes are mostly stunted, evergreen, and spiny.*

## Grassland

Australia contains vast areas of dry, open grassland, known as the "outback." The best grazing land for cattle and sheep is in Queensland and New South Wales. Scarce surface water is supplemented by underground water from artesian wells. Lush grassland covers the eastern side of New Zealand's South Island.

## Eucalyptus woods

Many kinds of gum trees, also known as eucalyptus, grow in Australia. There is a species of gum tree for virtually every environment, from cold, damp mountain tops to hot, dry inland areas. Gum trees are evergreens, with leathery leaves.

*Mountain gum leaves*

*Narrow leaves hang down to avoid drying out in the hot sun.*

*Sandstone is worn smooth and rounded by erosion.*

## Coastal climate

The coastal strip between Brisbane and Melbourne in southeast Australia is backed to the west by the peaks of the Great Dividing Range, including the Australian Alps. Warm breezes blow in from the Pacific Ocean, bringing rain to this green and fertile region. The long, sandy beaches and mild, pleasant climate make this the most populated region in Australia.

*Powerful waves create long, sandy beaches.*

Byron Bay, New South Wales

## Hot desert

The spectacular red Olgas rocks rise unexpectedly out of the arid flat expanse of Australia's scorching central desert. Situated near Uluru (Ayers Rock), this giant mass of boulders formed more than 570 million years ago and gradually eroded during the past 150 million years.

## Deciduous rain forest

The west coast of New Zealand's South Island is covered with deciduous forest. Trees such as oak, beech, and hickory thrive in the mild, damp climate.

**Beech forest in New Zealand's Fiordland National Park**

## People

The earliest inhabitants of Australasia were the Aboriginals of Australia and the Polynesians and Melanesians from the Pacific islands. White Europeans began colonizing Australia and New Zealand in the late 1700s. Since the 1970s, Australia has allowed many other peoples to settle there, including Chinese, Cambodians, and Vietnamese.

Australian children

## Resources

Land is a major resource for Australia and New Zealand and is used extensively for grazing cattle and sheep, and for growing wheat. Australia is rich in minerals and leads the world in the production of bauxite (aluminum ore), diamonds, and lead ore. The main resources of the Pacific islands are fish and coconut products, such as copra, coir (rope), and matting.

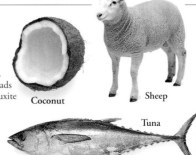

Coconut

Sheep

Tuna

 FIND OUT MORE    ABORIGINAL AUSTRALIANS    AUSTRALIAN WILDLIFE    CLIMATE    CORAL REEFS    DESERTS    EARTHQUAKES    FORESTS    ISLANDS    PACIFIC OCEAN    TREES    VOLCANOES

# AUSTRALIA

A COUNTRY and at the same time a continent, Australia is an ancient landmass and the smallest, flattest, and, after Antarctica, driest continent. It is the world's sixth largest country, yet only 18.9 million people live there, mostly along the coast. The center of the country consists of the desert or semidesert region called the outback. Australia has six states and two territories. It has strong trade links with the US, Europe, and Asia and makes significant contributions to international affairs. The population consists of a diverse ethnic mix, making Australia a truly multicultural society.

## Physical features

The center of Australia is covered by a vast, flat, arid plain called the outback – one of the hottest places on earth. Around the coast are tropical rain forests, snowcapped mountains, and magnificent beaches.

### AUSTRALIA FACTS

**CAPITAL CITY** Canberra

**AREA** 7,617,930 sq miles (2,941,283 sq km)

**POPULATION** 18,900,000

**MAIN LANGUAGE** English

**MAJOR RELIGION** Christian

**CURRENCY** Australian dollar

**LIFE EXPECTANCY** 79 years

**PEOPLE PER DOCTOR** 400

**GOVERNMENT** Multiparty democracy

**ADULT LITERACY** 99%

### Great Barrier Reef

Green Island forms part of the Great Barrier Reef, which stretches 1,243 miles (2,000 km) along the northeastern coast of Australia. Its coral is formed by layer upon layer of tiny anemonelike creatures, making it the largest living thing on earth. Thousands of tourists flock to see it each year, attracted by the clear, warm waters and more than 1,500 species of fish. Recent fears that divers and swimmers may be damaging the reef have led to its protection as a World Heritage Site.

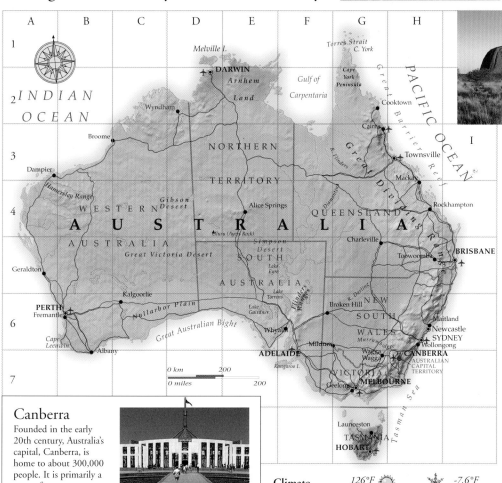

### Uluru (Ayers Rock)

This giant block of red sandstone that rises from the desert is more than 1.5 miles (2.4 km) long. Once known as Ayers Rock, Uluru, meaning "great pebble," is the original name given to it by the Aboriginal people, who regard it as sacred.

### Great Dividing Range

The Great Dividing Range is a series of high plateaus and low mountains that extends down the east side of Australia. It shields the arid interior of the country from the rainclouds that blow in from the Pacific Ocean. In winter, snow covers the higher peaks, and people can ski there.

## Canberra

Founded in the early 20th century, Australia's capital, Canberra, is home to about 300,000 people. It is primarily a center for government and has few industries. Official buildings include Parliament House, the Australian National University, the National Library, and the National Gallery.

**Parliament House**

## Climate

Most people live in the temperate zones that occur within 249 miles (400 km) of the coast in the east and southeast, and around Perth in the west. The interior, west, and south are arid. The north is hot, humid, and tropical.

126°F (52°C)  -7.6°F (-22°C)
68°F (20°C)  42°F (6°C)
25 in (629 mm)

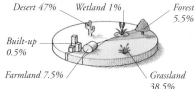

Desert 47%   Wetland 1%   Forest 5.5%
Built-up 0.5%
Farmland 7.5%   Grassland 38.5%

## Land use

Most of Australia's interior is inhospitable desert. Sheep and cattle are raised in the east and north, and wheat is grown in the fertile southwest and southeast. Some of the land is used to mine Australia's rich mineral deposits.

A

# People

Aboriginal people, Australia's first inhabitants, make up between one and two percent of the population. The rest is of mainly European origin, descended either from British settlers or from Europeans who emigrated to Australia after 1945. Recent years have also seen an influx of Asians.

**Multicultural society**
Australian society reflects the many different nationalities that have settled in the country. Aboriginal people, English, Irish, and central and eastern Europeans have all made their mark, and, since 1972, when immigration restrictions were lifted, the arrival of Chinese, Indo-Chinese, and Indonesian peoples has added new influences. Diverse languages, customs, foods, and festivals make Australia a varied and exciting society.

5 per sq mile
(2 per sq km)

85% Urban    15% Rural

# Farming

Less than five percent of the workforce farm, yet half the land is used for grazing cattle and sheep, and growing grapes and grains.

**Livestock**
Cattle roam the Australian outback, grazing on dry grass and drinking water drawn from artesian wells. They are raised on vast cattle ranches, mainly for their meat. Australia has seven times more sheep than people. They produce around one-third of the world's wool.

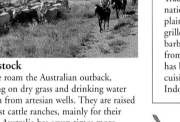

**Grain**
Although less than four percent of the land is suitable for farming cereal crops, Australia grows barley, millet, oats, and rice, and manages to rank highly in world production of wheat. Other crops includ sugarcane, fruit, and vegetables.

**Grapes**
The gentle climate of parts of southern Australia is ideally suited to growing grapes for winemaking. The Australian wine industry has grown by leaps and bounds in recent years, now producing about 495,000 tons (450,000 tonnes) of wine a year. Much is exported.

# Leisure

Australians love the outdoors. Because most live near the coast, many people enjoy water sports such as swimming, skindiving, surfing, and sailing. Cricket is a popular spectator sport, as are rugby and the unique Australian Rules football.

**Surfing**
The crashing waves of Australia's east coast attract thousands to try their luck at surfing. The aptly named Surfers' Paradise, in Queensland, is a favorite spot.

**Australian Rules Football**
One of Australia's national winter sports is Australian Rules football. It was invented in the 1850s and is based on Gaelic football. The only other country where it is played is Papua New Guinea.

# Food

Traditionally, Australians are a nation of meat eaters. They love plain foods such as fried eggs and grilled steaks, cooked on the barbecue. The influx of people from mainland Europe and Asia has brought a wide range of cuisine from China, Greece, Indonesia, and Italy.

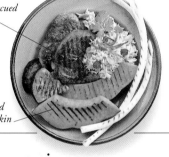

Barbecued lamb

Grilled pumpkin

# Transportation

With such a huge territory to cover, and the nearest countries so far away, Australians rely on airplanes for long-distance travel. Buses, cars, and trains are used for short distances in the cities. Trucks carry most intercity freight by road.

**Road train**
Heavy loads are often transported across the outback by road train. These huge trucks may pull five or six trailers over vast distances on deserted roads.

**Flying Doctor**
The Royal Flying Doctor Service was founded in 1928 to bring medical help to people living in the outback. Doctors are based at stations where emergency callers can contact them by radio and receive treatment quickly.

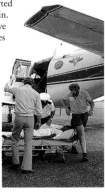

# Industry

Australia has a strong mining industry and is a major exporter of coal, iron ore, bauxite, lead, gold, copper, and diamonds. About 16 percent of the workforce is employed in manufacturing, and two-thirds is employed in services such as banks, tourism, and government.

Diamonds

Gold

**Gold and diamonds**
Australia is the world's top gold producer and exports more diamonds than any other country. Most of the diamonds are not gem quality and are used to make industrial cutting tools.

Quartz

**Tourism**
The spectacular scenery of the Hamersley Range in western Australia is popular with tourists, mostly from Japan, New Zealand, and Southeast Asia. About five million visitors visit Australia every year, providing a welcome addition to the country's foreign earnings.

**FIND OUT MORE**

ABORIGINAL AUSTRALIANS    AUSTRALIA, HISTORY OF    CARS AND TRUCKS    CONTINENTS    CORAL REEFS    DESERTS    FARMING    ROCKS AND MINERALS    SPORTS

# AUSTRALIA, HISTORY OF

Paddles for Aboriginal canoe

FOR THE LAST 40,000 YEARS, Australia was inhabited by Aboriginal peoples. The Aboriginals, who came from Asia, created a rich culture based on hunting and food gathering. Their peaceful existence was destroyed by the arrival of Europeans in the late 18th century. These settlers were convicts sent from crowded British prisons; later, farmers and miners drawn by the wealth of the country, joined them. In 1901, Australia became an independent nation, sending troops to fight in both world wars. Today it is a multicultural country with a rich economy and close ties with Asia, America, and Europe.

## First inhabitants
The first people to inhabit Australia were the ancestors of today's Aboriginals. They reached the country about 40,000 years ago after sailing across the shallow oceans that then separated Australia from Asia. As sea-levels rose, they moved inland, using stone axes to clear trees and build shelters of wood and bark.

**Outrigger canoe from Queensland**

*Outrigger made from solid wood*

*Canoe dug out of a whole tree trunk*

*String made of grass holds the outrigger to the main canoe.*

## Early sightings
In the 17th century, Spanish sailor Luis Vaez de Torres and Dutchman Willem Jansz explored the islands of Asia and the Pacific. Unplanned landings took place as ships were blown off course. In 1642–43 Dutchman Abel Tasman sailed around Australia without catching sight of it. He landed on an island he named Van Diemen's Land, now called Tasmania.

**Early map of Australia**

### Botany Bay
In 1770, the British explorer Captain James Cook sailed into an inlet in southeastern Australia. He named the place Botany Bay and claimed the entire east coast of Australia for Britain. Joseph Banks, one of the ship's naturalists, sketched and collected hundreds of plants, that had never before been seen by Europeans.

### Convict transportation
In 1787, the British decided to transport (ship out) prisoners to Australia. The first fleet, containing 759 convicts, arrived in Botany Bay in 1788. A penal settlement was established at nearby Sydney Cove, in Port Jackson. The last shipload of prisoners arrived in Australia in 1868.

*Convicts were often used as servants.*

## The 19th century
Some 90 years after the arrival of Cook, the major settlements were all on the coast, and few people traveled inland. The first explorers mapped the Murray and Darling rivers in the southeast, while others tried to reach the heart of Australia.

### Crossing the continent
The Royal Society of Victoria decided to send an expedition to cross the continent from south to north. Irishman Robert O'Hara Burke and Englishman William J Wills completed the trip in 1861, but died on the return journey. In July 1862 their rival, John Stuart, completed a similar journey, unaware that Burke and Wills had beaten him to it. He died in the attempt.

**Surveyor's chain used to measure land, 1800s**

**Prospectors' camp, Victoria**

**Banner for trade union**

### Gold rush
The discovery of gold in 1851 brought a rush of fortune-hunters. By 1860, the population had grown from 200,000 in 1840 to 1.1 million, and Australian gold accounted for 39 per cent of the world's total output.

### Growth
The colonies prospered in the last years of the 19th century. Industry grew quickly, especially in areas such as construction and manufacturing. Social policies were forward-thinking: for example, education for all was an early goal; trade unions were organized in many areas.

## Ned Kelly
Throughout the 19th century, parts of Australia were lawless. One of the most notorious outlaws, or bushrangers, was Ned Kelly (1855–80), who led a gang of robbers. The gang killed three policemen in 1878 and robbed several banks before Kelly was caught and hanged in Melbourne in 1880. His fight against the authorities made Kelly a national folk hero.

# Independent nation

In the early days, Australia consisted of six separate colonies. Each had its own government under the sovereignty of Britain. As the agricultural and mining industries grew in strength, the six colonies began to work closely together. In 1901, Australia gained its independence from Britain, and a federal government for the entire country was established with its capital in Melbourne. Today, the federal capital is at Canberra.

### Gallipoli

On April 25, 1915, ANZAC forces landed at Gallipoli at the mouth of the Black Sea, Turkey. They hoped to take Constantinople (modern-day Istanbul) and force Germany's World War I ally, Turkey, out of the war. The men showed extraordinary courage and spirit, but the campaign was a disaster. No important gains were made and more than 11,400 ANZAC troops lost their lives.

**Gallipoli memorial**

### Dominion status

When Australia became independent in 1901, it remained a Dominion of the British Empire and kept close links with its former ruler. But many people had few ties to the old "Mother Country." The threat of Japanese invasion during World War II led to closer links with the US as the only power that could defend Australia.

## ANZAC forces

**Anzac Monument, Sydney**

Australian and New Zealand forces fought for Britain in the Boer War (1899–1902) in South Africa and in both world wars. They fought together as the Australia and New Zealand Army Corps (ANZAC), sending a higher percentage of soliders per capita that other warring nations. The effort forged a strong sense of national identity.

*The Federation Flag was based on the state flag of New South Wales.*

**Federation Flag**

## Immigration

In 1902, the government passed the Immigration Restriction Act to limit Chinese immigration. The act required settlers to speak a European language, and began a White Australia policy that lasted until the 1970s. Britons, Greeks, and Italians flooded into Australia in the 1950s and 1960s, with immigration from Asia later increased

**Scottish emigrants leave for Australia.**

# Modern Australia

After World War II, Australia continued its military alliance with the US. The country sent troops to fight with the Americans in Korea during the 1950s and Vietnam in the 1960s. In recent years, those ties have weakened, and Australia has increasingly turned toward Asia, particularly Japan, for trade and investment. Today, Australia is an important trading partner with most of the powerful East Asian economies.

### National symbol

Sydney Opera House, with its bold concrete roofs, has become the most widely recognized symbol of Australia.

### Australian republic?

In 1992, the prime minister, Paul Keating, said he wanted the country to be a republic by the year 2000, with an Australian as the head of state, instead of the British monarch. Although Keating was defeated in 1996 elections, the debate continues.

**Skyscraper, Sydney**

**Chinese festival, Sydney**

### Multicultural Australia

Modern Australia is a multi-cultural state with large Chinese and Greek populations. However, the Aboriginals have waged a long battle to be included in society and to secure their land rights and civil liberties.

**Sailing in Sydney Harbour**

### Sports excellence

One way Australia has expressed its national identity is through a wide varieties of sports, ranging from cricket to yachting. For example, in 1983 Australia overturned a century of US dominance of the seas by winning the Americas Cup. Sydney was chosen as the site of the Olympic Games in 2000.

---

## Timeline

**c.40,000 BC** Aboriginals arrive in Australia.

**1642–43** Tasman names Van Diemen's Land (Tasmania).

**1770** Captain Cook lands at Botany Bay.

**1788** First British prisoners arrive.

**1828** Charles Sturt begins to explore Murray and Darling rivers.

**Wallaby**

**1851** Gold discovered in Victoria and New South Wales.

**1860–61** Burke and Wills cross Australia from south to north.

**1868** Britain abolishes the transportation of prisoners.

**Aboriginal women's digging sticks**

**1901** Australia becomes self-governing dominion in the British Empire.

**1902** Immigration Restriction Act establishes the White Australia policy.

**1914–18** 60,000 Australians are killed fighting for Britain in World War I.

**1927** Parliament meets for the first time in the new federal capital of Canberra.

**1970s** White Australia policy abolished.

**1993** Aboriginal land rights recognized by law.

**2000** Olympic Games held in Sydney.

**2001** Fierce bush fires cause immense damage.

---

**FIND OUT MORE**    ABORIGINAL AUSTRALIANS    CRIME AND PUNISHMENT    COOK, JAMES    EXPLORATION    OPERA    PREHISTORIC PEOPLE    WORLD WAR I    WORLD WAR II

# AUSTRALIAN WILDLIFE

AUSTRALIA HAS BEEN ISOLATED by water for more than 30 million years, resulting in the evolution of many unique animals and plants. Half of all marsupials, such as the koala and kangaroo, live only in Australia, along with the platypus and echidna, the world's only egg-laying mammals, or monotremes. Much of Australia is desert or scrub. The animals and plants that live here are adapted to the hot, dry conditions. There are also areas of tropical and temperate forests, which contain the greatest diversity of life in Australia.

## Desert wildlife

Australia's hot, dry, desert interior makes up half the continent. Drought-resistant vegetation, such as porcupine grass and acacias, grow here, providing a refuge for birds and insects. Many desert mammals rest in burrows by day to avoid the heat. Snakes and lizards are common desert animals.

### Emu
Emus are large flightless birds that can run at up to 30 mph (50 kmh), although they usually walk. They cover large distances in search of grasses, fruit, and flowers. They also eat insects. Males incubate the eggs and guard the young after they hatch.

### Porcupine grass
As its name suggests, porcupine grass is a spiny plant that grows in circular tussocks. It is adapted to dry desert conditions by having a thick outer covering (cuticle) to reduce water loss, and by having deep roots to reach water in the soil.

### Galah
The galah, or roseate cockatoo, is one of the most common parrots in Australia. Large flocks of these birds are found not only in dry areas but also in cities. Galahs eat seeds, leaf buds, and insects.

*Strong bill is used to dig up insects.*

### Thorny devil
This lizard's scales are drawn out into long spines. When temperatures fall at night, valuable water condenses on the spines and runs down tiny grooves towards the mouth.

*Spines protect against predators.*

### Mulgara
This carnivorous marsupial (pouched mammal) eats insects and small vertebrates, such as mice and lizards. It bites and shakes its prey to kill it. The mulgara digs burrows in sand, in order to escape the midday sun.

*Mulgara eats prey head first.*

*Grass forms a refuge for insects, lizards, and birds.*

*Long, strong legs*

*Lizard searches for ants.*

## Scrub and grassland wildlife

Covering about a third of Australia, scrub and grassland are hot and dry in summer and cooler in winter. Plants use occasional heavy rainstorms to blossom and produce seeds, and animals, such as frogs, emerge to reproduce.

*Canopy provides shelter for animals from the midday heat.*

### Bottle tree
These large trees get their name from their bottle-shaped trunks. The swollen trunk stores water that helps the tree survive periods of drought. The tree also provides food for many animals, including insects, and shelter for some birds and mammals. Other vegetation common in scrubland includes dry grasses and dwarf eucalyptus.

*Water is stored in bulbous trunk.*

### Short-beaked echidna
The short-beaked echidna is an egg-laying mammal found in Australia, Tasmania, and New Guinea. It uses its sticky tongue to extract ants and termites from their nests. If threatened, the echidna rolls into a ball, or digs down into the soil.

### Mallee fowl
The male mallee fowl builds a mound of vegetation and soil in which the female lays her eggs. As the vegetation rots, it releases heat that incubates the eggs.

*Male checks mound temperature with his beak, and by moving vegetation.*

### Water-holding frog
This frog survives drought by burrowing into the ground and forming a thin layer of skin around itself to conserve water. It also stores water in its bladder.

### Kultarr
This small, mouselike marsupial is nocturnal. It has large eyes to help it see in the dark and to catch insects and spiders. It moves by springing off its long hind feet and tail and landing on its front feet. During the day, it takes shelter in logs, hollow stumps, and burrows.

*Kultarr feeds on a spider.*

**A**

# Temperate forest wildlife

The temperate forests of southern and eastern Australia are hot and dry in summer, and cooler and wetter in winter. They are home to birds, such as parrots and kookaburras, marsupials, including the koala, and a variety of reptiles and insects. Many trees found here, such as eucalyptus, are unique to Australia.

## Silver wattle
The silver wattle, also known as mimosa, is a common plant in temperate forests. These trees, with their characteristic silver-gray leaves, can withstand dry periods and also the wet season.

*Bright yellow flowers provide food for insects and other animals.*

## Kookaburra
The kookaburra is the largest member of the kingfisher family. It is rarely found near water, however, preferring open woodland. Kookaburras swoop down from a tree branch perch to pounce on insects, lizards, snakes, and small birds and mammals. They defend their territory by making loud cackling calls that sound like human laughter.

*Male lyrebird sings a loud territorial song, mimicking other birds and animals.*

## Lyrebird
These ground birds use their large, lawed feet to turn over stones and break open logs in search of insects. The male lyrebird has a long tail shaped like a lyre, an ancient musical instrument. He performs courtship dances to attract females by vibrating his tail over his back.

*Flattened tail helps platypus swim.*

*Heavy beak kills reptiles and rodents.*

## Duck-billed platypus
This unusual-looking animal is an egg-laying mammal, or monotreme, that lives near rivers. The platypus feeds underwater on insect larvae and other food found by probing the stream bottom with its sensitive bill. It hunts mainly at night, spending most of the day in a burrow dug in the stream bank.

*Long tail feathers*

*Koalas spend most of their time in eucalyptus trees, using their sharp claws and strong legs to climb through the branches.*

## Koala
Koalas are bearlike marsupials that feed on the leaves of eucalyptus trees. They eat mainly at night, spending most of the day resting or sleeping in the fork of a tree.

## Tree kangaroo
The tree kangaroo is a marsupial adapted for life in the trees, by having rough paw pads and long claws for gripping. Its diet consists mainly of leaves and bark, but it sometimes descends to the ground to feed on shrubs and seedlings.

# Tropical rain forest wildlife

Despite occupying only a tiny part of northeastern Australia, the rainforests contain one-third of Australia's frog and marsupial species, and two-thirds of its butterflies. The wide variety of ferns and trees, such as breadfruit trees, provide shelter and food for these animals, and many birds, bats, and insects.

*Long tail helps balance in the trees.*

## Rainbow lorikeet
These brightly colored parrots live in screeching flocks of up to 20 birds in the upper rain forest canopy. They feed on pollen, nectar, flowers, seeds, and fruit.

## Trigger plant
When a bee lands on a trigger plant flower, the anther – the flower's male part – bends outward to dust pollen on the bee's hairy back. When the bee visits another flower the pollen sticks to the stigma – the female part of the flower, and pollinates it.

*Pink flowers attract bees.*

*Fangs are 0.5 in (1 cm) long so they can inject venom deep into their victims.*

*The male is brightly colored.*

## Taipan
This forest snake is active in the early morning and evening, and feeds mainly on rats and other small mammals. The taipan is one of the world's most poisonous snakes; a bite from its long fangs is often fatal to humans. Taipans normally retreat and hide when people approach, but they will become aggressive if threatened.

## Queen Alexandra's birdwing
Found in New Guinea, this is the largest butterfly in the world. The female is larger than the male and has a wingspan of up to 11 in (28 cm). Queen Alexandra's birdwing flies in the sunlight of the upper canopy, where it feeds on flower nectar.

*Brown coloration provides camouflage for taipan.*

| AUSTRALIA | BIRDS | BUTTERFLIES AND MOTHS | CAMOUFLAGE AND COLOR | FLIGHTLESS BIRDS | FROGS AND TOADS | KANGAROOS AND OTHER MARSUPIALS | REPTILES | TREES |

# AZTECS

A GREAT IMPERIAL power, the Aztecs came to dominate the Valley of Mexico in less than a hundred years. Egged on by bloodthirsty gods, they were a warlike people, outstanding for their military skill and well organized society. By the time the Spanish conquistador Hernán Cortés (1485–1547) arrived in 1519, the Aztecs and their allies were rulers of some 25 million people.

## Rise of the Aztecs

The Aztecs were one of many tribes who invaded the Valley of Mexico soon after the collapse of the Toltecs in the late 12th century. They dominated the valley after 1438.

**Human sacrifice**
When they won a war, the Aztecs killed many prisoners as offerings to their gods. Aztecs believed that human sacrifices were necessary in order for the universe to continue.

*Dish for human heart*

**Subject peoples**
The Aztecs ruled over a network of city states. Subject peoples made regular payments to their Aztec overlords, in the form of corn, cacao, or cotton. As long as this "tribute" was paid, the peoples of the Valley of Mexico were left to govern themselves and to keep their customs.

## Tenochtitlán

A city of canals and narrow streets, the Aztec capital was built on an island in Lake Texcoco. It was linked to the land by three narrow causeways. The city was home to 200,000 people – four or five times larger than any European city of the time. Most people lived in small houses in the narrow streets surrounding the temple precinct.

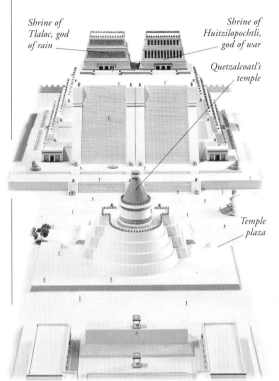

*Shrine of Tlaloc, god of rain*
*Shrine of Huitzilopochtli, god of war*
*Quetzalcoatl's temple*
*Temple plaza*

**The great precinct**
The center of Tenochtitlán was dominated by the Great Precinct, surrounded by a wall decorated with huge serpent heads. Inside the enclosure were the temples of the leading gods. A skull rack displayed the heads of countless victims of human sacrifice.

## Aztec society

Commoners lived in small mud houses and grew crops on the marshes. They dressed and ate simply. The nobles were warriors, tribute collectors, and judges; they were rewarded for their services with land.

*Mother of new baby*
*Chief priest*
*Three boys call out baby's name.*
*Midwife*
*School teacher*

**Customs**
Aztec customs included an elaborate naming ceremony for newborn babies.

## Aztecs on the eve of conquest

By the early 16th century, the Aztec Empire was showing signs of weakness. Shortly before the arrival of Cortés, priests and nobles were worried by a series of omens that seemed to forecast Aztec decline. These omens included the rumbling of the volcano Popocatépetl.

**Quetzalcoatl**
The Aztecs believed that the god Quetzalcoatl had been driven from his kingdom and would return to begin a golden age. When Cortés arrived, they thought he was the god. But the noise of Popocatépetl seemed to be an omen of defeat. **Popocatépetl**

*Quetzalcoatl, the feathered serpent*

## Montezuma II

The emperor Montezuma II (c. 1466–1520) was unsure if Cortés was Quetzalcoatl, and hesitated to repel the Spanish when they arrived. Cortés and his small army got as far as the capital, and Montezuma welcomed them there. But the Spanish seized the emperor and took him hostage. Montezuma died in prison, the last Aztec ruler.

## Conquest of the Aztecs

In April 1519, Cortés founded Veracruz on the coast of the Gulf of Mexico, inside the Aztec Empire. With his army of 600 men and 16 horses, he advanced toward Tenochtitlán, forging alliances with Aztec enemies. By August 1521, the Spanish had occupied Tenochtitlán after laying siege with the help of many local soldiers.

**Defeat by Tlaxcala**
The growing thirst for human sacrifice led Aztecs to wage constant war on the neighboring Tlaxcalans. Four years before the arrival of Cortés, the Tlaxcalans inflicted a heavy defeat on the Aztec armies, greatly weakening the empire.

FIND OUT MORE — CENTRAL AMERICA, HISTORY OF • MAYA • MESOAMERICANS • OLMECS

# Aztec life
## Everyday items

**Water jar** is made of glazed earthenware and has a narrow neck.

**Bowl** is decorated with bold abstract patterns in two colors.

**Ax heads** were often made of copper; they originally had wooden handles.

**Adze** was a woodworker's tool.

**Chisel** used by masons

**Flute** made of bone to play simple tunes

## Ritual items

**Flint knives**

**Obsidian hooked knife**

**Club** with obsidian blades

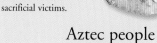

**Spear** with obsidian blades

**Tools** had blades of flint or obsidian, often with wood handles.

**Mask** may be made from skull of sacrificial victim.

**Greenstone mask** was left as an offering to the gods.

**Flint knives** may have been used to kill sacrificial victims.

**Feathered cloak** was worn by priest or warrior.

**Ritual vessel** was used in the temple.

## Aztec people

**Cleaner with broom**

**Boy carrying rushes**

**Mother and babies**

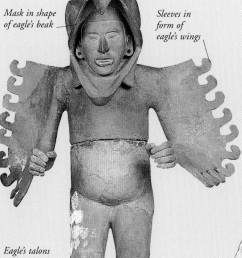

*Mask in shape of eagle's beak*

*Sleeves in form of eagle's wings*

*Eagle's talons on leg guard*

**Eagle warrior**

**Young woman**

**Weaver**

**Girl grinding corn**

**Boatman**

**Carpenter**

**Painter**

**Boatman**

**Musician**

**Schoolmaster**

**Jeweler**

**Goldsmith**

**Featherworker**

**Messenger**

# BABYLONIAN EMPIRE

ON THE EUPHRATES RIVER, nearly 4,000 years ago, an ancient settlement became the most magnificent city in the Near East. This city was Babylon, and when Hammurabi conquered Mesopotamia, he established his capital there. Over centuries, Babylonian fortunes rose and fell, as the city was invaded by the Hittites, Kassites, and Assyrians. The Assyrians destroyed Babylon in 689 BC. In 612 BC, the Babylonians retaliated by conquering the Assyrians and again made Babylon the world's greatest city. Babylonia's splendor continued after the Persian Empire absorbed it in 539 BC.

**The first Babylonian Empire**
By about 1770 BC, Hammurabi had conquered most of Mesopotamia. Babylon was established as the capital of the south for the duration of the Babylonian empire.

## King Hammurabi

Mesopotamia's wisest king, Hammurabi (r.1792–1750 BC), followed ancient tradition by issuing laws to protect his subjects. Using cuneiform script, he had 282 laws carved on a black stone pillar. The empire he founded collapsed in 1595 BC, when Hittites from Anatolia looted it. The Kassites from the mountains to the east of Babylon then invaded and took over.

**Kassites**
Between 1600 and 1190 BC, people called the Kassites ruled Babylonia. They are best known for their boundary stones (kuddurus), which marked property divisions and recorded gifts of land. These were often decorated with divine symbols. After the end of Kassite rule, Babylonia fell into a long period of chaos.

**Persian Empire**
In 539 BC, the Persian king, Cyrus II, took over the Babylonian kingdom and made Mesopotamia part of his empire. His son, Cambyses, was usurped by Darius I, also called "the Great," under whom the empire reached its greatest extent.

**Kudduru**

**Darius I (522–486)** introduced coinage.

## Literature and art

The Babylonian Empire was renowned for its great artistic and literary achievements. Literature, such as the legendary epic of Gilgamesh, a Sumerian hero, was written on clay tablets in cuneiform script. Artistic splendors included terra-cotta plaques, superb sculpture and glassware, and, above all, the lavish and decorative entrance to the city – the Ishtar Gate and Processional Way.

**Venus tablet, Kish**

**Science**
Babylonia was famous as a home of scientists and scholars. Babylonian astrologers studied the movements of planets and stars, recorded their findings on clay tablets, and used these to predict the future. Many texts are so detailed that modern astronomers can date ancient events from them. Ancient Greeks and Romans used the Babylonian system for naming planets.

*Cuneiform script*

*Magical spirit*

**The Ishtar Gate,** one of Nebuchadnezzar's most spectacular structures, was made from clay bricks which were molded and brilliantly glazed with color.

*Fortified tower*

*Stepped battlement*

**Religion**
The Babylonians inherited their religion from the Sumerians. They believed that gods and spirits controlled every aspect of the world. These gods included Anu, the sky god, who gave birth to some of the most important deities, including Ishtar, goddess of love and war (represented by the planet Venus), and Ea, god of wisdom and freshwater. Ea was the father of Marduk, the god of Babylon, who created the world and made humans by mixing earth with divine blood.

*Dragon, symbol of the god Marduk*

*Bull, symbol of Adad, god of the weather*

### Nebuchadnezzar

After the Babylonian king Nabopolasser defeated the Assyrian enemy, his son Nebuchadnezzar (r.605–562 BC) rebuilt the devastated Babylon on a grand scale. His works included the Ishtar Gate, and a temple and ziggurat tower. According to Greek tradition, he also built Hanging Gardens for his homesick wife, and these became one of the Seven Wonders of the World. In 596 BC, Nebuchadnezzar attacked the kingdom of Judah. Ten years later he returned, sacked Jerusalem, and took the Jews into exile in Babylon. They were not released until the reign of Cyrus II.

FIND OUT MORE

ARCHITECTURE | ASIA, HISTORY OF | ASSYRIAN EMPIRE | HITTITES | PERSIAN EMPIRES | SCIENCE, HISTORY OF | SEVEN WONDERS OF THE ANCIENT WORLD | SUMERIANS | WARFARE

**B**

# BADGERS, OTTERS, AND SKUNKS

THESE THREE GROUPS OF ANIMALS are members of the weasel family – Mustelidae. Their main characteristics are a long, low-slung body, short legs, and five toes on each foot. They are carnivores, although badgers have a mixed diet. The honey badger is especially fond of honey, as its name suggests. Most mustelids discharge a thick, oily, strong-smelling fluid called musk from their anal glands. They use this mostly to send scent messages to other members of the species, usually with their droppings.

**Skull**
A badger eats meat and plants, and its large canines and broad molar teeth are ideal for this diet. Its jaw muscles are fixed to a rigid bone on the top of its skull, giving the animal a powerful bite.

## Badgers

All badgers are thick set, with very powerful legs that they use to forage for food and to dig their often extensive burrows. They are nocturnal animals, spending the day underground with others of their social group. There are eight species of true badgers, plus the honey badger, which is classed in a subfamily of its own.

Short tail

Long, striped snout

Long, coarse hairs over a dense underfur

Badgers have a good sense of smell.

**Paws**
A Eurasian badger's track is unmistakable. Each foot has five toes with a kidney-shaped pad behind. The front claws usually leave marks because they are long.

Forepaw print

Hindpaw print

**Eurasian badger**
This is the largest badger and has the widest distribution. Females give birth to up to four cubs in February. They are weaned at 12 weeks, when they can forage for themselves.

## Otters

These semiaquatic mustelids live outside the polar regions on every continent except Australia. Some species are exclusively sea creatures, some use only freshwater, and others use both sea- and freshwater. Most have sleeping dens, or holts, on land.

European river otter

**Paws**
Although all otters swim, not all have webbed feet. The European otter has a large amount of webbing, while the Asian short-clawed otter has little webbing and uses its paws to find food by touch.

**Fur**
An otter's coat consists of two layers. A thick underlayer of fine hairs traps air for warmth, and longer, waterproof guard hairs keep the underfur dry.

Asian short-clawed otter

**Badger setts**
During the day, badgers live underground in a complex system of tunnels and chambers called a sett. A main badger sett is easy to spot because of the entrance with piles of soil outside.

**Honey badger**
The African honey badger, also known as the ratel, has a thick, loose skin. Predators can find it difficult to pierce its skin, and the badger can twist around inside its skin and bite back.

### Movement
With their long backs and heavy tails, otters can look clumsy on land. In the water they are graceful swimmers, propelling themselves forward by moving their hindquarters and tail up and down.

### Sprints
Otters secrete a powerful scent. They mark their territory by leaving their droppings, called spraints, which smell of this scent, on high points such as rocks.

## Skunks

There are 13 species of skunks, which all live in the Americas. They are best known for their ability to squirt a foul-smelling fluid from their anal glands. They aim this fluid at the eyes of an enemy, and it causes temporary blindness. Skunks search for insects and other small animals to eat, mainly at night.

**Markings**
Skunks have bold black and white coat markings. Like the yellow and black stripes of a wasp, these warn would-be predators of danger.

### EURASIAN BADGER

SCIENTIFIC NAME  *Meles meles*

ORDER  Carnivora

FAMILY  Mustelidae

DISTRIBUTION  Europe and a wide band across Asia

HABITAT  Mainly lowland farmland and woodland

DIET  Worms, insects, birds, and other small animals, fruit, cereals, fungi

SIZE  Length: 3.3 ft (1 m)

LIFESPAN  About 7 years

**FIND OUT MORE**

ANIMAL BEHAVIOR  LAKE AND RIVER WILDLIFE  NORTH AMERICAN WILDLIFE  POLLUTION  WEASELS AND MARTENS

*Formerly known as* **BALKAN STATES**

# SOUTHEAST EUROPE

SLOVENIA, CROATIA, Bosnia and Herzegovina, Yugoslavia, Macedonia, and Albania all lie in Southeast Europe. Ruled by Turkey for nearly 500 years, all the countries, with the exception of Albania, were united as Yugoslavia in 1918. It was, however, an uneasy peace, and, in 1991, Yugoslavia split up as a result of rival ethnic and religious tensions. War broke out, lasting until 1995. Since then, fresh conflicts have occurred and the region is still struggling to recover from war.

## Physical features

The west of this region is made up of limestone plateaus and steep mountain ranges separated by valleys. In the northwest are the flat plains of the Danube River.

73°F (23°C)     34°F (1°C)

34 in (870 mm)

### Regional climate
The inland plains and the coastal strip have a temperate continental climate, with hot summers and cold winters. Snow falls in the mountains in winter.

### Mountains
Mixed forests of deciduous trees and conifers cover the mountain slopes that dominate the north of the region. The Dinaric Alps are barren limestone ranges, or *karst*, that rise to about 5,905 ft (1,800 m) along the Adriatic Sea coast.

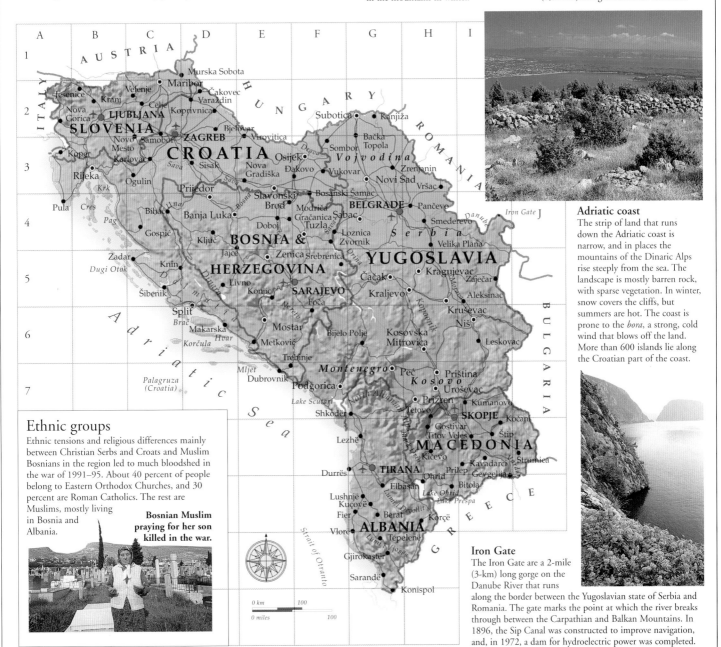

### Ethnic groups
Ethnic tensions and religious differences mainly between Christian Serbs and Croats and Muslim Bosnians in the region led to much bloodshed in the war of 1991–95. About 40 percent of people belong to Eastern Orthodox Churches, and 30 percent are Roman Catholics. The rest are Muslims, mostly living in Bosnia and Albania.

**Bosnian Muslim praying for her son killed in the war.**

### Adriatic coast
The strip of land that runs down the Adriatic coast is narrow, and in places the mountains of the Dinaric Alps rise steeply from the sea. The landscape is mostly barren rock, with sparse vegetation. In winter, snow covers the cliffs, but summers are hot. The coast is prone to the *bora*, a strong, cold wind that blows off the land. More than 600 islands lie along the Croatian part of the coast.

### Iron Gate
The Iron Gate are a 2-mile (3-km) long gorge on the Danube River that runs along the border between the Yugoslavian state of Serbia and Romania. The gate marks the point at which the river breaks through between the Carpathian and Balkan Mountains. In 1896, the Sip Canal was constructed to improve navigation, and, in 1972, a dam for hydroelectric power was completed.

B

B

# Slovenia

Historically and geographically, Slovenia has more in common with Austria than with other neighboring states. The country was ruled by Austria for almost a thousand years. Slovenia has many small farms and thriving businesses. Despite economic problems caused by the conflict in areas to the south, it is the region's wealthiest country.

### Resources
Slovenia mines mercury, lead, oil, and zinc for export. There are also deposits of brown coal and lignite, but they are poor quality and difficult to extract. One-third of the country's energy comes from a nuclear plant in Krsvo.

**Mercury ore**

### People
About 90 percent of the population are Slovenes who have kept their language and traditional culture despite centuries of Austrian domination. Workers earn more than in other Balkan states, and standards of education are high. One in seven Slovenes lives in the capital, Ljubljana, which has textile, electronics, chemical, and manufacturing industries.

### Tourism
Slovenia is slowly rebuilding its tourist industry, which suffered because of the war in Bosnia. Skiing, spa resorts, and lakeside scenery attract many visitors to the Alps in the north of the region.

*Lake Bled is a popular tourist destination.*

## SLOVENIA FACTS

| | |
|---|---|
| CAPITAL CITY | Ljubljana |
| AREA | 7,820 sq miles (20,250 sq km) |
| POPULATION | 2,016,000 |
| MAIN LANGUAGE | Slovene |
| MAJOR RELIGION | Christian |
| CURRENCY | Tolar |

# Croatia

Ruled by Hungary for more than 800 years, Croatia became part of Yugoslavia in 1918, gaining independence in 1991. Croatia's economy was damaged by the war with neighboring Bosnia, but it is fortunate in having important ports and rich resources, including oil, coal, and bauxite. The tourist industry is recovering.

### Zagreb
The cultural and industrial capital of Croatia is Zagreb, which grew out of two medieval settlements on the Sava River. The city has museums, art galleries, 13th-century buildings, and cathedrals, such as St Mark's and St Stephen's. Most people travel by streetcar and bus.

### Adriatic coast
Croatia's Adriatic coast has sandy beaches and hundreds of offshore islands that once attracted up to 12 million tourists every year. However, the outbreak of war in 1991 abruptly halted all tourism. There is still an active fishing industry, with an annual catch of about 27,500 tons (25,000 tonnes).

**Flax stalks**

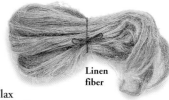

**Linen fiber**

### Flax
Fields of flax are cultivated in the fertile river valleys of northern Croatia. Flax fiber, obtained by crushing the stalks of the plant, is woven into linen and canvas, and its seeds yield linseed oil. Apricots, grapes, and plums are also grown in northern Croatia.

## CROATIA FACTS

| | |
|---|---|
| CAPITAL CITY | Zagreb |
| AREA | 21,830 sq miles (56,540 sq km) |
| POPULATION | 4,500,000 |
| MAIN LANGUAGE | Croatian |
| MAJOR RELIGIONS | Christian |
| CURRENCY | Kuna |

# Bosnia and Herzegovina

In 1991, bitter fighting broke out in the twin states of Bosnia and Herzegovina between the Roman Catholic Croats, Muslim Bosnians, and Orthodox Serbs. In all, about 300,000 people were killed, more than 2,000,000 fled the country, and many historic cities were devastated. A precarious peace has prevailed since 1995.

### Muslims
During the war, Serbs in Bosnia forced Croats and Muslims out of areas they regarded as their own. Thousands were killed, and many Muslims fled abroad. In 1995, a peace agreement split the country into two provinces: Bosnian-Serb and Muslim-Croat.

### Sarajevo
Straddling the Miljacka River, Sarajevo is the capital of Bosnia and Herzegovina. Under communist rule the city was transformed from a sleepy, Islamic town to a bustling, multi-cultural industrial center. During the civil war, however, it was shattered by 2,000,000 shells that killed tens of thousands of people. Serbs attacking the city were forced to withdraw in 1995.

### Farming
Bosnia and Herzegovina's main farming region lies in the southwest; the area has fertile, spring-fed soil and hot, dry summers. Crops include citrus fruit, grapes, corn, pomegranates, figs, olives, rice, and tobacco. Sheep are raised on the hill country.

**Figs**

**Pomegranates**

## BOSNIA AND HERZEGOVINA FACTS

| | |
|---|---|
| CAPITAL CITY | Sarajevo |
| AREA | 19,741 sq miles (51,130 sq km) |
| POPULATION | 4,000,000 |
| MAIN LANGUAGE | Serbo-Croat |
| MAJOR RELIGIONS | Christian, Muslim |
| CURRENCY | Marka |

# Yugoslavia

Two of the former Yugoslavia's states, Serbia and Montenegro, kept the name Yugoslavia in 1992. As a result of the part Serbia played in helping Serbs fight in Bosnia and Croatia, many countries imposed sanctions and refused to trade with the new Yugoslavia. Its disgraced former president Slobodan Milosevic was called to a war crimes tribunal.

## People

The people of Yugoslavia speak Serbo-Croat, which they write in the Russian-like Cyrillic alphabet. The largest minority group is Albanian (17 percent). Most people belong to the Serbian Orthodox Church.

**Raznjici**

*Cubes of grilled lamb* *Skewer*

## Food

A favorite Yugoslavian dish is *raznjici*, cubes of lamb grilled on skewers and served with yogurt. *Djuvetsch*, meat with rice and vegetables, is also popular. Desserts are made from honey and nuts. The national drink is *slivovitz*, plum brandy.

*Sveti Stefan was once a popular tourist destination.*

## Tourism

Before the war, the beautiful beaches and historic towns and villages on Montenegro's coast attracted millions of tourists. However, many beauty spots have been devastated. Yugoslavia only received 150,000 visitors in 2001 and is trying to rebuild its shattered tourist industry.

### YUGOSLAVIA FACTS

**CAPITAL CITY** Belgrade

**AREA** 39,506 sq miles (102,350 sq km)

**POPULATION** 10,600,000

**MAIN LANGUAGE** Serbo-Croat

**MAJOR RELIGIONS** Christian, Muslim

**CURRENCY** Yugoslav dinar

**B**

---

# Macedonia

The official name of the country is the Former Yugoslav Republic of Macedonia to appease the Greeks, who have a province called Macedonia. Landlocked, it is self-sufficient in energy, with efficient metal, chemical, textile, and food processing industries. Air pollution is a serious problem. Renewed ethnic conflicts broke out in 2001.

**Skopje**

Despite having been destroyed four times by earthquakes, most recently in 1963, Macedonia's capital, Skopje, is the hub of the country's communications and industry.

## Lakes

Lake Ohrid and Lake Prespa in southwestern Macedonia are two of Europe's most beautiful spots and, in peaceful times, they attract visitors for the scenery and the fishing. Ohrid is 964 ft (294 m) deep. Underground channels link the two lakes.

## People

The largest group of people is made up of Eastern Orthodox (Christian) Slav Macedonians who account for two-thirds of the population. Many ethnic Albanian refugees arrived from Kosovo in 1999.

### MACEDONIA FACTS

**CAPITAL CITY** Skopje

**AREA** 9,925 sq miles (25,713 sq km)

**POPULATION** 2,093,000

**MAIN LANGUAGES** Macedonian, Serbo-Croat

**MAJOR RELIGIONS** Christian, Muslim

**CURRENCY** Denar

---

# Albania

From 1944 to 1991, Albania was a one-party state with the most rigid communist regime in the world. It is now a democracy, but, in 1997, social unrest developed. Tirana, the capital, was founded in the 17th century and has light industries as well as government buildings.

## People

As a way of making the population grow rapidly, the communist government encouraged men and women to have large families. Under communism, Albania was the only official atheist state and, even today, many people are nonbelievers.

**Grapes**

**Tomatoes**

**Potatoes**

**Watermelon**

## Farming

About 24 percent of Albania is cultivated. Wheat, corn, potatoes, other vegetables, fruit, and sugar beet are the main crops. Sheep, goats, and cattle are raised for meat and milk, and donkeys are bred for transportation.

## Transportation

Communications are difficult. There are only 273 miles (440 km) of railroads, and 4,630 miles (7,450 km) of roads, 60 percent of which are not paved. There is only one car for every 50 people. Horses and carts are the main means of transportation.

### ALBANIA FACTS

**CAPITAL CITY** Tirana

**AREA** 11,100 sq miles (28,750 sq km)

**POPULATION** 3,100,000

**MAIN LANGUAGE** Albanian

**MAJOR RELIGIONS** Muslim, Christian

**CURRENCY** Lek

---

**FIND OUT MORE** CHRISTIANITY EARTHQUAKES EMPIRES EUROPE, HISTORY OF FARMING FISHING INDUSTRY ISLAM LAKES TEXTILES AND WEAVING TRADE AND INDUSTRY

# BALLET

ONE OF THE MOST beautiful of the arts, ballet is a combination of dance and mime performed to music. Many ballets tell a story; others are abstract and experiment with form and movement. Ballet began in Italy. It was taken to France in 1533 by Catherine de Médicis, a member of a famous Italian family, who married a French prince. In 1661, Louis XIV founded the first ballet school, L'Academie Royale de Danse. Today, children learn the basics in ballet schools around the world.

*Arms open wide*

*Both arms held in front*

*One arm in front, the other out to the side*

*One arm up, the other out to the side*

*Both arms up*

**First position** – heels together, feet turned out.

**Second position** – heels apart, feet turned out.

**Third position** – one foot crossed halfway in front of the other.

**Fourth position** (crossed) – one foot in front of the other.

**Fifth position** – Feet crossed and touching.

## Ballet positions

Every step in ballet makes use of the basic positions. It was at L'Academie Royale de Danse that the five basic positions of the feet were established. To achieve them, the whole leg has to be turned out from the hips. The position of the arms is known as *port de bras*.

### Benesh notation

For ballets to survive, the steps must be written down, or notated. One of the most popular notation methods was devised by Rudolf and Joan Benesh in the late 1940s. Symbols represent the position of the hands and feet.

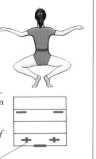

*Each line represents a part of the body: top of head; shoulder; waist; knee; floor.*

## Romantic ballet

In the early 1800s, the Romantic Movement, with its fascination with the supernatural, affected all the arts. One of the most important men in 19th-century ballet was the choreographer August Bournonville. His ballets were influenced by his years in Paris where Romantic ballet began.

**Marie Taglione**
Taglione (1804–84) was an Italian ballerina who created the role of *La Sylphide*. She perfected the art of dancing on the tips of her toes, or *en pointe*.

**Giselle**
The ballet *Giselle* is one of the most famous Romantic ballets. The story follows the romance between a peasant girl, Giselle, and Albrecht, a count. Giselle dies, but rises from her grave to dance with her lover.

*A scene from Giselle*

Nijinsky

**The Ballets Russes**
Many Russian choreographers and dancers became bored with Classical ballet. Organized by Serge Diaghilev (1872–1929), they formed the Ballets Russes and toured Europe. The dancers included Vaslav Nijinsky (1890–1950), famous for his jumps.

### Anna Pavlova
Russian ballerina Anna Pavlova (1881–1931) was the most famous dancer of her time. She danced with the Imperial Ballet, and also toured with the Ballets Russes. She formed her own company and toured all over the world.

## Ballet in Russia

In 1847, French dancer Marius Petipa went to Russia to work with the tsar's Imperial Ballet in St. Petersburg. With his assistant Lev Ivanov, he created Classical ballets – grand lavish ballets in three or four acts, designed to show off the brilliant techniques of the dancers.

**Classical ballets** contain dazzling dances for the hero and heroine to perform together.

*Partners have to trust each other.*

**Tchaikovsky**
Russian composer Pëtr Tchaikovsky (1840–93) wrote probably the most famous ballet music of all. He worked with Marius Petipa and Lev Ivanov on the three great classical ballets, *Sleeping Beauty* (1890), *The Nutcracker* (1892), and *Swan Lake* (1895).

*Moscow City Ballet in* Sleeping Beauty

## Ballet today

Almost every country has its own ballet company. The dancers perform Romantic and Classical ballets, ballets created by the Ballets Russes, and the works of more modern and contemporary choreographers.

**New York City Ballet**
The New York City Ballet (left) was founded by the Russian choreographer George Balanchine (1904–83). This is his ballet *Apollo*.

**The Royal Ballet**
Britain's Royal Ballet started as the Vic-Wells Ballet in 1931. It often dances works by past artistic directors Frederick Ashton and Kenneth MacMillan.

*Jumps require strength.*

*A character from Ashton's Tales of Beatrix Potter*

FIND OUT MORE

ART, HISTORY OF   DANCE   DRAMA   JAZZ   MUSIC   MUSICAL INSTRUMENTS   OPERA   STRAVINSKY, IGOR

# BALL GAMES

BALL GAMES OF EVERY VARIETY are played around the world with all shapes and sizes of balls; on fields, courts, courses, and tables; by teams and by individuals. In addition to various football games and racket games, there are bat-and-ball games such as cricket and baseball, stick-and-ball games such as hockey, hurling, shinty, and golf; and billiard-table games such as pool, snooker, and billiards. Other ball games include basketball, played on a court, volleyball, which is usually played on a court on the beach, and bowls, in which balls are rolled along the ground.

Batting gloves

Helmet

Bat made of willow

Wicket keeping pads

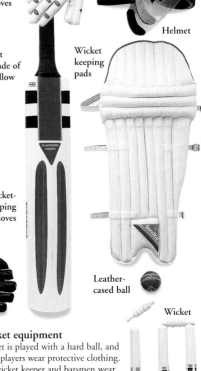

Wicket-keeping gloves

Leather-cased ball

Wicket

## Cricket

This game is played between two teams of 11, one team bowling and fielding against two on the batting side. The batsmen score runs by running between the wickets or hitting the ball over the boundary. The fielding side may dismiss the batsmen in several ways, including bowling at and knocking over the wicket with the ball.

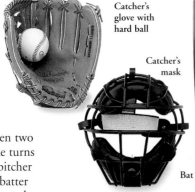

Sightscreen helps the batsman see the ball.

Pitch

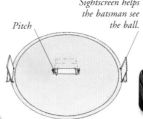

**Cricket field**
The field is usually oval but its size varies. The boundary is marked by a rope or white line. The pitch, situated at or near the middle of the field, measures 22 yd (20.12 m) between wickets and 10 ft (3.05 m) across.

**Cricket equipment**
Cricket is played with a hard ball, and many players wear protective clothing. The wicket keeper and batsmen wear special gloves and strapped-on leg-pads. Batsmen and close fielders may wear helmets with face guards.

---

Catcher's glove with hard ball

Catcher's mask

Bat

## Baseball

Baseball is played between two teams of nine which take turns batting and fielding. A pitcher throws the ball and the batter attempts to hit it and run to bases without being tagged or forced out before reaching home plate. The game has nine innings. An inning is over when six batters – three from each team – are out.

**Baseball equipment**
The catcher, who crouches behind the batter, wears a mask and body padding. Batters wear a helmet and fielders wear a padded mitt. The ball is made of cork wrapped in yarn and encased in leather.

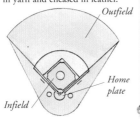

Outfield

Home plate

Infield

**Baseball field**
The field is made up of an infield, or "diamond," and an outfield. A pitcher throws from a mound at the center of the infield, which has a base at each corner. A batter stands at home plate.

### Babe Ruth

The sensational hitting of Babe Ruth (1895–1948) brought crowds to baseball in the 1920s. Originally a World Series-winning pitcher with the Boston Red Sox, he joined the New York Yankees in 1920 and slugged record after record, including his famous 60 home runs in 1927 and a lifetime total of 714.

---

Ball, traditionally white

## Field hockey

This is played between two teams of 11. Each player has a hooked stick, only the flat side of which can be used for playing the ball. The object of the game is to hit the ball into the opponents' goal. Goals may be scored only from inside a semicircle called the striking, or shooting, circle.

Goalkeeper's helmet

Stick

**Hockey equipment**
Players wear guards under their socks to protect their shins and ankles. The goalkeeper wears a helmet with a face mask, shoulder and elbow pads, padded gloves, substantial leg guards, and "kickers" over the boots to protect their feet when kicking the ball away.

**Hurling**
This is played, 15 on a side, with wooden sticks called hurleys, which are used to strike or carry a small, hard ball. Goals are like soccer goals with extended posts. Points are scored for hitting the ball under the crossbar (three points) or over it (one point).

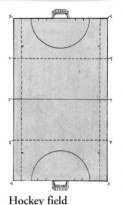

**Hockey field**
The pitch measures 100 yd x 60 yd (91.4 m x 54.9 m). Goals are 12 ft (3.66 m) wide and 7 ft (2.13 m) high. The shooting circles are joined quarter circles drawn from each post.

# Basketball

With five a side, basketball allows free substitution from as many as seven other players. The goal is to put the ball into the opposition's basket. Baskets, or field goals, are worth three points when scored from outside the three-point line, and two points when scored from inside the line.

*The player holds the ball in both hands when preparing to shoot.*

*Players can pivot and jump with the ball, as when shooting a "basket."*

*Three-point line*

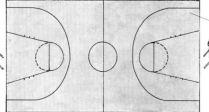

## Basketball court
A basketball court is 91.8 ft x 49.2 ft (28 m x 15 m). The baskets stand 10 ft (3.05 m) above the ground.

*Basketball*

*Ball is made of rubber encased in leather, rubber, or synthetic material.*

*Basket*

*Backboard*

## Basketball equipment
The main equipment needed for basketball is a ball and two baskets. Official time-keepers use clocks to keep track of the many time restrictions in the game, including the five-second limit on a player holding the ball.

*A moving player may take one stride with the ball.*

*High top sneakers are needed to support the ankles when turning and pivoting.*

## Netball
This is played by either seven women, or girls, on a side. The goal is to throw the ball into the opponents' net. Players must stay in certain areas of the court and may not move with the ball. They wear letters to show where they should be.

## Volleyball
Teams of six players aim to score points by propelling the ball over a net into the opponents' court so that they cannot return it. Players can play the ball with their hands or any part of the body above the waist. A team is allowed three hits to move the ball over the net.

# Golf

The goal in golf is to take as few strokes as possible to hit a ball a certain distance into a cup set in the ground. Players have a choice of clubs with which to strike the ball. The standard course has 18 holes of different lengths and configurations.

*Following through after contact*

*Starting a swing to hit the ball*

*End of follow-through*

*Tees*

*Golf balls*

# Bowls and bowling

Flat-green bowls is played on a flat lawn or indoors on a carpet. Players roll balls called woods, aiming to get them as close as possible to a smaller white ball called the jack. Tenpin bowling is played on indoor alleys. At each turn, bowlers have two goes to knock down as many pins as possible.

# Cue-and-ball games

Games played on billiards and pool tables include snooker and pool. Players use a stick called a cue to propel a white ball into colored balls to knock them into a pocket. Billiards is played with three balls – one white cue ball for each player and a red ball.

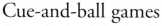

*Snooker balls*

## Playing a hole
Holes range from about 100 yd (90 m) to 600 yd (550 m). The first shot is played from the tee with either a wood, which is used for long shots, or an iron. Irons are used for the next shots until the putting green is reached, when the putter is used.

*Wood*

*Iron*

*Putter*

*Flat-green wood*

*Indoor bowls*

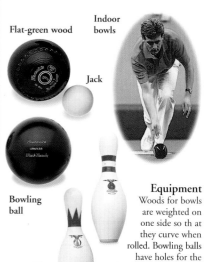

*Jack*

## Pool
Eight ball is the most widely played variety of pool. To win, one player must sink balls 1 to 7 in any order and then the 8, or black ball. The other player tries to sink balls 9 to 15 and then 8. Players take turns, remaining at the table until they fail to sink a ball, or commit a foul.

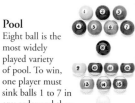

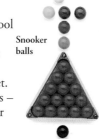

## Snooker
Players sink a red for one point, and then any color for two to seven points, depending on the color. The colors are replaced until no reds remain and are then sunk in order of their value.

## Golf equipment

Players are allowed up to 14 clubs, which they carry in a bag or trolley. Most players have three or four woods, nine or ten irons, and one putter. The ball is supported for the first stroke of each hole on a small stand, or tee. Players must wear studded shoes.

*Bowling ball*

*Pins*

## Equipment
Woods for bowls are weighted on one side so that they curve when rolled. Bowling balls have holes for the thumb and two fingers. The ten pins are cleared and reset automatically.

FIND OUT MORE    FOOTBALL    HEALTH AND FITNESS    OLYMPIC GAMES    SPORTS    TENNIS AND OTHER RACKET SPORTS

# Ball games

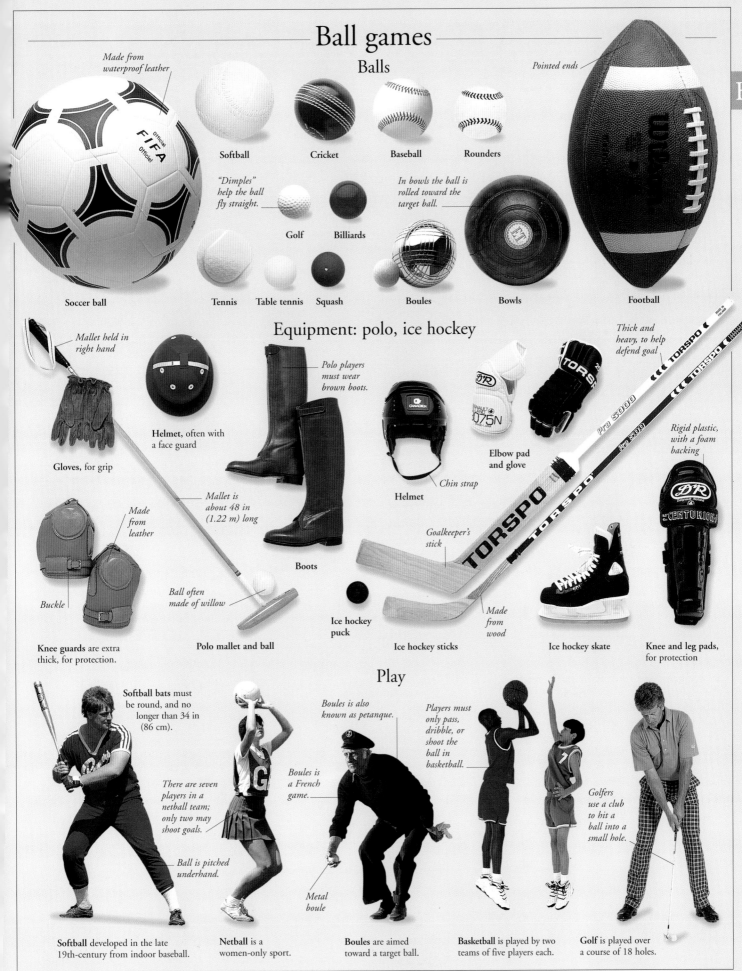

## Balls

*Made from waterproof leather*

*Pointed ends*

**Softball**

**Cricket**

**Baseball**

**Rounders**

*"Dimples" help the ball fly straight.*

*In bowls the ball is rolled toward the target ball.*

**Golf**

**Billiards**

**Soccer ball**

**Tennis**

**Table tennis**

**Squash**

**Boules**

**Bowls**

**Football**

## Equipment: polo, ice hockey

*Mallet held in right hand*

*Thick and heavy, to help defend goal*

**Helmet,** often with a face guard

*Polo players must wear brown boots.*

**Gloves,** for grip

*Rigid plastic, with a foam backing*

**Elbow pad and glove**

*Mallet is about 48 in (1.22 m) long*

*Made from leather*

**Helmet**

*Chin strap*

*Goalkeeper's stick*

**Buckle**

*Ball often made of willow*

**Ice hockey puck**

*Made from wood*

**Knee guards** are extra thick, for protection.

**Polo mallet and ball**

**Boots**

**Ice hockey sticks**

**Ice hockey skate**

**Knee and leg pads,** for protection

## Play

**Softball bats** must be round, and no longer than 34 in (86 cm).

*Boules is also known as petanque.*

*Players must only pass, dribble, or shoot the ball in basketball.*

*There are seven players in a netball team; only two may shoot goals.*

*Boules is a French game.*

*Golfers use a club to hit a ball into a small hole.*

*Ball is pitched underhand.*

*Metal boule*

**Softball** developed in the late 19th-century from indoor baseball.

**Netball** is a women-only sport.

**Boules** are aimed toward a target ball.

**Basketball** is played by two teams of five players each.

**Golf** is played over a course of 18 holes.

# BALTIC STATES AND BELARUS

THE THREE Baltic states of Estonia, Latvia, and Lithuania occupy a small area on the Baltic Sea coast to the west of the Russian Federation. Belarus, formerly known as "White Russia," sits between Russia, Poland, and Ukraine. All four countries were former Soviet republics; in 1991, after the breakup of the Soviet Union, they declared independence. Since then, they have suffered high inflation and environmental problems, but are now working to form a trade link between eastern and western Europe.

## Physical features

The Baltic states have a flat landscape of plains and low hills, with forests and swampy marshes. There are thousands of rivers and lakes; the largest, Peipus, at 1,400 sq miles (3,626 sq km), is shared between Estonia and Russia.

**Baltic coast and islands**
Estonia, Latvia, and Lithuania all have coasts and ports on the Baltic Sea, and ice covers much of the sea in winter. Estonia has the longest coastline, and the country includes more than 1,500 islands that form a barrier protecting the Gulf of Riga.

**Forests**
Dense deciduous and coniferous forests cover between 30 and 40 percent of the Baltic region. Belarus is dominated by lakes and thick forests full of wildlife such as deer and mink. The east of Latvia is forested.

Forested Ganja River valley, Latvia

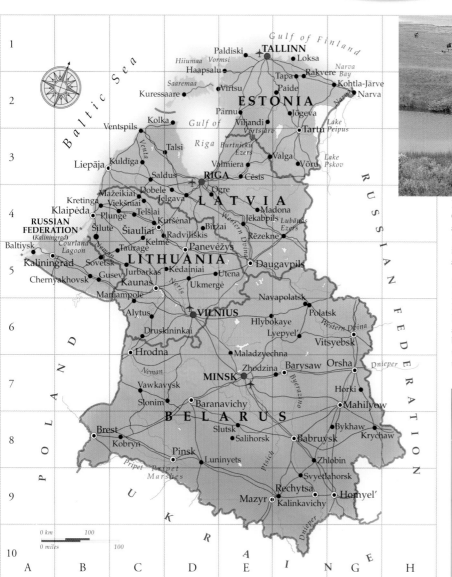

**Pripet Marshes**
Covering a vast area of southern Belarus, the Pripet Marshes are the biggest wetland area in Europe. They stretch for 15,000 sq miles (40,000 sq km), and are fed by several rivers including the Byerazino and Dnieper. The soils of the Pripet are clay or sandy, and large areas are waterlogged.

**Regional climate**
Estonia, Latvia, Lithuania, and Belarus have cold winters and cool, wet summers, because of their location on the Baltic Sea. Heavy snow falls during the winter throughout the region, particularly in Belarus.

63°F (17°C)    23°F (-5°C)

26 in (668 mm)

## Cultural diversity

Estonia, Latvia, and Belarus have large populations of Russians, who were resettled in the Baltic states under communist rule. Their presence causes racial tension with ethnic peoples in Estonia and Latvia. In Belarus, where most people are Russian speakers, and Lithuania, where 80 per cent are ethnic Lithuanians, there is social harmony.

**Folk dancer, Estonia**

# Estonia

The smallest and most northerly of the Baltic states, Estonia has a long coastline and beautiful scenery that attracts many tourists from Finland and Scandinavia. Under Soviet rule, its rural economy was transformed. It is now an industrial nation, and most people live in towns. Estonians are closely related to Finns and speak a similar language.

## ESTONIA FACTS

**CAPITAL CITY** Tallinn

**AREA** 17,423 sq miles (45,125 sq km)

**POPULATION** 1,400,000

**MAIN LANGUAGES** Estonian, Russian

**MAJOR RELIGION** Christian

**CURRENCY** Kroon

*Flax stems are used to make linen and ropes.*

### Flax
Textiles made from flax and cotton are among Estonia's leading exports. Flax is harvested at different times for various purposes: young green stems make fine cloth called linen; tougher fibers are used for ropes and mats.

### Tourism
More than one million tourists visit Estonia every year. The medieval buildings of Tallinn, Estonia's capital, are a major attraction, with a wealth of historical monuments. Summer regattas and boating and yachting in the sheltered waters of the Gulf of Riga are also popular.

# Latvia

Sandwiched in a central position between Estonia and Lithuania, Latvia is a flat country with about 12,000 rivers. Manufacturing, encouraged under Soviet rule, is the basis of the economy. Like the other states in this region, Latvia suffered high inflation during the 1990s. Farming, fishing, and timber are valuable sources of income.

## LATVIA FACTS

**CAPITAL CITY** Riga

**AREA** 24,938 sq miles (64,589 sq km)

**POPULATION** 2,400,000

**MAIN LANGUAGES** Latvian, Russian

**MAJOR RELIGION** Christian

**CURRENCY** Lat

### Farming
Latvia has a larger area of fertile land than the other Baltic states. Since independence, the huge state farms introduced by the Russians have been dismantled and are now privately owned. Most are dairy farms.

### People
About one-third of Latvians are of Russian origin and there are smaller numbers of Ukrainians and Belarussians. Just over half the population are ethnic Letts, or Latvians, who cling to their cultural heritage. They celebrate many traditional and religious festivals.

*Women wear traditional costumes in Latvia's Rites of Spring Festival.*

# Lithuania

Once a powerful nation, ruling lands that extended to the Black Sea, Lithuania sits south of Latvia. Most people live in the interior of the country, working in industry or farming. The short coastline, fringed with sand dunes and pine forests, is known for its amber. Since 1991, there have been disputes with Latvia over Baltic oil.

## LITHUANIA FACTS

**CAPITAL CITY** Vilnius

**AREA** 25,174 sq miles (65,200 sq km)

**POPULATION** 3,782,000

**MAIN LANGUAGES** Lithuanian, Russian

**MAJOR RELIGION** Christian

**CURRENCY** Litas

*Hill of Crosses, near Siauliai, a shrine to honor the dead.*

Yellow amber

### Amber
The Baltic states produce two-thirds of the world's amber, the fossilized sap of pine trees. Amber is used to make jewelry in shades of yellow, orange, and deep gold.

### Religion
By contrast to Estonians and Latvians, who are mainly Protestants, Lithuanians are mostly Roman Catholics. They managed to keep their faith even under Soviet rule, which discouraged religion.

# Belarus

Landlocked, and with few natural resources, Belarus suffers great poverty. In 1986, an accident at the Chernobyl nuclear reactor in the Ukraine severely contaminated farmland. Many areas remain unsafe. The shaky economy is based on the production of machines, cars, chemicals, and a large farming sector. Unlike the other Baltic states, Belarus has maintained close economic ties with Russia and is moving towards official union.

## BELARUS FACTS

**CAPITAL CITY** Minsk

**AREA** 80,154 sq miles (207,600 sq km)

**POPULATION** 10,320,000

**MAIN LANGUAGES** Belarussian, Russian

**MAJOR RELIGION** Christian

**CURRENCY** Belarussian ruble

### Ceramics
Belarus produces many beautifully crafted ceramic and porcelain items, such as vases and ornaments. The country is also known for its high-quality decorated glassware, made by heating sand with salt, limestone, and old glass, then molding the molten liquid glass.

### Food
The national dish of Belarus is *draniki*, made from fried, grated potatoes, and served with sour cream and pickled berries or beets. Soup made from beets is also a popular dish.

Draniki    Sour cream

---

**FIND OUT MORE**    CHRISTIANITY    FARMING    FESTIVALS    FORESTS    FOSSILS    GLASS    LAKES    NUCLEAR POWER    RIVERS    SOVIET UNION    TEXTILES AND WEAVING

B

# BANGLADESH AND NEPAL

NORTH OF THE BAY OF BENGAL, between India and Myanmar (Burma), is Bangladesh, a poor but fertile country with low-lying land that has repeatedly flooded, and largely dictated its fortunes. Nepal and Bhutan are small Himalayan states, ruled by kings, but slowly adopting democratic ideas. All three countries have a subsistence farming economy, and the majority of the people, who are a mix of Muslims, Hindus, and Buddhists, live in small, rural villages. Manufacturing industries are being developed.

### Himalayas
Nepal lies in the highest part of the Himalayas, a vast mountain range that stretches 1500 miles (2,400 km) between India and China. Mount Everest, the world's highest peak at 29,029 ft (8,848 m), is part of the range and several other peaks are more than 19,685 ft (6,000 m) high, including Ama Dablam in Nepal, at 22,493 ft (6,856 m).

## Physical features
Bangladesh is dominated by a low-lying plain created by soil caught up and carried on the great Ganges River and its tributaries. Much of the land is less than 50 ft (15 m) above sea level. By contrast, Nepal and Bhutan sit high in the mountains, with plunging forested valleys fed by many rapid streams.

73°F (23°C)    52°F (11°C)

*75 in (1,901 mm)*

### Regional climate
Bangladesh has a hot, tropical climate, and monsoon winds bring heavy floods to 67 percent of the country. Southern Nepal and Bhutan are hot and wet, but the Himalayas are cold and harsh, with much snow.

### Forests
About 70 percent of Bhutan is forested. Deciduous forests, which include hardwoods such as teak, grow in the south, while thick pine forests cover the steep mountains of central Bhutan. Bangladesh's flat landscape rises in the north and southeast to form wooded hills.

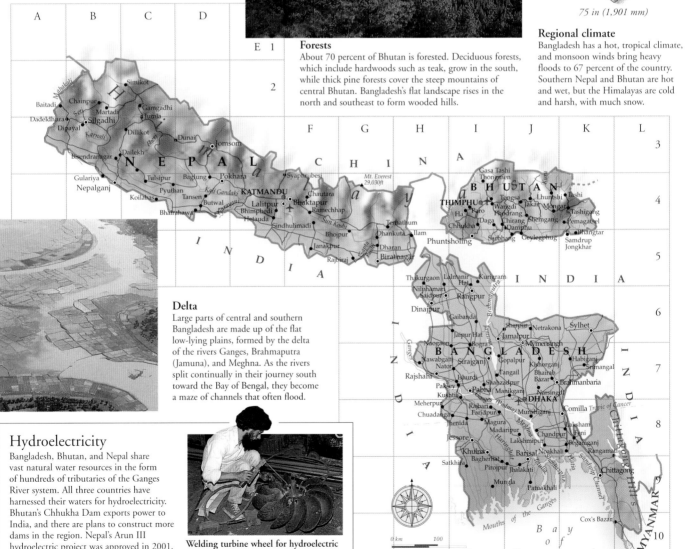

### Delta
Large parts of central and southern Bangladesh are made up of the flat low-lying plains, formed by the delta of the rivers Ganges, Brahmaputra (Jamuna), and Meghna. As the rivers split continually in their journey south toward the Bay of Bengal, they become a maze of channels that often flood.

## Hydroelectricity
Bangladesh, Bhutan, and Nepal share vast natural water resources in the form of hundreds of tributaries of the Ganges River system. All three countries have harnessed their waters for hydroelectricity. Bhutan's Chhukha Dam exports power to India, and there are plans to construct more dams in the region. Nepal's Arun III hydroelectric project was approved in 2001.

Welding turbine wheel for hydroelectric plant, Nepal

# Bangladesh

Formed in 1971 when it became independent of Pakistan, Bangladesh has a troubled political history. Democracy was restored in 1991, after a period of military rule. Bangladesh has one of the world's highest population densities and half of its people live in poverty. The country's vast water resources provide good farming conditions, but floods and cyclones wreak seasonal havoc.

**BANGLADESH FACTS**

**CAPITAL CITY** Dhaka

**AREA** 55,598 sq miles (143,998 sq km)

**POPULATION** 129,000,000

**MAIN LANGUAGE** Bengali

**MAJOR RELIGIONS** Muslim, Hindu

**CURRENCY** Taka

### Stilt houses
Many people live in houses that are built on stilts to protect them from the frequent floods. The country is overcrowded, and about 75 percent of the people live in rural communities. Most grow just enough rice to live on, and fish in the Ganges.

### Jute
Bangladesh is second only to India in the production of jute, a tough fiber used for sacking, rope, and carpeting. The country provides about 80 percent of the world's jute fiber. Jute products make up 13 percent of Bangladesh's exports.

*Jute rope*

*Silkworms spin a silky thread up to 0.6 miles (1 km) long.*

### Dhaka
The capital of Bangladesh, Dhaka, lies on the Buriganga River, which links ports around the country. It is a center of trade and commerce. The city contains more than eight million people, many of whom live in overcrowded slums.

### Textiles
Many Bangladeshis work in the textile industry, with cotton and silk the country's leading fabrics. Ready-made garments are the main product, totaling 60 percent of exports. Women are the backbone of the textile industry.

# Nepal

The Himalayas and their forested foothills cover most of this landlocked country. Nepal was an absolute monarchy until 1991, but now has a multiparty constitution. It is one of the world's poorest countries; the people are mostly farmers whose crops depend on the monsoon rains.

**NEPAL FACTS**

**CAPITAL CITY** Katmandu

**AREA** 54,363 sq miles (140,800 sq km)

**POPULATION** 23,900,000

**MAIN LANGUAGE** Nepali

**MAJOR RELIGIONS** Hindu, Buddhist, Muslim

**CURRENCY** Nepalese rupee

### People
There is a wide variety of peoples in Nepal, and most are of Indian or Tibetan descent. The Sherpas of the north are skilled, tough mountaineers. About 90 percent of Nepalese people are Hindus who combine their religion with Buddhism.

**Hindu holy man**

### Farming
Nepal is dependent on farming, which, with forestry, employs 90 percent of the workforce. Rice, corn, and sugar are grown on terraces cut into the mountainsides.

### Katmandu
Lying in a valley 4,500 ft (1,370 m) above sea level, Nepal's capital, Katmandu, is a city full of ornate temples and shrines. About 400,000 people live in the city, including the Newars of the valley, famed for their wood carving.

*Buddhist temple overlooking Katmandu*

### Trekking
Mountain climbing and trekking in the Himalayas attract 450,000 visitors to Nepal each year. Tourism attracts much-needed income, but seriously threatens the ecology.

# Bhutan

A small, isolated country, Bhutan is covered in forests and snowcapped mountains. Ruled by a monarch, known as the Dragon King, it is an isolated state, though there are plans for modernization. Three-quarters of the people are of Tibetan descent; the rest are Nepalese or Hindus. Farming, fishing, forestry, and light industry provide jobs.

Apricot · Cardamom seeds · Apple · Orange · Chili peppers

### Crops
Less than ten percent of Bhutan's land can be cultivated, but 90 percent of the people make a living from farming. Rice, corn, and potatoes are the staple foods, and cash crops, such as apricots, apples, chilies, cardamom, and oranges for export to other Asian countries are being developed in the fertile central valleys.

**BHUTAN FACTS**

**CAPITAL CITY** Thimphu

**AREA** 18,147 sq miles (47,000 sq km)

**POPULATION** 2,100,000

**MAIN LANGUAGE** Dzongkha

**MAJOR RELIGIONS** Buddhist, Hindu

**CURRENCY** Ngultrum

 **FIND OUT MORE** ASIA, HISTORY OF · BUDDHISM · DAMS · ENERGY · FARMING · HINDUISM · INDIA AND SRI LANKA · ISLAM · MOUNTAINS AND VALLEYS · RIVERS · TEXTILES AND WEAVING

# BARBARIANS

Huns ——
Goths and Vandals ——
Avars ——

TO THE ANCIENT GREEKS, all foreigners or outsiders were known as barbarians, but from the 3rd century on, this term was increasingly applied to nomadic mounted tribespeople from Asia, eastern Europe, and parts of Germany, such as the Huns and Goths. Organized into fearsome cavalry armies, these so-called barbarians caused havoc in their search for land, and were finally responsible for the collapse of the western Roman Empire.

## Who were the barbarians?
To most Europeans, barbarian tribes included Huns and Avars (from Asia), and Saxons, Vandals, and Goths (from Germany). Huns migrating from Asia into Europe caused fear among the resident Germanic tribes, who then poured in huge numbers across the Roman Empire's frontiers. In a short time, this migration led to the fall of the empire.

## Huns

The Huns were a nomadic Mongol people from the high plains, or steppes, of Central Asia who invaded southeastern Europe in c.370. Fierce in battle and famous for their skill on horseback, they conquered the Ostrogoths and drove the Vandals and other tribes westward. Under the leadership of Attila they reached the height of their influence, ravaging the Byzantine Empire and invading Gaul (modern France). In the 5th and 6th centuries, the White Huns, a related group, raided Persia (Iran) and northern India.

Huns made bows and arrows out of strips of bone.

Horse saddle

Hunting on the Steppes
by Chen Chii-Chung (Sung dynasty)

**Catalaunian Plains**
The Huns were deadly in battle as mounted archers. They made short bows of bone that were light and easy to use while on horseback. They also fought with sabers at close range. Under Attila, the Huns were victorious many times, but in 451, they were finally defeated by the Romans and their allies at the Catalaunian Plains, Gaul (now Chalons-sur-Marne, France).

### Attila the Hun
Attila (c.406–453) became king of the Huns in 434 jointly with his brother Bleda, whom he murdered in 445. Attila united his people into a vast tribe based in Hungary, then waged campaigns to win land and influence from the Roman and Byzantine empires. Short and crafty, the so-called "Scourge of God" was cruel to his enemies but fair to his own people. He died – possibly of poison – on his wedding night.

## Ostrogoths and Visigoths
The Ostrogoths were a Germanic tribe on the Black Sea who were related to the Visigoths from the Danube area. After the Roman Empire fell in 476, the Visigoths adopted Christianity and translated the Bible from Latin into a "Gothic" script that was used for centuries in German printing.

### Gothic architecture
Many medieval churches and cathedrals were built in the Gothic style. The highly decorative details, such as gargoyles, were believed by Renaissance artists to be "barbarous" when compared with the simplicity of older Roman buildings. So the artist named them after the Gothic tribes that overran Rome.

Notre-Dame gargoyles, Paris, France

## Saxons
"The barbarians drive us to the sea, and the sea drives us back to the barbarians; one way or another, we die." So wrote a group of 5th-century Britons to their former masters in Rome. The seafaring barbarians threatening them were Saxons, Angles, and Jutes – Germanic tribes of skilled craftspeople and farmers who conquered and settled stretches of fertile Britain from c.500.

Saxon shoulder clasp
Gold and enamel

Gold and garnet

Etched snake designs

Gold

Mosaic glass

Saxon purse lid

Saxon buckle

### Richborough Fort
The Romans built bases at Richborough and elsewhere on the southeastern English coast in the 3rd and 4th centuries. From these forts they could see and try to intercept Saxon raiders.

Walls were 4 ft (1.2 m) thick.

British ships destroying Chinese junks

### Barbarians in the East
People in other cultures also believed that outsiders were barbarians. The 18th-century Chinese looked down on "foreign devils" and insisted that all trade between China and the west take place only in the port of Canton. The Japanese actually stopped any foreigners from entering Japan for more than 200 years, until 1854.

FIND OUT MORE | ARCHITECTURE | ANGLO-SAXONS | ROMAN EMPIRE | WARFARE

# BATS

WITH ALMOST 1,000 species, bats are the second largest order of mammals after the rodents. They are the only mammals that can truly fly. The name given to their order is Chiroptera, meaning "hand wings." When bats are resting, they hang upside down. Most bats are nocturnal. They eat a variety of food, which they find either by scent and sight, as fruit bats do, or by using sound waves, a process called echolocation, as insect-eating bats do.

## Bat features

A bat's wing consists of an elastic membrane of skin that is stretched between the elongated fingers of its front limb, and back to its hind limb. Bats have lightweight bodies and strong clawed toes with which they cling to a suitable support.

*Insect-eating bats have large ears, which are needed when the animal uses echolocation.*

*Bats have a clawed thumb on the edge of each wing.*

*Furred body*

*Wing is formed by a membrane stretched over the bones of the fingers and forelimb.*

*Tail is used for balance and for braking in flight.*

*Bat catches insect in midair.*

*Clawed foot*

*"Fingers"*

**Greater horseshoe bat**

## Types of bats

Bats are divided into two groups. They are the Megachiroptera, or megabats, which are the old world fruit bats, and the Microchiroptera, or microbats, sometimes called insect-eating bats.

### Megabats

Fruit bats, or megabats, are also sometimes called flying foxes. They live in the tropical and subtropical parts of Africa, Asia, and Australasia. Most megabats eat fruit, but some also feed on flowers, nectar, and pollen.

*Large eyes and nose*

**Epauletted fruit bat**

*Ears are almost as long as the bat's head and body combined.*

**Long-eared bat**

### Microbats

The term insect-eating bats is a misleading name for these bats. Many feed on fruit, meat, fish, pollen, and even blood, as well as insects. Microbats live in both temperate and tropical regions, but in cooler climates they hibernate or migrate for the winter.

## Roosts

Bats need a variety of places to roost, or rest. At night they rest between bouts of feeding and often settle to eat large prey. During the day, they need somewhere to sleep and groom. Females choose a safe, warm place to give birth.

*Tent bats*

### Cave habitats

In warm climates, caves provide daytime and nursery roosts, where females give birth and look after their young. Bracken Cave in Texas has the largest colony in the world with up to 20 million bats.

*Free-tailed bats in Bracken Cave*

### Tree habitats

Microbats often roost in tree holes, such as old woodpecker nests, or cracks caused by storm damage. These Honduran white bats, also called tent bats, build a tent from large leaves.

## Hibernation

Bats need to hibernate somewhere cold but where they will be protected from frost, which would kill them. The place where they roost, called a hibernaculum, also has to be damp so that the bats do not dry out. Suitable sites include caves, loft spaces, and tree holes.

**Natterer's bat**

## Echolocation

To find objects in the dark, a microbat makes bursts of high-frequency sound. The sound bounces off objects, such as a moth, and the bat pinpoints the moth's position by listening to the returning echoes.

*Insect prey*

*Returning echoes*

**How a horseshoe bat catches prey**

*Horseshoe bats emit sounds through their noses.*

*Small eyes*

*Horseshoe bat*

1 The "horseshoe" on the bat's nose focuses the sound into a narrow beam. The bat sweeps its head from side to side as it flies along, scanning for insects.

*Broad, rounded wings*

2 The bat's large, mobile ears pick up vibrations made by the movement of an insect's wings. The bat can tell the size of an insect from the vibrations.

3 When the bat has located its prey, it scoops up the insect in its wings, often eating in midair.

*The bat uses its wing membrane to put food in its mouth.*

B

# Feeding

Bats have a wide variety of food sources. Most bats eat insects and can consume huge amounts in one night. The smaller bats, such as pipistrelles, catch tiny gnats and mosquitoes. Larger bats, such as noctules and serotines, feed on cockchafers and dung beetles. Some bats pounce on prey that is on the ground, and pick insects off leaves. Fruit-eating bats live mostly in the tropics, where they have a year-round supply of food.

*Bulldog bat*

*Fishing bats trail their long legs in the water to catch a fish.*

*False vampire bat*

*The bat finds its prey using echolocation.*

### Fishing bats
Some bats use echolocation to detect fish just below the water's surface. Fishing bats have long legs and they fly along the surface and catch the fish with long, sharp claws.

### Meat-eating bats
Many larger microbats catch and eat mice, rats, frogs, and lizards. False vampire bats from Asia and America carry their catch to a suitable perch to devour it, using their thumbs and wing membranes to hold the heavy prey.

### Vampire bats
True vampire bats feed on the blood of mammals or birds. Using their razor-like incisor teeth, they make a wound on an ear or ankle. As the blood flows, the vampire bat drinks it with a grooved tongue that acts as a drinking straw.

*Bat drinking from a donkey.*

*Incisor teeth*

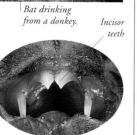

*Bats will only eat the pulp of the fruit.*

*Some nectar-feeding bats hover above the flower.*

### Fruit bats
These bats squash ripe fruit against ridges on the roof of their mouth. They spit out the rind and seeds that are difficult to digest. Fruit bats sometimes eat the fruit in the tree where they pick it, but they may carry it to a safe roost to eat.

*Spectacled flying fox*

### Nectar feeders
Trees that are pollinated by bats provide the animals with nectar and pollen as a reward for their services. The tongues of nectar-feeding bats have a brush-like tip which the bats use to lap up the nectar and pollen inside the flowers.

*Glossophagine bat*

# Nursery

Like all true mammals, a female bat carries her young inside her womb until she gives birth. Usually, only one bat is born at a time to minimize the extra weight a pregnant female has to carry in flight. Females gather, often in large numbers, to give birth in a nursery roost.

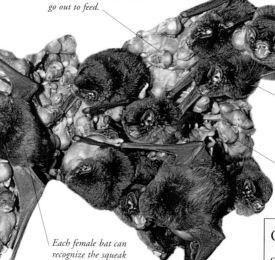

*Young bats hang upside down while their mothers go out to feed.*

*A large number of bats together keep each other warm.*

*Females suckle their young hanging upside down. The young cling to their mother with their teeth and claws.*

*Most young bats cannot fly until they are three weeks old.*

*This nursery roost is in the roof of a building.*

*Young bats are born pink and hairless, so they need warm surroundings.*

*Each female bat can recognize the squeak of her own young.*

*Ratsnake hunts at night.*

### Threats and predators
This red-tailed racer from Southeast Asia, also known as a mangrove ratsnake, catches bats in the tops of mangrove trees. Other animals that prey on bats include bat hawks, owls, and cats. Some of the greatest threats to the survival of bats around the world are habitat destruction, pesticides, and human vandalism. Many species are in danger of extinction.

### Largest and smallest
The largest bat is a Malaysian flying fox which can have a wingspan of up to 5.6 ft (1.7 m). The smallest bat is the bumblebee bat, also known as Kitti's hog-nosed bat. This tiny animal is only about 1 in (30 mm) long and weighs only 0.07 oz (2 g).

## GREATER HORSESHOE BAT

**SCIENTIFIC NAME** *Rhinolophus ferrumequinum*

**ORDER** Chiroptera

**FAMILY** Rhinolophidae

**DISTRIBUTION** Central and southern Europe, North Africa across to Japan

**HABITAT** Woodland, pasture, human settlements

**DIET** Insects

**SIZE** Length: 2.4–2.75 in (6–7 cm)

**LIFESPAN** Up to 30 years

FIND OUT MORE

CAVE WILDLIFE • CONSERVATION • HIBERNATION • MAMMALS • WHALES AND DOLPHINS

# Bats

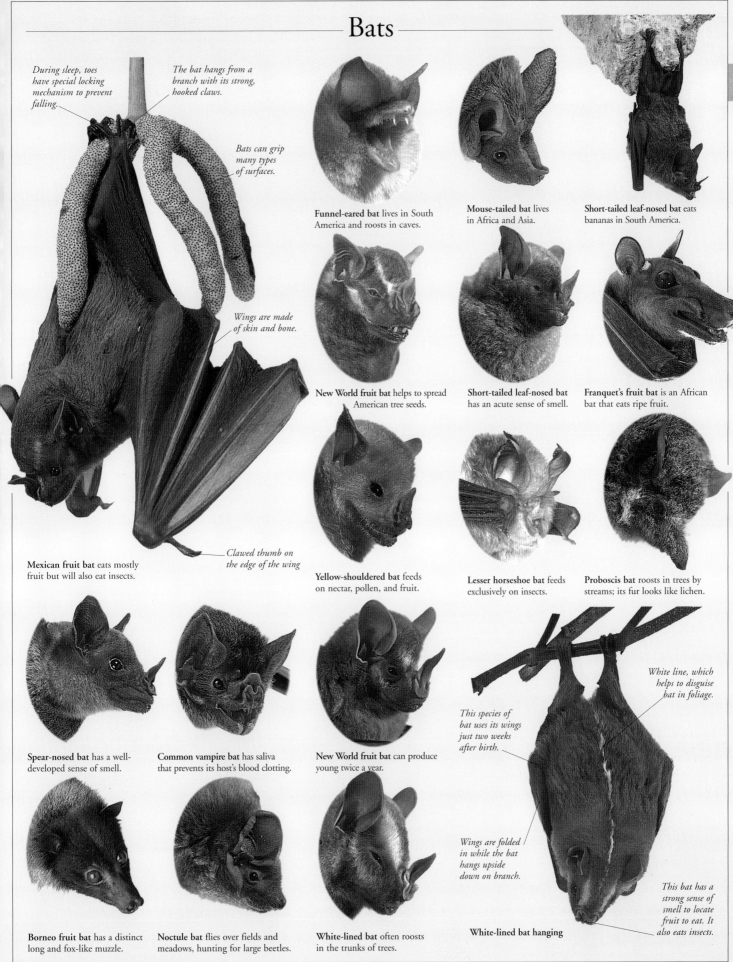

During sleep, toes have special locking mechanism to prevent falling.

The bat hangs from a branch with its strong, hooked claws.

Bats can grip many types of surfaces.

Wings are made of skin and bone.

Clawed thumb on the edge of the wing

**Mexican fruit bat** eats mostly fruit but will also eat insects.

**Funnel-eared bat** lives in South America and roosts in caves.

**Mouse-tailed bat** lives in Africa and Asia.

**Short-tailed leaf-nosed bat** eats bananas in South America.

**New World fruit bat** helps to spread American tree seeds.

**Short-tailed leaf-nosed bat** has an acute sense of smell.

**Franquet's fruit bat** is an African bat that eats ripe fruit.

**Yellow-shouldered bat** feeds on nectar, pollen, and fruit.

**Lesser horseshoe bat** feeds exclusively on insects.

**Proboscis bat** roosts in trees by streams; its fur looks like lichen.

**Spear-nosed bat** has a well-developed sense of smell.

**Common vampire bat** has saliva that prevents its host's blood clotting.

**New World fruit bat** can produce young twice a year.

This species of bat uses its wings just two weeks after birth.

White line, which helps to disguise bat in foliage.

Wings are folded in while the bat hangs upside down on branch.

**Borneo fruit bat** has a distinct long and fox-like muzzle.

**Noctule bat** flies over fields and meadows, hunting for large beetles.

**White-lined bat** often roosts in the trunks of trees.

**White-lined bat hanging**

This bat has a strong sense of smell to locate fruit to eat. It also eats insects.

# BEARS

THERE ARE SEVEN species of bears, plus the giant panda, which has recently been classified as a primitive bear. The polar and brown bears are the largest meat-eating land animals alive today. All bears rely heavily on their acute senses of smell and hearing to find food and to locate predators. Bears that live in cool climates hibernate in dens during the winter, but those in warmer areas are active all year round.

*Brown bears have a large hump of muscle and fat.*

North American brown bear

## Brown bears

There are nine subspecies of brown bears. The largest is the Kodiak bear, found on islands in Alaska. It may stand 12 ft (3.5 m) tall on its hind legs and is one of the most powerful animals in North America. The grizzly bear, also of North America, has white-tipped fur, giving it a "grizzled" look. The other brown bears live in Europe and temperate Asia.

*Large canine teeth and powerful jaws*

### Fishing
North American bears have a plentiful source of salmon when the fish swim up rivers to spawn. The bears are able to catch fish in the air as they leap up a waterfall.

Asian black bear feeding

## Diet

Bears belong to the order of mammals called carnivores, meaning meat-eaters. They catch and kill other animals for food and eat carrion, but they will take almost any kind of food they can find, including insects. About three-quarters of most bears' diet comes from non-animal sources, such as fruits, nuts, roots, and shoots.

### Paws
There are five clawed toes on a bear's paws. The animals use their forepaws to gather food and manipulate small food items. They can kill another animal with one blow from a paw, or use their long claws to dig up roots and open bee nests.

### Kermodes bear
Most American black bears are black, but some are brown, beige, or blue-black. Small isolated populations of white black bears, called Kermodes bears, live on the coast of British Columbia, Canada.

## Types of bears

**Brown bear** This bear lives across the northern hemisphere, but in small populations only. It has disappeared from many areas.

*Shaggy black fur*

### Sloth bear
A long-coated bear from India and Sri Lanka, the sloth bear eats mainly termites, which are sucked up through its lips.

### Sun bear
This bear from Southeast Asia is the smallest bear. It has short, dense fur, with a yellow mark on its chest. It has a long tongue with which it licks up ants and termites.

**Spectacled bear** The only South American bear, this rare animal lives on the wooded slopes of the Andes. It eats mostly plant material, especially fruit, but will eat meat if it is available.

*A crescent of white fur accounts for this bear's other name – moon bear.*

**Polar bear** This white-coated bear is the most carnivorous, eating mainly seals and fish. It lives on the Arctic coast.

**Asian black bear** An agile climber, this bear lives in woods of Southeast Asia, from Afghanistan to China, and Japan.

**American black bear** Found across North America, this bear will raid garbage cans, tents, and cars for food.

*Cubs' games are practise for adult conflicts.*

### Cubs
A female bear gives birth to her cubs in a den, where she will stay with them for up to two or three months. Each litter usually contains one to three cubs, which are born helpless and weigh only a tiny percentage of their mother's weight. They develop quickly, but will stay with their mother until nearly full-grown – two or three years in the case of the larger bears. Female bears make good mothers and will defend their cubs against any enemy ferociously.

## GRIZZLY BEAR

| | |
|---|---|
| SCIENTIFIC NAME | *Ursos arctos horribilis* |
| ORDER | Carnivora |
| FAMILY | Ursidae |
| DISTRIBUTION | Northwestern North America |
| HABITAT | Mountains, forests, wilderness |
| DIET | Almost anything, including berries, leaves, roots, small animals, fish, and carrion |
| SIZE | Length: 6–9 ft (1.8–2.8 m) Weight: 350–500 lb (160–230 kg) |
| LIFESPAN | 25–30 years |

FIND OUT MORE

ASIAN WILDLIFE    HIBERNATION    NORTH AMERICAN WILDLIFE    PANDAS AND RACCOONS    POLAR WILDLIFE

# BEATLES, THE

JOHN LENNON PLAYED rhythm guitar, Paul McCartney played bass, George Harrison played lead guitar, and Ringo Starr played the drums. Together they formed The Beatles – the most famous and influential group in the history of popular music. Their songs dominated the 1960s, when people believed that music could change the world, and the songwriting skills of Lennon and McCartney have ensured that their music lives on. Their songs still influence many musicians today.

### Early life
All four Beatles were born in the English port of Liverpool and played in various rock and roll groups in the late 1950s. In 1960–61, John, Paul, George, and drummer Pete Best played at the Star Club in the German port of Hamburg, where they learned about live performance. Back in England, The Beatles played regularly at Liverpool's Cavern Club. In 1962, their manager, Brian Epstein (1934–67), replaced Best with Ringo Starr as drummer.

## Live performances
The Beatles began by playing live in clubs in and around Liverpool, UK. Their lively performances were an exciting contrast to the staid and solid players who dominated popular music at the time. The Beatles' reputation was based on the songwriting abilities of John Lennon and Paul McCartney. At first they both wrote traditional rock-and-roll songs about friendship and love, but as the pair developed, their subjects became more varied.

*The Beatles play a football stadium in the US*

### Beatlemania
In January 1964 "I Want To Hold Your Hand" reached the top of the American music charts. A new word, "Beatlemania," entered the language, as thousands of screaming fans mobbed the group wherever they went. In months, The Beatles were the biggest music group in the world.

## Recording
In 1966, The Beatles stopped performing live and spent more time in the studio. There they experimented with different instruments, such as string orchestras and sitars, and with new recording techniques. Their masterpiece, *Sgt. Pepper's Lonely Hearts Club Band*, took many months to produce and made use of techniques such as tapesplicing and multitrack recording.

*Plates with pictures of The Beatles*

### Memorabilia
The Beatles were one of the first bands to be featured on a host of souvenirs and memorabilia. The four were immortalized on everything from mugs and T-shirts to buttons, badges, posters, and other souvenirs. Many fans bought everything that featured their four favorite musicians.

*Toy guitar with pictures of The Beatles*

*"Please Please Me"*

*"Sgt. Pepper"*

### Last albums
By 1969, the band was under strain as conflicts grew among the four Beatles and their musical interests took new directions. Their last albums to appear were *Abbey Road* (1969) and *Let It Be*, which was released in 1970 but recorded before *Abbey Road*. The Beatles disbanded later that year. All four continued their careers as solo musicians.

*The Beatles recording tracks for* Let It Be

### George Martin
British producer George Martin (b.1926) produced almost all The Beatles' records, having accepted their first demonstration tapes at EMI in 1962. Martin was a record producer with a background in both classical and popular music. He helped The Beatles get the most out of the recording studio and the wide range of instruments used in their records, translating many of their ideas into polished musical form.

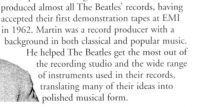

### THE BEATLES

**1940** John Lennon and Richard Starkey (Ringo Starr) born.

**1942** Paul McCartney born.

**1943** George Harrison born.

**1957** John and Paul form first group, The Quarrymen.

**1962** First record with EMI; Ringo Starr joins as drummer.

**1964** Beatles top charts in US.

**1967** *Sgt. Pepper's Lonely Hearts Club Band* released.

**1970** *Let It Be* released; Beatles disband.

**1980** John Lennon shot dead.

**1997** Paul McCartney knighted.

**2001** George Harrison dies.

**FIND OUT MORE**    MUSIC    ORCHESTRAS    ROCK AND POP    SOUND RECORDING

# BEES AND WASPS

THEIR STINGS USUALLY bring these insects to our attention. However, by pollinating crops and killing pests, bees and wasps play vital roles in our world. There are 115,000 species of bees and wasps. Most, such as carpenter bees, are solitary, but some, including common wasps and honeybees, are social insects, living in complex colonies. People keep honeybees in hives to produce honey and wax.

## Features of bees and wasps

Bees and wasps are similar in appearance, with narrow waists between the thorax and abdomen. Most species have two pairs of wings and are excellent fliers. They have two compound eyes and three small eyes, giving them good eyesight. Bees are hairier than wasps, and are normally herbivores, while wasps are generally carnivores.

## Stings

The females of most species of bees and wasps have stings. The sting evolved from the egg-laying tube. Wasps have unbarbed stings that they can use repeatedly for defense or to kill prey. Bees have barbed stings that cannot be extracted, causing the bee to die. Consequently, bees only sting if provoked.

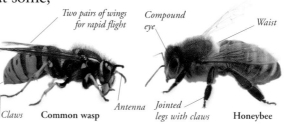
*Two pairs of wings for rapid flight* *Compound eye* *Waist* *Pointed abdomen* *Claws* **Common wasp** *Antenna* *Jointed legs with claws* **Honeybee**

**Bee sting** *Abdomen* *Poison sac* The sting may be painful and sometimes fatal.

## Queen

Social bees and wasps have a queen in their colonies who lays eggs and runs the colony. Honeybees have one queen per hive; if two appear at the same time they fight to the death. Queens produce queen substance, a chemical that stops full sexual development of the workers.

*Worker* *Queen is larger than workers.*

## Life cycle of a honeybee

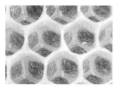
1 The queen bee spends most of her day checking cells and laying single eggs in them. She lays more than 2,000 eggs a day when there is a plentiful food supply. After 1–2 days, larvae hatch from the eggs.

2 Workers feed the larvae honey, pollen, and royal jelly. If fed extra royal jelly, larvae become queens. The larvae grow and molt, and on day 5 they spin a silk cocoon and pupate. Workers seal the cell with wax.

3 By about day 21, pupation is complete, and the adult bees chew their way out of the cells. Once the external skeleton has hardened and they can walk, the bees begin their tasks within the nest.

**Common wasp's nest**
*Protective layers of paper* *Pupae in cocoons* *Hole in nest is repaired.* *Old worker wasps gather wood, chew it up, mix in saliva, and use the mixture to build nest walls.*
**Fertilized eggs** develop into workers and queens.
**Unfertilized eggs** become drones.
**Worker** wasps spend the first week of their adult life cleaning the nest. Once able to fly, they leave the nest and hunt for insects to feed to the grubs (larvae) in the nest.
*Eggs are glued into cells, since the cells face downward.*
*Entrance is below.*
**Nest walls** are striped because the wood is collected from many sources.

## Nests

Common wasps' nests have the texture of paper and are made out of chewed-up wood, saliva, and water. Nests are built in hollow trees or below ground. Some other types of wasps, such as oriental stenogaster wasps, build nests out of mud. Honeybee nests are made out of wax produced from glands on the bees' abdomens. Wasps' and bees' nests usually contain combs, layers of six-sided cells in which the young grow.

## Colonies

Social wasps and bees live in large groups called colonies. Each member of the colony has a specific duty and works for the whole nest. Wasp colonies may contain more than one million individuals; bees' nests can exceed 70,000 in number, consisting of one queen, about 69,000 workers, and 300 drones. Both queen wasps and queen bees run their nests; drones are fertile males who mate with the queen and die soon after; workers perform all other tasks. Drones appear before swarming time, when new queens leave the nest, mate, and set up nests on their own.

## Food supplies

Wasps eat fruit and insects that they also feed to their young. Adult and larval bees feed on nectar and pollen that the adults collect from flowers. Bees do a dance to tell other bees the location of the flowers and navigate there by using the Sun.

*Pollen carried on legs*

**Pollen, nectar, and honey**
Bees carry pollen on hairs on their legs and store nectar in their stomachs. At the nest, they regurgitate the nectar. Water evaporates, concentrating the nectar to form honey. Honey and royal jelly, a high-protein substance made by workers, are also fed to the larvae.

## Types of bees and wasps

**Parasitic bees**
These solitary bees abandon their eggs in other bees' nests. The young then destroy the original eggs and wait to be fed by the host.

**Hornets**
Hornets are among the largest of the social wasps. They live in large colonies and defend their nests aggressively.

**Hunting wasps**
These solitary wasps paralyze other insects with a sting and lay their eggs on them. The young hatch and feed on the live host.

### HONEYBEE

**SCIENTIFIC NAME** *Apis mellifera*
**ORDER** Hymenoptera
**FAMILY** Apidae
**DISTRIBUTION** Worldwide
**HABITAT** Nests are built in hollow trees in the wild; also cultivated in hives
**DIET** Pollen and nectar from flowers
**LENGTH** Workers: 0.4–0.6 in (10–15 mm); queen: 0.6–0.8 in (15–20 mm)
**LIFESPAN** Workers live for 2–3 months; queen lives for 3–5 years

**FIND OUT MORE** ANIMAL BEHAVIOR • ANTS AND TERMITES • ARTHROPODS • EGGS • FLIGHT, ANIMAL • FLOWERS • INSECTS • NESTS AND BURROWS • WOODLAND WILDLIFE

# BEETHOVEN, LUDWIG VAN

FROM HIS BIRTH in Bonn in 1770 to his death in Vienna in 1827, Ludwig van Beethoven lived during a time of revolution and transformation. Despite a tragically unhappy life beset with family problems and deafness, he became the major composer of his time. His symphonies, sonatas, and chamber music expanded the Classical forms, introducing exciting new musical ideas that ushered in the fiery Romantic style. Unlike previous composers, Beethoven tried to remain independent, writing for himself rather than for a single rich patron. Independence allowed him to develop his own personal expressive musical style.

Beethoven's birthplace

### Early life
Beethoven was born in Bonn, Germany. His childhood was not a happy one. His father, himself a musician, forced Ludwig to practice and perform in public at an early age, hoping he would become a child prodigy. When his mother died and his father lost his job, young Ludwig had to provide for the whole family.

## Vienna

Beethoven's first visit to Vienna was cut short by his mother's illness, but he returned in 1792 to study with the composer Haydn. He soon established himself as a pianist and teacher, and settled there for the rest of his life. However, as his deafness worsened, he suffered from depressions and raging tempers, and withdrew from social life. He found consolation in composing music that expressed both his despair, and his optimism and joy.

### Performance
Until the onset of deafness, Beethoven earned his living as a teacher and performer. He was a superb pianist, whose emotional performances could move his audience to tears. Many of his piano compositions, especially the sonatas and concertos, explore the expressive capabilities of the instrument and are among his finest works.

### Deafness
In his late twenties, Beethoven's hearing began to fail. By 1820, he was almost totally deaf. Unable to hear what he was playing, he could not earn a living from performing. Instead, he concentrated on composing.

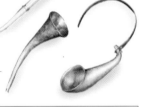
Hearing aids

### Notebooks
We can get a good idea of how Beethoven worked by looking at his manuscripts and notebooks. They show how he revised his work until he was completely satisfied with it. He wrote quickly and furiously, often crossing out and rewriting whole sections of the music.

Beethoven's Broadwood grand piano

## The symphonies

Symphonies before Beethoven's time were orchestral works that followed a fairly set pattern, but in his nine symphonies Beethoven developed the form into a large and expressive work. From the third symphony, the *Eroica*, on, these works became longer and more adventurous, using new instruments and even vocalists and a choir in the ninth symphony.

Manuscript of the *Pastoral* symphony

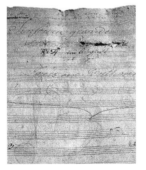

### LUDWIG VAN BEETHOVEN

**1770** Born in Bonn, Germany

**1792** Moves to Vienna, studies with Joseph Haydn

**1796** Begins to go deaf

**1802** Writes a letter, known as the "Heiligenstadt Testament," to his brothers, describing his unhappiness about his deafness

**1803** *Eroica* symphony

**1808** *Pastoral* symphony

**1809** Piano Concerto No. 5, "The Emperor"

**1824** *Choral* symphony

**1827** Dies in Vienna, Austria; some 10,000 people attend his funeral

### Chamber music
Much of Beethoven's music is for small groups, such as the string quartet. This chamber music was often written for amateur players, but Beethoven found it provided an ideal way of expressing his new musical ideas.

### Pastoral symphony
This symphony is unusual because it describes a scene: the countryside around Vienna where Beethoven loved to walk. It is full of the sounds of the country, including imitations of birdsong and a thunderstorm.

### Eroica symphony
Beethoven originally dedicated this symphony to his hero Napoleon, but was disgusted when Napoleon proclaimed himself emperor. He scratched out the dedication, but kept the title *Eroica* (heroic).

**FIND OUT MORE**

MOZART, WOLFGANG AMADEUS   MUSIC   MUSICAL INSTRUMENTS   NAPOLEON   ORCHESTRAS

# BEETLES

THERE ARE AT LEAST 350,000 types of beetles. They make up 30 percent of all animals and 40 percent of all insects. They range in size from the 0.08 in (2 mm) long battle d'or beetle to the giant timber beetles, that grow up to 6 in (150 mm) long. Beetles live almost everywhere, from hot deserts to snowy mountaintops, but they are most numerous in the tropics. They eat a wide range of food, including crops, and are considered pests, but they perform a valuable role by breaking down dead animals and plants and returning the nutrients to the soil.

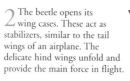

*Jointed legs* — *Thorax* — *Claws*
*Abdomen is below elytra.* — *Large mandibles to cut up food*
*Elytra* — *Compound eye*

**Chafer beetle**

## Features of a beetle

Beetles have three body parts – the head, thorax, and abdomen. They have compound eyes, and antennae used for touch and smell. Their forewings have developed into hard wing cases, or elytra, that protect the hind wings. The wings, elytra, and six legs are fixed to the thorax.

**Cockchafer beetle**

*Wings beat during flight.*

2 The beetle opens its wing cases. These act as stabilizers, similar to the tail wings of an airplane. The delicate hind wings unfold and provide the main force in flight.

*Elytra raised*

*Outstretched hind legs help streamline the beetle.*

*Feathery antennae spread to sense the air currents.*

*Beetle often opens and shuts elytra several times before taking off.*

### How a beetle flies

1 Large beetles, such as this cockchafer beetle, take a few seconds to get airborne. First the beetle pumps air into its body by expanding its abdomen.

*Wings unfurling, ready to beat*

3 The cockchafer beetle pushes off with its legs and starts to beat its hind wings. Within a few seconds the hind wings reach the 200 beats per second needed for takeoff, and the wing cases help provide lift. During flight, the beetle uses 100 times more oxygen than it does at rest.

---

## Wood-boring beetles

Some beetles remain larvae for many years. Jewel beetle larvae may live in wood for more than 40 years. They eat the wood, making tunnels through it, leaving small holes.

**Jewel beetle**

## Reproduction

Most beetles undergo complete metamorphosis. Larvae hatch from eggs laid by an adult female. This is the main feeding stage in a beetle's development. Once the larvae have finished growing, they turn into pupae. Inside, they change, or metamorphose, into the adult beetle that will eventually emerge from the pupa.

*Mealworm beetle larva*

*Inside – the larva's body breaks down and changes into the adult.*

*Pupa develops for about 6 weeks.*

*Adult beetle has emerged.*

**Giant mealworm beetle**

## Fighting

Male beetles often fight with each other over a possible mate. They use their mandibles (mouthparts) as weapons. Stag beetles have huge, but not very powerful mandibles, which they use mainly to impress rivals. Despite their size, the mandibles do little harm. In this way, fighting is more symbolic, and both beetles live to fight and mate again.

*The beetle clasps his rival in his huge jaws and tries to throw it on its back.*

**Stag beetles fighting**

---

## Feeding

Beetles' feeding habits, like beetles themselves, are diverse. Many, including spider beetles, feed on decaying leaf litter; others consume both living and dead wood. Some beetles, such as tiger beetles, actively hunt for live food. Scavengers, such as hide beetles, feed on rotting vegetation, dead animals, and dung. Some beetles, for example, rove beetles, are even parasites, living on creatures such as bats.

*Ladybug feeding on an aphid*

### Ladybugs

Ladybugs are found worldwide. They prey on small insects, such as aphids and scale bugs. In this way they are helpful animals to have in the garden and can be used to control pests in place of chemicals.

### Defense

Well-armored external skeletons and camouflage protect many beetles from predators. The bombardier beetle has an ingenious method of defense. It ejects a hot mixture of potent chemicals from its rear with an audible pop.

**Bombardier beetle**

### Water beetles

Many beetles live in water. Diving beetles use their oarlike legs to push themselves through the water after their prey. Whirligig beetles scavenge for food that floats on the water's surface. They have special eyes that are split in two. One half looks downward for fish, while the top half scans the air for predatory birds.

**Whirligig beetle**

### COCKCHAFER BEETLE

**SCIENTIFIC NAME** *Melolontha melolontha*

**ORDER** Coleoptera

**FAMILY** Scarabaeidae

**DISTRIBUTION** Europe and western Asia

**HABITAT** Gardens and woods

**DIET** Adult feeds on sap and nectar; the larvae feed on the roots of plants, such as rose and oak

**SIZE** Larvae: 1.6 in (4 cm) in length; adults: 0.8–1.2 in (2–3 cm) long

**LIFESPAN** Larvae take about 2 years to become adults; adults live for about 2–3 months

---

**FIND OUT MORE**  ARTHROPODS  DESERT WILDLIFE  GRASSLAND WILDLIFE  INSECTS  WOODLAND WILDLIFE

# Beetles

## Carnivores

*Predators are scared by these beetles being the same color as wasps.*

**Saber-toothed ground beetles** stalk fast-moving crickets.

**Great diving beetles** are the fastest underwater insects.

**Rove beetles** hunt for small carrion-eating animals.

**Common tiger beetles** have sharp jaws to rip prey apart.

**Violin beetles** are flat and can chase prey into small holes.

**Tropical tiger beetles** can catch fast-moving prey.

## Herbivores

*White elytra camouflage the beetle on white sand.*

**Leaf beetles** eat flowers and leaves; their young eat roots.

**Click beetles** make a clicking sound when they jump.

**Darkling beetles** live in the deserts of south-western Africa.

**Dung beetles** feed on the dung of herbivores. They roll the dung into balls.

**Malaysian timberworm beetles** have long heads.

*Antennae may be four times as long as the body.*

**Jewel beetles** are usually bright and shiny.

**Tortoise beetle** larvae hide under their parents' wings.

**Chafer beetles** eat nectar, giving them the energy to fly fast.

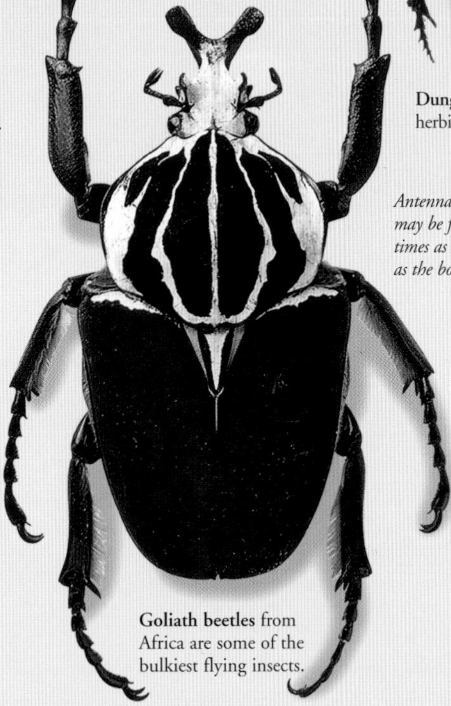

**Goliath beetles** from Africa are some of the bulkiest flying insects.

**Longhorn beetles** eat the sap of plants; their larvae eat wood.

*Strong legs help them cling to mate.*

**Lamellicorn beetles** eat nectar and sap, despite their huge jaws.

**Golden beetles** live only in Costa Rica in Central America.

**Weevils** are beetles that have a snout, or rostrum, with small biting jaws at the tip.

**Malaysian frog beetles** feed on sweet plants.

**Stag beetles** are the largest British beetles.

B

125

# BELGIUM

THIS SMALL, DENSELY POPULATED country in northwestern Europe borders France, Germany, and the Netherlands. Its current borders were settled in 1919, after World War I (1914–18). Today, Belgium is a highly developed industrial nation with a thriving economy. As a founding member of the European Union since 1957, and of the Benelux alliance (with the Netherlands and Luxembourg), Belgium plays an important role in European and international affairs.

## Physical features

In the north of Belgium is a flat plain stretching from Flanders to the Dutch border. The central plateau is bounded to the south by the Meuse and Sambre rivers. The Ardennes Plateau extends into Luxembourg and France.

### Ardennes Plateau
The Ardennes Plateau covers 3,860 sq miles (10,000 sq km) in southern Belgium, Luxembourg, and northern France. Crossed by deep river valleys such as the Semois and Meuse, this upland area is rocky and heavily wooded and has spectacular limestone caves.

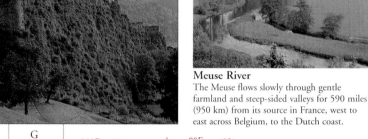

**Meuse River**
The Meuse flows slowly through gentle farmland and steep-sided valleys for 590 miles (950 km) from its source in France, west to east across Belgium, to the Dutch coast.

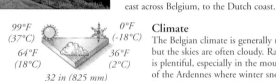

99°F (37°C)    0°F (-18°C)
64°F (18°C)    36°F (2°C)
32 in (825 mm)

**Climate**
The Belgian climate is generally mild, but the skies are often cloudy. Rainfall is plentiful, especially in the mountains of the Ardennes where winter snow lingers. Summers tend to be short.

**Land use**
Much of Belgium is built-up and densely populated. Farmers produce cereals, fruit, vegetables, and sugar beets, and raise cattle, sheep, and horses. Belgium has few natural resources and uses over 60 percent nuclear power.

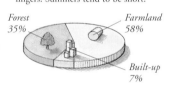

Forest 35%    Farmland 58%
Built-up 7%

**People**
In southern Belgium people speak Walloon, a dialect of French. In the north people speak Dutch, formerly called Flemish. A few people in the east speak German.

**805 per sq mile (311 per sq km)**    **97% Urban**    **3% Rural**

### Brussels
With about a million inhabitants, Belgium's capital, Brussels, is the center of government and trade. With three languages – Dutch, French, and German – it is a truly international city and the administrative headquarters of the European Union.

**Gothic buildings in Brussels's Grand Place**

### Industry
Belgium has highly developed business and service industries, such as banking and insurance. The once-thriving coal and steel industries on the Meuse and Sambre rivers are now in crisis and are being rapidly replaced by new industries producing pharmaceuticals, chemicals, electrical equipment, and textiles. Belgium is one of the world's largest exporters of chocolate, and produces fine beers.

**Belgian chocolates**

## Luxembourg

This tiny country shares borders with Belgium, Germany, and France. Its people enjoy low unemployment and Europe's highest living standards. It is known as a banking center.

**Finance center**
Despite its tiny size, Luxembourg is a key member of the European Union. The headquarters of the European Parliament and the European Court of Justice are based in Luxembourg City.

**FIND OUT MORE**    EUROPE    EUROPE, HISTORY OF    EUROPEAN UNION    FARMING    NETHERLANDS    TRADE AND INDUSTRY    WORLD WAR I

B

# BENIN EMPIRE

ESTABLISHED IN THE 11TH CENTURY, Benin was a powerful West African kingdom that flourished in the forests west of the Niger River. The wealth of Benin was based on trading: trans-Saharan trade with African savanna kingdoms linked the Benin Empire with the Mediterranean and the Middle East, and, coastal trade linked the empire with Europe. Benin's obas, or kings, controlled the trade networks. They wielded immense power and lived in the royal palace in the capital city of Benin. In 1897, the British conquered Benin and ended the empire.

## Empire boundaries

The Benin Empire was in modern Nigeria, where Benin City now stands. Both it and the modern republic west of Nigeria take their name from the old empire.

Sahara Desert

• Benin City

B

### Benin City

The empire of Benin was centered in the capital, Benin City. It was an impressive city. A wide road ran through it, and a huge dirt wall surrounded the city. The wall acted as a defense and took many years to build. Its size alone stood as a symbol of the influence held by Benin's oba. The city housed the oba's royal palace, and special areas called wards where the craftspeople lived.

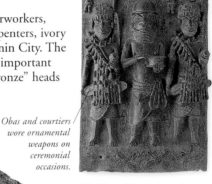

Engraving of Benin City

## Craft guilds

Guilds of craftspeople, such as leatherworkers, blacksmiths, drummers, weavers, carpenters, ivory carvers, and brass casters, lived in Benin City. The brass casters formed one of the most important guilds. They made the distinctive "bronze" heads and plaques for the royal palace.

*Spikes to support ivory carving*

*Only obas wore neck rings.*

### Bronze head

Benin "bronze" heads are actually made of brass. They commemorated dead obas and their family members, court ceremonies – even European traders. Carved ivory adorned the heads, which were kept in shrines in the royal palace.

**Memorial head of an oba**

*Obas and courtiers wore ornamental weapons on ceremonial occasions.*

*Carvings often told of the oba's wealth and military strength.*

**Oba flanked by two courtiers**

### Brass plaques

Carved plaques decorated the wooden pillars that supported the oba's palace roof. They depicted court life and important events, such as the presentation of gifts from the oba to his courtiers.

### Ivory carving

Ornately carved ivory tusks were among Benin's luxury goods. All trade in ivory was controlled by the oba. If elephant hunters killed an elephant, they had to give one tusk to the oba before they could sell the other.

*Carved human figures*

**Carved elephant's tusk**

## Trade

For centuries, Benin traded with African kingdoms to the north, including the Songhai Empire. The arrival of the Europeans in the 1400s disrupted these traditional relationships and established new trading outlets.

*Brass manilla*

### Brass manillas

In Benin, merchants used bracelet-shaped objects called manillas to buy expensive purchases, but they used tiny, white cowrie shells for smaller items.

### Merchants

Traveling by sea, Portuguese traders bought slaves, peppers, cloth, gold, and ivory from Benin, and paid with manillas, cowrie shells, and guns.

*Portuguese flag*

*Ship, called a caravel*

### British conquest

In 1897, in revenge for an attack on a British party, the British burned and looted Benin City, exiled the oba, and brought Benin under colonial rule.

## Oba Ewuare the Great

The warrior-king Ewuare (r.1440–80) rebuilt Benin City and, under his rule, the surrounding territory reached its greatest extent. Ewuare also established a tradition of secure hereditary succession.

**Ewuare's leopard-shaped arm ornament**

## Timeline

**11th century** Benin Empire founded in the forests of Nigeria.

**1450** Peak of Benin Empire.

**1486** First European to visit Benin is Portuguese explorer Alfonso d'Aveiro; shortly afterward a Benin chief establishes a trading store for the Portuguese.

**Benin ornamental sword**

**1500s** English, Dutch, and French merchants start to trade with Benin Empire.

**Early to mid-16th century** King of Portugal sends Christian missionaries to Benin to convert Oba Esigie and build churches.

**1688** Dutchman Olfert Dapper writes a history of Benin.

**1700s** Empire weakened by succession struggles.

**1897** Britain takes Benin City by force.

**1960** Nigeria, including the old Benin Empire, gains independence.

**FIND OUT MORE**    AFRICA, HISTORY OF    EMPIRES    EXPLORATION    METALS    SONGHAI EMPIRE

# BICYCLES AND MOTORCYCLES

FUN AND ENVIRONMENTALLY correct, the bicycle is the simplest form of mechanical transportation. A bicycle, or bike, is a two-wheeled machine that converts human energy into propulsion; a motorcycle is a bicycle with an engine. Modern motorcycles are complex, with engine sizes ranging from 50cc (cubic centimeters) to more than 1,000cc. In many countries, such as China, most people travel or transport goods by bicycle. In other parts of the world, bicycles and motorcycles are used primarily for sport and leisure.

Cannondale SH600, hybrid

## Reducing drag

Drag is the resistance of air that can slow down a bicycle or motorcycle and its rider. It is reduced by creating a streamlined shape for the air to flow around – some competitive bicycle riders even shave their legs to eliminate as much resistance as possible

**Time-trial bike**

## Parts of a bicycle

All bicycles, from a mountain bike to a racing bike or hybrid (a cross between the two), are designed to be easy to pedal and comfortable. Their weight is very important because it affects the speed at which the bike can be propelled.

**Saddles** are adjustable, moving up and down to accommodate different riders.

**Gears**, operated by levers, move the chain between different-sized gear wheels to change the speed at which the wheels turn.

*Handlebars may be dropped for riding with less wind resistance.*

**Brakes** are controlled by pulling levers on handlebars that force brake blocks against wheel rims to slow the bicycle down.

**Frame**, made from metal tubes, supports the rider.

*Seat post slides in and out of frame to adjust seat level.*

*Brake cable*

*Chain wheel*

**Spokes** are arranged to create a strong, but lightweight, wheel.

**Pedals**, attached to the chain wheel, are pushed to create the force that turns the wheel.

*Wheel hub secures the wheel to frame.*

**Tires** fitted on a metal wheel rim give a smooth, quiet ride over small bumps; mountain bikes have fatter tires to handle rough and rocky terrain.

## Parts of a motorcycle

Like a bicycle, a motorcycle has a frame, a rear wheel that drives it along, a front wheel for steering, and controls on the handlebars. Like a car, it has an internal combustion engine and a suspension system. The suspension supports the motorcycle's body on the wheels, and stops it from being affected by bumps on the road.

**Two-stroke engine** with one cylinder. Larger motorcycles have more cylinders.

*Lightweight frame*

*Fuel tank*

**1992 Yamaha FZR1000 Exup**

*Three-spoke alloy rear wheel, supported by suspension strut*

**Motorcycle** tires grip the road even when the motorcycle leans into turns. These are smooth, treadless, "slick" racing tires.

*Speedometer*

*Indicator and warning lights*

*Ignition switch*

*Engine rev counter*

**Motorcycle instrument panel**
Motorcycles have an instrument panel in the center of the handlebars. Control switches for lights and indicators can be operated with hands on the handlebars.

*Front suspension*

## Riding a motorcycle

A motorcycle rider changes speed by twisting the right handlebar grip and changes gear by flicking a foot lever up or down. The front brakes are operated by hand and the rear brakes by foot. To go around a corner, the rider turns the handlebars and leans with the motorcycle.

*Small engine for speed and economy*

*Open "step in" frame*

**SFX moped**

## Mopeds and scooters

Small motorcycles used for short journeys in towns and cities are called mopeds or scooters. They have small engines, so they cannot go very fast, but are very economical. Mopeds, restricted to a 50cc engine, have pedals that the rider can use on steep hills.

## Timeline

**1839** Kirkpatrick Macmillan, a Scot, invents a lever-driven bicycle.

**1863** The French Michaux brothers build the first pedal-powered bike, a velocipede.

**1868** The Michaux brothers add a steam engine to a bike, creating the first motorcycle.

**1885** In England, James Starley makes modern-style bicycles.

**1885** German Gottlieb Daimler builds an engine-powered tricycle (below).

**1901** The 1901 Werner is the first practical motorcycle.

**1914–18** Motorcycles used extensively in World War I.

**1963** Dutchman Van Wijnen designs what will become the Ecocar, covered pedal-powered transportation.

**FIND OUT MORE** | AIR | CARS AND TRUCKS | ENERGY | ENGINES AND MOTORS | FORCE AND MOTION | MACHINES, SIMPLE | MOTOR SPORTS | POLLUTION | SPORTS | TRANSPORT, HISTORY OF

# Bicycles

**Criterium racer** allows the rider to pedal round corners easily, especially in races.

**5-speed Peugeot** is a traditional "ladies" bike – without a crossbar.

**Mountain bikes**, ideal for off-road cycling, have rugged frames and fat tires.

**BMXs (Bicycle Motocross) bikes** are used for rough terrain and tricks, such as wheelies."

**Tricycles** have three wheels for additional balance.

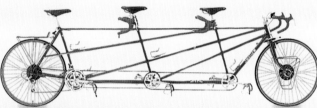

**Triple tandems** have three sets of pedals for three riders, linked by a chain to the back wheel.

**Pedicabs** are pedal-powered taxis. This one was made in 1980 in Bangladesh.

**Kingcycle Bean**, 1990, is designed to reduce drag for extra speed.

**French Velocar, 1933,** is a recumbent, which allows the rider to sit back while pedaling.

# Motorcycles

**Harley Davidson**, 1942, was adapted for military use, but was based on the civilian model.

**Harley Davidson Knucklehead 61E**, 1936, took the lead in American design; its engine resembled a clenched fist.

**Harley Davidson Hydra Glide**, 1951, has a classic chopper look with the machine stripped down to the bare essentials.

**Heinkle Perle**, 1956, has all the wires and cables running from the handlebars through the frame.

**BMW R/60**, 1956, has links to vary the angle between the "Steib" sidecar and the bike.

**"Mod" scooters** were popular in the 1960's: the more mirrors and lights, the more fashionable they were.

**BMW R75/5**, 1971, is a touring bike that combines reliability with comfort.

**Honda GL1500/6 Gold Wing**, 1991, has a 1500cc engine, an extra pair of cylinders, and luxuries such as a cassette player.

**Husqvarna Motocross TC610**, 1992, is a racing motorcyle for driving through fields or mud.

# BIG BANG

AN INCREDIBLE EXPLOSION called the Big Bang is believed to have created the Universe. Observations of galaxies and heat radiation from space have helped confirm this theory. Astronomers are now working to explain exactly what happened from the point of the Big Bang explosion, which created everything in today's Universe – matter, energy, space, and time – to the present Universe, with its galaxies, stars, planets, and us.

## Steady State theory

In the late 1940s and the 1950s, the Steady State theory was as popular as the Big Bang theory. It proposed that the Universe looked the same at any place and at any time. Although expanding, it would stay unchanged and in perfect balance. Material was being continuously created to keep the density of the Universe constant. As scientists found proof for the Big Bang, the Steady State theory was largely abandoned.

**A Steady-State** universe now (left) and later in time (right). The galaxies have moved apart, but new ones (coded orange) have been created to take their place. The density stays the same.

## Georges Lemaître

In 1931, Belgian cosmologist Georges Lemaître (1894–1966) was the first to put forward the theory that the Universe started from a dense, single unit of material in a big explosion. The name Big Bang followed in 1950, introduced by Fred Hoyle, a British astronomer and supporter of the Steady State theory.

## Origin of the Universe

One of the most difficult problems facing scientists in the 20th century was to explain how the Universe was created. The Universe is changing, but from what and to what? The Steady State theory suggested that the Universe had no beginning or end. The alternate, and now generally accepted, theory is the Big Bang. It proposes that the Universe was created in an explosion 15 billion years ago. From very small and simple beginnings it has grown vast and complex.

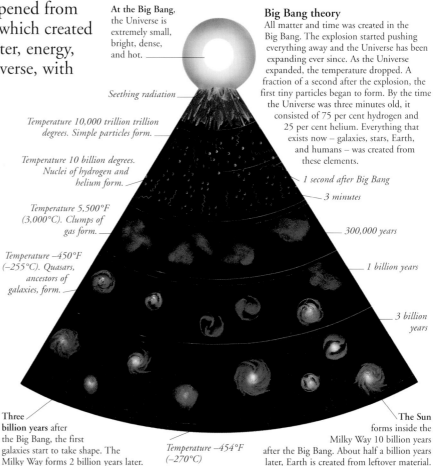

**At the Big Bang,** the Universe is extremely small, bright, dense, and hot.

*Seething radiation*

*Temperature 10,000 trillion trillion degrees. Simple particles form.*

*Temperature 10 billion degrees. Nuclei of hydrogen and helium form.*

*Temperature 5,500°F (3,000°C). Clumps of gas form.*

*Temperature –450°F (–255°C). Quasars, ancestors of galaxies, form.*

### Big Bang theory

All matter and time was created in the Big Bang. The explosion started pushing everything away and the Universe has been expanding ever since. As the Universe expanded, the temperature dropped. A fraction of a second after the explosion, the first tiny particles began to form. By the time the Universe was three minutes old, it consisted of 75 per cent hydrogen and 25 per cent helium. Everything that exists now – galaxies, stars, Earth, and humans – was created from these elements.

*1 second after Big Bang*

*3 minutes*

*300,000 years*

*1 billion years*

*3 billion years*

**Three billion years** after the Big Bang, the first galaxies start to take shape. The Milky Way forms 2 billion years later.

*Temperature –454°F (–270°C)*

**The Sun** forms inside the Milky Way 10 billion years after the Big Bang. About half a billion years later, Earth is created from leftover material.

## Expanding Universe

In the 1920s, analyzing starlight from galaxies showed that the galaxies are moving away from Earth. This is true of galaxies in every direction from Earth. Over time, the Universe is becoming larger and less dense. The idea that the Universe started in an explosion from a single point grew out of observations that the Universe is expanding.

### Background radiation

The heat produced by the Big Bang has been cooling ever since. It now has a temperature of –454°F (–270°C), detected as microwave radiation from all over the sky. The false-color map shows variations in the temperature 300,000 years after the Big Bang. The blue (cooler) patches are gas clouds, from which the galaxies formed.

**Redshift:** The faster a galaxy is moving away, the longer the wavelength of its starlight becomes. The starlight is said to redshift.

*The lines are shifted toward the red end of the spectrum.*

**More distant** galaxies are speeding away faster than closer ones. Their light has a greater redshift.

*Lines on the spectrum reveal a galaxy's speed.*

## Future of the Universe

Nobody knows for certain what is going to happen to the Universe. At present, it is getting larger and less dense. Most astronomers believe there will be a time when it stops expanding. But there is disagreement about what happens then: will the Universe live on forever, wither and die, or start to contract?

### Big Crunch

The Universe may end in a Big Crunch if it starts to contract until it is hot and dense once more. But even this may not mean the end of the Universe. The Big Crunch might be followed by another Big Bang explosion, and the whole process could start over again.

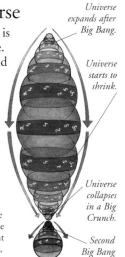

*Universe expands after Big Bang.*

*Universe starts to shrink.*

*Universe collapses in a Big Crunch.*

*Second Big Bang*

**FIND OUT MORE**
ASTRONOMY    BLACK HOLES    GALAXIES    GRAVITY    STARS    TIME    UNIVERSE

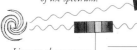

B

# BIOLOGY

WHEN YOU LOOK at a running horse, you know immediately that it is alive; a beach pebble, by contrast, is nonliving. What distinguishes the two is life, or the state of being alive. Biology is the study of life and living things, and it can be divided into two main fields: zoology and botany. People who study biology are known as biologists; the living organisms they study range from animals such as horses to microorganisms such as green algae. All use energy obtained from food and released by respiration in order to fulfill their natural processes.

## Classifying living things

There are about 2 million species of living organisms, and biologists classify them into groups. The largest and most general group is called a kingdom. There are five kingdoms: Monera (bacteria), Protista (protozoa and algae), Fungi, Plantae (plants), and Animalia (animals).

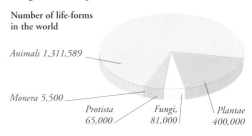

**Number of life-forms in the world**

Animals 1,311,589

Monera 5,500

Protista 65,000

Fungi, 81,000

Plantae 400,000

## Branches of biology

Biology covers a number of different studies. Ecology examines how living things interact and where they live. Physiology looks at how organisms work. Genetics is concerned with how characteristics inherited from one generation pass to the next. Other branches include anatomy, taxonomy, microbiology, and parasitology.

**Bird skeleton**

*Anatomists study skeletons to understand how an organism functions*

### Anatomy
Anatomy is the study of the structure of living organisms. Anatomists investigate the shape and form of the parts that make up organisms. This analysis allows them to figure out things such as how bats and birds are able to fly.

Case displays butterflies and moths.

### Taxonomy
The science of classifying the millions of living things into groups of related organisms is called taxonomy. Scientists called taxonomists identify and name organisms, and then group them together according to the characteristics they share and their common ancestry.

### Microbiology
Microorganisms are living things that are too small to be seen without a microscope. Microbiology is the study of all aspects of the biology of these tiny organisms, which include bacteria, viruses, protists, and some types of fungi such as yeasts.

### Parasitology
Parasites live in or on another organism and exist at its expense; the study of parasites is called parasitology. Fleas are parasites that suck blood from their host. Tapeworms live and feed in their host's intestine.

**Compound microscope**

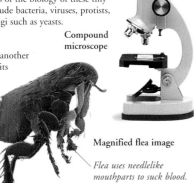

**Magnified flea image**

*Flea uses needlelike mouthparts to suck blood.*

## Zoology

Zoology is the branch of biology that is concerned with the study of animals. Animals are an amazingly diverse group of living organisms and encompass everything from sponges, spiders, and earthworms to lobsters, cats, and chimpanzees. Zoologists study the structure of animals, how their bodies function, and how they live and behave in their natural environment.

*Lorenz*

*Ducklings imprinted on Lorenz instead of their mother.*

### Ethology
The study of animal behavior is called ethology. Austrian zoologist Konrad Lorenz (1903–89) helped establish the science of ethology. He discovered imprinting, a rapid learning process that occurs early in life. Imprinting to food, surroundings, or the mother happens instinctively during a short, fixed timespan early in life.

**Kew Gardens, London, England**

### The work of a biologist
Biologists are trained in all branches of biology, but usually focus on one specific area. Their research might involve observing animal behavior, investigating plant photosynthesis, or studying ecosystems.

*Petri dishes contain control samples.*

**Biologist at work in a laboratory**

## Botany

Botany is the study of plants. Plants are diverse organisms, encompassing everything from mosses and ferns to trees, cacti, and flowers. They make their own food by a process called photosynthesis, which transforms sunlight into energy. Botanists are concerned with all aspects of the structure, function, and ecology of plants.

### Rachel Carson
In 1962, the American marine biologist and writer Rachel Carson (1907–64) published a book called *The Silent Spring*. In it, she warned that the indiscriminate use of pesticides and weedkillers was poisoning the natural world. Her pioneering book was fundamental in starting the environmental movement and in making ecological information accessible to the public.

**FIND OUT MORE**  ANIMAL BEHAVIOR • ANIMALS • ECOLOGY AND ECOSYSTEMS • GENETICS • MICROSCOPIC LIFE • PARASITES • PHOTOSYNTHESIS • PLANTS

B

# BIRDS

IN THE LIVING WORLD, only birds, insects, and bats are capable of powered flight. Birds are the largest and fastest of these flying animals, and are the only ones that have feathers. There are about 9,000 species of bird and they live in a huge range of different habitats – from deserts to the open oceans. They eat a variety of food, which they find mainly by sight. All birds reproduce by laying eggs. Most look after their young until they can fend for themselves.

*Wings almost touch during the upstroke.*

*Pigeon in flight*

*Fanned tail feathers act as a brake.*

*Flight feathers are spread out as the bird prepares to land.*

*Feet are held against the body during flight.*

## Bird features

Birds have a lightweight skeleton and their feathers give them a smooth outline, that helps them move easily through the air. They do not have any teeth; they have a hard beak instead. Birds use their beaks for eating, and also for many tasks that other animals carry out with their front legs and feet, such as grasping items, or tearing up food.

*Internal airspace with reinforcing struts*

**Wings**
The bones in a bird's wing are similar to those in a human arm. Most birds use their wings to fly. Strong muscles pull the wings downward when the bird flies; other muscles fold them up when not in use.

**Legs and feet**
A bird's feet and lower legs are usually covered with scales. Muscles that move them are close to the body. The feet are shaped according to their use.

**Beak**
A bird's beak is covered with keratin – the same substance that makes up human fingernails. The keratin keeps growing so that the edges of the beak do not wear away.

**Bone structure**
Most of the larger bones of a bird are hollow and lightweight. They contain air spaces that connect to the special air sacs the bird uses when it breathes. Some diving birds have solid bones to make diving easier.

**Skeleton**
Birds have fewer bones than reptiles or mammals, and many of the bones are fused together. A large flap called the keel sticks out of the breastbone and anchors the muscles that power the wings.

## Feathers

Birds use their feathers to fly, and also to keep warm and dry. Each feather is made of fine strands called barbs that carry rows of smaller barbules. In some feathers, the barbules lock together with hooks to produce a smooth surface needed for flying through the air. In others, they stay partly or fully separate. These feathers are soft and fluffy for warmth.

*Microscopic hooks lock barbules together.*

*A hollow quill anchors the feather in the bird's skin.*

*Macaw flight feather*

*Curved tip with interlocking barbules*

*Continuous curved surface*

*Central quill*

**Breeding colors**
Male birds often have bright colors that attract mates. In some species, these colors disappear at the end of the breeding season when the birds molt and a new set of feathers grows. In other species, such as pheasants, the colors are permanent.

**Down feathers**
These short, fluffy feathers do not have hooked barbs. They form an insulating layer next to a bird's skin. They trap air to stop heat from escaping from the bird's body.

**Body feathers**
The tips of these feathers overlap like tiles on a roof, giving the bird a smooth shape. The fluffy base of each feather is close to the body and conserves heat.

**Flight feathers**
These feathers are strong but flexible. They provide lift when the bird is airborne. Birds have to preen them carefully to keep them in good condition.

**Tail feathers**
A bird uses its tail feathers for steering and braking. Some male birds have long or brightly colored tail feathers. These play an important part in courtship.

B

# Breeding

Birds lay their eggs either directly on the ground or in a nest. One parent – or both – keep the eggs warm by sitting on them, or incubating them. Young birds hatch from eggs at different stages of development. Some can look after themselves almost immediately; others rely on their parents for food and protection.

**Eggs**
Birds' eggs have a hard shell. Ground-nesting birds often lay eggs that match their background. Birds that nest in trees often lay plain eggs.

**Helpless young**
Tree-nesting birds usually produce poorly developed young without feathers. The young stay in the nest until they are ready to feed themselves.

**Well-developed young**
The young of most ground-nesting birds can feed within hours of hatching. They soon leave the nest and follow their mother.

**Foster parents**
Brood parasites are birds that trick others into raising their young. Here a reed warbler is feeding a cuckoo that hatched in its nest.

# Senses

For most birds, vision is by far the most important sense. It guides them to their food and helps them avoid their many enemies. Hearing helps birds communicate, and is important to birds that hunt in the dark. The sense of smell is far less vital to birds than it is to many other animals, although some birds, such as the kiwi, use it to find food.

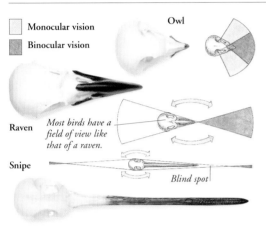

Monocular vision
Binocular vision
Owl
Raven
*Most birds have a field of view like that of a raven.*
Snipe
*Blind spot*

**Vision**
Birds that hunt, such as owls, have eyes at the front. This restricts their field of view, but they can judge distances accurately. Shorebirds, such as the snipe, have eyes at the side. They can spot danger in any direction, including the rear.

**Crane**
Like most birds, a crowned crane has keen eyesight. Its eyes are so big that they almost meet in the center of the skull. Its ear openings are at the base of its crown, but they are hidden by short feathers. Its nostrils are in its beak.

*Crown of spiky feathers*
Crowned crane

# Flight

This complex way of moving requires superb coordination. Some birds stay airborne almost entirely by flapping, but others hold their wings out and glide through the air using the natural curve of their wings to provide lift. During flight, a bird adjusts the shape of its wings to alter its speed and height.

*A pigeon's wings allow good maneuverability when extended, and fast flight when partially closed.*

*A kestrel's large wings provide lift as the bird flaps them nonstop while it hovers in the air.*

*A grouse's wings are shaped for load-bearing rather than speed. A grouse flies only in short bursts.*

*A peregrine falcon's slender wings partially fold up when it dives out of the sky on its prey.*

**Wing shapes**
Birds have evolved a variety of wing shapes that enable them to fly in different ways. Some wings provide lots of lift but do not work well at speed. Others create as little friction as possible when they cut through the air, allowing a bird to fly faster.

**Flightless birds**
During the course of evolution, some birds gave up the ability to fly. Flightless birds do not need a light body, and although some are quite small, they include the biggest birds that have ever lived.

*The flightless rhea comes from South America.*

## Largest and smallest
The world's heaviest bird is the ostrich. It weighs up to 275 lb (125 kg). This is about 80,000 times heavier than the rare bee hummingbird, the smallest bird. This tiny bird's eggs are the size of peas.

# Feeding and diet

Birds spend much of the time looking for food. To be able to fly, birds need food that provides them with lots of energy. Many of them eat small animals, which they catch either on land, in the air, or in water. Others visit plants and eat fruits, seeds, nectar, and pollen. Some have a mixed diet. Unlike mammals, only a few birds eat grass or the leaves of other plants.

**Fish eaters**
The great blue heron catches fish by stabbing them with its beak. Other fish eaters snatch their prey with talons, dive-bomb them from above, or chase them through the water.

**Seed eaters**
Different birds eat different seeds. They usually crack open the seed's husk before eating the food inside. The goldfinch is a typical seed eater. It feeds on thistles.

**Insect eaters**
Insect-eating birds search for their food on the ground or on plants, or snap it up in midair. The goldcrest often feeds high up in trees. Like other small insect eaters, it is expert at spotting insects hidden on leaves or bark.

**Meat eaters**
Many birds eat small animals, but owls and birds of prey specialize in hunting larger animals, such as mammals, reptiles, and other birds. A hooked beak allows them to tear up their food before swallowing it.

FIND OUT MORE | ANIMAL BEHAVIOR | BIRDS OF PREY | EGGS | FLIGHT, ANIMAL | FLIGHTLESS BIRDS | NESTS AND BURROWS | OWLS AND NIGHTJARS | SKELETON | SONGBIRDS

# Birds

## Fish and meat eaters

*Large eyes*

**Black-crowned night heron** hunts for fish mainly after dark.

**Inca tern** flutters in the air before diving down to snatch fish from the surface of the ocean.

**Spectacled owl** has keen eyesight and hearing for catching small animals.

**Harris's hawk** uses its hooked beak to tear off meat before swallowing it.

**Flamingo** feeds with its head down, trailing its beak through the water.

**Kookaburra** is a member of the kingfisher family and feeds in woodland and forests.

## Seed eaters

*Scarlet eyestripe*

**African pygmy goose** uses its broad beak to collect seeds floating on the water.

**Patagonian conure** lives in open grasslands of Argentina and Chile.

**Mourning dove** feeds on the ground in North America.

**Eurasian goldfinch** has a fine beak and extracts seeds from flowers.

**Common waxbill** is a common African finch that feeds in open grassland.

**Sparrows** have short, stout beaks that can crack the husks from small seeds.

## Insect eaters

*Bushy crest*

**Kentucky warbler** has a narrow beak ideally shaped for picking up small insects.

**Ocher-bellied flycatcher** chases after insects and catches them on the fly.

**Flycatchers** wait on a perch for insects to fly by that they can catch.

**Didric cuckoo** of Africa specializes in feeding on hairy caterpillars.

**Striated yuhina** of Asia picks insects off leaves, and often searches under the leaves.

**Racquet-tailed roller** often feeds on ants and termites from the ground.

## Nectar eaters

*Bright yellow throat*

**Blue-crowned hanging parrot** has a brush-tipped tongue that helps it to collect nectar and pollen.

**Duyvenbode's lory** feeds on the flowers of New Guinea forest trees, lapping up nectar with its tongue.

**Yellow-fronted woodpecker** feeds on fruit, probing deep into flowers to reach their nectar.

**Rufous hummingbird** pumps nectar into its mouth with its tongue.

**Booted racquet-tail** has a rather short beak, and feeds at flowers with spreading petals.

## Fruit eaters

*Bill has serrated edges.*

**Eurasian bullfinch** feeds on buds and fruit, using its short, powerful beak.

**Bearded barbet** feeds mainly on figs, and uses its heavy bill to dig nest holes in wood.

**Chestnut-eared aracari** uses its long bill to reach for fruit on the end of long branches.

**Fire-tufted barbet** of Malaysia eats both insects and fruit.

**Splendid glossy starling** gathers in isolated trees that carry ripe fruits.

**Long-tailed starling** searches for fruit in trees along forest edges.

## Mixed food eaters

**Eurasian jay** feeds on acorns in fall and winter, but many foods during the rest of the year.

**Alpine chough** eats small animals and seeds, and also scavenges animal remains.

**Blue magpie** eats seeds, fruits, and small animals, including lizards and snakes.

**Swainson's thrush** eats insects, spiders, and fruit, particularly in winter.

**Red-capped manakin** hovers in front of plants to eat the fruit, and also eats insects.

**Red-throated ant tanager** catches flying insects, and also eats fruit.

# BIRDS OF PREY

MOST BIRDS OF PREY, INCLUDING EAGLES, hawks, and falcons, kill and eat live animals. They soar high above the ground or dart among trees, using their excellent eyesight to search for prey. Once they spot a victim, they attack with their sharp talons, then tear up their food with their hooked beaks. Not all birds of prey feed in this way. A few species eat unusual foods, such as snails or nuts. Vultures eat carrion – animals that are already dead. They often wait for another animal to make a kill and then swoop down to the ground to feed on the remains of the carcass.

*At the end of a dive, the falcon opens its wings to slow down.*

*The falcon controls its flight by moving its long wing feathers.*

*Long broad wings with finger-like tips*

## Eyes
Birds of prey have superb eyesight for spotting prey on the ground from high up. Their eyes face forward, which makes the birds good at judging distances. This is essential for a bird such as the lanner falcon, because it has to know exactly when to brake as it hurtles toward its prey.

## Beak
Birds do not have teeth, so they cannot cut meat into pieces before they swallow it. Instead, birds of prey tear up their food with their beaks. Despite the ferocious appearance of a bird of prey's beak, it is hardly ever used as a weapon.

*Widely spread flight feathers brake the falcon's descent when it makes an attack.*

## Bird of prey features
With their forward-facing eyes, sharp claws, or talons, and hooked beak, birds of prey are perfectly adapted for hunting and feeding on meat. Most species have feathers covering the upper legs for warmth and protection.

## Lanner falcon
This falcon lives in desert and savanna areas of southern Europe, Africa, and the Middle East. Like other falcons, it catches prey by folding its wings back and falling on it in a steep dive. Falcons also attack birds in midair by diving on them from above.

*Tail feathers are used to steer in flight.*

## Talons
Birds of prey have large feet with long toes. Each toe ends in a talon that stays sharp by flaking into a point as it grows. The birds use their talons to kill food and carry it away. Many species can lift more than half their own weight.

*Chukar partridge is prey of the falcon.*

*Splayed feathers reduce air turbulence.*

**Flight path of kestrel**

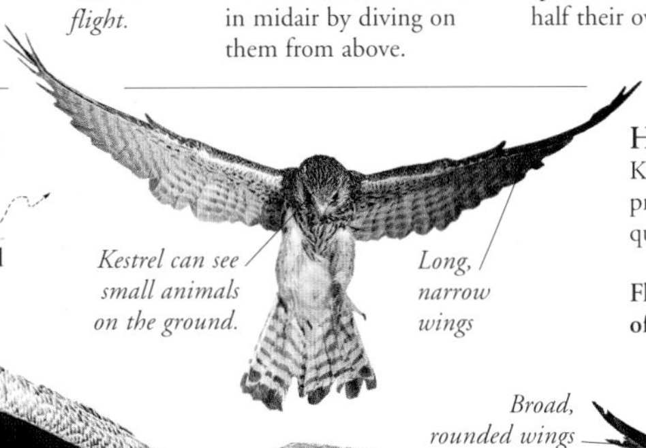

*Kestrel can see small animals on the ground.*

*Long, narrow wings*

## Hovering
Kestrels hover close to the ground while looking for prey. They use a lot of energy, but they can dive quickly on anything that moves below them.

**Flight path of goshawk**

*Broad, rounded wings*

*Long, broad wings*

## Flying styles
Most large birds of prey, such as eagles, look for food while soaring on currents of rising air. This uses little energy, allowing the birds to fly long distances every day. Smaller species, such as hawks, usually fly in short bursts. Kestrels are unusual in being able to hover in the air.

## Soaring
Eagles, buzzards, and vultures soar by riding on currents of rising air. They spiral around slowly as they soar upward, keeping their wings straight and steady.

## Low-level flight
Hawks usually hunt by flying in short bursts. They are highly maneuverable and can swerve between trees and over hedges, using surprise to catch small birds.

**Flight path of eagle**

## Roosting
These turkey buzzards from North America have gathered in a tree to roost, or settle for the night. Many vultures roost high in trees or on rocky ledges, making it easier for them to take off and become airborne when the day begins.

*Vulture guards carrion while compnion eats.*

*Long neck enables the vulture to reach into a carcass.*

Vultures feeding on carrion

### White-backed vulture
With a wingspan of more than 8 ft (2.5 m), this huge vulture soars high over open country in southern Europe, Asia, and Africa. Like most other vultures, it has a bare head and neck. If it had feathers there, they would become soaked with blood from the meat torn with its beak from inside a carcass.

*Bare head and neck for ease of cleaning*

## Carrion eaters
Instead of hunting live animals, vultures feed on the remains of ones that are already dead. They live in open places such as deserts, grasslands, and mountains, and find their food by soaring and looking for animal carcasses from the air. Vultures have large beaks, but their talons are weak.

### Feeding
Vultures have good eyesight. If one vulture spots a carcass and drops down to feed, others quickly follow. Soon vultures arrive from all around. The largest species usually feed first, leaving the smaller species to fight over the scraps.

## Specialized eaters
Over millions of years of evolution, some birds of prey have developed very specialized diets and techniques to deal with their food. Most of these feeders eat animal food, but a few are vegetarians. Some species have learned to live alongside humans, and they eat the variety of food scraps that people throw away.

### Egyptian vulture
The Egyptian vulture is one of only a few birds that uses tools to obtain food. It eats ostrich eggs, which it breaks open by picking up stones and hurling them against the shell until it breaks. In addition to Egypt, it lives in other parts of Africa, Europe, and Asia.

Egyptian Vulture

Secretary bird

*Eyes face to the side instead of the front.*

*Slim, athletic build for hunting on the ground in open country*

*Feathery quills, like those once used for writing, give the secretary bird its name.*

*Long tail feathers provide balance.*

*Secretary bird raises its crest of black feathers to attract a mate*

### Snail kite
The snail kite lives in marshy places from the southern US to Argentina in South America. It feeds almost entirely on freshwater snails, which it snatches from the water with one of its feet. It then scoops out the snail's body with its long, slender beak.

### Palmnut vulture
The diet of this African vulture is based mainly on the fruits of oil palms, but it eats some small animals. Unlike other vultures, it does not have to fly long distances in search of food, and spends most of its time in trees.

### Secretary bird
This highly unusual bird of prey from Africa hunts on the ground. It has long, strong legs and kills animals by stomping them to death. The secretary bird often feeds on snakes, and when attacking them uses its wings like a shield to protect itself.

## Largest and smallest
The Andean condor is the largest bird of prey, with a wingspan of more than 10 ft (3 m). It is a carrion eater. The smallest birds of prey are pygmy falcons and falconets, which feed mainly on flying insects. Some are only 6 in (15 cm) long.

### LANNER FALCON
**SCIENTIFIC NAME** *Falco biarmicus*

**ORDER** Falconiformes

**FAMILY** Falconidae

**DISTRIBUTION** Southern Europe, Africa, and the Middle East

**HABITAT** Scrub and desert

**DIET** Birds, small mammals, and lizards

**SIZE** Length, including tail: male – 14.5 in (37 cm); female – 18.5 in (47 cm)

**LIFESPAN** About 10 years

**FIND OUT MORE**   AFRICAN WILDLIFE   BIRDS   DESERT WILDLIFE   FLIGHT, ANIMAL   MOUNTAIN WILDLIFE   OWLS AND NIGHTJARS

# Birds of prey
## Eagles, hawks, and falcons

*Large, broad wings*

*Tail is fanned out to provide lift as the kestrel hovers.*

**Common kestrel** hovers to find its prey, instead of chasing it like other falcons.

**Tawny eagle** is a scavenger, feeding on carcasses, and even human garbage. It also steals from other birds of prey.

**Goshawk** hunts in forests and often catches birds in midair.

**Black eagle** is from southern Asia. It flies over forests and often snatches birds from their nests.

*Feathers down to the toes as in all true eagles*

**American kestrel** is a small falcon. It often feeds on insects.

**Golden eagle** lives in remote places throughout the northern hemisphere.

**Harris's hawk** sometimes hunts in groups, which is unusual for a bird of prey.

**Imperial eagle** is rare. It lives in Spain, eastern Europe, and Asia.

**Caracara** has long legs and toes that enable it to hunt on the ground.

**Peregrine falcon** is the fastest bird in the world.

**Bateleur** is almost tailless. This African eagle has an unusual zigzagging flight.

## Vultures

**Black vulture** lives in the Americas. Like the turkey vulture, it has slender legs and toes.

**Turkey vulture** has an immense range, stretching from Canada to Tierra del Fuego at the tip of South America.

*Collar of white feathers around the base of the neck*

*Huge flight feathers allow effortless soaring.*

*Worn feathers will be replaced when the vulture molts.*

**Andean condor** is the largest bird of prey. As its name suggests, it lives in the Andes Mountains of South America.

*Feet are too weak for catching food.*

**White-backed vulture** has only a few feathers on its neck and a bare head like all vultures.

*A bare neck is easy for the vulture to clean after feeding.*

# BLACK DEATH

IN THE 14TH CENTURY, a deadly epidemic swept the world. The Black Death, as it became known, was bubonic plague, a terrible disease that begins with fever, causes agonizing black swellings in the glands, and leads to death, usually within a few days of infection. Millions died. Terrified people fled infected areas and carried the plague with them. In towns the doors of plague carriers were marked with a cross to warn people to keep away. The dead were collected in carts and buried in mass graves. In Europe about one-third of the population died; a similar number probably died in Asia.

## Progress of the plague

The plague reached the Black Sea from Asia in 1346. From there, it was carried by Italian traders to ports on the Mediterranean. It then spread up rivers and land routes into northern Europe. By 1350, most of Europe was affected.

*Plague-free areas*

Black Sea
Prague
Paris
Milan
Constantinople
Bordeaux
Genoa
Florence

| | |
|---|---|
| | c.1351 |
| | Dec. 1350 |
| | June 1350 |
| | Dec. 1349 |
| | June 1349 |
| | Dec. 1348 |
| | June 1348 |
| | Dec. 1347 |

**Plague-free areas**
Some areas, such as modern-day Poland and Milan, escaped the plague, but the reason for this is still a mystery.

## Disease carriers

Plague is caused by a bacterium that lives on rodents. The disease was caught by black rats in Asia, which then traveled in ships to Europe and spread the disease among people there. An infected person could also pass the plague through the air by coughing.

**Plague bacterium**
The bacterium is called *Yersinia pestis*, after the Swiss biologist Alexander Yersin, who discovered it. It is common in wild animals such as field mice, ground squirrels, and marmots.

**Flea carriers**
The plague bacterium lives in the digestive system of a flea and causes a blockage there. When the flea feeds, the blockage makes it vomit the newly eaten blood back onto its host, along with plague bacteria, which then infect the host.

**Animal carriers**
The black rat lived in towns and on ships, and scavenged in food stores and garbage dumps. Rats carry fleas, and when plague-carrying rats died of the disease, their fleas searched for other hosts. If these new hosts were people, they, too, caught the plague.

**Human carriers**
The plague turned into an epidemic so rapidly because human travelers helped spread it. Mongol nomads and Asian merchants carried it across Asia. The traders of the great Italian cities, such as Genoa and Venice, carried it around Europe in their ships.

## Effects of the plague

The disease was so widespread that many left their families and took to the road to try to escape death. Some thought the plague was God's punishment for the sins of people, and mercilessly whipped themselves in the streets to show repentance.

**Labor force**
By the end of the 14th century, the smaller population of Europe meant that life was better for those who had survived. Because there were fewer peasants, they got higher wages and there was more food to go around. But recurring peasant rebellions showed that they still had grievances.

20M

8M

Black Death

World War I

**Population decline**
When Pope Clement VI asked how many people had died from the plague, he was told at least 20 million people in Europe, and 17 million in Asia. By comparison, around eight million soldiers died in World War I.

= 2 million dead

## Dealing with the plague

Some people tried to fend off the plague by using herbal remedies, bleeding by leeches, fumigation, and even bathing in urine. A 14th-century poem, called the Dance of Death (which states that death comes for people of every rank) was often enacted and painted to remind people that death – and the plague – could strike at any time.

Lungwort    Mint    Rose

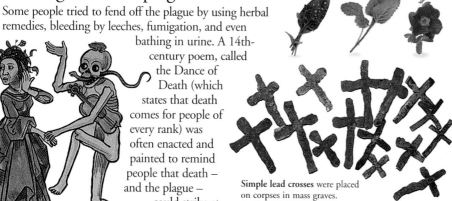

**Simple lead crosses** were placed on corpses in mass graves.

**Tombs**
During the plague, people faced death every day. Death is often realistically shown on 14th-century tombs, where images of skeletons and decaying corpses are common.

**Chantries**
People often left money for masses to be said for their souls. These masses were said in special chapels inside churches known as chantries. This chantry is at Winchester, England.

| FIND OUT MORE | ASIA, HISTORY OF | DISEASES | EUROPE, HISTORY OF | MEDIEVAL EUROPE | MICROSCOPIC LIFE |
|---|---|---|---|---|---|

# BLACK HOLES

ASTRONOMERS HAVE SPENT much time analyzing the life cycle of stars. One problem was to explain what happens to the most massive stars when they die. In 1967, the term "black hole" was used to describe what is left when such a star dies. Four years later, a powerful source of X rays, Cygnus X-1 was discovered; the first black hole candidate had been identified.

A massive star dies in a huge explosion, leaving a very dense core that then collapses.

## Detecting a black hole

Black holes appear black because nothing, not even light, can escape from their powerful gravity. Astronomers cannot detect them directly, but can "see" them because of the effect their gravity has on everything around them, such as gas from a nearby star. The boundary of the black hole is called the event horizon. Material pulled in toward the hole is swirled around by the gravity, forming a disk, before crossing the horizon.

**Gravity** increases as the core of the dying star shrinks.

*Event horizon*

**Anything** trying to pull away from the gravity must travel almost at the speed of light, as the core approaches the size of the event horizon.

**Once** the core is smaller than the event horizon, not even light can escape.

**The core** continues collapsing until it takes up virtually no space. The star is a singularity, a point mass of infinitely high density inside a black hole.

## Stellar collapse

Massive stars can end their lives in an explosion called a supernova that leaves behind a central core. If the core is made of the equivalent of more than three Suns, it becomes a black hole. Gravity forces the core to collapse. As the core shrinks, its gravity increases. At a certain point it reaches the critical size of the event horizon.

*Event horizon*

**Gravity**
Black holes have incredibly strong gravity that attracts anything that comes close enough. Anything pulled in beyond the event horizon is squashed to near infinite density and never escapes.

*Gas is torn from a nearby star.*

*Close to the black hole, the gas glows with heat.*

*Black hole*

*Gravity pulls the gas toward the black hole.*

*Accretion disk*

### Accretion disk
The material that swirls around a black hole forms a rapidly spinning accretion disk. As the material is pulled closer to the hole, it travels faster and faster, and becomes very hot from friction. Close to the hole, the material is so hot that it emits X rays before crossing the event horizon and disappearing forever.

**A black hole** is black because no light or other radiation can escape and a hole because nothing that crosses the event horizon can get out.

## Falling into a black hole

1 At the start of the fall, everything appears normal.

*Astronaut becomes distorted.*

2 As the astronaut approaches the hole, he starts to be stretched.

3 Light is also stretched to a longer wavelength, so the astronaut appears red.

4 Gravity stretches the astronaut until, close to the hole, he is torn apart.

**Galaxy NGC 4261** in the constellation of Virgo has what appears to be a huge accretion disk – 30 million light-years across – swirling around a huge black hole.

## Inside a black hole

Space and time are highly distorted inside a black hole. Anyone who fell into one would be "spaghettified" – stretched to resemble spaghetti as gravity pulled harder on the feet than the head. An observer watching a person fall would also see time running slower as the person fell toward the event horizon.

## Supermassive holes

Some galaxies have very active centers that emit lots of energy. An object that has powerful gravity, such as a supermassive black hole, could be the cause of the activity. Such a hole would be a hundred million times more massive than the Sun.

### Roger Penrose
The English mathematician Roger Penrose (b.1931) theorizes on the nature of space and time. He has shown that a massive collapsing star inevitably becomes a black hole, and that all black holes have a singularity – a point, occupying virtually no space, that contains the entire mass of the dead star. Penrose believes the singularity is always hidden by an event horizon.

FRICTION    GALAXIES    GRAVITY    STARS    SUN AND SOLAR SYSTEM    UNIVERSE

# BOLÍVAR, SIMÓN

SIMÓN BOLÍVAR WAS the brilliant charismatic leader who led South America to independence from 400 years of foreign rule. Together with other generals, he overthrew the Spanish in just 12 years. As president of the federation of Gran Colombia, he wanted to rule the whole continent, but this dream came to nothing. To this day, he is still known as "The Liberator," and one of the South American nations, Bolivia, is named after him.

## Early life

Bolívar was born into a rich family in Caracas, Venezuela, in 1783. His parents died when he was young, and he was educated by private tutors, such as Simón Rodríguez, a teacher who taught him about European ideas such as liberty.

## Fighting for independence

At the start of the 19th century, all of South America except Brazil and Guiana was under the rule of the Spanish king Ferdinand VII. Many South Americans resented this and wanted to govern themselves. In response, independence movements broke out all over South America. Bolívar, eager to work in the independence movement, returned to South America and fought the Spanish in Venezuela.

Bolívar's storms to victory at the Battle of Carabobo

### Bolívar in Europe

In 1799, Bolívar was sent to Madrid to live with relatives and improve his education. While in Europe, Bolívar learned of an attempt in 1806 by Francisco de Miranda to liberate Venezuela from Spanish rule. The rebellion failed, but inspired Bolívar to fight for independence.

Ferdinand VII of Spain

### The Angostura Congress

At a congress held in Angostura, now Ciudad Bolívar, Bolívar was elected president of Venezuela. The congress also proposed the formation of Gran Colombia, a federation that included present-day Venezuela, Colombia, Ecuador, and Panama. Between 1819 and 1822, Bolívar won a series of victories against Spain, confirming the independence of Colombia and Venezuela, and liberating Peru.

### The first republic

In 1810, Francisco de Miranda returned from exile in Europe and was made president of the new republic of Venezuela. In 1811, it became the first South American country to declare independence from foreign rule. Bolívar joined the rebel army, but the republic collapsed. He carried on the struggle, going to Colombia to fight the Spanish there.

Francisco de Miranda in prison

### The Liberator

From 1811 onward, Bolívar was the focus of independence movements across South America. In 1813, he defeated the Spanish and entered Caracas, where he was given the title of "The Liberator." In 1819, he put together an army of 2,500 men and marched them across the continent to Boyacá, Colombia. He won the resulting battle, and Colombia gained its independence.

Bolívar and Sucre

### Ecuador and Peru

In 1822, one of Bolívar's most talented generals, Antonio José de Sucre, defeated the Spanish at Pichincha to win Ecuador's independence. Two years later, Bolívar made a deal with the Argentinian liberator José de San Martín, whose forces were active in Peru. As a result, Sucre defeated the Spanish at Ayacucho, bringing independence to Peru. As a result of Bolívar's influence, another large area of South America was liberated.

## Bolivia

In 1825, Bolívar dispatched Sucre to conquer Alto Perú, in west central South America, which was still under Spanish control. Once the Spanish were defeated, the newly independent country was named Bolivia in honor of the Liberator. By now, every South American state except Uruguay had won its independence.

Bolívar's statue at government buildings, La Paz, Bolivia

### SIMÓN BOLÍVAR

| | |
|---|---|
| 1783 | Born in Caracas, Venezuela. |
| 1799 | Sent to Europe. |
| 1811 | Venezuela declares its independence; Bolívar becomes a military leader. |
| 1812 | First republic is defeated. |
| 1813 | Bolívar enters Caracas as "The Liberator," but is soon defeated. |
| 1819 | Angostura Congress. |
| 1819 | Bolívar wins Battle of Boyacá to win Colombian independence. |
| 1821 | Bolívar wins Battle of Carabobo to win Venezuelan independence. |
| 1822 | Ecuador wins independence. |
| 1825 | Bolivia named in his honor. |
| 1830 | Dies of tuberculosis. |

FIND OUT MORE — CENTRAL AMERICA, HISTORY OF • NAPOLEON BONAPARTE • SOUTH AMERICA, HISTORY OF • SPAIN, HISTORY OF

# BOLIVIA AND PARAGUAY

BOLIVIA AND PARAGUAY are the only landlocked countries in South America. They are also two of the poorest in the continent, reliant on their neighbors for access to the sea. In a bitter war between them over ownership of the Gran Chaco, (1932–35) Bolivia lost, but both countries suffered political turmoil. Under Spanish rule between the 1530s and 1820s, Bolivia and Paraguay still bear its legacy: Spanish is an official language, and more than 90 percent of the region's population is Roman Catholic. Many people farm and, in Bolivia, some grow and sell coca, for cocaine, a drug that the government has taken steps to banish.

## Physical features

The Altiplano dominates the west of Bolivia, while the east is covered by a lowland plain called the Oriente. Paraguay is divided north to south by the Paraguay River. In the west is the Gran Chaco, a region of grass and scrub; the east is covered in grassy plains and forests, and drained by the mighty Paraná River.

### Altiplano
At about 12,467 ft (3,800 m) above sea level, the Altiplano, a vast, windswept, almost treeless plateau, lies between two ranges of the Bolivian Andes. Despite its cold, arid climate, more than half of Bolivia's population lives here, growing a few crops and raising animals such as llamas and alpacas.

### Lake Titicaca
The clear blue waters of Lake Titicaca cover 3,200 sq miles (8,288 sq km) at a height of 12,500 ft (3,810 m) above sea level, making it the highest navigable lake in the world. It is the last surviving stretch of an ancient inland sea known as Lago Ballivián.

### Aymara
The Aymara are a group of Native South Americans who have farmed on the Bolivian Altiplano for hundreds of years, strongly resisting cultural change. With the Quechua, another Indian group, they make up more than half Bolivia's population, but suffer discrimination and do not contribute to politics or the economy. The state has successfully persuaded many Aymara to move into towns.

**Aymaras farmers, Altiplano, Bolivia**

### Gran Chaco
The flat, dry plain that covers southeastern Bolivia and northwestern Paraguay is called the Gran Chaco. Since so few people live in this area of coarse grass, cactus, and thorny shrubs, a range of plants and animals thrive.

### Regional climate
Bolivia's Altiplano has a cool, crisp, dry climate. The eastern part of the country is warm and humid, as is most of Paraguay. The Chaco is hot, with 20–40 in (50–100 cm) of rain a year, although it often has droughts in winter.

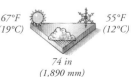

67°F (19°C)    55°F (12°C)

74 in (1,890 mm)

B

# Bolivia

The highest and most isolated nation in South America, Bolivia is named after Simón Bolívar, who, in the 1800s, led wars of independence against the Spaniards. Despite rich natural resources, exporting is difficult because of Bolivia's position. About half are Native Americans; the rest are Spanish or mixed blood *mestizos*.

## Music
Bolivian music has Incan, Amazonian, Spanish, and African influences. Rural Aymara orchestras are often composed entirely of panpipes, called *chuqui*. Other instruments include drums, flutes, and the *phututu*, made from a cow's horn.

Chuqui

*Pipes are made from a local reed. The longer the reed, the deeper the sound.*

## La Paz
Although Sucre is Bolivia's official capital, the country is governed from La Paz, which also has capital status. At 11,913 ft (3,631 m) above sea level, La Paz is the world's highest capital and Bolivia's largest city, with a population of about 2,515,000, of whom over half are Native Americans. La Paz has chemical and textile industries, but unemployment is generally high.

## Deforestation
Tropical rain forests in Bolivia are being cut down at the rate of 772 sq miles (2,000 sq km) a year, mostly for cattle ranching or growing coca for cocaine. Chemicals used in the manufacture of cocaine are discharged directly into the rivers of Amazonia, many of which have high pollution levels that damage plant and tree life.

Tin

## Metal mining
Bolivia is rich in mineral deposits. Its tin mines lie high in the Andes mountains and it is the world's largest producer of tin. It is also a leading exporter of antimony and silver. Other mineral deposits include zinc, gold, and lead.

### BOLIVIA FACTS

| | |
|---|---|
| CAPITAL CITIES | La Paz, Sucre |
| AREA | 414,162 sq miles (1,098,580 sq km) |
| POPULATION | 8,300,000 |
| MAIN LANGUAGES | Spanish, Quechua, Aymara |
| MAJOR RELIGION | Christian |
| CURRENCY | Boliviano |

Potatoes

Corn

Barley

## Crops
Bolivian farmers living on the Altiplano grow potatoes, soybeans, barley, and wheat for themselves and their families. Rice, corn, bananas, and plantains are grown in the lowlands. Cash crops include sugarcane, cocoa beans, and coffee, although the profits from illegal coca crops greatly exceed all legal farming produce combined.

# Paraguay

The Paraguay River, from which the country takes its name, divides the land in two. To the east lie the fertile hills and plains that are home to 90 percent of the people. The vast majority are *mestizos*, people of mixed European and Native American ancestry; the rest are Guaraní or Europeans. To the northwest is the Gran Chaco, large areas of which Paraguay won from Bolivia in the 1930s. Only five percent of the people live in the Chaco, including 10,000 Mennonites, farmers of German descent who retain their culture.

Macá bag

## Beef
The main industry in Paraguay's Gran Chaco is cattle ranching. Herds of animals roam the flat grasslands, tended by skilled Paraguayan cowboys called *gauchos* who round the cattle up on horseback. The farms are called *estancias* and are some of the only buildings in this open landscape.

### PARAGUAY FACTS

| | |
|---|---|
| CAPITAL CITY | Asunción |
| AREA | 157,046 sq miles (406,750 sq km) |
| POPULATION | 5,500,000 |
| MAIN LANGUAGES | Spanish, Guaraní |
| MAJOR RELIGION | Christian |
| CURRENCY | Guaraní |

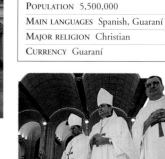

## Jesuits
In 1588, Spanish missionaries from the Jesuit order of the Roman Catholic Church arrived in Asunción. They converted the local Guaraní people to Christianity, and taught them trades such as weaving. The Jesuits built large stone churches.

## Macá Indians
The Macá are a small group of Indians who follow a traditional lifestyle in the Gran Chaco. They make a living from farming. Macá women also weave bags and cloth for the tourist trade.

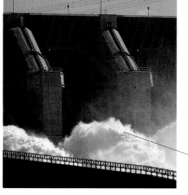

## Itaipu Dam
With a reservoir 1,255 sq miles (3,250 sq km) and 722 ft (220 m) deep, the Itaipu Dam, on the Paraná River, was undertaken as a joint project with Brazil. It provides water for the world's largest hydroelectric plant and generates enough electricity to make Paraguay self-sufficient in energy.

*Dam generates 13,320 megawatts of electricity – enough to supply New York City.*

## Exports
Soybean flour and cotton make up around 50 percent of Paraguay's exports. The country also sells timber from its forests, vegetable oils, and processed meat. Leading trading partners include Brazil, Argentina, and the Netherlands.

**FIND OUT MORE** BOLIVAR, SIMON   CHRISTIANITY   DAMS   DRUGS   ENERGY   FARMING   MUSIC   NATIVE AMERICANS   ROCKS AND MINERALS   SOUTH AMERICA, HISTORY OF   TEXTILES AND WEAVING

# BOOKS

FROM ENCYCLOPEDIAS TO NOVELS, books are a vital record of human life and achievement. They store the thoughts, beliefs, and experiences of individuals and societies, preserving them after the author's death. There are many kinds of books, from religious works, such as the Qur'an, and non-fiction, such as dictionaries and educational books, to fiction such as plays and stories. The Chinese invented printing in the 9th century; it arrived in Europe during the 15th century. Printing made it possible to mass-produce books, and knowledge was spread more widely. Today, publishing is a global industry.

Early Chinese book, made of fragile bamboo strips

## Early books
The first books were not made of paper. Long before 3000 BC, the Sumerians wrote on clay tablets. Around 1300 BC, the Chinese began making books from bamboo strips bound together with cord.

## Making books
Much preparation goes into making books and some take several years to produce. For example, making an encyclopedia will involve a team of people that includes authors, editors, designers, picture researchers, illustrators, photographers, and IT experts, as well as printers.

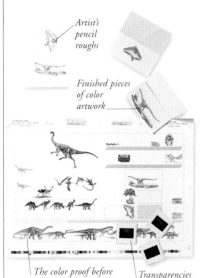
*Artist's pencil roughs*
*Finished pieces of color artwork*
*The color proof before text is added to page*
*Transparencies are a high-quality image format.*

### Illustration
The designer draws a detailed plan, showing the position of each illustration. The artist makes rough sketches, which are checked, then paints each picture separately. The artwork is photographed, and carefully positioned on the page using a computer, until the design is perfect.

### Author
The author is the first person to start work, researching and writing the contents of the book. The author advises the designer on suitable images for the book and works closely with the editorial team throughout the project.

*Papyrus plants grow by the Nile.*

### Paper
The ancient Egyptians wrote on scrolls made from papyrus, which grew by the Nile River. Later civilizations in the Middle East wrote on parchment made from animal skin. Modern paper was probably invented in China around AD 150. It was made by pulping flax fibres, then flattening and drying them in the sun. The Chinese kept this process a secret for 500 years before they passed it on to the rest of the world.

### CD Roms
There is a limit to how big any book can grow before it becomes too heavy and cumbersome to be practical. Now, modern technology is developing compact alternatives to traditional books. One CD Rom can contain as much text as a shelf of encyclopedias. Text and pictures from CD Roms can be read and transmitted by computer.

CD Rom

*The printed color matches the original artwork as closely as possible.*
*The spine of the book holds the pages in place.*
*The editor checks the author's text for mistakes and adjusts length of text if necessary.*
*Pictures and text are perfectly integrated.*

### Finished book
At last the book is finished, and fitted with a hard cover and a protective jacket. It is now ready to sell. An illustrated book may take several years to make, although new technology is speeding up this process.

### Text
The text is edited on a computer screen, and then produced as a page called a proof. The proof is matched with the artwork to make sure that words and images fit exactly, before going to the printer.

### Paperbacks
A paperback book contains the same text as a hardback, but has a soft cover. The first modern paperback books were published in London by Penguin, in 1935, priced sixpence (about 25 cents). They are cheaper than hardbacks, and many more people can buy them.

## Timeline
**c. 285 BC** Egyptian pharaoh Ptolemy I establishes a library at Alexandria, Egypt.

**AD 300s** Books with pages first invented.

Gutenberg Bible

**c.1440** Johannes Gutenberg invents the metal type.

**1789** French Revolutionaries proclaim the fundamental public right to print without fear of censorship.

**1796** Lithography (a technique for printing illustrations) invented.

**1811** First totally mechanized printing press invented, US.

**1935** First paperback books published for mass market by Penguin in UK.

**1980s** Electronic books for the computer published in CD Rom format.

**1990s** Books first published on the Internet.

FIND OUT MORE | CHILDREN'S LITERATURE | COMPUTERS | DRAMA | EGYPT, ANCIENT | LITERATURE | POETRY | PRINTING | WRITING

# BRAIN AND NERVOUS SYSTEM

B

EVERY THOUGHT YOU HAVE, every emotion you feel, and every action you take is a reflection of the nervous system at work. At the core of the nervous system are the brain and spinal cord, known as the central nervous system (CNS). The most complex part of the CNS is the brain; it constantly receives information from the body, processes it, and sends out instructions telling the body what to do. The CNS communicates with every part of the body through an extensive network of nerves. The nerves and the CNS are both constructed from billions of nerve cells called neurons.

## Nerves

Nerves form the "wiring" of the nervous system. Each nerve consists of a bundle of neurons (nerve cells) held together by a tough outer sheath. Nerves spread out from the brain and spinal cord and branch repeatedly to reach all parts of the body. Most nerves contain sensory neurons that carry nerve impulses toward the CNS, and motor neurons that carry nerve impulses away from the CNS.

**Inside a nerve**

*Sensory neuron*

*Motor neuron*

*Bundle of neurons*

*Blood vessels*

*Outer sheath of nerve*

### Nerve endings
At the ends of sensory neurons there are nerve endings called sensory receptors. If you touch an object, a sensory receptor in the skin is stimulated, nerve impulses travel to the brain along the sensory neuron, and you feel the object. In this way, visually impaired people can "read" Braille language with their fingertips.

**Brain** is the body's control and co-ordination center.

*Cranial nerves*

*Cervical nerves*

*Brachial plexus*

**Spinal cord** relays information to and from the brain and the rest of the body.

**Radial nerve** controls the muscles in the arm and hand.

*Thoracic nerves*

*Lumbar plexus*

*Lumbar nerves*

*Sacral plexus*

*Sacral nerves*

**Sciatic nerve** controls the muscles in the leg and foot.

**Tibial nerve** controls the muscles of the calf and foot.

## Nervous system

The nervous system is made up of the CNS and the peripheral nervous system, which consists of the nerves. The peripheral nervous system has two sections: the somatic system, which controls voluntary actions, and the autonomic nervous system, which controls automatic functions such as heart rate.

## Neurons

Neurons are long, thin cells adapted to carry electrical signals called nerve impulses. There are three types of neurons: sensory neurons, motor neurons, and association neurons. The most numerous are association neurons, which transmit signals from one neuron to another and are found only inside the CNS.

### Nerve impulses
Nerve impulses are the "messages" that travel at high speed along neurons. Impulses are weak electrical signals that are generated and transmitted by neurons when they are stimulated. The stimulus may come from a sensory nerve ending, or from an adjacent neuron. Nerve impulses travel in one direction along the neuron.

*Synapse*

*Cell body*

**Association neuron**

*Dendrite is a filament that carries signals to cell body.*

*Cell body*

*Axon of sensory neuron*

**Motor neuron**

*Axon of motor neuron*

**Sensory neuron**

*Neuromuscular junction*

*Direction of nerve impulse*

*Touch sensor in skin*

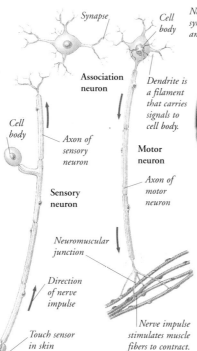

*Neuromuscular junction is a synapse between motor neuron and muscle fiber.*

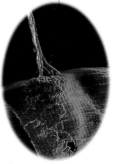

*Nerve impulse stimulates muscle fibers to contract.*

### Synapses
A synapse is a junction between two neurons. At a synapse, neurons do not touch. Instead, there is a tiny gap. When a nerve impulse reaches a synapse, it triggers the release of chemicals, which travel across the gap and stimulate the second neuron to generate a nerve impulse.

### Reflex actions
If you touch something sharp, you automatically pull your hand away without thinking about it. This is a reflex action. A sensory neuron carries impulses to the spinal cord, where an association neuron transmits impulses to a motor neuron, and the arm muscle contracts.

*Receptors in hand detect the prick of a pin and send signal to spinal cord.*

*Brain*

*Sensory receptors*

*Motor neuron*

*Muscle*

*Sensory neuron*

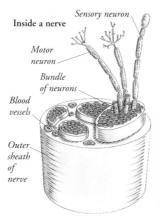

### Santiago Ramón y Cajal
Spanish anatomist Santiago Ramón y Cajal (1852–1934) pioneered the study of the cells that make up the brain and nerves. He developed methods for staining nerve cells so they could be seen clearly under the microscope. His work revolutionized the examination of brain tissue.

# The brain

The brain is the body's control center. Your brain enables you to think and to have a personality, and also regulates all your body processes. It has three main regions: the forebrain, the cerebellum, and the brain stem. The forebrain consists of the cerebrum (which is made up of two halves or hemispheres), the thalamus, hypothalamus, and the limbic system, which controls emotions and instinctive behavior.

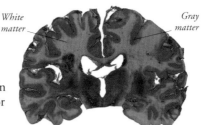

*White matter*

*Gray matter*

Section through brain tissue

## Gray and white matter

Each cerebral hemisphere has two layers. The outer layer, the cerebral cortex, consists of gray matter containing cell bodies of neurons that form a communication network. The inner layer, or white matter, consists of nerve fibers that link the cerebral cortex to the other parts of the brain.

B

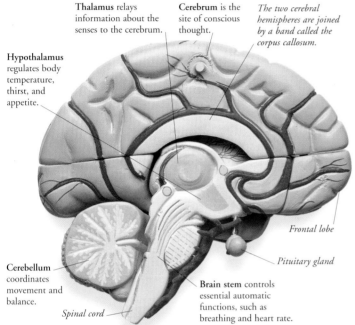

**Thalamus** relays information about the senses to the cerebrum.

**Cerebrum** is the site of conscious thought.

*The two cerebral hemispheres are joined by a band called the corpus callosum.*

**Hypothalamus** regulates body temperature, thirst, and appetite.

**Cerebellum** coordinates movement and balance.

*Spinal cord*

*Frontal lobe*

*Pituitary gland*

**Brain stem** controls essential automatic functions, such as breathing and heart rate.

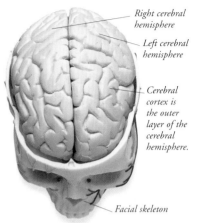

*Right cerebral hemisphere*

*Left cerebral hemisphere*

*Cerebral cortex is the outer layer of the cerebral hemisphere.*

*Facial skeleton*

## Left and right brains

The left cerebral hemisphere controls the right side of the body, and the right cerebral hemisphere controls the left side of the body. Although both hemispheres are used for almost every activity, each hemisphere has its own special skills. In most people, the left hemisphere is involved in spoken and written language, mathematical ability, and reasoning, while the right hemisphere controls the appreciation of art and music, insight and imagination, and shape recognition.

## Brain cells

The brain consists of hundreds of billions of nerve cells. Many of these are association neurons that are constantly receiving and transmitting nerve impulses. Any one of these neurons can have links to over 1,000 other neurons, producing a complex network. The brain also contains other nerve cells, called glial cells, which hold the neurons in place.

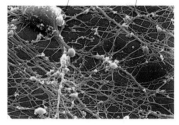

*Association neuron in brain*

*Glial cell*

## Brain areas

Certain areas of the cerebrum are involved with particular body functions. These areas can be highlighted on a brain map. Motor areas of the brain, such as the speech and basic movement areas, send out instructions to control voluntary movement. Sensory areas, such as the hearing, taste, smell, touch, and vision areas, receive information from sensory receptors around the body. Association areas, such as the frontal lobe, deal with thoughts, personality, and emotions, analyse experiences, and give you consciousness and awareness.

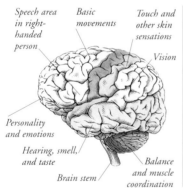

*Speech area in right-handed person*

*Basic movements*

*Touch and other skin sensations*

*Vision*

*Personality and emotions*

*Hearing, smell, and taste*

*Balance and muscle coordination*

*Brain stem*

# Brain waves

The brain's neurons are constantly sending out and receiving nerve impulses. This process produces electrical signals that can be detected using a machine called an electroencephalograph (EEG). Electrodes linked to the EEG can be attached to a person's scalp in order to record the brain's electrical activities as a series of patterns called brain waves.

## Sleep and dreams

As you sleep, you move repeatedly between phases of light REM (rapid eye movement) sleep and phases of deeper NREM sleep. These shifts can be detected using an EEG.

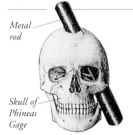

*Metal rod*

*Skull of Phineas Gage*

## Personality

The frontal lobe of the brain plays a major role in deciding personality. The case of an American worker, Phineas Gage, proved it. In 1848, an accident sent a metal rod through Gage's cheek and frontal lobe. He survived, but his personality changed from being friendly to being aggressive.

# Spinal cord

The spinal cord relays information between the brain and the rest of the body and is involved in many reflex actions. It is a flattened cylinder of nervous tissue, about 17 in (43 cm) long and as thick as a finger. It runs from the base of the brain to the lower back, surrounded by the backbone.

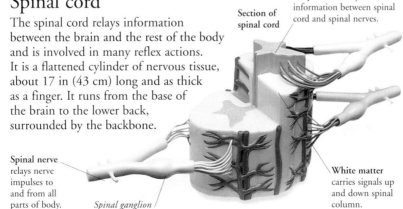

*Section of spinal cord*

**Gray matter** relays information between spinal cord and spinal nerves.

**Spinal nerve** relays nerve impulses to and from all parts of body.

*Spinal ganglion*

**White matter** carries signals up and down spinal column.

## Pierre Paul Broca

French anatomist and surgeon Pierre Paul Broca (1824–80) demonstrated that a specific region of the brain controlled a particular body function. Broca found that a small area coordinated the muscles in the mouth and throat that produce speech. This area is now called Broca's area, or the speech area. Broca made his discovery when treating a patient who could not talk after damage to part of his brain.

FIND OUT MORE    CELLS    EYES AND VISION    HORMONES AND ENDOCRINE SYSTEM    HUMAN BODY    MUSCLES AND MOVEMENT    SKIN, HAIR, AND NAILS    SMELL AND TASTE

# BRAZIL

THE LARGEST COUNTRY in South America, Brazil is a land of opposites. Watered by the second longest river in the world, the Amazon, it has the world's largest rain forest, arid desert in the northeast, and rolling grassland in the south. Crowded cities contrast with remote areas that have never been explored. The country has many well-developed industries and a huge, successful agricultural base, but many people live in poverty. Brazilian society is a vibrant, diverse mix of cultures.

## Physical features

The Amazon Basin and its forests, some mountainous, occupy northern Brazil. The southeast is a region of plateaus that vary from sunburned arid scrublands to rich fields and pastures.

### BRAZIL FACTS

**CAPITAL CITY** Brasília

**AREA** 3,286,472 sq miles (8,511,970 sq km)

**POPULATION** 170,000,000

**MAIN LANGUAGE** Portuguese

**MAJOR RELIGION** Christian

**CURRENCY** Réal

**LIFE EXPECTANCY** 68 years

**PEOPLE PER DOCTOR** 769

**GOVERNMENT** Multiparty democracy

**ADULT LITERACY** 85%

### Highlands

The Brazilian Highlands extend from the Amazon Basin to the coast, rising to 10,000 ft (3,000 m). About 60 percent of the country is dominated by the plateau, where landscape ranges from tropical forest to dry, rocky desert.

### Amazon rain forest

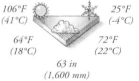

More than half of Brazil is cloaked in dense rain forest. The Amazon River, 4,007 miles (6,448 km) long, runs through the north of Brazil, giving life to more than 40,000 different species of plants and animals in the forests.

106°F (41°C)   25°F (-4°C)
64°F (18°C)   72°F (22°C)
63 in (1,600 mm)

### Climate

All except the extreme south of Brazil lies in the tropics, so temperatures are always high. The Amazon rain forest receives about 157 in (4,000 mm) of rain every year. By contrast, droughts are common in the northeastern corner. Farther south, summers are hot and winters can be cold with frosts.

## Brasília

Brazil's modern capital city, Brasília, lies on the extreme northern edge of the plateau region. Planned in the 1950s on the site of a felled rain forest, the city replaced Rio de Janeiro as the capital. Its inland location has helped develop new areas away from the coast. There are many imaginative, futuristic buildings, including the spectacular cathedral.

**Brasília Cathedral**

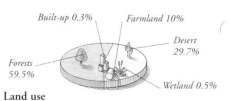

Built-up 0.3%   Farmland 10%
Desert 29.7%
Forests 59.5%
Wetland 0.5%

### Land use

Thick forests cover the majority of the land, but are being cleared at an alarming rate to make way for farmland and roads. The fertile southeast, especially around São Paulo, is permanently farmed. Much of the land is desert.

# People

The Brazilian people have a diverse ethnic background. There are large groups of Africans, Europeans, and Asians and the original inhabitants of Brazil form only a tiny percentage of the population. Many families are tight knit, fiercely loyal, and strictly Roman Catholic. The majority live in towns clustered along the southeastern coast.

**52 per sq mile (20 per sq km)**

**81% Urban** **19% Rural**

**Indian groups**
Some native Brazilians still live in the rain forests, following traditional ways of life. However, about 14 groups now shelter in Xingu National Park, set up when their forest home was destroyed.

# Leisure

The mainly Roman Catholic people of Brazil celebrate many religious festivals, such as the Rio and Bahía carnivals. Sports, including soccer, basketball, and water sports along the coast, are the chief leisure activities for millions of Brazilians. The samba, one of the world's most popular dances, originated in Brazil.

**Rio Carnival**
Known as one of the world's largest and most spectacular festivals, the Rio Carnival, in Rio de Janeiro, is held just before Lent every year. During the carnival, processions of brightly decorated floats and a myriad of colorful singers, musicians, and dancers with imaginative costumes, fill the streets.

**Soccer**
Many Brazilians have a passion for soccer, either as players or spectators. The national team has won the World Cup more times than any other team. Its star player, Edson Arantes do Nascimento, known as Pelé, was the world's leading player in the 1960s and is regarded by fans as a living legend.

# Farming

Brazil has immense natural resources. About 22 percent of the labor force works on the land, growing all Brazil's own food, with a vast surplus for export. The best farmland is around Rio de Janeiro and São Paulo, where water is plentiful and the climate is frost free. About 150 million cattle are raised on large ranches in this region.

**Cattle ranch, São Paulo**

**Orange**

**Coffee leaves and berries**

**Soybeans**
*Each berry contains two beans, which are washed, dried, and roasted.*

**Meat production**
Brazil is one of the world's largest producers of beef and veal. Cows graze on the rich green pastures of central Brazil. Large areas of tropical rain forest are cleared to create new cattle ranches, but the soil is soon exhausted and more forest has to be felled.

**Bananas**

**Crops**
Brazil is a leading producer of cocoa beans, coffee, oranges, and sugarcane, and one of the largest growers of soybeans and bananas. About 22 percent of the world's coffee comes from Brazil, and millions of oranges are picked every year. These crops grow successfully in the warm, fertile soil of central and southern Brazil.

# Forest products

The plants and trees of the Amazon rain forest have long been used for food, housing, and medicine by the people who live there. Some of the products, such as rubber and Brazil nuts, are now known worldwide. Other lesser-known plants are quinine, taken from the bark of chinchona and used to treat malaria; ipecac, an ingredient of cough medicine; and curare, once an arrow poison, now a life-saving muscle relaxant used in operations.

**Brazil nuts**

# Transportation

A vast network links Brazil's main centers, but only nine percent of the 1,031,693 miles (1,660,352 km) of roads are paved. Brazil has one of the world's largest national air networks. Cities with rapid growth, such as São Paulo, are expanding their subways.

# Industry

The manufacturing industry employs about 15 percent of the Brazilian workforce. Machinery, textiles, cars, food products, industrial chemicals, and footwear are the main export products. Brazil has large mining, oil, and steel industries, but has suffered high inflation.

**Mining**
Brazil is a leading producer of gold, manganese, and tin ore. The country is noted for its precious stones, such as amethysts, diamonds, and topaz, but the quest for mineral wealth has led to much forest destruction.

**Steel**
South America's top steel maker, Brazil ranks highly in world production. This, and cheap labor, has attracted many carmakers to invest in the country.

**"Green" cars**
About one-third of all Brazil's cars are run on so-called "green gas," or ethanol, which is made from fermented sugarcane. Because it produces less carbon monoxide than gas when it is burned, it is less harmful to the environment and is reducing pollution.

---

**FIND OUT MORE** CHRISTIANITY · CRYSTALS AND GEMS · FARMING · FESTIVALS · FORESTS · NATIVE AMERICANS · RIVERS · ROCKS AND MINERALS · SOCCER · SOUTH AMERICA, HISTORY OF

# BRIDGES

CURVING MAJESTICALLY across rivers and valleys, bridges are some of the most spectacular structures engineers have ever created. They are also some of the most useful, because bridges can speed up journeys by cutting out ferry crossings, long detours, steep hills, and busy junctions. The first bridges were probably tree trunks laid across streams. Wooden beam bridges and stone or brick arches were the main types of bridge from Roman times until the 18th century, when iron became available to engineers. Most modern bridges are made of steel and concrete, making them both strong and flexible.

## Types of bridges

On a trip, you may see many different shapes and sizes of bridge, but there are really only a few main types: arch bridges, beam bridges, cantilever bridges, suspension bridges, and cable-stay bridges. The type of bridge used depends on the size of the gap it must span, the landscape, and traffic that will cross it.

### Arch bridge

The arch is used to build bridges because it is a strong shape that can bear a lot of weight. To bridge a wide gap, several arches of stone or brick are linked together.

### Beam bridge

In a beam bridge, the central span (or beam) is supported at both ends. Very long beams are impractical, because they would be liable to collapse under their own weight.

### Cantilever bridge

A beam fixed at one end and stretching out over a gap is a cantilever. Balanced cantilever bridges have several supports, each with two beams that reach out from either side.

### Suspension bridge

The deck of a suspension bridge hangs from cables slung over towers and anchored to the ground at each end of the bridge. Such bridges have spans of up to 0.62 mile (1 km).

## Building a bridge

A cable-stay bridge is a type of suspension bridge with a deck hung from slanting cables that are fixed to pylons instead of the ground. Once the pylons are in place, the bridge is built outward in both directions from each pylon. This ensures that the forces on the pylons balance, so that there is no danger of the pylons collapsing.

*Pylon*
1 The foundations are laid, and the two pylons are erected. The concrete side spans, which will link the bridge to the shore, are assembled. *Side span*

2 The deck sections are hung from cables attached to the pylons, and the bridge begins to stretch across the river from each shore. *Cables*

3 The central deck spans are lifted by crane off river barges, welded into place, and attached to cables. *Crane*

4 When the last deck section is in place, the bridge is complete. The cables transfer the weight of the deck to the pylons.

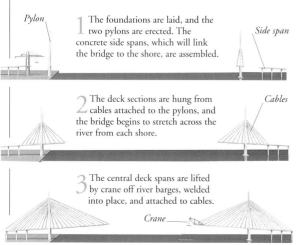

*23 pairs of cables attach to either side of pylon.*
*Model of the Pont de Normandie*
*Bridge carries 4 lanes of traffic.*
*Pylon of reinforced concrete*
*Deck is 170 ft (52 m) above water.*
*Piers support side spans.*
*Steel cables are coated in plastic to prevent rusting.*
*Foundations of pylons extend 164–197 ft (50–60 m) below ground.*

### Isambard Kingdom Brunel

English engineer Isambard Kingdom Brunel (1806–59) was a genius of bridge design. Brunel designed and built two of the earliest suspension bridges. He also planned and built railroads and several huge steamships.

## Aqueducts
Not all bridges carry roads or railroad tracks. An aqueduct is a bridge that carries water. The Romans built aqueducts to supply water to the baths and drinking fountains in their cities. More recent aqueducts carry canals over steep-sided valleys in order to keep the canal level. This avoids having to build long flights of locks.

**Aqueduct on the River Dee, Wales**

## Timeline
**200 BC** Roman engineers build arch bridges of stone or wood, and aqueducts.

**1779** The first bridge made of cast iron is built at Ironbridge, England.

**1883** In the US, New York's Brooklyn Bridge is the first bridge to be supported by steel suspension cables.

**1930** Switzerland's Salginatobel Bridge is constructed of reinforced concrete (concrete strengthened with steel).

**Sydney Harbour Bridge, Australia**

**1932** Australia's Sydney Harbour Bridge opens, carrying a road and rail tracks suspended from a huge steel arch.

**1998** The Akashi Kaikyo suspension bridge over Japan's Akashi Strait has the longest main span in the world.

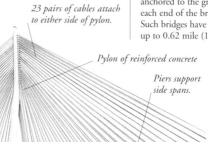

**FIND OUT MORE**  BUILDING AND CONSTRUCTION • IRON AND STEEL • RIVERS • ROADS • ROMAN EMPIRE • SHIPS AND BOATS • TRAINS AND RAILROADS • TRANSPORT, HISTORY OF • TUNNELS

# BRONTË SISTERS

THREE OF THE FINEST writers of the 19th century, Charlotte, Anne, and Emily Brontë, were brought up in solitude in a small town in northern England. In spite of many difficulties, including being far away from the world of publishing in London, they produced some of the most popular novels of the period. The books portrayed characters with a new frankness and showed how difficult life could be for women of that time. Their stories still enthrall readers of today.

## Haworth parsonage

The Brontë sisters were brought up in the small town of Haworth in Yorkshire, northern England. Their father was the curate (priest) at the local church, so they lived at the parsonage (clergyman's house). It was a grim stone building with a view over the graveyard.

**The Brontë family**
Charlotte, Emily, and Anne lived with their father, Patrick Brontë and their brother, Branwell. Their mother, Maria, died when the children were young and two other children died in infancy, so the sisters were brought up by their aunt. They had a lonely life. They mixed little with other children and had to make their own entertainment.

## Education

Charlotte and Emily were sent away to Cowan Bridge school. The conditions were poor and made Charlotte ill. Lowood school, in *Jane Eyre*, is based on her time there. All three sisters later worked as teachers, or governesses – one of the few jobs then open to educated young women.

*Cowan Bridge school*

*Manuscripts are still preserved at Haworth parsonage*

*Poetry manuscript by Charlotte Brontë at around the age of 14*

**Manuscripts and illustrations** completed by the Brontë sisters in their teenage years

## The novelists

In 1846, the Brontës started to get their works published. They began with a volume of poems, but only two copies were sold. In the following two years Emily's *Wuthering Heights*, Charlotte's *Jane Eyre*, and Anne's *Agnes Grey* were published. At the time it was not thought proper for the daughters of clergymen to write fiction, so the sisters used false names, or pseudonyms, to keep their identities secret. Lots of people bought the books and wanted to find out about the authors.

### The Bell brothers
The Brontë sisters published their books under three male names – Acton, Currer, and Ellis Bell, the initials of which matched those of the sisters' own names. To begin with, even their publishers did not know who the "Bell brothers" really were.

WUTHERING HEIGHTS

A NOVEL.

BY

ELLIS BELL.

IN THREE VOLUMES.

VOL. II.

LONDON:
THOMAS CAUTLEY NEWBY, PUBLISHER,
72, MORTIMER St., CAVENDISH Sq.
1847.

**Jane Eyre**
Charlotte Brontë's first novel tells the story of Jane Eyre and her struggle to be an independent woman in a hostile society. Working as a governess, she falls in love with her employer, Mr Rochester, only to discover terrible secrets in his past. The novel was considered radical in its time.

**Wuthering Heights**
Emily Brontë's novel follows a series of tragic relationships across the generations and is especially famous for its depiction of Catherine and Heathcliff. Set against the background of the Yorkshire countryside, the novel deals with issues of social change and industrialization.

## Angria and Gondal

To amuse themselves in the bleak moorland rectory, the Brontë children invented two imaginary lands, called Angria and Gondal. They wrote many stories and poems about these lands, which were peopled with heroes and heroines who lived exciting and tragic lives.

### CHARLOTTE BRONTË

| | |
|---|---|
| **1816** | Born Yorkshire, England. |
| **1822–32** | Educated at Cowan Bridge School and Miss Wooler's School, Roe Head, Yorkshire. |
| **1846** | Publishes her poems. |
| **1847** | Publishes *Jane Eyre*. |
| **1849** | Publishes *Shirley*. |
| **1853** | Publishes *Villette*. |
| **1854** | Marries Arthur Nicholls. |
| **1855** | Dies. |

FIND OUT MORE    BOOKS    CHRISTIANITY    DICKENS, CHARLES    FILM AND FILMMAKING    LITERATURE    UNITED KINGDOM, HISTORY OF    WRITING

# BRONZE AGE

IN ABOUT 3000 BC, prehistoric people began to use bronze – an alloy of copper and tin – instead of stone, to make tools, weapons, and ornaments. The dates for this development, which is known as the Bronze Age, vary from culture to culture, but the earliest bronze workers probably lived in Mesopotamia (modern Iraq). These people initially used pure gold and copper, which was easy to hammer into shape, before discovering how to make bronze. They were also responsible for developing the world's first civilizations. The Bronze Age was followed by a time when people learned to smelt and shape iron ore to produce stronger tools and weapons. This period is known as the Iron Age.

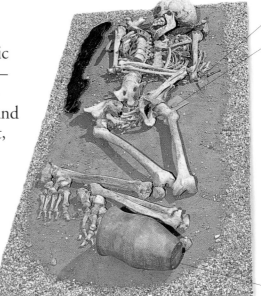

*Stone wristguard with gold screws*

*Copper dagger blade*

*Pottery beaker for use in the afterlife*

The Barnack grave, c.1800 BC

## The first metalworkers

In the early days of the Bronze Age, metalworkers used gold, copper, and bronze for luxury items or for high-status weapons, such as the dagger in the Barnack grave, England. People still made tools from stone, because stone was harder than bronze.

*Prongs for lifting meat from a cauldron*

Flesh hook

## Making bronze

People learned how to extract metal from ores by heating the rock. The metal could then be used to make useful or decorative objects.

### Ore

This common type of copper ore was fairly easy for people to spot on the ground.

*Yellow chalcopyrite*

*Blue bornite*

### Smelting

To extract the metal, Bronze Age people heated the ore to a high temperature. When the metal in the ore reached the melting point, they collected it in a round, stone crucible.

## Casting

Bronze Age people cast objects by pouring hot, molten bronze into a mold. When the metal had cooled and set, the mold was opened, revealing the finished item. Casting was used to produce decorative items.

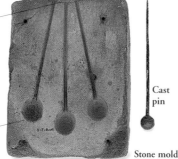

*Molten metal was poured through holes.*

*The mold was carved to the shape of the item.*

Cast pin

Stone mold

### Mold

This is one half of a stone mold for casting pins. It was made in Switzerland in c.1000 BC. To use the mold, the two halves were fastened together and metal poured in through the holes at the top.

### Cast pin

Bronze pins like this were cast in the stone mold. The mold used to make this pin was carved to create the delicate pattern on the pinhead.

## Copper

The royal family of the city of Ur in Mesopotamia used copper for jewelry, as well as for everyday items, such as this flesh hook. They used gold to make beautiful vessels for special occasions.

**Bronze swords** were sometimes cast, although they were stronger when the bronze was beaten into shape. This Danish sword is polished to show the original golden color of bronze.

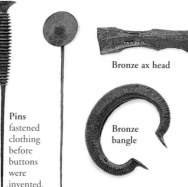

Ornate French sword

Bronze ax head

Danish bronze sword

**Pins** fastened clothing before buttons were invented.

Bronze bangle

Bronze pendant

### Bronzeware

Bronze was prized for its beauty. In Europe, the nobles liked to wear bronze jewelry, such as bangles and pendants, and bronze pins in their clothing. Bronze swords were high-status weapons.

### Ingots

Early metalworkers discovered how to add molten tin to copper to make bronze. Liquid bronze was poured into round molds and left to set. The blocks of bronze were called ingots.

*Trace of an ingot*

## Timeline

**3800 BC** The earliest known metal objects are produced by smelting. Copper is the main metal smelted in Tepe Yahya, Iran.

**3000 BC** Bronze objects are used throughout western Asia, where copper is being combined with tin.

**2500 BC** Bronze is used in the cities of Mohenjo-Daro and Harappa, Indus Valley.

**2000 BC** Bronze-working comes to the civilizations of the Minoans on Crete and the Myceneans in mainland Greece. These Aegean cultures trade in Europe for copper and tin.

**1900 BC** Iron Age starts in western Asian areas, such as Turkey, Iran, and Iraq.

**1800 BC** Bronze Age reaches European areas, such as modern Slovakia.

**800 BC** Early Iron Age starts in central Europe.

**Shaft-tube ax, Hungary**

**FIND OUT MORE**   GREECE, ANCIENT   INDUS VALLEY CIVILIZATION   METALS   MINOANS   POTTERY AND CERAMICS   STONE AGE   SUMERIANS

# BUDDHA

BUDDHISM IS A WORLD faith that has changed the lives of millions of people. It began in Sakya, a small kingdom in northeast India. The founder of Buddhism was a prince, named Siddhartha Gautama, but today he is known simply as the Buddha, a title meaning "the enlightened one." When he was a young man, Siddhartha began a search for an understanding of suffering. By the end of his life, he had become the Buddha, founded the Buddhist faith and already had many followers.

*Siddhartha, later called the Buddha*

*Maya, mother of the Buddha*

### Early life
According to tradition, Siddhartha was born while his mother, Maya, was on her way to visit her parents. She died soon afterward. His father was told that the boy would become either a great ruler or a Buddha. The king was afraid that Siddhartha would leave the court to become a holy beggar, so confined him to the palace grounds. But eventually he left to search for the true meaning of suffering.

*The Buddha meditating*

*Buddha sat under a holy fig or bo tree*

## Enlightenment
When Siddhartha left the palace, the suffering he saw around him made him decide to become a holy man. He spent six years depriving himself of food and sleep, and learning about spiritual matters. Eventually he realized that this ascetic lifestyle made him too weak for deep reflection, so he meditated under a tree. Here he made the breakthrough understanding of the truth known as enlightenment.

*Mara, the demon*

*Buddha*

### Temptations
While Siddhartha was meditating, a demon named Mara sent his beautiful daughters to tempt him from his chosen path. Mara also whipped up a storm and hurled thunderbolts at Siddhartha. But the young man continued to meditate, unmoved. He meditated for a whole night before understanding the truth, which he called *dharma*, and reaching peace, or *nirvana*, in his heart.

## Teaching
After experiencing enlightenment, the Buddha set out to teach others what he had learned. Many were converted, and the Buddha sent them off as wandering missionaries. Later, the Buddha returned to his father's court to teach his own people what he had learned. His father was among the first to be converted.

*Buddha*

*King Bimbisara*

### Sarnath
At Sarnath, near Varanasi, the Buddha preached his first sermon to five men who had previously sought enlightenment with him. He taught them that suffering is caused by desire, and to end suffering they must give up desire. Sarnath became the site of one of the greatest Buddhist shrines.

### Bimbisara
Even during his own lifetime, the Buddha commanded so much respect that many people left their homes to follow him and form orders of monks and nuns. When King Bimbisara gave the Buddha a generous gift of land – "the gift of the bamboo grove" – Buddha's followers built the first Buddhist monastery there.

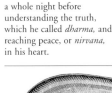

*Death of Buddha*

*Pilgrim*

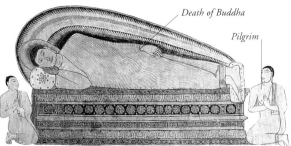

## Later life
When the Buddha was 80 years old, he ate some food that had been accidentally poisoned, and died at Kusinagara in India among his disciples. Many people came to pay homage to him. His body was cremated, and the remaining bones were placed under stone mounds that have since became holy places of pilgrimage for Buddhists.

### THE BUDDHA

Earliest records of Buddha's life were written more than 200 years after he died, so details are hard to verify. The following dates are accepted by most authorities.

**563 BC** Siddhartha Gautama, son of King Suddhodana of the Sakya, born in northeastern India.

**533 BC** Siddhartha leaves his father's court to become a holy man.

**527 BC** Siddhartha attains enlightenment, and becomes the Buddha.

**483 BC** Buddha dies at Kusinagara, in Oudh, India.

**FIND OUT MORE**    BUDDHISM    CHINA AND TAIWAN    INDIA, HISTORY OF    MAURYAN EMPIRE    MONASTERIES    SHRINES

# BUDDHISM

THE BUDDHIST FAITH was founded by an Indian nobleman named Gautama Siddhartha in the 6th century BC. Gautama, who became known as the Buddha, or the "Enlightened One," told people how to achieve fulfillment. He taught that fulfillment is reached by meditation, wisdom, and correct behavior in all aspects of life. Buddhists also believe in reincarnation, in other words that a person can be reborn after death. The Buddha is revered by his followers, but not worshiped as a god. For this reason, Buddhism exists side-by-side with other religions in many countries. There are about 320 million Buddhists worldwide, although the majority live in Asia.

## Rites and ceremonies

Ceremonies at Buddhist temples are usually simple. They involve reciting extracts from Buddhist scriptures and making offerings to the Buddha. A monk may give a sermon. Some Buddhist rituals also involve candlelit processions and music-making. The Buddhist year is enlivened with festivals, most of which take place at full Moon. The most famous festival is Wesak, at New Year, which celebrates the birth, enlightenment, and death of the Buddha.

**Hand gestures on a statue of the Buddha**

*The Buddha touches earth as witness to his worthiness for Buddhahood.*

*This gesture shows the Buddha actively turning the wheel of law.*

*The Buddha reassures an approaching person.*

## The Buddha

Statues of the Buddha are kept in temples and homes to inspire Buddhists to live as he did. Buddhists bow before the statues to show their respect. They also carry out the ceremony called "Going for refuge," in which they recite texts that show their dedication to the Buddha, to his teaching (the Dharma), and to the community of Buddhists (the Sangha).

## Teachings

The Buddha taught the Four Noble Truths, which explain the Buddhist attitude toward suffering and how fulfillment can be achieved. The Truths say that suffering is always present in the world; that the human search for pleasure is the source of suffering; that it is possible to be free from these desires by achieving a state called nirvana; and that the way to nirvana is through the Eightfold Path.

*Wheel of law*

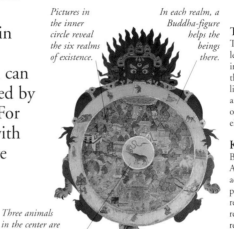

*Pictures in the inner circle reveal the six realms of existence.*

*In each realm, a Buddha-figure helps the beings there.*

*Three animals in the center are symbols of ignorance.*

**Wheel of Life**

### The Eightfold Path
The Path teaches that the way Buddhists lead their lives should be correct in eight important aspects: understanding, thought, speech, action, means of livelihood (work), effort, recollection, and meditation. The eight-spoked wheel of law shown above represents each of the eight stages of the Path.

### Karma
Buddhists believe in the law of karma. According to this law, good and bad actions result in fitting rewards and punishments, both in this life and in later rebirths. The Wheel of Life is a symbol of rebirth. When people die, they are reborn into one of its six realms of existence.

### Offerings
Buddhists regularly make offerings to the Buddha, such as flowers and food. Burning incense or candles and scattering petals around the Buddha's statue are ways of making an offering that also beautifies the temple. The light of the candles is the light of the Buddha's great wisdom, and the smoke from incense wafts the truth of the doctrine toward the devotees.

*The Buddha's topknot is a sign of his princely wisdom.*

*His face has the serene expression of meditation.*

*Long earlobes symbolize his nobility.*

*Eyes cast down show that he is meditating.*

*Colored sash is changed for each season.*

**Candles**

**Incense**

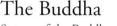
**Lotus flowers**

### Meditation
Buddhists meditate in order to purify their minds and free themselves from thoughts about material things. In this way they hope to achieve "perfect mindfulness," one of the stages in the Eightfold Path. One way in which they meditate is to concentrate on feeling their breath going in and out. Concentration empties the mind of selfish thoughts – the person becomes calmer and the mind clearer.

*Buddha's cross-legged position is called the lotus position.*

B

# Branches of Buddhism

From its beginnings in India, Buddhism spread around eastern and Southeast Asia, where the majority of the world's Buddhists still live. There are also Buddhist communities in other parts of Asia, and in the West. Buddhism has two main strands – Mahayana and Theravada – but other forms of Buddhism with distinctive features have also developed.

### Theravada

This branch of Buddhism is closest to the teachings of the Buddha himself. It is dominant in Southeast Asia (Myanmar, Cambodia, Laos, Sri Lanka, and Thailand). Theravada Buddhists revere the Buddha and do not worship other figures. They aim to become "perfected saints" by following the Eightfold Path and tend to believe that people can reach the state of nirvana only through their own efforts.

### Mahayana

This form of Buddhism prevails in China, Korea, Japan, Mongolia, Nepal, and Tibet. A follower's first goal is to become a bodhisattva, an enlightened being who does not pass into nirvana but remains in this world in order to help others to enlightenment. Mahayana Buddhists therefore place a high value on charity.

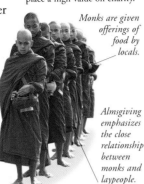

*Monks are given offerings of food by locals.*

*Almsgiving emphasizes the close relationship between monks and laypeople.*

**Chinese bodhisattva head**

### Zen

This form of Buddhism originated in China and spread to Japan in about the 13th century. Zen Buddhists aim to lead a simple life, close to nature, using everyday actions as a means of meditation. Zen Buddhists meditate in a way that tries to see beyond logical patterns of thought and preconceived ideas.

### Tibetan Buddhism

A form of Mahayana Buddhism is found in Tibet. Here, special value is placed on the Buddhist virtues of meditation and wisdom. Tibetan Buddhists have their own rituals, such as repeating sacred sayings, or mantras. Since the Chinese invasion of Tibet in the 1950s, few Buddhist monasteries remain in Tibet.

**Mantra**

*Inside a prayer wheel is a mantra that the monk repeats while spinning the wheel.*

*A Zen monk tidies a garden.*

---

# Monasticism

Buddhist monasteries began when the Buddha's followers built permanent settlements to live in together during the rainy season. Today there are many monks (and some nuns) who devote themselves to explaining the Buddha's teachings and setting an example by the way they lead their lives.

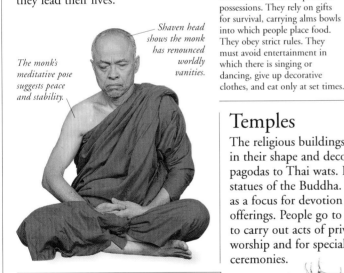

*The monk's meditative pose suggests peace and stability.*

*Shaven head shows the monk has renounced worldly vanities.*

**Sharpening stone**

*Alms bowl lid is also used as a plate.*

**Needle and thread**  **Razor**  **Water strainer**

**Alms bowl lid**

### Living as a monk

Monks live apart from their families and have few personal possessions. They rely on gifts for survival, carrying alms bowls into which people place food. They obey strict rules. They must avoid entertainment in which there is singing or dancing, give up decorative clothes, and eat only at set times.

**Alms bowl**     **Belt or girdle**

# Sacred texts

Buddhism has sacred texts made up of sayings and sermons, many of them attributed to the Buddha. One of the most important books of writings is the Dharmapada, which forms part of the Pali Canon, the oldest collection of Buddhist scriptures.

*In Tibetan-style libraries, manuscripts are wrapped in cloth and placed between boards.*

**Library in Shey Monastery, Ladakh, India**

# Temples

The religious buildings of Buddhism vary widely in their shape and decoration, from Japanese pagodas to Thai wats. But all contain statues of the Buddha. The statues act as a focus for devotion and for offerings. People go to the temples to carry out acts of private worship and for special ceremonies.

*Wat Benchamabophit, in Thailand's capital, Bangkok, is known as the marble temple.*

*Stepped roofs symbolize stages of spiritual development.*

*Devotees gather with their offerings on the grounds of the temple.*

## The Dalai Lama

The Dalai Lama is the spiritual and political leader of Buddhists in Tibet, who believe that each Dalai Lama is a reincarnation of the previous one. The present Dalai Lama, Tenzin Gyatso, was born in 1935. In exile since 1959 following the Chinese takeover, he is still Tibet's most important leader.

 FIND OUT MORE    ASIA, HISTORY OF    BUDDHA    CHINA, HISTORY OF    FESTIVALS    MAURYAN EMPIRE    RELIGIONS    SHRINES    SIGNS AND SYMBOLS    THAILAND AND MYANMAR

# BUFFALO AND OTHER WILD CATTLE

THE FIVE SPECIES OF BUFFALO, and all other cattle, are members of the family Bovidae. They have split, or cloven, hooves, and both sexes have horns. Wild cattle use their horns for defense against predators, and also live in herds for protection. Only the anoas are solitary animals. Cattle were among the earliest animals to be domesticated. The Asiatic buffalo, yak, banteng, and gaur are examples of cattle that have been domesticated. The loss of habitat, hunting, and disease has drastically reduced the world's wild cattle. Nine of the eleven species are in danger of extinction.

*Broad hooves support the weight of the buffalo.*

## Bison

Plains bison

Often incorrectly called buffalo, there are two species of bison. The American bison is a grassland animal which appears in two forms – the plains bison and the woods bison. The European bison, or wisent, is a forest dweller. Bison are massive animals standing more than 5 ft (1.5 m) tall and weighing more than a ton (910 kg).

**American bison**
The head, neck, and forequarters of the American bison are covered with long hair, which, with the large hump, makes the forequarters appear much bigger than the hindquarters. The horns are short and curved, and are grown by both sexes.

**European bison**
The wisent lives in Poland's Bialowieza Forest. It is taller than the American bison, has a longer, less barrellike body, and longer legs. Its hindquarters are also more powerfully built.

## African buffalo

The buffalo is the only species of wild cattle found in Africa. Cape buffalo bulls are up to 5 ft (1.5 m) at the shoulder and weigh more than 1,800 lb (816 kg). Their horns have a span of up to 5 ft (1.5 m) and form a massive helmet, or boss, across the head. A smaller subspecies, the forest buffalo, lives in equatorial forests.

**Asiatic buffalo**
There are four species of Asiatic buffalo – the water buffalo (shown here), the lowland and mountain anoa, and the tamarau. The water buffalo lives in both domestic and wild herds, although only a few wild herds survive. Its horns are semicircular and sweep outward and backward.

**Endangered tamarau**
Confined to the highlands on the island of Mindoro in the Philippines, this dwarf buffalo has been relentlessly hunted. Only about 100 survive today.

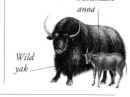

**Largest and smallest**
Wild cattle range in size from the wild yak, which is more than 6.5 ft (2 m) high at the shoulder, to the mountain anoa, which is no more than 30 in (76 cm) high.

*Mountain anoa*

*Wild yak*

## Oxen

The group of wild cattle commonly called oxen contains four species – the yak, the banteng, the gaur, and the kouprey. Domestic cattle also belong to this group. Most breeds of domestic cattle are descended from the now-extinct aurochs, which at one time inhabited the plains and woodlands of Europe and Asia in great numbers.

**Yak**
Largest of the wild cattle, the wild yak lives in herds high up on the Tibetan Plateau in Central Asia. Yaks have long, shaggy black hair reaching almost to the ground, with a thick undercoat that protects them against the bitterly cold climate.

**Banteng**
Found in Southeast Asia, Java, and Borneo, the banteng is a shy animal. Females and young are a brick-red color; adult males are black.

### CAPE BUFFALO

| | |
|---|---|
| **SCIENTIFIC NAME** | *Syncerus caffer* |
| **ORDER** | Artiodactyla |
| **FAMILY** | Bovidae |
| **DISTRIBUTION** | Africa, south of the Sahara |
| **HABITAT** | Grassland and woodland savannas, but seldom far from water |
| **DIET** | Mainly grass, occasionally supplemented with foliage |
| **SIZE** | 5 ft (1.5 m) at the shoulder |
| **LIFESPAN** | About 20 years |

**FIND OUT MORE**    DEER AND ANTELOPE    FARMING    NORTH AMERICAN WILDLIFE    SHEEP AND GOATS

# BUGS

THE WORD BUG is often used to describe any crawling insect or a disease-causing germ. The true bugs are a group of insects that have long feeding tubes specially adapted for sucking fluids out of plants and animals. Bugs, such as shield bugs, are often brightly colored, and, as a group, they are remarkably varied in shape. There are about 55,000 species of bugs, including large, solitary insects such as giant water bugs and cicadas, and tiny creatures, such as scale insects, bedbugs, and aphids. It is the smaller bugs, such as aphids and leaf hoppers, that create problems for farmers because of the severe damage they do to crops.

## Features of a bug

All bugs have specialized mouths with cutting implements for piercing and needlelike tubes held within a protective sheath for sucking. Some bugs, such as lantern bugs, have their membranous wings exposed when at rest; others have forewings that are partially thickened and used not for flight, but as a protective cover for the delicate hind wings.

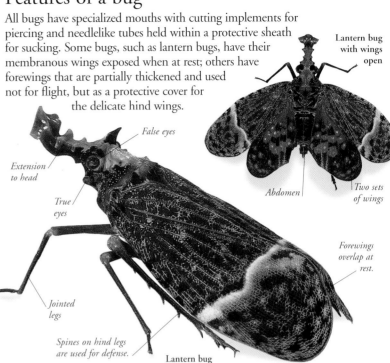

Lantern bug with wings open

False eyes

Extension to head

True eyes

Abdomen

Two sets of wings

Jointed legs

Forewings overlap at rest.

Spines on hind legs are used for defense.

Lantern bug

## Reproduction

Bugs attract a mate in many ways, such as emitting scent or vibrating the surface of water. Male cicadas attract females with their loud song, produced by drumlike organs on the abdomen. During mating, male and female bugs are often attached for hours. Females usually lay hundreds of eggs. These hatch into nymphs – tiny versions of their parents – and molt many times before reaching adult size.

### Parthenogenesis

Aphids multiply rapidly, because they can reproduce without mating. Females produce a succession of identical female offspring from unfertilized eggs, each of which later produces more of the same, a process called parthenogenesis.

### Shield bugs

Shield bugs are found virtually worldwide. They are also called stink bugs since they can give off a bad smell. Females protect their eggs and young from attack.

*Young shield bug nymphs being guarded by their mother.*

## Feeding

Bugs use their mouths to cut a hole in their food and pierce the soft parts inside. They inject enzymes and digestive juices through a pair of tiny tubes to break down solids and suck up the resulting fluids. In this way, predatory bugs, such as assassin bugs, can suck their victims dry. Bedbugs are parasites that suck the blood of birds and mammals, including humans. Some bugs feed only on plant juices.

### Assassin bugs

Assassin bugs are carnivores. Most prey on other invertebrates, such as millipedes. Some steal prey already caught in spiders' webs. Assassin bugs can squirt toxic saliva at would-be predators.

Feeding tube

*Assassin bug feeding on a cockroach*

### Leaf hoppers

Leaf hoppers are herbivores. They are often considered pests because they cut holes in the leaves of plants to suck out the sap, thereby weakening the plants.

## Defense

Small bugs face many enemies. To deter would-be attackers, bugs have evolved a range of defenses. Some bugs, such as tree hoppers, have developed elaborate camouflage; others, such as stink bugs, emit bad smells. The larvae of spittle bugs, also known as frog hoppers, hide within a frothy substance called cuckoo spit. Aphids employ ants to protect them by providing the ants with a nutritious sugary secretion.

### Tree hoppers

*Tree hoppers camouflage themselves with cuticles that resemble thorns.*

### Water bugs

Some bugs live in water. Water-striders skim over water on their dainty legs, while back swimmers dart below the water using paddle-shaped limbs. Underwater bugs either come to the surface to breathe, or carry around an air bubble.

Water-strider

## RED-BANDED LEAF HOPPER

| | |
|---|---|
| SCIENTIFIC NAME | *Graphocephala coccinea* |
| ORDER | Homoptera |
| FAMILY | Cicadellidae |
| DISTRIBUTION | Eastern US and eastern Canada |
| HABITAT | Meadows and gardens |
| DIET | Plant juices |
| SIZE | Length 0.4–0.5 in (8–11 mm); wingspan 0.5–0.6 in (12–16 mm) |
| LIFESPAN | Adults: up to 4 months |

**FIND OUT MORE**

ARTHROPODS    CAMOUFLAGE AND COLOR    FARMING    FLIGHT, ANIMAL    INSECTS    LAKE AND RIVER WILDLIFE    PARASITES    PLANTS, DEFENSE

# BUILDING AND CONSTRUCTION

THE SIMPLEST BUILDING is a permanent structure with a roof and four walls. Buildings come in a huge variety of shapes, sizes, and appearances – from skyscrapers and factories to schools, hospitals, houses, and garden sheds. Despite these differences, all buildings have the same basic purpose – to provide a sheltered area in which people can live, work, or store belongings. The engineers, surveyors, and construction workers who plan and build these structures also work on other projects, such as roads, bridges, dams, and tunnels.

### Early building
Since the beginning of history, people have built shelters to protect themselves from the weather, wild animals, and their enemies. The first buildings were simple, single-story structures made of materials such as wood, stone, and dried grass and mud. The first large-scale stone constructions were temples for the worship of gods and goddesses, and palaces in which powerful leaders lived. About 6,000 years ago, people discovered how to bake clay bricks. In time, engineers developed new building methods that enabled them to build higher and lighter structures.

*Walls are made from mud and bricks dried in the sun's heat.*

**Ancient tower house, Sana, Yemen**

## Anatomy of a building

Most buildings have certain features in common, such as walls, a roof, and floors. A large modern building, such as this airport terminal, also has a strong internal frame. Underneath this are the solid foundations on which the whole structure rests. The building is equipped with services, such as electricity and water supplies, as well as escalators, stairs, or elevators to give access to different stories, and fire escapes that enable people to leave the building rapidly in the event of an emergency.

### Roof
A roof is a protective covering over a building. Roofing materials include thatch, clay tiles, slate, glass, and steel. Roofs in wet climates are shaped to make rainwater run off; in cold countries, they slope steeply to stop snow from building up; and in dry climates, they are often flat. Sloping roofs are held up by supports called roof trusses.

*Roof trusses sit on frame.*  *Roof truss*

*Steel beams*  **Overhead cutaway of roof**

**Kansai Airport, Japan**

*Glass wall lets in a lot of light.*

*Roof is clad with shiny steel panels.*

*Floor rests on columns, which are part of frame.*

### Foundations
A building's foundations spread its huge load evenly into the ground, stopping the building from sinking under its own weight. Pile foundations are columns that rest on hard rock; raft foundations are concrete platforms that rest on soft rock. The foundations form the base on which the building's frame is constructed.

### Internal frame
The "skeleton" of a large building is its internal frame, which supports the roof, the walls, and the floors. Frames can be made of wood, steel, or reinforced-concrete columns and beams joined together.

*Foundations extend underground.*

*Basement houses service machinery.*

### Walls and floors
In a house, the walls – which may be made of wood, stone, or brick – are strong enough to hold up the floors, ceilings, and roof trusses. In a larger structure, however, the frame supports the building's weight, and the walls simply hang from the frame. The floors in a large modern building are reinforced-concrete slabs.

## Structural engineers

Long before the construction of a building is under way, structural engineers begin working on the design of the building with an architect. They calculate how strong the building's structure needs to be and draw up detailed plans, usually on a computer. When the building work commences, they make sure that everything happens safely, on time, and within the financial budget.

**Structural engineer on a building site**

### Surveyors
Accuracy is extremely important in construction work if the completed building is to have vertical sides and level walls, and be structurally safe. Even small errors in the design or assembly can result in parts not fitting together properly. People called surveyors check the building at every stage of its construction, using special instruments, such as theodolites and spirit levels, to take accurate measurements.

*Hard hat*

**Theodolite** is an instrument that measures angles to find distances, lengths, and heights.

**Surveyor using theodolite**

# Building sites

The different stages in the construction of a large building must always take place in a certain order, starting with the preparation of the site. Materials and machinery must arrive just when they are needed: if they are too early, the site may get too crowded; if they are too late, the building work may be delayed.

### Site clearance and excavation
The building site must first be cleared, which may involve demolishing other buildings, removing vegetation, and leveling the site. Holes are excavated (dug) for the foundations and basement.

### Foundation laying
The next stage is to build the foundations. This involves driving steel beams, called piles, into the ground, or pouring liquid concrete into a deep pit to form a solid base that will support the building.

### Frame building
The building's frame soon rises from the foundations. The frame is built either by bolting together steel beams, or by pouring concrete into molds crossed by steel rods. A shell of metal poles and wooden planks, called scaffolding, is temporarily erected around the building so that workers can reach all parts.

*Completed building is ready for use.*

### Completion
With the frame in place, work starts on the floors, walls, and roof. Services such as water and waste pipes, heating and air-conditioning ducts, and electricity and telephone cables are installed on each story. Finally, the windows are inserted, and the interior is decorated.

# Equipment

Some of the tasks on a building site, such as plastering a wall or laying bricks, are done by tradespeople using hand tools. Other tasks, such as erecting the building's frame or lifting heavy objects, may require large, specialized machines. Together, these machines are known as construction plant.

*Plumb line*

*Set square*

*Spirit level*

*Trowel*

**Bricklayer's tools**

### Hand tools
Each tradesperson involved in building and construction uses special tools. A bricklayer, for example, uses a trowel to spread mortar onto bricks, a plumb line to ensure that a wall is vertical, and a spirit level and a set square to check that it is horizontal.

### Construction plant
Powerful machines, such as cranes and cement mixers, can do jobs in a few minutes that would take manual workers hours or even days. Other machines include pile-drivers to hammer steel piles into the ground, bulldozers to level building sites, and excavating diggers.

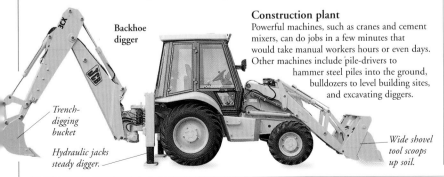

**Backhoe digger**

*Trench-digging bucket*

*Hydraulic jacks steady digger.*

*Wide shovel tool scoops up soil.*

# Building materials

Some building materials, such as steel, concrete, and bricks, are structural – that is, they make up the basic structure of the building. Other materials, such as ceramics and glass, are mainly decorative. Traditional materials, such as stone and wood, have been used for many centuries and are often found locally.

**Building site materials**

*Steel rods for reinforced concrete*

*Wooden planks for scaffolding*

*Steel girders for frame*

**Types of concrete**

### Concrete and steel
Most modern buildings contain concrete, steel, or a combination of both. Concrete is a mixture of cement, water, and small stones (called aggregate) that hardens like rock when it sets. Steel is iron that contains a tiny amount of carbon. Concrete strengthened by steel rods is called reinforced concrete.

### Wood
Some houses have floors made of wooden planks and wooden beams for roof trusses. Scaffolding may have walkways of wooden planks.

### Bricks
Blocks of hardened clay, called bricks, are laid in rows and joined together with mortar – a mixture of cement and sand.

### Local materials
Many buildings throughout the world are built from materials that occur naturally in the surrounding area. These local materials may include straw, mud, stone, wood, and even animal dung. They can do just as good a job as modern manufactured materials, which are usually more expensive and have to be imported from elsewhere.

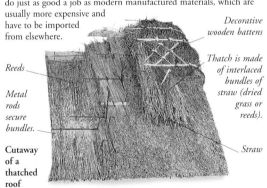

*Decorative wooden battens*

*Reeds*

*Metal rods secure bundles.*

*Thatch is made of interlaced bundles of straw (dried grass or reeds).*

*Straw*

**Cutaway of a thatched roof**

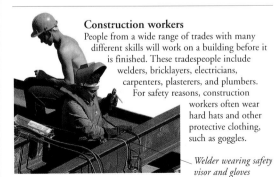

### Construction workers
People from a wide range of trades with many different skills will work on a building before it is finished. These tradespeople include welders, bricklayers, electricians, carpenters, plasterers, and plumbers. For safety reasons, construction workers often wear hard hats and other protective clothing, such as goggles.

*Welder wearing safety visor and gloves*

**FIND OUT MORE**   ARCHITECTURE   BRIDGES   CHURCHES AND CATHEDRALS   DAMS   HOUSES AND HOMES   IRON AND STEEL   ROADS   TUNNELS

# BUTTERFLIES AND MOTHS

SCALY WINGS AND A COILED feeding tube set butterflies and moths apart from other insects. Together, they form a single group of about 170,000 species, of which 90 percent are moths. Both have four stages to their life cycle in which they change from a caterpillar to an adult with wings. They feed on plants and rely on camouflage, irritating hairs or spines, or poisons in their body for protection against predators.

*Scales overlap like the tiles on a roof.*

**Wing scales**
Scales on the wings contain colored pigments. Some scales produce colors by reflecting the light.

*The front and back wings of a moth are hooked together.*

*Moth's bright colouring indicates it is poisonous*

## Moths

Zygaenid moth

Most moths fly at night. They tend to have drab colors, and have a fatter body and longer, narrower wings than butterflies. When resting, moths usually hold their wings open or fold them flat over their back.

**Swallowtail butterfly**

## Butterflies

In most cases, butterflies are more brightly colored than moths and have a thinner body. Unlike moths, they hold their wings upright when resting. The front and back wings are loosely joined together by a lobe on the back wing that grips the front wing. Butterflies are usually active by day rather than at night.

*Wings are made of a tough membrane supported by a network of rigid veins.*

*Proboscis is rolled up when not in use.*

*Moth antennae have a large surface area for picking up scents.*

**Feeding tube**
Adult butterflies and moths suck up liquid food, such as flower nectar, through a tube called a proboscis. A few moths have no proboscis because they do not feed as adults.

**Antennae**
Insects use their antennae for smelling, touching, and tasting. Butterfly antennae are clubbed; moth antennae range from single strands to feathery branches.

### Henry Bates

Henry Walter Bates (1825–92) was a British naturalist and explorer who studied camouflage in animals. He found that some harmless insects look the same as a poisonous insect so that predators leave them alone. This is now called Batesian mimicry after Henry Bates.

**Life cycle**
Butterflies and moths start life as an egg that hatches into a caterpillar. This feeds and grows until it turns into a pupa. The adult develops inside the pupa. This process of change is called metamorphosis.

*Pupa protects developing adult.*

*Adult butterfly emerges.*

*Butterfly pumps blood into its wings to expand and stiffen them.*

**Adult Blue Morpho**

## Defense

To escape from predators, butterflies and moths often fly away or hide. Some have irritating hairs or spines, or are poisonous. Bright colors may warn predators that a butterfly or moth is poisonous. Poisons often build up in a caterpillar from the plant it eats. These then remain in the adult.

**Camouflage**
Many butterflies and moths blend in with their surroundings at some stage of their life cycle. Camouflaged like this, they may escape predators.

**Eye spots**
False eyes on the wings can startle predators or stop them from pecking the real eyes. A damaged wing is not as serious as an injury to the head.

**Mimicry**
Some butterflies and moths gain protection by looking like another species of butterfly or moth. The top butterfly shown here is poisonous; the bottom one is not.

**Wing color**
When a butterfly is resting, only the underside of its wings shows. This is often colored for camouflage. The colors of the upper side help attract a mate.

### SWALLOWTAIL BUTTERFLY

**SCIENTIFIC NAME** *Papilio palinurus*

**ORDER** Lepidoptera

**FAMILY** Papilionidae

**DISTRIBUTION** From Burma to the islands of Borneo and the Philippines in Southeast Asia

**HABITAT** Tropical rain forest

**DIET** Flower nectar

**SIZE** Wing span: 3.75 in (9.5 cm)

**LIFESPAN** Varies (The adults of most butterflies live for only a few weeks or months)

FIND OUT MORE    CAMOUFLAGE AND COLOR    INSECTS    FLIGHT, ANIMAL

# Butterflies

Owl butterfly

Japanese emperor

Great spangled fritillary

Viceroy

Peacock

Blue morpho

Chequered skipper

Swallowtail

African giant swallowtail

Cairns birdwing

Brown-veined white

Orange-barred giant sulphur

Great orange tip

Common opal

Common blue

Small copper

Hewitson's blue hairstreak

# Moths

African moon moth

Hornet moth

Verdant sphinx

Goat moth

Magpie moth

Hoop pine moth

Oak eggar

Madagascan sunset moth

Buff-tip

Provence burnet moth

Garden tiger

Owl moth

Giant agrippa

Pale tussock

Hieroglyphic moth

# BYZANTINE EMPIRE

IN 395, THE GREAT ROMAN EMPIRE split into eastern and western sections. The western half – still called the Roman Empire – was centered in Rome. The eastern half became the Byzantine Empire with a center at Constantinople. The Greek character – in language, customs, and dress – of Constantinople contrasted with Latin Rome. Despite efforts on the part of emperors to reunite the two halves of the old empire, the Byzantine Empire gradually grew away from Rome. The Roman Empire collapsed in 410, but the Byzantine Empire existed until 1453, when the Ottoman Turks captured it.

**Extent of Byzantine Empire, c.565**
Because of its fabulous wealth, superb shipbuilding facilities, and strategic position between Asia and Europe, the Byzantine Empire was under almost constant siege by its powerful neighbors – Persia, Arabia, Turkey, and some states of the Christian west.

*Mosque*

## Byzantium to Constantinople

The ancient Greek port of Byzantium stood on the Golden Horn, a strip of land surrounded by sea on three sides. Constantine the Great (AD c.274–337) redesigned the city and re-named it Constantinople in AD 330. Soon it was one of the world's most beautiful cities.

**Bridge over the Bosporus Strait, linking Asia and Europe**

## Art and religion

Byzantine churches were famous for their interiors. They were lavishly decorated on a huge scale, with painted icons and intricate mosaic images of Christ, the Virgin, and saints.

**Icons**
In the 8th century, the empire was racked by arguments over whether it was idolatrous to worship beautiful religious statues and paintings, known as icons. Finally in 843, worship of icons was declared to be legitimate, and their production increased. Later, icons were collected by Renaissance artists.

## East versus west

By the 9th century, the Byzantine form of Christianity was changing from the western, or Roman, form. Greek had replaced Latin as the official language, and the Roman pope and Byzantine patriarch argued over church ritual, united only by their fear and hatred of the non-Christian Turks and Arabs.

**Great Schism**
In 1054, representatives of the Roman and Byzantine churches excommunicated each other. This religious split, or schism, destabilized political links between east and west, and caused mutual suspicion and hostility.

**Orthodox priest**

*St. Gregory of Nazianzus*    *Virgin and Child*    *St. John Chrysostom*

**Triptych icon, 12th century**    *Gilt covering*

**Hagia Sophia**
The biggest church in the eastern empire, Hagia Sophia was built in only five years (532–37). The Ottomans converted it into a mosque in the 16th century, and today it is a museum.

**Fall of Constantinople**
Constantinople was conquered twice: once by the west and once by the east. In 1204, it was ransacked by Christians on their way to the Holy Land. In 1453, Ottoman Turks overran it, and it became a Muslim stronghold.

**Fall of Constantinople, 1453**

**Mosaics**
Byzantine artists pressed cubes of tinted glass, marble, or precious stones into beeswax or lime plaster to make a mosaic. The artists often decorated the images with gold and silver leaf.

**Christ Pantokrator, 11th century**

## Timeline

**395** Roman Empire divided into west (Roman) and east (Byzantine).

**867–1056** Empire reaches its peak.

**The Good Shepherd mosaic, 5th century**

**529–34** Justinian I introduces his Roman Law Code.

**1054** Great Schism: Byzantine church breaks with the Roman church and forms the Eastern Orthodox church.

**976–1025** Basil II, known as "the Bulgar-slayer," gains more land than any emperor since Justinian I.

**1096** First Crusade: European army joins Byzantine army at Constantinople.

**1204** Fourth Crusaders sack Constantinople.

**1453** Ottoman Turks capture Constantinople, ending the empire.

## Emperor Justinian I
Justinian I (r.527–565) expanded the empire in the west by conquering North Africa, southern Spain, and Italy, while holding off the Persian threat in the east. In addition Justinian built Hagia Sophia, and his Codex Justinianus, or Roman Law Code, still forms the basis of the legal system in many European countries.

**FIND OUT MORE**     ART, HISTORY OF    CHRISTIANITY    OTTOMAN EMPIRE    PERSIAN EMPIRE    ROMAN EMPIRE

# CAESAR, JULIUS

JULIUS CAESAR WAS A BRILLIANT general and ruler of the Roman world. He is one of the most famous controversial figures in history. He transformed the Roman world, expanding Rome's territory into Gaul and suppressing many revolts. He was a fine administrator, reforming the Roman calendar and Roman law and bringing strong government to the republic. Caesar was also a great writer and orator. But he could be unscrupulous in pursuit of his own interests and made many enemies during his career.

### Early life
Caesar was born in Rome in about 100 BC. A member of a rich family, he had a successful military and political career, rising through various offices to become Pontifex Maximus, or high priest, in 64 BC. In 61 BC, he became Governor of Further Spain, one of the most important jobs in the Roman republic.

## Triumvirate

In the years leading up to 60 BC, rival politicians competed to gain power. Order was restored when Caesar, the financier Marcus Crassus, and the army commander Pompey set up a three-man committee, or triumvirate, to rule Rome. In 59 BC, the triumvirate allowed Caesar to be elected consul, one of the two magistrates who held supreme power. As consul, Caesar strengthened and reformed the government.

### Pompey
Gnaeus Pompeius Magnus (106–48 BC), known in English as Pompey, was a Roman general who conquered Palestine and Syria, and did much to get rid of opposition to Roman rule in Spain and Sicily. Although he was a member of the triumvirate and he married Caesar's daughter, he was always Caesar's rival.

**Pompey the Great**

## Gallic wars

From 58–50 BC, Caesar waged a series of wars that led to the incorporation of Gaul (modern France and Belgium) into the Roman republic. Caesar displayed great military ability in the Gallic Wars, and was ruthless with any tribes who tried to resist conquest. Caesar recorded his achievements in his famous memoirs of the campaign.

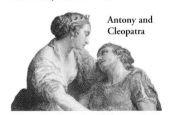

**Roman legionary's helmet**

## The civil war

After the death of Crassus in 53 BC, rivalry between Caesar and Pompey reached new heights. Pompey became sole consul in 52 BC and, with the support of the Roman senate (parliament), declared Caesar an enemy of the people. In 49 BC, Caesar crossed the Rubicon, the river dividing Italy from Gaul, and marched on Rome in triumph. In 48 BC, he defeated Pompey. By 45 BC, Caesar had removed all opposition, becoming master of the Roman world.

**Roman catapult bolts**

Roman cavalry spur

### Cleopatra
Caesar followed Pompey to Egypt and remained in the country after Pompey's death. He befriended and lived with Cleopatra, queen of Egypt, and helped establish her firmly on the throne. When Caesar returned to Rome in 47 BC, Cleopatra came with him. After Caesar's death, the Egyptian queen had twin sons with the Roman soldier and politician Mark Antony (c.82–30 BC).

Caesar as soldier

Caesar crosses the Rubicon.

### Pharsalus
Caesar showed his military skills when, in 48 BC, he defeated the much larger army of Pompey near the Greek town of Pharsalus. Caesar's strategic sense and better location enabled his small force to overwhelm Pompey's army, which was routed. Pompey himself fled to Egypt, where he died.

**Battle of Pharsalus**

**Antony and Cleopatra**

### JULIUS CAESAR

| | |
|---|---|
| c.100 BC | Born in Rome |
| 80 BC | First military service in Turkey |
| 60 BC | Forms triumvirate with Crassus and Pompey |
| 59 BC | Elected consul |
| 58–50 BC | Conquers Gaul |
| 50 BC | Roman senate declares him an enemy of the people |
| 49 BC | Starts civil war against Pompey |
| 48 BC | Defeats Pompey and follows him to Egypt |
| 44 BC | Assassinated in the senate in Rome by rival senators |

## Dictator

In 45 BC, Caesar was appointed dictator for life. He reformed the living conditions of the Roman people by passing new agricultural laws and improving housing. He also made the republic more secure from its enemies.

### Assassination
Despite his reforms, Caesar's dictatorial rule created enemies for him in Rome. On March 15, 44 BC, the Ides of March, Caesar was stabbed to death in the senate house by rival senators, including Cassius and Brutus. Caesar's work lived on in his adopted son, Octavian, who later became emperor.

**Assassination of Caesar**

FIND OUT MORE

ARMIES · FRANCE, HISTORY OF · ITALY, HISTORY OF · ROMAN EMPIRE · UNITED KINGDOM, HISTORY OF

# CAMELS

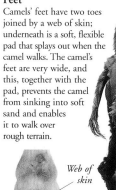

WELL-SUITED TO DESERT LIFE, camels can withstand extreme conditions. There are two main types: the one-humped dromedary, which lives in Africa and Arabia and is usually domesticated; and the two-humped Asian Bactrian, some of which still roam wild in the Gobi Desert. Closely related to camels are four animals without humps – llamas, alpacas, guanacos, and vicunas. All six species, called camelids, belong to the artiodactyls, a group of herbivorous, even-toed mammals that also includes cattle.

## Features of a camel

Camels are the largest of the even-toed mammals, standing up to 8 ft (2.4 m) at the shoulder. They have long legs and walk at an ambling pace. Camels have a split upper lip, which allows them to eat dry, spiky plants. Their lips and upright heads have given camels a reputation for arrogance. In reality this is nonsense. However, camels may spit at or bite humans if annoyed or frightened. During the mating season, male camels often fight, biting their rivals when competing for females.

### Feet
Camels' feet have two toes joined by a web of skin; underneath is a soft, flexible pad that splays out when the camel walks. The camel's feet are very wide, and this, together with the pad, prevents the camel from sinking into soft sand and enables it to walk over rough terrain.

**Thick fur** keeps camel warm during cold desert nights and helps prevent overheating in the day.

### Hump
Contrary to popular belief, the camel's hump is not filled with water, but is a fat store that provides the camel with energy when food is scarce. Because fat is stored in the hump, there is less fat under the rest of the skin, enabling the camel to lose heat more easily in hot conditions.

*Long eyelashes*

*Slitlike nostrils*

*Split upper lip*

**Head of dromedary camel**

### Eyes and nostrils
Camels have long eyelashes that protect their eyes from fierce sandstorms and enable them to see under difficult conditions. They can close their slitlike nostrils to reduce the amount of sand and dust blowing up the nose and minimize moisture loss from the nasal cavity.

*Web of skin*

*Large, wide feet with soft pads allow camel to walk on sand.*

*Shaggy fur*

*Long legs help camel walk long distances.*

*Long, curved neck allows camel to reach desert vegetation.*

**Foot of dromedary**

**Bactrian camel**

**Dromedary camel**

## Ships of the desert
Camels are the only animals that can carry heavy loads long distances in extreme heat and with little water. Nomadic peoples survive in deserts by using camels as pack animals as well as for meat, milk, and skins.

**Salt-laden caravan, Taoudenni, Mali**

## Water loss
Camels can exist for long periods without water, but make up the loss quickly when water is available. Camels are also adapted to reduce water loss by producing dry feces and small amounts of syrupy urine. In addition, their body temperature can rise to 104.9°F (40.5°C) during the day, reducing the need to keep cool by sweating, a process that also causes water loss.

*During long periods without drinking, a camel can lose 40 percent of its body mass as water.*

*Within 10 minutes, camels can drink sufficient water to make up huge losses.*

## Types of camelids
Related to camels are two species of domesticated camelids, the llama and alpaca, and two wild species, the vicuna and guanaco; all live in or near the Andes mountains in South America. Small herds of guanaco feed on grass and shrubs in shrub land and savanna up to heights of 13,900 ft (4,250 m) from southern Peru to southern Argentina.

*Vicunas are a protected species.*

*Alpacas' wool may be black, brown, or white.*

*The wool, milk, and meat of llamas are all used.*

**Vicuna**
Vicunas, the smallest of the camelids, live in family groups at high altitudes.

**Alpaca**
The highland people of Peru and Bolivia breed alpacas for their long, soft wool.

**Llama**
Llamas are used as pack animals to carry loads of up to 220 lb (100 kg), at altitudes of 16,400 ft (5,000 m) over long distances.

### DROMEDARY CAMEL

**SCIENTIFIC NAME** *Camelus dromedarius*

**ORDER** Artiodactyla

**FAMILY** Camelidae

**DISTRIBUTION** Domesticated in North Africa, Middle East, southwestern Asia; feral populations in Australia

**HABITAT** Desert

**DIET** Any type of desert vegetation, including thorny twigs and salty plants that other animals avoid

**SIZE** Head and body length 10 ft (3 m); shoulder height 6.5 ft (2 m); weight up to 1,320 lb (600 kg)

**LIFESPAN** Up to 50 years

FIND OUT MORE    ANIMALS    ASIAN WILDLIFE    DESERTS    DESERT WILDLIFE    MAMMALS    PIGS AND PECCARIES    SOUTH AMERICAN WILDLIFE

# CAMERAS

A LIGHTPROOF BOX with a hole or lens at one end, and a strip of light-sensitive film at the other, is the basic component of a traditional camera. To take a photograph, the photographer points the camera at an object and presses a button. This button very briefly opens a shutter behind the lens. Light reflected from the object passes through the lens and on to traditional film or a digital chip to produce an image.

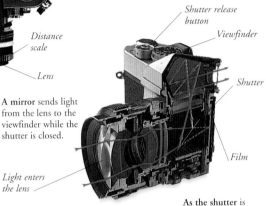

*Shutter release button*

*Shutter and film speed dial*

*Self-timer lever*

*Lens*

*Lens release button*

*Shutter and film speed dial*

*Connection for flash*

*Film rewind knob*

*Shutter release button*

*Aperture scale*

*Distance scale*

*Lens*

*Movable flash head*

*Flash light sensor*

## Parts of a camera

The quality of a photograph is controlled by adjusting the film and shutter speed dials, flash, and aperture scales. This is because the final image will depend on the type of film in the camera, the amount of light that enters the lens, and the length of time that the film is exposed to light.

**35mm cameras**
The most popular cameras are the 35mm, named after the width of the film they use. These cameras are small and easy to manage. They often have in-built features, which adjust automatically to variations in light and distance, to ensure that a clear photograph is taken every time.

*Shutter release button*

*Viewfinder*

*Shutter*

*Film*

**A mirror** sends light from the lens to the viewfinder while the shutter is closed.

*Light enters the lens*

**As the shutter** is released, the mirror slips up allowing the light to reach the film (shown by the dotted line).

## Digital cameras

Digital cameras contain no film. Instead, the image is captured on a photosensitive chip. Photos are displayed instantly on a screen on the camera and can be deleted if not liked. Images can be loaded into a computer and printed out.

**Computer imaging**
After an image has been stored on a digital camera, it can then be fed into a computer. From here it is printed out on photo paper or sent over the Internet. Special software allows the picture to be manipulated and gives the photographer a lot of control over the image.

*Images are set to high or low quality.*

*Some cameras can also record tiny video clips.*

*Batteries inside supply power.*

Digital camera

### Flashes
A flash provides the extra light needed for taking pictures after dark, or in dim conditions. The flash is electronically controlled to go off at the moment the shutter opens.

### Single-lens reflex camera
Unlike other cameras, the view through a single-lens reflex (SLR) camera is that of the actual image that is recorded on the film. Mirrors in the viewfinder correct the upside-down image sent from the lens.

## Lenses

Different lenses achieve different visual effects. A wide-angle lens allows more of the scene to appear in a photograph than a normal lens. A telephoto zoom lens can take a close-up shot of a distant object. The fisheye lens distorts images for dramatic effect. These lenses are detachable from the camera.

Normal lens

Wide-angle lens

Telephoto zoom lens

Fisheye lens

## Film types
Today, plastic film comes in various sizes and speeds, in a colour or a black and white format, packaged as rolls or plates. The speed, given in ASA/ISO or DIN numbers, indicates how quickly the film reacts to light. A new device, the Electronic Film System, fits into a 35mm camera and holds up to 30 digital images which can be transferred to a computer.

110mm film

35mm film

Plate film

## George Eastman

An American inventor, George Eastman (1854–1932), formed the Kodak company. In 1884, he produced the first roll film and in 1888 the first box camera, making photography an accessible hobby. In 1889, he used clear celluloid film on which the first movie pictures were taken.

## Timeline

**4th century** BC The "camera obscura" is developed; it consists of a darkened room into which an image is projected.

**1822** Frenchman Joseph Niepce takes the first photograph on a sheet of pewter, coated with bitumen.

**1839** Niepce's colleague, Louis Daguerre, announces process for recording images on copper.

**1839** William Fox Talbot, an Englishman, invents a process that allows photographs to be copied.

**1895** The Lumière brothers of France patent their original camera/projector using celluloid film with sprocket holes at the edge.

**1948** American inventor Edwin Land develops the first instant camera, which is marketed by the Polaroid Corporation.

**1956** A camera that records onto reel-to-reel magnetic videotape, rather than plastic film, is invented.

**1980s** First digital cameras prototyped.

**1986** Disposable camera launched.

**1992** The jpeg, a compressed file format for storing digital images, is introduced.

FIND OUT MORE   COLOUR   FILMS AND FILM-MAKING   GLASS   INVENTIONS   LIGHT   PHOTOGRAPHY   PLASTICS AND RUBBER   TELEVISION   VIDEO

# Still cameras

## Early cameras

*Image projected upside down*

**Fox Talbot's** camera of 1835 required exposure times of over an hour.

**Daguerreotype** camera of mid-1800s was the first model sold to the public.

*Shutter operated by a cord*

**Kodak Autographic Special** of 1918 was an early roll-film camera.

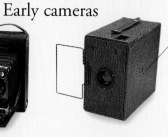

**Ensign** of the 1930s, with a side viewfinder: was popular in sports photography.

*Box made camera sturdy*

**Brownie Hawkeye** of the 1940s reflected the new use of plastic in design.

*Upper lens is for viewing*

**1950s Duaflex** was modeled on the superior twin-lens cameras of the time.

## 35mm cameras

*Shutter and film speed dial*

**Manual SLR** camera needs to be focused and wound manually.

*Shutter release button*

**Automatic SLR** camera has an automatic film loading and winding mechanism.

**Basic compact** camera has a fixed length lens and built-in flash.

**Advanced compacts** are often fitted with a zoom lens, giving extra flexibility.

*Zoom controlled by motor*

**Leica cameras** were the first to use the small-format 35mm film.

*Image is seen here*

**Waist-level viewfinder** allows photos to be taken from waist height.

## Medium- and large-format cameras

**6 x 4.5 cm camera** is a small, light, medium-format camera.

**6 x 6 cm camera** produces a square image and is used by many professionals.

**Direct vision** camera has range finder–focusing lenses, reducing size and weight.

**6 x 7 cm camera** produces a rectangular image ideal for landscape photography.

**6 x 9 cm camera** produces large images that make very clear enlargements.

**Large-format camera** uses individual sheets of film for each image.

## Special cameras

*Large viewfinder*

**Underwater camera** has large easy-to-read dials for use in deep water.

**Panoramic camera** rotates to take a view of up to 360° in one exposure.

**Bellows camera** allows for a very wide range of image magnifications.

*Moving bellows along track alters magnification*

*Film exit slot*

**Polaroid camera** produces a finished photo seconds after taking the picture.

*Built-in flash*

**Disposable camera** is simple and light, and is used only once.

# Movie cameras

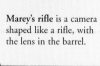

**Marey's rifle** is a camera shaped like a rifle, with the lens in the barrel.

*Trigger works like a shutter release*

**Debro pavro** was an early movie camera. The handle was turned to start filming.

*Magazines hold three strips of film separately*

**Technicolor three-strip camera** produces good, but expensive films.

*Matt-box keeps stray light out of the lens*

**Cine 8** takes still photographs in rapid succession.

*Images are recorded directly on video tape*

**Camcorders** are handheld video cameras used by many individuals.

C

# CAMOUFLAGE AND COLOR

ANIMALS HAVE EVOLVED different colors, shapes, and patterns that help them survive. Some, such as birds of paradise, are brightly colored to attract a mate; others, such as the fire salamander, use colour to advertise that they are poisonous to eat. Animals, such as lapwings and polar bears, are camouflaged – colored or patterned – in such a way that they blend with their surroundings. Camouflage helps animals hide from predators, but it can also help predators creep up on their prey.

*Bright colors of male make him stand out and attract females.*

*Newly hatched lapwings match color of straw.*

**Young lapwings in nest**

## Types of coloration

Coloration falls into two main categories: cryptic and phaneric. Cryptic colors and patterns help conceal an animal, thus helping protect it from enemies, or assisting in the capture of its prey. The factors that cryptic species suppress – color, movement, and shape – are exaggerated in phaneric species. Phaneric coloration makes an animal stand out. It can include the conspicuous display of brilliant colors, shapes, and actions, as demonstrated by birds of paradise.

### Cryptic coloration

Cryptic coloration is common among birds. The plumage of many desert species blends perfectly with the ground color of their habitat. Birds of the forest canopy, such as parrots, are frequently green to match the dense foliage in which they live. Not all members of the same species are always of cryptic colors. Sometimes the female or nestlings, which are generally in greater need of concealment, have cryptic color, while the male is conspicuously colored to attract a mate.

**Redheaded gouldian finch**

### Phaneric coloration

Phaneric coloration used by animals such as macaws and mandrills makes them stand out and be noticed. It is used between male and female in courtship displays, between parent and young and members of a group for purposes of recognition, between rival males in threat displays, and between predators and prey to warn, bluff, or deflect attack. Long ear and head plumes, fans, elongated tail feathers, wattles, and inflatable air sacs are all used to attract attention.

## Camouflage

For concealment to be effective, the color and pattern of an animal's coat or skin must relate closely to those of its background. A bird's color often harmonizes with its nest; some ground-nesting birds choose a nest site with surroundings of a color similar to that of their eggs to conceal them. Color and posture can be a highly effective form of camouflage. The many types of concealment include disruptive coloration, disguise, and immobility.

### Disruptive coloration

Irregular patches of contrasting colors and tones of an animal's coat divert attention away from the shape of the animal, making it harder to recognize. Tigers and giraffes show disruptive coloration.

**Tiger camouflaged in long grass**

**Giant spiny stick insect**

### Disguise

Cryptic coloration aims to disguise rather than conceal. The combination of color, form, and posture can produce an almost exact replica of a commonplace object associated with the habitat. Stick insects, for example, resemble small twigs, while nightjars, when lying down, look like stones or wood fragments.

### Mimicry

Mimicry is an extreme form of concealment. It occurs when a relatively defenseless or edible species looks like an aggressive or dangerous species. The mimic not only takes on the appearance of the object it is mimicking, but also adopts its behavior, assuming characteristics that are completely alien to it. For example, harmless milk snakes resemble poisonous coral snakes so that other animals will not attack them. The monarch, a poisonous butterfly, is mimicked by a non-poisonous species, the viceroy, which is indistinguishable from it.

**Coral snake**

**Milk snake**

*Milk snakes have stripes of the same color as coral snakes, but in a different order.*

### Immobility

Effective camouflage is possible only if an animal remains still. Many animals react to danger by freezing. For example, if confronted with danger, reedbuck crouch down with their necks outstretched, and, by remaining motionless, become hard to distinguish from their surroundings. Some birds, particularly ground-nesting birds such as nightjars, squat down to reduce the shadow they make.

**Reedbuck**

### Assassin bug

Many species of assassin bugs resemble the insects on which they feed. This enables them to get close to their prey without being detected, before seizing it and injecting a toxic fluid. One species of assassin bug, *Salyavata variegata*, lives in termite nests. It camouflages itself by covering its body in debris, including the bodies of termites, and then enters the nest unnoticed, and feed on the inhabitants.

*Assassin bug covered in debris by termites' nest*

*Termite*

C

# Social displays

Social displays take many different forms, from threat display to courtship and bonding. Both cuttlefish and octopuses can change color; darkening and flashing different colors to intimidate rivals or enemies. The male Uganda kob, a type of antelope, establishes territorial breeding grounds by displaying along the boundary of his territory. Lowering his head, he makes a mock attack with his horns, warning rival males to keep out of his territory, while at the same time, inducing other females to join his harem.

## Courtship

Many animals use courtship displays to attract a mate. The fiddler crab, for example, waves his outsize claw, the elephant seal inflates his nose, and the grouse spreads his tail and inflates his air sacs. Among the most impressive courtship displays are that of the male peacock, which spreads his brilliantly colored tail plumage, and the elaborate rituals of birds of paradise and bowerbirds. These involve vibrating the body, fanning feathers, puffing out plumage, decorating nesting areas, and calling loudly.

*Tail feathers overlap and rest on the ground when relaxed.*

**Peacock**

*Peacock starts to erect tail plumage.*

*Male calls as he starts to display.*

## Signaling

Signs and signals help animals maintain contact, preserve the social hierarchy, and intimidate rivals and enemies. The signals have to be conspicuous and unmistakable. The ring-tailed lemurs of Madagascar raise their long black and white tails to waft scent at their rivals and to enable all members of a group to maintain contact. The black rings encircling the cheetah's white-tipped tail enable the cubs to follow their parent, which would otherwise be invisible in the long grass. The young of ringed plovers have a white neckband that helps the parents keep the brood together.

**Ring-tailed lemurs signaling with raised tails**

*Strong feathers at the rear, attached to muscles, are used to raise the long feathers.*

**Peacock with tail feathers raised**

## Henry Walter Bates

The English naturalist and explorer, Henry Bates (1825–92) spent 11 years exploring the Amazon, returning with 8,000 species of previously unknown insects. In 1861, he published a paper on mimicry that made an important contribution to the theory of natural selection. He suggested that some harmless insects looked like harmful ones to discourage predators from attacking them.

**Red and black froghopper**

## False warning

Many animals employ bluff as a means of defense. In birds, this may take the form of fluffing up feathers, spreading wings, and clacking beaks. Many frogs and toads puff themselves up to make them appear larger; the hawkmoth caterpillar looks like a snake to intimidate enemies; and the Australian frilled lizard erects its frill and hisses loudly to intimidate intruders.

# Warning signals

Animals use many methods to frighten off other animals. Warning colors make prey appear unpalatable to discourage predators. Many poisonous and venomous animals do not need to be camouflaged; they advertise themselves with bright colored patterns of red, yellow, and black which, are recognized warning colors. Skunks' black and white coats warn they can squirt foul-smelling spray.

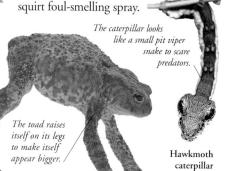

*The caterpillar looks like a small pit viper snake to scare predators.*

*The toad raises itself on its legs to make itself appear bigger.*

**European common toad**

**Hawkmoth caterpillar**

## Seasonal change

Some Arctic animals, such as the polar bear and snowy owl, remain white throughout the year; others undergo a seasonal change. In far-northern latitudes, the stoat becomes completely white in winter, except for the tip of its tail, which remains black. In the warmer parts of its habitat, it can retain its russet coloration, become particolored, or change to white as needed. This ability to change color provides the stoat with effective camouflage throughout the year.

**Stoat with dark summer coat**

**Stoat with pale winter coat**

| **FIND OUT MORE** | BIRDS | BUGS | DEER AND ANTELOPE | FROGS AND TOADS | LIONS AND OTHER WILDCATS | MONKEYS AND OTHER PRIMATES | OWLS AND NIGHTJARS | POISONOUS ANIMALS | SNAKES |

# CAMPING AND HIKING

ONE OF THE MOST popular types of vacation, camping offers people the chance to enjoy the great outdoors at close quarters. For many people, their first experience of camping is as children, setting up a tent in their own backyard. But it is also a popular activity with adults, who enjoy getting away from cities to explore the countryside, and perhaps even learning survival skills in the wild. Camping offers the freedom to choose to stay at one campsite through a holiday, or to set up camp at a different site each night. Whatever the type of vacation, it is important to take the appropriate clothing, food, and equipment.

An ideal campsite

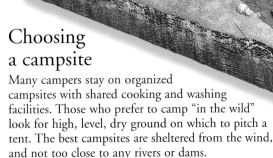

*Prevailing winds*

*Trees provide shelter from the wind.*

*River is a source of water for drinking and washing.*

*Ground is level and there is no danger of flooding.*

## Choosing a campsite

Many campers stay on organized campsites with shared cooking and washing facilities. Those who prefer to camp "in the wild" look for high, level, dry ground on which to pitch a tent. The best campsites are sheltered from the wind, and not too close to any rivers or dams.

## Fire ingredients

**Tinder**

**Kindling**

**Small fuel**

**Main fuel**

**Large fuel**

### Making a tepee fire

Fires provide warmth and a means of cooking, but they can also be dangerous. Campers must make certain that a fire is permitted, safe, and will not harm their tent or the surroundings. They are especially careful if a strong wind is blowing.

1 The camper gathers the fuel he or she needs (ranging in size from twigs to branches), cuts out a square of earth, and puts a layers of sticks in the hole.

*Make sure the fuel is dry.*

2 The camper then balances four sticks to meet at the top in a tepee shape, making sure the tepee has enough space for tinder inside the sticks.

3 Gradually, the camper adds more sticks, making the tepee as sturdy as possible, and puts some tinder, such as leaves and dry grass, inside.

*Hole for putting in tinder*

4 Having set light to the tinder, the camper gradually adds more tinder, then twigs and larger pieces of fuel. He or she takes care not to knock the tepee over. When the teepee burns, it will collapse and create embers that can be used for cooking.

*Keep a flashlight at the head of the sleeping bag.*

*Unpack things only as needed.*

*The head of a sleeping bag should face the door.*

### Living in your tent

There is very little room inside a tent, so campers need to be well organized, or they may lose things and be uncomfortable. To stop damp seeping in from the soil under a sleeping bag, campers put a waterproof sheet on the ground beneath the tent.

## Things to take camping

It is better to take only the basic items of equipment camping. These include all the tools needed to set up a camp, in addition to cooking and eating utensils. In addition, campers should take durable clothes to protect them against all types of weather.

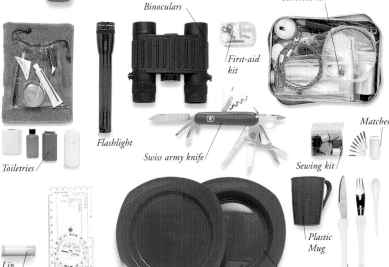

*Binoculars*

*Survival kit*

*First-aid kit*

*Flashlight*

*Swiss army knife*

*Matches*

*Sewing kit*

*Toiletries*

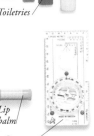

*Lip balm*

*Compass*

*Plastic Mug*

*Plastic plate and bowl*

*Cutlery*

C

# Food and water

For healthy eating, campers aim to maintain a balanced diet, including fruit and vegetables, bread, and food containing protein, such as fish and meat. If it is difficult or impossible for campers to buy food while they are away, they take tinned or freeze-dried foods, which will not perish. Campers should only drink water from approved sources. If necessary, they take water purifiers or a portable water filter.

## Meals for a day on the trail
When campers are going on a long hike, they plan their meals before they set out, sorting food into labelled plastic bags. They eats main meals at the start and end of the day, and nibble snacks during the day for energy.

*Hot drink*

**Breakfast** *Oatmeal*

*Keep water containers spotlessly clean.*

*Water*

**Snacks**

*Tea*

*Chocolate and cookies*

*Sugar*

*Herbs*

*Fruit and nuts*

*Hot soup*

**Lunch**

*Soaked lentils*

*Soup*

*Stew*

**Evening meal**

*Peach juice*

*Peaches*

*Freeze-dried meal is dehydrated, leaving the texture of food intact.*

## Dried foods
Dried meals are useful for hikers. They are portable and are prepared simply by adding hot water. This saves time and fuel. If meals are prepared in their bags and resealed, hikers can eat them on the trail.

*Rice*

*Curry*

*Foil bags*

*Egg*

## Food for traveling

**Boiled candies**

**Kidney beans**

**Bouillon cubes**

**Salami**   **Pasta meal**

**Sardines**

**Frankfurters and baked beans**

### Portable foods
To keep their backpack easy to carry, experienced campers put as much of their food as possible into bags. When they do take tins, these are small enough for the camper to eat the contents in one go.

### Canoe hiking
In some parts of the world, people can go hiking in canoes. They travel along rivers and spend the nights camping on the riverbank. Where the river is too dangerous for canoeing, they move to the land and carry their canoes. The canoes used are light and easy to carry

# Camping with trailers

Trailers are like compact homes on wheels, and can be towed by a car, or any vehicle, to a campsite. Trailers usually have several rooms and are more comfortable to live in than tents, most trailers have stoves, beds, and toilets, and some may even have refrigerators and showers. Some campsites have permanent, fixed trailers that you can rent for your vacation if you do not have your own.

# Hiking

Walking through the countryside, for a few hours or for up to several weeks, is a form of exercise enjoyed by people of all ages. Hikers walk in groups, so that if an accident occurs, at least two can go for help together, and one can stay with the injured member of the party. Hikers should be fully equipped for the sort of trip they are making and should tell someone where they are going.

*Ice pick*

*Windproof jacket with a hood.*

*Ice hammer*

### Mountain walking
The most difficult and dangerous form of hiking is mountain climbing. Mountain climbers enjoy testing their strength and skill on steep rock faces. They need to be particularly fit, and use special climbing equipment.

*Crampon*

*Tent poles and stakes in the same bag*

*Keep the pack full so that heavy items stay at the top.*

*Sleeping bag at the bottom*

### How to pack your sack
To keep the contents of a backpack dry, line it with a plastic bag and put everything in separate plastic bags. Pack the lighter, bulkier things at the bottom and the heavier things at the top. Spare clothes can be packed down the back to protect the spine.

*Shoulder straps can be adjusted to fit.*

### Backpacking
A comfortable way to carry belongings, backpacks range from light day packs to large packs that have space for everything needed for several days' hiking. They sit as high as possible on the shoulders, to distribute weight.

### Using a compass
Hikers take a map and a compass when they go on a long walk, so that they can follow the route and not get lost. A protractor compass, shown here, is popular because it is light, reliable, and accurate.

**FIND OUT MORE**   EXPLORATION   ENERGY   FIRST AID   FIRE   FOOD   HEALTH AND FITNESS

# CANADA

THE WORLD'S SECOND LARGEST country, Canada covers the northern part of the North American continent and is made up of ten provinces and three territories. Canada borders Alaska and the Pacific Ocean to the west, and the Atlantic Ocean to the east. Winters in the northern third of the country, much of which lies within the Arctic Circle, are so severe that very few people can live there. About 80 percent of Canadians live within 200 miles (320 km) of the US border. Canada has huge forests, rich mineral resources, and open, fertile farmland.

## Ottawa

Canada's capital sits on the south bank of the Ottawa River and has a population of 921,000. The city has clean, wide streets, many lined with parks. The Rideau Canal, part of a complex of lakes and canals linking Ottawa with Lake Ontario, freezes in winter, becoming the world's longest skating rink.

**Skating on the Rideau Canal**

## Physical features

Covered with lakes, rivers, and forests, Canada has one-third of the world's freshwater. Frozen islands lie in the Arctic, high mountains in the west, and vast prairies in the south.

113°F (45°C)    -81°F (-63°C)

70°F (21°C)    12°F (-11°C)

34 in (871 mm)

### Climate

Most of Canada has a continental climate with long, bitterly cold winters and hot, humid summers. Coastal areas are generally mild, especially the Pacific west coast. The glaciers and ice-caps of the north are permanently frozen.

Built-up 0.5%   Wetland 2%   Grassland 1%

Forest 59%   Tundra 27%

Barren 5.5%   Farmland 5%

### Land use

Canada's vast prairies are used for growing wheat. The forests support a thriving timber industry. Only five percent of Canada's land area is cultivated.

### Rocky Mountains

The snowcapped Rocky Mountains dominate western Canada, extending south into the US. Canada's highest mountain is Logan, at 19,551 ft (5,959 m).

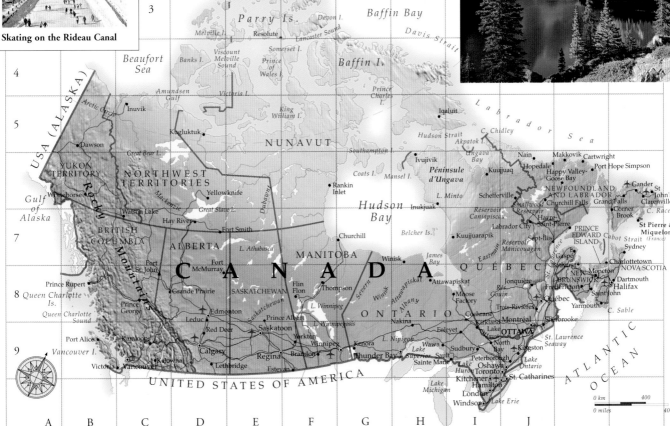

# People

Most Canadians have European ancestors who emigrated to Canada from the UK, France, Germany, Scandinavia, and Italy. There are large numbers of Ukrainians, Indians, and Chinese. The native people of Canada form only four percent.

**8 per sq mile** | **77%** | **23%**
(3 per sq km) | **Urban** | **Rural**

### Inuit
The Inuit are one of the country's indigenous groups, and almost 50,000 Inuits live in northern Canada. One-quarter are settled on Baffin Island, in the eastern Arctic, and speak their own language, *Inuktitut*. In 1999 the Inuit homeland of Nunavut was made a territory.

# Leisure

Many Canadians enjoy outdoor activities. In the summer, people sail, raft, canoe, or simply enjoy one of Canada's many well-kept parks. The major spectator sports are hockey, baseball, and soccer.

### Winter sports
Plentiful snow makes skiing and ice-skating popular with many Canadians. Ice hockey is played everywhere, from frozen backyards to national stadiums. Calgary hosted the 1988 Winter Olympics.

### Calgary Stampede
One of the world's largest rodeos, the Calgary Stampede attracts one million visitors every year. Held in July, the 10-day rodeo is an exciting re-creation of the Wild West, where people dress up in cowboy outfits and try their luck at calf roping, chuck wagon racing, and bronco riding.

*Hardwood stick*

*Tough rubber puck is hit into the goal.*

# Farming

Five percent of Canada's land is arable, and the country is a top exporter of wheat, oats, corn, and barley. Forest products and fish are also key exports. Cattle and pigs are raised on the pastures of the southeast. Farming employs three percent of the workforce.

**Apple**

**Cranberries**

### Niagara Fruit Belt
The land between lakes Ontario and Erie is called the "Niagara Fruit Belt" because the soil and climate are ideal for growing soft fruit such as cherries and peaches. Apples and cranberries flourish in British Columbia. In the east, the maple tree (its leaf is Canada's national emblem) yields rich syrup, a favorite served with sweet pancakes.

**Maple leaves**

### Wheat
Canada's main grain crop is wheat, and on the eastern prairies, around Saskatchewan, wheat farming is a way of life. About half of the 32,930,000 tons (29,870,000 tonnes) grown every year are exported.

# Transportation

The 5,000-mile (8,000-km) Trans-Canada Highway links the east and west coasts. The St. Lawrence Seaway provides trade links for the eastern provinces. Airways, railroads, rivers, and the lakes are also used for transportation.

### St. Lawrence Seaway
Opened in 1959, the St. Lawrence Seaway links the Great Lakes with the St. Lawrence River and the Atlantic. Over 450 miles (725 km), a series of locks enables oceangoing ships, from all over the world, to sail inland.

### Snowplow
Canada's long, cold winters bring heavy snow and ice to the country, making traveling by road difficult and dangerous. Snowplows work through the day and night to keep roads clear. Most Canadian roads are wide to allow room for snow to be piled up on either side.

# Industry

The center of Canada's industry is at the western end of Lake Ontario, a region known as "the Golden Horseshoe." Canadian factories process foods, assemble cars, and make steel, chemical products, and paper. The service industries are thriving, and tourism now employs one in ten Canadians.

**Nickel**

**Zinc**

### Mining
Minerals have been one of the major factors in the growth of Canada's economy. The country is the world's largest producer of zinc ore and uranium, and second of nickel and asbestos.

### Forestry
Canada's abundant forests have made it the world's second largest exporter of softwood (fir and pine) and wood pulp. Ten percent of Canada's labor force work in the lumber industry, using timber as a raw material. British Columbia, Québec, and Ontario are the major timber-producing provinces.

# Québec

At the heart of French Canada, Québec City has many stone houses and 17th-century buildings, and its old town was declared a World Heritage Site in 1985. The province of Québec is home to nearly 7,500,000 people. More than three-quarters of the people are of French descent; they keep the French language and culture alive. There have been many attempts by the province to claim independence from Canada.

**Château Frontenac, Québec old town**

**FIND OUT MORE** | CANADA, HISTORY OF | FARMING | FISHING INDUSTRY | FORESTS | LAKES | NATIVE AMERICANS | PORTS AND WATERWAYS | ROCKS AND MINERALS | TUNDRA | WINTER SPORTS

# CANADA, HISTORY OF

FOR MOST OF ITS history, Canada has been home to Native Americans and Inuits. They were descendants of the first people to settle there during the Ice Age, and built advanced cultures based on hunting and trapping fish and animals. In 1497, the first Europeans visited the country, establishing settlements in the early 1600s. In the 18th century, French and British armies fought for control of the entire country. The British won, but a sizable French community has remained in Québec to this day.

## The first Canadians
The first inhabitants of Canada were peoples from northern Asia who crossed a land bridge from Siberia and moved south through America more than 20,000 years ago. The Inuits lived in the Arctic regions; other Native American peoples occupied the plains and coastal areas. They all developed their own distinctive cultures. For example, the tribes of the northwest coast recorded their family history on totem poles, carving out representations of the family spirits on the trunks of cedar trees.

## Fur trading
European settlers were attracted to Canada by the wealth to be made from furs and skins of animals trapped in the forests. The English-owned Hudson's Bay Company, established in 1670, and other trading companies set up fortified trading posts to trade furs and other goods with local Indian tribes. Québec (established 1608) and Montreal (1642) became important centers of the fur trade.

*Traders traveled by canoe in order to reach the trading post.*

*Missionaries built churches to convert Native Americans.*

*Wigwams made of birch wood covered with skins or bark.*

**Trading post**

*Houses and walls were built with wood from the forests.*

## Jacques Cartier
The French sea captain Jacques Cartier (1491–1557) was hired by Francis I of France to look for a northwest passage to China above North America. In 1534, he sailed into the Gulf of St. Lawrence and, in 1535, discovered the St. Lawrence River. As he sailed up the river, he stopped at two Indian villages – Stadacona (modern Québec) and Hochelaga (Montreal). As a result, French immigrants began to settle by the St. Lawrence River.

## Capture of Québec
In 1759, British forces led by General James Wolfe attacked Québec, capital of the French colony of New France. Wolfe captured the city, arriving from the Gulf of St. Lawrence

**Wolfe's flotilla arrives in Québec**

with a flotilla of 168 ships that carried over 30,000 men. However, both he and the French commander, Louis, Marquis de Montcalm, were killed. All of French North America came under British control.

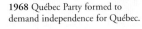

*Northwest Territories, 1870*
*Saskatchewan, 1905*
**Canadian provinces**
*Nunavut, 1999*
*Ontario, 1867*
*Alaska*
*Québec, 1867*
*New Brunswick, 1867*
*Yukon Territory, 1898*
*Newfoundland 1949*
*British Columbia, 1871*
*Nova Scotia, 1867*
*Alberta, 1905*
*Manitoba, 1870*

## Independence
In 1867, Canada became an independent dominion (nation) within the British Empire. At first, the new country consisted only of parts of Ontario, Québec, and two provinces on the Atlantic coast. Gradually, the other provinces joined. By 1905, most of Canada had joined the Dominion.

## Immigration
At the end of the 19th century, Canada's economy expanded and several transcontinental railroads improved communications. Canada became an attractive place for European emigrants, and between 1891 and 1914, over three million people came to Canada in search of work and a new life. Canada's government encouraged Europeans to emigrate, promising future citizens health and wealth in their new home.

**Canadian government poster**

## Timeline

**1497** John Cabot, an Italian sailor, claims Newfoundland for Britain.

**1534** Jacques Cartier explores the St. Lawrence River for France.

**1605** French establish the first European colony at Port Royal, Nova Scotia.

**1754** French and Indian War between Britain and France. France forced to relinquish Québec to Britain.

**1846** Oregon Treaty confirms present borders with USA

**1949** Founder member of NATO

**1968** Québec Party formed to demand independence for Québec.

**1989** UK transfers all power relating to Canada in British law.

**1998** Government apologises to Native Americans over land.

**Canadian flag**

## Québec
Canada recognized both its English- and French-speakers as equal, but in the 1960s, many people in French-speaking Québec began to press for their province to become independent. In 1982, Québec was given the status of a "distinct society," but referendums seeking independence were defeated in 1980 and 1995.

**FIND OUT MORE**  EXPLORATION  FRANCE, HISTORY OF  NATIVE AMERICANS  NORTH AMERICA, HISTORY OF  UNITED KINGDOM, HISTORY OF  UNITED STATES, HISTORY OF

# CARIBBEAN

HUNDREDS OF ISLANDS lie in the Caribbean Sea, east of the US and Central America and stretching west into the Atlantic Ocean. These Caribbean islands, also known as the West Indies, take their name from the Caribs, the original inhabitants of the region, until the Spanish arrived in 1492. Most islanders today are descendents of African slaves brought to work on plantations between the 16th and 19th centuries. The islands have a tropical climate, turquoise waters, and fine beaches, and have developed a booming tourist industry. However, many people are poor, and live by farming.

**Volcanic islands**
Many Caribbean islands are made of volcanic rocks that emerged from the ocean millions of years ago. Some, such as the St. Lucian Gros Piton, 2,619 ft (798 m), and the Petit Piton, 2,461 ft (750 m), are the remains of ancient volcanoes that rise up from the sea on the west coast, near the town of Soufrière. Several are still active, such as La Soufrière, at 4,000 ft (1,219 m), on St. Vincent.

## Physical features

Long, sandy beaches, tropical seas, and fine natural harbors have earned the Caribbean islands a reputation for beauty. Most of the islands are forested and mountainous. Some are volcanic in origin, others are founded on coral reefs. Hurricanes, earthquakes, and active volcanoes shake parts of the region from time to time.

**Coral islands**
The warm, tropical seas of the Caribbean provide ideal conditions for coral. Some of the Caribbean's volcanic islands, such as Barbados and the Cayman Islands, are fringed with coral reefs, which protect them against the lashing waves. The 700 islands and 2,300 islets of the Bahamas are entirely built up of coral, which can be viewed from the bridge that links Nassau with Paradise Island.

**Hurricanes**
Powerful tropical storms called hurricanes sweep the Caribbean between May and October every year, often causing great damage and economic hardship. They begin as thunderstorms that are whipped up by high winds and warm waters to form destructive storm clouds. These clouds swirl around a single center at up to 220 mph (360 kmh). A hurricane can last for up to 18 hours.

**Regional climate**
The countries of the Caribbean all enjoy a warm, tropical climate. Mountainous islands, such as the Windwards, receive three times as much rainfall as lower areas. Most islands have a wet, hurricane-prone season between June and November. From January to March, it is generally dry and pleasant.

82°F (28°C)   73°F (23°C)
46 in (1,167 mm)

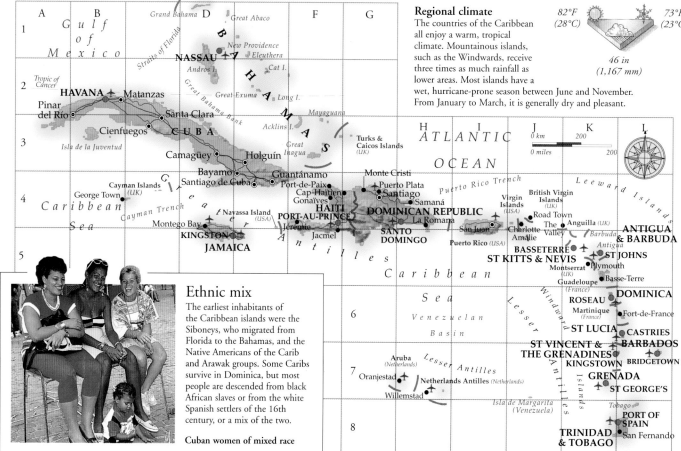

**Ethnic mix**
The earliest inhabitants of the Caribbean islands were the Siboneys, who migrated from Florida to the Bahamas, and the Native Americans of the Carib and Arawak groups. Some Caribs survive in Dominica, but most people are descended from black African slaves or from the white Spanish settlers of the 16th century, or a mix of the two.

**Cuban women of mixed race**

172

# Cuba

The largest island in the Caribbean, Cuba has fertile lowlands set between three large mountainous regions. Sugar, rice, tobacco, and coffee are grown on the lowlands, and chromium and nickel are mined. Formerly a Spanish colony, Cuba has been a communist state since 1959. Hostile politics caused the US to impose a trade embargo, which has disabled Cuba's economy and kept it agricultural.

*Sugar is extracted from the cane.*

### Sugar
With an annual production of 55,000,000 tons (50,000,000 tonnes), sugarcane is Cuba's largest crop. It is grown around Havana and processed in the city's factories. Cuba is one of the world's largest producers but suffered a decline in the 1990s following the collapse of one of its main customers, the Soviet Union.

### Havana
Situated in a natural harbor, Cuba's chief port and capital, Havana, was founded by the Spanish in 1515. Its old town has many ancient buildings and cobbled streets. There are no shantytowns here, unlike many capitals in the region, but of its 2,328,000 people, half live in substandard houses.

### Communism
The only communist state in the Caribbean, Cuba is led by Fidel Castro (b. 1926), who led the revolution in 1959. Under Castro, and with Soviet help, Cuba made considerable social and economic progress, although living standards suffered with the breakup of Soviet communism in 1991. US policies remain hostile.

## CUBA FACTS

| | |
|---|---|
| CAPITAL CITY | Havana |
| AREA | 42,803 sq miles (110,860 sq km) |
| POPULATION | 11,200,000 |
| MAIN LANGUAGE | Spanish |
| MAJOR RELIGION | Christian |
| CURRENCY | Peso |

### Cigars
Cuba's fertile soil and warm climate are ideal for growing high-quality tobacco. Havana cigars are popular all over the world and are made from a blend of at least five different types of tobacco. Cigars are still rolled by hand at long wooden tables.

# Bahamas

Located to the northeast of Cuba, the Bahamas extend south for about 600 miles (965 km). Of the 3,000 coral islands and islets, only 30 are inhabited. Most of the people are black, but on Spanish Wells Island, there are about 1,200 white descendants of Puritan settlers. Tourism, fishing, and financial services flourish on the islands.

### Festival
Music and dancing are everywhere in the Caribbean, but especially so at the Junkanoo Festival in the Bahamas. Held at the end of every year, Junkanoo is a lively celebration with street dancing, music, and colorful parades where people wear wild costumes and blow whistles. The festival has roots in the celebrations of a slave leader called John Canoe, and slaves' days off at Christmas.

## BAHAMAS FACTS

| | |
|---|---|
| CAPITAL CITY | Nassau |
| AREA | 3,864 sq miles (10,010 sq km) |
| POPULATION | 307,000 |
| MAIN LANGUAGE | English |
| MAJOR RELIGION | Christian |
| CURRENCY | Bahamian dollar |

# Jamaica

The third largest island of the Caribbean, Jamaica is a land of springs, rivers, waterfalls, and sandy beaches. A few wealthy families dominate the island, but the slum areas around Kingston are controlled by violent gangs. Many of the people of those areas are Rastafarians, worshipers of the former emperor of Ethiopia. Jamaica is a prosperous country, with booming tourist, mining, and farming industries. Cricket is a popular game.

### Reggae
Jamaica's distinctive form of popular music, reggae, began in the 1960s as an offshoot of rhythm and blues, with songs calling for social and political change. Bob Marley (1945–81), whose band became very popular in the 1970s, is a reggae icon, and his birthday is celebrated by all Jamaicans.

**Okra**

**Breadfruit**

### Vegetables
Jamaicans grow a wide range of vegetables. *Dasheen*, or *taro*, is a staple vegetable. The roots and leaves are eaten. There are more than 1,000 varieties of *dasheen* and it is also used for medicinal purposes. Okra are green pods that are used in "pepperpot stews." Breadfruit, with a creamy, pulpy texture, grow to 5 in (13 cm) wide, and are eaten baked or roasted.

**Dasheen or taro**

### Women
The Caribbean women's rights movement began in Jamaica, and many Jamaican women hold senior posts in economic and political life. An increasing number of women prefer to be single mothers, especially those who have careers. Women also dominate the growing data-processing industry, largely because they work for lower wages than men.

## JAMAICA FACTS

| | |
|---|---|
| CAPITAL CITY | Kingston |
| AREA | 4,243 sq miles (10,990 sq km) |
| POPULATION | 2,600,000 |
| MAIN LANGUAGE | English |
| MAJOR RELIGIONS | Christian, Rastafarian |
| CURRENCY | Jamaican dollar |

### Bauxite
Jamaica is the world's third largest producer of bauxite, the ore from which aluminum is made. Refineries produce alumina, the next stage in producing the metal, worth ten times as much as the ore. Aluminum provides half of Jamaica's export income, and accounts for 10 percent of global output.

C

# Haiti

Occupying the western third of the island of Hispaniola, Haiti is one of the most mountainous countries in the Caribbean. It is also the poorest. About 95 percent of its people are descendents of black slaves. The country is overcrowded and has suffered deforestation, soil erosion, and desertification, as well as a turbulent political history.

## Voodoo

A Haitian blend of West African religions and Christianity, voodoo uses drumming, singing, and dance. Its followers believe that through worship of spirits, they can live in harmony with nature and their dead. Many celebrations coincide with Christmas and the Mexican Day of the Dead.

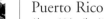
*Voodooists on Gede, or All Saint's Day*

**HAITI FACTS**

| | |
|---|---|
| CAPITAL CITY | Port-au-Prince |
| AREA | 10,714 sq miles (27,750 sq km) |
| POPULATION | 8,200,000 |
| MAIN LANGUAGES | French, French Creole |
| MAJOR RELIGIONS | Christian, Voodoo |
| CURRENCY | Gourde |

## Port-au-Prince

Modern hotels have lured many visitors to Haiti's capital, Port-au-Prince. The city has two cathedrals, a university, and many government buildings. However, it also has the worst slums in the Caribbean, most of which are found north of the city. They have no sewage system and are overcrowded.

## Puerto Rico

About 994 miles (1,600 km) southeast of Miami, the crowded island of Puerto Rico is a self-governing territory of the US. It is home to more than 3.8 million people, of African and Spanish descent, of whom half live in the capital, San Juan. An old walled city, it has colonial buildings.

**Balconies, old San Juan**

# Dominican Republic

Lying 600 miles (966 km) southeast of Florida, the Dominican Republic spreads across the eastern two-thirds of Hispaniola. It has the Caribbean's highest peak, Pico Duarte, 10,417 ft (3,175 m), and also its lowest point, crocodile-infested Lake Enriquillo, 144 ft (44 m) below sea level. Nickel, amber, and gold mining are important industries, and vacationers flock to the island for its long pearly beaches, modern hotels, and wildlife.

## People

With a higher standard of living than neighboring Haiti, the Dominican Republic provides good health care for its people. The mixed race middle classes form about 73 percent of the population. The minority of blacks work as farmers, selling their produce at market.

## Farming

About 24 percent of the labor force works on farms located in the north and east of the country, and in the San Juan valley. Sugar, tobacco, and cocoa are main crops, and although the market has slowed, most are exported to the US.

*Tobacco leaves are hung upside down to dry and then made into cigars and cigarettes.*

**DOMINICAN REPUBLIC FACTS**

| | |
|---|---|
| CAPITAL CITY | Santo Domingo |
| AREA | 18,815 sq miles (48,730 sq km) |
| POPULATION | 8,500,000 |
| MAIN LANGUAGES | Spanish, French Creole |
| MAJOR RELIGION | Christian |
| CURRENCY | Dominican republic peso |

## Tourism

The Dominican Republic is the largest tourist destination in the Caribbean, attracting two million each year. The industry brings in half of the country's earnings and provides much-needed jobs.

# St. Kitts and Nevis

The two islands of St. Kitts (or St. Christopher) and Nevis sit in the northern part of the Leeward Islands. Both are mountainous and their idyllic palm-fringed beaches attract many tourists. Most people are descendents of black Africans, and nearly all work in farming or tourism.

**ST. KITTS AND NEVIS FACTS**

| | |
|---|---|
| CAPITAL CITY | Basseterre |
| AREA | 139 sq miles (360 sq km) |
| POPULATION | 41,000 |
| MAIN LANGUAGE | English |
| MAJOR RELIGION | Christian |
| CURRENCY | Eastern Caribbean dollar |

## Sugarcane

The main crop on St. Kitts is sugarcane, which accounts for 25 percent of exports and provides 12 percent of jobs. Low world prices and hurricane damage have created problems.

# Antigua and Barbuda

The largest of the Leeward Islands, Antigua has two dependencies: Barbuda, a small coral island bursting with wildlife, and Redonda, an uninhabited rock with its own king. The blue lagoons and corals that surround Antigua teem with tropical fish.

**ANTIGUA AND BARBUDA FACTS**

| | |
|---|---|
| CAPITAL CITY | St. John's |
| AREA | 170 sq miles (440 sq km) |
| POPULATION | 66,400 |
| MAIN LANGUAGE | English |
| MAJOR RELIGION | Christian |
| CURRENCY | Eastern Caribbean dollar |

## Yachting

The harbor at St. John's has an annual Sailing Week that attracts many visitors. Throughout the year, cruise ships and luxury boats call at the 18th-century Nelson's Dockyard.

# Dominica

The largest and most mountainous of the Windward Islands, Dominica has some of the finest scenery in the Caribbean, with rain forests containing 200 wildlife species. Bananas and coconuts are principal exports; shrimp farming is proving successful.

## DOMINICA FACTS

CAPITAL CITY  Roseau

AREA  290 sq miles (750 sq km)

POPULATION  73,000

MAIN LANGUAGES  English, French

MAJOR RELIGION  Christian

CURRENCY  Eastern Caribbean dollar

### Carib reservation

In the 1900s, the British forced the Caribs to move to a reservation. Today, the Carib reservation, on the east coast of the island, is home to more than 2,000 Caribs, descendants of the original inhabitants. Within the reservation – a popular tourist attraction – Caribs follow traditional lifestyles, although their language has died out. Many Carib craftspeople make a living selling bags made from banana leaves and grasses.

# St. Lucia

The beautiful island of St. Lucia has clear seas, sandy beaches, and striking volcanic mountains. Most people work in farming, tourism, or industry. Each year, 165,000 tons (150,000 tonnes) of bananas are exported.

## ST. LUCIA FACTS

CAPITAL CITY  Castries

AREA  239 sq miles (620 sq km)

POPULATION  156,300

MAIN LANGUAGE  English

MAJOR RELIGION  Christian

CURRENCY  Eastern Caribbean dollar

### Ecotourism

St. Lucia's lush rain forests, hot springs, and twin Piton peaks are attractions that lure visitors to the island. Aromatic tropical plants, trees, and flowers grow everywhere.

# Barbados

Known as the "singular island," Barbados lies 100 miles (160 km) east of the Caribbean chain. Barbados retains a strong English influence, and many Britons retire to the island. The people of Barbados, called Bajans, enjoy some of the Caribbean's highest living standards.

## BARBADOS FACTS

CAPITAL CITY  Bridgetown

AREA  166 sq miles (430 sq km)

POPULATION  270,000

MAIN LANGUAGE  English

MAJOR RELIGION  Christian

CURRENCY  Barbados dollar

### Tourism

Barbados has one of the Caribbean's most well-developed and lucrative tourist industries. About 556,000 people visit the island every year.

# St. Vincent and the Grenadines

The quiet island of St. Vincent is fertile and volcanic, while its 100 tiny sister islands of the Grenadines are flat coral reefs. Both are exclusive vacation resorts and their clear waters are popular with yachts-people. Bananas are the main export.

## ST. VINCENT AND THE GRENADINES FACTS

CAPITAL CITY  Kingstown

AREA  131 sq miles (340 sq km)

POPULATION  115,500

MAIN LANGUAGE  English

MAJOR RELIGION  Christian

CURRENCY  Eastern Caribbean dollar

### Arrowroot

St. Vincent is the world's largest producer of arrowroot, a starchy liquid that is removed from the arrowroot plant. It is used as a thickening agent in foods and, more recently, as a fine finish for computer paper. Arrowroot is St. Vincent's second largest export.

**Arrowroot**

**Arrowroot powder**

# Grenada

The most southerly of the Windwards, Grenada rises from a rugged coast to a high forested interior. Formerly a British colony, Grenada has built its economy on agriculture and tourism. Its people are of African or mixed origin.

Nutmeg

Ginger

Cinnamon

## GRENADA FACTS

CAPITAL CITY  St. George's

AREA  131 sq miles (340 sq km)

POPULATION  99,500

MAIN LANGUAGE  English

MAJOR RELIGION  Christian

CURRENCY  Eastern Caribbean dollar

### Spices

Grenada is described as the "spice island." It grows about two-thirds of the world's nutmeg and, with Indonesia, dominates the market. Large quantities of cloves, mace, cinnamon, ginger, bay leaves, saffron, and pepper are also cultivated on the island.

# Trinidad and Tobago

The low-lying island of Trinidad and its smaller partner, Tobago, lie just off the coast of Venezuela. The islands have a vivid, cosmopolitan culture, home to people from every continent. Both have fertile farmland, fine beaches, and abundant wildlife.

## TRINIDAD AND TOBAGO FACTS

CAPITAL CITY  Port-of-Spain

AREA  1,981 sq miles (5,130 sq km)

POPULATION  1,317,000

MAIN LANGUAGE  English

MAJOR RELIGIONS  Christian, Hindu, Muslim

CURRENCY  Trinidad and Tobago dollar

### Steel bands

Trinidad and Tobago are the home of steel bands, calypso, and limbo dancing. The first drums, or *pans*, began as empty oil containers. Today, drums are hand-decorated and tuned so that melodies can be played on them. They provide the beat for lively calypso songs.

FIND OUT MORE    CARIBBEAN, HISTORY OF    CHRISTIANITY    FARMING    FESTIVALS    ISLANDS    MUSIC    RELIGIONS    ROCKS AND MINERALS    SLAVERY    VOLCANOES

C

# CARIBBEAN, HISTORY OF

FOR CENTURIES, the Caribbean islands were home to the Carib and Arawak peoples. Their way of life was abruptly disturbed when Europeans arrived in the 1490s. Within 100 years, most had been wiped out by new European rulers who brought thousands of Africans into the Caribbean to work on sugar plantations. The sugar-based economy continued until its decline in the late 19th century. From the mid-1960s, the islands gradually gained independence from European control.

### Original inhabitants
The Caribs were expert navigators, traveling great distances in wooden canoes. The Arawaks were skilled craftsworkers, who produced baskets and furniture.

Arawak-style wooden seat from the Bahamas

### Spanish conquest
The arrival of the Spanish-sponsored navigator Christopher Columbus in the Caribbean in 1492 transformed the region. Convoys of galleons laden with gold and other treasures from the Spanish empire in South America soon crossed the sea on their way back to Spain. Within a few years, Spanish armies had conquered and settled almost every island. Most of the Caribs were killed by the invaders.

Columbus's ship, the *Santa Maria*

## European settlement
In the 16th century, with unofficial government backing, English, French, and Dutch pirates raided Spanish treasure ships. They also captured many of the smaller islands. Settlers from Europe arrived, and by 1750 most of the islands were under British, French, or Dutch rule

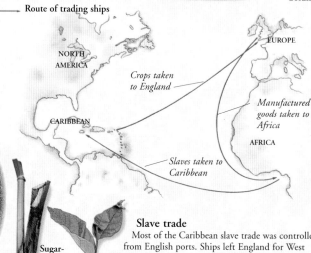

Route of trading ships

NORTH AMERICA

EUROPE

*Crops taken to England*

*Manufactured goods taken to Africa*

CARIBBEAN

AFRICA

*Slaves taken to Caribbean*

### Toussaint L'Ouverture
Ex-slave Toussaint L'Ouverture (1743–1803) led a revolt of slaves in French-ruled Haiti in the 1790s. He declared the country a republic, but the French regained control and took him to France, where he died.

### Plantations
Europeans set up plantations to satisfy demand for sugar and tobacco in Europe. African slaves worked on the plantations. By 1750, the Caribbean produced most of the world's sugar.

Sugar-cane

Tobacco

### Slave trade
Most of the Caribbean slave trade was controlled from English ports. Ships left England for West Africa with goods to barter for slaves. The slaves were shipped across the Atlantic. Sugar, tobacco, and other crops were then taken back to England for sale.

## Rastafarians
Many Jamaicans are Rastafarians. They believe that the last emperor of Ethiopia, Ras Tafari, or Haile Selassie, was the new messiah who would one day lead his people back to Africa.

### Cuban War
In 1895, following an earlier, unsuccessful uprising, the Cubans rose in revolt against their Spanish rulers. In 1898, the US declared war on Spain, and freed Cuba.

### Emigration
After World War II, many people left the Caribbean in search of work and a better standard of living in Europe. In 1948, the *Empire Windrush* took 492 emigrants from Kingston, Jamaica, to London. Over the next 20 years, thousands of Caribbean islanders emigrated to Britain.

### Fidel Castro
In 1959, Fidel Castro (b.1927) became the President of Cuba and introduced many social reforms. The US government tried to depose him in 1961, and he turned to the USSR for help. When Soviet nuclear missiles were installed in Cuba in 1962, the world came close to nuclear war.

## Timeline
**1300s** Caribs drive out Arawak people from the eastern Caribbean islands.

**1492** Christopher Columbus lands in the Bahamas.

**1500s** The Spanish take control of the Caribbean.

**1700s** French, British, Dutch, and Danes capture many islands.

**1804** Haiti becomes first Caribbean island to achieve independence from European rule.

**1898–1902** Cuba under rule of US.

**1933** Fulgencio Batista becomes ruler of Cuba.

**1948** *Empire Windrush* takes first emigrants to Britain.

Capturing a slave

**1959** Cuban Revolution; Fidel Castro takes power.

**1962** Cuban missile crisis brings the US and the USSR to the brink of nuclear war.

**1983** US overthrows left-wing regime in Grenada.

**1962** Jamaica is first British Caribbean colony to win independence.

**1962–83** Most British islands win independence; Dutch and French islands remain tied to Europeans.

Flag of Jamaica

**1994** US intervenes to secure democracy in Haiti, after years of dictatorship on the island.

FIND OUT MORE

AFRICA, EAST    COLUMBUS, CHRISTOPHER    EMPIRES    EXPLORATION    FRANCE, HISTORY OF    GOVERNMENTS AND POLITICS    SLAVERY    SPAIN, HISTORY OF

# CARNIVOROUS PLANTS

PLANTS THAT catch and "eat" insects are called carnivorous plants. These plants fall into two groups. Some species, such as the Venus flytrap, have active traps with moving parts. Other species have passive traps, catching their victims on a sticky surface or drowning them in a pool of fluid. Carnivorous plants live in areas where the soil is poor in nitrates and other nutrients, such as bogs, peatlands, and swamps. They obtain extra nutrients by catching insects, which are digested by special juices.

Monkey-cup pitcher plant

*Tendril*

**Pitcher plants** from Southeast Asia form traps that hang from their leaves.

*Hanging pitcher*

## Passive traps

Most carnivorous plants have passive traps. Usually the leaves of these plants have evolved to catch insects in a variety of ways. Some are sticky, others form pit-fall traps with fluid at the bottom and are called pitcher plants.

*The lid and the smooth rim are often brightly colored to attract insects.*

*Rim of the pitcher contains nectar.*

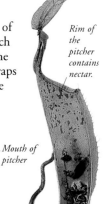

*Mouth of pitcher*

*Lid stays closed while the pitcher develops.*

*Insects fall into the liquid and are digested.*

### Development of a pitcher plant

1 A young leaf tip extends into a tendril.

2 An upturned swelling appears at the end.

3 The swelling develops into a pitcher.

4 The lid opens when the pitcher is mature.

## American pitcher plants

Although they catch their prey in the same way as other pitcher plants, American pitcher plants grow up from the ground rather than hanging from leaves. The inside of the pitcher is slippery and lined with downward pointing hairs which prevent the insects from escaping. The liquid below drowns and slowly digests them.

### Pitcher plant

*Pitcher is made of leaves joined at the edges.*

## Butterworts

These small plants have sticky leaves. Small flies are attracted to their smell and get stuck. The leaves slowly roll up, and the insects are digested by juices that ooze out of the leaf.

**Common butterwort**

*Leaf*

*Sundew flowers develop at the end of a long stalk.*

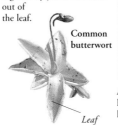

**A fly stuck to the hairs on a sundew leaf**

**Cape sundew**

## Active traps

Any trap with moving parts is called an active trap. These include plants such as sundews and butterworts, and the Venus flytrap.

### Sundews

The upper surface of a sundew leaf is covered with red hairs that secrete drops of clear, sticky liquid. Insects get stuck, then the edges of the leaf slowly roll inward enclosing the insect, and the plant secretes juices that digest it.

*Sticky leaf*

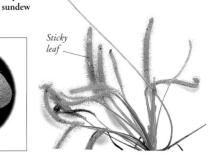

## Venus flytrap

The most spectacular of the carnivorous plants is the Venus flytrap. It is related to the sundews but has evolved a more elaborate trap. The Venus flytrap grows wild only in one small patch of marshy ground on the border of North and South Carolina, US. Its trap springs closed when an insect touches the hairs on its surface.

*Closed trap*

## Bladderworts

These are rootless water plants. Their leaves and stems bear tiny bladders with a lid covered in sensitive hairs. If a creature brushes the hairs, the lid of the bladder flips open. Water rushes in, carrying the victim with it.

**Greater bladderwort**

*Stimulation of at least three trigger hairs sets off the mechanism that closes the trap.*

*Surface of the trap*

**Venus flytrap**

**Magnified view of a trigger hair**

## How a Venus flytrap works

1 An insect lands on a leaf, touching the sensitive trigger hairs.

2 The leaf closes, and the spines interlock, trapping the insect.

3 The trap is fully closed in 30 minutes, and digestion begins.

*Trigger hair*

*Trap is fringed with long spines.*

*Insect is trapped in one-fifth of a second.*

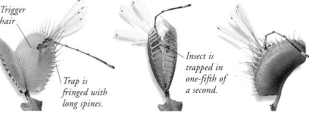
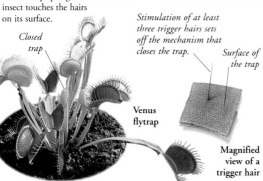

**FIND OUT MORE**
ASIAN WILDLIFE | FLOWERS | INSECTS | NORTH AMERICAN WILDLIFE | PLANTS | PLANTS, ANATOMY | PLANTS, DEFENSE | PLANTS, REPRODUCTION | SOUTH AMERICAN WILDLIFE

C

# CARS AND TRUCKS

A Benz Motor
Wagen of 1886

OF ALL THE DIFFERENT FORMS of transportation, cars have the biggest effect on our lives. Cars give people the freedom to go where they like, when they like – with some types of car you don't even need a road. Trucks are used for long-distance haulage and for performing many specialized tasks, such as fire-fighting. In parts of the world where there are no railroads, trucks offer the only way of transporting goods. But cars and trucks create pollution. Because there are now so many of them on the roads, the world's cities have become clogged with traffic, and the air that many of us breathe is poisoned with traffic fumes.

## Early cars

Early cars were called "horseless carriages." They were made by manufacturers of horse-drawn carriages and coaches, and had the same large wheels, high driver's seat, and suspension. They were powered by a single-cylinder gasoline engine, which could reach a top speed of 9 mph (15 kmh).

## Modern cars

Efficiency, safety, and comfort are the most important features of a modern car, as well as minimal air pollution from exhaust fumes. To be efficient, cars need engines that use as little fuel as possible, and a streamlined shape to reduce air resistance. In some cars, electronics help efficiency and safety. Modern cars are built with the help of computers and robots in high-tech, automated car plants.

### Henry Ford

American engineer Henry Ford (1863–1947) formed the Ford Motor Company in 1903. In 1908 Ford launched the Model T. It was made cheaply on a factory assembly line and sold by the million.

*Stiff body* is made from thin sheets of steel pressed into shape and welded together. It is chemically treated and painted to protect against rusting.

*Windshield* of toughened glass protects driver and passengers from wind and rain. If hit by a stone, the windshield cracks but does not shatter.

*Side windows can be lowered.*

*Padded seats*

*Engine* burns fuel and uses the energy stored within the fuel to propel the car along.

*Hood is raised to examine engine.*

*Radiator* circulates water around the engine to cool it.

*Luggage is stored in trunk.*

*Rear bumper*

**Exhaust pipe** carries waste gases away from the engine and expels them at the rear of the car.

*Hub-cap covers the center of the wheel.*

**Suspension** spring allows the wheel to move up and down as the car travels over bumps in the road, protecting passengers against uncomfortable jolting.

**Driveshaft** connects the transmission to the rear wheels, which are driven around by the engine.

**Transmission** contains intermeshing gear wheels which allow the engine to drive the road wheels at different speeds.

**Pneumatic (air-filled) tires** grip the road and help give a smooth ride.

*Front bumper*

---

*Car has plenty of room for luggage.*

**Family sedan**

*Aerodynamic design enhances speed performance.*

**Sports car**

**Minivan/MPV**

*Three rows of detachable seats*

**Formula 1 racer**

*Wing*

*Driver's cockpit*

## Types of cars

The most popular car is the sedan, which has an enclosed passenger compartment and a separate rear space for luggage. Hatchbacks are sedans with a large rear door and a folding back seat for extra luggage space.

### Sports cars

Sports cars are designed to be stylish, fast, and fun. Some sports cars are convertibles, which have a flexible roof that can be folded down so that passengers can enjoy driving in the open air. Luxury convertibles have roofs that open and close automatically.

### Minivan

One of the latest types of car is the minivan, or multi-purpose vehicle (MPV). This vehicle is a cross between a sedan car and a van. People carriers are very versatile, with at least six seats and plenty of space for luggage. They are perfect for outings or vacations.

### Racing car

Some cars are custom-built for racing. They have a very powerful engine, wide tires, and a low, wide body for stability around fast corners. An aerodynamic "wing" on the back helps keep the car on the road at high speeds. Sedans can be converted into racing or rallying cars.

# Trucks

Trucks are used for carrying cargo along roads. Their journeys can range from a few miles on local deliveries to thousands of miles across continents. The first trucks were built in the 1890s, and were driven by steam engines. Since then, trucks have grown ever larger. In Australia, trucks called road trains tow hundreds of tons of cargo across long distances in several full-sized trailers. Some trucks are "rigid," which means, built in one piece. Articulated trucks are built in two sections: a tractor unit and a semitrailer, which is designed to carry specialized loads. Great skill is required to drive an articulated truck.

## Modern trucks

At the heart of most modern trucks is a powerful diesel engine, using diesel oil, a type of gasoline. Some diesel engines are turbocharged for extra power. The engine powers the truck, and operates any hydraulic parts, such as the lifting arms of a dumper. Some trucks, such as military vehicles, have chunky tires and strong suspensions, to enable them to travel off-road in rough terrain.

*Some trucks have up to 20 forward and 10 reverse gears.*

**A tractor unit and semitrailer**

## Inside a truck cab

Long-distance truck drivers spend many hours in the cabs of their trucks. Cabs are designed for comfort, and some of the controls, such as the steering and brakes, are power-assisted to make them easy to use. Many cabs have a small rear room, with a bunk, washing facilities, and television. To help prevent accidents, some countries have introduced tachometers to record how many hours the truck is on the road. It is illegal for the driver to go beyond a certain number of hours.

**Heating controls** (temperature selector and fan speed selector) keep cab at a comfortable temperature in hot or cold weather.

**Cassette, radio,** and CB (citizens' band) radio provide entertainment on the road. Drivers may use CB to warn each other of traffic jams.

**Adjustable nozzles** allow fresh air into the cab.

**Warning indicators** light up if anything goes wrong with the truck.

**Gauges,** such as the speedometer, show speed, engine temperature, and the amount of fuel left.

**Large diameter steering wheel** is easy to turn with power assistance. This is known as power steering.

*Gear selector*    *Clutch pedal controls gears.*    *Brake pedal*    *Accelerator pedal*

## Karl Benz

In 1886, German engineer Karl Benz (1844–1929) patented his first car, using an internal combustion engine. The car had electric ignition, three wheels, differential gears, and was water-cooled. In 1926, his company merged with Daimler to become one of the leading car and truck producers in the world.

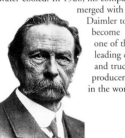

# Research and development

Modern research aims at improving car economy, safety, and ecology. Because gasoline reserves are limited and its use is environmentally unsound, research is taking place into new fuels from sustainable sources, such as plant oils. Researchers are also experimenting with new materials for car parts, including plastics for car bodies. Car manufacturers are aware that making cars cleaner and safer is likely to improve sales.

*Crash test dummy*

**Testing airbag inflation**

## Catalytic converter

Cars and trucks are gradually becoming "cleaner," which means they create less pollution. Most new cars have a catalytic converter that removes carbon monoxide, nitrogen oxides, and other poisonous chemicals from the exhaust gases.

**Catalytic converter from car exhaust**

## Safety features

Manufacturers are constantly developing new safety features, such as airbags that inflate automatically in the event of an accident. They are also working on new ways of preventing accidents, such as antilock brakes.

# Types of truck

Most trucks start life as a standard chassis and cab. Car manufacturers can then add the body, which determines the function of the truck. Common specialized trucks include garbage trucks, flat trailers to transport large items such as cars, tankers, fire engines, and vehicles modified to carry animals, such as horse trailers.

**Garbage truck**
This truck has a closed container for garbage and a garbage-can elevator that empties a pail into the body through a protective shield.

**Car transporter**
A car transporter is used to convey cars to showrooms. There are ramps at the back that fold down at the rear so that the cars can be driven on and off. The trailer of a car transporter can carry up to 18 vehicles.

*Storage space above the cab.*

**Horse trailer**
This truck carries horses to shows. The horse enters the truck via a door at the rear that folds down to make a loading ramp.

 **FIND OUT MORE**    BICYCLES AND MOTORCYCLES    ENGINES AND MOTORS    FORCE AND MOTION    OIL    POLLUTION    ROADS    TRANSPORT HISTORY OF    TRAVEL    UNITED STATES, HISTORY OF

# Cars

*Known as the "Silver Ghost"*

*Introduced front wheel drive*

**Rolls Royce 40/50,** UK; launched 1907; top speed 55 mph (88 kmh)

**Model T Ford,** US; launched 1908; top speed 42 mph (68 kmh)

**Citroën Traction Avant,** France; launched 1934; top speed 70 mph (113 kmh)

*Best-selling car ever produced*

*An icon of 1950s' America*

**Volkswagon Beetle,** Germany; launched 1939; top speed 82 mph (132 kmh)

**Jaguar XK120,** UK; launched 1949; top speed 126 mph (203 kmh)

**Ford Thunderbird,** US; launched 1955; top speed 114 mph (183 kmh)

*Famous "gullwing" doors*

*Nicknamed "the shark"*

**Mercedes-Benz 300SL,** Germany; launched 1954; top speed 165 mph (265 kmh)

**Fiat 500 D,** Italy; launched 1957; top speed 59 mph (95 kmh)

**Citroën DS,** France; launched 1960; top speed 116 mph (187 kmh)

*A sporty, compact car*

*Won the Le Mans 24-hour race four times in a row*

**Austin Mini Cooper,** UK; launched 1963; top speed 100 mph (161 kmh)

**Ford Mustang,** US; launched 1964; top speed 127 mph (204 kmh)

**Ford GT40,** US; launched 1964; top speed 200 mph (322 kmh)

*Streamlined shape*

*Classed as a passenger van*

*Micro-car is ecologically designed and easy to park.*

**Porsche Carrera 911 RS,** Germany; launched 1972; top speed 150 mph (243 kmh)

**Toyota Previa,** Japan; launched 1990; top speed 111 mph (180 kmh)

**Smart car,** France/Germany; launched 1998; top speed 87 mph (139 kmh)

# Trucks

*Front, tractor section*

*So heavy and wide, it can use only major roads*

*18 wheels*

**Pickup or utilities truck:** useful for carrying small loads, these popular trucks have open, flat backs

**Semitrailer:** a monster truck suitable for a wide range of bulk or heavy goods

# CARTOONS AND ANIMATION

CARTOONS, OR ANIMATED FILMS, are movies in which drawings or models seem to come to life. The effect is achieved by slight changes to the drawing or model between each frame of film. Animated films first appeared in the 1900s, and the art has developed alongside motion pictures; computer animation is now used to create amazing special effects in movies. Cartoons usually have a comic theme, although animation can also be a thought-provoking medium for a serious message.

## Direct animation

With this method the animator creates characters from clay or other media. The characters are slightly repositioned before the camera between each frame of film, creating the effect of movement.

Scene from *A Close Shave* (1995)

**Clay model in an animated sequence**

*Step 1: figure starts out with his back to the camera.*

*Step 2: position is manually altered before next frame is shot.*

*Step 3: a sequence has been created which shows him turning around.*

### Wallace & Gromit
Wallace & Gromit are the creations of British animator Nick Park and have starred in several award-winning films. The plasticine puppets are less than 6 in (15 cm) high. It took a budget of $1.9 million and a crew of 25 animators, modelmakers, and camera operators to make *A Close Shave*.

### Key shapes
Traditionally, one of the most difficult areas of direct animation has been to show a character talking. Specific mouth and lip positions, called "key shapes", must be created for every word spoken. Today, computers can aid this process.

### Chuck Jones
US animator Chuck Jones (1912–2002) drew the rabbit Bugs Bunny and many other famous characters in Warner Brothers' "Looney Tunes" cartoons. He directed his first animated film in 1938 and made 300 films in his lifetime, winning three Academy Awards.

## Computer animation

Animators use computers to draw the images between the start and end of an action, or to improve or alter hand-drawn images. Computers can now generate an entire film, as in *Toy Story* (1996), as well as breathtaking special effects.

### Aladdin
*Aladdin* (1992) was one of Disney's first major computer-animated films. Although the characters were hand-drawn, three-dimensional software was used to create dramatic effects in lighting, texture, and movement, such as the lava sequence.

© Disney

### Hanna-Barbera
The US animators Bill Hanna (1910–2001) and Joe Barbera (b.1911) created many of the most popular TV cartoon characters. Their first film, called *Puss Gets the Boot*, was released in 1940 and starred Tom and Jerry, the cat and mouse rivals. Other Hanna-Barbera characters include Yogi Bear and the Flintstones.

## Cel animation

In cel animation, animators produce at least 12 drawings for each second of action. The background, which usually does not move, is drawn on paper. The animator draws the moving characters on layers of cel (clear plastic film), so there is no need to redraw the parts that do not move between frames. The background shows through the clear areas of cel.

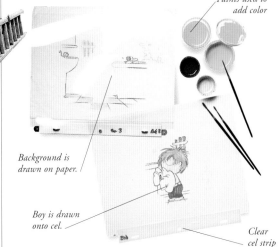

*Paints used to add color*

*Background is drawn on paper.*

*Boy is drawn onto cel.*

*Clear cel strip*

### The Simpsons
Matt Groening created *The Simpsons* while still at school, publishing them as a newspaper comic strip. The animated series made its debut on US television in 1989 and has since become one of the world's most popular shows. The quirky storylines centre on Bart and his family.

*Homer* *Marg* *Maggie* *Lisa* *Bart*

**The Simpson family**

MATT GROENING

FIND OUT MORE | CAMERAS | DISNEY, WALT | FILMS AND FILM-MAKING | NEWSPAPERS AND MAGAZINES | PAINTING AND DRAWING

# CASTLES

IN MEDIEVAL EUROPE, castles acted as both home and military stronghold. They were occupied by a lord, his family, servants, and sometimes an army of professional soldiers. They provided refuge for local people in times of war. Local lords could control the surrounding land from their castles, which meant they were a very important part of feudalism. Castles were built to be defended, with walls strong enough to keep out an enemy while allowing the occupants to shoot at any attackers. Designs changed as builders invented better methods of defense, or adapted new ideas from castles in the Islamic world.

**The Chapel**
Every castle had its own chapel. It was usually in an upper room in one of the towers. This is the chancel of the chapel at Conwy. The altar would have been beneath the windows, and there would have been enough room for everyone in the castle to gather together.

*Northwest Tower*
*Outer Ward*

**The Great Hall** was the center of activity. There was a high table for the lord and lady, and lower tables for everyone else.

**The Kitchen** was where food for the whole castle was prepared. There were wood fires, oak tables, and alcoves.

**The Stockhouse Tower** got its name when stocks for prisoners were made here in the 1500s.

**The Inner Ward** was the last refuge in time of attack.

**Machicolations**, or overhanging parapets, allowed defenders to pour boiling water on their opponents.

*Chapel Tower*

**The Prison Tower** had a deep, dark dungeon.

*Bakehouse Tower*
*King's Tower*

**Conwy Castle, Wales, in the 13th century**

**The King's Tower**
This room on the first floor close to the royal apartments has a stone fireplace and a recessed window. The recess means a person looking out remains safe from any enemy fire. The original floors have been removed.

*Chapel*
*King's Tower*

## Parts of a castle

Early castles had a keep, which contained the lord's rooms, hall, chapel, storerooms, and a well-defended gatehouse. Later castles abandoned the keep and replaced it with a Great Hall, which was built against the castle walls. The lord's rooms were sometimes built into the gatehouse, but in Conwy they are in the Inner Ward, which was the heart of the castle, and most easily defended.

**The East Barbican** was the first line of defense against attack by sea, and was also a good position from which to fire. Defenders could isolate the enemy in this area.

*Lookout Tower*

## Timeline

**1066** The Normans erect wooden motte-and-bailey castles during the conquest of England. These are quick to build, and the motte, or tower on top of a mound, is easy to defend. Most buildings are in the bailey, or courtyard.

**Krak des Chevaliers, Syria**

**1142** Krak des Chevaliers in Syria, one of the most easy-to-defend Crusader castles, has concentric stone walls.

**1127** Rochester Castle has a great hall, chapel, and storerooms. The entrance is well protected, and defenders can shoot at attackers.

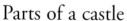
**Great Tower, Rochester, England**

**1150** Many French lords build castles along the Loire River. Examples built (or enlarged) during this period include Loches, Chinon, and Montreuil-Bellay.

**1200** The German lords of Liechtenstein build their castle on a high crag for extra defense.

**1238** The Muslim rulers of medieval Spain begin the castle-palace of the Alhambra.

**1271** Concentric castles, such as Caerphilly, become popular. They have rings of walls and sometimes water defenses (moats).

**Caerphilly, Wales**

182

# How castles were built

Building a castle required many skilled workers. A master mason drew up plans and supervised the work, and senior masons carried out the building. Carpenters did the woodwork, and metalworkers made hinges and door fasteners. In a large castle, some specialists stayed on permanently to do the maintenance work.

### Wood and earthwork
The Normans chose a site where there was a water supply, built a mound and a wooden castle on top, and surrounded the structure with a wooden fence, or palisade. Most were replaced with stone constructions.

Motte-and-bailey

### Stonework
Building a stone castle took decades, but the result was a strong castle that would withstand attack well. The important structures, such as the outer walls, mural towers, and keep, were all made of stone. Buildings in the castle courtyard were still made of timber and had thatched roofs.

# Windows

Most castle windows were narrow or cross-shaped slits. They usually had a large alcove on the inside of the wall. This alcove allowed an archer to stand aside and avoid missiles while preparing to shoot.

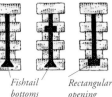

*Fishtail bottoms*    *Rectangular opening*    *Crosslet*    *Round-ended cross*    *Gun loop*

**Arrow slits** developed that were large enough for a defender to shoot an arrow out, but too small for an attacker's missiles. Later, the gun loop developed, with a circular hole to fit a gun barrel.

# Edward I
In the early years of his reign, Edward I (r.1272–1307) conquered Wales and built an "iron ring" of castles in strategic Welsh towns to keep the country under his control. Many of these Welsh castles, such as Harlech and Beaumaris, were built on the concentric plan, which meant they had both inner and outer walls for defense. Concentric castles were very difficult to attack successfully.

# Asian and African castles

Castles have been built in many different places. There was a strong tradition of castle-building in the Islamic world, and medieval soldiers took Muslim ideas about fortification to western Europe when they returned from the Crusades.

### Himeji Castle, Japan
Seventeenth-century Japan had a feudal system similar to that of medieval Europe, and Japanese lords also lived in castles. Tall towers with pagodalike roofs had narrow window openings through which soldiers could shoot. The towers were surrounded by courtyards and walls.

### Fasilidas Castle, Ethiopia
The central stronghold shows many features in common with western castles, including thick walls of stone, round corner towers, and battlements. The remains of the outer curtain wall can be seen in the foreground to the right.

### Van Castle, Turkey
Built on a rocky outcrop, Van Castle was begun in 750. It was later enlarged, and was occupied by the Seljuk and Ottoman Turks before being taken over by Armenian Christians.

# Attack and defense

Attackers could fire arrows, hurl missiles using catapults, break down doors or walls with battering rams, climb the walls using ladders, or try to demolish the walls by tunneling under them (mining). In addition to defense features, such as thick walls and doors, moats, and machicolations, a castle also needed plenty of storage space for food so that the stronghold could withstand a long siege.

*Arm*

*Sling pouch*

*Rope to pull arm down again*

*Hauling rope*

*Ropes to pull arm down*

*Throwing arm*

*Wooden cup for missile*

*Handle to turn ropes*

### Crossbow
Crossbows were powerful but slow to reload. Despite this they could be useful in defending castles, where they could be reloaded behind the safety of the stone walls.

### Catapult
The soldiers used a handle attached to a rope (made from a skein of twisted rope) to pull the throwing arm down. They then released it, and the arm flew up, releasing its missile, usually a rock, from a wooden cup.

### Traction trebuchet
This siege engine was like a giant catapult. When soldiers pulled down on the ropes, the end of the arm flew upward, and the sling opened to release a missile, which usually weighed about 100–200 lb (45–90 kg).

---

### Pfalzgrafenstein, Germany
**1338** Many German castles are built on the Rhine because of the river's importance as a trade route.

### Bodiam, England
**1385** Bodiam Castle has a curtain wall around a courtyard, which contains the hall and chapel.

### Real de Manzanares, Spain
**1416** By this time many French castles, such as Saumur on the Loire River, have conical towers, strong defensive walls, and luxurious rooms.

**1435** The elaborate Real de Manzanares is built.

**1642** In Traquair, a Scottish tower-house, turrets, and battlements are more for decoration than defense.

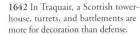

Traquair House, Scotland

**1600s** Many castles were built by local lords in Japan, like Himeji.

FIND OUT MORE    ARCHITECTURE    EUROPE, HISTORY OF    FEUDALISM    MEDIEVAL EUROPE    NORMANS

# CATS

DOMESTIC CATS are related to wild cats such as lions and tigers, and they are able to fend well for themselves. They are excellent hunters and their eyes, ears, nose, and whiskers are well adapted to their natural preference for hunting at night. Cats are affectionate and respond well to humans. They were domesticated about 4,000 years ago to keep people company and to kill pests.

## Kittens

Cats have an average of four or five kittens in a litter. Kittens love to stalk, chase, and pounce on things. This playful behavior helps make them strong and develops the skills they will need as adults.

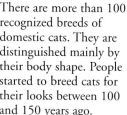

## Domestic cats

There are more than 100 recognized breeds of domestic cats. They are distinguished mainly by their body shape. People started to breed cats for their looks between 100 and 150 years ago.

White    Lilac    Red    Blue    Chocolate

## Fur

Cats can be divided into long- and shorthaired breeds. The texture of their fur varies. Common coat colors are gray-blue, black, brown, white, red, and mixtures of these, such as silver and lilac.

Siamese    British shorthair    Persian longhair    Devon Rex

## Head shapes

Cat head shapes range from large and round, like that of the British shorthair, to wedge-shaped, like that of the Siamese. Some breeds have special characteristics. The Scottish fold has ear tips that bend forward.

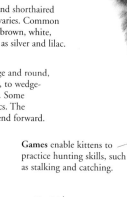

**Games** enable kittens to practice hunting skills, such as stalking and catching.

1 If a cat suddenly falls, balance organs in its ears tell it which way is up.

*Loose-fitting skin gives freedom of movement.*

*Flexible spine allows the cat to twist its body.*

## Balance

A cat's long, flexible tail helps it balance. Cats will almost always land on their feet, even when falling from a great height. They have very quick reflexes and can twist and turn their body the right way up in a fraction of a second.

### Grooming

Cats are very clean animals and spend at least an hour a day grooming, using their tongue as a "comb." The tongue has tiny hard spines called papillae on its surface. The licking helps keep the fur clean and waterproof, and also spreads the cat's scent all over its body.

*Papillae*

2 The cat turns its head around first so that it can see where it is falling, and where it is going to land.

3 Then the cat turns the rest of its body. By the time it reaches the ground, it will land on its feet.

*Back paws are brought forward.*

## Senses

Cats can see well in low light and can focus on small objects at a distance. Their super-sensitive hearing picks up sounds that we cannot hear and can also take in two sounds at once, such as a mouse in a thunderstorm. Whiskers are sensitive to touch. Cats use them to feel their way in the dark and to measure whether spaces are wide enough for them to fit through.

*Ears are funnel-shaped to draw sounds inside the ear.*

*Long, flexible ears can turn toward sounds.*

*Cats rely more on eyesight than smell when hunting. They have the largest eyes in relation to their size of any animal.*

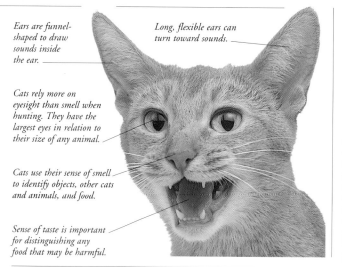

4 The cat stretches out its front legs to absorb the impact of landing.

## Claws

Cats use their claws to defend themselves and to climb. At other times, the claws are drawn in, or retracted, for protection. They are covered by a bony sheath that is an extension of the last bone of each toe and fit inside pockets in the skin.

*Cats use their sense of smell to identify objects, other cats and animals, and food.*

*Sense of taste is important for distinguishing any food that may be harmful.*

Narrow pupils in the light

Large pupils in the dark

### Changing pupils

A cat's pupils expand enormously in the dark to let in as much light as possible. A layer of cells at the back of the eyes called the tapetum reflects light back into the eye and helps cats see in the dark.

**FIND OUT MORE**

ANIMAL BEHAVIOR    EYES AND VISION    LIONS AND OTHER WILDCATS    MAMMALS    MOUNTAIN WILDLIFE

# Cats
## Longhaired

Turkish van (auburn) has a chalky white coat. *Long, silky fur*

Persian longhair (blue) has a short, bushy tail. *Flattish, round face*

Birman (seal tabby point) has pure white paws. *M-shaped tabby marking*

Somali (sorrel) was bred from the Abyssinian.

Ragdoll (blue mitted) goes limp when it is stroked. *Matching mittens*

Turkish angora (blue-cream) has fine, silky fur. *Tufted ears*

Balinese (blue tabby point) has a long, well-plumed tail.

Javanese (cinnamon) is graceful and lithe – a typical Oriental cat.

Somali (silver) has ticking (bands of color) on each hair. *Longer fur forms a ruff.*

Maine coon (brown classic tabby) is a large, hardy cat.

Color pointed longhair (chocolate point) has thick fur.

## Shorthaired

American wirehair (brown mackerel tabby) is active. *Crimped coarse fur feels like lamb's wool.*

Burmese (chocolate) has glossy fur with a satin feel.

Scottish fold (tortie and white) has folded ears. *Ears are folded forward and downward.*

Exotic (blue) is playful and affectionate. *Massive round head on a thick neck*

Manx (red classic tabby) is bred to have no tail. *Thick undercoat with longer top coat*

American shorthair (silver classic tabby) has thick fur. *Widely spaced ears with rounded tips*

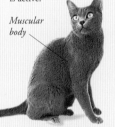

Korat (blue) is a playful cat. It has close-lying fur. *Muscular body*

Japanese bobtail (red and white) is usually patterned. *4-in (10-cm) long inflexible tail*

Egyptian mau (silver) has a spotted coat. *Dorsal stripe*

Siamese (seal point) has an angular face and large ears. *Color gets darker with age.*

California spangled (gold) has well-defined spots.

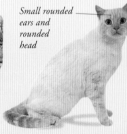

Color pointed British shorthair (cream point). *Small rounded ears and rounded head*

Oriental shorthair (foreign red) is a sleek, slender cat with fine, glossy fur.

British shorthair (chocolate) has a solid build with a round face and short nose.

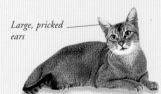

Abyssinian (usual) is an elegant cat and looks like the cats of ancient Egypt. *Large, pricked ears*

Cornish rex (cinnamon silver) has a short wavy coat, patterned over the whole body. *Flat skull and large ears*

Russian shorthair (blue) has a graceful, long body with abundant, fine fur. *Coat has a silvery sheen.*

Chartreux (blue-gray) is an old French breed. All Chartreux are this color.

Oriental shorthair (Havana) was developed from a chocolate point Siamese.

Tonkinese (cream) is a Burmese and Siamese cross. It is active and affectionate.

# CAUCASUS REPUBLICS

THE COUNTRIES of Georgia, Armenia, and Azerbaijan lie just within Asia, on a narrow plateau sandwiched between the Greater and Lesser Caucasus Mountains. They are often collectively called Transcaucasia or the Caucasus Republics. To the west of the region lies the Black Sea, and to the east, the landlocked Caspian Sea. All three countries were part of the former Soviet Union and gained their independence in 1991. Since the end of communist rule, growing ethnic and religious tensions have caused civil unrest throughout much of the region.

## Physical features

Much of the land is mountainous and rugged, with large expanses of semidesert in the Armenian uplands. The Kura is the longest river, flowing 848 miles (1,364 km) from central Georgia, through the fertile lowlands of Azerbaijan, to the Caspian Sea. The low Black Sea coastal area in western Georgia is lush and green. The area suffers earthquakes.

### Regional climate

79°F (26°C)    32°F (0°C)

15 in (375 mm)

The varied landscape of this region gives rise to a wide range of climates. Georgia's Black Sea coast is warm and humid, while Armenia is generally dry with long, cold winters. The lowland areas of Azerbaijan have long, hot summers and cool winters. Winters in the mountains are bitterly cold.

### Ararat Plains

Most of Armenia is a high plateau with large expanses of semidesert. In the southwest, the land drops toward the Aras River, which forms the border with Turkey and drains most of Armenia. Known as the Ararat Plains, this fertile, sheltered strip is used for growing vegetables and vines.

### Lake Sevan

Once valued for its pure waters and stunning setting, Armenia's Lake Sevan is at the center of an ecological crisis. Tragically, irrigation and hydroelectric projects begun in the 1970s have caused the water level to drop by up to 53 ft (16 m).

### Greater Caucasus Mountains

The Greater Caucasus stretch for about 745 miles (1,200 km) from the Black Sea to the Caspian Sea, effectively separating Europe from Asia. Rich in copper, iron, and lead, the mountains also shelter the Caucasus Republics from the icy winds that blow down from Russia in the north. The highest mountain is Mount El'brus at 18,481 ft (5,633 m), just over the Russian border.

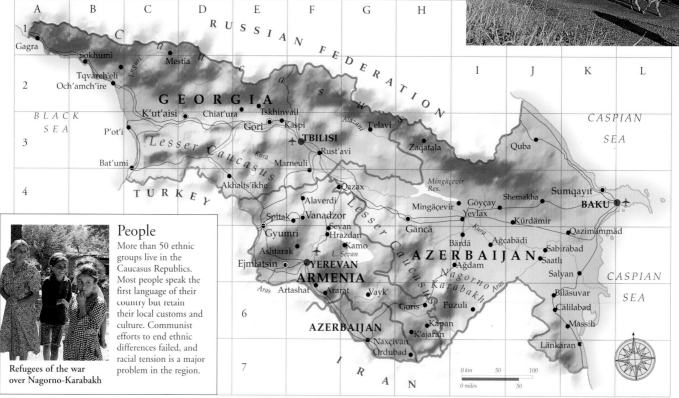

### People

More than 50 ethnic groups live in the Caucasus Republics. Most people speak the first language of their country but retain their local customs and culture. Communist efforts to end ethnic differences failed, and racial tension is a major problem in the region.

Refugees of the war over Nagorno-Karabakh

# Georgia

Georgia is the westernmost of the three republics. About 70 percent of the people are ethnic Georgians, most of whom belong to the Christian Georgian Orthodox Church. In recent years, the economy has suffered as a result of civil wars and ethnic disputes in the regions of Abkhazia and South Ossetia, which are trying to break away. War has damaged the Black Sea tourist industry.

### Textiles
Georgia produces fine silk cloth and grows mulberry bushes, used to feed silkworms. Bright cotton fabrics are used to make the scarves worn by Georgian women.

*Gold threads enhance bright patterns.*

C

### People
More Georgians claim to live for over 100 years than any other nationality in the world. Contributing factors are thought to be a healthy diet, regular exercise, a clean environment – and a genetic predisposition to longevity. Claims for ages over 120 have not yet been proved.

### Tbilisi
Situated on the banks of the Kura River, Tbilisi, Georgia's capital since the 5th century, is a multicultural city of 1,200,000. Home to most of Georgia's Armenian minority, it has places of worship for many religions.

### Tea and wine
More than 90 percent of the tea sold in Russia is grown in Georgia, which produces about 250,000 tons each year. Georgia also has extensive vineyards and produces excellent red wines.

# Armenia

Landlocked and isolated from its neighbors, Armenia is the smallest of the Caucasus Republics. The only way out of the country is by difficult road and rail routes over the mountains to Georgia. The people, mostly ethnic Armenians, speak a unique language. The country exports fruit, brandy, and minerals such as copper.

# Azerbaijan

The largest of the Caucasus Republics, Azerbaijan also has the most extensive area of farmland. Ninety-three percent of the population are Muslims. Most other people are Christian Armenian and Russian. Nazçivan, a separate part of Azerbaijan, lies within Armenian territory.

*Cubes of meat are separated by peppers and onions for flavor.*

*Metal skewer allows cooking meat to be turned.*

### Food
Lamb is the main meat, often served as kabobs, with a variety of vegetables. Cooks use pine nuts and almonds for flavoring. Local cheeses and rich desserts are specialties.

### Oil industry
Natural gas and oil are extracted from the Caspian Sea. Pipelines link Baku, which is the center of the industry, with Iran, Russia, Kazakhstan, and Turkmenistan. Other oil-related industries include the production of chemicals and oil-drilling equipment.

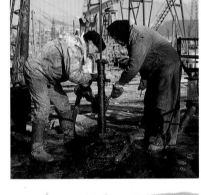

### Yerevan
Armenia's capital, Yerevan, is also its largest city. Situated on the Razdan River, it is a major cultural and industrial center. Market traders sell fruit, vegetables, and rich, colorful rugs woven locally from silk and wool.

### Territorial conflict
Nagorno-Karabakh, an enclave in southern Azerbaijan, has been the subject of armed conflict with Armenia since 1988. Most of the people here are Armenians, and Armenia claims the territory. A ceasefire was negotiated in 1994 and continues to hold today.

### Farming
Agriculture, mainly in the Aras River valley, employs 30 percent of the workforce and is the country's main source of wealth. Crops include grains and fruit such as apricots, grapes, olives, and peaches.

Soldiers on parade, Karabakh

### People
Communal drinking of hot, sweet tea from tiny glasses is a typically male ceremony. As in neighboring Georgia, the Azerbaijanis have a reputation for longevity, and it is not uncommon for people to continue working into their eighties.

**FIND OUT MORE**  ASIA, HISTORY OF   CHRISTIANITY   ENERGY   FARMING   ISLAM   MOUNTAINS AND VALLEYS   OIL   SOVIET UNION   TEXTILES AND WEAVING   TRADE AND INDUSTRY

# CAVES

BENEATH THE GROUND, there is a network of large holes, or caves. Caves are naturally occurring chambers formed out of rock. There are many different cave types, some housing hidden lakes and waterfalls; caverns are extensive networks of giant caves. Some caves are no bigger than a closet, but others are huge. The Sarawak Chamber in Malaysia is 2,296 ft (700 m) long and 164 ft (50 m) high; the world's biggest sports stadium, the Louisiana Superdome, could fit into it three times over. Damp and dark, caves have distinctive features, such as stalactites and stalagmites.

## Types of caves

The biggest and most common cave systems are found in carbonate rocks such as dolomite and limestone, but small caves form in all kinds of rock. Caves are found in many terrains, from the sea to glaciers, and can have different formations.

**Sea cave**
Small caves form in sea cliffs; waves force water into cracks, blasting the rock apart. The hole may emerge as a blow-hole on the cliff-top.

**Fissure cave**
The movement and force of an earthquake can create deep fissures, long, narrow openings, and caves.

**Ice cave**
Greeny-blue tunnel caves form under glaciers after spring meltwater carves out passages under the ice.

**Lava cave**
Tunnellike caves form in lava – surface layers harden, and molten lava flows underneath.

**Limestone cave**
Most caves form in limestone. This rock has many joints and its calcium content is vulnerable to the acid in rainwater.

## How a cave forms

Most of the world's biggest caves are formed by water trickling down through soluble rocks such as limestone. The water widens joints or cracks by dissolving the rock. Rainwater is dilute carbonic acid, and wears away the rock, creating a cave.

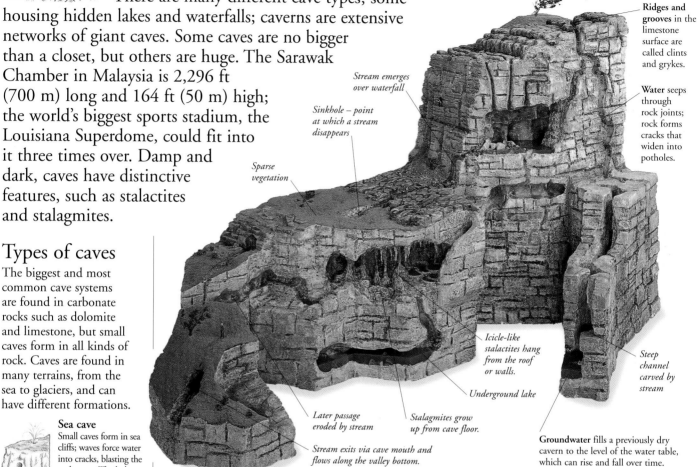

**Ridges and grooves** in the limestone surface are called clints and grykes.

**Water** seeps through rock joints; rock forms cracks that widen into potholes.

Stream emerges over waterfall

Sinkhole – point at which a stream disappears

Sparse vegetation

Icicle-like stalactites hang from the roof or walls.

Steep channel carved by stream

Underground lake

Later passage eroded by stream

Stalagmites grow up from cave floor.

Stream exits via cave mouth and flows along the valley bottom.

**Groundwater** fills a previously dry cavern to the level of the water table, which can rise and fall over time.

## Cave features

Formed over thousands of years, stalactites and stalagmites are found in caves. Droplets of water partially evaporate to form calcium deposits (calcite); drips create hanging stalactites on the roof, and upright stalagmites where they fall to the floor. Spiraling drips form twisted helictites. Flowstone is solidified calcite on the cave floor or walls.

Stalagmite

**Stalagmites and stalactites**
Stalactites can form in different ways – a long, thin curtain stalactite is formed when water runs along the cave roof. When stalactites and stalagmites meet in the middle, they form a column. The biggest stalactite, 33 ft (10 m) long, is in Pruta do Janelão, Minas Gerais, Brazil; the biggest stalagmite is over 105 ft (32 m) tall in the Krasnohorska Cave in Slovakia.

Merged stalactites

Stalactite

Stalactite with ring marks

Curtain stalactite

## Spelunking

Spelunks are the vertical pipes that lead down to many extensive cave networks. Today, spelunking is a popular but dangerous sport. Exploring and discovering caves can unearth historic treasures. The caves at Lascaux, France, for instance, which contain a wealth of prehistoric wall paintings and tools were discovered by spelunkers.

FIND OUT MORE    CAVE WILDLIFE    COAST    EARTHQUAKES    FOSSILS    PREHISTORIC PEOPLE    ROCKS AND MINERALS    SPORTS

# CAVE WILDLIFE

A DEEP CAVE is a world of its own, with conditions far removed from those outside. Deep inside a cave there is no light. No day and night pass, and the temperature hardly changes with the seasons. Without light, plants cannot grow, yet animal life can exist in the dark. Some animals enter caves for shelter or to hunt for prey; others spend their entire lives in this environment and have adapted to moving around and sensing food in the dark.

## Caves

Caves occur in sea cliffs, around volcanoes, and under glaciers, but the most spectacular are those formed when rainwater hollows out fissures in limestone rock. Limestone caves contain various habitats for wildlife, including narrow tunnels, chambers, streams, pools, and the partly lit entrance. Some caves, especially those in the tropics, are teeming with life. Bat colonies live in the roof, and an army of invertebrates consumes their droppings on the floor below.

Limestone cave

### Plants

No plants can grow deep in a cave because there is no light. But the cave entrance is often framed by plants – such as liverworts, mosses, ferns, and algae – that have adapted to damp, shady conditions. Many plants grow without soil, sending out small roots that grip the bare rock.

Fern

Moss

## Invertebrates

Caves are often full of invertebrate life. Beetles, spiders, snails, worms, and crayfish survive in large numbers in caves. They feed on debris brought in by running water or dropped by animals that feed outside.

Touch-sensitive spikes

Long antennae

### Cave cricket

Scavenging cave crickets use their long, wiry antennae to feel their way past objects in the dark and toward food on the cave floor. Alert for the merest brush against them, they try to out-maneuver prey such as cave centipedes. Cave crickets, like cockroaches and other invertebrates, feed on debris dropped by bats and cave birds. They also eat the fallen carcasses of these animals when they die.

### New Zealand glowworm

These glowworms are gnat larvae that live at the entrances to caves. They have evolved an ingenious method of catching food. The larvae spin dangling sticky threads that they illuminate with a light produced from their own bodies. In the darkness of a cave, the glowing threads lure and then snare small flying insects that the larvae haul up and devour.

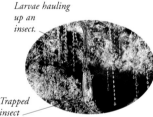

Larvae hauling up an insect.

Trapped insect

Eyes

Transparent legs

### Cave crab

Tropical caves are often home to some small species of crab that use their pincers to pick food debris from underground streams or the cave floor. Like many cave dwellers – among them millipedes, spiders, salamanders, and shrimps – cave crabs have lost their pigmentation and are almost colorless. Some animals also lose their sight because of the lack of natural light.

### Birds

Some birds, such as barn owls and swifts, make nests inside caves. The oilbird of South America nests deep within caves and uses rapid tongue clicks to navigate by echolocation. Colonies of oilbirds fly outside the cave at night to feed on fruit in the surrounding forests. The birds' droppings litter the cave floor below the birds' roosting ledges, and bring nutrients into the cave from far and wide.

Oilbird

## Mammals

Some mammals make temporary or permanent homes in caves. The American black bear sometimes takes shelter in caves during the winter months, as do some foxes. Many species of bats roost, rear their young, or hibernate in the security of caves, some forming colonies of thousands. Hanging from the roof by their hind feet, the bats are out of reach of almost all predators.

### Lesser horseshoe bat

The lesser horseshoe bat is found in large numbers in caves all over Europe, Asia, and northern Africa, where it hibernates during the winter months. Like other bats, it navigates in the dark by using echolocation. It emits high-pitched calls and listens for echoes that bounce back from the cave walls, stalactites, and other obstructions.

Wings made of elastic skin supported by bones.

## Fish

A number of fish species have adapted to living in subterranean streams that flow inside cave systems throughout the world. Most are sightless, with only remnants of eyes underneath their lids, because nothing can be seen underground.

### Blind cave characin

Sightless cave animals compensate for their lack of vision with a highly refined sense of touch. Most fish have a lateral line along their sides – a row of sense organs containing nerve endings. The blind cave characin of Mexico has a very prominent lateral line with which it can sense vibrations from passing prey.

Row of dark scales is the lateral line.

---

FIND OUT MORE    BATS    BIRDS    CAVES    CRABS AND OTHER CRUSTACEANS    FERNS    FLIES    FISH    GRASSHOPPERS AND CRICKETS    HIBERNATION    MOSSES AND LIVERWORTS

# CELLS

ALL LIVING ORGANISMS are made of self-contained units of life called cells. Some, such as the amoeba, consist of a single cell, while others, such as humans, are made up of billions of cells. Each cell has a nucleus, which contains the genetic material DNA; DNA provides the instructions the cell needs to maintain itself. Surrounding the nucleus is the cytoplasm, which contains the matter that makes the cell function. Forming a layer around the cytoplasm is the cell membrane which forms the cell's boundary.

## Specialized cells

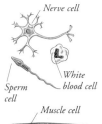

*Nerve cell*

*Sperm cell*

*White blood cell*

*Muscle cell*

Most plants and animals consist of many cell types, each specialized to perform a specific task. Neurones are long cells that carry nerve impulses around an animal's body; guard cells are rigid box-like structures filled with fluid. They open and close pores on the surface of plant leaves.

### Palisade mesophyll cell

These cells are found in the upper layer of the middle part, or mesophyll, of plant leaves. They are packed with chloroplasts, which contain the green pigment chlorophyll which harnesses the energy in sunlight.

Palisade mesophyll cell

### Liver cells

The human liver has over 500 functions related to controlling the chemical balance of the body. These functions are carried out by cells called hepatocytes. For instance, some liver cells remove poisons from blood.

Liver cell

### Abnormal cells

When cells divide inside an organism they do so in a controlled way. Sometimes, cells become abnormal and start dividing uncontrollably, leading to the production of growths called tumors. The presence of these abnormal cells and tumors causes a number of different forms of a disease called cancer.

Cancer tumor cell (yellow) being attacked by a T-lymphocyte cell (green).

### Marie François Bichat

French pathologist Marie François Bichat (1771–1802) showed that an organ, whether a leaf of a plant or a kidney of an animal, is made of different groups of cells. He called each group a tissue, and showed that the same tissues could appear in different organs. His research formed the basis of histology – the study of organs and tissues.

## Cell structure

Most cells have similar structures. They consist of a fluid called cytoplasm, a surrounding cell membrane, and a nucleus. Cytoplasm contains structures known as organelles. Plant cells, unlike animal cells, have a tough outer wall and chloroplasts.

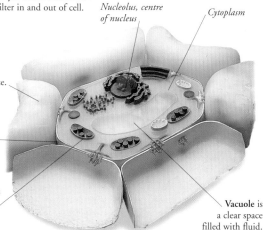

Model of an animal cell

Endoplasmic reticulum is a maze-like network of membranes that make and store chemicals.

Golgi apparatus sorts and stores proteins.

Nucleus is the cell's control center.

Vacuole is a small and temporary space where food and waste is stored.

Glycogen granules are food reserves or insoluble waste.

Pinocyte allows substances to filter in and out of cell.

Plasma membrane is the thin flexible layer surrounding the cytoplasm.

Mitochondrion generates energy from sugars and fatty acids.

Cytoplasm forms the bulk of the cell and gives it its shape.

Organelles are any structures that live in the cytoplasm and control special functions.

Model of a plant cell

Cellulose cell wall is a tough outer jacket mainly made of cellulose.

Plasma membrane is selectively permeable or semipermeable and receives stimuli.

Chloroplast is an organelle present in green plants; it converts light energy into food by photosynthesis.

*Nucleolus, centre of nucleus*

*Cytoplasm*

Vacuole is a clear space filled with fluid.

## Cell division

Cells reproduce by dividing. During cell division, the nucleus divides first, followed by the cytoplasm. There are two kinds of cell division: mitosis and meiosis. Mitosis produces cells needed for growth and to replace dead cells. Meiosis produces sex cells for reproduction.

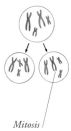

*Mitosis*

### Mitosis

This produces two daughter cells that are identical to the parent cell. The cell's chromosomes (genetic material) make copies of themselves. These separate and move to opposite ends of the cell to form two new nuclei. The cytoplast splits, and two new cells are formed.

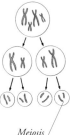

*Meiosis*

### Meiosis

This takes place in sex organs and involves two cell divisions. It makes four sex cells that differ from the parent cells because they have half the normal number of chromosomes. These sex cells are called sperm in males and ova in females.

## Studying cells

Cells are so small that they must be studied with a microscope. Both the light microscope and the electron microscope have revealed cells' external and internal structure. For this study, cells must be carefully prepared to see their details clearly.

Chemical dyes used for staining cells

### Staining cells

When cells are seen under a microscope, they are often transparent, showing little detail. For that reason, they are colored with chemical stains to pick out details such as the nucleus.

**FIND OUT MORE**

BIOLOGY    GENETICS    HUMAN BODY    MICROSCOPES    MICROSCOPIC LIFE    PHOTOSYNTHESIS    PLANTS, REPRODUCTION    REPRODUCTION

# CELTS

PROUD WARRIORS AND SKILLED METALWORKERS, the Celts were among Europe's oldest peoples. The first tribes lived in camps in central Europe, but by 400 BC, they also dominated the British Isles, Spain, Italy, and France, and had settled as far as western Asia. Unique and decorative Celtic arts spread, as did their mythology and religion, via trade routes, but the Celts showed no interest in building an empire by unifying all their territories. By 50 BC, the mighty Romans and Germanic peoples had squeezed the Celts into Europe's fringes, where they converted to Christianity. Today, Celtic culture and language survive in Ireland, Scotland, Wales, and parts of France and England.

**Celtic world c.200 BC**
The first phase of Celtic society probably developed around Hallstatt (now in Austria) between 1200 and 750 BC. From 500 to 50 BC, there was a second phase known as La Tène, after its center in modern France.

## Celtic society

Celtic tribes were made up of three main classes: warriors, druids, and farmers. Warfare was an important part of life, so the warriors, armed with their sophisticated iron weaponry, formed an aristocracy. Druids were religious leaders who often held the power of life and death over other tribe members. Farmers, who reared cattle and cultivated crops using iron tools, kept the economy going. Celts lived in fortified camps called hillforts. Though built for defense, hillforts were also places of trade and religious worship – some even grew into towns. Each pagan Celtic tribe had its own king, and maybe even its own gods. Skilled metalworkers probably had high status.

*Thatched roof*

*Timber fence*

*Wooden frame supports roof.*

*Ditch*

*Mud walls*

*Souterrain, or underground passage, used for storage or defense*

Celtic hillfort

**Celtic horse**
The horse played a major part in early Celtic warfare and religion. A horse-goddess called Peon was worshiped first by the Celts, but then also by cavalrymen in the Roman army. There are several chalk figures cut into the rock in former Celtic areas. Some resemble the horse figures that appear on surviving Celtic coins.

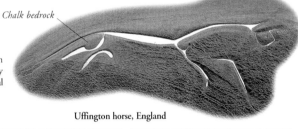

*Chalk bedrock*

Uffington horse, England

## Druids

The druids were holy men in pagan Celtic society. The earliest record of them comes from Julius Caesar, who reported that they acted as judges, led rituals in forest clearings, and used golden sickles to cut mistletoe from sacred oak trees. Druids were skilled in herbalism and kept oral records of their tribe's history. Occasionally, they performed human and animal sacrifices. Those wanting to become druids had to study for up to 20 years.

Oak leaves

**Ritual**
The druids left no written records, so their rituals are shrouded in mystery. Celts worshiped many gods and spirits, particularly of trees, rocks, and mountains. One of the oldest gods, Cernunnos, is known as the lord of the beasts. He is often portrayed either wearing antlers or with horned animals, such as stags. He is also often shown wearing golden torques, and seems to represent fertility and abundance.

*Stags are often shown with Cernunnos.*

*Horned animals symbolize aggression and vitality.*

Detail from Gundestrup Cauldron

**A stone head** with three faces is called a triple head.

**Cult of the head**
The human head was very important to the pagan Celts, as was the number "3." One custom was to cut the head off a dead enemy, hang it from a horse bridle, then put it on public display. Druids may have believed that a person's soul was in his head, and it had to be defeated, too.

### Boudicca

Boudicca (d.61 AD) was queen of the Iceni, one of Britain's Celtic tribes. When the Romans conquered Britain after 43 AD, the Iceni joined forces with them to defeat a rival tribe. However, the Romans then seized Iceni lands and flogged Boudicca. She led a huge revolt, destroying the Roman settlements at St. Albans, Colchester, and London. The Romans finally defeated the rebels, and Queen Boudicca killed herself by taking poison rather than risk being captured.

## Art and decoration

The Celts were a warlike people, but they were gifted craftworkers and artists, too. Celtic metalworkers excelled at decorative weapons, jewelry, vessels, and mirrors. After the conversion to Christianity, Celtic monks in the British Isles illustrated holy books with great detail. The Lindisfarne Gospels (c.700) feature 45 different colors – all made from finely ground minerals or vegetable dyes.

*Red glass inlay*

*Circular boss*

*Curved patterns*

*Curves (made with compasses)*

**Battersea shield**

### Battersea shield
Many of the most beautiful bronze Celtic shields were too lightweight to be used in battle and were purely ornamental. The Battersea shield was probably used only for military parades. It was found in the Thames River, London, in 1857.

### Torque
According to the ancient Greek writer Strabo, Celts loved to dress in colorful clothes and wear jewelry in gold, silver, or electrum (an alloy of gold and silver): "They wear torques around their necks, and bracelets on their arms and wrists," he wrote. Many gold, bronze, and silver torques have been found in Celtic graves.

**Electrum torque**

*Amber*

*Gold wire*

*Enamel*

**Tara brooch**

### Tara brooch
Brooches, such as the Tara, date from the 8th century – the early Christian era in Celtic Ireland. Only 3.5 inches (9 cms) in diameter, the Tara brooch is a magnificently detailed piece of jewelry, featuring filigree, gilt chip-carvings, enameled glass, amber, and gold wire.

### Sculpture
Animals and birds often figured in Celtic art and decoration. Certain animals were sacred, such as pigs and boars, which often appear in Celtic legend. The legendary King Arthur himself was known as "the Boar of Cornwall."

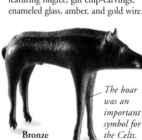

*The boar was an important symbol for the Celts.*

**Bronze boar**

### Metalworking
As well as sophisticated iron weaponry and farming tools, skilled Celtic metalworkers produced elaborate goods for chieftains and highly decorated items for trade throughout Europe. In Gaul (modern France) the smiths even had their own god – a smith-god known as Sucellos.

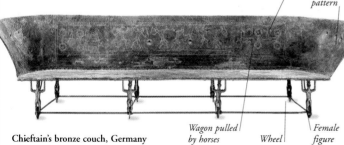

**Chieftain's bronze couch, Germany**

*Sword and shield*

*Swirling abstract pattern*

*Wagon pulled by horses*

*Wheel*

*Female figure*

## Christianity

During the Roman occupation, Christianity came to Britain – but failed to take hold among the people. However, one convert, St. Patrick, converted pagan Celtic Ireland in the 5th century. The Celts then adopted this religion with gusto, and Ireland became a Christian stronghold for the next three centuries.

**Celtic cross**

### Monks
Celtic Christianity was famous for the harshness of the monks' lives and the enthusiasm of its devotees. From c.500, monasteries ranged from simple cells for single monks to communities the size of towns.

**Early Christian church, Ireland**

### Missionaries
After Irish Christians set up monasteries in Britain, France, and northern Italy, they started to convert the native peoples. The monks loved learning and helped keep culture alive in Europe during the chaos that followed the decline of the Roman Empire. Irish monks operating from the island of Iona, off western Scotland, produced the beautiful *Book of Kells*, c.800, with its extraordinary illuminated (decorative) lettering.

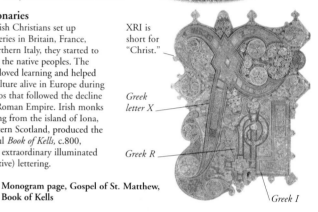

*XRI is short for "Christ."*

*Greek letter X*

*Greek R*

*Greek I*

**Monogram page, Gospel of St. Matthew, Book of Kells**

## Myths

The pagan Celts had a rich oral tradition. Their stories included myths about mighty gods, such as the Welsh Bran the Blessed and the Irish Dagda (Father of All); legends about fearless warrior-heroes, such as Cuchulain and King Arthur; and tales of the "shape-changers" – magical creatures from the Underworld. Since the Celts had no written language, monks later wrote down the stories for future generations.

### Merlin
The first written legends of the Welsh wizard Merlin said that he was a Celtic boy whose father was the devil. At an early age, he found he could predict the future. In later stories, he appeared as the wizard and mentor of King Arthur of England.

**A still from the modern film, *Excalibur***

### Languages
Two types of Celtic languages continue to be spoken and written today: Brythonic (Breton, Welsh, Cornish) and Gaelic (Irish, Scots Gaelic, Manx). They may all be traced back to a common, ancient Indo-European language.

**Modern Irish**

*"Hill"*

*"Beach"*

# CENTRAL AMERICA

SEVEN SMALL COUNTRIES make up Central America, a tapering neck of land that connects northern North America to South America. The Pacific Ocean lies to the west, and the Caribbean Sea, an arm of the Atlantic Ocean, lies to the east. The two oceans are connected by the Panama Canal, a shortcut that saves ships months of travel time. The original peoples of Central America were Native Americans, conquered by the Spaniards in the 1500s. Since gaining independence, these countries have had periods of turbulent politics and unstable economies.

## Physical features

Central America has a backbone of rugged volcanic peaks and massive crater lakes that run from Guatemala down to Costa Rica. The Pacific coast is flat and fertile, and the eastern lowlands, stretching to the Caribbean Sea, are wild, empty swamps and rain forests, with little cultivation.

**Tropical rain forest**
The hot, tropical climate and high rainfall of Central America's Caribbean coast supports vast areas of dense rain forest, particularly in Belize and Guatemala, and on Nicaragua's Mosquito Coast. Economic pressure is forcing people to cut and clear parts of the forest for crops.

**Sierra Madre**
The Sierra Madre is the highland region of Guatemala and El Salvador and is a continuation of the Sierra Madre of Mexico. It includes Tajumulco, an extinct volcano, which, at 13,845 ft (4,220 m), is the highest peak in Central America. Most Guatemalans live in this cooler region.

**Lake Nicaragua**
Covering an area of 3,060 sq miles (7,925 sq km), Lake Nicaragua is the only freshwater lake in the world to contain sea fish, including sharks, which swim up the San Juan River from the Caribbean Sea. The lake is dotted with 310 islands, the largest of which is Ometepe.

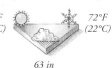

**Regional climate**
Throughout Central America the climate is tropical and hot, with a distinct rainy season from May until November or December. Mountain and upland areas are cooler. Rainfall is higher along the Caribbean coast than on the Pacific side, and can be as high as 260 in (6,600 mm) per year.

77°F (25°C)   72°F (22°C)

63 in (1,615 mm)

## Pan-American Highway

The Pan-American Highway runs the length of Central America, providing an important link between North and South America. In the north, the road connects with the US highway network, and in the south, it extends as far as Chile – a total distance of about 5,593 miles (9,000 km) from the Mexican border.

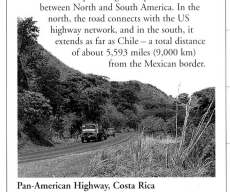

Pan-American Highway, Costa Rica

# Guatemala

 Once the hub of the Mayan civilization, modern Guatemala is Central America's largest and most populated country and has the biggest manufacturing sector. Guatemalan factories produce foods, textiles, paper, pharmaceuticals, and rubber goods. Plantations in the south grow coffee, bananas, cotton, and sugarcane for export.

### Farming

About half of Guatemala's people are of Mayan descent. Most live in the western highlands, growing crops and rearing animals, which they trade at local markets. People from distant hamlets use weekly markets as a chance to socialize and keep abreast of local news.

## GUATEMALA FACTS

| | |
|---|---|
| CAPITAL CITY | Guatemala City |
| AREA | 42,043 sq miles (108,890 sq km) |
| POPULATION | 11,400,000 |
| MAIN LANGUAGES | Spanish, Quiché, Mam, Kekchí, Cakchiquel |
| MAJOR RELIGION | Christian |
| CURRENCY | Quetzal |

### Tikal

Tourism is a growing industry in Guatemala, and each year about 500,000 people visit the country's Mayan ruins. Tikal, once a great Mayan city, was founded in about 600 BC and flourished until about AD 890, when it was suddenly deserted. The city once had about 40,000 inhabitants.

# Honduras

A small, poor country, Honduras relied for many years on bananas and timber as its main sources of income. However, since the banana industry was devastated by Hurricane Mitch in 1998, coffee, flowers, and fruit now supply the country's income. Unemployment is high, and most people live in small villages.

## HONDURAS FACTS

| | |
|---|---|
| CAPITAL CITY | Tegucigalpa |
| AREA | 43,278 sq miles (112,090 sq km) |
| POPULATION | 6,350,000 |
| MAIN LANGUAGES | Spanish, English Creole, Garifuna |
| MAJOR RELIGION | Christian |
| CURRENCY | Lempira |

### People

About 90 percent of Hondurans are *mestizos*, of mixed European and Native American descent. Along the Caribbean coast are settlements of the Garifuna people, descendants of black slaves who swam ashore more than 350 years ago when ships from Nigeria were shipwrecked off the coast.

### Hurricane Mitch

The vast banana plantations in the northeast of the Honduras were wiped out by Hurricane Mitch in 1998. The storms caused $3 billion worth of damage and the deaths of 5,600 people. Bananas comprised 40 percent of the country's exports, but have since been replaced by coffee, shrimp, and melon.

# El Salvador

The smallest country in Central America, El Salvador has a rugged landscape that includes more than 20 volcanoes. A thick layer of volcanic ash and lava on the highlands provides ideal conditions for growing coffee. El Salvador is poor as a result of a civil war that raged from 1979–1992 and a devastating earthquake in 2001.

## EL SALVADOR FACTS

| | |
|---|---|
| CAPITAL CITY | San Salvador |
| AREA | 8,124 sq miles (21,040 sq km) |
| POPULATION | 6,300,000 |
| MAIN LANGUAGE | Spanish |
| MAJOR RELIGION | Christian |
| CURRENCY | Colón and US dollar |

### People

El Salvador is Central America's most densely populated country. There are now about 788 people per sq mile (304 per sq km) and the population is growing at about two-and-a-half percent a year. Almost 90 percent are *mestizos*, and three-quarters are Roman Catholics. More than half are farmers who scrape a living in the highlands.

### Deforestation

Today, only about five percent of El Salvador is still forested. Vast tracts of forest, including cedar, oak, and mahogany, have been felled for export and to clear land for farming cash crops such as coffee.

# Belize

Most of Belize is dense rain forest; most of its small population lives along the Caribbean coast. The two largest groups are the *mestizos* and Creoles, who also have African blood and are descended from black slaves who were marooned in Belize in the 17th century.

### Barrier reef

Protecting Belize's swampy coastal plains from flooding is the world's second largest barrier reef, 190 miles (290 km) long. The reef supports a wide variety of colorful fish.

## BELIZE FACTS

| | |
|---|---|
| CAPITAL CITY | Belmopan |
| AREA | 8,865 sq miles (22,960 sq km) |
| POPULATION | 200,000 |
| MAIN LANGUAGES | English, English Creole, Spanish, Maya, Garifuna |
| MAJOR RELIGION | Christian |
| CURRENCY | Belizean dollar |

### Belmopan

Belize City, the country's chief port, was the capital for many years. In 1960, a hurricane and tidal wave caused severe damage, so in 1970, a new capital, Belmopan, was built in the center of the country, far from coastal storms. Its population is only 4,000, mostly civil servants.

CENTRAL AMERICA

# Nicaragua

Occasionally called the land of lakes and volcanoes, Nicaragua lies at the heart of Central America. Earthquakes frequently shake the country, and Hurricane Mitch caused severe damage in 1998. In 1978, Nicaragua experienced a violent civil war between the left-wing Sandinista government and right-wing "contras," backed by the US. The war ended in 1990.

Delivery of sugarcane

### Farming
Agriculture employs about one-quarter of the workforce, growing cotton, coffee, sugar, bananas, and meat for export. The country has also developed related industries, such as sugar refineries and canning factories that process agricultural produce.

### People
*Mestizos* make up 70 percent of Nicaraguans. The rest are whites or blacks, descended from Africans who were taken to Nicaragua as plantation workers in the 18th century. Three-quarters of the population is below the age of 30. Families are tight-knit and up to three generations may live together.

Black pepper
Garlic
Onion
Chili pepper
Scallions
Hot chili sauce

### Food
Nicaraguans enjoy corn roasted on the cob. Meat and bean dishes are spiced with pepper and garlic and scooped up in thin pancakes called tortillas, made from corn flour. Food is often topped with hot chili sauce.

## NICARAGUA FACTS

CAPITAL CITY Managua
AREA 50,193 sq miles (130,000 sq km)
POPULATION 5,100,000
MAIN LANGUAGES Spanish, English Creole, Miskito
MAJOR RELIGION Christian
CURRENCY Córdoba oro

# Costa Rica

Unlike its neighbors, Costa Rica is a stable and peaceful country with a democratically elected government. The army was abolished in 1949. Costa Ricans enjoy excellent schools and hospitals. Most people are *mestizos* of Spanish origin. In the Puerto Limón area on the east coast, one-third are English-speaking blacks, descended from plantation slaves.

*Costa Rica has more than 750 species of birds – more than the whole of the US.*
*Dark-roasted coffee beans have a deep, rich taste.*

### San José
Founded in 1737, San José became Costa Rica's capital in 1823. With many parks and a mix of traditional and modern Spanish architecture, San José is a commercial center and has food-processing factories. It has rail links with Pacific and Caribbean ports and lies on the Pan-American Highway.

### Tourism
More than 20 percent of Costa Rica has been set aside to create a network of national parks, including volcanic peaks and undisturbed tropical forest rich in plant and animal species. Many ecotourists are attracted by the country's resident wildlife, such as jaguars, giant sea turtles, crocodiles, and armadillos.

### Coffee
Costa Rican coffee is some of the world's finest and fetches a high price. It grows in the rich black volcanic soil near the capital, San José. Costa Rica was the first Central American country to grow the beans. Bananas are the other leading cash crop.

## COSTA RICA FACTS

CAPITAL CITY San José
AREA 19,730 sq miles (51,100 sq km)
POPULATION 4,000,000
MAIN LANGUAGES Spanish, English Creole, Bribri, Cabecar
MAJOR RELIGION Christian
CURRENCY Colón

# Panama

Occupying the southernmost and narrowest part of Central America, Panama is cut in two by the Panama Canal, which links the Atlantic and Pacific Oceans. A country of swamps, mountains, and grassy plains, Panama has some of Central America's wildest rain forest.

*Some 14,000 ships pass through the canal every year, earning Panama valuable toll fees.*

### Financial centers
At opposite ends of the Panama Canal, Colón and Panama City are important business centers, providing banking, financial, and insurance services. A free trade zone in Colón enables goods to be imported and exported duty free.

### Panama Canal
Linking the Caribbean Sea with the Pacific Ocean, the Panama Canal was built by the US and opened in 1914. It is more than 40 miles (65 km) long and passes through three sets of locks. The length, which is the distance between deep-water points of entry, is 51 miles (82 km).

### Shrimp
Panama has a busy and important fishing fleet. The leading catch is shrimps, which form 11 percent of the country's exports. Anchovetas, small anchovies used for fish meal, make up three percent of exports. Other catches include herring and lobsters.

## PANAMA FACTS

CAPITAL CITY Panama City
AREA 29,761 sq miles (77,080 sq km)
POPULATION 2,900,000
MAIN LANGUAGES Spanish, English Creole, Indian languages
MAJOR RELIGION Christian
CURRENCY Balboa

FIND OUT MORE
CENTRAL AMERICA, HISTORY OF  COLUMBUS, CHRISTOPHER  CORAL REEFS  EARTHQUAKES  FARMING  FISHING INDUSTRY  FORESTS  MAYA  NATIVE AMERICANS  PORTS AND WATERWAYS  TRAVEL

C

# CENTRAL AMERICA, HISTORY OF

RICHLY ENDOWED WITH natural resources, Central America has had a violent history, with civil wars, revolutions, and terrible repression. The area was home to the great Mayan civilization, but the Spanish arrived in the 16th century and began to conquer and settle Mexico and the lands to the southeast. As a Spanish colony, the area was called the Captaincy General of Guatemala and had its capital in Guatemala City. After gaining independence in the 1820s, the region split into separate nations ruled by a few rich families. During the 20th century, the United States often intervened in Central American politics with aid and arms.

### Maya
Mayan civilization was at its peak in the tropical forest lowland area of Guatemala from about AD 250 to 900. Here, the Maya built cities, with steep pyramids. Around AD 900, the Toltecs from the north conquered the Maya. The Maya revived around 1200, but were in decline by the time of the Spanish conquest.

Mayan pottery bowl

## Independence
In 1821, following the example of Mexico, Central America declared independence. A federation of new states was proposed, but politicians disagreed over what form it should take. The disputes led to war and, in 1838 the break-up of the area into five self-governing republics.

### The Captaincy General
A small group of wealthy Spanish merchants born in Central America dominated the rich trade in indigo dye, and also the political life of the colony. The area was ruled by a Captain General of Guatemala and his council at Guatemala City.

### Panama Canal
With military support from the US, Panama separated from Colombia in 1903. US engineers built a great canal linking the Atlantic and the Pacific. The Panama Canal, which runs across the south of the country, opened in 1914. After this, the Panamanian economy came to depend almost entirely on the US.

### Coffee
In the 1850s, there was a high world demand for coffee. Rich landowners began to grow coffee in large quantities, forcing local people off their land. Coffee export enabled Costa Rica and El Salvador to achievesome stability in the late 19th century, but changes in coffee prices brought problems later.

Coffee growing, El Salvador

Coffee beans

## Modern Central America
Immense differences between rich and poor, combined with the strong economic, political, and cultural influence of the United States, made Central America a turbulent region in the 20th century. Many rulers were dictators and governments changed rapidly, giving little chance of political stability. There were many revolutions, which were often suppressed with huge loss of life.

### US intervention
During the twentieth century, the United States was closely involved in the affairs of Central America. In 1909, the US supported a right-wing revolution in Nicaragua, and US marines occupied the country until 1933 when, after a guerrilla war, Augusto Sandino (1895–1934) forced them to withdraw. Later, the US intervened to stop left-wing revolutions and to prevent the spread of communism during the Cold War. More recently, the US supported the Contras (right-wing guerrillas) in Nicaragua and, in 1989, invaded Panama to oust corrupt ruler General Manuel Noriega.

Students in El Salvador erect a statue of Augusto Sandino

### Somoza family
Anastasio Somoza and his sons ruled Nicaragua from 1937–79. The economy grew under their rule, but there was widespread corruption. In 1979, an uprising led by the Sandanistas (a left-wing group named after the former socialist leader Augusto Sandino) ousted the Somozas from power.

### Daniel Ortega
Socialist politician Daniel Ortega (b.1945) became the Nicaraguan head of state in 1981 and won free elections in 1984. He failed to free his country from the conflict between the right-wing politicians backed by the US and his own left-wing allies.

## Oscar Romero
Archbishop Oscar Romero (1917–80) was head of the Catholic church in El Salvador. His reading of the Bible led him to demand better conditions for the poor. Many Catholics began to get involved in social activism in the 1970s. This annoyed the government, which employed death squads to kill priests. When Romero declared that armed struggle was the only option left, he, too, was shot dead.

FIND OUT MORE | AZTECS | CENTRAL AMERICA | CHRISTIANITY | EXPLORATION | MAYA | RELIGIONS | SOUTH AMERICA, HISTORY OF | SPAIN, HISTORY OF | UNITED STATES, HISTORY OF

# CHARLEMAGNE

ON CHRISTMAS DAY, 800, a remarkable emperor was crowned in Europe. His name was Charles, and he was known as Charles the Great, or Charlemagne. He was king of the Franks of northern France and managed to create a large empire after the turmoil that followed the fall of Rome. Under Charlemagne, Europe enjoyed a period of peace and unity it had not had for 400 years. Yet the king was illiterate and brutal, and held his empire together only by force.

### Early life
Charlemagne was born in Aachen in what is now Germany in about 742. He was the oldest son of Pepin, king of the Franks, and inherited his kingdom in 768 jointly with his brother, Carloman. When Carloman died in 771, Charlemagne became sole ruler of the Franks.

## Carolingian Empire

In order to control his vast territory, Charlemagne installed bishops and counts in each district to run both the religious and the secular affairs of the empire. He supported an educational system based on the monasteries, and introduced a legal system that owed much to the Roman Empire.

### The marches
In order to protect his vast empire, Charlemagne established marches, or buffer zones, along the southern border of Muslim Spain and the eastern border of the various Germanic tribes. Troops of armored horsemen patrolled the marches to protect the empire against raids across its lengthy borders.

### Extent of the empire
By the time of his death in 814, Charlemagne controlled an empire that stretched from Hamburg in northern Germany to south of Rome, and from the Atlantic Ocean to the Danube River. He converted the warlike Saxons to Christianity, and subdued the Lombard kingdom of northern Italy.

Charlemagne's realm

Frankish lands, 714

Adjoining territories

— Empire of Charlemagne

*Charlemagne used cavalrymen to protect the borders of his empire.*

Double-edged blade

Socket to attach shaft

**Carolingian spearhead**

## A new Roman emperor

In the 8th century, the Pope's security as head of the Christian church was threatened by the Lombards from northern Italy. In 773, Charlemagne conquered Lombardy. To recognize his support, the Pope gave Charlemagne the title of Emperor of the Romans.

**Coin of Charlemagne**

### Coronation
Charlemagne visited Rome in 800, and Pope Leo III crowned him and paid him homage. For the first time since the Roman Empire was united, and the idea of a Holy Roman Empire was born.

## Dark Ages

For centuries, historians talked of the time after the fall of the Roman Empire as the Dark Ages. But we now know that the period was a time of great achievement in scholarship and the arts. This activity reached its height under Charlemagne.

### Aachen
At his capital of Aachen (Aix-la-Chapelle), Charlemagne created a brilliant court where art flourished. He built a vast palace and chapel that some visitors thought of as a "second Rome."

### Scholarship
Scholars came from all over Europe to Aachen to work for Charlemagne. They rescued classical Latin learning from oblivion, and ensured that future generations could learn about the Roman Empire.

### CHARLEMAGNE

c.742 Born in Aachen.

768 Succeeds to Frankish Empire with his brother Carloman.

771 Takes sole control of empire.

772 Begins conquest of Saxony in northern Germany.

773 Subdues Lombards in Italy.

778 Conquers Bavaria in southern Germany.

795 Establishes Spanish march to protect his kingdom from Muslim Spain.

800 Crowned Emperor of the Romans by Pope Leo III.

814 Dies and is buried at Aachen.

FIND OUT MORE

FEUDALISM • FRANCE, HISTORY OF • GERMANY, HISTORY OF • HOLY ROMAN EMPIRE • KNIGHTS AND HERALDRY • ROMAN EMPIRE • SPAIN, HISTORY OF • WRITING

# CHAVÍN

FROM THE 10TH to the 1st centuries BC, a brilliant civilization flourished in Peru. It is known today as Chavín, after the important town of Chavín de Huántar in central Peru. Its people produced large temples, fine textiles, and created religious art in a distinctive style. They were also the first people to unify the flat coastal region of Peru with the high Andes Mountains beyond. By doing this, they prepared the way for other important Peruvian civilizations such as the Inca.

Chimú
Huari
Tiahuanaco
Chimú and Huari

**Civilizations**
Other cultures, such as the Chimú, grew up in the Andes region after the Chavín declined.

## Chavín de Huántar

The main city of the Chavín civilization was built at a natural transportation interchange. It lay on the Mosna River next to two passes into the mountains. The city was well placed for trade, with food such as chili and salt coming down to the city through the mountain passes.

**Castillo**
The people of Chavín de Huántar built stone temples at the center of their city. The famous Old Temple or Castillo was a complex stone structure containing many intricate passages. Some of these were probably drainage ducts, designed to channel away water from the temple. The adjoining rooms may have been storerooms for offerings and religious equipment.

## Art

Chavín art was highly elaborate. Chavín artists made carved stone reliefs, statuettes in precious metals, and beautiful textiles, some of which have survived. Their favorite subjects were gods and goddesses, and the priests, birds, and animals that attended them. Many works of art, such as the textiles and gold statuettes, were small and easily portable. They were traded far and wide in South America, and later cultures copied their styles.

**Kennings**
Chavín sculptors liked to use the kenning, a type of visual pun, to represent parts of the body. Instead of carving a person's face realistically, they made up their features using repeated elements such as eyes or snakes. Many Chavín carvings, like this stone relief of a god, are therefore intriguing but difficult to understand.

Jaguar vessel

Animal-figure bowl

**Pottery vessel**
Andean peoples such as the Chavín made highly decorated pottery with tall, curved handles. This example, from Chavín de Huántar, has the face of a jaguar god with a gold nose ornament and large, dangling earrings.

**Ornate bowl**
This bowl in the shape of an animal is another example of the skill of the Chavín potters' art. It may have been used in a religious ceremony, or adorned the table of a wealthy member of the Chavín nobility.

*God carries shield with cross design in his left hand.*

**El Lanzón**
This was probably the main god of the Old Temple. Its statue is found in one of the innermost rooms in the building. It was a human figure that had catlike teeth, suggesting that it was part-human, part-jaguar, like many ancient gods of South and Central America.

*God carries staff in his right hand.*

## Religion

The Chavín people had several gods, including a creature called El Lanzón, or "the smiling god." His statue was placed in a central room in the temple at Chavín de Huántar. Above the statue was a hole. A hidden person could speak through this hole, giving the impression that the god himself was speaking.

**The staff god**
Another important Chavín deity is known as the staff god. This figure is shown in carved reliefs waving a long staff. He was often shown with crops such as cassava, gourds, and peppers, and was thought to be the provider and protector of these valuable foodstuffs.

## After the Chavín

Several civilizations dominated the Andes after Chavín declined. Tiahuanaco, another highland culture, and its neighbors the Huari, flourished from AD 500 to 900. On the coast, the Chimú were the dominant people from the 10th to 15th centuries until they were conquered by the Incas.

**Vessel from Tiahuanaco**

**Tiahuanaco**
This highland empire was a strong, centralized state based in a city on a high plain some 13,100 ft (4,000 m) above sea level. Its monuments included the Gateway of the Sun, which was carved out of a single block of stone.

*Face of Sun god*

*Carved lintel*

*Typical square-headed opening*

**Gateway of the Sun**

**FIND OUT MORE**

GODS AND GODDESSES

INCAS

POTTERY AND CERAMICS

SOUTH AMERICA, HISTORY OF

# CHEMISTRY

THERE IS MORE TO CHEMISTRY than experiments in laboratories – doctors use it to fight disease, chefs use it to cook food, and farmers use it to increase the growth of their crops. Chemistry is the branch of science that studies the structure of different elements and compounds. It also investigates how they change and interact with each other during processes called chemical reactions.

## Chemical change

When a pile of orange ammonium dichromate crystals is heated by a flame, a chemical reaction occurs. Heat, light, and gases are given off, and a mound of gray-green ash is left behind. The ash not only looks different from the crystals, but it also has a different chemical makeup – it has changed into the substance chromium oxide.

*The reaction is so vigorous that a cloud of ash is hurled into the air.*

*Pile of crystals is lit by a flame.*

Ash    Ammonium dichromate crystals

### Antoine and Marie Lavoisier

The French chemist Antoine Lavoisier (1743–94) showed that burning is a chemical reaction, that air is a mixture of gases, and that water is a compound of hydrogen and oxygen. His wife, Marie (1758–1836), translated and illustrated many of his scientific works.

$$2H_2 + O_2 \longrightarrow 2H_2O$$

### Chemical equations

Scientists write equations to describe what happens during reactions. The equation above shows how hydrogen ($H_2$) and oxygen ($O_2$) react in the ratio of 2 to 1 to make water ($H_2O$).

## Rates of reaction

Reactions can be sped up by making the reacting particles come into contact with each other more often. One way of doing this is by increasing a reactant's surface area. Sulfuric acid reacts more rapidly with powdered chalk than with chalk pieces because the powder has more surface area.

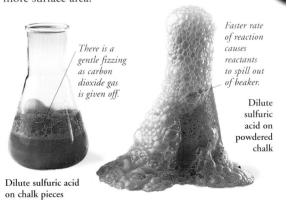

*There is a gentle fizzing as carbon dioxide gas is given off.*

*Faster rate of reaction causes reactants to spill out of beaker.*

**Dilute sulfuric acid on powdered chalk**

**Dilute sulfuric acid on chalk pieces**

### Catalysts

Compounds called catalysts speed up a chemical reaction by helping substances react together. The catalysts are left unchanged by the reaction. Many cars are equipped with a catalytic converter to remove polluting gases from engine fumes. The converter forces the gases into close contact with catalysts. The catalysts make the gases react rapidly with each other, producing less harmful gases that escape out of the exhaust.

## Chemical reactions

During a chemical reaction, substances called reactants break apart and new substances called products form. Energy is taken in to break the bonds between the reactants' atoms. As the atoms link up again in different combinations to make the products, new bonds form and energy is given out.

**Exothermic reactions**
In an exothermic reaction such as burning, more energy is given out than is taken in from the surroundings.

**Endothermic reactions**
Most of the reactions that occur in cooking are endothermic, meaning that more energy is taken in than is given out.

### Oxidation and reduction

When iron rusts, a reaction occurs between the iron and oxygen in the air. The iron gains oxygen, and an orange-brown compound called iron oxide forms. A reaction in which a substance gains oxygen is called oxidation. When oxidation occurs, there is a simultaneous reaction called reduction, in which a substance loses oxygen. When iron oxidizes, the air is reduced as it loses oxygen to the iron.

*Coating of iron oxide forms on the metal.*

**Rusting iron**

### Reversible reactions

Many chemical reactions permanently change the reactants, but reversible reactions can go both forward and backward. For example, when nitrogen dioxide is heated, it breaks down into nitrogen monoxide and oxygen. Cooling this mixture makes the two gases react to form nitrogen dioxide again.

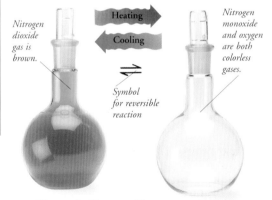

*Nitrogen dioxide gas is brown.*

**Heating**

**Cooling**

*Symbol for reversible reaction*

*Nitrogen monoxide and oxygen are both colorless gases.*

**Nitrogen dioxide**    **Nitrogen monoxide and oxygen**

## Chemical industry

The chemical industry is one of the world's largest and most important industries. It involves taking raw materials – such as air, oil, water, coal, metal ores, limestone, and plants – and using chemical reactions to change them into useful products. These products include food, clothing, medicine, pesticides and fertilizers, paints and dyes, soaps and detergents, plastics, and glassware.

1 A container of whole milk is allowed to stand for a day or so. The curds are removed and then heated.

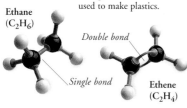

*Acetic acid*

2 Acetic acid is added to the warm curds. A white, rubbery material called casein forms in the liquid.

# Organic chemistry

The study of carbon compounds is called organic chemistry, because all living organisms depend on carbon compounds for their existence. Today, chemists can also create synthetic carbon compounds. Natural and synthetic carbon compounds occur in a wide range of materials, such as food, fuel, paint, textiles, and plastics. This experiment shows how paint can be made from casein – an organic compound derived from milk.

*Casein forms in curds.*

3 The casein is removed by straining the liquid, It is kneaded in warm water and then dried.

*Casein hardens as it dries.*

4 Casein can then be mixed with other materials to form paint. The casein is used to bind the pigment to the surface.

*Casein-based paint*

## Aliphatics
Organic compounds containing a chain of carbon atoms linked by single, double, or triple bonds are called aliphatics. The aliphatic ethane occurs in natural gas, and ethene is used to make plastics.

**Ethane ($C_2H_6$)**

*Double bond*

*Single bond*

**Ethene ($C_2H_4$)**

## Aromatics
The strong-smelling organic compounds called aromatics contain a ring of six carbon atoms. Benzene, the simplest aromatic, is a colorless liquid obtained from coal, natural gas, and petroleum. Aromatics are used to make vivid dyes called anilines.

*Carbon atoms (black)*

**Benzene ($C_6H_6$)**

*Hydrogen atoms (white)*

## Fats and oils
Liquid vegetable oil is an unsaturated fat – a type of fat in which some of the carbon atoms are linked by double bonds. When the oil reacts with hydrogen, the double bonds break and the carbon atoms link up with extra hydrogen atoms, forming a solid fat such as margarine. Solid fats contain only single bonds between their carbon atoms. These fats are said to be saturated because they cannot bond with more hydrogen atoms.

**Liquid oil**

**Solid fat**

## Polymers
Polymers are giant molecules that consist of winding chains of thousands of small organic molecules called monomers. Fats, starches, and proteins are natural polymers; plastics and artificial fibers are made of synthetic polymers. Polythene contains polymers made of many ethene monomers joined together.

*Plastics, such as polythene and PVC, are made up of polymers.*

**Plastic products**

# Electrochemistry

The study of the relationship between electricity and chemical substances is called electrochemistry. Many compounds consist of electrically charged particles called ions, which form when atoms lose or gain electrons. A battery uses a chemical reaction to generate an electric current.

*Electrons flow toward copper plate.*

**Simple battery**

*As the zinc dissolves in the acid, the zinc atoms lose electrons and become ions.*

*Dilute sulfuric acid*

*Current lights bulb.*

*Electrons flow through wire as an electric current.*

## Electrolysis
The process of splitting up a compound by passing an electric current through it is known as electrolysis. Two metal or carbon rods called electrodes are placed in the compound and connected to a battery. As electricity flows through the compound, positive ions are attracted to the negative electrode (the cathode), and negative ions are attracted to the positive electrode (the anode), causing the compound to split.

*Chlorine gas collects at top of tube.*

*Deposits of copper metal form as copper ions move to cathode.*

*Chlorine ions move to anode and form chlorine gas.*

**Electrolysis of copper chloride solution**

**Research into respiration**

**Geochemist examining rocks**

## Biochemistry
The study of the chemistry of living organisms and the chemical processes, such as respiration, that take place within them is called biochemistry. The discoveries of biochemists are used in industry, medicine, and agriculture.

## Geochemistry
The Earth's composition and the chemical structure of rocks are studied in geochemistry. The findings of geochemists give us a greater knowledge of the Earth's history and help us find ores, minerals, and other resources.

## Alfred Nobel
The Swedish chemist Alfred Nobel (1833–96) invented the explosives dynamite in 1867 and gelignite in 1875, which made him very rich. On his death, he left his vast wealth to pay for a series of annual awards – the Nobel Prizes – for achievements in science, art, and medicine.

# Timeline

**2 BC** Egyptian alchemists try to change "base" metals such as lead into gold.

**1661** Robert Boyle, an Irish scientist, realizes that chemical reactions can be explained by the existence of small particles.

**1770s** Antoine Lavoisier investigates compounds such as air and water.

**1807** Englishman Humphry Davy uses electrolysis to discover the element sodium.

*Davy's equipment*

**1808** English scientist John Dalton proposes that each element has its own unique type of atom.

**1830s** German chemists focus on studying carbon and its compounds.

**1909** American Leo Baekeland makes the first fully synthetic plastic – Bakelite.

*Bakelite radio set*

**1939** Linus Pauling, an American chemist, explains the nature of chemical bonds between atoms and molecules.

**FIND OUT MORE**

ACIDS AND ALKALIS · ATOMS AND MOLECULES · DYES AND PAINTS · ELECTRICITY · ELEMENTS · GLASS · MEDICINE · MIXTURES AND COMPOUNDS · PLASTICS

# CHESS AND OTHER BOARD GAMES

BOTH CHILDREN AND ADULTS enjoy games, whether for the challenge of perfecting a skill, the excitement of competition, or simply for fun. Board games, in which competing players move pieces on a special board following rules agreed in advance, are particularly popular. They have a long history and exist in every culture. They range from demanding games of skill and strategy, such as the ancient game of chess, to more simple games of chance, like snakes and ladders, where a throw of the dice determines the winner.

## Strategy games

Games of strategy are challenging, for superior skill, concentration, and tactics decide the winner. Chance plays no part. In most strategy games two players aim to cross the board, or to encircle or capture their opponent's pieces.

### Go
Go, also known as *wei-ch'i*, is at least 4,300 years old. It is extremely popular in China, Japan, and Korea. Players capture areas of the board by surrounding them with their own pieces.

## Chess

Chess is a war game. Two players aim to capture, or take, the other's pieces, ultimately trapping the opponent's king. This situation, known as checkmate, occurs when the king cannot be protected by his own pieces, and cannot move without being taken. The word checkmate comes from the Persian *shah-mat* (the king is dead). Chess can be enjoyed at all levels: by beginners, or by grandmasters in international competition.

*The board has 64 squares.*

*Each player starts with 16 pieces.*

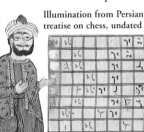

Illumination from Persian treatise on chess, undated

Kasparov vs. the supercomputer

### History of chess
It is thought that chess originated in China or India more than 1,400 years ago. It spread to North Africa and was introduced to Europe after the Muslim conquest of Spain. Early pieces were based on an Asian army, with elephants, chariots, and foot soldiers.

### Pieces
Chess pieces consist of eight pawns, two bishops, knights, and rooks (castles), a king, and a queen. Each piece has its distinctive moves: pawns, for instance, can only move one space forward, while the queen can move in any direction, as far as is needed.

### Computer chess
Computers can be programmed to play chess against humans. In 1997, the chess world was shocked when a supercomputer beat the Russian world champion Gary Kasparov (b.1963) in a match. A vast memory for the tactics of past games gives computers an edge.

## Race games

Many board games are races, in which the winner is the first player to reach a certain part of the board or remove all their pieces. Some race games depend on luck, when a throw of the dice decides how quickly a player moves. This allows players of different ages or levels to compete fairly against each other.

Starting position for mancalah

### Mancalah
There are many varieties of this ancient game of skill from Africa. Two or more players compete to clear their side of the board. Each takes turns to pick up a pile of pebbles, dropping them one by one in the hollows.

### Pachisi
In India, pachisi is a popular game. Four players race counters around a cross-shaped board; they throw dice or shells to see how many spaces to move. Many other games, such as ludo, are based on pachisi.

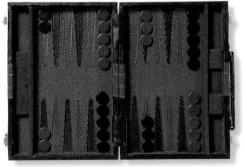

Starting position for backgammon

Men playing pachisi, India

### Backgammon
Invented 5,000 years ago in Asia, backgammon is a fast-paced game for two players. It draws on both skill and chance, and is most popular around the Mediterranean. The first player to remove all his or her "men" from the board wins.

### Playing cards
Card games do not need a special board, but must be played on a flat surface. Generally, games are for two or four players. Some games, such as bridge, require concentration and skill, and are played at international competition level; games such as poker, which rely more on luck are often played by gamblers for money.

*A pack of cards contains 52 cards divided into four groups known as suits.*

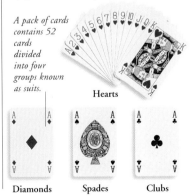

Hearts

Diamonds     Spades     Clubs

FIND OUT MORE    CHINA AND TAIWAN    COMPUTERS    INDIA AND SRI LANKA    JAPAN    SPAIN, HISTORY OF

# Chess and other board games
## Chess pieces

**King** moves one square at a time in any direction.

**Bishop** moves diagonally across the board.

**Rook** travels in straight lines but not diagonally.

**Pawn** moves forward one square at a time.

**Knight** can jump over other pieces to new position.

**Queen** can move in any direction, but cannot jump.

## Board games

Game accessories

*Draught piece*

**Draughts** is a game of skill that was played in ancient Egypt.

**MONOPOLY**
Společenská hra o obchodování s nemovitostmí

*Pieces move around board collecting pies.*

Monopoly tokens

**Trivial Pursuit**, introduced in 1982, is available in a range of editions.

*Players build up words from letter blocks.*

*Each player chooses a character.*

**Monopoly**, patented in 1935, can be adapted to show streets of any major city in the world.

**SCRABBLE**
*Original*

Harry Potter

**Harry Potter**, launched in 2000, is based on JK Rowling's children's book series of the same title.

Cluedo
Das klassische Detektiv-Spiel

*Marbles are used as pieces.*

**Solitare** is game of skill that is played by only one person.

**Scrabble**, originally known as Criss-Cross, is a word game that was devised in 1931.

Scrabble letters

**Cluedo**, a detective game played around the world, was created in 1944.

LUDO · SNAKES&LADDERS

LUDO

SNAKES & LADDERS

**Ludo**, a game for two to four players, originated from an ancient Indian game called pachisi.

**A compendium** is a collection of different board games contained in one box.

**Snakes and Ladders** is a game of chance. Players move their pieces up ladders or down snakes.

# CHILDREN'S LITERATURE

WRITTEN LITERATURE has existed for more than 3,000 years, but it is only in the past 300 years that literature has been created especially for children. Before then, children listened to oral fables and folktales. Early children's books were educational, but in the 19th century many new forms, or genres, developed such as adventure and fantasy stories, and picture books.

## Fables

A short story that illustrates a moral or lesson is called a fable. Fables usually feature animals with human characteristics, such as wisdom or carelessness, and have traditionally been read or told to children in order to encourage good behavior. A fable may, therefore, end with a proverb such as "look before you leap."

### Aesop's Fables
The most famous collection of fables are attributed to a Greek called Aesop who is thought to have lived in the 6th century BC. There are many stories about him; he is often described as a slave who gained freedom to become a royal adviser. The stories attributed to Aesop were first passed on orally, and then written down in the 4th century BC.

The *Tortoise and the Hare* is one of Aesop's fables.

## Modern fables

Some modern children's stories have been strongly influenced by ancient fables. English author Beatrix Potter (1866–1943) wrote a story about a squirrel called Nutkin whose naughty behavior ended in punishment.

### Uncle Remus
The *Uncle Remus* stories by American author Joel Chandler Harris (1848–1908) are fables based on the stories of plantation slaves in the United States. Told in African-American dialect, the tales are narrated by a wise, genial black man to the son of a plantation owner, and feature characters such as the trickster Brer Rabbit.

Brer Rabbit and Brer Fox

### James Thurber (1894-1961)
In *Fables for Our Time* (1940), American author James Thurber reworked traditional stories, such as fairy tales, into fables that were relevant to the 20th century. For example, in Thurber's reworking of the tale of *Little Red Riding Hood*, the girl recognizes the wolf and shoots him dead.

*Finnish*
*French*
*German*
*Japanese*
*Russian*
*Swedish*
*Italian*
*Iranian*

## Books

Children's books are produced in more styles, shapes, and sizes than any other form of literature. They range from pop-up books to picture storybooks. Books for younger readers have large type, and use pictures to help explain the story. As readers get older, their books become longer and the stories more complex.

## Folk- and fairy tales

These are among the most popular types of stories, particularly for young children. All cultures have created their own stories about magical beings and events, and the same folk story may occur in many places. For instance; the tale of an orphaned girl with a wicked stepmother is found in most societies.

A scene from *Cinderella*, by the London City Ballet

### Monkey King
The daring Monkey King is one of the best known folk heroes in Chinese literature. The Chinese writer Wu Cheng'en used many oral folktales as source material in his novel about the Monkey King's adventures, *Journey to the West* (1500s).

Monkey battles with the White-Bone Demon

An illustration from Andersen's *The Snow Queen*

### Hans Christian Andersen
Danish writer Hans Christian Andersen (1805–75) was one of the first authors to write new fairy tales. His first collection, *Fairy Tales,* was published in 1835. By the time of his death, he had published more than 160 stories; most of them, such as *The Ugly Duckling*, are still read today.

### Charles Perrault
Frenchman Charles Perrault (1628–1703) was the first person to write down oral folktales. His *Tales of Past Times* (1697) included *Cinderella*, but his version was less violent and bloody than the original.

### Grimm Brothers
German brothers Jakob (1785–1863) and Wilhelm (1786–1859) Grimm were the editors of *Grimm's Fairy Tales*, which included *Snow White*, and *Hansel and Gretel*. Because of their scholarly approach to collecting folktales from Europe, their versions of these ancient stories are often regarded as definitive.

Wilhelm Grimm        Jakob Grimm

## Fantasy stories

Until the mid-19th century, most of the stories written for children were concerned with the teaching of morals and good behaviour. However, the enormous success of Hans Christian Andersen's fairy tales encouraged many writers to produce wild fantastic stories which celebrated the imagination above all else.

### Alice in Wonderland
Written in 1865, English author Lewis Carroll's (1832–98) fantasy revolutionized children's literature with its fantastic plot, bizarre characters, and absence of any moral. The half dream, half nightmare world that Alice encounters when she plunges down the rabbit hole shows the limitless possibilities of the fantasy story.

*Tenniel illustration of the Mad Hatter*

### Peter Pan
English author JM Barrie (1860–1937) originally wrote *Peter Pan* as a play in 1904. Peter, a motherless half-magical boy, takes the Darling children to Never Land.

### Wonderful Wizard of Oz
American author L Frank Baum (1856–1919) wrote this fantasy in 1900. Dorothy is carried by a whirlwind out of Kansas to the magical Land of Oz, where she befriends the Scarecrow, Tin Woodman, and Cowardly Lion. In 1938, it was made into a popular film, ensuring that people world-wide know the story, even if they have never read the book.

### The Hobbit
JRR Tolkien (1892–1973) published the tale of the Hobbit, Bilbo Baggins, in 1937. The trilogy that followed it, *The Lord of the Rings*, is one of the most popular stories ever published.

*Peter Pan*

*Still from the 1938 film of The Wizard of Oz*

*The Hobbit*

## Adventure stories

The 19th century saw the beginning of great adventure stories for children. The books celebrated bravery, daring, and excitement, although the heroes were often boys rather than girls. Some books, such as *Treasure Island*, described imaginary lands while others, such as *Huckleberry Finn*, were about adventures close to home.

*Huck and Jim*

### Treasure Island
Scottish author Robert Louis Stevenson (1850–94) told a story of piracy. The tale is told by Jim Hawkins, who acquires a map showing hidden pirate gold. He has to defeat the pirates before he can claim the treasure.

### Huckleberry Finn
American author Mark Twain (1835–1910) set his novel on the banks of the Mississippi River. One of its themes, black slavery, is illustrated by Huck's friendship with the runaway slave Jim.

*A scene from the 1950 film of Treasure Island*

## School stories

School is part of children's experience, and often features in literature. The first and most famous school story was called *Tom Brown's Schooldays* (1857) by Thomas Hughes (1822–96). It was based on the author's own time at boarding school in England. Today's school stories usually reflect the experiences of most children.

### Harry Potter
Author JK Rowling published the first in the Harry Potter series in 1997, *Harry Potter and the Sorcerer's Stone*. The book won several literary awards and was followed by equally popular sequels. The stories centre on Harry, an orphan who is sent to live with his aunt and uncle and discovers the Hogwarts School of Witchcraft and Wizardry. By 2002 the series had sold 100 million books in 46 languages.

**Daniel Radcliffe played Harry Potter on screen.**

### Roald Dahl
British author Roald Dahl (1916–90) is known for his fantasy stories, which include *James and the Giant Peach* (1961), *Charlie and the Chocolate Factory* (1964), *Matilda* (1988), and *The BFG* (1989). His popularity is partly due to his skill in describing adults' frightening peculiarities in such a way as to make them laughable.

## Family stories

Children's literature often takes as its theme family life. Stories of family life date back to the 19th century; one of the first was *Little Women* (1869) by Louisa May Alcott. Today's family-based stories look at the difficulties that children may experience, such as divorced parents, bereavement, or abuse.

*Illustration from Tom Brown's Schooldays*

### Little Women
Louisa May Alcott's (1832–88) novel about life in a small town in New England, was one of the first books that presented children in a realistic fashion. The story of the March family, Meg, Jo, Beth, Amy, and their mother, Marmee, was in part autobiographical. It inspired many other American writers to produce stories about family life. Alcott wrote several sequels to *Little Women* including *Little Men* and *Good Wives*.

*A scene from the 1949 film of Little Women*

# Picture books

Children's picture books have a long history; from the *Orbis Pictus* in 1658 there have been picture books for children. Babies and young children can enjoy books in which pictures are just as important as words. The illustrations tell stories and help teach concepts such as colors, shapes, and the names of things. Many talented artists now make books for children.

### Visible world

Even the earliest books included illustrations. However, the first picture book that was especially designed for children was called *Orbis Pictus,* or *Visible World* (1658), by John Amos Comenius. It used pictures in order to help the translation of German into Latin.

### Merchandising

Successful children's books are now big business. Popular characters soon appear as toys, games, and even ceramics. The image of the characters can be found printed on clothing and books.

### Beatrix Potter

The first master of the picture storybook was Beatrix Potter (1866–1943). She was a lonely child who taught herself to draw and became skilled at painting animals. Her first book, *The Tale of Peter Rabbit,* was published in 1901. The books of Beatrix Potter are still popular throughout the world.

*Pierre Lapin*

**Beatrix Potter** books are printed in many languages.

*Jug*

*Cuddly Peter Rabbit toy*

**Beatrix Potter merchandise**

*Teapot*

*Mug*

*Board game*

### Where the Wild Things Are

When this book was published by the American writer Maurice Sendak (b.1928) in 1963, many people thought it was too scary for children. It tells the story of a boy called Max, who sails away to the land of the Wild Things, where after many adventures, he becomes their king.

### Dr. Seuss

The American artist Dr. Seuss (Theodore Geisel 1904–90) created many classic picture books. Stories such as *The 500 Hats of Bartholomew Cubbins* (1938) are built around strange and improbable situations. Dr. Seuss was one of the first authors to make rhyming storybooks that helped teach children to read. In *The Cat in the Hat* (1958), a cat visits two children and creates rhyming chaos while their mother is away.

# Children's poetry

Verse for children dates back to the songs and ballads of the oral tradition, and children still memorize rhymes and songs and pass them on among themselves. Children's poetry has been written in every style imaginable, from humoros fantasies and nonsense limericks to powerful social commentary.

### Nursery rhymes

Spoken rhymes are found all over the world, and many are ancient. Little Bo Peep is linked to a hide-and-seek game called Bo-Pepe, which is more than 600 years old. Around the Rosey describes the symptoms of the plague, which left rose-like marks on its victims.

### Limericks

The English artist Edward Lear (1812–88) wrote many nonsense rhymes. His limericks generally involve all sorts of people in very odd situations.

"**There was** an old man of Whitehaven, who danced a quadrille with a raven."

# Prizes

Today, more children's books are being published than ever before. To encourage good writing and illustration, prizes are awarded for the best books. There are awards for everything from teenage fiction to picture books. Some prizes are nominated by children.

### Newbery Medal

The American Library Association awards this prize for the year's best children's book. It is named after John Newbery (1713–67), who opened the world's first children's bookshop.

### Carnegie Medal

This prize has been awarded by the British Library Association since 1936. It takes its name from American millionaire Andrew Carnegie (1835–1919), who founded libraries in Britain and the US.

## Timeline

**15th century** Chapbooks (crime and miracle stories) published. Courtesy books tell children how to behave.

**1745** John Newbery sells *Little Goody Two-Shoe*s in the first children's bookshop.

*Little Goody Two-shoes*

**1877** English author Anna Sewell publishes *Black Beauty.*

**1883** *Pinochio* by Italian author Carlo Collodi (1826–90) published.

**1894** *The Jungle Book* by Rudyard Kipling (1865–1936) published.

**1908** Kenneth Grahame (1859–1932) publishes *The Wind in the Willow*s.

**1922** The first Newbery Medal for children's literature awarded.

**1926** *Winnie-the-Pooh* by A. A. Milne (1882–1956) published.

**1929** *Emil and the Detectives* by German author Eric Kästner (1899–1974) published.

**1931** *The Story of Babar* by French artist Jean de Brunhoff published.

**1952** E. B. White (1899–1985) publishes *Charlotte's Web.*

**1968** *The Pigman* by Paul Zindel (b.1936) published.

**1975** *Forever,* one of the first books for young adults, by American author Judy Blume (b.1938) published.

**1997** JK Rowling publishes the first book in the *Harry Potter* series.

**FIND OUT MORE**   BOOKS   DRAMA   EDUCATION   LITERATURE   MYTHS AND LEGENDS   POETRY   PRINTING   WRITING

# CHINA AND TAIWAN

THE WORLD'S THIRD LARGEST COUNTRY, after Russia and Canada, China covers a vast area of eastern Asia. It has, by far, the largest population in the world and contains about 36 percent of Asia's people. China has a long Pacific coastline to the southeast, but also borders 14 countries inland. Closely associated with China are Taiwan, an independent island, and the two former European colonies of Hong Kong and Macao. China is ruled by a communist government that is working to continue the country's economic boom of the 1990s.

## Great Wall

More than 2,200 years ago, 300,000 slaves built the Great Wall of China to keep out invaders from the north. Stretching from Central Asia to the Yellow Sea, the wall's total length is 3,980 miles (6,400 km), and is the world's longest human-made structure.

Soldiers walking along the Great Wall

## Physical features

China's vast land area includes rugged hills, subarctic regions, deserts, and tropical plains, and is watered by many river systems. High mountains, mainly in the north and west, dominate one-third of China's land.

### Huang He

Two mighty rivers flow in eastern China, the Chang Jiang and the Huang He. At 3,395 miles (5,464 km), the Huang He is known in English as the Yellow River, or "China's Sorrow," after the yellow soil left behind by its devastating floods.

### Guilin Hills

China's agricultural heartland is in the south and center of the country. The Li river is used to irrigate land that can be intensively farmed. Here at Guilin, the river supports fishermen and their families, who make a living from its rich waters. The steep Guilin Hills rise up behind the river.

### Climate

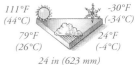

China has two main climates. More than half of the country is arid or semiarid, and in the north and west, deserts and mountains experience extreme temperature variations. The winters are bitterly cold and summers are hot and dry. The summer monsoon brings rain from the Pacific to areas nearer the sea, particularly the south and east, where conditions are wet, warm, and often humid.

111°F (44°C) -30°F (-34°C)
79°F (26°C) 24°F (-4°C)
24 in (623 mm)

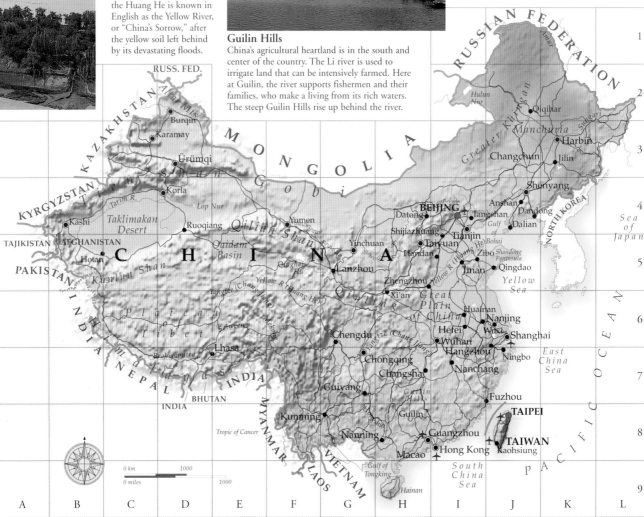

# China

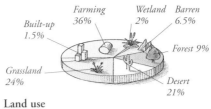

Ruled by the Communist Party since 1949, China is divided into 22 provinces, five autonomous regions, and three special municipalities. Although technically governed from Beijing, many of these are becoming increasingly independent. About 93 percent of China's people are Han Chinese, and around 60 percent follow no religion, because the communist rulers discourage religious beliefs. Although fertile land is in short supply, farming is often intensive and employs two-thirds of the work-force. The Olympic Games will be held in Beijing in 2008.

*Schoolchildren in Beijing*

### Land use

Built-up 1.5% / Farming 36% / Wetland 2% / Barren 6.5% / Forest 9% / Desert 21% / Grassland 24%

The majority of China's farmland is in the east and south of the country. Much of the desert and mountain regions is uninhabitable. China has large mining areas in the Shaanxi and Sichuan basins, and is the world's largest coal producer.

## People

About 80 percent of Chinese live in less than half the country's land area, mostly in small villages. However, more than 30 of China's cities have more than one million inhabitants. China's population is growing by 15 million a year, so the government has asked families to have only one child, and fines those who have more. Known as "Little Emperors," single male children are often spoiled.

335 per sq mile (137 per sq km) — Urban 32% — Rural 68%

## Food

Chinese food varies greatly from region to region. Rice is the basis of all dishes in the south, where it grows; in the north, wheat noodles are the staple food. Both noodles and rice are usually served with stir-fried vegetables and meat. Cantonese food is reputed to be the most exotic in China, using rare meats such as snake and turtle. Fish and duck are also served frequently. The Chinese eat with chopsticks held in one hand.

*Chopsticks*
*Fried noodles*

## Beijing

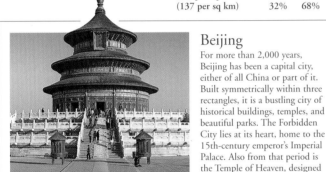

For more than 2,000 years, Beijing has been a capital city, either of all China or part of it. Built symmetrically within three rectangles, it is a bustling city of historical buildings, temples, and beautiful parks. The Forbidden City lies at its heart, home to the 15th-century emperor's Imperial Palace. Also from that period is the Temple of Heaven, designed in the Chinese pagoda style.

*Temple of Heaven, Beijing*

### New Year

China's most important festival is the celebration of New Year, which begins in January or February at the second new Moon of winter. People celebrate with colorful processions and dragon dances and close all shops and offices. Each year is named after an animal.

### Leisure

City dwellers, who have no gardens, are encouraged to take exercise in the well-kept parks. On weekends and summer evenings, neighbors meet to play board games such as *mah jong*.

## Rice farming

Many women work in flooded paddy fields in southern China. Rice is the main crop, and in a good year two yields can be harvested as is one of vegetables. When the crop is ready for harvesting, it turns golden. The women cut and tie the stalks into bundles for threshing, which separates the grain and its protective husk from the stalk.

## Shanghai

A leading center of trade and industry and a busy harbor, Shanghai is China's largest city and home to 16,000,000 people. The city has traditional pagodas and glittering skyscrapers alongside the Chang Jiang River.

## Industry

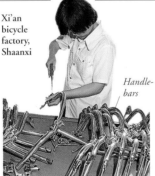

*Xi'an bicycle factory, Shaanxi*
*Handle-bars*

China has well-developed heavy industries such as iron and steel. Since the late 1970s, growth has been concentrated in Special Economic Zones in eastern China, where joint Chinese and foreign trade and enterprise are encouraged.

*Tibetan monk pours Chang beer at hosar festival.*

## Tibet

The mountainous region of Tibet became a part of China in 1965. Most Tibetans are devout Buddhists, but under Chinese rule their religious and civil liberties were taken away. Opponents of the government were exiled, and some Han Chinese were resettled in the area, causing tension. The monks still practice their faith and carry out ceremonies, such as offering beer to Buddha in a *hosar*, or New Year, ritual.

C

# Hong Kong

Hong Kong is a special administrative region in southeast China, made up of 236 islands and a mainland area. It has a busy port and is a leading financial centre. More than six million people live there. A former British colony, Hong Kong was returned to China in 1997. It experienced economic setbacks after the transition, but is now recovering.

### Gambling
Gambling is a popular activity in Hong Kong. Playing mahjong, a traditional game, with friends and family is a way of socializing. Horse racing is a big industry, with many people placing bets online.

### Houseboats
Some Hong Kong fishing families live in houseboats called sampans, which are moored in the harbours. The fishermen are now facing increasing competition from more efficient deep-sea trawlers.

# Macao

A tiny peninsula in southeast China, Macao became a Portuguese colony nearly 450 years ago and was returned to China in 1999. Situated about 40 miles (64 km) west of Hong Kong, Macao is a popular tourist destination, with fragrant woods, and a sandy coastline onto the South China Sea.

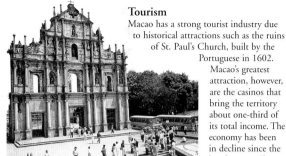

### Tourism
Macao has a strong tourist industry due to historical attractions such as the ruins of St. Paul's Church, built by the Portuguese in 1602. Macao's greatest attraction, however, are the casinos that bring the territory about one-third of its total income. The economy has been in decline since the handover to China.

# Taiwan

Often referred to as a "Little Dragon", Taiwan has one of Asia's most rapidly expanding economies. However, it is not recognized by the UN and lies at the centre of a debate over ruling rights. China claims Taiwan to be a province of Beijing, although the Taiwanese have governed here since the communists gained control of China in 1949. Despite tension, Taiwan has established global trading markets, and its people enjoy high living standards.

### People
About 84 percent of Taiwanese are Han Chinese, who moved to Taiwan when the communists took power in 1949. They live in extended family groups, following traditional customs. Taiwan's native peoples of Indonesian origin now make up only two percent of the population. The Ami, of the eastern mountains, are the largest group. Expert potters and farmers, their women rule the household.

### Opera
Traditional Chinese opera was brought to the island with settlers from China. The operas are based on traditional stories. Stage sets are basic, but the costumes are elaborate, made from richly coloured silks with delicate embroidery. Make-up is used to highlight emotions.

*Fishermen unload their catch.*

### Sun Moon Lake
Taiwan's scenic Sun Moon Lake, known as *Jih-yüeh Tan,* is surrounded by the Central Mountains. The two parts of the lake, Sun Lake and Moon Lake, supply a hydroelectric plant that produces four percent of the country's power. The tranquil, forested area is known for its ornate buildings, including the Buddhist Wen Wu Temple.

### Taipei
The high-tech capital in the north of the island is the fastest growing city in Asia, having expanded to four times its original size. Many of the three million inhabitants ride to work on motor scooters, causing pollution and jams.

### Industry
Few natural resources have forced Taiwan to develop a booming, highly specialized industry. Backed by an educated, ambitious workforce, the country exports electronic equipment, such as computers and television sets, machinery, textiles, sports equipment, toys, and watches. Profits are invested, or used to buy oil for energy. Farming and fishing ensure self-sufficiency in food.

### Fishing
Taiwan's fishermen land 1,290,793 tons (1,171,000 tonnes) of fish annually from the rich fishing grounds surrounding the island. Some Taiwanese fishermen have been accused of plundering Atlantic fishing grounds. Much of the catch goes to supply the huge Japanese market. Freshwater ponds are used for farming carp.

FIND OUT MORE    ASIA, HISTORY OF    BUDDHISM    CHESS AND OTHER BOARD GAMES    CHINA, HISTORY OF    FESTIVALS    FISHING INDUSTRY    GARDENS    OPERA    PORTS AND WATERWAYS    TRADE AND INDUSTRY

# CHINA, HISTORY OF

CHINA IS THE WORLD'S oldest continuous civilization. For more than 2,000 years, from 221 BC to AD 1911, it was united as a single vast empire under a series of all-powerful rulers. During this period, borders changed, capitals shifted, and the country was invaded by fierce tribes, including the Mongols. However, for most of its history, China led the world in art and technology, with inventions including paper, porcelain, and gunpowder. Despite its huge size, a unique system of government and a strong sense of national identity have helped to maintain a united China.

Shang bronze ritual cauldron

Shang bronze staffhead

### Ancient China
The first known Chinese dynasty, the Shang, ruled from about 1500 to 1027 BC. The rulers of the Shang were believed to be semi-divine, and were called the Sons of Heaven. It was their duty to maintain good relations between earth and the heavenly realm.

## Qin Shi Huangdi

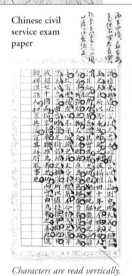

When Zheng (258–210 BC), the leader of the victorious Qin army, took control of China in 221 BC, he took the title of First Sovereign Qin Emperor, or Qin Shi Huangdi. The First Emperor treated his subjects harshly, and his dynasty was overthrown by a peasant rebellion in 207 BC. The name China comes from Qin.

Chinese civil service exam paper

## Han Dynasty

In 207 BC, a new dynasty took power. The Han emperors, who ruled until AD 220, set up a national civil service to run the country. Officials studied the teachings of the philosopher Confucius (551–479 BC), and were selected by a rigorous examination system. The structure of the civil service remained largely unchanged for 2,000 years. The Han reign marked a period of peace and prosperity.

*Characters are read vertically.*

Each soldier has a different face and is modeled on a real soldier.

Hollow body

## Unification

By 400 BC, central government had broken down, and many small kingdoms fought among themselves. In 221 BC, the state of Qin emerged victorious, uniting all the rival kingdoms under the rule of the First Emperor. The Great Wall was built at this time, using slave labor.

### Terra-cotta army
The First Emperor's tomb was guarded by thousands of life-size terra-cotta warriors with horses and chariots, whose job was to protect the emperor in the afterlife. This terracotta army was found in 1974 by men digging a well. The tomb lies near to the modern-day city of Xian.

Great Wall

Qin Empire

*The soldiers once carried real weapons made of bronze, but these were stolen by grave robbers.*

### First empire
Protected by the Great Wall, the Qin empire covered northern and eastern China. The Qin built the wall as a defence against hostile tribes from Central Asia.

*Solid legs*

## Inventions

Throughout Chinese history, emperors encouraged the development of science and technology. Paper and printing, gunpowder, harnesses for animals, the magnetic compass and stern rudder, and the wheelbarrow were all invented in China.

15th-century gun

Shield protects soldier.

Bronze "knife coins"

Multiple gun fires a hail of bullets.

### Paper money
The Chinese perfected papermaking in about AD 105, using pulped silk waste. In later years, hemp, bark, or bamboo were used. The development of printing followed, and paper money was first circulated in China in the 9th century. By this time, the Chinese were also printing books using carved wooden blocks.

### Gunpowder
Chinese scientists first produced gunpowder in the 9th century, and soon adapted their technology to make fireworks and weapons. Early Chinese rockets, fueled by gunpowder, were in use by the 13th century. The Chinese also invented the gun, the bomb, and the mine.

Chinese character, or symbol that translates to mean "happiness and good fortune"

### Three perfections
The Chinese call calligraphy, poetry, and painting "the three perfections." From the Song dynasty (960–1279) onward, the combination of these three disciplines in a single work of art was considered to be the height of artistic expression, and to be skilled in them was seen as the greatest accomplishment of an educated person. Calligraphers spent many months practising the brushwork of just one or two characters.

C

Ming roof tile decorated with horse

# Ming dynasty

In 1368, Hong Wu, a peasant who had led revolts against China's Mongol rulers, managed to drive the Mongols out and create a new dynasty, the Ming. He built a new capital at Beijing and established peace, prosperity, and good government. To make society more equal, he abolished slavery, confiscated big estates, gave land to the poor, and taxed the rich.

## Admiral Zheng

As part of the policy of restoring Chinese prestige, the Ming emperors sent Admiral Zheng He (1371–1433) to visit foreign rulers. Zheng made seven voyages in Southeast Asia and the Indian Ocean, sailing as far west as East Africa. He was accompanied by a fleet of 317 oceangoing junks.

Oceangoing junk

*Tile would have decorated the ridge of a roof.*

## Foot binding

The Chinese believed that tiny feet were a vital part of female beauty. Young girls from rich families had their feet tightly bound to prevent them from growing. This process was very painful. Adult women were also forced to wear platform shoes. In 1902, the emperor issued an order banning foot binding, although it continued for years.

*Platform shoes made the wearer take tiny steps.*

Opium pipe

# Decline of the empire

During the last 250 years of the Chinese empire, the throne was occupied by the Manchus, a non-Chinese people from north of the Great Wall. The first Manchus were enlightened rulers, but later emperors feared that change might lead to rebellion and they clung to old traditions. In 1911, the Chinese overthrew the feeble Manchus, and established a republic.

Boxer rebels

## Boxer Rebellion

In 1900, a secret group called the Society of Harmonious Fists (Boxers) rose up in protest at European involvement in China. The rising was swiftly put down when an international force captured Beijing, but it weakened China's government.

*Japanese troops in Manchuria*

## Opium wars

In 1839, the Chinese tried to stop the British opium trade in Canton. The British went to war, forcing the Chinese to open ports to foreign trade and to cede Hong Kong to the British. France, Russia, and later Japan, made similar demands.

## Japanese invasion

Civil war and a communist uprising weakened the new republican government. In 1931, the Japanese took advantage of the chaos to invade the northern province of Manchuria. Six years later they invaded the rest of China, capturing cities and ports.

# Communist China

In 1949, the Communist party led by Mao Zedong (1893–1976) finally took control of China after years of civil war. The new government nationalized industry and the land, and began a series of five-year plans to transform the country into a major industrial power.

*The red star, a Communist symbol from the Chinese flag*

# Modern China

After the death of Mao Zedong in 1976, the Chinese began to modernize their economy by introducing some western ideas and technology. Central government control over the economy relaxed, and this led to an economic boom as new industries were established.

## Tiananmen Square

In 1989, students took to the streets of Beijing demanding democratic reform. Many students occupied Tiananmen Square, Beijing. On June 4, the army entered the square, killing more than 3,000 people. After this massacre, the pro-democracy movement was ruthlessly suppressed.

*Troops in Tiananmen Square*

# Timeline

c.1650–1027 BC Shang dynasty rules northern China; bronzeworking and Chinese writing are developed.

221 BC First Emperor, Qin Shi Huangdi, founds the Qin dynasty and unites the country.

221 BC–AD 618 Great Wall of China built.

589–618 Short-lived Sui dynasty builds the Grand Canal linking major rivers.

618–906 Tang dynasty brings great prosperity to China; art and trade flourish.

960–1279 Industrial revolution occurs under the Song dynasty.

1279 Mongols under Kublai Khan conquer China; trade with Europe flourishes along the Silk Road.

1368–1644 Ming dynasty establishes China as world power.

1644–1911 Manchu dynasty.

**Mao Zedong**

1911 Chinese republic declared.

1949 Communists declare the People's Republic of China.

1966 Mao Zedong heads Cultural Revolution.

1997 Deng Xiaoping dies. Hong Kong handed back to China by the UK.

1999 Portugal hands back Macao to China.

Shang bronze halberd (dagger)

 **FIND OUT MORE**

ASIA, HISTORY OF    CHINESE REVOLUTION    GUNS    INVENTIONS    MONGOL EMPIRE    POTTERY AND CERAMICS    WRITING

# Chinese arts and crafts
## Jewelry and adornment

**Belt and garment hooks,** worn by men, could be beautifully decorated.

**Gilded hair comb** has prongs of silver; it was probably used by a high-ranking woman.

**Gilded sleeve weight** helped wide sleeves hang properly.

**Gold buckle** is decorated with carved patterns.

**Belt and garment hooks** were sometimes inlaid with turquoise and gold.

**Silver and gilt belt plaque** is decorated with a pattern of fruit.

**Gold and silver nail guards** were used to decorate and protect the long fingernails of rich men and women.

## Status artifacts

**Jade buckle plaque** with dragon design

*Rich, gilded decoration*

*Fish is Buddhist symbol representing spiritual freedom.*

*Decoration made by pushing enamel paste into gaps between metal.*

**Box** is made of lacquer, carved with leaves.

**Cup** is carved from jade, a precious gemstone.

**Jade pot** was used for washing writing brushes.

**Elephant ornament** is made of gold and ivory, inlaid with gems.

**Box** is made of lacquer, carved with peony flowers.

**Fish vase** is decorated with enamel paste and gilded metal.

**Camel** ornament is made of glazed earthenware.

**Jade pot** is adorned with carving of man and house.

**Inlaid lid** for writing brush

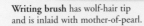

**Writing brush** has wolf-hair tip and is inlaid with mother-of-pearl.

*Extremely detailed work*

# CHINESE REVOLUTION

THE CHINESE REVOLUTION refers to the bitter struggle for control of China between the Kuomintang, or nationalists, led by Chiang Kai-shek, and the communists, led by Mao Zedong. The struggle began in the 1920s when the nationalists expelled the communists from their movement; it ended in 1949 when the communist party took power and Chairman Mao proclaimed that China was a People's Republic. Under Mao's leadership China was transformed from a backward peasant society into one of the most powerful nations in the world.

### 1911 Revolution
In 1911, a nationalist revolution overthrew the Manchu dynasty and created a republic in southern China. Sun Yat-sen (1866–1925) was elected provisional president of the republic, but the lives of the peasants did not improve and real power remained with warlords (military leaders).

## Kuomintang
In 1926, a Kuomintang general named Chiang Kai-shek (1887–1975) defeated the warlords, helped by the communist party. Chiang set up a government in Nanking but, once in power, he threw the communists out of the government and massacred many communist leaders.

## Long March
In 1931 Mao and a small band of communists set up China's first communist state in Jiangxi, southern China. The Kuomintang attacked them constantly, and in 1934 Mao was forced to withdraw. The following year he led 100,000 people, mostly peasants, over 6,000 miles (9,000 km) of some of the world's roughest terrain, to a new base in Shaanxi province in the north. The Long March crossed 18 mountain ranges, 24 rivers, and passed through 11 provinces and 62 cities.

**Only 30,000 marchers** out of the original 100,000 reached their destination.

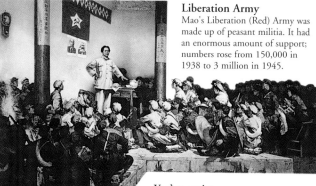

### Liberation Army
Mao's Liberation (Red) Army was made up of peasant militia. It had an enormous amount of support; numbers rose from 150,000 in 1938 to 3 million in 1945.

**Mao Zedong** addressing followers at the Yan'an soviet during the early days of the revolution.

### Yan'an soviet
In 1935, Mao set up new headquarters in northern China – his Yan'an soviet, or base. He and his followers lived in caves around the city of Yan'an, and went into the countryside where they recruited a huge following among the peasantry.

*Cap featuring red star*

*Epaulets show rank*

*Green wool pants*

**Red Army uniform**

**Little Red Book**

## Cultural Revolution
In 1966, in an attempt to introduce revolutionary zeal, Mao introduced a socialist cultural revolution to attack the four "olds": old ideas, old culture, old customs, and old habits. Those accused of "revisionism" (rejecting the revolution) were publicly humiliated in "struggle meetings." The Cultural Revolution ended in 1969, but its excesses nearly led to civil war.

### Red Guard
Radical students, trained as Red Guards, were the main participants in the Cultural Revolution. Using the *Little Red Book* containing the thoughts of Chairman Mao, the Red Guard attacked anyone they believed guilty of betraying the revolution.

## Mao Zedong
The son of a peasant, Mao (1893–1976) followed the nationalist ideals of Sun Yat-sen. In 1921, he helped found the Chinese communist party. Convinced that revolution should come from the peasants, not from the industrial workers, he built a massive following among them. After victory against Chiang Kai-shek, he became chairman of the new republic.

## Timeline

**1911** Nationalist revolution ends rule of the Manchu dynasty. A republic is formed.

**1921** Chinese communist party formed.

**1926** Northern Expedition: communists and nationalists unite to fight warlords.

**1927** Kuomintang under General Chiang Kai-shek attacks and executes hundreds of communists.

**Chairman Mao**

**1931** Japan invades Manchuria.

**1934–5** Long March. Communists march to Shaanxi.

**1937–45** Japan invades China. Communist guerillas harass Japanese and liberate most of northern China by 1945.

**1945–48** Civil war between Kuomintang and Communists after Japanese surrender in World War II. Mao's communists gain control and set up government in Beijing (Peking). Nationalists and Chiang Kai-shek flee to Taiwan.

**October 1, 1949** People's Republic of China is declared.

**FIND OUT MORE**
CHINA, HISTORY OF    COLD WAR    GOVERNMENTS AND POLITICS    JAPAN, HISTORY OF    RUSSIAN REVOLUTION    SOVIET UNION

# CHRISTIANITY

CHRISTIANS BELIEVE that Jesus of Nazareth was the son of God, who came to Earth as promised in the Old Testament, and through whose life, death, and resurrection, believers are freed from their sinful state. Christianity began in the first century AD in the area now known as Israel and Palestine, which was then a part of the Roman Empire. The faith gradually spread throughout the Mediterranean, promoted by followers of Christ such as Saint Paul.

## The cross

Christ's death on the cross and his resurrection were the two key events in his life on Earth. The cross has therefore become the most important Christian symbol. Every church is marked by a cross, and crosses are placed on altars and in other prominent places in churches. During worship, Christians make the sign of the cross.

*The cross symbolizes Christ's resurrection from the dead.*

*This elaborate gold cross is ornamented with precious stones.*

## The Christian world

In the early years there were few Christians, and they were persecuted by the Romans because they refused to worship the Roman gods. But in AD 394, Christianity became the official religion of the Roman Empire after the conversion of the emperor Constantine. The faith spread quickly throughout the empire. Today's Catholic church is still based in Rome and claims to be the descendant of the early church in the Mediterranean. There are now nearly 1.6 billion Christians worldwide.

Shading shows worldwide distribution of Christians.

*Christianity is the largest world religion.*

Stained-glass window showing St. Luke and St. John teaching the gospel

### Spreading the word

Jesus preached the coming of God's kingdom, but his message was rejected and he was put to death. On the third day after Christ's death, God brought him back to life. Christ met his followers and told them to spread the word. Since then, Christianity has been spread by preachers and missionaries. From Europe, colonists took the faith with them to Africa and the Americas.

*God the Father*

*The holy spirit is shown as a white dove, the symbol of peace.*

*Christ on the cross is a symbol of death and salvation.*

*Beneath Christ's feet is a globe representing the Earth.*

### The Holy Trinity

Christians believe that God exists as three persons: God the Father is the creator; God the Son is Jesus Christ; and God the Holy Spirit is the presence of God on Earth. It is the Holy Spirit that inspires prophets and acts as a means of divine revelation. Although there are three persons in the Holy Trinity, they exist as one substance, so Christians believe in one God.

## Branches of Christianity

Two important groups have split from the Roman Catholic church: the Protestant churches that broke away during the Reformation of the 16th century, and the Eastern Orthodox church that is strong in eastern Europe and western Asia.

### Roman Catholicism

Catholics make up the largest Christian denomination. They stress the importance of the church's role in interpreting the scriptures and the authority of the Pope as the leader of the church. They believe in the doctrine of transubstantiation – that the bread and wine used in the Mass are actually converted into the body and blood of Christ.

*A Protestant service in London, UK*

*Bare walls without paintings or statues*

### Protestantism

There are many different Protestant churches around the world, especially in North America. To a greater or lesser extent, they all stress the authority of scripture itself, rather than the clergy's interpretation of the text of the Bible. These branches do not believe in the doctrine of transubstantiation. Although there is great variation in their rituals, Protestants have simpler church buildings and less elaborate ceremonies than the Catholic and Orthodox churches.

*Orthodox Christians pray to icons, such as this image of St. George.*

### Orthodoxy

Like the Roman church, the Eastern Orthodox church stresses the importance of the sacraments. Orthodox Christians do not recognize the authority of the Pope: the highest authority is the church's Ecumenical Council.

*In Catholic churches, incense is burned to release scented smoke.*

*Charcoal is put into the censer and lit to heat the incense.*

Medieval censer

# Ceremonies

The most important Christian ceremonies are the sacred rites known as sacraments. The Roman Catholic and Orthodox churches recognize seven sacraments: baptism (the rite of entry into the church), confirmation (a further initiation ceremony), the Eucharist (Mass), penance (turning to God after sin), extreme unction (preparation for death), ordination (becoming a priest), and marriage. The Protestant churches recognize baptism and the Eucharist.

## Baptism
This ritual is an act of ceremonial cleansing before becoming a member of a church. In some cases, holy water is splashed on the head of the infant. In other cases, an adult entering the church is totally immersed in water.

## Marriage
Christians believe that marriage symbolizes the relationship of Christ with his church. Marriage marks the beginning of a new family and a new generation.

## Eucharist
At his last supper with his disciples, Christ identified the bread and wine as his body and blood. Christians remember this at the Eucharist (or Mass), at which a priest consecrates bread and wine and distributes it among the worshipers.

*Head of saint*

*A priest blesses the wine in a chalice.*

**Sixteenth-century silver chalice**

*An Amish couple in Pennsylvania travel in a horse-drawn carriage.*

# Festivals

The most important Christian festival is Easter when believers commemorate Christ's crucifixion and resurrection. The celebration of Christ's birth, Christmas, is an important festival. Ancient pagan festivals merged with Christian festivals so that old fertility rites are linked with Easter and winter festivals with Christmas.

## Christmas
Christ's nativity (birth) is traditionally celebrated in December. The Christmas story tells of his birth in a stable in Bethlehem. The many Christmas customs include giving presents, decorating trees, lighting candles, singing special hymns (or carols), and eating elaborate meals.

*This nativity painting shows the worship of the Magi, the three Wise Men who came bearing gifts.*

*The Adoration of the Magi,* by Botticelli (1444–1510)

*In the Middle Ages, saints' relics were kept in reliquaries.*

## Amish
The Amish are a Protestant sect founded in the 17th century. Its followers live separately from the rest of society and believe that salvation can only be reached within the community. In the US, Amish communities follow a simple lifestyle with strict rules. They reject modern technology and wear traditional clothing, such as vests and hats and bonnets and capes.

## Saints' days
Christians who have lived outstanding lives or who were killed for their beliefs are revered as saints. Each saint has his or her own special day, and these are often marked with processions, celebrations, and church services. Festivals on saints' days are particularly popular in Catholic countries.

**Reliquary of St. Eustace, an early Roman Christian martyr**

## Easter
The celebration of Easter can involve many moods, from the solemn prayers of Good Friday, when the crucifixion is remembered, to joy at the resurrection three days later. A spring festival, Easter is a time when new life is celebrated. Christ's resurrection is reflected in the new growth of plants and crops, and is celebrated by children when they hunt for decorated eggs.

*Christians carry a statue to symbolize Christ carrying the cross.*

*An Easter procession in Granada, Spain*

# The Bible

The sacred text of the Christian religion is the Bible. Its first part is the Old Testament, a group of books inherited from the Jews, among whom Christianity originally took root. Second comes the New Testament, which is made up of books dealing with the early history of Christianity. The New Testament includes the four gospels, the Acts and Epistles (giving details of the spread of Christianity), and the Book of Revelation (containing prophecies for the future).

**The Dead Sea Scrolls**

## The gospels
The first four books of the New Testament are called the gospels, from a word meaning "good news." They tell the story of the life of Christ. Three of the four gospels (those of Matthew, Mark, and Luke) are very similar; they are known as the synoptic gospels. John's gospel is quite different from the others, and its author may not have known the other three texts.

## The Dead Sea Scrolls
These scrolls of parchment were discovered in caves near Qumran on the Dead Sea in the 1940s and 1950s. They contain writings that include texts of parts of the Old Testament in versions earlier than any previously discovered. They were hidden in AD 68.

## St. Paul
Originally opposed to Christianity, Paul converted when he had a vision of Christ. He began to preach Christianity and spread the faith on four arduous missionary journeys through Greece and Asia Minor. His role was central to the early development of the church. He wrote several of the New Testament books in the form of letters to the Christian communities he visited. He died c. AD 64-68.

**FIND OUT MORE** CHURCHES AND CATHEDRALS · CRUSADES · EUROPE, HISTORY OF · FESTIVALS · HOLY LAND, HISTORY OF · JESUS CHRIST · MONASTERIES · MOTHER TERESA · REFORMATION · RELIGIONS

# CHURCHES AND CATHEDRALS

CHURCHES AND CATHEDRALS are Christian places of worship. Early churches were small, with only enough room for an altar and a small congregation. As Christianity spread, larger churches, with separate areas for the clergy and the followers, were built. A cathedral is a church in which a bishop presides; he organizes the day-to-day running of local parishes.

## The first churches

Christianity began in the Mediterranean during the time of the Roman Empire. Early churches were modeled on the public buildings of ancient Rome, especially basilicas, where meetings and law courts were held. The congregation sat in an area called the nave, and the altar was housed in a smaller area, the sanctuary.

**St. Sabina, Rome**
Founded in AD 422, this early church has a wide nave and small, semicircular sanctuary.

## Parts of a cathedral

Many cathedrals and churches are designed in the shape of a cross. The "arms" of the cross, the transepts, contain small chapels. The altar lies to the east to face the rising sun; the nave lies toward the west.

**Columns and vaults**
The interior has decorative stone ceilings, called ribbed vaults, supported on columns of local Purbeck marble. Each column is surrounded by four shafts (smaller columns), which create a light, delicate effect.

*404-ft (123-m) spire*

**Bell towers** have openings to allow the sound of the bells to escape.

**The large nave** can accommodate big congregations.

**Cathedral interior**
The great nave, with its high, vaulted ceiling, is made to appear larger still by aisles on either side. Light comes in through stained glass windows.

*Intricately carved west front*

*Main entrance*

**Salisbury Cathedral**
This 13th-century Gothic cathedral has slender walls and pointed arches and windows. These features help make it elegant and delicate in spite of its huge size. The 14th-century spire is the tallest in England and can be seen from far away.

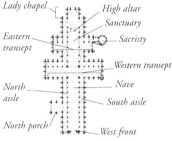

*Lady chapel* — *High altar*
*Sanctuary*
*Eastern transept* — *Sacristy*
*Western transept*
*North aisle* — *Nave*
*South aisle*
*North porch* — *West front*

**Floor plan**
The cross shape symbolizes the wooden cross on which Christ died.

*Western transept* *Eastern transept*

*Sanctuary*

**Pointed arches** are a typical feature of Gothic architecture.

*Lady chapel*

**Buttresses** (supports) help bear the weight of heavy vaults.

## Church decoration

Many churches and cathedrals are richly decorated with symbols of the Christian religion, including images of Christ, angels, the saints, and crosses. Protestant churches tend to be less elaborately decorated than Roman Catholic and Eastern Orthodox churches.

**Fan vaulting**
This delicate fan vault can be found at Canterbury Cathedral, England.

**Gargoyle**
Devils and grotesques were carved on church exteriors during the Middle Ages to represent evil outside the church.

**Statuary**
Representations of the Madonna and Child are found in Roman Catholic churches. This Renaissance-style statue, which was finished in 1896, is in the church of the Sacré-Coeur, Paris.

**Mosaic**
Mosaics were an early form of decoration in Mediterranean churches. This 9th-century mosaic is in the Santi Nereo e Achilleo, Rome.

**Triptych**
The finest decoration of all is usually close to the altar, such as this triptych in St. Peter's Basilica, Rome.

**Stained glass windows**
Beautiful colored windows that decorate churches often illustrate Bible stories told by Jesus and his disciples.

## Churchyards

Churchyards separate a church from noisy streets and provide land to bury the dead. Burials also take place in large cemeteries.

**Celtic cross**
This cross in Ireland combines two Christian symbols: the cross and the circle, a symbol of eternity.

**Columbarium**
A Columbarium houses the ashes of cremated people.

**Burial tombs**
Some tombs tell the lives of those buried inside. This tomb of much-imprisoned French revolutionary Raspail is in the form of a prison.

**FIND OUT MORE**   ARCHITECTURE   CHRISTIANITY   FESTIVALS   GLASS   MEDIEVAL EUROPE   RELIGIONS

# CITIES

LESS THAN 200 YEARS AGO, most people lived in villages. Today, about one-half of the world's population lives in cities. During the 19th century, towns and cities expanded as people moved away from rural areas to work in new industries. Cities have continued to grow haphazardly, in contrast to the carefully-planned cities of the ancient world.

*Hole in roof instead of door*

*Walls made of mud*

**Çatal Hüyük**

*Early cities had no streets.*

## First cities

Settlements in western Asia, such as Jericho (Israel), Çatal Hüyük (Turkey), and Ur (Iraq), started to expand around 4000 BC. At this time, craftsworkers began to trade goods outside their local areas, creating new wealth that was used to build palaces, large temples, and strong walls for defense. These towns grew in importance and emerged as the first cities.

## Modern cities

The world's cities have grown rapidly in modern times but inadequate planning has contributed to poor living conditions and poverty in many urban centers. Poor areas, wealthy neighborhoods, and areas dominated by one particular ethnic group are all features of city life. Most cities offer many people a wide choice of jobs, houses, and recreational facilities.

**Gardens, parks, and squares** give people the chance to escape the bustle of city streets.

**Entertainment** is a feature of most cities. Cities are usually cultural centers with theaters, museums, galleries, and music venues, such as Sydney's striking Opera House.

**Residential**
There are different residential areas in cities. Older houses and apartments are close to the city center, while modern developments extend outwards, clustering around railroad lines and major roads.

**Business** is always located close to the heart of the city. Nowadays, the business area is usually dominated by skyscrapers.

*Apartment building*

*Skyscraper*

*Converted loft*

*Brownstone*

*Underground*

*Services*

**Sydney, Australia**

**Roads**, railroads, boats, and airlines bring people into the city center.

**Manufacturing**
Small factories and light industry were once at the heart of cities. Today, large industrial complexes are usually built farther out, reducing pollution.

### New York
The city of New York contains some of the world's tallest skyscrapers. It also has large apartment buildings, low-rise commercial sites (some of which have been converted into homes called lofts), 19th-century brownstone (a type of sandstone) houses, and smaller, modern houses. Steps lead to underground subways and shops.

## Villages

A traditional village is a small, rural settlement, often by a stream or river. In most parts of the world, people still live and work in villages, farming the surrounding countryside and trading with nearby settlements.

**Masai village, Kenya**
Many of the Masai people live in groups of thatched, mud houses surrounding a central cattle enclosure.

**Stilt village, Sumatra**
In many Southeast Asian villages, houses are raised on stilts to keep out unwanted animals, like snakes.

**Gold rush town**
Towns grew around 19th century gold mines. Abandoned as the gold ran out, some still stand as "ghost towns".

### Forbidden City
The Forbidden City in Beijing, China, was built in the 15th century. Only the emperor, his family, and his officials were allowed in.

## Timeline

**8000 BC** Strong walls and a stone tower are built at Jericho.

**3500 BC** City-states such as Ur develop in Mesopotamia (modern Iraq).

**5th century BC** Greeks plan and build the elegant city of Athens.

**1st century BC** The Roman Empire expands, and new European cities are built.

**12th century AD** Stone walls, such as those at Carcassonne, France, are built to protect medieval towns and cities.

**1421** Construction starts on Forbidden City, Beijing, China.

**15th century** Renaissance architects lay out classical cities, such as Florence and Siena in Italy.

**19th century** Industrialization stimulates growth of towns and cities in Europe and America.

**Siena, Italy**

**1950s** Brasilia designed and constructed as new capital of Brazil.

**1990s** Skyscrapers dominate most city skylines.

 **FIND OUT MORE**  ARCHAEOLOGY  ARCHITECTURE  BUILDING AND CONSTRUCTION  INDUSTRIAL REVOLUTION  IRON AND STEEL  RENAISSANCE  SOCIETIES, HUMAN  TRAINS AND RAILROADS

# CLIMATE

WEATHER CAN CHANGE from moment to moment. Over a long period of time, a region's characteristic weather, however changeable, is called its climate. Climates are generally warm near the Equator, the imaginary line around the middle of the Earth, and cool at the poles. Other influences on the three broad climate types – warm tropical, cold polar, and mild temperate – include the distance from an ocean and the position within a continent. Climate determines a region's animal and plant life.

Polar
Mountain
Tundra
Temperate
Mediterranean
Dry grassland
Desert
Subtropical
Tropical

**Climate zones**
Close to the equator, the Sun's rays are strong as the sun climbs high in the sky at midday. Closer to the poles, the Sun's rays are weaker – it climbs less high. Climatic zones, which affect vegetation, can be further classified by physical features.

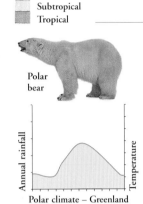
Polar bear

Polar climate – Greenland
Annual rainfall / Temperature

## Polar climate
Towards the ice-capped poles, the Sun is always low in the sky, and in winter barely rises at all. Summers are brief. Winter temperatures in the tundra regions around the North Pole are below -76°F ( -60°C).

## Tropical climate
Weather in a tropical climate, such as Brazil, is always warm, often with heavy rainfall. Some tropical climates, such as deserts, are hot and dry; others, such as rain forests, are warm and moist.

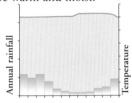
Parrots

Tropical climate – Brazil
Annual rainfall / Temperature

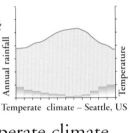
Oak sprig

Temperate climate – Seattle, US
Annual rainfall / Temperature

## Temperate climate
In mid-latitude (imaginary lines parallel to the Equator) areas such as the US, summers are warm and winters cool, with regular periods of rainfall. A Mediterranean climate, with dry summers and warm, damp winters, is a type of temperate climate.

### Mountain climate
High altitude causes the air to cool, thus creating a cold climate. Exposed mountaintops also make mountain climates very wet and windy. Above a certain height called the snow line, there is always snow.

Oceanic and continental climate zones

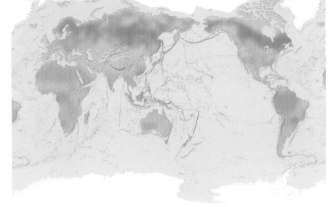

## Oceanic and continental climate
Coastal regions have wet, changeable weather. Summers are cooler and the winters are warmer than inland areas, because the ocean heats up and cools down more slowly than the land. Places in the continental interior, such as Moscow, have cold winters.

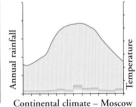
Continental climate – Moscow
Annual rainfall / Temperature

### Desert climate
Over a fifth of the world's land surface is desert, where there is typically an annual rainfall of less than 4 in (100 mm). In the tropics, desert temperatures frequently climb above 122°F (50°C).

### Monsoons
These are warm, tropical climates with wet and dry seasons. In India, it is dry from October to May as the winds blow out to sea, and very wet from June to September as the monsoon winds blow inland.

---

*Each tree ring shows one year's growth: a wide ring means the weather was warm and the tree grew well.*

## Climate change
Over long periods of time, climate fluctuates. Signs of massive ice formation for instance, show that the world was once much colder. We now live in an interglacial period. Subtle changes in the climate's recent past are revealed by variations in the sizes of tree rings.

### Global warming
Pollution may be warming the Earth's climate. Certain gases trap the Sun's heat in the Earth's atmosphere. Rising levels of these gases, such as carbon dioxide, which come from burning oil or forest land, may trap so much heat that the Earth's climate could warm up by 7.2°F (4°C) over the next 50 years, in what scientists call the greenhouse effect.

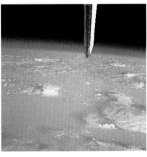

**FIND OUT MORE**    DESERTS    MOUNTAINS AND VALLEYS    OCEANS AND SEAS    POLLUTION    RAIN    WEATHER    WEATHER FORECASTING    WINDS

# CLOTHES AND FASHION

PEOPLE HAVE ALWAYS WORN clothes, either as protection from the weather, or out of modesty. Yet throughout history, people have also chosen clothes to impress or attract others, or to reflect their job, social status, or religious beliefs. Clothes send out signals about the wearer's lifestyle and the type of society he or she lives in: for instance, during the 20th century, the emancipation of women was reflected in the more practical clothes they wore.

## Clothing design

Designers choose the fabric, color, and shape of a garment. Their decisions are influenced by the function of the item and who will eventually wear it. A work shirt, for example, must be made from durable fabric; a high-fashion shirt can be made from less practical silk or linen.

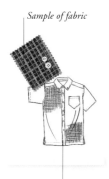

*Sample of fabric*

*Sketched design*

**Design**
Some designers sketch their ideas for a new style on paper. Others work directly with the fabric, draping it over a dressmaker's mannequin and pinning it until the right shape emerges.

**Pattern**
Once the design has been created, it is made into pattern pieces of paper or cardboard. These are used as a guide for cutting out the fabric. The pattern pieces are made in different sizes and sent to the cutting room.

## Daily wear

The popular informal outfit of shirt, jeans, and sneakers can be seen in many parts of the world, worn by both sexes at all ages. This casual outfit is an example of the changing attitudes to clothes seen in the 20th century. For the first time, everyday clothing crossed barriers of age, gender, and social class.

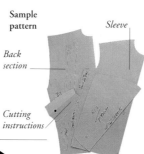

**Sample pattern**

*Back section*

*Sleeve*

*Cutting instructions*

## Hat

*Sports caps are popular everyday wear.*

In the early and mid-20th century, adults usually wore hats in public. The way people dress has become less formal since then, and the hat's importance as an accessory has declined.

*Belt*

## Shirt
In medieval Europe, shirts were worn beneath a tunic. Over the years, more and more of the shirt was allowed to show. Now it is regarded as an outer garment. Everyday shirts are usually made of durable fabric and are easy to put on.

## Jeans
Bavarian-born retailer Levi Strauss (1829-1902) sold the first blue jeans – Levis – to miners in the 1850s. They have been popular ever since because they are long-wearing and easily adapted to changes in fashion.

## Sneakers
Sneakers were originally made for tennis or basketball players – the rubber soles stopped them from slipping. They have since become fashionable "street" wear.

*Rubber sole*

*Leather or fabric upper*

*Cotton*

*Computerized control panel*

*Needle*

## Clothing industry

The clothes manufacturing industry is massive and employs millions of people worldwide. Some designs are exclusive, produced by the great fashion houses. Most clothes, known as ready-to-wear, are manufactured in standard sizes and mass-produced in factories.

**Cutting**
Up to 150 layers of fabric are spread out on long tables. The pattern pieces are then laid on top and the material is cut, using either a mechanical knife or a laser.

**Sewing**
The cut pieces are carried to the person whose job it is to match them up for the sewing machinist. Each machinist concentrates on a particular part of the garment, such as the sleeves.

**Pressing**
Once the clothes are sewn together, they are laid on large, flat tables to be pressed. Then a final inspection is made to check the quality of the finished garment before it is sold to a wholesaler.

## Sewing machine
To make a stitch, a sewing machine must loop one thread around another. The latest models are computerized: touching a panel changes the type of stitch. Home sewing machines can make about 1,000 stitches a minute; industrial machines are ten times faster.

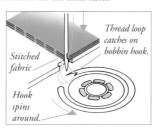

*Thread loop catches on bobbin hook.*

*Stitched fabric*

*Hook spins around.*

1 As the needle pokes through the fabric, it makes a loop of thread that is picked up by a bobbin hook beneath the needle plate.

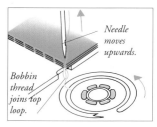

*Needle moves upwards.*

*Bobbin thread joins top loop.*

2 The loop is pulled around thread drawn from within the bobbin, joining the top thread as a stitch. Both threads are then released.

# Traditional clothing

The clothes worn in some parts of the world combine modern lifestyles and traditions thousands of years old. Traditional national costumes often reflect the dress of peasants, whose garments were suited to the local climate and the kind of work they performed.

*Traditional jacket (parka) in modern fabric*

*Insulated boots*

**Canada**
Inuit people dress to protect themselves against cold weather: in northern Canada, it snows from October to May.

*Shaved head*

*Silk jacket*

*Rubeka*

**Tanzania**
The Maasai wear vivid pieces of cloth called *rubeka*. Young women who are old enough to marry wear special headdresses.

*Scarf*

**South Korea**
This traditional silk costume is called *hanbok,* meaning "Korean clothing." It is worn on special occasions.

*Sneakers (not traditional)*

*Embroidery*

*Hang pen*

**Vietnam**
The traditional outfit of the Dao people, a hill tribe, is a *lamchu:* a scarf, skirt, jacket, and *hang pen*, wound around the legs.

**India**
The most popular dress for Indian women is the *sari*, which is usually made from a length of silk or cotton.

*Elegantly draped sari*

## Tying a sari

The sari is a length of material between 15 and 30 ft (5 to 9 m) long and just over a yard wide. It is worn over a bodice called a *choli*, and a long petticoat. When the weather gets hot, the sari can be adjusted to let in cool air.

*Choli, worn beneath sari*

*Sari fabric*

**1** First, the material is wrapped around the body once, then tucked into the petticoat.

**2** The sari fabric is pleated, then tucked into the petticoat again.

**3** The extra fabric is draped over the shoulder.

## Coco Chanel

The French designer Gabrielle "Coco" Chanel (1883–1971) had a powerful influence on Parisian and world fashion for almost 60 years. Her designs stressed simplicity and comfort at a time when clothes tended to be restrictive and uncomfortable. Many of her innovations are now fashion classics, such as bell-bottomed pants, practical suits, and the "little black dress."

# Body decoration

Every culture has practiced some form of body decoration, ranging from scarring and tattooing, which are permanent, to makeup and body paint, which last only a few hours. One of the oldest forms of body decoration is jewelry, worn to show wealth and status, for protection and healing, or for beauty. Examples include rings, necklaces, earrings, bracelets, and brooches.

*Glass necklace*

*Dress clips*

*Bracelet*

**Jewelry**
Beads, berries, feathers, shells, bone, glass, precious stones, and metals have all been used to make jewelry. Most costume jewelry is made from cheap materials, such as plastic, because it is worn only for a short time.

*Plastic brooch*

**Body painting**
People paint their faces and bodies to mark a religious occasion, celebrate important events in their community, or ward off illness. Sikh brides, for example, paint ornate, beautiful patterns on their hands using dye from the henna plant.

*Body paint in Papua New Guinea*

# Fashion

Following fashion (the changing trends in clothing) was once so expensive that only the wealthy could afford it. Today, however, advances in manufacturing and the invention of synthetic fabrics have made clothes more affordable. Styles have changed faster than ever before and fashion has become big business. Shows by fashion houses such as Dior (France) or Ralph Lauren (US) attract buyers from all over the world.

*High-fashion wedding dress*

# Hats and shoes

Through the ages, hats and shoes have come in many styles: hats have ranged from headdresses to berets, shoes from simple leather sandals to chunky platform boots.

*Riding hat*

*Chin strap*

*Badge*

**Police officer's cap**
Hats may stand for authority. Here, the police officer's cap is part of the uniform.

**Hard hat**
People who are at risk of head injuries, such as construction workers, wear hard hats to protect themselves.

**Shoe**
Shoes must suit people in different climates as well as follow fashion. They are commonly made from durable leather, but rubber, plastic, silk, and canvas are also used.

*Lining*

*Tongue*

*Thin upper encloses foot.*

**Cross-section of shoe**

*Steel shank supports arch of foot.*

**FIND OUT MORE**    DYES AND PAINTS    GLASS    INDIA AND SRI LANKA    METALS    PLANTS USES    TEXTILES AND WEAVING

# Fashion in the 20th century

*Corset pushes chest forward and hips back.*

**Daywear**, typical S-bend silhouette, 1900s

**Daywear**, narrow, tailored line, 1910s

*Shirt collar is turned down, a recent fashion development.*

*Wrapover skirt*

**Lounge suit**, single-breasted, 1910s

*Orange-blossom headdress*

**Wedding dress**, with new, shorter skirt, 1920s

*Wide knicker-bockers, or "plus-twos"*

**Three-piece suit**, for country wear, 1920s

*"Modesty" skirts feature on both costumes*

**Wool bathing costumes** (knitted one-piece), 1930s

*Bias cut fabric clings to the body*

**Crepe evening dress**, full-length, 1930s

*Boxy style, economical with fabric*

*Felt trilby*

**Daywear** from World War II, 1939–45

*Tightly fitted bodice*

*Long, full skirt*

**Suit**, in style of French designer Christian Dior, 1950s

*Mini-skirt*

**Minidress**, "Space Age" influence, 1960s

*"Ethnic" styles influence fashion*

*Flared (wide-leg) pants*

**"Hippy" fashion**, 1970s

*Pants*

**Daywear**, 1990s

## Underwear, hats, and shoes

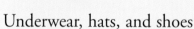

**Cotton camisole** with lace inserts, 1900s

**Brassieres** from the 1920s and 1930s

**Girdle**, worn from the 1930s to the 1950s

**Underwear** in easy-care nylon, 1960s

**One piece** in polyester, 1980s

*1920s "Long Johns"*

*Cotton shorts, 1950s*

*Brief cotton pants, 1980s*

**Men's underwear**

**Boater**, worn on the river and as informal wear, 1900s

**Silk hat** on wire-frame base, 1920s

**Cloche**, bell-shaped hat with small brim, 1920s

**Bowler**, worn on horseback, 1920s

**Felt hat**, with shallow crown, 1930s

**Silk hat**, with glass berries, 1950

**Shoes** with steel beading, early 1900s

*Kid boots*, possibly worn for cycling, early 1900s

**Reptile-skin shoes**, popular in the late 1920s

**Lace-up shoes** with a wedge heel, 1940

*Boots* with black and gold thread woven into fabric, 1960s

**Platform soles**, high fashion in the 1970s

# CLOUDS

WHEN YOU LOOK UP at the sky, you usually see clouds. In temperate or mild climates, there are at least a few clouds on most days, and sometimes cloud cover is total. Clouds are dense masses of water drops or ice crystals so light and small that they float in the air. Clouds form when rising air cools and can no longer contain its water vapor, and so the vapor condenses. There are three basic forms, or shapes, of cloud – puffy cumulus, layered stratus, and feathery cirrus – but there are many different types of clouds. The type of a cloud depends on how high the air rises and on its temperature.

## Cloud formation

Clouds form by the condensation or freezing of water vapor. The way they form depends on the amount of vapour in the air and the speed of upward air movement. When pockets of warm air rise rapidly, clouds form in huge puffs (cumulus). When air rises slowly and evenly over a large area, clouds form in layers (stratus).

### Making a cumulus

The sun-warmed ground creates thermals – rising currents of warm air. The air cools as it rises. Eventually, it becomes so cool that water droplets condense and a cloud forms. The cloud continues to build up as long as the thermal continues to supply water vapor.

**Formation of a cumulus cloud in three stages**

### Luke Howard

An astute amateur meteorologist, and a pharmacist by profession, British-born Luke Howard (1772–1864) kept detailed weather logs that provided valuable meteorological data before official records were kept. Howard used Latin names to identify each cloud by shape. His classification of clouds is still used today.

## Cloud types

There are 10 distinct types of cloud. Cirrus, cirrostratus, and cirrocumulus clouds form 3–7 miles (5–11 km) above sea-level. Altocumulus, altostratus, and nimbostratus clouds form 1–4 miles (2–7 km) above sea-level. Stratocumulus and stratus form at 1 mile (2 km ) or under above sea-level. Cumulus and cumulonimbus clouds form over a wide range of heights.

**Cirrus clouds** form at high altitude where air is cold and strong.

**Cirrostratus** is a high level veil of cirrus cloud.

**Altostratus** is a thin watery sheet of cloud.

**Cirrocumulus** are clouds of ice crystals with a varied appearance.

### Cloud cover

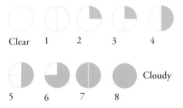

| Clear | 1 | 2 | 3 | 4 |
| | | | | Cloudy |
| 5 | 6 | 7 | 8 | |

The amount of sunlight reaching the ground depends on how much sky is covered by clouds. This is measured in "oktas" (eighths). One okta means one-eighth of the sky is covered in cloud; two oktas equals two-eighths of cloud cover in the sky, and so on.

**Cumulonimbus** is created by strong updrafts, bringing heavy thunder and rain.

## Fog and mist

When water vapor in the air condenses near the ground, it forms fog and mist. "Radiation" fog forms on cold, clear, calm nights when the ground rapidly loses the heat it has absorbed during the day and cools the air above to its dew point. "Advection" fog forms when warm, moist air flows over a surface so cold that the water vapor in the air condenses.

**Altocumulus** are puffs or rolls of clouds at medium height.

**Cumulus** are fluffy white clouds, often short-lived.

*A cloud puff that floats around a mountaintop is called a banner cloud.*

### Sea mist

When warm moist air flows over cold water, water vapor in the air may condense to form a kind of advection fog called a sea mist. These mists usually form on early summer mornings when the air is calm.

**Beachy Head, Sussex, England**

**Nimbostratus** are layers of dark rain clouds.

**Stratus** are cloud layers, often giving long periods of rain.

**FIND OUT MORE**   ATMOSPHERE   CLIMATE   RAIN   STORMS   WEATHER   WEATHER FORECASTING   WINDS

# COAL

MORE THAN two hundred million years ago huge trees grew in the warm, humid swamps that covered vast regions of the world. They captured the Sun's energy to make their wood. When they died, their trunks became buried and gradually changed into coal. When we burn coal today, we release the energy the trees captured all those years ago. Because of its origin, coal is called a fossil fuel. It was the first fossil fuel to be used by people, and is today second only to petroleum in importance for energy production worldwide.

## Coal mining

Almost 5 billion tons of coal are mined a year. China and the United States mine the most coal, with annual outputs exceeding 1.6 billion tons. Coal deposits can be up to about 66 ft (20 m) thick, but they average less than 10 ft (3 m). Some deposits are found on the surface, but most lie underground between layers of rock.

*Piles of dead plant material accumulate in swampy regions.*

### How coal is formed
Coal began to form in swampy forests about 350 million years ago, during the Carboniferous period. Decaying plants were buried under layers of mud. As heat and pressure increased, plant remains slowly converted into coal. Today, there are three main grades of coal – lignite, bituminous coal, and anthracite.

**Peat** represents an early stage in coal formation. It is soft, fibrous, and moist, but still gives off heat when burned.

**Lignite**, or brown coal, is a low-grade fuel containing up to about 60 percent carbon, along with plant remains and moisture. It is soft and crumbly.

**Bituminous coal** is a better quality fuel, comprising more than 80 percent carbon. It is the most common solid fuel used in industry. It is hard, but dirty to the touch.

**Anthracite** is the highest grade coal, containing more than 90 percent carbon. It is shiny black, clean to touch, and burns with little smoke.

**Collecting coal at a strip mine**

### Strip mining
One method of surface, or opencast, mining is called strip mining. The coal is excavated in a series of long strips. Any soil above each strip is used to fill in the trench created when the coal has been removed from a previous strip.

**Drilling coal in a shaft mine**

### Shaft mining
Coal seams deep below the surface are reached by a system of vertical shafts and horizontal tunnels. The coal is dug out by powered coal-cutters and hydraulic tools.

## Coal products

Coal can be processed into valuable products by a method called destructive distillation. Coal is heated in coke ovens to 2,400 °F (1,300 °C) without air. A mixture of liquid vapors and gases escapes and is then separated into coal gas, ammonia liquid, and coal tar. The solid left behind is called coke.

### Coke
This solid, porous substance is, like coal, an excellent fuel that contains more than 80 percent carbon. It is widely used in industry, mostly in blast furnaces for making iron. In the furnace it also acts as a chemical agent in the iron-extraction reaction.

### Coal tar
Coal tar is a black oily liquid that is a rich source of mostly organic chemicals, such as benzene, phenol, and creosote. These can be processed into a variety of materials including dyes, paints, and drugs.

**Coal tar soap**

### Mine safety
Mines are dangerous places because of the risk of rock slides and the build-up of explosive gases such as methane. One safety device was invented by an English scientist, Humphry Davy, in 1815. His safety lamp was able to detect dangerous levels of poison gases.

**Davy lamp**

## Power

About 25 percent of the world's energy supply is generated from coal. In coal-burning power stations, the coal is first pulverized (powdered) and then ignited in a furnace. The hot gases produced pass over tubes containing water and turn it into steam. The steam drives powerful turbogenerators that produce electricity. The electricity is then transmitted through a national grid network.

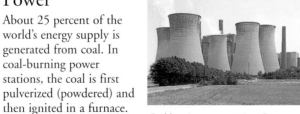

**Coal-burning power station, Germany**

### Domestic fuel
Until the mid-1900s, coal was the fuel most used in Western homes. Each room was heated by open coal fires, and cooking was usually done on a coal-burning stove. Today, few modern homes have coal fires, because people heat their homes with oil or gas. Some cities and towns allow only nonpolluting fuel to be used for energy.

**Burning smokeless fuel keeps pollution low**

**FIND OUT MORE**    CHEMISTRY    DYES AND PAINTS    ELECTRICITY    ENERGY    FIRE    INDUSTRIAL REVOLUTION    IRON AND STEEL    OIL    PLASTICS AND RUBBER

# COASTS

A COAST IS SIMPLY defined as the boundary between the land and sea – an area that may range from a rocky cliff to a sandy beach. This boundary is always shifting as the sea continues its relentless assault on the land – waves roll up and down, and tides ebb and flow. The action of the sea creates distinctive landforms, such as a cliff, created by eroding (wearing away) rock; a shore (an area between low tide levels and the highest storm waves); or a beach, built up by shore deposits. Wind and rain erosion also contribute to the changing aspect of coastlines.

## Evolution of a coast

Waves crash against a shore with great force, wearing away rocks by pounding them with water and hurling rocks and stones at them. On high coasts, the waves undercut the base of the slope, creating a cliff. The model below shows the gradual effect of waves and seawater on the coast.

## Beaches and sandbars

Material worn away from rocky coasts is pounded by waves into sand and shingle and deposited elsewhere as beaches and sandbars – an offshore strip of sand or shingle. A spit resembles a sandbar, with one end attached to the land; a tombolo is a spit that links an island to the mainland.

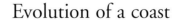

*Sea erodes into the cliffs, sculpting patterns of rock, such as this arch.*

*Waves eat back inland, leaving a wave-cut platform that juts out beyond the cliff.*

*Eroded material accumulates at the shoreline, forming beaches.*

*Stack, or lone pillar*

*Cliffs are attacked by storms; sea arch roof collapses, leaving a stack; another arch appears behind.*

*Cliff retreats farther as rocks fall.*

*Rough seas continue to erode coastline, spurting through a blowhole, a crack in the cliff.*

*Storm waves eat away at cliff base.*

*Stack is worn down.*

*Cave mouth*

*Cliff face marked with crags and gulleys where boulders fall.*

*Coastline has moved backward with erosion of cliffs.*

## Types of coasts

Coasts vary according to their composition and structure. Whether the coast is high or low, and made of soft or hard rock, affects whether it has been formed largely as a result of erosion or by deposition.

### Bay-head beach
This is formed when material eroded from headlands (high land jutting into the sea) is washed into a bay, a coastal inlet between the headlands.

*Wave direction*

### Drowned coast
Where the sea level has risen or the land sunk, valleys are flooded to form narrow inlets, or rias. Where the valleys are glacial, the inlets are called fjords.

### Highland coast
Where the sea meets a highland coast, it generally wears away the rocks, creating cliffs, small coves, and wave-cut rock platforms.

*Wave direction*

### Lowland coast
Broad beaches, saltmarshes, and estuaries are features of lowland coasts.

*Raised beach*

*River slopes toward new sea level.*

## Waves

The wind whips the sea's surface into waves. Waves travel across the water, but the water in them circulates on the spot. When waves reach the shore, the bottom touches the beach and slows down; the top spills on, causing the wave to "break".

**Wave formation**

*Top spills over; wave breaks.*

*Circular motion is upset as the wave hits the beach.*

*Waves grow steeper as they approach the shore.*

*Water circulates in the wave in orbital paths.*

### Coastal protection
When waves strike a beach, they wash the sand or pebbles across the beach at an angle. This repeated process is known as longshore drift. Fences or groines may be built, to slow down such reshaping of the beach.

Coastal fences

## Beach material

Fine sand and silt are usually found lower down a beach; bigger storm waves wash gravel and pebbles higher up. On some beaches, there is a ridge of pebbles, called a storm beach, that has been flung up beyond the high-tide mark by violent storms.

*Pebbles and stones*

*Fine sand*

*Gritty sand*

**FIND OUT MORE**    CAVES    CORAL REEFS    GLACIATION    MOUNTAINS AND VALLEYS    OCEANS AND SEAS    ROCKS AND MINERALS    SEASHORE WILDLIFE

# CODES AND CIPHERS

A CODE IS ANY SYSTEM of prearranged symbols, words, or numbers that is used in communication. For example, the flags that are used to send messages at sea are a naval code. We use codes to simplify, organize, and communicate complex information, for instance, in area and zip codes, or bar codes that describe goods in a way that machines can read. Not all codes have an everyday use. Ciphers (secret codes) hide the true meaning of a message. Banks use them to keep financial deals private, and spies or criminals use them to avoid getting caught.

## Ciphers

In a cipher, each letter is represented by a different letter or symbol. For instance, it is easy to encipher a message by jumbling the alphabet, changing C into M and M to C. It is easy to break such a simple cipher, but computers can create ciphers that are impossible to read without the key (a long number that unlocks the meaning).

### Spies

A spy is a secret agent who collects information for a government or organization. A spy's work often involves stealing the secrets of rival governments. Spies use ciphers to scramble data when they send it to their employers.

*Spy codesheet*

### Cipher disks

These devices create ciphers by replacing letters of a message on the outer ring with the letters alongside them on the inner ring.

*Cipher disk*

### Cipher machines

The Enigma cipher machine was used in World War II. It had a typewriter keyboard with electrical connections that scrambled letters. Each letter was coded separately, making the cipher hard to break.

*Metal cover plate fits over rotor cylinders.*

*Viewing window shows code letters.*

*Rotor cylinder*

*Coding rotor*

*Keyboard*

*Plugboard setting is altered to change cipher.*

*Klappe schließen*

*Filter dims lights.*

German Enigma cipher machine, World War II

## Uses of codes

Codes make messages quicker to send. They are used for many reasons. Sailors, for example, have used flag codes to communicate for more than 1,000 years. By flying the three flags standing for the letters NKA, a warship sends a message meaning "I have not sighted any vessels since leaving my last port." A code book carried on every ship translates the codes.

### Computer codes

Special codes are used to program information inside computers, where letters and punctuation marks are represented by binary numbers. Ciphers can also be also used to protect e-mail (mail sent between computers) so that it can only be understood by the sender and the addressee.

E-mail can be encrypted so that only the addressee, who holds a secret "key" (a long number), can read it.

### The alphabet in Morse code

| | | | |
|---|---|---|---|
| A | • — | N | — • |
| B | — • • • | O | — — — |
| C | — • — • | P | • — — • |
| D | — • • | Q | — — • — |
| E | • | R | • — • |
| F | • • — • | S | • • • |
| G | — — • | T | — |
| H | • • • • | U | • • — |
| I | • • | V | • • • — |
| J | • — — — | W | • — — |
| K | — • — | X | — • • — |
| L | • — • • | Y | — • — — |
| M | — — | Z | — — • • |

### Morse code

The telegraph was invented in the 19th century; it used electricity to send messages quickly over long distances for the first time. The system could not transmit speech, so to communicate operators used an alphabetic code devised by US artist Samuel Morse (1791–1872). Letters were represented by dots and dashes (long and short pulses of power). Operators tapped a key to turn the electric current in the telegraph wires on and off. Morse code is still in use.

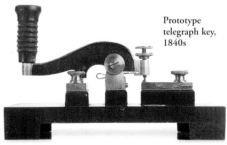

Prototype telegraph key, 1840s

## Smoke signals

Fire beacons and smoke codes were used to send signals by the people of ancient China, Egypt, and Greece. Native Americans, such as the Cheyenne, Comanche, and Sioux, communicated over distances using smoke signals, shaping smoke with an animal hide or blanket. There were a few generally understood signals – two puffs meant "all's well" – but each group also had secret codes that they shared only with people they wanted to read the messages.

Frederic Remington, *Smoke Signals*

## William Friedman

Russian-born American William Friedman (1891–1969) decrypted secret messages for the US government in World Wars I and II. In 1940, William led the team that discovered the key to the Japanese Purple cipher. A message in this cipher warned of the Pearl Harbor attack.

**FIND OUT MORE** FLAGS • INFORMATION TECHNOLOGY • LANGUAGES • NATIVE AMERICANS • SIGNS AND SYMBOLS • WORLD WAR II

# COLD WAR

IN 1945, THE ALLIED FORCES of the US, Britain, France, and the USSR – now known once again as Russia – gained victory over Germany in World War II. Within four years, the allies had become enemies, and a new war had broken out. This was not a military war, but a "cold" war – a political and diplomatic battle between communist Eastern Europe and capitalist Western Europe. The rival blocks expressed hostility by backing opposing sides in conflicts such as Korea and Vietnam. The Cold War ended in 1990 when Eastern Europe's communist governments fell.

Winston Churchill, FD Roosevelt, and Josef Stalin, Yalta Conference

## Yalta Conference

In 1945, the British, American, and Soviet leaders Churchill, Roosevelt, and Stalin, met in the Russian resort of Yalta to determine the shape of post-war Europe. The conference agreed Soviet control over Eastern Europe. This started the political division of Europe into east and west that was to last until 1990.

## Iron Curtain

By 1949, there was a clear division in Europe between the communist states in the east that followed Russia, and the capitalist states in the west that followed the US. Both east and west became secretive and hostile. In 1946, the British Prime Minister Winston Churchill described this polarization as "an iron curtain ... (descending) across the continent."

Iron Curtain

*Austria was divided until 1955.*

*Switzerland was neutral during the war.*

Capitalist    Communist

Mig-15 jet

### Korean War

In 1945, Korea was divided between a communist north and an American-backed south. In 1950, North Korea invaded the south; the USA supported South Korea, while the USSR and China supported North Korea. War raged until an armistice was agreed in 1953. Korea remains divided to this day.

### Red Scare

In the early 1950s, fear of communism in the US led to a witch-hunt against known Communist Party members and possible sympathizers. Senator Joe McCarthy led a government committee that created a "Red Scare" in the US, and caused hundreds of innocent people to lose their jobs.

## Spies

Technological information was very important during the Cold War. In order to find out what the other side was planning, both sides of the Iron Curtain employed spies. Spies worked undercover in civilian and defense jobs, passing vital military secrets back to their own governments.

*Spies used invisible powder to help identify each other.*

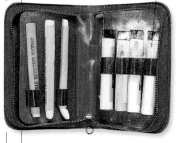

Chemical detection kit

Soviet ship returning to the USSR

## Cuban missile crisis

In 1962, Soviet ships delivered nuclear weapons to the Cuban government. The US – only 90 miles (145 km) from Cuba – blockaded the island, which caused a crisis between the USA and the USSR. After several days of tension, the USSR withdrew its missiles.

## Détente

In the 1960s, tension between east and west began to ease. In the 1970s, Willy Brandt, West Germany's leader, negotiated treaties with Poland and the USSR. In the late 1980s, Mikhail Gorbachev began to reform the USSR, which eventually led to the fall of communism in Eastern Europe.

Anticommunist poster

Berlin Wall is dismantled, 1989

## Timeline

1945 Europe divides into eastern and western blocks.

1949 Western nations set up NATO (North Atlantic Treaty Organization).

1950–54 McCarthy era, in US.

1950–53 Korean War.

NATO symbol

1955 Warsaw Pact establishes military alliances between communist countries.

1961 Berlin Wall divides East from West Berlin (and East from West Germany).

1962 Cuban missile crisis marks the peak of the Cold War; its resolution slowly leads to détente.

1989 Fall of the Berlin Wall begins the fall of communist governments throughout Eastern Europe.

1990 Reunification of East and West Germany.

1991 Gorbachev resigns; collapse of communism in USSR.

## Mikhail Gorbachev

Gorbachev (b.1931) became leader of the USSR in 1985. He attempted to reform the country, and negotiated arms reduction agreements with US President Reagan. Despite his success, he failed to improve the living standards of the Soviet people and resigned in 1991.

 FIND OUT MORE    EUROPE, HISTORY OF    RUSSIA, HISTORY OF    SOVIET UNION    UNITED STATES, HISTORY OF    WARFARE    WEAPONS    WORLD WAR II

# COLOR

A WORLD WITHOUT COLOR would be dull and uninspiring. Color is a form of light. Light is made up of electromagnetic waves of varying lengths. The human eye detects these different wavelengths and sees them as different colors. White light – like that from the Sun – is a mixture of all the different wavelengths. Objects look colored because they emit or reflect only certain wavelengths of light.

## White light spectrum

Passing white light through a transparent triangular block called a prism separates the different wavelengths of light. The prism refracts (bends) each wavelength by a different amount, forming a band of colors called a white light spectrum, or visible spectrum. The seven main colors are red, orange, yellow, green, blue, indigo, and violet. Red has the longest wavelength and violet the shortest. Here, a convex lens combines the colors back into white light.

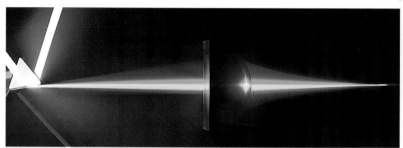

## Rainbow

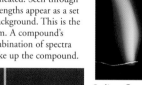

A rainbow at dawn

If it rains on a sunny day, you may well see a rainbow if you stand with your back to the Sun. A rainbow is a curved white light spectrum that forms when light is reflected and refracted by raindrops in the sky.

### How a rainbow forms

The white sunlight passes through a raindrop, the raindrop acts like a tiny prism, refracting the light and splitting it up into its separate colors. The colors fan out and emerge as a spectrum. A rainbow is made up of spectra from millions of raindrops.

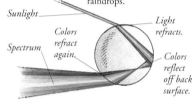

*Sunlight*

*Colors refract again.*

*Spectrum*

*Light refracts.*

*Colors reflect off back surface.*

## Color and temperature

Objects at room temperature emit (give out) electromagnetic waves, but these waves are too long for human eyes to see. Heating an object, such as this steel bar, makes the waves short enough to be seen, and the bar begins to glow. As the bar's temperature rises, it glows with different colors.

Steel bar at 1,170°F (630°C )

Steel bar at 2,790°F (1,530°C)

## Spectroscope

*Light source*

*Diffraction grating*

An instrument called a spectroscope is used to analyze the light emitted by hot substances. Inside the spectroscope, a prism or diffraction grating (a glass slide scored with fine lines) splits light from a glowing substance into its component wavelengths.

### Emission spectrum

Each chemical element gives out a unique range of light wavelengths when heated. Seen through a spectroscope, these wavelengths appear as a set of bright lines on a dark background. This is the element's emission spectrum. A compound's emission spectrum is a combination of spectra from the elements that make up the compound.

Emission spectrum of a sodium flame

Sodium flame

### Cone cells

At the back of the eye are special cells called cones that enable humans to see colors. There are three types of cones, called red, green, and blue cones. Each type of cone is sensitive to a different range of light wavelengths. White light stimulates all three types of cones.

Cone cells

*Sensitivity of red cones*

*Sensitivity of green cones*

*Sensitivity of blue cones*

*Visible spectrum*

Sensitivity of cone cells in the human eye

*Glowing white*

*Glowing red*

*Visible spectrum*

### Red hot and white hot

As the steel bar gets hotter, it emits more and more of the visible spectrum. At about 1,170°F (630°C), it is "red hot" and emits light from the red end of the spectrum. At about 2,790°F (1,530°C), the "white hot" bar emits the entire white light spectrum.

### Hot stars

The color of a star gives a clue to its age. To the naked eye, most stars look white, but their true colors can be seen through a telescope. Young stars are hot and glow with white light. Older stars are relatively cool and glow red or orange.

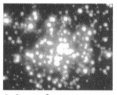

A cluster of young stars

## Joseph von Fraunhofer

The German physicist Joseph von Fraunhofer (1787–1826) became interested in the nature of light while training as a mirror maker and lens polisher. His training enabled him to make spectroscopes of great precision. From 1814–17, he used them to make the first scientific study of the Sun's emission spectrum.

## Munsell color system

Describing colors exactly using words alone is not easy. To avoid confusion, manufacturing industries use standard color-identification systems. The Munsell system is used to specify colors for dyes and pigments. It defines a color by its value (brightness), its chroma (strength), and its hue (position in the spectrum).

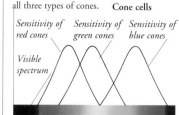

### Color matching systems

Graphic designers use swatches of color cards to match the colors in their work with those available from printers. The designer supplies the printer with the reference number of the color, so the printer knows exactly what is wanted.

*Each color has a reference number.*

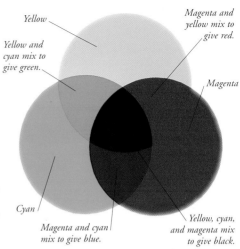

Green

Red and green light mix to give yellow.

Green and blue light mix to give cyan.

Red, green, and blue light mix to give white.

Red

Blue

Red and blue light mix to give magenta.

# Colored lights

Different amounts of red, green, and blue light can be mixed to form light of any other color. This process is called color addition. Unlike paints, red, green, and blue are the primary colors of light. Equal amounts of any two primary colors give a secondary color (yellow, cyan, or magenta). When all three primaries are mixed in equal amounts, white light is produced.

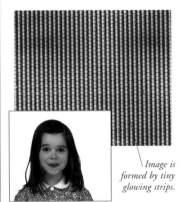

**Color television**
The principle of adding colored lights is used in color television. The screen is covered with tiny strips that glow with red, green, or blue light. They are so small that, at normal viewing distance, the human eye mixes the light coming from them. By adjusting the intensity of these three colors, the sensation of any other color is produced.

*Image is formed by tiny glowing strips.*

**Painting with dots**
"Pointillism" is a style of painting in which an artist uses thousands of tiny colored dots to build up a picture. When viewed close up, the colors of the individual dots are clearly visible. Like the colored strips on a television screen, the dots are too small to be seen from farther away. When viewed from a distance, the dots seem to merge, giving areas a single color.

## Thomas Young

The English doctor and physicist Thomas Young (1773–1829) carried out many experiments to prove that light travels in waves. He realized that colors are light waves of different lengths and that interference colors occur where light waves meet and combine. Young also investigated color vision. In 1801, he proposed that the human eye contains three types of color sensors (now called cone cells), sensitive to blue, red, and green light.

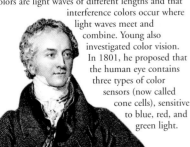

# Pigments

A pigment is a chemical that absorbs only certain colors from white light. This process is called color subtraction. Yellow, magenta, and cyan are primary pigments. Each absorbs one of the primary colors of light and reflects the other two. For example, a yellow pigment absorbs blue light but reflects green and red, which mix to give yellow. An equal mix of all three pigments absorbs all the colors from white light, giving black.

Yellow

Magenta and yellow mix to give red.

Yellow and cyan mix to give green.

Magenta

Cyan

Magenta and cyan mix to give blue.

Yellow, cyan, and magenta mix to give black.

**Color printing**
To print a color picture, three single-color images are printed on top of each other – one in cyan, one in magenta, and one in yellow. Each picture is made up of tiny colored dots. The dots overlap and absorb the right wavelengths of light to give all the other colors required. A black image is then added to make the picture sharper.

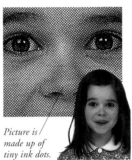

*Picture is made up of tiny ink dots.*

**Mixing paints**
Paints are pigments mixed with water or oil. Any color except white can be made by mixing the three primary pigments. Mixing paints has the effect of evenly mixing the pigments, and absorbing more of the white light spectrum.

# Scattering and interference

Two other processes, called scattering and interference, can remove colors from the spectrum. Interference occurs when light from two sources meets and combines. In scattering, some parts of the spectrum are briefly absorbed by particles of matter and then radiated out again in all directions.

**Blue sky**
Sunlight includes all the colors of the spectrum. The sky appears blue during the day because air molecules in the atmosphere scatter light from the blue end of the spectrum in all directions.

**Soap bubble**
When white light strikes a soap bubble, it reflects off both the inner and outer surfaces of the bubble. The reflected light rays interfere, canceling out some colors but making others appear bright.

*Interference creates a pattern of bright colors and dark bands.*

**Using interference**
Stress is a force that can stretch or bend objects. Engineers shine light through plastic models of their designs to test their ability to withstand stress. The plastic molecules make the light rays split up and interfere. The interference patterns show the points of greatest stress.

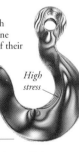

*High stress*

# Reflecting colors

Objects have color only when light falls upon them, because colors do not exist in total darkness. An object that appears one color in white light may look different when illuminated by colored light. The yellow pot in this sequence of pictures appears yellow only in white light.

**White light**
The yellow pot reflects the red and green parts of the white light spectrum, but absorbs the blue part.

**Red light**
The yellow pot reflects red light, and therefore appears red when illuminated by red light.

**Green light**
When illuminated by green light, the yellow pigment reflects the green light and appears green.

**Blue light**
When only blue light is available, the yellow pot absorbs the blue light, making it look black.

 **FIND OUT MORE**

DYES AND PAINTS    EYES AND VISION    LIGHT    PHOTOGRAPHY    PRINTING    TELEVISION

# COLUMBUS, CHRISTOPHER

CHRISTOPHER COLUMBUS was the first European since the Vikings to visit America. In the 1400s, Europeans did not know that America existed – they thought that Asia faced Europe across the Atlantic Ocean. In 1492, Columbus set sail from Spain across the Atlantic. He hoped to open up a trade route to Asia that would be quicker than the old land journey. He found some islands he believed were the East Indies, off what was presumed to be the Asian mainland. What he had really discovered was a continent soon to be known as America by the Europeans.

The port of Genoa in the sixteenth century

### Early life
Columbus was born in the port city of Genoa, Italy, in 1451 and was named after St. Christopher, the patron saint of travelers. His father was a weaver, and Christopher had little formal education. As a boy, he went to sea and later worked in Lisbon, Portugal, where he drew sea charts for Portuguese sailors.

## Crossing the Atlantic

While the Portuguese and other sailors were trying to find a sea route to Asia by sailing south and east around Africa, Columbus believed that, since the world was round, he could reach Asia from the opposite direction by sailing west across the Atlantic. In 1492, he persuaded the king and queen of Spain to finance his voyage, and set sail with three ships, the largest of which was the three-masted *Santa Maria*. At his first attempt, he landed in the Bahamas. Columbus, however, thought these islands were off the coast of Asia.

The *Santa Maria*

Columbus's four voyages
— 1492
→ 1493
— 1498
→ 1502

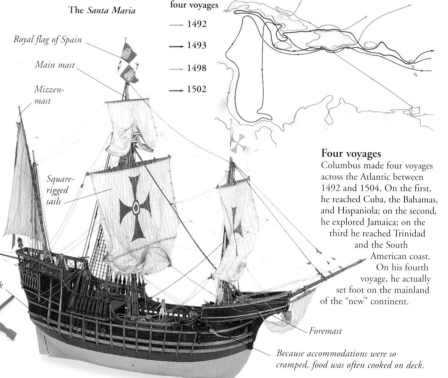

*Royal flag of Spain*

*Main mast*

*Mizzen-mast*

*Square-rigged sails*

*Room for 40 crew below deck*

*Foremast*

*Because accommodations were so cramped, food was often cooked on deck.*

### Navigation
Columbus had few instruments to help him navigate across the ocean. He used a crossstaff and astrolabe to calculate the ship's latitude, but had no way of knowing its longitude. Despite this lack of information, he managed to navigate successfully back home to Europe.

*Astrolabe*

*Using the crossstaff*

*Crossstaff*

### Four voyages
Columbus made four voyages across the Atlantic between 1492 and 1504. On the first, he reached Cuba, the Bahamas, and Hispaniola; on the second, he explored Jamaica; on the third he reached Trinidad and the South American coast. On his fourth voyage, he actually set foot on the mainland of the "new" continent.

## West Indies

Columbus was amazed by the beauty and lush vegetation of the Caribbean Islands, but he was disappointed that he had not found the rich trading cities of Asia. However, his discoveries encouraged other Europeans to visit the area in the coming centuries, founding colonies and opening up new trade links between Europe and the Caribbean.

Columbus arriving at the island of Hispaniola

### New discoveries
While in the West Indies, Columbus and his crew tasted new foods, such as pineapple, potatoes, and sweet corn. They saw people sleeping in hammocks, and observed the Arawak peoples of Cuba rolling up dried tobacco leaves and smoking them.

### Later life
In 1493, Columbus was made governor-general of all the lands he discovered, but he was a poor administrator. In 1500, there were complaints about his rule of Hispaniola. As a result, Columbus was arrested and sent back to Spain in chains. He retired to Seville, where he died in 1506.

### CHRISTOPHER COLUMBUS

|  |  |
|------|-------|
| 1451 | Born in Genoa, Italy |
| 1476 | Becomes a map maker in Lisbon, Portugal |
| 1479 | Marries Filipa de Perestrello e Moniz |
| 1484 | Becomes master mariner in Portuguese merchant service |
| 1492 | First voyage: sails across Atlantic Ocean in search of new route to Asia |
| 1493–96 | Second voyage |
| 1493 | Establishes European colony on Hispaniola |
| 1498–1500 | Third voyage |
| 1502–04 | Fourth and final voyage |
| 1506 | Dies in Seville, Spain |

**FIND OUT MORE**    CENTRAL AMERICA, HISTORY    EXPLORATION    NAVIGATION    SHIPS AND BOATS    SOUTH AMERICA, HISTORY    SPAIN, HISTORY

C

# COMBAT SPORTS

FIGHTING SPORTS, which had their origins in ancient Greece, developed in different ways. Judo and the other martial arts, such as karate, kung fu, tae kwon do, and aikido, evolved in the East, often as a way of life or connected with religion. Only since the 1950s have their secrets become known in the West and their popularity as sports spread. The chief Western combat sports are boxing, wrestling, and fencing. These have Eastern counterparts in kick boxing, sumo, and kendo respectively.

*The judo suit, or "judogi," is a loose-fitting cotton jacket and pants.*

*Players grip an opponent by the jacket.*

## Judo

Judo means "the gentle way," and players try to use their opponent's weight and strength against them. Players can use more than 40 recognized throws to put their opponents on their backs. Or, in groundwork, they try to pin their opponent's back on the mat with a hold. In competition, a referee awards points for throws and holds.

*The arm is used to absorb the impact of a throw.*

**Scoring**
A perfect throw or 30-second hold-down earns *ippon*, worth 10 points, and wins the contest outright. Near-perfect throws or shorter hold-downs earn *waza-ari*, worth seven points, and two of these win a contest. If the contest goes its full length, other scores and penalties count.

*The shoulder is pinned to the ground during groundwork.*

**Performing a hip throw**

Red
Black
Brown
Blue
Green
Orange
Yellow

**Belts**
The color of the belt a player wears around the jacket indicates his or her grade. Judo grades range from *kyu*, meaning student, to the advanced *dan* grades when the player wears a black belt or red for ninth or tenth dan.

## Fencing

In fencing, points are scored by registering "hits" on the opponent's target areas. These vary according to the weapon used: the upper body, including the arms for a saber; the trunk only for a foil; and the whole body for an épée. A bout lasts until one player has scored the agreed number of hits or the time limit has been reached.

*Scoring a hit*

**Weapons**
A foil and saber must not weigh more than 17.5 oz (500 g), an épée not more than 26.9 oz (770 g). The foil and épée have a 35.4-in (90-cm) blade and must strike the target with the point. The edges of a saber's 34.7-in (88-cm) blade may be used for a hit.

**Gauntlet**

**Wired vest**

**Fencing kit**
Fencers wear protective clothing on the body, a mask of steel or plastic mesh, and a padded gauntlet on their sword hand. In competition, target areas may be electrically wired to register hits, signaled by lights.

Foil
Épée
Saber
Mask

## Boxing

Boxers fight in a raised, square "ring" bounded by ropes. Amateur boxing is staged over three three-minute rounds. Professional fights last up to 12 rounds (15 in title fights). Fights may be won by a knockout, by the referee stopping the fight, or on points.

### Muhammad Ali

Arguably the most colorful figure in sports, Muhammad Ali (b.1942) was the first boxer to regain the world heavyweight title three times. Born Cassius Clay, he won the Olympic light-heavyweight title in 1960, turned professional, then gained the world heavyweight crown with a surprise win over Sonny Liston in 1964. He changed his name when he joined the Black Muslims.

## Other combat sports

Like judo, most of the other Eastern combat sports come from Japan, including karate, sumo wrestling, and kendo.

**Karate**, meaning "empty hands," uses kicks and strikes by the hands, elbows, and head.

**Sumo wrestling** is steeped in the ritual of the Shinto religion. Each contestant tries to throw his opponent or push him out of the ring.

**Kendo** pays tribute to the samurai fighters of feudal times. "Swords" are bamboo sticks.

Amateur's headgear
Padded gloves
**High-top boots**

**FIND OUT MORE** GREECE, ANCIENT | JAPAN, HISTORY OF | OLYMPIC GAMES | RELIGIONS | WEAPONS

# COMETS AND ASTEROIDS

COMETS AND ASTEROIDS ARE LEFTOVERS from when the nine planets formed in the Solar System 4.6 billion years ago. Comets are fragile balls of snow and dust found at the edge of the Solar System in the Oort Cloud. Some leave the cloud and travel toward the Sun. The Sun's heat melts the snow and the comet appears to grow in size many times over. Asteroids are made of rock and are found mainly between the orbits of Mars and Jupiter.

*Thin, straight gas tail*

**Comet West** passed Earth in 1976. It had two distinctive tails.

*Broad dust tail*

*Nucleus* | *Coma*

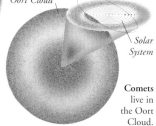

*For most of its orbit, a comet is a dirty snowball.*

*Tail develops as comet approaches Sun.*

*Tail is longest near Sun.*

*Tail shrinks as comet moves away from Sun.*

## Anatomy of a comet

At the center of a comet is the nucleus – a dirty ball of snow and dust that is just a few miles across. If a comet is close to the Sun, the snow becomes gas, and gas and dust are released, forming a vast cloud of material – the coma – and one or two tails.

### Halley's Comet

Halley's Comet is the only comet that has been observed close to. Five spacecraft went to investigate when it traveled through the inner Solar System in 1986. The space probe *Giotto* took this image of its dark, potato-shaped nucleus.

### Edmond Halley

Comets are usually named after their discoverer, but one is named after the English scientist Edmond Halley (1656–1742). He was the first person to show that comets can be periodic and follow orbits that return them again and again to Earth's sky.

### Periodic comets

When a comet leaves the Oort Cloud it can travel on an orbit which returns it again and again to the inner Solar System. This is a periodic comet. About 150 are short-period comets; they return to appear in Earth's sky in periods of less than 200 years. Halley's Comet passes Earth every 76 years.

*Oort Cloud*

*Solar System*

**Comets** live in the Oort Cloud.

### Oort Cloud

Surrounding the Solar System is the Oort Cloud, made up of 10 trillion comets. Although the cloud is large, it is so distant that the comets cannot be seen. Comets only become visible when they travel within the inner Solar System. Astronomers have seen about 700 comets in Earth's sky.

## Meteoroids

Tiny pieces of dust and chunks of rock travel through space. They are meteoroids and originate from two main sources: comets and asteroids. About 220,000 tons (tonnes) of such material enter Earth's atmosphere a year. The smallest meteoroids produce meteors. Larger pieces reach Earth and land on its surface. These are meteorites.

### Meteors

Tiny meteoroids burn up as they travel through Earth's atmosphere, producing streaks of light known as meteors. When Earth travels through a concentration of meteoroids, a meteor shower is produced. The meteoroid material is left by comets as they pass close to the Sun.

### Meteorites

More than 3,000 meteorites land on Earth every year. Most fall in the sea, but a handful are seen to fall on land. There are three main types of meteorites: stony, iron, or stony-iron.

**Nakhla meteorite**

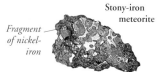

**Stony-iron meteorite**

*Fragment of nickel-iron*

### Rock from Mars

Eight meteorites are known to have come to Earth from Mars. The Nakhla meteorite fell in Egypt in 1911. It is 13 million years old. Such meteorites tells us that Mars once had running water.

### Impact crater

When a meteorite lands on Earth, it can create a crater. Earth was once bombarded by meteorites but its surface has since changed, removing the evidence. Today, about 150 impact craters can be identified, including Wolfe Crater in Australia.

*Wolfe Crater*

## Asteroid belt

Between the orbits of Mars and Jupiter is the asteroid belt – a doughnut-shaped ring made of millions of asteroids, pieces of rock, and metal. The smallest are specks of dust; the biggest, Ceres, is more than 550 miles (900 km) across.

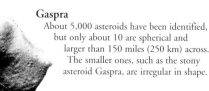

**Gaspra**

About 5,000 asteroids have been identified, but only about 10 are spherical and larger than 150 miles (250 km) across. The smaller ones, such as the stony asteroid Gaspra, are irregular in shape.

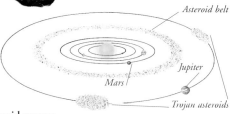

*Asteroid belt*

*Jupiter*

*Mars*

*Trojan asteroids*

### Asteroid groups

Not all asteroids are in the asteroid belt. About 10 percent travel in groups away from the belt. The Trojans travel along Jupiter's orbit, one group in front and one group behind the planet. The Amor, Apollo, and Aten groups all follow orbits closer to Earth.

**FIND OUT MORE**    ASTRONOMY    PLANETS    SPACE EXPLORATION    SUN AND SOLAR SYSTEM    UNIVERSE

# COMPUTERS

WITH LIGHTNING SPEED, a computer carries out millions of calculations each second. Sets of instructions called programs tell the computer what to do. The hard disk unit is the heart of a computer. It contains the central processing unit (CPU), which controls all of the operations of the computer. The hard disk, monitor, keyboard, and other connected devices are called hardware. The programs that enable it to function and carry out specific tasks are known as software.

## Personal computer

A personal computer (PC) is a compact computer that can be operated by only one person at a time. It consists of a hard disk, to which hardware called peripherals is connected so that data can be either input or output. Keyboards and printers are examples of peripherals. Interfaces are electronic circuits that allow the hard disk to communicate with each peripheral.

**Hard disk** contains the memory, the CPU, and the disk drives.

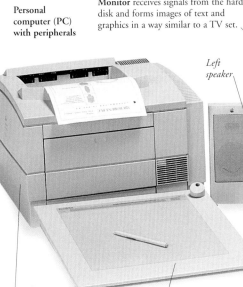

**Personal computer (PC) with peripherals**

**Monitor** receives signals from the hard disk and forms images of text and graphics in a way similar to a TV set.

*Left speaker*

*Right speaker with controls*

*Mouse mat*

**Keyboard** consists of numbers, letters, and special function keys that allow data to be typed directly into the computer.

**Mouse** controls pointer on screen; inside the mouse is a ball that rotates as the mouse moves, and the ball's movement sends signals to the computer.

**Scanner** copies an image and translates it into on-off pulses of electricity that are fed into the computer so that the image can be displayed on the monitor screen.

**Printer** receives data from hard disk and produces printout of documents and graphics.

**Graphics tablet** enables images to be "drawn" on the monitor screen as a stylus moves over its surface.

## Motherboard

A motherboard is a large circuit board in the hard disk to which the computer's key electronic components are attached. These components are linked together by strips of metal called "buses" on the underside of the motherboard. Also attached to the motherboard are the interfaces that link the hard disk to the peripherals, as well as expansion slots, to which other circuit boards can be added to improve the computer's performance or capabilities.

### Memory

A computer's electronic memory allows it to "remember" how to function. There are two parts to the memory: the random access memory (RAM) and the read-only memory (ROM). Both consist of circuits called microprocessors, or silicon chips.

**PC motherboard**

*Video card controls operation of monitor screen.*

*Expansion slots for extra circuit boards*

*Sockets called ports allow peripherals such as a modem or printer to connect to the hard disk.*

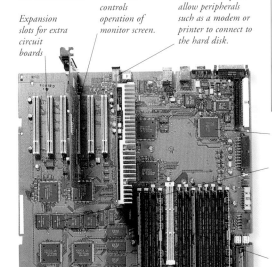

*Buses carry signals around the computer.*

*Battery controls computer's internal clock.*

*Central processing unit (CPU)*

**ROM (read-only memory)** chips store important programs, such as the disk-operating system, with content that cannot be changed.

**RAM (random-access memory)** chips store data fed into the computer on disks or via the keyboard, which can then be retrieved and changed as desired.

## Charles Babbage

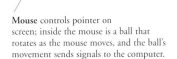

English mathematician Charles Babbage (1791–1871) built a mechanical computer called the Difference Engine that consisted of hundreds of gear wheels. It could do complicated sums more quickly than doing the same calculations by hand.

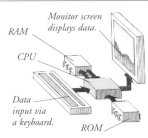

*Monitor screen displays data.*

*RAM*

*CPU*

*Data input via a keyboard.*

*ROM*

### Central processing unit (CPU)

The CPU is a single microprocessor that holds a large number of circuits. The CPU receives data from the ROM, RAM, and keyboard. It sends data to the RAM for storage, and to output devices, such as the monitor.

# Computer disks

Programs and data can be stored on computer disks. Magnetic disks record data as magnetic patterns in tiny iron particles that coat the disks' surfaces. A hard disk is a stack of magnetic disks inside a computer. Other types of disk include compact discs (CDs) and magneto-optical disks. A device called a disk drive is used to store data on disks and retrieve it.

*Sector boundary*
*Concentric tracks*
*Sector*

**Floppy disk**
*Recording surface*

### How a disk drive works

Disks arrange data into divisions called tracks and sectors. A disk drive has a magnetic read-write head that "reads" data from, or "writes" data to, a specific sector and track on the disk. In CD and optical disk drives, the read-write head is a laser beam.

**Types of computer disk**

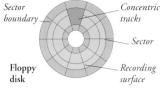

**SyQuest disks** are large magnetic disks able to store more data than floppies.

**Magneto-optical disks** store data magnetically, but are read by a laser beam.

**Compact discs (CDs)** store data as tiny pits in the surface of the disk.

**Floppy disks** are small magnetic disks.

**Optical mini-disks** are small magneto-optical disks.

*Operating system allows this girl to use a program for learning Spanish.*

## Operating system

Every computer has a program called an operating system (OS) that controls its basic functions. The OS is always at work "behind the scenes" when other applications are running. A graphical user interface (GUI) often forms part of a computer's OS. The GUI allows the computer operator to use a mouse to move information or to run programs.

## Steve Jobs and Steve Wozniak

The Apple Computer company – one of the world's largest – was founded in 1976 by Steve Jobs (b. 1955) and Steve Wozniak (b. 1950), who wanted to make computers affordable to ordinary people. Their 1977 Apple II computer was the first PC made for the mass market. It was hugely successful, because users of the Apple II needed no prior knowledge of electronics or computing.

# Types of computer

Most schools and many homes have personal computers, but there are many other types of computer, both larger and smaller than a PC. Some computers enable people to work while they are travelling; others are designed purely for entertainment. Large, powerful, high-speed computers are often used to process information for many people at once, or perform many tasks simultaneously.

**Dedicated computer**
While some computers can carry out many different tasks, others are "dedicated", meaning that they are designed for one specific purpose. A familiar example of a dedicated computer system is a games computer.

**Laptop**
Many business people take small, portable PCs called laptops with them when they travel. A laptop contains rechargeable batteries that allow it to function on trains, buses, outdoors – in fact, almost anywhere.

**Mainframe**
Most large organizations have a mainframe computer that can be used by many people at once, each working at a separate monitor, or terminal. A mainframe must be kept in a cold, dry environment.

**Supercomputer**
The most powerful computers are supercomputers. They are used to perform very complex tasks, such as forecasting future weather systems or analysing gravity and black holes in space. The first supercomputer was launched in 1976 by Cray.

## Timeline

**1642** Blaise Pascal invents the first mechanical adding machine.

**1834** Charles Babbage designs a mechanical computer, which he calls the Difference Engine.

**1939** John Atanasoff, an American, completes the first electronic computer.

**Commodore personal computer, 1970**

**1945** ENIAC, the world's first automatic computer, is built in the US.

**1967** Keyboards are used for data entry.

**1970** Floppy disks appear.

**Late 1970s** Mass-produced PCs are introduced.

**1975** The first portable computer is introduced.

**Late 1970s** The Xerox Corporation invents the graphical user interface.

**1983** The mouse is first used on an Apple computer.

**1985** Computer CDs appear.

**Assorted software programs**

**1980s** Sales of PCs soar.

**1990** IBM Pentium PC performs 112 million instructions per second.

**2000** Mobile phones and other handheld devices are designed to include computing facilities, software, and Internet.

**FIND OUT MORE**    ATOMS AND MOLECULES    ELECTRONICS    INFORMATION TECHNOLOGY    LASERS AND HOLOGRAMS    MATHEMATICS    NUMBERS    SOUND RECORDING    WEATHER FORECASTING

# CONFUCIUS

TWO THOUSAND YEARS AGO, China was in a state of turmoil and warfare. Strong imperial government had collapsed and civil order had broken down. One man learned the lessons of this disorder. Confucius devised a moral code based on respect, kindness, and the strength of the family. He believed people could be taught to behave themselves as members of a well-ordered community. This vision, although based on a traditional view of Chinese society, is still influential in China today.

## Early life

Confucius was born in Lu province in northeast China in about 551 BC. His name was Kong Qiu. His father died when he was three and he was raised by his mother. He became known as K'ung Fu-tse, or "great master kong." In the West he was called Confucius, the Latin form of this title.

## Confucius' teaching

Confucius learned to develop his new moral outlook from his experience in government. He taught that a good ruler should set an example by dealing fairly with his subjects, using force only as a last resort. In return, subjects had a duty to respect and obey their ruler.

### Zhou dynasty

Between 1027–256 BC, most of northern China was ruled by the Zhou dynasty. The early Zhou emperors ruled well, but later, as a result of pressure from powerful local lords, China split into a number of warring states. Confucius looked on the early years of the Zhou as a golden age of social harmony.

### Political career

For some years, Confucius worked as an adviser to the Duke of Lu and other local rulers. He attempted to promote good government by advising respect for the existing social order and fostering political stability. But his severe lifestyle and strict views were not popular, and Confucius eventually left Lu province.

*Handle in the form of mythical beast*

**Ritual vessel, Zhou period**

### Ancestor worship

In all his teachings, Confucius encouraged ancestor worship because it strengthened family ties. As a result, the Chinese people came to see themselves as part of a great national family that included not only living people but also the dead and those people who were still to be born. Many of the traditional Chinese gods and goddesses were believed to be ancestors who once lived as ordinary people in China and who, after their death, could influence everyday life.

**The traditional goddess Kuan Yin**

### Analects

Most of what we know about the teachings of Confucius can be found in a book of his sayings, the *Lun Yü*, or Analects. These sayings were collected by Confucius' followers after his death. Confucius is also said to have compiled or edited five classic books known as the *Wu Ching*. The most famous of these, the *I Ching*, or Book of Changes, provides a method of revealing the future through the use of 64 patterns of broken and unbroken lines.

### Chün-tzu

According to the writings of Confucius, the ideal gentleman, or Chün-tzu, was a person who was compassionate, self-controlled, respectful of superiors, and concerned for the welfare of others. As a result, he was against slavery and human or animal sacrifices. Under the influence of Confucius, it became common to bury pottery figures in tombs, rather than living animals or slaves.

**Chinese characters written by a later follower of Confucius**

**Bronze tomb model of a rhinoceros**

## Mencius

After Confucius' death, a number of his followers carried on his work. The most famous was Mencius (c.371–c.288). He believed that people are basically good, and that it is the duty of the ruler to insure the prosperity, education, and moral well-being of his subjects. His pupils wrote down his thoughts and sayings in *The Book of Mencius*.

## Impact

Although Confucius did not found a religion, his teachings are still influential throughout the world, especially in China, where the traditional values of the family are still based heavily on his views. The moral code taught by Confucius fits well with such established religions as Buddhism, Taoism, and Shinto, while his writings and classic texts are still widely studied in the West.

**Chinese family, 19th century**

## CONFUCIUS

1027 BC  Zhou dynasty takes control of northern China.

c.551 BC  Confucius born in Lu.

532 BC  Confucius marries.

531 BC  Confucius' son born.

517 BC  Confucius goes into exile for the first time.

501–496 BC  Holds important post in Lu province.

483 BC  Returns to Lu province after many years of wandering.

c.481–221 BC  China splits into seven warring states.

c.479 BC  Death of Confucius.

 FIND OUT MORE    BOOKS    CHINA, HISTORY OF    PHILOSOPHY    RELIGIONS    SOCIETIES, HUMAN    WRITING

# CONSERVATION

CONSERVATION ENSURES the survival of life in all its forms and variety. Conservationists do not want natural resources to be used beyond their capacity for renewal but to continue for the benefit of future generations. Conservation requires an understanding of ecology – the interrelationships of the different plants and animals (including our own species) with each other, and with their environment. Concern for the health of the environment is steadily increasing, as can be seen from the growth of conservation organizations on almost every continent.

## Why we need conservation

Ever increasing human populations lead to an increase in the demand for natural resources. This demand causes deforestation, habitat loss, pollution of air and water, and extermination of species. Poaching animals for meat, fur, and medicinal components reduces their numbers. Conservation is an means of slowing down or reversing these practices, in an attempt to safeguard the environment and all living things within it.

### Endangered species
As human numbers increase, more land is needed to grow food, so forests are cut down and habitats destroyed. Without its habitat, wildlife cannot survive. Human pressure and hunting are causing many species, such as the white rhino, to become rare or endangered, some to the point of extinction. It is too late for animals such as the Tasmanian wolf, but others, such as the gray whale, have been saved from extinction.

*Rhinos are hunted for their horns.*
White rhino

*Grizzly bears stand 10 ft (3 m) high.*

**Grizzly bears** are the largest and most powerful of the animals living in Yellowstone National Park.

*When displaying, male lifts tail into a fan.*

**Sage grouse** are the most spectacular of the North American grouse. When displaying, the male struts around vibrating his wings and emits a booming sound.

*Wingspan may reach 3.5 in (9cm).*

**Phoebus butterflies** appear in the Rockies in midsummer.

*Males use antlers to fight.*

**Wapitis** live in the forests of Yellowstone. They are larger than the red deer of Eurasia, but behave in similar ways.

## Conservation
Conservation means wise use of resources recognizing that they are there to be used, as long as they are not exploited beyond their capacity for renewal. Conservation is concerned with the survival of life in all its forms, and with maintaining organic life at the optimum rate of productivity.

*Forests are home to wapitis.*
**Yellowstone National Park**

### Preservation
Preservation differs from conservation in that preservation means strict protection of resources, without regard for the consequences. The first area of land that was preserved was Yellowstone National Park, where animals such as grizzly bears and wapitis thrive in this undisturbed environment. Over-protection can lead to an increase in the animal numbers, causing habitat destruction and the starvation and decline of the animals. This can be avoided by good management and controlling animal numbers.

## Environmental organizations
Hundreds of organizations are concerned with safeguarding the Earth's resources. The International Union for Conservation of Nature and Natural Resources (IUCN), and the Worldwide Fund for Nature (WWF), carry out conservation projects worldwide.

**Park rangers, WWF, Tsavo National Park**

## Methods of conservation
The establishment of national parks and wildlife sanctuaries is an effective method of conserving natural areas and their wildlife. Other methods include education, breeding programs, using renewable energy such as solar, wind, and wave power, and legislation. Some developing countries have agreed to safeguard areas of natural habitat, in return for a reduction in their foreign debt.

### Legislation
The Convention on International Trade in Endangered Species (CITES), controls trade in rare species, such as tigers; other groups control fishing and pollution.

*Tiger bones are used to make oriental medicines.*
**Siberian tiger remains**

### Education
The importance of educating young people about conservation and the effect it has on their lives cannot be overstated. The need for education is as vital in the west as in the developing world. For conservation to be effective, it must have the support of the local people.

**Game ranger teaching children**

### Breeding programs
The best chance of survival for some animals close to extinction lies in breeding them in captivity for eventual return to their natural habitat. In one of the earliest breeding programs, the few remaining Arabian oryx were captured, bred in the US, and later successfully reintroduced to Oman.

*Pale fur helps conceal oryx in the desert.*
**Arabian oryx**

**FIND OUT MORE** BEARS · DEER AND ANTELOPE · ECOLOGY AND ECOSYSTEMS · ENERGY · LIONS AND OTHER WILDCATS · POLLUTION · RHINOCEROSES AND TAPIRS · ZOOS

# Endangered animals

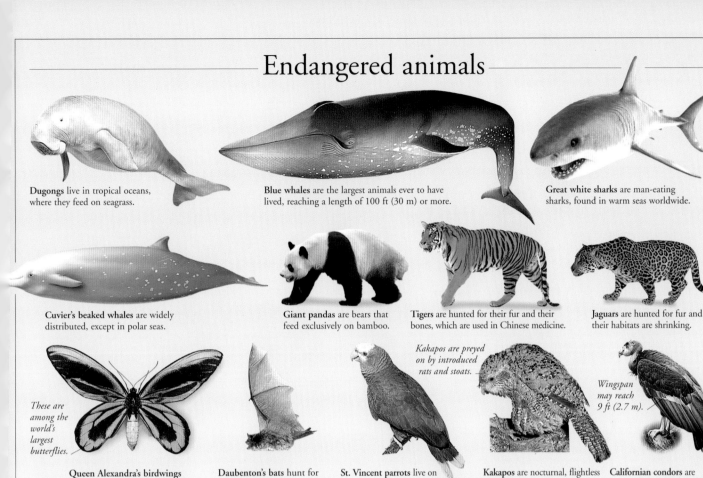

Dugongs live in tropical oceans, where they feed on seagrass.

Blue whales are the largest animals ever to have lived, reaching a length of 100 ft (30 m) or more.

Great white sharks are man-eating sharks, found in warm seas worldwide.

Cuvier's beaked whales are widely distributed, except in polar seas.

Giant pandas are bears that feed exclusively on bamboo.

Tigers are hunted for their fur and their bones, which are used in Chinese medicine.

Jaguars are hunted for fur and their habitats are shrinking.

*These are among the world's largest butterflies.*

Queen Alexandra's birdwings live only in Papua New Guinea.

Daubenton's bats hunt for insects over ponds and rivers.

St. Vincent parrots live on the island of St. Vincent.

*Kakapos are preyed on by introduced rats and stoats.*

Kakapos are nocturnal, flightless birds from New Zealand.

*Wingspan may reach 9 ft (2.7 m).*

Californian condors are among the largest living birds.

Great crested newts are the largest of the European newts, at up to 6 in (15 cm) long.

*This weta is among the largest insects in the world.*

Golden mantellas from Madagascar are threatened by habitat destruction.

Stephen's Island weta is confined to a small island off the coast of New Zealand.

Przewalski's horses are extinct in the wild, but have been bred in captivity.

Gorillas are endangered; their rain forest habitat is being destroyed.

Père David's deer, extinct in its native China, has been bred in captivity.

White rhinos are scarce in Zaïre, but more abundant in South Africa.

# Endangered plants

*Insects are trapped when the two lobes of the leaf snap shut.*

*This plant is threatened by the arrival of goats.*

*Cactus shrinks back into the ground for part of the year.*

Dawn redwoods were rediscovered in China.

Venus's flytraps feed on insects.

Silverswords live on the volcanic islands of Hawaii.

Knowlton cacti are among the world's rarest cacti.

New Zealand brush lilies are eaten by introduced possums.

Japanese sago palms are slow-growing evergreens.

# CONTINENTS

THE WORLD'S SEVEN great land masses are known as continents. The seven continents are North America, South America, Africa, Europe, Asia, Antarctica, and Australia. Although you may not realize it, the continents are crunching together and drifting apart even as you read this page. This is because the Earth's outer shell, or crust, is made up of a number of vast, ever-moving slabs of rock called tectonic plates. The continents are embedded in these plates, which move very slowly – Europe and North America, for example, are drifting apart by just 1.5 in (4 cm) each year. Over millions of years, however, the continents have shifted this way and that across the globe, dramatically changing the face of the planet time and time again.

## Tectonic plates

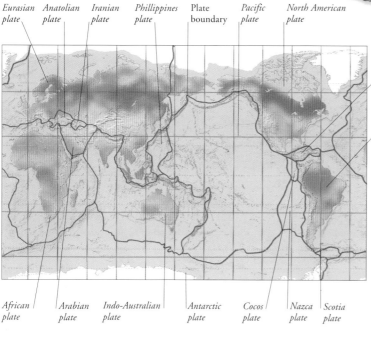

There are nine major tectonic plates and a number of smaller ones. They fit together like the pieces of a jigsaw, covering the whole of the Earth's surface. The continents are carried by continental plates, such as the Eurasian plate. Oceanic plates, such as the Pacific plate, form most of the seafloor; the rest is made up of the fringes of the continental plates, which lie underwater.

Eurasian plate · Anatolian plate · Iranian plate · Phillippines plate · Plate boundary · Pacific plate · North American plate · Caribbean plate · South American plate · African plate · Arabian plate · Indo-Australian plate · Antarctic plate · Cocos plate · Nazca plate · Scotia plate

The major plates of the Earth's crust

## Continental drift

If you study a world map, you will notice that the east coast of South America looks as if it would fit neatly into Africa's west coast. This is because 220 million years ago Africa, South America, and all the other continents formed a single giant "supercontinent", now called Pangaea. Eventually, Pangaea split up into smaller land masses that drifted over the Earth's surface, giving the arrangement of continents that appears on your map today. Earth scientists call this theory continental drift.

**200 million years ago:** Pangaea, the single land mass, begins to break up.

**135 million years ago:** the South Atlantic opens up, pulling Africa and South America apart; India moves towards Asia.

Asia · Africa · South America · India · Europe · Australia · South Atlantic · North Atlantic · North America · Antarctica

**10 million years ago:** Antarctica and Australia drift apart; the North Atlantic opens up, moving North America away from Europe.

### Evidence for continental drift

*Glossopteris* fossil · Fossilized *Lystrosaurus* skull

Identical fossils of land-based plants and animals, such as the fern *Glossopteris* and the mammal *Lystrosaurus*, have been found in continents now widely separated by the sea. The only plausible explanation is that the continents were once linked together.

### Alfred Wegener

German meteorologist and geophysicist Alfred Wegener (1880–1930) devised the theory of continental drift. As evidence, he cited the continents' matching coastlines, similar rock strata in continents separated by huge oceans, and fossil discoveries. Although widely accepted now, his ideas were ridiculed at the time.

### Triple junctions

At places called triple junctions, a column of magma – hot, molten rock from the Earth's interior – burns its way through a continental plate. This splits the plate three ways, producing huge rift valleys between the fragments of the plate. The Great Rift Valley in East Africa was formed in this way. The fragments of the plate are forced further apart over millions of years, creating new continental land masses. As the rift valleys widen, new oceans form between the pieces of the fragmented plate.

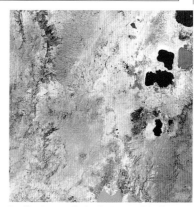

Satellite image of Africa's Great Rift Valley

# Diverging plates

At some places beneath the world's great oceans, the tectonic plates that make up the Earth's surface are slowly diverging. These places are called constructive margins. As the plates pull apart, molten rock called magma wells up through the crack between the plates and emerges as lava. When the lava cools, it adds new material to the seafloor. This process is known as seafloor spreading.

## Mid-ocean ridge

As two plates pull apart, the lava emerging from the Earth's interior solidifies and builds a line of undersea mountains along the crack. This is called a mid-ocean ridge. There is such a ridge beneath each of the world's great oceans. In Iceland, the North Atlantic Ridge rises above sea level and can be seen as a long gash in the landscape.

**North Atlantic Ridge, Thingvellir, Iceland**

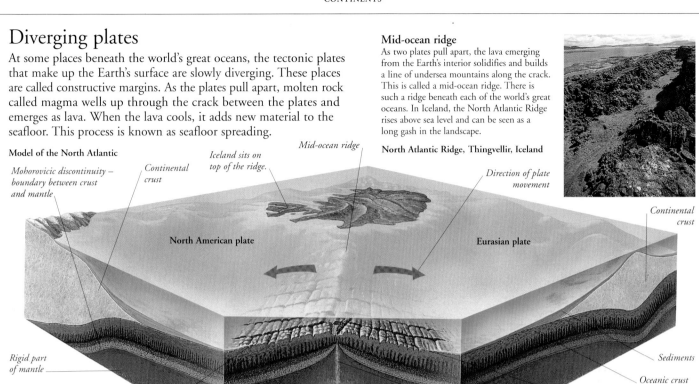

**Model of the North Atlantic**

*Mohorovicic discontinuity – boundary between crust and mantle*

*Continental crust*

*Iceland sits on top of the ridge.*

*Mid-ocean ridge*

*Direction of plate movement*

**North American plate**

**Eurasian plate**

*Continental crust*

*Rigid part of mantle*

**Transform faults** are sideways tears along a mid-ocean ridge caused by the curve in the Earth's surface.

*Sediments*

*Oceanic crust*

*Rising magma*

**Median valley** is a long trough, or rift, which runs along the ridge.

# Converging plates

In many places the tectonic plates are converging, or moving against one another. In places known as destructive margins, oceanic plates are drawn underneath the continental plates. The oceanic plate is pulled down into the layer of the Earth's interior called the mantle, where it is destroyed by intense heat. This process is called subduction. In other places called collision zones, the edges of two continental plates may crumple as they collide. This process creates great mountain ranges such as the Alps and the Himalayas.

## Transform

In some places where tectonic plates meet, the plates neither collide nor pull apart, but simply slide past each other in opposite directions. These places are called transforms, or conservative margins. Perhaps the most famous transform is the San Andreas Fault in California, where the Pacific and North American plates grind slowly past one another. As the plates move, they often snag and shudder, setting off violent earthquakes.

**San Andreas Fault, California**

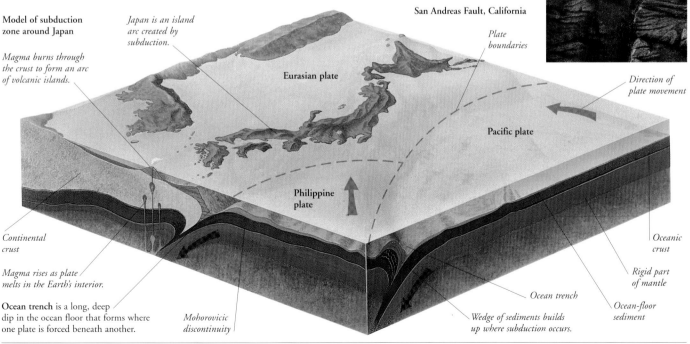

**Model of subduction zone around Japan**

*Magma burns through the crust to form an arc of volcanic islands.*

*Japan is an island arc created by subduction.*

*Plate boundaries*

**Eurasian plate**

*Direction of plate movement*

**Pacific plate**

**Philippine plate**

*Continental crust*

*Magma rises as plate melts in the Earth's interior.*

**Ocean trench** is a long, deep dip in the ocean floor that forms where one plate is forced beneath another.

*Mohorovicic discontinuity*

*Wedge of sediments builds up where subduction occurs.*

*Ocean trench*

*Oceanic crust*

*Rigid part of mantle*

*Ocean-floor sediment*

| FIND OUT MORE | EARTH | EARTHQUAKES | FOSSILS | GEOLOGY | MAGNETISM | MOUNTAINS AND VALLEYS | OCEAN FLOOR | OCEANS AND SEAS | VOLCANOES |

# COOK, JAMES

UNTIL THE MID-18TH CENTURY, European explorers were motivated by trade or plunder. James Cook, a British naval captain, began a new form of exploration – he was more interested in scientific research. From 1768 to 1779, he made three voyages to the South Pacific, applying scientific methods to navigation for the first time, and making astronomical observations that would help future sailors. He also carefully recorded everything he saw, bringing back many specimens and drawings of previously unknown flora and fauna.

**Early life**
James Cook was born in the town of Marton-in-Cleveland, near Whitby, England, in 1728. He went to sea as a boy, sailing in the Baltic before joining the British Royal Navy in 1755. Cook rose quickly through the ranks and was given command of his first ship in 1759, during the Seven Years' War with France.

*The port of Whitby, England*

## The Endeavour

During the 1760s, Cook mastered the skills of navigation. These were put to good use when he was asked, in 1768, to sail to Tahiti in the South Seas to observe the transit of the planet Venus across the sky. His choice of ship was unusual: a converted Whitby collier familiar to Cook and known for its toughness and ability to carry a heavy cargo.

*The Endeavour*

*Mainmast*

*Mizzenmast*

*Foremast*

*Cook's explorations*

*Red ensign (British naval flag)*

**Cook's sextant**

**Navigation**
Navigation during Cook's time was primitive but effective. Cook used a chronometer to determine longitude (position east-west) and a quadrant or sextant to determine latitude (position north-south).

**Lemons and limes**

**Diet**
Cook was the first sea captain to take measures against scurvy – a disease caused by lack of vitamins – and supplied his crew with fresh fruit, meat, and vegetables wherever possible.

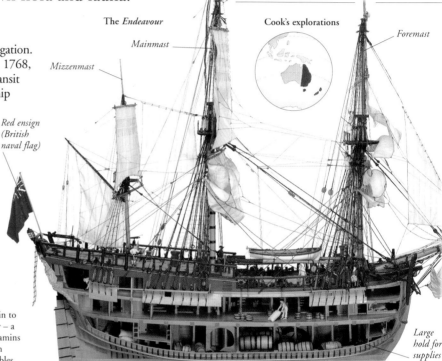

*Large hold for supplies*

## Mapping the Pacific

Cook made three voyages around the Pacific, circumnavigating New Zealand, mapping the east coast of Australia, and exploring many islands. He guessed correctly that there was an area of frozen land around the South Pole, and confirmed that Australia was a large island and not part of any southern continent.

**Joseph Banks**
Cook took with him botanist Joseph Banks, artist Sydney Parkinson, and a team of scientists. They discovered many species, such as the breadfruit and the kangaroo, previously unknown to Europeans. One area yielded so many new species that they called it Botany Bay. It is now a suburb of Sydney, Australia.

**Joseph Banks**

*Some of Parkinson's illustrations*

**Death of Cook**
On his third voyage, begun in 1776, Cook came across the Hawaiian Islands, which he named the Sandwich Islands. He spent the winter of 1778–79 in Hawaii, learning much about the inhabitants, and he returned in the spring of 1779, after exploring the west coast of America. This time, however, the local people were less friendly, and after a quarrel broke out, Cook was stabbed to death.

**Cook is killed fighting the Hawaiian islanders.**

*Hawaiian clubs, used against Cook*

### JAMES COOK

**1728** Born in Marton-in-Cleveland, Yorkshire, England.

**1755** Joins Royal Navy.

**1759** Takes command of his first ship.

**1768–71** Sails to the Pacific Ocean to observe the transit of Venus: explores Tahiti, New Zealand, and Australia.

**1772–75** Second voyage; maps many of the Pacific islands and sails south toward Antarctica.

**1776–79** Third voyage: sails into North Pacific; looks for inlet into Arctic Ocean.

**1779** Stabbed to death in Hawaii.

FIND OUT **MORE**    AUSTRALIA    AUSTRALIA, HISTORY OF    EXPLORATION    NAVIGATION    SHIPS AND BOATS

# CORAL REEFS

TEEMING WITH WILDLIFE from shrimps to sharks, coral reefs are some of the most beautiful underwater structures. A coral reef takes thousands of years to form; it is composed of the living and dead skeletons of colonies of tiny animals called corals. Corals have flourished and built reefs in shallow, tropical seas for more than 440 million years. Corals are related to sea anemones and jellyfish, and belong to the group of animals called coelenterates. Australia's Great Barrier Reef is 1,240 miles (2,000 km) in length but is under threat from increased pollution.

*Corals compete for light and food-bearing water currents.*

## Coral reefs

Coral reefs cover 239,015 sq miles (619,000 sq km) of the Earth's surface. Fringing reefs grow along coastlines; atolls are reefs that grow around extinct volcanoes; and cays are complete islands made of coral. Coral comes in all colors from red and yellow to blue and green, and grows in a variety of shapes and sizes, including delicate fan corals, upright staghorn corals, and dome-shaped brain corals. Many animals hide in the holes and crevices within the reef.

Staghorn coral releasing eggs

### Reproduction
Corals reproduce asexually to form colonies of genetically identical polyps. They also reproduce sexually, releasing eggs and sperm into the water. The fertilized eggs turn into larvae that join the plankton, which is carried on the currents, ensuring wide distribution.

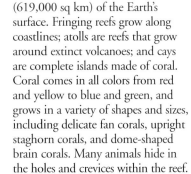

*Symbiotic algae* live in corals and give them their bright colors.

Coral polyps open at night

Coral polyps close in the day

### Coral polyp
Coral reefs are made up of many individual animals called coral polyps. They normally live in large colonies, but a few species are solitary. Soft corals have a rigid inner layer for support; hard corals secrete a cup-shaped chalky skeleton from their jellylike bodies. A circle of tentacles, armed with stinging cells, immobilizes prey and pushes it through the mouth into the stomach. Coral polyps close up during the day, but at night the reef comes to life when the corals extend their tentacles into the water currents to trap prey.

## Fish

Coral reefs are home to fish of all shapes and sizes. Solitary giant groupers and wrasse up to 6 ft (1.8 m) long lurk in reef caves and recesses. Shoals of tiny damselfish graze the fronds of seaweed on the top of the reef. Some, such as the moray eel, are vicious predators; others, such as parrot fish, feed on coral.

*Tubular mouth*

*Sea horses often hide within seaweed.*

*Prehensile tail grasps seaweed.*

### Sea horse
Sea horses are pipefish with upright S-shaped bodies and prehensile tails. They eat small crustaceans, such as shrimps, and suck them into their tubular mouths. Females lay eggs in the males' brood pouches; the young develop and later emerge.

*Spine can be raised.*

### Mandarin fish
The most poisonous fish of the reef are the various scorpion fish, such as the mandarin. Their bodies are protected by bony plates and poison-tipped spines. Mandarin fish swim slowly. They live near the ocean floor, waiting for prey to pounce on.

### Black tip reefshark
The largest inhabitants of the reef are the black tip reefshark and its distant relative the giant manta ray. They patrol the seaward side of reefs, looking for potential fish prey that stray too far from the protection of the reef. By contrast, mantas are filter feeders attracted to the reef by the growth of plankton.

*Eyes close when eating.*

*Black tip of fin*

*Jaws contain sharp teeth.*

*Gills*

*Streamlined body for speed*

*Powerful tail*

*Flippers*

*Wide feet to help it paddle in water.*
**Green turtle**

### Reptiles
Sea turtles and sea snakes are reptilian inhabitants of reefs. Both need to surface to breathe air, but while turtles have to move to land, such as oceanic island reefs, to breed, sea snakes can give birth to live young at sea. Some turtles prey on other animals, while others feed on grass. Sea snakes are good swimmers and are the most venomous snakes in the world. They prey on the abundant reef fish.

## Invertebrates

Reefs provide a variety of habitats for invertebrates such as sea slugs, sea cucumbers, and sea urchins. The reef protects delicate filter feeders, such as sponges, from the impact of the waves. Some bivalve mollusks nestle in crevices; others such as mussels, anchor themselves to the coral with rootlike hairs. Many crustaceans, such as shrimps, scavenge among the corals.

*Strong suckers help octopus grip rocks.*

### Common octopus
The reef is an ideal environment for the octopus to hide in – its soft body slips easily into crevices. A stealthy hunter, it grabs prey with sucker-covered tentacles. When in the open, its ability to change its skin's texture and tone provides excellent camouflage.

### Giant clam
This biggest living shellfish grows 3 ft (1 m) long and, like corals, is inhabited by symbiotic algae. A clam opens its shell to feed on plankton and closes it if danger threatens. Giant clams stay in one place once they are adults.

*Shell is made of two halves.*
*Siphon for waste*

*Algae*

**FIND OUT MORE** • AUSTRALIA • FISH • OCEAN WILDLIFE • OCTOPUSES AND SQUIDS • SHARKS AND RAYS • TURTLES AND TORTOISES

# CRABS AND OTHER CRUSTACEANS

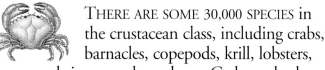

THERE ARE SOME 30,000 SPECIES in the crustacean class, including crabs, barnacles, copepods, krill, lobsters, prawns, shrimps, and sow bugs. Crabs and other crustaceans share characteristics, including two pairs of antennae, mandibles, and a shell. In size they can range from microscopic freshwater fleas to giant Japanese spider crabs, which have a claw-to-claw span of 11 ft (3.6 m). Most crustaceans live in the sea, others prefer freshwater, and a few, such as the sow bug, live on land. Some are parasitic – they live on or in other animals.

*Pincers*
*Smooth legs*
*Bumps on front legs*
*Carapace, or hard shell*
*Spikes protecting carapace*
*Mouth and eyes under edge of carapace*
*Jointed legs*
*Walking legs*
**Spiny spider crab**

*Teeth*

## Defense
Although they get protection from their shells, crabs can also defend themselves using their enlarged claws, or pincers, which often have a sharp, serrated (toothed) edge. Some crabs, such as decorator crabs, camouflage themselves by fixing seaweed to their shells and blending into their surroundings. Even with these methods of defense, crabs are still eaten by octopuses, fish such as bass, shorebirds, and mammals.

**Claw of Japanese spider crab**

## Features of a crab
Crabs belong to the Decopoda (10-legged) order. They have four pairs of jointed walking or swimming legs, plus an extra modified pair called pincers. They have two pairs of antennae, gills, and a segmented, calcareous shell, or carapace. As they grow, crabs shed the carapace and grow a new one.

*Seaweed and shells attached to crab*
**Decorator crab**

## Feeding
Crabs, such as the hermit crab, are generally omnivorous and can be either predators or scavengers. Hermit crabs catch their prey in their pincers. The crab then uses the pincers like a fork to pass the food to its mandibles (specialized jaws). The crab chews its food, then uses two pairs of adapted limbs to push the food farther into the mouth.

*Fish*
**Hermit crab**

## Breeding
After the male has fertilzed the female's eggs, she may carry them in a brood pouch until ready to hatch, or release them into the sea. Some crustaceans hatch as tiny adults, but crabs go through a larval stage and spend their early life as plankton.

*Eyes on stalks*
*A colorfully enlarged pincer attracts females.*
**Fiddler crab**

## How a crab moves
Crabs walk slowly forward or backward on their jointed legs when exploring their surroundings underwater, but scuttle sideways across the ground when threatened. Some crabs, such as velvet crabs, are able to swim because their hind legs have been adapted into flattened paddles, also known as swimmerets.

*Pincers* *Crab crouching in defense.* *Crab starts to turn to its left.*
**Shore crab turning.** *Missing limb* *Small, flaplike abdomen* *Fully turned crab can scuttle away.*

## Barnacles
Young barnacles float in the sea until they find any stable surface, such as a rocky shore. They then attach themselves to the surface, and secrete a calcium-based substance that forms protective plates around them. They leave an opening for feeding that closes when the animal is exposed to the air at low tide. Barnacles are hermaphrodites – that is, both sexes exist in one individual.

*Goose barnacles attach themselves to driftwood with long stalks.*
**Goose barnacles**

## Feeding
Most barnacles feed themselves using their feet. When covered with water, these fine, feathery, curly limbs protrude from the barnacle's opening. The feet trap food as it floats past, filter it from the seawater, and transfer it into the barnacle's mouth. Goose barnacles do this while floating in the ocean.

## Sow bugs
Sow bugs are the only true land-living crustaceans. A sow bug's "shell" consists of flat, waterproof plates that protect its back. Sow bugs can dry out, so some species, such as the pill bug, have developed the ability to roll up and reduce water loss.

*Waterproof plates*

# Lobsters

Lobsters, crabs, shrimps, prawns, and crayfish are all known as crawlers because of the way they move. They live on the seashore, seabeds, and in streams. Lobsters have large pincers for defense and feeding. The male's pincers are usually larger than the female's. The biggest species is the blue lobster, which weighs up to 55 lb (25 kg). Crayfish, close relatives of the lobster, live in freshwater and tend to be smaller.

### Environments
Lobsters prefer an environment featuring many nooks and crannies. Their ideal hiding place is a sandy burrow under a rock.

*Lobster backs into its burrow.*

*Large antennae sense food and danger.*

*Second pair of legs has claws.*

*When threatened, the lobster's large pincers open.*

C

### Defense
Lobsters can escape capture by discarding a limb. There is a special "breaking plane" near the base of the leg that, when twisted, causes the leg to snap off. The wound soon heals and a new limb starts growing immediately.

*Small antennae* *Eyes*

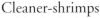

**Common lobster adopting a defensive pose**

### Lobster march
In an extraordinary event known as the lobster march, hundreds of lobsters gather and walk one after the other for more than 60 miles (100 km) across the ocean floor. It is possible that they are looking for a suitable area to settle, with an adequate supply of food. The lobsters make sounds during their migration and it is thought that these are noises of communication that help coordinate the journey. This event has not been seen in any of the other larger crustacean groups.

**Spiny lobsters**

### Water fleas
Water fleas, a group that includes brine and fairy shrimp, all breathe through leaf-shaped gills on their feet. Brine shrimp live in saline pools; water fleas inhabit freshwater. Fairy shrimp live in temporary puddles. When these dry up, their eggs become airborne and then fall into another pool.

**Daphnia water flea**

## Cleaner-shrimps
Brightly colored and easy to see, cleaner-shrimps remove external scale and gill parasites from passing fish, such as the goby – and even remove unswallowed food particles within the fish's mouth. Both animals benefit from this association, known as "cleaner symbiosis." Other symbiotic relationships exist between shrimps and sponges, sea anemones, and corals.

**Cleaner-shrimp**

# Shrimps

The world's oceans are full of scavenging shrimps and prawns. They look similar, but prawns have a pointed rostrum (a sawlike structure at the front of the body) and two pairs of pincers, while shrimps have only one pair. Krill, small shrimplike animals that live in the Antarctic oceans, form the main food of whales.

### Growth of shrimps
Most crustaceans, including shrimps, are unable to grow because their exoskeleton (shell) is inflexible, so they molt their shell at regular intervals. The new, soft, exposed skin underneath hardens quickly to form another, larger hard shell.

*Shrimps have flatter bodies than prawns.*

**Strawberry shrimp**

### Mussel shrimp
The tiny mussel or seed shrimp (so-called because its carapace is made up of two shells, like that of a mussel) produces the largest sperms in the animal kingdom. The 0.01-in (0.3-mm) long male of one species produces sperm 20 times its own length.

# Copepods

These tiny creatures are an important part of plankton, which provides most of the world's fish with food. One species, *Calanus finmarchicus,* forms the staple diet of open-sea fishes, such as herring, sprat, and mackerel. Others, however, are parasitic and live in or on worms, mollusks, other crustaceans, fish, and whales.

*Long, fringed tentacles*

*Legs are extended for food gathering.*

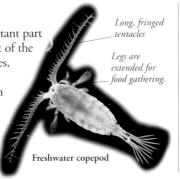

**Freshwater copepod**

### Gribble
Able to digest wood, the gribble bores into the submerged wooden supports of jetties, wharfs, bridges, and pilings. It can turn these structures into a pulpy mass, causing them to collapse.

*Segmented shell*

### SPINY SPIDER CRAB

SCIENTIFIC NAME *Machrocheira kaempferi*

SUBCLASS Malacostraca

ORDER Decapoda

DISTRIBUTION Oceans around Japan

HABITAT On the ocean floor

DIET Scavenges anything edible from the ocean floor – an omnivore, it eats meat and plant matter

SIZE Span, claw-to-claw, 11 ft (3.6 m)

LIFESPAN Unknown, but lobsters, a relative, have lived up to 70 years in captivity

**FIND OUT MORE**

ARTHROPODS    CAVE WILDLIFE    CORAL REEFS    OCEANS AND SEAS    OCEAN WILDLIFE    SEASHORE WILDLIFE

# CRAFTS

BASKET MAKERS, WOOD CARVERS, and stonemasons are craftspeople; they make objects by hand that are both useful and attractive. Unlike other art forms, crafts are concerned with function as well as beauty: they are made to be used. Before the Industrial Revolution, craftspeople made furniture for the home and tools for the workplace. Today, these items are mass-produced in factories, so hand-crafted objects are valued for their individuality and because they often come from a tradition that is centuries old.

*Goggles for protection*

**Stonecutter at work**

*Taps chisel gently to cut stone to pattern*

*Carpet to protect edges of stone*

*Plaster-of-Paris holds stonework steady.*

*Banker, or workbench*

## Early craftspeople

Medieval craftspeople made their living from being skilled in one particular craft, such as coopering (barrel making), dyeing cloth, leather work, or goldsmithing. Each craft had its own guild, which was an association of the workers. The guilds fixed prices and standards of work, and supported members who fell on hard times.

**Dyers**

**Judging a masterpiece**

### Apprentices
Boys between the ages of 10 and 15 who wanted to learn a trade, would pay to start work as an apprentice to a craftsworker. They spent between four and seven years learning every aspect of their craft from a master.

### Masterpieces
At the end of his term as apprentice, each boy was required to produce an object that showed he had learned his craft. It was called a masterpiece, because it was judged by a master craftsman.

**Mallet**

**Hammer-head chisel**

**Mallet-head chisels**

## The craft workshop

Many craftspeople have a workshop where they keep tools and materials. People who produce crafts objects for a living often sell goods from their workshop so they can work when they are not helping customers.

### Stonework
The craft of cutting and shaping stone for building is centuries old. Medieval masons prepared the stone to build churches, dams, and bridges; stonecutters prepared ornamental finishes.

### Shaping the stone
The stonecutter begins by drawing a design onto a piece of acetate. The design is then transferred to a block of stone as a guideline for cutting or carving. The stonecutter uses a toothed tool (claw) to gouge out the basic design.

*Stone, trimmed (cut) into a small block*

*Marked out design*

### The finished article
A variety of chisels and carving gouges further defines the shape of the carving, removing the worst of the marks left by the claw in the process. Finally, a double-ended file, called a riffler, is used to smooth the marks left by the chisels. It takes years to master ornamental carving.

*This piece links the ribs that support stained glass in cathedral windows.*

*Cusp (from the Latin cuspis, or "spearhead")*

## Types of crafts

Almost any material can be used in crafts, from wood, stone, and metal, to beads, reeds, and shells. A craftsperson may sell work to earn a living, but crafting is also a popular leisure activity.

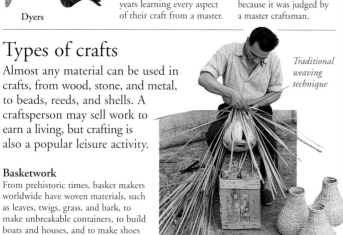
*Traditional weaving technique*

*Finished baskets*

**Basket maker, Spain**

### Basketwork
From prehistoric times, basket makers worldwide have woven materials, such as leaves, twigs, grass, and bark, to make unbreakable containers, to build boats and houses, and to make shoes and hats. Machines cannot yet match the fine technique displayed in a handwoven basket.

*Silk thread used for wings*

*Gold thread used for outline*

### Embroidery
Embroidery, where designs are stitched onto fabric, decorates everyday clothing and furnishings, as well as costumes for festive occasions. The embroiderer either draws the design onto the fabric before stitching into the cloth, or develops it while she or he is working on the embroidery.

**Butterfly detail, embroidered sleeve, China**

**African beadwork**

### Beadwork
Beads, made from materials such as wood, bone, shell, seeds, plastic, and glass, have been used to decorate material for centuries. The geometrical designs of Native American beadworkers are featured on leather clothing, bags, and shoes. African beadwork decorates festive costumes and jewelry.

*Papier-mâché items, such as this bowl, can be simple to make.*

### Papier-mâché
Some people take up a craft as a hobby. One popular example is papier-mâché. Named after the French word meaning "chewed paper," it involves building up layers of paper and paste over a mold. When the paste dries, the paper is firm and can be painted and varnished.

**FIND OUT MORE**

INDUSTRIAL REVOLUTION    MEDIEVAL EUROPE    POTTERY AND CERAMICS    UNIONS, TRADE    TEXTILES AND WEAVING

# Crafts
## Basketwork

**Shopping basket,** rope detail decoration, England

**Sewing basket,** bamboo handles, Canada

**Basket,** traditional design, Thailand

**Sisal basket,** Kenya

**Willow potato basket,** wire base, France

## Stone and woodcarving

*Mason's tools*

**Decorated vault,** Italy

**Roof decoration,** carved fruit and leaves, Britain

**Ballflowers decoration,** Britain

**Flowing tracery,** medieval Britain

**Wall ornament,** medieval Britain

**Carved panel,** 16th century, Britain

**Church roof detail,** medieval Britain

## Embroidery and beadwork

**Tobacco pouch,** North America

**Beaded gourd,** Africa

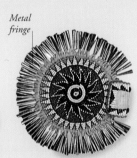

**Necklace,** South Africa

*Metal fringe*

**Tobacco pouch,** North America

**Zulu beadwork,** Africa

**Flask,** made from gourd fruit, Africa

*Charm to ward off evil*

**Amulet,** North America

**Cradleboard,** North America

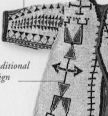

*Imported glass beads*

*Traditional design*

**Child's coat,** North America

*Colorful embroidery*

**Masquerade costume,** Africa

**Deerskin moccasin,** North America

*Colorful geometric pattern*

**Embroidered sandals,** North Africa

# CRIME AND PUNISHMENT

A CRIME IS A FORBIDDEN ACT, punished by law because it may harm a society or injure its members. The type of act that constitutes a crime varies from culture to culture, changing as societies and attitudes develop. For example, in some parts of the Middle East, it is a crime to drink alcohol, but a man may have more than one wife. In the United States, alcohol is not illegal, but having more than one wife is against the law.

*Bronze cat from ancient Egypt, dedicated to the cat goddess Bastet*

**Killing cats**
The ancient Egyptians honored cats as sacred animals, depicting them in paintings and sculptures. As a result, killing a cat was seen as a serious crime. The punishment was usually instant execution.

## Types of crimes

Some acts, such as murder and theft, have been crimes in all civilized societies for thousands of years and are known as *malum in se* (the Latin phrase for "bad in themselves"). Other crimes, such as driving a car without license plates, are *malum prohibitum* (bad because the law says they are).

Murder

**Crime against the person**
When one person intentionally kills another, that person has committed murder. It is a crime against the person, and does not respect the individual's right to live his or her life without fear of attack and violence. Assault, rape, and kidnapping are other such crimes. Killing someone in self-defense, or killing an enemy of your country in times of war, is not considered to be murder.

**Crime against property**
Laws exist to protect people's right to own property. It is a criminal act to take or damage the property of another against the owner's wishes. Examples of such crimes include theft, forgery, arson, and vandalism.

Silverware
Antiques

Jewelry

Stolen property

Electronic goods

## Organized crime

Organized crime consists of large-scale activities by groups of outlaws, sometimes known as gangsters. They make much of their money by providing illegal goods, including drugs, and services, such as gambling or prostitution.

**Crime syndicates**
Secret criminal organizations exist across the world, such as the Mafia, which originated centuries ago in Sicily. During the 1920s a powerful crime syndicate grew up in Chicago, run by brutal gangsters, such as the notorious Al Capone (1899–1947).

Al Capone

## Punishment

Theories about punishment have developed since the 18th century when even minor offenses were harshly punished to deter others from committing crime. Around the world, law-breakers are punished in various ways: in the UK, for instance, criminals are usually fined or sent to prison.

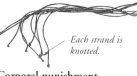
Cat-o'-nine tails whip

*Each strand is knotted.*

**Corporal punishment**
In some countries, people are whipped for certain minor crimes. This is corporal punishment. It was once common, and beatings took place in public as a warning to deter others from committing crimes.

## Prison

Someone who commits a crime may be sent to prison for a length of time reflecting the seriousness of their crime. Prison is mainly a punishment, but it also offers criminals a chance to reform. It acts to deter other people from crime and keeps dangerous criminals away from the public.

*High-security cell in a European prison*

*Barred window*

*Window for keeping a watch on prisoners*

*Prisoners can send only one letter a week.*

*Simply furnished*

*Very few personal belongings are allowed.*

**Men and women** go to separate prisons. As inmates, they may spend as much as 23 hours a day locked in their cell, which they usually share with one or two others. They must wear prison uniforms.

**Alcatraz**
A maximum-security prison was built on the island of Alcatraz in San Francisco Bay. It was in use from 1933 to 1963; in that time, not one prisoner escaped alive. Of the 23 that tried, five were shot dead, six drowned, and 12 were recaptured.

**High-security cell**
Criminals convicted of serious crimes are sent to high-security prisons. Inmates are allowed to leave their cells only to eat, work, or for study periods. People who commit lesser crimes may be sent to prisons where they have more freedom.

**Capital punishment**
The ultimate penalty for a crime is death, or capital punishment. Hanging, gassing, and the electric chair are some of the methods that have been used. Many people now argue that capital punishment is morally wrong. In the US, this issue is hotly debated; many Western nations have now abolished the death penalty.

Electric chair

FIND OUT MORE    EGYPT, ANCIENT    HUMAN RIGHTS    LAW    POLICE    SOCIETIES, HUMAN

# CROCODILES

SUBMERGED BELOW water, crocodiles lie in wait ready to attack almost any animal that strays too close. Crocodiles belong to the group of reptiles, called the crocodilians, which has remained largely unchanged for more than 140 million years. This group contains crocodiles, alligators, caimans, and gharials, which, apart from small differences, such as snout shape and tooth arrangement, are all very similar. All are effective freshwater predators and are well adapted to their semi-aquatic life.

## Eyes

A crocodile's eyes protrude above its snout, providing 25° overlapping vision to judge distance. A third eyelid slides from side to side for underwater vision. Special pupils allow more light to reach the retina in low light levels and protect the retina from bright light. The retina itself has a layer of night-seeing cells that glow red in bright light.

*Third eyelid moves from side to side.*

*Transparent eyelid converts eye for underwater vision.*

## Crocodiles

Crocodiles are tropical reptiles found in freshwater habitats around the world. There are 14 species ranging from the 7 ft (2 m) long dwarf crocodiles of western Africa to the huge man-eating 25 ft (7.5 m) long Indo-Pacific crocodiles. The American, Nile, and Indo-Pacific crocodiles can live in the ocean as well as in freshwater. The Cuban and Siamese crocodiles are endangered because of habitat destruction and hunting.

C

*Nostrils and eyes are high on head so crocodile can breathe and see when almost submerged in water.*

*Huge cone-shaped teeth line the long jaw.*

Nile crocodile

*"Tail walking" involves pushing the body up using the tail.*

## Snout shape

Alligators and caimans have broad, rounded snouts, while gharials have very narrow snouts. Crocodiles have broad or narrow snouts. They also have an externally visible fourth tooth. This distinguishes them from alligators in which this tooth is concealed.

Caiman

Alligator

Crocodile

Gharial

## Breeding

Loud bellowing preceeds mating underwater. One month later females lay up to 90 leathery-shelled eggs that they incubate for 2–3 months in nests. Some species lay eggs in several locations to avoid total loss by flooding or predation. High temperatures during incubation result in more males than females. A hatchling breaks out of the eggshell by pipping with an egg tooth on the tip of its snout and calls its mother with squeaks.

*Mother carries young to a nest, where she will guard them until they become independent.*

*Baby crocodile pushing itself out of its egg*

Nile crocodile with eggs

## Movement

On land crocodiles may slide along on their bellies, scooting with their feet. Sometimes they adopt the "high walk" and raise their bodies fully off the ground. Crocodiles run or "gallop," with their tails in the air, usually when being chased. The "tail walk" is used to snatch prey from branches above the water. In water, crocodiles swim using powerful sweeps of their tails.

*High walking*

Dwarf crocodile

## Feeding

After lying hidden for hours, a crocodile suddenly seizes prey from riverbanks and drags it below water until it drowns. Crocodiles cannot chew, so prey is dismembered by shaking and spinning. The whole animal is eaten. Strong juices and pebbles in the stomach help break down the food.

*Topi*

*The jaws close with tremendous force, splintering bone and crushing tissue.*

## Alligators

There are two true alligators. The American alligator from the southeastern United States is up to 18 ft (5.5 m) long. It is the only crocodilian that is not endangered. The Chinese alligator from the Yangtze River, eastern China, is smaller, at up to 7 ft (2 m). Alligators are subtropical, and are more widely distributed than other crocodilians.

*Regular-sized scales*

American alligator

*Thick, muscular tail*

## Caimans

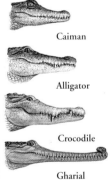
*Spectacled caiman*

Caimans are South American alligators. There are six species, ranging from the 5 ft (1.5 m) long dwarf caiman that lives in forest creeks to the 15 ft (4.5 m) long black caiman of larger rivers. The spectacled caiman has ridges around the eyes resembling spectacle frames.

*Stocky body*

## Gharials

There are two species of gharials, which have long narrow snouts. The Ganges gharial lives in India, Bangladesh, Pakistan, Nepal, and Burma. It reaches 23 ft (7 m) in length. Some males have a bulbous swelling on the end of their snout. The other species, the tomistoma, lives in Indonesia and Malaysia. It reaches a length of 15.5 ft (4.7 m).

*Widely spaced teeth line the forceplike jaw.*

*Ganges gharial*

## NILE CROCODILE

| | |
|---|---|
| SCIENTIFIC NAME | *Crocodylus niloticus* |
| ORDER | Crocodylia |
| FAMILY | Crocodylidae |
| DISTRIBUTION | Africa south of the Sahara, excluding the Kalahari; Madagascar. Now largely extinct in the Nile River in Egypt |
| HABITAT | River systems, lakes, marshes, estuaries, and mangrove habitats. Also able to swim out to sea |
| DIET | Fish, frogs, reptiles, wading birds, and mammals up to the size of water buffalo. Humans are also sometimes victims |
| SIZE | Length: 20 ft (6 m) |
| LIFESPAN | 25–100 years |

FIND OUT MORE

| CONSERVATION | EGGS | LAKE AND RIVER WILDLIFE | MARSH AND SWAMP WILDLIFE | REPTILES | RIVERS |

# CROWS

CROWS AND THEIR RELATIVES are intelligent and noisy birds that usually live alone or in pairs, but are sometimes found in flocks. They live mainly in the northern hemisphere and are common in woods and farmland. Some species can be found in gardens and backyards. Birds in the crow family are not specialized for one particular way of life, allowing them to make the most of different kinds of food. Many of them will eat almost any kind of food they find, including young birds.

## The crow family

There are about 113 species in the crow family. These include ravens, jays, magpies, rooks, and jackdaws. Most species are almost jet black, but many jays and magpies are brightly colored. Members of the crow family are classified as songbirds, but they communicate mainly by harsh chattering calls or croaks.

**Carrion crow**
This widespread crow lives throughout Europe and much of Asia. Like most crows, it is an opportunist and often feeds on the remains of dead animals that have been run over on roads.

*Glossy black plumage*

*Broad wings used for soaring high*

*Powerful legs covered with large scales*

**Blue jay**
Measuring 11 in (28 cm) long, this brightly colored bird is one of the smallest species in the crow family. It lives in eastern North America.

**Common raven**
Ravens are the largest members of the crow family. They live in remote places, such as mountains and rocky coasts, and have a deep, croaking call.

*Powerful beak can tear open the bodies of dead animals.*

## Feeding

Crows have strong beaks, but unlike many birds, they are not fussy about what they eat. They are fond of seeds, worms, and insects, and in spring they sometimes eat the eggs and nestlings of other birds. They are determined feeders. Farmers try to scare them off with scarecrows or shotguns; small birds have more difficulty keeping them away.

**Seed eaters**
Unlike most members of the crow family, some jays live mostly on the seeds of oaks, pines, and other trees. They collect seeds during the fall, and then bury them. These seed stores provide food for the winter.

**Nest robbers**
Magpies make life difficult for small birds by raiding their nests. Magpies are cumbersome and, despite their large size, quite timid. They rarely plunder nests that are constantly guarded.

**Jackdaw hierarchy**
These small but boisterous crows come from Europe and western Asia. They live in groups in which there is a strict hierarchy. They are good at living near humans and often nest on buildings.

## Social groups

Ravens, jays, and magpies often live on their own or in pairs, but some members of the crow family spend their lives in large flocks. Group living makes it easier for the birds to defend themselves against predators, and also increases their chances of finding food.

**Carrion eaters**
Ravens search for food by flying high over open ground, just like birds of prey. Instead of killing animals, they usually eat ones that are already dead.

*Long tail gives the magpie maneuverability in the air.*

**Azure-winged magpie**
This magpie lives in two different areas of the world: China and Japan, and Spain and Portugal. Some people think it was brought to Europe from Asia long ago. Others think it once lived all over Europe and Asia but disappeared from many areas because of climate changes.

**Rooks**
These birds build their nests at the tops of high trees, and they gather together as the sun begins to set. These nesting sites are called rookeries. The same name is used to describe breeding groups of many other animals, from penguins to seals.

### COMMON RAVEN

| | |
|---|---|
| **SCIENTIFIC NAME** | *Corvus corax* |
| **ORDER** | Passeriformes |
| **FAMILY** | Corvidae |
| **DISTRIBUTION** | North America, Europe, northern and central Asia |
| **HABITAT** | Mountains, fields, and rocky coasts |
| **DIET** | Seeds, small animals, and animal remains |
| **SIZE** | Length: 25 in (64 cm) |

**FIND OUT MORE** ANIMAL BEHAVIOR • BIRDS • BIRDS OF PREY • FLIGHT, ANIMAL • PENGUINS • SEALS • SONGBIRDS

# CRUSADES

JERUSALEM HAD LONG been a place of pilgrimage for Christians from Europe, but by the 11th century, the area was ruled by devout Muslim Turks, and pilgrims were often attacked. In 1095, Pope Urban II called for a crusade, or Holy War, to conquer Jerusalem for the Christians – the First Crusade. Over the next two centuries, a pattern emerged: Christians attacked and captured cities, such as Jerusalem and Damascus, and the Muslims recaptured each one, until finally the Crusaders lost all their territory and retreated from the Holy Land (Palestine) for the last time.

## Crusaders

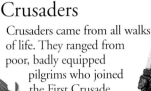

Crusaders came from all walks of life. They ranged from poor, badly equipped pilgrims who joined the First Crusade under the preacher Peter the Hermit, to well-equipped, mounted knights. In between were thousands of foot soldiers. Only the better-equipped soldiers stood a chance against the strong forces of the Seljuk Turks.

**Crusading knight**
With his shield, flat-topped helm, and coat of mail, the crusading knight was well protected against enemy swordsmen.

**Turkish warrior**
One dynasty of Turks, the Seljuks, were formidable defenders of Muslim lands, helped by expert marksmen.

## Land and sea routes

The route from western Europe to Syria and Palestine was long and hazardous. Many travelers died from disease and hunger and never saw the Holy Land. Sea travelers relied on trading cities such as Venice and Genoa to provide ships. The sea route was also far from safe – the Holy Roman Emperor Frederick I drowned while leading the Third Crusade.

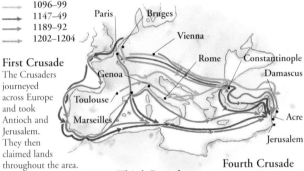

- → 1096–99
- → 1147–49
- → 1189–92
- → 1202–1204

Paris, Bruges, Vienna, Rome, Constantinople, Genoa, Damascus, Toulouse, Marseilles, Acre, Jerusalem

**First Crusade**
The Crusaders journeyed across Europe and took Antioch and Jerusalem. They then claimed lands throughout the area.

**Second Crusade**
After their earlier defeat, the united Muslims attacked Christians in the east. They captured Damascus and routed the new French and German Crusaders.

**Third Crusade**
In 1187, the great Saladin reconquered Jerusalem. Crusaders from England, France, and the Holy Roman Empire retaliated, but managed to capture only Acre.

**Fourth Crusade**
Sponsored by the pope, Crusaders sailed to Constantinople, looted the city, and installed Baldwin of Flanders as emperor. They did not go on to the Holy Land.

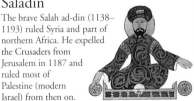

**Children's Crusade**
In 1212, thousands of children marched from the Rhineland to the Mediterranean. Most died of hunger or disease, or were caught and sold as slaves.

## Military orders

The military orders were founded during the 12th century. They were monks who took religious vows but, unlike other monks, also bore arms and fought against Muslims. They included the Knights of St. John, the Templars, and the Teutonic Knights (a German order).

**Knights of St. John**
The Knights of St. John, or the Hospitalers, used their medical skills to care for wounded Crusaders and sick pilgrims. They eventually settled in Malta, where they continued to fight for the Christian cause.

## The spread of knowledge

The Crusades increased contact between East and West and helped take Islamic science and technology to Europe. Western medicine and architecture improved, although these changes may also have been due to contact with Muslims living in Spain.

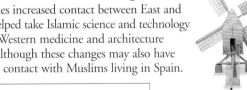

**Windmills**
Wind power was used in the eastern Mediterranean to provide power to grind corn, and Crusaders may have taken the idea back to Europe with them. The first European windmills appeared in France in 1180.

**Balm of Gilead**

**Myrrh**

**Islamic medicine**
Islamic medicine was well developed, and the writings of the Arabian physician Avicenna, or Ibn Sina (979–1037), were influential. Herbs were used as medicines. Myrrh was used for various infections, while balm of Gilead was used for chest and throat diseases.

**Templars**
In 1118, a group of knights who protected Christian pilgrims established themselves in the Holy Land. They became a religious order and took their name from their headquarters near the Temple of Jerusalem.

### Saladin

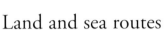

The brave Salah ad-din (1138–1193) ruled Syria and part of northern Africa. He expelled the Crusaders from Jerusalem in 1187 and ruled most of Palestine (modern Israel) from then on.

### Richard I

King Richard I of England (the Lionheart) spent most of his reign (r.1189–1199) abroad. Despite some victories on the Third Crusade, he never captured Jerusalem. After the Crusades, he was imprisoned, ransomed, and spent his last years in France.

## Timeline

**1096–9**
First Crusade: The victorious armies establish first bases in the Holy Land.

**1147–9** Second Crusade: Muslims retake Damascus; Crusaders fail to retrieve it.

**1189–92** Third Crusade: Christians take Acre, but Muslims keep Jerusalem.

**1202–1204** Fourth Crusade: armies conquer Egypt and loot Constantinople.

**1218–21** Fifth Crusade: Crusaders capture land in Egypt, but fail to keep it.

**1228-9** Muslims and Christians negotiate a truce that lasts 10 years.

**1248–70** Seventh and Eighth Crusades.

**1291** Muslims recapture the city of Acre, the last Christian stronghold in the Holy Land.

**FIND OUT MORE** | BYZANTINE EMPIRE | HOLY LAND, HISTORY OF THE | KNIGHTS AND HERALDRY | MEDIEVAL EUROPE | MEDICINE, HISTORY OF

# CRYSTALS AND GEMS

THE WORLD AROUND US is made of tiny crystals. Much of the Earth's surface is made of rocks that contain minerals which are, in turn, formed from crystalline particles. A crystal is a solid substance that has grown in a regular, geometric form, with a smooth, plane surface, or face, and straight edges. Crystals have many different properties, and are used in industry, and for decoration. Most gemstones are crystals prized for their beauty; they are usually cut and polished to enhance their appearance.

### Crystal structure
Crystals are usually made from a single mineral. They are built up from a regular lattice, or framework, of atoms. Each atom has its own special position and is tied to others by bonding forces. The atoms of each mineral always bond together in the same way to form crystals of that mineral.

Limescale crystals that form in a kettle

### Cecil Rhodes
Known as the "King of Diamonds", British imperialist and businessman Cecil Rhodes (1853–1902) made his fortune after staking a claim in a diamond mine in Africa in 1871. By 1888 he had secured a virtual monopoly of the African diamond industry.

Cartoon of Rhodes as "King of Diamonds"

## Crystal systems
Well-formed crystals have regular, symmetrical shapes. The geometrical shapes in which minerals crystallize are grouped into seven crystal systems. Within each of these systems many different forms are possible, but all the forms can be related to the symmetry of that system.

**Cubic** system contains cube-shaped crystals, and also includes 8- and 12-sided crystals.

**Hexagonal and trigonal** are two systems with similar symmetry.

**Tetragonal** systems are generally more elongated than the cube.

**Triclinic** is one of the least symmetrical of the crystal systems.

**Orthorhombic** system has prisms and flattened tabular forms as its most typical features.

**Monoclinic** has less symmetry than the cubic system.

### Crystal habit
Crystals form as molten magma cools, or as a liquid evaporates from a solution containing a dissolved mineral. Crystals rarely form perfectly. The conditions under which crystals grow affect their shape. The general shape of crystals is called their habit.

**Prismatic** crystals are prism-shaped.

**Massive** crystals grow in a mass in which individual crystals cannot be seen.

**Acicular** crystals have slender, fragile needlelike masses.

**Dendritic** crystals have tree or plant shapes.

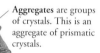
**Aggregates** are groups of crystals. This is an aggregate of prismatic crystals.

**Bladed** crystals look like the blade of a knife.

## Gems
Highly valued and used in jewelery, most gemstones are beautiful, rare, and durable inorganic crystals. A few gems are organic, such as amber, jet, and pearls. Others, called synthetics, are produced in laboratories. They have similar appearances and properties to natural gemstones but are cheaper to buy.

*Diamond in kimberlite*

### Diamonds
The world's hardest substance, diamonds are sought after not only for their unique luster but also for use in drill bits and glass cutters.

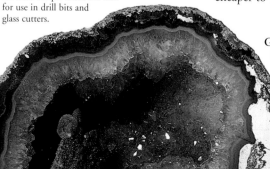

### Geode
Many gemstones are found in geodes, round rock-hollows lined with crystals. These are formed from the bubbles of hot gas and mineral-rich fluids in magma. They are prized by collectors.

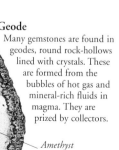
*Amethyst crystals in geode*

### Gem cutting
Most rough crystals have to be cut and polished to remove surface imperfections and to reveal their true brilliance. Before this happens the lapidary, or cutter, studies the rough stone through a loupe (lens) to see if it is suitable for cutting.

### Quartz
Quartz is "piezo-electric." This means that when an electric current passes through quartz, it resonates at such regular intervals that it can be used to keep time very accurately.

*Quartz watch*

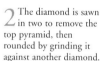
1 The cutter identifies the natural grain and flaws, then marks where the diamond should be cut and ground.

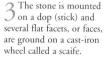
2 The diamond is sawn in two to remove the top pyramid, then rounded by grinding it against another diamond.

3 The stone is mounted on a dop (stick) and several flat facets, or faces, are ground on a cast-iron wheel called a scaife.

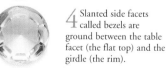
4 Slanted side facets called bezels are ground between the table facet (the flat top) and the girdle (the rim).

5 The stone is turned over and faceted in the same way. It is then finished by a brillianteer who adds 40 small facets.

**FIND OUT MORE** ATOMS AND MOLECULES · CLOTHES AND FASHION · ROCKS AND MINERALS · TIME · SOLIDS

# Gems

## Precious stones

*Drop-shaped morganite*

*Black precious opal*

*Sapphire*

*Brilliant-cut diamond*

*Pendeloque emerald*

*Octagonal aquamarine*

*Cushion-cut ruby*

**Morganite,** which is colored by manganese, is the pink form of beryl.

**Opal** is hardened silica gel. Precious opal is iridescent.

**Sapphire** is a precious form of corundum. It is usually blue.

**Diamonds** are made from carbon placed under extreme pressure.

**Emerald** is a green variety of beryl.

**Aquamarines** are a blue-green variety of beryl.

**Ruby** is the red, precious form of corundum.

## Semiprecious stones

*Crystallization progresses towards center of cavity*

*Quartz crystals are built-up in layers.*

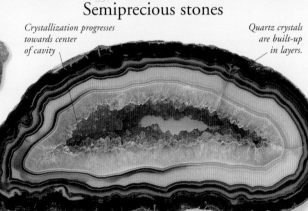

**Smoky** quartz crystals joined together in a twisted group.

**Amazonite** is a blue-green type of microline.

**Amethyst** is a purple form of quartz.

**Rose quartz** is best used for carvings and shaping into beads.

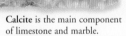

**Calcite** is the main component of limestone and marble.

**Chalcedony** is a massive variety of quartz made from tiny fibers, or grains, of silicon dioxide.

**Rose quartz** is usually found in great lumps – single crystals are very rare.

*Turquoise is usually intense blue or green.*

*Some people believe crystals have healing properties.*

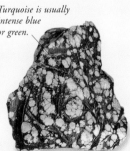

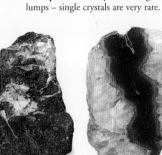

**Labradorite** can be multi-colored and has a sheen.

**Rhodochrosite** gets its color from manganese.

**Turquoise** is valued because of its amazing colors.

**Rock crystal** is an almost colorless form of quartz.

**Lapis lazuli** contains several different minerals.

**Carnelian** is a red variety of chalcedony.

## Organic gems

*Coral carving*

*Polished amber bead*

*Ivory relief*

*Shell pill box*

*Cut and polished jet*

*Pearls*

*Jet containing fossils*

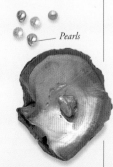

**Coral** is the calcium carbonate skeleton of colony-living sea creatures. It is usually pink.

**Amber** is the fossilized resin, or sap, of trees. It is usually translucent.

**Ivory** comes from the teeth and tusks of mammals. The best ivory comes from the African elephant.

**Mother-of-pearl** lining of shells is prized for its iridescence.

**Jet** is a fine-grained black stone formed from very hard coal.

**Pearls** are tiny pellets of calcium carbonate that form inside some shellfish.

C

# CURIE, MARIE

THE PHYSICIST MARIE CURIE was a pioneer in the science of radioactivity – the study of powerful rays emitted by certain rare materials. Her work changed physics and chemistry and formed a basis for later research in nuclear physics. She discovered two previously unknown elements and also founded an important research institute. In 1903, she shared the Nobel Prize for physics with her husband Pierre, with whom she worked, and French scientist Henri Becquerel. In 1911, she was awarded the Nobel Prize for chemistry. She died after suffering for years from an illness caused by exposure to radiation.

### Early life
Marie Curie was born in Warsaw, Poland. After finishing school, she worked as a governess to save up money to go to college in Paris. In 1891, she left to study at the Sorbonne. She was top ranked there, even though she sometimes fainted from hunger in class.

### Poland
At the time that Marie was born, Poland was under the rule of neighboring Russia, and the best jobs and education went to Russians. After she had finished her schooling, Marie began to go to secret meetings of the "Floating University," a group of Polish people who met to read books that the Russians banned because they thought they might stir up rebellious ideas.

## Radioactivity

In 1895, the German physicist Wilhelm Röntgen discovered invisible "penetrating rays," which he called X rays, coming from an electric tube in one of his experiments. The following year Becquerel discovered similar rays coming from the metal uranium. The Curies devoted the rest of their lives to studying these rays.

### Her equipment
For much of her life, Marie Curie worked under difficult conditions. Her laboratory was in an unheated shed and much of her equipment was homemade. Pierre helped her design and build some of her equipment, including a device called an electrometer, which measured the strength of radiation coming from uranium compounds.

*Electrometer measures electric current.*

*Piezo-electric quartz plate measures radioactivity.*

*Ionization chamber contains radioactive substance.*

### Pierre Curie
Born in Paris and educated by his father, Pierre Curie (1859–1906) began work as a laboratory assistant in Paris. He made several important discoveries before he met Marie in 1894. After they married, he spent the rest of his life working with her. He made some of her equipment and worked beside her in the laboratory. He was killed in a street accident in 1906.

### Isolating radiation
The Curies noticed that pitchblende, the ore from which uranium is extracted, was many times more radioactive than uranium itself. They realized that pitchblende must contain other radioactive substances, so they processed tons of pitchblende to extract these other radioactive elements.

*Tripod stand*

### Pitchblende
The Curies spent about 12 years separating the radioactive elements in pitchblende. They found there were two substances. One they named polonium, after Marie's home country, and the other they called radium.

### X-rays
When World War I (1914–18) broke out, Marie Curie raised funds to set up mobile X-ray units to be used on the battle front. She supervised the conversion of around 200 vans for this purpose. These became known as "Little Curies."

## MARIE CURIE

| | |
|---|---|
| **1867** | Born Manya Sklodowska in Warsaw, Poland. |
| **1891** | Goes to the Sorbonne, Paris; changes first name to Marie. |
| **1895** | Marries Pierre Curie. |
| **1898** | Discovers the elements polonium and radium. |
| **1903** | Awarded Nobel Prize for physics. |
| **1910** | After 12 years of work on pitchblende, she produces pure radium for the first time. |
| **1911** | Awarded Nobel Prize for chemistry. |
| **1918** | Radium Institute opens after delay caused by World War I; Marie becomes research director. |
| **1934** | Dies in France. |

## Radium Institute

In 1912, the Sorbonne and the Pasteur Institute decided to found a Radium Institute in Paris, devoted to research into radiation and the medical uses of radioactivity. Marie became a director of the Institute and spent much of her time supporting scientists in their work and raising money for research.

### The Joliots
Marie Curie's daughter, Irène, was also a scientist. She and her husband, Frédéric Joliot, worked together, much like Marie and Pierre. They discovered how to make non-radioactive substances radioactive by bombarding them with radioactive rays. In 1935, they were awarded the Nobel prize for chemistry.

**FIND OUT MORE**   CHEMISTRY   ELEMENTS   MEDICINE, HISTORY OF   PASTEUR, LOUIS   RADIOACTIVITY   WORLD WAR I   X RAYS AND THE ELECTROMAGNETIC SPECTRUM

# CYCLING

CYCLE SPORTS are held on tracks, roads, and crosscountry circuits. Races range from 1,000-m (1,094-yd) sprints on an indoor track to multistage events over hundreds of miles that last a week or more. Special courses are prepared for off-road racing, which includes cyclocross and mountain-bike racing. Racers ride specialized bikes for the different races. Some need to be be as light as possible; others need to be strong, and the top riders have bicycles made for them to their own specifications.

## Track racing

Track races take place on indoor tracks, with banked sides, or flat outdoor tracks. Races include sprints, where riders jockey for position before making a last-lap dash, and pursuits, where riders start on opposite sides of the track, the race won by the fastest rider or when one rider overtakes the other.

*Riders crouch over the handlebars in a streamlined position.*

*Disk wheels are more efficient indoors because there is no crosswind.*

*Track bicycles have no gears or brakes.*

Pursuit bicycle

*Saddle is set high for more pedaling power.*

Criterium bicycle

Composite wheel

### Types of wheels
The design and material of wheels are constantly being improved to suit particular uses. Weight and shape are the important factors. Using spokes saves weight, but increases drag.

Spoked wheel

### Team pursuit
In team pursuit, riders take turns leading their group of four. The time of the third rider in each team determines the result. One rider usually makes an all-out effort near the finish before trailing off.

British cyclist Chris Boardman on his revolutionary Lotus bike

### Time trials
In time trials, competitors ride as fast as possible, on their own, over a set distance or for a fixed time. Time-trials are some of the hardest races and require continuous effort.

## Road racing

Races take place on courses set along ordinary roads. There are single-stage races and multistage events such as the Tour de France, in which the total time determines placings. In individual and team time trials on the road, the riders start at intervals. Criterium races are 25–62 miles (40–100 km) long. They take place over short courses with many laps, along city streets and through parks.

### Tour de France
The world's leading road race is the Tour de France, which lasts about three weeks. The overall leader on total time wears the famous yellow jersey for the next stage.

## Off-road racing

Bicycles for off-road races have chunky tires for the rough terrain. Cyclocross is the original form of cross-country cycling, with world championships since 1950. Mountain biking is now the most popular form, with world championships since 1990 and Olympic recognition in 1996.

### Cyclocross
In cyclocross, races take place over laps of a cross-country course. Riders often find it quicker to dismount and carry their bikes over obstacles such as fences, gates, and ditches, and may have to run up steep hills or wade through water with them.

*For log hopping, the rider must learn to shift her weight.*

### Mountain biking
Mountain bikes are built to survive rough handling. Most have steel-alloy frames, straight handlebars, and flat knobbly tires. Courses for races have many climbs and descents, with routes over fields and gravel pits.

*Rider brings her weight over the front wheel.*

*Weight is kept over the front wheel until the hop has been completed.*

*Weight over the rear wheel*

### Miguel Indurain
Spanish road racer Miguel Indurain (b. 1964) became the first cyclist to win the Tour de France in five successive years (1991–95), equaling the record number of wins. In 1996, he took first place in the Olympic road time trial.

FIND OUT MORE — BICYCLES AND MOTORCYCLES · FRANCE · HEALTH AND FITNESS · MOTOR SPORTS · OLYMPIC GAMES · SPORT

# DAMS

IN MANY AREAS of the world, people rely on dams for their water and electricity supplies. A dam is a barrier that holds back water. The dam itself and the surrounding hills form a bowl in which water collects to form an artificial lake called a reservoir. Most dams are built across a river valley to catch the river's flow, but some dams create reservoirs into which water is pumped for storage. How strong a dam needs to be depends on the depth of the water in the reservoir. Some dams are enormous: the Grand Coulee Dam in Washington State weighs nearly 9 million tons.

## Types of dam

There are three main types of dams: arch dams, gravity dams, and buttress dams. The type of dam that engineers decide to build depends on the geography of the location. Factors affecting the decision include the width and depth of the river valley and the type of rock around the site.

**Buttress dam**
A buttress dam is a huge concrete wall that leans into a reservoir of water. The wall is made up of concrete slabs that are supported on the downstream side of the dam by concrete projections known as buttresses.

**Arch dam**
An arch dam is built across the entrance to a narrow valley, so that the height of the dam is greater than its width. The dam's curved shape holds back water because it transfers the push of the water to the rock of the valley sides.

**Gravity dam**
A gravity dam is a huge embankment of earth or rock. Leakage is prevented by a waterproof clay core or a concrete skin on the upstream side of the dam. The dam's immense weight prevents the water from pushing it over.

Water from reservoir enters intake towers.

Arched concrete wall

Sides of river valley

Reservoir

Highway across top of dam

Water flows through pipes in dam to hydroelectric power station.

Model of an arch dam

Spillway lets excess water flow into river, so that dam does not overflow.

## Anatomy of a dam

This model shows an arch dam that creates a reservoir for supplying water and electricity to nearby towns and cities. The dam is made of thin concrete strengthened by thousands of steel bars. Water flowing through pipes in the dam drives electricity generators in the hydroelectric power station at the foot of the dam.

## Flood control

On large rivers, dams help prevent flooding by holding back surges of flood water and releasing them downstream slowly. A flood barrier is a movable dam built across a tidal river. The barrier has gates that are usually open to allow the river to flow freely, but which can be closed when dangerously high tides threaten to surge upstream.

### Environmental effects

A river dam and the reservoir it forms can harm the environment. Huge areas of countryside are drowned by the reservoir, and the dam disrupts the river's natural flow, affecting wildlife and irrigation downstream. A dam also prevents fish from moving freely up and down the river.

### Tidal barrage

A barrage is a dam across a river estuary that generates hydroelectric power. The dam holds back the tide as it ebbs and flows. The water is forced through pipes inside the barrage, where it drives electricity generators.

**La Rance barrage, France**

### Weir

A weir is a low river dam that controls the flow of water by creating a stretch of deeper water upstream. Deep water makes the river navigable for boats.

Weir in Middlesex, England

Model of Thames Flood Barrier, UK

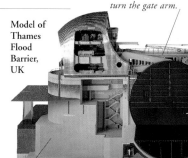

Hydraulic rockers turn the gate arm.

Circular gate arm opens and closes gate.

Steel-plated roof

Water level

Concrete pier

Gate open; when gate closes, it rotates into its vertical position, blocking the flow of water.

Barrier gate is a hollow semicircle plated with high-strength steel.

Steel piles sunk into riverbed.

FIND OUT MORE | BUILDING AND CONSTRUCTION | ELECTRICITY | ENERGY | FARMING | LAKES | RAIN | ROADS | OCEANS AND SEAS | RIVERS

# DANCE

WHEN PEOPLE MOVE in time to music they are dancing. People have a natural urge to move in time to rhythms. Children jump up and down when they are excited; babies move naturally to rhythms they hear or feel. In dancing, these natural movements are organized into rhythmic and visual patterns. Different dances have developed all over the world, and are performed for different reasons. Dancing can be both an art form and recreation. It can express an emotion, tell a story, or set a mood.

**Masai dancers**
The Masai of East Africa move in straight lines as they dance, and include high jumps in their routines. As happens in all African dance, they are accompanied by rhythmic, exhilarating drumbeats.

## African dance

Dancing is an essential part of life to many Africans, and important events, such as births, deaths, and initiation to adulthood, are all observed by dancing. African dances can last for many hours. The dances for men are usually very energetic, and include a lot of stamping and leaping. Women tend to do more gentle dances, clapping and swaying to the music or rhythm.

## Origins

Dancing is probably the oldest art form. The first dances may have evolved from spontaneous stamping steps. These steps were later given rhythms and shapes and accompanied by grunts and shouts.

**Ceremonial dance**
Early people found that rhythmic movements had a strong effect on the mind, and felt that dancing must have magical powers. They began to dance to ward off evil spirits, heal people, and ensure good crops.

**Australian Aboriginals performing the Corroboree**

## Asian dancing

The main influence on dance styles in Asia comes from India. Many Asian dances make use of stylized hand movements, particularly those from countries such as India, Sri Lanka, Myanmar (Burma), Thailand, and Cambodia.

*Headdress*

**Indian dances**
Indian classical dancers mime out stories from Indian mythology, and include sequences of more abstract dance movements.

*There are six styles of Indian classical dance.*

*Bent-back fingers*

**Dragon**
The mythical dragon is a very important symbol in Chinese culture. Dragon dances are performed to celebrate festivals such as the Chinese New Year.

*Dancers wear a dragon costume.*

## Dance as entertainment

The ancient Egyptians were the first known to use dancing simply as a form of entertainment. Professional dancing girls entertained the pharaoh and his guests at banquets, performing dances that included running, high kicks, and sensual hip movements.

**Ancient Egyptian dancing girls**

**Southeast Asian dances**
Classical dance in Southeast Asia typically includes slow, controlled movements, with many graceful hand and arm gestures. Dance-dramas, performed by highly trained dancers, are particularly popular in Indonesia and Thailand. Throughout the region there is a wide variety of traditional folk dances.

**Royal Thai classical dancer**

## European folk dancing

Every European country has its folk dances, which are now essentially social. Some of them have been taken to other countries by settlers. The dances are often performed in traditional costumes, and many of them involve people forming simple patterns, such as lines and circles.

## Flamenco

Perhaps the most famous of all Spanish dances is the flamenco. This dance is a mixture of both the Spanish and Arab cultures. The men use complicated footwork, while the women weave patterns with their arms. The dancers are accompanied by fast, dramatic guitar music.

*Flamenco dancers also use their voices.*

**Chorus depicted on a Greek vase**

**Dance as theater**
The ancient Greeks made dance the basis of all their theater. The chorus in a Greek play was a group of actors who danced and sang a commentary on the action.

## Irish dancing

Irish jigs are usually performed either by pairs or by individuals, but large groups also perform Irish dances. The jig is based on simple steps, but the dancers can elaborate and perform complicated leaping steps. They hold their upper body still and their arms straight down at their sides or hold hands. The dances are usually accompanied by the fiddle or bagpipes.

# South American dancing

The dances of Central and South America reflect the cultures not only of the native peoples who have long occupied the region, but also of the European colonists and their African slaves. Many dances that have originated in this region, such as the tango and samba, have become popular all over the world.

### Macumba

The Macumba dance was taken to Brazil by African slaves as a form of voodoo-worship in which the dancer is believed to be possessed by a god. Macumba dancers worship Yemannjah, a goddess of the sea. Like all voodoo dances it involves shaking of the head and shoulders.

### Tango

This dance originated in Argentina about 200 years ago. It had to be "cleaned up" before it became fashionable in Europe in the 1900s, because it was considered too immodest for the dance halls.

### Modern dance

This style has no fixed technique. Dancers express their feelings in their movements. Modern dance began at the start of the 20th century, when US dancer Isadora Duncan broke away from ballet and developed her own style.

### Samba

The samba was first danced in Brazil, especially at Carnival time, and became extremely popular in the United States and Europe in the early 1940s. It is danced by couples who perform simple backward and forward steps, swaying their bodies. In Brazil, there are many versions of the dance, each with a different rhythm, tempo, and mood.

# Ballroom dancing

Developed in the courts of Europe, many ballroom dances, such as the waltz and samba, were adapted from folk dances. They were danced on flat, polished floors, which allowed for elegant gliding movements, rather than the jumping and stamping which folk dancers developed to cope with the rough floors or grass on which they danced.

*Dancing the waltz*

*In competions dancers dress formally.*

*The couple progress around the dance floor in an anticlockwise direction.*

*Partners dance in close contact with each other.*

### Waltz

When the waltz first became popular with the aristocracy, in the 1700s, it caused a scandal because the couple was expected to dance close together. It was originally a simple Austrian peasant dance, but by the 19th century it was highly fashionable and composers such as Austrian Johann Strauss the younger (1825–99) specialized in writing waltz music.

*Professional dancers require strong ankles and a fit body.*

*Dancers adopt a flirtatious carnival mood.*

*There is no body contact in the samba.*

*A tilting pelvic action is required in many figures.*

*Dancers compete in the Rio de Janeiro Carnival every February.*

*Couples progress around in an anticlockwise direction.*

*Dancing the samba*

## Gene Kelly

American dancer Gene Kelly (1912–96) made film musicals popular with his athletic dance style. His films include *For Me and My Gal* (1942), *An American in Paris* (1951), and *Singin' in the Rain* (1952).

US dancer and actor Fred Astaire

### Tap dance

In 19th-century America, black slaves combined African rhythms with the jigs of English and Irish settlers. Tap dance was thus created and became very popular.

### Jazz dance

When jazz music became popular in the 1920s, an energetic, expressive form of dance developed with it. Today, jazz dancing is the main form of dancing in musicals and films.

### Disco

Disco dancing became popular in the 1970s. The name comes from the clubs called discotheques in which records were played for dancing. Couples usually dance facing, but not touching, each other, using simple repetitive movements.

FIND OUT MORE    BALLET    DRAMA    FILMS AND FILMMAKING    JAZZ    MUSIC    OPERA    ROCK AND POP

# DARWIN, CHARLES

THE BRITISH NATURALIST Charles Darwin is best known as the man who developed the remarkable theory of evolution by natural selection. The theory, which describes how one species can develop or evolve into another, caused a revolution in biological science. Darwin was not the first person to suggest a theory of evolution, but was the first to present a solid body of evidence for the idea. He also wrote books about his travels, coral reefs, barnacles, the pollination of flowers, and insect-eating plants.

### Early life
Darwin was born in 1809, in Shrewsbury, England. His grandfather, Erasmus Darwin, had put forward his own theory of evolution in the 1790s. To begin with, Charles Darwin did not believe in the idea of evolution. He trained as a priest before studying geology and biology.

D

## Galápagos Islands
Darwin studied thousands of plants and animals all around the world on the *Beagle's* journey. The most interesting part was the few weeks spent in the Galápagos Islands, about 600 miles (1,000 km) from the coast of South America. Darwin noticed that the species there were different from those elsewhere in the world.

Notebooks used by Darwin in Galápagos

*List of species*

*Map pasted into notebook*

*Galápagos Islands*

### Notebooks
During his voyage on the *Beagle*, Darwin made careful, copious notes of everything he saw, gaining him the nickname "the old philosopher" from the ship's officers. The wealth of information he gathered helped him later when he was developing his theory of evolution.

### Darwin's finches
When he got home, Darwin realized that the finches on the Galápagos Islands had different beaks depending on which island they inhabited. He decided that the birds had developed beaks that were best suited to the diet on their particular island.

## The Beagle
At Cambridge, Darwin made friends with John Henslow, the professor of botany. Henslow suggested that Darwin would be a good choice as official naturalist on the naval survey ship HMS *Beagle*, which was about to sail around the world on a five-year scientific cruise. The trip lasted from 1831 to 1836.

Darwin's watch

Darwin's telescope

### Fossil finds
When he landed in South America, Darwin found fossils of extinct animals, such as the giant sloth (now called *Mylodon darwini*), that closely resembled modern species. This suggested that animals had gradually changed to suit their environments.

*Bones of* Macrauchenia, *a prehistoric mammal found by Darwin*

Rock hammers

## The Origin of Species
Darwin returned to England and wrote an account of his travels. He spent years studying the specimens he had collected and the notes he had made. Gradually, he developed his idea that species evolved as animals adapted to suit their environments. He published his findings in his book *On the Origin of Species by Means of Natural Selection*. The work caused an outcry because it challenged the story of creation in the Bible.

### Wallace
The British naturalist Alfred Russel Wallace (1823–1913) drew up a theory of evolution by natural selection quite independently of Darwin. He wrote to Darwin for advice, and the men wrote a paper about evolution together.

### The naturalist
After his voyage, Darwin spent the rest of his life studying specimens, doing experiments, and writing up his findings. He never left England again, and for much of the rest of his life he was too ill to leave his home. Illness did not stop him from working on subjects ranging from earthworms to the pollination of plants.

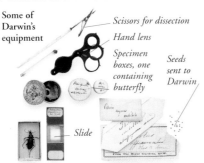

Some of Darwin's equipment

*Scissors for dissection*

*Hand lens*

*Specimen boxes, one containing butterfly*

*Seeds sent to Darwin*

*Slide*

### Natural selection
Parents produce many offspring, all different from each other. Only those best suited to their environment will survive, passing on some of their features to their offspring.

*Lesser black-backed gull*

*Herring gull has same ancestor as Lesser black-backed, but has evolved separately.*

### CHARLES DARWIN

**1809** Born in Shrewsbury, England

**1831** Sets sail on the *Beagle*

**1836** Returns to England

**1858** Wallace writes to Darwin about his evolutionary theory; they produce a paper on evolution together

**1859** Darwin publishes his *Origin of Species*

**1871** Publishes *The Descent of Man*, on human evolution

**1875** Publishes *Insectivorous Plants*, which describes how the sundew traps insects

**1880** Publishes *The Power of Movement in Plants*, which shows how light influences the direction of plant growth

**1882** Dies in Downe, England

FIND OUT MORE

BIOLOGY   DINOSAURS   EVOLUTION   FOSSILS   GEOLOGY   HUMAN EVOLUTION   SCIENCE, HISTORY OF

D

# DEER AND ANTELOPE

DEER AND antelope look alike and are both herbivorous, hoofed animals. However, they belong to different families: deer to a family of their own; antelope, which include gazelles, duikers, and spiral-horned antelope, to the same family as cattle. What distinguishes deer and antelope is their headgear: deer have branched antlers that are shed, antelope have unbranched horns that are permanent.

*Female red deer have no antlers.*

**Fringe-eared oryx**
Oryx live in the arid grasslands of Tanzania and Kenya in Africa. They obtain water from roots and tubers.

**Red deer**
This is the most common deer. It is found throughout Europe and Asia to Japan and on to the Himalayas.

*Both sexes have long, straight horns.*

**Stages of antler growth in a fallow deer**

*Growing antlers*

*Fully grown antlers*

*Peeling velvet*

**Antlers**
The larger a stag's antlers, the more females it will attract. While the antlers are growing, they are protected by a velvety skin, richly supplied with blood vessels and nerves. At the end of the deer's breeding season, the blood supply to the antlers is cut off, causing the velvet to dry out and peel off in strips.

## Deer

There are 38 species of deer spread over most of Europe, as well as Asia, North Africa, and the Americas. Some have been introduced into Australasia. Most species live in herds that split up in the breeding season. Most male deer, or stags, bear multibranched antlers, which are shed and regrown every year.

## Antelope

Most of the 60 species of antelope live in Africa. Some, such as the blackbuck and the Tibetan antelope, are Asian, and a few species have been introduced to other countries. Antelope range in size from the giant Derby eland to the pygmy and royal antelope, which are no bigger than rabbits.

## Antelope horns

All male antelope have horns, as do some females. The males use their horns to intimidate their rivals and to defend their territory.

*Horns are hollow.*

*Front view of hartebeest horns*

*Front view of greater kudu horns*

**Browsing antelope**

**Grazing gazelles**

**Four-horned antelope**
Males have two pairs of horns, making the deer a sought-after trophy for hunters. The front pair of horns is smaller than the back pair.

**Nyala**
The nyala, found in southeast African forests, has dark brown with a white tip. These can be up to 31 in (78 cm) long, with usually one open curve.

**Hartebeest**
Both male and female hartebeests have curved horns. Each has about 12 ridges but a smooth tip. Seen from the front the horns are angular.

**Greater kudu**
The triple-spiraled horns of the male greater kudu are among the most imposing horns of any living animal. They grow up to 5 ft (1.5 m) long.

**Roan antelope**
Males and females have horns. About 22 in (55 cm) long, they have deep ridges and curve gradually backward.

**Browsers and grazers**
Antelope include both grazing and browsing species. In Africa, for example, some species, such as Thomson's gazelle, graze on grass. Other species, such as the gerenuk, browse the leaves and shoots of trees. Grant's and dorcas gazelles browse and graze, according to what is available.

## Largest and smallest deer
The largest of all deer is the moose of North America, known as the elk in Europe. An adult male moose may stand 6 ft (1.8 m) at the shoulder and weigh 1,200 lbs (545 kg). The smallest deer is the South American pudu, which stands only about 16 in (40 cm) at the shoulder and weighs about 20 lbs (9 kg).

## Père David's deer
This deer once roamed wild in China. Then, for 3,000 years, it lived only in zoos. In 1865, the missionary Père David saw the last surviving herd. This herd was later wiped out, but the Duke of Bedford established a herd in England. In recent years, deer bred in captivity have been sent to China and reintroduced into their native habitat.

D

## Rutting

For most of the year, red deer stags remain apart from the females, or hinds, and their young. During the breeding season, known as the rut, males collect harems of hinds that they vigorously defend by roaring or, if necessary, by fighting.

## Breeding

Most species of antelope and deer give birth when the weather is warm and food is abundant. Young caribou are born in early June when the herd is migrating. The calves can follow their mother within minutes of birth. The young of some species are left alone. Their mothers come to suckle and clean them several times a day until they are strong enough to join the herd.

### Caribou

The Eurasian reindeer and the North American caribou are the same species. They live in large herds and migrate long distances every year to find food. The reindeer has been domesticated by, among others, the Lapps of northern Europe.

*Female reindeer are the only female deer that grow antlers.*

*Females in a herd give birth within two weeks of each other.*

*A calf can run with the herd when only an hour old.*

*A reindeer calf weighs about 9 lb (4 kg) at birth.*

**Reindeer with calf**

## Antelope habitats

Antelope are found in most kinds of tropical and subtropical habitats. Most are creatures of the open plains and forests, but others have adapted to live in deserts, wetlands, and mountains. Grazing antelope live where there is plenty of grass, whereas the browsers tend to inhabit woodland.

### Woodland inhabitant

Also called the chousingha, the shy, solitary, four-horned antelope lives in wooded, hilly country. Hunting has greatly reduced its numbers, but it still survives in several wildlife reserves in India and one reserve in Nepal.

*Sitatunga hoof*

### Swamp inhabitant

The sitatunga lives only in swamps and marshes. It has evolved long hooves that help it walk on marshy ground. When in danger, it submerges itself in water with only its nostrils exposed.

---

*Pointed antler*

## Defense

Some deer and antelope may sometimes use their antlers and horns to defend themselves, but usually their headgear is not strong enough for that purpose. Most deer and antelope rely on their excellent eyesight and acute sense of hearing to detect potential enemies, and on speed to escape if they are threatened.

*Muntjak head*

*Tusklike teeth*

*Muntjak skull*

### Self-defense

If attacked, a muntjak's first defense is to run away. If trapped, males thrash with their antlers. These are mounted on "stalks" of bone as long as the antlers themselves. Males also have two tusklike teeth used mainly in battles with rivals.

### Camouflage

Some deer and antelope avoid predators because they blend into their surroundings. Kirk's dik-dik is an African antelope that lives in dry bush country where the thick underbrush protects it.

## Pronking

The springbok of Africa runs fast to escape a predator. Like most gazelles, it will often leap high into the air, with legs stiff, hooves close together, and back arched. Called pronking or stotting, this action may warn the herd, confuse predators, or simply give the gazelle a better view of its escape route.

### RED DEER

| | |
|---|---|
| SCIENTIFIC NAME | *Cervus elaphus* |
| ORDER | Artiodactyla |
| FAMILY | Cervidae |
| DISTRIBUTION | Europe and Asia. Introduced into Australia, New Zealand, and South America |
| HABITAT | Woodland and open country |
| DIET | Grass, leaves, shoots, flowers (it both grazes and browses) |
| SIZE | Height at the shoulder: 4 ft 6 in (1.4 m) |
| LIFESPAN | 12–15 years |

FIND OUT MORE

AFRICAN WILDLIFE    BUFFALO AND OTHER WILD CATTLE    GRASSLAND WILDLIFE

# DENMARK

THE SMALLEST, flattest, and most southerly country in Scandinavia, Denmark occupies the Jutland peninsula, the islands of Sjaelland, Lolland, Falster, and Fyn, and more than 500 smaller islands. The Faeroe Islands and Greenland in the North Atlantic are self-governing Danish territories. A prosperous, environmentally conscious, and progressive nation, Denmark offers its population high living standards and was one of the first countries to set up a welfare system in the 1930s.

## DENMARK FACTS

| | |
|---|---|
| CAPITAL CITY | Copenhagen |
| AREA | 16,629 sq miles (43,069 sq km) |
| POPULATION | 5,300,000 |
| MAIN LANGUAGE | Danish |
| MAJOR RELIGION | Christian |
| CURRENCY | Danish krone |
| LIFE EXPECTANCY | 76 years |
| PEOPLE PER DOCTOR | 345 |
| GOVERNMENT | Multiparty democracy |
| ADULT LITERACY | 99% |

## Physical features

Denmark's flat landscape is broken by low, rolling hills and gentle valleys with shady beech forests. There are also extensive areas of heathland, a beautiful lake district, and a coastline of cliffs, dunes, and broad sandy beaches.

### Jutland
The Jutland peninsula makes up about 70 percent of Denmark's land. Its west coast is edged with beaches and the southwest has a sandy plain. Strong winds sweeping across the land turn windmills to generate electricity.

### Baltic islands
The steep chalk cliffs on the Baltic island of Møn contrast with the gentle dunes on other islands. The Danish take great care of their environment and beaches.

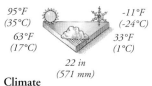

95°F (35°C)  63°F (17°C)  -11°F (-24°C)  33°F (1°C)  22 in (571 mm)

### Climate
Denmark's usually mild and damp climate is dominated by stiff westerly winds. In many coastal areas, to prevent sand in the dunes from blowing over the land, the Danes have planted conifers as windbreaks.

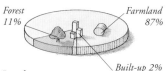

Forest 11%  Farmland 87%  Built-up 2%

### Land use
Over four-fifths of Denmark is farmland, including lush pasture for grazing cattle and for raising pigs. Denmark's land yields few natural resources, although high winds are harnessed to produce power.

### People
Only four percent of the population is foreign – mainly European. The only minority groups are Turks and Inuits from Greenland. The Danish have progressive lifestyle policies, with a high divorce rate. Today, 47 percent of all children are raised by unmarried couples or single parents. Three-quarters of all women work, and the country has the best childcare system in the world.

Danish pigs

### Map legend (Denmark)

Skagen, Hirtshals, Hjørring, Løkken, Frederikshavn, Hanstholm, Brønderslev, Fjerritslev, Åbybro, Læsø, Thisted, Ålborg, Limfjorden, Nissum Bredning, Mørs, Lemvig, Skive, Hobro, Struer, Viborg, Randers, Grenå, Holstebro, Gudenå, Ringkøbing, Ikast, Silkeborg, Ebeltoft, Ringkøbing Fjord, Herning, Brande, Århus, Samsø, Skjern, Give, Horsens, Varde, Grindsted, Vejle, Endelave, Sejerø, Esbjerg, Kolding, Fredericia, Kalundborg, Roskilde, Tastrup, Ribe, Brørup, Middelfart, Otterup, Slagelse, Køge, Ringsted, Rømø, Haderslev, Årup, Odense, Korsør, Store Heddinge, Tøftlund, Fåborg, Ringe, Kvaerndrup, Næstved, Åbenrå, Tønder, Troense, Svendborg, Præstø, Gråsten, Sønderborg, Nakskov, Vordingborg, Maribo, Sakskøbing, Møn, Lolland, Nykøbing, Gedser

DENMARK, Rønne, Bornholm, Baltic Sea, Helsingør, Hillerød, Hørsholm, COPENHAGEN, Sjaelland, The Sound, GERMANY, Kiel Bay

Skagerrak, Jammerbugten, North Sea, JYLLAND, Fyn, Lillebælt, Storebælt, Langelandsbælt, Falster

## Copenhagen
Denmark's capital is also its most important port and Scandinavia's largest city. Crisscrossed with a network of canals, quaint alleys, and bicycle paths, Copenhagen has many historic buildings and churches. It also boasts the Tivoli Gardens, an amusement park that attracts millions every year.

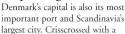

Tourist boat on canal

Danish family visiting Legoland on Jutland

324 per sq mile (125 per sq km)

85% Urban  15% Rural

### Farming and industry
Danish farming is efficient and often run by cooperatives. Only about four percent of the workforce is employed in farming, mainly of dairy cattle and pigs, yet agriculture accounts for much of the country's export income. Denmark also has successful fishing, manufacturing, and food industries for processing bacon and dairy products. Service industries employ 79 percent of workers.

**FIND OUT MORE** — ATLANTIC OCEAN · ENERGY · EUROPE · EUROPE, HISTORY OF · EUROPEAN UNION · FARMING · FOOD · SCANDINAVIA, HISTORY OF · TRADE AND INDUSTRY · VIKINGS

# DESERTS

FEW PLACES ON EARTH are as stark and hostile as deserts. Deserts are vast areas where very little rain falls – typically under 3.9 in (100 mm) a year. Any rain that does fall quickly evaporates. Few plants can survive, and soil cannot develop in such a dry and barren or arid environment. The landscape is bare sand, gravel, or rock. Clear skies and sparse vegetation leave the ground exposed to extremes of temperature. In the tropics, cloudless skies create hot deserts with daytime temperatures that often exceed 122°F (50°C). Deserts at higher latitudes can be extremely cold.

*Areas thought to be at risk of desertification (shown in orange)*

*12% of land is covered with desert.*

**Desert regions**
The world's great deserts lie deep within continents far from the moisture of the oceans. They are also along the Tropics of Cancer and Capricorn, on either side of the equator, where sinking air creates stable dry weather.

D

## Desert landforms and dunes

Strong winds, sudden flash floods, and exposure to extreme temperatures create distinctive desert features. The wind piles sand up in dunes or sandblasts rocks. Flash floods carve canyonlike valleys. The desert heat creates corrosive chemicals that sculpt rocks into bizarre shapes.

*Wadi – gorgelike, generally dry valley*

*Mesa – isolated, flat-topped, steep-sided mountain*

*Parabolic dunes are also common on coasts.*

*Butte – eroded mesa*

**Oasis**
An oasis, such as the Azraq oasis in Jordan (above), is a fertile area within a desert that lies near an underground stream or a spring. Crops such as date palms can grow, and desert dwellers can live supported by the land. Artificial oases can be created through irrigation.

**Seif dunes** form where sand is sparse and wind comes from two directions.

*Oasis is a pocket of water.*

**Zeugen,** or mushroom, rocks are produced by weathering.

**Hamada is** an area strewn with boulders and stones.

**Playa is** a salty lake into which desert streams and wash flow.

*Eroded arch*

*Bolson is a drainage basin.*

**Barchan dune** is shaped like a crescent and its tips usually point downwind.

*Transverse dune – ridge lying across the wind*

**Bajada is** a ramp of sand deposited by rivers along mountain edges.

### Mirage
Sometimes the desert heat is so intense that desert travelers believe they can see water. This is an optical illusion (a trick of the eye) caused by the reflection of a faraway object that gives the false appearance of a sheet of water.

## Types of deserts

Climatic conditions create different types of deserts. In Africa, the Sahara has vast areas of erg (sand seas), hamada (stony plateaus), reg (pebble plains), rocky deserts, canyons, and cliff deserts. In the Antarctic, there are ice deserts, while in the deserts of the western USA the heat evaporates rain so quickly that it leaves behind dissolved minerals in a hard, salty crust.

*Rocks brought to desert by flood water*

**Sandy desert**
In flat areas, vast sand seas, or ergs, develop. After a rainfall, water rushes along a wadi, a dry riverbed. The sandstone cliffs on either side are gradually worn away by the heat, wind, and rain.

**Rocky desert**
Many of the world's deserts are strewn with boulders that have been washed there by flash flooding. These rocks are gradually eroded by the action of wind and weather.

## The shifting desert

As climatic conditions change, deserts shrink and expand. In the past, the Sahel, the southern edge of the Sahara, was watered by summer rains moving up from the south. In recent years, the lack of rain in the Sahel has caused drought and famine in places such as Sudan and Ethiopia.

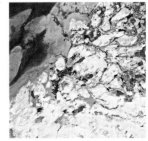

**Desertification**
The effect of drought and heavy grazing by cattle, sheep, and goats destroys vegetation cover, turning the area permanently to desert. This process is known as desertification.

**FIND OUT MORE**   CLIMATE   DESERT WILDLIFE   ECOLOGY AND ECOSYSTEMS   ROCKS AND MINERALS   WEATHER

# DESERT WILDLIFE

THE DRIEST PLACES ON EARTH are known as deserts. Food is scarce, and there is little shelter from the sun and wind. Deserts are among the most inhospitable of all places in which to live. In spite of this, many remarkable animals survive and even thrive in these hostile surroundings. Birds, mammals, insects, arachnids, amphibians, and reptiles are all represented, together with some equally remarkable plants.

## Deserts

Many different types of deserts exist in different parts of the world. Some are mountainous and rocky; others are pebbly or full of sand dunes. Some become baking hot by day; others have bitterly cold winters.

### Sahara
Stretching across North Africa, the Sahara is the greatest of all deserts. It is a vast wilderness of sand and rock, with only scattered palms and bushes to offer shade from the searing daytime sun. Most of the animals that live there find shelter under rocks or in burrows.

### Oases
Oases provide reliable sources of drinking water for wildlife in the desert. They form in the few places where springs bubble up from underground, or where rainwater from neighboring mountains collects in hollows.

## Birds

Though some desert-dwelling doves and finches forage for seeds, the most well-known birds of arid lands are predators. They probe vegetation and scour the ground for prey, obtaining all the moisture they need from the bodies of their victims.

*Pale-colored fur reflects heat.*

### Dwarf hamster
Only about 3.3 in (8.5 cm) long, this hamster lives in the deserts of Mongolia, Siberia, and China. It has thick fur, that helps to keep it warm in the bitterly cold winters.

*Long, bushy tail can be curled around the body to keep it warm during the night.*

## Mammals

Desert mammals show a remarkable ability to cope with conditions that would be dangerously hot and dry for most animals. Some, such as camels, can tolerate steep rises in their body temperature and long periods of dehydration. Others have special means of securing shade, obtaining moisture, finding food, and avoiding danger in the wide-open terrain.

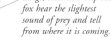

*Large, erect ears help the fox hear the slightest sound of prey and tell from where it is coming.*

### Fennec fox
The fennec fox is small with large, pointed ears. The large size of the ears helps the fox lose excess heat from its body during the heat of the day. The fox has thick fur that keeps it warm on cold nights.

### Bactrian camel
Camels are perfectly adapted for life in deserts. They can roam about for days without drinking or sweating. The two humps of the Bactrian camel act as fat reserves that nourish the animal. The shaggy coat protects the camel during the cold winters in Asia's Gobi Desert.

*Humps flop over when the fat is depleted.*

### Gila woodpecker
The Gila woodpecker forages for insects in the deserts of Mexico and the US. Typically, it hammers out nest holes in the stems of large cacti.

### Roadrunner
Roadrunners seldom fly, but they are extremely fast, agile runners. They often prey on desert snakes, which they subdue with a series of lethal stabs from their sharp beaks.

*Falcons can spot prey from a great height.*

### Lanner falcon
This darting bird of prey nests among rocks and cliffs in the Sahara. It hunts small birds, which it chases and snatches in midair or on the ground. It also preys on smaller animals, such as gerbils, lizards, and locusts.

### Red kangaroo
In Australian deserts, red kangaroos browse on bushes. They produce dry dung as a way of saving moisture, but still make regular trips to waterholes to replace moisture lost through sweating.

### Kalahari ground squirrel
These burrowing rodents eat seeds and other plant material in the Kalahari Desert of Africa. During the day, they hold their bushy tails over their bodies for shade.

*Long fur covers the upper surface of the feet.*

D

D

# Reptiles and amphibians

Both snakes and lizards are tolerant of dry climates, and these reptiles are among the most common of desert animals. Amphibians are much more in danger of drying out, but a few species do appear on the desert surface, especially after rare periods of rain.

*Sandviper buries itself tail first.*

*Snake descends vertically into the sand.*

### Sandviper
The sandviper has perfected an efficient way of disappearing on desert dunes. It wriggles down into the loose sand, becoming buried within seconds. It does this to escape danger and to be ready to attack prey.

### Fringe-toed lizard
This lizard forages in sandy deserts. When the surface becomes too hot, it stands on two legs to help keep cool. Projections between its toes spread its weight and stop it from sinking into the sand.

*Lizard can close its nostrils to prevent sand getting into its air passages.*

*Smooth scales*

### Water-holding frog
For months, this frog lies dormant underground in a waterproof cocoon. It emerges to feed and breed only after heavy rains, swelling its body with water before it returns into the soil.

### Sandfish
The sandfish is a lizard that makes its home on desert sand dunes. It is named after the way it moves across and through the sand, pushing sideways with its flattened toes as if it were swimming. Like other small lizards, it hunts mainly for insects.

### Gila monster
The Gila monster is a fearsome lizard. Large, with a venomous bite, it leaves its burrow at dawn to hunt rodents and raid birds' nests. Fat stored in its thick tail provides nourishment when prey is scarce.

### Yucca moth
The yucca moth of American deserts has evolved a close relationship with the yucca plant. The moth pollinates the plant; the yucca flowers give shelter to the moth larvae.

### Desert cricket
An inhabitant of the deserts of India and Pakistan, the desert cricket can bury itself quickly in the sand. It digs a hole directly beneath itself with its star-shaped feet and sinks down.

# Invertebrates

Few insects and other invertebrates can withstand the full force of the desert Sun. Those that can have an especially tough, waxy covering, or cuticle, that prevents them from drying out. Other invertebrates take shelter during the day.

*White spots warn off predators.*

### Domino beetle
This domino beetle lives in the dry lands of northern Africa through to the Middle East. During the day, it hides under rocks and in holes made by other animals. At night, it emerges to hunt insects and other small prey.

### Scorpion
Scorpions are among the hardiest of desert invertebrates, able to tolerate strong sunshine though they normally hunt at night. Armed with strong claws and a lethal sting, they ambush foraging insects such as locusts, as well as spiders and other scorpions.

*The venom of this scorpion is strong enough to kill a person.*

*The scorpion holds its prey in its large claws.*

# Plants

Only the hardiest of drought-resistant plants can survive all year in the desert. Among these are cacti and yuccas. Seeds of more fragile plants lie dormant in the soil. After rain, they sprout and flower before the moisture evaporates.

### Desert holly
Some desert plants, such as the desert holly, have dusty-looking leaves. Salt secreted through leaf pores forms a fine whitish powder that reflects some of the sun's rays. The leaves stay cool, preventing excessive evaporation of moisture.

### Cacti
Many different kinds of cacti grow in American deserts. All store water in their green swollen stems. They do not have leaves, and this prevents excess moisture loss. Sharp spines deter animals from biting the succulent stems.

*Seeds develop after the vine's flower has been pollinated by insects.*

*A welwitschia plant may live for 1,000 years or more.*

### Welwitschia
This plant has two ribbonlike leaves that trail across the sand. Each leaf has millions of pores that extract moisture from the sea fogs that sweep the Namib Desert in Africa.

### Little snapdragon vine
Rains in the Mexican desert bring the seeds of snapdragon vines to life. The vines quickly grow, trailing over the soil and curling around other plants. They flower and set new seed before they die as the conditions get dry again.

*Each leaf grows up to 6.5 ft (2 m) long.*

*Leaves usually split into several strips.*

FIND OUT MORE   AFRICAN WILDLIFE   AMPHIBIANS   ASIAN WILDLIFE   BIRDS   BIRDS OF PREY   DESERTS   INSECTS   MAMMALS   PLANTS   REPTILES

# DESIGN

ORIGINALLY A DESIGN was an artist's first sketch for a work of art; but today design plays a broader role in our lives. Before any object can be made, it must be designed. Most things around us have been designed to carry out a particular job. The design of objects is known as product design; other areas of design include fashion, garden, housing interiors, and computer graphics. Changing tastes can result in popular design movements, such as art nouveau and Bauhaus.

## The design process

The first stage in the design process is writing a description that outlines the functions and features of the finished object. The designer then does a first sketch. This sketch is transformed into a rough model, or prototype, which is repeatedly tested and revised as needed. The design process of making numerous small changes is called an iterative process. Finally, the actual product is made.

1 The designer does a first sketch on a drawing board or computer. This sketch shows a vacuum cleaner.

## Product design

In order to design an object, the designer has several factors to consider. He or she must create a shape that suits the object's purpose, but also consider other factors, such as the material to be used, the cost of manufacturing the product, the safety and durability of the product, and how it will finally look. Product design usually aims to be both functional and stylish.

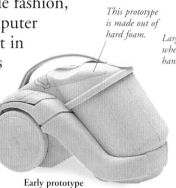

*This prototype is made out of hard foam.*

**Early prototype**

2 A series of prototypes is made out of different materials to test the design. The final prototype is handmade and painted to look like the final product.

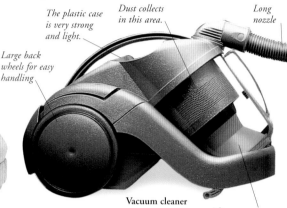

*The plastic case is very strong and light.*

*Dust collects in this area.*

*Long nozzle*

*Large back wheels for easy handling*

**Vacuum cleaner**

3 The final product is made to the revised design sketch. Designs can be patented (protected by copyright law) to prevent someone copying an original design.

*This vacuum cleaner uses a unique suction system to pick up dirt.*

*This bottle's shape is easily recognizable.*

*A can's tab opening is designed to open easily.*

**Classic design**
Some product designs so successfully combine functionality with a strong sense of style that they are timeless. The distinctive shape of the Coca-Cola® bottle, for example, is a classic design that has hardly changed since 1915.

**Coca-Cola® bottle**

*Headlights and bumpers are chrome.*

*Large steering wheel*

*The MGB is compact but stylish.*

**MGB Tourer**

**Classic cars**
Some classic designs express certain ideals perfectly. The sleek lines of a sports car's body, such as this MGB, are intended to suggest speed and freedom. Launched in 1962, the MGB became the best-selling single model sports car ever, with 512,000 owners worldwide.

## Graphic design

Graphic designers use words and images to communicate a strong visual message. We are surrounded by graphic design, in magazines and books, on posters, on street signs. Designers use letters in different sizes and typefaces, often with colors and patterns, to make an impact.

**London Underground map**
The London Underground map is a good example of design. By distorting the distances between stations, it is possible to see the entire London Underground at a glance.

**Shell Oil logo**

**Logos**
Logos are graphic designs that aim to communicate a message without words. Companies design logos to be easily recognized by the public. The simple shape and strong colors of the logo shown above advertise the Shell Oil Company worldwide.

**Computer-aided design**
Increasingly, much of the design process is carried out on computer. Using computer-aided design, the designer creates a three-dimensional model, such as a car, on screen, which can then be rotated and viewed from all angles.

**Walter Gropius**
In 1919, the German architect Walter Gropius (1883–1969) founded the Bauhaus design school. It taught the importance of functional design and of using materials such as steel, glass, and concrete. Bauhaus influenced the development of the arts. Gropius (on right) is shown with the French architect Le Corbusier (1887–1965).

**Art nouveau**
Design movements are trends in design, some of which have a lasting influence. Art nouveau was a design movement beginning in Europe in the 1880s that aimed to make ordinary objects, such as buildings, furniture, and jewelry, beautiful.

*This art nouveau window in Paris, France, shows typical decorative curves based on organic forms.*

**FIND OUT MORE** ARCHITECTURE · ART, HISTORY OF · BUILDING AND CONSTRUCTION · CARS AND TRUCKS · CLOTHES AND FASHION · FURNITURE · GARDENS · PAINTING AND DRAWING · PRINTING · TRADE AND INDUSTRY

# DICKENS, CHARLES

CHARLES DICKENS IS one of the greatest writers in the English language. He was a household name in his own lifetime. His lively descriptions of 19th-century Britain combine with a superb gift for depicting people and their eccentricities, a social conscience, and compassion for the problems faced by ordinary people. He brought to the English novel the ability to portray an entire society in one book. His novels are still loved by readers of all ages.

### Early life
Charles Dickens was born in Portsmouth, England, in 1812. His father was a clerk in the Royal Navy pay office and worked for a time in the royal dockyards in Chatham, Kent, where Charles spent much of his childhood. When his father was imprisoned for debt in London's Marshalsea Prison, Charles, then aged 12, had to take a series of menial jobs in factories and offices. He later used these painful experiences in some of his novels.

## "Boz"

Scrooge meets the Ghost of Christmas Past

As a young man, Dickens was a journalist, covering Parliament for the *Morning Chronicle.* In 1833, he began to write a series of articles, mostly about London life, using the pseudonym "Boz." These were collected and successfully published as *Sketches by Boz* in 1836. Dickens was then commissioned to write some humorous short stories. These appeared in 1836–37 as *The Posthumous Papers of the Pickwick Club* and made Dickens the most famous writer of his day.

*David Copperfield*

### David Copperfield
In 1849–50, Dickens wrote *David Copperfield*, a partly autobiographical novel in which he used his own experiences of an impoverished childhood and menial employment to great effect. Of all his books, it was Dickens' favorite. The novel features Mr. Micawber, who is loosely based on Dickens' father. Always in debt and waiting for "something to turn up," Micawber is one of the great characters of English literature.

### Household Words
From 1850, Dickens edited and contributed first to the magazine *Household Words*, and then, from 1859, to *All The Year Round*. He used these monthly magazines to publish his latest novel in installments, reaching a far wider readership than he would have done by simply publishing a book. Both magazines featured works by other famous writers of the time, such as Elizabeth Gaskell and Wilkie Collins. Dickens also included articles about social problems, such as substandard housing and factory accidents.

### A Christmas Carol
Ebenezer Scrooge, who refused to celebrate Christmas, and his impoverished clerk, Bob Cratchit make, *A Christmas Carol* (published in 1843) one of Dickens's most popular novels. Scrooge changes his ways when he witnesses a series of visions, including his own death and the ghosts of Christmas Past, Present, and Future.

**In a scene from *Oliver Twist*, Oliver asks for more porridge.**

### Oliver Twist
The story of Oliver tells of a pauper child of unknown parentage who was brought up in a poorhouse and dared to ask for more food. *Oliver Twist* was first published as a book in 1838. The book was later made into a successful musical and film. The story was the first by Dickens to explore the dark side of London life in the 19th century, and the fact that thousands of children were living on the streets or in inhuman poorhouses.

## Dickensian London

In Dickens's time, London was a rich city at the center of the biggest empire the world had ever seen. But many people lived in poverty, making a living from whatever work they could find. Dickens described their suffering, but he loved London – its sights, sounds, and atmosphere pervade his books.

### Social reforms
Dickens often spoke in public about the plight of the poor, the need for educational reform, and the importance of good sanitation to remove the threat of disease. His speeches and novels helped raise awareness of the need for radical reforms, and led to many changes in the law.

**London street, 19th century**

### Public readings
Dickens went on three tours of Britain and one of America, reading selections from his novels. He poured a huge amount of energy into these readings, adapting his works specially for public performance and reading all the parts himself. In 1869, he set out on a fourth British tour, but his health began to fail, and he died the following year.

### CHARLES DICKENS

| | |
|---|---|
| 1812 | Born in Portsmouth, England. |
| 1824 | Father imprisoned for debt. |
| 1836 | Marries Catherine Hogarth; publishes *Sketches by Boz.* |
| 1836–37 | *Pickwick Papers* |
| 1838 | *Oliver Twist* |
| 1839 | *Nicholas Nickleby* |
| 1850 | *David Copperfield* |
| 1853 | *Bleak House* |
| 1857 | *Little Dorrit* |
| 1858 | First reading tour |
| 1859 | *A Tale of Two Cities* |
| 1861 | *Great Expectations* |
| 1864 | *Our Mutual Friend* |
| 1870 | Dies and is buried in Westminster Abbey. |

**FIND OUT MORE**   BOOKS   EMPIRES   INDUSTRIAL REVOLUTION   LITERATURE   UNITED KINGDOM, HISTORY OF   WRITING

# DIGESTION

**D**

THE BODY NEEDS THE nutrients in food to grow, maintain its structure, and provide energy. But the food we eat cannot be used by the body until it is processed by the digestive system, essentially a long tube running from the mouth to the anus. As food passes along the digestive system, it is chewed and crushed, and then broken down chemically by enzymes. As it passes through the small intestine, food resembles a thin soup, and simple food molecules can be absorbed into the body itself through the bloodstream.

## Swallowing

Once food is chewed, the tongue pushes the ball of food, or bolus, to the back of the mouth. As it touches the throat, the bolus triggers a reflex action and passes into the esophagus. A flap called the epiglottis closes the entrance to the trachea (windpipe) to stop food from entering the lungs.

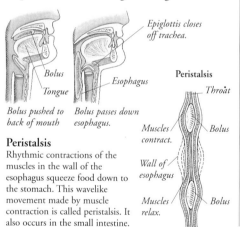

*Epiglottis closes off trachea.*

*Bolus*

*Tongue*

*Esophagus*

*Bolus pushed to back of mouth*

*Bolus passes down esophagus.*

**Peristalsis**

*Throat*

*Muscles contract.*

*Bolus*

*Wall of esophagus*

*Muscles relax.*

*Bolus*

**Peristalsis**

Rhythmic contractions of the muscles in the wall of the esophagus squeeze food down to the stomach. This wavelike movement made by muscle contraction is called peristalsis. It also occurs in the small intestine.

## Digestive process

The digestive process has four stages: ingestion, digestion, absorption, and egestion. Ingestion happens when you eat food and is followed by digestion. Absorption is the transfer of food molecules into the bloodstream, and egestion is the removal of waste as feces.

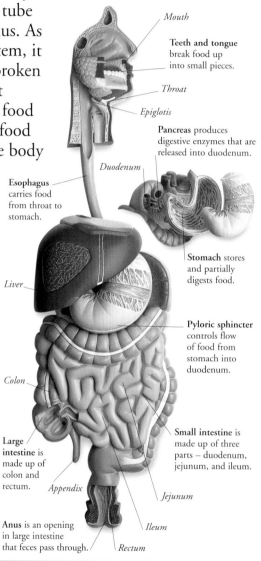

*Mouth*

**Teeth and tongue** break food up into small pieces.

*Throat*

*Epiglottis*

**Pancreas** produces digestive enzymes that are released into duodenum.

*Duodenum*

**Esophagus** carries food from throat to stomach.

*Liver*

**Stomach** stores and partially digests food.

**Pyloric sphincter** controls flow of food from stomach into duodenum.

*Colon*

**Large intestine** is made up of colon and rectum.

*Appendix*

**Small intestine** is made up of three parts – duodenum, jejunum, and ileum.

*Jejunum*

**Anus** is an opening in large intestine that feces pass through.

*Ileum*

*Rectum*

## Liver, pancreas, and gall bladder

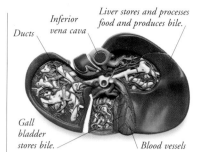

*Inferior vena cava*

*Ducts*

*Liver stores and processes food and produces bile.*

*Gall bladder stores bile.*

*Blood vessels*

These three organs take part in digestion even though, since they have other body functions, they are not part of the digestive system. The liver produces bile, which is stored in the gall bladder and helps digest fats. The pancreas produces digestive enzymes that are released into the small intestine.

## Absorption

Simple food molecules are absorbed into the bloodstream across the wall of the small intestine. Tiny fingerlike projections called villi (singular: villus) greatly increase the surface area over which food can be absorbed.

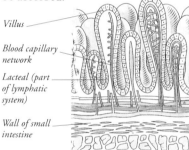

*Villus*

*Blood capillary network*

*Lacteal (part of lymphatic system)*

*Wall of small intestine*

## Imaging the intestine

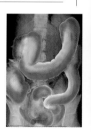

A special liquid is introduced into the large intestine to show clearly its position and internal shape. This type of X ray enables doctors to detect signs of disease inside the large intestine without having to operate.

## William Beaumont

The US Army surgeon William Beaumont (1785–1853) was the first to observe how food was digested in the stomach. In 1822, Beaumont treated a patient who had shot himself in the side and was left with an opening into his stomach. Through this opening, Beaumont was able to observe the stomach's movements during digestion and to record his findings.

## Food and enzymes

Enzymes are biological catalysts that speed up the conversion of one substance into another. Digestive enzymes speed up the breakdown of the complex carbohydrates, fats, and proteins that make up most of our food.

**Carbohydrates**

The body's main fuel, carbohydrate, comes in the form of sugars and complex carbohydrates, which include starch. Enzymes break starchy foods down into sugars such as glucose.

*Glucose molecules*

*Starch molecule chain*

*Fat droplets*

**Fats**

Fats provide the body with energy. Foods rich in fats include eggs and meat. Fats are broken down by enzymes in the small intestine to form fatty acids.

*Fatty acids*

*Protein*

**Proteins**

Proteins are needed for growth and maintaining the body. Protein-rich foods are meat, fish, and nuts. Proteins are broken down into amino acids.

*Amino acids*

FIND OUT MORE

CHEMISTRY   FOOD   HORMONES AND ENDOCRINE SYSTEM   HUMAN BODY   IMMUNE AND LYMPHATIC SYSTEM   TEETH AND JAWS

# DINOSAURS

FOR 150 MILLION YEARS, from the Triassic Period until the end of the Cretaceous Period, 65 million years ago, dinosaurs lived on Earth. Their remains have been discovered on every continent, including Antarctica. They formed a varied group of land-living reptiles. People who study prehistoric life, called paleontologists, divide them into two main groups – the Ornithischia and the Saurischia. There were meat eating and plant eating dinosaurs. Some dinosaurs, were huge; others were only the size of chickens.

Iguanodon skull

### Iguanodon skull
Gideon Mantell, an English doctor, named *Iguanodon* in 1825, noting the similarity between its teeth and those of the modern iguana. *Iguanodon*'s teeth were shaped to fit tightly together. They wore down as the dinosaur chewed its food of tough vegetation with the help of a hinged jaw.

D

Iguanodon tooth

### Iguanodon
This was one of the first dinosaurs to be discovered. Modern reconstructions give it an outstretched tail and forelimbs that can reach the ground.

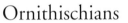

Iguanodon

Iguanodon foot

## Ornithischians
The Ornithischia, or bird-hipped dinosaurs, such as *Iguanodon*, were all herbivorous. They had a huge number of teeth – *Corythosaurus* had 2,000 – and a hinged upper jaw that allowed them to chew.

### Iguanodon foot
The feet of *Iguanodon* had small hooves on the toes instead of claws, and would have made recognizable three-toed prints with rounded digits. *Iguanodon* probably walked on its toes, which must have been strong to carry the animal's great weight.

*Tyrannosaurus*

## Saurischians
The Saurischia, or lizard-hipped dinosaurs, include the meat eating theropods, such as *Tyrannosaurus*, that walked on two toes, and the plant eating sauropods, such as *Diplodocus*, that walked on four legs. The sauropods were the largest ever land animals.

### Tyrannosaurus tooth
Carnivorous dinosaurs had curved, pointed teeth. The sharp edges often had serrations, which helped the dinosaurs to slice through skin and meat. Paleontologists still have to be careful when handling these teeth.

*Long, hollow tubular crest*

*Tail was used for balance.*

Pubis bone — Ischium bone

### Tyrannosaurus skeleton
*Tyrannosaurus* may have hunted as well as scavenged on other dinosaurs. It had a massive skull with powerful jaws, supported by a short, flexible neck. This flexibility allowed the animal to twist its head around to wrench flesh from its prey.

Ischium bone

Pubis bone

*Rounded, hooflike claws*

Skeleton of *Parasaurolophus*, an ornithischian

*Toothless jaws*

*Tyrannosaurus tore off the flesh of its prey with its teeth and claws.*

### Tyrannosaurus
Although not thought to be the largest of the carnivorous dinosaurs, *Tyrannosaurus* was still an extremely fearsome predator. It walked on its hind legs with its back level and head raised. It could run very fast, its tail balancing the weight of its huge, heavy body.

### Fossil dung
Preserved pieces of dung are called coprolites. They contain the remains of what dinosaurs ate, such as bone fragments, fish scales, or plant remains. Scientists can study these to find out about the diet of dinosaurs.

### Hips
Dinosaurs fall into one of the two main groups according to the structure of their hip bones. The bird-hipped dinosaurs (ornithischians), such as *Parasaurolophus*, had a pubis bone in their hip girdle that sloped backward, parallel to the ischium bone. The lizard-hipped dinosaurs (saurischians), such as *Gallimimus*, had a pubis bone that sloped forward away from the ischium.

Pubis bone

*Long foot bones suggests Gallimimus could run fast.*

Skeleton of *Gallimimus*, a saurischian

D

Orodromeus *laid up to 24 eggs.*

*Orodromeus* nest

**The first dinosaurs**
One of the earliest dinosaurs was *Eoraptor*, meaning "early plunderer." It was no bigger than a large dog and lived 225 million years ago (mya). As with all the early dinosaurs, it was a carnivore and walked on two legs.

*Eoraptor* skull

# Breeding

Dinosaurs laid hard-shelled eggs as some reptiles do today. Many dinosaurs laid a clutch of eggs in a hollowed-out nest in the ground. Several fossilized nests have been found close together, which suggests that some dinosaurs nested in colonies. The chicks developed rapidly and may have left the nest soon after hatching. Many were cared for by the parent dinosaur until they were able to look after themselves.

## Richard Owen

Born in Lancaster, England, Richard Owen (1804–92) became the Hunterian Professor of the Royal College of Surgeons in 1836. In addition to being an anatomist, he was a paleontologist. He was the first to use the term "dinosaurs," which means "terrible lizards," in a report in 1842. He noted that these animals had pillarlike legs, rather than the sprawling legs of modern reptiles, and should be classified separately.

# Defense

Dinosaurs protected themselves against attack from predators. Different dinosaurs developed a variety of powerful defenses. For example, *Triceratops* had horns on its head, *Euoplocephalus* had a tail club, and *Tuojiangosaurus* had a spiky tail. Some of these adaptations may have had several functions, but one of them was likely to have been defense. Scientists cannot say exactly how these animals defended themselves, but it is easy to imagine.

*Euoplocephalus had thick bone plates and spikes over its back, with a large shoulder spike for added protection.*

**Reconstruction of *Iguanodon* hand**

## Tuojiangosaurus
The flanks and belly of *Tuojiangosaurus* were vulnerable to attack. Near the tip of its tail were four bony spikes. These pointed up and out, producing a formidable defense when the dinosaur swung its tail. This animal was a type of bird-hipped dinosaur called a stegosaur. It lived in China 157-145 mya.

*Tuojiangosaurus*

*Defensive spikes*

*All stegosaurs had a double row of plates running down their back.*

*Small, narrow head with a walnut-sized brain*

*Short front limbs*

*Thumb spike*

*Raised nodules for protection*

## Iguanodon spike
When *Iguanodon* was first reconstructed, its large spike was placed on its beak. It is now known that the spike was on its thumb and may have been used as a defensive weapon against predators. The spike could have pierced the belly, throat, or eye of an attacker. The dinosaur may also have used it in fights for status with other *Iguanodons,* and even to help it feed.

## Dinosaur skin
Occasionally, the skin or skin impression of dinosaurs is preserved. From these fossils we can tell that the skin of many dinosaurs was not smooth, but nodular and rough to give some protection against the claws and teeth of predators. This is the skin of *Polacanthus.*

*Euoplocephalus*

*Club was made out of several bones fused together.*

## Euoplocephalus
This armored ornithischian had a large, bony club at the tip of its muscular tail. It could have swung this with great force, disabling a predator.

*Claw*

*Brow horn*

*Frill anchored the jaw muscles.*

*Nose horn*

## Triceratops
The ceratopsians, or horned dinosaurs, were ornithischians. Most of them had brow horns and nose horns. *Triceratops,* the largest ceratopsian, had two long horns on its brow, a short nose horn, and also a bony neck frill protecting its neck. Its head was nearly one-third of its length. It probably used its horns to fend off predators, and males used them to deter rivals in the herd, mostly by display, but also by fighting.

*Triceratops* skull – side view

*Triceratops* skull – front view

## Dinosaur discoveries
Removing dinosaur fossils from surrounding rock is tricky. Some need to be protected in a jacket made of plaster or polyurethane foam before they are taken to a laboratory. Fossils are found every year, and each discovery teaches us more about these extinct animals.

**Finding dinosaur bones**

| FIND OUT MORE | ANIMALS | ANIMAL BEHAVIOR | EVOLUTION | FOSSILS | PREHISTORIC LIFE | REPTILES | SKELETON |

# Dinosaurs
## Ornithischians

*Six long spikes*

**Iguanodon** could walk on two or four legs.

**Styracosaurus** was a short-frilled ceratopsian.

**Heterodontosaurus** was one of the first bird-hipped dinosaurs. It lived about 205 mya.

**Corythosaurus** had a tall crest on its head.

*Scelidosaurus* was the oldest-known armored dinosaur.

*Spiky tail for defense*

*Long thigh compared to the rest of the leg*

*Swinging tail club*

*Body built for speed*

**Hypsilophodon** was once thought to have lived in trees, but its limbs were not built for climbing.

**Stegoceras** was a pachycephalosaur, and had a thick-domed skull.

**Stegosaurus** was the largest stegosaur at 30 ft (9 m) long. It had large plates along its back.

**Euoplocephalus** had body armor and a tail club to protect it against attack.

## Saurischians

*Stiff tail helped with balance.*

**Deinonychus** was a meat eater and may have hunted in packs.

**Gallimimus** was shaped like an ostrich and was one of the fastest running dinosaurs.

*Toothless beak*

**Dilophosaurus** had two high crests on top of its large head.

*Flat, crocodile-like jaws*

*Tail was used for balance and speed.*

*Long neck enabled Barosaurus to reach leaves at the top of trees.*

*Ankle joint*

*Long, clawed fingers*

*Hands could be used to grasp food.*

*Long foot bones increased the length of the leg.*

**Baryonyx** had a huge 12-in (31-cm)-long claw on each hand.

*Whiplash tail used in defense.*

**Anchisaurus** may have eaten both meat and plants.

*Daggerlike teeth*

*Body like Archaeopteryx, the first bird*

*Two-clawed fingers on each hand*

*Large hind legs were needed to bear the weight of the body.*

*Small arms with two-fingered hands*

**Compsognathus** was small – only 2.5 ft (74 cm) long.

**Herrerasaurus** was a carnivore that lived in Argentina 228 mya.

**Barosaurus** resembled *Diplodocus*. It was about the same size with a shorter tail and longer neck.

**Tyrannosaurus** was one of the largest known land-living carnivores, weighing up to 6.6 tons.

# DISEASES

JUST LIKE A MACHINE, the human body works smoothly and efficiently most of the time, but sometimes it breaks down. The body may receive an injury, such as a broken bone, or it may develop a disease. Diseases occur because the body has been infected by a pathogen (germ), as in the case of influenza or food poisoning, or because of problems arising inside the body, such as heart disease or diabetes. Some diseases can be controlled and cured by the body's immune system. More serious diseases may require drug treatment or surgery to aid the body in fighting illness.

*Epidemiologist tests samples in laboratory.*

### Epidemiology
Epidemiology is the study of diseases as they affect groups of people. Epidemiologists are concerned with why diseases occur in a population, and their control and prevention. They have discovered links between disease and diet, environmental factors, and lifestyle. Epidemiologists first discovered the link between smoking and lung cancer.

## Noninfectious diseases
If a disease is noninfectious, it is not caused by a pathogen and cannot be passed from one person to another. Noninfectious diseases include circulatory system diseases, such as heart attacks, strokes, and cancer, and respiratory diseases, such as bronchitis and emphysema.

### Nutritional diseases
Nutritional diseases are caused by a lack of a balanced diet, causing a deficiency of vitamins and minerals. A child not getting enough vitamin D may suffer from rickets, where the skeleton does not form properly.

*Rickets may leave sufferer bowlegged.*

**Miners may develop lung problems.**

## Infectious diseases
Infectious diseases are those, such as the common cold or pneumonia, caused by pathogens that invade the body. Common pathogens are bacteria and viruses, although some diseases, such as yeast infections, are caused by fungi, and some, such as malaria, by tiny organisms called protists. They are normally destroyed by the body's immune system. Those that are not can often be destroyed by drug therapy.

**Bacteria are in water, air, and soil, as well as many plant and animal tissues.**

### Bacteria
Bacteria are single-celled microorganisms. Most bacteria are not harmful to humans. However, some multiply inside the body and produce toxins that cause disease. Bacterial diseases include typhoid and scarlet fever. Most can be treated with drugs called antibiotics.

*Chicken pox causes an itchy rash that, when scratched, can leave scars.*

### Viruses
Viruses are tiny infective particles, not usually classed as living things. They take over a body cell's genetic material (DNA) and make copies of themselves that infect other cells. Human viral infections include colds, measles, and HIV.

### Industrial diseases
Work situations may affect a person's health. Industrial processes can create harmful environments or use chemicals that cause diseases. Some miners develop a lung disease called pneumoconiosis.

## Spreading infection
Most diseases are acquired from other people by skin-to-skin contact, breathing in droplets when someone sneezes or coughs, or by sexual contact without the use of condoms. Infection can also be spread through infected food, contaminated water, and insect bites. Drug users who share needles risk infections of the blood, such as hepatitis and HIV.

### Sanitation
Human feces contain bacteria and viruses that cause disease. If there is poor sanitation and human waste is discharged into rivers, people may catch diseases such as dysentery or cholera through contact with polluted water.

### HIV and AIDS
The human immunodeficiency virus, or HIV, causes AIDS (Acquired Immune Deficiency Syndrome). HIV infects and destroys the cells that form part of the body's immune system – the body's defenses against diseases. HIV is transmitted by some bodily fluids, such as blood and semen. The system becomes progressively weaker, and the person becomes infected with various diseases, known collectively as AIDS.

*HIV*

*Some mosquitoes carry strains of malaria that are resistant to drugs.*

### Insects
Insects such as mosquitoes and fleas feed on human blood and can carry disease. A mosquito transmits the malaria microorganism if it feeds on an infected person's blood.

**Keeping rivers clean** prevents diseases that can be caught if people drink, wash, or grow food in the water.

### Preventing disease
Disease prevention is an important part of modern medicine. Diseases can be prevented by better sanitation, immunization, and improving food hygiene. Eating a balanced diet and exercising may also prevent disease.

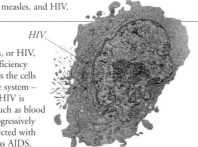

**Syringes** that are not properly sterilized after use can spread disease.

**Pills** contain measured amounts of drugs.

**Bottled water** assures that water is safe in certain countries.

**FIND OUT MORE**

BLACK DEATH    CELLS    CURIE, MARIE    DRUGS    HUMAN BODY    IMMUNE AND LYMPHATIC SYSTEM    PASTEUR, LOUIS

# DISNEY, WALT

IN 1901, A MAN WAS BORN who would change the face of entertainment. Walt Disney became interested in animation as a schoolboy; by the time he was 20 he was making short animated films. But it was his later work that changed the history of the movies. He created a string of cartoon characters that have been favorites ever since – Donald Duck, Goofy, and, above all, Mickey Mouse. Walt Disney also made the first feature-length animated film, *Snow White and the Seven Dwarfs* (1937), which was followed by many other screen successes.

## Early life

In 1906, Disney's father, Elias, bought a farm in Marceline, Missouri. This was where young Walt first saw animals. He also became interested in drawing. The first drawing he ever sold was of the local doctor's stallion, for which the doctor paid Disney a nickel.

### Early animation

Disney began to make animated films in 1920. These films featured characters which were made by cutting figures out of paper. The figures could be moved while they were photographed with a hand-cranked camera.

*Disney with a hand-cranked camera*

## Hollywood

Disney moved to Hollywood in 1923. There were no animation studios, so he set up his own. He was soon in the forefront of technical innovation, pioneering the use of synchronized sound and the three-color Technicolor process.

### Mickey Mouse

*Steamboat Willie,* the first cartoon to feature Mickey Mouse, appeared in 1928. This was also the first cartoon with sound. Disney himself supplied Mickey's voice, and the film was an instant success. Mickey has since appeared in many other films. He has become the instantly recognizable Disney symbol and has appeared on countless Disney merchandise products.

**Walt Disney with Mickey Mouse and Donald Duck**

Snow White with the seven dwarfs

### Snow White

In the 1920s, cartoons were usually shown before a full-length live-action film. But in 1935, Disney had the idea of producing a full-length cartoon, *Snow White and the Seven Dwarfs* (1937). Hundreds of animators worked on the film, which was followed by many other full-length animated features.

### Mary Poppins

From the 1950s onward, Disney produced many live-action films. Some of these, such as the musical fantasy *Mary Poppins* (1964), also included animated sequences.

Julie Andrews in a scene from *Mary Poppins*

## The Mickey Mouse Club

Disney was the first major US studio to create locally produced children's programming such as The Mickey Mouse Club, and is the only studio to maintain a worldwide network of production offices. This network produces more than 40 weekly Disney programs that reach more than 300 million viewers.

Mickey Mouse Club logo

## Disneyland

For many years, Walt Disney wanted to re-create the sets and characters of his films in a recreational park. The result, Disneyland, opened in 1955 in Anaheim, near Los Angeles, California. This theme park is one of the world's most popular attractions. Other parks have since opened: Walt Disney World in Florida and Disneyland ® Paris.

Disneyland

## WALT DISNEY

| | |
|---|---|
| 1901 | Born in Chicago, US. |
| 1919 | Begins to make animated films. |
| 1923 | Moves to Hollywood. |
| 1928 | *Steamboat Willie,* featuring Mickey Mouse. |
| 1937 | *Snow White and the Seven Dwarfs,* the first feature-length animated film. |
| 1940 | *Pinocchio.* |
| 1940 | *Fantasia.* |
| 1942 | *Bambi.* |
| 1955 | Disneyland opens. |
| 1964 | *Mary Poppins.* |
| 1966 | Walt Disney dies. |

FIND OUT MORE    CARTOONS AND ANIMATION    FILMS AND FILMMAKING    TELEVISION

# DOGS

DOGS HAVE LIVED with people for more than 12,000 years. They may have started to stay near humans for food and warmth. Then people began to train dogs to work for them. They bred certain types of dog for herding and guarding other domestic animals, then for hunting and for companionship. Gradually, different types of dog developed, but it was not until the end of the 19th century that specific breeds were classified. Today, there are about 200 dog breeds throughout the world. They are more varied in their appearance and behavior than any other domestic animal.

Siberian husky

English setter

Shetland sheepdogs

Chihuahua

Scottish terriers

Bloodhound

## Dog groups
The people of ancient Egypt and western Asia were the first to breed distinct types of dog for different purposes. By Roman times, dogs were kept for much the same reasons as they are today. There are six main groups – (from left to right) top row: working, sporting, herding; bottom row: companion, terriers, and hounds.

## Domestic dogs
All breeds of domestic dogs, from the great dane to the chihuahua, are descended from the wolf and have inherited the wolf's instincts. Like wolves, dogs are pack animals. They treat humans as part of their pack and can be trained to accept their owner as the pack leader and to follow his or her commands.

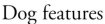

*Borzois have sharp eyesight and hunt by sight.*

*The borzoi was bred in Russia in the 13th century and used first to hunt wolves.*

*Long, strong legs and a flexible body for speed*

## Dog features

The wolf is designed to chase, capture, kill, and eat its prey. It is agile, with strong legs for running long distances. Domestic dogs retain many of the features of a wolf, but through selective breeding now exist in many shapes, sizes, and colors.

### Coats
There are three main types of dog coats – long, short, and wiry. Most breeds have an outer coat of guard hairs and an undercoat of shorter hairs. They molt, or shed their fur, changing their coat in spring and fall.

### Feet
Dogs walk on their toes rather than the soles of their feet. Their paw pads help with grip, as do their claws, which do not retract.

Shorthair    Longhair    Wirehair

### Senses
Dogs have highly developed senses of hearing and smell. They use these to communicate and to track down their prey. The police use dogs to sniff out explosives, criminals, and drugs. The dogs can see well in the dark and are good at seeing movement in the distance.

*Beagles were bred to hunt hares.*

## Reproduction

A female dog is pregnant for about nine weeks, then gives birth to several puppies known as a litter. At birth, puppies are blind and deaf. Their eyes open after about 10-12 days and they are able to hear after 13-17 days. Teeth start to grow between three and five weeks of age.

*A young puppy is defenseless.*

*All puppies are born with short legs and a little tail.*

*Eyes are fully open.*

1 After one week, a puppy spends most of its time sleeping and feeding by suckling from its mother.

2 After two weeks, the puppy takes its first wobbling steps and begins to explore. Its eyes are now open and it can hear.

3 After three weeks, the puppy may start to eat solid food. At first, its mother will regurgitate meat for it.

4 After six weeks, the puppy no longer feeds from its mother. It can soon be taken away from her to a new home.

**FIND OUT MORE**    ANIMALS    ANIMALS, BEHAVIOR    CATS    GRASSLAND WILDLIFE    MAMMALS    POLICE    WOLVES AND WILD DOGS

# Dogs

## Working dogs

**Great Dane** makes an excellent family pet.

**Mastiff** existed in Britain in ancient Roman times.

**Boxer** is a lively and affectionate dog.

**German shepherd dog** is intelligent and enthusiastic.

**Dalmatian**, used to deter highwaymen in the 1800s.

**St Bernard** exists in wire- and smooth-haired forms.

## Companion dogs

*"Papillon" refers to the shape of the ears.*

*Large head*

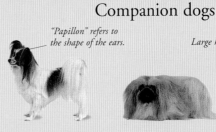

**Papillon** is named after the French for "butterfly."

**Pekingese** has a flattened face, with a broad nose.

**Bulldog** is a strong but affectionate dog.

*Thick, harsh-textured coat*

**Miniature poodle**, world's most popular dog in the 1950s.

**Cavalier King Charles spaniel**, bred in 1900s.

**Pug** has a soft coat and a curled tail.

## Terriers

*Up to 24 in (60 cm) tall*

*Coat comes in a variety of colours.*

**Airedale terrier** is the largest terrier breed.

**Border terrier** was first bred for hunting rats.

**Staffordshire bull terrier** is loyal and devoted.

*Tail carried upright*

**Boston terrier** originated in Boston, Mass., in the 1800s.

**Smooth fox terrier** is alert and tireless.

**Parson Jack Russell terrier** has a mostly white coat.

*Long body for its height*

**Yorkshire terrier** is a small but spirited guard dog.

**Cairn terrier** has a shaggy, water-resistant coat.

**Australian terrier** is capable of tackling a snake.

## Hounds

*Slightly curved tail*

*Long body and short legs*

*Strong back*

**Basset hound** is an agile and single-minded hunter.

**Dachshunds** can be long-, smooth-, or wire-haired.

**Whippet** was bred in the 1800s for racing.

*Muscular neck*

**Rhodesian ridgeback** has a ridge of hair on its back.

**Afghan hound** needs plenty of exercise.

**Greyhound** is built for speed.

*Powerful hindquarters*

*28–35 in (71–90 cm) tall*

**Lurcher**: individuals vary considerably within the breed

**Saluki**, fast and agile, was once used to hunt gazelles.

**Irish wolfhound** is the tallest dog in the world.

## Herding dogs

*Deep muscular chest*

*Hair falls over the eyes.*

**Australian cattle dog** has great stamina.

**Border collie** is an outstanding sheepdog

**Old English sheepdog** has a thick, shaggy coat.

## Sporting dogs

*Obvious stop on the muzzle*

*Water-resistant coat*

**Pointer** is agile, athletic, and needs much exercise.

**English springer spaniel** is one of the largest spaniels.

**Curly-coated retriever** is one of the oldest breeds.

271

# DRAMA

DRAMA HAS BEEN DELIGHTING people for at least 2,500 years. A Broadway musical, a play by Shakespeare, and a television soap opera are different forms of drama. What they have in common is the presence of actors, who perform a story (the play) in a theatrical setting to entertain an audience and make them think. Dramatists (writers of drama) use their art to entertain and thrill their audiences or, more seriously, to explore human character and raise questions about the nature and meaning of life.

## Renaissance and 17th century

The traditions of ancient Greek drama were revived in Renaissance Italy and spread through Europe. Many plays were written in verse. Drama thrived in the 16th and 17th centuries, the age of English playwright William Shakespeare (1564–1616) and his contemporaries.

*Lope de Vega*

### France

The French dramatist Jean Racine (1639–99) wrote plays that were heavily influenced by Greek tragedy and often based on Greek mythology. Many featured women in title roles, an unusual practice then. Another great dramatist of the era, Molière (1622–73), developed French comedy with plays that mocked the middle classes.

*Phèdre (1677), by Racine*

### Spain

The 17th century was the Golden Age of Spanish theater. The Spanish dramatist Lope de Vega (1562–1635) wrote some 1,500 plays; his play *Fuenteovejuna* was one of the first to deal with ordinary working people. The other great Spanish dramatist of this time was Pedro Calderón de la Barca (1600–81), who produced many tragedies and historical plays.

## Early drama

Western drama originated in ancient Greece, where plays were staged to honor the gods. The Greeks invented two of the most enduring dramatic forms, tragedy and comedy, which were later imitated by the Romans.

### Classical Greek drama

The ancient Greeks held regular drama festivals, at which dramatists competed for prizes. Their tragedies were based on characters from Greek mythology. Their comedies ranged in style from uproarious satires to more realistic dramas.

*Statuette of muse, holding a mask from Greek comedy*

### Medieval drama

Western drama went into a decline at the end of the Roman Empire, but revived in the 10th century, with the rise of Christian religious drama. Amateur players produced plays enacting stories from the Bible, performed over a number of days. The audience watched outdoors in markets and other public spaces.

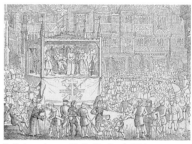
*Religious drama, York, England, 13th century*

## Realism and 20th century

From the mid-18th century onward, drama became increasingly realistic, with playwrights portraying middle-class characters in familiar situations. Theaters were fitted with picture-frame stages and realistic sets. It was fashionable for plays to deliver a direct moral message. During the 20th century, dramatists experimented with dialogue and plot structure that challenged "realism" or gave plays a symbolic meaning.

*A Doll's House (1879), by Ibsen*

### Realistic drama

Dramatists such as Norwegian Henrik Ibsen (1828–1906) and Swede August Strindberg (1849–1912) produced plays that attacked the narrow social attitudes of their time and sometimes shocked audiences with their frankness.

### Bertolt Brecht

In his plays, the German writer Bertolt Brecht (1898–1956) explored serious socialist messages. He constantly reminded his audience that they were watching a play to make them think about the socialist ideas in his works and look more closely at the world outside the theater.

## Types of drama

The many types of drama include tragedies (serious plays that deal with the downfall of a flawed but heroic individual) and lighthearted comedies (plays with happy endings). Other types include historical plays, thrillers, and musical theater.

*The stage is empty, except for a single tree.*

**Waiting for Godot** (1955), by Irish writer Samuel Beckett (1906–89), is a type of modern drama known as the "Theater of the Absurd": the plot seems to lead nowhere, suggesting life has no point.

*Mother Courage (1941), by Brecht, is set during the Thirty Years' War.*

*The heroes wait for someone who does not arrive.*

### Broadway

A street in New York at the heart of the city's theater district, "Broadway" is world renowned, and synonymous with the commercial theater in North America. Broadway productions need a big budget and guaranteed audiences, so more experimental plays often appear in theaters "off-Broadway" first, and transfer to a Broadway theater if successful.

# Broadcasting

Anyone with access to a television or radio can now enjoy drama every day. Sometimes these are productions of works originally written for the stage and adapted. More common are dramas specially written for broadcasting. Many of these are run as series, so that every week, or even every day, people can watch or listen to another episode of their favorite drama. Some forms of television drama have proved especially popular, such as crime stories, adventure series, and soap operas.

O Maraja, *satirical Brazilian soap opera*

**Soap operas**
Immensely popular, these serialized television dramas usually deal with the lives and loves of "ordinary" people. Soap operas are so-called because they were at first sponsored by commercial companies such as soap manufacturers.

# Actors

The skill of the actors is vital to the success of a drama. Using the right tone of voice, facial expression, or gesture, an actor creates the illusion that the audience is watching or listening to real people and events on stage or screen. Many actors study at drama schools before becoming professionals, paid to appear on stage.

**Chinese opera**
Traditional Chinese, or Beijing, opera retells stories from historical events and Buddhist stories. The action comprises arias and recitations, mime, song, and dance, with music from an orchestra of traditional instruments, such as the lute, clappers, gongs, and drums.

**Farewell My Concubine** is a film about Chinese opera.

**Noh theater**
In traditional Japanese Noh drama, actors wear elaborate costumes and masks, but perform on a bare stage. They move slowly and make special, meaningful gestures. They chant their lines, accompanied by music. Plays are performed in groups, the whole program lasting an entire day.

**Javanese shadow puppet**

In shadow plays, puppets are used to tell traditional stories.

*Made from leather*

*The operator uses thin rods to move the puppet.*

# World drama

Many non-Western cultures have produced their own distinct traditions of drama that draw on local customs and skills. In Asia, for example, drama draws on local mythology and tales of gods and goddesses. Such drama also uses local craftworkers to produce striking costumes and masks, and may be accompanied by music played on traditional instruments.

*Noh mask*

**Noh masks** represent five groups: male, female, old people, the gods, and monsters.

**Ritual drama**
In parts of Africa, Asia, and Melanesia, traditional drama forms an important part of religious ritual. A high priest or shaman puts on a mask and costume that completely disguises him and, as he dances to music, people believe that he actually becomes the spirit he is imitating.

**Papua New Guinea Trobrianders:** ritual religious drama

**Drama festivals**
Drama festivals are held around the world so that theater-goers can celebrate the best in acting and writing. Plays range from traditional productions to experimental works from new writers. The Edinburgh International Festival, held annually, is world famous.

*At a festival held each year in Salzburg, Austria, actors reenact a medieval religious drama.*

**Circuses**
A circus is a form of entertainment that combines a number of different skills, such as juggling, acrobatics, clowning, and magic. Circuses date from the end of the 18th century. Animal acts once formed part of circus routines, but these are now less popular in the West.

**Moscow State Circus**

# Puppetry

Puppetry is a type of drama that involves puppets, figures that seem to come to life when a human operator moves them. It is one of the oldest types of drama, dating from at least the 5th century BC. One example is shadow puppetry, popular in Southeast Asia. A light is used to cast a shadow from the puppet onto a translucent viewing screen. The puppet then acts out a play.

# Robert Lepage

The Canadian playwright and director Robert Lepage (b. 1957) has achieved world status for his experimental work. Giving everyday objects symbolic meaning, and working closely with actors, he has taken risks that, while not always a critical success, expand the boundaries of drama.

# Timeline

**5th century BC** The Greeks pioneer tragedy and comedy.

**11th to 15th centuries AD** Religious drama becomes popular in Europe.

**Statue of comic actor from Roman drama**

**1580–1642** In England, the Elizabethan and Jacobean dramatists revitalize English drama.

**1600–80** The Golden Age of Spanish drama.

**1782** Friedrich von Schiller (1759–1805) stages *The Robbers*, one of the plays that inspires the German Romantic movement in the 18th century.

**c.1800** In Vietnam, Hat Boi theater dramatizes tales of war and suffering.

**Late 1800s** "Realist" drama develops, exploring modern social issues.

**1960s** The "Theater of the Absurd" subverts the conventions of the theater.

**1990s** Musicals are the most popular type of plays.

FIND OUT MORE    FESTIVALS    FILMS AND FILMMAKING    GREECE, ANCIENT    LITERATURE    MEDIEVAL EUROPE    OPERA    RENAISSANCE    SHAKESPEARE    THEATERS

# DRUGS

A DRUG IS ANY SUBSTANCE that, when put into the body, alters its normal workings or body chemistry. Natural body hormones, such as insulin, can act as drugs when taken in concentrated form. Medical drugs have many uses. Some, such as cough suppressants, may relieve symptoms; others, such as analgesics, deaden pain; while others, including antibiotics, treat the cause of disease. Drugs may also be taken for nonmedical reasons, such as steroids to enhance sports performance and bodybuilding. The abuse of such drugs may be illegal, and can cause physical harm.

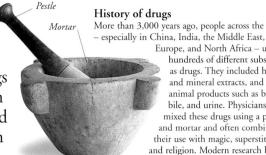

*Pestle*
*Mortar*

## History of drugs

More than 3,000 years ago, people across the world – especially in China, India, the Middle East, Europe, and North Africa – used hundreds of different substances as drugs. They included herbal and mineral extracts, and animal products such as blood, bile, and urine. Physicians mixed these drugs using a pestle and mortar and often combined their use with magic, superstition, and religion. Modern research has discovered that some are effective.

## Types of drugs

Drugs can be grouped by their medical uses or effects. For example, antibiotics kill bacteria, analgesics deaden pain, anti-inflammatories reduce swelling, antipyretics lower body temperature, and anticoagulants help prevent unwanted blood clots. Some drugs, such as aspirin, can be placed in more than one category.

## How drugs work

Drugs change the processes within the cells of the body. Their effectiveness depends on the dose (quantity) and method of administration (or route into the body). These routes include: absorption through the skin from a cream or a skin patch; injections into a muscle, vein, or under the skin; inhalation; eye- or eardrops; or the oral route, where medication is swallowed as tablets, pills, capsules, or liquid.

### Antibiotic

These drugs kill or disable germs (harmful microbes) known as bacteria. Most come from chemicals made either by fungi or by other bacteria.

**Antibiotic cream**

### Analgesic

Painkillers come in two types: narcotics, such as morphine, codeine, and other opiates originally from the opium poppy; and non-narcotics, such as paracetamol, which have a different origin.

### Cytotoxic

The name means "cell-poisoners," but cytotoxic drugs are designed to affect only the out-of-control cells in tumors and malignancies (cancers), while leaving normal body cells unharmed. They are one type of anticancer drug. They are very powerful and their doses and uses must be carefully supervised.

**Syringe containing cytotoxic drugs**     **Tablets and capsules**

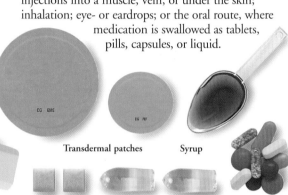

**Pressurized inhaler**

**Transdermal patches**     **Syrup**

**Chewing gum**     **Suppositories**     **Pills and tablets**

### Drugs from nature

Half of modern drugs originate from plants, fungi, animals, or microbes. In ancient times, people were unable to separate the actual drug – the active ingredient – from its source. As chemistry became more sophisticated, scientists identified and purified these ingredients, making the drug safer. Some drugs extracted originally from nature are now made from genetically engineered microbes.

*Fresh leaves*

**Witch hazel**     *Resin*   *Dried parts*

### Paul Ehrlich

The German scientist Paul Ehrlich (1854–1915) dreamed of finding a substance that would act as a "magic bullet," by destroying invading germs while leaving healthy body cells unaffected. He pioneered synthetic drugs (chemical agents made in the laboratory, rather than extracted from natural sources). The first of these was Salvarsan, a laboratory-made drug containing arsenic; it was effective against syphilis and related infections.

## Drug research

In the laboratory, scientists analyze potential new drugs. They perform tests on the drug to establish its chemistry, and how it affects the body's processes. Then they test it on tissues and cells in the laboratory, on animals, and finally on human volunteers in clinical trials.

**Drug research laboratory**

**Brand name** – the name by which manufacturers sell a drug, e.g. Bayer.

**Generic name** – the name by which the active ingredient is known, e.g. aspirin.

**Common chemical name** – showing the chemical subgroups, e.g. acetyl-salicylic acid.

**Chemical formula** – lists the atoms and their numbers in the drug, e.g. $C_9H_8O_4$.

**Aspirin**

# Pharmacies

The science of drugs is known as pharmacology. Pharmacy refers to both the practice of preparing and dispensing drugs, and the place where this happens. A person qualified in pharmacology is called a pharmacist. The dispensing pharmacist can advise which drugs to use for minor ailments.

Pharmacist at work

## Prescription

Some drugs, known as controlled substances, are only available with a doctor's permission. A prescription is a written and signed instruction from a doctor that authorizes a pharmacist to dispense a controlled substance. Prescriptions include the name and dosage of the drug, how often the patient must take it, and any other relevant instructions.

Hospital pharmacy

## Over-the-counter drugs

Over-the-counter drugs are available without a prescription. They can be bought at super-markets and pharmacies, and are usually less powerful than prescription drugs. They have fewer side effects or contra-indications (health problems that warn against their use), but they can still be misused. Pharmacists are qualified to recommend certain drug preparations, although they cannot diagnose or prescribe treatment.

D

# Nonmedical drugs

Some drugs can be taken for their non-medicinal effects on the mind and body. These effects may include the stimulation or sedation of the mind, a temporary boost to physical performance in sports, or a feeling of emotional well-being.

*Caffeine is found in coffee, tea, and soda.*

Wine and brandy

## Sedatives

These drugs sedate (slow down) bodily functions, including physical activity and mental agility. Sedatives can make the user feel relaxed and peaceful for a short time. They include sleeping pills, antihistamines (which suppress allergic reactions), antidepressants, and alcohol, which is probably the most widely used nonmedical drug in the world.

## Stimulants

Coffee

These drugs temporarily stimulate (speed up) bodily functions and mental processes. However, they can have side effects, such as depression. Stimulants include caffeine, nicotine (in tobacco), and cocaine.

## Jonas Salk

Vaccines are substances that give the body resistance or immunity to certain infecting germs. In the 1950s, American microbiologist Jonas Salk (1914–95) developed the first effective vaccine against the crippling disease of poliomyelitis (polio). It spread into world-wide use from 1955 onward. From 1960, an oral form of the vaccine, Sabin, gradually replaced the Salk injection.

# Drug abuse

This is the improper nonmedical use of legal or illegal drugs for physical or psychological reasons. The feelings and mental state experienced by the taker are often very different from that person's actual behavior. After too much alcohol, a drinker may feel bright and witty, while onlookers see someone slurring their words.

Tobacco store

Customs official arresting a drug trafficker

## Illegal drugs

Some drugs are so powerful and dangerous that they are illegal almost everywhere in the world. These include LSD and mescaline, known as Schedule I drugs, amphetamines, cocaine, and narcotics, or Schedule II drugs. Supplying these illegal drugs to users has become a vast international business.

## Legal drugs

The legality of drugs varies greatly all over the world. In addition to the drug's strength and effects, legality often depends on tradition, religion, and availability. One of the most powerful and addictive drugs is alcohol. Alcohol is fully legalized in some countries, partly legalized (for people over 18 or 21) in others, and completely banned in others. Nicotine, in the form of cigars, cigarettes, chewing tobacco, and snuff, is also legal in most countries.

Group therapy session

## Dependence and addiction

A person may come to depend on addictive drugs in order to function. Addiction – intense craving – is hard to control. If the user stops taking the drug, his or her body undergoes a "withdrawal" that includes symptoms, such as headaches, sweating, hallucinations, and mood swings. People trying to stop using addictive drugs often find support groups are helpful.

# Timeline

**1840s** Anesthetics used during surgery.

**1881** Artificial vaccine used against anthrax.

**1910** Paul Ehrlich introduces chemo-therapeutic drugs.

Fresh witch hazel

**1922** Frederick Banting and others treat diabetes using insulin, a natural body hormone.

**1936** Treatment of infections improves with the advent of Prontosil, the first sulfa drug.

**1940s** Howard Florey and Ernst Chain make penicillin available as an antibiotic. It is used widely in World War II.

**1956** Oral contraceptives (birth control pills) are introduced, using the natural female hormones, estrogen and progestogen.

**1967** Fertility drugs help couples conceive.

**1983** Cyclosporin, an immuno-suppressant, helps prevent rejection of transplanted organs.

**1990s** AIDS drugs tested.

Tablets and capsules

FIND OUT MORE

FIRST AID　　HOSPITALS　　MEDICINE　　MEDICINE, HISTORY OF　　PASTEUR, LOUIS　　PLANTS USES

# DUCKS, GEESE, AND SWANS

MOST DUCKS, GEESE, AND SWANS spend their life on or near water. They belong to a family of birds called waterfowl and are closely related to each other. They have broad beaks and short legs with webbed feet. They are good swimmers and have waterproof plumage that keeps them dry and also helps them float. There are about 160 species of waterfowl in the wild. Some species of ducks and geese have been domesticated and are often raised on farms.

Khaki Campbell – a domestic duck

## Ducks

Ducks are the smallest and most varied waterfowl. Males are often brightly colored and females are usually drab, which helps camouflage them when they are sitting on their eggs. Some ducks live in coastal waters, but most live on rivers, lakes, and ponds.

*Webs stretched open*  *Webs closed*

*Mute swan has a black knob at the base of its beak.*

### Swimming
A duck's webbed feet work like paddles to push it through the water. When it pushes its feet backward, it spreads its toes to stretch out the webs between them. When it pulls its feet forward, it closes its toes to shut the webs, which then offer less resistance to water.

### Plumage
Ducks produce a waterproof oil from a gland near the base of their tail. When they preen their feathers, they spread the oil over them. This oil is so effective that a duck stays dry even when it dives beneath the surface.

*A Mandarin duckling leaves the nest in response to its mother's call.*

## Swans

The largest waterfowl are swans, with a wingspan of up to 7.5 ft (2.3 m). Most of the eight species are white, but the Australian black swan has a black body and white flight feathers. A swan spends a lot of its time on water. It uses its long neck to reach plants below the surface.

*With its wings held wide, the duckling jumps.*

*Big feet and stubby wings work like parachutes to slow the duckling's fall.*

*A tree duckling must jump before it is a day old to find food.*

*Mute swan egg is an oval shape.*

**Swan egg**

### Young swans
Young swans, or cygnets, stay with their parents for a whole year, which is a long time for a bird. When they develop their adult plumage, their parents drive them away.

### Nesting swans
Swans nest on the ground close to the water's edge. The female incubates the eggs for up to 38 days, and she hisses loudly at anything that comes too close. If her warnings are ignored, she attacks. Her powerful beak and wings make formidable weapons.

### Tree-nesting ducks
Most ducks nest on the ground, but a few lay their eggs in holes in trees. Soon after the young have hatched, their mother leaves the nest and calls to them to follow her. The ducklings are too young to fly; instead they jump to the ground.

### Swan takeoff
Swans can weigh up to 28.5 lb (13 kg), which makes them among the world's heaviest flying birds. Swans cannot take off from a standing start. Instead, they have to run across the water to get enough speed for takeoff.

*The duckling walks away on landing.*

## Geese

Unlike most waterfowl, geese usually feed on land. They eat grass, gripping it in their beaks and pulling it up with a tug. Many geese breed in the tundra of the far north. These white-fronted geese, seen here in western Scotland, fly north to Greenland after the winter.

### MUTE SWAN
**SCIENTIFIC NAME** *Cygnus olor*
**ORDER** Anseriformes
**FAMILY** Anatidae
**DISTRIBUTION** Western Europe, parts of central Asia; also introduced into other parts of the world, including North America, Australia, and New Zealand
**HABITAT** Lakes and rivers
**DIET** Water plants
**SIZE** Length: 60 in (152 cm)
**LIFESPAN** About 20 years

**FIND OUT MORE**  ANIMAL BEHAVIOR  BIRDS  EGGS  FARMING  FLIGHT, ANIMALS  PENGUINS  SEABIRDS

# DYES AND PAINTS

DYES AND PAINTS are substances that are used to stain or give color to a range of objects, from textiles and paper to buildings and machinery. The substances that give color to dyes are called dyestuffs, which, when dissolved in water, penetrate the fibers of fabrics by means of a chemical reaction. Pigments form the color in paints. They are held in place using a varnish-like substance called a vehicle, or binder, which also binds the pigment to the surface being painted. Throughout history, people have created color; first by means of natural dyes and pigments, and today by using synthetic ones.

## Early pigments

The first materials used as pigments were probably colored clays, which were mixed with water or animal oils to make paint. Dyes made from plants and animals were later used to color textiles. Common plant dyes included woad, madder, saffron, and turmeric. Animal sources included cochineal (beetle) and the Murex sea snail.

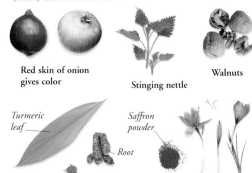

Red skin of onion gives color

Stinging nettle

Walnuts

Turmeric leaf

Root

Powder

Turmeric

Saffron powder

Saffron crocus

## Dyes

Some natural dyes still exist, but most used today are synthetic. These are organic chemicals produced by processing petroleum and coal-tar chemicals such as benzene. Most dyes are used in the textile industry, but are also used in the leather, paper, food, and cosmetics industries. The dyes can be applied to the fiber or fabric using either a direct or indirect process.

**Wool** can by dyed using a mordant dye, but this dye is now avoided in Western countries due to its use of potentially harmful chemicals.

### Indirect dyeing

In some dyeing processes, a number of steps are needed to dye the fiber. In one process, a chemical called a mordant is first added to the fiber, which is then dyed. The mordant molecules fix the dye to the fabric.

Fabrics can be colored using a range of dyes.

### Direct dyeing

In most industrial dyeing processes today, dyes can enter the fiber and color it in one step, without the need of a mordant. The dye is dissolved in hot water, strained, and then added to the fabric. Sometimes the dye is mixed with salt to help fix the color.

*The T-shirt on the left shows how the dye has faded.*

*This T-shirt shows how the color has remained fast.*

### Color fastness

Two of the most important properties demanded of a dye by clothes manufacturers are its abilities to resist being washed out, and not to fade in the light. The color fastness of a fabric also varies according to the dyeing process that is used and the type of material that is being dyed.

## Paints

Paint comes in many colors and can be used as a coating on rigid structures such as houses, bridges, ships, and cars. Finer paints are used by artists to produce imaginative and colorful works of art. The pigments used to make the paints may be natural, such as rutile (titanium dioxide), or synthetic, such as phthalocyanine blue.

*Oil paints usually come in tubes so that users can squeeze out the exact amount of paint needed.*

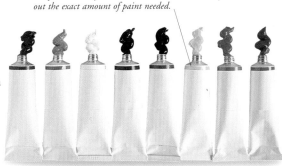

Oil paints

### Artists' paints

Artists use a variety of types of paint to achieve different effects, including watercolors, oils, and acrylics. The pigments in watercolor paints are mixed with a water solution of gum arabic, in oils they are mixed in a slow-drying oil, such as linseed oil, while in acrylics the pigments are mixed with a synthetic-resin vehicle.

### Industrial paints

Industrial paints are custom-made for specific jobs. Some paints contain powdered metal and metal oxides, so that the paint can protect exposed structures, such as iron bridges. Paints such as those used on cars are designed to withstand rusting and high temperatures.

Paint-spraying car body

### Domestic paints

Most decorating paints are made for easy application. Nondrip paints are jelly-like in the can, but flow easily when applied. Emulsion paint uses water as its vehicle, so splashes can be removed and brushes easily cleaned.

**Can of nondrip paint and brush**

## William Henry Perkin

British chemist William Henry Perkin (1838–1907) accidentally produced the first synthetic dye, mauve, in 1856. He was attempting to make the drug quinine from coal-tar chemicals, but instead produced a purple liquid dye. This was the start of the synthetic-dye industry.

**FIND OUT MORE** — ART, HISTORY OF · CHEMISTRY · CLOTHES AND FASHION · COAL · COLOR · MIXTURES AND COMPOUNDS · MONET, CLAUDE · PAINTING AND DRAWING · TEXTILES AND WEAVING

# EARS AND HEARING

WHEN A BEE BUZZES, a soprano sings, or a jumbo jet takes off, each generates invisible vibrations called sound waves that enter the ears, the body's organs of hearing. The sound waves travel deep inside the skull to the part of the ear that does the hearing. Here, sound waves are converted into nerve impulses that travel along nerves to the auditory, or hearing, area on each side of the brain. In the brain, the impulses are interpreted as sounds. Our ears can pick up a wide range of sounds and, with our eyes, they help us make sense of our surroundings.

## Anatomy of the ear

Mostly concealed within the skull, the ear is divided into three parts. The outer ear consists of the pinna (ear flap) and the auditory canal. The middle ear is filled with air and contains three tiny bones called ossicles. The inner ear is fluid filled and contains the cochlea and the semi-circular canals.

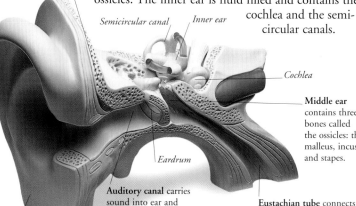

*Temporal bone*

*Semicircular canal*    *Inner ear*

*Cochlea*

**Middle ear** contains three bones called the ossicles: the malleus, incus, and stapes.

*Eardrum*

**Auditory canal** carries sound into ear and produces wax that keeps the ear free of dust and debris.

*Pinna*

**Eustachian tube** connects middle ear to throat to equalize air pressure inside and outside the ear.

## Hearing sounds

Sound waves channeled into the auditory canal cause the eardrum and the ossicles to vibrate. These vibrations travel through the fluid-filled cochlea. Inside the cochlea, sensory hair cells convert the vibrations into nerve impulses. These are carried by the cochlear nerve to the brain.

### Eardrum
The eardrum, or tympanic membrane, is a taut piece of skin that separates the auditory canal from the middle ear. When sound waves hit the eardrum, it vibrates like a drum and transmits its vibrations to the ossicles of the middle ear.

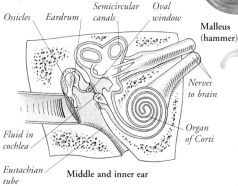

*Ossicles*  *Eardrum*  *Semicircular canals*  *Oval window*

**Malleus (hammer)**    **Incus (anvil)**    **Stapes (stirrup)**

*Nerves to brain*

*Fluid in cochlea*

*Organ of Corti*

*Eustachian tube*    **Middle and inner ear**

### Ossicles
The ossicles are the three smallest bones in the body. The malleus, incus, and stapes connect the eardrum to the cochlea by way of the oval window.

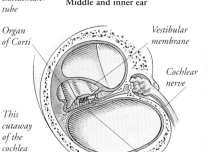

*Organ of Corti*    *Vestibular membrane*

*Cochlear nerve*

*This cutaway of the cochlea shows its three chambers.*

*Basilar membrane*

### Cochlea
The cochlea is a long, coiled tube in the inner ear that is filled with fluid. It is divided by two membranes into three chambers that run lengthwise. The middle of these three chambers, the cochlear chamber, contains the spiral organ of Corti, which consists of over 20,000 sensory hair cells that send nerve signals to the brain.

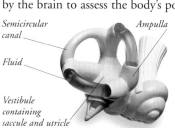

### Air pressure
You hear most clearly when the air pressure inside the middle ear is the same as the air pressure outside your body. If the air pressure outside changes suddenly, you may not be able to hear properly. This can happen if you are a on a plane that is taking off or landing, or if you are traveling on a fast train.

## Balance

Part of the inner ear helps you with balance. Sensors inside the three semicircular canals detect movements made by the head and the rest of the body. Sensors inside two adjoining chambers, the saccule and utricle, detect whether the body is upright, upside-down, or in between. Nerve impulses from the semicircular canals are analyzed by the brain to assess the body's position.

*Gymnast's outstretched arms help balance.*

*Semicircular canal*    *Ampulla*

*Fluid*

*Vestibule containing saccule and utricle*

### Semicircular canals
The three semicircular canals in each ear are filled with fluid. At the base of each canal is a bulge called an ampulla that contains sensory hair cells that send impulses to the brain. The three canals are set at 90° to each other so they can detect movement in any direction.

### Bartolomeo Eustachio
Italian anatomist Bartolomeo Eustachio (1520–74) studied the detailed anatomy of the ear, as well as other body organs and systems, while he was a professor in Rome. He wrote the first full description of the ears in his book *The Examination of the Organ of Hearing*, published in 1562. Included in this was the first detailed description of the tube that links the middle ear with the throat, later named the Eustachian tube.

### Hearing ranges
The pitch of a sound depends on the frequency of the sound waves that produced it. High-pitched sounds have a high frequency, and low-pitched sounds have a low frequency. Frequency is measured in units called Hertz (Hz). Our hearing ability decreases as we get older, from 20,000 to 12,000 Hz.

*Bats' ears can hear very high-pitched sound waves called ultrasound.*

**20–20,000 Hz**        **1,000–120,000 Hz**

**FIND OUT MORE**    BRAIN AND NERVOUS SYSTEM    HUMAN BODY    MUSIC    SOUND

# EARTH

WE LIVE ON A GIANT BALL OF ROCK spinning around the Sun, which we call the Earth. The Earth is one of nine planets in the Solar System and one of the four made of rock. However, the Earth is unique, because it is the only planet in the Solar System – and perhaps even in the Universe – that can support life. The distance of the Earth from the Sun makes it neither very hot like Venus, nor icy cold like Pluto, enabling liquid water to exist on its surface. The Earth also has an oxygen-rich atmosphere. These two substances – water and oxygen – are the key factors that allow life to flourish on the Earth.

## Structure of the Earth

By recording the way vibrations from earthquakes reverberate through the Earth, scientists have discovered that the Earth has an egg-like structure. At its center is a "yolk" of metal, surrounded by an "egg white" of soft rock called the mantle, and an outer "shell" of hard rock called the crust.

*The Earth's crust consists of a number of interlocking slabs of rock called tectonic plates.*

## Earth's ingredients

Although more than 80 elements (basic substances) occur naturally on the Earth, the bulk of the Earth is made of iron (35%), oxygen (28%), magnesium (17%), and silicon (13%). The following elements are present in significant, but small, amounts: nickel (2.7%), sulfur (2.7%), calcium (0.6%), and aluminum (0.6%). Tiny proportions of other elements make up the remainder (0.6%).

### Investigating Earth's composition

By taking rock samples from the Earth's interior, geologists have been able to understand the Earth's chemical makeup. Analysis of meteorites – solid pieces from an exploded planet – has led some geologists to believe that the Earth may have formed from the same space debris of which meteorites are made.

*Solid iron*

*Molecule of oxygen gas*

*Magnesium ore (magnesite)*

*Locket containing crystal of silicon.*

*Nickel ore (nickeline)*

*Sulfur crystals*

*Calcium-rich chalk*

*Aluminum ore (bauxite)*

*Chondrite meteorite*

### Meteorites

Meteorites are natural objects that fall to the Earth from space. They are made of iron, stone, or a mixture of both. The two main types of meteorite are called chondrites and achondrites.

*Achondrite meteorite*

*The Earth's structure*

**Atmosphere** is a thin surrounding layer of gases about 400 miles (640 km) deep.

**Crust**, Earth's outer layer of rock, varies in thickness: beneath the oceans, it is 4–7 miles (6–11 km) thick, but it stretches up to 43 miles (70 km) under mountain ranges.

**Mohorovicic discontinuity**, or Moho, is the boundary between the crust and the mantle.

**Mantle** is a partially molten layer beneath the crust, extending to a depth of about 1,800 miles (2,900 km) and made largely of a rock called peridotite.

**Gutenberg discontinuity** is the boundary between the mantle and the core.

**Outer core** reaches to a depth of about 3,050 miles (4,900 km) and is made of molten iron and nickel – magnetic metals that give the Earth its magnetic field.

**Inner core**, like the outer core, is made of iron and nickel, but although temperatures reach 6,690°F (3,700°C), the pressure is so great that the metal remains solid.

### Richard Oldham

By examining the seismographic recordings of earthquakes, the British geologist Richard Oldham (1858–1936) discovered that earthquakes produce two different kinds of vibration. He called them primary (P) waves and secondary (S) waves. Oldham's analysis revealed that P waves travel more slowly through the core of the Earth than through the mantle. He concluded that Earth's core must be liquid, which is partly true.

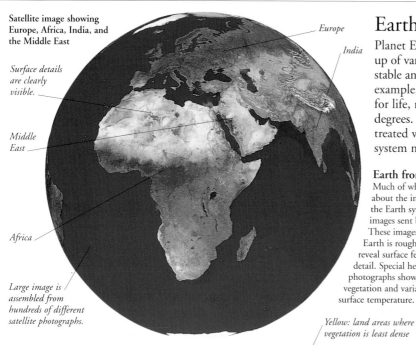

Satellite image showing Europe, Africa, India, and the Middle East

*Surface details are clearly visible.*

Europe

India

*Middle East*

*Africa*

*Large image is assembled from hundreds of different satellite photographs.*

# Earth system

Planet Earth seems to operate like a vast, complex system made up of various interconnected processes that keep conditions stable and suitable for life. The atmosphere's unique makeup, for example, ensures that the Earth stays at an ideal temperature for life, never heating up or cooling down by more than a few degrees. Scientists now realize that the environment must be treated with care, because a change to one part of this complex system may have unpredictable repercussions in other parts.

## Earth from space

Much of what scientists know about the interrelated parts of the Earth system comes from images sent back by satellites. These images show us that the Earth is roughly spherical and reveal surface features in clear detail. Special heat-sensitive infrared photographs show the distribution of vegetation and variations in the Earth's surface temperature.

## Energy regulation

The Earth system exchanges energy with its surroundings, but there is no overall gain or loss of energy. The Earth receives heat, light, and other forms of energy directly from the Sun. Some of this energy is reflected back by the clouds, oceans, land, and atmosphere; the rest is absorbed and then released back into space. The total energy the Earth gives out equals the total energy it receives from the Sun.

**Infrared image of temperature variations in the Atlantic Ocean off the eastern coast of the US**

## Biosphere

Between the atmosphere's lowest layers and the ocean floor is a rich diversity of life, from tiny ocean organisms called plankton to the largest trees and animals. Together, these organisms form the biosphere – the living part of the planet. Satellite images can help scientists understand the complicated links between living things and the Earth.

*Yellow: land areas where vegetation is least dense*

*Green: land areas where vegetation is most dense*

*Red: ocean areas where plankton is most dense*

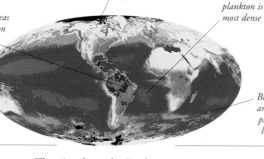

**Infrared image of vegetation and plankton distribution**

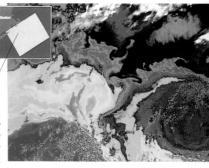

*Locator map*

*Blue: ocean areas where plankton is least dense*

# Gaia theory

British scientist James Lovelock (b. 1919) suggests that the Earth and all the life-forms upon it function as if they were a single living organism. He calls this "organism" Gaia, after the Greek goddess of fertility. Like any other organism, he says, Gaia is self-regulating, meaning that it will naturally change its environment to maintain the right conditions for life – even if humans make the Earth unfit for themselves by polluting it and using up its limited resources.

**Greek statue of Gaia, 450 BC**

## Theories about the Earth

There have been many theories about the Earth that may seem strange to people today, but which were widely believed at the time. The ancient Egyptians, for example, thought that the Earth was a flat square under a pyramid-shaped sky, and people in medieval Europe believed that it was the Sun that revolved around the Earth, and not vice versa. Similarly, before technology enabled scientists to understand more about the interior of the Earth, people suggested that the Earth was hollow.

*People assumed the Earth had a vast, empty core.*

**Hidden lands** and oceans, complete with plants and animals and warmed by a subterranean Sun, were thought to lie within the centre of the Earth.

**Hollow Earth theory**

## Search for another Earth

Astronomers have recently detected signs of the existence of planets beyond the Solar System. Wobbles in the movements of the stars 47 Ursae Majoris, 70 Virginis, and 51 Pegasi suggest that they may be orbited by planets – perhaps even ones similar to the Earth. Astronomers have found other stars with solar systems forming around them.

*The yellow-and-red area may be another solar system forming around Beta Pictoris.*

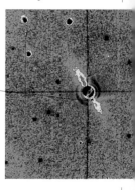

**False-color satellite image of the star Beta Pictoris, about 50 light years away**

# Timeline

**c.4,600 mya** The Earth and the other planets form as parts of a vast cloud of hot gas and dust circling the Sun begin to cluster together.

**c.4,300 mya** The Earth's crust forms.

**c.4,200 mya** As the Earth cools, gas bubbles and water vapor rise from the interior to form a cloudy atmosphere.

**Gneiss rock**

**c.4,000 mya** The crust and mantle separate; rain begins to fall; the atmosphere clears.

**c.3,800 mya** The first organisms are single-celled bacteria.

**c.3,000 mya** The atmosphere becomes oxygen-rich as ocean plants absorb sunlight and release oxygen into the air.

**c.1,500 mya** Protists, such as amoeba, are the first complex living cells; later, protists join up to form sponges – the first multicelled organisms.

**c.570 mya** A huge variety of complex life-forms develops in the Earth's seas and oceans.

**Sponge**

**c.440–400 mya** Land-based plants and animals become widespread.

**c.220 mya** There is a single, vast land mass, now known as Pangaea, which later breaks up into the smaller land masses we today call continents.

**c.200–70 mya** The era of the dinosaurs.

**c.100,000 ya** First modern humans appear.

**FIND OUT MORE**

ATMOSPHERE    CONTINENTS    EARTH SCIENCES    ELEMENTS    FOSSILS    GEOLOGY    MAGNETISM    PREHISTORIC LIFE    PLANETS    SUN

# EARTHQUAKES

FROM A GENTLE RIPPLE to terrifying and violent movements in the earth, earthquakes literally rock the world. Earthquakes are tremors in the ground created by the sudden movement of tectonic plates – huge slabs of rock that make up the earth's crust. The majority of earthquakes are so gentle that no one notices them, but some are so violent they destroy whole cities. An earthquake's effect and intensity are measured on different scales. In earthquake-prone countries, planning minimizes the damage earthquakes cause.

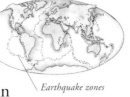

## Earthquake zones
Although earthquakes can occur anywhere, they are more frequent in earthquake zones. These zones, such as Japan and California, lie near the moving edges, called fault lines, of the tectonic plates.

*Earthquake zones*

## What is an earthquake?
Tectonic plates usually slide past each other, but sometimes they get stuck together. The stress on the rocks builds up until they fault (crack). The tectonic plates then jolt past each other, sending shock waves through the ground. These vibrations, known as seismic waves, cause the earth to quake.

## Epicenter
The point at which an earthquake occurs is known as the focus. Above the focus is the epicenter – the point on the earth's surface where the effects of an earthquake are most devastating. The focus may be as much as 185 miles (700 km) below the epicenter. In 1985, an earthquake in Mexico City, with its epicenter in the Pacific Ocean, left 9,500 people dead. It measured 8.1 on the Richter scale.

*Destruction diminishes as shock waves travel away from the epicenter, recording a lower number on the Richter scale.*

*Earthquake that causes small object to fall rates V on the Mercalli scale.*

The **Mercalli scale** rates an earthquake according to its effect on a scale of I–XII: a swinging lightbulb measures I; extensive structural damage measures XII.

*Folds form in the ground as the earth moves.*

*Epicenter*

## Seismometer
Seismometers show seismic waves, and measure an earthquake's location and intensity on the Richter scale. The height of each line shows the wave's force.

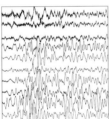

**Reading from Kobe, Japan**

## Tsunami
These are huge waves that start when an earthquake or volcanic eruption shakes the ocean floor. Tsunamis roll along the ocean floor as fast as a jet plane. When they reach shallow coastal waters, they form waves about 100 ft (30 m) high. Many tsunamis occur in the Pacific Ocean, such as the one in Hawaii, 1964 (left).

The **Richter scale** measures the force of an earthquake on a scale from 1–10 taken from seismograph readings of the seismic waves. Each figure represents a force 10 times greater than that of the next lowest figure.

*Focus*

*Shock waves radiate outward in circles from focus.*

## Earthquake proofing
Technology cannot prevent earthquakes but it can help limit their damage, particularly in building design. Most loss of life is caused not by the shaking ground, but by the collapse of buildings and roads, and by fires started when electrical equipment is damaged.

### Building design
Pyramid-shaped, curved, and fire-resistant buildings and structures, such as this staircase in California, bend rather than break during an earthquake. Mounting foundations on rubber also helps absorb some of the earthquake shocks.

## Timeline
**1556** Reports of an earthquake in the region of Shaanxi, China. Almost a million deaths.

**1755** Lisbon, Portugal, is destroyed by an earthquake and the subsequent flood.

**1883** Krakatoa Island destroyed by earthquake and tsunami.

**1906** San Francisco, California, is flattened by an earthquake.

**1964** Alaska is hit by an earthquake of 9.2 on the Richter scale.

**1964** Earthquake in Alaska generates a tsunami, which causes damage as far away as California, USA.

**1976** Earthquake in China kills 255,000.

**1990** In Iran 40,000 people die in quake.

**1995** Kobe, central Japan, is devastated by an earthquake.

**1999** Turkish quake kills 20,000 and makes 200,000 homeless.

**2001** Earthquake in Gujarat, India, leaves 30,000 people dead.

**FIND OUT MORE**

BUILDING AND CONSTRUCTION  CONTINENTS  EARTH  GEOLOGY  OCEAN FLOOR  RADAR AND SONAR

E

# EARTH SCIENCES

FOSSILS PROVIDE CLUES to the ages of rocks; the atmosphere provides clues to tomorrow's weather. Among others, these elements are studied within the discipline of Earth sciences, the study of the planet's physical characteristics, from volcanoes to raindrops. The different branches of Earth sciences cover all of the Earth's dynamic systems, except for life forms, which are studied within biology. Knowledge about the Earth's history and formation also informs us about its needs, which will help ensure the future survival of the planet.

## Branches of Earth sciences

The term Earth sciences has been used since the 1970s. It covers the range of subjects that were previously bracketed under the term "physical geography". Although each of the Earth sciences is a distinct study focusing on one aspect of the Earth, each is also a key element of the inter-related study of Earth sciences.

Pebbles

Anthracite, a form of coal

Granite

### Paleontology
Fossils, the remains of once living organisms preserved in sedimentary rock, are studied within the branch of Earth science called paleontology. From fossils, scientists can estimate the ages of rocks and develop a picture of the history of plant and animal life on Earth over billions of years.

Fossil of a sea creature

*Earth sciences cover many different areas of study.*

### Geology
The oldest branch of the Earth sciences, geology is the study of the Earth's history, structure, and composition. Although it focuses on rocks and the composition of the Earth's crust, geology also relates to the other Earth sciences, except for meteorology.

### Volcanology
The study of volcanoes and the reasons why they erupt is known as volcanology. Volcanologists sometimes have to work very close to an erupting volcano. The scientists wear special clothing to protect them from the hazards of gas, heat, and flying lava bombs.

Volcanic bomb

### Geomorphology
The study of landforms and the processes that shape them is known as geomorphology. This includes landforms ranging from mountains and valleys to rivers and glaciers, and the effects of different shaping processes upon them, such as the erosion caused by weathering.

### Oceanography
Oceanography covers ocean chemistry, the ocean bed and currents (shown above by satellite), and marine animal and plant life.

### Geography
The study of the Earth's surface, human geography looks at world patterns of human activity. Physical geography studies the Earth's physical environment.

### Meteorology
The discipline of meteorology focuses on the Earth's atmosphere, on the processes that make the weather, and on weather forecasting. Climatology is the study of weather patterns.

## Surveying the Earth

Earth scientists can learn very little about the Earth from laboratory studies. Instead, they must make observations, collect data, and test their theories in the outside world. They do this by climbing mountains or braving earthquakes. Satellite photography has provided a vast new source of data, but most information continues to come from fieldwork.

## Earth resources

The Earth provides all the materials we need for living, from the food we eat and the water we drink, to the bricks we use for building. Earth sciences help us identify the location of these resources. They also show what damage we may be doing to them by exploiting them thoughtlessly.

Fruit

Squid

### Air
We need air to breathe every second of our lives. However, this vital resource is becoming increasingly damaged by human pollution.

### Food
Food is provided by things living on the Earth's surface. These depend on the mineral resources, water, and air provided by the Earth.

### Survey equipment
Earth scientists sometimes need to use specific survey equipment. This laser equipment helps to monitor the movement of earthquakes.

Tourmaline gemstone

### Minerals
From metal for cars to concrete for buildings, nearly everything we make comes from minerals or chemicals taken from the Earth's crust. Gems are another of its rich resources.

### Water
All forms of life are dependent on water. Patterns of human activity are controlled by the need to be near a source of clean water.

### Energy
Ninety percent of the energy we use comes from a finite supply of minerals – oil, coal, and gas – extracted from the Earth's crust.

FIND OUT MORE    CLIMATE    EARTH    FOSSILS    GEOLOGY    OCEANS AND SEAS    ROCKS AND MINERALS    VOLCANOES    WEATHER

# ECOLOGY AND ECOSYSTEMS

NO LIVING THING exists in isolation. It interacts with other living things and with its physical surroundings. The study of these relationships is called ecology. Ecologists consider all the organisms that live in one area as an interdependent community. All plants and animals rely on, and influence, vital factors in their environment, such as the supply of nutrients, food, and water. A community and its environment is called an ecosystem.

## Communities
Wildlife communities exist almost everywhere you look, on land, in rivers, and in the oceans. A typical community contains a mixture of plants, various animals that feed on them or hunt one another, and organisms that burrow through the soil below.

*Trees offer shelter for animals, and food in the form of leaves, berries, seeds, and blossoms.*

*Insects feeding on flowers help pollinate them.*

## Habitats
The habitat of a species is the surroundings in which it lives, including the rocks, soils, water, and plants. Different habitats are suitable for different species and have a certain type of community.

*Mice eat seeds, and are hunted by bigger animals.*

*Dense undergrowth provides shelter for small animals.*

*Most of the tadpoles that hatch out from the frog spawn will be food for other animals.*

*Rotting wood is home to fungi and invertebrates.*

*Snails feed on the leaves of plants and are food for some birds such as thrushes.*

*As ferns grow, they take nutrients from the soil.*

*Frogs live in both land and water habitats.*

## Biomes
The biggest ecological units are biomes, such as deserts, rain forests, and lakes, across which similar climatic and other conditions create similar ecosystems. The plants and animals may differ across a biome, but they make up the same kinds of communities with the same ecological features.

### Seashores
Battered by waves and flooded by tides, seashores have few plants other than seaweed. Animals include shellfish, tide pool fish, and wading birds.

### Deserts
Cloud-free, dry climates create deserts that are home only to plants and animals that are able to adapt to the dryness and range of temperature.

### Grassland
Grassland is found in places where there is a long dry season. Grassland supports grazing animals, some preyed on by swift-running predators. The savanna of East Africa is one of the best-known areas of grassland.

### Rain forests
In hot, humid climates, dense forests develop that are home to a large variety of animal life. Tropical rain forests cover only 10 percent of the Earth's land surface, but contain more than half of all animal and plant species.

## Ecosystems
An ecosystem contains several different wildlife communities and their habitats. Ecologists use the term to mean all the complicated interactions that take place among living and non-living things in an area. The various components of the ecosystem include sunshine, water, nutrients in the soil, bacteria, plants, and animals.

### Freshwater
Lake- and river-dwelling communities include floating or submerged plants, freshwater plankton, and fish. Different species live in different parts of a river or lake, depending on the conditions that they tolerate. This is Bow Lake in the Canadian Rockies.

E

# Ecological interactions

The components of an ecosystem interact with each other in different ways. Rain, for example, provides water for plants. Plant growth and decay influence the texture and richness of soil. Soil provides a home for worms, and worms, as they crawl, change the structure of the soil.

*Toucans live high in the crowns of trees.*

*Puss moth larva cuts and chews leaves using its sharp jaws.*

## Food chain

Perhaps the most obvious way in which living species affect one another's lives is by feeding. In the food chain, most things are food for something else. Caterpillars eat leaves but are themselves food for birds. The birds, in turn, are food for other animals, and so on up the food chain.

## Transportation

Animals can move around; plants cannot. Plants therefore use various methods that make sure animals carry their seeds and pollen, so that the plants can reproduce. Bumblebees carry pollen on their legs as they move from flower to flower.

*Honey fungus*

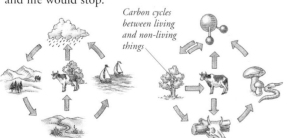

*Young stinkhorn fungus*

## Shelter

The cover and shelter that trees and vegetation provide offer much more security than bare, open ground. In a rain forest, the large trees provide toucans with shelter from the weather, a place where they can raise their young in relative safety, and protection from predators.

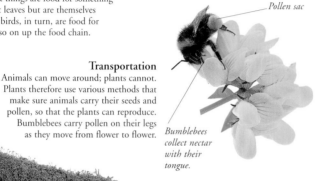

*Pollen sac*

*Bumblebees collect nectar with their tongue.*

## Parasites

Animals, plants, and fungi that live off other living things are called parasites. Nearly all animals and plants are host to parasites of some kind. A parasitic relationship exists between a honey fungus and a tree. The fungus steals food from the tree, usually harming it in the process.

# Symbiosis

When two species have a close relationship in which both benefit, it is called symbiotic. Symbiosis often involves giving shelter in return for protection or food, and it occurs among a variety of organisms.

## Clownfish

Clownfish find shelter among the stinging tentacles of sea anemones, which do not harm them. The fish may lure in other fish for the anemones to eat.

*Clownfish stay where they are protected.*

# Adaptation

All plants and animals adapt to the living conditions in their particular habitat. How they adapt is the key to evolution. How and where a species lives, how it gets its food, what it eats, and how it interacts with other species is known as its ecological niche.

## Cacti

A cactus has adapted in many ways to desert life. For example, its leaves have adapted into spines to prevent water evaporating too easily. When rain does fall, a cactus stores as much water as possible in its stem.

*Spines protect the swollen stem.*

# Cycles in nature

Nature automatically recycles the substances that are vital for life. Oxygen, nitrogen, carbon, and water are constantly exchanged between the air, the soil, the oceans, and living things. If substances were not continuously put back into the ecosystems to be used again, the supply for organisms would soon run out and life would stop.

*Carbon cycles between living and non-living things*

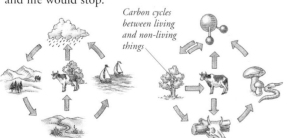

## Water cycle

Water lost by evaporation from plants, rivers, and oceans forms clouds in the atmosphere. This falls back as rain, runs into rivers and oceans, and is soaked up from the soil by the roots of plants.

## Carbon cycle

Organisms release carbon dioxide into the air. Carbon is also released when organisms decay or when fuel is burned. Plants absorb carbon from the air, and this is passed to animals that eat them.

# Ecological change

Ecosystems may change over time. If an event changes a particular habitat, for example, a fire burns a forest to the ground, new seeds take root, grasses and herbs grow, then shrubs cover the area until trees begin to grow once again.

*The process of change from grassland to woodland is called succession.*

*Land erosion in Madagascar*

## Human impact

People's actions also change ecosystems and sometimes the impact is so great that nature cannot repair the damage. For example, poor farming techniques sometimes cause so much soil depletion that plants cannot grow and the vegetation never recovers.

 FIND OUT MORE    ANIMAL BEHAVIOR    EVOLUTION    FOOD WEBS AND CHAINS    POLLUTION    SOIL

# ECUADOR AND PERU

TOGETHER ECUADOR AND PERU form the western side of equatorial South America, lying between Colombia to the north, Chile to the south, and Brazil and Bolivia to the east. The dominant influences in the west of the region were the Incas, who ruled until the 1500s, and the conquering Spaniards, who imposed their own culture and language. About 40 percent of the population are *mestizos*, who are people of mixed blood resulting from intermarriage between Spaniards and Incas. Many Native Americans still live in remote Amazonian villages.

## Physical features

Lying on South America's Pacific Coast, Ecuador and Peru are dominated by the jagged volcanic peaks of the Andes, with eastern slopes that descend to hot, humid, tropical rain forest and wetlands in the Amazon Basin. To the west is the coastal strip. Peru's coast is largely arid desert, but Ecuador's coast is hot, swampy, or forested.

### Mount Cotopaxi

A perfect cone capped with snow, Cotopaxi, at 19,345 ft (5,897 m), is the world's highest active volcano and Ecuador's second highest peak. It lies in the Andes, which form the backbone of Ecudor and Peru. Ecuador has 15 major volcanoes, ten of which are active. The area is occasionally shaken by earthquakes, which cause damage to cities.

### Amazon Basin

The steamy Amazon Basin occupies the eastern regions of Ecuador and Peru. The forest is not an uninterrupted mass of trees, but contains pockets of grassland and swamps. The headwaters of the Amazon originate in this region. Much of this area is disputed territory awarded to Peru in 1942.

### Regional climate

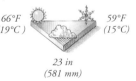

66°F (19°C)     59°F (15°C)

23 in (581 mm)

Ecuador is hot and humid along the coast, cool and dry in the Andes, and hot, with heavy rainfall, in the Amazon Basin. Peru has a more mixed climate. The coastal region is dry, and kept cool by the cold waters of the Peru Current. The western part of the Peruvian Andes is fairly dry, but the eastern Andes and tropical Amazonia have heavy rainfall.

### Coca

The Incas used to chew coca leaves to relieve fatigue and hunger. Today, in remote areas, coca is grown illegally to produce the powerful and dangerous drug cocaine for supply to the international drug trade. Governments are offering farmers money to destroy their coca crops and grow bananas, cocoa, or coffee instead.

**Picking coca leaves, Quillabamba, Peru**

### Map

(Map of Ecuador and Peru with grid references A–H and 1–11)

Esmeraldas, Ibarra, QUITO, Equator, Santo Domingo de los Colorados, Latacunga, Cotopaxi 19,342, Manta, Portoviejo, Ambato, Montecristi, Babahoyo, Riobamba, Milagro, Guayaquil, Cuenca, Gulf of Guayaquil, Machala, Loja, Sullana, Piura, Chiclayo, Moyobamba, Tarapoto, Cajamarca, Trujillo, Pucallpa, Chimbote, Huaraz, Huánuco, Cerro de Pasco, Tarma, La Oroya, Callao, LIMA, Huancayo, Machu Picchu, Ayacucho, Cusco, Ica, Nazca, San Juan, Juliaca, Puno, L. Titicaca, Arequipa, Mollendo, Moquegua, Tacna

COLOMBIA, Aguarico, Napo, Putumayo, Amazon Basin, Iquitos, Amazon, Ramón Castilla, Marañón, Ucayali, Apurímac, Madre de Dios, BRAZIL, BOLIVIA, PERU, Andes, PACIFIC OCEAN, CHILE

0 km 250
0 miles 250

### Lake Titicaca

At more than 106 miles (170 km) long, Lake Titicaca is South America's largest lake. The Uros people live here on islands that they make from the *totora* reed. They also make reed boats.

E

# Ecuador

The third smallest, most densely populated independent country in South America, Ecuador is also one of the most geographically varied and politically stable. Agriculture and oil dominate the economy. About 630 miles (1,000 km) off Ecuador's Pacific coast, the lonely Galápagos Islands, known for their unique wildlife, are part of Ecuador.

*Quechua woman gathering gladioli for market*

### Oil
Since the 1970s, oil, piped from the eastern lowlands, has been the mainstay of Ecuador's economy and accounts for 40 percent of exports. Other exports are balsa wood, shrimp, processed fish, and textiles. Most goods are exported via Guayaquil, Ecuador's main port and largest city.

### Crops
Beans, corn, and potatoes are the main crops grown in the Andes. Bananas, cocoa, rice, coffee, oranges, and wheat are cultivated on the coast, mostly for export. Roses, carnations, gladioli, and statice (sea lavender) are grown for markets.

### People
Indians make up 25 percent of the people, and *mestizos*, who have a mix of European and Indian blood, make up more than half. The rest are white, black, or Asian. At least 93 percent of people are Roman Catholic, and some people blend Catholicism with traditional beliefs.

*Bold rug designs, often with an animal theme, are woven from homespun wool fiber.*

### Otavalo market
The small town of Otavalo lies high in the Andes, north of the capital, Quito. Local Indians weave brightly colored ponchos and rugs to sell at the famous Otavalo market, which dates from pre-Inca times.

### Panama hats
Originally made in the 1800s in Ecuador to protect the heads of travelers, panama hats are constructed from the fibers of the toquilla plant. A panama can be rolled up for packing – a good one squeezes through a finger ring.

| ECUADOR FACTS | |
|---|---|
| CAPITAL CITY | Quito |
| AREA | 109,483 sq miles (283,560 sq km) |
| POPULATION | 12,500,000 |
| MAIN LANGUAGES | Spanish, Quechua |
| MAJOR RELIGION | Christian |
| CURRENCY | US dollar |

# Peru

Four hundred years ago, Peru was at the heart of the Inca Empire, of which ruins still survive high in the Andes. The country has great mineral resources, yet most Peruvians are poor farmers, growing potatoes, corn, rice, and grain for their own use, and cotton and coffee for export. Political terrorism by the Maoist Shining Path group has forced military rule in some areas.

### Railroads
Peru has two unconnected railroad systems – the Central and Southern Railroads – both of which go from the coast to the highlands. A branch of the Central Railroad linking Lima and Huancayo in the Andes reaches 15,806 ft (4,818 m) above sea level, making it the highest standard-gauge line in the world.

### Machu Picchu
Peru's greatest tourist attraction is the ruined Inca city of Machu Picchu in the Andes. The ruins, hidden by dense forest vegetation, were discovered in 1911, when American archaeologist Hiram Bingham stumbled upon them, almost by accident. The ruins are made of stone and were built without mortar.

### People
About half the people in Peru are Indian, and one-third are *mestizo*. The most populated areas are the highlands and the coastal plain. Only five percent of people live in the Amazon Basin. Here, in remote areas, there are about 70 small ethnic Indian groups.

*Jivaro Indian man*

| PERU FACTS | |
|---|---|
| CAPITAL CITY | Lima |
| AREA | 496,223 sq miles (1,285,220 sq km) |
| POPULATION | 24,700,000 |
| MAIN LANGUAGES | Spanish, Quechua, Aymara |
| MAJOR RELIGION | Christian |
| CURRENCY | Nuevo sol (new sol) |

### Fishing
The cold waters of the Peru coastal current bring rich nutrients that attract large numbers of herring, sardines, tuna, and other fish, making fishing a major industry in Peru. However, every few years, the arrival of the El Niño current raises the temperature of the water, driving away the fish and causing great hardship to the fishermen.

*Sardines*

### Mining
Peru is a leading producer of copper, lead, tungsten, silver, and zinc and has reserves of gold, iron ore, and oil. However, low world mineral prices and industrial problems have badly affected mining.

**Above-ground lead mine in the Andes**

**FIND OUT MORE**    FARMING    FISHING INDUSTRY    INCAS    NATIVE AMERICANS    OIL    PACIFIC OCEAN    ROCKS AND MINERALS    SOUTH AMERICA, HISTORY OF    TEXTILES AND WEAVING    TRAINS AND RAILROADS    VOLCANOES

# EDISON, THOMAS

ONE OF THE GREATEST INVENTORS of all time, Thomas Alva Edison produced a number of inventions that changed the world – electric lighting, sound recording, and an early form of moving pictures, among many others. He had little formal schooling, but he was fascinated by science. He worked extremely hard, and would spend days, months, or even years experimenting in order to make something work. He often slept fully clothed on one of his worktables so that he could start work again first thing in the morning.

### Early life
Edison was born in 1847 in a small town in Ohio. His teachers thought he was stupid, so his mother taught him herself, inspiring his interest in science. In 1869, after moving to New York, he improved the "ticker," a machine for relaying information about the stock market. The machine earned him $40,000.

E

## Menlo Park

In 1876, using the money from his stock "ticker," Edison built an "invention factory" at Menlo Park, 24 miles (39 km) from New York City. This barnlike two-story building was the world's first research laboratory, where a staff of scientists helped Edison develop his ideas into devices that actually worked. In the six years that Edison worked at Menlo Park, he patented more than 400 different inventions.

### Research work
At Menlo Park, Edison would come up with rough ideas and sketches. These would be refined, built, and tested by his assistants. They often had to build inventions again and again to find out why they did not work. Edison, when asked about his success, stressed the importance of these setbacks. "I failed my way to success," he said.

*Organ, for experiments on sound*

*Edison watches to see how strongly the bulb glows.*

*Bench contains chemicals and other scientific equipment.*

## Electric light

Perhaps Edison's most important invention was the electric lightbulb. He saw that a bulb with a glowing thread or filament would work, using little electricity. It took him thousands of experiments before he discovered that the best material for the filament was carbonized cotton thread. British scientist Joseph Swan (1828–1914) invented a lightbulb at the same time as Edison, and the two men later joined forces.

*Carbon filament*

Patent drawing for the lightbulb

*Carbon filament*

**Swan's electric lightbulb**

*Glass bulb*

Edison's electric lightbulb

### Lighting the city
Having developed the lightbulb, Edison went on to create a complete electric lighting system, powered by a central generator. His first power plant opened in 1882, serving 85 satisfied customers. Soon, whole cities were lit with electricity.

## Other inventions

Edison patented 1,093 inventions in his lifetime. He helped make the first successful typewriter, a dictating machine, and an improved telephone mouthpiece. He came close to inventing radio and predicted the use of atomic power.

*Recording cylinder*

*Mouthpiece*

Edison's phonograph

*Handle to turn cylinder*

### Phonograph
The phonograph, a device for recording and playing back sounds, was Edison's favorite invention. He sketched the machine and gave it to an assistant to build. It worked, but Edison did not realize this because he had poor hearing.

**Recording the voice**

### Kinetoscope
In 1889, Edison invented the kinetoscope, a projector with a peepshow-type viewer to go with it. Kinetoscopes were installed in special viewing parlors in the US, and customers paid to see short films.

### THOMAS EDISON

|  |  |
|---|---|
| 1847 | Born, Milan, Ohio. |
| 1869 | Improves the "ticker," for relaying prices on the stock market. |
| 1876 | Moves to Menlo Park. |
| 1877 | Creates the phonograph. |
| 1877 | Invents the carbon microphone for use in telephone mouthpieces. |
| 1879 | Patents the electric lightbulb. |
| 1882 | Power switched on at the Pearl Street generating station, New York. |
| 1883 | Edison and Swan form an electric company. |
| 1889 | Invents the kinetoscope. |
| 1931 | Dies, aged 84. |

FIND OUT MORE    ELECTRICITY    FILM AND FILM-MAKING    INVENTIONS    PHYSICS    SCIENCE, HISTORY OF    SOUND RECORDING    TECHNOLOGY

# EDUCATION

FOR A SOCIETY TO SURVIVE and progress, each generation must pass its knowledge, skills, and values on to the next. This process is called education. Passing on knowledge is so vital that most countries have established formal systems of education for teaching children by sending them to schools and colleges. Throughout our lives, we are also educated informally by parents, friends, or the media. Education provides society with doctors, teachers, and scientists, gives industry a capable workforce; and helps maintain law and order by instructing people in social values.

## Early education

In prehistoric times, elders taught children the survival skills they needed, such as how to hunt or make fire. As civilizations developed and writing was invented, formal institutions of learning – schools – were created so that some people could learn to read and write.

### The ancient world

As happens today, education in the ancient world reflected the state's needs and attitudes. In warlike Sparta, for example, education was geared towards producing good soldiers. Throughout the ancient world and medieval Europe, women and the poor did not have the same acccess to education enjoyed by the male, ruling classes.

**Teacher and pupil, Romano-Germanic period**

## Theories of education

Some theories state that people learn by practice; others, that pupils must work things out themselves in order to learn; and some suggest that pupils learn by following their emotional needs and acquiring the skills and knowledge to fulfil them. Most people probably learn in all three ways.

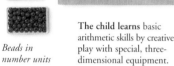

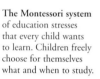

*Beads in number units*

**The child learns** basic arithmetic skills by creative play with special, three-dimensional equipment.

**The Montessori system** of education stresses that every child wants to learn. Children freely choose for themselves what and when to study.

$5 \times 2 =$

**Multiplication board**

## Types of education

Different types of education cater to different needs. The best-known example is the general education that schools and colleges provide, in subjects such as reading, writing, and arithmetic.

### Vocational

Vocational education prepares people for specific jobs; it is available through courses at school, or training at specific colleges. Skills or crafts are also passed on informally, perhaps from parent to child, when a trade is passed on from one generation to the next.

*Mother teaches sewing skills to children*

### Adult education

Adult education is for those who, although not full-time students, choose to continue an aspect of their education, or learn something new. The courses keep adults up-to-date, improve job prospects, and bring new interests.

**Learning computer skills**

### Special needs

Wealthy nations can afford to provide some schools where education is tailored to the special needs of certain children, such as the physically challenged or the highly gifted.

**Disabled boy learns sailing skills.**

## Socialization

The first form of education a child receives starts from birth by his or her caregivers. It is known as socialization and includes not only learning such basic skills as speaking, but also teaches the child how society expects him or her to behave. The child learns from instruction and by imitating others. Socialization also takes place at school, and through cultural influences such as television.

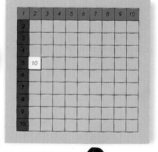

*Table manners are a learned form of social behavior.*

## Maria Montessori

The Italian educator Maria Montessori (1870–1952) developed teaching methods that encouraged children to work things out for themselves through practical activity, rather than simply obeying instructions. She developed her ideas while working with children with learning difficulties.

## Timeline

c.3100 BC Sumerians invent writing.

3rd century BC The Greek thinker Plato (c.427 BC–c.347 BC) proposes that all education should be run by the state.

1524 German priest Martin Luther (1483–1546) advocates education be made available for all, so that everyone is able to read the Bible.

1762 French philosopher Jean Jacques Rousseau (1712–78) argues education should prepare children to be adults.

1763 Prussians introduce compulsory schooling from the ages of 5 to 13.

1899 US educator John Dewey (1859–1952) publishes *The School and Society*, an influential analysis of the social function of education.

1945 World War II ends: with the desire to build a better world, many countries reform school systems to make secondary education available to all.

1990s Education is fully recognized as vital to social and economic growth.

**FIND OUT MORE**

CRIME AND PUNISHMENT
SCHOOLS AND COLLEGES
SOCIETIES, HUMAN
TRADE AND INDUSTRY
WRITING

# EGGS

MANY ANIMALS, from earthworms and insects to fish and birds, reproduce by laying eggs. An egg is a single living cell complete with a supply of food. After the egg is laid, the cell starts to divide, and gradually a young animal's body takes shape. When the animal is ready to start life in the world outside, it breaks out of the egg, or hatches. There is a great variety of eggs – large and small, with shells and without. Some animals lay just a few eggs each time and look after them carefully. Others lay thousands or millions of eggs and leave them to develop on their own.

## Types of eggs

Some eggs are so small that they can be seen only under a microscope; others are as big and heavy as a coconut. Animals that live in water usually lay jellylike eggs. Animals that live on land, such as insects, reptiles, and birds, lay eggs with a hard or leathery shell. The shell prevents an egg from drying out.

*Cockroach egg package contains 16 eggs.*

**Packages**
When cockroaches and praying mantises lay their eggs, they surround them with a special froth. The froth dries and hardens, forming a package like a tiny purse. This package protects the eggs, and the female carries it around on the end of her abdomen until the eggs are ready to hatch.

**Mermaids' purses**
Sharks lay some of the most unusual eggs. Instead of being round, these eggs can be flat, or even spiral. Dogfish, which are small sharks, lay eggs called "mermaids' purses." These have long tendrils with which the dogfish anchors the eggs to underwater plants.

**Eggs without a shell**
Frogs' eggs do not have a shell. Instead, they are surrounded by a layer of jelly. The jelly swells up when the eggs are laid, forming a floating mass that can be more than 12 in (30 cm) across.

**Eggs in strings**
The common toad lays eggs like those of frogs, but they are laid in strings up to 10 ft (3 m) long. As the female lays the eggs, she winds them around underwater plants. The tadpoles hatch after about two weeks.

*Leopard gecko's egg*

**Leathery eggs**
Lizards and many other reptiles have eggs with a leathery shell. Unlike amphibians, reptiles can lay their eggs in dry places because the shell helps keep the inside of the egg moist.

*American robin's egg*

**Chalky eggs**
The shell around birds' eggs is reinforced with a substance like chalk. To hatch, most young birds peck open their shell, but some kick their way out.

*Leatherhead's egg*

## Egg development

After an egg has been laid, a young animal starts to develop inside it. With some insects, such as the housefly, development takes less than a day, but with birds it may take more than a month. Eggs develop more quickly if they are warm, and most birds keep their eggs warm by sitting on them. This is called incubation.

**Mallee fowl**
Instead of sitting on its eggs, the Australian mallee fowl buries them in a huge compost heap that it makes out of dead leaves. Heat from the giant heap keeps the eggs warm.

### Development of a bird's egg
A bird's egg is divided into two main areas – the white and the yolk. The white is made of a substance called albumen. It stores water and cushions the developing chick from any sudden jolts. The yolk contains a store of food, which the chick uses up as it develops.

1 When the egg has just been laid, the part that will become the chick looks like a tiny pale spot. It lies on the upper surface of the yolk.

2 Within a day, cells in the spot start to divide to form an embryo. A network of blood vessels fans out over the yolk and supplies the embryo with food.

3 Three days after the egg was laid, the embryo is growing fast. Its eyes start to form, and tiny buds grow that will soon develop into wings and legs.

4 After seven days, the embryo has become a chick, and a special bag has formed to collect its waste. In three weeks, the chick's development will be complete.

## Egg clutches

Some animals, such as queen termites, lay a steady stream of eggs, but most animals produce eggs in groups called clutches. The number of eggs in a clutch is closely linked to their size. For example, a wandering albatross has very big eggs, but it produces only one egg every two years. By contrast, a sunfish has tiny eggs, but it releases millions each time it breeds.

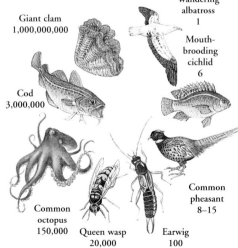

Giant clam 1,000,000,000
Wandering albatross 1
Mouth-brooding cichlid 6
Cod 3,000,000
Common octopus 150,000
Common pheasant 8–15
Queen wasp 20,000
Earwig 100

# Eggs
## Non-passerine birds

**Glossy ibis** eggs are not camouflaged.

**Willow grouse** eggs are laid on the ground where they are camouflaged.

**Plains wanderer** lays eggs in a grass-lined hollow.

**Jamaican tody** eggs are almost spherical and have an extremely thin shell.

**Black shouldered kite** eggs often have marks concentrated at one end.

**Guira cuckoo** eggs are, unusually for cuckoos, incubated by the parents.

**Common guillemot** eggs are sharply pointed.

**Limpkin** eggs are camouflaged to blend in with dead leaves of waterside plants.

**Nacunda nightjar** eggs have brown blotches.

**Prairie chicken** lays up to 16 eggs in each clutch.

**Southern cassowary** eggs have a grainy surface created by raised bumps.

**Manila nightjar** lays its eggs on bare ground.

**Elegant tinamou** eggs have a glossy sheen.

## Passerine birds

**Olive sunbird** eggs have a distinctive ring of marks.

**Yellow-streaked greenbul** eggs have sparse markings formed just before the egg is laid.

**Scarlet minivet** eggs have variable patterns.

**Black-capped mockingthrush's** eggs are mottled with red spots.

**Black and yellow grosbeak's** eggs have streaks that may help break up their outline.

**Cetti's warbler** eggs are reddish-brown.

**Bokmakierie** eggs are blue with red spots.

**Cape crow** eggs have lots of red spots or speckles on them.

**Paradise riflebird** eggs have dark streaks that look like brush marks.

**Black-headed weaver** eggs are variable and laid inside a woven nest.

# EGYPT, ANCIENT

ABOUT 5,000 YEARS ago, the great civilization of ancient Egypt grew up on the banks of the Nile River. It lasted virtually unchanged for 3,000 years. During this time the Egyptians built the first large stone buildings, invented one of the earliest forms of writing, and created a cult of the dead unlike anything known in any other culture. This cult involved preserving dead bodies and burying them with their possessions. As a result, people today know a great deal about the ancient Egyptians.

### Tilling the soil
Egyptian farmers used a lightweight plow pulled by oxen. The plow had a wooden blade and a handle so that the farmer could steer it, and was effective enough to cut a furrow in the light Egyptian soil.

Models of everyday activities, such as tilling the soil, were often found in tombs.

Egyptian farmer, c.2000 BC

## Nile River

The Nile River was the lifeblood of the whole region. Every year the river flooded, depositing dark silt on the banks. This silt made the soil fertile and, because of this, most Egyptians lived by the river. When the Nile flooded and work in the fields was impossible, many people helped on the great royal building projects, such as the Great Pyramid at Giza.

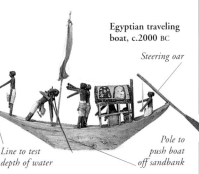

Mediterranean Sea
Nile delta
Giza
Memphis
Saqqara
Thebes
Nile River
Extent of floodplain

3,000-year-old bread found in a tomb

Pomegranate

Grapes

Figs

### Crops
The Egyptians cultivated wheat and barley, from which they made bread and brewed beer. The hot climate also allowed them to grow many different kinds of fruit, including figs, dates, pomegranates, and grapes.

Egyptian traveling boat, c.2000 BC

Steering oar

Line to test depth of water

Pole to push boat off sandbank

### Sailboats
The Nile was the main highway of Egypt. Wooden boats carried passengers and heavy cargo up and down the river. Water transportation was especially useful for heavy loads, such as stones for the pyramids. Egyptian boatbuilders were among the first to attach sails to their craft.

## Pharaohs

Ancient Egypt was ruled by kings called pharaohs. The pharaohs had absolute power, and the Egyptians believed that they joined the gods in the next world when they died. For this reason, the Egyptians took special care when burying their pharaohs, building splendid tombs.

### Pharaoh's court
A pharaoh was surrounded by officials, high priests, and ambassadors, all of whom helped him run the kingdom. The court was also the home of entertainers and the women of the royal harem. The pharaoh and courtiers lived in great luxury. They took pride in their appearance, dressing in fine linen. The women used black eye makeup and had elaborate hairstyles.

### Rameses II
Rameses II (r.1304–1237 BC) was famous for his military campaigns and great building projects. He defended Egypt against the Hittites, signing a peace treaty with them. His many buildings included the mortuary complex at Thebes on the west bank of the Nile, and the temple at Abu Simbel.

## Gods

The Egyptians believed in many different gods. Some were local gods, who represented each district of Egypt. Others had more general powers, such as Thoth, the god of wisdom.

Anubis, the god of death

Amun-re, king of the gods

Osiris, the god of the underworld

Bast, the cat goddess

### Temples
Karnak at Thebes was the greatest of the Egyptian temples. Temples were run by priests, who maintained the building and left offerings for the gods. The most important temples had large estates and rich treasuries, so high priests were very powerful.

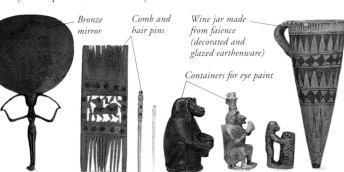

Bronze mirror

Comb and hair pins

Wine jar made from faience (decorated and glazed earthenware)

Containers for eye paint

## Timeline

**3000 BC** Ancient Egyptian civilization begins; early Dynastic Period. The two kingdoms of Upper and Lower Egypt are united under Narmer.

**2650 BC** Step Pyramid of Zoser is built at Saqqara. It is the first pyramid and the first large-scale stone structure.

**2500s BC** Largest of the pyramids is built for Khufu at Giza.

**2100 BC** Middle Kingdom begins. Funerary (funeral) customs spread from royalty to other classes.

Giza

Saqqara

# Mummification

Ancient Egyptians believed in life after death. They thought that people had a spirit as well as a body, and for the person to live in the next world, the spirit had to be reunited with the body. They therefore preserved the body of the dead person in the form of a mummy.

## Mummy cases

The Egyptians placed the mummy inside a coffin or case, and put a cover on top. By the time of the Middle Kingdom (c.2100–1550 BC), they used two coffins to give added protection from tomb robbers and animals. The coffins were decorated with writing, images of the gods, and sacred amulets, or lucky charms.

## Book of the Dead

This is a series of prayers, written on papyrus, that were meant to help the dead person travel to the next world.

**The Weighing of the Heart** ceremony, in which the dead person is judged by the gods

**Thoth, the god of wisdom,** writes details of the person's actions when alive.

## Making a mummy

The Egyptians first removed the organs and dried out the body with natron. They filled the body with sawdust or dry leaves, then wrapped the body in bandages.

*Plate to cover the cut in the body*   *Embalming tools*

*Dish of natron, a natural salt used to dry out the body*

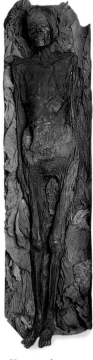

*Red straps usually indicate a priest.*

*Linen wrappings*

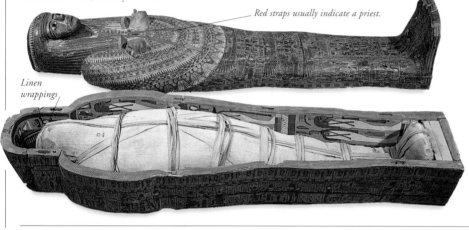

**The body's organs** were placed in containers called canopic jars.

**Unwrapped mummy,** showing how well-preserved the body is

---

# Writing

Ancient Egyptians developed a complex system of writing, called hieroglyphics, in which simple pictures represented objects. Some pictures also stood for letters. Ideas that were too complicated to be shown by one picture were written as groups of hieroglyphs.

## Hieroglyphs and hieratic script

Hieroglyphs were slow to write, so the Egyptians used them mainly for sacred texts and tomb carvings. They used another, faster script, called hieratic, for business and literary texts. Later, they invented a third script, called demotic.

*Royal door plate inscribed with the name of Amenhotep*

*Hieratic script*   *Hieroglyphs*

## Rosetta Stone

For hundreds of years, no one could read hieroglyphs. Then, in 1799, a stone slab called the Rosetta Stone was discovered. It contained the same text in hieroglyphs, demotic, and Greek. Scholars could read and understand Greek, so they could work out the meaning of the hieroglyphs.

# Daily life

For most Egyptians, life consisted of hard work in the fields and on the great building projects. They ate mainly vegetables and bread, and drank beer. High officials and royal courtiers lived a much more leisurely life.

*Ax head*   *Ax*   *Chisel*   *Carpenter's saw*

## Houses

Ancient Egyptians built houses of sun-dried mud-bricks. They covered the walls with smooth plaster. Small, high windows let in the breeze, but kept out the sun. The house pictured above belonged to a royal official, and had a garden with fruit trees.

## Work

Most ancient Egyptians worked at producing their own food. Others were craft workers, making items for the home from wood, pottery, and metal. Their tools, such as saws and chisels, were very similar to the hand tools used by craftspeople today.

---

**1550 BC** New Kingdom founded. Height of Egyptian civilization.

**1503–1482 BC** Reign of Queen Hatshepsut. She sends expeditions to the mysterious land of Punt to buy incense.

**1379–63 BC** Reign of Akhenaten. This pharaoh, with his queen Nefertiti, encourages realistic art and changes Egyptian religion by banning all gods except the sun god.

**Nefertiti**

**1363–52 BC** Brief reign of Tutankhamun, who restored the old gods. He is most famous for the riches discovered in his tomb.

**Tutankhamun**

**1304–1237 BC** Reign of Rameses II, who builds Abu Simbel.

**30 BC** Death of Cleopatra VII; the Romans take over.

**Abu Simbel**

---

FIND OUT MORE

BUILDING AND CONSTRUCTION

FARMING, HISTORY OF

GODS AND GODDESSES

HITTITES

PYRAMIDS

WRITING

# Ancient Egyptian amulets

## Funerary amulets

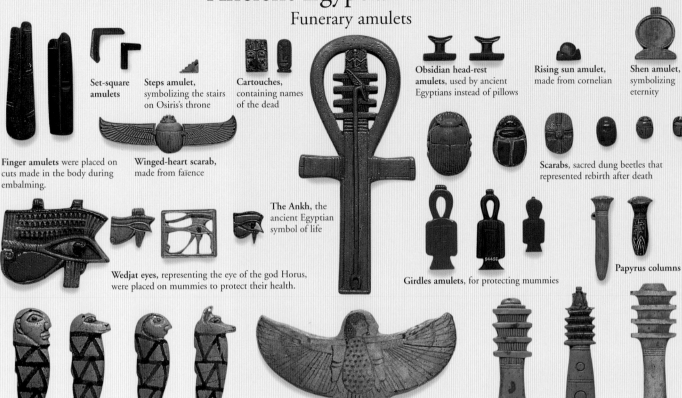

Set-square amulets

Steps amulet, symbolizing the stairs on Osiris's throne

Cartouches, containing names of the dead

Obsidian head-rest amulets, used by ancient Egyptians instead of pillows

Rising sun amulet, made from cornelian

Shen amulet, symbolizing eternity

Finger amulets were placed on cuts made in the body during embalming.

Winged-heart scarab, made from faïence

Scarabs, sacred dung beetles that represented rebirth after death

The Ankh, the ancient Egyptian symbol of life

Wedjat eyes, representing the eye of the god Horus, were placed on mummies to protect their health.

Girdles amulets, for protecting mummies

Papyrus columns

Sons of Horus amulets guarded the canopic jars, which held the vital organs removed from a mummy.

Soul-bird amulet

Djed pillars, amulets representing the backbone of Osiris, were thought to give the mummy strength after death.

## Ushabti figures

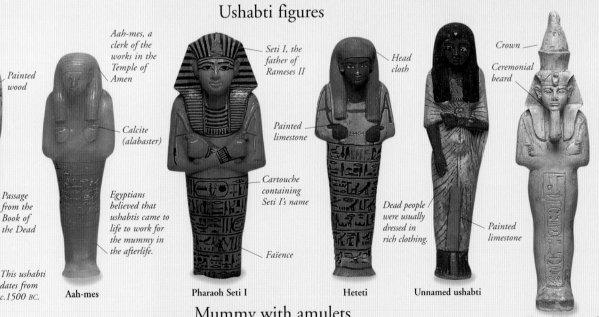

Aah-mes, a clerk of the works in the Temple of Amen

Seti I, the father of Rameses II

Head cloth

Crown

Ceremonial beard

Painted wood

Passage from the Book of the Dead

This ushabti dates from c.1500 BC.

Rensenb

Calcite (alabaster)

Egyptians believed that ushabtis came to life to work for the mummy in the afterlife.

Aah-mes

Painted limestone

Cartouche containing Seti I's name

Faïence

Pharaoh Seti I

Dead people were usually dressed in rich clothing.

Heteti

Painted limestone

Unnamed ushabti

Pharaoh Merenptah

## Mummy with amulets

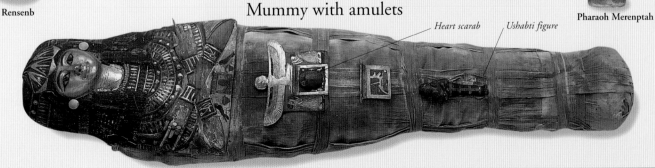

Heart scarab

Ushabti figure

# EINSTEIN, ALBERT

$$E = mc^2$$

ALBERT EINSTEIN WAS a scientific genius who changed the way we view our universe. In 1905, he united space and time in one mathematical description. Ten years later he proposed a complete theory of gravity which explains how the universe works, relating mass and energy in the famous equation $E = mc^2$. Many people doubted his theories, but later investigation proved that Einstein's theories are correct. As well as transforming the science of physics, Einstein's work paved the way for the creation of nuclear weapons.

### Early life
Einstein was born in Ulm, Germany, and studied in Switzerland before graduating from Zurich's Institute of Technology in 1900. He did not fit in at school because he asked many difficult questions, and found no work until he began a job in the Patent Office in Bern in 1902.

## Special Theory of Relativity
In the early 1900s, Einstein developed the Special Theory of Relativity, according to which time is relative: it passes differently for individuals, depending on how fast or slowly they move. The faster anything travels, the slower time seems to pass. If one person travels into space close to the speed of light and another stays on Earth, time is slower for the person in space. On the traveler's return, the stay-at-home will be older.

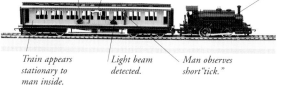

Light beam sent by device on floor.

Light bounces off mirror on ceiling

Train acts as "light clock" – the time taken by light, moving at constant speed, to go along train, acts as one "tick" of the clock.

Train appears stationary to man inside.

Light beam detected.

Man observes short "tick."

Light emitted from device on floor.

Woman sees long "tick."

Train has moved forward by time light beam hits mirror

Train has moved still farther by time light beam hits detector on floor.

### Moving clocks
According to the special theory, time measured by a moving clock will run more slowly than if measured by a stationary clock. This can be demonstrated by light beams carried on a train traveling at nearly the speed of light. A person on the train sees the light travel a short distance; an observer on the platform sees it travel farther because of the train's movement.

This light represents a pulsar.

This light represents a neutron star.

The twin stars make a double dent in space time.

These lines represent peaks and troughs in gravitational waves.

## General Theory of Relativity
Einstein developed the General Theory of Relativity that explains gravity and the nature of space. He explained that as light travels the shortest path through space, when it bends space must be curved. Planets that travel round the Sun are thus following as straight as possible a path through curved space.

### Making waves
Stars in a binary pulsar rotate round each other. As they move, they make waves in space. The waves carry energy from the stars, causing the stars to slow down as they lose energy. The rate that a pulsar slows in its orbit exactly matches Einstein's theory, though the first pulsar was not discovered until 1968.

### Ripples in space
Einstein's theory predicted that objects jiggling around in space – such as two stars in a binary pulsar system – would make ripples in space. These ripples can be detected as gravitational waves. Subsequent experiments have proved Einstein's theory correct.

Stars rotate counterclockwise.

Neutron star moves around pulsar.

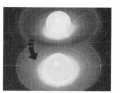
Stars' positions change in relation to observer.

Stars continuously swap places.

## Mileva Einstein
Einstein married his first wife Mileva, a mathematician and scientist in 1903. They had a daughter and two sons. Mileva worked closely with her husband and helped with his research, though to what degree she influenced his work is unknown. They were divorced in 1919.

Mileva and her son Hans Albert

## Political life
In 1933, Einstein moved to America to avoid Nazi persecution as a Jew, and campaigned for a Jewish state. He realized that his theories made possible the creation of nuclear weapons, but campaigned against such weapons after World War II. In 1952, he was offered the presidency of Israel, but declined the offer.

### The bomb
In the late 1930s, Einstein feared that Nazi Germany would use nuclear weapons in war so he wrote to President Franklin D. Roosevelt in 1939, urging the US to begin constructing atomic weapons to counter this threat.

Explosion of atomic bomb

### ALBERT EINSTEIN

| | |
|---|---|
| **1879** | Born in Ulm, Germany. |
| **1896–1900** | Studies at Institute of Technology, Zurich, Switzerland. |
| **1902–09** | Works in Patent Office, Bern, Switzerland. |
| **1905** | Obtains doctorate; writes Special Theory of Relativity. |
| **1914** | Moves to Berlin. |
| **1915** | Writes General Theory of Relativity. |
| **1921** | Awarded Nobel Prize for Physics. |
| **1933** | Moves to the US. |
| **1952** | Offered presidency of Israel. |
| **1955** | Dies in Princeton, N.J. |

**FIND OUT MORE**  NUCLEAR POWER  PHYSICS  SCIENCE, HISTORY OF  WORLD WAR II

# ELECTRICITY

A FLASH OF LIGHTNING is striking evidence of the invisible energy called electricity. This energy is produced by the movement of electrons – tiny particles found in atoms of matter. Every electron carries an identical negative electric charge. When electric charge builds up in one place, it is called static electricity. If the charge flows from place to place, it is called current electricity.

## Electric circuit

The path around which current electricity flows is called a circuit. In the circuit shown here, electricity from the battery lights the bulbs. Two bulbs connected one after the other are described as being "in series." Bulbs in separate branches of the circuit are said to be "in parallel."

*Ammeter measures current from battery.*

*Battery*

*Series circuit*

*Parallel circuit*

*Bulbs in series share the voltage, so they glow dimly.*

*Bulb in parallel gets the full voltage and glows brightly.*

*Voltmeter measures voltage across the bulb.*

## Electric current

Electrons pushed through the wires of a circuit form an electric current. The push on the electrons is called electromotive force (e.m.f). Voltage is a measure of e.m.f. The greater the voltage, the more current flows through the circuit.

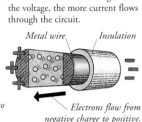

*Metal wire*  *Insulation*

*Electrons flow from negative charge to positive.*

### Battery

A battery is a source of electric current. A chemical reaction between materials in the battery separates electrons from their atoms. The battery's e.m.f makes electrons flow out of the negative terminal, around a circuit, and back to the positive terminal.

*Positive terminal (+)*

*Ammonium chloride paste*

*Carbon rod*

*Zinc casing*

*Negative terminal (–)*

## Static electricity

Rubbing two materials together can transfer electrons from one material to the other. A material that loses electrons gains a positive charge of static electricity, and a material that gains electrons gets a negative charge.

### Attracting and repelling

A positively charged balloon attracts electrons to the surface of nearby hairs, giving them a negative charge. Opposite charges attract, so the hairs are pulled toward the balloon. Charges of the same type repel (push each other away).

### Lightning

A tremendous charge of static electricity builds up inside a storm cloud. A flash of lightning occurs when this charge is suddenly released as a powerful electric current.

*Steel is a good conductor.*

*Plastic blocks current.*

### Conductors

Current can flow only through materials called conductors. Conductors have electrons that are bound loosely to their atoms, so they can move easily through the material.

### Insulators

Current cannot flow through materials called insulators, whose electrons are bound firmly to their atoms.

## Generator

Most of the electricity used in homes and factories is produced by devices called generators. Inside a generator, coils of wire spin rapidly in a magnetic field. The magnetism moves electrons through the wire, creating an electric current. In this simple version, bar magnets produce the magnetic field.

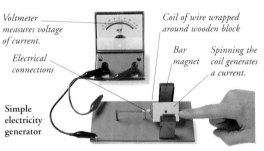

*Voltmeter measures voltage of current.*

*Electrical connections*

*Simple electricity generator*

*Coil of wire wrapped around wooden block*

*Bar magnet*  *Spinning the coil generates a current.*

### Electricity supply

Electric current produced by generators in power stations reaches consumers via cables buried underground or carried by tall towers called pylons. The current alternates, which means that it changes direction many times each second. A battery produces direct current, which flows in one direction only.

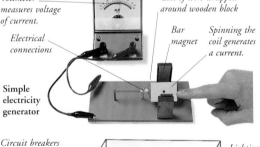

*Circuit breakers cut off the electricity if the voltage gets dangerously high.*

*Meter records how much electricity is consumed.*

*Earth wire*

*Lighting circuit*

*Wall socket*

*Main circuit*

### Electricity in the home

Separate circuits in the home supply different voltages for different purposes. An electrical appliance takes power from the circuits through a plug that fits into a wall socket. The sockets are linked to the ground outside by an earth wire. If an electrical fault occurs, the current is diverted safely into the ground.

### Michael Faraday

In 1831, the English scientist Michael Faraday (1791–1867) built the first generator after noticing that moving a magnet in and out of a wire coil made a current flow through the wire. Faraday also invented the electric motor and pioneered electrolysis (using electricity to break down substances).

## Timeline

**500s BC** The ancient Greeks discover static electricity when they notice that amber (fossilized tree sap) attracts small objects if rubbed with wool.

**Charged amber attracting feather**

**1752** American scientist and politician Benjamin Franklin proves that lightning is an electrical phenomenon.

**1799** Italian physicist Alessandro Volta makes the first battery.

**Volta's battery**

**1831** American physicist Joseph Henry and English Michael Faraday independently build "induction coils" – the world's first electricity generators.

**1868** French chemist Georges Leclanché invents the Leclanché cell, the forerunner of modern zinc-carbon batteries.

**1897** English physicist Joseph John Thomson discovers the electron.

**FIND OUT MORE**  ACIDS AND ALKALIS  ELECTROMAGNETISM  ENERGY  FRICTION  MAGNETISM  STORMS

# ELECTROMAGNETISM

AT THE FLICK OF A SWITCH, an invisible force turns the drum of a washing machine 1,600 times every second. This force is called electromagnetism. It is a form of magnetism produced by electricity. When an electric current flows through a wire, it produces a magnetic field around the wire. Making the wire into a coil increases the strength of the magnetic effect. Winding the coil around an iron bar makes the magnetism even stronger. Any device that exerts electromagnetic forces is called an electromagnet.

*Connections to battery*

*Compasses show magnetic field around coil.*

*Coil*

### Solenoid
A coil of current-carrying wire forms a type of electromagnet called a solenoid. The magnetic field around the coil is the same as that around an ordinary bar magnet. The field's strength depends on the number of turns in the coil and the amount of current flowing through the wire.

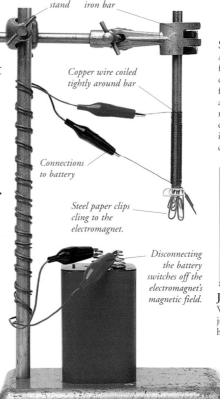

*Clamp stand*

*Clamp holding iron bar*

*Copper wire coiled tightly around bar*

*Connections to battery*

*Steel paper clips cling to the electromagnet.*

*Disconnecting the battery switches off the electromagnet's magnetic field.*

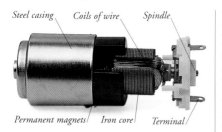

*Steel casing*   *Coils of wire*   *Spindle*

*Permanent magnets*   *Iron core*   *Terminal*

## Electric motor
Inside an electric motor are wire coils surrounded by permanent magnets. Electricity flowing through the wire produces a magnetic field around each coil. The magnetism of the coils interacts with the magnetic fields of the permanent magnets. They push and pull on each other, making the coils rotate. This movement is used to drive machines such as electric drills.

## Electromagnet
Most electromagnets consist of a coil of wire wrapped around an iron bar. When an electric current flows through the wire, a magnetic field forms around the electromagnet. The magnetism can be switched off by disconnecting the electricity supply.

### Junkyard electromagnet
Waste metal is moved around a junkyard by a crane carrying a huge electromagnet. When the electromagnet is switched on, it picks up metal scraps containing iron. The metal is moved to a different place and then dropped by switching off the electromagnet.

### Electric drill
An electric drill can quickly make a hole in wood, stone, and even some metals. Inside the body of the machine, gears harness the rotation of a powerful electric motor to drive the drill at high speed. A cooling fan prevents the drill from overheating.

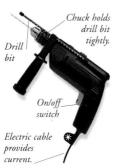

*Chuck holds drill bit tightly.*

*Drill bit*

*On/off switch*

*Electric cable provides current.*

## Uses of electromagnetism
Some electrical appliances contain electric motors that use electromagnetism to produce movement. But electromagnetism is also used in many other ways, such as to make sound or detect hidden objects.

### Loudspeaker
A loudspeaker contains a paper or plastic cone that vibrates and creates sound waves in the air around it. The cone is attached to a wire coil surrounded by a permanent magnet. The magnetic fields of the coil and the magnet interact. This causes the coil to move rapidly to and fro, making the cone vibrate.

*Cone vibrates as electricity flows through coil.*

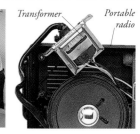

*Transformer*

*Portable radio*

### Metal detector
Inside the arch of an airport metal detector are large coils of wire carrying an electric current. Any person who walks through the arch passes through the magnetic field produced by the coils. A hidden metal object will affect the strength of the field and trigger an alarm.

### Transformer
Many electrical devices use a transformer to alter the voltage of an electrical supply. Inside a transformer are two wire coils. When a varying current flows through one coil, it produces a varying magnetic field. This field causes an electric current to flow through the second coil, but at a different voltage.

## Hans Christian Oersted
The Danish physicist Hans Christian Oersted (1777–1851) discovered electromagnetism in 1820. He placed a compass near a wire carrying an electric current and noticed that the compass needle was deflected and no longer pointed north. Oersted realized that the current had produced a magnetic field around the wire.

## Timeline
**1799** Italian physicist Alessandro Volta invents the battery, which allows scientists to experiment with electric currents.

**1820** Oersted's discovery of electromagnetism opens the way for the development of the electric motor and the electromagnet.

**1821** English scientist Michael Faraday makes an electric motor, in which a current-carrying wire rotates around the pole of a magnet. It has no practical use.

*Faraday's electric motor*

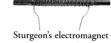

*Sturgeon's electromagnet*

**1828** English scientist William Sturgeon builds the first electromagnet – a coil of wire around an insulated iron bar.

**1883** Croatian-born physicist Nikola Tesla invents the "induction motor" – the first practical motor.

**1885** American engineer William Stanley invents the transformer.

FIND OUT MORE    ELECTRICITY    ENGINES AND MOTORS    FORCE AND MOTION    MAGNETISM    MACHINES, SIMPLE    SOUND

# ELECTRONICS

THE ELECTRONICS REVOLUTION is rapidly changing our world: whether we are at home, at work, or out shopping, we are surrounded by electronic machines and equipment. Electronics involves using devices called components to control electric current, the flow of tiny, electrically charged particles of matter called electrons. An electronic circuit is an arrangement of linked components – such as transistors and diodes – that manipulates current in order to carry out a specific task, such as adding numbers in a calculator.

## Circuit board

The components for an electronic device such as a radio are attached to a circuit board, a flat base with metal tracks running along its underside. The components are secured to the tracks using an alloy called solder. The tracks link the components to form a circuit.

Inductors are wire coils that produce magnetic fields when current passes through them, creating a resistance that restricts the flow of current.

Variable capacitors can be adjusted to store varying levels of charge; in radios, they are used to select radio stations.

Diodes allow electric current to pass through them in one direction only.

Transistors can be used to amplify electrical signals (make them stronger) or switch circuits rapidly on and off.

Resistors allow only a fixed amount of electric current to flow through a circuit.

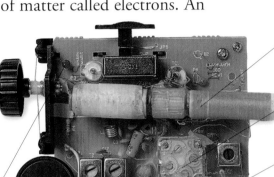

Light Emitting Diodes (LEDs) glow when current passes through them and are used to indicate that a device's power supply is on.

Variable resistors allow the level of current flowing through a circuit to be adjusted.

Radio circuit board and components

Capacitors are components that store electric charge; electrolytic capacitors can store more charge than ceramic ones.

Electrolytic capacitors

Ceramic capacitors

Power cables

Integrated circuits consist of a plastic case containing a complete circuit etched onto a tiny silicon chip.

### William Shockley

US physicist William Shockley (1910–89) was part of a three-man team that invented the transistor in 1947. The transistor made it possible to build tiny electronic circuits and develop more compact electronic devices.

**Remote control**

Pressing a button on the remote control of a TV – for example, to change channels – makes an LED flash pulses of infrared light to the TV set. The TV set decodes the pulses and obeys the instruction.

## Semiconductors

The element silicon is a type of material called a semiconductor, because it conducts electricity only under certain conditions. The properties of a semiconductor can be altered by adding chemical impurities to it in a process called doping. Doped semiconductors are used to make diodes, transistors, and many other electronic components.

Silicon crystal

## Uses of electronics

Electronic circuits are either analog or digital. Analog circuits deal with continuously varying electric currents, such as television and radio signals. Digital circuits process information in the form of thousands of on-off pulses of electric current every second.

Pocket calculator

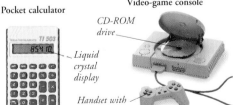

Video-game console

CD-ROM drive

Liquid crystal display

Handset with control keys

### Microprocessors

Many electronic devices including computers – are controlled by circuits called microprocessors, or "silicon chips." A microprocessor is made from a single slice of doped semiconductor. The circuit, which may contain thousands of components, can carry out many complex tasks.

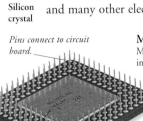

Pins connect to circuit board.

Silicon chip sealed under metal cover

Ceramic casing

### Calculator

A calculator's digital circuits split up a calculation into a series of simple steps, each of which is performed at high speed.

### Video game console

Digital circuits inside the console control the play. The console sends an analog signal to a TV screen, which displays a picture of the game.

Television controls

Liquid crystal display

Timer and clock controls

Number keypad

Video recorder controls

TV/video remote control

FIND OUT MORE   COMPUTERS   ELECTRICITY   ELEMENTS   INFORMATION TECHNOLOGY   METALS   TELEPHONES   TELECOMMUNICATIONS   VIDEO

# ELEMENTS

AN ELEMENT IS a substance composed of only one type of atom. Elements are the most basic substances in the Universe and cannot be split into anything simpler. There are 109 elements – 91 of which occur naturally, and 18 of which can be made artificially. All life on Earth is based on the element carbon, which is vital to the functioning of living cells. Oxygen is the most plentiful element on Earth. It occurs in air, water, and even rocks.

## Elements in nature

Only a few of the naturally occurring elements can be found in their pure state. Most elements combine, or react, with other elements to form more complex substances called compounds. Pure gold can be mined directly from the ground because it is unreactive – that is, it does not readily form compounds.

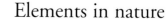

Gold veins in quartz rock

Quartz rock is a compound of the elements silicon and oxygen.

Pure gold.

## Groups of elements

Just as the members of a human family share the same characteristics, there are "families" of elements that have similar properties. An element's chemical properties are determined by the structure of its atoms. Elements in the same group have similar atomic structures.

Calcium gives bones their hardness.

### Alkaline-earth metals
Calcium and magnesium belong to the group of elements called the alkaline-earth metals. They are so named because they form alkaline solutions in water, and their compounds occur widely in nature. Calcium, for example, occurs in seashells, bones, teeth, milk, and chalk. Magnesium occurs in the substance chlorophyll, which plants use to make food by photosynthesis.

### Alkali metals
Potassium (which is used in fertilizers) and sodium (which occurs in salt) are both alkali metals. All the elements in this group are soft, extremely reactive metals. They react violently or even explosively with water to form alkaline solutions.

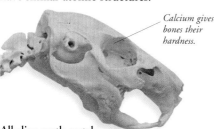

Reaction of potassium in water

### Allotropes

It may seem difficult to believe, but hard, sparkling diamonds are made of the same types of atoms as soft, black graphite. Diamonds and graphite are allotropes of carbon, meaning that they are different physical forms of the same element. Their atoms link up in different ways to make them look and behave differently.

Graphite pencil

Diamonds consist of carbon atoms linked strongly to each other in a rigid framework.

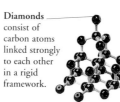

Only weak bonds hold sheets together.

Graphite is made up of sheets of carbon atoms that can slide over each other easily.

### Artificial elements

New elements can be created by bombarding existing elements with high-speed subatomic particles in a device called a particle accelerator. Since 1937, scientists have made 18 new elements, some of which only exist for a few millionths of a second.

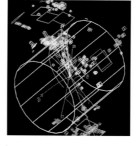

Computer image of a particle accelerator collision

Iron compounds are often red, black, or brown.

Iron sulfide

Iron carbide

Iron oxide

Colored compounds of iron

### Transition metals
The transition metals are a large group of hard, dense elements that conduct electricity and heat well, form colored compounds, and some of which (iron, cobalt, and nickel) are magnetic. Other transition metals include copper, gold, chromium, titanium, platinum, and tungsten.

### Noble gases
Multicolored street signs often contain noble gases, because each of these gases glows a different color when electricity flows through it. Neon, for example, glows red, helium yellow, and argon blue. The noble gases are unreactive nonmetals that rarely form compounds.

Iodine    Bromine    Chlorine

### Halogens
Swimming pools smell the way they do because the halogen chlorine is put in the water to kill germs. Compounds of fluorine, another halogen, are put in water and toothpaste to prevent tooth decay. The halogens, which also include iodine, bromine, and astatine, are all strong-smelling, highly reactive nonmetals.

### Hydrogen
The element hydrogen makes up 90 percent of all the matter in the Universe. It was the first element to form when the Universe was created in the explosion known as the Big Bang. Hydrogen is a tasteless, colorless, odorless, nontoxic gas. It is the simplest of all the elements, with atoms containing just one proton orbited by a single electron. Hydrogen gives acids their acidic properties.

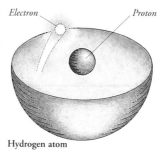

Electron        Proton

Hydrogen atom

### Dmitri Mendeleyev
In 1869, the Russian chemist Dmitri Mendeleyev (1834–1907) devised a chart called the periodic table, which classified the 63 elements then known into different groups. He used the table to predict the existence of three new elements, all of which were discovered a few years later.

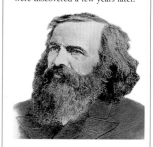

FIND OUT MORE    ACIDS AND ALKALIS    AIR    ATOMS AND MOLECULES    BIG BANG    MATTER    METALS    MIXTURES AND COMPOUNDS    SKELETON    TEETH AND JAWS

# ELEPHANTS

THE AFRICAN AND ASIAN elephants are the only two living species of a once much larger family that was found on every continent. The African elephant is the largest land mammal, but despite its size and power it is a gentle creature. Elephants are highly intelligent, very sociable animals that live in close family units. The African and Asian elephants are descended from different ancestors; the Asian elephant is more closely related to the mammoth than to the African elephant.

## Features of an elephant

Everything about an elephant is oversized. Its most conspicuous feature is the long, flexible trunk – an elongation of the nose. The huge tusks are overgrown incisor teeth. Besides hearing, the large ears are used as fans to cool the elephant. They also make the animal appear larger than it really is, and spreading the ears helps intimidate a rival or a potential enemy. Soft fatty cushions on the underside of the feet spread as the elephant walks.

E

### Teeth
The elephant has only four teeth, one in each quarter of the jaw. Each tooth is about 12 in (30 cm) long. As one wears down, another pushes in from behind. This can happen only six times, after which the supply of teeth is exhausted. Without teeth, the elephant can no longer eat, so it dies of starvation.

### Tusks
A tusk is a specialized type of tooth growing from either side of the upper jaw. Tusks are used mainly as tools and weapons. The heaviest pair of tusks ever recorded weighed 225 lb (102 kg) and 240 lb (109 kg). The longest pair measured 11 ft (3.35 m) and 11 ft 5 in (3.5 m).

### Skin
The skin is very wrinkled. Deep crevices increase the surface area of the skin and allow greater heat loss. The crevices also help trap water, which then takes longer to evaporate, and helps keep the elephant cooler for longer.

*Large ears*

*Elephant using tusks to dig into ground*

*Tusks*

*Trunk*

*Diamond-shaped ridges*

*Pads under large feet expand when stepped on.*

*Tail*

## Trunk

The elephant's trunk is highly flexible and serves much the same function as a human arm and hand. It combines great strength with delicacy, and is so versatile that it can pluck a single leaf as easily as it can lift a heavy log. Because the elephant has a trunk, it does not need to lower its head while feeding, which allows it to remain alert. Its trunk also allows the elephant to graze on leaves that are out of the reach of most other animals.

*The elephant uses its trunk to feed.*

*Fingers are used to hold objects.*

### Nostrils
Located at the tip of the trunk, the elephant's nostrils can be raised high above its head, like a periscope, and turned in any direction to pick up traces of scent carried on the wind. The elephant relies on its sense of smell more than its other senses. In deep water, the trunk may be lifted above the surface and used as a snorkel.

*Picking up scent on the wind*

### Fingers
In addition to the nostrils, the tip of the trunk has fleshy "fingers." The African species has two opposing fingers, but the Asian elephant has only one, which it uses to grip against the wide underside of the trunk. Fingers enable the elephant to perform precise movements and pick up very small objects.

*Upper finger*

*Lower finger*

*Fingers of the African elephant trunk*

## Ivory trade
The elephant's only enemy is humans, who kill for the tusks. In recent years, the demand for ivory has led to killing on a vast scale. From 1979 to 1989, the number of elephants in Africa was reduced from 1.3 million to 609,000.

*Ivory is made into carvings and trinkets.*

## Types of elephants

### Asian elephant
The Asian elephant, found in forests in India and Southeast Asia, has been domesticated for at least 2,500 years. It is used for ceremonial purposes and forestry work. Of the 34,000–56,000 elephants remaining in Asia, 10,000 are working animals.

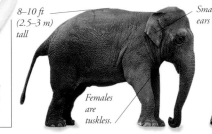

*8–10 ft (2.5–3 m) tall*

*Small ears*

*Females are tuskless.*

### African bush elephant
The African bush elephant lives in open country and woodland in Africa south of the Sahara. It is larger, with much larger ears and a more concave back, than the Asian elephant. Both males and females have tusks. Unlike the Asian elephant, it has never been domesticated.

*Large ears*

*Elephant reaching up with its trunk*

*Small, rounded ears*

*13 ft (4 m) tall*

### African forest elephant
The forest elephant is a smaller subspecies of the African bush elephant, with smaller, more rounded ears. It does not need such large ears to help it keep cool, because it lives in the tropical rain forests of the Congo basin in equatorial Africa. Its tusks are slender and point downward.

E

# Family group

The elephant's social organization is based upon a group of 10–12 females and their calves, led by a mature female. Harmonious relationships often develop between individual members of the group. Friendships can last for decades, as elephants often live for up to 80 years. Elephants show great affection for their young, but discipline is strong, and any lapse of acceptable behavior is dealt with firmly. Family groups often seek shade during the heat of the day, preferring to feed and drink in the cool of the evening. Elephants graze on leaves and shoots, but they also eat grass. They spend about 18 hours a day feeding, to satisfy their huge appetites.

### Herd gathering
Separate family groups associate closely with each other. They often live only a few hundred yards apart, constantly coming together and drifting apart again. Occasionally, many family groups congregate in an exceptionally large herd of more than a thousand animals.

### Young
Females normally conceive every four years and give birth to a single calf after 22 months' gestation, the longest gestation period of any animal. The newborn calf stands about 33 in (84 cm) high. Other calves from previous matings remain with their mother after the new calf is born. The older calves help take care of their younger siblings.

### Water holes
Elephants like to drink every day. They also enjoy bathing and spraying themselves with water. As the dry season advances, food and water become scarce, and they may have to walk up to 50 miles (80 km) between watering and feeding grounds. They also dig holes in some riverbeds to reach water below the surface, thereby providing water for other animals.

### Matriarch
Leadership of the family unit rests with the oldest and most experienced female, the matriarch, who is usually the mother or grandmother of the whole group. Each member of the group knows its position in the hierarchy and respects matriarchal authority without question.

*Secretion shows bull is in musth.*

# Bulls

Only immature bull calves are allowed in the family group; as soon as the bulls reach maturity they are expelled. They live alone or in small bachelor groups. Mature bulls briefly rejoin the herd when any of the cows are ready for mating.

### Musth
By 25 years of age, bulls come into musth once a year. Musth is a period of aggressive behavior in which a bull picks fights with other bulls searching for a female ready to mate. A thick secretion from the temporal gland indicates he is in musth.

### Fighting
Young bulls often have mock battles to test each other's strength. They are usually harmless affairs in which they clash tusks and grapple with each other's trunks. Older bulls, especially those in musth, may sometimes fight to defend territory or to establish dominance.

*Young bulls sparring*

### Threat displays
Differences between elephants are generally resolved peacefully. Displeasure is indicated by head-shaking, ear-spreading, trunk-twirling, and foot-shuffling, called a threat display. If this behavior fails to deter, the elephant may make a full-scale charge. This is a rare event in which the elephant covers ground at rapid speed, with its trunk raised and ears outstretched, while trumpeting furiously. Threat charges are rarely carried through; the elephant usually halts or turns at the last moment.

*Ears spread wide to intimidate an enemy.*

# Communication

Touch is an important way of communicating in elephant society. When elephants meet, they greet each other by entwining trunks and touching each other's face and body. At rest, they often stand together, head to head. If a young calf misbehaves, its mother may actually use her trunk to smack it. When a calf is frightened, other elephants help calm it by standing close and caressing it with their trunks.

*Elephants standing face to face and touching each others' heads and trunks*

### Rumbling
Elephants maintain contact by means of rumbling sounds from the throat, back of the nose, and trunk. A sudden cessation of rumbling warns the herd of possible danger. Elephants are also capable of communicating over substantial distances, with low-frequency sounds that humans cannot hear.

### AFRICAN ELEPHANT

| | |
|---|---|
| **SCIENTIFIC NAME** | *Loxodonta africana* |
| **ORDER** | Proboscidea |
| **FAMILY** | Elephantidae |
| **DISTRIBUTION** | Africa south of the Sahara |
| **HABITAT** | Open savannas and forests |
| **DIET** | Grasses, leaves, shoots, twigs, and other shrubs |
| **SIZE** | Height at shoulder: 13 ft (4 m); weight: 6.7 tons (6.1 tonnes) |
| **LIFESPAN** | 70–80 years |

**FIND OUT MORE**    AFRICAN WILDLIFE    ANIMAL BEHAVIOR    ASIAN WILDLIFE    CONSERVATION    ECOLOGY AND ECOSYSTEMS    GRASSLAND WILDLIFE    MAMMALS    RAIN FOREST WILDLIFE

# ELIZABETH I

FOR THE 45 YEARS from 1558–1603, a truly remarkable woman governed England. By force of personality and political skill, Queen Elizabeth I united her divided country and presided over one of the greatest periods in the arts and culture. Yet she had to struggle all her life: her mother died when she was only three, her sister later put her in prison and, as an adult, she was a single woman in a world dominated by men. But she overcame every adversity, and when she died in 1603, she left England one of the most prosperous and powerful nations in Europe.

Elizabeth I's accession to the throne, at the age of 25

### Early life
Elizabeth was the daughter of Henry VIII (r.1509–47) and his second wife, Anne Boleyn. She was born in Greenwich Palace on September 7, 1533. Elizabeth's mother was executed for treason when Elizabeth was just three years old. The future queen was imprisoned briefly while her Catholic half sister Mary was crowned queen. Elizabeth took the throne on November 17, 1558, after Mary's death.

## Church and state
Elizabeth's father Henry VIII broke with the Roman Catholic Church in 1534, establishing the Protestant Church of England. Her half sister Mary I (r.1553–58) tried to return England to Catholicism, but Elizabeth introduced the Anglican faith, as a compromise between Catholicism and extreme Protestantism.

### William Cecil
Cecil, later Lord Burghley, served Elizabeth first as her Chief Secretary of State and, after 1572, as Lord Treasurer. He introduced many reforms and was an able adviser to the queen. He died in 1598, and his son became chief minister.

### Mary, Queen of Scots
Mary was Elizabeth's heir, but also a Catholic. She became the center of many plots against Elizabeth, notably one led by Mary's page Anthony Babington. Elizabeth reluctantly had Mary tried and executed for treason in 1587.

## Spanish Armada
As leader of Catholic Europe, Philip II of Spain, husband of Elizabeth's half sister Mary, was a threat to Protestant England and encouraged plots against the queen. After the execution of Mary, Queen of Scots, Philip decided to invade England. In 1588, he sent a huge Armada of 130 ships carrying 20,000 soldiers. Harried by English ships, attacked in the English Channel, and wrecked by severe storms, the Armada was forced to return, in defeat, to Spain.

English fire ships are sent to meet the Spanish fleet.

Spanish ships escape toward the North.

### Francis Drake
Between 1577 and 1580, in his ship the *Golden Hind*, Francis Drake became the first Englishman to sail around the world. He delayed preparations for the Spanish Armada by attacking the fleet while it was at anchor in Cadiz Harbor in 1587, and played an important part in its defeat the following year. He continued to attack Spanish shipping until his death off the coast of Panama in 1596.

## Phoenix emblem
Elizabeth created a strong public image of herself by adopting the phoenix as her emblem. The "Phoenix Jewel," dated around 1574, shows a bust of Elizabeth, with a reverse image of the mythical phoenix rising from flames.

The renowned "Phoenix Jewel"

### Virgin Queen
Elizabeth spent her life surrounded by suitors, yet she never married. Powerful foreign monarchs courted Elizabeth throughout her life, eager for a stake in her flourishing kingdom, but she played her suitors off against each other for political gains. Elizabeth gloried in her role as the Virgin Queen, using it to create a national self-confidence that fueled a flowering of the arts, distinguished by William Shakespeare, the poet Edmund Spenser, and composers such as Thomas Tallis.

Elizabeth stands on a map of her kingdom.

### ELIZABETH I

1533 Born in Greenwich Palace near London, England.

1536 Elizabeth's mother, Anne Boleyn, executed for treason.

1554 Elizabeth put under house arrest by half sister, Mary.

1558 Succeeds to the throne; appoints William Cecil as Secretary of State and Matthew Parker as Archbishop of Canterbury.

1559 Act of Supremacy makes her head of Anglican church.

1588 Spanish Armada defeated.

1603 Dies in Richmond Palace.

FIND OUT MORE

CHRISTIANITY    DRAMA    HOUSES AND HOMES    REFORMATION    SHAKESPEARE, WILLIAM    THEATERS    SPAIN, HISTORY OF    UNITED KINGDOM, HISTORY OF

# EMPIRES

E

A LARGE SUPER-STATE under a single ruler is called an empire. There have been many different empires throughout history, from the ancient Roman Empire to the great empire of the Incas in Peru. The largest ever was the British Empire. Most empires have an army to conquer territory and suppress revolts, and a government to carry out the day-to-day running of the empire and collect taxes. No empire lasts forever – though the effect on the occupied countries may be permanent. Empires perish for many reasons, including internal rebellion, economic decline, or the sheer difficulty of uniting many peoples under one leader.

Ottoman sword and scabbard

## Growth of empires

Empires grow because ruling powers want extra income from trade or taxes, or they may have territorial ambitions, or they may want to convert a conquered people to a religion. Empires always need a strong army.

Imperial cross

### Ottoman Empire
The Ottoman Turks expanded their empire by military might. At their height in the 17th century, they dominated the Mediterranean coast from present-day Greece to Tunisia.

### Holy Roman Empire
Based in Germany, the leaders of this empire saw themselves as heirs to the Roman emperors. The emperors wanted to wield religious power over all western Christians and to exert political power over the other European rulers, such as the German and Italian princes.

## British Empire

The largest empire the world has ever seen had its beginnings in the 18th and early 19th centuries, when Britain acquired Australia, Canada, and a range of territories from Honduras to Hong Kong. The "jewel in the crown" of the empire was India, which Britain dominated through the East India Company. Queen Victoria (r.1837–1901) took the title Empress of India in 1876. The British Empire had a lasting influence on its territories – for both good and bad. British-style administration provided a model for local governments when territories gained independence. On the other hand, the British exploited local labor forces on a massive scale.

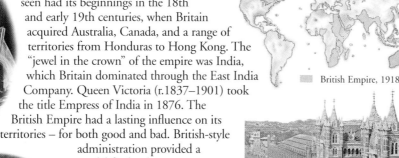
British Empire, 1918

### Extent of the empire
After winning the Napoleonic Wars, and with the decline of the older empires of Spain, Portugal, and the Netherlands, Britain was clearly one of the world's strongest countries. As the 19th century wore on, the already vast British Empire added parts of Africa and Southeast Asia. By 1918, the empire had reached its peak.

Victoria Station Bombay, India

### Gordon of Khartoum
In 1884, two years after Egypt became part of the empire, General Charles Gordon (1833–85) came to Sudan to aid Egyptians defending their garrisons against a local revolt. Gordon was cut off in the city of Khartoum and withstood a 10-month siege, but was finally killed. There was an outcry that a relief force had not been sent quickly enough to save Gordon, and he became a hero of the empire.

### Resources of the empire
Britain had limited resources but an expanding industry, so the British used their empire as a source of raw materials and as a market for goods. The far-flung empire provided raw materials such as cotton, gemstones, hard wood, tea, rubber, tin, copper, and wool.

Timber

Cotton    Emerald

### Public works
The British built the major towns of the empire in the style of British cities. They sent British engineers and architects all over the world to build government headquarters, churches, railroad stations, art galleries, and public buildings. Former imperial cities, such as Bombay, still have Victorian-era administration and transportation centers.

## Timeline

**509 BC–AD 476** Roman Empire dominates much of Europe, western Asia, and northern Africa.

**221–206 BC** Qin emperor unites China.

**321–187 BC** Mauryans rule much of India.

**324–1453** Byzantine Empire established in the eastern territory of the Roman Empire.

**962–1806** Holy Roman Empire dominates central Europe.

Conquistador's helmet

**1206–1405** Mongols create an empire, including most of Asia.

**1345–1521** Aztec emperors hold power in Mexico.

**1521–1825** Spain builds large empire in southern America.

**1580–1931** British Empire increases in size.

**1930s** British Empire starts to decline. By the 1940s, territories are claiming independence.

## Imperialism

The economic domination from the 17th century of Asia, North America, and Africa by Europe, the United States, and Russia is known as modern imperialism. Ancient imperialism peaked with the Roman Empire.

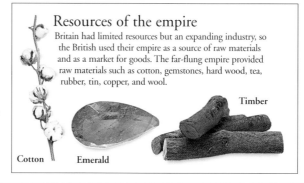

The bear, symbol of Russia, 1888

# ENERGY

WE RELY ON THE ENERGY stored in food to keep us alive and on the energy locked within fuels to drive our machines and industries. Energy is the ability to make things happen, whether it is moving something, heating it up, or changing it in some way. Energy exists in many different forms, including electricity, sound, heat, and light.

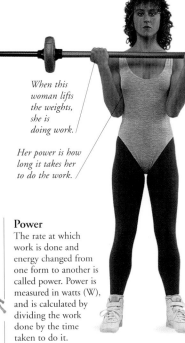

*When this woman lifts the weights, she is doing work.*

*Her power is how long it takes her to do the work.*

*Weights gain potential energy.*

## Work

When a force moves an object, energy changes from one form to another and work is the result. This woman does work as she lifts weights. The force she applies converts the kinetic energy of her moving arms into the potential energy of the raised weights. Multiplying the force by the distance through which the object moves gives the amount of work done.

## Types of energy

All energy is either kinetic or potential. Kinetic energy is the energy of moving objects, while potential energy is energy that is stored, ready for use. Energy is measured in units called joules (J).

*When this frog leaps through the air, it has kinetic energy.*

### Kinetic energy

All objects in motion – from atoms to aircraft – possess kinetic energy. The higher the object's speed and the greater its mass, the more kinetic energy the object has.

### Power

The rate at which work is done and energy changed from one form to another is called power. Power is measured in watts (W), and is calculated by dividing the work done by the time taken to do it.

### Potential energy

An object may gain potential energy if its position or condition alters. A bungee-jumper standing on top of a bridge has potential energy – that is, the potential to fall back to Earth. When he jumps, his bungee rope gains potential energy as it stretches, because it has the potential to pull him back up again.

*The jumper's potential energy changes to kinetic energy as he falls.*

*1.1 lb (500 g) peas*
*3 oz (90 g) beef*
*1.8 oz (50 g) sugar*
*1.1 lb (500 g) peeled oranges*
*1 oz (30 g) butter*
*1.8 oz (50 g) cheese*

### Chemical energy

Foods and fuels contain energy stored within chemical compounds. This is a type of potential energy called chemical energy. Some foods store more energy than others. All the foods above contain the same amount of energy, but you would have to eat 1.1 lb (500 g) of peas to get as much energy as you would from just 1 oz (30 g) of butter.

**100 W fan**
**1,000 W iron**

### Electrical power

Every electrical appliance is given a power rating. If a fan has a power rating of 100 W, the rating shows that the fan changes 100 J of electrical energy into kinetic energy each second. Similarly, a 1,000 W iron changes electricity into heat at the rate of 1,000 J per second.

*Both bulbs give out the same light.*

**60 W bulb (incandescent)**
**15 W bulb (fluorescent)**

*Fluorescent bulb uses less electricity.*

### Efficiency

Out of every 100 J of electrical energy used by a 60 W incandescent bulb, only 10 J are changed into light; the rest are lost as heat. The bulb has an efficiency of 10%. A 15 W fluorescent bulb is 40% efficient. It gives the same light using a quarter of the electricity.

## Energy transfer

The Law of Conservation of Energy says that energy is always conserved – that is, it can be neither created nor destroyed. This law means that when objects gain or lose energy, the energy simply transfers from place to place, or changes into a different form.

*Harvested wheat*
*Bread is made from wheat.*
*Friction occurs between brake and wheel.*

1 Tremendous temperatures at the Sun's surface cause it to give out light and other forms of energy, some of which reach the Earth.

2 When sunlight falls on plants, some of the light energy transfers to the plants by a process called photosynthesis. It is stored as chemical energy.

3 Eating whole-grain foods such as bread enables you to break down the stored chemical energy in the food and transfer it to your body.

4 Riding a bicycle changes the chemical energy into kinetic energy. If you brake, friction changes this energy into heat as you slow down.

### James Joule

The unit of energy, the joule, is named after the English physicist James Joule (1818–89), who helped to develop the Law of Conservation of Energy. Joule noticed that if he rotated a set of paddles in water, the water soon became warm. He realized that the work of turning the paddles changed their kinetic energy into heat, proving that heat is a form of energy.

### Timeline

**1829** French physicist Gustave Coriolis introduces the term "kinetic energy."

**1843** James Joule's experiments show how heat, work, and power are related.

**1847** Joule and German physicists Hermann von Helmholtz and Julius Meyer independently state the Law of Conservation of Energy.

**1853** Scottish scientist William Rankine devises the concept of "potential energy."

**1881** The world's first electricity-generating power plant opens in Surrey, UK.

**1884** Irish engineer Charles Parsons invents the steam turbine.

*Parsons' turbine*

**1905** German physicist Albert Einstein suggests that matter is a form of energy, and vice versa.

**1980s** Declining fossil fuel reserves and pollution bring calls for machines and industries to be more energy efficient.

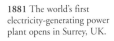

303

E

# Power plant

Most of the energy used in homes, offices, and factories is electricity produced by power plants. Inside a coal- or oil-fired power plant, chemical energy stored within fuel turns into heat energy as the fuel burns in a furnace. The heat is used to boil water into steam, which drives turbines linked to electricity generators. The electricity reaches consumers by a network of cables called a grid.

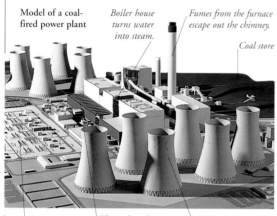

Model of a coal-fired power plant

Boiler house turns water into steam.

Fumes from the furnace escape out the chimney.

Coal store

Connections to electricity grid

The turbine house contains the turbines and generators.

Cooling towers turn steam from the boiler back into water.

The turbine blades revolve about 3,000 times each minute.

The generator uses the motion of the turbine to produce electricity.

Turbine-generator unit in a coal-fired power plant

## Turbine

A turbine is a machine powered by the force of moving liquid or gas. It consists of a set of angled blades mounted on a shaft. In a power plant, jets of high-pressure steam strike the turbine blades and make them revolve at high speed. The turbine shaft is connected to an electricity generator. As the shaft spins, it turns an electromagnet inside the generator, producing an electric current.

# Renewable energy

Energy that is produced without permanently using up the Earth's limited resources is called renewable energy. Apart from biomass fuels, which produce smoke and other fumes when burned, renewable energy sources are pollution free, because they harness the energy of natural phenomena such as winds and waves. As the Earth's fossil fuel reserves are gradually used up, people will have to rely much more on renewable energy sources.

## Geothermal power

Below the Earth's surface, water is turned into steam by geothermal energy – that is, the energy of hot, molten rocks. By drilling a well, this steam can be harnessed to drive generators. Electricity produced in this way is called geothermal power.

## Wind power

A wind turbine is a tall tower with propellerlike blades that converts the kinetic energy of the wind into electricity. As the wind blows, the turbine's blades rotate and drive a small generator. A group of wind turbines is called a wind farm.

## Hydroelectric power

A hydroelectric power plant converts the kinetic energy of falling water into electricity. The power plant sits under a dam at the end of a reservoir. Inside the power station, turbines and generators are driven by water rushing down with tremendous force from the reservoir above.

## Wave power

Towers such as the one above stand in coastal waters and use the movement of the ocean's waves to produce electricity. As the waves rise and fall, they push a column of air inside the tower up and down. The to-and-fro motion of the air turns a turbine and drives a generator.

## Solar power

Electricity produced from sunlight is called solar power. A "solar furnace" uses a vast bank of mirrors to focus sunlight onto water. The water boils into steam, which drives turbines and generators.

## Biomass fuels

Plant material is called biomass. Millions of people around the world burn peat, wood, animal dung, and other biomass fuels to heat and light their homes and to cook food. Burning biomass fuels releases chemical energy stored within the plant material.

## Tidal barrage

At high and low tides, huge amounts of water move up and down river estuaries. A tidal barrage is a dam across an estuary. As the tides come in and go out, some water is allowed to pass through tunnels in the dam. The tidal flow drives electricity generators built into the dam.

# Fossil fuels

Coal, oil, and natural gas are called fossil fuels because they formed underground over millions of years from the fossilized remains of plants and animals. The Earth has limited supplies of these fuels – they cannot be replenished once exhausted.

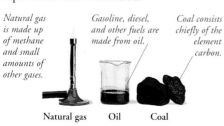

Natural gas is made up of methane and small amounts of other gases.

Gasoline, diesel, and other fuels are made from oil.

Coal consists chiefly of the element carbon.

Natural gas          Oil          Coal

## Charles Parsons

The engineer Charles Parsons (1854–1931) was born in London, England, of Irish parents. He is best known for inventing the steam turbine in 1884. Power plants around the world still use steam turbines based on Parson's designs. In 1897, his boat *Turbinia* became the first to use a steam turbine to power its propellers.

# World energy use

Around 90 percent of all the energy used comes from fossil fuels, which give out a lot of energy when burned, but release polluting gases into the air. Nuclear power is an alternative to fossil fuels, but produces dangerous radioactive waste. Hydroelectric power is the only form of renewable energy that is used in any significant amount.

Oil 40%

Nuclear power 6%

Hydroelectric power 7%

Gas 22%          Coal 25%

**FIND OUT MORE**          COAL          ELECTRICITY          FOOD          HEAT AND TEMPERATURE          LIGHT          NUCLEAR POWER          OIL          SOUND          X RAYS AND THE ELECTROMAGNETIC SPECTRUM

# ENGINES AND MOTORS

EVERY MACHINE THAT MOVES OR HAS
moving parts needs an engine or a motor
to make it work. A motor is a machine
that converts some form of energy, such as
fuel or electricity, into motion. An engine is a
kind of motor. Engines and motors, both huge
and tiny, are everywhere – in vehicles from
motorcycles to airliners and railroad locomotives,
and in appliances around the home, in
industrial machines, and in power stations.

## Early engines

The first engines,
developed in the
middle of the 18th century,
were steam-powered. During the
19th century, a new form of engine was
developed: the internal combustion engine,
which was lighter and had more practical
uses than its predecessor.

*Early four-cylinder
gasoline engine*

E

## Modern engines

Fuel efficiency, plenty of power for
its low weight, and little need for
maintenance are the hallmarks of the
modern car engine. Many engines
have electronic components that
further increase their fuel efficiency.

**Internal combustion engine**
Most cars are fitted with internal combustion
engines – so-called because they combust, or
burn, fuel inside a cylinder. The power this
combustion produces is
harnessed by pistons
and used to power
the engine.

**Exterior of internal
combustion engine**

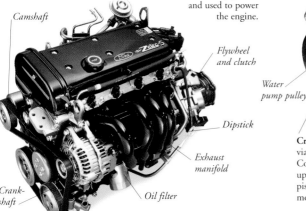

*Camshaft*

*Flywheel
and clutch*

*Crank-
shaft*

*Dipstick*

*Oil filter*

*Exhaust
manifold*

**Camshaft** controls the opening and
closing of the valves. There are
separate camshafts for fuel
inlet and exhaust valves.

**Timing belt**
drives the
camshaft.

*Spark plug*

**Combustion chamber**
is where fuel burns to
force the piston down.

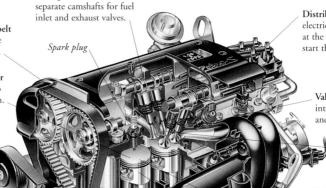

**Sectioned view of a petrol-fuelled
internal combustion engine**

**Distributor** feeds a spark of
electricity to each cylinder
at the right moment, to
start the fuel burning.

**Valves** let fresh fuel
into each cylinder,
and spent gases out.

*Valve
assembly*

*Exhaust manifold
channels waste gases
and heat to exhaust pipe.*

*Cylinder
and piston*

**The pistons** slide up
and down in the
cylinders, providing the
driving force that keeps
the engine running. The
number of cylinders in
an engine varies; there
are usually at least four,
and sometimes more.

*Water
pump pulley*

*Oil filter*

*Sump reservoir
for lubricating oil*

**Crankshaft** turns the wheels
via the clutch and gearbox.
Connecting rods turn the
up-and-down motion of the
pistons into the circular
motion of the crankshaft.

**Lubricating oil** is
pumped around the engine,
continuously covering the
moving parts with a thin film
of oil that stops them rubbing
together and wearing out.

## How engines work

This sequence of diagrams
shows what happens in one
cylinder of a gasoline engine
while the engine is running.
During the sequence, the
piston goes down, up, down,
and up again. This is called a
four-stroke cycle. The cycle is
repeated over and over again –
up to 50 times a second when
the engine is turning at high
speed. In an engine with more
than one cylinder, the cylinders
fire one after the other to
provide continuous power.

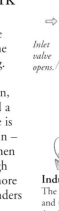

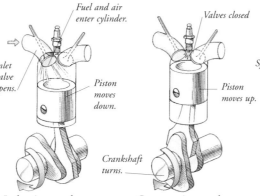

*Fuel and air
enter cylinder.*

*Inlet
valve
opens.*

*Piston
moves
down.*

*Crankshaft
turns.*

*Valves closed*

*Piston
moves up.*

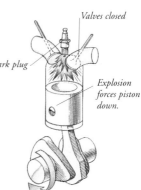

*Valves closed*

*Spark plug*

*Explosion
forces piston
down.*

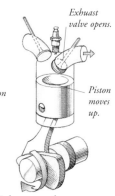

*Exhaust
valve opens.*

*Piston
moves
up.*

**Induction stroke**
The piston moves down
and the inlet valve opens.
A mixture of fuel and air is
sucked into the cylinder.

**Compression stroke**
The valve closes. The
piston moves up again,
squeezing the fuel and air
into the top of the cylinder.

**Power stroke**
The spark plug flares
and ignites the fuel
which explodes, pushing
the piston back down.

**Exhaust stroke**
The piston moves up,
pushing waste gases out of the
cylinder. The exhaust valve
opens to let exhaust gases out.

E

# Diesel engine

A diesel engine is a four-stroke engine without spark plugs. The engine's cylinder has a piston, which rises and falls, squashing the fuel-and-air mixture in the cylinder into a tiny space. The mixture gets so hot, it explodes.

Eight-cylinder diesel truck engine

## Using diesels

Diesel engines are very fuel-efficient. They are used for driving electricity generators, and in vehicles that need to keep going for long periods without refuelling, such as lorries, taxis, trains, ships, and boats. Many modern cars are also fitted with diesel engines.

*The heated air turns the turbine blades at rear.*

*Burning fuel heats the air in the combustion chamber.*

*Air is sucked in the front.*

# Gas turbine engines

In a gas turbine, burning fuel makes a stream of hot gas that spins a set of turbine blades very fast. A shaft attached to the turbine drives a compressor that sucks air into the engine so the fuel burns.

## Jet engine

High-speed aircraft have a type of turbine called a turbojet or turbofan. The stream of hot air and gases created in the engine turns the turbine, then shoots out of the back of the engine, pushing the aircraft forward.

## Turboshaft engine

Some turbine engines make ship or aircraft propellers spin. The spinning turbine turns a shaft connected to the propeller. Large hovercraft have turboshaft engines to create their air cushion and to drive their propellers. Large helicopters also have turboshaft engines to turn their rotors.

SR.N4 ferry hovercraft

# Steam engine

The pistons of a steam engine are moved up and down in their cylinders by steam under high pressure. The pistons are connected to rods that turn the wheels. The steam is made outside the cylinders by heating water in a coal-fired boiler, which is why steam engines are called external combustion engines.

## Using steam

Until the middle of the 1900s, most railway locomotives and ships were powered by steam engines. Steam also drove many early trucks and buses. The first steam engines were used for pumping flood water out of mines, and to work industrial machines.

*Steam leaves train via a funnel.*

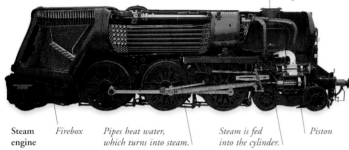

Steam engine | Firebox | Pipes heat water, which turns into steam. | Steam is fed into the cylinder. | Piston

# Electric motors

An electric motor produces movement from electricity. Inside it are electromagnets – wire coils that become magnets when an electric current flows through them. The electromagnets are turned on and off in sequence to pull a magnetic shaft around and around. Motors are used in household appliances.

Hairdryer

## Blow

The electric motor in a hairdryer turns a fan to blow air that is heated by hot wire coils. A switch adjusts the speed of the motor. The larger the current it allows through, the stronger the magnets become, and the faster the motor spins.

## Suck

A vacuum cleaner has a powerful electric motor that turns an air pump. The pump sucks air through the machine, where the dust is removed from it. The motor has to generate a lot of power, so it needs electricity from the mains to drive it.

Vacuum cleaner

## Turn

Many kitchen gadgets, such as food processors, have an electric motor that moves their working parts. Gears slow the speed of the motor, so the parts turn slowly. The electricity comes either from the mains or from batteries.

Food processor

# Solar power

Petroleum and coal are fossil fuels, formed from decayed prehistoric organisms. They are expensive to produce, and create harmful gases when they burn. Solar energy is energy from the Sun. It can be used to heat houses, run air conditioning, and to generate electricity to power lightweight vehicles.

## Solar panels

Sunlight can be turned into electricity by solar panels. These are made from many photovoltaic cells. The bigger the area of photovoltaic cells, and the brighter the sunlight, the larger the electric current the solar panel will produce.

Solar-powered car

## James Watt

British engineer James Watt (1736–1819) improved the design of steam engines, and produced the first effective one in 1765. In 1774, he and Matthew Boulton began building steam engines for pumping water from mines. The unit of power, the watt, is named after him.

# Timeline

**1st century** AD Hero of Alexandria, a Greek inventor, makes a novelty toy that is turned by steam.

**1698** Englishman Thomas Savery (c.1650–1715) builds the first machine to provide power by using steam.

**1815** British engineer George Stephenson (1781–1848) builds the first steam-powered locomotive.

Gears

**1876** In Germany, Nikolaus Otto (1832–91) develops the first four-stroke petrol engine. It is a great commercial success.

**1892** The diesel engine, used for driving machines, is patented by German engineer Rudolph Diesel.

**1894** The *Turbinia*, the first ship with a steam-turbine engine rather than a piston engine, is demonstrated in England.

**1937** The first jet engine is demonstrated by the British jet-power pioneer Frank Whittle (b. 1907).

AIRCRAFT    CARS AND TRUCKS    ELECTRICITY    FORCE AND MOTION    INDUSTRIAL REVOLUTION

# ETRUSCANS

A PIRATE PEOPLE OF MYSTERIOUS ORIGIN, the Etruscans dominated the Mediterranean world from the 8th to the 4th centuries BC and formed a league of 12 city-states in what is now modern Tuscany, Italy. Though many of these cities – possibly the first in the area – have been lost over the centuries, superb painting and statuary remain. Etruscan fortunes, based on trade and conquest, started to decline after c.500 BC when the Romans, who had lived under Etruscan rule for a century, began to absorb their former masters into their own expanding empire.

### Expansion
From their base in Etruria, the Etruscans' influence spread between the northern Alps and Naples. From 616 BC, the Tarquins, an Etruscan dynasty, ruled Rome itself.

## Art

Vivid wall paintings have survived in tombs at the ancient cities of Orvieto, Veii, and Tarquinia – some dating to c.600 BC. Scenes often show dancing, religious observances, or the underworld. Etruscan art was influenced by the Greeks in subject matter and style, but as the Etruscan civilization grew, it developed its own bold, colorful, and naturalistic style.

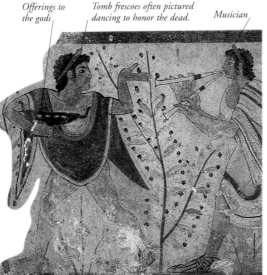

Offerings to the gods

Tomb frescoes often pictured dancing to honor the dead.

Musician

Wall painting, Tomb of the Leopard, Tarquinia

### Cities of the dead
Rich Etruscans were buried in underground tombs, some of which were carved from rock to resemble rooms. These cities of the dead contained frescoes, furniture, and lavish ornaments that tell us much about daily life.

Etruscan rock-cut tombs, Sovana

### Bronze sculpture
The best sculptures were made in metal, especially bronze. Early sculptors made copies of imported Syrian or Phoenician objects, but then Greek styles became more popular.

Pan, the liveliest Greek god, in Etruscan style

### Statuary
Etruscan sculptors made statues of terra-cotta – a brownish-red, unglazed, fine pottery. The sculptors were particularly skilled at creating realistic human faces and figures, such as those at the precinct of Apollo in the city-state of Veii.

## Pirates and traders

For centuries, Etruscan ships dominated the area of the Mediterranean called the Tyrrhenian Sea. Feared at first as pirates, Etruscans later turned to legitimate and prosperous trade with the Phoenicians, Greeks, and Egyptians, until they were eclipsed by the Romans.

Etruscans adopted the letters of the Greek alphabet.

Bronze coin

### Trade
Etruscan agriculture, industry, and commerce all flourished in the period before the rise of Rome. Mineral deposits in the area allowed the Etruscans to trade metal products, such as jewelry and bronze figurines, as far away as Scandinavia and England.

Etruscan jewelers were especially good goldsmiths; surviving pieces show originality and artistry. Much gold jewelry was made for trade with Greece.

Semi-precious stones

Gold bead

Necklace

Gold medallion

### Language
Though examples of Etruscan writing survive on coins and tablets, the language remains a mystery. It is believed to be the last spoken language before modern European languages took over. The first six numbers were *mach, zal, thu, huth, ci, sa,* but no one has determined which of them match the numbers 1, 2, 3, 4, 5, 6.

Fragment of marble statue

Sheep livers and cloud patterns were thought to reflect the will of the gods.

### Relationship with Rome
The last Etruscan king was overthrown in 510 BC, as Rome took over the Etruscan cities one by one. Many practices, such as predicting the future by studying sheep entrails, lived on in the new Roman republic. Leading Roman families were proud of their Etruscan ancestry.

Flowers

Fruit

Naturalistic human features

Gold earrings

Gold wreath hair ornament

### City people
No one can be sure exactly which 12 walled cities formed the original Etruscan league. Ancient walls still surround modern Tuscan towns, such as Orvieto. The original cities were built haphazardly and were dominated by temples.

FIND OUT MORE
ART, HISTORY OF    ARCHITECTURE    GREECE, ANCIENT    ITALY, HISTORY OF    METAL    RELIGIONS    ROMAN EMPIRE    SCULPTURE

# EUROPE

THE SECOND SMALLEST of all the continents, Europe nevertheless has the third largest population. Rich, fertile soils, a variable but hospitable climate, and abundant natural resources have made it easy for people to live in Europe for thousands of years, establishing more than 40 nations and considerable wealth. Shifting land borders and inhabitants of wide ethnic diversity have caused conflict, but Europe is politically stable and is a major world power.

## Physical features

Europe's landscapes range from frozen tundra and coniferous forests in the north to the balmy Mediterranean coast and arid semidesert of central Spain. The high mountains of the Pyrenees, Alps, Carpathians, and Urals give way to the low-lying North European Plain. Rivers provide communication and transportation.

**Ural Mountains**
The Ural Mountains in Russia separate Europe from Asia. They stretch 1,500 miles (2,400 km) from the Arctic Ocean to the Caspian Sea. The highest mountain is Narodnaya at 6,214 ft (1,894 m).

**North European Plain**
The vast, rolling North European Plain extends from southern England, across France and Germany, and into Russia as far as the Urals. Rich in coal, oil, natural gas, and fertile farmland, this is Europe's most densely populated area.

**Alps**
The high Alps dominate western Europe. Stretching 932 miles (1,500 km) from southern France, through Switzerland, Germany, Italy, Austria, and Southeast Europe, this vast arc of mountains separates northern Europe from the warmer south. The highest point is France's Mont Blanc at 15,774 ft (4,808 m).

## Cross-section through Europe

Fertile farmland on France's Atlantic coast rises to the plateau of the Massif Central and the Alps at more than 13,125 ft (4,000 m) above sea level. It then drops down to the Hungarian plain before climbing upward again to the Carpathians and down into the Black Sea.

Bay of Biscay — Massif Central — Mont Blanc — Alps — Plain of Hungary — Carpathian Mountains — Black Sea

A          Approximately 1,500 miles (2,400 km) from A to B          B

## EUROPE FACTS

| | |
|---|---|
| **AREA** | 4,000,000 sq miles (10,400,000 sq km) |
| **POPULATION** | 704,900,000 |
| **NUMBER OF COUNTRIES** | 43 |
| **BIGGEST COUNTRY** | Russian Federation |
| **SMALLEST COUNTRY** | Vatican City |
| **HIGHEST POINT** | Mt. El'brus 18,481 ft (5,633 m), Caucasus Mountains |
| **LOWEST POINT** | Volga Delta 92 ft (28 m) below sea level, Caspian Sea |
| **LONGEST RIVER** | Volga |
| **BIGGEST FRESHWATER LAKE** | Lake Ladoga |

# Climatic zones

Europe's position and varied landscape greatly affect its climate. Apart from the far north where it is always cold, European winters are generally cool, and summers warm or hot. Europe's west coast is milder because of the Gulf Stream that brings warm waters north. Mountains, such as the Alps and Pyrenees, form a natural barrier, protecting the south from the rain and cold winds that blow from the north.

Polar, Coniferous forest, Tundra, Wetland, Deciduous forest, Scrub, Mountain, Grassland, Desert

*Only shallow-rooted plants can survive the cold.*

## Tundra
The extreme north of Europe lies inside the Arctic Circle and has a polar climate. The vegetation there is tundra, treeless plain where much of the subsoil is permafrost, permanently frozen ground. Only in summer does the topsoil thaw and plantlife flourish.

## Deciduous forest
Broad-leaved woods and forests are found in many parts of Europe. The trees, which lose their leaves in winter, include the quick-growing birch and ash, and the slower, longer-lived beech, chestnut, maple, plane, and oak. Today, few truly ancient forests survive, and most of these trees have been planted.

**Oak leaves and acorns**

*Beech trees lose their dead leaves in spring when the new buds sprout.*

*Straight trunks provide timber for making paper, furniture, and boards.*

## Taiga
In Russian, the word taiga means a marshy forest. The trees in the forests of northern Europe are mainly conifers, such as fir, larch, and pine. They keep their needlelike leaves even during the cold winters when they may be covered with snow for many months.

**Pine-needles and cone**

## Grasslands
Large areas of Europe, such as the central *meseta* region of Spain and the steppes of southern Russia and southeastern Ukraine, are covered in vast expanses of dry grassland. Much of this land is used for grazing animals and growing crops. Drought can be a problem in extreme summer temperatures.

*Many plants have small leathery leaves to conserve water in the summer heat.*

*Ice, rain, and wind make it impossible for plants to survive on the peaks.*

*In the spring, the grass is lush and green, but becomes scorched as summer wears on.*

## Garrigue
The warm, dry hillsides close to the Mediterranean Sea in countries such as Spain, Greece, and France are covered with thorny, often aromatic plants and low bushes. In limestone soils this vegetation is called *garrigue*, elsewhere it is *maquis*.

## Pyrenees
The Pyrenees form part of a vast arc of comparatively young mountains that stretch almost continuously across southern Europe and join with the Himalayas in Asia. Unlike the ancient mountains in Britain and Scandinavia, their shape is still changing because of plate movements beneath the Earth's crust. Mount Aneto is the highest peak at 12,962 ft (3,404 m).

## People
Most Europeans live in densely populated towns and cities, many of which lie on the fertile North European Plain. Living standards are generally high compared with other parts of the world, and Europeans benefit from plentiful food and good healthcare. Many countries have sizable ethnic minorities, usually from former colonies. The majority of Europeans are Christian.

**Finnish girl**   **Greek boy**   **French girl**

## Resources
Europe is rich in natural resources. More than half the land is used for farming a wide variety of food crops, from grains such as wheat, barley, and oats to grapes, olives, citrus fruits, and salad vegetables. Europe mines 40 percent of the world's coal and around 33 percent of its iron ore. There are also great reserves of oil and natural gas, and lead, zinc, and other metals. Many of the rivers supply hydroelectric power.

**Grapes**

**Coal**

**Wheat**

**FIND OUT MORE**   CLIMATE   CONTINENTS   EUROPE, HISTORY OF   EUROPEAN WILDLIFE   FARMING   FORESTS   MOUNTAINS AND VALLEYS   ROCKS AND MINERALS   TREES   TUNDRA

# EUROPE, HISTORY OF

EUROPE HAS PLAYED a much more important role in world history than its small population or size would suggest. The Greeks and Romans colonized large parts of North Africa and western Asia, and from the 15th century, European nations established trading empires that spanned the globe. The Industrial Revolution of the 18th century gave Europe an economic strength that allowed it to dominate world trade, and both World Wars began in Europe. Since 1945, Europe's global influence has declined, as wealth and military power has shifted to North America and Asia.

### Prehistoric Europe
The first settlers in Europe were primitive hunters, who moved around in search of food. By about 5000 BC, people learned to farm and settled in villages. Bronze-working, and later iron-working, spread across the continent.

**Prehistoric "Venus" figurine from Lespugue, France**

## Civilizations of Europe
After 900 BC, four peoples made their successive mark on Europe. The first were the Greeks, who created powerful city-states. They were followed a century later by the Etruscans in Italy. By 200 BC, the Celts had settled across Europe. Finally, the vast and powerful Roman Empire spanned the continent, reaching its height in AD 117.

## Christian Europe

In the 4th century, Christianity became the official religion of the Roman Empire, and over the next 700 years the faith spread throughout Europe. With the breakup of the Roman Empire by 476 and the lack of any strong political force afterward, Christianity became the single unifying force across the continent, and the church gained great power.

**Papal ring**

### Papacy
As head of the Roman Catholic Church, the popes had enormous spiritual power. Vast landholdings also gave the popes much political power, which led to many conflicts between the papacy and the leading rulers of Europe.

### Greek Europe
The independent city-states of ancient Greece got most of their wealth from trade. Their merchants sailed around the Mediterranean and established colonies from Spain to the Black Sea. The most powerful Greek cities were Athens and Sparta.

**Ionic-style capital from ancient Greek temple**

### East and west
Attempts by the pope in Rome to establish his jurisdiction over the entire Christian Church were resisted by the Orthodox Churches of eastern Europe, centred around the ancient city of Constantinople. In 1054, this schism (split) became final, leading to a religious division in Christian Europe that survives to this day.

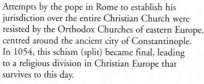

*College built around a central quadrangle*

**Merton College, one of Oxford's earliest colleges**

**Orthodox icon of the Archangel Gabriel**

### Growth of education
The Church dominated education, at first through the monasteries and then the universities. The first university in Europe, specializing in medicine, was established at Salerno in southern Italy in the 9th century; others, such as Bologna, Paris, and Oxford, followed later.

**Latin inscription from a Roman tomb**

### Roman Europe
From its foundation in c.753 BC, the city of Rome gradually expanded its power until, by the first century AD, it controlled most of Europe. The Romans gave Europe a network of roads, a common language (Latin), and a legal system, all of which survived long after the fall of the empire in the 5th century.

## Nation state

By the 16th century, centralized national governments had emerged right across Europe, from Spain in the west to Russia in the east. The Holy Roman Empire had began to break up, and in countries such as England power was concentrated in the hands of the monarch who ruled with the support of a parliament, composed of members of the aristocracy and church.

**The royal coat of arms of Philip II of Spain decorates the cover of one of his books.**

### Religious wars
The creation of new Protestant Churches in the 16th century divided western Europe. Roman Catholic and Protestant states fought for supremacy in a series of bitter wars that lasted until the middle of the next century.

**Henry IV of France was raised Protestant, but later converted to Catholicism.**

**Basilica in Goa, India**

### Overseas empires
In the 15th century, European nations built up empires. Spain and Portugal colonized Central and South America; Britain, France, and the Netherlands colonized North America and the Far East.

E

# World imperialism

The Industrial Revolution began in Britain in the mid-1700s, and it transformed world politics and economics. Within a century, European nations were strong and rich enough to set up colonies all around the world. Only the United States was able to resist European influence.

Diamonds

Hemp

Cotton

## Global economy

In the 19th century, European steamships took raw materials from their colonies to factories in Europe, and shipped out finished goods to markets abroad. The huge industrial cities of Europe gained vast wealth, but at the expense of poor producers in African and Asian colonies.

## Nationalism

During the 19th century, many of the peoples of Europe struggled to obtain their freedom from outside rulers. In one year, 1848, Italians, Germans, Hungarians, Poles, Irish, and others fought for independence or fairer forms of government.

Fighting at Catánia, Italy, 1848

# World wars

*Austrian officer's hat*

*Scottish private's cap*

Soldiers' hats, 1914

Twice in the 20th century, European conflicts led to war on every continent. In 1914, national rivalries resulted in a four-year war that cost 22 million lives. Germany was defeated and dissatisfied with the peace treaty. Again, war broke out in 1939. By the end of that war in 1945, Europe was exhausted. Two superpowers, the USA and the Soviet Union, now dominated international affairs.

## End of empires

World War I led to the defeat of four great European empires – Germany, Austro-Hungary, Russia, and Turkey – and weakened both Britain and France. After World War II, Europe's overseas colonies fought successfully for independence, with only France retaining sizeable overseas possessions.

**The double-headed eagle symbol of Germany**

Flag of Nazi Germany

## Rival ideologies

Communism was established in Russia after 1917 and in Eastern Europe after 1945, while Fascism and Nazism took hold in Italy, Germany, and Spain in the years up to 1945. By 1990, parliamentary democracy, at first weak in Europe, was the dominant form of government.

## Iron Curtain

After World War II, Russian troops occupied much of Eastern Europe. A clear border, known as the Iron Curtain, emerged between the Russian-dominated east and American-dominated west. The border split Germany into two countries.

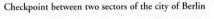

**YOU ARE LEAVING THE AMERICAN SECTOR**
**ВЫ ВЫЕЗЖАЕТЕ ИЗ АМЕРИКАНСКОГО СЕКТОРА**
**VOUS SORTEZ DU SECTEUR AMÉRICAIN**
**SIE VERLASSEN DEN AMERIKANISCHEN SEKTOR**

**Checkpoint between two sectors of the city of Berlin**

# Modern Europe

After World War II, French and German politicians worked together to overcome their old hostilities. Economic collaboration between the two countries developed into a formal European Union that grew to include many other western European countries. With the collapse of communism and the rise of market economies in Eastern Europe, many former communist countries lined up to join the EU.

## Collapse of Communism

During the late 1980s, Russia withdrew its military and economic support from its communist allies in Eastern Europe. Popular protests then overthrew communism in every East European nation by 1990, but by the late 1990s, there was deep unrest in many of these countries.

**Revolution on the streets of Romania**

## Willy Brandt

Willy Brandt (1913–92) was born in Lübeck, Germany, but lived in Norway during World War II, where he was active in the Resistance. As Chancellor of West Germany from 1969–74, Brandt worked to improve east-west relations and made treaties with Poland and the USSR. He was awarded the 1971 Nobel Peace Prize.

# Timeline

c.1250 BC Mycenaean culture flourishes in Greece.

c.900 BC Greek city-states gain power.

c.753 BC Rome is founded.

c.200 BC Celts spread across Europe.

**Bronze statue of Roman legionary**

AD 117 Roman Empire is at its height.

1054 Christian Church splits into Orthodox east and Roman Catholic west.

1500s European nations use their navigation skills to explore and colonize large parts of the globe.

1914–18 World War I.

1939–45 World War II.

Mid–1700s Industrial Revolution begins to transform the European economy.

1871 The map of Europe is transformed as Germany and Italy become unified nations.

**Flag of European Union**

1940s–80s Europe gives up most of its colonies.

1957 EEC is set up.

1989–91 Communism falls.

1994 Outbreak of war in Southeast Europe.

2001 Euro is launched.

**FIND OUT MORE**   CELTS   COLD WAR   EMPIRES   GOVERNMENTS AND POLITICS   GREECE, ANCIENT   HOLY ROMAN EMPIRE   MEDIEVAL EUROPE   ROMAN EMPIRE   WORLD WAR I   WORLD WAR II

# EUROPE, CENTRAL

LYING AT THE HEART of Europe on the North European Plain, central Europe consists of four countries: Poland, the Czech Republic, Slovakia, and Hungary. With poor defenses because of the flat terrain, this historically troubled region has often been invaded by neighboring powers and its country borders redrawn. At one time or another, French, Germans, and Russians have all dominated the area. After World War II (1939–45), the countries of central Europe became communist states closely tied to the former Soviet Union. Since their independence in the late 1980s, many have struggled to compete on the world market.

## Roman Catholicism

In spite of repeated invasions of the area, and half a century of antireligious communist rule, Roman Catholicism remains the dominant religion of central Europe. Throughout the region, colorful processions celebrate saints' days and other religious festivals.

**Religious procession, Kraków, Poland**

## Physical features

Most of central Europe lies on the vast North European Plain and is largely flat, rolling farmland, broken by the low Sudeten and Carpathian Mountains in the south. In the north, rivers flow into the Baltic; in the south, they flow into the Danube on its way to the Black Sea.

**Tatra Mountains**
The Tatra Mountains between Poland and Slovakia are the highest part of the Carpathian Range. Their breathtaking scenery makes them popular with walkers in summer, and in winter the snow-covered peaks attract skiers.

**Forests**
Poland's Bialowieza National Park is the largest area of woodland in northern Europe. Some woods have survived for thousands of years, but acid rain now threatens them. One quarter of central Europe is forested.

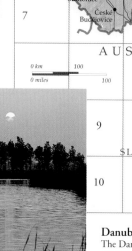

**Danube River**
The Danube is 1,775 miles (2,857 km) long and links Germany and the Rhine River to the Black Sea. It is Europe's greatest waterway and is used for carrying freight and generating hydroelectric power in Slovakia.

**Regional climate**
Central Europe has a temperate climate with hot summers and cold winters. Winters tend to be milder in the south, except in the Carpathian Mountains and other upland areas where heavy snow falls. The summer months are often the wettest.

68°F (20°C)     13°F (-2°C)

22 in (553 mm)

# Poland

This country of medieval towns and scattered farms and villages has a history of invasion and occupation by foreign powers. From 1945 to 1989, Poland was a communist state. Since the collapse of communism, however, Poland has been experiencing massive economic, social, and political change. Poland has a strong strategic position between eastern and western Europe and joined NATO in 1999.

## People
Like the neighboring Czechs and Slovaks, Poles originate from the Slavic peoples of Europe. Poland has few ethnic minorities, and more than 95 percent of the people are Polish-speaking Roman Catholics. Many Poles have a traditional way of life; local folk arts and crafts flourish. These include wood carving and colorful embroidery.

POLAND FACTS

CAPITAL CITY Warsaw

AREA 120,720 sq miles (312,680 sq km)

POPULATION 38,800,000

DENSITY 330 per sq mile (127 per sq km)

MAIN LANGUAGE Polish

MAJOR RELIGION Christian

CURRENCY Zloty

LIFE EXPECTANCY 73 years

PEOPLE PER DOCTOR 435

GOVERNMENT Multiparty democracy

ADULT LITERACY 99%

## Warsaw
Poland's capital since the 1500s, Warsaw was almost completely destroyed during World War II (1939–45). Working from original plans, paintings, and photographs, the Poles have rebuilt the city, restoring its ancient landmarks and treasured buildings. Today, the reconstructed buildings line wide streets and squares.

**Old Town Square**

Beet

Potato

## Root crops
Poland is a major producer of rye, and also of root crops such as potatoes, sugar beets, and beets. Nearly half the land is used to grow crops or raise livestock, particularly pigs. State farms account for about 10 percent of this land. Most privately owned farms are small, producing some crops to sell, and the rest to feed farmers' families. Farming employs about a quarter of Poland's workforce.

Sugar beet

## Wheat
Poland's leading grain crop is wheat, although yields are poor. Two-thirds of the wheat is fed to livestock, some, with potatoes, is used to distill vodka, and with the rest, farmers bake bread.

## Industry
About one-fifth of Poland's labor force works in industry, but production in the huge old Soviet-style factories is inefficient. In order to compete on the free market, the government is slowly privatizing industry. Shipbuilding is an important industry on the Baltic Coast, and the Gdansk shipyard is one of several. Poland has a thriving iron and steel industry, and big reserves of coal, lignite (brown coal), copper, lead, silver, and zinc.

# Czech Republic

The Czech Republic consists of the two ancient states of Bohemia and Moravia, which once formed part of the Holy Roman Empire. From 1918, it was part of Czechoslovakia and only emerged as an independent country in 1993, when Czechoslovakia was partitioned. The Czech Republic is central Europe's most industrialized nation, and manufacturing employs 40 percent of its workforce.

## Farming
Only five percent of the Czech workforce is employed in farming. Much of the land is controlled by large farms owned by the state or cooperatives. Czech farms have some of the highest grain yields in central Europe, but most is fed to livestock because the Republic specializes in meat and milk production.

CZECH REPUBLIC FACTS

CAPITAL CITY Prague

AREA 30,260 sq miles (78,370 sq km)

POPULATION 10,200,215

DENSITY 335 per sq mile (129 per sq km)

MAIN LANGUAGE Czech

MAJOR RELIGION Christian

CURRENCY Czech koruna

LIFE EXPECTANCY 76 years

PEOPLE PER DOCTOR 333

GOVERNMENT Multiparty democracy

ADULT LITERACY 99%

## Prague
One of the most beautiful capital cities in Europe, Prague has remained virtually unchanged for centuries. Today, it plays host to an increasing number of visitors who come for both business and pleasure. However, air pollution caused by nearby factories poses a major problem.

**St. Nicholas's Church**

## Bohemian glass
Since the 1300s, the Bohemians of the south have made beautifully decorated glass from the fine sands found in this region. Bohemian glass is prized for its high quality, elegance, and delicacy.

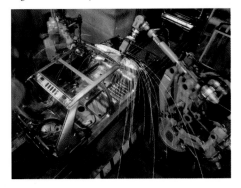

## Beer
Czech beers are popular all over the world, and Budweiser, Budvar, and Pilsner are household names. Brewing traditions go back hundreds of years.

## Industry
The breakup of the communist regime led to the privatization of many Czech companies. However, some of the very large factories, such as the Skoda works at Plzen, remain under state control. Czech factories are able to produce about 200,000 cars a year. As well as cars, Skoda produces locomotives, machine tools, and weapons. The Czechs also produce iron and steel, machinery, and transportation equipment, although there is a trend to move away from heavy industry into consumer goods such as textiles.

# Slovakia

Slovakia was the rural and poorer half of Czechoslovakia, and after its independence in 1993, the country suffered economically. Much of the land is mountainous and forested. About half is used for crops or grazing, but industry now employs a large number of workers. Most people are Slovaks, speaking their own language, but there are also some Roma and Czechs, as well as a nine percent Hungarian minority.

### SLOVAKIA FACTS

| | |
|---|---|
| CAPITAL CITY | Bratislava |
| AREA | 19,100 sq miles (49,500 sq km) |
| POPULATION | 5,400,000 |
| MAIN LANGUAGE | Slovak |
| MAJOR RELIGION | Christian |
| CURRENCY | Koruna |

### Bratislava

From 1536 to 1784, Bratislava was the capital of Hungary. Now it is the capital of an independent Slovakia. The city was founded in the 10th century, and has had a university since 1467. The new parliament buildings were once the home of an archbishop. Bratislava is a Danube river port and a rail center. Its factories make chemicals and engineering goods.

### Rural life

The Slovakian countryside is a mixture of mountain villages, ancient walled towns, and castles. There are still many large state-run farms, but about 20 percent of the land is farmed by tiny, family-run concerns. The main crops are potatoes, sugar beets, and grains. Rural life is hard, and poverty is common, driving increasing numbers of young people to towns in search of work.

### Folklore

Folk traditions are strong in Slovakia, where puppet shows are popular. The former Czechoslovakia is acknowledged as the original home of European puppetry. The Slovakian people enjoy folk festivals where they can dress in regional costumes and sing and dance to traditional music.

**Wooden puppet**

# Hungary

Hungary was formed about a thousand years ago by the Magyars, an ethnic group from Russia that makes up 90 percent of today's population. Hungary was communist from 1945 until 1990, and since then its industries have had to compete on the world market. The country's skilled scientists and engineers have succeeded in attracting foreign investment.

### Thermal springs

Hungary has hundreds of hot thermal springs; their warm mineral waters are said to have medicinal properties. The country has more than 150 spring baths, which are open to the public.

### HUNGARY FACTS

| | |
|---|---|
| CAPITAL CITY | Budapest |
| AREA | 35,919 sq miles (93,030 sq km) |
| POPULATION | 10,000,000 |
| DENSITY | 280 per sq mile (108 per sq km) |
| MAIN LANGUAGE | Hungarian (Magyar) |
| MAJOR RELIGION | Christian |
| CURRENCY | Forint |
| LIFE EXPECTANCY | 71 years |
| PEOPLE PER DOCTOR | 286 |
| GOVERNMENT | Multiparty democracy |
| ADULT LITERACY | 99% |

### Wine

Hungary is a world-class wine producer and exports a wide range of high-quality red and white wines. The best known Hungarian wine is Tokay, pronounced tok-eye. It is a sweet, rich, golden wine, widely believed to be healthful. Another well-known Hungarian wine is Bull's Blood, so-called for its dark blood-red color.

### Paprika

Hungarians grow more than 40 percent of the world's paprika, a sweet, bright-red pepper used in cooking. One town, Kalocsa in southern Hungary, even has a museum devoted entirely to this spice. Paprika originally came from Central America. Hungarian farmers also grow rye, corn, wheat, barley, sugar beets, and potatoes, as well as grapes, olives, and figs. Sunflowers are grown for their oil.

*Goulash is a traditional Hungarian stew.*

### Goulash

Hungary's most famous dish is goulash, a stew of beef with vegetables, flavored and colored with paprika. A pork version is called *pörkhölt*. Other traditional dishes with paprika include bacon and potato casserole, and chicken paprikash.

### Budapest

Straddling the Danube, Budapest is two cities in one – Buda on the hilly right bank, and Pest on the low-lying left bank. Buda was the old royal capital of Hungary, and has fine old buildings and the remains of a Roman town. Pest is the country's administrative and industrial center.

**The Parliament buildings in Pest, viewed from Buda**

### Horse breeding

Hungary has a long tradition of horse breeding, located at the great stud farms at Mezöhegyes and Bábolna. The best-known Hungarian breeds are the Nonius and Furioso, which were developed at Mezöhegyes, and the Shagya Arab at Bábolna. Today, these stud farms develop horses for taking part in shows.

**Hungary's oldest stud farm at Mezöhegyes**

 FIND OUT MORE   CHRISTIANITY   EMPIRES   EUROPE   EUROPE, HISTORY OF   FARMING   GOVERNMENTS AND POLITICS   HOLY ROMAN EMPIRE   HORSES   SOVIET UNION

# EUROPEAN UNION

FIFTEEN COUNTRIES have joined together to form the European Union (EU). But Europe was not always at peace. Between 1870 and 1945, France and Germany were at war three times. Determined to ensure their two countries never fought each other again, the French and Germans decided to link their coal and steel industries so their nations would be forced to work together. The creation of the European Coal and Steel Community (ECSC) in 1951 led to today's European Union.

## The euro
On 1 January 2002, a single currency, the euro, was fully launched in 12 countries of the European Union (EU). The notes and coins of this new currency replaced the national currencies of those nations. The only EU countries to stay out of the monetary union were Britain, Denmark, and Sweden.

E

## Uniting Europe
In 1957, the ECSC evolved into the wider European Economic Community (EEC). Ten years later, this became the European Community (EC). In 1991, EC leaders signed the Maastricht Treaty, which started Europe towards full economic and monetary union. When the treaty came into force in 1993, the EC became the European Union (EU).

**The growing union**
The European Union has 15 members. A further 13 states have applied for membership, with more considering joining. Trade and cooperation agreements are already in place between the EU and many applicants. Switzerland has close trade links with the EU, but a national referendum in 2001 rejected joining.

1 Netherlands
2 Belgium
3 Luxembourg
4 Slovenia

*More countries in central and eastern Europe are intending to apply.*

Date of joining
- [ ] 1957
- [ ] 1973
- [ ] 1981
- [ ] 1986
- [ ] 1995
- [ ] Membership applications

Members of the EU, 2001

## Structure of the EU
The EU has three main institutions. The Commission, based in Brussels, Belgium, is the civil service that runs the EU; the Parliament, in Strasbourg, France, and Brussels, provides control over the EU; while the European Court of Justice, in Luxembourg, makes sure EU laws are applied properly.

**European Parliament**
Every five years, adults throughout the EU go to the polls to elect 626 Members of the European Parliament (MEPs) to represent their interests. Although it does not have the same powers as a national parliament, the European Parliament advises the Commission and supervises its work and annual budget.

## What the EU does
The European Union has many different roles covering economic, financial, commercial, political, industrial, agricultural, social, and cultural matters. Its two main achievements have been to establish free trade between the member states by abolishing customs duties, and to set up a common agricultural and fisheries policy.

**EU aid**
The EU provides subsidies to the less well off regions of Europe, for projects such as developing new industries. Much EU aid is targeted toward improving transportation links in Europe, such as building roads, so all regions can share the benefits of the single market.

*The EU has sponsored a common European passport.*

**Agricultural policy**
In order to guarantee food supplies and increase agricultural productivity, the EU runs the very complex Common Agricultural Policy (CAP). It has established free movement of farm produce throughout the EU.

**Social policy**
The EU tries to improve employment for unemployed workers and young people by investing in education and training in deprived regions. It has also established the Social Chapter of Workers' Rights.

## Jean Monnet
Jean Monnet (1888–1979) was a French economist who convinced the French foreign minister, Robert Schuman (1886–1963), that the only way to avoid another war between France and Germany was to integrate their coal and steel industries. The ECSC was set up with Monnet as its first president. His vision led directly to the development of today's EU.

## Timeline

**1951** European Coal and Steel Community (ECSC) is set up.

**1957** The ECSC nations sign the Treaty of Rome, setting up the European Economic Community (EEC); a separate treaty establishes the European Atomic Energy Community (Euratom).

**1967** ECSC, EEC, and Euratom merge to form the European Community (EC).

**1979** European Monetary System set up to link currencies.

**1991** Maastricht Treaty sets out timetable for full economic union.

**1993** EC becomes the European Union (EU).

**2002** The euro replaces existing currencies in 12 EU countries.

**FIND OUT MORE** | EUROPE, HISTORY OF | FARMING | FISHING INDUSTRY | FOOD | MONEY | TRADE AND INDUSTRY | WORLD WAR II

# EUROPEAN WILDLIFE

EUROPE IS A landmass that contains many different habitats, ranging from the Arctic tundra, through broad-leaved forests, and mountainous areas, to dry, hot regions around the Mediterranean. Only deserts and tropical forests are missing from the list. European wildlife is not as rich as it once was; human intervention in the form of agriculture and forest clearance, as well as the sheer size of the human population, has diminished the number of plants and animals. Yet in undisturbed forests and wetlands, a large diversity of wildlife remains.

## Broad-leaved woodland wildlife

Broad-leaved woodlands extend across Europe. The trees within them, such as oaks and sycamores, are broad-leaved, or deciduous trees, which means they lose their leaves in winter. In spring and summer, when the leaves reappear and plants bloom, woodlands support many insects, birds, and mammals, such as squirrels and mice.

*Dappled coats help to camouflage deer as they graze on grass.*

### Oak tree
Commonly found in broad-leaved woodlands, oaks provide homes and food for many animals. Insects, for example, feed on leaves and other parts of the tree, while they themselves are food for larger animals, such as birds. Acorns, the fruits of the oak, appear in late summer.

*Once acorns have fallen to the ground, they provide a nutritious meal for birds, squirrels, and mice.*

*Female nut weevil drilling into acorn with her mouthparts.*

*Rostrum*

### Red fox
Red foxes live on their own or in small family groups in underground dens. They are most active at night when they hunt for rabbits, rodents, and worms. They may also eat fish and fruit.

*Females flick their large, bushy tails to warn cubs of danger.*

### Fallow deer
Woodland provides cover and food for fallow deer. Females and young live in small herds. Males have antlers, and are solitary or live in small groups. Males and females meet during the mating season in the autumn.

### Nut weevil
This beetle lives on oak trees, feeding on buds and leaves. It has a snout-like rostrum, at the end of which are its jaws. In late summer, the female makes holes in the oak's acorns. In each hole she deposits an egg. The larva that hatches from the egg feeds on the acorn.

*Bulrushes provide nesting sites for birds.*

*Flower head*

### Bulrushes
These tall grass-like plants grow at the fringes of lakes and ponds. Their roots are often in wet soil or submerged in water, while their stems and leaves extend above the water. Bulrushes have dark, compact, cylindrical flower heads.

## Wetland wildlife

Europe's wetlands are rich in wildlife. Reeds, bulrushes, and marsh plants provide food and shelter for wetland animals, such as voles and otters. Insects and other invertebrates are a food source for fish and frogs, which themselves are eaten by many water birds.

### European kingfisher
This small bird hunts for fish and other water animals from a perch along the banks of streams and lakes. Once prey is spotted, the kingfisher plunges into the water, grabs it with its long, pointed beak, and returns to the perch to eat its meal.

### European otter
Otters are strong swimmers, adapted for rapid movement in water. An otter's body is long and streamlined, its dense, glossy fur is water-repellent, and it has webbed feet. Otters hunt underwater, catching prey such as fish, water birds, and frogs. They are equally agile on land, and catch water voles and other animals that live on riverbanks.

### Water vole
Water voles are good swimmers. They build tunnels in banks next to lakes and slow-moving rivers. These tunnels have chambers for food storage and nesting, and entrances that open above and below the waterline.

*Water voles feed on plants, roots, and bulbs.*

### Edible frog
Edible frogs live in marshes and lakes, sometimes emerging at night to feed on land. They catch insects with their long, sticky tongues. Larger prey, such as newts and small fish, are caught in the jaws and pushed into the mouth with the feet.

E

### Alpine chough
In summer, choughs live in flocks above the tree line. They walk over rocky ground, probing under vegetation and in crevices for insects and snails. They glide on air currents, coping easily with the strong gusts of wind found at high altitudes.

# Mountain wildlife
The Alps and the Pyrenees are the major mountains of Europe. Vegetation changes with increasing altitudes; each zone has its characteristic wildlife. Animals tend to move to lower altitudes during the cold winter months when food becomes scarce.

### Mouflon
The mouflon is a wild sheep that lives in remote, mountainous regions. It feeds on grasses and other plants during the day, and rests at night. The mouflon is surefooted, moving easily over rough terrain. Males bang their heads and horns together when competing for mates.

### Alpine meadow
Alpine meadows are found above the tree line and below the snow line. In summer, they are covered in a blanket of bright flowers and dwarf shrubs. These provide food for hordes of insects, which in turn are eaten by birds. Meadow vegetation is also eaten by grazing animals.

*Bears eat rodents, deer, insects, salmon, carrion, roots, and berries.*

*Cubs are born in dens in mid-winter.*

### Brown bear
These large bears live in remote forested areas of mountains and as far north as the tundra. They have no natural enemies apart from humans. In winter, brown bears usually retire to a den for a period of dormancy.

# Coniferous forest wildlife
Coniferous forests of evergreen trees, such as spruce and pine, extend across northern Europe. They are thick and dark, with few ground plants. Summers are warm; winters are cold, with heavy snowfalls. Many animals eat the leaves and seeds of conifers.

### Norway spruce
Norway spruces have reddish trunks and dark green crowns, and grow up to 180 ft (55 m) in height. These seeds of the spruce, as well as the bark, buds, and needlelike leaves, provide food for forest animals.

*Triangular outline prevents snow from piling up and snapping branches.*

### Pine marten
Pine martens hunt in the morning and evening, using their excellent hearing and sight to locate birds, squirrels, rabbits, and rats.

*Pine martens climb trees, resting by day in tree hollows.*

### Common crossbill
The common or red crossbill lives in the forest canopy and is rarely seen on the ground, except when it lands to drink. Its crossed beak provides the bird with a strong "tool" for prying open the scales of pine and spruce cones. It then uses its tongue to extract the seeds.

*Upper and lower parts of bill are crossed.*

### Arctic hare
The arctic hare lives in the forests and tundra of the far north. Its fur turns from brown in summer to white in winter, to conceal it from predators such as foxes.

*Bright yellow flowers are strongly scented.*

# Mediterranean wildlife
The Mediterranean region of Europe has hot, dry summers, and milder and wetter winters. Aromatic plants, such as thyme, and trees such as cedar grow here. Many animals survive by sheltering in midday heat; others migrate.

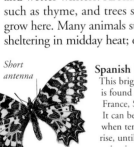

*Black, bristly feathers give it its other name: bearded vulture.*

### Lammergeier
The lammergeier lives in mountainous areas. It eats carrion, including the bones, which it drops on to rocks from midair to smash them and expose the soft marrow.

*Short antenna*

### Spanish festoon butterfly
This brightly patterned butterfly is found on the coasts of France, Spain, and Portugal. It can be seen from late winter, when temperatures start to rise, until early summer, when mating is complete.

*Zig-zag wing pattern*

*Ear tufts are used to signal to other lynxes.*

### Common lizard
A common sight in southern Europe during the summer, this lizard sunbathes in the morning to increase its body temperature, making it more active when searching for insects.

### Broom
This shrub can survive the hot, dry conditions of the Mediterranean summer. The seed pods produced by the flowers dry in the sun, and split open to scatter the tiny seeds.

### Spanish lynx
This cat, once found all over Spain, is now restricted to the pine forests, scrub, and sand dunes of the Coto Doñana National Park in southwestern Spain. Lynx feed on rabbits and hare, deer fawns, and ducks.

**FIND OUT MORE**    BIRDS OF PREY    FORESTS    LAKE AND RIVER WILDLIFE    MARSH AND SWAMP WILDLIFE

E

# EVOLUTION

THE TERM "EVOLUTION" refers to the theory that existing animals and plants have evolved, or developed, through a process of continual change from previous life-forms. Some scientists argue that by looking at fossil evidence, we can find out more about the past. Fossils have shown that primitive life-forms appeared more than 3.8 billion years ago, and that vertebrates existed at least 500 million years ago. Over generations, better adapted organisms have developed.

## How a species evolves

An organism may undergo change due to a number of processes, such as natural selection and adaptation, induced by the environment in which it lives. For example, selection may have promoted larger and faster horses adapted for living on open grassy plains. In some cases, a subspecies can change so much that it becomes very different from the rest of its species.

*Hyracotherium,* the first in a long line of horses, appeared approximately 55 million years ago.

*Four-toed hoof*

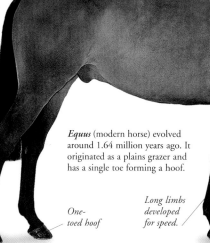

*Equus* (modern horse) evolved around 1.64 million years ago. It originated as a plains grazer and has a single toe forming a hoof.

*One-toed hoof*

*Long limbs developed for speed.*

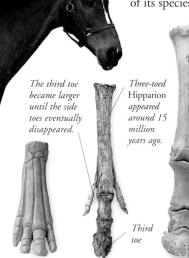

*The third toe became larger until the side toes eventually disappeared.*

*Three-toed Hipparion appeared around 15 million years ago.*

*Third toe*

Foot of early four-toed *Hyracotherium*

Foot of three-toed *Hipparion*

Hoof of modern horse, *Equus*

## Natural selection

The theory of natural selection suggests that environmental factors may favor some members of a species over others, enabling the fittest to survive. Experiments with the carnivorous plant, sundew, backed this theory. Plants that were fed meat produced more flowers and seeds than plants that were not.

*Plant fed meat produces flowers.*

*Unfed plant has fewer flowers.*

### Heredity
Heredity studies how characteristics of certain individuals are passed on from one generation to the next. This process often involves the expression of a parent's dominant gene, which may mask the effect of the recessive gene.

**Russian hamsters**

*Recessive albino gene*

*Dominant gray gene*

### Variation
Variation refers to the differences within a species. Certain variations, such as shell color, may give certain individuals advantages over others. These individuals will have a greater chance of surviving and reproducing.

**Banded snails**

*Shell colors allow snail to adapt to local habitat.*

### Mutations
Occasionally during reproduction, the process of replicating genetic material (DNA) goes wrong and produces an accidental mutation. Normally, these mutants do not live, but some survive as an important source of variation on which selection operates.

*Fuller's mutant teasel has curved spines allowing easier seed dispersal.*

**Teasel plant**

### Sexual selection
Some animals choose their mates by means of sexual selection. A male, may have elaborate features, such as bright feathers, to attract a mate. Characteristics such as these, which may be beneficial to the species, are passed to the next generation.

**Peacock**

## Adaptation

The process of adaptation occurs when an organism evolves in a certain way to make it better suited to its environment. Some people believe that this can lead to a new species, and that an animal or a plant will adapt to its surroundings so that it has a better chance of survival.

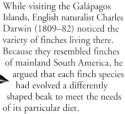

**Plant-feeding finch**

**Insect-feeding finch**

### Darwin's finches
While visiting the Galápagos Islands, English naturalist Charles Darwin (1809–82) noticed the variety of finches living there. Because they resembled finches of mainland South America, he argued that each finch species had evolved a differently shaped beak to meet the needs of its particular diet.

**Monarch butterfly**

**Viceroy butterfly**

### Mimicry in butterflies
Mimicry is a form of adaptation where one species has developed a resemblance to another as a means of protection. Birds find the monarch butterfly distasteful, but also avoid the similarly colored viceroy, even though it is palatable.

# Intermediates

Intermediates are thought to be the "halfway" species that should exist if one group of organisms has evolved from another. In 1861, discovery of the earliest fossil bird, *Archaeopteryx*, provided important support for this theory. The fossil clearly combines the reptile characteristics of a dinosaur in its skeleton, but at the same time has the uniquely bird-like feature of feathers.

**Lungfish**

### Living intermediates

The lungfish can breathe oxygen directly from air and has paired fleshy fins for swimming. Lungfish arose about 380 million years ago when animals first stepped on land; it is thought that the first land-going tetrapods (four-footed animals) evolved from lungfish-like intermediates.

# Human impact

For centuries, humans have had an impact on animal and plant habitats. For example, some animals have had to adapt to new environments created by human settlement and industry. Also, by selective breeding, scientists have altered the genetic makeup of some plants and animals to create superior crops and meat for human consumption. Fruits, such as grapes and oranges, have been bred so that they no longer have seeds and are therefore easier to digest.

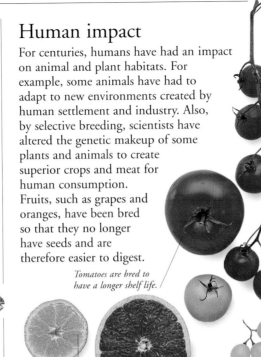

*Tomatoes are bred to have a longer shelf life.*

*Seedless orange*

*Seedless grape*

### Artificial selection

Scientists can manipulate the genetic makeup of plants and animals by artificially selecting particular strains according to need. For instance, genetically altered products such as tomatoes with enhanced flavor are already on sale. Dog breeders, too, can alter the temperament, shape, size, and color of dogs. The ability to alter genetic makeup raises many ethical questions.

**Shar-pei dog**

### Impact by pollution

It was discovered that during the Industrial Revolution, light-colored peppered moths, previously camouflaged from bird predators, became vulnerable on soot-blackened trees. However, darker colored peppered moths did survive and went on to breed more dark moths.

**Peppered moths**

# Evidence

Much of the evidence for evolution is based on fossils. These show how life originated from simple forms in the sea and then evolved to occupy land, freshwater, and air. Study of the common characteristics of organisms suggest how they could be related. Also, investigations into genetics and its molecular basis have led to a greater understanding of how evolution works.

**Fossil of fern plant**

### Fossil evidence

Fossils of animals and plants show that there have been significant changes throughout geologic time. Fossils show how the first land- living plants appeared some 440 million years ago, but were not sufficiently well established to form forests until about 320 million years ago.

### Molecular evidence

Often, if two new species evolve from a common ancestor, their DNA begins to change. For example, both the red and gray squirrel feed on acorns. However, the red squirrel lacks the digestive enzyme that breaks down chemicals in the acorn. This has led to a decline of red squirrels in the British Isles.

**Gray squirrel population outnumbers that of the red squirrel in Britain.**

### Creation theories

Evolutionists believe that life on Earth has evolved progressively over thousands of millions of years, originally from nonliving materials. However, some people argue that all life-forms on the Earth were created by design, in or close to the form in which they exist today. Although creationists as a group reject the theory of evolution, many accept that life-forms on Earth can change. They believe that God created various kinds of creatures that have diversified within each kind until the present day.

**19th-century caricature of Charles Darwin**

### Jean-Baptiste de Lamarck

French naturalist Jean-Baptiste de Lamarck (1744–1829) proposed a theory of evolution that broke the prevailing idea of the fixity of species. He claimed that by striving to fit into their natural surroundings, organisms changed in bodily form, and that such transformations were passed on to their offspring. According to his theory, the giraffe developed a long neck by stretching to eat leaves from trees.

*The sturdy armadillo limb is adapted for digging.*

**Armadillo forelimb**

*Wrist bone*

*Finger digits*

*The chimpanzee's arm is very similar to the basic vertebrate bone pattern.*

*Upper arm*

**Chimpanzee's arm**

**Bones of bat's wing**

*In bats, the hand and finger bones developed into supports for the membranes of the wing.*

### Comparative anatomy

French naturalist Georges Cuvier (1769–1832) demonstrated that the function of the vertebrate skeleton reflects the way in which the animal lived. Since vertebrates have a common ancestry, the structure of the skeleton has a similar plan. Armadillo limb bones may be directly compared with the arm bones of a chimpanzee, and those of a bat's wing.

**FIND OUT MORE**    ANIMALS    BIG BANG    DARWIN, CHARLES    DINOSAURS    FOSSILS    GENETICS    HUMAN EVOLUTION    PREHISTORIC LIFE    PREHISTORIC PEOPLE

# EXPLORATION

SINCE THE EARLIEST TIMES, people have been curious about the world in which they live. For more than 3,000 years, explorers have charted most of Earth's surface by land and sea. Often these brave pioneers went out into the unknown inspired by more than mere curiosity. Sometimes they went in search of riches, or to find new and less crowded places to live, or in a quest for scientific knowledge. In the course of mapping the world, explorers destroyed many myths – but brought back true stories that seemed even stranger than fiction.

## Ancient exploration

In ancient times, peoples such as the Phoenicians explored new regions in their quest for trading partners. The Greeks and Romans also discovered more about the world as their empires expanded. People began to read about distant lands in books by Classical geographers such as Strabo (c.63 BC–c.AD 21).

### Xuan Zang

The Buddhist monk Xuan Zang (602–664) was one of the greatest travelers of ancient China. In 629 he set off alone on the famous Silk Road to visit India, Nepal, Sri Lanka, and Pakistan, making friends for China and studying as he went. He returned in 654 with the finest Asian artworks. After Xuan Zang's death, the emperor Gaodong built the Xingjiao monastery outside Xi'an to honor him.

## Exploration for trade

After the Ottomans captured Constantinople in 1453, European rulers paid sailors to find alternatives to the land route to Asia. It was soon proved quicker and cheaper to ship luxury goods such as spices and silks by sea.

*Han dynasty (206 BC–220 AD) figurine*

**Chinese jade horse**

*Chinese dragon*

**Ivory imperial seal**

**Chinese silk**

*Bolts of silk were traded throughout the Silk Road.*

### Silk Road

In ancient and medieval times, there was a 4,000-mile (6,400-km) overland trade route between China and Europe known as the Silk Road. It fell into disuse when Asian and European traders adopted new east-to-west sea routes in the 15th and 16th centuries.

### Marco Polo

The Venetian pioneer trader Marco Polo (c.1254–1324) traveled overland to China, and served the emperor Kublai Khan as a diplomat for 17 years. Back in Europe, while in prison for debt (1296–98), he dictated a book about life in the Far East that became very popular. Centuries later, it helped inspire Columbus to find a new westward sea route to the East.

**Kublai Khan and Marco Polo**

*Mongol emperor Kublai Khan*

*Marco Polo*

**Clove tree**

### Spice Islands

Europeans knew that valuable spices, such as cloves, grew wild in the East, and some of the greatest explorations were efforts to find the Spice Islands, which are today known as the Moluccas. Portuguese, Spanish, Dutch, and British navigators all fought to control this valuable source of trade for their countries.

## Vasco da Gama

Portuguese navigator Vasco da Gama (c.1469–1524) became the first European to sail to India when he landed at Calicut (Calcutta) in 1498. Da Gama returned twice; in 1502 to avenge the deaths of some Christian traders, and for the last time in 1524, as Viceroy of India. He died shortly after this appointment.

**Aztec sacrificial knife**

## New World

From 1492 Europeans tried to reach India by sailing west. When they discovered that America was in their path, they hailed this continent as a "new world." But as they explored it, they brutally plundered and destroyed the rich empires of the Aztec, Inca, and Maya.

**Aztec portrait beaker**

## Southern Continent

For centuries Europeans believed that there was a Terra Australis Incognita – or Unknown Southern Continent. In the 17th and 18th centuries Dutch and British navigators, such as James Cook (1728–79), began to explore it, and the great continent became known as Australia.

### Robert O'Hara Burke and William J. Wills

Early European settlement of Australia was coastal. Burke (1820–61) and Wills (1834–61) made the first journey, from Melbourne across the continent's parched interior to the northern coast. On the way back, they died of starvation in the outback.

**Death at Cooper's Creek**

E

# Exploration tools

In the days before radar, radio, and satellites were invented, navigators and explorers used a variety of hand-operated tools. Compasses, sextants, and other devices calculated positions at sea and measured distances on land. Exploration led to more accurate charts and maps.

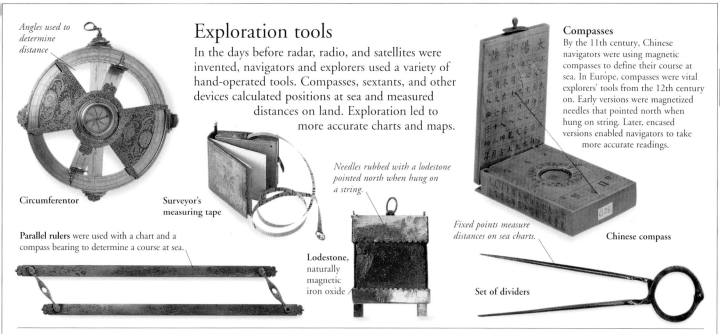

*Angles used to determine distance*

**Circumferentor**

**Surveyor's measuring tape**

*Needles rubbed with a lodestone pointed north when hung on a string.*

**Parallel rulers** were used with a chart and a compass bearing to determine a course at sea.

**Lodestone,** naturally magnetic iron oxide

*Fixed points measure distances on sea charts.*

**Set of dividers**

## Compasses
By the 11th century, Chinese navigators were using magnetic compasses to define their course at sea. In Europe, compasses were vital explorers' tools from the 12th century on. Early versions were magnetized needles that pointed north when hung on string. Later, encased versions enabled navigators to take more accurate readings.

**Chinese compass**

## Pundits
In the 19th century, the British in India trained Indian surveyors, known as pundits, to make maps of the central Asian territories of Karakoram, the Hindu Kush, and the Himalaya. In 1863, one of the earliest pundits, Muhammad-i-Hameed, made the first recorded trip over the Karakoram range to Chinese Turkestan. He died after spending six months in Yarkand, but his surveying equipment and notebook containing vital topographical information were sent back to India.

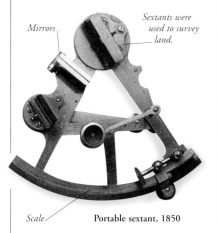

*Mirrors*

*Sextants were used to survey land.*

*Scale*

**Portable sextant, 1850**

# Empire building

From the 15th century, the Spanish, Portuguese, Dutch, British, and French created huge empires outside Europe. After a nation's explorers, traders, and settlers had made links with an overseas territory, it might easily come under that nation's rule as a colony. Africa, Australia, parts of Asia, and the Americas, were all colonized by Europeans at one time.

## Livingstone and Stanley
Dr. David Livingstone (1813–73), a Scottish missionary, made three great expeditions through parts of Africa previously unknown to Europeans. He disappeared when trying to find the source of the Nile River and was feared dead. New York journalist H.M. Stanley (1841–1904) found him on the shores of Lake Tanganyika, greeting him with the famous words, "Dr. Livingstone, I presume?"

**Stanley's hat**

## Charles Sturt
Despite the presence of two great rivers, the Murray and the Darling, Australian settlers could find no river mouths on the southeastern coast, so explorers searched for an inland sea. In 1828–30, Sturt (1795–1869) mapped these river systems for 994 miles (1,600 km). In 1844, he explored the Australian interior, or outback, and finally proved there was no inland sea.

# Final frontiers

In 1909 and 1911, the first-ever expeditions reached the north and south poles. Since then there have been few places on Earth left to map, but with technological advances, scientists have been able to extend exploration to include investigations of the oceans and space. In 1969, explorers landed on the Moon for the first time.

## Mary Kingsley
Few women took part in the first explorations of the world. It was generally believed that only men had the courage to venture into uncharted foreign lands. However, English naturalist Mary Kingsley (1862–1900) proved that this was untrue when she traveled through West Africa in 1893 and 1894, collecting fish and beetle specimens for the British Museum and making a study of African religions. In 1900, she returned to Africa to nurse soldiers in the Boer War, and died there.

## Hubble Space Telescope
Astronomers can now explore time as well as space. The *Hubble Space Telescope*, launched in 1990, orbits Earth at a distance of 370 miles (600 km). From this distance it collects images traveling through space from millions of years ago.

*Equipment box*

*Solar panel*

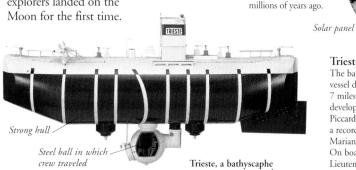

*Strong hull*

*Steel ball in which crew traveled*

**Trieste, a bathyscaphe**

## Trieste submarine
The bathyscaphe *Trieste* – a manned diving vessel designed to reach depths of up to 7 miles (11 km) in the ocean – was developed by the Swiss scientist Auguste Piccard (1884–1962). In 1960 it dived to a record 35,815 ft (10,916 m) in the Mariana Trench of the Pacific Ocean. On board were Piccard's son Jacques and Lieutenant Donald Walsh of the US Navy.

# EYES AND VISION

YOUR EYES ENABLE you to see by stimulating the creation of images in your brain. Each of the two eyeballs is a sphere measuring 2.5 inches (6.25 cm) in diameter. Eyeballs contain sensory cells that, when stimulated by light, send messages to the brain that are interpreted as images. Reflex mechanisms control the amount of light entering the eye and enable the eye to focus on objects whether they are near or distant. Much of the eyeball is hidden because it is protected within the orbit, a bony socket in the skull. The delicate outer surface of the eye is also protected by the eyelids.

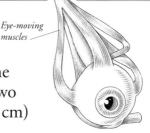

**Moving the eye**
Your eyes move constantly, even when you are staring. Six muscles move each eyeball and hold it in place inside its skull socket. Each muscle pulls the eye in a different direction, enabling the eyeball to move up and down, from side to side, and diagonally. Your brain controls these movements to make sure that both eyes move together.

*Eye-moving muscles*

*Eyeball*

## Seeing

The eyes gather light from whatever you look at. The cornea and lens focus this light on the retina to produce an upside-down image. Cells inside the retina, called rods and cones, respond to light by sending nerve impulses along the optic nerve to the brain. The brain interprets these impulses so you see the image the right-side up.

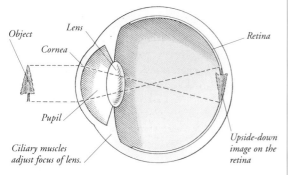

*Object*
*Lens*
*Cornea*
*Retina*
*Pupil*
*Ciliary muscles adjust focus of lens.*
*Upside-down image on the retina*

## Inside the eye

The transparent cornea at the front of the eye helps focus light as it enters. Behind the cornea are the iris, which controls the amount of light entering, and the lens, which fine-focuses light on the retina. Two liquids, aqueous and vitreous humor, maintain the shape of the eyeball.

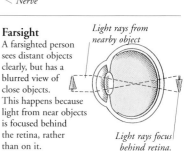

**Tear gland** moistens and protects eye.

**Optic nerve** sends messages from retina to brain.

**Choroid** supplies inside of eye with blood.

**Eyeball** lies within a protective bony socket.

**Lens** changes shape to focus light.

*Iris*

**Pupil** is an opening that channels light.

**Retina** is a membrane at the back of the eye.

**Sclera** is the tough, white, outer coat of the eye.

*Nerve*

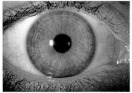

### Iris and pupil
The iris controls the amount of light entering the eye. Muscles in the iris alter the size of the pupil, the opening that allows in light. In dim light, the pupil widens; in bright light, the pupil gets smaller.

### Rods and cones
There are about 120 million rods and 7 million cones in the retina. Rods work best in dim light. Cones are responsible for color vision and enable you to see things in detail.

### Tears
Tears are released by lacrimal (tear) glands above the eye. When you blink, tears spread over the eye's surface. Tears keeps the cornea moist, wash away dust, and kill germs. After flowing over the eye, tears drain through two small openings at the side of the eye into the lacrimal duct, and then into the nose.

## Vision defects

The most common vision problems are farsight and nearsight. In both cases, the eye does not focus light properly on the retina. Some people, mainly males, have color blindness and cannot distinguish between certain colors, most often red and green.

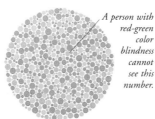

*A person with red-green color blindness cannot see this number.*

**Farsight**
A farsighted person sees distant objects clearly, but has a blurred view of close objects. This happens because light from near objects is focused behind the retina, rather than on it.

*Light rays from nearby object*

*Light rays focus behind retina.*

**Nearsight**
A nearsighted person can see close objects clearly, but sees distant objects as a blur. Nearsightedness is usually caused by the eyeball being longer than normal. This means that light entering the eye from distant objects is focused in front of the retina, rather than on it.

*Light rays from distant object*

*Light rays focus in front of retina.*

**FIND OUT MORE** — BRAIN AND NERVOUS SYSTEM · CAMERAS · CELLS · COLOR · GENETICS · HUMAN BODY · LIGHT · MEDICINE, HISTORY OF

# FARMING

BY CULTIVATING CROPS and raising animals, farms produce food and other products. Ten percent of people in developed nations, and 60 percent in developing countries, make their living from farming. In the West, technology makes the land highly productive, producing abundant, cheap food and requiring fewer workers. In developing countries, farms have much lower yields because the soil or climate are often unsuitable for agriculture, and farmers, unable to afford new machines and chemicals, must rely on labor-intensive methods.

## Crops

Ancient farmers bred crop plants by collecting and sowing the seed from the healthiest wild plants: the first cultivated crop was probably a kind of wheat. Today's major food crops are wheat, rice, corn, and potatoes; major non-food crops include cotton and tobacco. The types and quantities of crops a farmer can grow are determined by soil and climate.

*Cotton bolls (seedpods)*

### Cotton
The cotton crop provides fibers and oil. The main producers of the world's cotton are China and the United States.

### Rice
Rice is a cereal crop, and the main food of half the world's people. Asia produces 90 percent of the world's crop. Plants are grown in warm climates, usually on flooded "paddy" fields. Rice is a labor-intensive crop, meaning that people do most of the work, not machines.

*Rice seedlings*

| 2 days old | 2–3 weeks | 4–5 weeks |
|---|---|---|

*Harvesting rice by hand*

*Terraced fields*

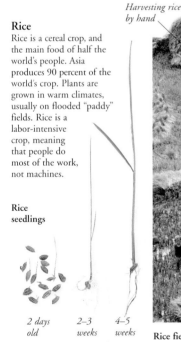

*Plants are cut down and left in bundles to dry out.*

*Rice field, China*

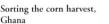
*Sorting the corn harvest, Ghana*

### Corn
Corn is a kind of grass. There are many varieties, which can be ground into flour, eaten as a vegetable, made into oil, or used as animal feed. Corn is a major crop in the United States, Brazil, southern Africa, and parts of Asia.

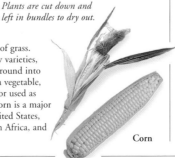
*Corn*

## Types of farms

In the developed world, mixed farms were once common; farmers grew a few different crops and kept some livestock. Today's technology makes it advantageous for farms to specialize, raising just one kind of crop or animal with very high output. Such farming is big business. Some farmers, concerned by the possible effects on the environment, have changed to organic farming, and do not use artificial fertilizers and pesticides.

*Shepherd shakes seedpods from a tree to feed sheep.*

### Subsistence farming
Subsistence farmers produce only enough to feed their household, with little or no surplus to sell. This is more common in developing nations, where many farmers cannot afford the chemicals or machinery that would increase their yield, and rely on centuries-old farming methods.

*Subsistence farming, Kenya*

### Commercial farming
Commercial farmers farm animals and crops intensively. They aim for a high yield and sell their produce for profit. In many countries, farmers produce too much food. When surplus crops and animals force food prices down, damaging the food industry, governments pay farmers to grow less.

*Cattle fair, Argentina*

## Livestock

Farmers rear livestock (animals) for meat, milk, eggs, skins, and wool. In some cases, livestock is reared intensively, with many animals kept indoors under artificial conditions to encourage fast growth. By contrast "free-range" animals are reared outside; they live in a more natural setting, but their products are more expensive.

*Sheep's milk*

**Farmers** kept goats and sheep for milk long before cattle.

**Butter,** from cow's milk

**Cheese,** from goat's milk

### Dairy farming
Dairy farming is the breeding of animals for their milk and milk products. Cows are the main dairy animals, producing an average of 2.6 to 4 gallons (10 to 15 liters) a day. Sheep and goats are also raised for their milk.

### Sheep
The versatile sheep produces meat, wool, and milk. Sheep do not need such rich pasture as cattle: they can survive on poor quality land and in dry or cold climates.

**Sheepshearing** takes place in late spring.

F

# Farming technology

Ever since the Agricultural Revolution in the 18th century, scientific advances in agriculture have rapidly raised farms' productivity. Artificial fertilizers, pesticides, research into selective breeding, and genetic engineering keep the increasing Western populations fed. Selective breeding programs improve crops and livestock by combining the strengths of each parent in their offspring. By modifying genes directly in the laboratory, scientists can achieve the same results as selective breeding in a fraction of the time.

*Vegetables* can be bred to be regular in shape, and so more attractive to shoppers, even though there is no difference in taste.

*Intensively farmed*

*Irregular shape*

## Chemicals in farming

Fertilizers enrich the soil with the minerals essential for plant growth. Animal manure is an organic fertilizer; science has also developed inorganic (artificial) fertilizers. Pesticides are chemicals that control the pests that attack crops. While these chemicals improve productivity, some chemicals get into the water supply, possibly harming human health.

**Cattle raised in zero-grazing pen**

## Intensive rearing

Intensive farming maximizes the production of crops and livestock with chemicals and machines. Shoppers prefer cheap food: to produce this, the cost of raising livestock must be kept to a minimum. Cattle, pigs, and other animals live in controlled conditions. for example, pigs live in units and are fed a prescribed mix of nutrients that makes them put on the most weight in the least time.

# Machinery

During the 20th century, new machinery increased farm productivity in industrialized nations, and also cut labor requirements. Tractors, motor vehicles that pull farm machinery, quickly replaced horses as the source of pulling power on the farm. The tractor's power allowed farmers to plant and harvest crops over vast areas.

*Tractors were first built in the late-19th century.*

*Coulter cuts into soil.*

*Share digs soil up.*

*Moldboard turns soil over.*

**Tractor, pulling plow**

**Because combine harvesters** work so quickly, they reap a crop at its best.

## Harvesters

Machines can speed the harvest. A combine harvester both cuts a crop of wheat and separates the grain from the stalk. In less than an hour, a machine with one driver can turn five acres of wheat into grain. Sugar, potatoes, and peas are other crops harvested by machine.

## Equipment

Milking machines have changed the face of dairy farms, with farmers now able to keep much larger herds of cattle. Farmers operate machines that milk cattle twice a day, although in the Netherlands robotic machines have been introduced that milk cows whenever the cows want it. The robots place vacuum cups on the cows' teats to draw out their milk. Each cow wears a radio collar that tells the robot where to look for the udder.

**Robotic milking barn, the Netherlands**

## Preparing the land

To prepare the soil for sowing seeds, farmers first plow the fields. The blade of a plow cuts a deep furrow in the soil and turns it over, burying weeds, which rot to enrich the soil. Harrows and cultivators are then used to break up large lumps of earth before the seed is sown.

# The farmer's year

The changing seasons set the pace of a farmer's work. On a livestock farm, for instance, spring is the time when lambs or calves are born. The arable (crop growing) farm is busiest during the spring-to-fall growing season. Apple growers must carry out different tasks through the year to produce the best crop.

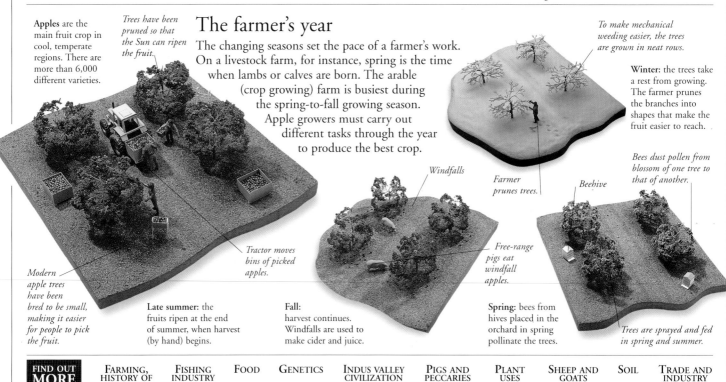

**Apples** are the main fruit crop in cool, temperate regions. There are more than 6,000 different varieties.

*Trees have been pruned so that the Sun can ripen the fruit.*

*Modern apple trees have been bred to be small, making it easier for people to pick the fruit.*

*Tractor moves bins of picked apples.*

**Late summer:** the fruits ripen at the end of summer, when harvest (by hand) begins.

*Windfalls*

**Fall:** harvest continues. Windfalls are used to make cider and juice.

*Farmer prunes trees.*

*Free-range pigs eat windfall apples.*

*To make mechanical weeding easier, the trees are grown in neat rows.*

**Winter:** the trees take a rest from growing. The farmer prunes the branches into shapes that make the fruit easier to reach.

*Beehive*

*Bees dust pollen from blossom of one tree to that of another.*

**Spring:** bees from hives placed in the orchard in spring pollinate the trees.

*Trees are sprayed and fed in spring and summer.*

**FIND OUT MORE** | FARMING, HISTORY OF | FISHING INDUSTRY | FOOD | GENETICS | INDUS VALLEY CIVILIZATION | PIGS AND PECCARIES | PLANT USES | SHEEP AND GOATS | SOIL | TRADE AND INDUSTRY

# Farming

## Animals farmed for produce

**Chickens** are bred for eggs and meat.

**Peacocks** are bred for their exotic plumage.

**Ducks** are farmed for feathers, eggs, and meat.

**Sheep** are bred for milk, meat, skins, and wool.

**Geese** are kept for meat, down, and eggs.

**Red deer** are bred for their meat, called venison.

*Jerseys are farmed for their very rich milk.*

*Angora goats have a coarse undercoat and a curly wool outer coat.*

*Cattle are the world's most numerous farm animals.*

**Cattle** are farmed for milk and meat.

*Herefords were first bred in Britain and are now farmed in 50 countries.*

**Goats** are farmed for milk, meat, and wool.

*Goats can feed on scrubby grass and thorny branches.*

*Almost every part of a pig can be eaten.*

*Now scarce in the wild*

*Udders*

*Pigs are versatile feeders.*

**Ostrich chick:** farmed for meat and feathers

**Saanen goats** are bred in Europe for their milk.

**Chinchillas,** rodents bred for their soft, delicate fur

**Pigs** are farmed for pork, bacon, other meat products, skins, and bristles.

## Animals bred to work

*Long, erect ears*

*Well-muscled leg*

*Poitou donkeys are the world's largest.*

*Elephants pull heavier loads than any other animal.*

**Camels** are used as pack animals, and also farmed for wool, milk, hides, and meat.

**Heavy horses,** used where a farmer has no tractor

**Donkeys** carry large loads on little food or water.

**Mules** are interbred from horses and donkeys.

**Elephants** are used as draft (pulling) animals in Southeast Asia.

F

325

# FARMING, HISTORY OF

TEN THOUSAND YEARS AGO, the first farmers began to grow crops and breed animals for food. Before that, nomadic hunter-gatherers fed on berries, plants, and wild beasts they encountered on their travels. With the emergence of farming, however, people were able to produce a reliable food supply, and to settle permanently in one place, giving rise to the world's earliest civilizations in Mesopotamia, Egypt, India, and China. Farming methods continued to evolve slowly until, in the 18th century, a so-called agricultural revolution led to dramatic changes. Since then, farming has become more mechanized and feeds ever greater numbers of people.

## Early farmers

The first farmers tamed wild animals, kept them in herds, and used them for meat, milk, skins, and wool. By contrast, nomadic herders moved their animals constantly in search of new pastures.

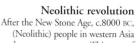
Flint sickle in wooden handle

Rice farming

### Neolithic revolution
After the New Stone Age, c.8000 BC, (Neolithic) people in western Asia began to grow crops. This type of farming supported 10 times more people than hunting and gathering.

### Irrigation
Early farmers needed water for their crops. Rivers and artificial canal systems played a vital role in the ancient agricultural civilizations of Egypt, the Indus Valley, and China.

## Agricultural revolution

From about 1750, a series of major changes ushered in the era of modern farming. Key developments included large-scale farming, the intensive breeding of livestock, and the improvement of a number of agricultural techniques – such as four-field crop rotation – all of which were first developed in Britain.

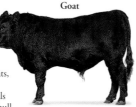
Goat

### Selective breeding
Robert Bakewell (1725–95), the fifth Duke of Bedford (1765–1802), and other British stock breeders during the agricultural revolution, used selective breeding on their farms and estates to develop larger, healthier animals, such as cattle, goats, sheep, and turkeys, with a higher milk or meat yield. Later breeders used the same system to develop animals for a particular purpose. For example, the Camargue bull is bred only for fighting.

Camargue bull

### Crop rotation
During the agricultural revolution, farmers found that if they grew certain crops, such as turnips, clover, barley, and wheat in successive years, they did not need to let the land lie fallow for a year. Root crops, such as turnips, improved the soil and therefore the quality of the next harvest.

Turnips and wheat

Black Norfolk turkey

### New farm machinery
Machines, such as the thresher (formulated in 1786 by Scots inventor Andrew Meikle), eased workloads and improved productivity. Threshers, which separated the grain from the stalk, became more effective after 1850 when farm workers attached steam engines to power them.

## Medieval farming

Farmers in medieval Europe divided the land around their village into three fields. Each family had one 12-hectare strip of land in each field. Everyone followed the same three-year farming cycle: one field was left fallow (unused) each year to restore the soil's nutrients, and the other two grew barley, oats, rye, or wheat.

### Enclosures
From the 1500s, English landowners enclosed open land with ditches or hedges, and made it private property. As a result, the cooperative medieval system of farming gave way to a system of private ownership in which landowners made all the decisions about what to farm.

Book of Hours, 1416

## Charles "Turnip" Townshend

A main forerunner of the agricultural revolution, Viscount Townshend (1674–1738) retired from a brilliant career in politics to concentrate on farming. He popularized a four-field rotation of crops, and pioneered "marling" (using lime as fertilizer). His widespread cultivation of the turnip – as a fodder crop to keep animals fed during the winter – earned him his nickname.

### Green Revolution
In the 1960s, a Green Revolution took place. New "high-yield" crop varieties were developed to increase wheat and rice production, particularly in highly populated countries such as India, and China. Critics claimed this process damaged the environment by using too much fertilizer and concentrating on only a few species. Recently farmers have been rediscovering traditional farming methods and using organic fertilizers and insecticides.

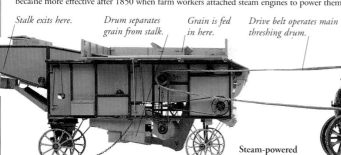

Stalk exits here.

Drum separates grain from stalk.

Grain is fed in here.

Drive belt operates main threshing drum.

Drive wheel rotates to turn drive belt.

Coal stored here.

Steam-powered threshing machine

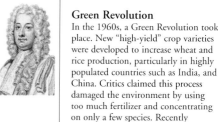
Seaweed, an organic fertilizer

**FIND OUT MORE**   BRONZE AGE   CHINA, HISTORY OF   EGYPT, ANCIENT   EUROPE, MEDIEVAL   FARMING   INDUSTRIAL REVOLUTION   INVENTIONS   KHMER EMPIRE   STONE AGE   SUMERIANS

# FERNS

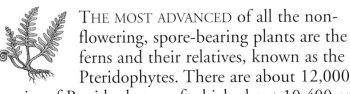

THE MOST ADVANCED of all the non-flowering, spore-bearing plants are the ferns and their relatives, known as the Pteridophytes. There are about 12,000 species of Pteridophytes, of which about 10,400 are ferns. The others include horsetails and club mosses. Pteridophytes are vascular plants, that is, plants whose stems contain tissues that transport water and food around the plant internally. They flourish best in warm, damp environments, but also grow where it is cool or dry.

## Ferns

A typical fern plant has underground stems, or rhizomes, from which grow roots, and leaves called fronds. Upright rhizomes produce a fern with a short radiating crown of fronds, while long horizontal rhizomes produce a spreading fern. Ferns grow in a variety of places, but all have a two-stage life cycle. The gametophyte is a small, short-lived plantlet that produces sex cells. After fertilization, a female sex cell grows into a sporophyte, which is the fern plant.

**Male fern**
Ferns similar to this male fern, so-called because of its vigorous growth, are found in woods all around the world. This species has stiff, bright green fronds. Each blade is divided into "leaves" called pinnae (singular: pinna), each of which is further divided into pinnules.

*The frond continues to lengthen as the lower parts unfurl.*

*A developing male fern plant*

*Pinna and pinnules*

*A full-grown frond may be as much as 5 ft (150 cm) long.*

*Young frond*

*Stipe is the "stalk" of the fern.*

*Rhizome*

*Root*

1 Frond buds develop on the rhizome. Each bud produces just one frond. It takes up to three years for a bud to develop and a frond to start growing.

2 A frond can grow rapidly because all the cells of the stalk and leaflets are fully formed, though very small. They just have to expand.

3 A male fern produces tall fronds, each carried on a scaly stipe. Fertile fronds are the last to unfurl, so that the spores are released in the summer.

### Epiphytic ferns
An epiphytic fern grows on the bough or trunk of a tree. It takes no nourishment from its host, but obtains moisture and minerals from rain and debris that become trapped among its roots.

*Fronds hang clear of the branch.*

*Radiating fronds*

### Tree ferns
Tree ferns have woody, fibrous trunks topped with a crown of fronds. They are found in all climates, most frequently in the tropics and subtropics. The tallest species reaches 65 ft (20 m).

*Base of dead fronds*

### Water ferns
Some ferns are aquatic. They either root into mud in fresh water, or float free. This *Azolla* species floats. Its tiny roots dangle in the water below a mat of fronds.

## Club mosses
These small plants grow on damp ground or on rain forest trees. Their creeping stems are covered with tiny leaves arranged in a spiral. Spores are borne in modified leaves on fertile stems.

## Horsetails
The stiff, upright stems of horsetails grow in dense patches from underground stems. Branches are arranged in whorls, although fertile stems often have no branches. Tiny brown leaves grow in rings around the stems and branches. Spores are borne in conelike structures on the tip of fertile stems.

**Sterile stem**  **Fertile stem**

## The life cycle of a fern

*Dry weather causes the sporangium to burst at a weak spot.*

*Sex organs are carried on the underside of the gametophyte.*

*Archegonium containing female sex cells*

*Antheridium containing male sex cells*

*New fern plant – the sporophyte*

*Sori*

*Pinna*

*Sorus*

*Sporangia*

*Gametophyte is a thin green plantlet.*

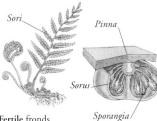

**Fertile** fronds have sori (singular: sorus), usually on the lower surface of each pinna.

**Within** each sorus are clusters of sporangia, which contain the spores.

**Sixty-four** spores develop inside each sporangium. The sporangium then bursts, releasing all the spores.

**A spore** landing on damp soil germinates into a gametophyte. This bears male and female sex organs.

**Male** sex cells swim in a film of soil moisture to the female sex cells and then fertilize them.

**The first** female sex cell to be fertilized grows into a fern plant.

FIND OUT MORE · MOSSES AND LIVERWORTS · PLANTS · PLANTS, ANATOMY · PLANTS, REPRODUCTION · RAIN FOREST WILDLIFE · TREES

# FESTIVALS

ALL OVER THE WORLD, people set aside special days each year to enjoy themselves at festivals. These public celebrations are held for many reasons: they may be linked to a community's religious beliefs, mark the changing seasons, or honor important events in a country's history.

*Streamers are hung from a pole.*

### Day of the Dead
On November 1, Mexicans celebrate the Day of the Dead to honor people who have died. Families have picnics by the graves of their relatives, decorate the streets with flowers and carved skeletons, and eat candy shaped like skulls and coffins.

**Papier-mâché skeleton**

## Calendar festivals

The majority of festivals are held at the same time each year. Many religions have adapted the celebrations of early peoples to their own ends: the Christian Christmas and the Hindu Diwali are held around the same time as ancient feasts marking the onset of winter.

### Children's Day
To mark Children's Day (May 5) in Japan, streamers in the shape of carp are hung out. The strong, energetic fish are seen as good role models for young children.

## Harvest festivals

Ancient peoples thought that thanking the gods would ensure a good crop the next year, and people still celebrate festivals based on this idea. There are many festivals in Africa and Papua New Guinea that celebrate the yam crop, and the Oktoberfest beer festival in Germany began as thanks for the crop of hops.

**Radishes**
On Christmas Eve, citizens of Oaxaca, Mexico, celebrate their radish crop by carving large, recently harvested radishes into elaborate shapes that they use to decorate market stalls and restaurants. Food is served on chipped plates that are saved for the occasion and ritually smashed at the end of the night.

### Corn
In England, people often used the last of the year's corn to make a figure called a corn dolly. The dolly kept the corn spirit alive through the winter, ensuring another good harvest the next year.

**Traditional English corn dolly**

## Carnivals

Originally, carnivals were pagan festivals to celebrate the rebirth of nature in spring. Later, they became associated with the Roman Catholic festival of Lent. The start and duration of the carnival season varies from country to country.

### Carnival in Venice
This famous Italian carnival first began in the 11th century. Traditionally, many revelers wore masks to hide their faces while they misbehaved.

*Float pulled by tractor.*

**Mardi Gras float**

### Caribbean carnival
Carnival in the Caribbean combines African and European traditions; dance, costume, and music are important parts of African religious beliefs.

### Mardi Gras
In many Roman Catholic countries, carnival is by tradition a last chance for merrymaking before the start of Lent, the weeks of fasting that come before Easter. Thousands of people enjoy the week-long Mardi Gras carnival in New Orleans. Mardi Gras is French for "Fat Tuesday," the day before Lent begins, which is also known as Shrove Tuesday. On this day all the fats in the home must be used up to prepare for the fasting period.

## Modern festivals

Most festivals set up today mark non-religious events. The Olympics celebrate excellence in sports; the Edinburgh festival in the UK promotes the performing arts.

**Mime artist, Edinburgh Festival**

### Roskilde
Thousands of fans attend this summer rock music festival in Denmark.

## Political festivals

Significant political dates, such as a leader's birthday, are often the cause for annual celebration. In the US, President's Day in February marks the birth month of two great presidents: Lincoln and Washington.

### May Day
Once a springtime fertility festival, May 1 is a now a public holiday to honor workers. In Russia, May Day is marked with parades.

**FIND OUT MORE**    CHRISTIANITY    FILM AND FILMMAKING    FOOD    HINDUISM    SPORT    UNIONS, TRADE

328

# FEUDALISM

IN PARTS OF MEDIEVAL ASIA and Europe, a system arose for organizing society known as feudalism. In the feudal system, the king gave land to powerful barons, who then gave land and protection to lesser lords, and so on through to the peasants. Each level was then expected to fight to protect its overlords whenever needed. European feudalism started in the late 9th century, and spread all over the continent. Outside Europe, the feudal system operated in Palestine during the Crusades, and also in Japan, where samurai gave military service to their overlords in return for land.

## How feudalism began

The great emperor Charlemagne insisted that all his nobles swear loyalty to him. This bond beween lord and warrior began the feudal system. Over the next two centuries, feudalism spread through France, Germany, northern Italy, the Slav countries, and finally the British Isles and Sicily.

### Mounted warriors
Warriors riding horses to war became more common after 950. These warriors were the first knights. They had great prestige, and became an important part of the feudal system.

## Lords and vassals

In the European feudal system, the only person who actually owned land was the king. When the king granted land to a baron, the baron knelt and pledged to be the king's vassal (servant). Lesser lords swore a similar oath to the barons and became their vassals, and peasants swore allegiance to the lords. Bishops were also the king's vassals, and held nearly as much power as the barons.

*Derisive image of king with cat, not crown, on his head*

### King
Although the king owned the land, he could rarely afford to keep an army. He was often in conflict with the barons, on whom he relied for his warriors.

### Barons
The most powerful of all the nobles, the barons got their lands directly from the king. Because they provided the royal army, they had great power and prestige.

### Local lords
Local knights got their land (or manor) from the barons. In return, they fought for the barons when needed. As time went on, local lords often paid a tax called scutage (shield money) instead of fighting, and the king used this money to hire professional soldiers. In peacetime, they farmed and kept order.

### Peasants
The peasants, at the bottom of feudal society, got their plots of land from the local lord of the manor. He allowed them to farm this land; in return, they paid rent in produce and money. The peasants also contributed several days' labor on "public" projects such as road- and bridge-building.

## The manor

Farmland and its ownership was the most important part of feudalism, and the manor was the administration center of the system. The lands surrounding the manor house were divided into the demesne (for the lord's own use), the arable (granted in parcels to the peasants), and the meadow lands (used by everyone for livestock).

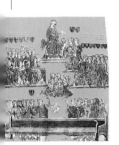

### Feudal counsel
Kings and barons often asked for advice, or counsel, from their vassals when making any important decisions. This 14th-century French manuscript shows Philip VI of France judging Robert of Valois, helped by the bishops on his right hand and the barons on his left.

### Feudal contract
The people owed their loyalty to the monarch. This "contract" meant that Philip VI could – and did – tax his subjects heavily to finance the Hundred Years War.

Ightham Mote, England

### The manor house
Every manor house had a hall. This acted as the dining and living room for the family, and also as a general reception room where the peasants paid their rent. The kitchen was at one end of the hall, beside a pantry and buttery (store room for drinks). Buildings in the courtyard outside included workshops and cattle-sheds. The whole complex was often surrounded by a moat for protection.

**The Hall, Ightham Mote**

## Domesday Book

For the feudal system to work well, the ruler needed detailed information about the land and who lived on it. William of Normandy, who introduced feudalism to Britain, had a complete record made of all land ownership in England in 1085–86. This became known as the Domesday Book.

*The book is the most complete record of land-holding in medieval Europe.*

### William I
The illegitimate son of Duke Robert I of Normandy, William (c.1028–1087) conquered England in 1066. He introduced the feudal system to the island, and replaced Saxon nobles with Norman lords.

**FIND OUT MORE**  CHARLEMAGNE  HUNDRED YEARS WAR  KNGHTS AND HERALDRY  MEDIEVAL EUROPE  NORMANS  SAMURAI AND SHOGUNS

# FILMS AND FILMMAKING

IN 1895, THE Lumière brothers held the first public film screening in a room below a Parisian café. The black and white images flickered dimly on a silent screen, yet the audience was enthralled. The magic of the movies has continued ever since. Technology developed rapidly: sound arrived in 1927, color in the 1930s, and today's films often involve computer-generated special effects. Film production is now an international industry, generating great wealth and employing thousands worldwide.

## Preproduction

Filmmaking begins long before the cameras start to turn. After a studio (a filmmaking company) agrees to make a movie, a script is prepared, the budget drawn up, actors and skilled crew hired, and the entire production planned to the last detail.

### The producer
A producer decides which film to make, finds the money to finance it (often millions of dollars), and brings together the stars, script, and director.

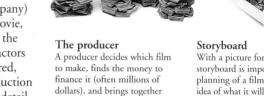

*Pictures represent each shot.*

### Storyboard
With a picture for each shot, a storyboard is important in the planning of a film and gives an idea of what it will look like. Notes outline the action and dialogue.

## Casting
It is vital to the success of a movie to cast (hire) actors who suit their parts artistically. Audiences have their favorites, so the choice of a popular star can turn a promising film into a huge box-office success.

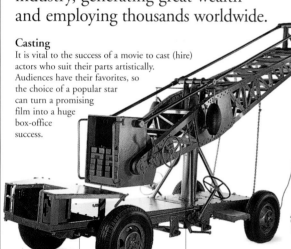

*Focus puller has a seat on top of crane, to adjust the focus of the camera lens.*

*The set designer uses sketches and models to design the set.*

### The set
The film scenery, or set, is often built to create a scene or location without the film crew leaving the studio. An actor who, on screen, seems to swagger into a saloon in the Wild West, may, in fact, be on set in a studio in Bombay, Hollywood, or Paris.

*The set decorator finds props and decorates set.*

*Powerful light*

*Boom holds microphone close to actor but out of shot.*

*Boom operator sits here to position the microphone.*

RAMIREZ SALOO

*Crane raises the camera above the actors' heads.*

*The camera and camera equipment on the set are moved by the grip.*

*The camera operator sits here to work the camera during shooting.*

*Director's folding chair is placed next to camera.*

*When the actors move, grips push the stand to move the microphone.*

## Production
When filming begins, a movie set is crowded with equipment, and each piece is the responsibility of a specific crew member. Between takes (sequences of filming), everyone works frantically to ensure that everything is adjusted exactly as the director wants. Off the set, props, wardrobe, and makeup directors have their own staff on hand.

### The director
Responsible for the artistic side of the filmmaking process, the director is the most important person on the set. Directors judge how well each take brings the script to life. They consult with experts in each department, such as the director of photography, who is responsible for the way the film looks.

*Screen to view the film*

*Loudspeaker plays back soundtrack*

*Editing table*

### Motion pictures
The continuous action on a movie screen is, in fact, an illusion. What we are watching are thousands of still photographs, taken rapidly one after the other. A film camera shoots 24 photographs (frames) every second, and when the images are projected at the same rate, our eyes 90 ft (27 m) of film is shot for just one minute of action.

## Postproduction
Separate scenes in a film are shot in whatever order suits the crew. Then the director chooses the best sections and the film editor links them in the right sequence to tell the story. While working closely with the director and other technicians, the editor carefully aligns the soundtrack and pictures, and adds the special effects.

### Editing
The editor cuts up the disjointed sequences of film, cutting between frames, and splices them together. Cuts are viewed at an editing table.

### Soundtrack
Music, the actors' dialogue, and any background sound effects are recorded separately and then combined to make the soundtrack.

# Types of film

From a short cartoon to a full-length feature with an all-star cast, films cover every subject. There have been notable films on many topics, but some of the most successful movies have been in areas where film can add an extra dimension, such as the vivid settings of fantasy and space adventures or western movies, the special effects of science-fiction and horror films, or the singing and dancing of American musicals.

*Babe is a piglet who believes he is a sheepdog.*

*Babe, 1995*

### Comedy
The first films were silent, yet the comic antics of the actors made audiences roar with laughter. Today, comedies range from biting social commentary to the gentle humor of an animal film such as *Babe*.

### Charlie Chaplin

Chaplin (1889–1977) moved to the US from London as a young man. He is one of the best-loved comedians of the silent screen, and appeared in more than 60 short films and 11 full-length comedies, including *City Lights* and *Modern Times*. His characterization of a tramp, who keeps a sense of humor despite great hardship, was based on observation of poor people on the London streets.

### Romance

*Jean-Louis Barrault  Arletty*

*Les Enfants du Paradis, 1944*

Love stories are always popular. The romantic *Les Enfants du Paradis* was made in German-occupied France during World War II; in 1979, French critics voted it the best French film ever made.

### Horror
German filmmakers were the first to realize that audiences like being frightened: directors were making horror movies in Germany by 1913. By the 1930s, horror had caught on in Hollywood, where it has been popular ever since. *Frankenstein* appeared in 1931. More than 100 films have been based on the same theme since.

*Boris Karloff as Frankenstein's monster*

# Going to the movies

By the 1930s, going to the movies was popular entertainment, but in the 1950s television took over and the film industry declined. Recently, movie-going has grown popular again. Today, multiplex theaters screen many films at the same location, offering audiences a wide choice of viewing.

# Special effects

Anything can happen on film, thanks largely to the special effects department, a complex and skilled area of filmmaking. Effects may range from animals that seem to talk to horrific dripping wounds or people appearing to fly through the air.

*Eyes, nose, and mouth operated by motors.*

*Dog, from* The Storyteller

*Motor*

### Makeup
Actors wear makeup to look natural under the bright film lights. Makeup also helps when an actor must look unnatural. A makeup artist can make an actor look much older, or, by using latex rubber and lining colors, can add dreadful wounds. In horror and science-fiction films, makeup is used to turn people into aliens.

*Makeup in* Terminator 2

### Movie models
Where it is too costly, dangerous, or impossible to use the real thing, film-makers may turn to models. Tiny models stand in for massive spacecraft in science-fiction films. A talking animal may be a puppet, or an actor in costume whose mask is operated by a puppeteer using remote control. This kind of puppetry is called animatronics.

### Picture palaces

*Le Grand Rex movie theater, Paris, France*

*Dramatic lighting*

Following the arrival of sound in 1927, movie theaters were built in most towns in North America and Europe. With their impressive architecture, these theaters of the 1920s and 1930s were sometimes known as picture palaces.

*Neon sign*

### Hype and merchandise
The enormous cost of making a film means it is vital to make the public eager to see it so that the producers can earn back their investment and make a good profit. Publicists work hard to sell a film before it opens. They inform journalists, and arrange for the actors to appear on television talk shows. This process is known as hype. Selling items that tie-in to the movie, such as socks or a mug, is a way of gaining extra publicity and making more money.

*Batman logo*

*Batman tie-ins*

™ & © 1996 DC Comics

### Blue screen
To create the illusion that a character is flying, an actor is filmed in front of a blue screen. Wind machines make his clothes flutter, as if air is moving past. An optical printer then combines the sequence with footage shot from a plane, or of a simulated space environment. The printer rephotographs images from each film onto a single frame to blend the two films seamlessly.

*Actor held by wires*

### Computers
Computers can manipulate images to create extraordinary special effects. Programs also allow operators to draw and animate characters on screen. Changes are much easier to make here than in animation that has been hand-drawn frame by frame.

*Disney's* Toy Story *is a computer-generated film.*

© Disney

# Timeline

**Academy Award (Oscar ®)**
© A.M.P.A.S. ®

**1895** The Lumière brothers open first public movie theater in Paris, France.

**1913** By this date, Hollywood, Calif., is the center of the US film industry.

**1920s** Russian director Sergei Eisenstein (1898–1948) introduces cross-cutting, showing bursts of action one after the other so they seem to happen simultaneously.

**1927** The Academy of Motion Picture Arts and Sciences is set up; in 1929, it honors film-makers for the first time.

**1927** *The Jazz Singer*, starring Al Jolson, is the first full-length film with sound.

**1932** The "three strip" process is introduced by the Technicolor company, and color films, originally developed much earlier, begin to take off.

**Technicolor three-strip camera**

**1941** US actor-director Orson Welles (1915–85) releases *Citizen Kane;* it explores new techniques in lighting, dialogue, and the use of camera lenses.

**1952** The CinemaScope process introduces wide-screen filming.

**1960s** *Nouvelle Vague* ("New Wave") filmmakers in France introduce influential new techniques.

**1980s** The VCR allows people to see films at home.

**1990s** Special effects techniques are advanced.

FIND OUT MORE    CAMERAS    CARTOONS AND ANIMATION    EDISON, THOMAS    VIDEO

# Film posters

## United States

The Gold Rush (US, 1925), a classic silent film, is touching yet very funny.

Raging Bull (US, 1980) is seen as one of the most influential films of the 1980s.

Blade Runner (US, 1982) portrays a bleak Los Angeles in 2019.

Do the Right Thing (US, 1989) develops from comedy to social commentary.

## Europe

The Battleship Potemkin (USSR, 1925), commissioned by Soviet leaders to put across a powerful political message, is still referred to as a masterpiece of filmmaking.

Metropolis (Ger., 1926) is a disturbing vision of an "ideal" city in the year 2000.

Pelle the Conqueror (Den./Swe., 1987) won top international awards.

## Oceania

Once Were Warriors (NZ, 1994): a great success critically and at the box-office.

Four Weddings and a Funeral (UK, 1994) is a light-hearted, appealing romance.

Women... (Spain, 1988) is a manic farce from talented director Pedro Almodovar.

The Piano (Aust., 1993), directed and written by Jane Campion, won three Oscars.

## Africa

Yeelen (Mali, 1987) tells the story of the struggle between a father and son.

The Sixth Day (Egypt, 1986), directed by Youssef Chahine, starred actress Daleeda.

In Yaaba (Burkina, 1989), a friendship develops between a boy and an old woman cast out by other villagers.

## Asia

Pather Panchali (India, 1956) brought its director, Satyajit Ray, world recognition.

Ran (Japan, 1985) is based on King Lear by Shakespeare; the battle scenes are superbly staged and shot.

Raise the Red Lantern (HK, 1991) looks at a woman's life in 1920s China.

# FINLAND

A LAND OF LAKES AND FORESTS, Finland is bordered by Russia on the east, the Baltic Sea on the south, and Sweden and Norway on the west and north. Finland shares government of Lapland, in the Arctic Circle, with Sweden and Norway. Finland was ruled by Russia until 1917, and, as a result, Finns have more in common culturally with the east than with their Scandinavian neighbors. A wealthy, progressive nation, Finland was the first European country to give women the vote.

## FINLAND FACTS

| | |
|---|---|
| CAPITAL CITY | Helsinki |
| AREA | 130,552 sq miles (338,130 sq km) |
| POPULATION | 5,200,000 |
| MAIN LANGUAGES | Finnish, Swedish |
| MAJOR RELIGION | Christian |
| CURRENCY | Euro |
| LIFE EXPECTANCY | 77 years |
| PEOPLE PER DOCTOR | 333 |
| GOVERNMENT | Multiparty democracy |
| ADULT LITERACY | 99% |

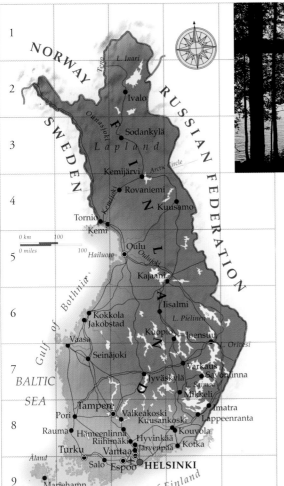

91°F (33°C)
62°F (17°C)
-42°F (-41°C)
21°F (-6°C)
24 in (618 mm)

## Lakes and islands

Finland has more than 60,000 lakes, mainly in the southeast, carved out by glaciers in the last Ice Age. Many islands are scattered in the lakes and off the warm southwestern coast, including 6,000 of the Åland Islands.

## Climate

Finland has short, bright summers and long, cold winters when lakes often freeze up to 1 ft 3 in (1 m) deep. The Arctic north sees midnight sun in its 73-day summer.

## People

Almost half of the population lives around Helsinki. Families are close-knit, and most homes have a sauna, or hot, steamy relaxation room. Women enjoy equal rights and about 50 percent pursue a career.

Cooling off after the sauna

44 per sq mile (17 per sq km)

67% Urban   33% Rural

## Physical features

From the air, Finland is a patchwork of lakes, peat bogs, and trees. Forests dominate the land, and water covers ten percent of the country. There are some 98,000 islands within the lakes, and 30,000 off the coast. The Arctic north, including part of Lapland, is a bleak area of rocky tundra.

## Forests

Pine, spruce, and birch trees cover 80 percent of Finland, making it the ninth most forested country in the world. The forest is most dense just south of the Arctic Circle and is often covered in snow.

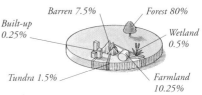

Barren 7.5%     Forest 80%
Built-up 0.25%              Wetland 0.5%
Tundra 1.5%                 Farmland 10.25%

## Land use

Dense forests and a maze of lakes, rivers, and peat bogs mean only 11 percent of Finland's land can be used for crops or grazing animals. Despite this, farmers produce all of the country's dairy foods. The forests support a valuable timber industry, and waters is used for fishing and hydroelectric power.

Kirkniemi paper mill

## Farming and industry

Finland produces all of its own food. Most crops are grown in the southwest and on the sunny Åland Islands. The country is a world leader in the production of plywood, wood pulp, and paper, and these alone make up 30 percent of the total exports. Furniture and high-tech manufacturing compete in world markets and, with the service sector, employ the majority of the workforce.

## Helsinki

Standing on a peninsula and several islands in the Gulf of Finland, the vibrant capital of Helsinki has about 770,000 inhabitants. Tree-lined avenues and a colorful market line a busy harbor. Only half of the city's area has been developed, leaving parks for the residents to enjoy.

The bustling Helsinki harbor

FIND OUT MORE

| ARCTIC OCEAN | ENERGY | EUROPE, HISTORY OF | FISHING INDUSTRY | FORESTS | GLACIATION | LAKES | PAPER | SCANDINAVIA, HISTORY OF | TRADE AND INDUSTRY | WINTER SPORTS |

# FIRE

BURNING OUT OF CONTROL in forests or cities, a fire leaves a trail of destruction. Yet life without the benefits of fire is unimaginable. We use fire in power stations, car engines, and kitchens, to provide electricity and transportation, or to cook food. Early humans realized the value of fire about half a million years ago – perhaps when lightning set a tree on fire. Learning to control and use the flames helped them hunt, clear land for farming, survive in colder climates, and eat foods that were inedible when raw. No wonder some religions still worship fire as a hungry god.

*Flame is a glowing gas, produced when fuel burns.*

## Combustion or burning

Fire is the heat and light that is produced when fuel burns. This process is known as combustion. Fuel is any kind of flammable material (one that can catch fire). The material must first be heated up to its ignition temperature and then it will burst into flame. As a fire gets hotter, more fuel ignites, and the flames spread. Gases and vapors burn most quickly; liquids and solids take longer to burn.

## Using fire

To make fire do useful work, the supply of air or fuel must be controlled to keep the flames burning evenly. Furnaces, cooking stoves, and power plants use fire for the heat energy it produces. Heat is not always the main purpose of creating fire. In a car engine, fuel burns explosively. Expanding gases drive the vehicle; the heat produced is wasted.

*Welder at work*

### Welding

Many industrial processes rely on combustion. In the welder's torch, oxygen and acetylene gas mix and produce a flame hot enough to melt steel.

*Fire-engine with hydraulic platform, used to reach awkward spaces*

*Some booms are up to 203 ft (62 m) long.*

*Rescue platform*

*Arm, or boom*

*Built-in hose*

*Leg for support*

### Cooking

Many foods must be cooked before they can be eaten. When food is heated, chemical changes take place that improve its taste and make it easier to digest. Early people ate raw food until they discovered cooking, probably by accident.

## Making a fire

In the past, there were two basic methods of starting a fire: raising the temperature until flames appeared, or striking sparks to light tinder. Pocket lighters still start fires by using the spark of flint on steel.

*Mouthpiece steadies drill*

*Wooden drill*

*String*

*Modern model of bow drill*

*Hearth*

### Bow drills

Rapidly turning the string of a bow drill causes friction at the tip, which starts flames.

*Piston handle is pumped to compress air.*

**A fire piston** works like a bicycle pump: compressing air in the tube raises the temperature until the tinder (flammable material) inside catches fire.

*Tinder stored in box*

*Lid with candle holder*

*Flint*

*Steel*

**A tinder box** contains flint, which makes sparks when struck against metal (the steel).

### Matches

Invented in 1827, these wooden splinters were tipped by chemicals. They were ignited by the heat that was generated by rubbing the tip against sandpaper. Safety matches burn only when rubbed against a specially coated strip on the matchbox.

## Myths about fire

The power and danger of fire made ancient peoples wonder about its origin. Myths that explain how people learned to tame flames occur in many different cultures. Most fire myths involve a hero who brings fire to the world.

### Prometheus

In Greek mythology, the chief god, Zeus, hid the secret of fire from mortals (humans) to punish them for a trick that a lesser god, Prometheus, had played on him. But Prometheus snatched a glowing ember from the Sun, and brought fire to the Earth.

*Prometheus*

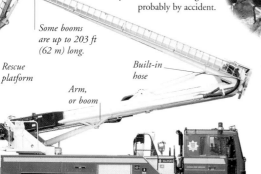

*Cooking with fire*

## Fighting fire

Fires feed on fuel, air, and heat; removing any one of these puts out the flames. Firefighters spray a blaze with water to remove heat and create a blanket of steam that chokes off the air supply.

FIND OUT MORE    FOOD    HEAT AND TEMPERATURE    INVENTIONS    LIGHT    PREHISTORIC PEOPLE

# FIRST AID

FIRST AID RANGES from cleaning a small wound and covering it with a bandage, to dealing with serious injuries at a major disaster. But its purpose is the same: to save life, prevent the victim from getting worse, promote healing and recovery, and arrange for expert help if needed. Recently, first aid has advanced greatly through a better understanding of the body's needs in serious injury or disease, improved medical equipment, and mobile communications. It now plays an even more vital role in saving lives, and promoting recovery.

Scene of a motorcycle accident

## At the scene

Effective first aid – the temporary treatment of injury or illness while waiting for medical aid – relies on correctly assigning priorities. At an accident, one of the first priorities is to summon emergency services.

**Assessing conditions**
Experienced first aiders know that noisy victims are not necessarily the most hurt. At a multiple accident, they assess quickly the condition of all victims, then concentrate available first aid on the most seriously injured. In hospitals, this assessment is known as triage.

**Sending the alarm**
A telephone call is usually the best way to get help. Special telephones are located in areas such as highways, but calls to emergency services are free on all telephones. Shouting, waving flags, or firing flares are alternative methods.

Spanish public telephone

**Further danger**
First aiders should never place themselves or others in danger. Before treating the victim, they should try to make the area safe. Fire, traffic, electricity, and unsafe structures are some of the hazards that may delay treatment.

Fire extinguisher

## ABC of first aid

ABC stands for the body's three vital needs. "A" stands for airway: the airway needs to be open so that oxygen-containing air can enter the lungs. "B" stands for breathing, by which the body inhales fresh air and expels stale air. "C" stands for the circulation of the blood, which distributes oxygen around the body. When dealing with an unconscious person, the first aider must check that the victim has a clear airway, is breathing, and has a pulse that indicates blood circulation.

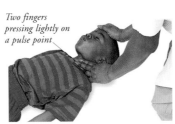

*Two fingers pressing lightly on a pulse point*

**Checking for a pulse**
The heart pumps blood around the body, causing a pulse. A first aider can check that the heart is still beating by feeling for this pulse in arteries located in the neck or wrist.

**Airway**
Inhaled foreign bodies or fluid can block the airway. By tipping the head back and straightening the airway, a first aider can look for blockages.

**Breathing**
If breathing stops, the first aider may blow air at regular intervals through the victim's mouth into their lungs. This is called artificial respiration.

**Circulation**
If a pulse is absent, the first aider may carry out heart massage (external chest compression) to try to stimulate the heart into action.

## First-aid kit

In many countries, the law requires workplaces and schools to keep first-aid kits. The contents should be kept in a clean, marked container and be restocked regularly. Because there is a danger of misusing drugs, the contents of some kits are restricted to sterile wound dressings.

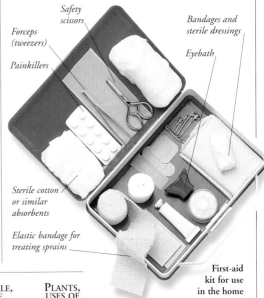

*Safety scissors*
*Forceps (tweezers)*
*Painkillers*
*Bandages and sterile dressings*
*Eyebath*
*Sterile cotton or similar absorbents*
*Elastic bandage for treating sprains*

First-aid kit for use in the home

---

*Bent leg and arm in front of body prevent victim from rolling onto front.*

*An extended head and neck keeps the airway open and prevents the tongue from blocking throat.*

**Recovery position**

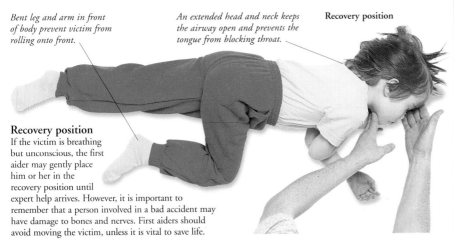

**Recovery position**
If the victim is breathing but unconscious, the first aider may gently place him or her in the recovery position until expert help arrives. However, it is important to remember that a person involved in a bad accident may have damage to bones and nerves. First aiders should avoid moving the victim, unless it is vital to save life.

---

FIND OUT MORE

DRUGS　HOSPITALS　MEDICINE　MEDICINE, HISTORY OF　NIGHTINGALE, FLORENCE　PLANTS, USES OF

# FISH

THE FIRST FISH appeared in the seas 470 million years ago. Today, more than 20,000 species have been described, ranging from the great whale shark to the pygmy goby. Fish live in freshwater streams, rivers, and lakes, and in saltwater seas and oceans. A few, including eels and salmon, migrate from salt to freshwater. Some fish are fierce predators, and because they are, many others have evolved various methods of defense. Although most fish leave their eggs and young to take care of themselves, some species protect their young.

### Fins
Most fish have a dorsal fin, paired pectoral and pelvic fins, and a tail for movement. In some fish, fins have become specialized as lifting foils, walking legs, suckers for holding on, or poisoned spines for protection.

### Scales
Most fish have a covering of backward-facing scales that help to streamline them. Bony fish have either flat, oval, or square overlapping scales, while sharks have toothlike structures buried in the skin.

*Dorsal fin*

*Caudal, or tail, fin*

*Operculum (gill cover)*

*Pectoral fin*  **European carp**

*Anal fin*

*Pelvic fin*

### Fish features
Fish have a number of features in common. They breathe through gills, and are generally streamlined in shape with paired body muscles along each side. They have a tail for propulsion, fins for steering, and scales for protection. Their heads contain paired eyes and an obvious mouth with teeth.

### Gills
Almost all fish have gills for breathing. The sharks and rays have paired gills in the throat, with openings to the outside known as gill slits. Bony fish have paired gills at the back of the head, with one opening covered by a flap of skin known as the operculum.

### Swim bladder
Bony fish have a swim bladder containing air, and they are able to fill and empty it at will. In many bony fish the swim bladder controls buoyancy, allowing the fish to move up and down in the water.

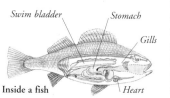

*Swim bladder*   *Stomach*

*Gills*

**Inside a fish**   *Heart*

### Flatfish
Flatfish spend most of their lives lying on their sides, half buried and camouflaged in the sand on the seabed. Like most fish, the young develop in eggs. They hatch into normal larval fish that swim "the right way up" in the plankton.

**10 days old**

**17 days old**

**35 days old**

1 The larval fish has an eye on either side of its head.

2 One eye gradually "migrates" to the other side of the head.

3 An adult flatfish lies on one side. Its eyes are on top.

### Fish groups
The fish are divided into three groups: jawless and primitive fish (cyclostomes), which include the lampreys and hagfish; cartilaginous fish (elasmobranchs), which include the sharks, rays, and ratfish; bony fish (teleosts), which include the more familiar fish, such as herring, cod, flounder, trout, eels, goldfish, sticklebacks, and guppies.

*Caudal fin*   *Dorsal fin*

**Great white shark**

*Gill slits*

*Pectoral fin*

*Sharp teeth*

### Jawless fish
Hagfish and lampreys have funnel-shaped mouths. Lampreys attach themselves to other fish with their mouths and rasp away flesh with their teeth. Hagfish are scavengers.

**Sea lamprey**

**Pike**

### Bony fish
These fish are divided into two groups – those with jointed, bony fin rays, such as most fresh- and saltwater fish, and those with fleshy fin lobes, such as lungfish.

### Cartilaginous fish
Sharks and rays have large mouths with many teeth in rows that are continually being replaced. Their skeletons are made of cartilage (gristle), instead of bones.

### Where fish live
There are fish living wherever there is water. Some fish live in oceans, the largest numbers living in the shallow seas of the continental shelf. The most brightly colored fish live on coral reefs. Other fish live on muddy, sandy, or rocky seashores, in estuaries, in rivers and streams, and even in temporary puddles.

### On land
Inhabitants of Indo-Pacific mudflats and mangrove swamps, mudskippers are able to leave the water. They can stay on land for hours, absorbing oxygen through the mouth and pharynx. They have eyes on top of their heads for all-round vision.

**Mudskipper**

**Red mullet**

**Rainbow trout**

### Oceans
The oceans provide a range of habitats for fish. Light-producing fish live in the deepest ocean trenches, while other fish live near hot volcanic vents. Some, such as sharks, roam the open oceans searching for smaller fish to eat.

### Freshwater
Fish live in fast-flowing streams, slow-moving rivers, ponds, and lakes, and are suited to their habitat. Some have to be powerful swimmers or have suckers for holding onto stones. Others live in shoals or are camouflaged to avoid predators.

F

F

# Protection

As well as scales, fish use color, camouflage, or poisonous spines to protect themselves. The spiny puffer fish can take in water or air and swells up to more than twice its size. Some eels use an electric discharge, while other fish live in shoals, making it difficult for a predator to pick out any one individual.

Clown fish

Flounder

Weever fish

### Cutting blade

The surgeon fish has a formidable cutting blade that lies in a groove. This defensive structure is a developed scale and is as sharp as a surgeon's scalpel. If attacked, the fish erects the blade and slices its opponent with a blow from its tail.

*Cutting blade in a groove in the body*

*Blade extended*

Surgeon fish

**Surgeon fish's blade** folds in when not in use

### Color

Fish use color to warn other fish that they are poisonous. Color also helps some fish hide from predators. The fish's color depends on its lifestyle. Cave fish have no color; deep-sea fish are black; open-sea fish are silvery.

### Camouflage

Some fish look like the plants among which they live. The triple tail looks like a mangrove leaf, and the leafy seadragon and sargassum fish look like seaweed. The flounder can change color to match the surrounding seabed.

### Poison

Several fish are poisonous. Weever fishes are extremely dangerous. They lie partly buried and camouflaged in sand, waiting for food. The spines on their gill covers and dorsal fin can inject poison into anyone who steps on one.

# Food

Many larger fish, including sharks, groupers, pikes, and barracudas, are predators that catch and eat their prey. Most smaller shoal fish feed on plankton, which floats in the water. Some fish are bottom feeders, such as flounder, while others are grazers, such as the parrot fish, which rasps organisms from rocks.

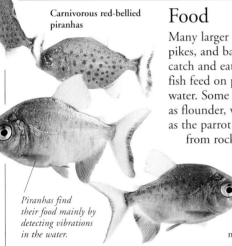

Carnivorous red-bellied piranhas

*Piranhas find their food mainly by detecting vibrations in the water.*

### Piranhas

These South American fish have strong jaws and sharp triangular teeth. A shoal of carnivorous piranhas can strip an animal to the bone in minutes. They are one of the most feared types of fish, but most eat mainly fruit and nuts.

### Cleaner fish

Fish called cleaners, such as some wrasses, have "cleaning" stations where they wait for customers. The customers allow the cleaners to remove bits of food and parasites from their skin, gills, fins, and even the inside of their mouths.

**Cleaner wrasse at work**

Angler fish with lure

### Angler fish

Angler fish usually live in deep water. They have a dorsal fin ray modified into a fishing line, with a lure on the end to attract their prey. They can swallow fish much larger than themselves.

# Reproduction

Most bony fish lay eggs in the water, and they are then fertilized by a male's sperm. The parents usually leave the eggs to their fate, but some species protect their young in their mouths, in pouches, or in nests. Some sharks, such as the dogfish, lay eggs in an egg case, while others bear live young.

*Male stickleback's underside turns red in the breeding season.*

### Sticklebacks

Male sticklebacks make a nest and attract females by doing a zigzag dance. The female lays her eggs in the nest, and the male fertilizes them. He then protects the nest from any intruder until the young hatch and are ready to fend for themselves.

**Male three-spined stickleback**

### Sea horses

Within 10 seconds of mating, the female sea horse transfers 200 fertilized eggs into the broodpouch of the male. The male carries them around with him for four weeks until they are ready to hatch. The male then "gives birth," and the young sea horses swim away.

Stickleback eggs

### Salmon

The Atlantic salmon lays its eggs in upland streams. The young, called parr, live there for three years; they are then called smolt. The smolt swim down-river to the sea and travel across the Atlantic. At maturity, the salmon return to spawn in the same stream where they hatched.

*Adult salmon will leap up waterfalls on their journey upstream to spawn.*

**FIND OUT MORE** | CAMOUFLAGE AND COLOR | LAKE AND RIVER WILDLIFE | MARSH AND SWAMP WILDLIFE | MIGRATION, ANIMAL | OCEAN WILDLIFE | POISONOUS ANIMALS | SHARKS AND RAYS

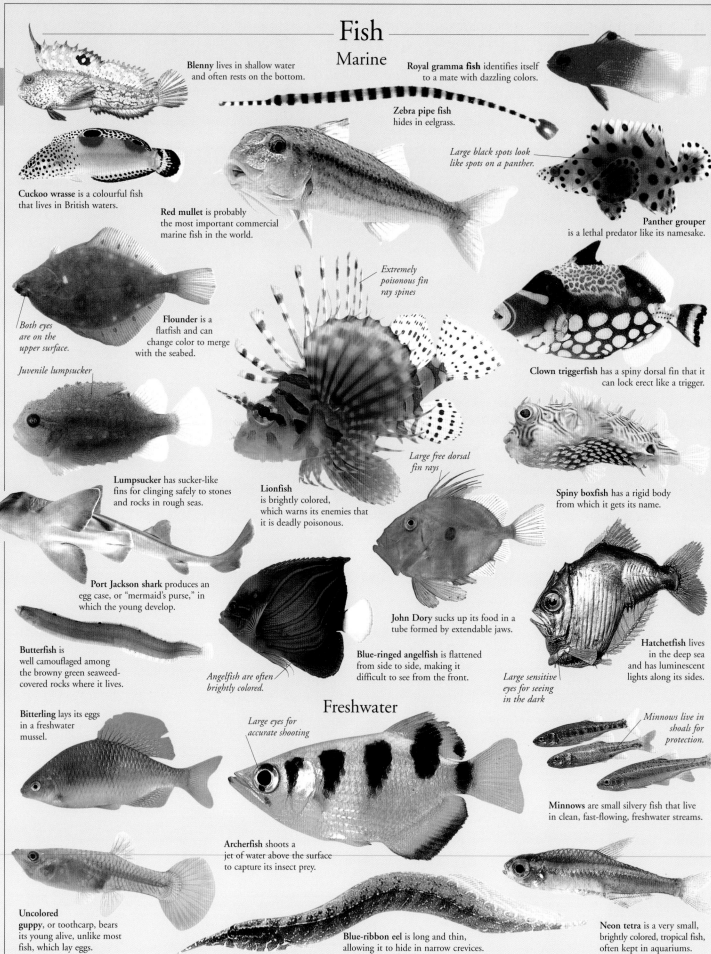

# Fish
## Marine

**Blenny** lives in shallow water and often rests on the bottom.

**Royal gramma fish** identifies itself to a mate with dazzling colors.

**Zebra pipe fish** hides in eelgrass.

*Large black spots look like spots on a panther.*

**Cuckoo wrasse** is a colourful fish that lives in British waters.

**Red mullet** is probably the most important commercial marine fish in the world.

**Panther grouper** is a lethal predator like its namesake.

*Extremely poisonous fin ray spines*

*Both eyes are on the upper surface.*

**Flounder** is a flatfish and can change color to merge with the seabed.

*Juvenile lumpsucker*

**Clown triggerfish** has a spiny dorsal fin that it can lock erect like a trigger.

*Large free dorsal fin rays*

**Lumpsucker** has sucker-like fins for clinging safely to stones and rocks in rough seas.

**Lionfish** is brightly colored, which warns its enemies that it is deadly poisonous.

**Spiny boxfish** has a rigid body from which it gets its name.

**Port Jackson shark** produces an egg case, or "mermaid's purse," in which the young develop.

**John Dory** sucks up its food in a tube formed by extendable jaws.

**Butterfish** is well camouflaged among the browny green seaweed-covered rocks where it lives.

**Blue-ringed angelfish** is flattened from side to side, making it difficult to see from the front.

*Angelfish are often brightly colored.*

*Large sensitive eyes for seeing in the dark*

**Hatchetfish** lives in the deep sea and has luminescent lights along its sides.

**Bitterling** lays its eggs in a freshwater mussel.

## Freshwater

*Large eyes for accurate shooting*

*Minnows live in shoals for protection.*

**Minnows** are small silvery fish that live in clean, fast-flowing, freshwater streams.

**Archerfish** shoots a jet of water above the surface to capture its insect prey.

**Uncolored guppy**, or toothcarp, bears its young alive, unlike most fish, which lay eggs.

**Blue-ribbon eel** is long and thin, allowing it to hide in narrow crevices.

**Neon tetra** is a very small, brightly colored, tropical fish, often kept in aquariums.

# FISHING INDUSTRY

LONG BEFORE FARMING BEGAN, people fed themselves by hunting fish and land animals. Today, the fishing industry continues this hunting tradition. Fishing vessels go to sea from every country with a coastline. Small boats, such as the stern trawler, have few crew members, and fish within a day's journey of their home port. The biggest fishing ships can stay at sea for months, and freeze their catch on board.

### Fishing with lines
To catch valuable tuna, fishing boats trail a line as long as 112 miles (97 nautical miles; 180 km). Branching off this line are 200 smaller lines, each ending in a baited hook. This arrangement is known as a drifting longline.

## Sea fishing

Most sea fish live within (165 ft) 50 m of the surface. They are concentrated in the shallow waters around the coasts of continents. In the past, the supply of sea fish appeared limitless. However, intensive fishing in areas that were once rich in fish, such as the Grand Banks of North America, has driven cod and other popular species to the edge of extinction.

Stern trawler

*Fish-finding equipment in pilothouse shows the crew where to find the biggest catch.*

*Deck winch drags the full net toward the boat.*

*Hoist lifts the net onto the boat.*

P40

*Crew launch the trawl net over the boat's stern.*

### Deep-sea fishing
To catch demersal fish (those that live near the ocean floor) fishing boats sink bag-shaped nets in the water. The fish are trapped by towing the net along the bottom (trawling) or drawing the neck of the net closed (seine fishing). The boat then hauls in the net to land the catch.

Lobster pot

### Traps
Bait lures lobsters into this basketlike "pot," which rests on the seabed in shallow water. Its funnel-shaped entrance makes escape impossible. Fish traps take many different forms: the Mediterranean tuna trap, for example, is like a maze of net corridors anchored to the seabed. There are even special aerial traps for catching flying fish.

Seine fishing

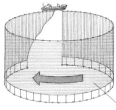

*Net closes like a purse, trapping fish.*

*Weighted net hangs down from floats.*

### Surface fishing
Many species of pelagic fish (those that live near the surface) swim together in large groups called shoals, and it is these shoals that fishing boats seek. They catch them by enclosing the shoal in a purse seine net, which is like a circular curtain. Pulling a line closes the bottom of the net, preventing the fish from escaping.

## Freshwater fishing

Only 5 percent of the world's fish catch comes from freshwater sources such as rivers and lakes. However, in nonindustrialized nations, freshwater fishing with lines and nets is a vital industry, especially on great lakes such as those in East Africa's Rift Valley. In industrialized nations, anglers have to pay to fish on the few remaining stretches of unpolluted water.

*Fur and feather make hook resemble an insect.*

Freshwater rods

*Barb*

*Point*

Double hook    Treble hook    Fly-fishing bait    Weight

### Ocean mammals
The oceans are also home to mammals. Fishing for whales, the world's largest mammals, has now almost stopped because their numbers fell so low. The fur of the seal makes it a target for hunters, and although few fishing vessels catch dolphins deliberately, many dolphins die because they become entangled in abandoned nets.

*In the past, whaling crews made beautiful carvings out of the bones and teeth of sea mammals.*

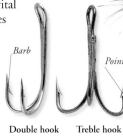

### Fish farming
Just as farming produces meat more efficiently than hunting, farming fish is more efficient than catching them. Fish farms breed fish carefully to give good-quality stock, and protect the young fish in ponds or enclosures from predators. Carp and trout are the main freshwater farm fish.

### Angling
Fishing for sport is known as angling and is as ancient as fishing for food. Anglers fix a hook to a thin line and then cast it into the water using a long, flexible rod. To lure fish, anglers bait the hook with worms or insects. They may also use a "fly," which is a hook disguised as an insect.

**FIND OUT MORE**    FARMING    FISH    FOOD    SHIPS AND BOATS    SPORTS    WHALES AND DOLPHINS

339

# FLAGS

FOR HUNDREDS of years, people have used flags as emblems, signals, or rallying points. Among the earliest flags were those flown in battle, so that soldiers could identify their leader and tell each side apart. The flag has since developed as a means of communication, used to send rapid signals, or as a symbol representing a nation or group. Every country has its own flag, as do many states and most political organizations.

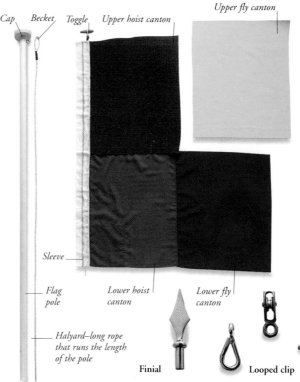

Cap  Becket  Toggle  Upper hoist canton  Upper fly canton

Sleeve

Flag pole

Lower hoist canton  Lower fly canton

Halyard–long rope that runs the length of the pole

Finial  Looped clip

## Parts of a flag

A flag is usually made from brightly colored fabric and is square or rectangular in shape – although more varied shapes, such as streamers, banners, and long, narrow pennons, were once popular. Flags are divided into four quarters (cantons); those near the pole are the hoist, and the others the fly. A special emblem often appears in the upper hoist canton.

### Flying the flag

In Europe, flags are attached to the pole by passing the toggle through a loop (becket) in another rope (halyard). In the US, flags have eyelets to which clips are attached. Inglefield clips have a quick-release mechanism, and are popular at sea. Parade flagstaffs are topped with decorative finials.

Toggle and becket

## First flags

Many ancient armies carried standards, carved symbols on the end of a pole. The Roman standard first introduced cloth flags. These hung from horizontal poles, to make them easy to carry on horseback.

### Homemade flag

The first flag was probably a piece of brightly colored cloth tied to a stick. A plain red flag signaled danger to early people, just as it does today.

Cloth dyed with natural earth pigment

Finial on top of pole could show legion badge.

Badge of legion

Name of legion

### Pride of a legion

The Roman standard was awarded to a military unit only as a reward for special effort.

## Uses of flags

Flags communicate across language barriers. At sea, the International Code of Signals is a system of signaling with flags: the meanings are the same in every language. In both sports and politics, flags also send messages that are understood universally.

Red Cross flag

Flag of the United Nations

The dove on the Greenpeace flag, a symbol of hope

### Rallying cries

Modern flags are developed to identify political movements, or international medical or environmental groups. The emblems and colors represent the organization's ideals: for instance, a white background stands for peace, while olive branches symbolize reconciliation.

Soccer flags are raised to signal when the ball has gone out of play.

Golf flags are attached to slender pins to mark the holes on a course.

### Sports flags

Flags are used in many sports for marking the area of play or signaling to participants.

Plastic marker flags

### Political symbols

An image on a national flag can symbolize political ideals that would otherwise take many words. The hammer and sickle symbol of the former Soviet flag represented the workers and farmers who took part in the Russian Revolution.

## Semaphore

This method of signaling with just two flags is still used at sea. Signalers can spell out a message quickly, simply by changing the position of their arms. Red and yellow flags are chosen because they can be seen at long distances.

A  B  C  D  E  F  G  H  I  J  K  L  M  N

O  P  Q  R  S  T  U  V  W  X  Y  Z

FIND OUT MORE    FOOTBALL    PEACE MOVEMENTS    ROMAN EMPIRE    SHIPS AND BOATS    SIGNS AND SYMBOLS    SOVIET UNION    UNITED NATIONS

# International Code of Signals
## Alphabet and single flag messages

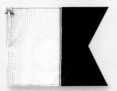

**A** I have a diver down; keep well clear at slow speed.

**B** I am taking in, or discharging, or carrying dangerous goods.

**C** Yes.

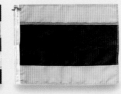

**D** Keep clear of me; I am maneuvering with difficulty.

**E** I am altering my course to starboard.

**F** I am disabled; communicate with me.

## Two-flag messages

**G** I require a pilot (or, I am hauling nets).

**H** I have a pilot on board.

**I** I am altering my course to port.

**J** I am on fire and have dangerous cargo on board; keep well clear of me.

**K** I wish to communicate with you.

**DX** I am sinking.

**L** You should stop your vessel instantly.

**M** My vessel is stopped and making no way through the water.

**N** No.

**O** Man overboard.

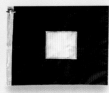

**P** All persons should report on board as vessel is about to proceed to sea.

**NG** You are in a dangerous position.

**Q** My vessel is healthy and I require free pratique [permission to trade].

**R** [No single letter meaning].

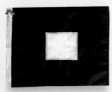

**S** My engines are going astern.

**T** Keep clear of me; I am engaged in pair trawling.

**U** You are running into danger.

**AC** I am abandoning my vessel.

**V** I require assistance.

**W** I require medical assistance.

**X** Stop carrying out your intentions and watch my signals.

**Y** I am dragging my anchor.

**Z** I require a tug.

**NH** You are clear of all danger.

## Numerals

ONE    TWO    THREE    FOUR    FIVE

SIX    SEVEN    EIGHT    NINE    ZERO

# FLIES

THEY MAY BE PESTS AT TIMES, but flies are remarkable insects. As their name suggests, they have mastered the power of flight. Fast and agile in the air, flies dart around, hover, and make lightning turns. There are about 90,000 different insects that we call flies. About 75,000 of these are true flies, which have only one pair of wings and belong to the insect group Diptera. The remainder form many other groups of insects with two pairs of wings. Unlike most other types of flies, the larvae of true flies are completely different from the adults. Often called maggots, they have simple bodies with no legs and are little more than eating machines.

## Feeding

Fly larvae feed on foods such as microscopic organisms, living flesh, plants, and dung. The mouthparts of adult flies are adapted for a liquid diet. They have extendible tubes to draw fluids into their bodies. The feeding habits of flies cause many health problems worldwide, from stomachaches to more serious illnesses, such as cholera.

*Abdomen swollen with blood*

**Tsetse fly**

### Bloodsuckers and predators
Bloodsuckers and flies that catch prey have piercing mouthparts that cut holes in their victims. They inject anti-clotting agents to keep blood flowing, or poison to kill the prey. Enzymes are also released to help break down the body contents.

**Hoverfly**

### Nectar and waste feeders
Flies that feed on nectar or decaying matter have soft pads on the ends of their sucking mouthparts, that help soak up liquid food. On solid food, flies deposit saliva, then suck up the partly digested juice that results.

## Features of a true fly

The body of an adult fly is clearly divided into three main parts: the head, thorax, and abdomen. The head consists of sucking mouthparts and a bulging pair of compound eyes, with antennae attached between the eyes. Attached to the thorax are the fly's six legs and its membranous wings. The abdomen contains most of the body organs.

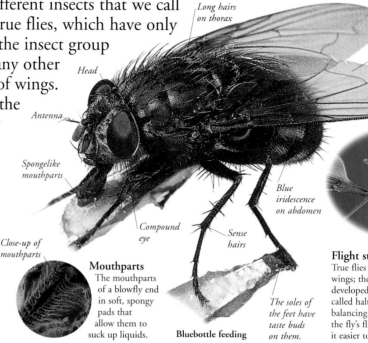

*Long hairs on thorax*

*Head*

*Antenna*

*Single pair of wings*

*Haltères of a crane fly*

*Spongelike mouthparts*

*Blue iridescence on abdomen*

*Compound eye*

*Sense hairs*

*Close-up of mouthparts*

**Mouthparts**
The mouthparts of a blowfly end in soft, spongy pads that allow them to suck up liquids.

**Bluebottle feeding**

*The soles of the feet have taste buds on them.*

### Flight stabilizers
True flies have a single pair of wings; the hindwings have developed into club-ended stubs called haltères. Haltères act as balancing organs that improve the fly's flight control and make it easier to change direction.

## Breeding

After mating, female flies lay hundreds of eggs on a suitable feeding site for the larvae that develop from the eggs. These sites may be in dung, soil, or water, or on leaves, dead bodies, or living animals. The larvae eat voraciously, then grow into pupae within which they change into their adult form.

**Robber flies mating**

**Bluebottle larvae**

### Mating
Before mating, flies may go through elaborate courtship rituals. Fruit flies dance on leaves, and gnats dance in the air. After mating, female robber flies usually eat their mates.

### Larvae
Fly eggs often hatch out into larvae on dead animals, which they begin to eat. The larvae, also called maggots, may live longer than the adult flies into which they develop.

## Aquatic larvae

Mosquitos and many other bloodsucking flies lay their eggs in water. The larvae that develop float upside down on the surface. They breathe through a tube attached to the abdomen, that pokes above the water. After pupation, the adult emerges to fly away.

*Tube takes in air.*

**Mosquito larva**

## Types of flies

In addition to true flies, many other kinds of flies exist that have two pairs of wings, such as dragonflies and mayflies. The young that emerge from the eggs of such flies have a more complicated body structure than the larvae of true flies – some even look like wingless versions of the adults.

### Dragonflies
Dragonflies are large predators. They dart around in seach of other insects which they catch in flight with their long legs. They lay their eggs in water.

*Giant compound eyes*

### Caddis flies
Adult caddis flies always live near water. Their larvae live underwater, and carry with them a protective case made of plant debris or sand.

*Long antenna*

### Mayflies
Young mayflies live below water. After growing wings, they leave the water and form swarms in the air. The adults mate, lay their eggs, then die a few hours later.

*Long, thin legs*

### Lacewings
Lacewings often hibernate in houses over winter. The adults and larvae prey on other insects such as aphids. They are weak fliers.

*Delicate wings*

## BLUEBOTTLE

**SCIENTIFIC NAME** *Calliphora erythrocephala*

**ORDER** Diptera

**FAMILY** Calliphoridae

**DISTRIBUTION** Europe

**HABITAT** Fields, meadows, houses, and buildings

**DIET** Rotting flesh, feces, and other decomposing organic matter; adults also eat nectar

**SIZE** Length 0.4 in (10 mm)

**LIFESPAN** Larvae: 7 days; pupae: 8–10 days; adults: unknown

**FIND OUT MORE**

ARTHROPODS    DISEASES    EGGS    FLIGHT, ANIMAL    INSECTS    MARSH AND SWAMP WILDLIFE

# FLIGHT, ANIMAL

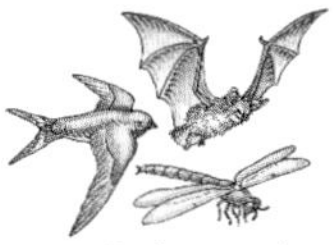

ALTHOUGH SOME ANIMALS CAN glide for short distances,only birds, bats, and insects are capable of powered flight. Flight is very useful. It helps the animals find food, escape from predators, and migrate long distances. Flying animals need wings, powerful wing muscles, a streamlined shape, and a lightweight body. They also need to eat lots of food to give them the energy to flap their wings.

## Birds

A bird's wings are an airfoil shape – curved on top and slightly hollow underneath. As the wings move through the air, the difference in air pressure above and below lifts the bird into the air. A bird steers by changing the angle of one or both wings, twisting its body, and spreading and twisting its tail.

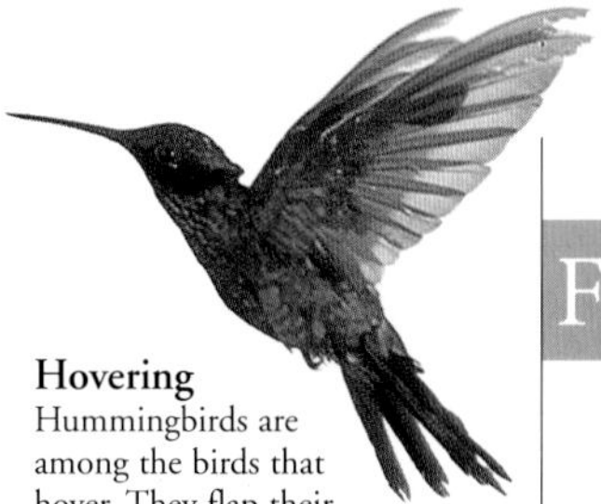

**Hovering**
Hummingbirds are among the birds that hover. They flap their wings in a figure-eight pattern, producing lift on both the upstroke and downstroke. They can also fly sideways, straight up and down, backward, and even upside down.

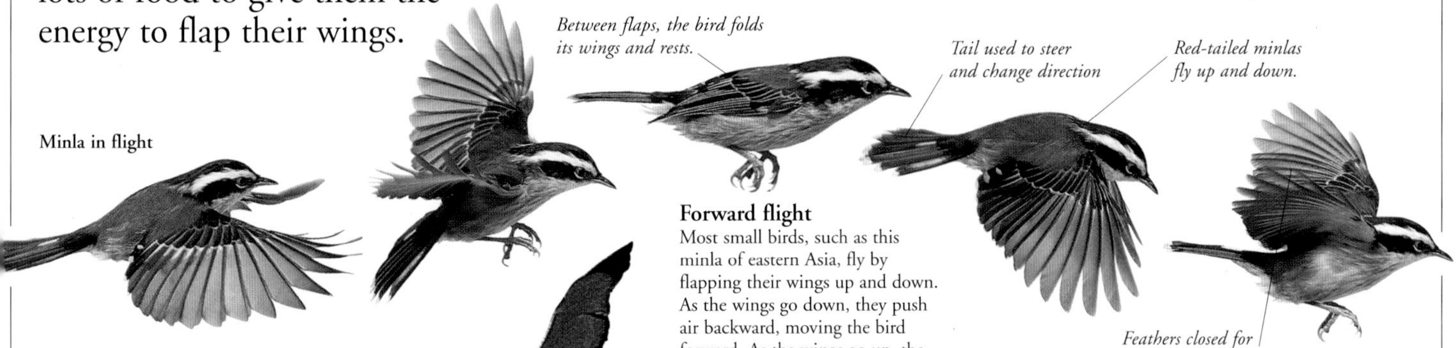

Minla in flight
Between flaps, the bird folds its wings and rests.
Tail used to steer and change direction
Red-tailed minlas fly up and down.
Feathers closed for the downstroke


**Forward flight**
Most small birds, such as this minla of eastern Asia, fly by flapping their wings up and down. As the wings go down, they push air backward, moving the bird forward. As the wings go up, the feathers at the wingtips move apart to allow air to slip through.

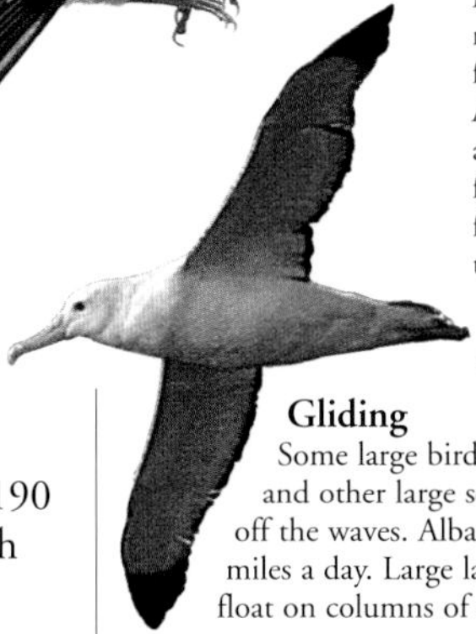

Gliding albatross

**Gliding**
Some large birds rarely flap their wings. Albatrosses and other large seabirds glide on strong winds rising off the waves. Albatrosses can travel for hundreds of miles a day. Large land birds, such as vultures and eagles, float on columns of rising hot air called thermals.

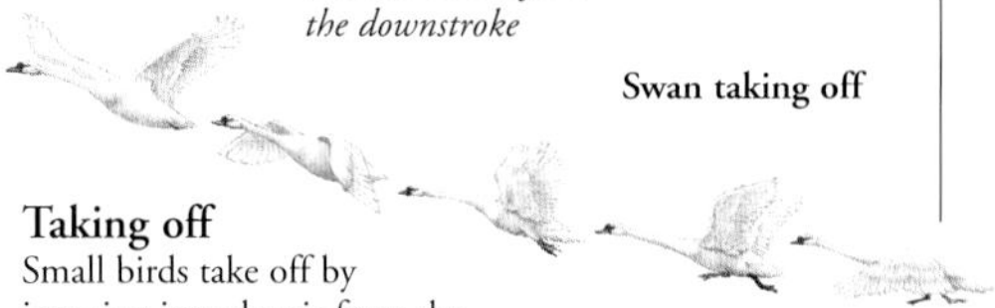

Swan taking off

**Taking off**
Small birds take off by jumping into the air from the ground or from a perch and flapping their wings. A large, heavy bird, such as a swan, cannot do this. It needs to run along the ground while flapping its wings to create enough lift for takeoff.

## Insects

A small insect, such as a mosquito, flaps its wings 1,000 times a second. Most insects flap about 520 times a second. Dragonflies are the fastest insect fliers, reaching nearly 190 mph (300 km/h). Some insects, such as flies, have one pair of wings. Others, such as bees, have two pairs.

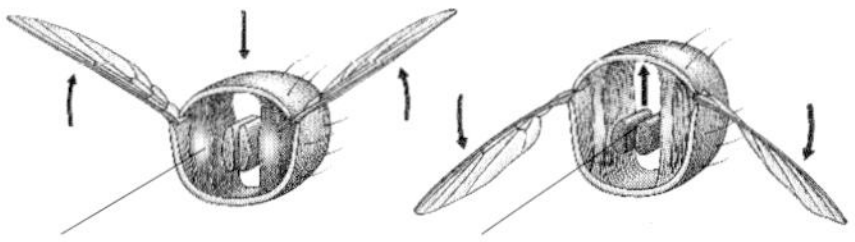

Vertical muscle contracts, moving the wings up
Horizontal muscle contracts, moving the wings down.


**Wing muscles**
Insect wings developed from their hard body covering. They are not modified legs, like the wings of birds or bats. Insects do not have any muscles on the wings. Instead, their wing muscles are inside the thorax, the middle part of the body.

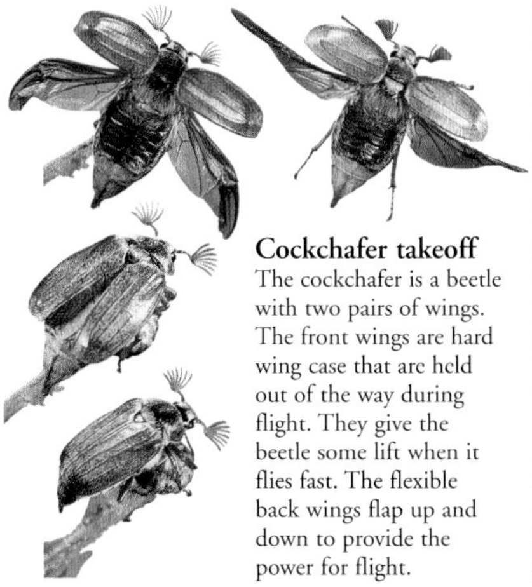

**Cockchafer takeoff**
The cockchafer is a beetle with two pairs of wings. The front wings are hard wing case that are held out of the way during flight. They give the beetle some lift when it flies fast. The flexible back wings flap up and down to provide the power for flight.

## Bats

The only mammals able to fly, bats are more acrobatic than birds. They have four large pairs of flight muscles and several smaller pairs, while birds have only two pairs. Each wing consists of skin stretched between four long fingers.

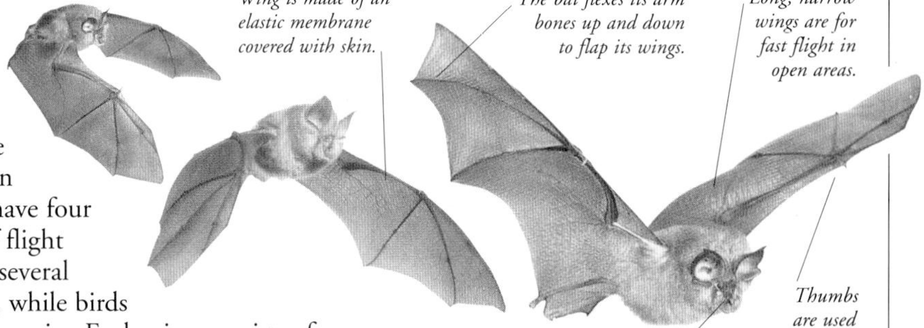

Wing is made of an elastic membrane covered with skin.
The bat flexes its arm bones up and down to flap its wings.
Long, narrow wings are for fast flight in open areas.
Thumbs are used for clinging to surfaces.
Horseshoe bats find prey by echolocation.


## Gliding animals

Some animals can glide slowly downward. They have developed large fins, or webs or flaps of skin, which they spread out to slow their fall. They have to be able to judge speeds and distances accurately.

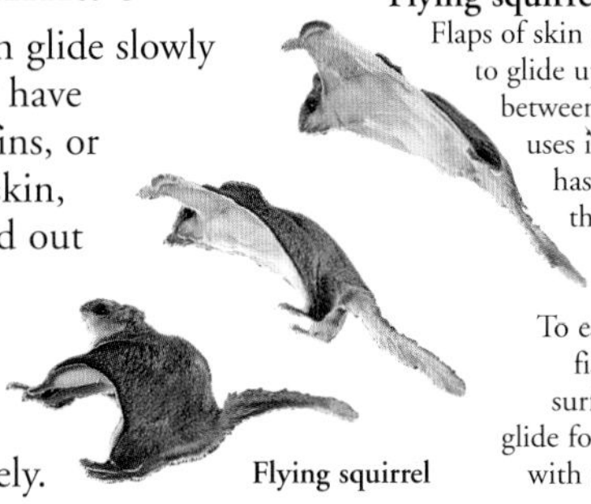

Flying squirrel

**Flying squirrel**
Flaps of skin allow a flying squirrel to glide up to 330 ft (100 m) between trees. The squirrel uses its tail as a rudder, and has sharp claws to grasp the surface on landing.

**Flying fish**
To escape predators, flying fish swim fast along the surface, then take off and glide for up to 160 ft (50 m), with their huge fins spread.

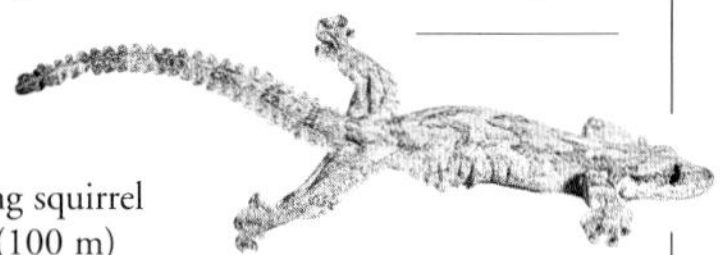

**Flying gecko**
The gecko (above) has flaps of skin along the sides of its body and tail. It spreads out the flaps to glide between trees. It has webbed feet to help it steer.

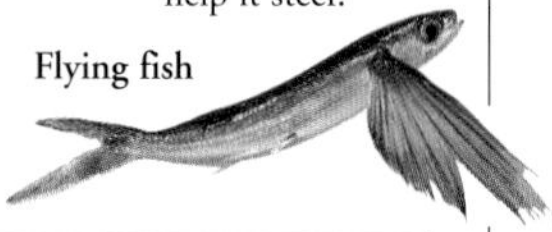

Flying fish


FIND OUT MORE
AIRCRAFT ANIMALS BATS BIRDS FLIGHT, HISTORY OF INSECTS MIGRATION

# FLIGHT, HISTORY OF

EVERY DAY, MILLIONS OF PEOPLE fly to destinations all over the world. Planes are a common sight in the skies, but despite their widespread use, they were first developed only about 90 years ago. The urge to fly is ancient, but by the start of the 20th century, the only flying machines were hot-air balloons, airships, and gliders. World War I stimulated the development of airplanes, and, by the end of World War II, advances were made in jets and rockets. Since then, flight technology has produced supersonic planes and space travel.

Flying machine designed by Leonardo da Vinci in the 15th century

## Copying the birds

Wings are the part of an aircraft that provide the upward lift needed to keep it in the air. Successful airplanes were impossible to build before people understood how wings worked. Early attempts at flight concentrated on copying the flapping action of birds, which proved to be impractical because a human's muscles are far too weak. Many "bird men" were killed trying to fly.

## First controlled flight

The first controlled flight of a powered aeroplane took place on December 17, 1903, in Kitty Hawk, North Carolina. The plane, *Flyer I*, flew 36 m (119 ft) in a flight that lasted under 12 seconds: it is nonetheless perhaps the most famous flight of all time. *Flyer I* was designed and built by the Wright brothers, Orville and Wilbur, after years of experiments with kites and gliders. It was powered by a gas engine they built themselves.

Flyer I *climbed to a height of 3 m (10 feet).*

Wilbur Wright watches his brother Orville take off.

## Warplanes

The military's interest in the potential of airplanes as weaponry was central to the advancement of flight technology. During World War I (1914–18), warplanes were transformed from being slow and vulnerable to being fast, easily maneuverable fighting machines. Huge bomber and fighter planes were made in this period.

Protective clothing worn by World War I pilots included leather flying helmet, goggles and gloves.

### Airships

Airships are held aloft by a vast gas-filled envelope and driven forward by engines with propellers. Airships were a popular form of passenger and military transportation until long-distance aircraft were developed in the 1940s.

### Amelia Earhart

American aviation pioneer Amelia Earhart (1898–1937) set several long-distance flight records. She was the first woman to fly solo across the Atlantic. In 1937, in a bid to fly round the world, she disappeared near New Guinea.

### Biplane

World War I pilots flew biplane (twin-winged) fighters. Built from wood and fabric, biplanes were sturdier than monoplanes, but flying them was little fun. The cockpit was open to the cold and wet, and to spits of oil from the engine. Larger fighters had a second cockpit for a navigator and gunner. Single seaters had a machine gun that fired through the spinning propeller.

Biplane of 1917

## Modern age

The basis for the modern airplane first appeared in the 1920s. It was a monoplane (single-winged) aircraft. The wing was made of metal, as was the fuselage. All aircraft had piston engines and propellers until the late 1930s, when a new type of engine, the jet, was invented.

Harrier GR5 jet fighter

### Jets

A turbojet engine allows aircraft to fly much faster and more quietly than a propeller engine. Jet aircraft were increasingly used after World War II and became standard for fighter aircraft and for long-distance passenger planes.

Ariane launch vehicle

Boarding pass

Airline ticket

### Passenger flight

Fast, comfortable, and affordable air travel had become accessible by the 1960s. Today, millions of passengers fly around the world in the Boeing 747, a so-called "jumbo jet" which has quiet, turbofan engines.

### Space flight

The first rockets powerful enough to reach space were built in the late 1950s. Today, modern launch vehicles and reusable spacecraft, such as the Shuttle, make going into orbit almost an everyday event.

**FIND OUT MORE**   AIRCRAFT   AIRPORTS   AIRSHIPS AND BALLOONS   LEONARDO DA VINCI   SPACE EXPLORATION   TRANSPORTATION, HISTORY OF   TRAVEL   WARPLANES   WEAPONS

# FLIGHTLESS BIRDS

FLYING IS A VERY USEFUL WAY of moving, but it does have drawbacks. It uses a lot of energy, and it is possible only for animals with a light body. Most birds can fly, but some have given up flight and the problems it brings. Instead, they run, or, as is the case with penguins, they swim; some can move extremely fast. There are about 40 species of flightless birds alive today, including kiwis, emus, and the world's biggest bird, the ostrich. Many more flightless species, including some record-breaking giants, existed in the past, and some of today's species are also in danger of extinction.

*Long neck with sparse feathers*

*Weak, fanlike wings used in courtship rituals*

*Females are slightly smaller than males, with brown plumage instead of black.*

*Two large, clawed toes on each foot*

**Ostrich crèche**
Young ostriches are guarded by an adult male. Several families of chicks gather together, forming a group called a crèche.

## Kiwis

These medium-sized birds are found only in the forests of New Zealand. Their wings are only about 2 in (5 cm) long, and their body is covered with a unique plumage that looks like hair. Kiwis are nocturnal and because they have poor eyesight, they find food mainly by smelling it.

## Ostrich

The ostrich is the world's largest bird. It can run at up to 40 mph (65 kmh), and uses its speed and stamina to outdistance most of its enemies. An ostrich's feet have two toes, and each toe ends in a large claw. If an ostrich is cornered, it uses these claws as deadly weapons to defend itself.

**Hatching**
The shell of an ostrich egg is thicker than a china mug, but not as hard. The young ostrich breaks out by kicking and pecking at the shell.

*Sensory, whisker-like feathers at the base of the beak*

**1** The chick turns its body as it pecks and pushes at the shell.

**2** Half the shell is in pieces, and the chick is almost free of the egg.

**3** The chick tumbles out and will soon start to look for food.

*Small wings are hidden under the body plumage.*

*Hard "helmet," or casque*

**Cassowaries**
These large, flightless birds live in dense forests in northern Australia and New Guinea. They use their claws as weapons and have been known to kill people.

*Rheas escape from danger by running away.*

**Rheas**
There are two species of rheas, both of which live on the open plains in South America. Young rheas have bright stripes, but the adults are grayish-brown.

*Strong legs with large feet*

*This egg is shown in proportion to the kiwi above.*

**Probing beak**
The kiwi has nostrils at the tip of its long, curved beak, instead of near its head. It uses its beak to find food on the forest floor.

**Kiwi egg**
The kiwi's egg is 5 in (13 cm) long, and is a quarter of the female's weight. Relative to her body, the female kiwi lays the largest eggs of all birds.

**Emus**
Found only in Australia, emus are the second largest birds in the world, after the ostrich. Emus live in large flocks and wander long distances in search of food. They can cause problems on farms by raiding crops.

| OSTRICH | |
|---|---|
| SCIENTIFIC NAME | *Struthio camelus* |
| ORDER | Struthioniformes |
| FAMILY | Struthionidae |
| DISTRIBUTION | Tropical western and eastern Africa, and southern Africa |
| HABITAT | Savanna and semi-desert |
| DIET | Fruit, seeds, leaves, small animals |
| SIZE | Height up to 8 ft (2.4 m); weight up to 340 lb (154 kg) |
| LIFESPAN | About 30 years |

**FIND OUT MORE**    AUSTRALIAN WILDLIFE    BIRDS    EGGS    FLIGHT    GRASSLAND WILDLIFE    PENGUINS    SOUTH AMERICAN WILDLIFE

# FLOWERS

THE FIRST flowering plants appeared about 120 million years ago. They are now the largest group of plants, and are found worldwide. Flowers are the advanced reproductive structures of plants. The majority of them are pollinated by the wind or by animals. Over millions of years, flowers and insects have coevolved to produce some very complex and interesting relationships.

## Parts of a flower

A plant's reproductive organs are inside the flowers. Male organs, called stamen, produce pollen. Female organs, called carpels, contain ovules, which develop into seeds. A ring of petals attracts pollinators, and sepals protect the flower when in bud.

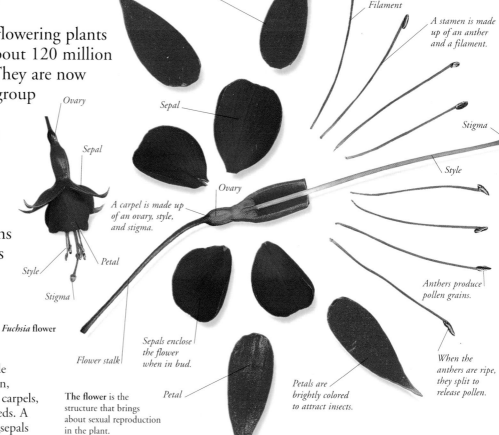

Petal

Anther

Filament

A stamen is made up of an anther and a filament.

Sepal

Ovary

Stigma

Style

Ovary

Sepal

Style

Petal

Stigma

A carpel is made up of an ovary, style, and stigma.

Anthers produce pollen grains.

*Fuchsia* flower

Flower stalk

Sepals enclose the flower when in bud.

The flower is the structure that brings about sexual reproduction in the plant.

Petal

Petal

Petals are brightly colored to attract insects.

When the anthers are ripe, they split to release pollen.

## Pollination

In order for seeds to develop, a flower has to be pollinated. Pollen from the stamens of a flower of the same species must stick to the plant's stigma. Cross-pollination occurs when pollen from one plant lands on the flowers of another. If a flower is pollinated by its own pollen, it is called self-pollination.

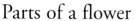

Bee at a *Narcissus* flower

**Insect pollination**
Flowers are usually pollinated by insects that are attracted by their petals, a scent, and a supply of nectar or pollen to eat. The pollen sticks to a flying insect and is deposited on another flower.

Freesia

Tobacco plant

Wattle

**Scent and color**
The color and scent of a flower attract insects or other animals. Drops of sugary nectar secreted at the base of the petals provide food for the insects, which are dusted with pollen while they drink. Flowers are often sweetly scented, but some smell unpleasant, especially those pollinated by flies.

**Water pollination**
Aquatic plants may have aerial, submerged, or floating flowers. A few use the surface film of water to carry pollen. The flowers float in shallow waves. The pollen slides into these and pollinates the flowers.

**Starwort**

**Wind pollination**
Some plants rely on wind to waft their pollen from one flower to another. Their flowers may have no petals, or only tiny ones. They are often arranged in catkins with conspicuous stamens and stigmas.

**Hazel catkins and pollen**

**Bird pollination**
Many flowers that rely on birds to pollinate them are red or orange – colors that attract birds. The flowers tend to be tubular so that when birds dip their beaks in, their heads touch the stamens, which then release pollen.

**Hummingbird at a thistle flower**

**Mammal pollination**
Important mammal pollinators include some species of tropical bats and many types of tiny Australian possums. They pollinate flowers as they feed on nectar and pollen.

**Pygmy possum feeding on a *Banksia* flower**

### Insect mimics

Many orchids have such specialized partnerships that only one type of insect serves as a pollinator. Some orchids look and smell so like a female insect that males of that species try to mate with them, picking up pollen as they do so.

**Bee orchid**

An orchid's pollen is produced in small clumps called pollinia.

The bee orchid can be pollinated by a bee, but is often self-pollinated by the wind.

Part of the flower looks and smells just like a bee.

 **FIND OUT MORE**   CARNIVOROUS PLANTS   FRUITS AND SEEDS   INSECTS   PLANTS   PLANT ANATOMY   PLANT REPRODUCTION   PLANT USES   TREES   WINDS

# Flowers

## Insect-pollinated

*Urn-shaped flowers*

**Bramble** pollinators include beetles and bees.

**Bell heather** is pollinated by short-tongued bees.

**Primrose** flowers appear in the spring.

*Brown lines on the petals guide insects to the nectar.*

**Hollow-stemmed asphodel** has hollow stems and leaves.

*Each flower contains a drop of nectar.*

**Red clover** has a head of tubular flowers.

**Greater periwinkle** is pollinated by bees.

*Domed hood*

**Mirror orchid** has pollen in clumps called pollinia.

**Anemone pavonina** is pollinated by insects.

**Magnolia** flowers have thick, waxy petals.

**Corn marigold** flowerhead has many tiny flowers.

**Fox and cubs** has strap-shaped ray florets.

**Bastard balm** attracts bees with its large petal.

**Dwarf elder** has small flowers clustered together.

**Early dog violet** has dark veins that guide insects.

**Wild pansy** is pollinated by long-tongued bees.

*Insects crawl into the bell-shaped flowers.*

**Foxglove** is pollinated by bumblebees.

*Umbels of tiny yellow flowers*

**Thorow-wax** has clusters of flowers called umbels.

**Marsh cinquefoil** has much larger sepals than petals.

**Red valerian** has tiny tubular flowers pollinated by moths and butterflies.

**Carline thistle** has yellow flowers surrounded by stiff, spiny bracts.

**Honeysuckle** has scented flowers that attract honeybees and hawkmoths.

**Cornflower** has scented flowers and is pollinated by flies and bees.

**Common rockrose** is pollinated by insects, but can be self-pollinating.

**Red campion** is pollinated by long-tongued bees and also by hoverflies.

## Bird- and mammal-pollinated

*Petals bend back so that birds are dusted with pollen.*

**Fuchsia** is pollinated mostly by birds.

**Passionflower** is pollinated by nectar-drinking birds.

**Silver wattle flowers** attract birds and opossums.

**Nasturtium** flowers are pollinated by birds.

*Stamens and stigmas on a long column*

**Hibiscus** dusts hawkmoths and birds with pollen.

**Urn plant** flowers are surrounded by spiny bracts.

## Wind-pollinated

*Spike of petal-less flowers*

**Broad-leaved pondweed** has a dense spike of flowers.

*Anthers protrude from the tiny green flowers.*

**Greater plantain** has purple anthers.

*Long, slender catkins*

**Armenian oak** has male flowers in yellow catkins.

**Sand couch** has flowers in stalkless spikelets.

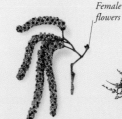

**Alder** has male flowers in long, dangling catkins.

*Female flowers*

**Stinging nettle** has catkins of male or female flowers.

# FOOD

WE ARE WHAT WE EAT: our bodies get the energy and nourishment they need from our daily diet. Not having enough of the right food, or eating too much of the wrong food, causes ill-health. Food and eating are important in other ways too. Many countries have a distinctive cuisine (cooking style), which reflects the eating habits of its people and the ingredients available locally. In many industrialized nations, cooking is a hobby as well as a necessary task. Today there is concern about levels of chemicals in food, and many people choose an organic diet.

Fast food is food that is mass-prepared and served quickly in takeaway outlets. The hamburger is a popular fast food in many western countries.

*A delicacy in France*

*Popular in Japan*

*Made with pig's blood*

*Jews and Muslims do not eat pork.*

Frog's legs  Seaweed  Black pudding  Snails  Pork sausages

## What is food?

Anything humans can digest counts as food. Worldwide, diets vary widely: food habits are influenced by availability, climate, and religious, moral, or social factors. Ideally, a daily diet should include staple, energy-giving carbohydrates, such as rice or pasta, plus proteins, fats, vitamins, and minerals. In reality, poverty or warfare make this impossible in many places.

## Processing and preserving

Even before they are cooked, most foods must be processed to make them ready for cooking: for example, wheat must be ground into flour before it can be baked as bread. Preserving food allows it to be stored for use later; this reduces the risk of shortages, and prolongs availability. A food industry has grown up to provide the food we eat, and process, preserve, and package it.

*Preparing cassava*

**Cassava**
Many foods are indigestible without processing but bitter cassava, the main food in many tropical areas, is actually poisonous. Grating, pressing, and heating the root removes the deadly cyanide it contains.

## Preparing food

Although some foods, such as salad vegetables and fruit, are delicious when raw, many foods need to be cooked first. Cooking makes food tastier and easier to digest. Cooking root vegetables, for instance, makes their starch grains absorb water, swell, and burst, releasing essential nutrients.

*Salad*

*Fennel*

*Orange*

*Steaming fish is a healthy way to cook it.*

**Cooking methods**
There are many cooking methods, such as simmering food in water, which heats it to just under 212°F (100°C). Only a few foods, such as eggs, cook at temperatures lower than this. Grilling or frying in oil heats food to a much higher temperature, cooking it faster.

**Food preservation:** freezing peas

*Viner*

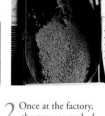

*Frozen peas*

1 Until frozen peas were invented, the only peas most people could eat were dried or tinned. A machine called a viner harvests the peas when they are sweet enough to be frozen. It tumbles them in a drum to remove the pods. These are ploughed back into the field as fertilizer.

2 Once at the factory, the peas are washed and blanched. They are then carried on a conveyor to the freezing chamber. On the way, jets of cold air prevent them sticking together. In the chamber, the peas are blast-frozen at a temperature of -2°F (-18°C).

3 Before packaging, the peas are assessed for quality and taste. Fresh vegetables begin to lose their nutrients as soon as they are picked. Because these peas have been frozen within two and a half hours, they are fresher than fresh peas in a shop.

## Hunger and famine

Each year, 800 million people cannot get enough food to lead healthy lives, despite food surpluses in other parts of the world. Children suffer most. Malnutrition in children severely damages their physical and mental development. Every year in the developing world, famine (widespread starvation) occurs when insects, plant diseases, drought, or warfare destroy crops, and a harvest fails.

*Cocoa beans*

**Chocolate**
Chocolate is a food product derived from the cocoa bean. The Aztecs of Mexico enjoyed a chocolate drink, flavoured with chilli. When the Spanish conquered Mexico in the 16th century, they introduced the drink to Europe. People began to eat solid chocolate from about 1630, but chocolate bars were a luxury until the 20th century.

**Frozen food**
Freezing food to preserve it dates from prehistoric times in cold regions. Following the appearance of home electric refrigerators in 1913, frozen vegetables first went on sale in the US in 1930.

*Peas in the pod*

*Frozen vegetables*

FIND OUT MORE    DIGESTION    FARMING    HEALTH AND FITNESS    TRADE AND INDUSTRY

# Food

## Types of food

*Uncooked rice*

*Puffed rice cakes*

**Rice** is a staple for Southern Asia and parts of Africa.

*Grains of wheat*

*Bread made with wheat flour*

**Wheat** is a staple in North America, Europe, Australia, and parts of Asia.

*Corn*

*Tortilla chips*

**Corn** is a staple in some African, Asian, and American countries.

*Potatoes*

*Lettuce*

**Starchy roots** are a good source of carbohydrates.

**Vegetables** are an important source of vitamins.

*Soybeans*

**Legumes** (beans and peas) are rich in protein.

*Coconut*

**Nuts and seeds** can be pressed to make oils.

*Watermelon*

**Fruits** are an important source of vitamins.

*Honeycomb*

**Sugars and honey** sweeten food.

*Duck*

*Lobster*

*Cheese*

*Olive oil*

*Chilies*

*Vanilla*

**Meat** is a major protein source.

**Fish and shellfish** are a low-fat protein source.

**Eggs** are a valuable source of protein.

**Milk and milk products** provide protein and important minerals.

**Fats and oils** store energy.

**Spices and herbs** add flavor to a meal.

## Country specialities

*Chicken*

**Australia:** meats grilled outdoors on a barbecue

**India:** vegetable curry and *roti* (wheat bread)

*Mussels*

*Prawns*

**Spain:** *paella*, rice simmered with chicken, seafood, and spices

**France:** *bouillabaisse*, fish soup, served with bread

*Salad*

**Mexico:** *buritto*, a pancake with chili, meat, and beans

**Vietnam:** spring rolls filled with pork, prawns, noodles

**Morocco:** chicken baked with spices

*Raw salmon*

**United States:** pork ribs with black-eyed peas

**China:** roast duck with an aromatic seasoning

*Parmesan cheese*

**Italy:** *fettucini*, a kind of pasta, in a tomato sauce

**Thailand:** *pad thai*, Thai fried noodles

**Japan:** *sushi*, extremely fresh, raw fish, with rice and seaweed

*Yorkshire pudding*

**United Kingdom:** roast beef, gravy, and roast potatoes

**Russia:** *borscht* (beet soup) with *blinis* (pancakes)

F

# FOOD WEBS AND CHAINS

THE LIVES OF DIFFERENT species in a wildlife community are linked together through the process of feeding. As plants and animals grow and are eaten by others, energy and food substances in their body tissues pass up a chain. These food chains interlink with one another and the resulting network is called a food web. The number of different animals and plants in a community are naturally balanced. If the balance is upset, the entire web is affected.

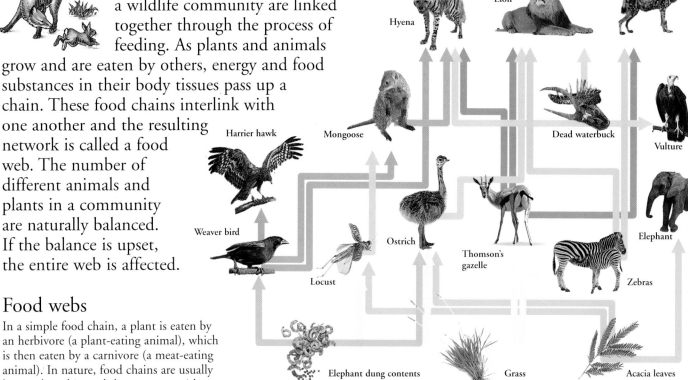

African hunting dog

Lion

Hyena

Harrier hawk

Mongoose

Dead waterbuck

Vulture

Weaver bird

Ostrich

Thomson's gazelle

Elephant

Locust

Zebras

Elephant dung contents

Grass

Acacia leaves

## Food webs

In a simple food chain, a plant is eaten by an herbivore (a plant-eating animal), which is then eaten by a carnivore (a meat-eating animal). In nature, food chains are usually longer than this, and they connect with other chains to form a web. The arrows in this diagram show how different plant foods on a typical African savanna are eaten by a variety of animals, which in turn provide food for various other animals.

**Decomposers**
Some animals, fungi, and bacteria feed on dead or waste plant and animal tissue. They turn it back into simple substances, that plants use to grow.

**Producers**
In ecology, plants are called producers. They start the food chain by using the sun's energy to produce food from simple substances.

**Consumers**
Animals are known as consumers because they get the biological material they need for life from the plants or other animals that they eat, or consume.

## Top predator

The tawny owl at the top of this food chain is known as the top predator. An owl needs to eat many weasels and rodents to meet its energy needs.

*The number of animals or plants represents the amount of energy available to the next level.*

## Trophic pyramids

Ecologists call each stage in a food chain a trophic level. These levels are represented as a pyramid. Animals use much of the energy they get from their food to grow. They also use energy to live, to move around, breed, feed, and avoid their enemies. The use of this energy means that at each trophic level there is less energy available to the next level.

### Secondary consumers
Weasels are secondary consumers because they get energy from the plants through other consumers. There are more weasels in a community than the owls that hunt them.

### Primary consumers
Mice and voles get energy directly from plants. They use a lot of energy; many are needed to support the weasels.

### Primary producers
Energy is stored in plants. It takes a large quantity to support the rodents.

## Population cycles

A change in the population of one species affects the population of other species in the food chain. The lemming population in the tundra and Arctic rises and falls on roughly a four-year cycle. When there are lots of lemmings, the Arctic foxes that hunt them breed more successfully, so their population increases too.

*Arctic fox*

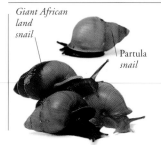

*Giant African land snail*

*Partula snail*

## Upsetting the balance
When the giant African land snail was taken to Pacific islands, the snails destroyed vegetation because there was nothing to prey on them. Another type of snail was released to eat their eggs, but these began to wipe out the native *Partula* snail instead.

 **FIND OUT MORE**   ANIMALS   AFRICAN WILDLIFE   ECOLOGY AND ECOSYSTEMS   ENERGY   FOOD   GRASSLAND WILDLIFE   PHOTOSYNTHESIS   RAIN FOREST WILDLIFE

# FOOTBALL

FOOTBALL, ALTHOUGH WATCHED WORLDWIDE on television, is played little outside the United States, but other forms of football are among the most popular sports to play and watch. Soccer is played in almost every country by men and women. Rugby games are less widespread, but the professional rugby union is becoming increasingly international. Other popular games include Australian football, played chiefly in the state of Victoria, and Gaelic football, an Irish game.

Helmet

Face mask made from unbreakable plastic coated in rubber

Shoulder pads

Upper arm pad

Rib pads tie to shoulder pads.

Hip pad

Breeches

Thigh pad

## Soccer

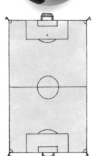

Soccer ball

Soccer is a kicking game played 11 on a side. Only the goalkeeper is allowed to handle the ball. The object is to propel the ball into the opposition's goal with a kick or with the head. A game lasts 90 minutes, with a 15-minute rest period plus, in some competitions, an extra 15 minutes each way.

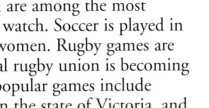

Soccer pitch

## Football

A handling game, American football is played 11 on a side with limitless substitution from 40 players or more. It is divided into short bursts of action as the attacking team advances in a series of "downs." Points are awarded chiefly for touchdowns and field goals.

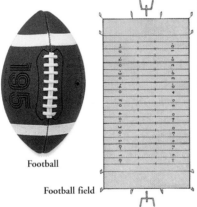

Football

Football field

### Equipment

To withstand the crunching tackles and blocks, players wear extensive protective padding under their uniform, the amount and type depending on their position. Players wear a number from 1 to 99 to identify them to coaches and fans.

### World Cup

The soccer World Cup is as popular as the Olympics. About 170 countries enter competitions to qualify for the 32 places in the finals, which take place every four years.

### Pelé

Brazilian soccer star Pelé (b. 1940) won universal acclaim when he inspired Brazil to win the World Cup for the first time in 1958. His performances in Brazil's 1970 triumph have gone down in soccer folklore. In an all-star career he scored 1,281 goals.

### Women's soccer

In 1991, the first women's soccer World Cup was held, and women's soccer was accepted as an Olympic sport in 1996. In many countries, girls now begin playing soccer at school.

### Australian football

Australian football is played 18 on a side on an oval field. Players kick, catch, and run with the ball, which must be grounded every 33 ft (10 m). A goal, kicked between the inner posts, is worth six points; a behind, kicked inside the outer posts, scores one point.

## Rugby

The rugby codes are rugby union and rugby league. They are handling games featuring running, hand-to-hand passing, tackling, and kicking. Points are scored for a try – touching the ball down over the opposition goal line, or a goal – kicking the ball over the crossbar and between the posts. The two codes have a slightly different ball and field.

Rugby union ball

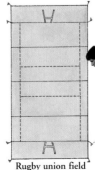

Rugby union field

### Rugby union

This is played 15 on a side with eight forwards, two halfbacks, four three-quarters, and one fullback. It features scrums (shown here), lineouts to restart play, and tactical kicking. Tries score five points; conversions two points.

### Rugby league

Rugby league is played 13 on aside. A tackled player may rise and kick the ball with his foot. After six successive tackles, a team must give up the ball to the other team. Tries score four points; goals one or two.

### Gaelic football

This is played 15 on a side with a round ball. It is a cross between soccer and Australian rules. The ball may be kicked, fisted, and passed hand-to-hand. Points are scored by kicking the ball between the posts, under the bar for three points; over for one point.

FIND OUT MORE

BALL GAMES    OLYMPIC GAMES    TENNIS AND OTHER RACKET SPORTS    SPORT

# FORCE AND MOTION

THE WORLD IS NEVER STILL – traffic and pedestrians rush along busy streets, clouds race across the sky, and the Earth turns on its axis and whirls around the Sun. Forces make all this motion, or movement, possible. A force is a push or a pull that causes an object to start or stop moving or to change its speed or direction. When forces combine, they can hold things still or make things balance. The study of the way objects move when forces act upon them is called dynamics.

## Combining forces

Equal forces acting on an object in opposite directions will have no effect. If the forces are not equal, or if they do not act in opposite directions, they will combine to give an overall force called the resultant.

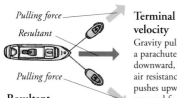

*Pulling force*
*Resultant*
*Pulling force*

**Resultant**
Two tugboats helping an ocean liner into port do not pull in the direction the ship needs to travel. They pull at an angle to each other so that the resultant force moves the ship straight ahead.

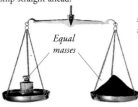

*Equal masses*

**Equilibrium**
An object is in equilibrium when the forces acting upon it balance. This set of scales is in equilibrium when two equal masses are placed on the pans, because gravity pulls on each pan with the same force.

**Terminal velocity**
Gravity pulls a parachute downward, but air resistance pushes upward with an equal force. There is no resultant, because the forces cancel each other out. The parachute cannot accelerate, so it falls to the ground at a constant speed, known as terminal velocity.

*"Flying buttresses" support the walls.*

**Statics**
Statics is the study of forces acting on stationary objects in equilibrium. It is important in building design, because a building will collapse if the forces acting upon it do not balance.

## Circular motion

A free-moving object will naturally move in a straight line. Centripetal force is needed for the object to move in a circle. This is a force that pulls an object toward the center of a circle, constantly changing its direction and stopping it from moving off in a straight line. A motorcycle uses centripetal force to travel around a bend.

*Friction between the tires and the road provides centripetal force.*

## Speed and acceleration

An object's speed is how far it moves in a period of time. Speed in a particular direction is called velocity. Acceleration is the rate at which an object's velocity changes.

*A sprinter who runs 60 meters in 12 seconds has an average speed of 5 m/s.*

*The sprinter's feet push against the starting blocks.*

*The force exerted by the sprinter's feet propels him forward.*

*A sprinter's acceleration is greatest during the first few seconds of a race.*

## Inertia

An object's mass makes it resist a force that tries to change its state of motion, whether it is moving or at rest. This resistance is called inertia. The greater an object's mass, the more inertia it has. For example, the same force will accelerate a small car more than a loaded truck because the car has a smaller mass and less inertia.

**Momentum**
When a moving object collides with a stationary one, the result depends upon a quantity called momentum. An object's momentum is calculated by multiplying its mass by its velocity. For example, a heavy bowling ball has more momentum than a light plastic ball moving at the same velocity because it has a greater mass.

*The mass of the bowling ball gives it enough momentum to scatter the pins.*

*The lighter plastic ball has a smaller mass and bounces off the pins.*

## Archimedes

Archimedes (c.287–212 BC) was a Greek mathematician and inventor who studied forces and how they could be used by simple machines. He founded statics, discovered why objects float and sink, and worked out the principles behind levers and pulleys.

## Newton's laws of motion

In 1687, English physicist Sir Isaac Newton devised three laws to summarize the principles of force and motion.

Force ➡    Motion ➡

**First law**
An object continues in a state of rest or constant motion unless a force acts upon it. The inline skater in the picture will keep on rolling at the same speed until a force, such as friction, stops him.

**Second law**
An object's acceleration is equal to the size of the force acting upon it divided by the object's mass. This inline skater's acceleration depends on how heavy he is and how hard he is pushed.

**Third law**
For every force there is an equal force acting in the opposite direction. Forces act in pairs, so when A pushes B, an equal and opposite force acts on A, making both inline skaters move apart.

A   B

**FIND OUT MORE**    FRICTION    GRAVITY    MACHINES    MAGNETISM    PRESSURE

# FORESTS

A THIRD OF THE WORLD'S land surface consists of forest – areas of land covered by dense tree cover. Each forest is an ecosystem – a group of animals and plants interacting with the physical environment and one another. More plants and animals live in forests than in any other environment. Forests differ according to the climate – boreal, temperate, or tropical. They help maintain the Earth's natural balance; trees absorb and release gases that regulate the climate.

Tropical forest
Temperate forest
Boreal coniferous forest

## Tropical forest

Tropical forests, or rain forests, tend to thrive in warm and wet climates. The porous soil is generally rich in aluminum and iron. In one acre there may be more than 400 species of trees, hundreds of birds, mammals, and reptiles, and thousands of insects.

*Emergent trees rise up to 197 ft (60 m).*

*Canopy of trees 50 ft (15 m) above the ground*

*Plants twine around branches.*

*Understory contains shrubs and young growth.*

**Tropical forest**

*Each forest has layers of vegetation. In a tropical forest emergent trees poke through the top. Below are the canopy, the understory, and the forest floor.*

*Broad leaves of deciduous trees grow rapidly in summer and are shed in winter.*

**Temperate forest**

*Downward-angled branches allow the trees in cold climates to shed the weight of the snow without breaking.*

*Forest floor is dark with little plant growth, but vegetation decay enriches the soil.*

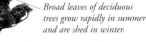

## Temperate forest

These forests are found in mild or temperate climates, where winters are cool and summers are warm. The majority of trees are deciduous, such as oak and beech. Many temperate forests have been cleared for farmland because the soil beneath is very fertile.

## Boreal coniferous forest

In cool, northern, or boreal regions, such as northern Asia, there are vast areas of boreal forests, sometimes known as taiga. These dense forests contain hardy coniferous or evergreen trees, such as spruce, pine, fir, and larch trees.

*Soil beneath these trees is acid and infertile.*

**Boreal coniferous forest**

## Afforestation

More people are becoming aware of the value of forests. In Southeast Asia, new forest land is created with tree-planting programs. Some forests are now conservation areas.

## Deforestation

Each year, forest land the size of the state of Washington is destroyed. Trees are cut down for farmland or timber. Deforestation can cause huge environmental problems, disturbing the soil and forest life. Fewer trees to absorb carbon dioxide may also disrupt the climate.

**Cattle ranching**
Huge areas of rain forest in Brazil are cut down for cattle-ranching, which exhausts the soil within a few years.

**Slash and burn**
Nomadic farmers slash and burn forests for farmland. After a few years, they move on to allow the soil to regenerate.

**Overgrazing**
A shortage of land forces nomadic farmers to stay in one place. The land is over-grazed and the soil dries up.

FIND OUT MORE    CLIMATE    ECOLOGY AND ECOSYSTEMS    PLANT USES    POLLUTION    RAIN FOREST WILDLIFE    SOIL    TREES    WOODLAND WILDLIFE

F

# FOSSILS

THE REMAINS AND TRACES of past life forms are called fossils. All living organisms are potential fossils, but only a few are preserved. The most common fossils are those of hard parts of animals and plants. Only rarely is soft tissue fossilized. Sometimes trace fossils, such as footprints, are found. The study of fossils, called paleontology, is crucial to our understanding of life.

Graptolite

Conodont

## Fossil dating
Some fossils, such as graptolites and conodonts, evolved and became extinct over geologically short periods of time. This makes them useful for dating the rocks in which they are found.

## How a fossil is formed
In order for something to fossilize, it must be buried quickly by sediment, such as sand or mud, before it decomposes. Fossils form in a variety of ways, depending on the environment in which the animal or plant lived, and the conditions after it was buried.

*The skeleton may be broken up.*

*Water deposits sediment.*

*Erosion of the rock brings the fossils closer to the surface.*

1 After death, the soft parts of a *Triceratops* decompose quickly, leaving just the hard skeleton and horns.

2 Over time, the bones are buried under thick layers of sediment and harden to form fossils.

3 The layers of sediment turn to rock, which may be pushed up or folded to form mountains.

4 Erosion exposes the bones. Paleontologists can then collect and study the dinosaur remains.

## Studying fossils
The study of the evolution of environments and natural communities is an important part of paleontology. This limestone contains fossils of different animals, such as trilobites and corals. It shows a community that existed on the ocean floor more than 400 million years ago.

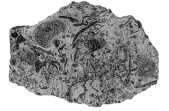
**Limestone from Much Wenlock, England**

### Coral
Fossil corals are common because they have a hard skeleton. Soft-bodied animals, such as sea anemones and jellyfish, would have lived in the same community but are unlikely to have formed fossils.

### Trilobite
Trilobites were arthropods that lived in the sea. They shed their shells regularly, as modern arthropods do, and these shells are often found as fossils. They are divided into three distinct parts, or lobes, hence the name "trilobite." A few fossils of soft parts have been found.

## Types of fossils
Fossils range from microscopic plants and animals to the huge bones of dinosaurs. They can be almost unchanged from the original or replaced by minerals.

### Amber
The fossilized resin of trees, called amber, often contains trapped insects and other small animals and plants. The trapped fossils are often preserved in great detail.

### Volcanic ash
This child's body was buried by volcanic ash at Pompeii, Italy, in AD 79. Ash turns to rock quickly. A buried animal or plant may rot away to leave a hollow, which, if filled with plaster, forms a cast.

### Trees
Fossilized trees, such as these *Lepidodendron* trunks and roots, can be preserved as internal molds of the bark. The inside rots away and is replaced by sand.

### Bones
Vertebrate fossils are made of many parts and are usually found as single pieces. If conditions are right, a skeleton can be preserved whole, as in this *Diplomystus*, an ancestor of the modern herring.

*Females were larger than males.*

*Ammonite shells replaced with iron pyrites, or "fools' gold"*

### Petrification
These monkey-puzzle cones have been turned to stone, or petrified. This happened when silica-rich waters crystallized within the cells of the cones.

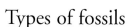

### Concretions
Hard lumps, or concretions, are often formed around fossils in sediment. This concretion reveals the fossil shell and mold of a clam.

## Georges Cuvier

A French zoologist, Cuvier (1769–1832) realized that the parts of the body were interrelated. For example, an animal that has hooves is an herbivore, and must have an herbivore's teeth. He identified a fossil as a marsupial from a jaw.

*Jurassic ammonite*

### Ammonites
These mollusks were abundant in the seas of the Mesozoic Era. Their shells were made of the mineral aragonite and were often replaced by other minerals during fossilization.

**FIND OUT MORE**

ARTHROPODS   DINOSAURS   EVOLUTION   GEOLOGY   PREHISTORIC LIFE

# Fossils

## Invertebrates

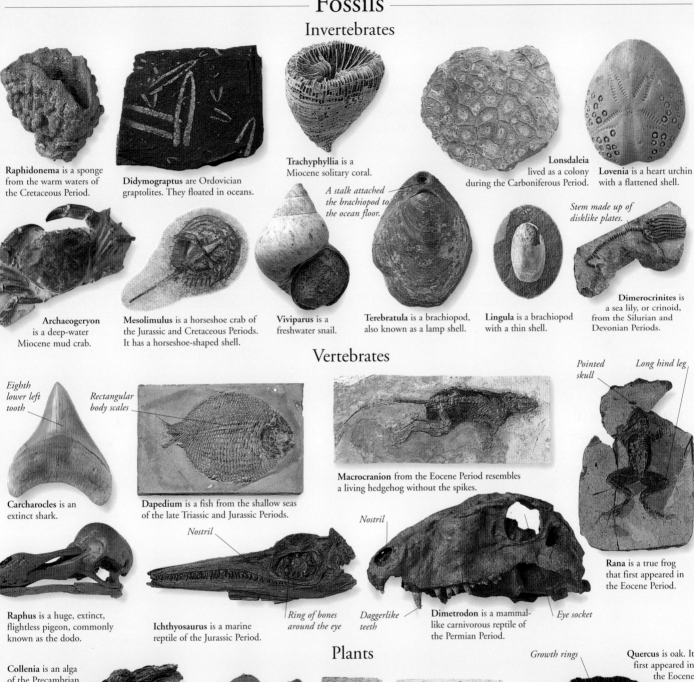

**Raphidonema** is a sponge from the warm waters of the Cretaceous Period.

**Didymograptus** are Ordovician graptolites. They floated in oceans.

**Trachyphyllia** is a Miocene solitary coral.

*A stalk attached the brachiopod to the ocean floor.*

**Lonsdaleia** lived as a colony during the Carboniferous Period.

**Lovenia** is a heart urchin with a flattened shell.

*Stem made up of disklike plates.*

**Archaeogeryon** is a deep-water Miocene mud crab.

**Mesolimulus** is a horseshoe crab of the Jurassic and Cretaceous Periods. It has a horseshoe-shaped shell.

**Viviparus** is a freshwater snail.

**Terebratula** is a brachiopod, also known as a lamp shell.

**Lingula** is a brachiopod with a thin shell.

**Dimerocrinites** is a sea lily, or crinoid, from the Silurian and Devonian Periods.

## Vertebrates

*Eighth lower left tooth*

*Rectangular body scales*

*Pointed skull*

*Long hind leg*

**Macrocranion** from the Eocene Period resembles a living hedgehog without the spikes.

**Carcharocles** is an extinct shark.

**Dapedium** is a fish from the shallow seas of the late Triassic and Jurassic Periods.

*Nostril*

*Nostril*

**Rana** is a true frog that first appeared in the Eocene Period.

**Raphus** is a huge, extinct, flightless pigeon, commonly known as the dodo.

**Ichthyosaurus** is a marine reptile of the Jurassic Period.

*Ring of bones around the eye*

*Daggerlike teeth*

**Dimetrodon** is a mammal-like carnivorous reptile of the Permian Period.

*Eye socket*

## Plants

*Growth rings*

**Quercus** is oak. It first appeared in the Eocene Period.

**Collenia** is an alga of the Precambrian and Cambrian Periods.

**Ficus** is a fig which first appeared in the Eocene Period.

**Porana** is a Miocene flower.

*Trapped spider*

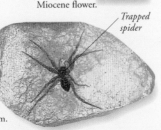

**Populus** is a poplar, almost identical to poplars today.

*Polished, petrified wood*

*Carved jet*

*Ribbed seed*

**Stigmaria** are the root-bearing branches of a Carboniferous club-moss.

**Amber** is fossilized tree resin or gum.

**Jet** is a type of fossilized wood.

**Trigonocarpus** is the seed of a Carboniferous seed fern.

# FRANCE

THE LARGEST COUNTRY in western Europe, France stretches from the Pyrenees in the south to the English Channel in the north. A founding member of the European Economic Community (now European Union), France plays a key role in world affairs. It is a leading industrial nation, although approximately five percent of the population works in farming. The first of the modern republics, France includes Corsica, Guyana, and various islands in the Caribbean and Pacific Ocean.

## FRANCE FACTS

| | |
|---|---|
| CAPITAL CITY | Paris |
| AREA | 212,930 sq miles (551,500 sq km) |
| POPULATION | 57,800,000 |
| MAIN LANGUAGE | French |
| MAJOR RELIGION | Christian |
| CURRENCY | Euro |
| LIFE EXPECTANCY | 78 years |
| PEOPLE PER DOCTOR | 333 |
| GOVERNMENT | Multiparty democracy |
| ADULT LITERACY | 99% |

### The Seine
From its source in the east, the Seine crosses Paris before winding its way north to the Atlantic Ocean. France's river network, which includes the Loire and the Rhône, is used for transportation and for irrigating farmland.

**The Seine in Normandy**

## Physical features
France's landscape varies from undulating fields in the north to sparse hills in the Massif Central, and mountains in the Alps to Pyrenees in the south.

### Corsica
With an area of 3,350 sq miles (8,630 sq km), Corsica is the third largest Mediterranean island. Fragrant, thorny scrub called *maquis* covers the slopes of towering granite peaks, and rich, fertile valleys are used to graze sheep and grow vines. The capital is Ajaccio.

**Corsican *maquis***

### Climate
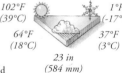

Northwestern France, particularly Brittany, is mild but damp. The east has hot summers and stormy winters. Summers in the south are dry and hot, and forest fires are common. In the Pyrenees and Alps, winter snowfalls are heavy, making these ideal areas for skiing.

102°F (39°C)  1°F (-17°C)
64°F (18°C)  37°F (3°C)
23 in (584 mm)

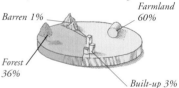

Barren 1%  Farmland 60%
Forest 36%  Built-up 3%

### Land use
France's fertile farmland includes gently rolling pastures and fields of wheat and sugar beet in the north, and vineyards and lavender fields in the south. Much of the Massif Central is pasture on which sheep graze.

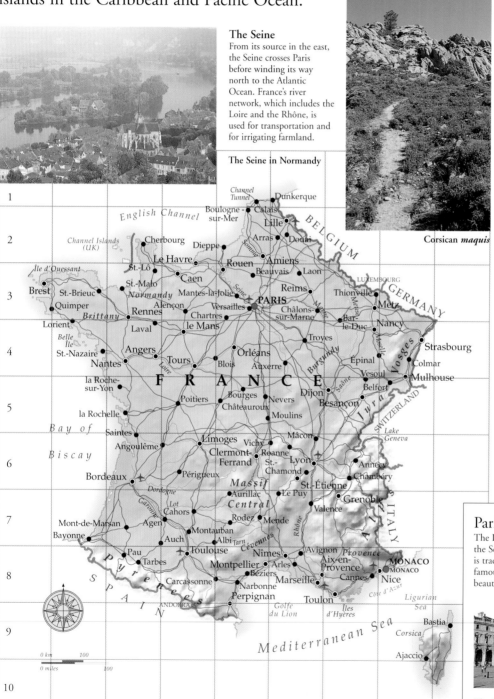

*Map of France with grid coordinates A–I (columns) and 1–10 (rows).*

Channel Tunnel, Dunkerque, Calais, Boulogne-sur-Mer, Lille, Arras, Douai, Cherbourg, Dieppe, Amiens, Laon, BELGIUM, LUXEMBOURG, English Channel, Channel Islands (UK), Le Havre, Rouen, Beauvais, St-Lô, Caen, St-Malo, Mantes-la-Jolie, Reims, Thionville, Metz, GERMANY, Île d'Ouessant, Brest, St-Brieuc, Normandy, Alençon, Versailles, PARIS, Châlons-sur-Marne, Bar-le-Duc, Nancy, Quimper, Rennes, Chartres, Brittany, Laval, le Mans, Troyes, Strasbourg, Lorient, Belle Île, Angers, Orléans, Auxerre, Épinal, Colmar, St.-Nazaire, Nantes, Tours, Blois, Burgundy, Vesoul, Mulhouse, FRANCE, Bourges, Nevers, Dijon, Belfort, Jura, SWITZERLAND, la Roche-sur-Yon, Poitiers, Châteauroux, Besançon, Moulins, Lake Geneva, la Rochelle, Bay of Biscay, Saintes, Limoges, Vichy, Mâcon, Angoulême, Clermont-Ferrand, Roanne, Lyon, Annecy, St.-Chamond, Chambéry, Bordeaux, Périgueux, Massif Central, St-Étienne, Le Puy, Grenoble, Dordogne, Aurillac, Valence, ITALY, Garonne, Lot, Cahors, Rodez, Mende, Rhône, Mont-de-Marsan, Agen, Montauban, Albi, Tarn, Bayonne, Auch, Cévennes, Nîmes, Avignon, Provence, MONACO, Pau, Toulouse, Aix-en-Provence, Cannes, Nice, Tarbes, Montpellier, Arles, Marseille, Carcassonne, Béziers, Toulon, Côte d'Azur, Pyrenees, SPAIN, Perpignan, Narbonne, Golfe du Lion, Îles d'Hyères, Ligurian Sea, ANDORRA, Bastia, Corsica, Ajaccio, Mediterranean Sea

0 km 100
0 miles 100

## Paris
The Louvre lies on the fashionable Right Bank of the Seine, which divides the city. The Left Bank is traditionally home to students, artists, and the famous Eiffel Tower. One of the world's most beautiful and most visited capitals, Paris is the cultural and political center of France.

**The Louvre**

F

# People

People of French descent make up about 94 percent of the population. Among these are several groups that speak their own languages and have strong independence movements. These include the Bretons of Brittany in the north, the Basques in the Pyrenees, and the Corsicans.

278 per sq mile
(107 per sq km)

75% Urban  25% Rural

### Ethnic groups
France's five million immigrants include mainly North African Muslims and economic migrants from South and Central Europe. Most live and work in the cities.

# Leisure

Soccer, rugby, cycling, and tennis are all popular sports in France, as are horse- and Formula 1-racing. The French Open is a major international tennis event.

### Tour de France
Each year, over a hundred of the world's leading professional cyclists compete in this famous bicycle race over a 2,113-mile (3,400-km) route in 24 one-day stages.

### Boules
Throughout France, groups of people playing *boules* are a common sight in the town or village square. *Boules* is France's national game and involves rolling heavy balls at a smaller target ball.

# Farming

The French grow a variety of crops, such as wheat, barley, sugar beet, and grapes for making wine. About a third of all the farmland is pasture for grazing cows and sheep, which are raised for their meat and milk.

Cantal

Livarot

St.-Nectaire

### Cheese
France produces more than 365 kinds of cheese, from cow, sheep, and goats' milk. These include St.-Nectaire, Cantal, and Livarot, as well as Brie, Camembert, and Roquefort. Milk and butter are also important exports.

### Grain
France's main crop is wheat, which grows on large farms in the north of France where the soil is fertile.

### Wine
The wines of the Rhône valley, Bordeaux, Burgundy, and Champagne make France the world's leading producer. Their quality is tightly controlled.

# Food

French cuisine is world famous, and words such as café, restaurant, paté, and quiche are common in many languages. Special French dishes include *bouillabaisse* (fish soup), *escargots* (snails), and *grenouilles* (frogs' legs).

Prawn

Slice of lemon

Snail

Lobster  Mussel

# Industry

France has strong chemical, steel, electronics, and manufacturing industries, and an active aerospace program. Nuclear power provides three-quarters of the country's electricity. Perfume and fashion are also a major source of income.

### Perfume
French perfumes, such as Chanel, are world famous. Many are made from the fragrant oils extracted from roses, jasmine, and lavender, which grow in the south of the country.

### Tourism
The fashionable resorts of the Côte d'Azur in southeastern France attract thousands of tourists every summer. With 75 million visitors annually, France is the number one vacation destination worldwide.

### Car production
Most French drivers buy French cars, such as this Renault Espace. Other names include Peugeot and Citroën. The French car industry ranks fourth in the world.

# Transportation

France boasts the world's fastest train, the TGV, which can travel at speeds of up to 186 mph (300 kmh). A direct service runs to England via the Channel Tunnel.

# Monaco

This tiny independent principality on the Côte d'Azur derives its income from tourism, banking, sales tax, and gambling. It has close ties with France.

### Grand Casino
The people of Monaco pay few taxes and earn more per capita than any other country in the world. The game rooms and roulette wheels of the Grand Casino in Monte Carlo are open to anyone with money to spend.

### MONACO FACTS

**CAPITAL CITY** Monaco

**AREA** 0.75 sq miles (1.95 sq km)

**POPULATION** 32,000

**MAIN LANGUAGE** French

**MAJOR RELIGION** Christian

**CURRENCY** Euro

FIND OUT MORE | CARS AND TRUCKS | CLOTHES AND FASHION | CYCLING | EMPIRES | EUROPE, HISTORY OF | EUROPEAN UNION | FARMING | FRANCE, HISTORY OF | TRADE AND INDUSTRY | TRAINS AND RAILROADS

# FRANCE, HISTORY OF

THE LARGEST COUNTRY in western Europe, France has dominated European history ever since the Franks conquered the country in the 5th century. Its vast natural wealth and large population have enabled a succession of rulers, such as Charlemagne in the 9th century, Louis XIV in the 17th, and Napoleon in the 19th, to create powerful empires that spanned Europe. Despite three bitter wars with Germany between 1870 and 1945, France emerged as one of the world's superpowers. Today, France is a leading member of the European Union, and one of the wealthiest countries in the world.

Horses heads, carved c.10,000 BC

### Prehistoric France
The first inhabitants of France were prolific artists. More than 20,000 years ago, they adorned caves at Lascaux and elsewhere with lifelike pictures of animals. They also carved likenesses of animal heads from bones, antlers, and rocks.

Samian ware bowl

*French potters made this type of ware in the Roman period.*

## Roman France
Between 58 and 51 BC, a Roman army led by Julius Caesar conquered France. The new province of Gaul was one of the richest in the empire. Trade flourished, and the Romans built many roads and bridges. They also introduced growing grapes for wine.

### Franks
In 486, the Franks from Germany routed the last Roman governor of Gaul and took control, giving France its name. At first the Franks continued with Roman customs, but their empire broke up in civil wars. The 8th-century kings Charles Martel, Pepin the Short, and Charlemagne restored order.

Charlemagne

## Medieval France
In common with other European rulers, the power of the French kings was always limited by the strength of local nobles. Despite this weakness, France became one of the richest countries in Europe during the 11th century. Major trade fairs in the Champagne region attracted merchants from all over Europe, and trade and commerce flourished.

### Angevin Empire
As a result of marriage and war, Henry II of England (r.1154–89) ruled much of western and northern France. His vast realm was called the Angevin Empire, after the county of Anjou. For years it was a threat to French unification.

Château Gaillard, Angevin castle

### Religious wars
The Reformation split France, with many Catholics becoming Huguenots (Protestants). In 1562, civil war broke out between the two sides; religious toleration was agreed by the Edict of Nantes in 1598, but tension remained high. In 1685, Louis XIV revoked the Edict, and many Huguenots fled to England and Holland.

## Renaissance France
Joan of Arc, who fought the English for independence, was burnt at the stake in 1431. During the 15th century, the French kings drove out the English, and united their country. They also crushed the power of the nobles. During the next century, the ideas of the Italian Renaissance entered France. New châteaus were built, and the arts flourished.

### Golden age
The 17th and 18th centuries were a golden age of the arts. Royal support led to the founding of the Gobelins tapestry works in 1602 and the royal pottery at Sèvres in 1756. The nobility supported artists such as Watteau and Fragonard, dramatists such as Racine, Molière and Corneille, the writer Montaigne, creator of the essay, and the fable-writer La Fontaine.

## Bourbons
Under the Bourbon kings, France emerged as the major power in Europe during the 17th century. Hapsburg-ruled Spain and Austria – enemies of France – were defeated, and all power was centralized under the king. Industry and commerce were supported, and France established colonies in North America and India.

### Palace of Versailles
In order to increase his own power and reduce that of the nobility, Louis XIV built this vast new palace outside Paris. Some 36,000 people worked on the building, decorating it with the best examples of French art and design. At the center was the king's bed chamber, where Louis received guests.

*Hand-painted figures*

*Gilded decoration*

Sèvres porcelain vase

### Louis XIV
During the long reign of Louis XIV (r.1643–1715), the power of the French kings reached its height. Louis believed in the divine right of kings to rule, and governed without parliament. He reorganized the army and expanded French territory. But his lavish lifestyle left France almost bankrupt.

F

F

# Monarchy and empire

After the defeat of Napoleon in 1815, France had a series of short-lived, weak governments. The restored Bourbon monarchy was overthrown in 1830 and King Louis Philippe lost his throne in 1848. The resulting Second Republic collapsed when its president, Louis-Napoleon (r.1852–70), became emperor. In spite of these problems, France grew prosperous.

### French Revolution
Revolution broke out in 1789, sweeping away the king and nobility. A new National Assembly was set up, and swore the famous "tennis court oath," that they would not disband until France had a proper constitution. Napoleon Bonaparte became Emperor in 1804, marking the end of the revolutionary period.

### Revolution of 1848
In February 1848, Parisians rose up against their ineffectual king, Louis Philippe. A republic was set up, with Louis-Napoleon, a nephew of Bonaparte, as president. Radical reforms were promised, but in 1852 Napoleon became emperor.

Revolutionaries in Paris, 1848

Infantryman's pack, Franco-Prussian War

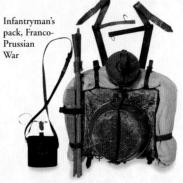

### Franco-Prussian War
Although successful at home, Napoleon III was no match for Bismarck, chancellor of Prussia. In 1870, rivalry between France and Prussia led to war, but the French armies were unprepared and were soon defeated. France lost the provinces of Alsace and Lorraine to Germany.

# Modern France

After the liberation of France from German occupation in 1944, a Fourth Republic was set up to govern the country. Like its predecessor, it was weak and was brought down by the unrest caused by the Algerian war in 1958. Charles de Gaulle then set up the Fifth Republic, aiming to restore French prestige and prosperity.

## Charles de Gaulle
Charles de Gaulle (1890–1970) trained as a soldier, rising to command an armored division. On the fall of France in 1940, he fled to Britain and called on French people to resist German occupation. As leader of the Free French, he did much to boost French morale during the war. In 1958 he became president, leading his country until he resigned in 1969.

J'Accuse...! LETTRE AU PRÉSIDENT DE LA RÉPUBLIQUE Par ÉMILE ZOLA

*J'Accuse*, writer Emile Zola's pamphlet supporting Dreyfus

# Third Republic

The Third Republic (1870–1940) was riven with internal disputes and conflicts between moderates, radicals, socialists, and royalists. Between 1918 and its collapse in 1940, there were 44 governments and 20 different prime ministers. Yet France stayed one of the leading states in Europe, with a worldwide empire and a strong economy.

### Dreyfus case
In October 1894, French army captain Alfred Dreyfus was court-martialed for treason, for passing military secrets to Germany. But a mistake had been made, and a campaign to free Dreyfus began. He was cleared in 1906, but the case split the nation between his supporters and those who refused to change the verdict.

### Vichy France
In 1940, German forces invaded France. French general and right-wing politician Marshal Pétain set up a government in Vichy, central France. This government collaborated with the occupying forces; opposition was led from London by Charles de Gaulle, leader of the Free French. Vichy France was occupied by the Germans in 1942.

*Cross of Lorraine*    Flag of the Free French

May 1968

### May 1968
In May 1968, students demanding more money for education demonstrated against high defense spending. Riots broke out in Paris and elsewhere, with fighting between police and students. A general strike ensued, and de Gaulle's government was weakened.

After the riots, Paris, May 1968

### Algerian war
In 1954, Algeria, one of several African countries colonized by France, demanded that it be granted its independence. This led to conflict with the many European settlers in the country. The French army supported the settlers in their wish to remain French and waged a vicious war against the Algerian rebels. Algeria finally won its independence in 1962.

# Timeline

**58–51BC** Gaul (present-day France) becomes part of the Roman Empire.

**AD 486** The Franks take control of the country.

**1337–1453** France and Britain fight the Hundred Years' War.

*Encyclopedie*, 1751

**1589** Henry IV becomes first Bourbon king.

**1643–1715** France reaches height of its power under Louis XIV.

**1789** Revolution breaks out in Paris.

**1848** After a revolution, the short-lived Second Republic is established.

**1870–71** Third Republic set up.

**1870s** Impressionist movement founded by Claude Monet and other French painters.

Claude Monet, *Waterlilies*

**1914–18** France fights Germany in World War I.

**1946** Fourth Republic established after World War II.

**1958** De Gaulle takes power and introduces Fifth Republic.

**1950s–90s** France is a leading member of European Union.

**FIND OUT MORE**    EUROPE, HISTORY OF    FRENCH REVOLUTION    GERMANY, HISTORY OF    MEDIEVAL EUROPE    NAPOLEON BONAPARTE    NAPOLEONIC WARS    ROMAN EMPIRE    WORLD WAR I    WORLD WAR II

# FRANKLIN, BENJAMIN

INVENTOR, PRINTER, PUBLISHER, writer, scientist, politician, diplomat, and an author of both the US Declaration of Independence and the US Constitution – there was nothing Benjamin Franklin did not turn his hand to. He was born into a poor family, but had a fertile mind very receptive to new ideas. He invented items such as the lightning conductor and bifocal lenses, but he is most respected for his contribution to the founding of the US. He is sometimes known as the "wisest American."

## Early life
Benjamin Franklin was born in 1706 in the American port of Boston. He was the son of a candle and soap maker, and left school at age 10 to help in his father's business. Later he worked for his half brother James, printer and publisher of a newspaper to which Benjamin contributed. After disagreements with James, he left Boston in 1723 to work as a printer in Philadelphia.

## Printer
Franklin prospered as a printer. As publisher of the popular *Poor Richard's Almanac* between 1732–57, he introduced numerous common-sense sayings that have since become part of the American language. He also set up an academy that later became the University of Pennsylvania.

*Bend caused by lightning.*

Lightning rod

## Scientist
In 1748, Franklin handed over his printing business to his foreman so that he could devote his life to science. He researched the nature of electricity, and this work led to his invention of the lightning rod, that protects tall buildings from lightning. He also worked out a theory of heat absorption and tracked the paths of storms across the sky.

### Lightning
In 1752, Franklin flew a kite in a thunderstorm to prove that lightning is electrical. Electricity from the thunderclouds flowed down the string to a metal key tied on it near the ground. Sparks flew from the key, showing the presence of the electrical charge in the sky.

**Franklin experimenting with a kite and lightning**

## Inventor
Franklin was a tireless inventor, using his scientific knowledge to devise a number of inventions that were designed to make human life safer and more comfortable. These ranged from bifocal eyeglasses – combining two lenses of different strengths in one frame to correct both close and distant vision – to a musical glass "armonica." Among his useful inventions were the lightning rod and an energy-saving stove still made today.

### Stove
Among Franklin's many inventions was a practical stove that made use of the heat that would otherwise have escaped up the chimney. Stoves like this were installed in many American houses.

*The armonica was played by rubbing the fingers gently on the edges of the glasses.*

### Armonica
In the early 1760s, Franklin built a musical instrument made up of a series of glass bowls, graduated in size and fitted one inside another. By rotating a spindle the edges of the bowls passed through a trough of water. Contact with the musician's fingertips produced a penetrating sound. Composers such as Mozart and Beethoven wrote music for this strange device.

## Constitution
In 1787, Franklin helped to write the new American constitution. Although his proposal for a single-chamber congress was rejected, he negotiated a compromise between the different authors that resulted in the constitution that survives today.

## Statesman
During the American Revolution, Franklin was a member of the committee that wrote the Declaration of Independence, which he signed in 1776. Later that year, he sailed to France to win diplomatic recognition for the new nation. When the war ended, he was one of the main US negotiators in the peace talks.

**Franklin (left) talks to the French king and queen (seated, right) and members of their court**

## BENJAMIN FRANKLIN

**1706** Born in Boston, MA

**1723** Begins work as a printer

**1732–57** Publishes *Poor Richard's Almanac*

**1752** Conducts famous experiment with lightning

**1776** Helps to draft Declaration of Independence

**1781** Chosen as one of the US negotiators with Britain

**1787** Member of group that draws up US constitution

**1790** Dies in Philadelphia

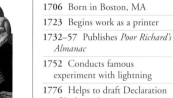

**FIND OUT MORE**

AMERICAN REVOLUTION    ELECTRICITY    EYES AND VISION    GOVERNMENTS AND POLITICS    INVENTIONS    MUSICAL INSTRUMENTS    UNITED STATES, HISTORY OF

# FRENCH REVOLUTION

IN 1789, REVOLUTION BROKE OUT in France when people rose up against poverty and injustice. The French Revolution swept away the power of the monarchy and ended the traditional social order. When the revolution began, poverty was widespread, the king was unpopular, and people resented the clergy and nobility. Following the formation of the National Assembly, France was declared a republic, the king was executed, and, for a while, terror reigned. In 1799, Napoleon came to power and the revolution ended.

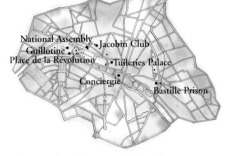

## Revolutionary Paris

The key events of the revolution occurred on the streets of Paris. Various political groups sprang up, such as the Jacobin Club, which relied on the Parisian *sans culottes* for support.

## National Assembly

In 1788, France ran out of money, and Louis XVI called the Estates-General, representing clergy, nobility, and middle classes. The Third Estate formed a National Assembly. They seized lands, ended feudal privileges, and drew up a constitution.

### Rights of Man

The National Assembly issued the *Declaration of the Rights of Man and the Citizen,* stating that "Men are born and remain equal." Women's rights were not included, but the ideals of "liberty, equality, and fraternity" inspired everyone.

### Storming of the Bastille

In 1789, angry demonstrators seized the Bastille, a prison that had been a symbol of oppression for many years. This act sparked a wave of rebellion. Outside Paris, peasants attacked the country houses of the nobility they hated.

**The bonnet rouge,** or red bonnet, symbolized freedom. It looked like the cap worn by freed Roman slaves.

*Coarse working blouse*

## Reign of Terror

By 1792, the revolution was under threat. There were food shortages, royalist uprisings in the countryside, and a threat by Prussia to invade and restore the monarchy. Extremists, known as Jacobins, grew in power, declaring a republic and executing the king in 1793. They set up the Committee of Public Safety, and a reign of terror began. Anyone suspected of being an enemy of the revolution was arrested and guillotined. Thousands died. By 1794, the leaders of the Committee were themselves executed, and the terror was over.

### Guillotine

Named after a French doctor, the guillotine consisted of a wooden frame with a sharp blade mounted on it that sliced off the victims' heads. This killing machine was quicker than previous methods of execution, and was therefore thought to be more humane.

*Sharpened blade fell on victims' necks.*

## Robespierre

A lawyer by profession, Maximilien Robespierre (1758–94) was one of the leaders of the revolution. He headed the Jacobin Club, and, by 1793, was leader of the Committee of Public Safety that conducted the Reign of Terror. In 1794, he, too, went to the guillotine.

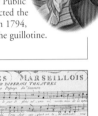

### Marseillaise

From 1792, revolution spread outside French borders. A soldier composed the *Marseillaise* as a revolutionary marching song. Today, it is France's national anthem.

### Revolutionaries

The revolutionaries were men and women from all social classes: lawyers, peasants, workers. Street revolutionaries were known as *sans culottes* (without breeches) because they wore striped pants. Two rival revolutionary groups emerged: the Girondins and the more radical Jacobins.

*White was the color of the royal family.*

*Red and blue were the colors of Paris.*

*Striped pants*

*Strong leather shoes*

## Timeline

**1788** France bankrupt. Louis XVI summons Estates-General.

**May 1789** Third Estate forms National Assembly,

Louis XVI

**July 14, 1789** Paris mob storms the Bastille; French Revolution begins.

**August 27, 1789** National Assembly issues *Rights of Man.*

**October 1789** Women march to Versailles from Paris to demand bread.

**1791** The revolution inspires a slave rebellion in Haiti.

**1792** National Assembly abolishes monarchy. France becomes a republic and goes to war with Austria and Prussia.

**1793** Louis XVI executed. Counterrevolution breaks out. Revolutionary war spreads across Europe.

**1793–4** Reign of Terror.

**1795** The Directory, a more moderate board of governors, is formed, and takes power.

**1799** Napoleon overthrows Directory and takes power.

**1798–99** Revolution inspires uprisings in Ireland.

FIND OUT MORE

| AMERICAN REVOLUTION | EUROPE, HISTORY OF | FRANCE, HISTORY OF | GOVERNMENT AND POLITICS | NAPOLEONIC WARS |

# FREUD, SIGMUND

ONE HUNDRED YEARS AGO, people viewed the workings of the human mind as a mystery. Sigmund Freud helped to make sense of that mystery. Because of his innovative ideas, he is often referred to as the father of psychiatry. Freud was an Austrian doctor who worked in Vienna almost all his life. He researched the meaning of dreams, how the unconscious mind works, and how events in our past influence the actions we take. In developing the science of psychoanalysis, he provided insights that have affected every aspect of modern life.

### Early life
Freud was born into a Jewish family in 1856 in Freiburg (Pribor), in what is now the Czech Republic. In 1859, his family moved to Vienna. Freud was a brilliant student, at the top of his class in school for six years. In 1873, he began to study medicine at Vienna, and, in 1881, he received his degree.

*Freud's couch*

## Psychoanalysis

In 1886, Freud began to specialize in neuroses, or nervous diseases. To find out what was causing his patients' illnesses, he used first hypnotism and then free association – instructing his patients to say whatever came into their head in the belief that they would reveal the cause of their illness. Freud published his ideas in 1895 in *Studies on Hysteria*, the first-ever account of psychoanalysis – the interpretation and treatment of mental disorders.

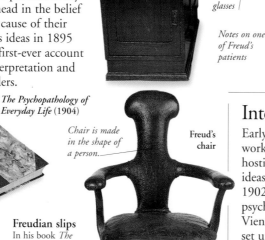

*Freud's glasses*

*Notes on one of Freud's patients*

### Analyst's couch
Much of Freud's work consisted of listening to his patients as they talked about themselves. The patient lay on a couch in Freud's study, and Freud sat at his desk, surrounded by his collection of ancient Egyptian statues, listening and taking notes. This technique, devised by Freud, is still used widely today. Many of Freud's books are made up largely of case studies – reports of the psychoanalytic sessions and the conclusions Freud drew from them.

*The Psychopathology of Everyday Life (1904)*

*Chair is made in the shape of a person.*

*Freud's chair*

*The Interpretation of Dreams (1900)*

### Interpretation of dreams
Freud believed that beneath our conscious mind is a submerged unconscious that governs much of our behavior. Dreams are the way in which the unconscious comes to the surface. He published this theory in *The Interpretation of Dreams* in 1900.

### Freudian slips
In his book *The Psychopathology of Everyday Life* (1904), Freud explained how slips of the tongue can reveal hidden, unconscious wishes. Freud made many connections between what we say and do and what we actually mean.

## International Psychoanalytical Association

Early in his career, Freud's work met with intense hostility, but gradually his ideas were accepted. In 1902, he established a psychoanalytical society in Vienna, and, in 1910, he set up the International Psychoanalytical Association (IPA) to promote his ideas. Regular IPA meetings and discussions helped Freud confirm his theories about the mind and spread them to a wider audience.

### Carl Gustav Jung
The Swiss psychiatrist C. G. Jung first met Freud in 1907 and they lectured together in the US in 1909. Jung was the first president of the IPA, but resigned in 1914 because he disagreed with Freud about the origins of neurosis. He later created his own school of thought about the workings of the mind.

## Later life
In the 1920s, Freud developed a new theory that the mind is made up of three parts – the id, which contains impulses, the ego, which represents reasoning, and the superego, the self-critical area. He was developing this theory when he left Austria in 1938, because it was occupied by Nazi Germany.

### Anna Freud
In 1938, Freud moved to London, where he died in exile the following year. His work was carried on by his youngest daughter, Anna (1895–1982). A certified teacher, she specialized in child psychiatry. She founded and directed a renowned clinic for child therapy in London and wrote several books.

### SIGMUND FREUD
**1856** Born in Freiburg, Moravia.
**1859** Family moves to Vienna.
**1886** Begins work as a specialist in nervous diseases.
**1900** *The Interpretation of Dreams.*
**1910** Sets up International Psychoanalytical Association.
**1923** Has his first operation for cancer of the jaw; publishes *The Ego and the Id.*
**1938** Leaves Vienna for London; publishes *An Outline of Psychoanalysis.*
**1939** Dies in London.

**FIND OUT MORE**   BRAIN AND NERVOUS SYSTEM   GERMANY, HISTORY OF   HOSPITALS   MEDICINE   MEDICINE, HISTORY OF

# FRICTION

DRAGGING A HEAVY OBJECT across the floor is difficult because of friction, a force that opposes motion. Friction occurs between any two surfaces that are in contact. Even smooth surfaces have microscopic ridges and troughs that make them grip one another. Friction is greater between rough surfaces than smooth ones. Static friction stops surfaces at rest from moving. Dynamic friction slows down surfaces in motion.

## Static friction

Friction acts between these two masses and the wooden slope. Static friction on the stationary block is great enough to prevent it from moving. The moving block has overcome static friction, but it then produces dynamic friction, which limits its speed.

Gravity makes the mass on the smooth surface overcome static friction and slide down the slope.

Smooth surface

Rough surface

The rougher surface increases the force of static friction and prevents the mass from sliding.

## Using friction

Friction can be useful. Without friction, no one would be able to walk or run. Friction helps people's shoes grip the ground and stops their feet from sliding out from under them. In the same way, friction enables a vehicle's tires to grip the road. Most brakes use friction to slow a vehicle down. Friction between surfaces always produces heat, and sometimes electricity.

The pattern on the soles of these shoes is designed to create friction to give maximum grip.

Balloon charged by friction

### Disk brakes
When the rider of this motorcycle applies the brakes, a pad presses against the metal disk fixed to the wheel. The rubbing action of the pad against the moving disk produces friction and slows the wheel enough to stop the motorcycle.

Brake pad unit

Disk

The brakes glow as the car slows down.

### Friction and electricity
Rubbing two objects together can produce a charge of static electricity. Friction between a T-shirt and a balloon will dislodge negatively charged electrons from the atoms of the shirt. The electrons transfer to atoms in the balloon and give it a negative charge, while the shirt becomes positively charged. Opposite charges attract, so the negatively charged balloon clings to the positively charged shirt.

### Friction and heat
In cold weather people often rub their hands together to warm them. Friction between two surfaces always produces heat. When a race car brakes at high speed, the brakes glow red as the energy of the car's movement is changed into heat.

## Reducing friction

If two moving machine parts rub together, friction will eventually damage them. Friction in machines generates heat and wastes a lot of energy. Most methods of reducing friction involve keeping the surfaces apart in some way.

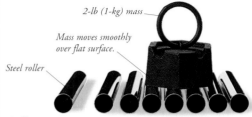

2-lb (1-kg) mass

Mass moves smoothly over flat surface.

Steel roller

### Rollers
The rollers under this 2-lb (1-kg) mass allow it to move smoothly over a flat surface. The mass and the surface are not in contact, so there is no friction between them. If the mass is pushed or pulled, the rollers will roll instead of drag over the surface.

Axle passes through center.

Outer ring attaches to wheel.

### Ball bearing
A ball bearing is a device used to reduce friction between a wheel and its axle. As the wheel turns, the steel balls in the bearing roll around and prevent the wheel and axle from rubbing together.

### Lubrication
Using a fluid such as oil to make machine parts move more smoothly and reduce wear is called lubrication. The oil coats the surfaces of the moving parts, preventing them from rubbing together.

### Air resistance
Dynamic friction between the air and a moving object is called air resistance. Streamlining gives an object a smooth shape so that air flows more easily around it. Here, smoke trails blown over a streamlined car show how the air moves over its surface.

### Hovercraft
A hovercraft overcomes the problem of friction by using high-pressure air as a lubricant. Fans pump air from the atmosphere into a flexible skirt around the craft's hull. This powerful downward jet of air allows the craft to hover over the water, keeping friction with the water's surface to a minimum. Large propellers on top of the craft move it quickly across the water.

### Christopher Cockerell

In 1953, English engineer Christopher Cockerell (1910–99) began working on ways to reduce the friction between a ship's hull and the water. His solution was to lift the vessel above the water practical hovercraft, called the SR-N1.on a cushion of compressed air. In 1959, after making successful models, he produced the world's first

F

# FROGS AND TOADS

THE CROAKING SOUNDS of frogs and toads are often heard in spring as they try to attract a mate. Frogs and toads are amphibians – cold-blooded animals that live both on land and in water. There are more than 2,600 species of frogs and toads, living in most parts of the world where there is freshwater. In some areas, they are easy to distinguish – frogs have slimy skins and live mainly in the water; toads have dry, warty skins, and live mainly on land. In the tropics, they are more diverse and harder to tell apart. Their habitats range from lakes and marshes to rain forests, mountains, and deserts.

## Features of frogs and toads

Frogs and toads have porous skin – water and air can pass through it – enabling them to breathe through their skin as well as their lungs. Most have sharp teeth, and can see and hear well. They have four legs, varying in length between species. Frogs range in size from a few inches long to the West African Goliath frog, which is 16 in (40 cm) in length. Some unusual species are the hairy frog – the male grows hair in the breeding season – and the Borneo flying frog, which glides between trees.

### Feeding

Most tadpoles are herbivorous, while adult frogs and toads are insectivorous or carnivorous. Prey includes insects, worms, spiders, fish, other frogs, or small reptiles, depending on species. Most species catch insects with their long, sticky tongues. Larger frogs and toads rely on ambush. Giant horned toads and bullfrogs have powerful jaws and wide mouths and can even eat mice.

*Warty skin*

*Sticky tongue is used to catch the worm.*

**Green toad**

*Short legs for hopping*

*Hind legs in full stretch*

*Feet push off from the ground.*

*Frog in a streamlined position in mid-flight*

*Eyes closed for protection*

*Webbed feet*

*Frogs swim by pulling their hind legs toward their bodies, then kicking them backwards to push themselves forward through the water.*

*Back legs are long and very powerful.*

*Front legs are held back.*

**Northern leopard frog**

### Leaping and swimming

Long-legged frogs, such as this Northern leopard frog, can jump more than 30 times their own length in a single leap. When swimming, its long, webbed toes help propel it through the water. Short-legged frogs walk, crawl, or do short hops. Some species, such as spade-foot frogs, have feet that can burrow into loose earth. Toads usually have short legs and can only hop weakly or walk. Some species, such as the natterjack toad, can run.

*Frogs use their front legs like brakes when they enter the water.*

## Reproduction

Most frogs and toads mate in water. The male fertilizes the eggs externally as the female lays them; a few species fertilize eggs internally. Some bear live young; others form "mating-balls" of a female and several males. The eggs develop into tadpoles, which live in water and breathe through gills. The tadpoles change into air-breathing adults with lungs.

*The dark dots develop into tadpoles.*

*The eggs stick together.*

*Tadpole uses its tail to swim.*

*Tiny buds from which front legs will grow*

*Back legs*

*Tail eventually disappears.*

### Life cycle of a common frog

**1** Eggs stick together to form frogspawn. Each egg contains a dark center that will become a tadpole. Many eggs are infertile and die, or are attacked by fungus or predators.

**2** The newly hatched tadpole lives in the water and breathes through external gills. Most species at this stage are herbivorous and feed on plants.

**3** By 6–9 weeks, the tadpole has grown considerably in size. The hind legs have developed. The tadpole now prepares to metamorphose, or change, into a froglet.

**4** At 12 weeks, the tail has almost receded. The tadpole has become a froglet. It is now ready to leave the water to begin its adult life – partly on land.

### Croaking

Frogs and toads croak to attract mates. Usually the males croak, using inflatable vocal sacs in the throat. Each species has its own distinctive croak that attracts mates of the same species. This also avoids mating between different species in regions where there are many similar frogs and toads.

**Painted reed frog**

*Vocal sac*

## Defense

Some frogs have poisonous skin that is brightly colored. Others such as tree frogs may secrete bad-tasting sticky substances. Many toads, including cane toads, have poison-secreting glands. Large species, such as horned toads, give painful bites.

### Poison dart frog

This South American frog is the most poisonous frog in the world. Its bright skin warns predators that it is poisonous to eat.

*Skin is highly toxic*

**Golden poison dart frog**

*Red belly*

### Fire-bellied toad

Fire-bellied toads in Europe have drab backs but bright red bellies. If threatened, the toad exposes its belly. This flash of color frightens away predators.

### Tree frogs

Tree frogs move easily in trees. They have sticky disks on their toes and an opposing thumb, enabling them to grip most objects, even smooth surfaces. Flying frogs are tree frogs with very large webbed feet that enable them to glide down from branch to branch.

*Sticky pads on their toes enable them to grip branches.*

**Red-eyed tree frog**

### NORTHERN LEOPARD FROG

| | |
|---|---|
| **SCIENTIFIC NAME** | *Rana pipiens* |
| **ORDER** | Anura |
| **FAMILY** | Ranidae |
| **DISTRIBUTION** | Northern and western US and Canada, as far south as New Mexico |
| **HABITAT** | Found in most habitats, even those far from water, which explains its other name of "meadow frog" |
| **DIET** | Insects |
| **SIZE** | Length 3.5–4.5 in (9–11 cm) |
| **LIFESPAN** | Up to 6 years (in captivity) |

**FIND OUT MORE**    AMPHIBIANS    CONSERVATION    EGGS    LAKE AND RIVER WILDLIFE    MARSH AND SWAMP WILDLIFE    POISONOUS ANIMALS    RAIN FOREST WILDLIFE    URBAN WILDLIFE    WOODLAND WILDLIFE

# Frogs

*Colors help camouflage frog in earth and leaf litter.*

**Asian painted frogs** are burrowers that emerge onto the surface at night and inflate themselves if touched.

**Foam-nesting frogs** lay eggs in self-made foam in trees above water, into which the tadpoles drop.

**Tomato frogs** from Madagascar live on land, but breed in slow-moving or stagnant water.

*Color varies from deep red to pale orange.*

*Eyespots look like eyes to confuse predators.*

*Large digital disks help it land after gliding.*

*Bright colors indicate it is poisonous to eat.*

*Long fingers and toes*

*A diet of tiny invertebrates makes skin poisonous.*

**Chilean four-eyed frogs** have eyespots on their backs that deter predators.

**Malayan flying frogs** cannot fly, but glide downward.

**Yellow and black poison dart frogs** live in cracks in riverside rocks.

**Paradoxical frogs** develop from tadpoles twice their length and shrink as they "grow."

**Green and black poison dart frogs** have toxic skin.

*Very wide mouth*

*These toads can reach 8 in (20 cm) in length.*

*Smooth, slimy skin*

**Golden mantellas** are poisonous frogs from Madagascar. They feed on small invertebrates.

**African bullfrogs** are large, carnivorous frogs that feed on other frogs, reptiles, and even mice and rats.

**Common frogs** are becoming rarer, partly due to the loss of wetland areas.

**White's tree frogs** are large Australian frogs.

*Sticky pads below fingers*

# Toads

*Smooth skin is unusual for a toad.*

*These toads run rather than hop.*

*Developing eggs*

*Fleshy horns project over eyes to enhance leaflike appearance.*

**Asian tree toads** have flat digital disks, enabling them to climb riverside trees.

**Natterjack toads**, also called running toads, are the rarest toads in Britain.

**Male midwife toads** carry their eggs on their backs until they hatch into the water.

**Asian horned toads** resemble dried leaves, to escape discovery on the forest floor.

*Narrow fingers used for feeding.*

*Warty skin*

*Ornate horned toads may even eat others of the same species.*

*Cane toads were originally from South America.*

**African clawed toads** are totally aquatic.

*Webbed feet*

**Ornate horned toads** from Argentina are large, aggressive toads with huge appetites.

**Cane toads** were introduced to Australia to control sugar cane pests, but have become pests themselves.

**Mexican burrowing toads** live in dry areas, rarely coming to the surface.

# FRUITS AND SEEDS

CHERRIES, TOMATOES, and pea pods are fruits, the part of a plant that contains and protects the seeds it needs for reproduction. A fruit forms after a flower has been pollinated. First the petals wither and fall, then the part of the flower called the ovary swells. This swelling becomes the fruit. Inside the fruit the seeds are supplied with nutrients through tiny stalks connecting them to the fruit wall. As the seeds grow, the fruit ripens. Some fruits are sweet and juicy and may be edible; others are inedible, or even poisonous.

## Parts of a fruit

In some fruits, the fruit wall, or pericarp, has three distinct layers – an outer epicarp, a middle mesocarp, and a hard, inner endocarp. These layers are easy to see in fleshy fruits, such as plums, but in other fruits the layers are not so easy to identify. The fleshy part of an apple, for example, is actually formed from the receptacle – the swollen tip of the flower stem.

*Remains of stamen*
*Pedicel (flower stalk)*
*Seed or pip (surrounded by endocarp)*
*Raspberries are made of clusters of drupelets.*
*Mesocarp*
*Epicarp (skin)*
*Receptacle*
*Drupelet*

Raspberry

Cross-section of a raspberry

## How a fruit develops

Once a flower has been pollinated and fertilization has taken place, its ovary becomes known as a fruit. This fruit and the tiny seeds within begin to develop and grow. Gradually the fruit enlarges, and as it matures, its shape, color, and texture also change. When a juicy, edible fruit such as this melon ripens, its flesh becomes very sweet and succulent.

## Parts of a seed

All seeds contain a tiny embryo and seed leaves called cotyledons, which are full of stored food. The seed also has an outer seed coat called a testa. The embryo has a minute root called a radicle and a tiny stem called a plumule. When the seed germinates, the food store provides nourishment for the tiny seedling.

*Testa (seed coat)*
*Embryo*
*Cotyledon (seed leaf)*
*Testa*

Apple seed

Cross-section of an apple seed

*The flower is brightly colored and attracts insects that will pollinate it.*

*After pollination, the ovary starts to swell.*

*The flower is no longer needed, so it shrivels up and dies.*

*The fruit begins to form.*

*The fruit grows larger as it ripens.*

*The fruit has ripened and contains hundreds of seeds deep inside.*

*A melon is a kind of berry.*

## Seed dispersal

Plants need to spread their seeds to reproduce. Seeds are dispersed by wind, water, and animals. In some plants, parts of the fruit wall or flowerhead also help spread the seeds. As the fruit dries, the fruit wall splits open and the seeds are scattered.

### Dispersal by burial
Seeds are a valuable source of food for mammals and birds. Squirrels and other rodents bury acorns and other nuts, then forget to dig them up. These forgotten seeds grow into plants.

Squirrel burying nuts

### Bird dispersal
Brightly colored orange and red berries attract birds. The birds swallow the berries whole but digest only the fleshy part. The seeds pass out, unharmed, in the bird's droppings.

Redwing

### Water dispersal
Some fruits and seeds float. Their fruit wall contains oil droplets or air to make them buoyant. Coconut palm fruits float in the ocean until they are washed up on a beach.

Coconut growing on a beach

### Wind dispersal
Light fruits and seeds are spread by the wind. The seeds of a columbine are scattered when the breeze shakes the seed head. Maple tree seeds have papery wings to carry them on the wind.

Columbine seed head

### Animal dispersal
Some seeds are encased inside hooked fruits that can easily snag in the fur of mammals. They are carried by the animals and drop off later in another place.

Bison with seeds trapped in fur

## Types of fruits

Simple fruits have a single ovary; compound fruits have more than one. When ripe, some fruits remain succulent; others become woody and hard, or dry and papery, such as larkspur. False fruits develop from other flower parts in addition to the ovary.

### Berries
Berries have a combined mesocarp and endocarp layer. They often have many seeds that each have a tough seed coat, or testa.

Grapes

### False fruits
In most false fruits, the receptacle swells to enclose the true fruit. Tiny true fruits may also be fixed to the surface of the receptacle.

Pear

### Drupes
Drupes, or stone fruits, have a thick, fleshy mesocarp and a woody endocarp – the stone. Fruits such as raspberries are made up of many tiny drupelets.

Plum

### Dry fruits
Dry fruits often have lids or seams that open to release the ripe seeds. This capsule has round openings called pores.

Love-in-a-mist capsule

FIND OUT MORE | BIRDS · FLOWERS · FOOD · MAMMALS · PLANTS · PLANTS, ANATOMY · PLANTS, REPRODUCTION · PLANT USES · RATS AND OTHER RODENTS

# Succulent fruits

## Berries

**Kiwanos** have a spiky rind to prevent animals from eating them until the seeds are ripe.

**Avocados** have a single large seed and oily flesh.

**Red currant** seeds are spread by birds.

**Persimmons** are juicy berries with many seeds.

**Grapes** each have a tiny stalk and grow in large clusters.

**Tomato** seeds are covered in a jelly layer that protects them while inside an animal's gut.

**Melons** are a firm-walled kind of berry called a pepo.

**Gooseberry** seeds are embedded in juicy flesh.

**Lemons** are citrus fruits with flesh made of juice-filled hairs.

**Litchis** have a fleshy layer that grows from the seed stalk.

**Rambutans** have very hairy skin.

**Kiwis** have black seeds embedded in firm green flesh.

## Drupes and drupelets

**Peaches** have juicy flesh and a single seed protected inside a woody stone.

**Cherries** have a single seed inside a hard stone.

**Apricots** are cultivated fruits that have a single seed inside a woody stone.

**Blackberry** fruits each consist of many single-seeded drupelets.

**Nectarines** are a cultivated variety of peach with a smoother skin.

**Damsons** are small plums. Their seeds are spread when animals eat the flesh.

**Mangoes** have a large, single seed and sweet flesh.

**Greengages** are a kind of plum with green or yellow flesh.

**Loganberries** are made up of many single-seeded drupelets.

**Plums** have juicy flesh and a single seed inside a stone.

**Sago palm** fruits have a corky layer that allows them to float.

**Coconuts** are the fruit of a palm tree.

## False fruits

**Rowanberries** are the swollen tips of the flower stem. They enclose the real fruit.

**Apple** flesh is the swollen tip of the flower stem, and the pips are the seeds.

**Fig** fruits are tiny, woody pips contained in a fleshy, swollen flower stem.

**Strawberries** consist of a red fleshy receptacle covered in tiny fruits.

**Quinces** have hard flesh and a seed-filled core.

**Breadfruits** have many fruits in a large, fleshy flowerhead.

# Dry fruits

**Honesty** has a papery fruit and flat seeds.

**Dandelion** fruits have hairs that help them float in a breeze.

**Goosegrass** fruits have hooks that cling to animals' fur.

**Maple** fruits have wings that carry them in the wind.

**Larkspur** fruits split open to release the seeds.

**Hogweed** fruits are papery and contain two seeds.

**Laburnum** pods split to release the hard seeds.

**Poppy** capsules contain masses of tiny seeds.

**Burdock** has a head of hooked fruits.

**Acorns** are nuts with a tough, woody fruit wall.

**Chestnuts** are enclosed in a spiny case.

**Beech** nuts are arranged in threes inside a rough case.

# FURNITURE

EVERY DAY, PEOPLE SIT on chairs, sleep in beds, and eat from tables. All these are items of furniture, the movable equipment of a home. At one time, furniture was handmade, so most homes contained only basic, functional pieces. A wide range of more affordable furniture became available when production was mechanized in the 19th century. Today, furniture design is largely determined by function, cost, size, and fashion.

*The chairs in this Roman sculpture are similar to modern chairs.*

### Antique furniture
Antiques are objects made more than 100 years ago. Antique furniture was usually handcrafted, using fine materials, in many different styles. Antiques are frequently considered valuable and are highly prized by collectors today.

### Early furniture
Different cultures have produced very similar furniture. The ancient Egyptians had folding beds, and the Romans had armchairs. The earliest furniture to survive was sealed in Egyptian tombs.

*An 18th-century cabinet*

## Types of furniture
Furniture made for use in a home is designed to be as comfortable as possible. Choices of shape and fabric let the buyer express personal taste. Office furniture is usually plainer and more functional. Furniture is found outdoors in the form of garbage cans, street lamps, and bus stops.

### Domestic furniture
Most homes have a bed or a futon. Originally created in Japan for modern, urban life, the futon saves space by serving as a bed at night and a sofa during the day.

### Office furniture
Modern office furniture, such as this adjustable desk lamp, is designed to be practical, sturdy, and long-lasting.

*The lamp head is easily adjusted.*

*The heavy base provides balance.*

### Street furniture
Despite having similar functions, street furniture looks very different all over the world. This elaborate public drinking fountain is in Paris, France.

## How an armchair is made
Most modern furniture is mass-produced by machine rather than handcrafted. Furniture such as sofas and armchairs have machine-made parts that are fit together by hand and then upholstered. This armchair is made from materials that have been built up around a wooden frame.

**Steel springs** attached to the frame help spread a person's weight evenly.

**Arms** are cushioned with foam padding and a fleece layer.

**Upholsterer** fits the fabric covering securely into position.

**Castors** are small wheels beneath the chair that allow it to be moved easily.

**Metal springs** make the chair comfortable to sit on.

**Layers of metal mesh and hessian** hold the springs in place.

### Upholstery
A layer of padding called upholstery covers the basic wooden frame of a chair. Upholstery also refers to the way in which fabric is fitted to the frame. The top layer of fabric is chosen from a range of colors, patterns, and textures.

**Cushions** are filled with foam or feathers.

**Fabric covering** is durable.

### Interior design
In furnishing a room, people try to choose colors, pictures, fabrics, and furniture that go well together. This process is known as interior design. It began in Europe in the 16th century, when furniture makers were first given charge of entire rooms to decorate as a unified whole.

**Soft furnishings** are materials such as rugs, cushions, and curtains. These materials are chosen to make a room comfortable and to help create its overall look.

*Cushions and wallpaper borders are coordinated.*

### William Morris
The British designer, artist, and socialist William Morris (1834–96) was active in many areas. He was influential in the design of furniture and fabrics, argued for a return to handcrafted furniture, and founded the Arts and Crafts Movement for design.

**FIND OUT MORE**   ARCHITECTURE   ART, HISTORY OF   CRAFTS   DESIGN   EGYPT, ANCIENT   HOUSES AND HOMES   MUSEUMS

# English furniture

## Lights

Iron candlestand,
late 17th century

Brass candlesticks,
early 18th century

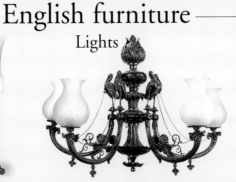

Bronze storm lamp,
early 19th century

Gilt gaslight chandelier,
mid 19th century

Glass electric chandelier
with brass edgings, c.1900

Floor lamp,
1930-40

## Chairs

Carved oak armchair,
c.1620

Walnut chair,
c.1680

Beech armchair with
caned seat, c.1815

Upholstered chair with beech
and walnut frame, c.1860

Ebonized beech
side chair, c.1890

Birch veneered
plywood chair, 1989

## Tables and cabinets

Pine and oak side table gilded
in Chinese style, c.1690

Mahogany and walnut table
on a tripod stand, c.1760

Rosewood side
table, c.1800

Combined games and
needlework table, c.1830

Mahogany table in
Moorish style, c.1895

Maple veneer side
table, late 1930s

Queen Anne cabinet on chest,
walnut veneer on a pine frame, c.1700

Shelves projecting
from back panel

Open shelf

Cupboard
with painted
panel set
into door

Painted panels
showing signs
of the zodiac

Moorish
style
decoration

Double
glazed doors

Mahogany cabinet with inset painted panels and
decoration, designed by Lewis F. Day in 1880

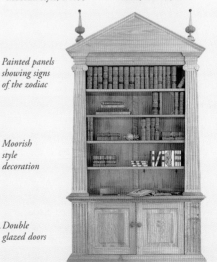

Oak bookcase with fluted columns,
handcrafted in a traditional style, 1993

# GALAXIES

A HUNDRED BILLION galaxies exist in the Universe. Each consists of a vast collection of stars, gas, and dust. They started life thousands of millions of years ago, slowly forming into distinctive shapes. Each galaxy can contain billions of stars. Gravity keeps the stars together and keeps the galaxies in clusters.

## Milky Way

About 500 billion stars make up the spiral-shaped Milky Way. The arms contain young, hot, bright stars; older, dimmer stars make up the nucleus. A thin halo of old stars surrounds our galaxy. The Sun is in one of the arms, about two-thirds of the way from the center. It orbits the center of the galaxy once every 220 million years.

*Spiral arm in profile* | *Central hub*

The **Milky Way** is about 100,000 light-years wide and 13,000 light-years through its central hub.

## Types of galaxies

Most galaxies have a central ball of stars, the nucleus, and many have a flattened disk that extends from it. Astronomers classify galaxies into three main types based on these features. No one knows why galaxies become a particular shape, but it may depend on how fast a galaxy spins and how quickly stars form inside.

### Elliptical
About 60 percent of galaxies are ball-shaped collections of old stars. They range in shape from round to flattened ovals. Astronomers describe their shape with the letter *E* followed by a number between *0* and *7* – the higher the number, the flatter the galaxy.

### Spiral
A hub of older stars is surrounded by a flattened disk with spiral arms containing younger stars. The shape of a spiral is described by the letter *S* followed by a letter between *a* and *d* to indicate how tightly wound the arms are and the size of the hub.

E0  E3  E5  E7   Sa   Sb        Sc

Classification of galaxies by shape

SBa   SBb   SBc

### Irregular
About 10 percent of galaxies are irregular. They are collections of stars with no distinctive shape or structure and do not fit into any of the classifications. They are smaller than the average galaxy and contain large amounts of gas and dust.

### Barred spiral
These galaxies consist of a central bar of older stars with arms containing younger stars coming from the ends of the bar. Barred spirals are described as *SB* followed by a letter from *a* to *d* to indicate how tightly wound the arms are and the size of the hub.

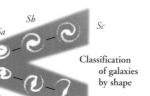

## Active galaxies

Unusually large amounts of energy are emitted from some galaxies. This energy may come from an object that is visible, such as a quasar, or from an invisible object, such as the lobes of a radio galaxy. How the energy is created is uncertain, but evidence suggests it could be from a supermassive black hole at the center of the galaxy.

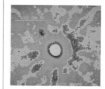

### Quasars
Quasars are the brightest, most distant, fastest moving, and youngest objects visible outside the Milky Way. Thousands are known, each emitting huge amounts of energy. They are found at the heart of large galaxies.

### Radio galaxies
Powerful radio energy is emitted by radio galaxies. The energy comes from lobes at either side of the visible core and is detectable with radio telescopes. Centaurus A is the nearest active galaxy: it is 16 million light-years away.

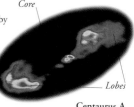

*Core* | *Lobes*

**Centaurus A**

### Colliding galaxies
Galaxies can collide as they move through space, as is happening (left) with two galaxies in the constellation of Boötes. Such collisions either change the shape of a galaxy or result in a merger.

## Edwin Hubble
In 1923, the American astronomer Edwin Hubble (1889–1953) proved that there are galaxies other than the Milky Way. The next year he classified galaxies according to their shape. He went on to show that galaxies are moving away from each other, and thus providing proof that the Universe is expanding.

## Galaxy clusters

Galaxies are grouped together in clusters. The Milky Way belongs to a cluster of about 30 galaxies called the Local Group. The Virgo Cluster (right) contains about 2,500 galaxies, mostly spirals.

## Superclusters
Clusters of galaxies group together into superclusters that spread across many millions of light-years. In turn, hundreds of superclusters group together to form huge walls and filaments, such as the Stick Man that stretches for hundreds of millions of light-years.

**The Stick Man** contains millions of galaxies.

FIND OUT MORE ASTRONOMY   BIG BANG   BLACK HOLES   GRAVITY   STARS   UNIVERSE

# GALILEO GALILEI

THE ITALIAN SCIENTIST Galileo Galilei was one of the greatest astronomers and physicists of all time. He was the first person to use a telescope to look at the heavens. He started a branch of physics called mechanics, showing that nature obeyed mathematical rules. His belief that science should be based on observation made him one of the first modern scientists. It also led him into trouble, because his views about the Solar System went against those held by the Roman Catholic Church.

### Early life
Galileo was born in Pisa, Italy, in 1564. After school he went to the University of Pisa to study medicine. But Galileo was more interested in mathematics and physics and left without a degree. By the time he was 25, he was back at the university – as professor of mathematics.

## Telescope
In 1609, Galileo heard of the invention of the telescope and made one of his own. He used it to look at the heavens and made many astronomical discoveries. He noticed that the planet Venus has phases like the Moon. This supported the theory of Nicolaus Copernicus that the planets went around the Sun.

## Moving bodies
In the 16th century, people believed that the Sun moved around Earth. Galileo did not agree with this, and developed Copernicus's theory of Earth moving around the Sun.

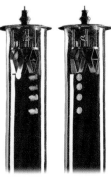

*Falling feather*

*Coin falls at same speed*

### Gravity
Galileo showed that all objects fall at the same speed, no matter what their weight. Previously, people had believed that heavier objects fell faster. There is a story that Galileo proved his theory by dropping objects from the leaning tower of Pisa, but this is probably not true. He certainly did an experiment similar to this: objects of different weights were dropped in identical jars from which the air was pumped out.

*Replica of Galileo's telescope, 1609*

*Artist's impression of the Milky Way*

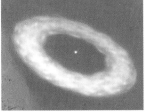

*Planet with two moons*

*Planet with ringlike formations*

*Galileo's drawings of Saturn*

### Milky Way
In 1610, Galileo built a telescope that could magnify 1,000 times. It enabled him to see thousands of stars that no human being had ever seen before. He trained his new telescope on the Milky Way and found that it was a vast collection of stars, clustered together in groups of various sizes.

### Planets and moons
Through his telescope, Galileo saw what he at first thought were two small moons orbiting the planet Saturn. He drew these "moons" in his notebooks, but he later decided that they were Saturn's now-famous rings. He also discovered the four moons that orbit the planet Jupiter, and was able to examine the craters on our own Moon.

### The Starry Messenger
In March 1610, Galileo published many of his discoveries in his book *The Starry Messenger*. The book also showed that Copernicus was right to say that the Earth moved around the Sun, and that the Roman Catholic Church's idea of an unmoving Earth at the center of the Universe was wrong. *The Starry Messenger* infuriated many churchmen.

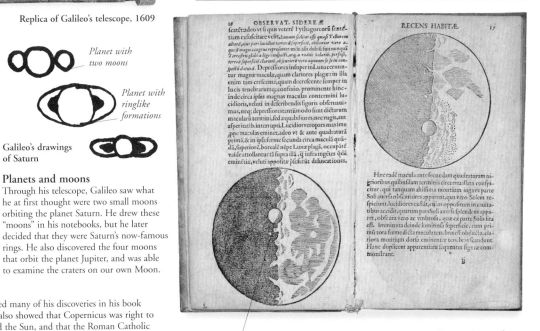

*Crater on Moon*

*Illustrated pages from The Starry Messenger, 1610*

## Inquisition
Galileo's support for Copernicus's ideas outraged the Catholic Church because the priests thought that the Earth should be at the center of the Universe. In 1633, the Church called Galileo to appear before its court, or inquisition, in Rome. The court ordered him to deny his beliefs under threat of torture. Galileo was forced to agree that Earth was the center of the Universe, but was heard to mutter, "Yet it *does* move."

*Trial of Galileo*

### GALILEO GALILEI

1564 Born, Pisa, Italy.

1589 Becomes Professor of Mathematics at Pisa University.

1609 Makes his first telescope.

1610 Publishes *The Starry Messenger*.

1632 Publishes *Dialogue*, explaining the two theories of the universe.

1633 Sentenced by the Inquisition.

1642 Dies under house arrest at Arcetri, Italy.

**FIND OUT MORE**    FORCE AND MOTION    PLANETS    SCIENCE, HISTORY OF    STARS    SUN AND SOLAR SYSTEM    TELESCOPES

# GANDHI, MOHANDAS

WHEN THE VAST AND HEAVILY populated nation of India gained independence from Britain in August 1947, one man more than any other was responsible for that achievement. Mohandas Gandhi united the different communities of India and led them to independence. He believed in nonviolent protest and despised the racial violence of his homeland. He became known as Mahatma, or "great soul." Although he did not live long enough to see the results of his work, Gandhi is remembered today as the instigator of three movements crucial in the 20th century: the campaigns against racism, colonialism, and violence.

### Early life
Mohandas Kamarchand Gandhi was born in Porbandar, India, in 1869. Educated in India and Britain, he trained in law and became a lawyer in 1889. In 1893, he moved to work in South Africa. While there, he edited a newspaper called *Indian Opinion* and campaigned against racial injustice, forcing the South African government to grant Indians rights of permanent citizenship in 1914.

## Indian nationalism

The British had controlled India since the 18th century, but many Indians wanted to govern themselves. In 1915, Gandhi returned from South Africa and became one of the leaders of the independence movement. He led many peaceful campaigns against British rule, using the tactic of nonviolent civil disobedience. He called this method Satyagraha ("holding to the truth"). It was copied by many civil rights leaders around the world.

Gandhi with Jawaharlal Nehru, leader of the socialist wing of Congress

### Congress
The Indian National Congress Party was founded in 1885. Its members wanted to increase Indian participation in government and represent all religions and cultures. During the 1920s, under the leadership of Gandhi and Jawaharlal Nehru, Congress took the lead in campaigning for Indian independence.

Gandhi's sandals

Gandhi's eyeglasses

Gandhi's watch

Gandhi lived a simple life, wearing plain clothes and keeping only a few possessions.

### Imprisonment
During his many campaigns, Gandhi was often imprisoned by the British for civil disobedience. But after each spell in prison, Gandhi emerged more powerful and more respected than before. His personal prestige was so high that people began to call him Mahatma, the "great soul." He alone seemed able to unite the diverse elements of the independence movement that represented the many different religions and cultures in the huge subcontinent of India.

### Salt march
The British controlled the production of salt in India. This monopoly forced up prices and was very unpopular. In 1930, Gandhi led a 200-mile (320-km) march to the sea to get his own salt, and thousands joined him on the way. Gandhi was imprisoned for civil disobedience, but the march showed the power of Satyagraha.

## Social reforms

In 1937, the Indian provinces received a large measure of home rule. The Congress Party took control of seven of the 11 provinces and began to reform the country. Gandhi pushed for social, economic, and educational improvements designed to rebuild India. He encouraged crafts such as spinning cotton, because he believed that small cottage industries could help India's villages.

Gandhi spinning cotton

## Independence

In 1947, India gained its independence. Hindus in the Congress Party wanted a united India, but Muslims wanted a country of their own. The country was, therefore, divided into India and Pakistan, a division Gandhi bitterly opposed.

### Assassination
Gandhi took little part in the independence talks, but threatened to fast to death to protest against the violence between Hindus and Muslims. In January 1948, he was assassinated by a Hindu fanatic who resented his concern for the Muslims.

Monument at the place where Gandhi died

### MOHANDAS GANDHI

| | |
|---|---|
| **1869** | Born in Porbandar, India. |
| **1889** | Becomes a lawyer in England. |
| **1891–93** | Works as a lawyer in India. |
| **1893–1915** | Works in South Africa. |
| **1920s** | Takes control of Congress Party with Nehru. |
| **1930** | Leads salt march to the sea. |
| **1942** | Launches Quit India campaign during World War II, and is interned until 1944. |
| **1945** | New British government promises independence by 1947. |
| **1947** | India gains its independence. |
| **1948** | Gandhi is assassinated. |

FIND OUT MORE

EMPIRES    HINDUISM    HUMAN RIGHTS    INDIA, HISTORY OF    SOUTH AFRICA, HISTORY OF

# GARBO, GRETA

SOPHISTICATED, SUPERIOR, scornful, and beautiful, Greta Garbo was everyone's idea of the perfect film star. The daughter of a poor laborer in Stockholm, Sweden, she conquered Hollywood in the 1920s and 1930s. Her audiences adored her, but at the height of her career she retired, becoming a recluse and never showing her face in public again. Yet this most celebrated actor received no Oscars, only a belated special award for her unforgettable films.

## Early life

Greta Gustafson was born in the Swedish capital of Stockholm in 1905. Her family was poor, and she worked from an early age in a barber's shop and a department store. Her first film part was in *How Not to Dress*, a publicity film for the store.

### Training

Early in her career, Garbo appeared as the female lead in a slapstick comedy, *Peter the Tramp*. She then applied for and won a scholarship to Sweden's Royal Dramatic Theater training school, where she was soon playing small parts on stage.

## Mauritz Stiller

While at training school, Garbo was spotted by the Swedish film director Mauritz Stiller. Stiller was best known for such films as the comedy *Love and Journalism,* and the sexually charged movie *Erotikon*. Stiller took a special interest in Garbo's career, gave her the surname Garbo, and made her a star.

Garbo and Mauritz Stiller

### First success

Garbo's first major film role was as the star of *The Atonement of Gösta Berling*. The film was a romantic tale about a priest set in the Swedish countryside. The premiere in Stockholm in 1924 attracted a huge audience and launched Garbo's film career.

Still from *Gösta Berling*

## Hollywood

In 1925, after the success of *Gösta Berling,* Garbo moved to Hollywood, the center of the US film industry. She signed a contract with Metro-Goldwyn-Mayer (MGM) and began filming *The Torrent*. Her first major success was *Flesh and the Devil*, made in 1926 and directed by Clarence Brown. By 1927, she was earning $5,000 a week from MGM. In all, Garbo made 24 films in Hollywood, and became one of the most famous, and highest paid, film stars in the world.

### Studio system

Filmmaking in Hollywood was dominated by a few large companies, such as MGM, Paramount, and Warner Bros. These and other studios held actors and directors to tight contracts, so that they could not work for a rival company. As a result, Garbo was forced to star in films she did not like.

### Anna Karenina

Garbo's reputation as a tragic heroine was established by *Anna Karenina* (1935), based on the novel by the great Russian writer Leo Tolstoy. The film won numerous awards and confirmed Garbo's reputation as the leading actress of her day.

### "Garbo talks!"

In 1930, the first sound film starring Garbo appeared. The publicity slogan was "Garbo talks!" The film, *Anna Christie,* had a heroine with a Swedish accent. The producers thought this would be an ideal role for Garbo. They believed that audiences might not otherwise accept her heavily accented voice.

### Garbo laughs

Garbo's reputation was as a serious, intense actress. In 1939, she astounded audiences with her relaxed performance in the romantic comedy *Ninotchka*. Publicity for the film made much of her laughter in this role.

### A life apart

In 1941, Garbo announced her retirement from making movies, because she did not want to grow old in front of her fans. Despite her success in Europe, her popularity was declining in the US. She became an American citizen in 1951 and led the life of a recluse, although she remained friendly with many famous people.

*"I want to be alone"* was Garbo's famous wish after her retirement in 1941.

### GRETA GARBO

| | |
|---|---|
| 1905 | Born in Stockholm, Sweden. |
| 1924 | Stars in *The Atonement of Gösta Berling,* her first major film. |
| 1925 | Moves to the US and signs contract with MGM. |
| 1930 | Has her first talking role, in *Anna Christie.* |
| 1935 | *Anna Karenina.* |
| 1938 | Nominated for an Oscar for *Camille.* |
| 1939 | *Ninotchka.* |
| 1941 | Retires from filmmaking. |
| 1954 | Honored at Academy Awards. |
| 1990 | Dies in New York. |

FIND OUT MORE   CAMERAS   FILMS AND FILMMAKING   LITERATURE

# GARDENS

LIKE LANDSCAPES in miniature, gardens are places to grow plants for pleasure and to provide beauty and relaxation. Gardens have a practical purpose, too. From ancient times, people have cultivated plants for food and medicine. Botanic gardens keep extensive collections for scientific study. Gardens provide an escape from pollution in cities, and a refreshing environment in a hot climate. A well-designed garden can enhance the finest building.

## Tools

Gardeners use a variety of tools. Some, such as forks, have hardly changed in hundreds of years. Mechanical aids such as the lawn mower, invented in 1832, are relatively new developments.

*Shears, for cutting hedges*

*Thick blades*

*Used for digging soil*

Spade and fork

Watering can

Trowel

Hand fork

## Development of gardens

Gardens have an ancient history. They were planted in Mesopotamia, China, Egypt, Persia, and Greece. The Romans spread knowledge of gardening to northern Europe during their rule of the Mediterranean lands. When Roman power declined in the 4th century AD, monks continued the tradition by cultivating plants in their monastery gardens. European gardens were enclosed by abbey or castle walls until the Renaissance.

### China and Japan
Gardens in China and Japan often have a religious significance, where nature itself is honored. This tradition is centuries old. For Zen Buddhists, landscaped gardens of raked gravel, where a rock may represent a mountain, are places of silent meditation.

**Temple garden, Kyoto, Japan**

*Gravel, raked into patterns*

*Clipped shrubs*

### Islamic gardens
North African Moors created shady courtyard gardens, with pools and fountains to reflect the sky and cool the air. When they conquered Spain in the 8th century, the Moors took the style to Europe, as seen in the Court of the Myrtles, the Alhambra, Spain.

### Renaissance formality
During the Renaissance in the 14th century, architects planned gardens as settings for the grand houses they designed. Fashionable gardens were formal, open, and regular, reviving a style established by the Romans.

**Villa Lante, Bagnaia, Lazio, Italy**

*This small classical temple, in a wooded glade, is typical of the Jardin Anglais style.*

### 18th-century naturalism
The Jardin Anglais (English garden) style spread throughout Europe during the 18th-century. The trend was begun by the English architect William Kent (1684–1748), who planned less formal gardens than had been common previously. He used an open style, which he believed to look more natural, to set off the formality of his buildings.

**Chiswick House, London, England**

## Botanic gardens

In botanic gardens, specimen plants are collected and cultivated for scientific study. They developed from the herb or physic gardens tended by medieval monks, where plants were grown for medicinal purposes.

### Plant collectors
From the late 1600s, European explorers returned from their world expeditions with many new and exotic varieties of plants. Serious plant-collecting expeditions began in the 18th century, bringing back specimens for scientific study and to decorate gardens.

*The peony, a native of China, was taken to Europe by plant collectors.*

### Roberto Burle Marx

Brazilian garden designer Roberto Burle Marx (1909–94) created stunning gardens for modern buildings in Brazil, using only plants native to his country. He made Brazilians more aware of the amazing plants found in their country.

### Wildlife gardens
In the 20th century, gardeners became more interested in the wild creatures that inhabited their plants, trees, and ponds. Instead of treating them as pests, they welcomed wildlife. Careful planting of a wildlife garden creates many different habitats, encouraging the widest possible range of animal visitors.

*Gardeners plant flowers that attract insects.*

**FIND OUT MORE**

ARCHITECTURE　　BUDDHISM　　ISLAMIC EMPIRE　　MEDICINE, HISTORY OF　　MONASTERIES　　PLANT USES　　RENAISSANCE

# GASES

WHEN YOU CATCH an unpleasant smell given off by a chemistry experiment, your nose is detecting the presence of a gas released by a chemical reaction. A gas is a type of matter with no fixed shape or volume. Not all gases have a smell, and many are invisible, but all are made of tiny, fast-moving particles that move rapidly and randomly.

## Gas particles

The forces between the speeding particles of a gas are too weak to hold them in one place, so the gas spreads out.

*Nitrogen dioxide gas soon escapes from the beaker and mingles with the air.*

*Copper and nitric acid react, releasing brown nitrogen dioxide gas.*

## Properties of gases

A gas quickly spreads out to fill any available space because its free-moving particles travel in all directions. The higher the temperature of a gas, the more energy its particles have and the faster they move. The pressure of a gas is linked to the number of collisions between the gas particles and the walls of its container: the more frequent the collisions are, the greater the pressure the gas exerts.

### Amedeo Avogadro

In 1806, an Italian lawyer named Amedeo Avogadro (1776–1856) gave up his legal career to devote himself to the study of physics. In 1811, Avogadro proposed that equal volumes of all gases at the same temperature and pressure will contain the same number of particles. This is now called Avogadro's Law.

## Condensation

Tiny droplets form on the inside of a cold window when water vapor in the air is cooled by the glass and turns into liquid water. The change of a gas to a liquid is called condensation. As a gas cools, its particles lose energy and slow down. The forces between the particles grow stronger and pull them together to form a liquid.

### Vapor

A gas normally forms when a liquid boils. However, a type of gas called a vapor sometimes forms when a liquid is below its boiling point. Paint, for example, dries when liquid particles at its surface gain enough energy to escape into the air as a vapor.

## Brownian motion

Dust particles can often be seen dancing in shafts of sunlight. Their random, jittery path is caused by tiny, unseen air molecules that bombard the dust particles. This motion – called Brownian Motion after Robert Brown (1773–1858), a Scottish biologist – shows that gas particles are constantly moving.

## Gas laws

The gas laws are a set of proven theories that allow scientists to predict how a gas will behave when there is a change in its volume, pressure, or temperature. The laws apply only when a gas is held in a sealed container.

### Charles's Law

This law, formulated by French physicist Jacques Charles (1746–1823), states that the volume of a gas at a constant pressure is proportional to its temperature. Thus, when the temperature of the gas halves, so does its volume.

1 When a gas-filled balloon is cooled in liquid nitrogen at -321°F (-196°C), the gas particles slow down.

2 The particles strike the balloon walls less often, so the gas volume shrinks, and the balloon collapses.

3 As the gas warms again in the air, the gas particles speed up, the volume expands, and the balloon reflates.

*The air molecules collide more often with the syringe walls, so the air pressure rises.*

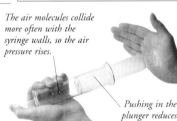

*Pushing in the plunger reduces the volume.*

### Boyle's Law

Put your finger at one end of a syringe, push in the plunger, and you will feel the air pressure in the syringe rising. The air obeys Boyle's Law, formulated by the Irish physicist Robert Boyle (1627–91). The law states that when a gas is at a constant temperature, its pressure is inversely proportional to its volume. In other words, if the volume halves, the pressure doubles.

*Pressure blows off the lid.*

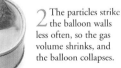

### Pressure Law

Heating a sealed can raises the air pressure inside the can until it is so great that the lid blows off. The air obeys the Pressure Law, which states that when the volume of a gas is constant, its pressure is proportional to its temperature. This means that if the temperature of the gas doubles, so will its pressure.

### Diffusion

When a jar of bromine gas and a jar of air are placed together, the gases quickly intermingle as their moving particles spread out to fill all the available space. This process is called diffusion. Aromas from the kitchen are smelled throughout the house when gas particles released by the food rapidly diffuse in the air. Diffusion also occurs when solids and liquids dissolve to form solutions.

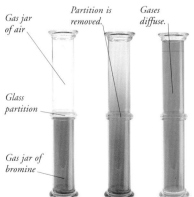

*Gas jar of air*

*Partition is removed.*

*Gases diffuse.*

*Glass partition*

*Gas jar of bromine*

# GENETICS

EACH PERSON IS UNIQUE, but he or she also inherits some characteristics and even appearance from his or her parents. The study of how characteristics are passed on from parents to offspring is known as genetics, and it affects all forms of life. At the center of the process is the deoxyribonucleic acid (DNA) molecule, which exists inside every living cell and contains a complex chemical "code" that controls the way in which life-forms are put together and operate. DNA is composed of genes and, DNA in turn, makes up chromosomes. All these microscopic structures are in the nuclei of cells.

## DNA

A DNA molecule contains all the information required to make and operate a specific organism. DNA is found in the nucleus of a cell and is a long structure that consists of two strands twisted together to form a double helix. The strands are linked by four chemicals called bases: thymine, adenine, cytosine, and guanine.

*"Backbone" of strand is made from sugar and phosphate molecules.*

Thymine
Adenine
Cytosine
Guanine

### Replicating DNA

DNA is unique in its ability to replicate, or copy, itself. When a cell divides (reproduces), DNA information is passed on unchanged. During replication, the DNA strands separate, and DNA building blocks, nucleotides, line up, matching the original sequence of bases to form two new and identical DNA molecules.

*New strand*

*Original strand*

*Cytosine–guanine base pair*

*Adenine–thymine base pair*

*Two strands coil round each other to form a double helix.*

*Nucleotide*

*Replication fork*

**DNA replication**

*Original double helix, or parent DNA molecule*

## Chromosomes

A chromosome is a thread-like structure found in the nucleus of a cell. Chromosomes store DNA and carry DNA molecules when a cell reproduces by dividing. Most human cells contain 46 chromosomes, divided into 23 pairs; 23 chromosomes are derived from each of the parents.

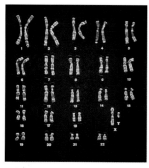

**Chromosomes, stained and paired**

### Chromosome defects

A chromosome defect can result from the wrong number of chromosomes, a missing piece of chromosome, or an unnecessary extra piece. Alternatively, there may be a "mistake" in part of the DNA. Any of these can cause a genetic disorder before or after birth, or later in life.

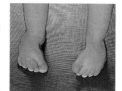

**Genetic defect causes malformed feet.**

*An albino squirrel is a mutation.*

### Mutations

A mutation is an accidental change in the structure of part of a DNA molecule, or sometimes in the number or shape of chromosomes. Mutations may result in new or unusual characteristics.

### Variations

While members of a species look similar, they are not identical, as we can see from people around us. Variation happens because each individual receives a unique combination of DNA from its parents during reproduction.

**Variations in types of flowers**

## Genes

A gene is the basic unit of inheritance, a small segment of a DNA molecule. There are about 100,000 genes in the 46 human chromosomes. Genes contain the instructions to construct proteins, which control cell activities. Therefore, genes help to determine the characteristics of an organism.

### Genotype and phenotype

The genotype is the overall genetic blueprint for an organism. The phenotype is what an organism actually looks like, based on genotype and environment.

### Alleles

Each gene has two or more forms called alleles. They control the same characteristic (for example, eye color) but different versions of it (for instance, blue or brown).

### Franklin, Watson, and Crick

The discovery of the DNA molecule was a collaborative effort. Rosalind Franklin (1920–58) completed groundbreaking work, which was consolidated in 1953 by Francis Crick (b. 1916), James Watson (b. 1928), and Maurice Wilkins (b. 1916). Watson, Crick, and Wilkins shared the 1962 Nobel Prize.

James Watson, American biologist

Rosalind Franklin, British biochemist

Francis Crick, British scientist

**Gray-blue eye,** round-shaped, with long eyelashes, and large eyelid

**Dark brown eye,** almond-shaped, with short eyelashes

**Medium-brown eye** with fine eyelashes, and small eyelid

*A length of DNA molecule*

# Heredity

Heredity is the transmission of characteristics from one generation to the next. These inherited characteristics, such as size, shape, and color, are determined by genes passed on by parents. When different forms of the same genetic characteristic meet (for example, blue and brown eye color), some genes are dominant (effective) and some are recessive (ineffective).

**Family inheritance**

*Children inherit genetic traits and characteristics from parents.*

*Each child is unique because it inherits a different mix of genes from its parents.*

*Each child resembles, but is not identical to, its parents.*

## Sex chromosomes

Whether an animal is male or female is determined by one pair of chromosomes called the sex chromosomes. In humans and other mammals, a female's sex chromosomes are identical and are called XX. In males, one chromosome is smaller, and the pair is called XY.

Human X chromosome

*Mutation in gene in this area causes a form of muscular dystrophy.*

*Mutation in gene here causes an eye disease.*

*Mutation in gene here causes cleft palate.*

*Mutation in gene here causes hemophilia, a disease that affects blood clotting.*

**Sex determination**
Sperm and eggs each carry one sex chromosome. Eggs carry an X chromosome, and sperm carry an X or a Y. When a sperm and an egg meet during fertilization, there is a 50:50 chance of producing a male (XY) or a female (XX), depending on which chromosome the sperm is carrying.

Most ginger cats are male.

Tortoise-shell cats are always female.

**Sex-linked inheritance**
Sex chromosomes also carry genes that determine characteristics other than an animal's sex. More of these sex-linked genes are found on X chromosomes than Y. So some characteristics are specific to only males or females.

---

*Parent's genotype: two dominant alleles*

*Sex cell genotype*

*Sex cell genotype*

*Parent's genotype: two recessive alleles*

RR

R

r

rr

**Pink flower**

R

*Sex cell genotype*

Rr

r

**White flower**

*Sex cell genotype: parent genotype divides during reproduction*

*Frame containing four offspring of pink parent with white parent*

Rr

Rr

Rr

Rr

### Dominant genes
If two forms of the same gene, alleles, are present in the same cell, only the dominant gene exerts its effect. In this case, R, the gene that controls pink flower color, is the dominant gene, so the color white remains recessive.

*Parent's genotype*

*Sex cell genotype*

*Sex cell genotype*

*Parent's genotype*

Rr

R

R

Rr

*Parent with one dominant gene and one recessive gene*

*Sex cell genotype*

r

RR

r

*Parent with one dominant gene and one recessive gene*

*Sex cell genotype*

*White flower color produced by two recessive genes*

Rr

Rr

rr

### Recessive genes
A recessive gene is one of a pair of alleles that, if present in a cell with its dominant partner, does not exert its effect. If two recessive genes are in the cell, however, they prove effective. In this case, r, the gene that controls white flower color, is recessive until it meets another recessive gene: together they are effective.

**Diagrams show fertilization between two parent flowers, and how genes determine color in offspring.**

---

## Genetic code

DNA contains the instructions to make the proteins that construct the cell and control its functions. Four chemical bases – adenine (A), cytosine (C), guanine (G), and thymine (T) – combine in pairs to form a sequence, or code. The cell then translates this code and produces a protein.

### Human Genome Project
The genome is the complete set of genes found in the nucleus of every body cell. In the 1980s the Human Genome Project set out to identify all of those genes by working out the sequence of bases. In 2001 they announced the existence of around 30,000 genes.

**Genetic codes are made up of bases (A, C, G, T).**

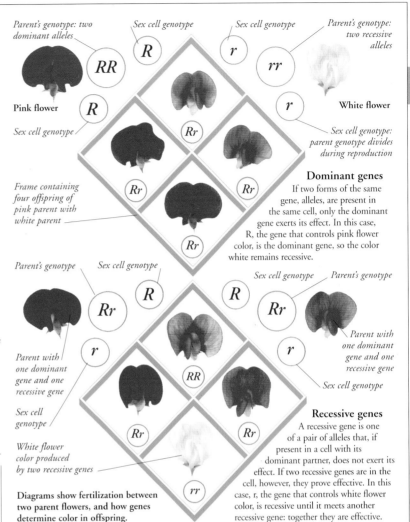

## Genetic engineering

Genetic engineering involves taking genes from one cell and inserting them into another cell. This gives the cell new characteristics, which are determined by the transferred gene. In the future, genetic engineering may be used on human cells, so that genetic disorders can be eliminated.

### Genetically engineered food
Food products can also be altered by genetic modification. For example, scientists can genetically engineer certain fruits and vegetables, so that they do not rot so quickly. There is much debate about the safety of genetically engineered foods.

Genetically engineered tomatoes

---

FIND OUT MORE    BIOLOGY    CELLS    DISEASES    FOOD    HUMAN BODY    PLANTS, REPRODUCTION    REPRODUCTION

# GEOLOGY

G

PEOPLE ONCE THOUGHT that the Earth was just a ball of rock. More recently geologists have shown that it is much more complex. Geology is the study of the Earth's history, structure, and composition. Originally only the study of rocks and rock structures, the subject of geology broadened after the discovery in the 1960s that the Earth's crust is made up of giant, continually moving plates. These plates affect everything from the creation of continents to the eruption of volcanoes. The science of geology also helps us locate mineral reserves and understand our environment.

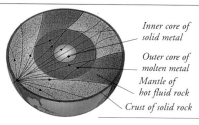

**Structure of the Earth**
Geophysicists and geochemists study the structure of the Earth. Geophysicists focus on its physical processes, such as the circulation of heat deep inside; geochemists study the Earth's chemical composition.

*Inner core of solid metal*
*Outer core of molten metal*
*Mantle of hot fluid rock*
*Crust of solid rock*

### James Hutton
Scottish-born James Hutton (1726–97) was the founder of modern geology. With his collection and analysis of rock formations, he proved that the Earth was more than just a few thousand years old and that all its rocks and landforms had been formed over millions of years.

**Seismographs**
The seismic waves, earthquake vibrations, are picked up by seismographs. These can reveal to geologists the structure of the rock they have passed through.

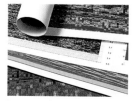

**Seismographs**

## Rock and field geology
Petrology is the study of rocks and minerals. Surveys and rock samples indicate the occurrence of different rocks beneath the landscape, their structure, and their history.

**The rock strata**
Many rocks were formed in strata (layers) of sediment deposited on the seabed. Stratigraphy is the study of these layers. A break in a sequence of rock layers is called an unconformity, shown as a red line on the models below.

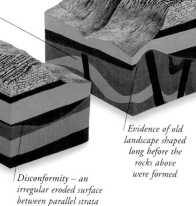

*Limestone pavement*

*Angular unconformity – the older rock strata below the unconformity are at a different angle to the new layers.*

*Parallel conformity – strata either side of unconformity dip at the same angle*

*Evidence of old landscape shaped long before the rocks above were formed*

*Disconformity – an irregular eroded surface between parallel strata*

**Rock strata models**

*Nonconformity – strata overlie eroded surface of igneous or metamorphic rock.*

Key to strata:
- ⬛ Shale
- ⬜ Conglomerate
- ⬛ Red Sandstone
- ╱ Unconformity
- ⬛ Igneous rock
- ⬛ Mudstone
- ⬛ Clay
- ⬛ Sandstone

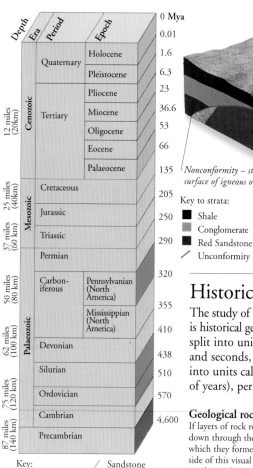

| Depth | Era | Period | Epoch | Mya |
|---|---|---|---|---|
| | | | | 0 |
| | | | | 0.01 |
| 12 miles (20km) | Cenozoic | Quaternary | Holocene | 1.6 |
| | | | Pleistocene | 6.3 |
| | | Tertiary | Pliocene | 23 |
| | | | Miocene | 36.6 |
| | | | Oligocene | 53 |
| | | | Eocene | 66 |
| | | | Palaeocene | 135 |
| 25 miles (40km) | Mesozoic | Cretaceous | | 205 |
| 37 miles (60 km) | | Jurassic | | 250 |
| | | Triassic | | 290 |
| 50 miles (80 km) | Palaeozoic | Permian | | 320 |
| | | Carboniferous | Pennsylvanian (North America) | 355 |
| 62 miles (100 km) | | | Mississippian (North America) | 410 |
| | | Devonian | | 438 |
| 75 miles (120 km) | | Silurian | | 510 |
| | | Ordovician | | 570 |
| 87 miles (140 km) | | Cambrian | | 4,600 |
| | | Precambrian | | |

Key:
- ╱ Mud
- ╱ Limestone
- ╱ Sandstone
- ╱ Shale
- ╱ Metamorphic

**Tools**
In order to examine the Earth's structure, geologists need some basic tools such as goggles to protect their eyes from flying rock chips and a hammer and chisel for collecting rock samples.

*Geologist's hammers*
*Chisels*
*Goggles*
*Club hammer for use with chisels*

## Historical geology
The study of rocks of the Earth's crust is historical geology. Just as the day is split into units called hours, minutes, and seconds, geological history is split into units called eras (lasting millions of years), periods, and epochs.

**Geological rock column**
If layers of rock remained undisturbed, a column cut down through the layers would reveal the sequence in which they formed. The rock types shown along the side of this visual representation of geological time are the predominant rocks of each period.

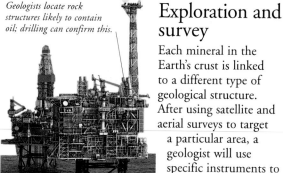

*Geologists locate rock structures likely to contain oil; drilling can confirm this.*

## Exploration and survey
Each mineral in the Earth's crust is linked to a different type of geological structure. After using satellite and aerial surveys to target a particular area, a geologist will use specific instruments to pinpoint the mineral.

**FIND OUT MORE** • EARTH • EARTHQUAKES • EARTH SCIENCES • FOSSILS • ROCKS AND MINERALS • VOLCANOES

# GERMANY

THE FEDERAL REPUBLIC of Germany lies at the heart of Europe, bounded by nine other nations and the Baltic and North Seas. Since the country was reunified in 1990, it is, more than ever, a link between east and west both economically and culturally. Germany is one of the world's wealthiest nations and Europe's leading industrial power. It was a founding member of the European Union and plays a key role in international affairs. Germany has the second largest population in Europe.

## Physical features

Germany has a varied landscape. It includes lakes, hills, and islands in the north, fertile pastures and great forests in the center and southwest, and great mountains such as the Bavarian Alps in the south.

## GERMANY FACTS

CAPITAL CITY Berlin

AREA 137,800 sq miles (356,910 sq km)

POPULATION 82,200,000

MAIN LANGUAGE German

MAJOR RELIGION Christian

CURRENCY Euro

LIFE EXPECTANCY 78 years

PEOPLE PER DOCTOR 286

GOVERNMENT Multiparty democracy

ADULT LITERACY 99%

### Rhine River
The Rhine is one of Europe's most important rivers. It rises in the Swiss Alps and flows into the North Sea at Rotterdam in the Netherlands. Its length is about 820 miles (1,320 km), nearly half of which is in Germany. Long barges regularly carry freight such as coal, grain, and timber. Many tourists visit the southern part of the Rhine to see the scenery, vineyards, and castles that are built on its banks.

### Black Forest
Germany's Black Forest lies in the southwestern part of the country. The name comes from the dark conifers that rise from its mountain slopes and provide timber for the traditional wooden houses. Tourists flock to the region, attracted by the beauty of the scenery, spa resorts, and nearby Lake Constance.

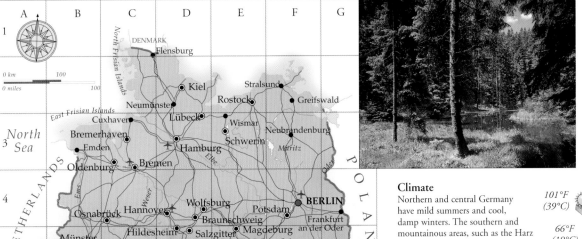

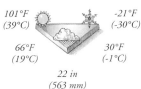

### Climate
Northern and central Germany have mild summers and cool, damp winters. The southern and mountainous areas, such as the Harz Mountains, the Black Forest, and Bavaria have much hotter summers and cold winters with heavy snow.

101°F (39°C)  -21°F (-30°C)  66°F (19°C)  30°F (-1°C)  22 in (563 mm)

### Land use
Germany has relatively few natural resources, and forest covers almost half the country. Most of the land is fertile and is used for growing crops or raising livestock.

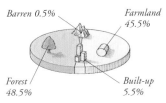

Barren 0.5%  Farmland 45.5%  Forest 48.5%  Built-up 5.5%

### Berlin
The Brandenburg Gate in Berlin symbolizes the reunification of Germany in 1990 when the Berlin Wall, built after World War II (1939–45) to separate East and West, was demolished. Always a thriving center of art and culture, and Germany's largest city, it is in the process of rebuilding.

Brandenburg Gate

G

# People

About 92 percent of the people are Germans. The total immigrant population in Germany is around 7,400,000. Turks, who came to Germany in the 1960s to boost the labor force, form the largest minority group and number around 2,100,000. Discrimination has caused social tension.

225 per sq km (583 per sq mile)   86% Urban   14% Rural

**Society**
German society prides itself on equal opportunities and a comprehensive social welfare system, with free education and health care. Germans are environmentally aware, and the influence of the Green Party has led to strict anti-pollution legislation.

# Leisure

The Germans love sports and outdoor activities. Many enjoy hiking and cycling in the countryside, or canoeing and sailing on the lakes and rivers. In winter, skiing and skating are popular. Germans also excel at soccer, tennis, and automobile racing.

**Skiing**
Snow-covered slopes in the Bavarian Alps provide Germans with plenty of opportunities to practice their skiing. Children begin the sport early. Many people also travel to nearby French and Swiss ski resorts.

**Soccer**
The German national team has won the World Cup three times, as well as the Euro '96 cup against the Czech Republic. Soccer is the most popular sport in Germany both for players and spectators, and there are many clubs.

# Farming

Only three percent of Germany's workforce farms, yet the country grows about two-thirds of all the food it needs. Crops include grains, potatoes, and other vegetables. Pigs and cattle are the main farm animals.

Grapes

**Crops**
Germany's chief grain crops are barley, oats, rye, and wheat. Sugar beet that is refined to make sugar is also widely grown. Grapes grow best in the areas bordering the Rhine and Moselle rivers, and are used for producing Germany's world-famous white wines.

Wheat

Sugar beet

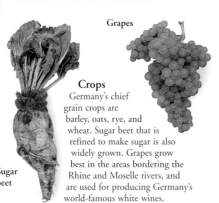

**Dairy**
The lush green pastures of Germany's Allgäu valley in the Alps are ideal for grazing dairy cattle for milk, butter, and cheese.

# Food

German people enjoy traditional smoked sausages, smoked meats and cheese, *sauerkraut* (pickled cabbage), and smoked and pickled fish, usually eaten with good sourdough bread and a glass of cold beer. They also make tasty soups, sweet and savory dumplings, and enjoy afternoon *Kaffee und Kuchen*, coffee with cakes.

*Lid keeps flies out of beer.*

*Gherkin*   *Salami*

*Wurst*

*Smoked sausage*

Beer stein   Selection of meats   *Bread*

# Industry

Over the last 50 years, Germany has become one of the world's leading industrial nations, and it is an important manufacturer of vehicles, electrical goods, ships, and chemicals. The heart of German industry lies in the Ruhr, once a coal-producing region.

**Cars**
Germany is one of the world's largest car manufacturers. Volkswagen is an internationally known make. Other famous makes are BMW, Mercedes-Benz, and Porsche.

# Transportation

Germany has an excellent transportation system with 14 international airports, major seaports in Hamburg and Bremen, and a highly efficient rail and road network. Rivers, such as the Rhine and Ruhr, carry as much freight as highways.

**Inland waterways**
Many of Germany's rivers are linked by canals, like the Danube-Main canal, creating a waterway that makes long distance freight hauling practical.

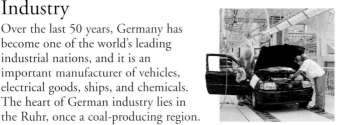

**Shipbuilding**
Hamburg, Germany's largest port on the mouth of the Elbe River, has a long tradition of shipbuilding, as has Bremen at the mouth of the Weser River. Germany leads the rest of Europe in shipbuilding and ranks highly in the world.

**Precision work**
Electronic devices such as calculators and computers, and electrical equipment like this drill, form a large part of Germany's industrial output. The country also produces precision optical equipment.

**Autobahns**
Germany has Europe's most elaborate highway system, stretching almost 7,084 miles (11,400 km), with no speed limit. The first *Autobahn* was built in the 1930s for military use.

**FIND OUT MORE**   CARS AND TRUCKS   EUROPE   EUROPE, HISTORY OF   EUROPEAN UNION   FARMING   FOOTBALL   GERMANY, HISTORY OF   PORTS AND WATERWAYS   SHIPS AND BOATS   WINTER SPORTS

# GERMANY, HISTORY OF

ALTHOUGH THERE HAVE ALWAYS been German speakers living in Europe, a single German country did not exist until 1871. For much of its history, Germany consisted of many small kingdoms, duchies, and other states, kept apart by rivalries. Unification was eventually achieved under the diplomatic and military leadership of the north German state of Prussia. German industrial strength allowed the new nation to dominate Europe, but defeat in two world wars left the country divided again. In 1990, Germany reunited, and once more became the major economic power of Europe.

### German tribes
In about 370, Huns from Asia swept into Germany, forcing native German tribes to pour into the neighbouring Roman Empire. Within a century, Rome had collapsed, and Germanic tribes such as the Visigoths and Franks controlled much of western Europe.

Brooch made by Germanic Lombard tribe

## Medieval Germany

In 962, Otto I of Saxony united the German kingdoms in the Holy Roman Empire. This empire was long-lasting but weak, as local rulers fought to protect and increase their own power. Despite this disunity, the country became increasingly rich. By the late 15th century, German cities such as Augsburg controlled European banking and finance.

Seal of Hamburg

### Hanseatic League
The cities of northern Germany worked together to support their trading interests. In 1241, Lübeck and Hamburg concluded a treaty that led to the growth of the Hanseatic League, a trading alliance that dominated commerce in northern Europe. At its height there were 160 cities in the League.

Ulm cathedral

### Coming of Christianity
From the 5th century onwards, individual Germans became Christian. Some churches, such as Ulm Cathedral, were founded in the early 7th century, but it was not until the mission of St Boniface in the early 8th century that most of the people converted to Christianity.

Isenheim Altarpiece, by Mathias Grünewald

### German Renaissance
In the 15th century, the Renaissance spread to Germany. Artists such as Albrecht Dürer (1471–1528) perfected the technique of the woodcut, Hans Holbein (1498–1543), working mostly in Switzerland and England, produced superb portraits, and Mathias Grünewald (1480–1528) painted religious masterpieces.

## Peasants' War

In the 16th century, there was much tension between Catholics and Protestants in Germany. In 1524, peasants in southern Germany exploited the confusion to rise up and demand social reforms. The revolt was crushed in 1526.

## Thirty Years' War

In 1618, a revolt broke out in the Protestant province of Bohemia against the rule of the Catholic Habsburgs. War spread through Germany as Protestant princes rebelled against the Habsburgs. Other nations, notably France and Sweden, entered the war on the Protestant side to end Habsburg domination of Europe.

*Inscription says that the owner "Fights for God".*

### Treaties of Westphalia
When the treaties ended the Thirty Years' War in 1648, German agriculture and commerce were in ruins, and the population had been reduced by half. The Habsburgs were seriously weakened by the years of conflict and Germany was more disunited than ever before, split into no fewer than 234 states and 51 independent cities.

German rapier of the 1630s

| Prussian by 1648 | ☐ |
| Prussian by 1772 | ▨ |

Prussian lands in Europe

### Rise of Prussia
Prussia was one of the few German states to emerge from the Thirty Years' War with increased power. Under successive rulers, Prussian territory expanded across most of northern Germany and, by 1795, also included western Poland.

### Frederick the Great
Frederick, King of Prussia from 1740–86, laid the foundations of later Prussian greatness. An inspired military leader, his diplomacy enabled Prussia to expand by outwitting Austria and Russia. At his death, Prussia was Europe's foremost power.

Peasant rebellion in southern Germany

# German unification

After Napoleon's defeat in 1815, many Germans wanted to unite as one nation. A confederation of states was set up, but it was too weak to last. In 1861, Wilhelm I became king of Prussia. Prussia's strength grew, and the other German states agreed to unite with Prussia. At last, in 1871, Wilhelm was made emperor of a united Germany.

### Prussian power
A strong army gave Prussia the power to defeat France in the Franco-Prussian War of 1870–71. Prussian strength also enabled the newly united Germany to negotiate a powerful and advantageous alliance with Austria-Hungary and Russia in 1881. This gave Germany great influence throughout the Continent.

Prussian army officer's helmet

## Bismarck

Otto von Bismarck (1815–98) became chief minister of Prussia in 1862. In a brilliant series of diplomatic and military campaigns, he removed all foreign influence from Germany, making Prussia the leading German state. He was chancellor of Germany for 19 years.

# Imperial Germany

Under Wilhelm I and Wilhelm II, Germany became the leading power in Europe. Germany sought its "place in the sun" by acquiring colonies in Africa, China, and the Pacific, but its aggressive foreign policy led to world war in 1914 and the collapse of its empire in 1918.

Factories, Ruhr Valley

### Industrialization
Between 1870 and 1914, Germany's population rose from 33 to 65 million, and its industrial output quadrupled. The Ruhr Valley became the center of large iron, coal, steel, and armaments industries. This industrial power helped Germany become the most powerful state in Europe by 1914, and helped provide resources and finances for World War I.

Chair by Bauhaus designer Marcel Breuer

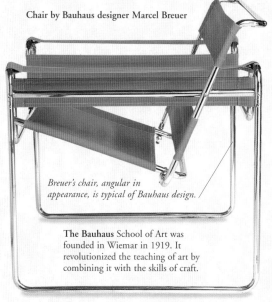

*Breuer's chair, angular in appearance, is typical of Bauhaus design.*

**The Bauhaus** School of Art was founded in Wiemar in 1919. It revolutionized the teaching of art by combining it with the skills of craft.

Nazi swastika and eagle badge

Badge of the SS, the Nazi security force

# Weimar Germany

In 1918, following its defeat in World War I, Germany became a republic. A new constitution was agreed in 1919 in the town of Weimar, where the National Assembly met until it moved back to Berlin in 1920. However, Germany was badly affected by economic problems in the 1920s and by 1932, over 5 million people were unemployed.

Statuette of soldier

### The rise of the Nazis
The unfavorable terms of the peace settlement after World War I, together with the economic failures of the 1930s saw Germany crippled by high unemployment and hyper-inflation, and led to a desire for change among the people. Support grew for the Nazis, an extreme nationalist party led by Adolf Hitler that took power in 1933. The Nazis promised to rebuild Germany's strength and power. It was Hilter's imperialist ambitions that were one of the causes of World War II.

# Modern Germany

After World War II, the country was occupied by French, British, US, and Russian troops. In 1949, Germany was divided in two, with a communist, Russian-backed state in the east and US-backed capitalism in the west. Living conditions in West Germany were much better than in the east.

Housing complex, East Germany

### Reunification
In the late 1980s, Russian control over East Germany weakened. The Berlin Wall, which divided the former capital, was taken down in 1989, and free access between the two countries was guaranteed for the first time. By October 1990, the two halves of Germany were politically united once more.

*People flocked to Berlin to see The Wall come down.*

Demolition of the Berlin Wall

# Timeline

The medieval castle of Pfalz

**962** Otto I of Saxony establishes Holy Roman Empire.

**1241** Hamburg and Lübeck combine to form Hanseatic League; German trade prospers.

**1517** German monk Martin Luther begins Protestant Reformation.

**1618–48** Thirty Years' War devastates Germany.

**1740–86** Frederick the Great rules Prussia.

**1815–66** German Confederation tries to unite Germany.

**1871** Wilhelm I is made German emperor.

**1871–90** Bismarck governs as chancellor.

**1914–18** Germany fights in World War I, is defeated, and empire collapses.

**1919** Weimar Republic is established.

Banknote, 1931

**1931** German economy crashes; prices rise, the currency becomes worthless, and many suffer unemployment.

**1939–45** Germany fights in World War II.

**1949** Germany divided into East and West.

**1990** East and West Germany reunited as a single state.

**FIND OUT MORE**  ARMIES  BARBARIANS  COLD WAR  EUROPE, CENTRAL  EUROPE, HISTORY OF  FRANCE, HISTORY OF  HOLOCAUST  HOLY ROMAN EMPIRE  WORLD WAR I  WORLD WAR II

# GERONIMO

A CENTURY AFTER the native people of North America fought the white settlers to stay on their land, one name is remembered above all others. As a fearless warrior, Geronimo had no equals. In his early 20s, he lost his entire family to Mexican raiders, and he determined to fight to the death to safeguard his Apache way of life. Only in old age, defeated by the armament of the US government, did he surrender. He ended his days as a wealthy farmer, revered by people across the US.

## Early life
Geronimo was born in about 1829 in Arizona. He was a member of the Mimbreño Apache tribe, and his Apache name was Goyanthlay. Spaniards called him Geronimo.

### Massacre
In 1858, a band of Mexican raiders killed Geronimo's mother, wife, and children. Geronimo was filled with a deep hatred of white people, and decided to spend the rest of his life fighting for his people.

Native American encampment

## Apaches
The Apaches lived among the arid mountains and deserts of the southwest. Because their land was unsuitable for farming, they earned a living hunting and raiding for food. This brought them into conflict with the many settlers who were moving into the area from Mexico and the eastern US.

### The young warrior
As a young warrior, Geronimo was trained to shoot, track enemies or wild animals across the land, map out a new and unfamiliar terrain, and survive for days away from camp. He also learned the skill of traveling through the countryside over vast distances without being observed. For recreation, he took part in Apache games such as the loop-and-pole game (left), arrow shooting, and wrestling.

## Reservations
As white settlers pushed west, Native Americans were forced into special areas called reservations. The Native Americans were therefore excluded from their traditional lands and prevented from roaming over vast areas as they had done before. In response, many tribes broke out and raided neighboring areas.

### San Carlos reservation
In 1877, Geronimo and 16 of his warriors were captured by US forces and marched 400 miles to the San Carlos reservation in Arizona. The new reservation was brutal and corrupt, with suppliers making vast fortunes at the expense of the native inhabitants. Many resentful and half-starved Apaches left the reservation to go on raids.

*Sharp metal blade*

*Bowl of pipe*

*Ornately carved wooden shaft*

### Warfare
Geronimo was a skilled warrior who sometimes had to fight for his life. With only a small group of followers, he managed to tie down large numbers of US law enforcers. His ability to move quickly and quietly across the land, thus avoiding detection, created great fear among local settlers. If he was followed, he and his men would split up. Their understanding of the country enabled them to vanish into the bush.

### Raiding
US officials tried to reform the San Carlos reservation, but Geronimo and his followers continued their raiding. Overwhelmed by the superior force of the US Army, Geronimo was forced to surrender in 1886.

Geronimo (far right) before his surrender

Apache tomahawk pipe

### Fort Sill
After his surrender, Geronimo was sent first to Florida, then Alabama, and finally, in 1894, to Fort Sill, Oklahoma. He sold native American handicrafts, became a farmer, adopted Christianity, and appeared at the 1904 St. Louis World's Fair, and in President Theodore Roosevelt's inaugural parade in 1905. To the end of his life, he hoped to return to his native southwestern mountains.

### GERONIMO

c.1829 Born in Arizona.

early 1850s Raiders kill his family.

late 1850s Accepts Cochise, head of the Chiricahuas, as his leader, and marries a Chiricahua wife.

1876 Retreats into the Sierra Madre mountains and raids both sides of the US–Mexican border.

1877 Confined to the San Carlos reservation, but continues to raid the surrounding lands.

1886 Surrenders; exiled to Florida.

1894 Confined to Fort Sill.

1909 Dies at Fort Sill.

FIND OUT MORE   HUMAN RIGHTS   NATIVE AMERICANS   UNITED STATES, HISTORY OF

# GIRAFFES

WITH ITS MASSIVE neck and long legs, the giraffe is the world's tallest animal. Despite its ungainly appearance, it is very graceful. Giraffes live in the savannahs of Africa – grasslands with a few trees and bushes. Their distribution closely follows that of the acacia trees on which they feed. They avoid open grassland because of their feeding habits and because their size makes them conspicuous in the open. There is only one species of giraffe, but eight subspecies, which differ mainly in the color and pattern of their coats.

*Thick, rubbery lips and saliva protect a giraffe's tongue and mouth from thorns.*

*An adult male giraffe can stand 17.5 ft (5.3 m) high.*

*Short mane*

*The giraffe's long neck has the same number of vertebrae as other mammals, but they are larger.*

*Hoof*

*Reticulated giraffe*

*Reticulated giraffes have regular russet-colored markings.*

## Grazing

The giraffe's great height is a specialized adaptation for grazing the upper branches of trees. Leaves and small twigs form the greater part of the giraffe's diet. It also eats shoots, flowers, fruit, seed pods, and even bark, but never grass. Many acacias and other trees have vicious thorns to discourage grazing, but the giraffe's tongue is well equipped to get past such strong defenses.

## Drinking

For an animal as tall as the giraffe, drinking presents special problems. To lower its head the giraffe has either to bend its knees forward or to extend its forelegs out to either side. This awkward posture greatly reduces the animal's field of vision, leaving it vulnerable to attack.

## Features of a giraffe

Massive shoulder blades carry the huge muscles that support the giraffe's head and long neck. Its hind legs are shorter than its forelegs, but the angle of the back makes them appear shorter than they really are. By breaking up its outline against its surroundings, a giraffe's coat markings help camouflage it.

## Herds

Giraffes usually live in small groups of up to about 12 females and their calves. Adult males live apart and visit the herd only for mating. Occasionally, giraffes gather together in large groups of up to 70 animals that stay together for a few days, or sometimes just a few hours.

*Giraffes have exceptionally good eyesight.*

*Standing still and staring toward a potential threat acts as a warning sign of danger.*

### Coat markings

Giraffe markings range from regular geometric patterns to irregular fuzzy-edged patterns. Old males darken with age and may become almost jet black.

Reticulated giraffe

Rothschild's giraffe

Masai giraffe

*Median horn*

*The horns are covered with hairy skin.*

*Horns grow on the crown of the head above the eyes.*

*Large nostrils*

### Horns

Giraffes of both sexes have a pair of short, stubby horns, about 12 in (30 cm) in length in an adult male. Some giraffes, such as the reticulated giraffe, have a third (median) horn in the middle. Rothschild's giraffe also has a small pair of horns behind the ears and is often called the five-horned giraffe.

### Necking

Necking is a form of ritualized sparring that determines dominance within a group. It begins with one bull challenging another by advancing toward it with its head held high, legs rigid, and neck erect. After much preliminary jostling, one bull swings its head in a huge arc in an attempt to strike its opponent's neck with its head.

*Giraffe's neck is very flexible.*

## Okapi

The giraffe's only living relative, the okapi, is a much smaller animal, with shorter limbs and neck. While the giraffe lives in herds for mutual protection and is active by day, the forest-dwelling okapi is a solitary animal, active by night. It lives in the tropical rain forests of Zaire. The okapi's vision is poor, but its hearing and sense of smell are acute and more useful in the forests, where visibility is limited.

*Only males have horns*

*Large ears*

*Deep chestnut-colored coat*

*Creamy white or light gray markings help camouflage the okapi.*

*Striped legs*

*Hoof*

### RETICULATED GIRAFFE

**SCIENTIFIC NAME** *Giraffa camelopardalis reticulata*

**ORDER** Artiodactyla

**FAMILY** Giraffidae

**DISTRIBUTION** Africa south of the Sahara

**HABITAT** The savanna

**DIET** Leaves, shoots, small twigs, flowers, and fruit

**SIZE** Height: males 17.5 ft (5.3 m); females 15 ft (4.5 m)

**LIFESPAN** 25 years

FIND OUT MORE

AFRICAN WILDLIFE   CAMOUFLAGE AND COLOR   GRASSLAND WILDLIFE   MAMMALS   PLANTS, DEFENSE   RAIN FOREST WILDLIFE

# GLACIATION

THE SHAPING OF THE LANDSCAPE by ice is called glaciation. All over the world there are landscape features that were formed during past ice ages by glaciers, huge moving rivers of ice, and even bigger mounds of ice called ice sheets. In cold places, such as the polar regions, glaciers and ice sheets are still present, and glaciation still continues. The landscape created by ice is dramatic. Glaciers carve out deep, troughlike valleys, ice sheets pile up huge quantities of debris, and the icy conditions can shatter rock into jagged peaks and razor-sharp ridges.

## How a glacier forms

Glaciers are created when layers of snow are compacted in icy mountain regions to form rivers of ice, which slowly creep downhill until they melt. The ice on the surface of a glacier cracks, forming deep crevasses, and both the surface and the underside of a glacier are covered with debris plucked away from the valley sides by the sheer weight of the passing ice.

### Valley glaciers

In high mountain ranges, such as the Alps and the Himalayas, glaciers form in valleys as snow slides from the peaks of the mountains. These are called alpine glaciers. Where these emerge from the mountains, they may cause piedmont glaciers, so called because they spread out in the shape of a foot.

*Cirque, the deep hollow where the glacier begins*

*Frost shatters rocky summits into jagged "horn peaks."*

Valley glacier, Norway

*Bergschrund, the deep crack at the head of a glacier*

*This glacially carved edge is called an arête.*

*Arête is frost-shattered and hence knife-edged.*

### Glacial erosion

Glaciers have immense erosive power. In some places, erosion works through abrasion; the moving ice acts like sandpaper, scraping away the rock with the huge amount of rock debris trapped in its base. Sometimes, it simply sweeps away loose rocks shattered by the cold. Occasionally, snow freezes around the rocks and literally picks them up.

*Frost-shattered rock falls onto the ice as lateral moraine along the side of the glacier.*

*Medial moraine – a band of moraine formed as two glaciers flow together*

*Ice fills the valley.*

*Crevasses fill with debris and water.*

*Debris is swept along beneath the glacier.*

### U-shaped valley

It takes many thousands of years, but over time a glacier can carve out a very distinctive, deep, U-shaped trough of a valley. If the valley reaches the coast and fills with seawater, it is called a fjord.

*Huge quantities of subglacial moraine are swept along underneath the glacier.*

*Ice fall, where the ice flows over a step in the valley floor*

### Traces of glaciation

Glaciers carry huge quantities of debris, called moraine, which either fall onto the glacier from the mountains above or are swept away from the rock beneath. The moving ice pushes this debris into giant piles, or leaves it scattered over the landscape when the ice melts.

*Lateral moraine forms terraces along the valley side.*

*Holes in the ice fill with debris left behind when the ice melts.*

*Subglacial streams often leave winding ridges of debris called eskers.*

*Meltwater lakes fill up behind debris in front of the glacier.*

*Terminal moraine is the band of debris across the snout of a glacier.*

*Lower end of the glacier*

*Melt-water chamber*

*Drumlins are half-egg shaped piles of subglacial moraine.*

### Fjords

Fjords are steep-sided, narrow coastal inlets, formed where glaciers have ground out deep valleys along existing riverbeds. When the ice melted, the sea level rose and flooded the valleys. The coast of Norway has many fjords.

**G**

## Snowline

Above a certain height, called the snowline, the air is so cold that the snow never melts. In the tropics, the snowline is well over 16,000 ft (5,000 m) but comes down to 1,900 ft (600 m) in Greenland and is at sea level at the north and south poles.

*Mount Kilimanjaro, Tanzania*

## Avalanches

The snow cover on steep slopes is often far from stable. If the layers are not well compacted, even a slight disturbance – a falling rock, a skier, or even a shout – can make an entire snowfield collapse in an avalanche.

*A powder snow avalanche such as this can produce shock waves powerful enough to explode buildings.*

## Ice sheets and caps

Ice sheets are huge layers of ice, thousands of feet thick, that may cover not just a single valley but an entire continent. Ice caps are smaller dome-shaped sheets of ice that cover a mountain. The sheets of ice over Antarctica and Greenland are also called ice caps. The ice deep within the polar ice caps first fell as snow many millions of years ago.

**Formation of an ice cap**
Ice caps form gradually by accumulation as snow falls, stays frozen, and is compacted by the addition of new snow. Some ice is lost by "ablation" (melting and evaporation), but if the ice is formed faster than it is lost, then the ice cap grows.

**1** An ice cap forms when the snow covering a peak remains frozen all year.

**2** Fresh snowfalls compact the snow beneath, turning it into dense crystals.

**3** Eventually the lower layers are compacted into solid opaque ice.

**Ice sheets** are thousands of feet deep but vary in extent between the seasons.

**Isolated mountaintops** jutting through the surface of an ice cap are called nunataks.

*Glacier moves by sliding over melted ice.*

*Rocks under glacier are slowly eroded.*

*Ice fall – crevasses form where glacier flows over steep rock.*

### Icebergs

Icebergs are huge chunks of ice that have broken off from the edge of an ice sheet or glacier to float in the sea. They are generally rounded or blocklike in shape. Icebergs float because ice is less dense than water, but it is only a little less dense, so one-eighth of the iceberg is visible above the surface.

*Around 10,000 icebergs a year break away from the glaciers in Greenland.*

**When Arctic glaciers** reach the ocean, the tides and waves heave the ice up and down, cracking bits off to float away as icebergs, a process known as calving.

*Only about 12 percent of an iceberg is visible above the surface of the ocean.*

**Icebergs** may be broad and tabular (flat). They are often hundreds of miles long and may last for years before melting.

*It is estimated that the average age of the ice in an iceberg is 5,000 years.*

### Titanic disaster

Because most of an iceberg is hidden below the surface, it can pose a real hazard to ships if one drifts across sea lanes. In 1912, the luxury liner *Titanic* sank after a collision with an iceberg. Over 1,500 passengers and crew died.

### Louis Agassiz

Swiss-American geologist Louis Agassiz (1807–73) realized that past ice ages had shaped the landscape. In 1836, he noted that glaciers are not static, but move, and found rocks that had been scoured by glaciers. He concluded much of northern Europe had at one time been covered by ice.

*The extent of the ice cover during the last ice age.*

### Ice Age

There is no doubt that ice ages have occurred several times in the Earth's past. Some geologists believe they are linked to the variations in the energy reaching Earth from the Sun as the Earth wobbles and tilts in its orbit. Others think there may be some other trigger for an ice age.

# GLASS

FEW MATERIALS have the same remarkable properties as glass. It is transparent, easy to shape and clean, does not rot, and resists attack by most chemicals. Glass is also cheap to produce because it is made from sand, one of the most common materials on Earth. When sand is heated with other materials, it turns into a liquid, which, when cooled, solidifies into glass. Although the glass looks crystalline, it still has the structure of a liquid, and is termed a "supercooled" liquid.

### Ancient glass

Decorative glass objects have been found in ancient Egyptian tombs dating back to 2500 BC. After the invention of the blowpipe in about 100 BC, glass was made across the ancient world, particularly in Rome.

**Roman glassware, dating from 1st century AD**

## Types of glass

Three main ingredients are used to make glass: pure silica sand, soda ash, and lime. These are heated in a furnace to about 2,500 °F (1,400 °C), to produce soda-lime glass. This is the ordinary glass we use to make bottles and windows. Different kinds of glass can be made by adding other ingredients.

### Lead glass
Also called crystal, lead glass contains lead oxide, which makes it easy to cut. The cut glass exhibits a diamondlike sparkle.

**Lead crystal**

### Optical glass
Optical lenses are made from pure glass. A variety of substances, such as lead and titanium, are added to give glass its optical properties.

**Eyeglasses**

**Magnifying glass**

### Heat-resistant glass
Boron oxide is sometimes added in the glassmaking process to produce heat-resistant borosilicate glass.

**Heat-resistant glass jug**

### Fiberglass
Glass may sometimes take the form of fibers, used for loft insulation, reinforcement for plastics, and fiber-optic cables.

**Fiberglass**

### Stained glass
Stained glass is normally used to create decorative windows using pieces of colored glass set in a lead framework. Medieval stained glass may seem richer to the eye because it is full of impurities.

**Stained-glass window**

## Working glass

Glass is easy to work, but only when it is in a molten state. The most common method of shaping glass is blowing by craftsworkers or machines. Other methods include pressing molten glass into a mold, a traditional technique still used today, and casting it into a mold to make lenses.

### Sheet glass

Sheet glass was originally made by drawing a ribbon of molten glass vertically upward. However, this caused distortion. Today, it is made by floating molten glass on a bath of molten tin. This float glass is of even thickness throughout and shows no distortion.

**Glass building**

### Glassblowing
Most glassblowing is done mechanically, but traditional methods, shown in the following sequence, are still used for making special objects.

*Molten glass*

*Iron rod*

*Strong shears*

1 An iron rod is dipped into the furnace to pick up a gob (lump) of molten glass. The glassblower cuts off the correct quantity of glass needed using special glass shears, and drops it into a measuring mold.

*Measuring mold*

*Shaping mold into which the shaped parison is fitted.*

*Layers of steam protect and cushion the glass.*

*The bottle shows no signs of the joint between the two halves of the mold.*

**Blowing glass**

*The semifinished glass shape is called a parison.*

**Bottles ready to be recycled**

### Recycling glass
Glass is an easy material to recycle because it melts easily. It is recycled, not for the purpose of conservation, but to save energy because the original glassmaking process requires such high temperatures. In Europe alone, about four million tons of glass are recycled each year.

2 The glassblower picks up the molten glass from the measuring mold on a blowing-iron, then blows air through the iron to shape the glass and form a parison.

3 With further blowing, the glass expands and takes its final shape inside the mold. At the same time, the rod is spun to stop the object showing signs of joints from the mold.

4 The glassblower removes the final object from the mold and smooths the mouth of the bottle by reheating it in the furnace and shaping it.

 **FIND OUT MORE** | ARCHITECTURE | CHURCHES | CRYSTALS AND GEMS | EYES AND VISION | PLASTICS AND RUBBER | POLLUTION | ROCKS AND MINERALS | ROMAN EMPIRE

# GODS AND GODDESSES

SINCE PREHISTORIC TIMES, humans have worshipped gods and goddesses – spirits that are believed to control nature and human destinies. The mythology that surrounds them attempts to explain the how and why of life, and account for forces that are beyond human control. The rituals associated with these supernatural beings, or deities, are a powerful force in binding societies together. The variety of gods and goddesses worshipped around the world reflects the diversity and power of human imagination.

*Venus figure, c.4000 BC*

## Mother goddess

Every culture had a mother goddess, one of the earliest deities, who represented nature and fertility. In ancient Egypt, she was called Isis and may have been a model for the Christian Madonna.

**Hades and Persephone**

**Persephone**
In Greek mythology, Hades, god of the underworld, abducts Persephone. She returns to the world for six months every year, bringing spring and summer.

**Durga**
In Hinduism, Durga is the powerful warrior-goddess. She is often represented with a beautiful face and 10 arms, each one holding a weapon.

## Gods

Much of what we know of gods and goddesses was passed down by men rather than women, so male gods – often gods of war – predominate in mythology. Many myths portray the struggle between good and evil. Some deities are kind and just, while others, such as the Norse god Loki, commit acts of evil and treachery on other gods or humans. Gods may be depicted either in human form, or as part-human and part-animal.

### Thor
In Norse mythology, Thor was the god of the sky, rain, thunder, and farming. Thor's hammer, known as Mjollnir, made thunder-bolts when the god threw it. Norse gods such as Thor and Odin were worshipped in parts of Scandinavia up until the 12th century.

*Thor fighting frost giants*

*Mars was popular in Rome.*

### Mars
Mars, god of war, was said to be the father of Rome's founder. Many Roman gods were equivalent to earlier Greek versions: Mars was called Ares in Greek myth-ology, and Demeter, goddess of spring, was Persephone.

## Sacrifices

A sacrifice is an offering of an animal, plant, possession, or even a human life, to please or pacify a deity. In ancient cultures, sacrifices were made to gods and goddesses on special days or at important ceremonies. Ancient Romans marked such occasions with a *suovetaurilia*, a special sacrifice involving a bull, a ram, and a pig – the most valuable items of Roman livestock.

**Wicker man**
Roman historians recorded that Celtic tribes in Gaul (France) placed human sacrifices inside wickerwork figures, then burnt them alive. Wicker figures are still burnt at festivals in Spain.

**Mountain-top sacrifice**
The Aztecs offered human sacrifices to the god of the Sun, Tezcatlipoca. This deity was the most feared of the Aztec gods and thousands, usually prisoners of war, were sacrificed in his name. The Aztecs carefully chose their victim, who was accorded great honours for one year. Then, on the day of the sacrifice, a priest cut open the victim's chest and offered his heart up to Tezcatlipoca.

*Aztec warrior and his prisoner of war*

## Priests

In many societies, priests are the human links between the natural world and the supernatural world of the gods. They are thought to have special, often magical power, and may carry out sacred rites.

*Priest in traditional costume*

**Priest's costume**
Costumes convey authority and represent tradition. The priest's costume of the Nkimba people of the Congo, West Africa, includes an ornate carved wooden mask and a grass net decorated with feathers.

**Shaman's mask**
The shamans of Native American tribes wore masks representing a guardian spirit. This showed the connection between the human and spirit worlds.

## Oracles

The term "oracle" describes a direct communication with a deity though the mouth of a priest. The most famous oracle was at Delphi in ancient Greece, at a temple to the god Apollo. In Greek mythology, the heroes Oedipus and Heracules consulted the oracle, whose replies to questions were always ambiguous.

**Delphi Oracle, Greece**

**FIND OUT MORE**  AZTECS  CELTS  EGYPT, ANCIENT  GREECE, ANCIENT  MAYA  RELIGIONS  ROMAN EMPIRE  WITCHES AND WITCHCRAFT

# Gods and Goddesses

## Nature

**Mayan** rain god

**Men** is an Anatolian Moon god.

**Aztec** agricultural god

*Luna drives a chariot across the night sky.*

**Luna** is the Roman Moon goddess.

**Syrian** river god

**Ceres** is the Roman corn goddess.

**Poseidon** is the Greek god of the sea.

**Silvanus** is the god of uncultivated land.

**Celtic** god of rivers

**Apollo** is the Roman Sun god.

**Hephaistos** is the Greek god of fire.

*Balls of thunder*

**Japanese god** of thunder and lightning.

## Love and Fertility

**Artemis** is the Greek goddess of fertility.

**Cupid** is the Roman god of love.

**Attis** is the Egyptian goddess of fertility.

*Aphrodite is the mother of Eros.*

*Eros is a god of love.*

**Priapus** is the Roman god of fertility.

## War and Death

**Proserpina** is the Roman queen of the underworld.

**Cerberus** is a dog that guards the underworld.

**Hades** is the Roman god of the underworld.

**Athena** is the Roman goddess of war.

*Ares is the father of Eros.*

**Venus** is the Roman goddess of love and beauty.

**Aphrodite** is the Greek goddess of love and beauty.

**Juno** is the Roman goddess of marriage and maternity.

**Ares** is the Greek god of war.

**Serapis** is an Egyptian god of the dead.

**Osiris** is the Egyptian god of the underworld.

**Antlered** Celtic goddess

# GOODALL, JANE

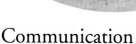

FROM 1960 TO 1995, Jane Goodall spent 35 remarkable years devoted to studying chimpanzees in the wild, and became one of the world's most respected and influential zoologists. She began her painstaking research alone in the middle of the tropical forest in Tanzania, East Africa, and steadily built up one of the foremost centers for field research on primates. Her observations and those of her colleagues revolutionized our knowledge of chimpanzee behavior and shed light on our own human ancestry.

### Early life
Jane Goodall was born in London, England, in 1934. As a teenager, she dreamed of studying wildlife in Africa, and the ambition never faded. In 1957, with savings from a summer job as a waitress, she embarked on a trip to Kenya. There she approached the famous anthropologist Louis Leakey, and told him she wanted to work in Africa. Leakey gave her a job as a secretary.

*Tool used to open bees' nests*

*Fishing stick*

*Wooden chisel*

## Research
In spite of Jane Goodall's lack of formal training, Louis Leakey decided to help her realize her dream. In 1960, he raised funds for her to begin a research program at Gombe, Tanzania. She has been based there ever since. In the 1960s, most primatologists studied captive animals in zoos. Goodall's task was different – to gain the confidence of the chimps and study them at close quarters in their natural environment.

**Goodall with one of the chimps at Gombe**

### Working methods
Goodall worked by spending day after day alone in the forest with the chimpanzees. Gradually, she won their confidence, and they accepted her. She filled her notebooks with descriptions of the chimpanzees, and wrote freely of the emotions, personalities, and intelligence of the chimps.

### Toolmaking
One of Goodall's most startling discoveries was that wild chimps are good toolmakers. They use objects as tools, modifying them to suit their purpose. She saw chimps stripping twigs to make probes for "fishing" termites from their nests, and chewing clumps of leaves to make sponges for getting water from shallow pools.

## Communication
Goodall was fascinated by the way the chimps used sounds, gestures, and expressions to communicate with one another. Every noise conveyed a different message, and gestures and body movements were also forms of communication.

### Displays
Goodall saw how body movements act as' visual displays of emotion and intent. Males issue threats to rivals by charging forward with their fur raised, often dragging branches or throwing stones. Early on, Goodall noted that groups of chimps would react to coming rainfall with an agitated "rain dance."

**Charging display**

### Touch
Goodall observed that chimps would often pat, embrace, or kiss as a way of calming distressed individuals. She also saw them grooming each other's fur. This has a calming effect and strengthens social bonds.

**In her lonely** observation posts in the jungle, Goodall made careful drawings of the chimps' use of tools and other behavior

**Two of Goodall's notebooks**

## Conservation
Goodall championed the cause of chimpanzee conservation and campaigned for better conditions for captive chimps. In 1977, she launched the Jane Goodall Institute for Wildlife Research, Education, and Conservation in the US. By the late 1990s, it had branches in the UK, Canada, and Tanzania.

**Goodall campaigning for chimpanzees**

### JANE GOODALL

| | |
|---|---|
| 1934 | Born in London, England. |
| 1957 | Travels to Kenya and meets Louis Leakey. |
| 1960 | Establishes research station at Gombe, Tanzania. |
| 1965 | Gains doctorate from Cambridge University. |
| 1971 | Publishes *In the Shadow of Man*, first of several influential books. |
| 1977 | Founds Jane Goodall Institute. |
| 1991 | Launches international youth environmental program, "Roots and Shoots." |
| 1995 | Receives Hubbard Medal. |

FIND OUT **MORE**   AFRICAN WILDLIFE   CONSERVATION   LEAKEY FAMILY   MONKEYS, AND OTHER PRIMATES

# GOVERNMENTS AND POLITICS

A GOVERNMENT IS an institution that makes the political decisions about running a country. Governments and politics are unique to each country because they reflect that country's history and culture. Despite the differences, systems of government and issues of political debate are similar everywhere, for they reflect each country's concern about what is best for the benefit of all its citizens.

*The orb symbolizes a monarch's spiritual authority over his or her subjects.*

German orb

*The crown symbolizes sovereignty.*

Russian imperial crown

Prussian scepter

*The crown jewels (crown, orb, and scepter) symbolize the monarch's authority.*

## Types of government

There are almost as many types of government as there are countries in the world. The three main types of government are republican, monarchical, and dictatorial, although these have many variations. Anarchists believe that governments are not necessary.

### Republic
Most countries in the world are republics in which electors vote for their head of state as well as for their government. The power of the president ranges from holding real political power, as in the US, to being a symbolic figurehead, as in India.

### Monarchy
In a monarchy, the head of the royal family is head of state and is succeeded by his or her closest relative in hereditary succession. In most monarchies, such as Britain and Japan, the monarch has little real power, but in countries such as Morocco, Saudi Arabia, and Jordan, the king holds considerable political power.

### Dictatorship
Many countries in the world have at one time or another been ruled by dictators, single rulers with absolute power. Most dictators gain power either through a military takeover or by seizing leadership from an existing ruler, as Saddam Hussein did in Iraq in 1979. Dictators eliminate any opposition to their rule.

## Democracy

In a democracy, electors vote for a government from a range of political parties. There are two main types of democracy: presidential, where voters elect the president, who then runs the government and may choose the prime minister; and parliamentary, where voters directly elect the government of their choice.

### Presidential
As the president of Ireland, Mary McAleese (b.1951), is the symbolic head of the nation. In France and Russia, the president chooses the prime minister.

**Old Parliament House, Canberra, Australia**

### Parliamentary
Parliamentary systems exist in both republics and monarchies. Parliament is made up of politicians from different political parties. Electors vote for the party or individual of their choice, and the government is drawn from the largest political party in parliament. The leader of this party becomes head of government. Most nations in the world are parliamentary democracies.

## How government works

Each country has its own system of government, often consisting of four separate parts. The executive governs the country, the legislature makes the laws, the civil service carries those laws out, and the judiciary ensures that laws are applied fairly.

### Legislature
The legislature is the place where laws are made and the executive is held to account for its actions in governing. The legislature is made up of elected representatives, and often consists of a lower house of parliament, where laws are made, and an upper house, which keeps a check on the lower house. The British upper house (the House of Lords) is unique in mainly consisting of hereditary not elected members.

**Parliament House, New Delhi, India**

### Civil service
The role of the civil service is to administer the country. Once the executive has proposed a law, and the legislature has passed it, the civil service implements it. Civil servants are nonpolitical and work for whichever government is in power. Their work ranges from local issues such as street lighting to national issues such as defense.

*Judge calls court to order with a gavel.*

### Judiciary
The judiciary makes sure that laws are carried out fairly. Judges sit in judgment in individual cases and also review the operation of the law or suggest changes to improve it. The judiciary is independent from the executive and legislature to maintain its neutrality.

### Executive
The executive's role is to govern the country. In parliamentary democracies, the executive consists of senior ministers and the prime minister, who sit in the Houses of Parliament. In the US, the executive, such as the Secretary of State, Colin Powell (b. 1937), is chosen by the president and is separate from the Houses of Congress.

Pentagon, US

# Elections

In a multiparty democracy, every four or five years voters go to the polls to elect their government, choosing from a list of candidates the politicians who will represent them. Elections are an opportunity for politicians to present their ideas for the government of the country, and for the electorate to debate and consider matters of interest and concern to them. In the past, elections were local, personal affairs, in which candidates for office tried to meet each voter in person. Today, most campaigning is carried out by advertising and television.

## Political parties

Political parties are formed to represent particular political beliefs, such as the Socialist Party in France or the Christian Democratic Party in Germany, or to represent particular areas of a country, such as the Scottish Nationalists, who wish to see Scotland become independent from Britain. Political parties are active at the local and national levels in getting their supporters out to vote and in attracting new voters to their cause.

Swedish Christian Democratic Party

French Socialist Party

## Politicians

People become politicians for different reasons. Some people run for election because they believe in serving the public, or have a particular skill that would be useful in government. Others run to represent a particular political viewpoint. In the US, the cost of a campaign sometimes restricts candidates' campaign strategies.

US Democratic Convention, 1996

## Voting

The electors vote in secret for the candidates of their choice by marking a ballot paper or pulling a lever. The votes are counted and the winning candidate is elected. In many countries, voters rank candidates in order of preference. Proportional representation then ensures that the candidates with the most preferences are elected.

## Politics

Politics is the organization of political debate and discussion in a country. That debate can take place in a formal setting, such as parliament, or informally. Any subject can be discussed, from major issues such as the economy or international relations, to local issues such as road-planning.

*Chamber of the House of Commons, London, UK*

# Political beliefs

Different political beliefs play a large part in determining how a country is governed. Left-wing ideologies, such as communism and socialism, favor a large role for the state acting on behalf of its citizens, while right-wing ideologies, such as capitalism, favor individual action and responsibility by citizens.

## Capitalism

Capitalism is the system in which wealth and profit in the hands of a few people drive the country's economy. Capitalism can lead to great differences in income between rich and poor.

## Socialism

Socialism is the system in which the economy is controlled by the state for the benefit of the whole community. Countries such as the Netherlands and Sweden aim for a more equal distribution of wealth.

## Fascism

Fascism is the system of government under which total authority resides in the leader of the country, who pursues nationalist and militarist policies. Like other far-right ideologies, fascism glorifies the state for providing strong national leadership.

## Communism

Communism is the system in which land and property are owned by the whole community and each person is paid according to his or her needs and abilities. China and North Korea are examples of communist countries.

# Public pressure

Everyone can participate in politics, from full-time politicians to individuals who are concerned about a particular issue or event. Apart from elections, individuals can put pressure on governments both by participating in public protest, such as strikes and demonstrations, and by joining interest groups that are set up to campaign for particular issues, such as protecting the environment or civil liberties.

## Protest groups

In order to force an issue into public debate, it is sometimes necessary to take direct action. Recently, protest groups have achieved success against the location of nuclear weapons and the proposed building of new roads.

## Interest groups

Interest groups play an important part in focusing attention on issues of public concern. Environmental interest groups, such as Greenpeace, raise public awareness on issues of pollution or environmental damage that cross national borders.

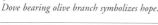

*Dove bearing olive branch symbolizes hope.*

## Machiavelli

Niccolò Machiavelli (1469–1527) was a civil servant in the Florentine Republic in Italy. He was a realist who observed the political chaos of his times and urged governments to pursue practical, realistic politics rather than lofty political ideals. In his book *The Prince* (1532), he described politics as the art of the possible and pointed out what a government can do rather than what it ought to do.

**FIND OUT MORE**   COLD WAR   EUROPE, HISTORY OF   EUROPEAN UNION   HUMAN RIGHTS   LAW   PEACE MOVEMENTS   UNIONS, TRADE   UNITED NATIONS   WARFARE   WOMEN'S MOVEMENT

# GRASSES, RUSHES, AND SEDGES

THESE THREE GROUPS of plants are all monocotyledons – flowering plants whose seedlings possess a single cotyledon, or seed leaf. In common with many other monocotyledons, grasses, rushes, and sedges have long, narrow leaves with parallel veins. They are all wind-pollinated and, therefore, do not have showy blossoms to attract animals. Instead, they have tiny flowers grouped in spikes or clusters. These produce large amounts of dry pollen.

*Flowerheads at the top of tall, leafy stems*

*Flower stem, or culm*

**G**

Yorkshire fog

## Grasses

There are about 9,000 species of grasses, including cereal crops such as wheat and barley. They are the most widespread flowering plants. Grass plants often grow close together to make a turf. Each plant has a mass of fibrous roots, leafy shoots, and flowerheads borne on long stems.

Cross-section of sedge flower stem

## Sedges

The sedge family includes true sedges, cottongrasses, club-rushes, and galingales, totaling about 4,000 species. Unlike grasses, sedges have leaves in tufts around the base of the stem. The flower stem is usually leafless and three-angled.

*Male flowers at the top of the spike have withered and fallen.*

*Fruits explode out of the ripe flower spike.*

*When these leaves are cut off, new shoots grow from the base of the plant.*

Cross section of rush stem

## Rushes

The 400 or so species of rushes are small to medium-size plants. They are found mostly in the damp habitats of temperate and mountain regions. Rushes have green, white, or brown flowers that turn into dry fruits called capsules. Leaves may be flat like grass leaves, or cylindrical. The stems of all rushes are circular in cross-section.

Ripe flower spike

*Tightly packed female flowers*

**Tillers**

The reason grasses can tolerate the pressures of constant grazing or mowing is that new leafy shoots rise from buds at ground level. This kind of branching is called tillering.

*Woody bamboo canes have many uses, from kitchen utensils to scaffold poles.*

*Soil particles are trapped and held by a network of rootlets.*

**Reed mace**

Often wrongly called bulrushes, these tall plants grow in shallow, slow-moving or still water. There are about 15 species in their own family. Each plant has a flower spike made up of densely packed flowers that splits open when ripe, releasing a mass of single-seeded fruits.

**Bamboo**

About 830 tropical and sub-tropical species of grasses have tough, woody stems. These are called bamboos. The tallest species reaches 115 ft (35 m) tall.

**Soil binding**

The roots of grass plants growing close together make a densely interwoven mat. This stabilizes loose, dry soil and prevents erosion of all kinds of soil.

**FIND OUT MORE** ECOLOGY   FARMING   FLOWERS   PLANTS   PLANTS, ANATOMY   PLANTS, REPRODUCTION

# Grasses

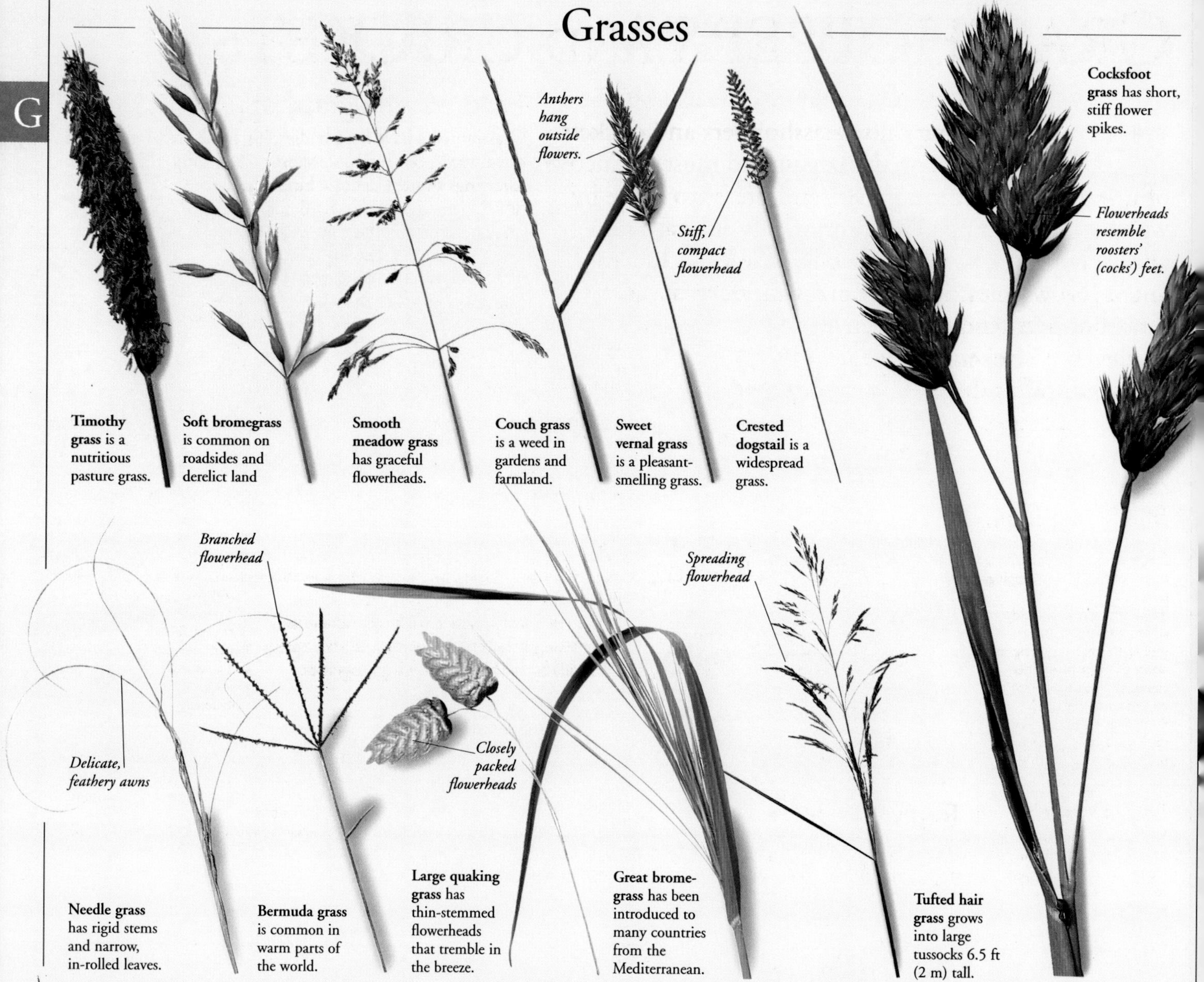

**Timothy grass** is a nutritious pasture grass.

**Soft bromegrass** is common on roadsides and derelict land

**Smooth meadow grass** has graceful flowerheads.

*Anthers hang outside flowers.*

**Couch grass** is a weed in gardens and farmland.

*Stiff, compact flowerhead*

**Sweet vernal grass** is a pleasant-smelling grass.

**Crested dogstail** is a widespread grass.

**Cocksfoot grass** has short, stiff flower spikes.

*Flowerheads resemble roosters' (cocks') feet.*

*Branched flowerhead*

*Spreading flowerhead*

*Delicate, feathery awns*

*Closely packed flowerheads*

**Needle grass** has rigid stems and narrow, in-rolled leaves.

**Bermuda grass** is common in warm parts of the world.

**Large quaking grass** has thin-stemmed flowerheads that tremble in the breeze.

**Great brome-grass** has been introduced to many countries from the Mediterranean.

**Tufted hair grass** grows into large tussocks 6.5 ft (2 m) tall.

# Rushes and sedges

**Soft rush** is a very common rush of bogs and marshes.

**Common sedge** spreads on creeping underground stems.

*Clusters of flowers borne up the stem*

**Hairy sedge** has hairy leaves and fruits.

**Woodrush** has fine hairs on the margins of its leaves.

**Greater tussock sedge** has stiff leaves with finely toothed edges.

**False fox sedge** has sharp-angled triangular stems.

**Pendulous sedge** has long, drooping flower spikes.

**Greater pond sedge** grows beside rivers and ponds.

# GRASSHOPPERS AND CRICKETS

FAMOUS FOR THEIR ATHLETIC LEAPS and chirping calls, grasshoppers and crickets are among the largest and most distinctive of insects. Most are weak fliers and prefer to move by walking or jumping. They live mainly in grasslands and rain forests, but some live in deserts and caves, and a few wingless species burrow underground. Grasshoppers tend to be active by day, but crickets are out and about after dark; in many parts of the world, their constant chirps fill the night air.

G

## Features of a grasshopper

Grasshoppers have long bodies, big heads, large eyes, and downward-pointing mouthparts. Their long, thickened forewings protect delicate hind wings, which they use mainly for flying. Grasshoppers use their powerful, long hind legs for leaping. Bumps on the hind legs rub against the forewings to make sounds.

*Wings outstretched during flight, before it lands*

*Grasshopper gains height by holding its wings back.*

*Compound eye*

*Grasshoppers may jump up to 1 ft (0.3 m) before opening their wings.*

*Hind legs held out almost straight behind*

*Front legs outstretched over eyes, ready to touch down*

### Leaping
Propelled forward by snapping their hind legs straight, grasshoppers can out-jump all other insects. If danger threatens or if the grasshopper wants to move to another clump of vegetation, it springs into the air, opens and flutters its wings to prolong the leap, and drops down as much as 3.3 ft (1 m) ahead.

*Long, strong back legs*

*Front legs*

*Grasshopper poised, ready to leap*

**Common field grasshopper**

## Crickets

Crickets are similar to grasshoppers but differ in some key features: their hearing organs are on their legs rather than abdomen; they have longer antennae, sometimes longer than their bodies; and they make sounds by rubbing their wings together.

*Long antenna*

**Bush cricket**

### Eardrum on legs
Crickets have a swelling below the knee that consists of a drumlike membrane, called a tympanum, on either side of the leg. This is the cricket's ear and is sensitive to sound vibrations.

**Cricket's leg showing tympanum**

## Locust swarms
Locusts are grasshoppers. After heavy rains, lush plant life grows, creating the right conditions for locusts to breed in large numbers. Swarms of up to 50 billion set out across the land. They devastate crops and plants, causing famine.

**Swarm of locusts in Ethiopia**

## Reproduction
During mating a male grasshopper or cricket transfers tiny packets of sperm to the female to fertilize her eggs. She then uses a spikelike ovipositor to place batches of up to 100 eggs at a time into the soil or into plant stems and leaves. Tiny nymphs – miniature versions of the parents – hatch from the eggs. They molt and grow many times until they reach adult size.

*Grasshopper rubs its legs rapidly against its wings to generate sounds.*

*Male has laid a sperm sac that is being taken up by the female.*

*Ovipositor*

**Bush cricket transferring sperm sac**

### Stridulation
The rapid rubbing sounds made by grasshoppers and crickets are known as stridulation. To amplify the sounds, crickets rub veins and ridges on both wings together; grasshoppers rub ridges on their legs against a tough vein on their wings. Breeding males produce stridulations to attract mates. Sounds are particular to each species and sounded at specific times of the day.

## Feeding
Most grasshoppers feed on leaves, buds, and other parts of plants that they chew with their mouthparts. Crickets have a more varied diet. Many eat plants but also catch and devour other insects – in fact, some bush crickets are dedicated hunters. Crickets that live in houses and caves scavenge on waste matter.

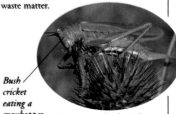

*Bush cricket eating a grasshopper*

**Great green bush cricket**

## Defense
Many grasshoppers and crickets are brown or green so they are less visible to predators. Others have brightly colored hind wings that they flash to warn off enemies. Some have elaborate camouflage, with body parts resembling leaves and plant stems.

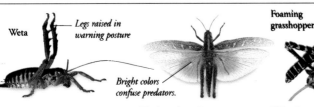

*Weta*

*Legs raised in warning posture*

*Bright colors confuse predators.*

*Foaming grasshopper*

### Posture
Large crickets, called wetas, have spines on their hind legs. If disturbed, they raise their hind legs into a threatening posture to frighten predators.

### Flash coloration
Only the outer wings are exposed when this grasshopper is at rest. If disturbed, the insect flashes its lilac inner wings to confuse predators.

### Warning coloration
This grasshopper eats poisonous plants and stores the poisons in its body. Its bright stripes warn predators that it is dangerous to eat.

## COMMON FIELD GRASSHOPPER

| | |
|---|---|
| SCIENTIFIC NAME | *Chorthippus brunneus* |
| ORDER | Orthoptera |
| FAMILY | Acrididae |
| DISTRIBUTION | Europe |
| HABITAT | Dry open areas with short grass |
| DIET | Grass and other low-lying plants |
| SIZE | Length: males up to 0.7 in (18 mm); females up to 0.9 in (23 mm) |
| LIFESPAN | 6–7 months |

FIND OUT MORE    ARTHROPODS    CAVE WILDLIFE    CAMOUFLAGE AND COLOR    GRASSLAND WILDLIFE    INSECTS    NORTH AMERICAN WILDLIFE

# GRASSLAND WILDLIFE

GRASSLANDS SUSTAIN MORE ANIMALS than any other type of land habitat. This is because each species eats a different type, or part, of the grass. In this way, the various species of herbivore can share the same habitat without competing for food. On the African plains, for example, zebras eat the tops of grasses, wildebeest prefer the middle layers, while Thomson's gazelles graze close to the ground. Tall grasses also provide shelter for myriad insects, and a refuge for small animals, such as birds and rodents, many of which live in burrows because there is no shelter from trees.

*Prairies of North America*

*Eurasian steppe*

*Pampas of South America*

*Savannas of Africa*

*Australian grasslands*

*Giraffes browse on trees.*

*Zebras and springboks graze on grass.*

Giraffes, springboks, and zebras grazing on the African savanna

## Grasslands

Grasslands cover 25 percent of the Earth's land surface. The world's principal grasslands are the Eurasian steppe, the savannahs of Africa, the pampas of South America, the prairies of North America, and the Australian grasslands. Grasslands are areas where it is too dry for many trees to grow, but tough grasses grow in abundance. Grasses can withstand constant grazing by animals, and recover quickly from damage by fire, flood, or drought.

## Mammals

Grasslands feed a wide variety of mammals, mainly herbivores, often in large numbers. The herbivores support a population of carnivores, while scavengers, such as hyenas, jackals, and vultures, dispose of their remains. Typical grassland mammals include zebras in Africa; prairie dogs and coyotes in North America; maned wolves in South America; marmots in Eurasia; and kangaroos in Australia.

### Blackbuck
Blackbucks are a type of antelope that once roamed the Indian grasslands in herds of up to 10,000. More recently, hunting has reduced their numbers, and there are now more blackbucks in Argentina and Texas, where they have been introduced, than in their original homeland.

*Males have slender, spiraled horns.*

*Huge ears and good sense of smell help locate prey.*

*Pairs of African wild dogs run down animals larger than themselves.*

### Patagonian hare
The Patagonian hare, or mara, looks like a hare but is closely related to the guinea pig. It lives in burrows in groups of 30–40, in the Argentinian pampas and the stony Patagonian desert.

*Long, thin legs help hare run fast.*

### American bison
The most characteristic animal of the Great Plains of North America, the bison once numbered 50–60 million. By the 1880s, the huge herds had been almost destroyed by hunters. Only 500 remained, but given protection, numbers rose to 25,000. The bison now live in herds of up to 50 animals.

### African wild dog
The wild dog lives in packs of up to 12 on the open savannas of Africa. It employs a very effective method of communal hunting; having singled out an animal, such as a zebra or gazelle, from the herd, a pair of dogs chases it until they are tired, when a fresh pair takes over. Relays of dogs continue in this way until the prey is exhausted, and the pack closes in for the kill.

## Invertebrates

Invertebrates are of great importance in tropical grasslands. They feed on dead vegetation, helping decompose it, and make nutrients available to plants. They also bring subsoil to the surface, keeping the soil healthy.

### Ant lion
Ant lion larvae build pits in sandy soil and wait at the bottom for an ant or spider to dislodge grains of sand. Once alerted, the larva squirts sand at its victim, making it slide into the pit where the ant lion seizes it in its powerful jaws.

### Termites
Tropical grasslands are dotted with termite nests, each containing several million of these insects. Termites are an important food source for many animals, especially echidnas, numbats, aardvarks, and pangolins.

### Dung beetle
Dung beetles roll dung into balls, which they lay eggs in, and push into holes. The larvae hatch and feed on the dung.

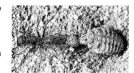

**Queen** termites have huge, swollen bodies and can lay up to 30,000 eggs a day.

*Termite nest may be 20 ft (6 m) high.*

# Reptiles

Many reptiles live in grasslands where they can tolerate the harsh conditions during the dry season. However, when the grass is short it provides little cover in which to hide, so reptiles need to be camouflaged. Many grassland snakes and lizards are dull colored, with brown or gray mottled markings that blend into the surroundings.

*Large claws help it catch prey.*

*Strong jaws and sharp, curved teeth help it catch snakes, rabbits, and birds.*

*The perentie can lash its huge tail from side-to-side in self-defense.*

### Perentie
Reaching a length of 7 ft (2 m), the perentie is the largest of the Australian monitor lizards. It lives in grasslands and among rocky outcrops in deserts. Like other monitors, the perentie is a carnivore with a voracious appetite. It also eats carrion. If threatened, it inflates its body, hisses, and lashes out with its tail.

### Grass snake
This small, non-venomous reptile lives in grasslands close to water. It is a strong swimmer, and catches much of its prey, such as fish, frogs, and newts, in water. If attacked, it releases a bad smell, or feigns death by lying on its back, with its tongue hanging out. Grass snakes hibernate in winter, usually in holes in the ground.

*Grass snakes usually lay a clutch of up to 30–40 eggs in decaying vegetation.*

### Puff adder
Hidden within the grass stems of the African savanna lurks the slow-moving, dangerous puff adder. Camouflaged in the grass, it lies in wait for prey. It produces a powerful venom for immobilizing prey, such as rodents and frogs, and as a means of defense, against mongooses, secretary birds, and eagles.

*Mottled markings break up outline against the grass.*

# Birds

Grasslands support many birds, among them bustards, guineafowl, francolins, long-legged seriemas, and the secretary bird. Many birds nest on the ground as there are few trees. The burrowing owl even goes underground and nests in burrows on the American prairies. Other birds, such as weaver birds, flock in droves to the same isolated tree to weave their basket-shaped nests.

### Greater bustard
A turkey-sized, ground-dwelling bird with a wing span of up to 8 ft (2.4 m), the greater bustard lives in the open grasslands of Asia and southern Europe. It is famous for the male's spectacular courtship display. He inflates the air sac on his throat, and twists his back and tail feathers forward, transforming himself from a drab grey color into a shimmering white mass.

*Long neck gives bustard a clear view over the grass.*

### Emu
The emu is the second largest bird in the world, after the ostrich. It is flightless and lives on the Australian grasslands, where it feeds on grasses, berries, fruit, and insects. Emus live in small, nomadic flocks, moving long distances in search of food and water. They are powerful runners, covering the ground in 9 ft (2.7 m) strides, reaching speeds of up to 30 mph (50 kmh) over short distances. Males incubate the eggs and look after the chicks.

*Long, shaggy feathers*

*Bare skin on neck*

### Indian white-backed vulture
Vultures are a group of carrion-eating birds of prey. They perform a vital role of scavenging and keeping the environment clean by disposing of waste. Indian white-backed vultures hunt by soaring on thermal currents from where they can spot a kill; once sighted, the vultures land to feed on the remains. The sight of vultures circling an area draws other scavengers to the kill.

*Long legs for running*

*Vulture feeding on a goat*

# Plants

Grasslands sustain numerous types of grass, among the best known are red oat grass in Africa and buffalo grass in America. Which species grow depends on altitude, temperature, soil type, and rainfall. Grassland trees often have deep roots to reach water supplies far below the ground, allowing them to survive during the dry season. Some trees can store water. The baobab tree can store about 2,400 gal (9,000 l) of water in its huge swollen trunk.

### Acacia tree
The characteristic tree of Africa's arid and semiarid grasslands is the flat-topped umbrella tree, *Acacia tortilis*. This tree is protected from grazing animals by sharp thorns, but these do not deter giraffes, which manage to pluck the leaves and blossoms. Acacias produce a mass of pods that fall to the ground providing food for many animals. Acacias also provide welcome shade for the animals of the savanna.

*Fluffy white seed heads*

### Pampas grass
The Argentine pampas extend from the foothills of the Andes to the Atlantic coast. Many of the grasses that grow there can be up to 8 ft (2.5 m) high.

*Petals and bracts are covered with small hairs.*

### Anemones
When the snow retreats on the Asian steppes, many wildflowers, including anemones and peonies, grow amidst the sea of grass.

| FIND OUT MORE | ANTS AND TERMITES | BIRDS OF PREY | BUFFALO AND OTHER WILD CATTLE | DEER AND ANTELOPE | GRASSES, RUSHES, AND SEDGES | PLANTS, DEFENCE | WOLVES AND WILD DOGS |

# GRAVITY

WITHOUT GRAVITY, we would fly off the spinning Earth and into space. Gravity is a force of attraction that acts between any two objects. The objects can be as large as galaxies or as small as subatomic particles. The strength of the gravity between two objects depends on their masses and the distance between them. Objects with large masses exert a strong force of gravity. Objects far apart attract each other weakly.

## Center of gravity

Every object consists of tiny particles of matter. Each of these particles has a small force of gravity acting upon it. Together, the forces act like a single force pulling downward at just one point, called the center of gravity. An object will balance when it is supported in line with its center of gravity. Balancing is easiest if the object has a low center of gravity.

*Center of gravity is directly below the string, making the object very stable.*

## Gravity in space

Gravity is a universal force because it acts between any two objects, wherever they are in the Universe. The force that keeps our feet firmly on the ground is the same one that holds huge clusters of stars together as galaxies.

**Galaxies**
A typical galaxy is about 100,000 light-years across. The stars are so massive that gravity can still act over this huge distance, preventing the stars from drifting off into space.

**Planetary orbits**
Gravity holds the planets of the Solar System in orbit around the Sun. Venus and the Earth have similar masses, but because Venus is closer to the Sun than the Earth, the force of gravity keeping it in orbit is greater.

*Path of orbit*
*Gravitational force on the Earth*
*Sun*
*Venus*
*Earth*
*Gravitational force on Venus*

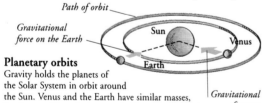

*Orbital path of Mercury over 4 years*
*Sun*
*Mercury*
*Orbit shifts over time.*

**General Relativity**
In 1915, German-born physicist Albert Einstein published his Theory of General Relativity. This theory sees gravity not as a force, but as a curvature of space caused by bodies of matter. In 1919, the theory was used successfully to explain why Mercury's orbit gradually varies over time.

## Weight

The force of gravity acting on an object is called weight. Like all forces, weight is expressed in units called newtons (N). An object's weight is directly related to its mass. On Earth, 2.2 lb (1 kg) of matter weighs about 10 N.

*Apple weighs about 1 N.*
*Newton meter measures weight and other forces.*
*Apple has a mass of 3.5 oz (100 g).*

*The force of gravity acting on the ball is constant.*

*Balls slow down as they are thrown upward.*

*Balls speed up as they fall.*

*Gravity tries to pull the balls downward.*

## Earth's gravity

Gravity always acts toward the center of the Earth, defining the "downward" direction at every point on the planet's surface. Gravity pulls a juggling ball toward the ground, slowing it as it rises and speeding it up as it falls. The ball also pulls on the Earth, but the Earth is so massive that the ball's gravity has no noticeable effect.

**Moon's gravity**
The Moon is smaller and has less mass than the Earth, so the force of gravity is weaker on the Moon. A hammer on the Moon weighs one-sixth of its weight on the Earth. It takes 1.1 seconds for a hammer to fall 3.3 ft (1 m) on the Moon, but only 0.44 seconds on the Earth.

Earth    Moon

## Aristotle

The Greek philosopher Aristotle (c.384–322 BC) believed that heavy objects fall faster than lighter ones. Aristotle's ideas were accepted until the Italian scientist Galileo Galilei (1564–1642) showed that gravity pulls all objects to Earth at the same speed.

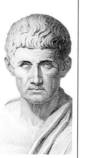

## Tides

Twice each day, the waters of the ocean rise a little and then fall back. This movement is called a tide, and it is caused by the pull of the Moon's gravity. The Sun also influences tides. When the Earth, Sun, and Moon are in line, their combined gravity produces tides that are higher than normal, called spring tides.

*Harbor at low tide*

## Timeline

**4th century BC** Aristotle proposes that stones fall to the ground simply because they are heavy, and that smoke rises because it is light.

**1604** Italian scientist Galileo Galilei investigates how objects fall to Earth.

**17th century** English physicist Isaac Newton publishes his Law of Gravitation, perhaps inspired by seeing an apple fall from a tree.

*Model showing how space curves around a planet.*

**1915** Einstein's Theory of General Relativity describes gravity as a curvature of space.

**1919** English astronomer Arthur Eddington (1882–1944) obtains proof of Einstein's theory by observing light, reaching the Earth from a distant star, being bent by the Sun's gravity.

**FIND OUT MORE**   EINSTEIN, ALBERT    FORCE AND MOTION    MATTER    MOON    NEWTON, SIR ISAAC    OCEANS AND SEAS

# GREAT DEPRESSION

ON OCTOBER 24, 1929, the world's financial heart – the New York Stock Exchange – stopped beating. Share prices crashed, consumers stopped investing, banks failed, and millions of people lost their jobs. Within a year, a severe economic depression gripped the world, and governments struggled to cope with the crisis. Ill-conceived economic policies led to social unrest and the rise of right-wing authoritarian governments in Europe. The Great Depression lasted for a decade; it ended when the threat of war resulted in the need for workers to produce armaments.

### Roaring Twenties
Once Western economies had recovered from World War I, they entered a period of rapid growth. High public confidence, low interest rates, and optimistic investments created a boom in the 1920s. Women enjoyed greater freedom, and people spent more on leisure and entertainment than ever before.

*A fashionable 1920s' "flapper"*

US magazine front cover, 1926

## Wall Street crash

In 1929, after years of rising share prices, the Stock Exchange on New York's Wall Street saw a dramatic crash (fall) in prices. The crash bankrupted many companies and private citizens.

### Soup kitchens
Many people lost their entire life savings after the Wall Street crash, and bankrupt companies had to lay off their workers. With no work and no social security system, millions of American families faced poverty and hunger. Every town opened soup kitchens to provide at least one good meal a day.

Bread line, New York, 1932

A family in the Texas Dust Bowl, 1938

Jarrow marchers on their way to London

### Jarrow March
By the early 1930s, the effects of the Depression had spread to Britain, Germany, and the rest of the world. Poverty was rife. In 1936, 200 unemployed workers marched 276 miles (444 km) from Jarrow, northeastern England, to the capital, London, demanding jobs. Almost 70 percent of Jarrow's workers were unemployed.

## Dust Bowl

In the United States, years of over-farming and drought caused dust storms throughout the mid-western states during the 1930s. Thousands of farmers, already hit hard by the Depression and suffering desperate poverty, were forced to abandon their land to seek work in the fruit farms of California. Few found it. Their plight was immortalized in John Steinbeck's classic novel *The Grapes of Wrath* (1939).

## Rearmament

From the 1930s, world leaders took action to combat unemployment: President Roosevelt started the New Deal to get people back to work. However, it was renewed war in Europe that ended the Depression. Armament factories producing airplanes and tanks created new jobs and revitalized the world economy.

### New Deal
In 1932, Franklin Roosevelt won the US presidential election against President Hoover. He pledged "a new deal for the American people," establishing agencies to regulate business, start public works projects, and build a series of hydroelectric power plants, such as the Hoover Dam, to provide employment.

### Franklin D Roosevelt
Roosevelt (1882–1945) was elected senator (Democrat) from New York in 1910, and Assistant Secretary to the Navy from 1913–1920. In 1921, he developed polio and was paralysed and confined to a wheelchair for the rest of his life. He returned to public life in 1928 as governor of New York, and won the 1932 presidential election. He promised "direct, vigorous action" against the Depression, and won reelection three times. He led the US to victory in World War II.

Italy's Fascist leader Benito Mussolini taking the salute at a rally

### Rise of Fascism
The Depression caused much tension. Socialists agitated for reform, but some countries looked to right-wing solutions. Italy had had a Fascist government since 1922; Germany got one in 1933, and Spain in 1936. Authoritarian governments across Europe quashed dissent from workers and left-wingers.

Hoover Dam, Nevada

### Timeline
1929 Wall Street Crash.

1930 World unemployment doubles.

1931 Britain forms national government to deal with crisis.

1932 More than 1 in 4 workers unemployed in US; unemployment in Germany triples to 5.6 million.

1933 Hitler comes to power in Germany with promises to get the country back to work through rearmament and national expansion.

1933 Slow recovery begins in US and Europe.

1939 Outbreak of war in Europe ends Depression as workers are employed in armament factories.

 FIND OUT MORE | GERMANY, HISTORY OF | UNITED STATES, HISTORY OF | WORLD WAR II

# GREAT ZIMBABWE

ONE OF AFRICA'S GREATEST archaeological mysteries is the walled city of Great Zimbabwe. This massive granite zimbabwe – a word literally meaning chief's court – was begun in the 13th century. By the 14th century, it had become the capital of a vast kingdom that stretched between the Zambezi and Limpopo rivers. The people of Great Zimbabwe were mainly farmers, but the city was also the main center for trade and religion. However, by 1450, Great Zimbabwe had been abandoned for reasons that remain a mystery. Today its ruins stand in modern Zimbabwe, the southern African country named after this remarkable walled structure.

**Rise of Great Zimbabwe**
Great Zimbabwe's first city started as a farming settlement, possibly as early as the 2nd century. In addition to raising and selling cattle, its people mined gold and copper on the Zimbabwe plateau. By the 12th century, long-distance trade based on gold and copper was passing through the city from the east coast of Africa. As Great Zimbabwe rose in importance and wealth, it was rebuilt in stone and increased in size.

## Great Enclosure

Built of massive granite blocks, the Great Enclosure is a huge, dry stone wall that surrounded the city, providing protection for Great Zimbabwe's people. Inside the enclosure, people lived in circular houses made from daga (a gravel-like clay) and roofed with thatch. There were also small oval enclosures – but, like the stone conical tower, their purpose remains a mystery. Near to the enclosure was a hill complex, which was used for religious rituals.

*The conical tower was 27 ft (9 m) high and made of solid stone.*

*Roofless oval enclosures*

*Masonry incorporates massive boulders.*

*Round thatched huts*

*Outside wall was 16 ft (5 m) thick at the base and 32 ft (9.75 m) high.*

*Chevron pattern decorated parts of wall.*

**Great Enclosure, Great Zimbabwe**

**Hill complex**

**Hill complex**
The religious center, where the ancestors' spirits were worshiped, was built on a hill near the Great Enclosure. At the front of the complex, there was a public space where the mambo (ruler) conducted sacred rites.

**Conical tower**
A massive and mysterious cone-shaped tower stands inside the Great Enclosure. Some archaeologists think it may be a monument celebrating the power and wealth of the rulers of Great Zimbabwe.

### Farming
Great Zimbabwe at its height had 10,000 people living in and around it. Most people were farmers in the surrounding areas. They herded cattle and grew millet, sorghum, and vegetables, which they sold to the many traders visiting the walled city.

**Zimbabwean cattle**

## Ancestor worship

The people of Great Zimbabwe worshiped the spirits of their dead rulers, known as ancestors. In sacrificial rites, they killed calves and offered the meat to ancestor spirits on beautifully carved soapstone dishes. They placed the dishes in sacred places outside the hill complex.

**Birds**
Eight carved soapstone birds have been found at Great Zimbabwe. They stood in sacred places on 3-ft (1-m) high soapstone columns. Each of the birds may represent a royal ancestor, and one of them is now used as the symbol of the modern state of Zimbabwe.

**Soapstone bird on column**

## Trade

The prosperous trading center of Great Zimbabwe was situated on one of the trade routes that linked southern Africa to the east coast. Traders from Sofala and Kilwa (in modern Mozambique) obtained gold and copper from Great Zimbabwe to export to Arabia and Asia.

**Metal exports**
The people of Great Zimbabwe mined gold, copper, iron, and tin on the Zimbabwe plateau. Cross-shaped ingots were exchanged for goods from Asia, such as beads, glassware, and ceramics.

**Copper ingot**

### Karl Mauch
A German self-taught geologist, Mauch (1837–75), traveled southern Africa from 1865 to 1872. During his nine months in Great Zimbabwe (1871), he drew diagrams of the ruins and sketched the carved stone and metal objects found there. Much of today's knowledge of the area is based on Mauch's diaries.

### Timeline
**c.900** Iron Age (Shona) people settle between the Zambezi and the Limpopo rivers in southern Africa.

**1100s** Trade passing through Great Zimbabwe to Africa's East Coast increases.

**1200s** Zimbabwean gold is exported to Asia.

**1250** Building in stone begins at Great Zimbabwe.

**Early 1400s** Great Enclosure is completed; and Great Zimbabwe contains its largest area.

**1450** Great Zimbabwe is abandoned, probably because its people leave to look for new and better farmland.

FIND OUT MORE — AFRICA, HISTORY OF — METALS — MALI EMPIRE

# GREECE, ANCIENT

MORE THAN 2,500 YEARS AGO, one of the world's most influential civilizations flowered in mainland Greece. From the 8th until the 2nd centuries BC, Greek writers, thinkers, and artists made a huge contribution to western culture – especially in politics, drama, mythology, architecture, and literature. Greek civilization declined when, after defeating the Persians and peacefully colonizing much of Europe, it was absorbed into the Roman Empire.

### Mycenaean civilization
The Mycenaeans formed the first great mainland Greek civilization (c. 2700 –1120 BC ) and were the forerunners of classical Greece. These Bronze Age traders and warriors ranged all over the Mediterranean area from their settlement at Mycenae. The gold mask was once thought to be of Agamemnon, a leader in the legendary Trojan War.

**The Parthenon**

*Red marble tiles covered the roof.*

*Colored frieze*

## Polis

Ancient Greece was made up of hundreds of separate city-states. Some were hardly bigger than villages, while others were based around great cities, such as Sparta or Athens. Each of these city-states was known as a polis (plural: poleis). Laws, festivals, and government systems varied, and there was often war between rival poleis, despite their common Greek background. The need for land led some poleis to colonize other parts of the Mediterranean between the 8th and 6th centuries BC, and in this way ancient Greece expanded.

*White marble columns*

*Reliefs decorated the exterior.*

*Temples were built on stepped platforms.*

Ancient Greece, c.4th century BC

### Sparta
Life in Sparta was disciplined and harsh. Spartans trained both girls and boys to excel at sports and feats of endurance. To strengthen military power, all the boys went on to become soldiers. After helping Athens defeat the Persians in 480 BC, Sparta conquered Athens in the Peloponnesian War (431–404 BC) and became master of Greece.

Spartan warrior

### Athens
From the 6th century BC, Athens was governed by a form of democracy (rule by the people) in which all male citizens voted. In the 5th century BC, thanks to its powerful navy, Athens had a maritime empire in the Aegean Sea, and its 250,000-strong population enjoyed a golden age of art and culture. After their triumph against the Persians, the Athenians celebrated by building a massive "fortified citadel" – the Acropolis. The Parthenon (447 and 432 BC) was the most important temple in the Acropolis and was dedicated to Athena.

### Clash of the Titans
The Greeks believed that the world was originally inhabited by giants called Titans. Their ruler, Cronos, swallowed his children alive so that they could not overthrow him. One son, Zeus, escaped this fate when his mother gave Cronos a cloth-covered stone to swallow instead. Zeus grew up in secret, made Cronos vomit up his siblings, defeated the other Titans in battle, and made himself king of the gods.

Cronos eating his children

### The Legend of Troy
Little of the ancient city of Troy (in modern Turkey) remains. Homer's *Iliad* says that a Greek army besieged Troy for 10 years in the late Mycenaean Age (c.1250 BC). According to legend, Athena advised the Greeks to smuggle their soldiers into the city inside a huge wooden horse. When they took her advice, they defeated the Trojans.

*Part of a trident*

Model of Trojan Horse

## Mount Olympus

Ancient Greeks believed that various deities (gods and goddesses) watched over ordinary mortals from a cloud-palace above the highest mountain in Greece – the snowcapped Mount Olympus. The deities who lived there were known as Olympians. Each Olympian had specific responsibilities: Poseidon was in charge of the sea, Athena of wisdom and the arts, Apollo of music and poetry, and Demeter of crops. The supreme god was Zeus, lord of sky and earth. Greek cities regarded different deities as their special protectors. For example, Athens was devoted to the cult of Athena.

### Oracle at Delphi
Ancient Greeks consulted the gods for advice or prophecies at holy places called oracles. The most famous oracle in Greece was at Delphi. People went there to ask questions at Apollo's shrine about religious or political matters. A high priestess went into a trance to give Apollo's answers. Most gods had their special shrine, but they competed with each other for the best ones. Legend has it that Athena won a competition against Poseidon over the Parthenon in Athens, the largest city in Greece, and he had to move his shrine to Attica.

*Poseidon was Zeus's brother and god of the sea.*

*Poseidon is usually shown holding a fish.*

### Homer
The Greek poet Homer probably lived in the 7th or 8th century BC. He is believed to be the author of two of the world's greatest epic poems: the *Iliad,* which is about the siege of Troy, and the *Odyssey,* which describes the wanderings of the hero Odysseus after the Trojan War. According to to later writers, Homer was blind.

Poseidon, god of the sea

# Culture

Ancient Greek art and science was of the highest standard, and set the standard for European culture for centuries. "Greece, though conquered," wrote the Roman poet Horace, "brought the arts to the uncivilized Latin peoples" (Romans) – and through them to modern Europe.

*Ceres, goddess of the harvest*

*Cloak*

*Chiton, or full tunic*

### Sculpture

Ancient Greek sculpture was famous for its naturalness, beauty, and perfect proportions. Statues related to all aspects of life, including religious worship and sport. Those of deities, such as Ceres, were popular among farmers, and were left at shrines to ensure a good harvest.

### Drama and architecture

The ancient Greeks learned much from the Egyptians about using stone in their architecture – but their theatres were spectacular and original. In the golden age of Athens (400s BC), dramatists, such as Aeschylus, Sophocles, and Euripedes wrote tragedies that are still performed.

**Epidaurus theater**

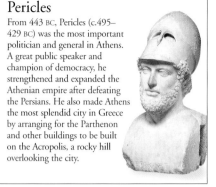

*Amphora*

*Human figures at a banquet*

**Art**

Red-figure painting replaced black-figure in c.530 BC. Most red-figure vases (amphorae) were made from Athenian clay. Subjects were usually male, and were often shown banqueting or engaged in athletics.

## Pericles

From 443 BC, Pericles (c.495–429 BC) was the most important politician and general in Athens. A great public speaker and champion of democracy, he strengthened and expanded the Athenian empire after defeating the Persians. He also made Athens the most splendid city in Greece by arranging for the Parthenon and other buildings to be built on the Acropolis, a rocky hill overlooking the city.

## Language and literature

Ancient Greek, like Latin, is known as a "classical" language. Many great works of Greek literature have survived by authors such as Hesiod and Appolonius (poets), Thucydides (a historian), and Plato (a philosopher).

*Greek inscription of thanks to Asclepius, the god of medicine*

### Alphabet

The word "alphabet" (used in many modern languages, including English) was formed by joining the first two letters of ancient Greek: alpha and beta. The Cyrillic alphabet of eastern Europe also grew out of the Greek alphabet.

## Greek-Persian wars

After 545 BC, the mighty Persian Empire took over Greek cities in Ionia, the easternmost part of Greek territory. When Athens tried to lend support to the cities (499–494 BC), the Persians invaded mainland Greece, but were driven back at Marathon. Ten years later, an alliance between Athens, Sparta, and other Greek cities defeated another massive Persian expedition on land and sea at Salamis.

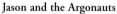

**The Treasury, Delphi**

**Battle of Marathon**

In 490 BC, a Persian force sailed across the Aegean Sea, and landed in Attica. On the plain of Marathon, against all odds, it was heavily defeated by an army of Athenians and their allies. The Athenians built a treasury at Delphi to mark this victory, filled it with Persian spoils, and dedicated it to Apollo, the god of war.

*Jason and the Argonauts*    *Poseidon*    *The Clashing Rocks*

**Battle of Salamis**

In 480 BC, the Persian emperor Xerxes the Great led a huge force along the shores of the Aegean Sea. As central Greece fell, the Athenians evacuated their city. A smaller Greek fleet then lured the Persians into battle in the straits between the mainland and the island of Salamis – and defeated them decisively.

## Philip of Macedon

Warrior-king Philip II ruled Macedon, a northern state in Greece, from 359 to 336 BC. A strong king and a great diplomat, Philip made Macedon the dominant power in the Greek world. He was murdered on the point of invading Persia, but by then had laid the foundations for his son, Alexander, to continue his military feats.

**Jason and the Argonauts**

Even today ancient Greek myths are rewritten, and made into plays and films. Few tales are as dramatic as the quest by Jason and his ship, the *Argo*, to steal the Golden Fleece of the Sun from a watchful dragon. On their journey, Jason and his crew (which included the hero Herakles) were helped and hindered by many gods, monsters, witches, and giants.

## Timeline

c.2700–1120 BC Myceneaen civilization flourishes.

c.750–550 BC Greeks colonize areas in Italy and Africa.

560–510 BC Athenian influence spreads.

**Detail from amphora**

510 BC Cleisthenes, an Athenian statesman, introduces democracy to Athens.

c.510–366 BC Peloponnesian League forms, led by Sparta.

499–494 BC Revolt against Persia by Ionian Greeks.

490 BC Battle of Marathon.

480–479 BC Greeks repel Persian invaders at Salamis and Plataea.

477 BC Athens and Ionian Greeks form Delian League against Persia.

459 BC Sparta defeats Athens in first Peloponnesian War.

443–429 BC Pericles dominant in Athens.

431–404 BC Sparta wins second, or Great, Peloponnesian War.

378–371 BC Thebes overthrows Sparta as leading Greek power.

359–323 BC Reigns of Philip II and his son Alexander the Great of Macedon.

**Hephaistos, god of fire**

 FIND OUT MORE    ALEXANDER THE GREAT    ARCHITECTURE    CITIES    ETRUSCANS    EUROPE, HISTORY OF    GODS AND GODDESSES    MINOANS    PERSIAN EMPIRES    ROMAN EMPIRE    SOCRATES

# GREECE and BULGARIA

ALTHOUGH Greece and Bulgaria share a border, mountains separate the two countries, making communication difficult. Greece and Bulgaria are quite different. Three-fifths of the Greek mainland is mountainous, and only one-third of the land is cultivated. By contrast, Bulgaria is much more fertile, with a strong agricultural tradition. Greece has a strong history of democratic government, while Bulgaria is only just emerging from almost half a century of communist rule.

## Physical features

Surrounded by sea on three sides, the country of Greece is made up of the mainland, the Peloponnese peninsula, and more than 2,000 islands. It is a mixture of tall mountains, dry, dusty plains, and dramatic coastlines. Land-locked on three sides, Bulgaria has broad fertile valleys, separated by the Balkan and Rhodope mountains.

### Regional climate

111°F (44°C)  -13°F (-25°C)
75°F (24°C)  43°F (6°C)
20.5 in (525 mm)

Greece has very hot, dry summers and cooler winters. The northern mountains have cold winters. Annual rainfall is low, and the country suffers from water shortages. Bulgaria, by contrast, has warm summers and cold, snowy winters, with a high rainfall – especially in the mountains.

### Danubian Plain

The mighty Danube River forms most of Bulgaria's northern border with Romania, flowing through the vast and fertile Danubian Plain, which spans the width of the country. This undulating farmland is used for grazing sheep, goats, and cattle, and for cultivating a variety of crops, including sunflowers, which are grown for their oil.

### Crete

The largest of the Greek islands – 3,235 sq miles (8,380 sq km), Crete lies 62 miles (100 km) southeast of the Greek mainland. More than 600,000 people live on the island, and one in three Cretans is a farmer. Many people work in tourism.

### Mount Olympus

Much of central and western Greece is made up of steep, rugged mountains, many of which are capped with snow for several months of the year. Mount Olympus is Greece's highest peak – 9,570 ft (2,917 m). Once thought to be the home of the gods, it is now a national park with busy ski resorts.

## Orthodox Church

Greece is the only official Christian Orthodox country in the world. Priests are responsible community figures and play an important part in national events. Most Greeks and Bulgars belong to the Eastern Orthodox Church, which split from the Roman Catholic Church in 1054. Each country has its own branch of the Church, which also flourishes in other parts of eastern Europe and Russia. Around one tenth of the world's Christians belong to the Orthodox Church.

**Greek Orthodox priest**

# Greece

One of Europe's oldest nations, Greece gained independence from almost 500 years of Turkish rule in 1830. Although it is the poorest member of the European Union, the country has a thriving tourist industry and a large shipping fleet. The Greek people have a strong national identity, based on their deep-rooted Orthodox religion, and a language that has remained in use for 2,700 years.

Parsley
Tomato  Cucumber
Eggplant
Olives

## Food

The Greeks love to eat outdoors in the warm summer months. Meals are simple and tasty and consist mainly of tomatoes, salad, olives, feta cheese, lamb, some fish, and yogurt made from sheep's milk. Retsina, a wine flavored with pine resin, is often served with meals.

## Farming

High mountains and poor soil make farming difficult in Greece. However, agriculture employs about 23 percent of the workforce, mainly on small, traditional farms. The main crops are olives, citrus fruits, grapes, vegetables, and tomatoes. Small herds of sheep and goats produce meat, and milk for cheese and yogurt. Greece is the world's third largest producer of olive oil.

### GREECE FACTS

| | |
|---|---|
| CAPITAL CITY | Athens |
| AREA | 50,961 sq miles (131,990 sq km) |
| POPULATION | 10,600,000 |
| DENSITY | 210 per sq mile (81 per sq km) |
| MAIN LANGUAGE | Greek |
| MAJOR RELIGION | Christian |
| CURRENCY | Euro |
| LIFE EXPECTANCY | 77 years |
| PEOPLE PER DOCTOR | 250 |
| GOVERNMENT | Multiparty democracy |
| ADULT LITERACY | 97% |

## Athens

Home to almost one-third of the Greek population, the capital of Athens is famous for its ancient buildings, such as the Acropolis and the 2,400-year-old ruins of the Parthenon. On certain days, cars are banned to protect the ruins. Nearby, pinewoods and mountains provide a retreat from the busy city.

Ruins of the Parthenon, a Greek temple

## Tourism

Each year, around 12,000,000 tourists visit Greece, attracted by its warm climate, ancient monuments, and beautiful islands. Tourism is the mainstay of the economy and employs thousands of Greeks each summer.

**Greek islander selling sponges to tourists**

## Shipping

Greece has the world's largest merchant fleet, and relies on ships to move goods between the many islands. The narrow Corinth Canal, built in 1893, links the Ionian and Aegean seas, providing important access to Athens.

# Bulgaria

From 1944 to 1989, Bulgaria was part of the Russian communist bloc. Since gaining independence, Bulgaria is slowly adapting to a democratic government and a western-style economy. About 85 percent of Bulgaria's population is Bulgar, with minorities of Turks, Macedonians, and Roma. The small groups have suffered discrimination, but are gaining power in parliament.

## Tourism

Bulgaria's Black Sea coast is becoming increasingly popular as a vacation spot, in particular the towns of Varna and Burgas. New airports serve western tourists, while Russians cross the Black Sea by ferry. Many new resorts have been built, and the natural beauty of the coastline, with its sandy beaches, pine forests, and old fishing villages, is often spoiled by high-rise hotels.

**Resort near Varna**

### BULGARIA FACTS

| | |
|---|---|
| CAPITAL CITY | Sofia |
| AREA | 42,822 sq miles (110,910 sq km) |
| POPULATION | 8,200,000 |
| DENSITY | 192 per sq mile (74 per sq km) |
| MAIN LANGUAGE | Bulgarian |
| MAJOR RELIGIONS | Christian, Muslim |
| CURRENCY | Lev |
| LIFE EXPECTANCY | 72 years |
| PEOPLE PER DOCTOR | 286 |
| GOVERNMENT | Multiparty democracy |
| ADULT LITERACY | 98% |

## Sofia

Bulgaria's capital is also its largest city, with more than one million inhabitants. Founded by the Romans, it is now the cultural and economic center, with one-fifth of the country's industry. The Alexander Nevsky Cathedral was built in the 1870s to celebrate liberation from Turkish rule.

Alexander Nevsky Cathedral

## Energy

Twenty-five percent of Bulgaria's electricity comes from the Kozloduy nuclear power station, built by the former Soviet Union in an earthquake zone. Increased safety measures have been introduced since 1990. Bulgaria imports 70 percent of its energy due to poor coal and oil resources, and has built a hydroelectric generator.

## Farming

Near the town of Kazanlúk in the Balkan Mountains, vast fields of roses are grown. The petals, picked at dawn in midsummer, are used to produce attar, the essential oil of roses, which is used in making perfume. Farther south, in the Maritsa valley, tobacco plants are grown and dried for cigarettes. Black grapes grown on the Danubian Plain are used for making high-quality red wine.

FIND OUT MORE

CHRISTIANITY  EUROPE, HISTORY OF  EUROPEAN UNION  FARMING  GREECE, ANCIENT  POLLUTION  PORTS AND WATERWAYS  SHIPS AND BOATS  SOVIET UNION

# GROWTH AND DEVELOPMENT

As THE HUMAN BODY grows and develops, it follows a regular sequence of changes. After birth, a human being passes through infancy, childhood, puberty, and adolescence, and into adulthood. The body grows at different rates at different times. Rapid growth, called a growth spurt, occurs during infancy and again at puberty. Growth is steady throughout childhood, but ceases in adulthood. In later life, the body ages and becomes less efficient. Eventually, one or more of the body's systems stops working, and a person dies.

## Changing proportions

Different parts of the body grow at different rates. Changing body proportions can be compared by fitting photographs of children and young adults into a panel that makes them appear the same height. The panel divides each body into eight equal parts. The head, for example, makes up one quarter of the height of a newborn baby, but only one eighth of the height of a 20-year-old.

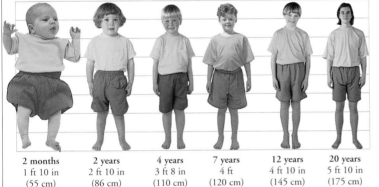

| 2 months<br>1 ft 10 in<br>(55 cm) | 2 years<br>2 ft 10 in<br>(86 cm) | 4 years<br>3 ft 8 in<br>(110 cm) | 7 years<br>4 ft<br>(120 cm) | 12 years<br>4 ft 10 in<br>(145 cm) | 20 years<br>5 ft 10 in<br>(175 cm) |

## From baby to child

During the first two years of life, a young human being grows and develops rapidly. A six-week-old baby is helpless and must have everything done for it, but by the age of two years, the baby can walk, talk, and feed itself. Growth and development is marked by a series of age milestones at which children have learned certain skills.

**6 weeks**
The baby sleeps when not being held or fed, and cries when distressed. She can follow objects with her eyes and listen to a person talking.

**6 months**
The baby can sit supported with her head up and back straight. She holds objects, squeals, and babbles.

**8 months**
The baby can sit up by herself, will try to crawl, and can stand if supported. She turns toward the sound of a familiar voice, and can imitate simple sounds.

**10 months**
The baby can crawl rapidly, pull herself up to a standing position, point to and pick up objects. She says her first words, usually "mama" and "dada."

*Toddler can walk a few steps on her own.*

*Child needs help getting dressed but can put on own shoes and socks.*

*Child can dress and undress herself.*

**14 months**
The child can stand alone and may walk without help. She speaks a few words, and tries to indicate what she wants.

**2 years**
She can run and jump, turn the pages of a book, identify pictures of familiar objects, and form a few short phrases.

**4 years**
The young girl now has good balance and can hop on one foot. She can draw simple pictures and copy some letters.

## Developing bones

The skeleton is formed before birth from flexible cartilage. During childhood, this is replaced by bone, as revealed by X rays. The skeleton continues to get larger and harder during the teenage years.

**A newborn baby's** skeleton is made of both bone and cartilage. Unlike bone, cartilage cannot be seen on an X ray.

**By the age of 6,** the wrist bones are forming so that there are now more bones. Other bones have become harder and bigger.

**By the age of 16,** the 27 bones that make up the fingers, palm, and wrist, are now mature, hard, and adult in size and form.

## Adolescence and puberty

Adolescence is the whole process of growing up from a child to an adult. During adolescence, changes occur to a person's body and in the way they think and feel. Puberty is part of adolescence during which the body grows rapidly and changes shape, and boys and girls become sexually mature and able to reproduce.

Puberty in boys          Puberty in girls

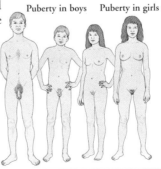

### Changes during puberty

In girls, puberty begins between the ages of 10–14. The body becomes rounder, breasts grow, and periods begin. In boys, puberty begins between the ages of 12–16. The body becomes more muscular, the testes produce sperm, and the voice deepens.

## Aging

Growing old is a normal part of life. Humans age because the body's cells gradually become less efficient. Signs of aging usually appear after 40 years of age. The body becomes less flexible, hair thins and turns gray, and the skin wrinkles. Bones become brittle and can break more easily. Exercise and a healthy diet can help slow down the aging process.

FIND OUT MORE | BRAIN AND NERVOUS SYSTEM | HORMONES AND ENDOCRINE SYSTEM | HUMAN BODY | MUSCLES AND MOVEMENT | REPRODUCTION | SKELETON

# GULF STATES

SAUDI ARABIA, Yemen, Oman, Kuwait, United Arab Emirates, Qatar, and Bahrain – make up the Arabian Peninsula. Six of these countries – all except Yemen – have coastlines on the Persian Gulf and are often called the Gulf States. As a result of the rich oil deposits in the region – about half the world's total – many of these countries are wealthy, and the region is politically very important. In the past 50 years, there has been great industrial and social change in what was an underdeveloped region. Even so, most of the land is uninhabited.

## Physical features

Nearly all of the Arabian Peninsula is dry desert, sandy or rocky, with some rugged, bare mountains near the coast. There are small fertile areas along the coasts, in some mountain regions, and at oases. Most of the fresh water for cities and industry comes from large desalination plants that remove salt from and purify seawater from the Persian Gulf.

**Red Sea**
The warm, salty waters of the narrow Red Sea, 1,243 miles (2,000 km) long, separate Africa from Asia. The Red Sea is connected to the Mediterranean Sea by the Suez Canal, which was built in 1869 to provide a route for ships between Europe and eastern Asia.

**Yemeni Mountains**
These rugged mountains in the west of Yemen reach a height of 12,336 ft (3,760 m). The western slopes are well watered by rain blowing in from the Red Sea and are extensively cultivated by terracing. The climate is ideal for growing coffee, grapes, and cotton.

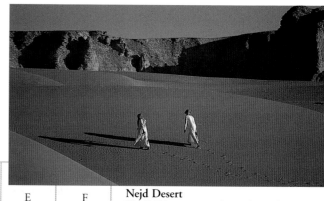

**Nejd Desert**
The Nejd is a vast area of stony desert plateau at the heart of Saudi Arabia. Some Nejdi people still live here, leading a seminomadic existence tending camels and sheep, although many are moving into towns. Saudi Arabia's largest desert is the uninhabited Rub' al Khali, in the south, known as the "Empty Quarter."

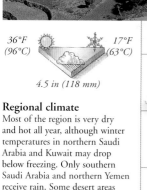

36°F (96°C)    17°F (63°C)

4.5 in (118 mm)

**Regional climate**
Most of the region is very dry and hot all year, although winter temperatures in northern Saudi Arabia and Kuwait may drop below freezing. Only southern Saudi Arabia and northern Yemen receive rain. Some desert areas have no rain for years at a time.

## Islam

For almost 1,500 years, Islam has been the dominant religion in the Gulf States. Muslims, the followers of Islam, believe in one god, Allah, and the prophet Muhammad, who was born in the Saudi Arabian town of Mecca. In many countries, life is interrupted five times a day while people pray.

Worshipers outside the mosque, Dubai

# Saudi Arabia

The largest and most important country in the Arabian Peninsula, Saudi Arabia is 95 percent hot, dry, and inhospitable desert. The most populated areas lie along the Gulf and Red Sea coasts. Founded in 1922 by Ibn Saud, Saudi Arabia has grown wealthy as a result of its vast oil reserves, discovered in 1938. It has major refining and petrochemical industries and spends freely on farming, education, and agriculture.

### People
Most Saudi people are Muslim Arabs. They take their religion seriously and interpret the Koran, the Islamic holy book, strictly. Women must wear veils and may not drive cars. However, about 33 percent of schoolchildren are girls, and women may take certain jobs, such as nursing and teaching.

*Cardamom pods are added to flavour the coffee.*

### Bedouin
Nomadic Bedouin roam the vast desert, grazing their camels, sheep, and goats in oases. They live in portable tents, but the government is trying to persuade them to give up their wandering life to settle in cities.

### SAUDI ARABIA FACTS

| | |
|---|---|
| CAPITAL CITY | Riyadh |
| AREA | 829,995 sq miles (2,149,690 sq km) |
| POPULATION | 21,600,000 |
| DENSITY | 26 per sq mile (10 per sq km) |
| MAIN LANGUAGE | Arabic |
| MAJOR RELIGION | Muslim |
| CURRENCY | Saudi riyal |
| LIFE EXPECTANCY | 71 years |
| PEOPLE PER DOCTOR | 588 |
| GOVERNMENT | Absolute monarchy |
| ADULT LITERACY | 77% |

G

## Riyadh
Saudi Arabia's capital since 1932, Riyadh is a modern city of about two million people. Lying among oases of orchards and palm groves, it is the center of Saudi Arabia's commerce and government. Buildings range from smart, modern skyscrapers, erected since 1950, to poor shacks.

**Saudi-Cairo Bank**

### Mecca (Makkah)
Every year, two million Muslims visit the Ka'ba shrine in the Great Mosque at Mecca, birthplace of Muhammed and Islamic holy city. All Muslims should make a pilgrimage, or *hajj,* to Mecca at least once in their lives.

**Lentils    Dates**

**Tomato**

### Farming
Massive irrigation projects using desalinated seawater to water vast, circular fields now make it possible for Saudi farmers to cultivate wheat, fruit, and vegetables. Farming employs one-eighth of the workforce.

*Giant pipes carry oil from wells to the coastal ports for export overseas.*

### Oil fields
Saudi Arabia has the world's biggest oil and gas reserves – one-quarter of the world's total – and is the leading oil exporter. Income from oil has greatly improved living standards.

# Yemen

Formerly two separate countries, Yemen was united in 1990. The north is mountainous, with a narrow, fertile, coastal strip on the Red Sea coast, where cotton and grapes are grown. The arid Rub' al Khali desert, or "Empty Quarter" covers the northeast. Yemen's main source of income is oil, some of which is refined in the port of Aden.

**Traditional Bedouin coffee pot**

### YEMEN FACTS

| | |
|---|---|
| CAPITAL CITY | Sana |
| AREA | 203,849 sq miles (527,970 sq km) |
| POPULATION | 18,100,000 |
| MAIN LANGUAGE | Arabic |
| MAJOR RELIGION | Muslim |
| CURRENCY | Yemeni riyal |

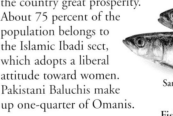

### Coffee
Yemen produces fine coffee beans, and coffee drinking is thought to have originated here. Mocha coffee is named after the port of Al-Makha from where it was exported. Yemenis chew *qat,* shoots of a narcotic shrub, with coffee.

### Sana
Yemen's modern capital, Sana, sits in the center of the country, 7,808 ft (2,380 m) above sea level. With a population of about half a million, it is a modern commercial and industrial center with historic buildings, markets, or *souks,* and ornately decorated mosques.

# Oman

Ruled by a sultan, the Sultanate of Oman is mostly desert, with a narrow fertile strip along the Gulf of Oman in the north, where most of the people live. Oil has brought the country great prosperity. About 75 percent of the population belongs to the Islamic Ibadi sect, which adopts a liberal attitude toward women. Pakistani Baluchis make up one-quarter of Omanis.

### OMAN FACTS

| | |
|---|---|
| CAPITAL CITY | Muscat |
| AREA | 82,030 sq miles (212,460 sq km) |
| POPULATION | 2,500,000 |
| MAIN LANGUAGES | Arabic, Baluchi |
| MAJOR RELIGIONS | Muslim, Hindu |
| CURRENCY | Omani rial |

**Sardines**

**Anchovy**

### Fishing
Omani fishermen catch 118,000 tons of fish a year in the rich waters of the Arabian Sea and Gulf of Oman. The main catches are anchovies, cod, cuttlefish, sardines, and tuna. The country exports dried fish and fish meal.

### City of the sands
Archaeologists have discovered the remains of a city, believed to have been built in about 3000 BC, buried beneath the sands of southern Oman. They think it may be the remains of the legendary lost Arabian city of Ubar.

G

# Kuwait

Oil has transformed Kuwait, a tiny desert country at the northern end of the Persian Gulf, into one of the world's most prosperous nations. Iraq's invasion of Kuwait, in 1990, was quelled by a United Nations force after a brief war. Since its liberation, Kuwait has built a wall to separate its territory from Iraq.

### Oil
Kuwait has about ten percent of the world's total oil

reserves. The oil industry, which attracts large overseas investment, accounts for more than 80 percent

### Kuwait City
The country of Kuwait is named after its capital city, which was founded in the 18th century. Situated on the shores of a natural harbor, Kuwait City is modern, built on a grid pattern with many attractive houses. The country's affluence is reflected in its glittering skyscrapers.

### KUWAIT FACTS

| | |
|---|---|
| CAPITAL CITY | Kuwait City |
| AREA | 6,880 sq miles (17,820 sq km) |
| POPULATION | 2,000,000 |
| MAIN LANGUAGES | Arabic, English |
| MAJOR RELIGION | Muslim |
| CURRENCY | Kuwaiti dinar |

### Free education
The revenue from the oil industry enables the Kuwaiti government to provide its children, both male and female, with free education, from nursery level to university. The Kuwaiti people have some of the world's highest salaries, pay no income tax, and receive free health care and social services.

# United Arab Emirates

The United Arab Emirates (UAE) is a federation of seven small states: Abu Dhabi, Ajman, Dubai, Fujairah, Ras al Khaimah, Sharjah, and Umm al Quaiwan. Each ruled by its own independent emir, or sheik, they unite for international matters and to sell the oil that has made them rich.

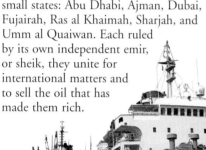

### Fishing
All the states bordering the Persian Gulf have busy fishing fleets. During midsummer they also send divers down to collect pearls from the pearl oysters. This industry has flourished for hundreds of years.

*Pearl develops from a grain of sand inside the shell.*

### Mina' Jabal 'Ali port
The UAE is one of the world's leading producers of natural gas and oil, both of which leave the country via Mina' Jabal 'Ali port, the world's largest artificial harbor. Since less than three percent of the UAE can be cultivated, the port is also used to import food products.

### UNITED ARAB EMIRATES FACTS

| | |
|---|---|
| CAPITAL CITY | Abu Dhabi |
| AREA | 32,278 sq miles (83,600 sq km) |
| POPULATION | 2,400,000 |
| MAIN LANGUAGES | Arabic, Farsi |
| MAJOR RELIGION | Muslim |
| CURRENCY | UAE dirham |

### Tourism
Hot sun, sandy beaches, and duty-free shopping make the UAE an attractive winter holiday resort for visitors from Europe and Japan (summer is too hot for tourism). The federation is gradually building up its tourism. Other attractions include trips into the desert, luxury hotels, and traditional markets.

# Qatar

A small peninsula in the Persian Gulf, Qatar, like other Gulf States, depends on natural gas and oil for its wealth. Although most of the country is desert, Qatar grows most of its own food by tapping reserves of underground water. Qatari women are free to drive cars and not wear veils.

### QATAR FACTS

| | |
|---|---|
| CAPITAL CITY | Doha |
| AREA | 4,415 sq miles (11,000 sq km) |
| POPULATION | 699,000 |
| MAIN LANGUAGES | Arabic, Farsi |
| MAJOR RELIGION | Muslim |
| CURRENCY | Qatar riyal |

### Foreign workers
Only 20 percent of the people are native-born Bedouin Qataris. The country has had to import workers from India, Asia, Iran, and other Arab countries to cope with the work produced by the oil industry. Almost 90 percent of the people live in the capital, Doha.

# Bahrain

Three inhabited islands and 30 smaller ones make up the small country of Bahrain. The oil reserves that made it rich are now running low, but the country has plenty of natural gas. Bahrain has a long history, and 4,000 years ago was a transit port for trade with India.

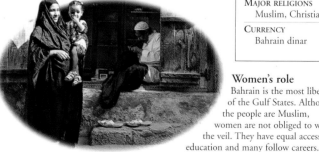

### BAHRAIN FACTS

| | |
|---|---|
| CAPITAL CITY | Manama |
| AREA | 263 sq miles (680 sq km) |
| POPULATION | 617,000 |
| MAIN LANGUAGES | Arabic, English |
| MAJOR RELIGIONS | Muslim, Christian |
| CURRENCY | Bahrain dinar |

### Women's role
Bahrain is the most liberal of the Gulf States. Although the people are Muslim, women are not obliged to wear the veil. They have equal access to education and many follow careers.

**FIND OUT MORE** ASIA, HISTORY OF · DESERTS · ENERGY · FARMING · FISHING INDUSTRY · ISLAM · ISLAMIC EMPIRE · MOSQUES · OIL · PORTS AND WATERWAYS

# GUNS

FROM A BOOMING cannon to a handgun, all firearms (guns) work on the same principle: a controlled explosion in one part of the gun propels a shell or bullet out of a tube or barrel. Firearms appeared in Europe in the early 14th century; although they were not powerful at first, in time they changed warfare forever. Armor could not stop bullets; castle walls could not withstand cannon balls. Without guns, no nation could resist invasion for long; armed with them, Europeans colonized most of the world.

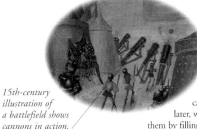

*15th-century illustration of a battlefield shows cannons in action.*

### Origins of guns
The first guns were cannons, known to have been used before 1326, when drawings of them appeared in a book. At first, smiths built the barrels from strips of iron. Safer, cast cannons came into use a century later, when bell-makers began to make them by filling a mould with liquid metal.

G

## Small arms

*.45-caliber bullet*

**Automatic Colt 1911 A1 pistol**

Soldiers carry small arms for individual use. These compact, lightweight weapons may have a stock for bracing the gun against the shoulder, or they may be fired from the hand. Most fire bullets rapidly from preloaded magazines. Some are very powerful: a modern rifle can fire a bullet more than 2,000 yards (1,800 m).

## Artillery

**Howitzer in use**

*Muzzle (front)*

*Shield protects gun crews*

*Breech (back), where ammunition is loaded.*

**Mountain howitzer**

A gun is described in terms of caliber, which is the width of the hole through its barrel, or the weight of the bullet it fires. The shells of artillery (heavy firearms) are big enough to destroy buildings. Artillery includes mortars, with a fairly short range, or longer-barrelled, long-range guns.

*Muzzle*    *Barrel*

### Pistols
A pistol is easy to hide under clothing and can be fired quickly. Its short barrel cannot be aimed accurately at distant targets, so it is used in close fighting or for self-defence.

*Trigger*

*Magazine rounds*

*Spring pushes bullets up.*

*Plastic hand guard*

**Submachine gun**

*30-round magazine is stored here.*

*Pistol grip*

### Automatic weapons
Set to automatic, many small arms will continue to fire as long as the soldier holds back the trigger.

**Sniper's rifle**    *Barrel*    *Stock*

### Rifles
Rifling (spiral grooves) inside the barrel of a gun makes the bullet spin in flight, improving accuracy. Self-loading rifles use the energy from firing a bullet to expel the cartridge case and load the next shot.

*10-round magazine*    *Rifles are fired from the shoulder.*

### Hiram Maxim

American-born inventor Hiram Maxim (1840–1916) developed the first practical automatic machine gun in 1884. Maxim guns fired so quickly that by World War I (1914–1918) soldiers no longer fought on horseback, but tried to hide from the bullets in trenches.

### Howitzers
A howitzer is a field gun, which may be towed or self-propelled to the battlefield. Its barrel and aim is midway between that of a mortar and a gun. Shells can be fired at a high angle so that they fly above hills or other defences before reaching enemy targets.

## Ammunition

The missile that a gun fires, the propellant (explosive charge), and the means of firing it are known together as ammunition. The first guns fired round stones, propelling them from the barrel with loose gunpowder, lit with a hot wire. From the mid-19th century on, following the introduction of rifled gun barrels, shells were long and pointed in shape. Today, in all but the biggest guns, a metal cartridge holds the missile, propellent, and means of firing together.

**Machine gun belt, World War I**

*250 rounds on the belt*

*Used by .22-in (5.56-mm) caliber gun*

**Rifle cartridge**    **Machine gun bullet**

*Armor-piercing shell, fired by anti-tank gun*

**Bullet, for .44 revolver**

### Gun control
A few civilians need to own guns for security, target shooting, pest control, and other uses. However, guns are dangerous and most countries control ownership. Many people believe these controls should be stricter to stop criminals getting hold of and using guns, and to reduce the number of shooting accidents.

**Gun safety poster, US**

FIND OUT MORE    ARMS AND ARMOR    WARFARE    WEAPONS    WORLD WAR I

# GUPTA EMPIRE

AT THE BEGINNING of the fourth century, India was made up of a number of separate kingdoms. In 320, Chandragupta I, ruler of Magadha, who was named after the warlike Mauryan rulers, took over neighboring kingdoms to found the Gupta Empire. Under his successors, the empire expanded to include much of India and became the greatest Asian country of the time, lasting about 150 years. It was a golden age of Indian painting, architecture, sculpture, and literature.

Magadha

Gupta Empire

## How the empire was run

The Guptas ran their empire as a group of small regions, or sub-kingdoms. Each sub-kingdom had its own ruler, but all were under the control of the emperor in Magadha. The first two Gupta emperors expanded the empire, while the later emperors had the task of holding the territory together.

Gupta coins had symbols, such as horses, instead of portraits.

**Chandragupta I**
In his short reign, the fierce Chandragupta I (320–330) expanded his territories by conquest and by his marriage to Princess Kumara Devi of the Lichchavi tribe.

**Samudragupta**
Chandragupta I's son (r.330–376) extended the empire into Bengal, central India, and the valleys of the upper Yamuna and Ganges rivers.

**Chandragupta II**
Named after his grandfather, the third Gupta had a long and peaceful reign (376–415), during which Indian art and literature began to flourish.

## Art and literature

Exteriors of the Buddhist cave-shrines at Ajanta, western India

During the Gupta period, Indian artists created some of their finest works. Magnificent palaces and temples contained the highest quality sculpture and paintings. Classical forms of music and dance, created under the Guptas, are still practiced all over Asia today.

Padmapani, the "lotus-bearer"

Bodhisattva

Musician with lyre

### Wall paintings
There are more than 30 Buddhist shrines and monasteries in the Ajanta hills. The walls of many of these were decorated with colorful frescoes, or wall paintings. Frescoes were a decorative style that continued for hundreds of years. The paintings show scenes from the life of the Buddha and other devotional subjects.

*The figures are dressed in Gupta-period costumes.*

*A procession of elephants*

*Wall paintings are a good source of information about life in the empire.*

**Painting from the Jataka stories, Cave 17, Ajanta**

### Sculpture
Lifelike sculptures adorned Gupta shrines and palaces. The most popular subjects were people who had made donations to the shrine, the Buddha and scenes from his life, and people known as Bodhisattvas (those who have reached the Buddhist goal of enlightenment and help others to do likewise). Many sculptures, such as the seated musician, were made of terra-cotta.

### The golden age of learning
Under the Guptas, universities expanded and became centers for the study of philosophy, medicine, and logic. The Sanskrit language was used to write epic stories. One of the finest writers of the period was Kalidasa, who lived during the reigns of Chandragupta II and Kumaragupta. His works include comedies, poems, and heroic plays that are still performed.

Sanskrit inscription

## Fa-Hsien

In 399, Fa-Hsien, a Chinese Buddhist, went to India to study the sacred writings of Buddhism. In the 10 years he was there, he wrote about life under the Gupta emperors. His writings form one of the most important sources for the history of this period.

### Cave-shrines

Many of the Buddhist cave-shrines in western India were cut out of the cliffs – a task that must have taken years of labor with the simple tools the Guptas used. The cave-shrines are dark but beautifully decorated with sculptures and paintings. The Buddha in this example is making the gesture known as *abhaya mudra*, or "have no fear."

## Timeline
**320** Chandragupta I founds the Gupta Empire.

**330–376** Samudragupta expands the empire from the Indus River to the Bay of Bengal and up into the northern mountains.

Bodhisattva

**376–415** Chandragupta II secures the empire and encourages trade.

**415–450** Kalidasa composes most of his poetry in the reign of Kumaragupta (415–455).

**c.450** Empire begins to collapse under pressure from invading Huns.

**554** The Gupta dynasty ends when the last emperor dies.

Silver Gupta horseman

**FIND OUT MORE**   BUDDHISM   HINDUISM   INDIA, HISTORY OF   MAURYAN EMPIRE   SHRINES

# GYMNASTICS

THERE ARE TWO MAIN BRANCHES of gymnastics – artistic and rhythmic. In artistic gymnastics, the gymnasts perform on fixed apparatus, such as bars and beams. In rhythmic gymnastics, they perform routines with apparatus such as hoops and balls. Other gymnastic sports include sports acrobatics and trampolining. In major artistic gymnastic competitions, the apparatus is set out on a large platform, or podium, and several events take place together. The competitors are awarded scores from one to 10 by a panel of judges.

## Men

There are six events in men's competitions. They are the floor, pommel horse, vault, rings, parallel bars, and high bar. Boys and men usually wear a jersey with shorts or white pants. Men's gymnastics calls for strength as well as balance and dynamic movement.

### Pommel horse
The pommel horse needs arm and shoulder strength. The gymnast moves back and forth along the horse, swinging his legs up and over, supporting himself on his hands only.

### Parallel bars
The bars are an all-around test for men. There is a wide choice of movements that a gymnast can perform, including swings and balances, and support and strength moves.

### Rings
During a routine on the rings, a gymnast must not swing the ropes. Some positions must be held for two seconds. Greater strength is needed than for any other apparatus.

*The ribbon is attached to a wand.*

*Ribon*

*Ball*

*Clubs*

*Rope*

*Hoops*

### Rhythmic gymnastics
Performed only by women and girls, rhythmic gymnastics consists of five individual exercises – ribbon, clubs, ball, hoop, and rope. There are also group exercises performed by a team, usually with two different pieces of apparatus.

*Holding a position to show strength*

### Floor
Men's floor exercises last 50 to 70 seconds and feature balances as well as somersaults and handsprings. Gymnasts must not step off the square mat.

### High bar
High bar routines contain continuous swinging moves. The gymnast circles around and around, with turns, twists, and changes of direction and grip.

### Vault
This is the shortest event. Boys and men perform only one vault. Until they are about 13, boys vault across the horse, but after that they vault along its length.

*The ribbon is made of silk.*

### Trampolining
This is an excellent exercise routine for practicing moves such as twists and somersaults, and it is also a sport in itself. There are solo competitions and synchronized pairs. Judges award marks for difficulty and how well a routine is performed.

## Women

There are four women's events – the floor, beam, asymmetric (uneven) bars, and vault. In competitions women enter all events. Women and girls usually wear one-piece leotards with short or long sleeves. Women's exercises call for balance and agility, and floor exercises include elements of dance.

### Beam
The beam is 16.4 ft (5 m) long and only 4 in (10 cm) wide. Gymnasts must perform deliberate movements and graceful balances. The leading gymnasts can perform somersaults and backflips.

*Springing into a back flip*

*One leg is brought over first.*

*Gymnast looks for the floor.*

### Floor
The women's floor routine is performed to music. Women and girls have from 60 to 90 seconds. Gymnasts are expected to include dance steps in their routine, as well as spectacular running somersaults.

*Women vault across the width of the horse.*

### Vault
Women and girls have two vaults in a competition; the higher of the two marks counts. Different turns and somersaults are used, especially as the gymnast thrusts off the horse before landing neatly.

### Asymmetric bars
This is possibly the most difficult of the women's apparatus. The gymnast must make full use of two bars 7.5 ft (2.3 m) and 5 ft (1.5 m) high, swinging and changing grip. The routine must have a flowing rhythm with no stops or hesitations.

## Nadia Comaneci

Romanian gymnast Nadia Comaneci (b.1962) became the first person to score a maximum 10 points in Olympic competition at the age of 14. She scored seven 10s in the 1976 Montreal Olympics, winning the overall gold medal as well as separate golds for the bars and beam.

### Sports acrobatics
This type of gymnastics comprises tumbling, pairs, and group events. Tumbling is like the floor exercises, but performed on a straight, sprung track. The routines in pairs (men, women, or mixed), the trio (women), and fours (men) are like those of circus acrobats.

*A mixed pair balance*

**FIND OUT MORE**

OLYMPIC GAMES

ROMANIA, UKRAINE, AND MOLDOVA

SPORTS

# Gymnastics
## Sports acrobatics

Clasps hands firmly

Leans back.

Keeps her body tensed.

The base rests much of his body on the floor.

Leg positions can be varied.

The top holds her body in a straight line.

The top keeps her body still.

The top lifts and straddles her legs.

The base carries his partner's weight on his legs.

**Counterbalance:** gymnasts use their weight against each other.

**Shoulder balance:** a simple, stable position

**Simple balance:** the base supports the top.

**Stag balance:** elegance contrasts with strength.

**Straddle lever balance:** an advanced position

## Rhythmic sequences

Gymnast performs to music.

Moves elegantly throughout the sequence.

Full side bend

The gymnast keeps her arm straight.

Graceful arm position

1 Swings hoop around the waist

2 Lets a side of the hoop drop

3 Jumps through the hoop

4 Carries hoop to the side

1 Carries the ball to one side

2 Circles the ball behind

3 Spirals to the other side

4 Rises into an arabesque

## Artistic, floor

This move is known as a Y-balance.

Legs held together and straight

Stretching his arms upward helps the gymnast stand.

Gymnast tucks his body down into a roll.

Keeps toes pointed

Gymnast presses legs together

Moves round in quarter turns

Gymnasts generally prefer to work barefoot.

The gymnast moves smoothly into each stage of the exercise.

Head tucked in

Spread fingers

1 Gymnast holds balance for two seconds.

2 Springs into a dive

3 Upward and forward into a dive roll

4 Lands on hands and rolls

5 Rolls onto feet and comes up to stand

6 Kicks up to a handstand, then turns around by moving his hands

## Artistic, beam

**The beam,** used only in women's gymnastics, is very difficult. For safety's sake, a gymnast must progress from floor skills to a low beam, then a practice beam.

The gymnast learns to walk, turn, and sit on a beam first.

Head up, back straight

Looking ahead

In competition, judges deduct points for wobbly or faulty landings.

The gymnast tries to jump as high as possible.

She bends her knees as she lands.

Toes pointed

1 Gymnast mounts the side or end of the beam.

2 Performs low move, known as V-sit

3 The gymnast begins a W-jump.

4 With one step, takes off from both feet

5 She points one leg forward and tucks the other behind.

6 Prepares to land

7 She keeps a steady balance.

G

# HEALTH AND FITNESS

IF A MACHINE is treated with care and given proper maintenance, it is more likely to function efficiently. Similarly, the human body is most likely to function best if it is kept fit and healthy. Health may be defined as the state of being well in body and mind. Fitness is an indication of how efficiently the body's muscles, heart, and lungs are working. If a person is fit, he or she can deal with stresses usually put on bodies by everyday activities such as walking and lifting, and also with sudden demands, such as sprinting for a bus. Mental health – the mind's fitness – is also important for a person's well-being.

## What is health?

When someone is in good health it means their body is working to its full potential and is not impeded by physical or mental diseases. People's health may suffer as they become older, if they eat a poor diet, if they are poor, if they are exposed to pollution, or work in a harmful environment.

Outdoor play contributes to the healthy development of children.

## Maintaining health

Many people in developed countries are overweight, take little exercise, and eat too much fatty food. This makes them unfit, and often unhealthy. Eating a balanced diet with plenty of fresh fruit and vegetables and not too much fat, combined with regular exercise, promotes better health.

### Diet
A healthy diet consists of the right amounts of protein, carbohydrate, fat, vitamins, minerals, and fiber. The energy it provides should keep the body at its ideal weight.

Fruit and vegetables are full of vitamins.

Fish provides energy, iron, and protein.

Dairy products provide protein and fat.

Meat is full of protein and vitamins.

Nuts and fungi contain protein and minerals.

Beans, rice, and pasta provide carbohydrates.

### Exercise
The human body requires exercise to improve fitness. Exercise makes the heart and lungs work more efficiently, and strengthens muscles and bones. This helps keep the body flexible.

*Stretching side lateral muscles and abdomen*

*Clothing is loose and comfortable.*

*Body weight is put on right leg to stretch left thigh.*

*All major muscle groups are stretched.*

Gentle stretching is a good way to start an exercise program

*Training shoes should be used.*

*Legs are stretched gently to prevent any strain.*

### Relaxation
Regular relaxation reduces stress and tension, increases a sense of well-being, and decreases the risk of disease. There are many ways to relax including massage, yoga, and meditation.

Yoga lotus position

## Mental health

Mental health is the fitness of the mind. Problems may be caused by heredity, or emotional problems triggered by relationships or lifestyle. Keeping fit, discussing problems, and seeking professional help can all improve a person's mental health. Some people are affected by mental illnesses that have been caused by chemical imbalances in the brain.

Doctors who look after mental health are called psychiatrists.

## Public health

Public health is concerned with the effect environment has upon a population's health, and how the health of a community can be improved. Workers in this field are interested in, for example, good housing, effective sanitation, reducing air pollution, and the immunization of children and adults against infectious diseases.

### Sanitation
Sanitation is the provision of clean drinking water, enclosed sewers, and drains. It stops food and water being contaminated by potentially fatal pathogens (germs) from human waste and helps stop the spread of disease.

Poor sanitation in slums in 19th-century England

Syringe

### Immunization
Immunization protects people from disease. It involves injecting them with small amounts of pathogens of a certain disease. This stimulates the body to produce antibodies that fight the disease, producing protection.

## Checkups
A doctor gives a checkup, or physical examination, to make sure that a person is healthy, and to look out for anything that may be wrong. During a checkup, the doctor will ask the patient how he or she feels, look at and feel the patient's body, use a stethoscope to listen to breathing and the heart, and measure blood pressure.

Doctor examines girl's throat.

FIND OUT MORE    DISEASES    DRUGS    FOOD    HUMAN BODY    MEDICINE    SOCIETIES, HUMAN    SPORTS

# HEART AND CIRCULATORY SYSTEM

THE HEART IS A FIST-SIZED muscular pump that beats nonstop, 24 hours a day, sending blood around the body. The blood travels along a massive network of tubes called blood vessels. Together, they make up the circulatory system. The larger blood vessels divide repeatedly to form smaller vessels that travel to every cell in the body, supplying oxygen from the lungs and digested food, and carrying away waste. Blood helps defend the body against infection and also distributes heat around the body, helping maintain the same temperature.

**Right atrium** receives oxygen-poor blood from body.

**Tricuspid valve** prevents blood flowing backwards from right ventricle into right atrium.

**Aorta** carries oxygen-rich blood from the heart to the body.

**Superior vena cava** carries blood from upper body into right atrium.

**Pulmonary trunk** carries oxygen-poor blood from heart towards lungs.

*Right atrium*

**Left atrium** receives oxygen-rich blood from lungs.

**Semilunar valve** stops blood from flowing back into right ventricle.

**Left ventricle** pumps blood to body.

**Right ventricle** pumps blood to lungs.

*Left atrium*

**Septum** is wall that separates ventricles.

**Coronary artery** supplies heart with blood.

*Right ventricle*    *Left ventricle*

## How the heart beats

The wall of the heart is made of cardiac muscle, which contracts automatically. The two halves of the heart beat together to pump blood around the body. Inside the heart, blood passes from the atria (upper chambers) to the ventricles (lower chambers). Valves ensure that blood cannot flow backward through the heart. Each heartbeat is not a single contraction, but consists of three stages.

## Heart

The heart consists of two muscular pumps, left and right, which lie side by side. Each pump is divided into a smaller upper chamber, or atrium, and a lower chamber, or ventricle. The left ventricle has a thicker wall because it has to pump blood around the body; the thinner-walled right ventricle pumps blood to the lungs.

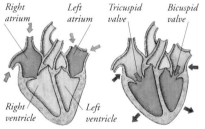
*Right atrium*  *Left atrium*  *Tricuspid valve*  *Bicuspid valve*
*Right ventricle*  *Left ventricle*

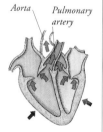
*Aorta*  *Pulmonary artery*

1 During the first stage (diastole), both the atria and the ventricles are relaxed. Blood flows into and fills both atria. The semilunar valves at the exit points of the ventricles are closed.

2 During the second stage (atrial systole), the tricuspid and bicuspid valves between the atria and the ventricles open. Both atria contract and squeeze blood into the ventricles below them.

3 During the third stage (ventricular systole), the ventricles contract to push blood out of the heart. The tricuspid and bicuspid valves close, while the semilunar valves open.

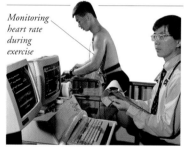
*Monitoring heart rate during exercise*

### Heart rate
The heart normally beats about 70 times per minute. This is your heart rate. It changes according to the oxygen demands of the body. If you exercise, heart rate increases to pump more oxygen-carrying blood to your muscles.

### William Harvey
English doctor William Harvey (1578-1657) was the first person to show that blood circulated through the body. Before Harvey, it was thought that blood ebbed and flowed along blood vessels rather like the tide coming in and going out. Harvey concluded that blood traveled in one direction only, and that it was pumped by the heart.

## Blood

Blood is a liquid transportation system that travels to every cell in the body. It supplies body cells with oxygen and nutrients, and carries away waste products. Blood consists of billions of blood cells floating in a yellowish liquid called plasma. There are three types of blood cells: red blood cells, white blood cells, and platelets. Red blood cells make up 99 percent of all blood cells. A soft tissue inside bones called red marrow produces blood cells.

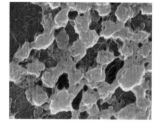
### Platelets
Platelets are cell fragments that prevent blood from leaking out of injured blood vessels. If a blood vessel is damaged, platelets gather at the site and stick to each other to form a plug.

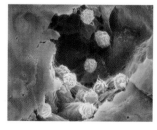
### White blood cells
White blood cells defend the body against infection. There are three main types. Granulocytes and monocytes engulf invading germs; lymphocytes release chemicals that destroy germs.

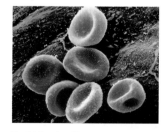
### Red blood cells
Red blood cells are packed with a red substance called hemoglobin. Hemoglobin picks up oxygen in the lungs and releases it as blood passes through other parts of the body.

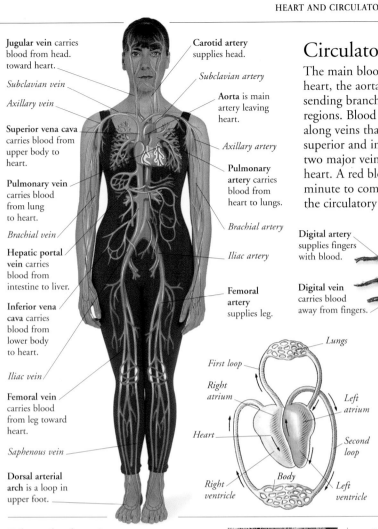

Jugular vein carries blood from head. toward heart.

Subclavian vein

Axillary vein

Superior vena cava carries blood from upper body to heart.

Pulmonary vein carries blood from lung to heart.

Brachial vein

Hepatic portal vein carries blood from intestine to liver.

Inferior vena cava carries blood from lower body to heart.

Iliac vein

Femoral vein carries blood from leg toward heart.

Saphenous vein

Dorsal arterial arch is a loop in upper foot.

Carotid artery supplies head.

Subclavian artery

Aorta is main artery leaving heart.

Axillary artery

Pulmonary artery carries blood from heart to lungs.

Brachial artery

Iliac artery

Femoral artery supplies leg.

Digital artery supplies fingers with blood.

Digital vein carries blood away from fingers.

# Circulatory system

The main blood vessel leaving the heart, the aorta, divides repeatedly, sending branches to major body regions. Blood returns to the heart along veins that join to form the superior and inferior venae cavae, the two major veins which reenter the heart. A red blood cell takes just one minute to complete its journey around the circulatory system.

## Circulation in the arm
The blood vessels of the arm show how the circulatory system works. The brachial artery divides into several branches, including the radial artery. Veins carrying blood from the hand and wrist unite to form the brachial vein leaving the arm.

Axiliary vein carries blood toward heart.

Cephalic vein

Basilic vein

Radial vein

Axiliary artery supplies arm with blood.

Brachial artery

Humerus

Radius

Ulna

Ulnar artery

## How blood circulates
There are, in fact, two parts to the circulatory system. The pulmonary circulation carries oxygen-poor blood from the right side of the heart along the pulmonary arteries to the lungs and back to the left side of the heart along the pulmonary veins. The systemic circulation carries oxygen-rich blood from the left side of the heart along the aorta to the body, and returns oxygen-poor blood to the right side of the heart.

Lungs

First loop

Right atrium

Heart

Right ventricle

Body

Left atrium

Second loop

Left ventricle

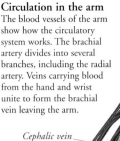

## Flushing
Exercise can cause a reddening of the face and body known as flushing. This happens when, to cool the body down, blood vessels near the skin's surface widen as blood flow increases to lose heat from the skin. The increased blood flow makes the skin redden.

# Blood clotting

When a blood vessel is damaged, clotting reduces the loss of blood. Platelets accumulate at the wound and stick together to form a plug. Red blood cells are trapped in threads of fibrin to form a clot. White blood cells prevent infection beneath a hard outer scab.

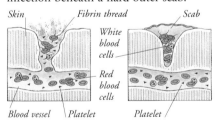

Skin

Fibrin thread

Scab

White blood cells

Red blood cells

Blood vessel

Platelet

Platelet

## Fibrin
Chemicals in the blood and damaged cells trigger the production of the protein fibrin. This forms strands that trap red blood cells into a clot. A hard crust, called a scab, forms over the clot to protect the wound.

# Blood vessels

There are three types of blood vessels: arteries, veins, and capillaries. Arteries divide into smaller vessels called arterioles, which themselves divide into a network of capillaries. Blood then passes to venules and veins.

## Arteries
Arteries carry blood away from the heart. They have thick, muscular walls that can withstand the high pressure produced when the heart beats. Arteries usually carry blood that is rich in oxygen.

## Veins
Veins carry blood toward the heart. They have thin walls because pressure inside them is low. They contain valves to prevent blood flowing backward.

Arteriole

Capillary network

Venule

Valve

Artery

Vein

Thick wall of artery

Thin wall of vein

## Capillaries
Capillaries are the tiny blood vessels that carry blood between arterioles and venules. They supply individual cells with food and oxygen and remove wastes.

## Karl Landsteiner
Austrian/American Karl Landsteiner (1868–1943) discovered the existence of blood types, and made safe blood transfusion a reality. In 1900, Landsteiner showed that red blood cells may clump together when blood from different people is mixed. He worked out the ABO blood type system, and was awarded a Nobel Prize.

# Blood types

People belong to different blood types, depending on the antigens (chemicals) that occur in their red blood cells. The ABO blood type system has two antigens, A and B. It has four blood types: A (carries A antigen); B (carries B antigen); AB (carries both antigens); and O (carries neither).

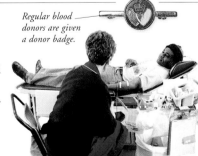

Regular blood donors are given a donor badge.

## Blood compatibility
Blood transfusion is the donation of blood by one person to another. People who share the same blood types can give or receive blood safely because their blood is compatible. In an emergency, however, people with type O blood can give blood to any other group.

FIND OUT MORE | CELLS | FIRST AID | HEALTH AND FITNESS | HORMONES AND ENDOCRINE SYSTEM | HUMAN BODY | IMMUNE AND LYMPHATIC SYSTEM | LUNGS AND BREATHING | MEDICINE | MUSCLES AND MOVEMENT

# HEAT AND TEMPERATURE

IN GREEK MYTHOLOGY, Icarus flew too close to the sun and fell to his death as the sun's heat melted his wings made of wax. Heat is a type of energy that can indeed melt wax, and many other substances. The temperature of a substance – how hot or cold it is – can be thought of as how much heat energy that substance contains. More precisely, temperature is a measurement of the energy possessed by the moving particles that make up a substance.

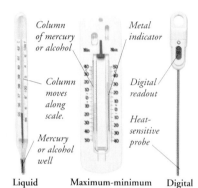

Column of mercury or alcohol

Metal indicator

Column moves along scale.

Digital readout

Heat-sensitive probe

Mercury or alcohol well

**Liquid**    **Maximum-minimum**    **Digital**

## Thermometers

A device that measures temperature is called a thermometer. A liquid thermometer contains a column of mercury or alcohol that expands and contracts as the temperature changes, moving up and down a scale. A maximum and minimum thermometer records the highest and lowest temperatures over a certain period using metal indicators that are moved by a liquid column. A digital thermometer contains a heat-sensitive electronic probe. The probe produces an electric current that varies with changes in temperature.

## Thermal expansion

Heating a substance gives its particles more energy so that they move faster and farther. The particles take up more room and increase the volume of the substance in a process called thermal expansion.

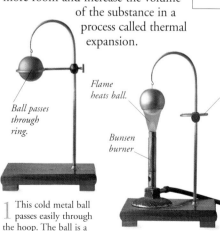

Ball passes through ring.

Flame heats ball.

Bunsen burner

Ring is moved away.

Hot ball is now too wide to pass through ring.

1 This cold metal ball passes easily through the hoop. The ball is a solid object, composed of millions of tightly packed, vibrating particles.

2 A hot flame heats the ball, giving its particles more heat energy.

3 The extra energy increases the size of the particles' vibrations, making them take up more space. The ball expands and will no longer pass through the ring.

## Temperature scale

Just as the scale on a ruler shows length in inches or centimeters, a temperature scale shows temperature in units called degrees Celsius (C), degrees Fahrenheit (F), or kelvin (K). Most temperature scales are defined by two "fixed points." The Celsius scale uses the melting and boiling points of water as its fixed points.

### Absolute zero

There is no upper limit to temperature, but there is a lower limit, called absolute zero (-459°F, -273°C, 0K), at which atoms and molecules are stationary. Scientists have managed to achieve temperatures within a millionth of a degree of absolute zero. The study of how matter behaves at very low temperatures is known as cryogenics.

**Cryogenics scientist at work**

212°F (100°C, 373K): water boils

136°F (58°C, 331K): highest recorded temperature on Earth

110.3°F (43.3°C, 316.3K): normal body temperature of a sparrow
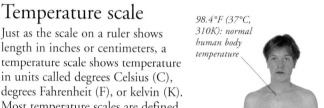

98.4°F (37°C, 310K): normal human body temperature

82.6°F (28.1°C, 301.1K): normal body temperature of echidna (spiny anteater)

64°F (18°C, 291K): normal room temperature (water is in its liquid state)

32°F (0°C, 273K): freezing point of water

**Fahrenheit scale**

## Producing heat

Heat can be produced in a number of different ways, including friction, chemical reactions, and an electric current.

Drilling machine

### Heat from friction

The American scientist Benjamin Thompson (1753–1814) discovered that friction produces heat. At his weapons factory in Germany, he noticed that when a brass gun barrel was drilled, friction between the drill and the gun barrel made the gun barrel extremely hot.

### Heat and chemical reactions

Athletes often use a device called a hot pack to treat a sprained limb. The pack contains powdered iron that reacts with oxygen from the air when the pack is shaken. The heat from the chemical reaction warms the joint and eases the pain.

### Heat and electricity

An electric current always produces heat. When current flows through an electric toaster, for example, the heat produced raises the temperature of the wire coil until it glows red hot and toasts bread.

Coil

## Refrigerator

A refrigerator is a machine that is used to chill food, drinks, and other items. A liquid called a refrigerant flows through pipes inside the refrigerator. The liquid absorbs heat from the refrigerator's contents and evaporates. The vapor is compressed and pumped into a tube on the outside of the refrigerator. As the vapor passes through the tube, it loses heat to the surrounding air and condenses back to a liquid.

Tube is called a condenser.

Refrigerant absorbs heat from inside refrigerator and loses it to air outside.

Insulated walls

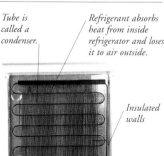

Pump circulates refrigerant

**Rear view of refrigerator**

Water molecules gain heat from the hot pan and vibrate faster.

Bubbles appear as the water molecules use heat from the flame to break free from each other and form steam.

## Latent heat

When a liquid is at its boiling point, an input of heat energy will not raise the liquid's temperature any further. Instead, the extra energy enables particles in the liquid to break free from each other and form a gas. This energy is called latent heat. The energy is released again if the gas condenses into a liquid. Latent heat is also absorbed when a solid melts, and released when a liquid freezes.

**Thermal motion**
All matter is made up of moving particles. This movement is called thermal motion. The temperature of an object is a measure of its thermal motion. Heating the object makes its particles vibrate faster and raises its temperature.

## Radiation

All objects give out energy in the form of infrared rays, which are similar to X rays. A hot object, such as a lightbulb, gives out a lot of infrared rays. These rays will heat up any object that absorbs them. Dull surfaces absorb infrared rays well; shiny surfaces reflect them. Infrared rays are invisible, but you can feel their effect. The closer you put your hand to a lightbulb, the warmer it feels because the radiation is more intense.

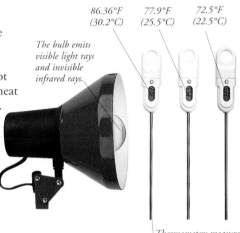

The bulb emits visible light rays and invisible infrared rays.

86.36°F (30.2°C)  77.9°F (25.5°C)  72.5°F (22.5°C)

Thermometers measure heat radiated by light.

**Propagator**
Seeds sprout and grow more rapidly in warm conditions, so they are often planted in a tiny greenhouse called a propagator. Sunlight passes through the propagator's plastic cover and warms the seeds and soil, which radiate the heat back out again as infrared rays. The rays cannot pass through plastic, so the heat is trapped inside and the temperature rises.

## Convection

The way heat travels as moving currents through a gas or a liquid is called convection. If a tank of water is heated from below, the warm water at the bottom will rise as it expands and becomes less dense. The cooler, denser water above sinks to take its place. Soon this cooler water also warms and starts to rise, creating a circulation of water called a convection current.

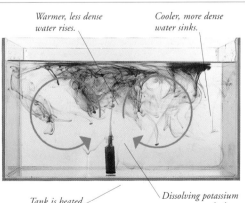

Warmer, less dense water rises.

Cooler, more dense water sinks.

Tank is heated from below.

Dissolving potassium permanganate crystals show the movement of the water.

## Heat conduction

When a substance is heated, its vibrating particles knock against neighboring particles and pass on some of their thermal motion, spreading heat throughout the substance. This energy transfer is called conduction. Heat conducts from warm substances to cooler ones. The warm air in a room can lose heat through a window. Heat conducts from the warm air to the window, and then to the cooler air outside.

Temperature outside is 65°F (18.3°C).

Temperature inside is 71°F (21.7°C).

Thermometer records temperature difference across window.

**Heat conductors**
Some materials – called conductors – conduct heat better than others. If you press wax on the ends of metal and plastic spoons in hot water, the wax on the metal spoon melts first. This is because metal is a better conductor.

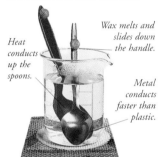

Heat conducts up the spoons.

Wax melts and slides down the handle.

Metal conducts faster than plastic.

**Hot or cold?**
A marble tile feels colder than a carpet at room temperature. Marble is a better conductor than carpet. Marble takes heat rapidly away from the body, making the marble tile feel much colder to the touch than the carpet.

Marble tile    Carpet

## Heat insulators

Poor conductors of heat, such as plastics, wood, cork, and air, are known as insulators. Using such materials to reduce heat loss from an object is called insulation. When these two jars are filled with water at 176°F (80°C) and left for 15 minutes, the jar covered in bubble wrap retains the most heat. Bubble wrap (plastic filled with pockets of air) is a good insulator.

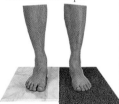

80.6°F (27°C)    108°F (42.4°C)

Bubble wrap

Uninsulated jar    Insulated jar

Airtight stopper

Hot or cold liquid

Vacuum between double walls of thermos

Shiny walls reflect heat radiation.

**Vacuum thermos**
A vacuum thermos keeps drinks hot or cold by stopping the transfer of heat to or from the liquid. Conduction can only occur through matter, so the flask has two walls with a vacuum between them to prevent conduction. Shiny walls reflect heat radiation, while the thermos is sealed with an airtight stopper made of a good insulator.

**FIND OUT MORE**  ELECTRICITY  ENERGY  FRICTION  GASES  LIQUIDS  MATTER  METALS  SOLIDS  X RAYS AND THE ELECTROMAGNETIC SPECTRUM

# HEDGEHOGS AND OTHER INSECTIVORES

THE ORDER INSECTIVORA, which means insect-eating, contains more than 370 species, including hedgehogs, moles, shrews, and tenrecs. Most of these mammals, especially the shrews, are highly active and have to eat almost constantly to sustain themselves. They have poor eyesight, but a good sense of smell. They rely on smell to find their prey of worms and snails as well as insects. Insectivores have sharp teeth for preying on invertebrates. The hedgehogs and some tenrecs are protected from predators by spines.

*The long snout has many highly sensitive whiskers that the hedgehog uses to navigate and also to find food.*

*A female hedgehog usually has two litters of young each year.*

*Ordinary fur grows on the chest and belly.*

## Hedgehogs

Like most insectivores, hedgehogs are nocturnal, solitary animals that associate only to mate. Each adult animal needs its own territory in order to find enough to eat. Not all hedgehogs are spiny, but the European and desert hedgehogs have a thick covering of spines on the top of the head and body to protect them against predators such as foxes.

*European hedgehogs build up a layer of fat during the summer to sustain them during the winter when they hibernate.*

*Young hedgehogs accompany their mother to find food.*

*Young hedgehogs stay with their mother until they are about seven weeks old.*

### Hedgehog spines

A European hedgehog has about 5,000 spines, which are actuallly hairs that grow into sharp, stiff tubes. Hedgehogs are born with their first coat of pale spines flat under the skin, but these grow out within a few hours. At two days old, the hedgehog's dark spines start to grow.

*When threatened, a hedgehog raises its spines.*

*Each spine is controlled by muscles in the hedgehog's skin.*

*Spines normally lie flat over the hedgehog's body.*

*For extra protection, a hedgehog can roll into a prickly ball.*

## Moles

Moles live underground in a system of tunnels that they dig through the soil. They are well adapted for this existence, with a compact body, short legs, tiny eyes, and no protruding ears. They are active day and night, looking for food such as worms, insect larvae, and beetles.

*Fur lies in no particular direction so that the mole can push backward or forward through its tunnels.*

### Molehills

Mounds of soil, often called molehills, are the result of a mole's tunneling activities. The mole pushes loose soil to the surface up short vertical tunnels.

*A nest under the mound*

*Strong claws for loosening the soil*

### Mole feet

The front paws are broad with large claws, that do the digging. The hind feet are narrower with sharp claws and are used to push soil to the surface.

## Shrews

These small mammals have a long snout and short legs. They are very active and need a constant supply of food to keep them alive. Shrews are extremely aggressive and will attack one another if they meet. Many predators avoid shrews because of a foul-smelling secretion that they can produce from scent glands.

*Shrews eat up to 130 percent of their body weight every day.*

## Tenrecs

The 30 species of tenrec live only on the island of Madagascar. Some swim, some climb, and others live underground. Some have spines, others look more like shrews. They bear many young. The common tenrec may have 34 in one litter.

### EUROPEAN HEDGEHOG

**SCIENTIFIC NAME** *Erinaceus europaeus*

**ORDER** Insectivora

**FAMILY** Erinaceidae

**DISTRIBUTION** Europe, east into Russia. Introduced to New Zealand.

**HABITAT** Farmland, suburbs, forests and mountains.

**DIET** Beetles, worms, caterpillars, other invertebrates, small mammals, and carrion.

**SIZE** Length: 10 in (25 cm)

**LIFESPAN** 4–7 years

FIND OUT MORE    ANIMALS    ANIMAL BEHAVIOR    HIBERNATION

# HERONS, STORKS AND FLAMINGOS

HERONS AND THEIR relatives are distinctive birds, with long, slender legs and a large beak. Most of them eat fish and other water animals, and can wade out into the water to look for food without getting their feathers wet. Herons hunt by stealth, and several species have developed remarkable fishing techniques. Flamingos catch their food by straining it through fibrous plates in their beak. Although storks have long legs, most of them do not wade, but catch their food on land. Many of these birds are sociable animals, living and nesting in large flocks or colonies. These groups give them some protection from predators.

*Neck is hunched at rest and in flight.*

*Herons often rest with one leg raised.*

## Herons

There are about 60 species of herons. They live all over the world, except Antarctica and the far north. Most live close to water, and they often nest in groups. They usually build their nests out of sticks and reeds in a tree or bush.

**Cattle egret**
This small heron lives near cattle and other grazers and feasts on the small animals that they disturb. In recent years, cattle egret have become one of the world's most commonly found birds.

**Bittern**
Bitterns live in dense reedbeds that camouflages it perfectly. When threatened, the birds point their beaks skyward and sway gently. They then look like the reeds moving in the wind.

**Juvenile goliath heron**

**Adult goliath heron**

*Long, straight legs*

**Black heron fishing**
The African black heron wades into the water and raises its wings like an umbrella. Its wingspan casts a shadow on the surface and probably helps the heron see any fish swimming below.

## Fishing

Many herons, including the goliath heron, catch fish by wading into the water and then keeping absolutely still with their necks hunched. When a fish swims by, the heron crouches down toward the surface, then suddenly stretches out its neck and stabs the fish with its beak. Other herons have developed different fishing techniques.

**Green heron**
This heron usually hunts at night when many small animals are active. It often perches, legs bent, on a low branch, ready to pounce on its prey.

**Flamingo skull**

**Marabou stork**

## Flamingos

Many of the five species of flamingos live in shallow, salty lakes where little else survives. They feed by turning their heads upside down, using their uniquely shaped beaks to filter tiny animals and plants from the water.

## Storks

There are 19 species of storks. Some feed by wading into water, but others live in dry habitats. The giant African marabou stork is a scavenger. It feeds on dead animals, much the way vultures do, but it will also eat live prey, such as insects, fish, rats, and small birds.

*This stork has one of the largest wingspans of all birds.*

*Long legs and toes*

**Fishing with bait**
The North American green heron throws small twigs or pellets into the water. It waits for fish to be attracted by this bait and catches them when they come within range.

**Colonies**
Flocks of flamingos can contain more than 2 million birds. They build moundlike nests with mud that they scrape up with their beaks.

**Nests**
White storks migrate long distances and return to the same place in Europe every year to breed. They are traditionally encouraged to nest on houses because they are supposed to bring luck.

### GOLIATH HERON

| | |
|---|---|
| SCIENTIFIC NAME | *Ardea goliath* |
| ORDER | Ciconiiformes |
| FAMILY | Ardeidae |
| DISTRIBUTION | Africa, Arabian peninsula, India |
| HABITAT | Coasts, lakes, rivers, marshy ground |
| DIET | Mainly fish |
| SIZE | Length: 59 in (150 cm) |
| LIFESPAN | About 25 years |

 FIND OUT MORE — BIRDS · BIRDS OF PREY · LAKE AND RIVER WILDLIFE · SHOREBIRDS

# HIBERNATION

DURING WINTER, as temperatures drop and food becomes scarce, some animals hibernate in order to survive the harsh conditions. Hibernation is a resting state in which the animal's body temperature falls to just above that of its surroundings, and its metabolic rate (the rate at which it consumes energy) drops dramatically. The animal resumes its active lifestyle in the spring. Hibernation is triggered by shorter days, falling temperatures, or by the animal's internal biological clock.

### Rodents
Rodents, such as dormice and woodchucks, form the largest group of hibernating mammals. Many smaller rodents living in the northern hemisphere hibernate in the winter months when the plants and small animals they feed on are in short supply. Some build nests in tree hollows or underground where they curl up to minimize heat loss and go into a deep sleep. Many species wake periodically either to eat, drink, or urinate to get rid of accumulated waste.

## Hibernation
Rodents, bats, and insectivores are mammals that hibernate. Their small size allows them to cool down and warm up quickly. Some animals eat more in early winter to build up fat stores to use while hibernating; others wake every few weeks to feed on food in their nest. A squirrel shows changes typical of a hibernating mammal; its metabolic rate drops to 1 percent of normal, and its body temperature falls from 99°F (37°C) to 39°F (4°C). When it wakes, its body weight will have fallen by 40 percent.

Natterer's bat

### Bats
Many temperate species of bats hibernate when their insect food disappears. They often hibernate in large numbers and cluster together to conserve warmth. The site where bats hibernate is called a hibernaculum; it may be a cave, mine, tree hollow, or a deserted building.

*Nest of straw and grass*

**Hibernating dormouse**

*Dormouse curled up in its nest*

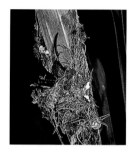

**Hummingbird**

### Birds
Most birds migrate to avoid cold winters; a few such as the whippoorwill enter a state of torpor and hibernate. Many hummingbirds hibernate every day. At night, their body temperature falls, enabling them to survive cooler conditions without consuming much energy.

## Dormancy
Some large mammals, such as bears and badgers that live in northern parts of North America and Europe, go into a resting state called dormancy during winter. Dormancy differs from hibernation; body temperature does not drop significantly, and the animal can wake quickly if danger threatens. However, this slight drop in body temperature, combined with a lack of activity, produces significant energy savings for the animal.

**European badger**
Badgers live in forests, where they dig extensive burrows called setts. In winter, badgers rarely leave their sett. They curl up in a nest and go into a dormant state, living off fat reserves they put on in summer and fall. Dormancy can last for seven months in Siberia.

*Bear feeds on berries to build up fat reserves.*

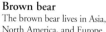

### Brown bear
The brown bear lives in Asia, North America, and Europe. In summer, it builds up fat on which it lives in winter. In the fall, the bear excavates a den, lines it with vegetation, and goes into its winter "sleep." Its body temperature falls by 9°F (5°C), and its metabolic rate drops by 50 percent. The bear emerges in spring weighing half what it did in the fall.

**Cabbage white butterfly pupa**

### Diapause
Diapause is the insects' equivalent of hibernation. Some insects enter diapause to survive adverse conditions, such as cold or lack of food. During diapause, growth and development are suspended, usually at the egg or pupa stage of the life cycle. For example, if the cabbage white butterfly lays her eggs in late summer, the pupal stage goes into diapause that winter, resuming development in spring.

### Estivation
Estivation is the state of dormancy animals such as African lungfish enter during hot, dry summers. Lungfish live in places that flood in the wet season and bake in the dry season. As river levels fall, the lungfish digs a burrow in the mud, ending in a chamber. The fish curls up in the chamber, secretes a protective mucus bag around itself, and remains there for up to six months until the rains come.

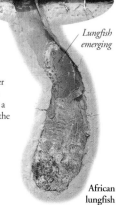

*Lungfish emerging*

African lungfish

**FIND OUT MORE**    ANIMAL BEHAVIOR    BATS    BEARS    HEDGEHOGS AND OTHER INSECTIVORES    MAMMALS    MIGRATION    RATS AND OTHER RODENTS

# HINDUISM

THE OLDEST OF THE GREAT world religions, Hinduism began in India at least 5,000 years ago. Hindus believe in one great power, or supreme god, called Brahman, that exists in everything. They believe in a cycle of death and rebirth – when we die, our souls live on in another person, animal, or plant. The goal of the Hindu is to live such a good life that the soul breaks this cycle and itself becomes part of Brahman. There are some 733 million Hindus, mostly living in Asia.

## Vishnu

Hindus know Vishnu as the preserver. They believe that when there is danger to the Earth, Vishnu protects it. His main task is to keep the balance between good and evil powers. To do this, he has visited the Earth in nine different human and animal forms, including the lord Rama and the god Krishna.

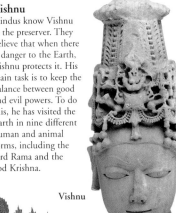

Vishnu

## Gods

Hindus worship many gods, each of which represents part of Brahman. Some of the gods can take different forms. Hindus can choose a favorite god; two of the most popular are Hanuman, the intelligent monkey-god, and Lakshmi, the goddess of beauty and wealth. But the most important of all is the holy trinity of Vishnu, Shiva, and Brahma. This group of three makes up Brahman, the supreme god.

## Shiva

Hindus know this god as the destroyer. Shiva destroys things that are no longer needed, but also allows new things to be created, so he is said to control life and death. He is shown in many forms. As Lord of the Dance, he brings the dance of life to an end so the new cycle of life can begin.

*Shiva beats a drum to summon up a new creation.*

*His left foot is a symbol of liberation.*

*Shiva bears a flame as a symbol of destruction.*

*The ring of flames represents the energy of the Universe.*

### Brahma

As the creator of the Universe, Brahma has four arms to symbolize the four points of the compass. He has four faces so he can look in all directions at the same time. These features also suggest that Brahma can be in all places at all times.

*These figures represent holy scriptures.*

*Shiva dances on the defeated figure of the demon of ignorance.*

### Ganesha

Ganesha, the elephant-headed god of wisdom and strength, is the son of Shiva and Parvati. Hindus worship him at the beginning of journeys because he is thought to remove obstacles.

## Sacred texts

Hinduism has many sacred books that explain the religion and instruct people as to how to lead their lives. The oldest texts are four books known as the *Vedas*. These contain hymns to the gods and texts telling priests how to carry out their duties. At the end of the *Vedas* are the *Upanishads*, which are philosophical discussions about religious belief. The *Puranas* are a series of books discussing and explaining the *Vedas*. The *Laws of Manu* provide teachings about everyday life.

*Indra is the Vedic god of conquest. He is a warrior and a destroyer of demons.*

*In the Bhagavad Gita, Krishna drives the warrior Arjuna's chariot.*

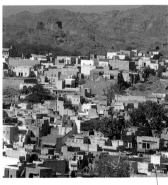

*Blue houses in Jodhpur were for Brahmins.*

### Rig Veda

The oldest and most sacred of the Vedas is the Rig Veda. It contains some 1,000 hymns of praise to 33 of the most important of the gods. Like the other Vedas, it was originally composed around 1200 BC, and passed on by word of mouth. The texts were written down in Sanskrit around AD 1400.

### The epics

Two great epic poems tell stories in which the gods come to Earth. The *Mahabharata* is probably the longest poem ever written. Its 100,000 verses tell of Vishnu visiting Earth as Krishna. It contains the text known as the *Bhagavad Gita*, the Song of the Lord. The *Ramayana* tells a story in which Vishnu comes to Earth as Lord Rama.

### Caste system

Hinduism divides people up into four separate groups, or varnas. The four groups are Brahmins (generally priests), Kshatriyas (soldiers and rulers), Vaishyas (traders and farmers), and Shudras (servants). These broad divisions are split into smaller groups called jatis or castes. Traditionally, people would not have anything to do with those in castes lower than their own, but today the caste system has broken down.

# Festivals

Throughout the Hindu year, festivals celebrate the gods in a variety of ways. At Janmashtami, Hindus commemorate Krishna's birthday with readings of the *Bhagavad Gita* and gifts of candies. Divali, the festival of lights, remembers the story of Lord Rama's victory over his enemies and his lamplit procession home.

*Pilgrims come to bathe in the Ganges River.*

*The sacred water is said to wash away one's sins.*

## Holi

The festival of Holi is held for two days in spring to celebrate the rescue of Krishna from the clutches of the demoness Holika, who was burnt to death by Vishnu. After worship a bonfire is lit to symbolize good overcoming evil. Dancing and processions take place.

## Pilgrimages

Going on a pilgrimage to a holy place is important for many Hindus. They may go to a shrine or to a place where one of the gods is said to have appeared on Earth, believing that their prayers are more likely to be answered if said at such a place. A favorite destination for a pilgrimage is a holy river, particularly the Ganges, in northwestern India. Varanasi on the Ganges is India's most sacred city.

*On the second day of Holi, people of all castes cover each other with colored powders.*

## Sacred cows

The white cow is a Hindu symbol of the soul, and cows are sacred in Hinduism. They are allowed to roam freely, and there are penalties for killing a cow. Hindus may drink milk and use cow dung as fuel, but must not kill cows for food. The cow's status is part of a wider respect for life and many Hindus are vegetarians.

*Daily traffic in the city of Delhi skirts around seated cows.*

# Worship

Since Hindus believe that god is in everything, any human activity, done well, can become an act of worship. But Hindus also perform special acts of worship at least once a day. They may worship in a temple, but the most common place for worship is in the home, in front of a shrine to a favorite god. Rituals include meditation and reciting sacred texts and prayers. Hindus light candles, make offerings to the gods, and waft incense around the shrine.

*Vishnu is the main image.*

*Krishna and his half-brother Balarama are shown with Vishnu.*

*Shesha the serpent protects Vishnu.*

## Shrines

The household shrine is the focus of daily worship. It may contain an image of one of the principal gods, plus pictures of other deities. It may also have a container full of water from the sacred Ganges River. Although some shrines are elaborately decorated, others may be as simple as a shelf or holy picture in the corner of a room.

## Puja

Before puja (worship) takes place, the image of the god is washed, dried, and anointed with turmeric or sandalwood powder. Offerings such as flowers, fruit, and cooked food are made to the god. The worshiper stands or sits in front of the shrine, reciting holy texts.

### Incense burner

*Burning incense welcomes the god to his shrine.*

### Kamal

*This scent shaker is shaped like the lotus flower, the symbol of creation.*

## Yoga

All Hindus strive to break the cycle of rebirth (samsara) and merge with Brahman. They believe that one way of achieving this state is through the physical and mental discipline of yoga. There are different types of yoga, but all aim to attain ultimate spiritual enlightenment.

*A Hindu carrying out yoga exercises.*

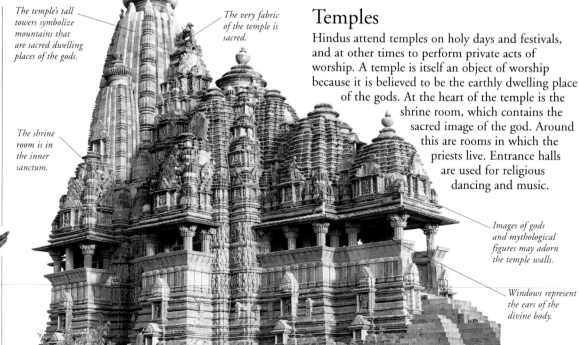

*The temple's tall towers symbolize mountains that are sacred dwelling places of the gods.*

*The very fabric of the temple is sacred.*

*The shrine room is in the inner sanctum.*

# Temples

Hindus attend temples on holy days and festivals, and at other times to perform private acts of worship. A temple is itself an object of worship because it is believed to be the earthly dwelling place of the gods. At the heart of the temple is the shrine room, which contains the sacred image of the god. Around this are rooms in which the priests live. Entrance halls are used for religious dancing and music.

*Images of gods and mythological figures may adorn the temple walls.*

*Windows represent the ears of the divine body.*

FIND OUT MORE    FESTIVALS    GODS AND GODDESSES    INDIA, HISTORY OF    INDUS VALLEY CIVILIZATION    LITERATURE    RELIGIONS    SHRINES    SIGNS AND SYMBOLS    WRITING

# HIPPOPOTAMUSES

SPENDING THE DAY submerged in water, hippopotamuses emerge at dusk to feed on nearby grassland. Well-used pathways lead to their feeding grounds. There are two species of hippos – the common hippo and the pygmy hippo – both of which live in the equatorial regions of Africa. The common hippo is the third largest land animal, after the elephant and the white rhino. Common hippos have a huge appetite and can consume vast quantities of grass. In places where they are numerous, they may destroy the vegetation for a considerable distance from the river or lake in which they live, sometimes causing serious soil erosion.

## School of hippos

The common hippo lives in groups of 20–100 animals called schools. A school spends the day partly submerged in water or wallowing in mud pools. Hippos establish a territory with males around the edge, and females and young in the center. Males are excluded from the female area except in the breeding season. Any male approaching too close will be attacked by the females.

## Common hippopotamus

The common hippo is a very large and aggressive animal. It is the second heaviest land animal after the elephant. Despite its huge size and legs that seem too short for its enormous, barrellike body, it can move at surprising speeds. Anything coming between it and the water is liable to be attacked. Hippos make a variety of noises, from bellowing to snorting.

### Skin

Hippo skin is smooth and almost hairless except for a few bristles on the nose, in the ears, and on the tail. Underneath the skin is a thick layer of fat. Pores on the skin exude drops of a thick pink fluid that acts as a sunscreen and a lubricant. The fluid is also thought to disinfect wounds sustained by males during fights.

*Scars are usually the result of sparring between adult males.*

*Small ears*

*Hippos feed on grass.*

## Young

Thirty-four weeks after mating, the female gives birth to a single young. Birth normally takes place on land, but occasionally in water. The newborn hippo can swim, walk, and run within a few minutes of being born. If a female temporarily leaves the territory, she puts her calf in the care of another female.

*Bristles on nose*

*Males open their huge mouths to display their large teeth and tusks.*

*Teeth*

*Prominant tusks project more than 24 in (60 cm) from the gums.*

### Threat displays

Males challenge each other by opening their mouths to maximum gape. If this fails to deter a rival, they may rise up out of the water and try to slash each other with their tusks. Ferocious fights often develop between rival males and may lead to serious injury.

*Eyes, ears, and nostrils appear above the water surface.*

*Hippos spend up to 18 hours a day submerged in water.*

### Hippo underwater

The common hippo, whose name means "river horse," is more at home in water than on land. When submerged, it can hold its breath and seal its nostrils and ears. Normally, it stays underwater for 3–5 minutes before having to surface to breathe, but, if necessary, it can remain submerged for considerably longer. It swims easily and may walk along the bottom of the riverbed.

*Hippo walking on the bottom of a riverbed*

## Pygmy hippopotamus

The pygmy hippo is about one-fifth the size of the common hippo. It swims well, but is less aquatic than the common hippo. It lives in marshland and swamp forest where it makes tunnellike tracks through the undergrowth. If alarmed it seeks refuge in dense undergrowth. The pygmy hippo is a shy, nocturnal animal living alone or in pairs. It spends most of the day resting and feeds during darkness on swamp plants, fruit, and leaves.

*Round head and body*

*Thick skin*

### COMMON HIPPOPOTAMUS

| | |
|---|---|
| SCIENTIFIC NAME | *Hippopotamus amphibius* |
| ORDER | Artiodactyla |
| FAMILY | Hippopotamidae |
| DISTRIBUTION | Tropical Africa |
| HABITAT | Rivers, lakes, and estuaries |
| DIET | Grass and aquatic vegetation – up to 100 lb (45 kg) per day |
| SIZE | Height: 5 ft (1.52 m); weight: 4.48 tons (4.06 tonnes) |
| LIFESPAN | 50 years |

**FIND OUT MORE**

| AFRICAN WILDLIFE | CONSERVATION | LAKE AND RIVER WILDLIFE | MAMMALS | MARSH AND SWAMP WILDLIFE |
|---|---|---|---|---|

# HISTORY

THE STUDY OF HISTORY is an attempt by people today to understand the lives of people in the past. Historians – the people who study history – look at primary sources – those writings and artifacts that have survived – and try to piece together a realistic picture of life in previous years. But not every piece of historical evidence survives to the present day; those that do can sometimes be interpreted in many different ways. As a result, history is a complex and sometimes controversial subject that excites considerable debate among historians and nonhistorians alike.

Parasaurolophus skull, a type of duckbill dinosaur

### Prehistory
Writing has existed for around 5,500 years. The period before written records is called prehistory. Archaeologists study material evidence, such as bones, fossils, and artifacts, to help them understand prehistoric periods, such as the Stone Age.

## Sources of history

What we know of history is based on material evidence, such as buildings, roads, tools, artwork, and clothes; written evidence, such as books; and oral evidence handed down through generations. All these sources provide valuable information about past societies and the people who created them.

Meroë pyramid, Sudan

### Material evidence
By piecing together material evidence, historians can discover much about the people of the time. The Bayeux Tapestry is the record of a known historical event – the Norman invasion of England (1066). But when historians study it more closely, they discover a wealth of information, not just about the event the tapestry is relating (such as which weapons were used) but about life of the time generally – and even about the women who made the tapestry.

English soldiers     Norman knights

**Normans attack the English, Bayeux Tapestry**

## Records of history

All primary sources, whether photographic or written, need careful study, because they may be biased, that is, illustrate a subjective (personal) viewpoint.

Lenin

### Propaganda
Historical evidence may be altered to serve political needs. The Soviet Union saw a power struggle between Josef Stalin (1879–1953) and Leon Trotsky (1879–1940) after the death of Lenin. When Stalin became leader, he had Trotsky removed from all official photographs.

**Trotsky appeared in the original of this photograph.**

### Dark Ages
Historians often label historical periods, though people of the time may not have agreed with the label. The chaotic period in Europe after the Roman Empire fell (c.500) is often called the Dark Ages, yet in places it was a time of culture and learning.

**The Book of Durrow, c.800**

### Written evidence
Books, diaries, poems, letters, account books, receipts, state documents, and newspapers are all written evidence and help historians in their work. But written evidence needs careful study, because it is often personal and has to be balanced against other accounts or other types of evidence to gain a picture of past events.

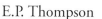
**Chinese letter, written on a scroll**    *The larger the document, the more useful it is to a historian.*

## E.P. Thompson

Edward Thompson (1924–93) was an important English social historian. His best-known work, *The Making of the English Working Class* (1965), studied the politics and protests of ordinary people as opposed to the history of political leaders.

### Oral history
Many societies know their own history, even though they have not written it down. In West Africa, storytellers known as *griots* record the history of their tribes through lengthy narrative stories set to music. In the 1960s and 1970s, there was more emphasis on sociological history, in which historians recorded the stories of people, such as women and the working classes, they previously ignored.

**Warrior's mother, Kenya**

## Timeline

c.400s BC Herodotus writes history of the Greek–Persian wars.

c.800 Monks begin the Anglo-Saxon Chronicle.

1380s Arab historian Ibn Khaldun writes *Kitab al-Ibar* to explain why civilizations rise and fall.

**Ammonite, prehistoric material evidence**

1800s History established as an academic subject, with the emphasis on primary sources rather than interpretation.

1860s Karl Marx (1818–83) argues a view of history in which economic factors determine events.

1930s French historians of the Annales school concentrate on social history.

1960s Historians focus on people previously ignored in accounts of history, such as women.

1992 US historian Frances Fukuyama argues that the fall of communism "ended" history.

**FIND OUT MORE**    ARCHAEOLOGY    MARX, KARL    RUSSIAN REVOLUTION    SEVEN WONDERS OF THE ANCIENT WORLD

# HITTITES

A WARLIKE PEOPLE known as the Hittites flourished from 1600 to 1200 BC, when they had one of the most powerful armies of the ancient world. They settled in Anatolia (central Turkey) around 2000 BC, then established control over the area from their great fortified capital at Hattusas. Gradually the Hittite kingdom expanded into Syria, where it clashed with Egypt and the growing might of Assyria. Despite their fearsome reputation, the Hittites were astute politicians and preferred diplomacy to armed conflict where possible. Eventually a series of attacks from outside forces, combined with famine, put an end to their ancient empire.

The Hittite Empire covered most of Turkey and Anatolia at its height, c.1300 BC.

### Chariot warfare

From 2000 BC the use of horses, the development of the bit, and strong, spoked wheels transformed the chariot from a humble cart pulled by asses into a dangerous weapon. It changed warfare in the Near East. The Hittites were masters of this weapon.

### Battle of Kadesh

The world's earliest battle that can be reconstructed was between the chariots of the Hittite king Muwatallis and the Egyptian Rameses II at Kadesh in 1286 BC. Chariots continued to be important to ancient armies for more than 2000 years.

### Diplomacy

The Hittites favored diplomatic marriages to secure peace, especially with Egypt. After the Battle of Kadesh, a Hittite princess was married to a pharaoh. On another occasion, an Egyptian queen, possibly Tutankhamun's widow, wrote to the Hittite king asking to marry one of his sons.

Rameses II

## Politics

Hittite rulers commanded the army and were chief judges and high priests. The greatest king was Suppiluliumas I (r.1380–1346 BC), who conquered all Syria between the Euphrates and the sea. Though he took this territory by military force, he kept it by bribing his Egyptian rivals with gold. Many Syrian gods were accepted by the Hittites as leading deities, including Teshub, who symbolized storms and the destruction of war.

### Ugarit

A wealthy trading city on the Mediterranean coast, Ugarit was a main area of conflict between the Hittites and the Egyptians. It was abandoned in the turmoil that destroyed the Hittite Empire. Archaeologists have unearthed one of the world's earliest cuneiform alphabets here.

Teshub was often portrayed holding a weapon.

A three-pronged lightning fork

Teshub, the Hittite storm god

## Art and literature

Hittite myths emphasize divine warfare and many feature Teshub defeating evil outside forces. In the remains of their hilltop capital at Hattusas (modern Boghazkoy, Turkey), stone reliefs in the city wall show helmeted warriors and some of the many Hittite gods. Tiny figures, crafted in gold, have been found. These depict kings and gods and wear the distinctive upturned boots of a mountain people.

Headdress, indicating high status

Short-sleeved tunic

Upturned boots, typical of a mountain people

Gold figurine, possibly of a Hittite king

Hittite wall relief

### Neo-Hittites

The Syrian city-states belonging to the empire adopted Hittite hieroglyphics and art. After the collapse of the empire, this influence continued and the cities became known as the Neo-Hittite states.

### Food and drink

The main crops were barley and wheat, which were used for making bread and brewing beer. The Hittites also grew fruits, such as apples, figs, and apricots, and they made wine from grapes. Bees produced honey, and farmers raised sheep, oxen, and cattle.

Apple

Figs

Apricots

## Timeline

Hittite warhorse

**1600–1400 BC**
The first Hittite kingdom is established in Anatolia.

**1595 BC** King Mursili I sacks Babylon, but does not remain.

**1550 BC**
The fortified Hittite capital is established at Hattusas.

**c.1460 BC**
Tudhaliyas II begins conquests that establish last phase of empire.

**1380–1346 BC**
Suppiluliumas commands a vast empire stretching from present-day western Turkey to northern Syria. Hattusas (modern Boghazkoy) is the cultural center of the area.

**1299 BC** One of the earliest known battles takes place between Hittite and Egyptian forces at Kadesh.

**1283 BC** Peace treaties are signed between Hittites and Egyptians.

**1200 BC**
The growth of the Assyrian Empire, forces invading from the north and west, and famine combine to destroy the Hittite Empire.

**FIND OUT MORE**    ASIA, HISTORY OF    ASSYRIAN EMPIRE    BABYLONIAN EMPIRE    EGYPT, ANCIENT    PERSIAN EMPIRES    SUMERIANS

# HOLOCAUST

H

BETWEEN 1939 AND 1945, six million European Jews were systematically murdered by the German Nazi regime. Some were killed in their own towns, but most died in concentration camps. This mass murder of Jews is known as the Holocaust, after a biblical term meaning "slaughter by fire." It was a deliberate national policy established by Adolf Hitler and his Nazi followers to wipe out all traces of Jewish life and culture. Jews have been persecuted throughout history, but the Holocaust, which slaughtered nearly 70 per cent of Europe's Jews, is history's worst example of anti-Semitism. Today, people still ask how such an atrocity was allowed to happen.

**Star of David**
From 1933, the Nazis began to segregate (separate) German Jews from the rest of the population. Jews had to wear the yellow Star of David to identify them, and they were banned from public places. Nazi propaganda encouraged hatred, and people attacked Jewish shops and homes.

Warsaw Ghetto

## Warsaw Ghetto

In 1939, Germany invaded Poland. The capital, Warsaw, was home to half a million Jews who were rounded up, forced to live in a ghetto (part of the city cut off from the rest), and given starvation rations. In 1943, the Jews made a brave and desperate attempt to fight back, but this uprising was mercilessly crushed. By the time Soviet troops liberated Warsaw in 1945, only 200 Jews remained alive.

## Concentration camps

Special concentration camps were built by the Nazis, to detain people considered "undesirable," particularly Jews. From 1941, many camps were set up throughout eastern Europe, including Chelmno, Treblinka, and Auschwitz. These were literally death camps, built to achieve Hitler's "final solution" of exterminating all European Jews. Thousands of men, women, and children were led into chambers where they were killed with a cyanide compound, Zyklon B, introduced through vents in the walls. Non-Jews were also killed, including gypsies and the disabled.

Entrance to Auschwitz

**Auschwitz**
One of the most feared death camps was Auschwitz (Oswiecim) in Poland, where some 12,000 victims a day were gassed and their bodies cremated. It was this burning in the death camps that gave the Holocaust its name.

*Main death camps*

France

Greece

Death camps were in eastern Europe

**Deportation**
Jews were rounded up from all over Nazi-occupied Europe, loaded onto trains in cattle cars, and deported to the death camps. Many of these were surrounded by local people hostile to Jews. Up to a thousand people were forced into each train and deprived of food and water. On arrival, survivors were sent to the gas chambers.

**Jewish resistance**
Despite the power of the Nazis, the Jews did resist oppression. During the war, there were revolts by Jews in ghettoes such as Warsaw, and even in the concentration camps, such as Sobibor. Elsewhere, small bands of Jews formed partisan groups that fought heroically in enemy territory, attacking Germans and destroying military stores and railroad tracks.

**Liberation**
From 1942, news of the death camps began to reach the West. It was only in 1945, however, that the full story emerged. When the Allied forces liberated the camps, they found, to their horror, huge mounds of skeletal people either dead or dying.

## Timeline
**1925** Adolf Hitler publishes *Mein Kampf* (My Struggle). In it, he states his anti-Semitism (hatred of Jews).

**1933** Hitler becomes Chancellor and begins the persecution of German Jews. First camp is built at Dachau.

**1935** Nuremberg Laws declare Jews to be second-class German citizens.

**Nov 9–10 1938** "Kristallnacht" (Night of Broken Glass), Germany. People attack more than 7,000 Jewish shops and homes, and 30,000 Jews are sent to concentration camps.

**1941** Hitler, Eichmann, and other leading Nazis announce their "final solution." Death camps are set up throughout Europe for mass slaughter.

**1943** Warsaw Ghetto Uprising: Nazis kill or deport more than 56,000 Jews in four weeks.

**1945** Allied forces liberate concentration camps in Eastern Europe.

**1962** First tree is planted in Israel's Avenue of the Righteous, which commemorates non-Jews who saved Jewish lives during World War II.

## Anne Frank
Born in Frankfurt, Anne Frank (1929–45) was a German Jew. In 1933, she and her family fled to Amsterdam, Holland, to escape persecution. In 1941, the Nazis invaded Holland, and from July 1942, Anne and her family were hidden by friends. While in hiding, she wrote a diary that is now world famous. In August 1944, the family was betrayed and sent to the concentration camps. Anne died in Bergen Belsen camp at age 16.

**FIND OUT MORE**    COLD WAR    EUROPE, HISTORY OF    GERMANY, HISTORY OF    JUDAISM    WORLD WAR II

# HOLY LAND, HISTORY OF

OVER THE CENTURIES, THIS VARIED region of mountains, deserts, and marshes has had shifting borders, various conquerors, and many names, including Canaan, Zion, Israel, Judah, and Palestine. The area is holy to three world religions: Judaism, Christianity, and Islam. Jews believe it is the Promised Land God gave them, and that Abraham, father of the Jews, settled there in about 1900 BC. The land is holy for Christians because Jesus Christ lived there; and for Muslims, Jerusalem is sacred as the site of many of Muhammad's activities. The Bible records mainly Jewish history in this region.

## The Holy Land

This crossroads between Europe, Africa, and Asia has been conquered by Babylonians, Persians, Greeks, Romans, Arabs, Byzantines, Ottomans, and British in turn. Today it includes Israel and parts of Jordan and Syria.

### Jericho

Excavations show that the walled city of Jericho may be the oldest settlement in the world. According to the Bible, it was destroyed many times in its history – once by Joshua, who led the Israelites after the death of Moses.

## Jerusalem

Over the centuries Jews, Christians, and Muslims have all fought for access to holy shrines, such as Solomon's Temple. This has caused many wars in one of the world's holiest cities.

### Solomon's Temple

This temple, completed by Phoenician craftsmen in 957 BC, housed the Ark of the Covenant and was the first permanent Jewish religious center. In 587 BC, the Babylonians destroyed the first temple. It was rebuilt in 37 BC but destroyed by the Romans in AD 70. All that remains today is the so-called Wailing Wall on the west side.

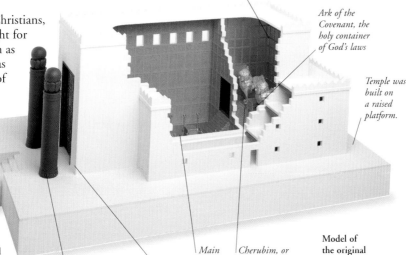

Holy of holies, inlaid with gold

Ark of the Covenant, the holy container of God's laws

Temple was built on a raised platform.

Jachim and Boaz, the bronze columns

Porch

Main hall

Cherubim, or sphinxes, flanking the Ark

Model of the original Solomon's Temple

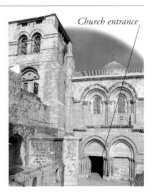

Church entrance

### Holy Sepulchre Church

In the 12th century, Crusaders rebuilt a Christian church on Mount Calvary, Jerusalem, where Jesus Christ was crucified. The church contains Greek Orthodox, Roman Catholic, and Armenian chapels. In a grotto underneath is the empty tomb of Jesus.

### Dome of the Rock

This massive rock is sacred to Muslims because Muhammad is said to have risen to heaven from this spot. It is sacred to Jews because Abraham is said to have prepared his son Isaac for sacrifice here.

## Philistines

The Philistines were part of a group of warriors also known as the Sea Peoples. In about 1100 BC, the Philistines threatened the Israelites, who had settled the southern coast of Palestine (in modern Israel). The Israelites lived subject to the Philistines for 200 years until the Israelite King David (r.1013–973 BC) managed to subdue them.

Slingshots.

### David and Goliath

Goliath, a huge Philistine leader, challenged the Israelites to present a man for one-on-one combat. No one dared respond until David, a young shepherd, volunteered. Against all odds, he knocked Goliath out with one slingshot and cut off his head. David went on to become Israel's greatest king and made Jerusalem a great political and religious center.

## Timeline

c.8000 BC Evidence of human settlement, Jericho.

c.1900 BC The patriarch Abraham settles in Canaan.

c.1200s BC The Exodus: Moses leads the Israelites out of slavery in Egypt.

**Holy Sepulchre Church**

1033–1013 BC Reign of Saul, first king of Israel.

1013–933 BC Reigns of David and Solomon.

587 BC Babylonians destroy first Jewish temple, Jerusalem.

AD 33 Romans crucify Jesus Christ in Jerusalem.

AD 70 Romans destroy the second Jewish temple at Jerusalem.

636 Muslim rule begins.

1096–1291 European Crusaders fight to control the territory.

1948 Declaration of the state of Israel.

## King Solomon

The son of King David and his wife Bathsheba, Solomon (r.973–930 BC) built the first temple at Jerusalem, and a number of cities. He was famous in ancient Israel for making profitable foreign alliances, and, during his reign, Israel reached the height of its influence and land holding. Myths present Solomon as very wise, but he was actually a rather harsh and despotic ruler.

**FIND OUT MORE**

ARCHITECTURE    CHRISTIANITY    CRUSADES    ISLAM    ISRAEL    MYTHS AND LEGENDS

# HOLY ROMAN EMPIRE

FOR MORE THAN 800 years, most of central Europe was part of a loose confederation called the Holy Roman Empire, an attempt to revive the old Roman Empire, with backing from the Christian Church. It was founded in 962. After 1273, the Hapsburg family of Austria captured the throne and dominated the empire. The emperors were elected by seven German princes and crowned by the Pope in Rome. The emperor had little power, but the title made him political leader of Europe.

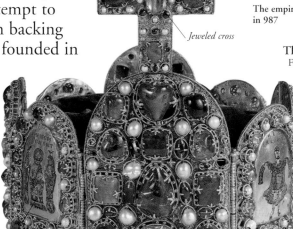

*Jeweled cross*

*Crown is set with enamel plaques.*

**10th-century imperial crown**

*Otto's German lands*

*The empire in 987*

*Emperors were also kings of Italy.*

### The empire

From its founding in 962 until the mid-13th century, the Holy Roman Empire included much of Germany, the Low Countries, Switzerland, Austria, and northern Italy. Over the next centuries, it shrank, but it remained centered in Germany.

### Otto I: the birth of empire

In 936, Otto, a descendant of Charlemagne, became king of Germany. He defeated the Magyar invaders at the battle of Lech in 955 and went on to conquer northern Italy. In 962, the Pope crowned him Holy Roman Emperor.

## Hapsburgs

The Hapsburgs took their name from a castle in Switzerland and held vast estates in Switzerland, Austria, and southern Germany. In 1273, a member of the Hapsburg family became Rudolf I of Germany and then the Holy Roman Emperor. With a few short breaks, the Hapsburgs ran the empire until its end in 1806. Under their rule, the interests of the empire were secondary to those of increasing Hapsburg family power.

*Maximilian I married Mary of Burgundy in 1477 and acquired Burgundy.*

*Philip I, son of Maximilian, married Juana of Castile and Aragon in 1496.*

*Mary of Burgundy*

*Charles' brother, Ferdinand I, married Anna and inherited Bohemia and Hungary.*

*Charles V, son of Philip, inherited Spain through his mother, Juana, and the Hapsburg lands from his grandfather, Maximilian.*

### Struggle for power

The emperor was the supreme secular (worldly) ruler of Christian Europe; the Pope was its supreme spiritual ruler. The two often clashed. In 1076, Pope Gregory VII deposed Emperor Henry IV. The conflict led to a decline in the power of the emperors over the next few centuries.

## Charles V

Hapsburg power in Europe reached its peak in 1519, when Charles V (1500–58) became emperor. He acquired vast lands from each of his grandparents, including Spain and its empire in America. Charles kept this empire together until 1556, when he gave up the throne and divided his empire between his brother Ferdinand. Charles, who became emperor on Charles' death in 1558, and his son Philip, who ruled Spain, Italy and the Low Countries.

## Imperial Vienna

The Hapsburg capital was the Austrian city of Vienna. It was one of the leading cities in Europe, with fine churches, palaces, and other civic buildings. The center of Hapsburg power was the Hofburg Palace, a vast complex including imperial apartments and government offices.

*Ornate Renaissance decoration*

**The Schweizertor, a gate to the Hofburg**

### Maria Theresa

In 1740, Emperor Charles VI died, leaving his daughter Maria Theresa on the throne. Prussia and France disputed her right to inherit the throne and declared war. Maria was an inspired leader and managed to keep her empire together, making Austria into a powerful, centralized state.

## Timeline

**800** Charlemagne crowned.

**962** Otto, king of Germany, becomes first Holy Roman Emperor.

**1076** Pope overthrows emperor Henry IV and establishes papal power over emperor.

**1273** Rudolf I becomes first emperor from the Hapsburg family.

**Imperial knight**

**1517** Reformation under Martin Luther results in a divide between German Protestant princes and the Catholic emperor.

**1519** Charles V is crowned emperor and becomes most powerful man in Europe.

**1556** Charles splits his empire between brother Ferdinand and son Philip; Hapsburg Austria dominates the Holy Roman empire.

**1806** Francis II abolishes the Holy Roman empire.

**FIND OUT MORE**   CHARLEMAGNE   CHRISTIANITY   GERMANY, HISTORY OF   REFORMATION   ROMAN EMPIRE

# HORMONES AND THE ENDOCRINE SYSTEM

H

THE ENDOCRINE SYSTEM is one of the body's control systems. It consists of endocrine glands, which produce chemicals called hormones that are then released into the bloodstream. The hormones act as chemical messengers and instruct specific areas of the body to carry out certain actions. Hormones usually work slowly and have long-lasting effects, regulating processes such as growth and reproduction.

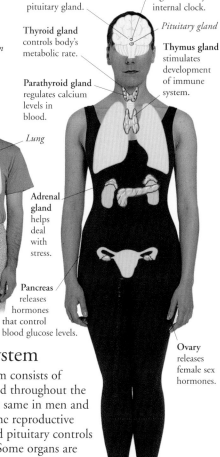

Hypothalamus is part of the brain that controls the pituitary gland.

Pineal gland regulates body's internal clock.

Pituitary gland

Thyroid gland controls body's metabolic rate.

Thymus gland stimulates development of immune system.

Brain

Parathyroid gland regulates calcium levels in blood.

Lung

Adrenal gland helps deal with stress.

Kidney

Testes release male sex hormones.

Pancreas releases hormones that control blood glucose levels.

Ovary releases female sex hormones.

## How a hormone works

The blood carries hormones throughout the body, but they only affect certain target cells within target tissues. The hormone attaches itself to a site on the surface of a target cell. This locking-on causes changes inside the target cells that produce the required action. For example, the pancreas releases the hormone insulin in order to reduce levels of glucose molecules in the blood. Insulin does this by stimulating the body cells to take in glucose.

Insulin stimulates liver to store glucose in blood.

Normal blood glucose

Glucose is obtained from digesting food.

Glucose in blood stimulates pancreas to release insulin.

### Hormone levels

Hormone levels in the blood are controlled by a feedback mechanism. For example, insulin is released from the pancreas in response to increased levels of glucose. Higher levels of insulin will then cause blood glucose levels to return back to normal. The lowered glucose levels "feed back" to the pancreas, which produces less insulin.

## Endocrine system

The endocrine system consists of many glands scattered throughout the body. Glands are the same in men and women, except for the reproductive glands. The pea-sized pituitary controls many other glands. Some organs are linked to the endocrine system because, as well as having other functions, they also release hormones. The pancreas, for example, produces digestive enzymes and releases hormones.

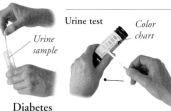

Urine test

Urine sample

Color chart

### Diabetes

Diabetes is a condition that occurs when blood glucose levels become very high because the pancreas cannot produce enough insulin. Doctors can monitor blood glucose levels by measuring the amount of glucose in a urine sample.

## Pituitary gland

The pituitary gland releases at least eight hormones. Some affect body functions directly, while the remainder stimulate other endocrine glands to produce hormones of their own. The pituitary gland has two parts, or lobes. The anterior lobe produces and sends hormones around the body; the posterior lobe releases hormones produced in the hypothalamus.

Hypothalamus

Nerves carry hormones from hypothalamus to posterior lobe.

Blood vessels carry hormones around body.

Tissues release hormones received from hypothalamus.

Anterior lobe

Posterior lobe

### Jokichi Takamine

Japanese chemist Jokichi Takamine (1854–1922) was the first person to isolate a pure sample of a hormone.
Using extracts of adrenal glands, he prepared crystals of a substance that increased blood pressure in animals. This substance was later called adrenaline.

### Prolactin

Prolactin is a hormone that is produced by the anterior lobe. It stimulates the production of milk when a woman breastfeeds her baby. When the baby sucks on the nipple, prolactin is immediately released from the mother's pituitary gland.

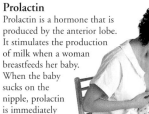

### Growth hormone

The anterior lobe produces growth hormone, which encourages the body to grow. It works by stimulating the body's cells to divide. Although growth hormone affects all tissues, its main targets are bones and skeletal muscles. Growth hormone is most active in childhood and adolescence.

### Adrenaline

If you have ever been frightened and felt your heart pounding, you have experienced the effects of adrenaline. It is a hormone that helps the body react to danger. When the adrenal glands release adrenaline, your breathing and heart rate speed up, and blood flows to your muscles so you can run from danger.

 FIND OUT MORE | BRAIN AND NERVOUS SYSTEM | DIGESTION | GROWTH AND DEVELOPMENT | HUMAN BODY | REPRODUCTION

# HORSE RIDING

PEOPLE RIDE HORSES for leisure and in competitions, which are often described as equestrian (from *equus*, meaning horse). These include show jumping, eventing, and dressage, all of which test the horse's ability to jump or perform special movements, and each of which appears in the Olympic program. Equestrian events also include racing events – track racing, steeplechasing, and hurdling – where jockeys ride specially bred horses called thoroughbreds. Other riding sports include polo, in which teams of riders compete to score goals.

**Riding**
Riders learn how to start, stop, steer and control the speed of a horse using their hands, legs, and body-weight. The natural gaits of a horse are the walk, trot, canter, and gallop.

*Hard hat is essential.*

*Bridle*

*Reins*

*Stirrup*

*Saddle*

*Horse breaks into a canter from a trot.*

## Show jumping

This involves riders taking their horses around a set course of jumps which may include artificial gates, a wall, and a water jump. Competitors receive faults if their horse refuses or knocks down a jump, or exceeds the specified time. The competitor with the fewest faults wins.

*Rider keeps looking ahead.*

*Rider's hands move up the reins to allow the horse to use his head and neck.*

*Rider leans forward from the hips.*

*Landing*

**Jumping a single pole**

*Horse draws up his hind legs and stretches to clear the jump.*

*Horse tucks up his forelegs.*

*Taking off*

**Puissance**
This show jumping competition tests the ability of the horse to jump high fences. From four to six fences are jumped, the number being reduced and the height raised for each round.

## Racing

Racing can be flat or over jumps. Some events such as the English Grand National – a steeplechase – are world famous and attract thousands of spectators and involve heavy betting on different runners. Horses may have to carry extra weights under the saddle, as well as the jockey (rider).

**Polo**
This game is played four on a side on a large field. Players mounted on polo ponies use mallets to strike a ball into their opponents' goal. A game consists of up to eight seven-minute periods called chukkers. Riders usually change ponies after every chukker.

## Dressage

In dressage, each competitor guides his or her horse through paces, figures, maneuvres, and halts (stops). Judges award points for the quality of the performance. Dressage is a formal sport and riders wear top hat and tails or military uniform; it needs a high degree of discipline and schooling.

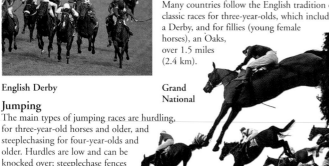

**English Derby**

**Jumping**
The main types of jumping races are hurdling, for three-year-old horses and older, and steeplechasing for four-year-olds and older. Hurdles are low and can be knocked over; steeplechase fences are larger and include ditches and water jumps.

**Track racing**
Horses are raced over distances from 5 furlongs (1 km) to 2 miles (3 km) or more. Many countries follow the English tradition of classic races for three-year-olds, which include a Derby, and for fillies (young female horses), an Oaks, over 1.5 miles (2.4 km).

**Grand National**

## Eventing

In three-day eventing, riders take their horses through a different discipline each day to test all aspects of the horse's abilities. Dressage tests a horse's obedience and show jumping its powers of recovery. There is also a four-phase endurance test which includes a steeplechase.

**Cross-country**
The cross-country phase may cover 4.3 miles (7 km) with about 30 fixed obstacles of all kinds. The course has to be completed in a set time to avoid time penalties. The jumps are often spectacular and include water, slippery grass banks, steps, solid walls, and drops.

### Mark Todd

A New Zealand eventer, Mark Todd (b. 1956) won the individual three-day event gold medal at the 1984 and 1988 Olympics on the horse Charisma. He was deprived of a third successive gold when his mount broke down on the second day after scoring well in the dressage.

**FIND OUT MORE**    EVOLUTION    HORSES    MAMMALS    MONGOL EMPIRE    OLYMPIC GAMES    SPORT

# HORSES

ALL MEMBERS OF THE HORSE family, which includes zebras and asses, are social animals. In the wild, they live in family groups that join to form a herd. People first tamed horses about 6,000 years ago, and today there are more than 300 breeds of domestic horses. They can be divided into three groups: heavy horses, light horses, and ponies, which are less than 14.2 hands high (4.8 ft or 1.47 m).

*A foal will drink its mother's milk until it is about one year old.*

*Five-week-old foal*

## The horse
Naturally grazing animals, horses in the wild eat grasses and shrubs. In each jaw, they have six incisor teeth for cutting and 12 molars for chewing. They rely on their sharp senses to survive, using taste and smell to check their food, and hearing and sight to detect danger. If they face possible danger, their first defense is to run away.

### Ear positions
Horses can move their ears separately to pick up sounds, and the position of their ears is a good indication of their mood. Ears forward show interest; one ear forward and one back means the horse is not sure; ears back indicate aggression or fear.

Dapple gray

Dun

Skewbald

Light bay

### Reproduction
A female horse carries her young in her womb for about 11 months. Within an hour of its birth, a young horse, called a foal, can stand and is soon able to run. In the wild, it has to keep up with the herd.

*Leg of modern horse*

*Leg of early horse*

*Side toe*

### Hooves and feet
Modern horses have one toe on each foot, protected by a hoof. It has taken 50 million years for them to evolve. The first horses, which were the size of small dogs, had a pad with four toes on the forefeet and three on the hind.

### Colors
Originally, the color of a horse's coat may have provided camouflage. Today, horses are bred in several colors. In some, the legs, mane, and tail are a different color from the rest of the body. Some horses have white markings on the head and legs.

## Movement
Horses can travel using four main patterns of leg movements, called gaits. These are the walk, trot, canter, and gallop. The gallop is the fastest, but a horse can gallop only short distances. Humans have bred horses to perform other gaits, such as the paso done by the Peruvian paso, and the tölt done by the Icelandic pony.

*The walk is a four-beat gait. The horse moves each leg in turn.*

*The trot has two beats. Opposite fore- and hind-legs move together.*

*The canter has three beats.*

*In the canter, one leg moves, then a diagonal pair, then the last leg.*

*All feet are off the ground together.*

*The gallop is like the canter, but paired feet go down separately.*

## Horse family
The horse belongs to the family of mammals called the *Equidae*. Also in this family are donkeys, zebras, the wild asses of Africa and Asia, Przewalski's wild horse of Mongolia, and the recently discovered Riwoche wild horse of Tibet.

### Zebras
There are three species of zebras, each with a different pattern of stripes. Herds of all species live wild in tropical Africa.

### Wild asses
The three species of wild asses are the African wild ass, and the onager and kiang of Asia. This kulan is a type of onager.

### Donkey
Descended from the African wild ass, donkeys have great strength and stamina.

### Przewalski's
An ancient breed of horse, it has been reintroduced into the wild.

## Herds
Members of a herd are close friends. They communicate using a variety of sounds, smells, and body language. For example, if a horse is startled, it will raise its head and tail, arch its neck, and flare its nostrils. This alerts the herd, which prepares to run.

Zebra

### Feral herds
These wild horses in Australia, called brumbies, are described as feral. They are domesticated horses now running wild.

**FIND OUT MORE**
EVOLUTION    FARMING    GRASSLAND WILDLIFE    HORSE RIDING    TRANSPORT, HISTORY OF

# Horses

## Light horses

*Strong build*

**Irish draft** was originally used for work on small Irish farms.

**Saddlebred** is an American horse with a high step. It is a beautiful show horse.

**Australian stock horse** has great endurance and stamina.

**Pinto** is also called the paint horse. It comes in a variety of types and sizes.

**Camargue** horses live in semi-wild herds in the Rhône delta, France.

*Strong, arched neck*

**Welsh cob** is a bold horse. It is extremely hardy and easy to keep.

*Compact body*

**Hackney horse** is often used in show-ring harness competitions.

**Lipizzaner** is used in the Spanish Riding School of Vienna, Austria.

*Long tail and mane*

**Morgan** descends from one stallion named Justin Morgan after his owner.

**Andalusian** is a Spanish breed from which the Lipizzaners derive.

**Tennessee walking horse** is good-tempered. It has three smooth gaits.

*Big joints*

**Hanoverian** is popular in Germany for showjumping and dressage competitions.

**Appaloosa** as a breed was first bred by the Nez Percé Indians of North America.

**Quarter horse** has great endurance and speed over short distances.

**Arabian** is the oldest breed and is accepted as the original source of all breeds.

**Orlov trotter** is a tall, lightly built horse. It was first bred in Russia.

**Thoroughbred** is the fastest horse breed, with almost perfect proportions.

**Barb** comes from Morocco in North Africa. It is one of the oldest horse breeds.

## Ponies

**Dartmoor** is noted for its long, low action.

*Good sloping shoulders*

**Connemara** is fast and a prized jumper.

**Exmoor** lives on Exmoor, southwestern England.

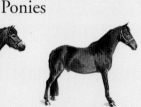

**American Shetland** is used mostly as a harness pony.

**Australian pony** has an excellent temperament.

*Compact body with depth through the girth*

**Welsh mountain pony** is hardy as well as beautiful.

**Shetland** is up to 40 in (102 cm) high, but can carry a person.

**Highland** is sure-footed, strong, and docile. It is known to be long-lived.

**Icelandic horse** can carry heavy weights at good speed over long distances.

**New Forest pony** is a friendly, comfortable riding pony.

**Fjord** comes from Norway and is descended from Przewalski's horse.

*Tail set low*

**Falabella** is a miniature horse standing only 7 hh (28 in/70 cm).

## Heavy horses

*Deep, strong neck*

**Suffolk punch** is very powerful. It was used as a general farm horse.

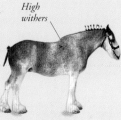

*High withers*

**Clydesdale** originated in the Clyde Valley, Scotland, in the 18th century.

**Shire** is the heaviest of the draft breeds. It is gentle and easy to handle.

**Percheron** is a French breed containing Arabian bloodlines.

*Short back*

**Ardennais** falls into two types – a lively, light draft, and a heavy type.

*Large, rounded quarters*

**Belgian draft** is also known as the Brabant. It is a very old breed.

# HOSPITALS

ANCIENT ROME HAD special places where sick people could receive medical treatment – the world's earliest hospitals. Today hospitals have additional responsibilities: patient care, health education, and medical research. Whether general or specialist, most hospitals have rooms for inpatients, clinics for outpatients, operating rooms for surgery, and pharmacies for dispensing drugs. Trained staff, such as doctors and nurses, care for patients using complex equipment, while non-medical staff, such as cooks, porters, cleaners, and engineers, are crucial in making the hospital function. In some poorer countries, there may be only one hospital for every million people.

## Specialist hospitals

Some specialist hospitals focus on groups of patients, such as women or children. Others concentrate on groups of diseases, such as eye problems, psychiatric disorders, or neurological (nerve and brain) diseases. Teaching hospitals train nurses, doctors, and other medical staff.

### Children's hospital

Hospitals specializing in the care of sick children use scaled-down equipment, such as surgical instruments, bandages, beds, and chairs. Rooms are bright and cheerful for the small patients, and there are toys and games. Parents are able to stay in nearby hospital rooms.

Child's teddy bear

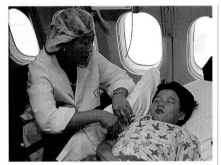
Flying eye clinic, China

### Eye clinics

Ophthalmology – the branch of medicine concerned with eye and sight problems – requires exceptionally detailed and precise equipment, and specialist facilities for patients who may be temporarily unable to see. In some large countries with remote regions, such as China or Australia, these facilities are provided in a mobile form – usually a small plane.

## Staff

Doctors usually work in different hospital departments for several years, to gain general training, before choosing a specialty. Nursing staff may also specialize, for example, in pediatrics (children), psychiatry, or intensive care. A hospital's staff usually includes radiographers, laboratory technicians, physiotherapists, and anesthetists.

### Nurses

Nurses attend to patients' comfort and daily needs, such as feeding and washing. They also carry out medical tasks, such as taking and recording pulse rate and body temperature, and giving medications.

General nurse

### Equipment

Modern equipment – especially that modified to be mobile – is crucial in hospitals. In an emergency, some of the most useful pieces include breathing apparatus (face masks or tubing), long syringes to administer fast-acting drugs, such as heart stimulants, and fluid products for intravenous infusions (drips).

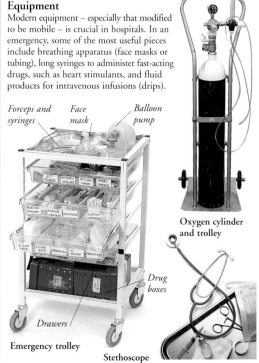

*Forceps and syringes*

*Face mask*

*Balloon pump*

*Drawers*

Emergency trolley

*Drug boxes*

Oxygen cylinder and trolley

Stethoscope

## General hospital

A general hospital provides medical facilities for a large area. Its staff cares for patients with common health problems. More complex cases are referred to a specialist hospital. General hospitals also arrange community services, such as visits by nurses.

*Chart*

Hospital beds in a room

### Wards

Inpatients usually stay in semi-private rooms. They are separated into medical and surgical groups of children, men, women, and the elderly. Patients with infective diseases usually stay in isolation rooms.

Ambulance, New York

### Accident and emergency

The emergency room receives medical emergencies, such as accident or heart-attack victims. The patient's problem is identified and stabilized, after which he or she may be sent home, or transferred to a suitable hospital room.

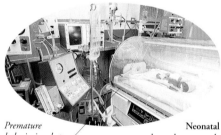

*Premature baby in incubator*

Neonatal intensive care unit

### Intensive care unit

In intensive care, expert staff attend gravely ill patients around the clock. Electronic equipment continuously monitors their vital processes, such as heartbeat and breathing.

Waiting room

### Outpatients

Outpatients attend the hospital to undergo screening tests or have minor surgery. They do not stay overnight.

FIND OUT MORE    DRUGS    FIRST AID    MEDICINE

# HOUSES AND HOMES

EVERYONE NEEDS A HOME, to provide comfort and shelter from the weather. It usually takes the form of a permanent house, although some people live in temporary structures, such as tents. Houses differ greatly around the world. They vary in what they are made of, because builders usually use local materials; in their structure, because their features must cope with local weather; and their plan. But they all provide a place for the inhabitants to sleep, eat, and cook.

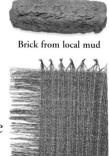

Brick from local mud

Straw woven into matting

*Overhanging thatched roof keeps off rain and provides shade.*

*Wooden poles support roof.*

### Early houses
From the earliest times, people built their houses out of materials that were available locally. Houses such as this African example have been made for thousands of years and are still built today. A wall of mud bricks is covered by a thatched roof supported by wooden pillars.

## Inside a house

A modern house includes many parts that are normally hidden from view. Many of them have to do with the services – such as running water, drainage, heating, and electricity – that are provided for the occupants. Water tanks are concealed in the roof space, pipes and wiring are hidden behind plaster, and drains are dug below ground level.

### Japanese house
Traditional Japanese houses have a timber framework. The gaps between the timber uprights are filled with wooden panels or sheets of paper to let through some sunlight. The rooms are designed to be covered by a set number of standard-sized straw mats called tatami mats.

### Construction
Modern houses in Europe and North America are commonly made of brick, timber, and concrete. A popular building method is to construct an inner wall, or "leaf," of concrete blocks, which are faced with an outer leaf of more attractive bricks. Wood is used for floors, doors, and roofing supports.

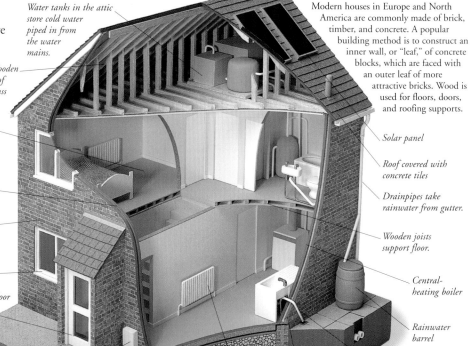

*Water tanks in the attic store cold water piped in from the water mains.*

*Wooden roof truss*

*Wooden floor*

*Inner leaf of concrete blocks*

*Outer leaf of bricks*

*Window, framed with wood or PVC*

*Wooden front door with porch*

*Box containing electricity meter*

*Concrete foundations*

*Central-heating radiator*

*Insulation cavity between wall leaves*

*Solar panel*

*Roof covered with concrete tiles*

*Drainpipes take rainwater from gutter.*

*Wooden joists support floor.*

*Central-heating boiler*

*Rainwater barrel*

*Pipe carries all waste to sewers.*

## Apartments

In towns and cities, where space is limited and many people want to live near the center, the answer is often to build upward, creating apartment houses. This type of home became common in the 19th century, when cities began to expand quickly and new devices such as steam cranes made it easier to lift building materials high up.

*In Ostia, the ancient Romans built apartments above shops.*

### Roman apartments
The ancient Romans were the first to build apartment houses. In cities such as Rome and Ostia, rising ground rents and growing populations encouraged the trend, and many brick and concrete five- or six-story apartment houses were built.

*Modern apartments made of concrete and steel, in France*

### Modern apartments
From Paris to New York, apartment houses are common in cities. The buildings have fire stairs or metal fire escapes to prevent residents from being trapped if there is a fire.

| FIND OUT MORE | AFRICA, HISTORY OF | ARCHITECTURE | BUILDING AND CONSTRUCTION | CITIES | CRAFTS | FURNITURE | INDUSTRIAL REVOLUTION | JAPAN | ROMAN EMPIRE |

# Houses and homes
## Permanent homes

**Troglodyte houses** hollowed out of rock, eastern Turkey

*Stilts protect occupants from vermin and floods.*

**Wooden stilt house** with thatched roof, Malaysia

**Adobe house** built from sun-dried clay bricks, New Mexico, US

*Thick walls and few windows keep house cool.*

**Decorated mud house**, Saudi Arabia

*Turf provides insulation.*

**Farmhouse** covered with turf and built into hillside, Iceland

*Stone-built palace*

*Small windows to help conserve heat.*

**Wooden house on stilts**, Canada

*Sloping roof to shed snow.*

**Wooden log house**, Switzerland

**Wooden log cabin** with overhanging roof, Wyoming, US

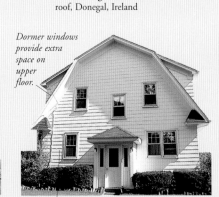

**Stone cottage** with thatched roof, Donegal, Ireland

*Large roof space for storage.*

*Wooden cross-braces add strength.*

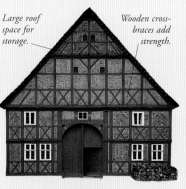

**Wood-framed house** with brick panels, Germany

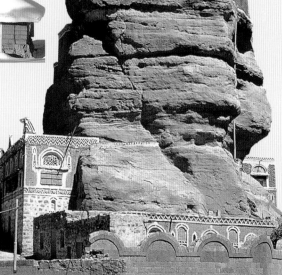

*Tall outcrop of sandstone*

**Summer Palace**, Wadi Dahr, Yemen

*Dormer windows provide extra space on upper floor.*

*Wooden panels give extra protection against weather.*

**Wooden house** with clapboard panels, US

## Temporary and movable homes

**Gypsy horse-drawn wagon**, UK

*Dome of compressed snow*

*Tunnel entrance*

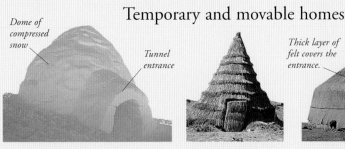

**Inuit igloo** built from blocks of snow and ice, Canada

*Thick layer of felt covers the entrance.*

**Shepherd's cabin** woven from bundles of straw, Spain

**Yurt** made from layers of felt lashed to a circular frame, Mongolia

*Wooden poles bound at top into a cone shape.*

*Circular entrance*

**Tepee** made of buffalo hides over poles, Arizona, US

# HUMAN BODY

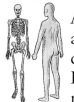

ALTHOUGH WE ALL LOOK different, we are identical in the way our bodies are constructed and the way they work. Each human body is built up from 12 major systems, including the digestive system, skeletal system, and muscular system. These systems interact to produce coordinated, active, intelligent humans. The study of the body's structure is called anatomy. Externally, the only consistent anatomical differences between humans are between males and females.

**Female** Narrower shoulders
**Male** Wider shoulders, Breasts
Wide hips / Narrow hips

## Anatomy

The human body is divided into the head and neck, the trunk (consisting of the chest, abdomen, and pelvic region), and the arms and the legs. Men and women differ in their external genitals and in the places where fat accumulates (shown in green).

## From cells to systems

The body's billions of cells are organized into tissues. Each tissue consists of similar types of cells. One or more types of tissues work together inside an organ, such as a bone or a lung. Organs are linked together to form a system that has one or more major roles. Together the systems are collected together to form the body.

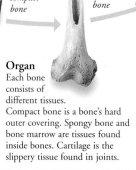

**Skeleton**
The adult skeletal system is made up of 206 bones. The skeleton provides a framework that supports the body, protects internal organs, and provides attachment points for muscles.

The skeleton is a framework of bones that supports the body.

The end of a bone is normally covered by cartilage.

The body is made up from hundreds of billions of cells.

Ligaments are strips of tissue that hold bones together at joints.

Compact bone
Thigh-bone
Spongy bone

Movable joints between bones make the skeleton flexible.

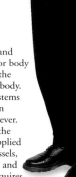

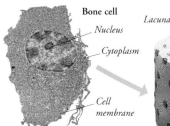

**Bone cell**
Nucleus
Cytoplasm
Cell membrane

**Compact bone**
Lacuna
Haversian canal
Circular layers of compact bone

### Cell
Osteocytes, or bone cells, are spider-shaped cells that make up the tissues that form a bone. Osteocytes are found in spaces called lacunae that are scattered around the hard matrix (material) found in bone tissue. Their job is to maintain the hard matrix.

### Tissue
Compact bone is one of the tissues that makes up a bone. It consists of layers of hard bone around a central tube called the Haversian canal. This carries blood vessels that supply the osteocytes with food and oxygen.

### Organ
Each bone consists of different tissues. Compact bone is a bone's hard outer covering. Spongy bone and bone marrow are tissues found inside bones. Cartilage is the slippery tissue found in joints.

### Body
The skeleton and the other major body systems form the living human body. The body's systems do not work in isolation, however. For example, the skeleton is supplied with blood vessels, lymph vessels, and nerves, and requires muscles to move it.

## Body systems

Each body system contributes to the body's normal functioning. Together, the body's systems are controlled by the nervous and endocrine systems. They enable us to move, talk, and perceive the world, while our internal processes run automatically.

 **Muscular**
The muscular system moves and supports the body. It consists of over 620 skeletal muscles attached to bones.

 **Nervous**
The nervous system controls the body's activities. It consists of the brain and spinal cord, and a network of nerves.

 **Circulatory**
The circulatory system transports material around the body. It consists of the heart, a network of blood vessels, and the blood.

 **Digestive**
The digestive system supplies the body with food. It consists of the mouth, esophagus, stomach, and intestines.

 **Integumentary**
The integumentary system is the body's outer, protective covering and consists of skin, hair, and nails.

 **Respiratory**
The respiratory system supplies the body with oxygen. It consists of the nose, throat, trachea, and lungs.

 **Urinary**
The urinary system removes waste. It consists of the two kidneys, the ureters, the bladder, and the urethra.

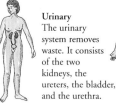 **Endocrine**
The endocrine system regulates many body processes. It consists of glands that make hormones.

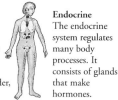 **Lymphatic**
The lymphatic system protects the body against disease. It consists of a network of lymph vessels.

 **Reproductive**
The reproductive system enables us to produce children. Male and female systems are different.

# HUMAN EVOLUTION

MUCH DEBATE HAS SURROUNDED the evolution of humans. However, most scientists are now agreed that modern humans, *Homo sapiens*, are the sole survivors of a number of human species that evolved from the common ancestor of humans and apes some six million years ago. Climatic changes forced our earliest ancestors out of the tropical forests and into open woodlands and grasslands. The challenge of these new habitats resulted in important changes, such as the ability to walk upright and an increase in brain size.

## Evolutionary tree

The evolutionary sequence from the earliest human ancestors is not a straight line, but is instead a "tree" with many dead ends. Because the fossil evidence is limited, scientists disagree about how many human species have existed and which were ancestors of others. This evolutionary tree provides a simple guide to relationships but does not necessarily indicate ancestry.

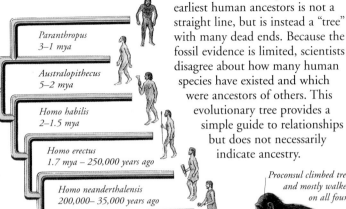

Common ancestors

*Paranthropus*
3–1 mya

*Australopithecus*
5–2 mya

*Homo habilis*
2–1.5 mya

*Homo erectus*
1.7 mya – 250,000 years ago

*Homo neanderthalensis*
200,000– 35,000 years ago

*Homo sapiens*
100,000 years ago

*Proconsul climbed trees and mostly walked on all fours.*

### Proconsul
*Proconsul* is the earliest known member of the hominoids, the group to which apes and humans belong. It lived in the tropical rainforests of East Africa between 24 and 18 million years ago. Compared to its ancestors, *Proconsul* had a large brain.

## Australopithecines

The Australopithecines are thought to be the earliest hominids (human-like people). Although ape-like, with a small brain and projecting jaws, *Australopithecus* stood upright and walked on two feet. This is known from its leg bones and backbone, and from 3.7 million-year-old footprints found at Laetoli in Tanzania.

### Lucy
"Lucy" is the name given to the most complete Australopithecine skeleton yet discovered, found in Ethiopia in 1974. It was an adult female, 3.18 million years old. Lucy was about 3 ft 6 in (1.1 m) tall.

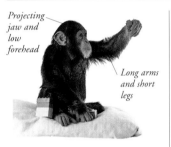

*Projecting jaw and low forehead*

*Long arms and short legs*

### Chimpanzees
The chimpanzee is our closest living relative. Chimpanzees and humans share over 98 percent of their DNA (genetic material). Chimpanzees and gorillas are known collectively as the African apes. About six million years ago, humans and African apes split from their common ancestor to evolve separately.

*Paranthropines had small brains and flattened faces.*

## Paranthropines

The Paranthropines were strongly built "man-apes" that lived in southern and eastern Africa between three and one million years ago. They were probably descended from the Australopithecines, but were not part of the evolutionary pathway that led to modern humans.

*A male Paranthropus was about 4 ft 4 in (1.35 m) in height.*

## Homo

*Homo* is the genus, or group of species, to which modern humans belong. It probably evolved from the Australopithecines between three and two million years ago, although there is no direct evidence for this. Early members of the genus showed increasing brain size and the ability to make tools.

### Homo habilis
"Handy man" is the earliest known species of *Homo*. It lived in the woodlands and savannas of Africa. *Homo habilis* had a brain size of 650 to 800 ml. It made and used simple stone tools, and was a successful forager and scavenger.

*Flat face and slender jaw*

*Reconstruction of Homo habilis*

### Homo erectus
*Homo erectus* was the first human to leave Africa and move to Europe and Asia. It had a sloping forehead, flattish face, and a brain size between 850 and 1100 ml. These humans exploited more habitats than their ancestors, and were the first to use fire.

### Neanderthals
*Neanderthals* were the first humans to have adapted to life in the cold climates of Europe and Asia. They had strong physiques and large brains. They wore clothes, made a range of tools, and used fire to keep warm. They were the first humans to bury their dead.

*Homo erectus skull*

*Neanderthal reconstruction*

### Homo sapiens
Modern humans first evolved in Africa. *Homo sapiens* has a large brain, considerable intelligence, and the ability to use language. Humans increasingly took control of their surroundings as they developed agriculture, societies, and technology.

*A modern human has an average brain size of 1400 ml.*

*Prominent brow*

*Face is straight rather than forward-jutting.*

FIND OUT MORE · ARCHAEOLOGY · BRONZE AGE · DARWIN, CHARLES · EVOLUTION · FOSSILS · GENETICS · HUMAN BODY · LEAKEY FAMILY · PREHISTORIC PEOPLE · SKELETON · STONE AGE

# HUMAN RIGHTS

MOST OF US BELIEVE that as human beings we have certain rights – to say what we want, to be treated fairly, and not be discriminated against because of our gender, color, age, religion, sexual orientation, or ethnic group. These and other rights are human rights we carry with us wherever we live. In many countries, these rights are written into national law, but in others they are denied. Recently, world attention has focused on countries that deny their citizens basic human rights. Despite this, abuses of human rights are still common.

Justice is often symbolized as a blindfolded figure, holding a pair of scales.

A fair trial is a basic human right.

### What are human rights?
Human rights are those rights and privileges that people possess regardless of the country they live in. Basic human rights include the right to freedom of speech, political liberty, and religious freedom. Some people believe that the right to the necessities of life, such as food and clean water, often lacking in areas of severe poverty, should also be viewed as basic human rights.

Clean water

## Bills of Rights

Many countries have incorporated a declaration of human rights into their constitutions. In France, for example, the Declaration of the Rights of Man and of the Citizen, written in 1789, today forms part of the constitution of the French Republic.

### The US Bill of Rights
The US Bill of Rights, made up of the first ten amendments to the US Constitution, includes the right to freedom of worship, the right to bear arms, and the Fifth Amendment (the right to remain silent to avoid self-incrimination); witnesses took "the Fifth" in the 1950s to protect themselves against investigations into "un-American activities."

Taking the Fifth Amendment, 1950s

## Modern human rights

The horrors of world war and countless atrocities in the 20th century have led people to believe that the only way to protect human rights is by setting an international standard to which all countries agree. Since 1945, many international agreements have been signed to protect the rights of oppressed people around the world.

### Universal Declaration
In 1948, the United Nations passed a Universal Declaration of Human Rights to serve as "a common standard of achievement for all peoples and all nations." Eleanor Roosevelt (1884–1962), chair of the UN Commission on Human Rights and widow of the former US president, was the person most responsible for getting the Declaration approved.

Eleanor Roosevelt

## Civil rights

Civil rights are those rights that people enjoy in individual countries and that are protected by law. Civil rights include basic human rights, as well as political rights such as the freedom to join a trade union. Where civil rights are denied, protests develop to repair the injustice.

### Amnesty International
Set up in 1961, Amnesty International is a global pressure group that campaigns for the release of people "detained anywhere for their beliefs, color, sex, ethnic origin, language, or religion."

The European Court ruled against corporal punishment in schools.

Amnesty symbol

### European Court of Human Rights
The European Court, which meets in Strasbourg, France, exists to hear human rights cases from the whole of Europe. Individuals can bring cases against their government if they believe their human rights are being violated.

© Amnesty International

### Freedom of expression
The right to express your views without fear of censorship or persecution, for example, in speaking against a government, is a fundamental human right. But it is denied in some countries, where newspapers and television are heavily censored and people are not allowed to demonstrate or express their views in public.

Amnesty leaflet against censorship

### Minority rights
The law is often used unfairly against certain groups of people whose culture has minority status within their society. Ethnic, religious, and other minorities have all had to protest in order to receive the rights already enjoyed by the majority of the population.

As a minority, homosexuals have had to campaign for equal civil rights in many countries.

## Rigoberta Menchu

Guatemalan human rights activist Rigoberta Menchu (b.1959) has campaigned since she was a teenager to secure and protect the rights of the native people in her country, who have been oppressed by Guatemala's military rulers. Menchu's own parents and brother were killed by the security forces. She was awarded the Nobel Peace Prize in 1992 for her work.

FIND OUT MORE

FRENCH REVOLUTION    PEACE MOVEMENTS    SLAVERY    SOCIETIES, HUMAN    UNITED NATIONS    UNITED STATES, HISTORY OF    WOMEN'S MOVEMENT

# HUNDRED YEARS' WAR

IN 1337 EDWARD III of England (r.1327–77) began a bitter war with France that was to last for over 100 years. Edward and his successors felt they had a claim to the French throne, but they also wanted to protect their inherited lands in southwestern France. In the beginning, under Edward III and his great-grandson Henry V, England seemed to be winning. Then, as the independent duchy of Burgundy abandoned the English and joined forces with the French army, fortunes changed, and France began to win. In the end, the French drove the English from their country, leaving Calais as the only English possession on the European mainland.

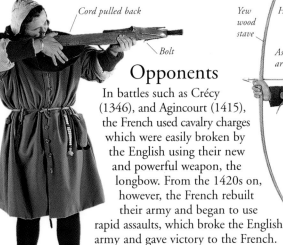
Cord pulled back
Bolt

French crossbowman

English longbowman
Yew wood stave
Hemp string
Ash wood arrow shaft

## Opponents

In battles such as Crécy (1346), and Agincourt (1415), the French used cavalry charges which were easily broken by the English using their new and powerful weapon, the longbow. From the 1420s on, however, the French rebuilt their army and began to use rapid assaults, which broke the English army and gave victory to the French.

### French crossbows
The crossbow was a slow but powerful weapon. After each shot, a lever or winder mechanism pulled back the string for the next shot. This took 30 seconds, during which time the bowman was open to attack.

### English longbows
The longbow was quicker to reload than the crossbow. An archer could shoot up to 12 arrows per minute. One arrow could pierce armour from as far away as 600 ft (180 m) – but they were not as accurate as the crossbow bolts.

## Early phases of the war

Helped by their Burgundian allies, the English had many successes until 1429, when the French, under the brilliant leadership of Joan of Arc, defeated them at Orléans. The French-Burgundian alliance of 1435 proved too strong for England, which steadily lost its French lands.

England
Calais
France
Aquitaine

**1340–1360**
The English inherited Aquitaine, and, in 1347, captured Calais. In 1359, they attempted to invade French territory. The French held them off, and the Treaty of Brétigny followed in 1360.

Burgundy
English allegiance
France

**1360–1429**
Although the English had lost Aquitaine by 1429, they had gained territory in northern France, including Normandy. Within 30 years they lost everything until by 1453 their only possession in France was the port of Calais.

## Joan of Arc

Joan of Arc (1412–1431) heard voices telling her to free France. At 17 she lead the French to victory against the English. Later, she was captured and sold to the English, who burnt her at the stake as a heretic. In 1920 she was declared a saint.

## Leaders of the war

The strong personalities and military skills of Joan of Arc and Henry V of England inspired their followers with courage and trust. The dukes of Burgundy were crucial for a different reason: they held the balance of power between England and France.

**The Black Prince**
Named because he wore black armor, Edward (1330–76) was the eldest son of Edward III. He fought at Crécy and Poitiers, and ruled Aquitaine in the 1360s.

**Charles VII of France**
Charles VII (r.1422–61) was not crowned King of France until 1429, after the victory at Orléans. He was then able to organise an army against the English.

**Philip the Good**
Philip (1396–1467), duke of Burgundy, was an English ally at first, but then changed sides and helped France to victory. He built his dukedom into one of the most powerful in Europe.

## Henry V

Henry V (r.1413–1422) of England captured major cities, such as Rouen, and led his men to many victories. Through his marriage to Catherine of Valois, he would have inherited the French throne from his father-in-law, King Charles VI of France, but he died before Charles. Shakespeare's play *Henry V* describes Henry's achievements.

## Timeline

**1346** Battle of Crécy: England builds up strength in France.

**1360** Peace of Brétigny: Edward III acquires Aquitaine, and gives up other French claims.

**1415** English victory at Agincourt; Henry V now controls Normandy.

**1420** Henry V named heir to French throne.

**1422** Charles VI and Henry V die.

**1429** Joan of Arc liberates Orléans, and escorts Charles VII to Reims to be anointed as the King of France.

**1431** Joan of Arc is sold to the English, and burnt at the stake as a heretic.

**1435** Council of Arras: Burgundy joins forces with the French army.

**1453** French victory at Castillon: England loses all her French lands, except Calais.

**FIND OUT MORE**
ARMS AND ARMOR
EUROPE, HISTORY OF
FEUDALISM
FRANCE, HISTORY OF
MEDIEVAL EUROPE

# HYENAS

THE EERIE CACKLING LAUGH of the spotted hyena is one of the characteristic sounds of the African savannah. There are three main types of hyenas – spotted, striped, and brown. The spotted hyena is the largest; all three have large, broad heads and powerful jaws. Their front legs and shoulders are larger and more powerful than their weaker hindquarters. Although hyenas look much like dogs, they are in fact more closely related to the cat family.

## Jaws
Bones and marrow form an important part of the spotted hyena's diet. Unlike any other carnivores, it will even eat hard tusks and horns. To cope with this diet, the spotted hyena's jaws and teeth are immensely powerful and capable of crushing the heaviest of bones.

Large, broad head with very powerful jaws

Sloping shoulders

Red-brown coat with dark spots

Forelegs are longer than hind legs.

Large, sharp canine teeth

Powerful, heavy jaws

## Spotted hyena
The spotted hyena is the most aggressive and most numerous member of its family. It is usually found in open country, but sometimes also on the forest fringes. Spotted hyenas' furtive movements and liking for carrion have given them a reputation for cowardice and dependence on the kills of other animals, but they are in fact predators in their own right. They have an important ecological role in keeping herds of hoofed animals moving. By forcing these animals to move to fresh grazing grounds, hyenas help conserve the habitat.

## Clan
Spotted hyenas live in clans of between 10–100 animals. They scavenge by day and hunt by night. Members of the clan work together and are capable of driving lions off their kill, and may even kill an old solitary lion. Females are larger than males, and the most dominant female presides over the clan.

## Feeding
Spotted hyenas scavenge the remains of other animals' kills, but also kill their own prey, frequently taking young gazelles, wildebeest calves, and zebras. They may hunt singly, but are more effective in packs. The pack size varies according to the availability of prey in their territory.

A pack of hyenas feeding on a carcass

## Young
Normally, two to three cubs are born in an underground burrow. They can see immediately. Several females often establish a nursery where they and their young live together communally. One female remains in the burrow to guard the cubs while the others go in search of food. The cubs are not fully weaned until they are 18 months old.

Cubs play together, but may also fight fiercely, to establish who will become dominant.

Long, wispy mane

Female hyenas nurse the young cubs.

## Types of hyenas
The hyena family consists of four species: the spotted, striped, and brown hyenas, and the aardwolf, which is sometimes placed in a separate family. The spotted and striped hyenas live in Africa and Asia; the brown hyena and the aardwolf are confined to southern Africa.

## Striped hyena
A much smaller animal than its spotted cousin, the striped hyena inhabits an area from India to the Middle East and southward to Tanzania. It is less predatory and less aggressive than the spotted hyena and tends to be more solitary by nature. It lives in rock clefts, caves, or burrows.

Striped body and legs

## Brown hyena
Essentially a desert species, the brown hyena is unaggressive, shy, and so secretive that it is seldom seen. At night it searches for the remains of other animals' kills. It lives in southern Africa, mainly in Namibia and Botswana.

Wispy brown coat

## Aardwolf
A timid animal, the aardwolf spends the day underground, often in another animal's abandoned den. It has weak jaws, small, widely spaced teeth, and a long, flexible tongue – adaptations to the termites and other insects on which it feeds. To deter predators it emits an evil smell from an anal gland.

Small head

Striped coat

### SPOTTED HYENA

SCIENTIFIC NAME *Crocuta crocuta*

ORDER Carnivora

FAMILY Hyaenidae

DISTRIBUTION Northern and eastern Africa and southern Asia

HABITAT Open grassland

DIET Mainly carrion, but is also an opportunist predator and will kill large animals, such as zebras, antelope, and gazelles

SIZE Height at shoulder: 31 in (79 cm); weight: 175 lb (80 kg)

LIFESPAN 20 years

FIND OUT MORE | AFRICAN WILDLIFE | ASIAN WILDLIFE | CATS | DESERT WILDLIFE | GRASSLAND WILDLIFE | MAMMALS

# IMMUNE AND LYMPHATIC SYSTEMS

EVERY DAY THE BODY IS INVADED by disease-causing microorganisms called pathogens, or germs. The immune and lymphatic systems are the body's defense against these pathogens. The immune system is a collection of cells that keep detailed records of invading pathogens so, if they reappear, they can be destroyed, making you immune to that disease. The lymphatic system drains fluid called lymph from tissues, filters out any pathogens, and returns the lymph to the bloodstream.

## Lymphatic system

The lymphatic system consists of a network of tubes called lymph vessels that reach all parts of the body, and several lymphatic organs. Lymph is carried by the vessels to the main lymph ducts, which empty into the bloodstream.

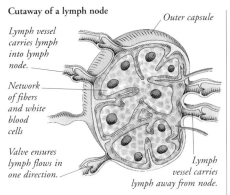

**Tonsils** guard throat against infections.

*Neck lymph nodes*

**Thoracic duct** empties lymph into a main vein.

*Heart*

**Spleen** is a lymph organ that also stores blood.

**Lymph node** removes pathogens from lymph.

*Groin lymph nodes*

*Knee lymph node*

*Network of lymph vessels*

## Lymph nodes

Lymph constantly leaves the bloodstream and flows through the spaces surrounding cells. It passes through lymph nodes, small swellings of the lymph vessels that clean and filter the lymph. Inside each lymph node is a network of fibers that supports large numbers of two types of immune system cells, lymphocytes and macrophages.

**Cutaway of a lymph node**

*Outer capsule*

*Lymph vessel carries lymph into lymph node.*

*Network of fibers and white blood cells*

*Valve ensures lymph flows in one direction.*

*Lymph vessel carries lymph away from node.*

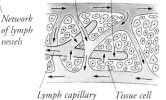

*Blood capillary*

*Tissue fluid passes into lymph vessel.*

*Lymph capillary*    *Tissue cell*

**Lymph vessels**
The smallest lymph vessels are capillaries. Excess fluid drains through the walls of lymph capillaries from the surrounding tissue. Lymph capillaries join to form larger lymph trunks.

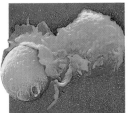

**Lymphocytes**
Lymphocytes, found in the lymph nodes recognize and destroy specific pathogens using chemicals that are called antibodies. Lymphocytes are also to be found circulating within the bloodstream.

**Macrophages**
Macrophages are cells with voracious appetites that detect, engulf, and destroy viruses, bacteria, cancer cells, and any other foreign material in the lymph that passes through the lymph node.

## Immunization

Immunization gives a person protection against a specific disease. There are two types of immunization. In active immunization, a vaccine containing some dead pathogens is injected into the body to stimulate the immune system to make antibodies. Passive immunization involves injecting antibodies and gives short term protection.

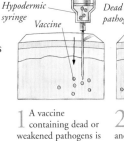

*Hypodermic syringe*    *Vaccine*    *Dead pathogen*    *Antibody locked onto pathogen*    *Real pathogen*    *Antibody*

1 A vaccine containing dead or weakened pathogens is injected into the body.

2 The immune system produces antibodies and keeps a "memory" of the pathogen.

3 If the real pathogens enter the body, large numbers of antibodies are released.

*Quilt for AIDS charity*

**AIDS**
Acquired Immune Deficiency Syndrome (AIDS) is caused by the Human Immunodeficiency Virus (HIV). A person with AIDS becomes infected with diseases that the body would normally fight off because HIV attacks and destroys immune system cells. In time, the immune system weakens and the person becomes unable to fight infections and eventually dies.

## Lady Mary Wortley Montagu

Lady Mary Wortley Montagu (1689–1762) was an English author who introduced an early form of immunization against smallpox to England. In Turkey, she had seen people scratching pus from small-pox blisters into the skin of healthy people to protect them from catching smallpox. She had her children "vaccinated" and publicized the method.

**Allergies**
If you have an allergy, it means that your immune system has wrongly identified a harmless substance, called an allergen, as being harmful. The body's reaction to these allergens produces symptoms such as sneezes and rashes. Common allergens include pollen, fur, dust, shellfish, and strawberries.

**Strawberry**

*A skin patch test is used to identify possible allergens.*

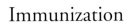
**FIND OUT MORE**    CELLS    HEALTH AND FITNESS    HEART AND CIRCULATORY SYSTEM    HUMAN BODY    MEDICINE    MEDICINE, HISTORY OF    PASTEUR, LOUIS

# INCAS

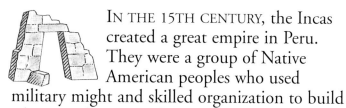

IN THE 15TH CENTURY, the Incas created a great empire in Peru. They were a group of Native American peoples who used military might and skilled organization to build what was then one of the world's biggest nations. Their empire took in most of the great mountain range of the Andes and huge areas of desert and rain forest. In 1532, Spanish adventurers conquered the Incas.

*Inca Empire* · *Peru* · Machu Picchu · Cuzco

## Cuzco

The Inca capital was called Cuzco, from the Inca word meaning "center." It is 11,000 ft (3,400 m) up in the mountains. Cuzco was an awe-inspiring city, made great by the emperor Pachacuti Inca. At the center of the city was the Temple of the Sun. Many Inca remains survive in the modern city.

*Farming terraces* · *Central plaza (square)* · *Palace* · *Temple of the Sun*

Machu Picchu

### Machu Picchu
The Incas built their cities using great blocks of rock so finely cut that they fit together without cement. Machu Picchu, high in the Andes Mountains, is the most spectacular remaining example of Inca architecture. Its stone buildings clinging to the mountain could accommodate thousands of people.

## Inca industry

The state collected manufactured goods, such as food, wool, and clothing, and kept them in storehouses. Every town had at least two storehouses: one for the ruler, one for the rest of the people. Llamas were used to transport goods along a large network of paved roads.

### Quipus
The Incas had no system of writing, but they kept records by knotting different colored strings onto a stick or cord known as a quipu. They could record figures such as the numbers of wool bales or the amount of births in a year, using this method.

### Agriculture
The Incas introduced terraced farming, which enabled crops to be grown on steep slopes. Bird droppings and fish heads were used as fertilizer. Most of the work was done collectively, and most of the land was owned in common by the local community.

## Inca society

At the top of society were the Inca ruler and his relatives. They could be identified because they were allowed to enlarge their ears with huge ornaments. Some of the nobles left their palaces in Cuzco to rule outposts of the empire. Ordinary people were organized into groups of villages called ayllus. Each ayllu was governed by an elected council of elders. Sometimes the emperors moved groups of people around the empire so that they could place loyal people in areas that were otherwise difficult to govern.

Cup with emperor's portrait

### Workers
Inca workers produced some goods for themselves, and some for the emperor and nobles. These provided the state with the resources for public works and other royal projects.

### Emperor
The Incas believed their rulers were descended from the Sun god, so they were worshiped as holy beings. This portrait of an Inca emperor decorates a cup used in religious rituals.

## Religion

Sun god

Chief of the gods was the creator Viracocha, who was worshiped by the Inca priesthood and nobility. Next in importance was the Sun god, Inti, claimed by royal Incas as their ancestor. Other Inca deities included gods of the Moon and stars. The earth god was also central, because the Incas relied on farming for wealth and food.

## Pachacuti

Pachacuti Inca was crowned in 1438. With his son, Topa Inca, Pachacuti enlarged the territory of the Inca state. He came to dominate many provinces, was a great organizer, and an effective administrator.

## Spanish conquest

Shortly before the Spanish ships reached Peru's coast, civil war broke out among the Incas. The Spaniards, led by Francisco Pizarro (c.1475–1541), took advantage of this division and captured the Inca Empire for the King of Spain.

Spanish coins

FIND OUT MORE

FARMING, HISTORY OF · GODS AND GODDESSES · SOUTH AMERICA · SOUTH AMERICA, HISTORY OF · SPAIN, HISTORY OF

# Inca arts and crafts
## Gold items

Gold figurines of gods were often left as offerings in the tombs of prominent Incas.

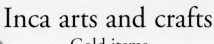

Small tomb figure was made of cast gold.

Belt ornaments were made of gold cut and hammered into shape.

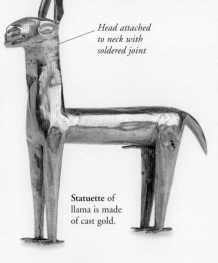

Head attached to neck with soldered joint

Statuette of llama is made of cast gold.

## Everyday items

Mouthpiece

Catlike head with bared fangs

Clay trumpet has twin catlike heads that may have represented a god.

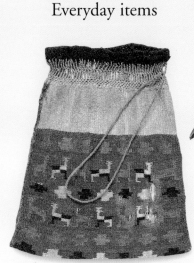

Drawstring bag is decorated with tapestry bearing design showing Peruvian llamas.

Alpaca-head handle

Stone container is made in shape of alpaca.

Pottery vessel has elaborate base; its exact use is unknown.

Pipes are made from quills.

Panpipes have different-length tubes for each note of the scale.

Flat-sided vessel could be hung on the back of a llama.

Stone bowl is decorated with a religious procession.

Jug is painted with simple geometric design.

Wooden beaker was made for Spanish conqueror Pizarro.

Copper chisels may have been used for woodcarving.

Tall, narrow neck

Carrying ring

Inca pots were often made in standard shapes; a common design had a conical base, long, flaring neck, and twin carrying handles; this type of pot was used for carrying water and beer.

Beaker decorated with Inca royal figures

# INDIA AND SRI LANKA

SEPARATED FROM other Asian countries by the Himalayas in the north, India forms part of a subcontinent that also includes Pakistan, Bhutan, Bangladesh, Nepal, and the island of Sri Lanka, which lies 20 miles (32 km) to the south. India is the world's seventh largest and second most populated country. Poverty is a serious problem, but India produces its own food, is increasingly industrialized, and is among the world's largest economies.

## Physical features

The Himalayan peaks form a natural border in northeastern India. The Indo-Gangetic Plain is drained by the Ganges and Indus rivers and stretches from Pakistan to Bangladesh. The Thar Desert is on the Pakistan border. The peninsula land slopes west from the Western Ghats across the Deccan Plateau to the Bay of Bengal.

**Western Ghats**
The Western Ghats Mountains stretch along India's west coast, rising to a height of 8,842 ft (2,695 m). Forests of tropical palms cover the lowlands west of the mountains and lush, evergreen rain forest, home to tigers and elephants, cloaks the slopes. To the east is dry, deciduous forest.

**Ganges**
At 1,678 miles (2,700 km) the Ganges is the longest river in India, flowing through a vast, highly populated plain. Its source is 13,779 ft (4,200 m) above sea level in an ice cave in the Himalayas. It ends in a huge delta that is mostly in Bangladesh. For Hindus, the Ganges is a sacred river.

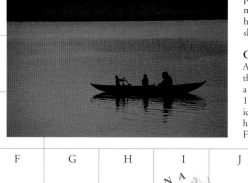

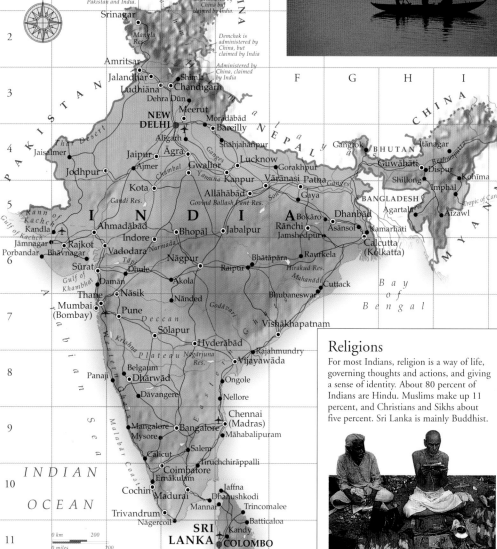

**Sri Lanka**
Just off the southeastern tip of India lies the island of Sri Lanka, a country in its own right. At the center of the island are high mountains surrounded by a low coastal plain. Like southern India, Sri Lanka has a tropical climate, with two monsoon seasons. However, the southwest has no dry season and is humid all year, while the northeast is drier, with open forest and grassland.

## Religions

For most Indians, religion is a way of life, governing thoughts and actions, and giving a sense of identity. About 80 percent of Indians are Hindu. Muslims make up 11 percent, and Christians and Sikhs about five percent. Sri Lanka is mainly Buddhist.

**Hindu priest**

115°F (46°C)  7°F (-14°C)
88°F (31°C)  57°F (14°C)
25 in (640 mm)

## Climate

Heavy and persistent monsoon rains soak India and Sri Lanka between June and September. The coolest season is from November to March. Winter temperatures rarely fall below 68°F (20°C) except in the high Himalayas, and may top 122°F (50°C) on northern plains in summer.

# India

With more than 450 million voters, India is the world's largest democracy. In 1947, the country became independent of Britain, and was left with a vast rail network, international ports, and working farms and factories, all of which have contributed to its industrial success. Today, India has many industries and large modern cities, although millions of people still live in extreme poverty. India has rich mineral resources, including oil, iron, bauxite, coal, and manganese.

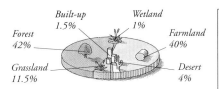

Forest 42%
Built-up 1.5%
Wetland 1%
Farmland 40%
Grassland 11.5%
Desert 4%

### Land use
Most of India's farmland is used for growing fruit and grain, and the country is largely self-sufficient in food. With such a large population to feed, demand for farmland is high, and many Indian forests have been felled to make way for crops. Some of the land is used for mining.

## People
Most Indians live according to the caste system, which indicates their role in society, who they can marry, and the work they can do. However, the caste system is now more flexible than in the past. Women have equal rights by law, but rarely in practice. Several measures to reduce India's rising population have been initiated by the state, but have remained largely unsuccessful.

883 per sq mile (341 per sq km)

28% Urban
72% Rural

Indian family

Movies are packed with stars, dancing, action, and romance.

### Filmmaking
India has a highly successful film industry and makes more movies than any other country, including the US. The center of the film industry is "Bollywood" – India's Hollywood – in Bombay.

### Music
India has a long and varied musical tradition. There are two classical forms of music: *Hindustani* and *Carnatic.* Both are based on the *raga,* a mixture of melody and scales. Typical classical instruments include the *sitar* and the *sarod* (lutes), flutes, drums, and the European violin. Folk music varies from region to region and is played on at least 500 different kinds of instruments.

Sitar

## Food
The traditional Indian food is curry, a sauce flavored with a subtle blend of spices, such as turmeric, cardamom, ginger, coriander, nutmeg, and poppy seed, eaten with meat or vegetables. Meat dishes, mainly lamb and chicken, are savored in the north. In southern India, vegetables and pulses such as *dhal* (lentils), coconut, and fresh sea food are enjoyed with curry. Rice and unleavened breads, such as *chapatis, parathas,* and *poori,* are eaten with meals.

Boiled rice

Vegetables in a spicy curry sauce

### New Delhi
Built by the British as India's capital, New Delhi has a population of 301,000 and lies 3 miles (5 km) from the old city of Delhi, with 16,000,000 people. Compared with Delhi's winding streets, temples, mosques, and bazaars, New Delhi has tree-lined boulevards and spacious parks.

Jama Masjid, Delhi

## Farming
About two-thirds of Indians are involved in agriculture. Many are poor farmers who grow just enough food to feed their families. Others work on plantations producing cash crops, such as tea, rubber, coffee, sugar, bananas, mangoes, cotton, and tobacco. India exports timber, including teak, sandalwood, and rosewood. Cattle are raised for butter and ghee, but not for beef, forbidden by the Hindu religion.

Sesame seeds

Bananas

Mango

## Industry
The country's economy is still based on small, cottage industries. But, aided by a large, cheap workforce, India's industry is growing rapidly. In the south, Bangalore is now a center for electronics, and many international companies have factories there. India also exports machinery, cut diamonds, textiles, clothing, and chemicals.

Electronics worker

### Kashmir
In 1947, Pakistan and India separated. Since then, they have disputed ownership of the former princely state of Kashmir. Part of Kashmir lies in the Indian state of Jammu and Kashmir. The rest is ruled by Pakistan, which claims it all because most of the people who live there are Muslims. Fighting breaks out from time to time.

## Transportation
Railroads in India total 39,030 miles (62,810 km). Every year they carry two-thirds of all the nation's freight and three billion passengers. India has 1,342,000 miles (2,160,000 km) of roads, only half of which are paved. Only one person in 300 owns a car, but buses are widely used and very crowded. In rural areas, oxcarts are common, and in cities, people ride bicycles or scooters.

Kashmiri winters are cold.

# Sri Lanka

 Known as Ceylon since 1796, Sri Lanka adopted a new name and constitution in 1972. It is separated from India by the Palk Strait, and is made up of one large island and the several coral islets of Adam's Bridge. In 1960, Sri Lanka became the world's first nation to choose a woman as prime minister, Sirimavo Bandaranaike. Since 1983, civil war has raged between the Sinhalese, who rule the government, and the Tamils, who are fighting for independence.

## Tamils

The Tamils, a mainly Hindu minority ethnic group, have been campaigning for an independent state in the northern peninsula of Jaffna since the 1980s. They object to the control of the government by the majority Sinhalese, most of whom are Buddhist. The Tamil Tigers, a ruthless guerrilla group, have fought many fierce battles in which up to 50,000 people have been killed.

Tamil man

### SRI LANKA FACTS

**CAPITAL CITY** Colombo

**AREA** 25,332 sq miles (65,610 sq km)

**POPULATION** 18,800,000

**MAIN LANGUAGES** Sinhala, Tamil

**MAJOR RELIGIONS** Buddhist, Hindu

**CURRENCY** Sri Lankan rupee

*Procession of decorated elephants in Kandy's Perahera Festival*

## Colombo

Sri Lanka's capital and chief port, Colombo, was developed by the Portuguese after 1507. The commercial capital is at Fort, which was a military garrison during Portuguese and Dutch occupation from the 16th to the 18th centuries. Today's city has a population of 2,241,000. It is a blend of old and modern buildings, with a busy bazaar area known as the Pettah. There are also Buddhist and Hindu temples and mosques.

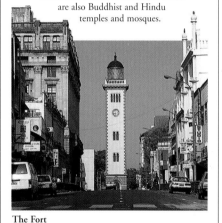

The Fort

## The Sacred Tooth

At the heart of Sri Lanka is the Buddhist holy city of Kandy, with a population of more than 100,000. There, in a gold casket inside the Dalada Maligawa (Temple of the Tooth), is a tooth that is said to have come from Buddha's funeral pyre (fire) in 486 BC. Every August, in the grand Perahera procession, the tooth casket is paraded on the back of a sumptuously decorated elephant.

## Education

At 92 percent, Sri Lanka has one of the highest Asian literacy rates. It has nearly 19,000 schools and 12 universities, including an Open University. Begun in 1980, it was modeled on the British Open University, a self learning system, aided by television, recordings, and correspondence courses.

Cloves – pungent

Chicory – bitter

Lemon – sour

Rock salts – salty

Sage leaves – astringent

Sweet potato – sweet

## Ayurvedic medicine

The traditional Hindu form of medicine called Ayurvedic medicine is practiced throughout Sri Lanka. Its name comes from the Ayurveda, an ancient treatise on healing that divides foods into six tastes. A healthy diet combines all of these. Disease can be cured by adjusting their intake. Sri Lanka also has an extensive national health service.

## Farming

Most Sri Lankans live in the humid southeast of the island. About 38 percent are poor farmers growing rice, sugarcane, cassava, and sweet potatoes for their own consumption, or working on plantations producing tea, rubber, and coconuts for export. Nearly 30 percent of the land is used for crops, and almost seven percent for grazing cattle, buffalo, and goats.

Coconut

Rice

Buddha figure carved from sapphire.

## Tea

Sri Lanka is the world's largest tea exporter. The tea is still marketed abroad as Ceylon tea. There are more than 2,000 tea estates. Their teas are described as high grown, medium grown, or low grown according to their height above sea level. The best quality comes from the cooler climate of the central highlands. The tea is handpicked, mostly by women, to preserve the delicate leaves. The pickers are paid by the basketful.

Dried tea leaves

Tea leaves

## Gemstones

Sri Lanka produces brilliant gemstones, which are found near Ratnapura, the "City of Gems," southeast of Colombo. It is especially noted for its sapphires. Other gems include deep yellow topazes, large rubies, and amethysts. Many are made into jewelry.

## Tourism

Despite the civil war, Sri Lanka's tourist industry is beginning to flourish. Increasing numbers of Europeans in search of winter sun visit the island's beautiful sandy beaches and coral reefs. Buddhists from all over the world make pilgrimages to the sacred Buddhist city of Kandy.

FIND OUT MORE | ASIA, HISTORY OF | BUDDHA | BUDDHISM | CRYSTALS AND GEMS | FARMING | FILMS AND FILMMAKING | HINDUISM | INDIA, HISTORY OF | MEDICINE | MUSIC

# INDIA, HISTORY OF

THE SUBCONTINENT OF INDIA has been home to some of the world's great civilizations. Dynasties such as the Buddhist Mauryans, the Hindu Guptas, and the Muslim Mughals spread their cultures and religions across India. As a result, India has remained dominated by a host of different cultures, a fact which has made it difficult to unify under one ruler. The Mughal empire declined in the 18th century, and the British added India to their empire, imposing strong rule from outside. India became independent in 1947, when the Muslim state of Pakistan was also created.

## Buddhist and Hindu empires

In 324 BC, Chandragupta Maurya, king of Magadha, eastern India, began to conquer northern India. He founded the Buddhist Mauryan empire, the first to unite the subcontinent. His dynasty was followed by the Guptas, a family of Hindu rulers who controlled India from AD 320 to c.700.

### Gupta Empire

India flourished under the Guptas. They promoted education, founding some of the earliest universities, and encouraged the arts of architecture, painting, sculpture, dancing, and music. The writers of the period produced books in the Sanskrit language which are still read today.

Nalanda University, founded during the Gupta period

Chola statue of a goddess

*Elaborate headdress shows high status*

### Imperial Cholas

The Cholas, from southeast India, were a Hindu people. In the late 9th century, they took over much of southern India and what is now Sri Lanka, ruling the area from the city of Tanjore. A seafaring people, their merchants sailed west to Arabia and east to China, organizing their trade efficiently and introducing India's first money.

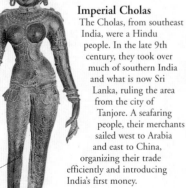

*Chola metalworkers cast bronze statues decorated with fine details*

**Statues** such as this were often commissioned from the artists of southern India by Chola merchants, many of whom were very wealthy.

*Mughal dagger*

*Sharp steel blade*

*Complex engraved decoration*

### Mughal Empire

The Mughals ruled India from 1526. Under their greatest emperor, Akbar, they brought prosperity to India, but after 1700 their power was weakened by opposition from Hindu southern India. Mughal emperors remained on the throne until 1858, but they had little power.

## Ancient India

People have lived in the Indian subcontinent for about 400,000 years. Some came to India from western Asia; others probably sailed on primitive boats from eastern Africa. By 2500 BC, the subcontinent's first civilization was developing on the banks of the Indus River.

Steatite seal from Indus Valley, 2500–2000 BC

### Indus civilization

This culture flourished from c.2500–1600 BC. It was based in large, well-planned cities near the Indus River (in what is now Pakistan). The people grew corn, wove cotton, and used a script we can no longer read.

### Aryan culture

Around 1600 BC, hordes of nomads moved out of the area between the Black and Caspian Seas. Some of them moved into the area around the Indus. Ancient religious texts called the *Vedas* describe their life, their gods, and their system of social castes or classes which later spread to the rest of India.

**Statue of Surya, a god of the Aryans**

## Coming of Islam

Between the 8th and 12th centuries, many Muslim invaders from Arabia and western Asia attacked India. By 1206, a Muslim sultan, based in Delhi, ruled the whole of the north Indian plain. Under the Delhi sultans and the later Mughal emperors, large areas of India were under Islamic rule. India's Muslim rulers built fine cities, but some were intolerant of other religious faiths.

Tomb of the Muslim emperor, Tughluq Shah, near Delhi.

### Delhi Sultanate

In the 13th and 14th centuries, the sultans of Delhi ruled much of northern India, from the Punjab in the west to Bihar in the east. But this empire was unstable. The sultans always had to fight opposition from Hindu states in southern India, and from the Mongols, who conquered Delhi in 1398.

### Aurangzeb

The last great Mughal ruler, Aurangzeb (1618–1707), became emperor in 1658. In 1678, there was a Hindu revolt against his rule and Aurangzeb began a series of costly wars against the Hindus. He expanded the empire, but bankrupted it with his wars, and it began to break up on his death.

**I**

## East India companies
In 1600, European countries founded East India companies to trade in India. England's company set up forts at Madras, Bombay, and Calcutta and began to trade in textiles. The English used the company to rule India, making alliances with local princes and driving out French colonists. Portugal also set up an Indian colony at Goa.

*Figure is finely carved and painted.*

*Gilt*

Statue of Portuguese East India Officer

# British India
In the late 1700s, the British East India Company defeated rival European colonists and established an empire based on the three "presidencies" of Bombay, Madras, and Bengal. By 1850, the company ruled some three-fifths of India, with the rest run by local princes who were subject to the British.

Indian soldier's belt

*Bullet pouch*

*Chain mail extension to protect hand*

*Powder flask*

*Fastens to arms with straps*

Tubular arm guard

*Double-edged blade*

*Handle made of steel*

*Recurved dagger*

### Indian mutiny
In 1857–58, there was a mutiny by Indian troops in the British army, arising from British insensitivity to Indian religions and customs. The rebels took large areas of India, but the British regained territory, restoring order by July 1858, after much bloodshed.

The British Parliament took a greater part in Indian government after the mutiny.

## British rule
After the Indian mutiny, the British disbanded the East India Company. The British adopted a more positive attitude towards the Indian people. A new government department was formed and an official called a Viceroy ruled on behalf of the crown. However, the Indian people remained far poorer than the British.

Building the railroad system in India

### Rise of industry
During the 19th century, India became an industrialized country. The British built Asia's largest railroad in India, and developed steamship and telegraph services. India exported raw materials to British factories, but also built its own steel and textile mills.

# Independence
In 1885, the Indian National Congress was founded to campaign for Indian rights. By the 1920s, under the leadership of Mohandas Gandhi, it was demanding Indian independence. A long campaign of resistance to British rule followed, but it was not until the end of World War II in 1945 that Britain agreed to make India an independent state.

India

Pakistan

Lahore

Delhi

Dhaka

Modern Bangladesh

*Indian Ocean*

*Indian Ocean*

Sri Lanka

## Pakistan
During World War II the Muslim League, led by Muhammad Jinnah, demanded a separate independent Muslim state on the Indian subcontinent. In 1947, the Muslim country of Pakistan was created, originally in two parts. In 1971, after a war between the two parts, East Pakistan became the independent state of Bangladesh.

### Nehru
Jawaharlal Nehru (1889–1964) was one of the leaders of the Indian National Congress and was imprisoned nine times for his political activities. In 1947, after India's independence, he became India's first prime minister. He funded industry and developed India's role as a superpower. Nehru's daughter, Indira Gandhi, became prime minister in 1966.

### Regional superpower
Under Nehru, India avoided alliances with major states. This policy of nonalignment gave India great power in its own right, power that increased when India supported East Pakistan in its civil war with West Pakistan in 1971.

Chemical works, India

First Indian National Congress

### Congress Party
The Indian National Congress had led India's independence movement. After 1947, it became the Congress Party. It controlled India for much of the period after independence, under the leadership largely of members of Nehru's family: Nehru himself (prime minister 1947–64), his daughter Indira Gandhi (1966–77; 1980–84), and her son Rajiv (1984–89).

## Timeline

c.2500 BC Rise of the Indus Valley civilization.

c.1600 BC Aryan nomads invade western India.

326 BC Alexander the Great invades the Punjab.

324–320 BC Mauryan dynasty.

320–c.700 Gupta Empire.

711 First Muslim invasions of India.

1206–1526 Sultans of Delhi rule northern India.

Terra-cotta Mother Goddess figure from Mohenjo-Daro, Indus Valley civilization.

1526–1707 The Mughal Empire is established and reaches its peak.

1600 British East India Company is founded.

1746 War between British and French colonists in India.

1858 Indian mutiny defeated; British impose direct rule.

Mohandas Gandhi, campaigner for independence

1917–44 Mohandas Gandhi leads campaign of resistance to British rule.

1947 India and Pakistan become independent.

1971 New state of Bangladesh formed.

1990s Efficient agricultural methods provide India with a healthier economy.

**FIND OUT MORE**   ALEXANDER THE GREAT   EMPIRES   GANDHI, MOHANDAS   GUPTA EMPIRE   INDUS VALLEY CIVILIZATION   MAURYAN EMPIRE   MUGHAL EMPIRE   UNITED KINGDOM, HISTORY OF